D1616047

Private Security
An Introduction to Principles and Practice

Charles P. Nemeth

CRC Press
Taylor & Francis Group
Boca Raton London New York

CRC Press is an imprint of the
Taylor & Francis Group, an **informa** business

CRC Press
Taylor & Francis Group
6000 Broken Sound Parkway NW, Suite 300
Boca Raton, FL 33487-2742

© 2018 by Taylor & Francis Group, LLC
CRC Press is an imprint of Taylor & Francis Group, an Informa business

No claim to original U.S. Government works

Printed by CPI on sustainably sourced acid-free paper

International Standard Book Number-13: 978-1-4987-2334-3 (Hardback)

Library of Congress Cataloging-in-Publication Data

Names: Nemeth, Charles P., 1951- author.
Title: Private security : an introduction to principles and practice / by
Charles P. Nemeth.
Description: Boca Raton : CRC Press, [2018] | Includes bibliographical
references and index.
Identifiers: LCCN 2017025019| ISBN 9781498723343 (hardback : alk. paper) |
ISBN 9781315157191 (ebook)
Subjects: LCSH: Private security services.
Classification: LCC HV8290 .N43 2018 | DDC 363.28/9--dc23
LC record available at https://lccn.loc.gov/2017025019

Visit the Taylor & Francis Web site at
http://www.taylorandfrancis.com

and the CRC Press Web site at
http://www.crcpress.com

To Mary Claire Nemeth—my youngest daughter—an artist who produces beauty. Soon to finish her MFA and make her artistic mark in a world desperate for creative work that is not only a wonder to gaze upon but more importantly uplifts and brings joy to those who encounter it.

To St. Thomas Aquinas No man is so wise as to be able to take account of every single case; wherefore he is not able sufficiently to express in words all those things that are suitable for the end he has in view. And even if a lawgiver were able to take all the cases into consideration, he ought not to mention them all, in order to avoid confusion: but should frame the law according to that which is of most common occurrence.

Summa Theologica at I–II, Question 96, Reply Objection 3

Contents

Preface: Introduction to Security

Before commencing this authorship, especially after so many years of involvement in the private security industry, in research, consulting, practice, and teaching, I thought I knew a great deal about the private security industry. After completing this text, I am not humbled into thinking otherwise. For sure, I had a strong experiential and intellectual base to work from in tackling this text—and considering my long advocacy of privatized services both as to inevitability and efficiency; I fully realized that the demand had long legs to run with. This was an industry not merely in growth mode—rather in a frenetic sort of dynamism that was unstoppable. Private security has now become a central player in nearly every facet of protection in terms of both people and assets. To be simplistic, the industry is everywhere and with everyone! So, tackling this industry is a major undertaking from every imaginable angle and sector. As a result, the text seems to know no bounds because the industry lacks boundaries as we project outward over the next decade or so. It is a growing organism and shows no signs of limitation. Therefore, the book that unfolds over the next 800 pages tries its best to cover everything and everyone, but it is ludicrous to think this even be realistic. However, the reader will be exposed to all the major threads of a powerful industry assuming more critical roles in the life and safety of a nation.

Chapter 1 lays out a full historical survey of private security with some provocative realities: first, that self-help and self-protection are more natural in the American experience than public policing, and second, that it appears that while public policing expanded over the last 100 years, that expansion appears to be coming to halt—while privatization and privatized services—the actual legacy of private security, is making a fierce comeback. The chapter delivers an overview on how the industry comes to play in the American historical experience and how industrialization, Western expansion, and social complexities triggered new models of policing.

Chapter 2 defines the idea of security from a host of perspectives such as private self-help, terror and defense, protection of the homeland, and the contrast between protection of assets and people. Special emphasis is given to the myriad of programs and protocols that provide security to business, industry, and individuals, and equal stress is evident when discussing how our homeland is now dependent on both public and private participation. The nature of security is viewed too through the eyes of an academic discipline, occupation's roles and functions, publications and professional journals, and its tendency to partner with public, governmental bodies.

Chapter 3 continues that definitional analysis by a comparative assessment of public policing and private security operations. Precisely what are the missions? Are they compatible or antagonistic? Is there cross-over and collaboration? To be succinct, the similarities are far greater than the contrasts in these two worlds and the text stresses the symbiotic relationship. Finally, the chapter targets the more dominant security positions witnessed in the occupational marketplace. In this way, we look to the common occupations that intersect with public policing and the private justice model and find a separation of the two impossible. The last portion of the chapter defines private security by its training and regulatory requirements both experientially and academically. Special attention is given to the many certifications and licensure programs for private security professionals. Only by these measures will a true understanding of the private security industry unfold.

Chapter 4 further defines the industry by its organizational structure—how it delivers its services, whether by contract or agreed proprietary services. In this light, a close look at the nature of an independent contractor status—a common event in the industry—is provided. The chapter additionally provides advice on how individual services are provided by consultancy or company and then features the usual deliverables. The last portion of the chapter focuses on corporate security with major emphasis on the CSO in the company decision-making.

In Chapter 5, the reader is exposed to the full array of legal principles applicable to the private security industry. Aside from minimizing legal liability, as to negligence, intentional torts, crimes, vicarious liability, and civil rights violations, the typical security company must be forever mindful of legal challenges. While not governed by constitutional principles as applied to public policing, this constitutional advantage does not negate all of the other forms of legal liability the industry can be slapped with. The chapter defines the many elements and components of these legal actions, and provides case law examples to edify the principles and factual scenarios to apply these legal theories to private security situations.

Chapter 6 expends all of its efforts on the nature of risk, hazard, threats, and vulnerabilities—constant preventive and mitigated realities for security managers and directors. Exactly what is risk and how do we measure it? What types of threats have the greatest significance for private security operatives? Is there any difference between natural or man-made threats and how does that impact company preparation? On top of these questions, the chapter looks at the typical natural disasters that both people and companies encounter; looks to ways of preventing, mitigating, responding to, and recovering from these disasters; and at the same time, calculates the reality of risks and threats aligned to terror—especially WMD challenges from the nuclear to the biological.

Chapter 7 targets the many facets of physical security—long-standing private sector responsibility. To protect people and assets, physical security plays a crucial and continuous role. The said security commences from the exterior—the perimeter—and ventures into the nooks and crannies of home and facility. The many types of physical security tools, from locks to lights, fencing to bollards, sensors to motion trackers, all are covered. The end part of the chapter looks to how crime prevention and environmental design go hand in hand and how surveillance is now part of the security fabric of protection.

The scope of chapter 8 rests firmly in the world of human personnel practices and the security that is so essential to assure integrity and safety in the workplace. The stresses in the chapter are many but mainly focused on background investigations—a province of the private security world for many generations—prevention and deterrence of crime and harm in the workplace with special emphasis on new and emerging challenges such as domestic violence, sexual harassment, and stalking as well as full coverage of active shooter protocols. Other coverage includes the world of executive and celebrity protection—another area of significant private sector involvement.

Chapter 9 targets the skills, characteristics, and both general and specific protocols for the private security operative conducting investigations. First in will be a full examination of the investigative method—precisely how and in what manner effective investigations can be done. Then, the chapter turns to specific applications in investigative practice, including but not limited to theft in its many forms, fraud in the retail and commercial exchange, employee scrutiny, and oversight for loss prevention purposes and other employee misconduct in need of particular proof. In the final portion of the chapter, the reader is exposed to investigative protocols that deal with workers' compensation, disability, and other insurance cases.

Covered next in Chapter 10 is the world of crisis and emergency response—a growing interplay for the security professional whose security work is now part and parcel of emergency planning and response. The thrust of the chapter is to lay out the more typical emergencies, accidents, and natural or man-made crises witnessed in the workplace, community, or other locale. Precisely how to plan for and respond to these events are central to the overall aim of the discussion. Hence, the reader is exposed to the myriad of potential harms and accidents encountered by employees, staff, or visitors to a location, including hazmat and contamination situations, accidents in the work environment, pandemic threats to communities and their infrastructure, natural disasters such as hurricane, flooding, and fire, and the full scope of WMD—whether biological or radiological, chemical, or bomb or other explosive.

Chapter 11 addresses the protection and care of critical infrastructure—a burgeoning area for private security professionals and companies. The broadest reach of critical infrastructure is part of the delivery, including the transportation sector, both air and rail; the maritime sector, which deals with ports, cargo, and shipping; food and agro-industry; and various utilities, including water, energy, and power and chemical plants. The overarching trend of the material highlights the significant role that private security plays in the protection of our critical infrastructure.

Moving to particular institutional practices encompasses the chief goal of Chapter 12. By institutional, we mean what the private security industry delivers to institutions such as art and cultural settings, educational facilities whether K-12 or at the college and university level, religious congregations and their respective houses of worship, and the full range of medical and hospital settings. Part of the chapter's direction includes practical suggestions, forms, and templates that target these institutional locales and at the same time highlight the professional best practices for their protection and the professional associations and groups, certification programs, and other advanced forms of continuing education, which assure the best possible methods for managing safety and security challenges.

Institutional safety and security continues in Chapter 13 where readers are exposed to a series of modes and best methods in hospitality, lodging and hotels, event facilities, mall and commercial properties, and the dynamically growing world of gaming and casinos. The chapter features forms, checklists, and other aids to assure safety and security in these specified environments. As in other sections of this work, the range of professional associations, educational opportunities, and certifications in these designated facilities is fully examined.

Chapter 14 highlights the infrastructure of cybersecurity—the virtual world where harm and injury are even more commonplace than what occurs on the street. Today's security professional must have exposure to the many complexities of the cyberworld, especially at the retail, commercial, and employment level. The coverage defines the various sectors of the cyberworld, and then delineates the type of crime and criminality often witnessed in this world. The latter portion of the chapter stresses countermeasures and other cyberdefense postures that are effective for the moment.

Chapter 15 prompts the reader to anticipate and imagine what the private security industry will be like in the next generation by identifying trends and movements. The content is futuristic by design and seeks to be prophetic about the direction of the industry. That privatization is an inevitable growth influence remains at the center of coverage. Overall, the chapter paints a picture of private security being on an unstoppable path to even further inroads in the once sacrosanct provinces of the public safety world. The chapter concludes that the future of the private security industry shows no signs of slowing down.

By the end of this long excursion into the world of private security, the reader has to be impressed with the magnitude of what this industry offers. Inside of this world are opportunities yet to be discovered or even thought of.

Acknowledgments

Any project of this magnitude depends on a cadre of professionals to bring to fruition. To be sure, the writing and composition is never easy when tackling the introductory text. My third edition of Homeland Security: Principles and Practices (CRC Press) once held the vaunted position of the most cumbersome and difficult book ever produced in my sphere of influence. Today, that status is fully vanquished by Introduction to Security—although both books share the same sort of pain. This is largely because the topical coverage of homeland security is vast with its tentacles reaching into every corner of the globe. In security, those tentacles extend ad infinitum and the end result accepting that homeland security is but one piece of the larger security puzzle. To cover everything, at a level that brings intellectual comfort, is simply impossible. One must settle with covering most of it in the best way possible.

Private security is so vast an industry that this work may likely turn into a multivolume set eventually and that is why the challenges of authorship, editing, and production are so, so strenuous. For that reality alone causes me great pause, especially to recognize those that bring this tome to life.

First, the editorial work starts with Hope Haywood whose brilliance at this end of the project can never be fully credited. I have often said that many of my works over the last 30 years would never have found a bookshelf without her very capable skills. That is truer today than it was 30 years ago. My gratitude is without measure for her unrivaled ability to keep the production moving.

Second, my gratitude to Mark Listewnik continues unabated for it is he who has the uncanny vision to know when something is missing in our academic disciplines. He has been a long and very rightful advocate for anything and everything homeland related but also just as energetic about the emerging influence of private security across the entire justice model. Not many editors at large presses understand the industry as Mark. I am most fortunate to have encountered his wisdom in these affairs. Finally, he also knows when any intellectual vacuum occurs in our world of private security and with the production of this text, we hope to deliver a meaningful work that introduces, explains, and edifies the dynamic world of private security.

Third, the environment at John Jay College is completely supportive of these scholarly endeavors and my special thanks extends to President Jeremy Travis and the Provost Dr. Jane Bowers—both of whom understand the role and critical importance of private security in the American justice system. At John Jay, an entire academic program, at both the undergraduate and graduate level, is dedicated to the private security industry. Security, at John Jay, is not a footnote or afterthought—it is rather central to its mission.

Thanks too to the many students at John Jay who assisted with research and other matters in the book's production.

My final John Jay connection is fully reflected in the insight, wisdom, and subject matter expertise of Dr. Marie-Helen Maras—an associate professor in Security, Fire and Emergency Management and the primary author of Chapter 14 on cybersecurity issues. Dr. Maras is a world-renowned expert in this area and to have her central involvement in the production of this chapter gives total credibility to its content. I am honored to have her input.

Finally, my love and affection for my family, who so often put up with my moody methods in writing—and the self-inflicted longing for text completion, remains steadfast. I can find few things in life that really give deep meaning and purpose—surely God, but also the importance of a family as patient and charitable with me as I trudge through this work. To Jean Marie, and our seven now very adult offspring, notably Eleanor, Stephen, Anne Marie, John, Joseph, Mary Claire, and Michael, I owe a life of purpose and abiding love. I am very fortunate to be a part of this wonderful family.

About the Author

Charles P. Nemeth is a recognized expert in homeland security and a leader in homeland security education. An educator for more than 30 years, Dr. Nemeth's distinctive career is a blend of both theory and practice. He has authored more than 40 books on law, security, law enforcement, and homeland security and is currently chair of the Department of Security, Fire, and Emergency Management at John Jay College in New York City. Dr. Nemeth is formerly the editor of the peer-reviewed journal *Homeland Security Review* and also currently serves as the director of the newly established Center for Private Security and Safety at John Jay College in New York City. He is a much sought-after legal consultant for security companies and a recognized scholar on issues involving law, morality, and ethics.

CHAPTER 1

Security origins and development

OBJECTIVES

After completing this chapter, the student will be able to

1. Review the concepts of private security, and law and order in the Greek and Roman civilizations.
2. Describe the concepts of self-help and self-protection evident in the feudal system of Europe.
3. Outline the evolution of public safety in England beginning with the Middle Ages and progressing through the eighteenth and nineteenth centuries.
4. Define "hue and cry," "watch and ward," and "posse comitatus" established by the Statute of Winchester of 1285.
5. Discuss the influence of the English culture and tradition on the American legal system evident in early colonial law enforcement.
6. Explain the ways in which private security is embedded in the nation's tradition and is an essential contributor to justice in modern America.
7. Identify the various classifications and functions of the private security industry in America.
8. Compare and contrast the many codes of ethics and statements of values in the private security industry today.

1.1 INTRODUCTION

Precisely how formal law enforcement engages the larger culture and community is a question of tradition, function, and necessity. Any reasoned analysis of "policing" usually begins with the public conception—that view that law enforcement is a function of government—of public officialdom. State and local police as well as federal authorities such as the FBI, DEA, and ATF capture our attention as if this method of delivering police services has always been intact. This knee-jerk conclusion, that policing is by nature governmental, has taken hold so deeply that most students of policing forget the governmental version be an aberration of sorts since policing in the community has been more a private affair than a public one over the last 3,000 years. By private policing, one assumes that the private citizen takes lead role in the delivery of protection services. How that private service is provided will vary depending upon a host of factors, historical conditions, and cultural tolerations. It could be a watch system, block committee, a posse comitatus, and the citizens' power to arrest and search as well as the conscious decision to defend property as individuals or a collective. In the latter case, the private citizen relies on self rather than some agency of government.[1]

Historically, the concepts of self-help and self-protection were considered foundational to security and the assurance of social order. Over the vast expanse of history, law enforcement functions were not delegated to professionals

---

[1] L. Zedner, Policing Before and After the Police: The Historical Antecedents of Contemporary Crime Control, 46 *Br. J. Criminol.* 78 (2006), at https://www.ncjrs.gov/App/publications/abstract.aspx?ID=234501.

or outside parties but retained and carried out by community members, volunteers, and designated parties who watched over the geography unique to a particular community. The private citizen was by most measures the chief party responsible for the safety and security of a community while public law enforcement does not appear until the late nineteenth century. Like any other type of institution, its practices and procedures are not fixed in a day, but emerge in an evolutionary sense.[2] Any clear and accurate assessment of private security and private sector justice begins at the beginning when most concluded that private protection is and was the preferred means of providing police services. Private protection, self-defense, personal protection of property, communal watches and wards, and neighborhood protection systems are not modern inventions but embedded historical practices, which undergird not only private security but also the public protection systems we now take for granted. These principles, derived from English law and the Anglo-Saxon tradition, and subsequently adapted to American jurisprudence, provide a panorama for how public and private protection systems not only emerged but legally operate. For example, what were the early parameters for protection of property? The right of self-help was first recognized within the common law and early codifications of English law. A man's home was indeed his castle, if he was fortunate enough to possess one. To protect his property and life, a person was entitled to use even deadly force. Eventually, these principles were codified or made applicable by case law determinations. Never has been a broad rejection of the private citizen's right to protect self and property, and by extension, these same rights were extended to collectives, to towns and cities, to neighborhoods and groups.[3] Self-help, self-determination, and self-defense are not foreign to our way of doing things; instead, these principles are deeply woven into our notions of policing and crime prevention.

To say the least, the modern idea of public safety cannot avoid its historical heritage.

1.2 SECURITY FROM ANCIENT TIMES

Early emanations of security and crime prevention can be traced to the earliest civilizations. For example, the maintenance of law and order in the Greek and Roman empires were primarily the function of the military and its command structure. Order was maintained in the empire not because of some formal entity, but because the power base was rooted in military authority.

> Although the word "police" has a classical origin—the Greek *politeuein* "to act as a citizen of a polis"—the metropolitan police forces we are accustomed to did not exist in the ancient world. A few cities had some form of institutionalized keepers of the peace—"magistrates of the peace"—but municipal police forces are a nineteenth century phenomenon: the British "bobbies" named for the Prime Minister Robert Peel appear in the 1830s.[4]

In Rome, the centerpiece of any protection system was the safety and well-being of the empire and emperor, a task that required a host of policing functions. The institution of the Praetorian Guard that kept vigil over Caesar could be construed as an early police system. Jones and Newburn coherently link the praetorian mission with traditional personal protection.

> [T]his imperial bodyguard was in charge of security of the palace and the imperial family. Splendidly uniformed for special occasions, they often appeared in civilian clothes with weapons hidden…Secondly, there were the three urban cohorts of 500 men each. Housed alongside the Praetorians, they apparently acquired daytime police duties and thus keep an eye out for ordinary street crime. Although they could be called out in the event of large-scale violence…on the whole they seem to have reacted to rather than sought to prevent crimes. There is no evidence that the cohortes urbanae patrolled on beat, and they were not detectives. Further, they do not seem to have been involved with "high-profile" crimes such as treason and murder.[5]

---

[2] For an interesting look at one side of the evolution, namely bounty hunting, see R.B. Fisher, The History of American Bounty Hunting as a Study in Stunted Legal Growth, 33 *N.Y.U. Rev. L. & Soc. Change* 199 (2009); see also J. Horwotz & C. Anderson, A Symposium on Firearms: The Militia and Safe Cities: Merging History, Constitutional Law and Public Policy, 1 *Alb. Gov't L. Rev.* 496 (2008).

[3] L.K. Stell, Close Encounters of the Lethal Kind: The Use of Deadly Force in Self-Defense, 49 *J. L. & Contemp. Probs.* 113 (1986), at http://scholarship.law.duke.edu/cgi/viewcontent.cgi?article=3827&context=lcp.

[4] F. Mench, Policing Rome: Maintaining Order in Fact and Fiction, at http://www.stockton.edu/~roman/fiction/eslaw2.htm, last updated July 25, 1999; see also T. Jones & T. Newburn, *Private Security And Public Policing* (Oxford, UK: Clarendon Press, 1998); J.F. Pastor, *Privatization of Police in America: An Analysis and Case* (Jefferson, NC: McFarland & Company, 2003).

[5] F. Mench, Policing Rome: Maintaining Order in Fact and Fiction, at http://www.stockton.edu/~roman/fiction/eslaw2.htm, last updated July 25, 1999.

Aside from the emperor, the Romans were masters at mass control and order maintenance due to the wise and efficient use of military units across its wide and sweeping empire. The justice model of the time knew nothing of correctional guards and police officers, psychologists and court appointed experts, but instead was driven by the military mechanics and ideology. For hundreds of years, Rome enforced in this way, as did their Greek counterparts.[6] For the Greeks, the idea of a formal, public justice system was utterly foreign.

As the Roman Empire disintegrated in the fifth century, the old dependable military paradigm was shaken to its foundation. Order and protection was threatened by nomadic bands of rogues and barbarians, territorial fiefdoms, and blood feuds. Anguished communities were held captive by hordes of intruders.[7] Without order and control, chaos emerged in the Dark Ages because the glory of Rome and the protection system it brought to its citizens lay in ruins. From this period forward, competing lords and land barons controlled the day. Here the concept of feudalism emerged, where the wealthy and powerful landowner gave protection to those who swore allegiance. In this system, small pockets of power developed, headed by lords and served by serfs, a quasi-slave in pure service to the landowner. The chief emphasis was on revenge and retribution when one citizen harmed another. In this way, justice was very primitive and certainly nonstructural. Radcliffe and Corss' analysis of the early English legal system paints an accurate picture.

> An injury done was primarily the affair of the party injured and of his kindred. It was for him and them to avenge the wrong on the wrongdoer and his kin, and to prosecute a "blood feud" against them until the wrong originally done was wiped out by retaliation.[8]

Feuding, blood lust, and tribal rivalries were the order of the day. In these times, the cultural psyche of neither the commoners nor the elite could envision outsiders addressing disputes. While the elite could depend on loyal servants and bureaucrats, the common person fended for themselves. Self-help and self-protection represented the only way of thinking.[9] Hence, protection, safety, and security were not assured by any formal policing mechanism or governmental authority, but by local landowners and warlords who controlled sectors. Although self-help in the protection of one's life and property was socially acceptable, other factors often dictated the practice as the only viable form of law enforcement.

For the majority of European and American history, sparsely populated areas, rugged geography, and a strong distrust of any proposed national police organization forced individual citizens and communities to enact and enforce the law through the best available means.

> Today's heavy reliance on government to control crime is a relatively recent phenomenon. Not too long ago, most protection of life and property in the United States and Europe was personal and private. There were no public prosecutions, and the police were public in name only, deriving most of their income from bounties and shares of revenues from fines.[10]

Oftentimes, private individuals acting on their own, or at the behest of communal interests, would be forced to take the law into their hands.

Although the self-help protection philosophy gave no clear-cut parameters as to what was fair and equitable justice, the origins of common law did develop from a notion of reasonable, nonlethal force in the protection of one's property. When criminal action threatened only property, the law did not condone the use of deadly, retaliatory force. The law rightfully considered human life more precious than mere property.[11] The issue of self-protection did not, however, exclude the use of deadly force in the protection of life. To be a legitimate use of deadly force, the use of force had to be justifiable, and not disproportionate to the force threatened.[12] A person, with justifiable cause, could use force in defense of family and self, and also in the defense of others.[13] Under the feudal system, the relationship between lord and vassal resembled the present-day system of contract security.

---

[6] See Plato, *The Laws of Plato*, trans. Thomas L. Pangle (Chicago, IL: University of Chicago Press, 1980), and Aristotle, *Nicomachean Ethics*, trans. David Ross (Oxford, UK: Oxford University Press, 2009).

[7] See G. Radcliffe, E.L. Corss, *The English Legal System* (London, UK: Butterworths, 1970); M. Radin, *Handbook of Anglo-American Legal History* (Holmes Beach, FL: Wm Gaunt & Sons, 1936); and W. Holdsworth, *A History of English Laws* (London, UK: Methuen, 1927).

[8] Radcliffe & Corss, at 6.

[9] F. Prassel, *The Western Peace Officer* 126 (Norman, OK: University of Oklahoma Press, 1972).

[10] National Center for Policy Analysis, Using the Private Sector to Deter Crime, at http://www.public-policy.org/~ncpa/w/w79.html, March 1994.

[11] R.M. Perkins, *Perkins on Criminal Law*, 2nd ed. 1926–1927 (Eagan, MN: Foundation Press, 1969).

[12] F.F. Russell, *Outline of Legal History* 93–94 (New York, NY: Russell, 1929).

[13] Holdsworth, at 313.

1.3 PRIVATE SECURITY IN ENGLAND

1.3.1 Middle ages

Although modern law enforcement, security organizations, and policing/security functions were not initiated during the Middle Ages, the need for "policing" and "security" function was self-evident. The sheer chaos of the early medieval period, with natural plagues, competing fiefdoms and tribal factions as well as developing political intrigues, drives the dialogue of the time. In many ways, this is a period of immense innovation, trying to find the proper mechanisms that assure order and tranquility. Medieval England and most of Europe tinkered with various versions of private, self-policing forces. For example, the vassal–lord relationship had developed a reciprocal self-help approach to the security of one's life and property whereby the "Lord" warrants his vassals, his serfs, and his followers, a protection system in exchange for work and the sharing of harvests. Later in these early feudal relationships, the concept of protection jumps from farm to the manors and villages, each responsible for their own protection. During the latter Middle Ages, the picture becomes far more formal. By 1160, the feudal system had evolved significantly enough to hearken for some protection and enforcement structure.[14] While the historical model of self-help and self-protection remained intact, feudal barons and landowners, along with loyal servants and vassals, required security to hold stable their various holdings. Land, as well as personal property, could continuously accumulate, and the competition for resources made crime a far greater reality in the European countryside. Real property served as the backdrop for the creation of the first, structural law enforcement model. Here, land owned by lords and others could be parsed up into various plots or lots known as a "tithing." Ten tithings were designated a "hundred," and in these surveyed descriptions emerged the responsibility for safety and security.

Each area was responsible for its own protection and the lord who controlled the land areas promised and pledged safety in return for crops, payment, or other enterprise.

> England was inhabited by small groups of Anglo-Saxons who lived in rural communities called tuns…Sometime before the year 700, they decided to systematize their methods of fighting by forming a system of local self-government based on groups of ten. Each tun was divided into groups of ten families, called a tithing…The tithings were also arranged in tens. Each group of ten tithings (or a hundred families) elected its own chief.[15]

When crimes occurred in the region, the citizens would give out the "hue and cry" to apprehend and prevent the escape of the perpetrator. The entire hue and cry system foundationally relies on the self-protection model. The cry is not for the local police to carry out the responsibility, but for the members of the community to band together to root out the perpetrator. As these areas continued to develop, usually into large manors and small villages, the need for a collective response for self-protection grew more urgent. The designation of constable emerges in the literature of the times and was primarily descriptive of a designated agent for the manor or small village. The constable assured the integrity of the hue and cry, assessed fines against those not carrying out expected duties, and rooted out those injurious to the land area under his supervision. While more formal, there is little doubt that the system just described is primarily "privatized."[16]

As growth continued, so did the sophistication of the security philosophy. As towns and villages multiplied, the truncated and individualized systems based in feudalism became inadequate. Specifically, in England, the king takes on a more active and formal role in the protection of his subjects. At the center was the king's promise to his subjects that he would institute a King's Peace across the land in exchange for their fidelity to both the king and his realm. These early English kings created a system of counties, then designated as "shires."

A "reeve" oversaw each shire; constables reported the activities of his tithings to the shire-reeve. The term has evolved into the occupational title sheriff.[17] "The shire-reeve seems to have developed from the king's reeve, the local official who looked after the king's business."[18] He was a royal representative, and it was intended that he would protect the royal interests if they conflicted with the local claims of anyone, including the lord of the county. Above all, the shire-reeve was the chief officer of the county.[19] Within a manor, an appointed officer known as a "constable" was responsible for

---

[14] P. Pringle, *Hue and Cry: The Story of Henry and John Fielding and Their Bow Street Runners* (New York, NY: William Morrow, 1955).

[15] National Sheriff's Association, History, at http://www.sheriffs.org/about/history/middle_ages.htm, 2001.

[16] C.P. Nemeth, *Private Security and the Law*, 4th ed. 2 (Waltham, MA: Elsevier, 2012).

[17] *Ibid.* at 3.

[18] Radcliffe & Cross, at 4.

[19] Radin, at 170–171.

dealing with legal matters. Both the shire-reeve and the constable were the forerunners of modern sworn police offi-cers.[20] This method proved effective, but only within the limited range of the feudal territory or lord's domain.

With each lord having his own system of security and no codified system of English law, the issue of national or regional security was a muddled mess of self-interests and conflicting jurisdictions. As the small manors of feudalism evolved into towns, villages, and eventually cities, the old system of self-help could not keep up with the rising crime rate.

> The system of English legal protection continued to expand and define itself more clearly. Under the Statute of Winchester of 1285 a system of "watch and ward" was established to aid constables.[21] The watch and ward system was comprised of a justice of the peace, constable, constable's assistants, and night watchmen whose primary function was the care and tend-ing of a designated area of a town or city known as a "ward."[22] Regular patrols of citizens were established to stand watch nightly and to arrest criminals and strangers found wandering at night. When an offender was caught in a criminal act, the "hue and cry" was raised.[23] It was then the duty of all men in the community, fifteen years and older, to rally at the scene and uphold justice. In addition, they were required by law to carry arms and form a *posse comitatus* to pursue criminals.[24] In these contexts, the predominant force in maintaining the king's peace and enforcing the law. While their emerging roles tethered to public officialdom, the security function remained a private responsibility.[25]

Although all men had the general duty and the right to make arrests, the constables and sheriffs had additional specific peacekeeping duties and powers. Unfortunately, the officers were ill-equipped to handle the urban growth that created cities with huge populations. Because constables were unpaid, ill-trained, and ill-equipped, English law enforcement was in dire straits. Lord Chancellor Bacon, in 1618, complained that constables were "of inferior stock, men of base conditions."[26] The towns and cities of England, especially London, fell into virtual anarchy because of the lack of publicly appointed and underpaid professional peacekeepers. Unfortunately, the bulk of the watchmen and constables lacked the essential qualities for success.[27] In his book, *Hue and Cry*, Patrick Pringle states thus:

> Such is our respect for institutions that when an established system breaks down we are quick to blame people and defend the system; but the lesson of history seems to be that systems must be made for people, because people cannot be made for systems. To be effective, any system—whether political, religious, economic, or judicial—must expect people to be base and selfish and venal.[28]

Owing to the rising crime rate, and the inability of the poorly organized English system of law enforcement to effectively combat it, private persons and businesses developed their own means of protection. As towns and cities expanded, merchants and artisans banded together for mutual protection. In his book *On Guard*, Milton Lipson relates how "[g]uild members united to perform the duty of watching their contiguous property in the heart of these medieval towns, serving as watchmen themselves, later assigning their apprentices and thereafter hiring special guards. In these practices are the visible roots of both modern insurance and private security."[29]

Other social, cultural, and economic forces played into the impetus for a more formal law enforcement system con-sisting of both public and private elements. The expanding trade and transportation of vital goods and services were temptations for criminals. It also demanded the need for protection of private interests, property, and self. From this arose the concepts of proprietary and contract security. Throughout the sixteenth century, different kinds of police agencies were privately formed. Individual merchants hired men to guard their property, and merchant associa-tions created Merchant Police to guard shops and warehouses.[30] The status of these private guards "was by no means uniform; some were sworn in as constables, while others continued in employment as private watchmen or guards.

---

[20] See generally 4 L. Radzinowicz, *A History of English Criminal Law* 105 (1968); and National Sheriff's Association, *supra* note 15.

[21] Holdsworth, *supra* note 5, at 6–7.

[22] Pringle, *supra* note 14, at 43.

[23] E. Reynolds, *Before the Bobbies: The Night Watch and Police Reform in Metropolitan London, 1720–1830* (Stanford University Press, 1998).

[24] T.A. Critchley, *A History of Police in England and Wales* 3 (Legend, 1966).

[25] See Reynolds, *supra* note 23; P.J. Stephens, *The Thief-Takers* (New York, NY: W. W. Norton, 1970); J.F. Richardson, *The New York Police* 38 (Oxford University Press, 1970); R. Lane, *Policing the City: Boston: 1822–1885* 7 (Atheneum, 1975); S. Bacon, *The Early Development of American Municipal Police* 44 (University Microfilms, 1939).

[26] Critchley, *supra* note 24, at 1.

[27] Reynolds, *supra* note 23, at 40–41.

[28] See Pringle, *supra* note 14.

[29] M. Lipson, *On Guard* 13 (Quadrangle/New York Times Book Company, 1975).

[30] G. Green, *Introduction to Security* 5 (Boston, MA: Butterworth, 1981).

There were also no general scales of payment, rules of conduct, or assigned duties for these newly created private security forces."[31] These areas were solely under the discretion of the employer. The essence of private security was born in the chaos of the Middle Ages, especially that of the "contract" variety, but the standardization of its organizational hierarchy, duties, and pay was yet to come.[32]

1.3.2 Eighteenth-century England and the rise of formal policing

While eighteenth-century London was regarded by many as one of the greatest cities in the world, its streets manifested a severe lawlessness and corruption that was rotting its foundation. But,

> [t]he problems were immense. London was a dirty, ill-lit place which in some quarters became lost in a tangle of impenetrable alleys and festering courts. This made the actual commission of crime easier; and of course it was not an environment conducive to high-minded civic virtue. Poverty, malnutrition, and squalor made life for a high proportion of London residents a short and unpleasant experience.[33]

"Watch and ward" and the constable model eventually became ineffective and set the stage for a major paradigm shift in the nature of public safety.[34] But even under the worst conditions, change comes slowly. Londoners, while sophisticated enough to understand the current dilemma of a corrupted system, lacked the understanding of the type of change that would resolve the problem. The very idea of a compensated police professional can only be described as foreign to the eighteenth-century citizen. To engineer an alternative model would require dramatic rethinking. Part of the problem was cultural as well as systematic. Londoners were nervous about the establishment of a police force because of potential negative impacts on cherished freedoms. To be free naturally implied resistance to governmental authority. A select committee of the House of Commons, in 1818, reported the general reticence Londoners had regarding the police force "in a free country."

> [S]uch a system would of necessity be odious and repulsive, and one which no government could be able to carry into execution. In despotic countries it has never yet succeeded to the extent aimed at by those theories, and among a free people the very proposal would be rejected with abhorrence; it would be a plan which would make every servant of every house a spy on the actions of his master, and all classes of society spies on each other.[35]

Even so, change had to push forward in the English city and countryside. Growth of urban areas, commercial economies, and a rising population were forces that moved the once comfortable paradigm.

The rise of highway robbery and petty thievery in the English culture could not be effectively addressed by a system of immobile and less than proficient constables. Nor could the watchmen keep up with these roving bands of vagabonds and thugs. Thus, the idea of incentive-based compensation tied to arrest, and subsequent prosecution of thieves and other criminals found a willing audience.[36] In addition, these historic private actors were entitled to the highwayman's property such as his horses, arms, money, and other items, unless those items were proven to have been stolen. The parliamentary rewards given by the government to the thief-takers eventually evolved into a sliding scale payment system depending on the type of apprehension.[37] Yet despite this innovation, the model of private security remained essentially intact. Thief-takers were hardly criminal justice professionals or on the public payroll. Too often these individuals were solely driven by the profit motivations, just as the bounty hunter is, and in some circumstances made minimal effort to catch the "true criminals." In fact, many worked with accomplices who colluded and invented various criminal operations for the mere purpose of collecting the stipend. Some thief-takers went as far as planting stolen goods and framing innocent people in order to secure convictions and receive rewards. Many of their prisoners were either framed or seduced into crime by thief-takers, in order for the thief-takers to claim a reward for

---

[31] 2 L. Radzinowicz, *A History of English Criminal Law* 205 (Macmillan Company, 1956).

[32] Pringle describes the situation in eighteenth-century London at pages 29–30 of *Hue and Cry*. See also P. Colquhoun, *A Treatise on the Commerce and Police of the River Thames* (J. Mawman, 1800); P. Colquhoun, *A Treatise on the Police of the Metropolis* (Arkose Press, 1796).

[33] P. Rogers, *Henry Fielding* 179 (New York, NY: Charles Scriber's Sons, 1979).

[34] Pringle describes the situation in 18th-century London at pages 29–30 of *Hue and Cry*. See also *A Treatise on the Police of Canada*.

[35] Reynolds, *supra* note 23, at 107.

[36] See Pringle, *supra* note 14, at 35.

[37] *Ibid.* at 35–36.

their services.[38] During the thief-takers' era, bribery was common where the justices, constables, and watchmen were concerned and any sense of professional ethics was a mere pipe dream.

As England yearned for law enforcement compatible with its cultural ideology and tradition, and fully accepted the need for alternatives, it was blessed with the like of Thomas De Veil. In 1729, De Veil was appointed to the Commission of the Peace for the County of Middlesex and the city of Westminster. From that day forward, his influence on police and security practice would be so dramatic that it would last a century. Although De Veil is not widely recognized in history, his philosophy clearly set the stage for the eventual institution of Robert Peel's municipal police force in 1829.[39] Even more critically, De Veil used his office as magistrate to perform particular functions that would eventually encompass the ideals of public police officers, detectives, investigators, and private security practitioners everywhere.

Magistrates, as today, were front-line, street-driven judges that contended with everyday crime and trifles between citizens as well as reconciled a myriad of legal issues common to urban living. De Veil was the head of the group of magisterial courts known as the Bow Street Magistrates. As the first Bow Street Magistrate, his authority extended to four counties, besides the city of Westminster. De Veil was in fact London's first Chief of Police, though the title was honorary since no police force had yet to be invented. Instead, he relied on the usual players—the inefficient constables, informers, and thief-takers. De Veil understood and reacted to the concept of crime more than any of his predecessors, engaging and suppressing criminals and crimes in ways previously not witnessed. He attacked the most powerful gangs, who had previously succeeded in intimidating other magistrates; he enforced unpopular and previously disregarded law, such as the controversial and unenforceable *Gin Act*. Most impressively, De Veil recast and extended the nature of his own position by turning justices and magistrates into activists in the field of public safety and crime prevention and detection. De Veil used informers, as well his own personal detective capabilities, to collect evidence against powerful criminal gang leaders of his time. His extraordinary successes came in his aggressive posturing and break up of London gangs. Within 6 years of his appointment, he was designated the leading magistrate and titled a Court Justice.[40]

Aside from these exceptional qualities, De Veil engaged in novel practices unheard of for his time and shifted the self-help model into a professional template. De Veil was also the first police magistrate in English history to go out of his district to assist in the investigation of a crime. According to Pringle, De Veil initiated the practice of giving expert detective help to other jurisdictions or authorities in need of professional advice. Before Scotland Yard ever existed, England depended on the Bow Street Magistrates. De Veil started the practice of undertaking investigations for private clients and received payments for restoration of a victim's losses, and in turn, set a precedent for the Bow Street Runners.

Soon after De Veil, Sir Henry Fielding's elevation to Bow Street continued the professional inquiry into what the term police/law enforcement means.[41] Faced with staggering rates of rising criminality, especially pickpockets, street robbers, highwaymen, gang robbing, defiance of authority, and prison breaks, Fielding began his tenure by scientifically examining both the results and methods of policing. Fielding was nominated to the Commission of the Peace for Westminster, accepted and assumed the task of creating the first police force of England, although unofficial and very limited in its capabilities. Fielding, who despised corruption, took his role seriously and often displayed a reformist's zeal. His entire vision can be best described as "criminological," his thrust being the search for root causes in criminality and its interplay with prevention, protection, and enforcement tactics and strategies.[42] Fielding believed that his office, and that of Bow Street itself, could play an integral role in the elimination of crime. Instead of solely apprehending, Fielding was in the business of predicting and deterring and posed some highly creative ideas that foretell modern criminology, including but not limited to

- Active cooperation of the public
- An institutional police force
- Crime causation and remediation
- Correction of conditions that cause crime

---

[38] See *Ibid.* at 36.
[39] See *Ibid.* at 36.
[40] See a full analysis of the ground-breaking career of De Veil in Pringle's *Hue and Cry* at 69.
[41] Rogers, *supra* note 33, at 232–233.
[42] *Ibid.* at 190.

Anticipating this need for public cooperation, Fielding utilized the media to convince the public that change was good. His office issued what can be best described as "Press Releases," which announced programs, plans, and recently enacted laws. As part of the continued effort to educate the public, Henry Fielding funded a small newspaper, the *Covent-Garden Journal* that included advertisements urging the public to report burglaries and robberies to Bow Street, in an effort to continuously educate the public as to what the criminal justice system was about. In 1759, his *Covent-Garden Journal* was renamed the *Public Adviser* and shortly thereafter became one of London's leading daily newspapers.

Even more significantly, Fielding reconstituted the ragtag constable group into a secret police force. This small plainclothed force eventually became known as "Mr. Fielding's people."[43] While not formally designated the "pubic police," Fielding's organization of the constables, coupled with training and preparation, signaled a new approach to police services. Fielding trained these men in tactics involving evidence collection as well as arrest and safe practices and provided professional insight into how to operate clandestinely in criminal circles. The existence of Fielding's "secret police" was kept confidential and never revealed until after he died.[44]

Fielding's reputation as a law enforcement thinker continued to grow unabated. In 1753, the Duke of Newcastle requested Henry Fielding propose a plan that would check the rising tide of murder and robbery in London.[45] It was within the confines of his study that the idea of a true public police system took shape. In place of the old reward-and-incentive-based system, the part-time justice operative, Fielding called for the professionalization of his Bow Street Runners, constables, watchmen, messengers, and informers.[46] Fielding was equally adamant about the allocation of resources to carry out the many tasks of public safety and law enforcement, using public revenues to halt and mitigate crime. Before these initiatives could be fully implemented, Sir Henry Fielding died of at the young age of 47. Shortly thereafter, his half-brother John, the "blind beak of Bow Street," took up his cause and held that office until 1780.[47] Although Henry Fielding outlined the plan and tinkered with the beginning stages of a public crime control paradigm, it was John Fielding who sought application in the practical realm.[48] Just as his brother, Sir John believed in the power of the press and public in the war on crime. He used the *Public Advisor* to print public notices letting citizens of London know that Bow Street's flying squad was able to respond to crimes within a "quarter of an hour's notice." Utilizing the success of Bow Street's more visible and notorious apprehensions, the younger Fielding again placed ads in the *Public Advisor* encouraging the citizenry to contact his Bow Street office with information of any crime. The "Runners" reputation evolved toward legendary status.[49]

John Fielding was just as prolific as his brother in using media sources to persuade the public and enlist their support. Publications on robbery prevention, most wanted lists with physical descriptions, and regular press briefings were part and parcel of his office's operation. As did his brother, Fielding investigated the correlation between crime and its causation.[50] He worked diligently to help boys and girls who lived off of the street and committed crimes and, in particular, girls who frequently turned to prostitution out of necessity. Once Fielding started interviewing the girls, he quickly discovered some of the underlying factors that led to the lifestyle.[51]

John Fielding promoted uniform standards for policing, which would eventually transform the Bow Street system into an organized police force. His plan included many creative components including an office for property and money receipt, a treasurer, and a legal advisor to employees. He stated that all fees and fines collected at different offices should be "collected into one fund," which could then be re-dispersed to pay for expenditures related to the public safety effort. Proposals for stricter licensing of establishments that sold alcohol, stringent controls for pawnbrokers, better street lighting, proper relief of a watchman, and establishment of foot patrols within specific hours were some of his other original recommendations that would surely influence the London police culture.[52]

---

[43] *Ibid*. at 180; Pringle, *supra* note 14, at 77.

[44] Pringle, *supra* note 14, at 97.

[45] *Ibid*. at 107.

[46] H. Goddard, *Memoirs of a Bow Street Runner* xi (Danvers, MA: Morrow, 1957).

[47] Pringle, *supra* note 14, at 114.

[48] Reynolds, *supra* note 23, at 212–216.

[49] See T.S. Surr, *Richmond: Scenes in the Life of a Bow Street Runner* vii (New York, NY: Dover Publications, 1976).

[50] Pringle, *supra* note 14, at 139.

[51] *Ibid*. at 144.

[52] Reynolds, *supra* note 23, at 46–50.

1.3.3 Nineteenth-century England and the Peelian revolution

Despite all the efforts to deter crime, England increasingly faced staggering rates of criminality. While the Bow Street system worked hard, it could not realistically be expected to fully tackle and thwart crime. Without personnel and resources, and given the complexities of urban and industrialized life, the demands for security continued. Self-help theory could not withstand the unceasing number of criminal acts. By the early nineteenth century, England's industrial base had become so sophisticated that cries for the protection of property, goods, and services had become very common. For example, commerce on England's central river, the Thames, had become big business in every sense of the word, and the infrastructure, which would assure its safe passage, did not exist at this time. One of law enforcement's most influential predecessors, Patrick Colquhoun (1745–1820), was the man of the hour on the Thames. His treatise, *The Commerce and the Police of the River Thames*, published in 1800, displays an uncanny understanding of the relationship of commerce and law enforcement.[53] His best-known work on policing is titled *Treatise on the Police of the Metropolis.*

By 1798, The River Thames was considered a center of international trade and one of the world's greatest trading ports. With more than 37,000 employees on the river, many of whom were less than desirable characters, and millions of dollars of goods and services traversing the waters, a system of policing and securing the river had to be established. Colquhoun and Captain John Harriet, who were both magistrates, along with the great utilitarian thinker Jeremy Bentham, a lawyer, devised a plan to implement policing for the River Thames known as the *Marine Police Establishment.*[54] In 1800, Parliament officially enabled the Marine Police granting it an initial seven-year charter. At this stage in law enforcement history, the integration of police and government first becomes apparent. The Marine Police dealt with crimes ranging from theft to murder. Eventually, the Marine Police would merge with London's founding police department—the Metropolitan Police.[55] It was operated for 30 years prior to the 1829 *Metropolitan Police Act*, a task assumed by Sir Robert Peel.[56]

Aside from this structural contribution, Colquhoun continued the criminological and behavioral tendencies evident in his precursors by dwelling on social problems and discussing the role of poverty and education in the rates of crime. As part of his prevention efforts, Colquhoun opened kitchens to feed the poor and maintained a fund to help workers retrieve the tools of their trade from pawnbrokers. Despite these innovations, the matter of security and protection in a complex world still weighed heavily on the ordinary citizenry. A revolution in the delivery of police and security services, led by Sir Robert Peel, was sufficient catalyst to assure change. Sir Robert Peel, the oldest son of a wealthy cotton manufacturer, was educated at Harrow and Oxford University.[57] See Figure 1.1.

A parliamentary seat was acquired for him with his father's money as soon as he became of age in 1809; one year later, he was appointed Undersecretary for War and Colonies, and two years later, he accepted the position of Chief Secretary for Ireland. It was during this term that he introduced the Act of Parliament, which would bring about the formation of the *Irish Peace Preservation Force*. Peel, widely known as the "father of policing," recognized the need for a more effective police force to replace the old watch and ward system as well as the limited capabilities of the Bow Street Runners. He set a standard that allowed the paradigm to continue its evolution in terms of solving problems, refining concepts, and clarifying detailed rules and regulations. Peel believed that by organizing a group of professionally trained full-time police officers, he would be able to reduce the level of crime through proactive prevention techniques instead of relying solely on prevention through punishment. To accomplish this evolutionary process, Peel promulgated new rules for police operations, some of which are included below:

- To prevent crime and disorder
- To recognize that the power of the police is dependent on public approval and respect
- To secure the respect of the public means also securing the cooperation of the public
- To seek and to preserve public favor by constantly demonstrating impartial service to law, without regard to the justice or injustices of individual laws, without regard to wealth or social standing; by exercise of courtesy and friendly good humor; and by offering of individual sacrifice in protecting and preserving life

---

[53] See Colquhoun, *A Treatise on the Commerce and the Police of the River Thames* and *A Treatise on the Police of the Metropolis.* (London, Joseph Mawman, 1800)
[54] Reynolds, *supra* note 23, at 89–92.
[55] *Ibid.* at 194–195.
[56] See *Ibid.* at 211.
[57] *Ibid.* at 211–213.

Figure 1.1   Sir Robert Peel.

- To use physical force only when necessary on any particular occasion for achieving a police objective
- To recognize always the need for strict adherence to police-executive functions
- To recognize always that the test of police efficiency is the absence of crime and disorder[58]

Like his predecessors, Sir Robert Peel passionately believed that it was better to prevent crime from occurring in the first place, then to catch and punish criminals postcommission. In the face of great opposition, Peel ultimately succeeded in getting the necessary laws passed and acquiring the necessary approval to develop London's first real police force on September 29, 1829. Peel's approach was clear and unmistakable when he stated thus:

> It should be understood at the outset that the principle objective to be achieved in policing is the prevention of crime…all the other objectives of a police establishment, will thus be better effected by prevention rather than by detection, apprehension and punishment of the offender as he has succeeded in committing the crime.[59]

This prevention mindset was clearly at the forefront of his policing theories. He was determined to establish a professional police force and ensure that it was an asset to the community. Maintaining the highest standards and implementing effective policies and procedures for his new officers soon followed. From this date forward, England would forego its self-help and protection heritage in favor of the new public bureaucracy, which to this day remains unchallenged. Across the Atlantic, the American experience would blend the Old World in ways unique to its geography, social order, and economic system.

1.4 PRIVATE SECURITY IN THE UNITED STATES

The influence of the English culture and tradition in America is quite evident in our legal system, and especially evident in early colonial law enforcement. Colonial America incorporated the systems of sheriff, constable, and watch as its earliest forms of law enforcement. With subsequent empire building, came further pressure to regularize and formalize the protection system. However, the concept of a uniform police force was still far in the future. George O'Toole contends in his book, *The Private Sector*, that

---

[58] See Reynolds, *supra* note 23.
[59] See *Ibid*.

police, public or private, are not one of America's oldest traditions: the Republic was nearly 70 years old before the first public force was organized, the infant nation had few laws to enforce, and the protection of life and property was largely a do-it-yourself matter in the tiny wilderness communities that made up the frontier.[60]

As in Medieval England and Europe, population and geographic factors in Colonial America favored a loosely structured communal law enforcement system. Generally, the sheriff served in unincorporated areas, and the constables in towns and villages.[61] In Colonial America, the sheriff was charged with the execution of all warrants directed to him, both civil and criminal. He shared with other peace officers special powers of arrest without warrant, but did not serve as an important agent in the detection and prevention of crime.[62] In 1607, the first constable was appointed in Jamestown, Virginia, becoming the first duly appointed law officer in the New World.[63] As in England, the constable's position was difficult to fill. His duties were many and varied, the pay was minimal, the hours were long, and the prestige associated with the job was low.[64] The constable was, however, the main law enforcement officer for the local American government in the 1800s.[65]

The watch system in America was derived as colonists coming to the New World banded together for mutual safety and business protection.[66] The first night watch formed in Boston in 1634.[67] Serving as a watchman was the duty of every male citizen over the age of 18. The tour of duty usually began at 9:00 or 10:00 p.m and ended at sunrise.[68] As in the selection of constables, finding men of high caliber to serve watch was difficult. The powers of the night watch were more limited than those of constables, and they had no policing power and limited arrest authority.[69]

Primarily, the early colonial need for security did not center on proprietary or commercial interests, but on the fear of fire, vagrants, and Indian attacks. As urban populations grew, the system of sheriffs, constables, and the watch proved inadequate in meeting law enforcement needs. The diversity of the original colonies did not promote any concept of uniform law enforcement practices or a national police. Even with increasing urban congestion and a rising crime rate, little would change in American law enforcement. "Watchmen remained familiar figures and constituted the primary security measures until the establishment of full-time police forces in the mid-1800s."[70] The seemingly unchanging organization of colonial American law enforcement was not so much a sign of social stability, but more likely a wariness of any public or national force controlled by a federal government. "The principle of states' rights had a profound and continuing impact upon law enforcement."[71] Americans, especially right after the American Revolution, were leery of any federal entity that sought to control and administrate over state and local matters. Law enforcement and security, like other facets of life, were to be controlled by state and local government, which reflected the "states' rights" mentality of the age and the supremacy of a decentralized federalism. Although local and state jurisdictions might have felt politically comfortable with the watch system of security, other factors necessitated a change in American security practices. As in England, the old systems of law enforcement became outdated and inadequate in facing the security problems of the growing nation. "The basic deficiencies of the watch and constable systems rendered them ill-prepared to deal with the unrest that occurred in many American cities during the first half of the nineteenth century."[72] New methods of organizing and defining public and private law enforcement were needed to combat urban problems.

---

[60] G.J.A. O'toole, *The Private Sector* 21 (W W Norton & Co Inc, 1975).

[61] G.G. Dralla et al., Who's Watching the Watchmen? The Regulation, or Non-Regulation, of America's Largest Law Enforcement Institution, The Private Police, 5 *Golden Gate U. L. Rev.* 442 (1975); see also Rogers, *supra* note 33, at 232–233; Goddard, *supra* note 46; Colquhoun, *supra* note 22.

[62] Lane, *Policing the City*, at 7; Visit the City of Boston Web location to experience the rich history of the Boston Police Department at http://bpdnews.com/history/, last accessed August 26, 2016.

[63] Green, *supra* note 30, at 8.

[64] Richardson, *The New York Police*, at 38.

[65] Lane, *Policing the City*, at 9.

[66] C.F. Hemphill, *Modern Security Methods* 5 (Prentice Hall, 1979).

[67] Bacon, *The Early Development*, at 44.

[68] Hemphill, *supra* note 66, at 5.

[69] Dralla et al., Who's Watching the Watchmen? at 443.

[70] National Advisory Commission on Criminal Justice Standards and Goals, Private Security Task Force Report 30 (1976).

[71] Green, *supra* note 30, at 9.

[72] Dralla et al., Who's Watching the Watchmen? at 443.

The first half of the nineteenth century saw a rise in urbanization, crime, and the need for better law enforcement.[73] Private security existed, but only on a small scale for business and merchant protection. Although private police greatly contributed to keeping the peace, it became obvious, particularly in the cities, that a centralized public police department was a necessity.

The early 1800s witnessed the birth of American policing as a viable peacekeeping force. New York City had started the rudiments of a police department in 1783, and by 1800 had established the first paid daytime police force. Daytime police forces were also started in Philadelphia (1833) and Boston (1838).[74] These early departments did not supplant the system of the watch but worked as the daytime counterpart. Since the day and night watches would prove inadequate in fighting crime, New York City became the first city to combine its day and night watches into a unified police force in 1844.[75] "Other large cities began to follow the lead—Chicago in 1851, New Orleans and Cincinnati in 1852, and Providence in 1864. The snowballing effect stimulated the modernization of American policing."[76]

The rapid development of the modern police force in no way sounded the death knells of private, self-help security. On the contrary, private security forces would continue to grow, expand, and complement other law enforcement agencies in fighting crime.[77] By 1850, the beginnings of a separation of the security function into two spheres of responsibility were taking place. Public police departments, with their sworn duties, were charged with maintaining law and order. The burden of security for private property, assets, and commercial interests, as well as private protection of the person, was assumed by the private security industry.[78] With public police forces centering their efforts on the enforcing of law and order, private security would expand and grow as guardians of the corporate, business, and industrial sector.[79] The growth of the commercial sector, the strained administrations of public law enforcement agencies, and the great westward expansion of America in the 1840s and 1850s led to this dramatic expansion. Public policing simply could not provide the level of protection services necessary for effective business and industry. With interests that often covered vast areas and multiple jurisdictions, businesses and commercial associations began to hire their own protective sources. Here the private sector finds the promise of both present and future opportunity—a place where private police would operate in a world, both different and distinct, from its public counterparts. Some business and commercial sectors felt the need for privatized police service more than others. A few examples of how certain sectors came so heavily to depend on the private sector industry follow.

1.4.1 Railroads, commerce, and the railroad police

The transportation industry, commencing with land-based delivery and courier services, was instrumental in developing the private security industry. For example, Henry Wells and William G. Fargo had established the American Express Company and Wells Fargo in the 1850s as protective services for commercial shipments both in the East and the Far West. Wells Fargo security measures included the use of armed guards, ironclad stagecoaches, and an expert investigative service. However, these services were short-lived as the next century's love affair with the railroad developed.

The railroad industry also had substantial security needs. As the greatest source of commercial transportation of the nineteenth century, railroads were also susceptible to criminal activity. Prior to the Civil War, the railroads contracted with private detective companies, namely the Pinkertons. After the war, the trend was toward developing company-owned internal police forces. The railroad police became instrumental in pursuing train robbers, watching out for petty theft and embezzlement, and securing the trains from unwanted vagrants.[80] On industry-wide problems, the security forces of different railroad companies often cooperated, increasing the security and efficiency of the industry as a whole. Railroad police, with their far-reaching jurisdictions and official powers, would represent the closest America, at this time in history, would ever come to a national police force. During the latter half of the

---

[73] For a fascinating look at entirely western law enforcement, see J. Boessenecker, *Lawman: The Life and Times of Harry Morse, 1835–1912* (Norman, OK: University of Oklahoma Press, 1998).

[74] E. Beckman, *Law Enforcement in a Democratic Society: An Introduction* 34 (Chicago: Nelson-Hall, 1980).

[75] Lipson, *supra* note 29, at 21.

[76] Beckman, *supra* note 74, at 34.

[77] *Ibid.* at 19.

[78] *Ibid.*

[79] E.E. Joh provides a good historical overview at The Paradox of Private Policing, 95 *J. Crim. L. & Criminology* 49 (2004); See also David A. Sklansky, The Private Police, 46 UCLA L. Rev. 1165 (1999).

[80] O'toole, *supra* note 60, at 21–22.

nineteenth century, only the railroad police agencies were with full police powers. In many areas, especially the West, the railway police provided the only security services until effective local government units were established.[81]

1.4.2 Industrialization, the labor movement, and Pinkertons

As the industrial revolution matured, economic interests for both company and worker solidified. To be sure, workers, whether in coal mines or steel works, no longer saw themselves as mere rabble to enrich the elites. Grumblings and rumblings of worker dissatisfaction were commonly heard, particularly in the industrial cities and centers for major industries.[82] Security firms were crucial players in this company–worker dynamic. Allan Pinkerton started the first contract private security agency in America.[83] Scottish immigrant and barrel maker by trade, Pinkerton developed an interest in detective work and had been named the city detective of Chicago in 1849. In 1850, he formed his own North-Western Police Agency, the first private detective agency in America. Capitalizing on the rapid growth of the country's railroad industry, Pinkerton began to contract his security forces to protect the railroads of the Midwest. The Illinois Central, Michigan Central, Michigan Southern and Northern Indiana, Chicago and Galena Union, Chicago and Rock Island, Chicago, Burlington, and Quincy Railroads all utilized Pinkerton's protective services.[84] It was through his association with the railroad industry that Pinkerton met George B. McClellan, vice-president and chief engineer of the Illinois Central Railroad, and later commander in chief of the Union Army during the Civil War. With the outbreak of the Civil War, McClellan would take Pinkerton and his detectives along as the United States' first military intelligence unit. See Figure 1.2.

Pinkerton's early success helped define the role and abilities of the private security industry.[85] For more than 50 years, the "Pinks" were the only officers involved in interstate activities such as the provision of security for transcontinental railroads and multilocation industrial concerns.[86] Pinkerton had definitely developed into the biggest protective service in the United States, but it would be in post–Civil War America where the greatest test for the fledgling industry would take place.

Figure 1.2   Allan Pinkerton.

---

[81] C. Chamberlain, A Short History of Private Security, 4 *Assets Prot.* 38 (1979).
[82] David A. Sklansky, The Private Police, 46 UCLA L. Rev. 1165, 1212 (1999).
[83] Chamberlain, *supra* note 81, at 21.
[84] Lipson, *supra* note 29, at 35.
[85] J.D. Horan, *The Pinkertons: The Detective Dynasty That Made History* 516 (New York, NY: Bonanza Books, 1968).
[86] Chamberlain, *supra* note 81, at 37.

Postwar industrial expansion, fed by an increasing flow of immigrants, also helped Pinkerton's business. With growth came labor unrest and movements to organize workers. In the strife that ensued, the use of private security guards to combat efforts to unionize became commonplace. Pinkerton and his company were used by industry, especially railroads and mining groups.[87]

As America was immersed in its industrial revolution, a growing consensus of American laborers, usually immigrants who toiled in the mines and mills, worked for the development of labor representation. In many instances, management refused to bargain with labor organizations and would send in strikebreakers to dismiss the mobs. On the other hand, labor unions and secret societies often used unethical tactics in their determination to change unfair labor practices. Pinkertons, Baldwin–Felts, and others were often hired by business management to disrupt and disband labor activities.[88]

One of the first labor disputes the Pinkerton Company contracted out for involved the Molly Maguires. The Molly Maguires was a secret society that originated out of nineteenth-century Ireland, a country then racked by poverty and hunger. Their life in America had improved little as they toiled in the coal mines of northeastern Pennsylvania. Pinkerton used undercover agents such as James McParland, who lived and worked with the Molly Maguires under the assumed name Jim McKennon, from 1873 to 1886. It was McParland's subsequent testimony in a murder trial, changing certain important players in the organization that effectively ended the Molly Maguires as an effective labor organization. At the same time in southern West Virginia, the Baldwin–Felts Detective Service was assigned by management to uphold justice and disband union experts in the coal mining towns.[89]

Another landmark labor-management dispute that involved the Pinkerton Agency was the Homestead Steel Strike of 1892.[90] In July 1892, workers at the Carnegie Steel Company in Homestead, Pennsylvania went on strike, protesting a proposed pay cut set forth by Carnegie Steel's new manager, Henry Clay Frick. Frick cited poor business as the reason for the designed wage cuts. Instead of acquiescence to management's demands, the striking steel workers blockaded and fortified the steel plant. In response, Frick secretly ordered his hired Pinkerton men to regain control of the plant. As 300 armed Pinkerton guards attempted to sneak up the river side of the plant, an estimated 10,000 angry steelworkers confronted the Pinkerton force. In the intense battle that ensued, eight were killed (three Pinkerton officers and five steelworkers). The Pinkerton officers were surrounded, forced to surrender, and were physically escorted to the railroad station. The Homestead Massacre was a debacle that ultimately hurt the image of private security agencies, and for a time the Pinkerton Company. The name Pinkerton became synonymous with labor spying and strikebreaking during the late nineteenth and early twentieth centuries. Its image was so badly tarnished that a House Judiciary Subcommittee began a formal investigation of Pinkerton and the private security industry in 1892. In 1893, the House passed the Pinkerton Law, which stated thus: "an individual employed by the Pinkerton Detective Agency, or similar organization, may not be employed by the government of the United States or the government of the District of Columbia."[91] In the aftermath of the Pinkerton Law, Pinkerton announced it would no longer take sides in any labor disputes. Again, the roles and parameters of the private security industry were being redefined. Strikebreaking was out and labor surveillance within legitimate bounds was in.

1.4.3 Private security and the expansion of the American West

With Pinkerton controlling the security and investigative services of the railroads, and Wells Fargo controlling the stages, law enforcement in the towns and territories of the American West was largely in the hands of sheriffs or private individuals. The ancient legal tenet of self-help saw its last vestiges of practice in the American West. As the guilds and businesses had done in a previous age, western businessmen, traders, bankers, and ranchers banded together for mutual benefit. "Business sponsorship of law enforcement started with the earliest days of the frontier… railroads, ranchers, mining concerns, oil field operators—all established their own investigating and law enforcement agencies."[92]

---

[87] Lipson, *supra* note 29, at 27.

[88] *Ibid.* at 28.

[89] Hadsell & Coffey, From Law and Order to Chaos Warfare: Baldwin-Felts Detectives in the S.W. Virginia Coal Mines, 40 *W. Va. Hist.* 268–286 (1979).

[90] Lipson, *supra* note 29, at 28.

[91] O'toole, *supra* note 60, at 21–22.

[92] Prassel, *supra* note 9, at 132.

In some cases, private security was provided by an association of businesses in the same area of commerce. A system of Merchant Police was formed in the towns and cities to safeguard mercantile interests. Cattle ranchers in the West joined forces to create associations that frequently employed agents to prevent and investigate cattle rustling.[93] These detectives, although paid by private groups, were often given official state or territorial recognition, and sometimes were given powers as official public law enforcement officers. Detective forces, each specializing in various forms of business and trade, appeared on the western scene in increasing numbers. F. Prassel's work, *The Western Peace Officer*, described their purpose: "At their worst, such security organizations constituted a combination of the protection racket and violence for hire…At its best, a private detective force could provide real services with integrity and discretion."[94]

By contemporary standards, western justice and law enforcement had less regard for procedural due process. Vigilantes, private individuals with no formal authority acting in self-interest or in the interests of a specific group, served as enforcers. The first American vigilantes, the South Carolina Regulators, appeared in 1767, but only really flourished after 1850.[95] Both the Los Angeles and San Francisco police departments originated as volunteer vigilante forces.[96] "The true vigilante movement was in social conformance with established procedures and patterns of structural leadership."[97] This was not often the case, as abuses of legal power became commonplace. Wyoming had such a distrust of private security forces as to adopt a statute in 1889, which stated thus: "No armed police force, or detective agency, or armed body, or unarmed body of men, shall ever be brought into this state, for the suppression of domestic violence, except upon the application of the legislature, or executive, when the legislature cannot be convened."[98] Other western states passed similar laws in attempts to curb abuses by private individuals or security forces. For many years, only private security forces served as the quasi-law enforcement agencies in the West. All major transportation systems and various commercial interests were protected by private security forces in one way or another.

1.4.4 Private security and World War II

World War II and the years that followed would have a profound effect on the type, organization, and need for American private security. The secrecy and vulnerability of war usually brings a demand for more internal security. With the dual need for fighting soldiers and security protection, the government could not solely rely on the depleted ranks of the local and state police. "Wartime requirements compelled local police establishments, already strapped because their young men had gone to war, to take on tasks beyond those it normally assumed. Industrial plants, drinking water and its sources, utilities and their transmission lines, and other vital services had to be guarded."[99]

With these massive security problems facing the United States, thousands of men and women served their country in the ranks of private security forces. By war's end, over 200,000 individual private security personnel had worked for the government.[100] With the end of World War II, the importance and usefulness of private security personnel would be a given, and the need for various forms of security increased dramatically. The Private Security Task Force of 1976 claims that, "after the war, the use of private security services and products expanded from an area of defense contractors to encompass all segments of the private-public sectors."[101]

The United States assuming the status of a world power heightened security problems and increased political and governmental suspicion and secrecy. Cold War reality and rumor led to an increased use of private security forces to protect government installations and secrets. Protection against information theft also became a growing security field. The fears of the 1950s allowed former FBI agent George R. Wachenhut and three other former agents to found the Wachenhut Corporation.[102] See Figure 1.3.

---

[93] *Ibid.* at 126–149.

[94] *Ibid.* at 133.

[95] L.M. Friedman, *The Development of American Law* 17 (Touchstone, 1979).

[96] *Ibid.* at 18–19.

[97] Prassel, *supra* note 9, at 131.

[98] See *Ibid.* for an interesting discussion.

[99] Lipson, *supra* note 29, at 42.

[100] Green, *supra* note 30, at 12.

[101] National Advisory Commission, *supra* note 70, at 35.

[102] O'toole, *supra* note 60, at 30; see also Wesley, Thirty Years of Security: An Overview, 4 *J. Sec. Admin.* 26 (1981); W.C. Cunningham, J.J. Strauchs, & C.W. Van Meter, *Private Security: Patterns and Trends* (National Institute of Justice, 1991); see also R. van Stedena & R. Sarre, The Growth of Private Security: Trends in the European Union, 20 *Sec. J.* 222–235 (2007).

Figure 1.3 Wachenhut badge.

With a long list of experienced personnel, the Wachenhut Corporation grew to be one of the largest private security contractors in the United States. Remarkably, Wachenhut was also able to skirt the previous legislative intention of the Pinkerton Law of 1893 by gaining security contracts for government installations, including NASA and the Department of Defense.

1.5 THE CONTEMPORARY STATE OF PRIVATE SECURITY

Since World War II and the Cold War, the private security industry has faced steady growth. "Private security personnel also significantly outnumber sworn law enforcement personnel and nonmilitary government guards by nearly 2 to 1."[103] Today, the public interacts with and depends upon a private sector model whose tentacles reach into every aspect of communal living. American Society for Industrial Security (ASIS) International sees the opportunities present in the field now and in the future, and states that the

> demand for heightened security is being increased by theft of information, workplace violence, terrorism and white collar crime. The security industry in the US is a $100 billion a year business and growing. Opportunities exist at all levels with the security industry. All businesses, no matter how small, have security concerns such as fraud, theft computer hacking, economic espionage or workplace violence.[104]

The developing complexity of the world marketplace, the technological evolution of goods, services, and the transference of money and other negotiable instruments, served as a catalyst to private security growth. By way of example, ponder the cyclonic revolution in the banking industry, from ATM machines to paperless checks, from wire transactions to credit card issuances. All of these practices are essentially novel, and at the same time, the subject of some inventive criminality. Here is where the future resides—in a system rooted in private prevention and protection, aligned with the public police model.[105] In the future, more collaboration will be witnessed in the crime scene, the terrorist investigation or the public facility. At present, the list of security functions assumed by the private sector

---

[103] Total private security employment in 1982 is conservatively estimated at 1.1 million persons (excluding federal, civil, and military security workers), 449,000 in propriety security and 641,000 in contract security. These rises continue unabated throughout the Western World. Our neighbors to the north have seen a shrinking to stagnant public police model replaced by a vibrant private policing system. See Government of Canada, Statistics Canada website, Table 1: Police Officers, Private Investigators and Security Guards, Canada 1991, 1996, 2001, and 2006, at http://www.statcan.gc.ca/pub/85-002-x/2008010/article/10730/tbl/tbl1-eng.htm, last accessed August 26, 2016.

[104] For more information, see American Society for Industrial Security, Professional Development—What is Security? at http://www.asisonline.org/careerwhat.html, last accessed October 10, 2002.

[105] The growth, internationally, has been equally dramatic. See J. De Waard, The Private Security Industry in International Perspective, 7 *Eur. J. Crim. Pol'y & Res.* 143, 1999.

continues its unabated growth. No longer will the public and community merely look only to the FBI, the ATF, or state and local police to carry out myriad tasks.

The private security industry possesses an unflappable inertia that will increasingly weave its way into areas of public safety and security.[106] Public policing and safety entities will welcome the assistance. In housing and apartment complexes, in state and federal installations, at military facilities and correctional locales, at traffic intersections and public transportation settings, and in executive protection details and arson/explosives assessments, this is an industry that scoffs at caricatures in the mold of rent-a-cops or retired, unenergetic police, donut in hand. Frank MacHovec calls all security services police functions that are not performed by police.[107] This is an industry on the cutting edge of technology and operational policy. This is industry public law enforcement now often envies.[108] Less burdened with regulation and free from excessive constitutional oversight and political interference witnessed in public law enforcement, and driven by efficiencies and corporate creativity, the security industry can only march forward.

Private security engages citizens even more than its public counterpart. And it has done so without the fanfare to match its astonishing rise. David Sklansky's, *The Private Police*, targets the central implications.

> For most lawyers and scholars, private security is terra incognita—wild, unmapped, and largely unexplored…Increasingly, though, government agencies are hiring private security personnel to guard and patrol government buildings, housing projects, and public parks and facilities, and a small but growing number of local governments have begun to experiment with broader use of private police.[109]

The Quiet Revolution[110] of private security could not have greater impact.[111] More than ever, the enormous public demands piled upon the private security industry call for professional planning and policy making, and a renewed dedication to the advancement of this dynamic industry. Combine technology with a rampant wave of economic crime, and the climate of accommodation to the private security industry could not be better.

Private sector police come into the equation with far less baggage and a willingness to respond rapidly. Herein is the genius of cooperation, the shared and mutually learned experience. Underlying this text's entire approach is the heartfelt belief that private security should be rooted firmly in the American system of law and order, not be treated as an afterthought where the bones and scraps of undesirable public police functions are tossed out. This enterprise ennobles both its members and constituents. The private sector allows an entire nation to exist and operate by fulfilling its public responsibility through private means.

Indeed, the private sector philosophy is part and parcel of the American tradition. Self-help, self-reliance, and self-protection are not mere slogans but a way of life in the American experience.[112] Self-help and self-protection signify the essence of free people who do not await public law enforcement's reaction to crime, but display the moral courage and will to protect their own. The greatness of a nation directly correlates to the willingness of its citizenry to stand up and resist the way of life that crime brings. This is true in the state, the nation, the neighborhood, and the business district.[113]

---

[106] C.P. Nemeth & K.C. Poulin, *The Prevention Agency: A Public Safety Model for High Crime Communities in the 21st Century* (California, PA: California University of Pennsylvania, 2004); C.P. Nemeth & K.C. Poulin, *Private Security and Public Safety: A Community-Based Approach* (Englewood Cliffs, NJ: Prentice Hall, 2004).

[107] F. Machovec, *Security Services, Security Science* 11 (Springfield, IL: Charles C. Thomas, 1992).

[108] Despite the envy from afar, status perceptions are often vastly different. Deborah Michael's study of security officer shows a negative self-image as "junior partners" when compared to public police officers. D. Michael, The Levels of Orientation Security Officers Have towards a Public Policing Function, *Sec. J.* 33 (1999).

[109] David A. Sklansky, The Private Police, 46 UCLA L. Rev. 1165, 1177 (1999).

[110] *Ibid.* at 1171.

[111] ASIS International, Groundbreaking Study Finds U.S. Security Industry to Be $350 Billion Market, August 12, 2013, at https://www.asisonline.org/News/Press-Room/Press-Releases/2013/Pages/Groundbreaking-Study-Finds-U.S.-Security-Industry-to-be-$350-Billion-Market.aspx.

[112] Nemeth, *supra* note 16, at 1.

[113] Carl F. Horowitz, in his work, An Empowerment Strategy for Eliminating Neighborhood Crime, highlights the power of the private sector on business and community and establishes the fundamental reason why the private sector is so vital to the control of crime: "Local residents, fearing crime, are unwilling to patronize neighborhood businesses during evening hours. Business owners may be willing to bear the risk of crime in order to attract evening customers, but if residents are too frightened to shop, many of the businesses will not survive. As a result, many inner city residents no longer enjoy the convenience of having neighborhood stores. A lengthy trip thus may be required for groceries, clothing, and other household goods."

In business and industry, the private security industry shines since it operates from the same vantage point. Firms that specialize in protection services can visualize how and why communities live and die, thrive, and disintegrate. By providing preventative and protective services to private interests, the private practitioner is ultimately securing the stability of the community. Few would argue this is not a primordial public responsibility. On top of this, there is an emerging preference for private sector involvement in American foreign policy. Throughout the Middle East, in Iraq and Afghanistan, the footprint of the private security industry could not be more apparent.[114] Labeled either as private military specialists or the "dogs of war" mercenaries will say much about the tension this new dimension causes. For those in favor, the private sector soldier provides "great flexibility, with an ability to create unique solution for each case, knowledge about the problem area and operational expertise, business integrity, secure confidentiality, and a generally apolitical nature."[115] Critics charge that the privatized military operations "exploit violence for personal gain, serve as agents for unsavory power, or happily promote repression, turmoil, and human rights violations…"[116] Neither of these cases is fully accurate, and the caricature that the Blackwater firm has turned into provides a poor illustration of this new and emerging dynamic.[117] The role of private security firms play in armed conflicts is a natural progression of mission and privatization.[118]

Whole-scale security systems in the war on terror have come to depend on the private sector system. The fit of private sector justice in the world of military action seems at first glance rather odd, yet the deeper the correlation is considered, the more sense it makes. Private security companies now "possess great flexibility, with an ability to create unique solutions for each case, knowledge about the problem area and operational expertise, business integrity, secure confidentiality and a general apolitical nature."[119] Put another way, the private security industry can provide a mercenary force that sees the problem dispassionately and as a result, is an agency more reasonable and rational in outlook.

This turning over of the guard, whether it be executive protection, private prison processing, community and neighborhood intelligence, diplomatic protection, to name just a few functions, manifests a change in the overall paradigm.[120] In both war and peace, one witnesses the staggering interlocking of a private justice model in public functions.

Privatization is now predictable nomenclature in the world of public policy and the delivery of governmental services. Coming full circle, legislators and policymakers now evaluate programs and their delivery in light of outsourcing, private contracts, delegable services, and partnerships with the private sector. No longer is this sort of thinking on the fringe. Although the shift has now become self-evident, the transition troubles many.[121] The National Institute of Justice has insightfully discerned the shift back to privatized justice in the form of nonpublic law enforcement:

> Such expanded use of private security and increased citizen involvement signals an increasing return to the private sector for protection against crime. The growth and expansion of modern police reflected a shift from private policing and security initiatives of the early nineteenth century. Now the pendulum appears to be swinging back. Despite the expanded role of the police in crime prevention in recent years, it appears that the private sector will bear an increased prevention role while law enforcement concentrates more heavily on violent crimes and crime response. Economic realities are forcing law enforcement to seek ways to reduce workloads.[122]

---

[114] E.L. Gaston, Mercenarism 2.0? The Rise of the Modern Private Security Industry and Its Implications for International Humanitarian Law Enforcement, 49 *Harv. Int'l L. J.* 221 (2008), at http://www.harvardilj.org/2008/01/issue_49-1_gatson.

[115] R. Mandel, The Privatization of Security, 28 *Armed Forces Soc.* 129, 132 (2001); see also J.S. Press, Crying Havoc over the Outsourcing of Soldier and Democracy's Slipping Grip on the Dogs of War, 103 *Nw. U. L. Rev.* 109 (2008).

[116] Mandel, The Privatization of Security, at 129.

[117] M. Calaguas, Military Privatization: Efficiency or Anarch? 6 *Chi.-Kent J. Int'l Comp. L.* 58 (2006).

[118] J. Cadieux, Regulating the United States Private Army: Militarizing Security Contractors, 39 *Cal. W. Int'l L. J.* 197 (2008).

[119] Mandel, The Privatization of Security, at 132.

[120] C. Kinsey, *Corporate Soldiers and International Security, The Rise of Private Military Companies* (Routledge, 2006); T. Jäger & G. Kümmel, *Private Military and Security: Companies Chances, Problems, Pitfalls and Prospects* (VS Verlag für Sozialwissenschaften, 2007).

[121] S.M. Sullivan, Private Force/Public Goods, 42 *Conn. L. Rev.* 853, 857–858 (2010); See also E. Dannin, Red Tape or Accountability: Privatization, Public-ization, and Public Values, 15 *Cornell J. L. & Pub. Pol'y* 111, 113 (2005); J. Freeman, The Contracting State, 28 *Fla. St. U. L. Rev.* 155, 170 (2000); C.P. Gillette & P.B. Stephan III, Constitutional Limitations on Privatization, 46 *Am. J. Comp. L.* 481, 490 (Supp. 1998); D.A. Super, Privatization, Policy Paralysis, and the Poor, 96 *Cal. L. Rev.* 393, 409–410 (2008).

[122] William C. Cunningham and Todd H. Taylor, Private Security and Police in America: The Hallcrest Report (Portland, OR: Chancellor Press, 1985).

In the final analysis, there is something empowering about this reality, and as some have described a "participatory democratic self-government."[123] In what greater sense does the citizen bear responsibility for the world around them than when that citizen assumes the responsibility of self-help and self-protection?

It appears private security's role in the administration of American justice is both multifaceted and entrenched. Its areas of service not only entail private, individual, or property security, but loss prevention, insurance, military intelligence, and related functions, as well as computer security. Security as a practice, process, and system is embedded in the nation's tradition and is an essential contributor to justice in modern America.

1.6 CLASSIFICATIONS AND FUNCTIONS OF THE PRIVATE SECURITY INDUSTRY

The private security industry weaves its threads into every corner of the American experience. Whether by individual delivery, proprietary service, or under a contractual agreement for services, private security touches every aspect of economic life. Contractual services, whereby money is paid for specific security services, promotes safety and security in a host of locales and settings.

> The "private contractual security services" industry encompasses guards, private investigative services, central-station alarm monitoring, armored transport and ATM servicing, security consulting and data security and private correctional facility management services. Niche markets also exist for a wide range of specialized security services, including: bomb sweeps and metal detection; drug testing; pre-employment screening; renting of site secure vaults; radon and hazardous gas testing; and guard dog services.[124]

Proprietary security services deliver similar results. The proprietary sector offers services directly to the public from property protection to private background checks, from fraud prevention systems to banking security controls. Propriety security reflects the ingenuity and brilliance of its inventors[125] with a surge of private investigators, computer and tech crime specialists, anti-terrorism practitioners, and executive protection specialists. The security industry, according to its premier professional association, the American Society of Industrial Security, breaks down the private security industry into four major disciplines:

Physical security focuses on the protection of people, property, and facilities through the use of security forces, security systems, and security procedures. Physical security personnel oversee proprietary or contract uniformed security operations, identify security system requirements, assess internal and external threats to assets, and develop policies, plans, procedures, and physical safeguards to counter those threats. Physical security can include the use of barriers, alarms, locks, access control systems, protective lighting, closed circuit televisions, and other state-of-the-art security technology.

Information security involves safeguarding sensitive information. Although information security has traditionally been associated with the protection of U.S. Government classified information, it can also include privacy data, proprietary information, contractual information, and intellectual property. Information security deals with issues such as who should access the data and how the data are stored, controlled, marked, disseminated, and disposed of.

Personnel security deals with ensuring the integrity and reliability of an organization's workforce. Personnel security encompasses background investigations, drug testing, and other pre-employment screening techniques, as well as adjudication of results and granting security clearances and other information access privileges.

Information systems security involves maintaining the confidentiality, reliability, and availability of data created, stored, processed, and/or transmitted via automated information systems. Information systems security personnel develop procedures and safeguards to protect against hackers and other unauthorized efforts to access data, viruses, and a number of other threats to information systems.[126]

---

[123] D.A. Sklansky, Private Police and Democracy, 43 *Am. Crim. L. Rev.* 89 (2006).

[124] P.S. Bailin & S.G. Cort, Industry Corner: Private Contractual Security Services: The U.S. Market and Industry, 31 *Bus. Econ.* 57 (Ap. 1996).

[125] See Pinkerton Security Services USA, at http://www.pinkertons.com/security/together.asp, last accessed 10/30/02, for information on the merger of Pinkerton, Securitas, and Burns Security.

[126] American Society for Industrial Safety, Professional Development—Security Disciplines, at http://www.asisonline.org/careerdisc.html, © ASIS.

Within the major areas, security breaks down into specialties and an endless array of subfields including but not limited to

- Educational institution security
- Financial services security
- Gaming/wagering security
- Government industrial security
- Healthcare security
- Information systems security
- Lodging security
- Manufacturing security
- Retail security
- Security sales, equipment, and services
- Transportation security
- Utilities security[127]

The National Criminal Justice Reference Service's recent study of the industry lays out the placement of security professionals by these and other classification. See Figure 1.4.[128]

Each sector has its own occupational needs and demands continuously seeking out those with specialized knowledge and experience in these diverse sectors. The private security industry can also be further classified and typed by its range of occupational roles and opportunities that service across many of these sectors, which will be discussed in more detail in Chapter 3. A cursory review is given in the following sections.

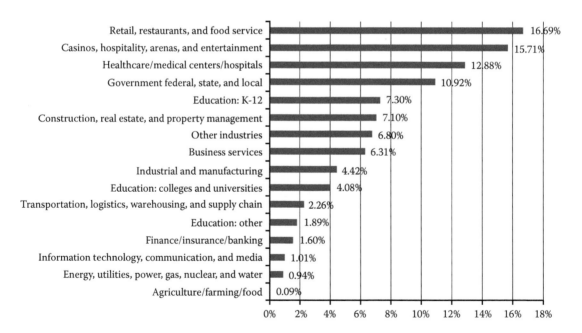

Figure 1.4 Number of proprietary security officers per employee by industry sector, 2009. (From Occupational Employment Statistics [OES] Survey [BLS, 2010c].)

---

[127] American Society for Industrial Safety, Professional Development—Security Specialty Areas, at http://www.asisonline.org/careerspecialty.html, © ASIS.

[128] K. Strom et al., *The Private Security Industry: A Review of the Definitions, Available Data Sources, and Paths Moving Forward* 4–12 (Washington, DC: Bureau of Justice Statistics, 2010).

Figure 1.5 ESA logo.

1.6.1 Unarmed officers

Whether in a business or a neighborhood community, private security professionals operate in a patrol capacity. Surveying, detecting, deterring, and integrating patrol, whether by foot, bicycle, or vehicle, open the door to communal and commercial life.

1.6.2 Alarm companies

Web Exercise: Find out about the many publications of the Electronic Security Association (ESA) at http://www.esaweb.org/?page=Pubs. See Figure 1.5.

1.6.3 Private investigators

The National Council of Investigation & Security Services is a collective of companies and associations that monitors the activities and advocates for the *investigation* and guard industries (Figure 1.6).

1.6.4 Campus law enforcement and educational institutions

Web Exercise: Visit the International Association of Campus Law Enforcement Administration at http://www.iaclea.org/.

1.6.5 Retail/industrial

In short, the retail and commercial interest remain at the heart of this magnificent enterprise and display little if no signs of change. Private sector justice protects assets in the free enterprise system.

1.7 ETHICAL ISSUES ENDEMIC TO THE SECURITY INDUSTRY

The true test of professionalism should be its unwavering dedication to ethical conduct, professional values, and occupational integrity. It is common knowledge that the industry has grappled with standards for a long time and

Figure 1.6 National Council of Investigation & Security Services logo.

has yet to announce or promulgate nationalized standards that are uniformly agreed to. While there are associations and governmental entities that issue general guidance, the diversity of approaches is quite dizzying for those hoping for uniform stands. Many states, within their larger oversight function, describe and outline conduct that is unlawful and thus unethical. Chapter 3 will examine a host of examples. At the association, professional member bodies and other groups appear the greatest opportunity for an ethical consensus. The industry's chief professional association, ASIS, has done an admirable though incomplete job in the matter of professional ethics. The ASIS International code of ethics is reproduced to demonstrate the continuing correlation between the professional duties and the framing of ethical standards. See Figure 1.7.[129]

The National Council of Investigators and Security Services publishe a well-rounded and reasoned code of ethics for security professionals. Its language and purpose gets right to the heart of the matter, forcing employees to think about how services are delivered both professionally and ethically.

National Council of Investigation and Security Services (NCISS) code of ethics

- A member shall provide professional services in accordance with local, state, and federal laws.
- A member shall observe, and adhere to the precepts of honesty, integrity, and truthfulness.
- A member shall be truthful, diligent, and honorable in the discharge of their professional responsibilities.
- A member shall honor each client contract, adhering to all responsibilities by providing ethical services within the limits of the law.
- A member shall safeguard confidential information and exercise the utmost care to prevent any unauthorized disclosure of such information.
- A member shall refrain from improper and unethical solicitation of business, including false or misleading claims or advertising.
- A member shall use due diligence to ensure that all employees and coworkers adhere to this same code of ethical conduct; respecting all persons, performing the job diligently, and working within the limits of the law.
- A member shall never knowingly cause harm or defame the professional reputation or practice of colleagues, clients, employers, or any member of the NCISS.
- A member shall never undertake an assignment that is contrary to the Constitution of the United States of America or the security interests of this country.[130]

On the employer front, companies play a critical role in setting out professional and ethical expectations. Securitas International, formerly Pinkerton's Security Inc., a massive security service provider, also publishes its values and ethics for its businesses and employees.[131]

Web Exercise: Visit Securitas to discover the full range of ethical insights the company urges its employees to adhere to at http://www.securitas.com/globalassets/com/files/csr/values-and-ethics/en/securitas-values-and-ethics.pdf.

At the other edge of the regulatory continuum will reside federal, state, and local regulatory authority, which promulgates instruction on acceptable professional behavior. Some governmental entities do this by regulatory boards, or by and through state police agencies or other agency. For example, the State of Maryland oversees the licensing

---

[129] American Society for Industrial Security, Code of Ethics, at https://www.asisonline.org/About-ASIS/Pages/Code-of-Ethics.aspx, last accessed August 26, 2016; see also R. Gallati, *Introduction to Private Security* 181–182 (Englewood Cliffs, NJ: Prentice Hall, 1983). © (2017) ASIS International, 1625 Prince Street, Alexandria, VA 22314. Reprinted by permission.

[130] National Council of Investigation and Security Services website at http://www.nciss.org/about-us/nciss-code-of-ethics.php, last accessed April 26, 2017.

[131] Securitas International website at http://www.securitasinc.com/en/who-we-are/about-securitas-usa/Mission-and-Values/, last accessed April 26, 2017.

Code of Ethics

Aware that the quality of professional security activity ultimately depends upon the willingness of practitioners to observe special standards of conduct and to manifest good faith in professional relationships, ASIS adopts the following Code of Ethics and mandates its conscientious observance as a binding condition of membership in or affiliation with ASIS:

ARTICLE I

A member shall perform professional duties in accordance with the law and the highest moral principles.

Ethical Considerations

1-1 A member shall abide by the law of the land in which the services are rendered and perform all duties in an honorable manner.

1-2 A member shall not knowingly become associated in responsibility for work with colleagues who do not conform to the law and these ethical standards.

1-3 A member shall be just and respect the rights of others in performing professional responsibilities.

ARTICLE II

A member shall observe the precepts of truthfulness, honesty, and integrity.

Ethical Considerations

2-1 A member shall disclose all relevant information to those having a right to know.

2-2 A "right to know" is a legally enforceable claim or demand by a person for disclosure of information by a member. This right does not depend upon prior knowledge by the person of the existence of the information to be disclosed.

2-3 A member shall not knowingly release misleading information, nor encourage or otherwise participate in the release of such information.

ARTICLE III

A member shall be faithful and diligent in discharging professional responsibilities.

Ethical Considerations

3-1 A member is faithful when fair and steadfast in adherence to promises and commitments.

3-2 A member is diligent when employing best efforts in an assignment.

3-3 A member shall not act in matters involving conflicts of interest without appropriate disclosure and approval.

3-4 A member shall represent services or products fairly and truthfully.

ARTICLE IV

A member shall be competent in discharging professional responsibilities.

Ethical Considerations

4-1 A member is competent who possesses and applies the skills and knowledge required for the task.

4-2 A member shall not accept a task beyond the member's competence nor shall competence be claimed when not possessed.

ARTICLE V

A member shall safeguard confidential information and exercise due care to prevent its improper disclosure.

Ethical Considerations

5-1 Confidential information is nonpublic information, the disclosure of which is restricted.

5-2 Due care requires that the professional must not knowingly reveal confidential information or use a confidence to the disadvantage of the principal or to the advantage of the member or a third person unless the principal consents after full disclosure of all the facts. This confidentiality continues after the business relationship between the member and his principal has terminated.

5-3 A member who receives information and has not agreed to be bound by confidentiality is not bound from disclosing it. A member is not bound by confidential disclosures of acts or omissions that constitute a violation of the law.

5-4 Confidential disclosures made by a principal to a member are not recognized by law as privileged in a legal proceeding. In a legal proceeding, the member may be required to testify to information received in confidence from his principal over the objection of his principal's counsel.

5-5 A member shall not disclose confidential information for personal gain without appropriate authorization.

ARTICLE VI

A member shall not maliciously injure the professional reputation or practice of colleagues, clients, or employers.

Ethical Considerations

6-1 A member shall not comment falsely and with malice concerning a colleague's competence, performance, or professional capabilities.

6-2 A member who knows, or has reasonable grounds to believe, that another member has failed to conform to Code of Ethics of ASIS should inform the Ethical

Standards Council in accordance with Article VIII of the Bylaws.

Figure 1.7 ASIS International code of ethics.

Maine Statutory Authority in Unlawful Conduct. Title 32, Section 9412.

1. *Acting without license; false representations.* It is a Class D crime for any person knowingly to commit any of the following acts:
   A. Subject to section 9404, to act as a security guard without a valid license;
   B. To publish any advertisement, letterhead, circular, statement or phrase of any kind which suggests that a licensee is an official police agency or any other agency, instrumentality or division of this State, any political subdivision thereof, or of the Federal Government;
   C. To falsely represent that a person is or was in his employ as a licensee;
   D. To make any false statement or material omission in any application, any documents made a part of the application, any notice or any statement filed with the commissioner; or
   E. To make any false statement or material omission relative to the requirements of section 9410-A, subsection 1, in applying for a position as a security guard with a contract security company.
2. *Failure to return equipment; representation as peace officer.* It is a Class D crime for any security guard knowingly to commit any of the following acts:
   A. To fail to return immediately on demand, or within 7 days of termination of employment, any uniform, badge, or other item of equipment issued to him by an employer;
   B. To make any representation which suggests, or which would reasonably cause another person to believe, that he is a sworn peace officer of this State, any political subdivision thereof, or of any other state or of the Federal Government;
   C. To wear or display any badge, insignia, device, shield, patch or pattern which indicates or suggests that he is a sworn peace officer, or which contains or includes the word "police" or the equivalent thereof, or is similar in wording to any law enforcement agency; or
   D. To possess or utilize any vehicle or equipment displaying the words "police," "law enforcement officer," or the equivalent thereof, or have any sign, shield, marking, accessory or insignia that may indicate that the vehicle is a vehicle of a public law enforcement agency.

Paragraph A does not apply to any proprietary security organization or any employee thereof.

3. *Representations as to employees; failure to surrender license; posting of license.* It is a Class D crime for any person licensed under this chapter knowingly to commit any of the following acts:
   A. To falsely represent that a person was or is in his employ as a security guard;
   B. To fail or refuse to surrender his license to the commissioner within 72 hours following revocation or suspension of the license; or after the licensee ceases to do business subject to section 9410;
   C. To post the license or permit the license to be posted upon premises other than those described in the license; or
   D. To fail to cause the license to be posted and displayed at all times, within 72 hours of receipt of the license, in a conspicuous place in the principal office of the licensee within the State.
4. *Other unlawful acts.* It is a Class D crime for any person licensed under this chapter, or for any employee thereof, knowingly to commit any of the following acts:
   A. To incite, encourage or aid any person who has become a party to any strike to commit any unlawful act against any person or property;
   B. To incite, stir up, create or aid in the inciting of discontent or dissatisfaction among the employees of any person with the intention of having them strike;
   C. To interfere with or prevent lawful and peaceful picketing during strikes;
   D. To interfere with, restrain or coerce employees in the exercise of their right to form, join or assist any labor organization of their own choosing;
   E. To interfere with or hinder lawful or peaceful collective bargaining between employers and employees;
   F. To pay, offer to give any money, gratuity, consideration or other thing of value, directly or indirectly, to any person for any verbal or written report of the lawful activities of employees in the exercise of their right to organize, form or assist any labor organization and to bargain collectively through representatives of their own choosing;
   G. To advertise for, recruit, furnish or replace or offer to furnish or replace for hire or reward, within or outside the State, any skilled or unskilled help or labor, armed guards, other than armed guards employed for the protection of payrolls, property or premises, for service upon property which is being operated in anticipation of or during the course or existence of a strike;
   H. To furnish armed guards upon the highways for persons involved in labor disputes;
   I. To furnish or offer to furnish to employers or their agents any arms, munitions, tear gas implements or any other weapons;
   J. To send letters or literature to employers offering to eliminate labor unions; or K. To advise any person of the membership of an individual in a labor organization for the purpose of preventing the individual from obtaining or retaining employment.
5. *Dangerous weapons at labor disputes and strikes.* It is a Class D crime for any person, including, but not limited to, security guards and persons involved in a labor dispute or strike, to be armed with a dangerous weapon, as defined in Title 17-A, section 2, subsection 9, at the site of a labor dispute or strike. A person holding a valid permit to carry a concealed handgun is not exempt from this subsection. A security guard is exempt from this subsection to the extent that federal laws, rules or regulations require the security guard to be armed with a dangerous weapon at the site of a labor dispute or strike.
6. *Class E crimes.* It is a Class E crime for any person licensed under this chapter or for any employee of such a person, to knowingly commit any of the following acts:
   A. To perform or attempt to perform security guard functions at the site of a labor dispute or strike while not physically located on property leased, owned, possessed or rented by the person for whom the licensee is providing security guards.

Figure 1.8   Maine statutory authority in unlawful conduct.

---

§ 3181. Unprofessional conduct

1. It shall be unprofessional conduct for a licensee, registrant, or applicant to engage in conduct prohibited by this section, or by 3 V.S.A. § 129a.
2. Unprofessional conduct means any of the following:
   a. Conviction of any felony or a crime involving fraud or dishonesty.
   b. Failing to make available, upon request of a person using the licensee's services, copies of documents in the possession or under the control of the licensee, when those documents have been prepared for and purchased by the user of services.
   c. Violating a confidential relationship with a client, or disclosing any confidential client information except:
      i. with the client's permission;
      ii. in response to a court order;
      iii. when necessary to establish or collect a fee from the client; or
      iv. when the information is necessary to prevent a crime that the client intends to commit.
   d. Accepting any assignment which would be a conflict of interest because of confidential information obtained during employment for another client.
   e. Accepting an assignment that would require the violation of any municipal, state, or federal law or client confidence.
   f. Using any badge, seal, card, or other device to misrepresent oneself as a police officer, sheriff, or other law enforcement officer.
   g. Knowingly submitting a false or misleading report or failing to disclose a material fact to a client.
   h. Falsifying or failing to provide required compulsory minimum training in firearms or guard dog handling as required by this chapter.
   i. Failing to complete in a timely manner the registration of an employee.
   j. Allowing an employee to carry firearms or handle guard dogs prior to being issued a permanent registration card.
   k. Allowing an employee to work without carrying the required evidence of temporary or permanent registration.
   l. Allowing an employee to use or be accompanied by an untrained guard dog while rendering professional services.
   m. Failing to provide information requested by the board.
   n. Failing to return the temporary or permanent registration of an employee.
   o. Failing to notify the board of a change in ownership, partners, officers, or qualifying agent.
   p. Providing incomplete, false, or misleading information on an application.
   q. Any of the following except when reasonably undertaken in an emergency situation in order to protect life, health, or property:
      i. practicing or offering to practice beyond the scope permitted by law;
      ii. accepting and performing occupational responsibilities which the licensee knows or has reason to know that he or she is not competent to perform; or
      iii. performing occupational services which have not been authorized by the consumer or his or her legal representative.
   r. For armed and guard dog certified licensees, brandishing, exhibiting, displaying, or otherwise misusing a firearm or guard dog in a careless, angry, or threatening manner unnecessary for the course of the licensee's duties.
3. After conducting a hearing and upon a finding that a licensee, registrant, or applicant engaged in unprofessional conduct, the board may take disciplinary action. Discipline for unprofessional conduct may include denial of an application, revocation or suspension of a license or registration, supervision, reprimand, warning, or the required completion of a course of action.

Figure 1.9 Vermont unprofessional conduct statute.

requirements through the office of the Maryland State Police.[132] Other governmental entities, such as New York, designate an actual agency that assures compliance.[133]

In the majority of American jurisdictions, the licensure process of the private security industry has been codified by actual legislation. Two examples of how the language of the law in Maine and in Vermont controls the licensure of private security employees are reproduced. Review Figures 1.8 and 1.9.

1.8 CONCLUSION

The road taken to arrive at a dynamic and bustling private security industry has been interesting. Concepts such as self-help and self-protection are especially prominent in the American psyche and hence, the undergirding for private sector justice, has always been a firmly entrenched alongside a developing public model. This chapter makes plain that before the public police model became entrenched, there were a host of other approaches generally inclined to the nongovernmental. As pressures and complexities mount in a developing America, the calls and clamors for a

---

[132] Maryland State Police, Licensing Division website, at http://mdsp.maryland.gov/Organization/Pages/CriminalInvestigationBureau/LicensingDivision.aspx, last accessed August 26, 2016.

[133] New York State, Division of Licensing Services website, FAQ-Security Guard, at http://www.dos.ny.gov/licensing/securityguard/sguard_faq.html, last accessed August 26, 2016.

professional police model, supported by public funds, surely takes hold until the present. However, the public model has since discovered that private participation is essential to its success. How these two systems interact and work together is still a work in progress.

Private security's road to professionalism has been fraught with difficulties as it balances efficiencies with professional standards, and the role of industry itself, the professional associations and groups, and governmental entities highlights the diverse approaches to regulating the industry. The security industry must take this professional sojourn seriously, if only because inaction will cause a more onerous legislative substitute. The future depends on a serious effort to upgrade and uplift this extraordinary contributor to American justice.

Keywords

1829 Metropolitan Police Act

American Express Company

Baldwin–Felts Detective Service

bobbies

Bow Street Magistrates

Bow Street Runners

code of ethics

Commission of the Peace for Westminster

constable

contract security

ethical standards

feudalism

father of policing

Homestead Steel Strike of 1892

hue and cry

hundred

industrial revolution

information security

information systems security

Irish Peace Preservation Force

justice of the peace

King's Peace

magistrate

Marine Police

Merchant Police

Metropolitan Police

Molly Maguires

night watchmen

North-Western Police Agency

personnel security

physical security

Pinkerton Law

Pinkertons

politeuein

posse comitatus

private contractual security services

private security

privatization

proprietary security

public law enforcement

quasi-law enforcement agencies

railroad police

reeve

self-help

self-protection

serfs

sheriff

shire-reeve

shires

South Carolina Regulators

specialized security services

strikebreakers

thief-takers

tithing

tun

urbanization

vassals

vigilantes

Wachenhut Corporation

watch and ward

Wells Fargo

Discussion questions

1. Discuss the emergence and evolution of security up to the eighteenth century in Europe.
2. Outline the impact the Bow Street Runners and Sir Henry Fielding had on the development of policing in England.
3. Describe the impact Sir Robert Peel had on the evolution of the modern police forces.
4. Summarize the impact the transportation industry in the 1900s had on the development of early American policing.
5. Relate the events that led up to the enactment of the Pinkerton Law in 1893.
6. Identify how private security's role in the administration of American justice is both multifaceted and entrenched.
7. Define the four major disciplines in the private security industry.
8. Explain the necessity of ethical codes and standards in the field of private security.

CHAPTER 2

Concept, context, and definition
Security

OBJECTIVES

After completing this chapter, the student will be able to

1. Discuss the various concepts and definitions of private security.
2. Outline the various areas of private security involvement in international terrorism, homegrown terrorism, and homeland security in general.
3. Identify the various laws, regulations, and executive orders that enable private security to carry out its aim and purpose.
4. Evaluate how specialized homeland security laws impact how security services are provided.
5. Recall the training and academic programs in homeland security sponsored by the Department of Homeland Security (DHS) as well as various colleges and universities.
6. Describe the interplay between private security and homeland security in the twenty-first century.
7. Explain how private sector security firms and personnel are central and integral in the defense of the nation.
8. Summarize how DHS formally encourages the interplay and cooperation between private sector justice entities and public law enforcement.

2.1 SECURITY IN CONCEPT AND DEFINITION

The idea of security takes on many meanings and connotations. To be secure is to be safe. The be in a secure state means that a party senses that threats and risks are in check or capably thwarted. The concept of security means other things as well—such as an exchange of collateral for a piece of property—to insure that a buyer or seller supports the transaction for it to have viability. Then too there is paper security or securities that represent a particular valuation which undergirds an ownership claim—seen in stocks, bonds, and other instruments.

Underneath all of these terms and definitions, there is an assurance that things will be right and orderly—that security provides the means to a safe and productive life for both the individual and the collective. Security is derived from the Latin noun "securitas," which means freedom from fear or care, safety, and a guarantor of conditions and circumstances. And in the final analysis, that aptly describes the security industry itself—existing to give assurances to others that things are safe and free from care. Whether it be the concert or the bridge, the courthouse or the gated neighborhood, the security business warrants safety and tranquility.[1]

These conceptions of security are macro and global by design for security cuts cross both the private and the public sector. For this text's purposes, the more piercing view of security will be how that intersection exists naturally, but

---

[1] K. Strom et al. *The Private Security Industry: A Review of the Definitions, Available Data Sources, and Paths Moving Forward*, NCJRS Document # 232781 (December 2010), at http://www.ncjrs.gov/pdffiles1/bjs/grants/232781.pdf.

also how the private sector justice system has taken on a life of its own. Security, when initially considered, does not rule out public activity to the express private domain. On the other hand, the term "private security" is common nomenclature, for that same term could not be construed as identically public. Public police are not spoken of as "public security." Instead, the term is reserved for the private sector rather than its public counterpart. Hence, there is a great deal of disagreement on precisely what private security really constitutes. On the one hand, the definition has some set meanings already noted, while on the other, it is clear that visions, expectations, and functions in this industry evolve by the moment. Put another way, private security is forever a work in progress because our under-standing of the industry adapts and modifies as new and novel ways of handling security issues emerge, and just as compellingly, the world confronts security challenges in literally every context of human exchange. When one speaks of terrorism, or threats or disasters, man-made and natural, it is normal for the idea of security to be part of that mix but precisely what portion is public versus private may be less obvious. It is equally fair to argue that the private security industry is often defined from long-term caricatures and stereotypes, so much so that even public officers see their operations as inherently superior—or real police rather than minimum wage rent-a-cop private actors.[2] All of these factors influence both definition and perception concerning private security.

The esteemed think-tank, the RAND Corporation defined private security as all types of private organizations and indi-viduals providing all types of security-related services, including investigation, guard, patrol, lie detection, alarm, and armored transportation.[3] This vision mirrors too tightly the public police dynamic—almost as if what the public police can do, so can private officers. But this outlook is far too elementary for private sector security engages the world is much broader terms. *Hallcrest I* defined security as those actions relating to protection including physical, information, and employment-related security. The Private Security Task Force (PSTF) adopted a definition that includes those self-employed individuals and privately funded business entities and organizations providing security-related services to specific clientele for a fee, for the individual or entity that retains or employs them, or for themselves, in order to protect their persons, private property, or interests from various hazards.[4] The PSTF also restricted its definition to organiza-tions with a profit-oriented delivery system and excluded quasi-public police organizations unless paid by private funds.

The broader view of the role of private security, which includes policing, personnel, technological, business and eco-nomic protection systems, and information and cyberspace, most accurately reflects the industry. American Society for Industrial Security (ASIS) International, the largest association of private security professionals in the United States, has defined security as

> The condition of being protected against hazards, threats, risks, or loss. In the general sense, security is a concept similar to safety. The distinction between the two is an added emphasis on being protected from dangers that originate from outside. The term *security* means that something not only is secure but that it has been secured.[5]

Security aspects are "those characteristics, elements, or properties which reduce the risk of unintentionally, inten-tionally, and naturally-caused crises and disasters that disrupt and have consequences on the products and services, operation, critical assets, and continuity of the organization and its stakeholders."[6]

ASIS further qualifies security in a larger context while simultaneously defines the concept of "private security" thus:

> An independent or proprietary commercial organization whose activities include safeguarding the employing party's assets—ranging from human lives to physical property (the premises and contents), responding to emergency incidents, performing employee background investigations, performing the functions of detection and investigation of crime and criminals, and apprehending offenders for consideration.
>
> The nongovernmental, private-sector practice of protecting people, property, and information, conducting investiga-tions, and otherwise safeguarding an organization's assets; may be performed for an organization by an internal depart-ment (usually called proprietary security) or by an external, hired firm (usually called contract security).[7]

---

[2] C.P. Nemeth, *Private Security and Law*, 4th ed. 301–329 (Elsevier, 2012).

[3] J.S. Kakalik & S. Wildhorn, *Private Police in the United States: Findings and Recommendations* 3 (Santa Monica, CA: Rand Corporation, 1971).

[4] Nat'l Advisory Committee on Criminal Justice Standards and Goals, *Private Security—Report of the Task Force on Private Security* (1976), at https://www.ncjrs.gov/App/Publications/abstract.aspx?ID=40543, last accessed August 27, 2016.

[5] ASIS International, Security Glossary, "S," at https://www.asisonline.org/Membership/Library/Security-Glossary/Pages/Security-Glossary-S. aspx, last accessed August 27, 2016.

[6] *Ibid.*

[7] *Ibid.*, "P," at https://www.asisonline.org/Membership/Library/Security-Glossary/Pages/Security-Glossary-P.aspx, last accessed August 27, 2016.

Experts attending a 2008–2009 ASIS Academic/Practitioner symposium provided a synthesis of core functions or elements that largely define the parameters of private security. Those included the following:

- Physical security
- Personnel security
- Information systems security
- Investigations
- Loss prevention
- Risk management
- Legal aspects
- Emergency/contingency planning
- Fire protection
- Crisis management
- Disaster management
- Counterterrorism
- Competitive intelligence
- Executive protection
- Violence in the workplace
- Crime prevention (general)
- Crime prevention through environmental design (CPTED)
- Security architecture and engineering[8]

Web Exercise: The influence of ASIS International on the day-to-day operations of security firms and personnel cannot be overstated. See the summary document of standards and practices at https://www.asisonline.org/Standards-Guidelines/Documents/SGquickReferenceGuide.pdf.

These core elements provide an inroad into understanding what private security means; what it dedicates its resources toward; and what coverage areas say about the industry itself. As it deploys its people into these sectors, the industry defines itself. Where it chooses to target its resources and energies goes a long way to defining the industry. Using a business model, the industry projects where the opportunities lie and what will be a lucrative investment strategy. *Security Magazine* tabulated location choices.[9] Responding organizations were self-selected among 16 industry sectors:

- Education (colleges and universities, K–12)
- Casinos, hospitality, arenas, and entertainment
- Finance/insurance/banking
- Government (federal, state, and local)
- Construction, real estate, and property management
- Energy, utilities, power, gas, nuclear, and water
- Business services
- Industrial and manufacturing
- Retail, restaurants, and food service
- Agriculture/farming/food
- Information technology, communications, and media

---

[8] ASIS International, *Compendium of the ASIS Academic/Practitioner Symposium* (1997–2008), at https://foundation.asisonline.org/FoundationResearch/Publications/Documents/1997-2008_CompendiumofProceedings.pdf, last accessed August 27, 2016.

[9] M. McCourt, The 2009 Security 500: Building Security's Future, *Security Magazine* (November 2009).

- Transportation, logistics, warehousing, and supply chain
- Diversified companies
- Ports and terminals: sea/land/air
- Healthcare/medical centers/hospitals

What is even more readily apparent is that security cannot deny its private and public qualities. An entanglement is unavoidable since so many of the services necessary for public safety are now being taken up by private sector companies. Thus, while the George Washington Bridge, which crosses the Hudson from New Jersey to New York, mostly relies on the services of the public police and metro authority for its safety, although an increasing presence of private security firms is obvious to those who ride across the river. Just as evident will be private security's presence at events and concerts, executive visitations and diplomatic events, energy facilities, water and sewer plants, and other critical infrastructure. Everywhere the eye can gaze, private security pops up in unique settings or side by side with public policing and safety counterparts. The implications of these shared services or distinctly different delivery systems are many—though none as pressing as the need for a shared knowledge base and protocols and professional practices that never work at odds with either system. The private model of security services should not be a foreign practice indiscernible to the public counterpart. These systems must work cooperatively and consciously in unison with a shared purpose.

In this sense, public and private conceptions of security inevitably merge together in a plethora of settings. The melding of these distinct systems inevitably takes place because the mission, aim, and purpose of the public and private realm are largely compatible. For these reasons alone, any meaningful understanding of security depends upon a shared knowledge base. All of these observations find their highest relevance when considering the impact of effect of 9/11 and past notions of what security means and is.

2.2 SECURITY, TERROR, AND HOMELAND DEFENSE

The concept of a threat to the homeland has historically taken many shapes. Terror and the terrorist are not new phenomena—they are a construction of the ages, seen throughout history in various guises. In recent years, the country has focused on domestic security and preventing acts of terrorism. Couple this perspective with a predictable national desire to protect one's homeland, and nothing here is unexpected. What is of greater utility in the discussion of security of the homeland will be how we arrived at our current position. Specifically, what did we do before the jihadist? What types of terror attacks did America experience? What motivated the terrorist? For example, the Ku Klux Klansman is hardly a jihadist, although his methods may be just as dastardly. How do we reconcile that difference? What of the military dictator, the tyrant, the leader who leads his country to ruin and grounds his enterprise on hate, such as the Third Reich. This too is terror by any reasonable definition. Terror is nothing new.

The acts of the terrorist have been with us since the dawn of recorded history. It is important to keep this in context in our interpretation of history. This chapter traces a whole host of acts and movements in the twentieth century that preceded the events of 9/11. All of the examples covered illuminate how and why terrorists do what they do. All of these illustrations, from the military machine that oppresses people and states, to the Weathermen that sabotage government installations, help to bring perspective to the discussion. When one scrutinizes the diversity of these acts and approaches, one can better understand the landscape of modern terrorism in a post-9/11 world.

While much can be written about the nature of threat and violence throughout U.S. history, it would appear that the best place to start in order to understand modern-day terrorism is the twentieth century—a century with complex conflicts and territorial challenges. From World War I to World War II (WWII), the concept of threats to the homeland was largely the result of country-to-country conquests, political disagreements, and imperial empire building. For example, the Third Reich's move into the Polish frontier, in the name of reclamation of Aryan races under the thumb of Polish authorities, is a land grab with eugenic flavor. Yet these wars and conflicts serve as an appropriate backdrop for how any nation seeks to maintain its territorial integrity. In a sense, the planes attacking the World Trade Center buildings were an assault on the country's sovereignty not unlike the way the German troops crossed into the Sudetenland. The means and motivation are clearly different, though the net effect is not completely dissimilar. The Nazi onslaught of WWII was, in a sense, the largest whole-scale terror campaign ever inflicted on a continent. The systematic extermination program was the subject of endless meetings and conferences, though admittedly the

Nazi leaders were quite effective in removing the paper trail. Similar arguments about Japanese imperialism can be posited, and for good cause. The Japanese intent was to dominate and rule the world using means far outside the mainstream of modern warfare. Survivors of Japanese occupation in the Philippines or of Japan's own concentration camps tell a story of brutality and degradation that seems inexplicable when one considers the modern democratic state of Japan.

Web Exercise: Visit the National Archives collection, which catalogs Japanese war crimes in WWII at http://www.archives.gov/iwg/japanese-war-crimes/select-documents.pdf.

As the victors of WWII set out to fashion a new Europe and continental framework, the Allies saw the world in distinct and sometimes incompatible ways. For sure, Britain and the United States shared the core values of freedom and democratic, republican principles. Contrasted by that was the starkly divisive approach of our Russian ally was fundamentally at odds with Western ideals. Dividing up countries such as Germany and replacing free democratic or monarchical countries such as Poland and Hungary with a Soviet-style socialist model, the Russian Bear flexed extraordinary muscle immediately after the end of the conflict. Concession after concession was made to the Soviet demand, much to the distress of Winston Churchill. In response, Churchill ultimately sounded a clarion call for halting the expansion of the Soviet empire in one of his finest speeches.[10]

> I have a strong admiration and regard for the valiant Russian people and for my wartime comrade, Marshal Stalin. There is deep sympathy and goodwill in Britain—and I doubt not here also—toward the peoples of all the Russias and a resolve to persevere through many differences and rebuffs in establishing lasting friendships.
>
> It is my duty, however, to place before you certain facts about the present position in Europe.
>
> From Stettin in the Baltic to Trieste in the Adriatic an iron curtain has descended across the Continent. Behind that line lie all the capitals of the ancient states of Central and Eastern Europe. Warsaw, Berlin, Prague, Vienna, Budapest, Belgrade, Bucharest and Sofia; all these famous cities and the populations around them lie in what I must call the Soviet sphere, and all are subject, in one form or another, not only to Soviet influence but to a very high and in some cases increasing measure of control from Moscow.

Web Exercise: To read Churchill's entire speech, titled "The Sinews of Peace," visit http://www.nato.int/docu/speech/1946/S460305a_e.htm.

A new war emerged—one not fought on the battlefield but in the sphere of territorial conquest and subliminal and direct attempts to destroy either side. This is the stuff of the Cold War, and it escalated very quickly. The United States quickly recognized these expansionist motivations. And this sort of expansionist mentality is nothing new under the sun nor has it evaporated from the current terror scene. ISIS (Islamic State of Iraq and Syria), the contemporary Islamic state group, also known as ISIL (Islamic State of Iraq and the Levant), operates on a similar mentality.[11]

The Cold War is not an illusory war by any means, but one with significant military and political consequences. By 1947, the Soviet Union commenced the construction of the Berlin Wall—separating the East from the West and trapping East Berlin in a dark, communist world. Ever the expansionist, the Soviet Union boldly expanded its sphere of influence into countries like Iran. In the wake of these actions, President Harry Truman discerned a meaningful and bona fide threat to free peoples. As a result, he made plain that the United States would not sit idly by while Soviet aggression spread throughout the world. In 1947, Truman enunciated what is now known as the Truman Doctrine. With the Truman Doctrine, President Truman established that the United States would provide political, military, and economic assistance to all democratic nations under threat from external or internal authoritarian forces. The Truman Doctrine effectively reoriented U.S. foreign policy, guiding it away from the usual stance of withdrawal from regional conflicts not directly involving the United States, to one of possible intervention in faraway conflicts.

Of course, the Truman Doctrine was cited in the Korean War, the Cuban Missile Crisis, and the Vietnam War. When President Kennedy confronted the Soviet government for its dispatch of long-range missiles to Cuba, the justification

---

[10] North American Treaty Organization, Winston S. Churchill, The Sinews of Peace, at http://www.nato.int/docu/speech/1946/S460305a_e.htm, last accessed August 27, 2016.

[11] T. Lister, ISIS: The First Terror Group to Build an Islamic State? CNN.com, at http://www.cnn.com/2014/06/12/world/meast/who-is-the-isis/index.html, last accessed December 27, 2015); Business Insider, These Maps Show the Progression of ISIS Control in Iraq and Syria, http://www.businessinsider.com/these-maps-show-the-progression-of-isis-control-in-iraq-and-syria-2015-8, last accessed December 27, 2015.

was the containment theory, the right of the Western hemisphere to be safe from this corrupt hegemony, and the insistence of Harry Truman that free peoples need not tolerate this political oppression.

Each of these unofficial wars was, at least in a legislative sense, efforts to contain the "threat" of communist takeover. Throughout the 1960s, 1970s, and into the early 1980s, the two opposing giants in the Soviet and American systems remained entrenched. Nuclear proliferation continued unabated. A lack of trust and cooperation remained standard operating procedures. Spy agencies, such as the CIA and the KGB, spent most of their energy engaged in the activities and efforts of the Cold War.

When President Richard Nixon visited China in 1972, a tectonic shift occurred in the Cold War. Nixon had brilliantly undercut the Sino–Soviet cooperation that appeared impenetrable for so many generations. Nixon made possible a new vision of cooperation on missile deployment, cultural exchange, and foreign relations. From this point forward, the Soviet system would be isolated and internally suffering from decades of misplaced investment in the military model over any other benefit for its people. The Soviet system was crumbling from within. By the time of President Ronald Reagan, the time was ripe for an end to the intolerable Cold War.

Reagan was an unabashed believer in the American way of life. He showed diplomacy in the background of negotiations and protocol, but publicly there was no greater critic of the Soviet system. On March 8, 1983, when he labeled the Soviet state an "evil empire," critics charged him with sensationalism. Those who supported Reagan felt he was defending the notion of freedom, believing that any government that dominated and oppressed its people was unjust in the eyes of history and its people. He was a strong proponent for the elimination of communism and, in particular, the Soviet-style system.

Just as the Russians were deemed the ultimate threat to the United States then, so too is the terrorist extremist currently considered the most immediate threat. To be sure, both have been at the forefront of our national security over the years. What we do know is that enemies are not permanent stations. They are subject to change. Experts at the time would never have imagined the United States and Russia having closer ties and working together. Yet the two countries have taken many diplomatic strides though it is too early to tell with the current political leaders in Russia with the reemergence of Vladimir Putin. Putin is often referred to as Russia's strongman and he works arduously to develop this caricature among his countrymen.[12] Putin has been vocal and transparent in many of his efforts to consolidate power although it is not the nation once ruled by the KGB but a populace that has tasted some element of a free society. The mass demonstrations of December 2011 say much about a Russian political system evolving.

While only time will tell in the matter of Russian political processes, it is a safe bet that once the citizenry experiences a bit of freedom, there is no going back. The prospects for increasingly improved Russian–U.S. relations appear a pipe dream at present. Current foreign policy decisions regarding the Middle East, especially in regards to Syria, were once thought to be a door opener for better relations.[13] Unfortunately, U.S. inactivity and Russian intervention in Syria have triggered the possibility of a new cold era. The Iran nuclear agreement, the Russian–Iranian partnership, has also added fuel to tension along with rising distrust. Other Middle Eastern countries may provide better avenues for reconciliation, such as Egypt and Jordan, but there is little doubt that the U.S. brand has suffered a miserable decline in most corners of Middle East under the Obama administration.[14]

2.3 SECURITY: THE BALANCE OF RIGHTFUL DEMONSTRATION AND THREAT

There is little doubt that the concept of terror resounded across the American landscape from the nineteenth century onward.[15] From the Black Panthers to the Ku Klux Klan (KKK), from the Workers Party to communist agitators, from Students for a Democratic Society (SDS) to the Weathermen of the Vietnam Era, the concept of terror against governing authority was entrenched into the political and social fabric of these organizations.

---

[12] E.D. Johnson, Putin and Putinism, 89 *Slavonic East Eur. Rev.* 788–790 (2011).

[13] M.R. Gordon, U.S. Begins Military Talks with Russia on Syria, *N.Y. Times Online* (September 18, 2015), at http://www.nytimes.com/2015/09/19/world/europe/us-to-begin-military-talks-with-russia-on-syria.html?_r=1, last accessed December 27, 2015; A. Tilghman, U.S., Russia resume military relations to 'deconflict' in Syria, *Military Times* (September 18, 2015), at http://www.militarytimes.com/story/military/pentagon/2015/09/18/russia-mil-to-mil/72395558/, last accessed December 27, 2015.

[14] Gordon, *supra* note 13.

[15] For an interesting analysis of the Ku Klux Klan as it rationalized its hatred with the fervor of false patriotism, see P.D. Brister, Patriotic Enemies of the State: A Cross Comparison of the Christian Patriot Movement and the 1920's Ku Klux Klan, 4 *Homeland Sec. Rev.* 173 (2010).

The internal, urban violence of the 1960s, triggered and prompted by generations of inequality and injustice, caused law enforcement not only to challenge their historic reactions to public protest, but also to see that "enemies" or protagonists of the government may actually be operating from a higher moral plane. The protest could also not be universally condemned because some were plainly justified. Certainly, the entire movement sparked by Dr. Martin Luther King Jr. challenged the status quo of police power and the remediation of injustice. Then too, those operating without moral advantage—groups such as the KKK or the SDS—posed real and meaningful threats against the internal security of the country by their egregious actions. In a sense, both lawful and unlawful protests shaped how the justice model reacted to protest and terror.

For example, during the Nixon era, ordinary citizens were perceived as troublemakers and seditionists for any protest to the policies of the president. Much has been written about the insular and almost paranoid perceptions of Nixon insiders as that government sought to squelch public protest concerning the war in Vietnam.[16]

Enemies of the state came in many shapes and sizes, some deserved and others not. In the midst of this era, the FBI posted its list of groups that were allegedly anti-American in design.[17] During this exceptionally turbulent time, politicians, government officials, and law enforcement professionals perceived events as a threat to our democratic process.

Web Exercise: Read about the Weatherman, a subversive antiwar, antigovernment, and anti-capitalist entity active all through the late 1960s–1980s at http://www.pbs.org/independentlens/weatherunderground/movement.html.

Throughout the centuries, even until the present day, we can see that terror is a tool for those wishing to maintain the status quo as well as those wishing revolution. Hence, it is imperative to remember that American justice policy has had an historic understanding and relationship with terror throughout most of its history. These acts of terror can be broken down into two essential categories: international and domestic.

Since the early 1960s, the threat of terror has sought to disrupt world economies, overthrow political structures, annihilate religious competitors, and assault value systems considered antagonistic to a perverted worldview. For most of the past 60 years, terror has been on the radar screen.

2.3.1 Security: The challenge of domestic terrorism—Pre-9/11

Domestic terrorism is considered that which is perpetrated by U.S. nationals and not the product of fringe Islamic extremists or jihadists. Terrorists can equally come from disenfranchised citizens, hate groups, or other extreme wings within the country. There have been some consistent players in terror activities across the American landscape, and surely the KKK fits the bill of consistency. Political upheaval and radical social change by any means whatsoever appropriately describe the KKK. For the KKK, terror was central to the mission of the rabid segregationist and promoter of inequality. Historic harassment and lynchings have been replaced by slick media and membership campaigns. Their official website, the "Official Knights Party of the KKK"[18] chastises those who see cross burnings as acts of terror and refers to the burnings as a theological exhortation. Regardless of the terrorist's mindset or rationale, history makes clear the motivation behind the tactics.

Domestic terror before the events of 9/11 occurred in a somewhat narrower or localized model in that the motive for attack was often not on a global scale. Just as the Klansman cares little beyond his or her myopic racism, the student radical, wishing the overthrow of the military complex, cannot see things in global terms. The student radical concludes that a group or a few assembled might wish to publicize their claims in every imaginable way—violence among its approaches. These operatives see the world in more myopic terms since it is the foundation of their movement that unites them and drives their relationship. In no sense does one justify the actions of the Black Panther or the Weathermen. This merely demonstrates a differing worldview exists when compared to the jihadist who ultimately desires the radical reconstruction of the entire planet while imposing a particular religious ideology and zealotry.

One of the more notable domestic terror attacks against the United States was the 1993 attack on New York City's World Trade Center. The boldness of the World Trade Center bombing shocked the intelligence community.

---

[16] R. Perlstein, *Nixonland: America's Second Civil War and the Divisive Legacy of Richard Nixon, 1965–1972* (New York, NY: Simon & Schuster, 2008).

[17] G.R. Stone, review of *Spying on Americans: Political Surveillance from Hoover to the Huston Plan*, by A. Theoharis, 8 *Rev. Am. Hist.* 134–138 (March 1980). For a full analysis of how the Weathermen worked, see Federal Bureau of Investigation, Weathermen Underground Summary Dated 8/20/76, at http://foia.fbi.gov/weather/weath1a.pdf.

[18] Official website of the Knights Party, United States, http://www.kkk.bz.

The sophistication of the plan, the potential for extreme damage and destruction, and the symbolism of the target itself attested to the determination of the terrorist movement long before 9/11.[19]

Presently, terror finds root in the ideology of religious fanaticism and the jihad. The statistical reality of jihadi motivation and Islamic extremism cannot be explained away by politically correct propaganda. Previously, terror was grounded in the ideology of politics and social movements. When the Communist Workers Party clamored for change, its advocacy dealt with the evils of excessive capitalism and the real need for collectivism in the distribution of goods and services. When the Black Panther Party set off violent action, it did so with a political revolution in mind and the whole-scale redress and payback for injustice based on race. Neither of these arguments can justify the violence that these groups offer up, but both groups attest to the dramatically different mindset when compared to the extreme and very radical Islamic fundamentalists who flew planes into the Twin Towers or the rationale for the Boston Marathon bombing that used jihad and Islamic radicalism as a warped rationale for the senseless killing of completely innocent people.[20]

Terrorism on the domestic front can be driven by diverse motivations. Race hatred, white supremacy, protests against governmental policy, and an inordinate desire to subvert and undermine the nature of the democratic state are just a few of the rationales employed. Timothy McVeigh's bombing of the Alfred P. Murrah Federal Building in Oklahoma City manifests the disproportionate dislike and distrust of government in any sense and the extreme alienation and isolation that certain terrorists seem to experience in light of the democratic process. That government may or may not be too intrusive cannot provide a sufficient justification for murder, but the level of distrust and flat-out antagonism toward government is a growing phenomenon in select quarters.

Ted Kaczynski (aka the Unabomber) also reflects this loner, antigovernment tradition of the terrorist. In his "manifesto," Kaczynski railed against most aspects of modern life, industrialization, the loss of freedom, and the invasiveness of government. Kaczynski's arrest, one of the FBI's most successful apprehensions, was celebrated and recollected in 2008.[21]

The array of terror groups include those advocating radical change involving racist ideologies, economic overthrow of existing governmental structures, and ideologies relating to the environment and animal rights. These groups are capable of inflicting extraordinary damage to the country, and must remain on the radar screen of those entrusted with the security of the United States and its citizens.

2.3.2 Security: The challenge of international terrorism—Pre-9/11

Just as in the United States, the international community had experienced a series of attacks from various constituencies. One of the more notable overseas terror attacks against the United States was at the Marine base in Beirut, Lebanon, in 1983, where 241 servicemen lost their lives. The attack in Lebanon, in a secure military environment, made plain the tenacity of the terrorist and the willingness of this enemy to tackle any target, no matter how formidable. This attack sent a vivid reminder to the government and military that terrorism was a growing and very dangerous reality.

During the 1980s, organized terrorist groups that we have come to know only too well—Al Qaeda, Hamas, and Hezbollah—gained foundational and organizational support from many quarters, in both a political and an economic sense. By the 1990s, Osama bin Laden had amassed a network of terrorists eager to carry out attacks. In Yemen and Somalia, Bin Laden funded, planned, and orchestrated acts that killed and injured a number of U.S. soldiers. Eighteen Special Forces members were attacked and killed in Somalia in 1993. In 1996, Bin Laden set out to attack the

---

[19] U.S. Fire Administration, *The World Trade Center Bombing: Report and Analysis* 15, ed. W. Manning (Washington, DC: U.S. Government Printing Office, 1993). For a comparison of the 1993 emergency reaction with that of 2001, see R.F. Fahy & G. Proulx, *A Comparison of the 1993 and 2001 Evacuation of the World Trade Center, Proceedings of the 2002 Fire Risk & Hazard Assessment Research Application Symposium* 111–117 (Quincy, MA: Fire Protection Research Foundation). For a close look at how World Trade Center bombings caused extraordinary upheaval from a social, behavioral and health perspective, see R.E. Adamsa, J.A. Boscarinoa, & S. Galeac, Social and Psychological Resources and Health Outcomes After the World Trade Center Disaster, 62 *Soc. Sci. & Med.* 176–188 (2006), at http://www.sciencedirect.com/science/article/pii/S027795360500239X.

[20] Reuters Boston Marathon Bombing archive, at http://www.reuters.com/news/picture/boston-marathon-bombing?articleId=USRTXYMXH, last accessed August 27, 2016.

[21] Federal Bureau of Investigation, History, *The Unabomber*, at https://www.fbi.gov/history/famous-cases/unabomber, last accessed August 27, 2016.

Khobar Towers in Saudi Arabia, where 19 American airmen died. In August 1998, Bin Laden and Al Qaeda bombed the embassies of Kenya and Tanzania, which resulted in death and injury of thousands of innocents. Al Qaeda and Bin Laden were getting even bolder as time progressed, carrying out a direct attack on a U.S. warship—the USS *Cole*—in Yemen in 2000. Using a small boat as a suicide projectile, Al Qaeda operatives displayed unparalleled methods in carrying out their attack.

None of these events occurred in a vacuum, but rather as a progressive series of events that eventually culminated in the single largest attack by a foreign enemy on American soil. Each attack displayed an evolving aggressiveness toward America, each attack employed a variety of tactics to keep the defenders off guard, and each attack manifested an increasing fanaticism in the Islamic extremist world. Succinctly, 9/11 did not occur out of the blue. Terror has a progressive history.

2.4 SECURITY: THE CHALLENGE OF 9/11 AND HOMELAND DEFENSE

To say the world changed on September 11, 2001 is an extraordinary understatement. As the assault on the Twin Towers and the Pentagon unfolded, people across the globe watched in stunned silence. Not only was the loss of life staggering, but the economic impact on the New York metropolitan area and the country was significant. Notions of security and safety within America's borders would be forever challenged and altered. Terms such as *WMD*, *dirty bomb*, *radical Islam*, *War on Terror*, *jihad*, and *man-made catastrophe* creep into the law enforcement lexicon without any notion of how much will be required to thwart these challenges. Nor did the system anticipate the shift from local act to a global panorama—for today's security is "transnational" yet at the same time now "homegrown." Sleeper cells and propagandized youth operating under the spell of a local Imam are now on the radar. Nothing in security remains a constant and undergoes constant reformation and adjustment. Confidence in our ability to withstand or detect attacks was severely undermined by the events of 9/11. Even to this day, it is impossible to measure the complete impact these events had upon the American psyche, the former invincibility of our home soil, and the pronounced reexamination of our entire approach to security and law enforcement in the nation.[22] At the same time, this yearning for a secure state of affairs has prompted a wide array of legal and moral challenges from privacy intrusions by phone and cell, metadata collection, generalized warrants sweeping in an entire population into to its application, and fuzzy boundaries of civilian prosecutions versus the logical demand by some that terrorists need nothing more than the military tribunal; these represent the challenges of a free people grappling with issues of internal and external security.

Side by side, public and private operatives suffer from a lack of coordination, and interagency cooperation, with the events of 9/11 manifesting that a wall did exist between the various agencies of government, as well as between the public and private sectors, was firmly erected. The CIA did not share with the FBI, the state and local police and private security companies did not communicate readily, and jurisdictional and turf issues often influenced policy making in the pre-9/11 world. "The absence of coordination and collaboration in the area of information and intelligence sharing contributed to the surprise of the attack."[23] After 9/11, it was blatantly obvious that a cooperative mentality had to be erected. Law enforcement, security, and emergency management authorities were forced to see the world in a post-9/11 mindset fully recognizing that what once was effective is now ineffectual. "There are significant changes not only in the daily lives of the American people but also in the function of the country's emergency management system."[24] In matters of command, communication, deployment, planning, and dispatch, traditional practices were challenged in ways never before envisioned. Nothing in the status quo could have operationally prepared these professionals for a post-9/11 world. And in a sense, that is exactly what the emergency, military, and law enforcement, and security communities have been doing since 9/11—searching for the best approach and adapting to the new reality. As law enforcement and fire personnel perished in the rubble of the Twin Towers and civilians in the airplanes plummeted to their deaths, the knowledge base of traditional safety was turned on its head.

Soon after 9/11, agencies developed and learned new strategies and tactics for prevention and mitigation. Soon after, the safety community began to reevaluate long-established practices in light of this tragedy. An extraordinary series

---

[22] For an interesting look into the cultural shifts in the intelligence community as it evaluated terrorism, see T.A. Gilly, Deconstructing Terrorism: Counter-Terrorism's Trajectory for the 21st Century, 5 *Homeland Sec. Rev.* 5 (2011).

[23] R. Ward et al., *Homeland Security: An Introduction* 57 (Cincinnati, OH: Anderson Publishing Co., 2006).

[24] J. Bullock et al., *Introduction to Homeland Security* 23 (4th ed., Oxford, UK: Butterworth-Heinemann, 2012).

of new approaches was implemented, many of which were implemented by a new Department of Homeland Security (DHS). Right from the start, state, local, and federal services rattled the cages of ordinary bureaucratic practices. From that tragic day until the following year, government moved at lightning speed.[25]

Not only was a new department erected, but so too a new policy and definitional approach. The term *homeland security* encompasses much of the emergency, military, and law enforcement and security sector once dedicated to a variety of relevant responsibilities in defense of a nation. DHS was created to unify the diverse functions and responsibilities of a homeland in need of protection. DHS is

> One department whose primary mission is to protect the American homeland;
> One department to secure our borders, transportation sector, ports, and critical infrastructure;
> One department to synthesize and analyze homeland security intelligence from multiple sources;
> One department to coordinate communications with state and local governments, private industry, and the American people about threats and preparedness;
> One department to coordinate our efforts to protect the American people against bioterrorism and other weapons of mass destruction;
> One department to help train and equip for first responders;
> One department to manage federal emergency response activities; and
> More security officers in the field working to stop terrorists and fewer resources in Washington managing duplicative and redundant activities that drain critical homeland security resources.[26]

Any conception of a government agency dedicated to the protection of the homeland takes time to develop and implement, though it is quite certain that the term "security" scales new heights of meaning. Security, under a DHS mantle, will forever mean a multitude of other factors than its historic and traditional definition.

U.S. DEPARTMENT OF HOMELAND SECURITY

Mission

We will lead the unified national effort to secure America. We will prevent and deter terrorist attacks and protect against and respond to threats and hazards to the nation. We will secure our national borders while welcoming lawful immigrants, visitors, and trade (U.S. Department of Homeland Security One Team, One Mission, Securing Our Homeland—U.S. DHS Strategic Plan [2008]).

Strategic goals

Awareness—Identify and understand threats, assess vulnerabilities, determine the potential impact, and disseminate timely information to our homeland security partners and the American public.

Prevention—Detect, deter, and mitigate threats to our homeland.

Protection—Safeguard our people and their freedoms, critical infrastructure, property, and the economy of our nation from acts of terrorism, natural disasters, or other emergencies.

Response—Lead, manage, and coordinate the national response to acts of terrorism, natural disasters, or other emergencies.

Recovery—Lead national, state, local, and private sector efforts to restore services and rebuild communities after acts of terrorism, natural disasters, or other emergencies.

Service—Serve the public effectively by facilitating lawful trade, travel, and immigration.

Organizational excellence—Value our most important resource, our people. Create a culture that promotes a common identity, innovation, mutual respect, accountability, and teamwork to achieve efficiencies, effectiveness, and operational synergies—U.S. Department of Homeland Security, Securing Our Homeland: U.S. DHS Strategic Plan (2004).

---

[25] President George W. Bush, *The Department of Homeland Security* 19–23 (Washington, DC: U.S. Government Printing Office, June 2002), at https://www.dhs.gov/sites/default/files/publications/book_0.pdf, last accessed August 27, 2016.
[26] *Ibid.* at 1.

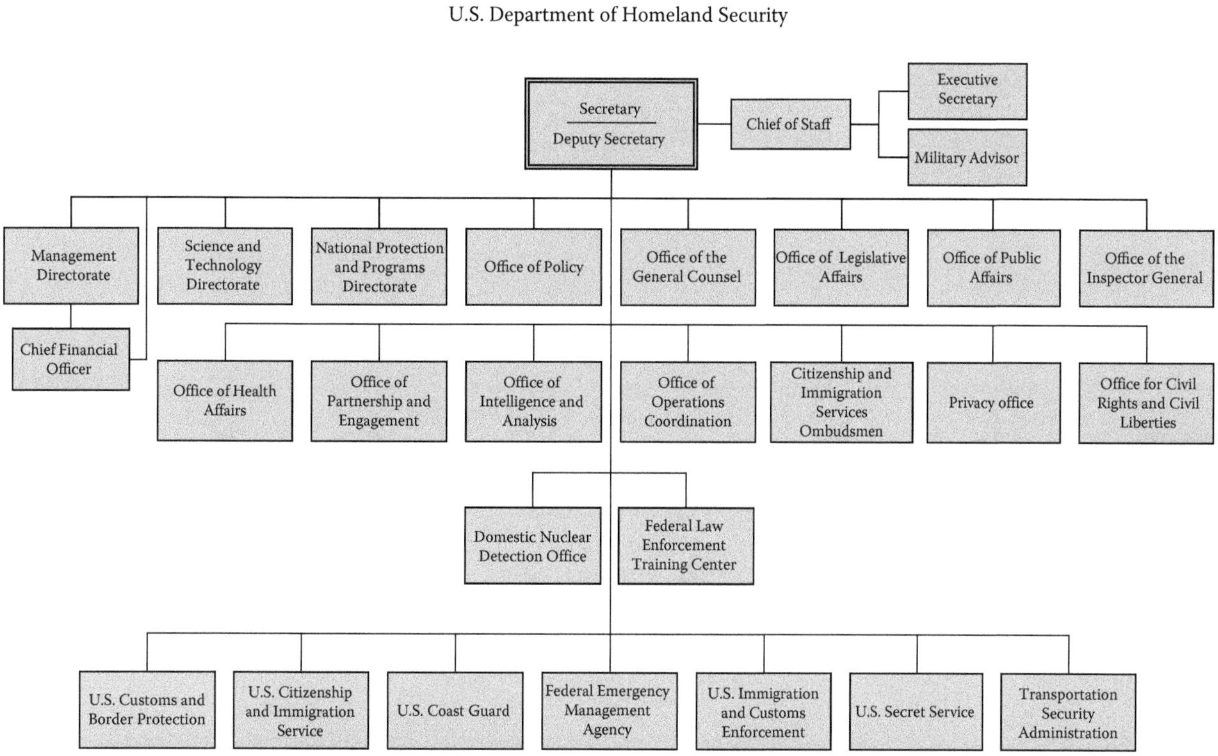

U.S. Department of Homeland Security

Figure 2.1   DHS organizational chart as of February 1, 2017.

The current structure of DHS is charted in Figure 2.1.

Over its short life span, the DHS has evolved vigorously, at least in a programmatic sense, but has taken to a slow mode of structural change. Despite this, the didactic about what security is and means in light of homeland policy and DHS mission has been anything but lethargic. During this last decade or so, the entire infrastructure of the public, military, and security culture has reexamined first principles about safety and security. Each agency added to the DHS mix, such as the Coast Guard or Immigration and Customs Enforcement, influences how professionals see the task of homeland security and safety in general. In 2003, a host of other external agencies were swept into DHS during the reorganization phase with inevitable consequences of how security should be defined, the entities being

- Federal Law Enforcement Training Center (FLETC)—The premier center for professional law enforcement training located in Glencoe, Georgia
- U.S. Customs and Border Protection (CBP)—The agency primarily responsible for the security of our borders
- U.S. Citizenship and Immigration Services—Administers the immigration and naturalization adjudication
- U.S. Immigration and Customs Enforcement (ICE)—The investigative arm of DHS that identifies and classifies threats at the borders
- U.S. Coast Guard—Protection of nation's ports and waterways
- Federal Emergency Management Agency (FEMA)—Manages hazards and threats and responds thereto
- U.S. Secret Service—Protection of the president, vice president, and other high-level officials; investigates financial crimes
- Transportation Security Agency (TSA)—Protects nation's transportation systems
- Domestic Nuclear Detection Office—Coordinates threat response related to nuclear materials

Each transference of authority and agency duty adds to a natural re-definition and worldview as to how security should be defined. Security, to illustrate, includes not only the protection of assets and persons, but borders, nuclear and energy facilities, protection of the president and other dignitaries, and our maritime interests and coastal resources, to name just a few. Security takes on the defense of a nation from a myriad of vantage points, and the structure and makeup of government agencies, such as DHS, as well as the aligned funding, press the definition to even broader boundaries. Security means far more than the sleepy guard watching bank customers journey to and fro. Security spreads its wings in diverse directions by tackling issues of safety in literally every aspect of daily life. In this way, the 9/11 revolution and the development of a homeland security infrastructure have bolstered and enhanced the definition of security.

DHS's intent was to combine, blend, and synthesize appropriate agency's functions with the appropriate office. For the most part, DHS has remained largely intact since these radical days of reorganization in 2003–2004. It was not only an administrative sweep that took place when these agencies moved from familiar locale to the DHS setting and new novel perspectives for what security means and demands were apparent in both mission and practice. For both DHS and the incoming agency, a change of outlook and culture was required—a larger, more macro vision of what security connotes in the larger culture. By change one means that a new prioritization of agency function had to occur; the former agency had to inculcate, acclimate, and become part of a new mission and mindset. To this day, there continue to be both challenge and unease in finding a universally agreed to definition of what security is and means. DHS, while clearly stimulating the parameters of the definition, has mixed a pot of function and policy with far too many ingredients and at dramatic cost—a state that cannot go on forever.[27]

2.5 FORMALIZING SECURITY IN THE HOMELAND: LAW, LEGISLATION, AND EXECUTIVE DECREE

Aside from philosophical and definitional considerations, the framework for "security" in a free society has long been a subject of debate in the American experience. By nature, Americans resist too much oversight and governmental control for the average citizen sees government as an entity in service to its constituents—though with limitations and controls. Government has never had unrestricted rights in the daily lives of its people. Since 9/11, the historic barrier has been tested in ways never witnessed and many practices once considered dangerously intrusive are sometimes justified under the security rationale. See Figure 2.2.

In this sense, the business and protocol of security has become more formalized in the last three decades. Before this period, security, in a nationalized sense, had more to do with spies and our Cold War enemies than the modern-day terrorist plot. Security was national as a defense to borders, and a military reaction to long-term enemies of democracy and freedom. Since 9/11, security and the agencies and entities entrusted with its assuring safety. Labor under a differing set of rules and principles. Security operatives today, while possibly still concerned about traitors and espionage, are far more concerned with the protection of particular infrastructure or industrial centers. Rather the Cold War plots to implant communist regimes in democratic governments, today's security professionals worry about the integrity of transportation systems, health and energy centers, colleges and high schools, and other points where a congregation of people is likely. And while much of this results from the changed landscape, a good portion of this shift to other priorities arises from laws, from regulations and administrative fiat from the many governmental bodies entrusted with these tasks. Federal lawmakers, seeking to assuage voters, cannot let a day pass without some other governmental intervention in the overall security of the United States. Hence, if one hopes to understand the current mindset in security, he or she must understand the laws which govern or give impetus to what occurs on the front lines. Laws, legislative enactments, and administrative regulations formalize what the security estate encounters.

Laws, regulations, and executive orders enable the agency so that it might carry out its aim and purpose. Many laws touch upon the functions of homeland defense, such as in matters of privacy, arrest, search, and wiretap, while other laws establish centers of research, operational funds for new initiatives, or primer for a new directive. Funding for DHS is a legislative decision as well. How Congress and the president eventually agree to fund DHS is an annual responsibility.

The power of DHS is derived from its legal authority. How that legal authority has sprinkled into the very culture of public and private policing becomes quite obvious when the content of these legal promulgations are weighed and evaluated. A cursory review of the more essential legal pronouncements follows.

---

[27] The Federal News Radio reports that support for consolidation is growing in the U.S. Senate. See http://www.federalnewsradio.com/?nid=108&sid=2545915, last accessed August 27, 2016.

Figure 2.2 Aerial view of the National Security Agency headquarters.

Soon after the September 11, 2001, attacks, President George W. Bush sought to establish an agency dedicated to the protection of the homeland, namely, the DHS.

2.5.1 Executive Order 13228: The origin of DHS

By executive order dated October 11, 2001, the president called for the establishment of DHS; outlined its mission, purpose, and aim; and set an early tone for how this agency would develop. See Figure 2.3.

2.5.2 Executive Order 12231: Protection of infrastructure

Shortly thereafter, President Bush issued another executive order that focused on the nation's critical infrastructure—those settings where significant damage could be inflicted, especially transportation infrastructure. In addition, the Chief Executive and Congress itself were rightfully concerned about other critical infrastructure such as water, energy and power plants, and other essential components of the American way of life. Executive Order 12231 (Figure 2.4), signed October 16, 2001, dealt directly with infrastructure.

The executive branch's view of infrastructure has been heightened over the term of President Barack Obama. In matters of funding and operational priorities, President Obama has repeatedly emphasized the interconnectedness of our infrastructure assets and urged agencies to prioritize the protection of our infrastructure in a more holistic way. By Presidential Proclamation 8607, President Obama declared that December 2010 was "Critical Infrastructure Protection Month" and noted that infrastructure is "essential to the security, economic welfare, public health and safety of the United States."[28]

2.5.3 Executive Order 13493 of January 22, 2009

Soon after his installation as president, Barack Obama reiterated his long-held view that the Guantanamo facility and its interrogation practices should be ended. In early 2009, he issued an order setting up a commission to end the status

---

[28] Federal Register, Friday, December 3, 2010, Vol. 75 No. 232, Proclamation 8607, pg. 75613.

Executive Order

Establishing the Office of Homeland Security and the Homeland Security Council

By the authority vested in me as President by the Constitution and the laws of the United States of America, it is hereby ordered as follows:

Section 1. Establishment. I hereby establish within the Executive Office of the President an Office of Homeland Security (the "Office") to be headed by the Assistant to the President for Homeland Security.

Section 2. Mission. The mission of the Office shall be to develop and coordinate the implementation of a comprehensive national strategy to secure the United States from terrorist threats or attacks. The Office shall perform the functions necessary to carry out this mission, including the functions specified in section 3 of this order.

Section 3. Functions. The functions of the Office shall be to coordinate the executive branch's efforts to detect, prepare for, prevent, protect against, respond to, and recover from terrorist attacks within the United States.

1. National Strategy. The Office shall work with executive departments and agencies, State and local governments, and private entities to ensure the adequacy of the national strategy for detecting, preparing for, preventing, protecting against, responding to, and recovering from terrorist threats or attacks within the United States and shall periodically review and coordinate revisions to that strategy as necessary.
2. Detection. The Office shall identify priorities and coordinate efforts for collection and analysis of information within the United States regarding threats of terrorism against the United States and activities of terrorists or terrorist groups within the United States. The Office also shall identify, in coordination with the Assistant to the President for National Security Affairs, priorities for collection of intelligence outside the United States regarding threats of terrorism within the United States.
   a. In performing these functions, the Office shall work with Federal, State, and local agencies, as appropriate, to:
      i. facilitate collection from State and local governments and private entities of information pertaining to terrorist threats or activities within the United States;
      ii. coordinate and prioritize the requirements for foreign intelligence relating to terrorism within the United States of executive departments and agencies responsible for homeland security and provide these requirements and priorities to the Director of Central Intelligence and other agencies responsible collection of foreign intelligence;
      iii. coordinate efforts to ensure that all executive departments and agencies that have intelligence collection responsibilities have sufficient technological capabilities and resources to collect intelligence and data relating to terrorist activities or possible terrorist acts within the United States, working with the Assistant to the President for National Security Affairs, as appropriate;
      iv. coordinate development of monitoring protocols and equipment for use in detecting the release of biological, chemical, and radiological hazards; and
      v. ensure that, to the extent permitted by law, all appropriate and necessary intelligence and law enforcement information relating to homeland security is disseminated to and exchanged among appropriate executive departments and agencies responsible for homeland security and, where appropriate for reasons of homeland security, promote exchange of such information with and among State and local governments and private entities.
   b. Executive departments and agencies shall, to the extent permitted by law, make available to the Office all information relating to terrorist threats and activities within the United States.
3. Preparedness. The Office of Homeland Security shall coordinate national efforts to prepare for and mitigate the consequences of terrorist threats or attacks within the United States. In performing this function, the Office shall work with Federal, State, and local agencies, and private entities, as appropriate, to:
   a. review and assess the adequacy of the portions of all Federal emergency response plans that pertain to terrorist threats or attacks within the United States;
   b. coordinate domestic exercises and simulations designed to assess and practice systems that would be called upon to respond to a terrorist threat or attack within the United States and coordinate programs and activities for training Federal, State, and local employees who would be called upon to respond to such a threat or attack;
   c. coordinate national efforts to ensure public health preparedness for a terrorist attack, including reviewing vaccination policies and reviewing the adequacy of and, if necessary, increasing vaccine and pharmaceutical stockpiles and hospital capacity;
   d. coordinate Federal assistance to State and local authorities and nongovernmental organizations to prepare for and respond to terrorist threats or attacks within the United States;
   e. ensure that national preparedness programs and activities for terrorist threats or attacks are developed and are regularly evaluated under appropriate standards and that resources are allocated to improving and sustaining preparedness based on such evaluations; and
   f. ensure the readiness and coordinated deployment of Federal response teams to respond to terrorist threats or attacks, working with the Assistant to the President for National Security Affairs, when appropriate.
4. Prevention. The Office shall coordinate efforts to prevent terrorist attacks within the United States. In performing this function, the Office shall work with Federal, State, and local agencies, and private entities, as appropriate, to:
   a. facilitate the exchange of information among such agencies relating to immigration and visa matters and shipments of cargo; and, working with the Assistant to the President for National Security Affairs, ensure coordination among such agencies to prevent the entry of terrorists and terrorist materials and supplies into the United States and facilitate removal of such terrorists from the United States, when appropriate;

Figure 2.3   Executive order establishing the DHS.   (*Continued*)

    b. coordinate efforts to investigate terrorist threats and attacks within the United States; and

    c. coordinate efforts to improve the security of United States borders, territorial waters, and airspace in order to prevent acts of terrorism within the United States, working with the Assistant to the President for National Security Affairs, when appropriate.

5. Protection. The Office shall coordinate efforts to protect the United States and its critical infrastructure from the consequences of terrorist attacks. In performing this function, the Office shall work with Federal, State, and local agencies, and private entities, as appropriate, to:

    a. strengthen measures for protecting energy production, transmission, and distribution services and critical facilities; other utilities; telecommunications; facilities that produce, use, store, or dispose of nuclear material; and other critical infrastructure services and critical facilities within the United States from terrorist attack;

    b. coordinate efforts to protect critical public and privately owned information systems within the United States from terrorist attack;

    c. develop criteria for reviewing whether appropriate security measures are in place at major public and privately owned facilities within the United States;

    d. coordinate domestic efforts to ensure that special events determined by appropriate senior officials to have national significance are protected from terrorist attack;

    e. coordinate efforts to protect transportation systems within the United States, including railways, highways, shipping, ports and waterways, and airports and civilian aircraft, from terrorist attack;

    f. coordinate efforts to protect United States livestock, agriculture, and systems for the provision of water and food for human use and consumption from terrorist attack; and

    g. coordinate efforts to prevent unauthorized access to, development of, and unlawful importation into the United States of, chemical, biological, radiological, nuclear, explosive, or other related materials that have the potential to be used in terrorist attacks.

6. Response and Recovery. The Office shall coordinate efforts to respond to and promote recovery from terrorist threats or attacks within the United States. In performing this function, the Office shall work with Federal, State, and local agencies, and private entities, as appropriate, to:

    a. coordinate efforts to ensure rapid restoration of transportation systems, energy production, transmission, and distribution systems; telecommunications; other utilities; and other critical infrastructure facilities after disruption by a terrorist threat or attack;

    b. coordinate efforts to ensure rapid restoration of public and private critical information systems after disruption by a terrorist threat or attack;

    c. work with the National Economic Council to coordinate efforts to stabilize United States financial markets after a terrorist threat or attack and manage the immediate economic and financial consequences of the incident;

    d. coordinate Federal plans and programs to provide medical, financial, and other assistance to victims of terrorist attacks and their families; and

    e. coordinate containment and removal of biological, chemical, radiological, explosive, or other hazardous materials in the event of a terrorist threat or attack involving such hazards and coordinate efforts to mitigate the effects of such an attack.

7. Incident Management. The Assistant to the President for Homeland Security shall be the individual primarily responsible for coordinating the domestic response efforts of all departments and agencies in the event of an imminent terrorist threat and during and in the immediate aftermath of a terrorist attack within the United States and shall be the principal point of contact for and to the President with respect to coordination of such efforts. The Assistant to the President for Homeland Security shall coordinate with the Assistant to the President for National Security Affairs, as appropriate.

8. Continuity of Government. The Assistant to the President for Homeland Security, in coordination with the Assistant to the President for National Security Affairs, shall review plans and preparations for ensuring the continuity of the Federal Government in the event of a terrorist attack that threatens the safety and security of the United States Government or its leadership.

9. Public Affairs. The Office, subject to the direction of the White House Office of Communications, shall coordinate the strategy of the executive branch for communicating with the public in the event of a terrorist threat or attack within the United States. The Office also shall coordinate the development of programs for educating the public about the nature of terrorist threats and appropriate precautions and responses.

10. Cooperation with State and Local Governments and Private Entities. The Office shall encourage and invite the participation of State and local governments and private entities, as appropriate, in carrying out the Office's functions.

11. Review of Legal Authorities and Development of Legislative Proposals. The Office shall coordinate a periodic review and assessment of the legal authorities available to executive departments and agencies to permit them to perform the functions described in this order. When the Office determines that such legal authorities are inadequate, the Office shall develop, in consultation with executive departments and agencies, proposals for presidential action and legislative proposals for submission to the Office of Management and Budget to enhance the ability of executive departments and agencies to perform those functions. The Office shall work with State and local governments in assessing the adequacy of their legal authorities to permit them to detect, prepare for, prevent, protect against, and recover from terrorist threats and attacks.

12. Budget Review. The Assistant to the President for Homeland Security, in consultation with the Director of the Office of Management and Budget (the "Director") and the heads of executive departments and agencies, shall identify programs that contribute to the Administration's strategy for homeland security and, in the development of the President's annual budget submission, shall review and provide advice to the heads of departments and agencies for such programs. The Assistant to the President

Figure 2.3 (Continued) Executive order establishing the DHS. *(Continued)*

for Homeland Security shall provide advice to the Director on the level and use of funding in departments and agencies for homeland security-related activities and, prior to the Director's forwarding of the proposed annual budget submission to the President for transmittal to the Congress, shall certify to the Director the funding levels that the Assistant to the President for Homeland Security believes are necessary and appropriate for the homeland security-related activities of the executive branch.

GEORGE W. BUSH
THE WHITE HOUSE,
October 8, 2001.

Figure 2.3   (Continued) Executive order establishing the DHS.

quo and seek transfer and other disposition of those residing in the facility. This promise was quite controversial and up to the present, its import utterly ineffectual. The Order posed in part:

Review of Detention Policy Options
By the authority vested in me as President by the Constitution and the laws of the United States of America, in order to develop policies for the detention, trial, transfer, release, or other disposition of individuals captured or apprehended in connection with armed conflicts and counterterrorism operations that are consistent with the national security and foreign policy interests of the United States and the interests of justice, I hereby order as follows:
Section 1. Special Interagency Task Force on Detainee Disposition.
(a) Establishment of Special Interagency Task Force. There shall be established a Special Task Force on Detainee Disposition (Special Task Force) to identify lawful options for the disposition of individuals captured or apprehended in connection with armed conflicts and counterterrorism operations.[29]

Executive Order on Critical Infrastructure Protection

By the authority vested in me as President by the Constitution and the laws of the United States of America, and in order to ensure protection of information systems for critical infrastructure, including emergency preparedness communications, and the physical assets that support such systems, in the information age, it is hereby ordered as follows:

Section 1. Policy.

a. The information technology revolution has changed the way business is transacted, government operates, and national defense is conducted. Those three functions now depend on an interdependent network of critical information infrastructures. The protection program authorized by this order shall consist of continuous efforts to secure information systems for critical infrastructure, including emergency preparedness communications, and the physical assets that support such systems. Protection of these systems is essential to the telecommunications, energy, financial services, manufacturing, water, transportation, health care, and emergency services sectors.
b. It is the policy of the United States to protect against disruption of the operation of information systems for critical infrastructure and thereby help to protect the people, economy, essential human and government services, and national security of the United States, and to ensure that any disruptions that occur are infrequent, of minimal duration, and manageable, and cause the least damage possible. The implementation of this policy shall include a voluntary public-private partnership, involving corporate and nongovernmental organizations.

Section 2. Scope. To achieve this policy, there shall be a senior executive branch board to coordinate and have cognizance of Federal efforts and programs that relate to protection of information systems and involve:

a. cooperation with and protection of private sector critical infrastructure, State and local governments, critical infrastructure, and supporting programs in corporate and academic organizations;
b. protection of Federal departments, and agencies, critical infrastructure; and
c. related national security programs.

Section 3. Establishment. I hereby establish the "President's Critical Infrastructure Protection Board" (the "Board").

Figure 2.4   Executive order on critical infrastructure protection.

---

[29] Federal Register, Tuesday, January 27, 2009, Executive Order 13493, 74 FR 4901, available at https://federalregister.gov/a/E9-1895, last accessed August 27, 2016.

The sum and substance of this decree was to find ways to end Guantanamo operations but the ambition met with the realities of being commander in chief and the president of the United States. While the president promised this policy during the campaign and the early days of his administration, the decree has never been realized. By 2015, he discovered that his worldview on the incarceration of terrorist's suspects had dramatically changed.

2.5.4 Executive Order 13567 of March 7, 2011

Disposing of some of the world's most suspect figures in the underbelly of terrorism can be quite a challenge. President Barack Obama, after nearly 26 months in office, essentially reverses himself on the closure of Guantanamo Bay by an order calling for periodic review and assessment of the prison's inhabitants.

The more pertinent part of the Order declares thus:

> Section 1. Scope and Purpose. (a) The periodic review described in section 3 of this order applies only to those detainees held at Guantanamo on the date of this order, whom the interagency review established by Executive Order 13492 has (i) designated for continued law of war detention; or (ii) referred for prosecution, except for those detainees against whom charges are pending or a judgment of conviction has been entered.
>
> (b) This order is intended solely to establish, as a discretionary matter, a process to review on a periodic basis the executive branch's continued, discretionary exercise of existing detention authority in individual cases. It does not create any additional or separate source of detention authority, and it does not affect the scope of detention authority under existing law. Detainees at Guantanamo have the constitutional privilege of the writ of habeas corpus, and nothing in this order is intended to affect the jurisdiction of Federal courts to determine the legality of their detention.
>
> (c) In the event detainees covered by this order are transferred from Guantanamo to another U.S. detention facility where they remain in law of war detention, this order shall continue to apply to them.
>
> Sec. 2. Standard for Continued Detention. Continued law of war detention is warranted for a detainee subject to the periodic review in section 3 of this order if it is necessary.[30]

At Section 2 of the Order, the president made plain that continued detention is within the discretionary authority of the United States under law of war principles. President Obama has been severely critiqued for essentially maintaining the policy of President George W. Bush. The American Civil Liberties Union has been less than kind about the determination holding the decree "shameless."[31]

2.5.5 Executive Order 13691 of February 13, 2015: Promoting private sector cybersecurity information sharing

The White House recently issued an executive order to encourage and promote sharing of cybersecurity threat information between the private sector and the government. Information sharing is an essential element of effective cybersecurity, because it enables U.S. companies to work together to respond to threats, rather than singularly operating and reacting to threats. Quick and expeditious identification of cyber threats is the chief aim of the order. See Figure 2.5.

Web Exercise: Discover the full range of cyber activities that DHS responds to at https://www.dhs.gov/topic/cybersecurity.

This executive order encourages the development of Information Sharing and Analysis Organizations (ISAOs), which become designated areas for cybersecurity sharing and dissemination. Information Sharing and Analysis Centers (ISACs) are already essential drivers of effective cybersecurity collaboration, and could constitute ISAOs under this new framework. In encouraging the creation of ISAOs, the executive order expands information sharing by encouraging the formation of communities that share information across a region or in response to a specific emerging cyber threat. The precise organizational qualities of the ISAO are wide open. Some states have banded together to create a multi-jurisdictional means of sharing and disseminating information. See Figure 2.6.

---

[30] Federal Register, Thursday, March 10, 2011, Executive Order 13567, 76 FR 13277, available at http://www.gpo.gov/fdsys/pkg/FR-2011-03-10/pdf/2011-5728.pdf, last accessed August 27, 2016.

[31] American Civil Liberties Union, President Obama Issues Executive Order Institutionalizing Indefinite Detention, March 7, 2011, at http://www.aclu.org/national-security/president-obama-issues-executive-order-institutionalizing-indefinite-detention, last accessed August 27, 2016.

Figure 2.5   President Barack Obama signing Executive Order 13691 on February 13, 2015.

Figure 2.6   Multi-State Information Sharing & Analysis Center logo.

2.5.6 Homeland Security Act of 2002

Not long after 9/11, Congress and President Bush, working swiftly and in concert, moved passage of the *Homeland Security Act of 2002*.[32] The act seeks to minimize the threat of another 9/11 and poses its mission in broad terms. Part of the act lays out the mission of DHS.

The primary mission of the department is to

- prevent terrorist attacks within the United States;
- reduce the vulnerability of the United States to terrorism;
- minimize the damage, and assist in the recovery, from terrorist attacks that do occur within the United States;
- carry out all functions of entities transferred to the department, including by acting as a focal point regarding natural and manmade crises and emergency planning;
- ensure that the functions of the agencies and subdivisions within the department that are not related directly to securing the homeland are not diminished or neglected except by a specific explicit act of Congress;
- ensure that the overall economic security of the United States is not diminished by efforts, activities, and programs aimed at securing the homeland; and
- monitor connections between illegal drug trafficking and terrorism, coordinate efforts to sever such connections, and otherwise contribute to efforts to interdict illegal drug trafficking.[33]

---

[32] Homeland Security Act of 2002, U.S. Code 6 (2002), § 101.
[33] Homeland Security Act of 2002, U.S. Code 6 (2002), § 101 (b).

The act further compartmentalized the agency into four main areas of responsibility, namely, border and transportation; emergency preparedness and response; chemical, biological, radiological, and nuclear countermeasures; and information analysis and infrastructure protection.

The significance of these categories cannot be overemphasized. In border and transportation, DHS assumed control over security services relating to our borders, territorial waters, and transportation systems. Immigration and naturalization, customs, coast guard, and animal protection issues are now DHS functions.

In emergency preparedness and response, there was a complete merger of FEMA operations into DHS. FEMA became an organization dedicated not only to natural disaster, but also to man-made events. Federal interagency emergency programs were subsumed into DHS as well as critical response units relating to nuclear and pharmaceutical events.

In matters involving prevention of chemical, radiological, and nuclear terror, DHS plays a central, coordinating role. Efforts here would be one of centralization and coordination of diverse department activities across the spectrum of government agencies. Guidelines regarding weapons of mass destruction were rapidly promulgated.

In the area of intelligence and threat analysis, DHS acts as a central repository for information pertaining to threats to the homeland. Data from traditional intelligence organizations such as the CIA, FBI, NSA, INS, and DEA are cataloged and disseminated as needed.

As for infrastructure, DHS is responsible for the evaluation and protection of the country's primary infrastructure, including food and water systems, health and emergency services, telecommunications, energy, chemical and defense industries, and common carrier transportation. Issues of infrastructure continue to be pressed by both the executive and the legislative branch. Since roads, bridges, tunnels, and other access points are not part of the infrastructure equation, President Obama has sought to designate homeland funding to its maintenance and repair. DHS continues to correctly dabble and identify infrastructure[34] with various programs such as

- Workshops on Aging Technology
- Rapid Visual Screening Tools for Buildings and Tunnels
- Collapse Mitigation
- Building Design Training Programs

Finally, DHS extended its program reach to state, local, and private sector justice agencies. One of the hallmarks of DHS is the cultivation of inter- and intra-agency cooperation. DHS saw the essential need for mutual trust and respect between competing agencies so that the mission of DHS might be implemented. DHS erected an "intergovernmental affairs office" to coordinate the numerous initiatives emanating from the agency.

2.5.6.1 The Homeland Security Act and Posse Comitatus

An often overlooked section of the Homeland Security Act makes reference to the *Posse Comitatus Act of 1878*. The Posse Comitatus Act, passed June 18, 1878, essentially outlines limits on the federal government's use of military forces for purposes of law enforcement. Section 886 of the Homeland Security Act refers to Posse Comitatus:

> SEC 886(b) SENSE OF CONGRESS.—Congress reaffirms the continued importance of section 1385 of title 18, United States Code, and it is the sense of Congress that nothing in this Act should be construed to alter the applicability of such section to any use of the Armed Forces as a posse comitatus to execute the laws.[35]

Section 1385 of title 18 is the reference to Posse Comitatus and, per November 11, 2002 remarks for then-President George W. Bush, essentially the Homeland Security Act and Section 886(b) "does not purport to alter, modify, or otherwise affect the Posse Comitatus Act or judicial interpretations of that Act, and the executive branch shall construe this provision accordingly."[36]

---

[34] Congressional Research Service, *Critical Infrastructures: Background, Policy and Implementation* (July 2011).

[35] Homeland Security Act of 2002, Public Law 107–296, November 25, 2002, at http://www.dhs.gov/xlibrary/assets/hr_5005_enr.pdf, last accessed August 27, 2016.

[36] President's Remarks at Homeland Security Bill Signing, Department of Homeland Security Official Home Page, November 25, 2002, at https://georgewbush-whitehouse.archives.gov/news/releases/2002/11/20021125-6.html, last accessed August 27, 2016.

This becomes relevant and creates an interesting debate; however, as on October 1, 2002, just past the one-year anniversary of 9/11, United States Northern Command (USNORTHCOM, or simply, NORTHCOM) was created. NORTHCOM is a Unified Combatant Command (UCC) of the U.S. military, meaning it has multiple branches of the military under a single command and its purpose is to provide command and control of DoD homeland defense efforts and to coordinate defense support of civil authorities. In recent years, there has been a growing debate among politicians, and government policy-makers and scholars over what role, if any, the U.S. military should take in domestic operations. Though not exempt when deployed under federal service, the National Guard is exempt during peacetime or when specifically called upon by state governors during crisis and disaster situations. The Coast Guard too is likewise exempt from Posse Comitatus.

Since its creation, NORTHCOM has aided in counter-drug operations as well as in response to Hurricane Katrina, multiple California and Colorado wildfires, and other similar regional domestic natural disaster events. It remains to be seen what the ultimate policy on and role of NORTHCOM will be in responding to natural disasters or mass civil disturbances in future.

2.5.7 USA Patriot Act

One of the most controversial pieces of legislation that arose from the turbulent post-9/11 period was the Patriot Act.[37] The Patriot Act was developed out of the belief that our intelligence was extremely poor prior to the attacks and it sought to remedy the perceived failures in intelligence to ensure such an attack would never occur again. Patriot Act proposals were quickly drafted and signed by President Bush on October 26, 2001. Given the intensity of the times, it is not surprising that such an important bill found formal approval in so short a span. The times influenced the aggressive nature of the bill and its inclination to expand or alter historic restrictions:

- Information sharing—The act liberalizes the sharing of intelligence information and removes most historical barriers to said sharing. Critics argue that the data will be used by other agencies for unrelated purposes or improper reasons.

- Roving wiretaps—The act permits the jurisdictional grant of one wiretap order that works or roves in multiple jurisdictions. Given the transiency of terrorists, and the difficulties of dealing with diverse jurisdictions, the policy makes sense. Critics claim it will lead to an open-ended form of electronic surveillance.

- Foreign intelligence and wiretaps—The act liberalizes the grant and extent of this activity. New standards for use have been enacted. Critics claim this will lead to abuse.

- Sneak and peek warrants—In criminal parlance, "exigent" circumstances have always permitted law enforcement to search a house without a warrant. The act permits quick searches, without notification, of a suspected terrorist place of abode under an "any crime" provision. Critics note that the historic standard of these types of searches relates to loss of evidence or other exigency.

- Material support—The act expands the definition of support to include advice and counsel. Historically "material" support related to economic or planning support that was central to the plot and plan. The idea of how one can support has been expanded. Critics claim this violates free speech.

The Patriot Act was reauthorized in 2006 despite significant controversy.[38] DHS publicly advocated for passage of the reauthorization since it had amassed concrete examples of how effective the act had been in the apprehension of terrorists and prevention of terror. In December 2005, DHS exhorted Congress to finish up its business relative to the act by noting,

The DHS benefits significantly from the USA Patriot Act and urges the U.S. Congress to reauthorize this proven tool in the global war on terror. The Patriot Act breaks down barriers to information sharing, enabling law enforcement and intelligence personnel to share information that is needed to help connect the dots and disrupt potential terror and criminal activity before they can carry out their plots. The broad information sharing provisions better

---

[37] Public Law 107-56—Uniting and Strengthening America by Providing Appropriate Tools Required to Intercept and Obstruct Terrorism (USA Patriot Act) Act of 2001.

[38] See K.L. Hermann, Reviewing Bush-Era Counter-Terrorism Policy After 9/11: Reconciling Ethical and Practical Considerations, 4 *Homeland Sec. Rev.* 139 (2010); see also C.L. Richardson, The Creation of Judicial Compromise: Prosecuting Detainees in a National Security Court System in Guantanamo Bay, Cuba, 4 *Homeland Sec. Rev.* 119 (2010).

enable CBP to screen international visitors and determine whether an apprehended alien presents a threat to security or public safety.[39]

During the 2010–2011 session, the Patriot Act was again reauthorized, and again the debate was highly contentious on both sides of the aisle. The dissent even crossed party lines as liberals construed the broad sweep of unchecked police powers while conservatives concerned about the constitutional implications reached similar conclusions.[40] In particular, the "roving wiretaps" provision, whereby investigators seeks court orders that allow changing phone number follow-ups without court scrutiny, was a stumbling block. The act reiterated its three-part requirement when seeking the court order, namely,

- Establishing probable cause that the target of the surveillance is a foreign power or agent of a foreign power;
- Probable cause that the device is being used or about to be used by a foreign power or agent of a foreign power; and
- That the actions of the target may have the effect of blocking their identification.[41]

The reauthorized act also retained the more liberal and flexible standard when seizing the business records of a suspected terrorist and instead of the historic "specific and articulable facts" requirement a court could issue an order based on a "relevancy standard."[42]

During the current congressional sessions of 2015, parts of the act are up for renewal—all of which is in flux at the moment. Debate about metadata collection, roving wiretaps and other surveillance tactics en masse are at center of the dispute.[43]

The U.S. House of Representatives have tried to rein in the potential for privacy abuse in the Patriot Act by offering up the U.S. Freedom Act—which would allow the full reauthorization of the Patriot Act as long as certain modifications were made, including

- End bulk data collection
- End NSA data collection in conformity with a recent legal ruling of a federal appeals court
- Strengthen privacy rights
- Curtail government surveillance[44]

The opposition to the reauthorization of the Patriot Act has been led by Senator Rand Paul. See Figure 2.7.

2.5.8 Specialized laws

Aside from the broader legislation and regulations covering the world of homeland security, there are many other laws and rules promulgated on behalf of or by administrative agencies and departments entrusted with functions in homeland protection. All of these laws impact how security services are provided at many locations. A few of the more prominent are discussed below.

2.5.8.1 The REAL ID program

Concerns over the legitimacy and integrity of driver's licenses resulted in the promulgation of a new DHS program—REAL ID.[45] The program sets minimal standards for the issuance of driver's licenses, including

- Information and security features that must be incorporated into each card
- Proof of identity and U.S. citizenship or legal status of an applicant

---

[39] U.S. Department of Homeland Security, *Fact Sheet: The USA Patriot Act—A Proven Homeland Security Tool* (December 14, 2005), at https://www.hsdl.org/?view&did=477077, last accessed August 27, 2016.

[40] C. Savage, Deal Reached on Extension of Patriot Act, *N.Y. Times* (May 19, 2011), at http://www.nytimes.com/2011/05/20/us/20patriot.html, last visited August 27, 2016.

[41] Republican Study Committee, *Legis. Bull.* (May 26, 2011).

[42] See USA Patriot Act, section 215 (2011).

[43] See D. Barrett, FBI Fears Loss of Surveillance Tools in Patriot Act, *Wall Street Journal* Online Edition (February 4, 2015), at http://www.wsj.com/articles/fbi-fears-loss-of-its-surveillance-tools-in-patriot-act-1423091243, last accessed August 27, 2016.

[44] See T. Risen, Freedom Act Passes House Despite Privacy Criticism, *US News & World Report* (May 13, 2015), at http://www.usnews.com/news/articles/2015/05/13/freedom-act-passes-house-despite-privacy-criticism, last accessed August 27, 2016.

[45] REAL ID Act of 2005, P.L. 109-13, U.S. Statutes at Large 119 (2005): 231, http://www.govtrack.us/congress/bill.xpd?tab=summary&bill=h109-418, last accessed August 27, 2016.

Figure 2.7   Senator Rand Paul.

- Verification of the source documents provided by an applicant
- Security standards for the offices that issue licenses and identification cards

Critics of the act claim it devises a national identity card program, but this criticism seems somewhat inaccurate. The provisions of the act reaffirm the preeminence of state governments in the matter of issuance and oversight. DHS posts a Q&A piece that deals with common misconceptions regarding REAL ID, shown in Figure 2.8.

Even the DHS fosters an ambivalent and less than supportive view of the program due to costs and implementation challenges. In its Inspector General report, the DHS remarked thus:

> Potentially high costs pose a significant challenge to states in their efforts to implement REAL ID. Specifically, state officials considered REAL ID implementation costs prohibitive because of requirements such as the reenrollment of all current driver's license and identification card holders and the new verification processes. Further, state officials in 17 of the 19 states we contacted indicated they needed more timely guidance from DHS to estimate the full cost of implementing REAL ID. State officials also said that REAL ID grants did not sufficiently mitigate the costs, and they viewed communication of grant information by DHS as ineffective.[46]

With nearly a decade of legislative life, the REAL ID program has yet to fully materialize on a state by state level. Implementation results have been dramatically mixed. By 2015, only 23 states had completely implemented the program.[47]

---

[46] Department of Homeland Security, Office of Inspector General, *Potentially High Costs and Insufficient Grant Funds Pose a Challenge to REAL ID Implementation* 1 (OIG-09-36) (March 2009).

[47] Center for Immigration Studies, *REAL ID Implementation: Less Expensive, Doable, and Helpful in Reducing Fraud* (January 2011), at http://cis.org/real-id, last accessed August 27, 2016.

Myth: REAL ID creates a national identification (ID) card

Fact: REAL ID simply sets minimum standards so that the public can have confidence in the security and integrity of driver's licenses and identification cards issued by all participating states and jurisdictions.

States and jurisdictions will maintain their ability to design and issue their own unique driver's licenses and identification cards. Each state and jurisdiction will continue to have flexibility with regard to the design and security features used on the card. Where REAL ID details the minimum data elements that must be included on the face of the card, most states and jurisdictions already include all or almost all of these data elements on their cards.

REAL ID identification documents will not be the only form of documentation accepted by the federal government or any other entity. You can still present another form of acceptable identification such as a U.S. passport, military ID, or government identification badge. If you do not have another form of acceptable documentation, however, you may experience delays at the airport due to the requirement for additional security screening.

Myth: REAL ID creates a national database of personal information

Fact: REAL ID requires that authorized DMV officials have the capability to verify that an applicant holds only one valid REAL ID. REAL ID does not grant the Federal Government or law enforcement greater access to DMV data, nor does it create a national database.

States will continue to manage and operate databases for driver's license and identification card issuance.

REAL ID does not create a national database or require additional personal information on your driver's license than is already required by most states. It simply verifies the documents an applicant presents at the DMV to confirm the individual's identity and ensure that each individual has only one valid REAL ID.

Personally identifiable information, beyond the minimum information necessary to appropriately route verification queries, will not be stored.

Myth: REAL ID will diminish privacy

Fact: The REAL ID final rule calls on states to protect personal identity information. It requires each state to develop a security plan and lists a number of privacy and security elements that must be included in the plan.

The DHS Privacy Office has also issued Best Practices for the Protection of Personally Identifiable Information Associated with State Implementation of the Real ID Act, which provides useful guidance to states on how to address the privacy and security of information related to REAL ID.

The REAL ID Act will not allow motor vehicle driver's data to be made available in a manner that does not conform to the Driver's Privacy Protection Act. Furthermore, with REAL ID, DMV employees will be subject to background checks, a necessary step to protect against insider fraud, just one of the vulnerabilities to a secure licensing system. These steps raise the bar for state DMVs beyond what was previously required.

DHS recognizes the importance of protecting privacy and ensuring the security of the personal information associated with implementation of the REAL ID Act.

Myth: DHS is creating a "hub" in order to gain access to Department of Motor Vehicle (DMV) information

Fact: An electronic verification hub will be designed to facilitate connectivity between the states and data owners to ensure that people applying for a REAL ID are who they say they are. The Federal Government will not gain greater access to DMV information as a result. Only authorized DMV officials and law enforcement will have access to DMV records.

REAL ID requires state DMVs to verify an applicant's identity document, date of birth, Social Security Number, residence and lawful status, as well as ensure that each individual has only one valid REAL ID. For example, the electronic verification hub will facilitate the state-to-state exchange of information to check for duplicate registrations in multiple states, therefore limiting the ability for persons to obtain multiple licenses for fraudulent purposes.

While DHS has pledged to fund the development and deployment of the hub, states will continue to manage and operate databases for driver's license and identification card issuance. DHS and the states will work together to ensure that security measures are in place to prevent unauthorized access or use of the information. Personally identifiable information, beyond the minimum information necessary to appropriately route verification queries, will not be stored.

Myth: REAL ID is an unfunded mandate

Fact: To date, approximately $90 million in dedicated grant funds have been offered by DHS to assist states with REAL ID implementation. This includes approximately $40 million in Fiscal Year (FY) 2006 and $50 million in FY 2008. An additional 20 percent of State Homeland Security Grant funds are discretionary and can be used for this purpose as well.

The President's Fiscal Year 2009 budget request includes up to $150 million in grants for states to implement REAL ID (up to $110 million from National Security and Terrorism Prevention Grants and again, 20 percent of the State Homeland Security Grants).

DHS requested $50 million in Fiscal Year 2009 appropriated funds for the establishment of a state-owned and operated verification system. Furthermore, DHS cut the total costs to states by more than $10 billion from an original estimate of $14.6 billion to approximately $3.9 billion, a 73 percent reduction. States will continue to have discretionary authority to use up to 20 percent of their Homeland Security Grant funds for REAL ID implementation.

In order to focus the first phase of enrollment on those persons who may present the highest risk, DHS outlined an age-based enrollment approach to REAL ID allowing other individuals to be phased-in later. Phased-in enrollment eases the burden on states to re-enroll their entire driver's license and identification card population by providing additional time to accommodate the re-enrollment process.

Figure 2.8   REAL ID FAQs.

Pace and commitment still differ among the states, but there is a noteworthy reduction in discussion as states are finding out implementation, on the whole, is not as expensive as they thought and is achievable. States like Maryland and Delaware, once committed, have completed implementation of the 18 benchmarks needed to fulfill material compliance with the law within a year for only twice the grant monies provided by the federal government. Extrapolated out, that puts total costs for implementing these key 18 REAL ID benchmarks in a range from $350 million to $750 million, an order of magnitude less than estimated previously. And with metrics in place, the story of REAL ID's value in securing against fraud is beginning to take shape as not simply theory, but reality.[48]

The card design requirements are estimated at 1.1 billion dollars.[49] See Figure 2.9 for an overview of state by state implementation.

While compliance dates have been extended three times, it appears unlikely that most states will be ever be compliant with the diverse requirements of the act. Critics have also called into question the constitutionality of this sort of federalized oversight in the matter of national identity.[50]

2.5.8.2 Office of Biometric Identity Management

The Office of Biometric Identity Management (OBIM; formerly the office of US-VISIT) resides in DHS was established to track the entry and exit of travelers to the United States by biometric means—digital fingerprints and photographs. The guiding principles of OIBM are the following:

- Enhance the security of our citizens and visitors
- Facilitate legitimate travel and trade
- Ensure the integrity of the immigration system
- Protect the privacy of our visitors

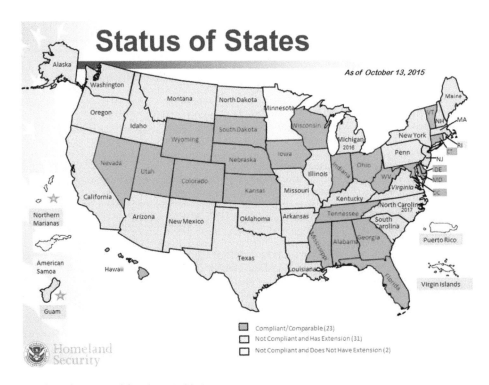

Figure 2.9   Status of the States as of October 13, 2015.

---

[48] *Ibid.*

[49] Department of Homeland Security, *supra* note 47, at 6.

[50] J. Harper, Florida's Implementation of the Federal Real ID Act of 2005 (February 24, 2011), at http://www.cato.org/pub_display.php?pub_id=12818, last accessed August 27, 2016.

The use of biometrics represents the cutting edge of identity assurance. By using unique physical characteristics, the agency can zero in on identity in a highly dependable way. OBIM uses biometric information for the following:

- To check a person's biometrics against a watch list of known or suspected terrorists, criminals, and immigration violators
- To check against the entire database of all of the fingerprints the DHS has collected since OBIM began to determine if a person is using an alias and attempting to use fraudulent identification
- To check a person's biometrics against those associated with the identification document presented to ensure that the document belongs to the person presenting it and not someone else

Upon a person's entry into the United States, a CBP officer uses inkless, digital finger scanners to scan both the left and the right index finger of the person. The officer also takes a digital photograph.

2.5.8.3 Chemical facilities

DHS has been actively involved in the oversight of chemical facilities due to their capacity to inflict widespread damage. Antiterrorism standards must be integrated in the design, plan, and operational security of designated chemical facilities. Congress, in passage of the 2007 Homeland Security reauthorization,[51] applied these standards because of the inherent risk to these facilities. DHS defines the risk as

- The consequence of a successful attack on a facility (consequence)
- The likelihood that an attack on a facility will be successful (vulnerability)
- The intent and capability of an adversary in respect to attacking a facility (threat)
- DHS established risk-based performance standards for the security of the country's chemical facilities. Covered chemical facilities are required to
- Prepare security vulnerability assessments, which identify facility security vulnerabilities
- Develop and implement site security plans, which include measures that satisfy the identified risk-based performance standards

DHS publishes both a list of chemical products of significant interest to the country and a list of assessment tools to ensure compliance.[52] Chemical facilities are construed as infrastructure.

2.5.8.4 The SAFETY Act

One of the Homeland Security Act of 2002s best kept secrets was its desire to promote innovation in antiterrorism efforts. Innovation in technology is always a risky business. When the potential legal liabilities are added to the process of invention, such as being open to lawsuit, the inventor is less aggressive. The *Support Antiterrorism by Fostering Effective Technologies Act of 2002 (SAFETY Act)*[53] provides a safe harbor for the inventor and the product developer. It also provides a certification process whereby DHS approves a product for usage in the fight against terrorism. As of 2015, hundreds of products and services have been approved. Here are some recent examples:

May 13, 2015—Centerra Group, LLC provides Security and Fire/Emergency Response Services (the "Technology"). The Technology is armed and unarmed guard services, specialized security forces, and fire protection and emergency response services for select government agencies. This Designation will expire on May 31, 2020.

May 13, 2015—Geo-Trans International, Inc. (d/b/a Boston Freight Terminals) provides a Certified Cargo Screening Facility (the "Technology"). The Technology is designed to aid in meeting the congressional mandate that 100% of cargo placed on passenger airplanes be screened. The Technology includes, and provides, screeners and programmatic personnel for the screening of cargo in accordance with the Transportation Security Administration ("TSA")'s Certified Cargo Screening Program at TSA-approved Certified Cargo Screening Facilities. This Designation will expire on May 31, 2020.

---

[51] Homeland Security Appropriations Act of 2007, P.L. 109-295, Section 550, U.S. Statutes at Large 120 (2006): 1355.

[52] For a complete list of chemicals subject to the administrative regulations, see Code of Federal Regulations, title 6, part 27 (2007), at http://www.dhs.gov/xlibrary/assets/chemsec_appendixa-chemicalofinterestlist.pdf, last accessed August 27, 2016.

[53] Code of Federal Regulations, title 6, section 25.7(j) (2004).

May 13, 2015—STT, LLC and STTARX, LLC provide STTarx™ (the "Technology"). The Technology is a software package designed to create secure, closed network environments using the public Internet in order to provide protection from cyber-attacks against networks, data, and communications. This Developmental Testing and Evaluation Designation will expire on May 31, 2018.

April 28, 2015—SecureUSA, Inc. provides the FutureWEDGE Series (the "Technology"). The Technology is a product line of active perimeter vehicle barricades that aid in delaying the entrance of unauthorized intruders to installations. The Technology also includes installation, maintenance, and service, depending on customer requests/requirements. This Designation will expire on May 31, 2020.

2.6 ACADEMIC AND TRAINING PROGRAMS IN HOMELAND SECURITY

The breadth, depth, scope, and coverage of training and academic programs in homeland security are simply mind-boggling. Not only do agencies of government at the state, local, and federal levels devise, design, and deliver training in all the affairs of homeland security, but so too a plethora of private companies, businesses, colleges, and universities. In a nutshell, training and education is a fast-growing business for both the public and the private sector. In the public sense, government agencies, in seeking to carry out their mission, educate the public and the professionals who must labor each day in the justice and emergency model. The DHS is the preeminent figure in the training modality and delivers programs to every imaginable sector. A partial list of the agency's more prominent programs is charted in Figure 2.10.

This section will provide an overview of some of the public and private training systems and educational programs.

2.6.1 Office of Grants and Training

DHS, in its quest for centralization and improved efficiency, recently blended a host of diverse offices into the Office of Grants and Training (G&T). The *Post-Katrina Emergency Reform Act of 2006* amended the Homeland Security Act and mandates some mergers and realignments. As part of this reorganization, major national preparedness components and functions, which include the G&T, the United States Fire Administration, National Capital Region Coordination, Chemical Stockpile Emergency Preparedness, and the Radiological Emergency Preparedness Program, while still operational under the DHS heading, were transferred to FEMA, effective April 1, 2007.

The new organization reflects the expanded scope of FEMA's departmental responsibilities. It strengthens FEMA's coordination with other DHS components, as well as agencies and departments outside of DHS. It also enhances

---

FEMA Training and National Domestic Preparedness Consortium—Direct training for state and local jurisdictions to enhance capacity and preparedness

The Federal Law Enforcement Training Center—Up-to-date, low or no cost training opportunities for state and local law enforcement officers

National Preparedness Network (PREPnet)—First responder information programming schedule, all open and available to the public

The National Fire Academy—Training and educational opportunities for members of the fire, emergency services and allied professionals

Noble Training Center—Hospital-based medical training in disaster preparedness and response

The Emergency Management Institute—Training to ensure the effectiveness of organizations and individuals working together in disasters and emergencies

National Integration Center (NIC)—Incident Management Systems Division Information, guidance and resources to assist state, local, tribal and federal agencies in adopting and implementing the National Incident Management System

National Incident Management System (NIMS) Online Training—Introduction to the purpose, principles, key components and benefits of NIMS

Comprehensive Haz-Mat Emergency Response Capability Assessment Program (CHER-CAP)—Resource to prepare for hazardous materials incidents

National Exercise Program—Training, exercising, and collaboration among partners at all levels

Homeland Security Exercise and Evaluation Program—Threat- and performance-based exercise activities of varying degrees of complexity and interaction

Lessons Learned Information Sharing—Best practices and lessons learned from actual terrorist events and training exercises

U.S. Fire Administration Publications—Free publications for emergency responders including manuals, reports & incident reports

---

Figure 2.10 Department of Homeland Security programs.

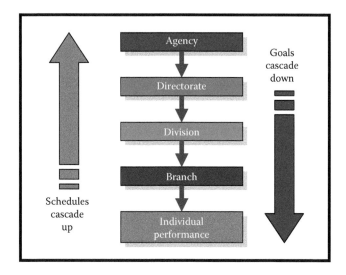

Figure 2.11 Strategy implementation chart.

FEMA's ability to partner with emergency management, law enforcement, preparedness organizations, and the private sector. Aside from this bureaucratic realignment, the G&T makes possible a bevy of training opportunities for homeland specialists. Its mission is multifaceted but directed primarily to those in the first responder category, such as fire and EMT, police, and paramedic.

Soon after these mergers, FEMA set out specific strategic goals that advance its grand vision to be the "Nation's Preeminent Emergency Management and Preparedness Agency."[54] FEMA sees the entire picture of grants and training in an agency–individual–employee horizon, making a noble effort to connect the larger purposes of the agency's purpose with the roles, tasks, and functions of its employees downstream. It labels this a "cascade up" or a "cascade down." Hence, the agency authors grant and training policies that compliment individual performance and the efficacy of the agency itself. See Figure 2.11.[55]

G&T fulfills this mission through a series of program efforts responsive to the specific requirements of state and local agencies. G&T works directly with emergency responders and conducts assessments of state and local needs and capabilities to guide the development and execution of these programs. Assistance provided by G&T is directed at a broad spectrum of state and local emergency responders, including firefighters, emergency medical services, emergency management agencies, law enforcement, and public officials.

G&T attends to this mission in a variety of ways by providing grants to states and local jurisdictions, providing hands-on training through a number of residential training facilities and in-service training at the local level, funding and working with state and local jurisdictions to plan and execute exercises, and providing technical assistance on-site to state and local jurisdictions. In many respects, the office fervently addresses Homeland Security Presidential Directive 8, which encourages all agencies of government to be prepared, train their personnel, and establish a national program and a multiyear planning system to conduct homeland security preparedness-related exercises that reinforce identified training standards, provide for evaluation of readiness, and support the national preparedness goal. The establishment and maintenance of the program will be conducted in maximum collaboration with state and local governments and appropriate private sector entities.[56]

The G&T supports cooperative partnerships among all relevant homeland constituencies. By and through the National Domestic Preparedness Consortium, the G&T identifies, develops, tests, and delivers training to state and local emergency responders. The G&T also funds equipment purchases for justice and emergency agencies. An approved equipment list is published by the department.

---

[54] FEMA, Grant Programs Directorate Strategic Plan, FY 2009-2001, at 9 (October 2008).
[55] *Ibid.* at 10.
[56] Office of the President, *Homeland Security Presidential Directive* 8 (December 17, 2003).

The G&T coordinates TOPOFF exercises and simulation programs. TOPOFF signifies "top officials" or higher-ups in the homeland supervisory chain. Officials from state, local, and federal agencies work collaboratively on a homeland problem, assess and evaluate the homeland dilemma, and publish best practices in dealing with the security question. The TOPOFF program has been replaced by what is now designated the "National Exercise Program" (NEP). The NEP allows federal, state, and local agencies to work collaboratively on all sorts of risks and hazards.

2.6.2 Center for Domestic Preparedness

The Center for Domestic Preparedness (CDP) operates within the FEMA construct and delivers key training and education in specialized fields. Located in Aniston, Alabama, the CDP is a fully accredited and comprehensive facility that provides both resident and commuter training in highly technical areas. Its specialty training relates to WMD. At the Chemical, Ordnance, Biological, and Radiological Training Facility (COBRATF), the CDP offers the only program in the nation featuring civilian training exercises using actual chemical agents. The advanced, hands-on training enables responders to effectively respond to real-world incidents involving chemical, biological, explosive, radiological, or other hazardous materials.

The CDP educates homeland professionals with graduated levels of sophistication and recognizes the most highly proficient practitioners. FEMA's CDP trained more than 93,500 local, state, and tribal responders from across the United States in preventing and responding to disasters and other terrorist threats involving chemical, biological, radiological, nuclear, and explosive materials.

2.6.3 Emergency Management Institute

The Emergency Management Institute (EMI), located in Emmittsburg, Maryland, is the lead national emergency management training, exercise, and educational institution. EMI is located on a pristine campus near Mt. St. Mary's College and shares its facilities with the U.S. Fire Administration's training center. EMI offers more than 510 courses covering all aspects of emergency preparedness in conjunction with its agency partners. The scope and influence of EMI has been significant since it has served an impressive number of customers including

- More than 2 million students annually, over all platforms.
- In 2010, the Disaster Field Training Operations trained 31,834 disaster response and recovery employees.
- In 2010, delivered 993 resident courses to over 24,000 individuals.
- EMI Independent Study program, a Web-based program open to the public, delivered online training of more than 180 courses to more than 1.9 million people.
- Courses are available in the following categories:
  - Integrated Emergency Management
  - Master Exercise Practitioner Program (MEPP)
  - Professional Development
  - Master Trainer Program
  - Mitigation Branch
  - Readiness
  - Disaster Operations and Recovery

EMI supports national and international emergency management with more than 50 countries participating in EMI's training and educational activities. EMI also enjoys close relations with several nationally recognized professional emergency management and related organizations, such as the International Association of Emergency Managers (IAEM), National Emergency Management Association (NEMA), Association of State Flood Plain Managers (ASFPM), American Public Works Association (APWA), American Society of Civil Engineers (ASCE), and American Society of Engineering Management (ASEM). EMI is fully accredited by the International Association for Continuing Education and Training (IACET) and the American Council on Education (ACE).

EMI conducts national-level conferences that are well received, including the National Preparedness Annual Training and Exercise Conference and the EMI Higher Education Conference. The conference collects and catalogs institutions, course materials such as syllabi and university texts, and programmatic directions in emergency management. EMI has also implemented a "School Program" that prepares elementary and secondary administrators for risk and threat.

The list of programs and initiatives launched by DHS is beyond the limitations of this text, but suffice to say, whether with transportation systems, maritime and cargo issues, pharmaceutical stockpiles and mass food storage, public health policy or contagious diseases, the federal influence on the security practice, for both the public and the private sector cannot be fully measured. Security is a worldwide series of protocols, practices, and targeted policies and each step taken by DHS causes ripples in the public and private justice systems.

2.6.4 The academic discipline of security management, security studies, and homeland security

Whenever an occupational profile translates into a new and emerging academic discipline or course of study, questions of depth of content, meaningfulness of social contribution, and diversity of career tracks are readily proven.[57] Security studies is a field of marked growth across many reputable universities, and plainly demonstrates the increased and steady demand for well-educated professionals. Sometimes housed in criminal justice departments as an individual major; other times a minor or secondary major for criminal justice and at other institutions, a free-standing academic program with all the rights and privileges of an academic major. Recent tallies show there are around 200 programs nationwide in the security management side, and an equal number in the emergent field of homeland security at both the graduate and the undergraduate level. In many ways, security studies and management resides in an early phase of its own inevitable development, much like criminal justice was in the 1950s. Often heard in debates about the field are those recurring critiques of vocationalism, occupationalism, and a lack of intellectual depth that used to be attributed to criminal justice. Is there something desirable in educating professionals and theoreticians in the justice system? Why is there an ongoing debate within various academic circles over the legitimacy of criminal justice and homeland security? These questions do not deal with semantic distinctions or academic turf protection regarding appropriate departments and disciplinary approaches. The questions are far broader than that—that is, is there function, is there purpose, is there value, is there a utility in the training of criminal justice professionals, including police and probation officers, and security managers and guard and other individuals who are responsible for the public and private order? George Felkenes, one of the most prolific writers and scholars within the discipline, notes,

> It is hardly surprising that in contemporary American education, a complex criminal justice program encounters controversy and even difficulty in defining its goals, objectives and often its very reason for being … There is a continuing dialog on the desirability of having training oriented programs located in educational institutions. The debate, sometimes acrimonious, sometimes filled with emotion, nevertheless is getting before the academic community and the public. The question of the basic desirability of having a field such as criminal justice recognized is an area worthy of study. It can also safely be said that as criminal justice educators began to question their own existence, the tendency developed to provide more and more specialized subdivision under the criminal justice rubric, each specialty required more and more time to master.[58]

Felkenes writes regularly about the inferiority complex that criminal justice has within the academic community, a complex fostered in part by the various constituencies it seeks to serve. A case in point is a police officer hardly enamored by the educational process described in "Does a Policeman Need to Have a College Degree to be a Professional?" The article states thus:

> So I again ask is a college degree needed? In most cases a police agency will train the officer on how to enforce the law, perform first aid and other related duties. I don't think college is going to change the officer's prejudices, emotional stability or personal feelings. To law enforcement I say, quit chasing a dream you are a professional.[59]

To many traditionalists in the police system and other criminal justice cynics, the view that education makes a good practitioner is blatantly naïve. Educators are viewed with some level of suspicion since they, in fact, often do operate from an ivory tower. In "Criminal Justice Education: Myths or Reality," the author comments insightfully.

---

[57] L. Stelter, Career Change Ahead, *Law Enforcement Technology* 14 (May, 2014).
[58] G. Felkenes, The Criminal Justice Component in an Educational Institution, 7 *J. Crim. Just.* 102 (1979).
[59] Gould, Does a Policeman Need to Have a College Degree to be a Professional? *Law & Order* 69 (February 1973).

The third issue in quality control involves the need to discover to what degree education training is functional. Educational institutions should not limit themselves only to the evaluation of the academic competencies of their students. They should also be concerned about the ability of the student to apply and use his education in a practical situation. Grades are no guarantee than an individual can or cannot function on the job … The question should be stated: How is the individual going to function on the job in relationship to his education.[60]

The answer to that query is cumbersome particularly since each educational institution may have a varied disciplinary approach, emphasizing training and vocationalism rather than the liberal arts, or strict cognitive analysis. What is demonstrable is that there is a segment of the practitioner population system that is suspicious of education. In short, education that does not constitute training is considered to be nonutilitarian. The key concepts of education and training summarize the conflict of interest between certain academics, theoreticians, and practitioners.

The antagonist position on education is a minority one. The overwhelming body of literature gives an extremely positive review of educational programs for police and other criminal justice professionals, and for a myriad of reasons. Most issues are problems of implementation and design rather than intentions. The consensus is more of a mandate from both scholarly and practitioner sources. For a plethora of reasons, education is something of value, utility, and function.

See "Academic Institutions Offering Degrees, Concentrations, or Certificates in Security Management"[61] for the ASIS's listing of academic programs in security management. It is not only the sheer number of programs that count but also the quality of the institutions sponsoring the academic department such as the John Jay College of Criminal Justice, George Washington University, Eastern Kentucky University, Northeastern University and Boston University.[62] Security studies has branched off into homeland security analysis as well.[63] In fact, growth has been quite significant.[64] The rise and constant escalation of homeland security programs, at both the graduate and the undergraduate level, should not be all that surprising given the market demands for trained professionals. The National Center for Education Statistics charts the decade-long comparison of homeland and other security-related programs. Growth is undeniable. See Figure 2.12.[65]

Web Exercise: Visit the EMI Web location which lists undergraduate and graduate programs in homeland security and emergency management by various traits at https://training.fema.gov/hiedu/collegelist/.

Some charge that "homeland studies" be conceptually insufficient to erect a full degree program and it would be wiser to keep that content within the framework of security management. Part of the movement, according to Steve Recca of the Naval Post Graduate School, was merely to get funding and meet a steady stream of demand—and for that the proponents get a "solid C."[66] Motivations for this emerging academic exercise must be more than that. Stanley Suspinski's "Security Studies: The Homeland Adapts" makes the point:

In many cases, academic institutions have built these programs for altruistic reasons, but market demands have also exerted a powerful influence. Institutions want to be on the cutting edge of education and support the needs of the job market, but they are also lured by the prospect of high volumes of paying students. The rush to take advantage of the demand has resulted in wide variations in program quality and curriculum, with courses, often taught by faculty with little or no direct professional experience of background.[67]

Pelfrey and Pelfrey pose a seminal question regarding the matter of academic sufficiency and it is reasonable to query whether there is a sufficient "essence" to the discipline since academics themselves and the academic institutions that

---

[60] Kuldau, Criminal Justice Education: Myths vs. Reality, 52 *Police Chief* 18 (1975); See also Erickson & Neary, Criminal Justice Education: Is It Criminal? 42 *Police Chief* 39 (1975).

[61] ASIS International, Academic Institutions Offering Degrees, Concentration, or Certificates in Security Management, Appendix A (2016), at https://www.asisonline.org/Membership/Library/Academic-Student-Center/Documents/Academic-Programs-in-Security.pdf, last accessed August 27, 2016.

[62] For an historic look at security as an academic discipline, see C.P. Nemeth, *A Status Report on Contemporary Criminal Justice Education* 151–154 (Lewiston, NY: Edwin Mellen Press, 1989).

[63] W.V. Pelfrey Sr. & W.D. Kelley Jr., Homeland Security Education: A Way Forward, 9 *Homeland Sec. Aff.* (February 2013).

[64] T. Dees, *Homeland Security Educational Programs* 40 (May, 2005).

[65] National Center for Educational Statistics, *The Condition of Education 2015*, Figure 2 at page 201 (2015).

[66] S. Recca, Homeland Security Education: Reading the Tea Leaves, 1 *J. Homeland Sec. Educ.* 2 (2012).

[67] S. Supinski, Security Studies: The Homeland Adapts, 7 *Homeland Sec. Aff.* The 9/11 Essays 3 (September 2011).

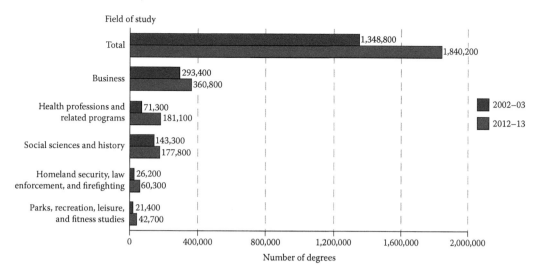

Figure 2.12 Number of bachelor's degrees awarded by postsecondary institutions in selected fields of study: academic years 2002–2003 and 2012–2013. *Note*: The first three fields of study shown were selected because they were the fields in which the largest number of bachelor's degrees was awarded in 2012–2013. The final two fields of study were selected because they were the fields with the largest increases in bachelor's degrees awarded between 2002–2003 and 2012–2013. Data are for postsecondary institutions participating in Title IV federal financial aid programs. The New Classification of instructional Programs was initiated in 2009–2010. The estimates for 2002–2003 have been reclassified when necessary to make them conform to the new taxonomy. For bachelor's degrees, "business" includes the business, management, marketing, and related support services field of study and the personal and culinary services field of study. Some data have been revised from previously published figures. (From U.S. Department of Education, National Center for Education Statistics, Integrated Postsecondary Education Data System (IPEDS), Fall 2003 and Fall 2013. Completions component. See *Digest of Education Statistics 2014*, Table 322.10.)

sponsor these program publish nothing that resembles a uniform approach.[68] Market demand drives a good deal of the decision-making in the world of homeland education and it is imperative that these conclusions be more than market driven but intellectually viable and supportive of a nation is desperate need of security professionals.

Web Exercise: Find out about whether or not a homeland security program is in the curricular mainstream or not by visiting the Center for Homeland Defense and Security at https://www.chds.us/c/academic-programs.

Despite these valid questions, homeland security programs appear to be permanent fixtures on many campuses and until and when that need is filled by other offerings, the future appears assured for the academic topic. Jobs for professionals, including working professionals teaching in an adjunct role, are consistently listed in mainstream magazines and on such websites as Highereducationjobs.com.[69]

2.7 THE PRIVATE SECTOR AND HOMELAND SECURITY

How the private sector contributes to the fight against terrorism and homeland defense is a story worth telling. And, as noted earlier, the synergies and connectedness of these public and private systems seem to most clearly coalesce when applied to the homeland. The public system is simply incapable of handling the draconian task of homeland security alone. Since 9/11, governmental agencies have urged the participation of not only state and local governments, but also the active input and involvement of the general citizenry.[70] On top of this, there has been a continuous push for private business and commercial entities to be involved and an expectation that much of the American

---

[68] W.V. Pelfrey Sr. & W.V. Pelfrey Jr., Sensemaking in a Nascent Field: A Conceptual Framework for Understanding the Emerging Discipline of Homeland Security, 4 *Homeland Sec. Rev.* 157 (2010).

[69] HigherEdJobs.com, Security Studies Faculty Search, at https://www.higheredjobs.com/faculty/search.cfm?JobCat=222, last accessed July 17, 2016.

[70] This approach has been repeatedly advanced by those arguing for private policing systems working side by side with public policing systems. See J.F. Pastor, Public-Private Policing Arrangements & Recommendations, 4 *Homeland Sec. Rev.* 71 (2010); see also C.P. Nemeth and K.C Poulin, *The Prevention Agency* (CUP Press, 2006); C.P. Nemeth & K.C. Poulin, *Private Security and Public Safety: A Community Based Approach* (Pearson Prentice-Hall, 2005); J.F. Pastor, *Terrorism and Public Safety Policing: Implications for the Obama Presidency* (CRC Press, 2010).

Figure 2.13   National Infrastructure Protection Plan 2013.

economy would need to be active players in the fight against terrorism. For example, America's chemical, water, utility, and nuclear sectors would have to be aggressively involved in the defense of their facilities, and thus the country itself.[71] Commercial interests could not simply wait for the government to do it all but instead had to jump into the mix of deterrence and prevention of terror. See Figure 2.13.

Infrastructure is largely owned by private enterprise and in need of a homeland defense plan. "Industries must plan to respond…and undertake recovery under severe conditions where much of the infrastructure of the surrounding area is unavailable and site access is limited."[72] Preparedness is an industrial and commercial concern. And it is also the private citizen that encompasses the private sector as well. The question of how much more prepared private homes and families can be is yet to be fully measured.[73]

---

[71] N. Santella & L.J. Steinberg, Accidental Releases of Hazardous Materials and Relevance, 8 *J. Homeland Sec. & Emerg. Mgmt* (2011).

[72] *Ibid.* at 11.

[73] M. Kano et al., Terrorism Preparedness and Exposure Reduction Since 9/11: The Status of Public Readiness in the United States, 8 *J. Homeland Sec. & Emerg. Mgmt* (2011).

Each facet of the private sector needs to understand

- How communities are impacted by terrorism
- How to create a plan of response consistent with state and federal standards
- How to mitigate loss in the event of catastrophe and disaster
- How to be active partners in the development of homeland policy
- How to work closely with public agencies
- How to add new programs in traditional Neighborhood Watch programs that focus on terrorism.[74]

The National Infrastructure Advisory Council, in its report on public–private sector intelligence coordination, identified 17 business and commercial sectors that need to step up in the fight against terrorism:

- Communications
- Chemical and hazardous materials
- Commercial facilities
- Dams
- Defense industrial base
- Energy
- Emergency services
- Financial services
- Food and agriculture
- Government facilities
- Information technology
- National monuments and icons
- Nuclear power plants
- Postal and shipping
- Public health and healthcare
- Transportation
- Water[75]

On a second front, the role of private sector security firms and personnel can only be described as central and integral in the defense of the nation. In the 2014 Quadrennial Homeland Security Review, DHS unreservedly elevates the importance of the private sector in its "Strengthening the Execution of Our Missions through Public-Private Partnerships." Private security is touted as a "partner" in this mission, as DHS declares,

> Homeland Security is achieved through a shared effort among all partners, from corporations to nonprofits and American families. Together, we can harness common interests to achieve solutions beyond what any of us could do alone. At a time when we must do more with less, two guiding principles help public-private partnerships maximize the investment by each partner and the success of the partnership: (1) aligning interests and (2) identifying shared outcomes.[76]

Overall, the role of private security interests can never be underestimated or underutilized for as a partner in homeland security, the government can

- Share information and data
- Coordinate with partners on targeted activities

[74] J. Fleischman, Engaging the Private Sector in Local Homeland Defense: The Orange County Private Sector Terrorism Response Group, *Sheriff* 33 (September/October 2004).
[75] National Infrastructure Advisory Council, *Public-Private Sector Intelligence Coordination: Final Report and Recommendations by the Council* 67 (July 2006).
[76] U.S. Department of Homeland Security, *2014 Quadrennial Homeland Sec. Rev.* 58 (2014).

- Link with diverse partners to achieve a stated goal
- Share the expenses of the operations while economically benefiting the providers
- Innovate and produce new strategies, products, methods, and means to security[77]

Such partnerships assure the ability to meet the many complex security challenges caused and fomented by the terrorist class.

The private sector portion of criminal justice operations grows at an almost immeasurable clip and as a result increasingly contributes to this national mandate for safety and security.[78] According to the Homeland Security Research Corporation, by 2011 the private sector "will trail only DHS in HLS industry procurement volume. This stems from the forecasted 50% private sector procurement growth from 2007–2011, totaling an accumulated $28.5B."[79] The face of private sector justice can be discovered across the DHS spectrum; from privatized forces seeking out terrorists in Iraq and Afghanistan to the protection of federal installations across the mainland, private sector justice makes extraordinary contributions in the defense of the country.[80] Private security forces may again be the predominant force in the transportation infrastructure as dissatisfaction grows with poor TSA performance.

Under the Screening Partnership program, airport authorities are turning to the private security force to conduct once sacrosanct TSA duties. In the just the last three years, contracts to delegate to private security firms have included:

- December 22, 2014—Awarded to VMD Systems Integrators for Portsmouth International Airport (PSM)
- December 5, 2014—Awarded to Trinity Technology Group for five airports in Montana: Havre CityCounty (HVR), Wokal Field (GGW), Wolf Point (OLF), Sidney (SDY), and Dawson (GDV)
- November 24, 2014—Awarded to Trinity Technology Group for Sarasota—Bradenton International Airport (SRQ)
- September 18, 2014—Awarded to Trinity Technology Group for Orlando Sanford International Airport (SFB)
- September 22, 2014—Awarded to BOS Security for Roswell International Air Center (ROW)
- May 29, 2014—Awarded to CSSI FirstLine for four Montana airports: Bert Mooney Airport (BTM), Bozeman Yellowstone International Airport (BZN), Glacier Park International Airport (GPI), and Yellowstone Airport (WYS)
- February 24, 2014—Awarded to Akal Security Inc. for Kansas City International Airport (MCI)
- August 16, 2012—Awarded to VMD-MT Security LLC for the Group 1 airports: Greater Rochester International Airport (ROC),

From Iraq to the local water facility, private sector justice operatives are engaged in a host of activities once exclusively reserved for the public sector. This trend, often labeled "privatization," assumes that the private sector, with its usual efficiencies and profit motivations, will carry out its task with greater effectiveness. Unions and entrenched government bureaucracies tend to be on the defensive with those promoting privatization. Those seeking greater accountability and freedom of operation tend to the privatized.[81] On paper, the concept is attractive, and in many cases, it is clear that the private sector can do a better job than the government in ensuring safety and security. It will all depend on the subject matter of that security and the corresponding costs. To illustrate, there are some who have argued that the TSA should never have been invented, but these same services should be subcontracted to private business. Of course, this is the model pre-9/11. Since 9/11, there has been a continuous debate over the preferability of public or private in the delivery of security services. What can be agreed upon is that both domains have essential responsibilities in combating terrorism—some exclusive, though most shared.

In this sense, private sector justice is driven by bottom-line considerations more than its governmental counterpart. It is motivated by efficiencies never weighed or evaluated in the public sector. And given this general motivation to the

---

[77] *Ibid.*

[78] Nemeth, *supra* note 2, at 12.

[79] Homeland Security Research Corporation, Private Sector to Become 2nd Largest Homeland Security Industry Customer by 2011, news release (April 9, 2008).

[80] For an examination of how these privatized practices prompt ethical concerns, see K. Carmola, *Private Security Contractors in the Age of New Wars: Risk, Law & Ethics* (New York, NY: Routledge Press, 2008).

[81] P. Starr, The Meaning of Privatization, 6 *Yale L. & Pol'y Rev.* 6–41 (1988). This article also appears in A. Kahn & S. Kamerman, eds., *Privatization and the Welfare State* (Princeton, NJ: Princeton University Press, 1989).

profit mentality, there are those who critique it as being willing to cut corners so that the bottom line will be brighter. Quality allegedly suffers. Indeed, many are suspicious of the qualifications of those entrusted with security responsibilities from the private sector. Do recent attempts to increase qualification and conduct legitimate background investigations on security officer applicants calm frayed nerves?[82] Ian Patrick McGinley, when critiquing federal legislation to ensure suitable licensure and background requirements for security officers, found that the industry is in a state of market failure.

Nevertheless, significant problems with leaving regulation to the market make this option unfeasible. For one, despite laudable attempts, the industry's self-regulation track record has been poor. Second, profit margins in the security industry are tight because many companies view security as a necessary evil. As a result, there is a race to the bottom—in terms of pricing and salaries—in order to gain a competitive advantage relative to other firms, resulting in less qualified officers.[83]

However, this argument does not pan out in so many governmentally operated entities. What of the public school system nationally? Are these systems not in crisis? What of public transportation systems? What of roads and bridges in near collapse? It is not difficult to discern where government fails to meet its mission. Privatization is evident everywhere—prisons, policing, and courts, to name just three, are examples of fields seeing these trends.[84] As the Bureau of Justice Assistance notes in its *Engaging Private Security to Promote Homeland Security*, private sector justice can jump in with feet first.

Private security can

- Coordinate plans with the public sector regarding evacuation, transportation, and food services during emergencies
- Gain information from law enforcement regarding threats and crime trends
- Develop relationships so that private practitioners know whom to contact when they need help or want to report information
- Build law enforcement understanding of corporate needs (e.g., confidentiality)
- Boost law enforcement's respect for the security field

Working together, private security and law enforcement can realize impressive benefits:

- Creative problem solving
- Increased training opportunities
- Information, data, and intelligence sharing
- Force multiplier opportunities
- Access to the community through private sector communications technology
- Reduced recovery time following disasters[85]

The National Defense Industrial Association (NDIA), another premier professional group for the private sector, argues as if the task of homeland is integral to any private security firm. Its mission unequivocally declares thus:

- To provide legal and ethical forums for the exchange of information, ideas, and recommendations between industry and government on homeland security issues
- To promote a vigorous, robust, and collaborative government–industry homeland security team
- To advocate for best-in-class, high-technology equipment, systems, training, and support for America's first responder community[86]

---

[82] Private Security Officer Employment Authorization Act of 2004, U.S. Code 28 (2004), § 534.

[83] I.P. McGinley, Regulating "Rent-A-Cops" Post 9/11: Why the Private Security Officer Employment Act Fails to Address Homeland Security Concerns, 6 *Cardozo Pub. L. Pol'y & Ethics J.* 145 (2007).

[84] C.P. Nemeth, *Private Security and the Investigative Process* 1–4 (3rd ed., 2010).

[85] Bureau of Justice Assistance, *Engaging the Private Sector to Promote Homeland Security: Law Enforcement-Private Security Partnerships* 11 (2003).

[86] National Defense Industrial Association, at www.ndia.org/Aboutus/pages/default.aspx, last accessed August 27, 2016.

And not only is it capable of carrying out its own mission in the world of homeland security, but it should do so with collaboration and collegiality in regards to its public partners. The world of public–private is not distinct or radically different; rather, these are compatible and complementary domains where a shared mission is obvious. Partnerships are what each should be looking for since the public and the private share 12 essential components:

- Common goals
- Common tasks
- Knowledge of participating agencies' capabilities and missions
- Well-defined projected outcomes
- A timetable
- Education for all involved
- A tangible purpose
- Clearly identified leaders
- Operational planning
- Agreement by all partners as to how the partnership will proceed
- Mutual commitment to providing necessary resources
- Assessment and reporting[87]

DHS formally encourages the interplay and cooperation between private sector justice entities and the public law enforcement function. Throughout DHS, policy making is the perpetual recognition that it cannot go it alone and that it needs the daily cooperation of the private sector. Within its Office of Policy, DHS has erected a Private Sector Office, its chief aims being

- To engage individual businesses, trade associations, and other nongovernmental organizations to foster dialogue with the department
- To advise the secretary on prospective policies and regulations and in many cases on their economic impact
- To promote public–private partnerships and best practices to improve the nation's homeland security
- To promote department policies to the private sector

The Private Sector Office focuses on two major functions: the Business Outreach Group and Economics Group. In the first instance, DHS affirmatively connects with the business and commercial sector fully realizing that cooperation and joint endeavors fare better than isolation or turf protection. The Outreach Group seeks input and advice from the business sector before the institution or implementation of policy. The Outreach Group

- Meets with private sector organizations and department components to promote public–private partnerships
- Promotes departmental policies
- Gathers private sector perspectives for use by the department

The Economics Group weighs policy in cost–benefit terms. Here, DHS displays a deaf ear regarding the costs of policy implementation since each new regulation or requirement does have a corresponding price tag. As a result, the group looks at the impact of policy from various directions, including

- Policy analysis—Evaluates the economic impacts of departmental policies on the private sector.
- Process analysis—Evaluates departmental processes that will allow the private sector to operate efficiently while meeting national security needs.
- Regulatory analysis—Provides a resource to the department on regulatory/economic analyses.
- Metrics—Promotes the use of metrics to identify successes and areas needing improvement.
- Benefits methodology—Actively works on the development of methodologies to quantify the benefits of homeland security investments.

---

[87] Bureau of Justice Assistance, *supra* note 85, at 13.

The Economics Group coordinates economic roundtables and publishes white papers and other studies that highlight cost–benefit.

Finally, DHS, not long after 9/11, instituted an advisory committee on private sector cooperation and collaboration. Members of the committee represent the full panoply of industry, corporate interests, and security firms with shared interests. From the outset of DHS, it was clear that policy making would not occur without the input of industry and commerce. It was equally evident that the skilled practitioners of private sector justice would be crucial contributors.

Web Exercise: The Private Sector Office publishes a variety of literature that encourages collaboration. See the key contact list authored by The Private Sector Office at http://www.dhs.gov/sites/default/files/publications/Policy-PSO/pso-appendix-a-key-contacts.pdf.

2.8 CONCLUSION

Any student or practitioner in the world of security and the private security industry must commence the journey with the basic definitions. First, what is security—what state of being is the secure person or asset? Second, does security deal, as is so often argued, with assets and commercial interests alone? Or is security something far more expansive and globally connected—whether it be individual persons or the collective itself? Third, is security a public responsibility to the exclusion of the private interest? Or is it a blend, an amalgam of both worlds—the public, governmental system joined to the private sector and private security industry itself? In order that security be understood, one must examine these profound questions for no longer is security something that the average citizen can merely rely on others to ensure. Security defines itself not only on the content of its coverage, which surely is both people and things, communities and governmental interests, but also on its eclectic nature being a simultaneous concern of public officialdom and the private sector.

Fourth, security can be defined and understood by what its professional groups and constituencies declare as its ultimate aim. Associations such as the International Association of Industrial Security, NASCO, and the PSTF, among others, lay out expectations for performance and appropriate fields of coverage. These same associations and groups fully define and delineate what security should be and in what sense their aim remains consistent with the overall purpose of a free, safe, and security nation.

Fifth, the subject matter of security can also be gleaned from the greater, more nationalized challenges this country faces, namely, the global challenge of homeland safety and security. The entire infrastructure of security services was turned on its head on 9/11 and what was once never considered becomes integral to a security plan and purpose. For example, after 9/11, the practice and protocols of defending critical infrastructure sweeps in the private sector and the private security industry. What was once the province of governmental authorities alone now consumes the private security industry complex. What security is depends upon what the global vision of homeland security is; whether it be in transportation, food and livestock, or energy and water supply, protection and safety in these diverse targets are now priorities. Notions of security are fully enveloped in the global defensive war that seeks to thwart threats against these and every other setting the terrorist sets his or her sights upon.

Sixth, the concept of security is further shaped by the laws, regulations, and promulgations relating to national security and its defense. Since the private sector is a major player in that defensive posture, precisely what is lawfully permissible under legislative designs and agency regulations goes a long way to shaping a definition of security and the industry itself. Throughout this chapter, the reader is introduced to various laws that target some sliver of security for self and the nation. Examples included the USA Patriot Act, the Real ID Act, and the enabling Homeland Security Act of 2002—all of which play a role in the formulation of a definition and context for security.

Seventh, any meaningful conception of security will depend upon some sort of academic formulation, which discerns whether there is a field of study or analysis under the broad title of "security studies." Is this a legitimate academic endeavor—and if it is, how does the academic sector define and design the field of security itself? What types of academic programs exist, at both the undergraduate and the graduate level in security management, homeland security, and related fields. Data on these trends with corresponding examples are fully delivered in this chapter.

Lastly, how has the partnership of the private security industry, with governmental authorities at the state and federal level, fostered clarity in the definition of security? Is a partnership between the public and private sector, particularly as to national defense and security, proof that the private security industry is now operating on a level playing field?

Is it fair to conclude that such partnerships give testimony to the extraordinary rise in the quality and integrity of the private security business? Or might it be argued that once sacrosanct lines of separation are giving way to a mutually, respectful association between two partners? Herein lies one of the more profound possibilities posed in this chapter—that the definition of private security may be closer to the public definition of security than at any time in recent memory. That when DHS erects a Private Sector Office dedicated to nurturing partnerships between the public and the private systems, the historic caste system where the private security operation was viewed as inferior to the public counterpart may finally be melting away. And in this sense, the definition of private security and its interest may align in near perfection with the public system it so ably serves.

Keywords

Al Qaeda

antiterrorism

Black Panthers

Cold War

communism

Cuban Missile Crisis

cybersecurity

domestic terrorism

Hamas

Hezbollah

homeland security

Homeland Security Act

Information Sharing and Analysis Organizations (ISAOs)

intelligence

international terrorism

ISIS/ISIL

Islamic extremism

jihadist

Korean War

Ku Klux Klan (KKK)

nuclear proliferation

manifesto

Office of Biometric Identity Management

Posse Comitatus Act

REAL ID Program

Students for a Democratic Society (SDS)

Support Antiterrorism by Fostering Effective Technologies Act of 2002 (SAFETY Act)

Third Reich

threat analysis

Truman Doctrine

Unified Combatant Command

United States Northern Command

U.S. Freedom Act

USA Patriot Act

Vietnam War

Weathermen

Workers Party

Discussion questions

1. Discuss the various factors that influence both the definition and the perception of private security.
2. List some of the ways private security is involved in the detection and prevention of both domestic and international terrorism.
3. Choose three executive orders or laws, and summarize them and their impact on the private security operative.
4. Select one of the government sponsored training programs, investigate their offering, and discuss how it would further one's training in the field of private security.
5. As a small group, list the pros and cons of a degree in homeland security for the private sector employee.
6. Outline the various ways in which private security can contribute as a partner in homeland security.

Chapter 3

Private security, public policing, and occupational roles

3.1 INTRODUCTION

Another approach to defining the private security industry is by a comparison with its public police counterpart—contrasting the distinct vision or outlook of either system. To say that the private security industry operates under similar principles as its public counterpart is both true and false. Both systems share much in common although there remain vast differences in approach and protocol. Both systems often merge in task and duty yet simultaneously find alternative avenues for dealing with crime and unrest. Understanding the nature of a security officer or private operative will depend on an understanding of how the private security system compliments the public policing infrastructure. When this task is completed, the ultimate definition of what security means and is can be further gleaned from the many occupational opportunities that exist in this dynamic industry. Jobs and professional opportunities abound in private security, and the depth, breadth, and range of professional opportunities speaks loudly about the system's day-to-day responsibilities and its ultimate goals.

3.2 PRIVATE VERSUS PUBLIC POLICING: A COMPARATIVE ANALYSIS

Side by side, two systems of law enforcement and maintenance control have long worked together. Everywhere across the globe, public police entities engage the private sector, governments employ private sector companies for security of facilities and asset protection, communities turn to both arms of the justice model, and the military industrial complex appreciates the value of private sector involvement in military operations. So entangled and intertwined are these two systems it is hard to imagine how society could function without the two systems. And yet, as these distinct operational systems carry out their tasks, the differences in approach and methodology can be quite marked. Private security is not public policing, although the lines and spheres of influence continue to merge. It is the commonality of interests that spur on this unbridled growth in cooperation. Despite the differences in legal powers, employers, and mission, private security officers and public police have many similarities.[1]

The historical legacy that characterizes the relationship between the public and the private justice systems is less than positive though continuously improving. In 1976, the Private Security Advisory Council, through the U.S. Department of Justice, delivered an insightful critique on the barriers to full and unbridled cooperation between the public and the private law enforcement systems. Struggling with role definition and resource deployment, the relationship has been an uneasy but steady one. The Council stressed the need to clarify role definitions and end the absurd and oft-practiced negative stereotyping.[2] The Council cited various areas of conflict and ranked them in order of importance.

1. Lack of mutual respect
2. Lack of communication
3. Lack of cooperation
4. Lack of security enforcement knowledge of private security
5. Perceived competition
6. Lack of standards
7. Perceived corruption[3]

Put another way, each side operates from a series of perceptions, some accurate, others not, though it is fair to say that police professionals appreciate the "the legitimate and lawful use"[4] of the private security industry. The *Hallcrest Report I*[5] decisively addressed this issue. In characterizing the police role as inclined toward crime detection, prevention, and control, security will always be to some extent the public police's antagonist. Private police give less attention to apprehension, crime detection, prevention, and technology than do their public counterparts. Comparatively, private security addresses similar subject matter but still dwells intently on the protection of assets, immediate deterrence, and commercial enforcement. Figure 3.1[6] provides a graphic illustration of the major distinctions between these two entities. Tables 3.1[7] and 3.2[8] further edify these occupational distinctions.

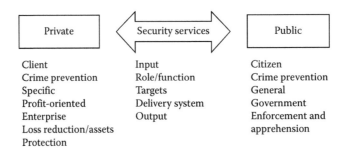

Figure 3.1   Comparison of private and public security services.

[1] A.J. Bilek, J.C. Klotter, & R.K. Federal, *Legal Aspects of Private Security* 180 (Anderson Pub. Co., 1980); J. Pastor, *Security Law and Methods* (Butterworth-Heinemann, 2006); J.F. Pastor, *Terrorism and Public Safety Policing: Implications for the Obama Presidency* (CRC Press, 2009).
[2] National Advisory Committee on Criminal Justice Standards and Goals, *Private Security: Report of the Task Force on Private Security* (1976); see also Operation Cooperation, *Guidelines for Partnerships between Law Enforcement & Private Security Organizations* 11 (2000).
[3] National Advisory Committee, *supra* note 2, at 2; see also Operation Cooperation, *supra* note 2.
[4] A. Harman, Private Security Use Debated, 48 *Law & Order* 125 (2000).
[5] W.C. Cunningham & T.H. Taylor, *Private Security and Police in America* (National Institute of Justice, 1986); see also Experts Salute Public & Private Sectors on Crime Reduction Collaboration, *Security Letter* (July 8, 2002); C.A. Bradford & C.A. Simonsen, The Need for Cooperative Efforts between Private Security and Public Law Enforcement in the Prevention, Investigation, and Prosecution of Fraud-Related Criminal Activity, 10 *Sec. J.* 161 (1998).
[6] W.C. Cunningham, J.J. Strauchs, & C.W. Vanmeter, *Private Security Trends 1970 to 2000: The Hallcrest Report II* 116 (Butterworth Heinemann, 1990); see also Operation Cooperation, *supra* note 2.
[7] Cunningham et al., *supra* note 6, at 120; see also Operation Cooperation, *supra* note 2.
[8] Cunningham et al., *supra* note 6, at 118.

Table 3.1   Security manager ranking of private security functions (rank ordered)

Proprietary managers	Contractual managers
Protection of lives and property	Protection of lives and property
Crime prevention	Crime prevention
Loss prevention	Loss prevention
Fire prevention	Fire prevention
Access control	Access control
Crime investigation	Order maintenance
Employee identification	Employee identification
Order maintenance	Crime reporting
Arrest/prosecution	Arrest/prosecution
Accident prevention	Information security
Crime reporting	Crime investigation
Information security	Accident prevention
Traffic control	Traffic control
N = 676	N = 545

Table 3.2   Law enforcement executive ratings of law enforcement function (rank ordered)

Protection of lives and property
Arrest and prosecution of criminals
Investigation of criminal incidents
Maintaining public order
Crime prevention
Community relations
General assistance to the public
Traffic enforcement
Traffic control
N = 384

A cursory assessment of these figures shows fundamental agreement on the protection of lives and property. Departure occurs in the upper classifications of law enforcement since the thrust of any public police department must be for the eventual arrest and prosecution of suspects. In contrast, the private justice function is still concerned with preventive activities in the area of crime loss, fire prevention, and other order-maintenance functions. In the security manager rankings, criminal investigation and arrest and prosecution show up in the lower rankings. This prioritization, in and of itself, is a telling distinction, though it should not be viewed as justification for a sharp division. If anything, both public and private law enforcement share a generic goal—namely, the general enforcement of laws. As Bill Strudal points out in his article, *Giving the Police a Sense of Security*,

> Our goal, usually not shared by police and security is law enforcement…if we accept the premise that police and security have the same goals, then why don't we work together on a regular basis? There are differences; nobody can deny that… there are many other gaps between the two forces, but none is insurmountable with good training and dialogue.[9]

The similarities between function, duty, and obligation are very apparent when the tasks of investigation are considered. The skills of the private sector are essentially identical to the public. Viewed from the private security industry perspective, the conceptions are far less negative with many security specialists seeing themselves as "socially beneficial" and as "teaming up" with their professional counterparts.[10] Employee theft, property crime, and access controls

---

[9] B. Strudel, The Private Security Connection: Giving the Police a Sense of Security, *Police Chief* (Feb. 1982), at 28–29; Law Commission of Canada, *In Search of Security: The Roles of Public Police and Private Agencies* (2002); G.S. Rigakos, *The New Parapolice* (2002).

[10] J. Manzo, How Private Security Officers Perceive Themselves Relative to Police, 23 *Sec. J.* 202–203 (2010).

Table 3.3 Private security contribution to crime prevention and control as rated by law enforcement and private security managers

	Law enforcement	Proprietary security	Contractual security
Overall contribution	2.2	1.5	1.2
Reduction in volume of crime	2.4	1.7	1.5
Reduction in direct dollar crime loss	2.2	1.6	1.5
Number of criminal suspects apprehended	2.6	1.9	2.0
Order maintenance	2.4	1.4	1.7
	N = 384	N = 676	N = 545

Scale: 1 = very effective; 2 = somewhat effective; 3 = not effective.

are the top concerns of security professionals. Computer and information security concerns continue to increase as the most important security-related concerns.

Another recurring stumbling block, at least perceptually, is public law enforcement's attitude of superiority. Table 3.3[11] indicates that traditional law enforcement takes a dim view of the contribution of proprietary and contractual security when compared to its own role, though the merger of functions and roles will likely shrink this chasm in the near future. But there is a road to travel.[12]

Unfortunately, slight differences in approach and methodology have increased the divide between these camps. And with these attitudes in place, it becomes a much more difficult task to partner and cooperate. A 2004 Policy Summit cosponsored by public and private law enforcement associations list the main reasons why these alliances falter.

- Egos and turf battles
- Lack of resources (funds, staff)
- Lack of a product
- Overemphasis on structure or resource needs
- Insufficient commitment and support from higher levels of participating organizations
- Overemphasis on the social aspect and underemphasis on business
- Unwillingness of partners to share information, especially information that would reflect poorly on the sharer
- Insufficient alignment of interests[13]

The U.S. Department of Justice's Community Oriented Policing Services confirmed this negative imagery of the private security industry by public police professionals declaring that collaboration can only be built on relationships of trust.

To the detriment of all, these petty differences continue to the present.[14] John Driscoll, in his article *Public and Private Security Forces Unite in Dallas*, asserts "this negative approach prevents the two similar entities from realizing their commonalities and capitalizing upon mutual cooperation."[15] Driscoll recounts the "Dallas Experiment" that stresses interaction between the parties in sharing "criminal information bulletins, recruit[ing] class training blocks, field training officer and security officer meetings, and additional joint information seminars."[16] The elitist attitude taken by public law enforcement fosters a polarization between the public and the private sectors. Though role conflicts and perceptual views of the public and private sectors are compelling arguments, there are other forceful explanations

---

[11] Cunningham et al., *supra* note 6, at 121; see also Operation Cooperation, *supra* note 2.

[12] International Chiefs of Police, National Policy Summit: Building Private Security/Public Policing Partnerships to Prevent and Respond to Terrorism and Public Disorder (2004), at http://www.cops.usdoj.gov/files/ric/Publications/national_policy_summit.pdf.

[13] International Chiefs of Police, *supra* note 12, at 18.

[14] J.E. Driscoll, Public and Private Security Forces Unite in Dallas, *Police Chief* (1988), at 48; see also S. Ronald Hauri, Public-Private Security Liaison: The Synergy of Cooperation, *Crime & Just. Int'l* (Oct. 1997), at 16; Operation Cooperation, *supra* note 2.

[15] Driscoll, *supra* note 15, at 48; see also Hauri, *supra* note 15.

[16] *Ibid.*

for the natural tension between these competing interests. What is undeniable is the march forward into the public realm, with examples so numerous it is now difficult to catalog. Private sector operatives now watch over airports and parks; act as first responders and protectors of federal and state installations; deliver safety and security to the Olympics and sporting events; and conduct surveillance and assess critical infrastructure. Even in the area of community policing where the rubber meets the road, private security forces are now assigned at street level.[17] It is inevitable that this transference of role and function occur, says Lt. Raymond Bechler,

> Privatized police ownership can become a reality. Economically, private policing makes sense and could be a financial victory for local governments… The benefits to local governments, communities, and to the law enforcement profession can be greatly enhanced by the competition of private police ownership.[18]

In the final analysis, the playing field will be leveled a little more each day by the ever-growing numbers of private security forces.[19] Public law enforcement is and has always been tasked with the needs of the public good. Few private security companies have to be concerned with domestic disputes, the transportation of the deceased, stray animals, or protection of the homeless and other downtrodden individuals.[20] The Private Security Advisory Council characterized police work as a public interest function. Public police have "a wide range of responsibilities to protect essentially public concerns and their efforts are closely tied to statutorily mandated duties and the criminal justice system."[21] The Advisory Council further relates that the police are burdened with constitutional limitations and must interpret and implement certain guidelines in the performance of their law enforcement duties. Additionally, public policing is further restrained by public budgeting and financing processes. Police management policies and an administrative hierarchy within most major police departments must evaluate and allocate their resources according to the needs and demands presently operating within their community structure.[22] For this reason alone, the cooperative venture with the private police system is bound to grow and flourish in the decades ahead. Public Police departments will more aggressively "leverage their existing resources"[23] by joining forces with the private sector police. Norman Spain and Gary Elkin, in their article, *Private Security versus Law Enforcement*, relate with precision:

> One of the traditional functions of the public police is to deter crime. In reality, their ability to do this is drastically limited. The primary reasons are that the police have little authority to change the conditions that foster crime and they have no authority to decide who will reside in their jurisdiction, whom they will police. Private security forces, on the other hand, may alter – at times drastically – the environment in which they operate. They can have walls and fences erected, doors sealed, windows screened, lights put up, and intrusion detectors installed. They can often play a decisive role in determining whom they have to monitor – who is to be an employee of the company – by conducting background investigations of potential employees.[24]

Such a supposition is difficult to dispute, since private security is primarily concerned with the private concerns of private property assets and particular individuals.

> Individuals and privately funded organizations and businesses undertake measures to provide protection for the perceived security needs which involve their private interests, not in the public domain. Private security is an option exercised to provide an additional or increased level of protection than that afforded by public law enforcement which must respond to the larger concerns of the public.[25]

---

[17] See, C.P. Nemeth and K.C Poulin, *The Prevention Agency* (2006); C.P. Nemeth & K.C. Poulin, *Private Security and Public Safety: A Community Based Approach* (2005).

[18] R.E. Bechler, *Private Police Ownership: Can It Possibly Happen?* (July, 2010), at http://lib.post.ca.gov/lib-documents/cc/47-Bechler.pdf.

[19] Operation Cooperation, *supra* note 2, at 11; see also Pastor, *Terrorism*, *supra* note 1; J.F. Pastor, *The Privatization of Police in America: An Analysis and Case Study* (2003).

[20] R.A. Lukins, Securing Training for the Guard Force, *Sec. Mgmt.* (May 1976), at 32.

[21] National Advisory Committee, *supra* note 2, at 5; see M.K. Nalla & D. Hummer, Relations between Police Officers and Security Professionals: A Study of Perceptions, 12 *Sec. J.* 31 (1999).

[22] National Advisory Committee, *supra* note 2, at 5; Hauri, *supra* note 15; Operation Cooperation, *supra* note 2, at 2–3.

[23] K. Hodgson, SIA Update (Oct. 14, 2011), at http://www.securityinfowatch.com/article/10506940/sia-update.

[24] N.M. Spain & G.L. Elkin, Private Security versus Law Enforcement, 16 *Sec. World* 32 (1979); see Nalla & Hummer, *supra* note 22; Hauri, *supra* note 15.

[25] National Advisory Committee, *supra* note 2, at 5.

Critics have long argued that this business myopia precludes full membership into the policing culture since "private sector security is always motivated by what is good for business."[26]As enticing an argument as this may be, it advances a skewed picture of exactly what private security police are doing—especially the range of services the industry now tackles. And this issue is evolutionary to say the least with professional tolerance at various levels of acceptance. Martin Gill, when assessing a group of senior police professionals as to their own vision of private security, categorizes reactions into *skeptics*, *pragmatists*, and *embracers*—the last designation signifying complete ease while the first continuing distrust.[27]

Another common critique of private sector policing is its lack of altruism when compared to public policing. Entrance into the vocation of public law enforcement is considered by most a moral and social commitment—a vocation rather than a mere job. This career distinction is generally not applied to individuals who commit their lives to the service of private security. But is such a viewpoint fair and rational? Is not the protection of assets, governmental facilities, communities, business interests, or private proprietary holdings, or contributions in military and security initiatives a noble endeavor? If private security was not involved, what would be the state of American industry and its physical plants, the security of courthouses and judicial centers, transportation facilities, and neighborhood associations? How would the dynamic of the battlefield change in foreign wars? How would the allocation of military personnel be impacted? For that matter, how many more employees would the public sector have to hire, on the backs of already beleaguered taxpayers, to cover the diverse functions of private sector justice? By what standards are these judgments of moral superiority or social importance designed? Critics and theoreticians who scathingly condemn the nature of private justice often forget the historical contribution private security has provided. Long before the establishment of a formal, publicly funded police department in pre- and postcolonial America, private security interests were the only entities providing protection for individual persons, assets, and business interests. Remember that the nature of a system of town watches, the "hue and cry," calling for posse formation and community cooperation, constables, and part-time sheriffs could hardly be characterized as public in design.[28]

Judgments about private sector justice cannot be made in a vacuum but evaluated in light of the range of services the industry provides a troubled world. To be more particular, who would protect the majority of federal installations? Who would protect the majority of American museums? What force or body would ensure safety and protection in the college and university environment? What other bodies would provide adequate crowd control at entertainment events? What cost would society incur to ensure a public police officer in each bank? Should taxpayers' money be spent in the transportation of money and other negotiable instruments? What police department would provide adequate security for American corporations? How far could city budgets be stretched to provide a secured environment for its multiple retail establishments if security services were absent?[29] When these queries are explored, public law enforcement's tendency to preach from a high moral pedestal is not as convincing. Richard Kobetz and H.H. Antony Cooper, in their article, *Two Armies: One Flag*, cogently state thus:

> It is no exaggeration to aver that without the aid of those presently engaged in the various tasks of private security, the resources of public law enforcement would have to be expanded far beyond the limits that the taxpayer could afford and would pay. Even those who do not contribute directly to the cost of providing private security services benefit to some notable extent from their existence. Private security is not a public luxury. It represents a substantial contribution to the general security of the community. In their impact on the community public and private law enforcement are one and indivisible.[30]

Predictably, a lack of respect between the public and the private sector leads to a lack of communication. The Private Security Advisory Council cogently concludes thus:

> Since many law enforcement personnel perceive themselves as having a higher degree of status than private security, and do not properly appreciate the role of private security in crime prevention, there will be a tendency to avoid communication with private security personnel. One might expect that private security would communicate freely with law

---

[26] M. Gill, Senior Police Officers' Perspectives on Private Security: Sceptics, Pragmatists and Embracers, 25 *Policing & Society* 289 (2015).
[27] *Ibid.*
[28] E.J. Criscuoli, Jr., Building a Professional Complement to Law Enforcement, *Police Chief* (1978), at 28; see also R.R. Rockwell, Private Guards: A Viewpoint, *Sec. Mgmt.*, 1975, at 5; Nalla & Hummer, *supra* note 22; Hauri, *supra* note 15.
[29] For an analysis of budget impact see A. Youngs, The Future of Public/Private Partnerships, *FBI Law Enforcement*, at 8.
[30] R.W. Kobetz & H.H.A. Cooper, Two Armies: One Flag, *Police Chief* (1978), at 28.

enforcement as a perceived higher status group. But the intensity of feelings expressed by private security and the ambiguity of their relationship with law enforcement…would seem to indicate an uncertainty as to the equality of status with law enforcement. Private security, then, would generally tend to avoid communication with law enforcement; without effective communication cooperation cannot be imposed.[31]

Another rationale often espoused by the public sector, which justifies its lack of communication, is functional separation. Some see no benefits to communication because of distinct occupational roles. The perception that private security protects only those interests that are strictly private is incorrect. Consider Table 3.4,[32] charting the public functions performed by the private justice sector.

Those asserting a limited public role for private security inaccurately portray the industry. Private security personnel have willingly taken on, been legislatively granted, or freely pursued these traditionally public functions:

- Community protection and services
- Public housing protection
- Parking authority control and security
- Enforcement of motor vehicle laws
- Natural resource activities
- Waterways and port services
- Air and rail protection
- Animal control
- Court security
- Governmental office security
- Private prisons
- Code violation inspectors
- Special event security
- Governmental investigations

The call for cooperation and professional interchange is earnest and well-grounded. Professional associations and groups such as the American Society for Industrial Security have formulated liaison committees. Additionally, The International Association of Chiefs of Police has emphasized the unique capacities of the security industry, stating that it should be viewed as a complement to public law enforcement.[33] Even the current structure and bureaucratic makeup of the Department of Homeland Security includes a Private Sector Commission that is considered a significant contributor in the war on terror.[34]

There can be little dispute that privatization of public services or contracting out of government responsibility to private employers is a major trend. Partnerships "gain more efficient use of funds and personnel… in addition to extending their reach and effectiveness. Properly defined and managed, a partnership with private enterprise can make the job of police officers more effective and rewarding and the results reported to voters more positive in the long run."[35] Not unexpectedly, much of this activity has been viewed with distrust and apprehension, particularly from those authorities that intend to ensure the vested interest of police. The *Hallcrest Report I* notes that this type of bickering and failure to communicate borders on the inane. The interest of the public will be better served through "constructive dialogue and creative planning by law enforcement and private security to facilitate contracting out of certain non-crime activities."[36] The report further notes that energy, time, and resources are being wasted in this debate and "could be better utilized in identifying areas for contracting out and developing tightly prescribed

[31] National Advisory Committee, *supra* note 2, at 12.

[32] Cunningham et al., *supra* note 6, at 275–276.

[33] Kobetz & Cooper, *supra* note 31, at 33.

[34] See C.P. Nemeth, *Introduction to Homeland Security: Principles and Practice* (CRC Press, 2010); see also K.C. Poulin & C.P. Nemeth, *Private Security and Public Safety: A Community-Based Approach* (Pearson Prentice Hall, 2004).

[35] Youngs, *supra* note 30, at 10.

[36] Cunningham & Taylor, *supra* note 5, at 185; see Nalla & Hummer, *supra* note 22; Hauri, *supra* note 15.

Table 3.4   Sites with experience in private provision of protection services

State	Jurisdiction	Type of service
Alaska	Anchorage	Parking meter enforcement
		Parking meter collection
		Parking lot security
Arizona	State	Parking lot enforcement
	Flagstaff	School crossing guards
	Maricopa County	Building security
	Phoenix	Crowd control
California	Federal	U.S. Department of Energy facility security
	Hawthorns	Traffic control during peak hours
	Los Angeles	Patrol streets surrounding private university
		Traffic and security for special events
	Los Angeles County	Building security
		Park security
	Norwalk	Park security
	San Diego	Housing project security
		Park security
	San Francisco	Building security
	Santa Barbara	Airport security
		Prison transport
Colorado	Denver	Building security
	Fort Collins	Building security
Connecticut	Hartford	Sport arena security
Florida	Dade County	Courts, building security
	Fort Lauderdale	Airport, building security
	Pensacola	Airport security
	St. Petersburg	Park security
Hawaii	State	Parking lot enforcement
Idaho	State	Regional medical center security
	Idaho Falls	School crossing guards
Kentucky	Lexington	Housing project security
Massachusetts	Boston	Hospital, courts, library security—city
		Library security—federal
Nevada	Federal	Nuclear test site security
New Jersey	Sport Authority	Sports arena security
New York	State	Response to burglar alarms in state office
	Buffalo	County security—federal
	New York City	Security compounds for towed cars
		Shelter security
		Human Resources Administration security
		Building security
		Locate cars with outstanding tickets
		Arrests for retail store theft
		Management training; police
		Campus security
Pennsylvania	State	Unemployment offices security
		Welfare offices security
	Philadelphia	Parking enforcement
	Pittsburgh	Court security—federal
		Patrol city park
		High-school stadium security
		School crossing guards
		Transfer of prisoners
Texas	Dallas/Fort Worth	Airport security including baggage checking
	Houston	Building security
Utah	State	Building security
		Training for transit police
Washington	Seattle	Building security
	Tacoma	Sports arena security
Washington, DC	District of Columbia Federal	Planning and management
		Building security

Table 3.5 Possibility of transferring responsibility to private security

Activity	Law enforcement executives (%)	Proprietary security managers (%)	Contract security managers (%)
Responding to burglar alarms	57	69	68
Preliminary investigations	40	88	68
Completing incident reports			
(a) Victim declines prosecution; for insurance purposes only	68	87	66
(b) Misdemeanors	45	81	63
Supplemental case reports	38	78	63
Transporting citizen arrests	35	32	38

contract specifications of performance."[37] The momentum of privatization makes public reticence to private sector justice even more unjustified. "But the trick to privatization is not only lowering costs, but also maintaining quality of service—particularly when the service in question is security."[38] The transference of public obligation to private interest is a trend likely to continue. See Table 3.5.[39]

The failure of public and private policing to communicate undermines and hinders the social order. Public law enforcement, in its own ignorance of the processes and functions of private law enforcement, simply chooses to disregard the reality of its professional counterpart. In the same vein, private security, particularly through its own internal decision-making, management, and personnel practices, has done little to dissuade its reputation that it is a business first and foremost. As one commentator states,

> Many problems are constant and intractable while the barriers remain; solutions become possible only as they fall away. Familiar roles are exchanged for others less accustomed. The experience is designed expressly to give practical insight into the domain and responsibility of others. It is a sobering feeling to have once in a while the privilege of walking a mile in someone else's moccasins. It is hoped that these shared experiences may be carried over into the day-to-day realities of professional life and provide a positive inspiration for cooperation and understanding.[40]

Failure of both the public and the private justice systems to communicate and cooperate is a staggering loss of human and professional resources. The Private Security Advisory Council revealed an exceptionally low level of interaction between the public and the private sectors. Its more salient findings included the following:

1. Less than one-half had conducted a survey to find out how many and what types of private security agencies operated in their areas.
2. Only one-third of the agencies stated that they had an office or officer to provide liaison with private security.
3. Only 25% of the agencies had policies or procedures for defining working roles of law enforcement in private security.
4. Only 25% had policies covering interchange of information with private security.
5. Less than 20% had procedures for cooperative actions with private security.[41]

Both law enforcement and the private security industry have a moral and legal obligation to open channels of communication and to cooperate professionally. On top of all this, private security brings to the forefront a "proactive" style of engagement—one driven by results and customer satisfaction—factors too often neglected in the public domain. The key is not simply to highlight the differences in style and approach but to identify "each other's strengths."[42] To maintain the current relationship is debilitating to efforts to reduce criminality and assure a safer

---

[37] Cunningham & Taylor, *supra* note 5, at 186.
[38] S.C. George, Privatization & Integration, 29 *Security* 5 (1992).
[39] Cunningham et al., *supra* note 6, at 272.
[40] Cunningham & Taylor, *supra* note 5, at 187.
[41] National Advisory Committee, *supra* note 2, at 14.
[42] R. Wurst, *Going Beyond Security*, at 62.

world. The continued practice of turf protection, stereotyping, and prejudicial analysis benefits no one. As Kobetz and Cooper relate,

> As soon as the essential unity of a mission is perceived and accepted, the special difficulties of responsibility and approach can be studied in detail. For too long, the other side – our common antisocial enemy – has seen matters in terms of "them versus us," is it not time that we, the public and the private providers of security, truly end this and in a practical and professional fashion begin to think of "us versus them"?[43]

Indeed, there appears to be a melting away of the once-entrenched divisions between the public and the private police systems. Aside from the insensibility of fostering division, the reality is that private police are acculturating into the public design by both intent and sheer accident. The future cannot support the separation since each system dabbles in similar content and responsibility. Ruddell, Thomas, and Patten correctly conclude thus:

> Thus, the crime-prevention and crime-fighting activities of security officers may reduce crime, as well as enable the police to be more efficient and selective by focusing on more significant problems, suspects and offences. Altogether, this study sheds light on the relationships between the police and private security, especially in regard to the formal and quasi-formal social control of urban areas. We find that the actions of private security officers augment the activities of the police, and it is likely that they will become a more important force in the future as the line between private and public policing becomes increasingly indistinct.[44]

Even acknowledging differing levels of inefficiency, it would be unfair to label the effort futile. On any given day, public police, with courage and zeal, have certainly reaped positive benefits for communities with its efforts in the areas of drugs and guns, by way of example. Patrolling city streets with uniformed officers in marked patrol cars may or may not equate to crime prevention. However, this same patrol will deter and will apprehend offenders and prevent other activities from taking place. While the police may not be the best protection from crime or the best prevention of crime, the police system is the most effective offense against it.[45]

On top of this are ridiculous expectations thrust upon the police model—not only expecting social services and social engineering from a law enforcement tenacity, but solutions to circumstances and conditions over which it has absolutely no control. In many circumstances, the sobering truth is that these issues need solutions that are well beyond the capabilities of police officers. The growing gap between rich and poor, the homeless, the blight of the inner city, racism and racial tensions, teen violence, teen pregnancy, substance abuse, lack of community ownership and involvement by its members, and a host of other difficulties are beyond the purview of the police system. Police can and do make remarkable differences in the lives contacted each and every day. To imply that no matter what is done is only marginal is harsh and inaccurate, for it is the police who are contacted when violations occur or emergencies are unfolding. 911 calls are routed to police officers not to social workers. Furthermore, it could be argued that the enforcement of many of our laws equates to active prevention of victimization. In other words, the enforcement model generates immediate and ongoing benefits for the whole community. For example, DUI arrests may prevent serious injury as does the intervention of police in an abusive spouse case. Each and every police interaction prompts rippling effects throughout the community, and in this way, positively impacts the life the community. But the reactive nature of the public police model will never be able to truly immerse itself into the community. Inevitably, public police will, knowingly or not, remain above the fray, outside the arena, and less integrated than the policing model suggested by the private security industry. Certainly, the private sector police have taken many, many cues from the public police methodology and the public sense of safety and "assurance" all the better for it.[46]

In the final analysis, each system offers much and can learn much from one another. Customer service, accountability, broken windows and community-based policy making, profit and efficiency, all represent the diverse approaches the public/private model brings to the table. Each system should maintain its fundamental mission yet at the same time, flourish by its own capacity to adapt and implement what works. For too long, the public police system operated

---

[43] Kobetz & Cooper, *supra* note 31, at 32.

[44] R. Ruddell, M.O. Thomas, & R. Patten, Examining the Roles of the Police and Private Security Officers in Urban Social Control, 13 *Int'l J. Police Sci. & Mgmt* 66 (Spring 2011).

[45] For an interesting study on how these two armies serve the urban populations with differing approaches, see Ruddell et al., *supra* note 45, at 54.

[46] See Rowland and Couple, *Patrol Officers.*

with a wallet never short on cash—those days are over. Today, police departments have to look strenuously at the bottom line in all operational settings. What better entity to learn from concerning cost and efficiency than the private sector police model?

Police departments talk about and even have gone as far as advocating the need to operate their agencies more like a corporation—one that is consumer friendly and results oriented. Given the nature of public police and the bureaucratic structure of departments, and the subject matter of usual business, is this plan possible? The public police system cannot equate its operational essence with that of the profit-driven corporation. While corporations are competition driven in budgeting, marketing, and strategic development, public police are functionally minded. Police departments are not in competition with others since competition does not exist in the public sector. Bruce L. Benson, in his book *To Serve and Protect*, insightfully recognizes this critical distinction:

> Police chiefs do not have to see that their departments make profits in order to survive, and they do not generally have to compete with other producers for the attention of consumers (they may have to compete for their appointment, of course, but their organization has a virtual monopoly over production of the service within its jurisdiction).[47]

To successfully operate like a corporation, police agency operations would have to undergo a draconian reformation. Budget dollars would be tied to productivity and effectiveness, promotion and staffing would be as apolitical as possible, and the utilization of civilians in key positions would be commonplace, especially in managerial and financial areas. Personnel deployment and shift decisions would also be altered. Instead of commanding, upper echelon police leaders would manage first, and order second. When contrasted with the operational philosophies of major security firms, the differences are stark. Corporations are proactive, while police departments naturally reactive toward crisis, crime, and emergency. The security giant Securitas rests its operational philosophy on a set of "core values," some of which public law enforcement may find foreign:

- Satisfy client needs
- Empower and respect our people
- Embrace high ethical standards
- Work as a team
- Reward innovation and constant improvement[48]

In these values resides a vastly different mentality. From training to education, from police academy requirements to promotion and job reviews, the culture of public police would have to shift dramatically. Private sector organizations, already rooted in the nonbureaucratic ideal, have a better chance of rising to the community policing challenge than their public counterpart.[49] Bickering about turf and jurisdictional lines would have to cease in the public model before any inroads into cost-efficient policing could occur. Private sector entities merge, consolidate, and reorganize for maximum effectiveness and in turn reduce costs or utilize excess revenues for the betterment of their service. Public law enforcement never willingly downsizes or streamlines its operational mandate. None of this is surprising to Bruce Benson, who fully appreciates the entrepreneurial nature of the private protection industry.

> This should come as no surprise, since private entrepreneurs – unlike public bureaucrats – are under constant competitive pressure to discover new ways to improve their products and services, including discovering new ways to improve community cooperation. Clearly, private entrepreneurs and the public they work with deserve much of the credit for falling crime rates.[50]

In the end, the public system will have little choice but to further adopt and integrate the private sector model into its operational design and just as compellingly will this occur in the private sector police setting as well. In the latter

[47] B.L. Benson, *To Serve and Protect.*

[48] Pinkerton Service Corporation, Core Values, at http://www.pinkertons.com/company/info/company_profile.asp, last accessed April 9, 2002.

[49] Private security can be said to labor under wholly different perceptions. For an interesting examination see, A. Micucci, A Typology of Private Policing Operational Styles, 26 *J. Crime Just.* 41 (January/February 1998).

[50] B.L. Benson, Growing Private Security Investments Help Crime Rates Tumble, *The Detroit News*, Editorials and opinions online edition, (December 16, 1999).

case, as transference and privatization of once sacrosanct public policing services continues its inevitable march to private delivery, the private security firm, the business and corporate firm will have to expand its operational vision.

As a result of all this change and transformation, the definition of security and its underlying business and industrial model will reflect this dynamic shift in how protection services are delivered.

3.3 DEFINING PRIVATE SECURITY BY CAREER ROLE AND OCCUPATIONS

The conceptual framework for private security is derived from many sources, including its historical heritage and place, its comparison with public sector policing, its role and involvement in homeland security practice, and its many roles and occupations. Private security can be fully understood and discovered when the many roles and occupational positions in the field are fully examined.[51]

Cast away any caricatures the industry has long been shackled with for this is a profession, a business and venture, and an entrepreneurial endeavor that long ago outlived the caricature. This is an industry operating in overdrive—with opportunities unmatched and growth unparalleled. The Bureau of Justice Statistics graphically portrays growth over nearly four decades. See Figure 3.2.[52]

Gone are the days of donut eating typecasts asleep at the wheel of responsibility. In its place a dynamic, changing private security.[53] Robert Meadows breaks down occupational opportunities in these categories in Figure 3.3.[54]

Security Magazine surveys the industry for its range of specializations. Sixteen areas comprise the list:

- Education (colleges and universities, K–12)
- Casinos, hospitality, arenas, and entertainment
- Finance/insurance/banking

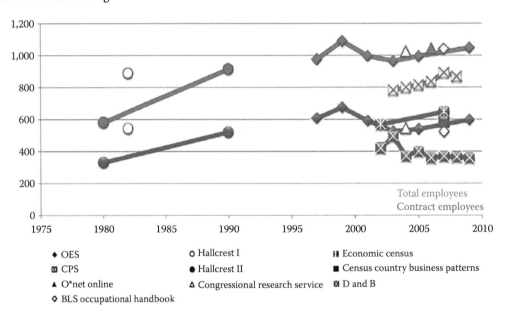

Figure 3.2 Total number of private security officers and contract security officers in the United States, 1980–2009. (From Bureau of Labor Statistics Occupational Outlook Handbook [BLS, 2009c]; Census County Business Patterns [2007]; Congressional Research Service [2004]; Current Population Survey [BLS, 2010b]; Dun and Bradstreet [2009]; U.S. Census Bureau, Economic Census [2002, 2007]; The Hallcrest Report I [Cunningham et al., 1985]; The Hallcrest Report II [Cunningham et al., 1990]; BLS [2010c]; O*NET OnLine [2006]; RAND [Bird et al., 1971].)

---

[51] Career planning need reflect the eclectic nature of the security industry. See *Developing Your Security Career Strategy*.

[52] K. Strom et al., *The Private Security Industry: A Review of the Definitions, Available Data Sources, and Paths Moving Forward* (December 2010), at https://www.ncjrs.gov/pdffiles1/bjs/grants/232781.pdf.

[53] See *Roundtable in Print: The Changing Role of Private Security*.

[54] R. Meadows, *Fundamentals of Protection and Safety*, at 10–11.

- Government (federal, state, and local)
- Construction, real estate, and property management
- Energy, utilities, power, gas, nuclear, and water
- Business services
- Industrial and manufacturing
- Retail, restaurants, and food service
- Agriculture/farming/food
- Information technology, communications, and media
- Transportation, logistics, warehousing, and supply chain
- Diversified companies
- Ports and terminals: sea/land/air
- Healthcare/medical centers/hospitals[55]

Coverage of the more crucial industry sectors follows.

Banking and Financial Institutions
  General Banking Institutions
  Bankcard centers
  Savings and Loan Companies
  Financial Centers
	Computer Security
	  Banks
	  Telephone Companies
	  Insurance Companies
	  Credit Card Companies
	  Crime Prevention

Credit Card Security
  Banks
  Retail Stores
  Gasoline Companies
	Restaurant and Lodging

Educational Institutions
  Universities
  Junior/Community Colleges
  Major School Districts
	Establishments
	  Large Restaurant Chains
	  Hotel and Motel Chains

Fire Resources and Management
  Small Communities
  Major, Firms, Aerospace
	Retail Stores
	  Department Stores
	  Grocery Stores
	  General Merchandise Stores

Health Care Institutions
  Hospitals
  Convalescent Homes
  Retirement Communities
  Pharmaceutical Firms
	Transportation and Cargo
	  Airlines
	  Trucking Firms
	  Special Couriers
	  Railroads
	  Ports/Maritime Security

Nuclear Security
  Production Facilities
  Power Plants
  Transportation Facilities
	Executive Protection
	  VIPs
	  Diplomats
	  Celebrities

Public Utilities
  Departments of Water and Power
  Telephone Companies
  Major Power Generating Facilities
	Community
	  Apartment Complexes
	  Afterschool Programs
	  Neighborhood Patrols

Figure 3.3 Security industry sectors and specializations.

[55] M. McCourt, Building Security's Future: Security 500, *Security* (2009, November), at 20–72.

3.3.1 Guard companies/security agency and security firm

At the base of private security operations are the sponsoring guard companies that provide officers, both armed and unarmed, for a host of activities, including crowd control at events, protection of public facilities, and safety and security at sports events and public gatherings as well as industrial and commercial asset protection. While a security officer may be an individually licensed person, the guard company, sometimes referred to as the agency or firm licensure, is entrusted with the oversight and delegation of larger numbers of officers to designated locations. *Security Magazine* annually lists the top security guard companies by personnel and revenue. Visit their website for the 2014 results.[56]

State by state rules and regulations govern the licensure of guard companies and firms.

3.3.2 Guards and private patrol officers

The classic stereotype of the security industry has long been its mainstay—the security officer or guard. While unarmed officers serve as the backbone of this dynamic industry, they are a subset among a series of occupational roles. Officers, according to the U.S. Bureau of Labor's *Occupational Handbook*, assume diverse functions in the protection end of the business. See Figure 3.4.[57]

Qualifications tend to be the least demanding. See Figure 3.5.

Guards or entry-level security officers are either licensed as "armed" or "unarmed." The definitional differences can be summed up as follows:

> What is an unarmed security officer? A person who performs the function of observation, detection, reporting, or notification of appropriate authorities or designated agents regarding persons or property on the premises he is contracted to protect, and who does not carry or have access to a firearm in the performance of his duties.[58]
>
> What is an armed security officer? A person employed to safeguard and protect persons and property or deter theft, loss, concealment of any tangible or intangible personal property on the premises he is contracted to protect, and who carries or has access to a firearm in the performance of his duties.[59]

The outlook for security guard positions is exceptional especially when one considers the impact of police privatization on the transference of services. The Bureau of Labor Statistics (BLS) concludes a very positive picture of employment until 2024. See Table 3.6.[60]

As security officers discover the many inroads to community service, their work in a patrol capacity is sure to increase in the years ahead. Whether in a business or a neighborhood community, private security professionals operate in a patrol capacity—surveying, detecting, deterring, and integrating the community, whether by foot, bicycle, or vehicle. Some jurisdictions have licensure requirements for the patrol functions. See Figure 3.6[61] for licensure requirements for a *private patrol operator or manager.*

3.3.3 Private investigators and detectives

Private investigators may investigate crimes, individuals, the cause of fire, losses, accidents, damage, or injury; search for lost or stolen property; and obtain evidence for use in court. Most investigators primarily investigate civil concerns. In some states, they may protect persons and property. Private investigators must be licensed and pass a criminal history background check through the Department of Justice and the FBI.

[56] *Security Magazine*, 11th Annual Top Guarding Firms Listing, at http://www.securitymagazine.com/ext/resources/SEC/2014/February/guard-chart-2014.pdf.

[57] Bureau of Labor Statistics, U.S. Department of Labor, Occupational Outlook Handbook, 2016-17 Edition, Security Guards and Gaming Surveillance Officers, at http://www.bls.gov/ooh/protective-service/security-guards.htm, last accessed July 17, 2016.

[58] Virginia Department of Criminal Justice Services, Unarmed Security Officer/Courier webpage https://www.dcjs.virginia.gov/licensure-and-regulatory-affairs/unarmed-security-officercourier.

[59] Virginia Department of Criminal Justice Services, Armed Security Officer webpage https://www.dcjs.virginia.gov/licensure-and-regulatory-affairs/armed-security-officer.

[60] Bureau of Labor Statistics, *supra* note 58.

[61] State of California, Bureau of Security & Investigative Services, Private Patrol Operator Fact Sheet, June 2015, at http://www.bsis.ca.gov/forms_pubs/ppo_fact.pdf.

What Security Guards and Gaming Surveillance Officers Do

Security guards and gaming surveillance officers patrol and protect property against theft, vandalism, terrorism, and illegal activity.

Duties

Security guards and gaming surveillance officers typically do the following:

- Protect and enforce laws on an employer's property
- Monitor alarms and closed-circuit TV (CCTV) cameras
- Control access for employees and visitors
- Conduct security checks over a specified area
- Write reports on what they observed while on duty
- Serve as witnesses for court testimony
- Detain violators

Security guards, also called security officers, protect property, enforce rules on the property, and deter criminal activity. Some guards are assigned a stationary position from which they monitor alarms or surveillance cameras. Other guards are assigned a patrol area where they conduct security checks.

Gaming surveillance officers and gaming investigators act as security agents for casinos. Using audio and video equipment in an observation room, they watch casino operations for suspicious activities, such as cheating and theft, and monitor compliance with rules, regulations, and laws. They maintain and organize recordings from security cameras, which are sometimes used as evidence in police investigations.

Guards and officers must remain alert, looking out for anything unusual. In an emergency, they are required to call for assistance from police, fire, or ambulance services. Some security guards are armed.

A security guard's responsibilities vary from one employer to another. In retail stores, guards protect people, records, merchandise, money, and equipment. They may work with undercover store detectives to prevent theft by customers and employees, detain shoplifting suspects until the police arrive, and patrol parking lots.

In office buildings, banks, hotels, and hospitals, guards maintain order and protect the organization's customers, staff, and property.

Guards who work in museums and art galleries protect paintings and exhibits by watching people and inspecting the contents of patrons' handbags.

In factories, government buildings, and military bases, security guards protect workers and equipment and check the credentials of people and vehicles entering and leaving the premises.

Guards working in parks and at sports stadiums control crowds, supervise parking and seating, and direct traffic.

Security guards stationed at the entrances to bars and nightclubs keep underage people from entering, collect cover charges, and maintain order among customers.

Security guards working in schools and universities patrol the buildings and grounds, looking for suspicious activity.

Figure 3.4   Security guard and gaming surveillance officers' roles and responsibilities.

Professional investigators need a wide array of personal and professional skills to be successful. Experience is also essential and the reason so many investigative positions are filled by former public police. While there are many qualities essential to the competent investigator, the following attributes are mandatory:

- *Communication skills.* Private detectives and investigators must listen carefully and ask appropriate questions when interviewing a person of interest.

- *Decisionmaking skills.* Private detectives and investigators must be able to think on their feet and make quick decisions, based on the limited information that they have at a given time.

- *Inquisitiveness.* Private detectives and investigators must want to ask questions and search for the truth.

- *Patience.* Private detectives and investigators may have to spend long periods conducting surveillance while waiting for an event to occur. Investigations may take a long time, and they may not provide a resolution quickly—or at all.

- *Resourcefulness.* Private detectives and investigators must work persistently with whatever leads they have, no matter how limited, to determine the next step toward their goal. They sometimes need to anticipate what a person of interest will do next.[62]

[62] Bureau of Labor Statistics, U.S. Department of Labor, *Occupational Outlook Handbook*, 2016-17 Edition, Private Detectives and Investigators, at http://www.bls.gov/ooh/protective-service/private-detectives-and-investigators.htm, last accessed August 27, 2016.

How to Become a Security Guard or Gaming Surveillance Officer

Most security guard jobs require a high school diploma. Gaming surveillance officers sometimes need experience with security and video surveillance. Most states require guards to be registered with the state, especially if they carry a firearm.

Education

Security guards generally need a high school diploma or equivalent, although some jobs may not have any education requirements. Gaming surveillance officers also need a high school diploma or equivalent and may need experience with video surveillance technology depending upon assignment.

Training

Although most employers provide instruction for newly hired guards, the amount of training they receive varies. Most guards, however, learn their job in a few weeks. During those few weeks, training from their employer typically covers emergency procedures, detention of suspected criminals, and proper communication.

Many states recommend that security guards receive approximately 8 hours of preassignment training, 8–16 hours of on-the-job training, and 8 hours of annual training. This may include training in protection, public relations, report writing, deterring crises, first aid, and other specialized training related to the guard's assignment.

Training is more rigorous for armed guards because they require weapons training. Armed guards may be tested periodically in the use of firearms.

For gaming surveillance officers and investigators, some employers prefer candidates with previous work experience in casinos or individuals with a background in law enforcement. Experience with video technology can also be helpful in using surveillance systems and software.

Drug testing may be required as a condition of employment and randomly during employment.

Licenses, Certifications, and Registrations

Most states require that guards be registered with the state in which they work. Although registration requirements vary by state, basic qualifications for candidates are as follows:

- Be at least 18 years old
- Pass a background check
- Complete training

Guards who carry weapons usually must be registered by the appropriate government authority. Armed guard positions have more stringent background checks and entry requirements than those of unarmed guards. Rigorous hiring and screening programs, including background, criminal record, and fingerprint checks, are required for armed guards in most states.

Some jobs may also require a driver's license.

Advancement

Some guards advance to supervisory or security manager positions. Those with experience or postsecondary education should have an advantage. Armed security guards have a greater potential for advancement and enjoy higher earnings.

Some guards with management skills open their own security guard business. Guards can also move to an organization that needs higher levels of security, which may result in more prestige or higher pay.

Important Qualities

Decisionmaking skills. Guards and officers must be able to quickly determine the best course of action when a dangerous situation arises.

Patience. Security guards and officers may need to spend long periods standing and observing their environment without distractions.

Observation skills. Guards and officers must be alert and aware of their surroundings, and be able to quickly recognize anything out of the ordinary.

Physical strength. Guards must be strong enough to apprehend offenders and to handle emergency situations.

Figure 3.5   Requirements for becoming a security guard or gaming surveillance officer.

Comprehensive security firms provide a full range of investigative services, but a significant portion of the investigator force is in the form of sole proprietors. See Figure 3.7.[63]

Some organizations and groups dedicated to the advancement of investigative practice in the security industry are as follows:

---

[63] *Ibid.*

Table 3.6   Bureau of Labor Statistics outlook for security guard positions through 2024

Occupational title	Security guards
Employment, 2014	1,095,400
Projected employment, 2024	1,150,900
Percent change, 2014–2024	5
Numeric change, 2014–2024	55,500

- American Medical Investigator's Association
- Council of International Investigators
- Institute of Professional Investigators
- National Association of Legal Investigators
- National Security Institute
- National Society of Professional Insurance Investigators
- International Association of Arson Investigators
- National Council of Investigation & Security Services, Inc.
- World Association of Detectives
- National Association of Investigative Specialists
- Global Investigators Network
- Private Eye International

Both the projected opportunities and compensation potential are quite good in the investigative end of security. The BLS charts compensation levels at significantly higher numbers than entry-level guards. See Figure 3.8.

3.3.4 Alarm services: Business and residential

Alarm companies sell alarms to protect the consumer's premises or business owner's facility; install, service, and monitor alarms; and respond to alarm activations. These companies must be licensed through the appropriate state entity. Retail stores that sell alarm systems only at the store may be exempt. Company operators, managers, and agents must pass criminal history background checks. An alarm company may hire another company to monitor alarms. Assurances must be made, verifying that the company is a licensed monitoring service. There are many home security alarm companies and many have expanded their services over the years. For example, ADT—one of the largest—provides temperature monitoring, flood monitoring, fire and smoke monitoring, carbon monoxide monitoring, and medical alert monitoring in addition to their traditional burglary alarm services.

Web Exercise: Discover the crucial role the Electronic Security Association plays in the promulgation of ethical standards for alarm companies at http://c.ymcdn.com/sites/esaweb.site-ym.com/resource/resmgr/ESA-Codes_ Standards/Code_of_Ethics.pdf.

Alarm services represent one facet of a much larger world, namely, security technology. Through technological advances, especially as to wireless access, remote capacity,and 24/7 GPS and other virtual services, the industry has been revolutionized over the last two decades. What is indisputable is the effective deterrence capability of the alarmed premises or business. A recent longitudinal study on the crime impact of alarmed communities, conducted by Rutgers University, confirms the efficacy of the alarmed model.[64]

3.3.5 Armed couriers

An armed courier elevates the requirements and obligations of those entrusted with carrying weapons and, at the same time, goods and valuables worthy of armed protection. Hence, the bank courier, who delivers funds from one branch to another, must be a person of the highest character. See Figure 3.9.

---

[64] See S. Lee, *The Impact of Home Burglar Alarm Systems on Residential Burglaries* (2008), at http://airef.org/wp-content/uploads/2014/06/ airef91808_exesummary.pdf.

PRIVATE PATROL OPERATOR OR QUALIFIED MANAGER
(FACT SHEET)

Requirements for Licensure

A private patrol operator operates a business that protects persons or property or prevents theft. In order for a company to seek licensure as a Private Patrol Operator, the applicant must have passed the licensing examination. In addition, each individual applicant, partner, or corporate officer must meet the following requirements:

- Be 18 or older.

- Undergo a criminal history background check through the California Department of Justice (DOJ) and Federal Bureau of Investigation (FBI); and

- Have committed no offense or violation of the Private Security Services Act that would be grounds for license suspension or revocation

- To apply for a company license, submit the $500 application processing fee, one recent passport-quality photograph and a Private Patrol Operator Live Scan form signed by the Live Scan Operator for each applicant, partner, and officer.

- Send your application to the Bureau of Security and Investigative Services, P.O. Box 989002, West Sacramento, CA 95798-9002.

If you do not have a qualified manager who already has a current qualification certificate, you must also submit the required forms listed on page 7 of the Private Patrol Operator and Private Patrol Operator Qualified Manager Licensing Packet for the qualified manager.

An additional $500 fee does not need to be submitted if you are applying for Private Patrol Operator license and Private Patrol Operator Qualified Manager certificate at the same time. A Qualified Manager who is also an applicant, partner, or officer should only submit one set of fingerprints or pay one fingerprint processing fee.

Insurance

ALL licensed Private Patrol Operators must maintain general liability insurance as a condition of licensure. Specifically, Private Patrol Operators are required to have commercial general liability insurance policies which provide minimum limits of one millions dollars ($1,000,000) for any one loss or occurrence due to bodily injury, including death, or property damage, or both.

The Bureau recommends that applicants wait until the Bureau provides the applicant with written approval of the Private Patrol Operator's business name to obtain a Certificate of Liability Insurance document since this information is required to be included on the document.

Private patrol operator applicants and licensees must submit a Certificate of Liability Insurance to the Bureau as proof that the insurance requirement is being met. The Certificate of Liability Insurance must include:

Figure 3.6 Fact sheet sample for private patrol operator or qualified manager.   (*Continued*)

Most states require armed couriers to be licensed. See the New York State licensure application in Figure 3.10.[65]

Web Exercise: Find out about The Brink's Company—one of the nation's largest courier firms at http://investors.brinks.com/CustomPage/Index?keyGenPage=107375001.

3.3.6 Loss prevention specialist

Theft prevention and asset protection has been the staple of the industry since its earliest days.[66] Commercial entities depend on the focused protection system security provides, and the future, both near and far term, does not manifest a decline in property pilferage. Richter Moore predicts property offenses once only dreamt of in science fiction.

---

[65] Armored Car Guard Application, NYS Department of State http://www.dos.ny.gov/forms/licensing/1351-f-l-a.pdf.
[66] *Hallcrest Report II*, at 115.

- Your company name;
- The insurance policy number; and
- The dates the coverage of insurance commenced and expires.

Qualified Manager

An individual, partnership, or corporation seeking a license as a Private Patrol Operator must specify in the application the individual who will manage the business on a day-today basis.

This individual is called the Qualified Manager. (An owner, partner, or corporate officer may serve as the Qualified Manager, or may hire someone to fill this role.) To be eligible to apply for licensure as a Qualified Manager, you must meet the following requirements:

- Be 18 or older.
- Undergo a criminal history background check through the DOJ and the FBI.
- Have committed no offense or violation of the Private Security Services Act that would be grounds for license suspension or revocation.
- Pass a two-hour multiple-choice examination covering the Private Security Services Act and other rules and regulations, business knowledge, emergency procedures, security functions, and use of deadly weapons. A copy of the Private Security Services Act is available through this link: http://www.bsis.ca.gov/about_us/laws/pssact.shtml
- Submit the Personal Identification Form with one recent passport-quality photograph, the Qualifying Experience Form, and a Private Patrol Operator Live Scan form signed by the Live Scan Operator. The Personal Identification Form and the Qualifying Experience Form can be found within the Private Patrol Operator and Private Patrol Operator Qualified Manager Licensing Packet located on the BSIS website.
- Send your application to the Bureau of Security and Investigative Services, P.O. Box 989002, West Sacramento, CA 95798-9002.

If you are applying only to become certified as a private patrol operator qualified manager you must include a $500 Examination Fee with the required forms previously listed.

To request an application for licensure as a Private Patrol Operator or qualified manager, call the Department of Consumer Affairs at (800) 952-5210, or visit our Web site: www.bsis.ca.gov.

Firearm Permit

You may **_not_** carry a gun on duty without a valid firearm permit or a screen print of the Bureau's approval obtained from the Bureau's web site. Also, a firearm permit issued by the Bureau **_does not_** authorize you to carry a concealed weapon. You may **_not_** carry a

Figure 3.6   (Continued) Fact sheet sample for private patrol operator or qualified manager.   (*Continued*)

Theft has always been the bane of private security. Loss prevention is a major responsibility of private security today. Its charge is to protect property from theft by outsiders or employees. Theft in the twenty-first century by criminal organizations will far exceed anything in the twentieth century in terms of sophistication and specialization. Piracy at sea, in the air, and at cargo terminals is a major concern of the transportation industry.[67]

---

[67] R.H. Moore, Private Security in the Twenty First Century: An Opinion, 18 *J. Sec. Admin.* 10 (1995).

concealed weapon on duty without a Concealed Weapons Permit (CCW) issued by local authorities, nor carry a caliber handgun not listed on your firearm permit.

To apply for a firearm permit, you must:

- Be a U.S. citizen or have permanent legal alien status.

- Pass a course in the carrying and use of firearms. The approximately 14-hour (8 hours classroom, approximately 6 hours range) training course covers moral and legal aspects, firearms nomenclature, weapon handling and shooting fundamentals, emergency procedures, and range training. The course must be given by a Bureau-certified firearms training instructor at a Bureau-certified training facility. Written and range exams are administered at the end of the course. Costs of training are determined by the training facility. For a list of certified training facilities, call (916) 322-4000. You can also access a listing of training facilities from the Bureau's webpage for firearm training facilities. Search by county for a listing of all the training facilities in that county.

- Submit a firearm permit application, pay the $80 application fee, and submit a Private Patrol Operator License with Firearm Permit Live Scan form signed by the Live Scan site operator, including ATI number.

- Send your application package to the Bureau of Security and Investigative Services, P.O. Box 989002, West Sacramento, CA 95798-9002.

Note: A firearms qualification card expires two years from the date it was issued. An applicant must requalify four times during the life of the permit: twice during the first year after the date of issuance, and twice during the second year. Requalifications must be at least four months apart.

Baton Permit

To carry a baton on duty, you must be a licensee or qualified manager and complete at least an eight-hour training course from a Bureau-certified baton instructor. For a list of certified baton training facilities, visit the Verify a License webpage. Search by county for a listing of all training facilities in that county.

"Protection of the public shall be the highest priority for the Bureau of Security and Investigative Services in exercising licensing, regulatory and disciplinary functions. Whenever the protection of the public is consistent with other interests sought to be promoted, the protection of the public shall be paramount."

Figure 3.6 (Continued) Fact sheet sample for private patrol operator or qualified manager.

Indeed, property offenses have taken on a cyber dimension for security specialists who labor to prevent credit card scams and copy, warehouse rerouting and fraudulent transfer to unauthorized parties, identity theft, and other attacks. So significant is the cyber threat to our retail and commercial systems that the FBI now posts a wanted listed of cyber thieves and criminals. See Figure 3.11.[68]

Aside from the technological challenges, the rates of retail and commercial theft continue unabated over the last five decades. To the chagrin of retailers, these entities now grapple with "organized" gangs and mobs that conspire to take large amounts of goods and property. Organized retail theft is now a 30-billion-dollar loss for American retailers.[69]

The most popular goods stolen are charted by the National Retail Federation. See Figure 3.12.[70]

Without private sector justice, our free enterprise system would be in jeopardy.

---

[68] FBI, Most Wanted, Cyber's Most Wanted, at https://www.fbi.gov/wanted/cyber, last accessed July 17, 2016.

[69] FBI, Organized Retail Theft: A $30 Billion-a-Year Industry, at https://www.fbi.gov/news/stories/organized-retail-theft, last accessed July 17, 2016.

[70] National Retail Federation, *Organized Crime Retail Study* 12 (2014), at https://nrf.com/sites/default/files/NRF%202014%20ORC%20report%20REV2.pdf, last accessed July 17, 2016.

What Private Detectives and Investigators Do

Private detectives must properly collect and document evidence so that it may be used in a court of law.

Private detectives and investigators search for information about legal, financial, and personal matters. They offer many services, such as verifying people's backgrounds and statements, finding missing persons, and investigating computer crimes.

Duties

Private detectives and investigators typically do the following:

- Interview people to gather information
- Search public or court records to uncover clues
- Conduct surveillance
- Collect evidence to present in court or to a client
- Verify employment and income
- Check for civil judgments and criminal history
- Investigate computer crimes and information theft

Private detectives and investigators offer many services for individuals, attorneys, and businesses. Examples are performing background checks, investigating employees for possible theft from a company, proving or disproving infidelity in a divorce case, and helping to locate a missing person.

Private detectives and investigators use a variety of tools when researching the facts in a case. Much of their work is done with a computer, allowing them to obtain information such as telephone numbers, details about social networks, descriptions of online activities, and records of a person's prior arrests. They make phone calls to verify facts and interview people when conducting a background investigation.

Investigators may go undercover to observe people and to obtain information.

Detectives also conduct surveillance when investigating a case. They may watch locations, such as a person's home or office, often from a hidden position. Using cameras and binoculars, detectives gather information on people of interest.

Detectives and investigators must be mindful of the law when conducting investigations. Because they lack police authority, their work must be done with the same authority as a private citizen. As a result, they must have a good understanding of federal, state, and local laws, such as privacy laws, and other legal issues affecting their work. Otherwise, evidence they collect may not be useable in court and they could face prosecution.

The following are examples of types of private detectives and investigators:

Computer forensics investigators specialize in recovering, analyzing, and presenting information from computers to be used as evidence. Many focus on recovering deleted emails and documents.

Legal investigators help prepare criminal defenses, verify facts in civil lawsuits, locate witnesses, and serve legal documents. They often work for lawyers and law firms.

Corporate investigators conduct internal and external investigations for corporations. Internally, they may investigate drug use in the workplace or ensure that expense accounts are not abused. Externally, they may try to identify and stop criminal schemes, such as fraudulent billing by a supplier.

Financial investigators may be hired to collect financial information on individuals and companies attempting to make large financial transactions. These investigators are often certified public accountants (CPAs) who work closely with investment bankers and other accountants. Investigators might search for assets to recover damages awarded by a court in fraud and theft cases.

Figure 3.7   Write-up about what private detectives and investigators do.

Given the growing complexities of loss prevention within the retail and commercial sectors, calls for increased training and certification have been common. The Loss Prevention Foundation sponsors both an entry-level and advanced course for loss prevention specialists. See Figure 3.13.[71]

Web Exercise: Find out about the Loss Prevention Foundation, an association dedicated to the professionalization of loss prevention specialists at http://www.losspreventionfoundation.org/membership.html.

Visit their LPC certification page at http://www.losspreventionfoundation.org/lpc-retail-loss-prevention.php.

---

[71] Loss Prevention Foundation, LPCertified website—About, at http://www.losspreventionfoundation.org/lpc-retail-loss-prevention.php, last accessed July 17, 2016.

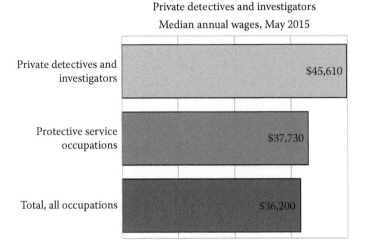

Figure 3.8 Median annual wages for private detectives and investigators. *Note*: All occupations includes all occupations in the U.S. economy. (From U.S. Bureau of Labor Statistics, Occupational Employment Statistics.)

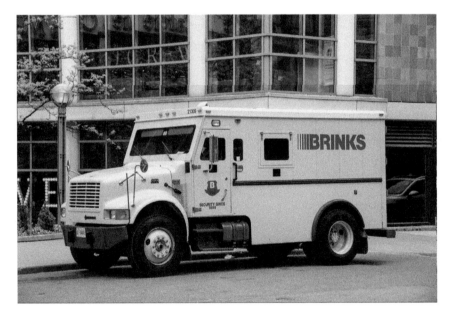

Figure 3.9 Armed vehicle.

3.3.7 College/university and school security

The private sector has a distinguished record of service to colleges and universities. Educational institutions tend to prefer a more humane, professional, and interactive approach than offered by traditional law enforcement, although a large number of public and private campuses employ police officers, per legislative acts. While larger state institutions maintain as visible a police presence as the surrounding community, smaller colleges and universities prefer private sector delivery. "Overall, 81% of public campuses had armed officers, compared to 34% of private campuses. Among campuses with 10,000 or more students, 89% of the public campuses had armed officers compared to 59% of the private campuses."[72]

---

[72] B.A. Reaves & A.L. Goldberg, *Campus Law Enforcement Agencies, 1995* iii (1996).

FOR OFFICE USE ONLY   CASH#: _____   FEE: **$50**

UID: _____   PREV. UID: _____   CLASS: _____   CODE: _____

Armored Car Guard Application

NYS Department of State
Division of Licensing Services
P.O. Box 22001
Albany, NY 12201-2001
Customer Service: (518) 474-7569
www.dos.ny.gov

INSTRUCTIONS: Forms must be completed in blue or black ink. Incomplete forms will not be processed.
Please refer to pages 4 - 6 for further instructions on completing this form.

APPLICANT INFORMATION

Social Security Number: ____ - ____ - ____   **Birth Date:** ____ - ____ - ____
(See Instructions-Privacy Notification)   M M   D D   Y Y Y Y

Applicant's Name: LAST NAME

FIRST NAME   MIDDLE NAME   NAME SUFFIX *(For example: Sr. / Jr. / III)*

Alias or
Maiden Name: LAST NAME

FIRST NAME   MIDDLE NAME   NAME SUFFIX *(For example: Sr. / Jr. / III)*

Gender: **Race:**
○ Male ○ Female   ○ White ○ Black ○ American Indian or Alaskan Native ○ Asian or Pacific Islander ○ Other ○ Unknown

RESIDENCE ADDRESS

STREET ADDRESS (Required) - P.O.Box may be added to ensure delivery   APT/UNIT/PO BOX

CITY   STATE   ZIP+4

COUNTY (Enter only if in New York State)   COUNTRY/NATION (Of above address)

DAYTIME PHONE (INCLUDING AREA CODE)   FAX NUMBER - IF ANY (INCLUDING AREA CODE)

E-MAIL ADDRESS (IF ANY)

DMV Consent Section - IMPORTANT INFORMATION Regarding Your Photo ID

The Department of State produces photo ID cards in cooperation with the NYS Department of Motor Vehicles (DMV). If you have a current NYS Driver License or Non-Driver ID card, please provide your 9-digit DMV ID Number in the space provided below. Then read the informed consent and sign this form. If you do not have a current NYS photo Driver License or Non-Driver ID card, please have your photo taken at any nearby DMV office BEFORE you complete this application. For more details, refer to our enclosed notice, "Request for Photo ID."

INFORMED CONSENT: I authorize the NYS Department of State and the NYS Department of Motor Vehicles (DMV) to produce an ID card bearing my DMV photo. I understand that DMV will send this card to the address I maintain with the Department of State. I also understand that the Department of State and DMV will use my DMV photo to produce all my subsequent ID Cards for as long as I maintain my license/registration with the Department of State.

DMV ID# ____ - ____ - ____

X _____   _____
        Applicant's Signature   *Date Signed*

DOS-1351-f-l-a (Rev. 06/14)   Page 1 of 6

Figure 3.10   New York State Armed Courier application.   *(Continued)*

Armored Car Guard Application

BACKGROUND QUESTIONS

Answer the following questions by checking either "YES" or "NO"

1. Are you currently an active duty police officer?
   → *IF "YES," you must submit certification of status.*

   ○ YES   ○ NO

2. Are you currently an active duty peace officer who has completed a required firearms training course?
   → *IF "YES," you must submit certification of status.*

   ○ YES   ○ NO

3. Have you ever been convicted in this state or elsewhere of a crime or offense that is a misdemeanor or a felony?
   → *IF "YES," you must submit with this application a written explanation giving the place, court jurisdiction, nature of the offense, sentence and/or other disposition. You must submit a copy of the accusatory instrument (e.g., indictment, criminal information or complaint) and a Certificate of Disposition. If you possess or have received a Certificate of Relief from Disabilities, Certificate of Good Conduct or Executive Pardon, you must submit a copy with this application.*

   ○ YES   ○ NO

4. Are there any criminal charges (misdemeanors or felonies) pending against you in any court in this state or elsewhere?
   → *IF "YES," you must submit a copy of the accusatory instrument (e.g., indictment, criminal information or complaint).*

   ○ YES   ○ NO

5. Has any license or permit issued to you or a company in which you are or were a principal in New York State or elsewhere ever been revoked, suspended or denied?
   → *IF "YES," you must submit an explanation.*

   ○ YES   ○ NO

6. Have you ever been discharged from a correctional or law enforcement agency for incompetence or misconduct as determined by a court of competent jurisdiction, administrative hearing officer, administartive law judge, arbitor, arbitration panel or other duly constituted tribunal, or resigned from such an agency while charged with misconduct or incompetence?
   → *IF "YES," you must submit an explanation.*

   ○ YES   ○ NO

7. Have you ever applied, in this state or elsewhere, for a registration/license as an armored car guard; armored car carrier; security guard; watch, guard or patrol agency; bail enforcement agent; or private investigator?
   → *IF "YES," please provide the UID # or Reg. # . _____*

   ○ YES   ○ NO

Figure 3.10   (Continued) New York State Armed Courier application.   (*Continued*)

Armored Car Guard Application

CHILD SUPPORT STATEMENT

You **MUST** complete this section. If you do **NOT** complete it, your application will **NOT** be processed.

I, the undersigned, do hereby certify that (You must "X" A or B, below):

A. ◯ **I am not under obligation to pay child support.** (SKIP "B" and go directly to **Applicant Affirmation**).

B. ◯ I am under obligation to pay child support   (You must "X" any of the four statements below that are true and apply to you):

    ◯ I do not owe four or more months of child support payments.
    ◯ I am making child support payments by income execution or court approved payment plan or by a plan agreed to by the parties.
    ◯ My child support obligation is the subject of a pending court proceeding.
    ◯ I receive public assistance or supplemental social security income.

APPLICANT AFFIRMATION

I affirm, under the penalties of perjury, that the statements made in this application are true and correct. I further affirm that I have read the provisions of Article 8C of the General Business Law and the rules and regulations promulgated thereunder.

X _____   _____
               Applicant's Signature   *Date Signed*

Print Name: _____

It is important that you notify the NYS Department of State of any changes in your address so you will receive renewal notices and any other notifications pertinent to your license.
Before mailing this application, please be sure to have included the appropriate documentation and the nonrefundable fee payable to the NYS Department of State. *(See the front of this application for the appropriate mailing address).*

Figure 3.10   (Continued) New York State Armed Courier application.   *(Continued)*

Armored Car Guard Application

INSTRUCTIONS

Read ALL instructions in this package carefully before completing the application. Incomplete forms will be returned. Any omission, inaccuracy or failure to make full disclosure may be deemed sufficient reason to deny a registration or may result in the suspension or revocation of an issued registration.

A COMPLETED APPLICATION MUST INCLUDE: *(Use this checklist to make sure you have included/completed all requirements.)*

☐ The completed, signed application;

☐ Signed DMV Informed Consent;

☐ Receipt that provides proof of electronic fingerprinting by an approved vendor

☐ $50 application fee payable to the NYS Department of State. See "Application Requirements -acceptable forms of payment;"

☐ Course completion certificate for 47 hours of firearms training (unless waived);

☐ Any additional documentation requested in response to specific questions on the application form

APPLICATION REQUIREMENTS:

Armored car guard duties:
An armored car guard, as defined in the General Business Law, is an individual employed by a licensed armored car carrier to: (1) provide secured transportation; (2) protect and safeguard valuable cargo from one place to another; *or* (3) provide cash services for automated teller machines, **all** by means of bullet resistant armored vehicles. Additionally, an armored car guard possesses or has access to a firearm.

Those armored car employees who may drive or accompany an armored car vehicle, but who do not carry or are not authorized to access a firearm, are not covered under the law and do not have to register.

Who must apply for an Armored Car Guard registration?
All persons who engage in armored car guard activities must complete appropriate training and be registered with the Department of State.

Required documents:
All applicants must submit an application and proof of completion of a 47-hour firearms training course in order to become registered as an armored car guard. Alternatively, the completion of the 47-hour firearms training course may be accomplished within 180 days after receipt of the guard application. Pending completion of firearms training, and freedom from relevant criminal convictions (verified by a report from DCJS after submission of fingerprints), the applicant will be issued a conditional letter of authority which will entitle him or her to work as an armored car guard.

Upon submission of proof of the 47-hour firearms training course, the individual will be issued a photo ID card signifying that they are authorized to perform armored car guard functions.

Firearms training requirements:
Armored car guards are required to complete training programs recognized by DCJS, including a 47-hour firearms course and an 8-hour firearms annual in-service course.

If you can demonstrate to the satisfaction of DCJS that you have already taken training which meets or exceeds the 47-hour firearms training, you may request a waiver from DCJS. Waivers may be requested from DCJS by contacting them directly at (518) 457-4135, or writing them at 80 South Swan Street, 3rd Fl., Albany, NY 12210-8002. If approved, they will provide a waiver letter to be submitted with the application.

Active duty police officers must register and complete training:
Active duty police officers must register with the Department of State to perform services as an armored car guard. Active duty police officers are not required to complete any firearms training. However, you must submit a certification of status with your application for armored car guard. This certifies that you are an active duty police officer in good standing. Certifications of status must be on official letterhead and be signed by either the chief or personnel officer.

Individuals previously employed as police officers are considered civilians. A police officer who has retired within the last five years, may qualify for a waiver from the 47-hour firearms training. Waivers may be requested from DCJS by contacting them directly at (518) 457-4135, or writing them at 80 South Swan Street, 3rd Fl., Albany, NY 12210-8002. If approved, they will provide a waiver letter to be submitted with the application.

Individuals who are no longer active duty police officers and do not qualify for a waiver, must complete the 47-hour firearms training course.

Figure 3.10   (Continued) New York State Armed Courier application.   *(Continued)*

Armored Car Guard Application

Peace officers must register and complete training:
Active duty peace officers must register with the Department of State to perform services as an armored car guard. Active duty peace officers may be exempt from further firearms training if you have already taken training which meets or exceeds the 47-hour firearms training.

Active duty peace officers who have completed the basic course for peace officers with long firearms may submit their basic course certificates with their applications.

A certificate for the basic course is valid for four years from the date of separation. Retired peace officers who have had the long firearms training, may qualify for a waiver. Waivers may be requested from DCJS by contacting them directly at (518) 457-4135, or writing them at 80 South Swan Street, 3rd Fl., Albany, NY 12210-8002. If approved, they will provide a waiver letter to be submitted with the application.

Individuals who are no longer active duty peace officers and do not have a valid basic course certificate, or do not qualify for a waiver, must complete the 47-hour firearms training course.

Fee and term of registration:
The nonrefundable application fee for an armored car guard registration is $50.00 payable to the NYS Department of State. The registration will be effective for two years. The renewal fee is $50.00, every two years.

Acceptable forms of payment:
You may pay by Money Order, Company Check or Cashiers Check made payable to the NYS Department of State. Personal checks or credit cards will not be accepted. Do not mail cash.

Note: Before mailing this application, please be sure you have included the appropriate documentation and the nonrefundable fee payable to the NYS Department of State. (See the front of this application for the appropriate mailing address.)

FINGERPRINT REQUIREMENTS:
Applicants have access to electronic fingerprinting through IdentoGo by MorphoTrust USA.

Electronic Fingerprinting Procedure:
Schedule Appointment: Applicants may schedule appointments with IdentoGo by MorphoTrust USA. To schedule an appointment at a location near you, visit their website at www.identogo.com or call 877-472-6915. For scheduling purposes, you must utilize the required ORI number NY922020Z.

What to bring to Appointment: Complete the request for NYS Fingerprinting Services - Information Form (pdf) and BRING it with you to the fingerprinting site.
Proof of electronic fingerprint completion: Upon completion of the fingerprint process, the vendor will provide you with two receipts as proof of fingerprint completion. Include one receipt with the completed application. The second copy of the receipt should be retained by your employer.
PLEASE NOTE: Fingerprint receipts are valid for 5 months from the date of fingerprinting. Please submit original application within 5 months from the date of fingerprinting. Failure to submit your application within this time period will require you to complete the fingerprinting process again.

Fingerprint fees:
All fees for fingerprinting are payable to MorphoTrust USA.
  • Division of Criminal Justice Services (DCJS) fee: $75.00
  • Applicable Fingerprint Vendor fee (Subject to change in January and July of each year)
    See "e-Fingerprinting" link on top right at www.dos.ny.gov/licensing.

Acceptable forms of payment:
Payment for fingerprint fees must be made in the form of check, money order or credit card payable to MorphoTrust USA.

Note: fingerprint fees are in addition to application fees.

ADDITIONAL REQUIREMENTS:

Child Support Statement:
A Child Support Statement is mandatory in New York State (General Obligations Law). The law requires you to complete this section — regardless of whether or not you have children or any support obligation.

Any person who is four months or more in arrears in child support may be subject to having his or her business, professional and driver's licenses suspended. The intentional submission of a false written statement for the purpose of frustrating or defeating the lawful enforcement of support obligations is punishable under §175.35 of the Penal Law. It is a class E felony to offer a false instrument for filing with a state or local government with the intent to defraud.

Figure 3.10   (Continued) New York State Armed Courier application.   (*Continued*)

Armored Car Guard Application

PRIVACY NOTIFICATION

The Department of State is required to collect the federal Social Security and Employer Identification numbers of all licensees. The authority to request and maintain such personal information is found in §5 of the Tax Law and §3-503 of the General Obligations Law. Disclosure by you is mandatory. The information is collected to enable the Department of Taxation and Finance to identify individuals, businesses and others who have been delinquent in filing tax returns or may have underestimated their tax liabilities and to generally identify persons affected by the taxes administered by the Commissioner of Taxation and Finance. It will be used for tax administration purposes and any other purpose authorized by the Tax Law and may also be used by child support enforcement agencies or their authorized representatives of this or other states established pursuant to Title IV-D of the Social Security Act, to establish, modify or enforce an order of support, but will not be available to the public. A written explanation is required where no number is provided. This information will be maintained in the Licensing Information System by the Director of Administration and Management, at One Commerce Plaza, 99 Washington Avenue, Albany, NY 12231-0001.

Figure 3.10   (Continued) New York State Armed Courier application.

Figure 3.11   FBI cyber division most wanted.

Health and beauty	Over-the-counter
Teeth whitening strips	**medicine**
Pregnancy tests	Allergy medicine
Razors	Diabetic testing strips
	Pain relievers
Electronics	Weight loss pills
GPS devices	
Laptops/tablets	**Clothing**
Cameras/recorders	Denim pants
Cell phones	Designer clothing/
	handbags
Home	
High-end vacuums	**Grocery**
High-end appliances,	Cigarettes
mixers, Children's	Energy drinks
electronic toys	High-end liquor
Laundry detergent	Infant formula

Figure 3.12   Top stolen goods by organized retail crime gangs.

However, given the rash of college and university violence, as evidenced at Virginia Tech and other mainstream colleges, there has been an increased emphasis on security forces that have ample police powers. To be sure, police officers and security personnel on college campuses are increasingly armed. A mix of public police personnel with private sector players is also now very common. See Figure 3.14.[73]

---

[73] B.A. Reaves, *Campus Law Enforcement, 2011–12* (NCJ 248028) 1 (January 2015), at http://www.bjs.gov/content/pub/pdf/cle1112.pdf; see also Bureau of Justice Statistics, *Survey of Campus Law Enforcement Agencies, 2011–12.*

Figure 3.13   LPCertified certification logo.

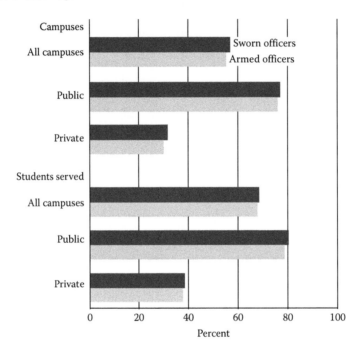

Figure 3.14   Use of sworn and armed law enforcement officers on four-year campuses with 2,500 or more students, 2011–2012. (From Bureau of Justice Statistics, Survey of Campus Law Enforcement Agencies, 2011–2012.)

The Bureau of Justice Assistance assessed the current state of campus-based policing in 2015 and reached the following conclusions concerning trends and directions:

- About 75% of the campuses were using armed officers, compared to 68% during the 2004–05 school year.
- About 9 in 10 public campuses used sworn police officers (92%), compared to about 4 in 10 private campuses (38%).
- Most sworn campus police officers were authorized to use a sidearm (94%), chemical or pepper spray (94%), and a baton (93%).
- Most sworn campus police officers had arrest (86%) and patrol (81%) jurisdictions that extended beyond campus boundaries.
- About 7 in 10 campus law enforcement agencies had a memorandum of understanding or other formal written agreement with outside law enforcement agencies.[74]

As a career option, working for a campus-based law enforcement entity can be economically satisfactory with salaries keeping pace with most public entities. See Table 3.7.[75]

---

[74] Reaves, *Campus Law Enforcement, 2011–12.*
[75] *Ibid.* at 18.

Table 3.7   Average base starting salary for selected positions in campus law enforcement agencies, 2011–2012

Type and size of 4-year campus	Sworn officers				Nonsworn officers			
	Chief/ director	Shift	Sworn officer with supervisor 5 years experience	Entry-level sworn officer	Chief/ director	Shift supervisor	Nonsworn officer with 5 years experience	Entry-level nonsworn officer
All campuses	$85,200	$48,900	$42,700	$36,700	$65,600	$37,400	$31,600	$27,500
Public	$86,800	$49,900	$43,100	$36,900	$65,800	$39,600	$32,500	$28,500
15,000 or more	$103,400	$55,100	$47,300	$40,400	$92,700	$47,800	$35,800	$33,300
10,000–14,999	$84,600	$49,500	$42,000	$36,400	$64,300	$39,200	$32,200	$28,200
5000–9999	$78,200	$46,900	$41,100	$35,100	$63,700	$36,600	$31,500	$29,500
2500–4999	$69,000	$42,500	$37,400	$32,800	$50,200	$32,100	$31,000	$26,600
Private	$78,800	$45,100	$40,800	$35,800	$65,600	$37,100	$31,400	$27,300
15,000 or more	$121,000	$61,900	$52,800	$44,000	$94,500	$44,300	$36,600	$28,800
10,000–14,999	$108,000	$50,400	$48,800	$39,400	$74,900	$40,100	$33,800	$29,400
5000–9999	$80,000	$46,800	$44,300	$37,200	$73,700	$43,000	$36,300	$31,300
2500–4999	$65,400	$38,100	$34,300	$31,700	$60,900	$34,600	$29,500	$26,000

Note: Salaries are rounded to the nearest hundred dollars.
Source: Bureau of Justice Statistics, *Survey of Campus Law Enforcement Agencies, 2011–2012.*

Campus security programs are prime illustrations of how public/private cooperation works—and works well. William Best and Galen Ash, respective Directors of Campus Safety at Bowling Green State University and the Bowling Green Police Department, feel confident that they have mastered the art of interaction. They have listed various essential elements in the recipe for successful cooperation:

1. A mutual assistance agreement
2. Support from the courts
3. Shared training programs
4. Efficient communications (technical)
5. On-going administrative working relations
6. Police/advisory committee participation
7. Shared crime prevention programs
8. Cooperative investigations and sharing of information
9. College educational programs
10. Informal daily contacts

The International Association of Campus Law Enforcement Administration (IACLEA) serves as lobby center for private sector justice in educational institutions. For more information on this group, see their website at http://www.iaclea.org.

Primary and secondary schools are part of security's landscape. With school violence capturing national attention,[76] the industry has been called upon to assure safety in the facilities. See Figure 3.15.[77]

See Figure 3.16,[78] which highlights the activities of the National Association of School Resource Officers.

---

[76] Family First, Kids and Violence—A National Survey and Report (1991); see also NCES Fast Facts: School Crime, at https://nces.ed.gov/fast-facts/display.asp?id=49, last accessed July 21, 2016.
[77] U.S. Department of Education, National Center for Education Statistics, *Indicators of School Crime and Safety: 2013* (NCES 2014-042) (2014).
[78] National Association of School Resource Officers website, https://nasro.org/about/.

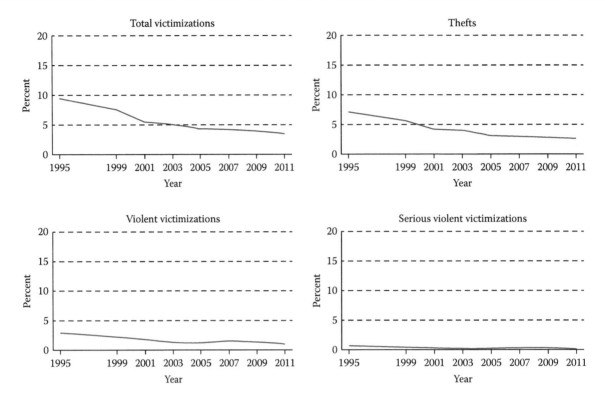

Figure 3.15 Percentage of students ages 12–18 who reported criminal victimization at school during the previous six months, by type of victimization: selected years, 1995–2013. (From U.S. Department of Education, National Center for Education Statistics [2016]. Indicators of School Crime and Safety: 2015 [NCES 2016-079].)

The National Association of School Resource Officers (NASRO) is dedicated to making schools and children safer by providing the highest quality training to school-based law enforcement officers.

NASRO, the world's leader in school-based policing, is a not-for-profit organization founded in 1991 for school-based law enforcement officers, school administrators and school security and/or safety professionals who work as partners to protect schools and their students, faculty and staff members.

NASRO developed the "triad" concept of school-based policing. It divides the school resource officer (SRO) responsibilities into three areas: teacher, informal counselor and law enforcement officer. By training law enforcement to educate, counsel and protect school communities, the men and women of NASRO continuously lead by example and promote a positive image of law enforcement to school children and school communities.

School-based policing is the fastest-growing area of law enforcement. With more than 3,000 NASRO members around the globe, NASRO takes great pride in being the first and most-recognized organization for law enforcement officers assigned to our school communities. NASRO is available to assist communities and schools districts around the world that desire safer schools and effective community partnerships in developing the most effective programs for their communities.

SRO programs across the globe are founded as collaborative efforts by police agencies, law enforcement officers, educators, students, parents and communities. The goal of NASRO and SRO programs is to provide safe learning environments, provide valuable resources to school staff members, foster a positive relationship with students and develop strategies to resolve problems that affect our youth with the goal of protecting all children, so they can reach their fullest potential.

Figure 3.16 About the National Association of School Resource Officers (NASRO).

3.3.8 Federal law enforcement and security

The role of private sector justice in federal service has been one of steady and continuous growth. Under the larger banner of the Federal Protective Service (FPS), FPS provides security and law enforcement services at U.S. federal government facilities. FPS plays a leading role in the protection of our nation's critical infrastructure and ensures a safe and secure working environment for federal workers and visitors in approximately 9,000 federal facilities nationwide.

FPS is a leader in physical security and strategic planning as to those facilities. The chief tasks of the FPS include but are not limited to the following:

- Conducting comprehensive security assessment of vulnerabilities at facilities
- Developing and implementing protective countermeasures, based on the latest risk management tools and technology
- Installing alarm systems, x-ray and magnetometer equipment, and entry control systems
- Monitoring systems at federal facilities for proper performance and security breaches
- Providing uniformed police response and investigative follow-up
- Contracting for security guard services
- Performing hazardous materials preparedness and response operations
- Managing K9 explosive detection operations
- Providing critical security services and logistical support at high-profile public events
- Coordinating vital emergency services and disaster response during and after natural disasters
- Engaging federal facility tenants through crime prevention seminars, facility security surveys, intelligence-gathering operations, and more

Most security-oriented jobs at the federal level involve the protection of government installations, courthouses and official offices, military bases, and transportation hubs. Many of these career options are readily discoverable at usajobs.com—a sample page reproduced in Figure 3.17.[79]

Of course, the extent of private security in matters involving homeland security continues its dynamic trek. In the area of airports, the transference of authority from Transportation Security Administration (TSA) to private companies now has occurred at 21 airports. See Figure 3.18.

TSA is no longer the sole provider of security services in the nation's primary travel industry. See Figure 3.19.

Today, security firms are increasingly assuming these once-entrenched roles and providing strong customer service to the airline consumer.

Web Exercise: Find out about the Screening Partnership Program between the TSA and the private security industry at https://www.tsa.gov/stakeholders/screening-partnership-program.

3.3.9 Moonlighting and merger: The public/private connection

That current or former public police officers and other law enforcement officers play a central role in the security industry is not much of a secret.[80] Many occupational activities in private security and public law enforcement blur their once-distinct lines. Examples include a private security officer who has been granted a special commission license or privilege by the state to perform clearly delineated activities. Certain jurisdictions designate individuals as "special policeman" or use other terminology to grant private security personnel public arrest privileges and rights.[81] This type of state involvement may meet the burden of 42 U.S.C. § 1983s color of state law standard. The fundamental premise behind the legislation is that the claimant must amply demonstrate an affirmative link between the private officer's conduct and the state or other governmental authority that involves itself directly or indirectly in the conduct.[82]

---

[79] USA Jobs search page, at https://www.usajobs.gov/Search?Keyword=security&Location=&search=Search&AutoCompleteSelected=False.
[80] Police Moonlighting Revisited: The Case of 'Pay Duty' in Three Canadian Police Services, 7 Policing 370–378 (2013), first published online November 11, 2013.
[81] *See* People v. Omeel, 166 N.W.2d 279 (Mich. App. 1968); Williams v. U.S., 341 U.S. 97 (1951); Tarref v. State, 512 P.2d 923 (Alaska 1973).
[82] *See* Ohio Rev. Code Ann. §§ 4973.17.

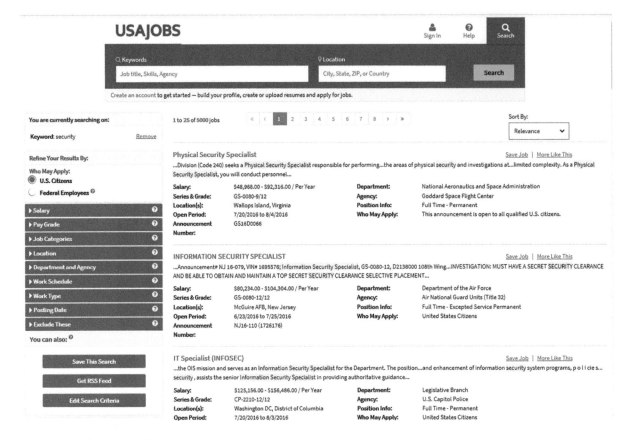

Figure 3.17 USAJobs search page.

A classic merger of public and private interest occurs when public police officers moonlight within the security industry.[83] The *Hallcrest Report II* sees significant dual occupational roles in the private sector:

> These surveys revealed that 81% of the law enforcement administrators indicated that their department's regulations permit officers to moonlight in private security, while 19% prohibited or severely restricted private security moonlighting. Law enforcement administrators estimated that about 20% of their personnel have regular outside security employment to supplement their police salaries. Nationally, the Hallcrest researchers estimated that at least 150,000 local enforcement officers in the U.S. are regularly engaged in off-duty employment in private security. The three most common methods of obtaining off-duty officers for security work, in rank order, are: (1) the officer is hired and paid directly by the business, (2) the department contracts with the business firm, invoices for the officer's off-duty work, and pays the officer, and (3) off-duty security work is coordinated through a police union or association.[84]

The lines between these two camps continue to erode due to various forces. First, privatization continues unabated and more and more public policing functions are being transferred to private sector operatives. Second, the partnership between private and public forces has long been a reality only furthered by the sharing of resources. Third, retirement for many public officers is at an early age, which thereby triggers the desire for a second career that the security industry happily provides.[85] Finally, the skill set developed and honed by the public officer finds a natural home in the private security system. For these and other reasons, the blending of public–private policing shows no signs of slowing down.

While the transitional move from public to private policing upon retirement or personal choice has few ethical or organizational issues to resolve, the active duty public officer's participation in the private system tends to create a

---

[83] Payton v. Rush-Presbyterian-St. Luke's Medical Center, 184 F.3d 623 (7th Cir. 1999).

[84] Cunningham et al., *supra* note 6, at 290.

[85] See J. Hawkins, *Transition into Private Security*.

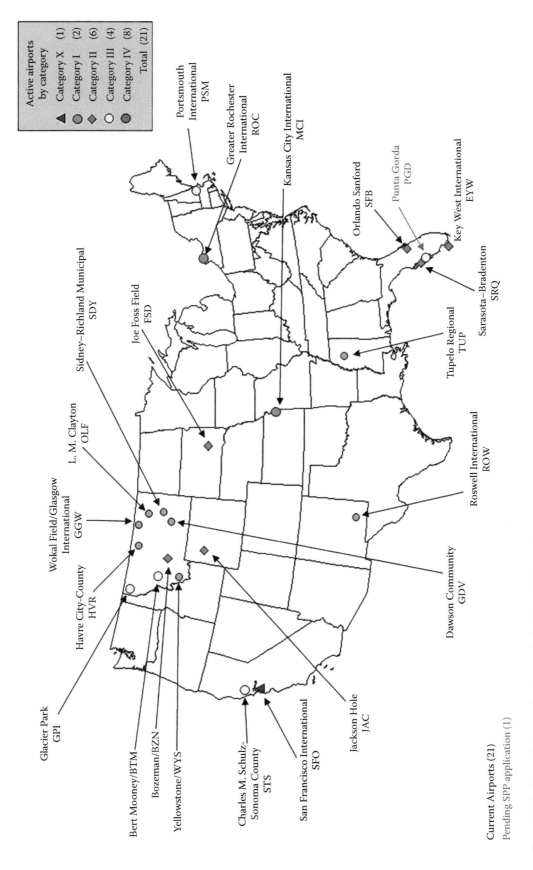

Figure 3.18 Map of airports that have switched from TSA to private security companies.

Figure 3.19 TSA logo.

few ethical thickets. In his or her public capacity, the constitutional requirements imposed on public officers may or may not be pertinent to the private officer. Next, the occupational lines of responsibility and even time charting, that is being on or off duty, may or may not generate conflicts. Public police—working in a private capacity, may cause legal dilemmas in terms of liability since public police enjoy immunity privileges while private police do not. Lastly, the mission of private security may conflict with the stated goals of the public program. Moonlighting police officers may make sense in some quarters, but in others, they cause enormous operational difficulties.

Web Exercise: Read the performance audit of the City of Pittsburgh, which was recently scandalized by secondary, moonlighting types of employment, at http://apps.pittsburghpa.gov/co/Performance_Audit_Public_Safety_Secondary_Employment_Oct2013.pdf.

3.4 SECURITY EDUCATION, TRAINING, CERTIFICATION, AND REGULATIONS

Questions regarding the substantiality of private security requirements as to education, training, and certification requirements have been long-standing when compared to the public police counterpart. Critics of the industry label private security as an underclass when compared to public requirements in these areas. While much time and energy has been expended in the professionalization of public law enforcement,[86] the pace, the lack of uniform standards, and the general reticence to invest in personnel have dogged the security industry. And while the private security industry continues its unabated growth, the matter of training and preparation for placement in the industry is far from settled. The Private Advisory Council expounds that these attitudes

> are based on incorrect assumptions that private security personnel perform the same job duties as patrol officers and investigators in law enforcement, and that a broad generalization can be made about the nature and personnel of all components of proprietary and contractual security—guards, private patrol services, private investigators, armored car guards and armed couriers, and alarm response runners and installers. Certainly, the security industry and private justice practitioners must concede there is a distinction between the level of training and qualifications for certification. The security industry has been its own worst enemy in this area by failing to promote high level, sophisticated standards of educational requirements.[87]

---

[86] See generally C.P. Nemeth, *Status Report on Contemporary Criminal Justice Education* (discussing education and its correlation to police professionalism) (1988).

[87] National Advisory Committee, *supra* note 2, at 11.

In response to the call for increased state and local regulation of the private security force, Richard Lukins, in his article *Security Training for the Guard Force*, castigates the industry for its lack of action.

> This trend has not caught the affected components of the private security industry—the guard services and proprietary security managers—completely by surprise but it does not appear that they were totally prepared either. And certainly no one can say that our industry has established an imposing record of self-regulation.[88]

Lukins further relates that the present impression of a security guard as not more than "half a cop" will be deleterious to future professionalism in the security industry.[89] The quest for professionalism requires more than rhetoric. Regulation, licensing, and qualifications, the road to professionalism is filled with impediments. Those impediments—a lack of educational discipline or cogent body of knowledge, an accepted code of ethics, a prestige or status consensus on occupational roles, or a seal of social and governmental legitimacy—are all attainable goals.[90] To get beyond the characterization that a private security practitioner is nothing more than a play policeman, the industry will have to aggressively implement the standards of professionalism. For example, ASIS International publishes professional expectation on specific security practices in its "Published Standards." Within these guidelines, minimum knowledge expectations are published for the industry. With said publication, the security provider is encouraged, in order to be compliant with the standard, to prepare his personnel properly by mirroring the standards. At present, ASIS International has posted standards for the following topics:

- Auditing Management Systems: Risk, Resilience, Security and Continuity—Guidance for Application
- Business Continuity Management Standard
- Chief Security Officer—An Organizational Model
- Conformity Assessment and Auditing Management Systems for Quality of Private Security Company Operations
- Investigations
- Management System for Quality of Private Security Company Operations—Requirements with Guidance
- Maturity Model for the Phased Implementation of a Quality Assurance Management System for Private Security Service Providers
- Maturity Model for the Phased Implementation of the Organizational Resilience Management System
- Organizational Resilience: Security, Preparedness and Continuity Management Systems—Requirements with Guidance for Use Standard
- Quality Assurance and Security Management for Private Security Companies Operating at Sea Guidance
- Risk Assessment
- Security Management Standard: Physical Asset Protection
- Supply Chain Risk Management: A Compilation of Best Practices
- Workplace Violence Prevention and Intervention Standard[91]

With uniform practices, the industry may eliminate or at least mitigate the usual rub on a lack of professionalism in the industry. On the other hand, much of that judgment is the result of prejudice and stereotype.

> Private security is aware of this status differential imposed by many law enforcement personnel and deeply resent it since they feel that law enforcement neither understands nor empathizes with their crime prevention role. This in turn leads to a lower level of esteem by private security for law enforcement personnel.[92]

Petty bickering and class warfare do little to advance a professional model in the private sector. Constructive suggestions regarding increased standards and performance objectives are more in order.

---

[88] Lukins, *supra* note 21, at 32.

[89] *Ibid.*

[90] *Ibid.* at 34; see also Pastor, *Terrorism*, *supra* note 1; Pastor, *Privatization*, *supra* note 20.

[91] ASIS International Website, Standards & Guidelines https://www.asisonline.org/Standards-Guidelines/Standards/published/Pages/default.aspx.

[92] See generally Private Security Advisory Council, *Codes of Ethics for Private Security Management and Private Security Employees* (1976); Private Security Advisory Council, *Model Security Guard Training Curricula* (1977); Private Security Advisory Council, *Report on the Meeting of April 21–23, 1976* (1976); Nemeth, *supra* note 18.

3.4.1 Education and training standards

Professionalism for the security industry remains an empty promise without a commitment to education, scholarly research and development, and academic rigor. Regulatory bodies throughout the United States have been placing heightened emphasis on education and training as part of the minimum qualifications of an applicant.[93] The *Private Security Advisory Council*,[94] a federally funded consortium of public law enforcement specialists and private security experts, has made numerous recommendations concerning the upgrading of educational standards. The Council notes eloquently:

> [W]hile private security is a vast crime prevention and reduction resource, it will for the most part remain only a potential resource until steps are taken to eliminate incompetence and unscrupulous conduct. Many private security personnel are only temporary or part-time employees who are often underpaid and untrained for their work. The protection of lives and property is an awesome societal responsibility, and the public interest demands that persons entrusted with such responsibilities be competent, well-trained, and of good moral character.[95]

In the early 1990s, the *National Private Security Officer Survey* portrayed an industry pool in need of higher educational achievement, reporting that most positions require a high-school diploma.[96] The requirements seem to be elevating on some levels. The *2002 Virginia Security Officer Study* reported that over 55% of the survey respondents possessed at least some college level education.[97] See Figure 3.20.

From the lowest echelon employee in a security organization to the highest supervisory personnel, education and training is inexorably tied to occupational development.[98] A 1973 study, *Private Police in the United States: Findings and Recommendations*, heralds education as a remedy to deficiencies in the security industry. Insisting on minimums, the study relays the following:

- All types of private security personnel should receive a minimum initial training program of at least 120 hours.

- Federal funds should be made available to develop appropriate training programs, including curricula, materials, and methodology.

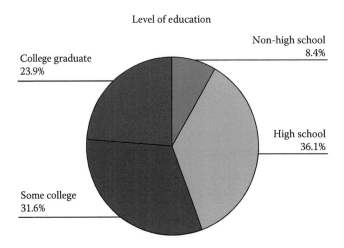

Figure 3.20 Statistics indicating education level for security officers.

---

[93] C.P. Nemeth & K.C. Poulin, *Private Security and Public Safety: A Community Based Approach*, Ch. 9 (2005); Nemeth, *supra* note 87; T. Savage, Security Officers: New Demands Require New Training, 150 *Safety & Health* 64 (1994); J. Maahs & C. Hemmens, Train in Vain: A Statutory Analysis of Security Guard Training Requirements, 22 *Int'l J. Comp. & Appl. Crim. Just.* 91–101 (1998); J. Akasie, Thwarting Terrorists, *Forbes* (September 21, 1998), at 162; C. Leatherman & D.K. Magner, Notes on the Curriculum, *Chronicle Of Higher Education* (March 9, 1994), at A19; see also Pastor, *Terrorism*, *supra* note 1; Pastor, *Security Law*, *supra* note 1; Pastor, *Privatization*, *supra* note 20.

[94] Private Security Advisory Council, *Guidelines for the Establishment of State and Local Private Advisory Councils* (1976).

[95] *Ibid.* at 7.

[96] Note, Survey Yields New Results on Officer Turnover, Training, 29 *Security* 71 (1992), at 72.

[97] R.A. Castle, *A Study of the Security Officer* 10 (2002).

[98] A.L. Baro, Law Enforcement and Higher Education: Is There an Impasse? 10 *J. Crim. Just. Ed.* 57 (1999).

- State regulatory agencies should require minimum training programs—in terms of quality, curriculum, and hours of instruction for all types of private security personnel.

- Appropriate higher education, such as a bachelor's degree in police science and administration should also be a substitute for part of the minimum experience requirements.[99]

The Private Advisory Council, as well as a RAND Study on private security,[100] critiques the paucity of the education and training provided to security personnel. The RAND Study concludes thus:

> 65% of private security personnel had no training at all prior to commencing job assignments. Approximately one-half of private security personnel carried firearms, but less than 20% had ever received any firearms training in their present job.[101]

The National Association of Private Security Industries, Inc. of Dallas, Texas, confirms the urgent need for training and education for the contract guard firm. A recent report by the National Association of Private Security Industries stated that contract guard firms want their officers to be trained in liability avoidance, documentation and reports, patrol techniques, mid-level security supervision, laws of arrest, and first aid.[102]

The call for increased education and training has been broad-based.[103] "In security, as in other functions of an organization, the higher an executive climbs, the broader is his need for education."[104] Education of public and private law enforcement can "dismiss prior notions or opinions, that is, to motivate them to think on a factual basis. The appalling lack of knowledge of the law can be corrected by immersing the officer in a study of the legal problems. Topics such as powers and restrictions on private police, law of arrest, search and seizure procedures, electronic eavesdropping, civil liabilities, and licensing statutes can be studied. Perhaps through an educational experience, an officer may not allow enthusiasm to overcome judgment in his daily rounds."[105]

The National Association of Security Companies (NASCO) corroborates the urgent need for educational preparation for the industry and concludes the causal connection between professionalism and education.

> The National Association of Security Companies (NASCO) is the nation's largest contract security trade association, representing private security companies that employ more than 400,000 of the nation's most highly trained security officers servicing every business sector. NASCO is leading efforts to set meaningful standards for the private security industry and security officers by monitoring state and federal legislation and regulations affecting the quality and effectiveness of private security.[106]

See Figure 3.21.

At the collegiate and university level, the development and legitimization of the academic discipline of security studies has been both steady and impressive. Currently, there are 1,476 institutions in the United States that offer some coverage of security and protective studies, though most do not offer full-fledged degrees.[107] Some of the institutions offering degrees and courses in the field are as follows:

- Alabama State University

- American University

- Auburn University—Montgomery

---

[99] J. Shane Creamer, Private Police in the United States: Findings and Recommendations, 10 *Sec. World* 66 (1973), at 68.

[100] National Advisory Commission on Standards and Goals, *Private Security: Report of the Task Force Report on Private Security* (1976).

[101] Private Security Advisory Council, *supra* note 95, at 8.

[102] Note, Security Endorses Campus Incident Reporting; Divided on Same for Business, 28 *Security* 8, 9 (1991).

[103] For example, The Law Enforcement and Industrial Security Cooperation Act of 1996, H.R. 2996 calls for increasing training and cooperation between public and private entities. See Strom et al., *supra* note 53.

[104] J. Fletcher & H. Borokawa, Non-Security Education, 1 *J. Sec. & Pri. Police* 14 (1978); see also Savage, *supra* note 94; Maahs & Hemmens, *supra* note 94; Akasie, *supra* note 94; Leatherman & Magner, *supra* note 94.

[105] J. Kostanoski, The Private Police and Higher Education, 1 *J. Sec. Admin. & Pri. Police* 26 (1978); see also Savage, *supra* note 94; Maahs & Hemmens, *supra* note 94; Leatherman & Magner, *supra* note 94.

[106] National Association of Security Companies (NASCO) (2016), at http://www.nasco.org.

[107] Data from a search conducted using the National Center for Education Statistics College Degree search tool at http://nces.ed.gov/ipeds/cool/Search.asp.

Figure 3.21   NASCO logo.

- Baylor University
- California State University—various locations
- California University of Pennsylvania
- Eastern Kentucky University
- Fairmont State College
- Farleigh Dickinson
- George Washington University
- Jackson State University
- Jersey City State University
- John Jay College of Criminal Justice
- Marquette University
- Sam Houston State University
- Seton Hall University
- Texas A&M University
- Xavier University

How security studies grows and evolves is likely a parallel story to how the academic discipline of criminal justice came to be. Criminal justice education illustrates the long and sometimes vicious battle for legitimacy within traditional academic circles. Now an academic discipline firmly entrenched in more than 1,100 colleges and universities, criminal justice's search for legitimacy in stodgy academic environs may soon be over.[108] Security training has been an integral course within criminal justice studies but is in its seminal stage at the undergraduate and graduate levels. "Growth in security academic programs has been significant. Nationwide, there were 33 certificate and degree programs 15 years ago. By 1990, the total had increased to 164."[109]

Web Exercise: Visit the ASIS International Directory of Colleges and Universities offering undergraduate and graduate degrees in security-related studies at https://www.asisonline.org/Membership/Library/Academic-Student-Center/Documents/Academic-Programs-in-Security.pdf.

In a degree-granting framework, there has been steady growth particularly at the graduate level.[110] ASIS International, through its Foundation, established a master's degree in security management at Webster University.

---

[108] C.P. Nemeth, *Directory of Criminal Justice Education, Including Criminology, Law and Justice Related Education* (1991); Nemeth & Poulin, *supra* note 94; Nemeth, *supra* note 87; Pastor, *Terrorism, supra* note 1; Pastor, *Security Law, supra* note 1; Pastor, *Privatization, supra* note 20.

[109] Cunningham et al., *supra* note 6, at 322–323.

[110] Richard Post notes in his article, Toward Rational Curriculum Development for Private Protective Services, First National Conference on Private Security (1978) that there are around 119 degree granting programs; see also Dr. Norman Bottom's annual compilation of security education programs in his *Journal of Security Administration*, showing around 165 programs. See also Pastor, *Terrorism, supra* note 1; Pastor, *Security Law, supra* note 1; Pastor, *Privatization, supra* note 20.

The Webster curriculum features a Master of Arts (MA) and a Master of Business Administration (MBA) option and reflects current security theory and practice. The program, guided by the Foundation, will be frequently revised to better meet the needs of students and will reflect input from university studies, corporate surveys and other assessments.[111]

Its core curriculum contains seven required business courses, including statistical analysis, business accounting systems, business information systems, financial planning, operations and production management, and economics for the firm and business policy. The program also requires eight security courses, which are the same courses required for the MA degree covering legal and ethical issues in security management, management and administration courses, asset protection, information systems security, emergency planning, and an integrated studies course.[112] At John Jay College of Criminal Justice, graduate degrees in the interdisciplinary field of protection management are offered as well as a national, online master's in security management. Both curricular are cutting edge in that the programs integrate traditional security conceptions with emergency and fire content. In addition, both programs value managerial skills to train future supervisors and directors. The programs are housed under the Department of Security, Fire, and Emergency Management.[113]

Jim Calder of the University of Texas argues that as long as protective security studies is so heavily tethered and entangled with criminal justice, its growth will be slower than expected:

> Security Studies must move from separate-but-equal status to total interaction with other aspects of criminal justice education. My premise is that the criminal justice system cannot reduce property crime profoundly (because of social structural limitations) and thus must rely more heavily on security forces.[114]

There has been discussion about whether security studies need to exist independently or as an aligned subject matter with criminal justice. Christopher Hertig, CPP, remarks that

> Security curricula exist on many campuses today, and an increasing number of criminal justice programs include courses in security, loss prevention, or safety. While many people dispute the wisdom of having security courses attached to criminal justice programs, the reality is that the majority of courses are within criminal justice curricula. This is not likely to change anytime soon. I believe that working with an existing program is generally more productive than idly wishing for something that may never be.[115]

The argument for security education and training is compelling, particularly when coupled with the drive toward professionalism. One certainly cannot exist without the other as Richard Post lucidly poses:

> Is security a profession? No, probably not to the extent that law enforcement or many of the other areas of criminal justice are professions… But, we have made a start. Things are beginning to move forward, and it is entirely possible that security may be considered the profession of the future.[116]

Education and training can take many forms, such as that mandated in Arizona. Figure 3.22[117] outlines the training topics that security companies are required by law to provide to their personnel.

From all perspectives—academically, legislatively, and industrially—there is a major push for increased education and training. The industry and its participants recognize the need to upgrade their image as a professional occupation and the parallel necessity of increased educational requirements. CPP Lonnie Buckels understands the interrelationship between education and professionalism:

---

[111] Note, ASIS in Action, 35 *Sec. Mgmt.* 116 (1991).

[112] P. Ohlhausen, Invest in Security's Future, 35 *Sec. Mgmt.* 49, 50 (1991).

[113] John Jay College of Criminal Justice, Department of Security, Fire & Emergency Management Website at http://www.jjay.cuny.edu/department-security-fire-and-emergency-management.

[114] J. Calder, The Security-Criminal Justice Connection: Toward the Elimination of Separate-but-Equal Status, 3 *J. Sec. Admin.* 25 (1980).

[115] C.A. Hertig, What Course Should We Take? 35 *Sec. Mgmt.* 218 (1991).

[116] Richard Post notes in his article, Toward Rational Curriculum Development for Private Protective Services, First National Conference on Private Security 6 (1978); see also Savage, *supra* note 94; Maahs & Hemmens, *supra* note 94; Akasie, *supra* note 94; Leatherman & Magner, *supra* note 94.

[117] Ariz. Rev. Stat. § 32-2613, § 32-2632 (2010); see also S.C. Code ANN. § 40-17-40 (2010).

Arizona Department of Public Safety

Unarmed Security Guard
8 Hour Training Syllabus
February 2, 2007

This syllabus was developed by the DPS Security Guard Licensing Unit and meets the **mandatory 8-hour pre-assignment training requirement** that must be completed prior to submitting a security guard license application. All training must be conducted by an authorized instructor – Training may not be performed using videos alone, however, they may be used to supplement the instructor's training.

- **Trainers:** Training shall be **at least 8-hours** in duration and **does not** include a lunch break. Ten minute breaks each hour are permissible and will not count against the 8-hours. Establish and maintain (5 years) a sign-in roster for each class.
- The agency shall ensure the application and training verification has been signed by the instructor or designee.
- Guards **may not** work a security post until they are in possession of a valid security guard card and are wearing the DPS **approved** uniform (as applicable).

1.   **Orientation - Introduction to Security**

2.   **Criminal Law / Laws of Arrest** (Legal Authority) *The law and legal portion of this course is a vital block of instruction for security guard applicants. Instructors must cover all topics listed below. References include ARS Title 13 and the AZ DPS website: Arizona Department of Public Safety-Licensing Unit. Much of the text "Legal Issues Relating to the Use of Deadly Force" by Michael Anthony (found on the AZ DPS CCW website) is also applicable, however, this text was primarily designed for the CCW course, not security guards. Edit out specific references to CCW issues. References to specific section numbers (bold - within parenthesis) are for use with the "Legal Issues Relating to the Use of Deadly Force" text, which security guard instructors may find useful.*

A.   Authority and Responsibility of a Security Guard

1) Definitions

2) ARS Title 32, Chapter 26, Security Guard Regulation. *Sections 2632.D, 2633, 2634, 2635, 2636, 2637, 2638, 2639.D, and 2642. Additionally, specifically state that security guards may not work a post unless they are physically in possession of a valid guard card and in the proper uniform – guards working under a "pending" application are in violation of State law.*

3) ARS Title 13, Chapter 4, Justification: *All relevant subsections to include 401, 402.B.2, 403.3, 403.4, 403.6, 404, 405, 406, 407, 408, 409, 410, 411, 412, 413, 416, 417, 418 & 419 (Section V). Subsections that do*

1

Figure 3.22   Arizona Department of Public Safety Unarmed Guard training courses syllabus.   (*Continued*)

The designation of professional has to be earned. For example, look at the medical profession. For decades, practicing medicine was thought to be part of the black arts. In some regions of the world it still is. However, after years of hard work, coupled with agonizingly slow technical advancements, medical practitioners are honored professionals. We have made steady progress in our quest for professional designation in the security industry. But we must continue this progress and be patient—professionalism takes time.[118]

The form and substance of training curriculum for the security industry widely vary and while there is a continuous push for nationalized standards, that reality is far from present reach. Private Security Advisory Council's recommended training program for armed security officers is reproduced below.

---

[118] L.R. Buckels, Professionalism—An Impossible Task? 35 *Sec. Mgmt.* 108 (1991).

not pertain to security guards carrying weapons may be omitted. This chapter is the most crucial section of the law and legal training requirement and all instructors must be thoroughly knowledgeable of this section.

B.   Laws of Arrest

1) Interface with Law Enforcement/Assisting Law Enforcement (Be a good witness but do not physically assist law enforcement unless asked).

2) A.R.S. 13-3801, Preventing offenses; aiding officers (Briefly Discuss)

3) A.R.S. 13-3802, Right to command aid for execution of process; punishment for resisting process (Briefly Discuss)

4) A.R.S. 13-3881, Arrest

5) A.R.S. 13-3882, Time of Making Arrest

6) A.R.S. 13-3884, Arrest by Private Person

7) A.R.S. 13-3889, Method of Arrest by Private Person

8) A.R.S. 13-3892, Right of Private Person to Break into Building

9) A.R.S. 13-3893, Right to Break a Door or Window to Effect Release

10) A.R.S. 13-3894, Right to Break into Building in Order to Effect Release of Person Making Arrest Detained Therein

11) A.R.S. 13-3895, Weapons to be Taken from Person Arrested

12) A.R.S. 13-3896, Arrest After Escape or Rescue; Method of Recapture

13) A.R.S. 13-3900, Duty of Private Person After Making Arrest (Call the Police)

C.   Search and Seizure

1) 4th Amendment Rights (Briefly Discuss)

2) Unlawful Search and Seizure, A.R.S. 13-3925 (Briefly Discuss)

D.   Criminal Law and Recognizing Crimes *(Security guards should be able to identify these crimes):*

1. Briefly discuss ARS Title 13, Chapter 11, Homicide **(Section III.A)** *13-1102, 1103 (Use of force aspects relating to security guards)*

2

Figure 3.22   (Continued) Arizona Department of Public Safety Unarmed Guard training courses syllabus.   *(Continued)*

3.4.1.1 Minimum training standards for armed security officers
3.4.1.1.1 Preassignment training

Prior to assuming any actual duty assignment, each new security officer should receive at least eight hours of formal classroom training and successfully pass a written examination on the subjects.

Orientation and overview in security—two hours

Criminal justice and the security officer, including legal powers and limitations—two hours

Emergencies—two hours

General duties—two hours

2. Briefly discuss ARS Title 13, Chapter 12, Assault and Related Offenses *(Section III.B) 13-1201, 1202, 1203, 1204.*

3. Briefly discuss ARS Title 13, Chapter 15, Criminal Trespass and Burglary *(Section III.C) Cover aspects that pertain to security guards.*

4. Briefly discuss ARS Title 13, Chapter 16, Criminal Damage to Property *Cover aspects that pertain to security guards.*

5. Briefly discuss ARS Title 13, Chapter 17, Arson *Cover aspects that pertain to security guards.*

6. Briefly discuss ARS Title 13, Chapter 18, Theft *1802, 1803, 1804, 1805, 1816, and 1817- Cover aspects that pertain to security guards.*

7. Briefly discuss ARS Title 13, Chapter 19, Robbery *Cover aspects that pertain to security guards.*

8. Briefly discuss ARS Title 13, Chapter 24, Obstructing Government Operations *Chapters 2402, 2403, 2404, 2406, 2409, and 2411 Cover aspects that pertain to security guards.*

9. Briefly discuss ARS Title 13, Chapter 29, Offenses Against Public Order – Disorderly Conduct *(Section III.D) 2904, 2905, 2907, 2907.01, 2908, & 2911).*

10. Briefly discuss ARS Title 13, Chapter 31 Weapons and Explosives *(Section III.E) 13-3101, 3102, 3107. Cover aspects that pertain to security guards.*

11. Briefly discuss ARS Title 4, 4-244.29 *Patrons may not bring firearms into commercial establishments that serve alcohol for consumption on the premises (except peace officers).*

12. Request students visit the AZ DPS Licensing website at: http://www.azdps.gov/license/default.asp.

3.   **Uniform and Grooming**

    A.   Arizona Law Pertaining to Uniforms

        1) Authorized Uniform by Law and Agency

        2) Responsibility to Wear the Authorized Uniform

    B.   Basic Hygiene Policy

3

Figure 3.22   (Continued) Arizona Department of Public Safety Unarmed Guard training courses syllabus.   *(Continued)*

3.4.1.1.2 *Weapons training*

Prior to being issued a firearm or taking an assignment requiring the carrying of or having access to a weapon, the security officer should receive at least six hours formal classroom training, successfully pass a written examination on the subjects and successfully complete an approved 18-hour firearms target shooting course.

Classroom:

Legal and policy restraints on the use of firearms—three hours

Firearms safety, care, and cleaning—three hours

4. **Communications**

    A.   Written

        1) Report Writing

        2) Note Taking

        3) Steps in Writing a Report

        4) Grammar and Spelling

        5) Report Forms

    B.   Human Relations / Communications

        1) Verbal Control

        2) Physiological Responses to Stress

        3) How to Bring Down Stress

        4) Bridging Barriers of Communication

    C.   Use of Force / Levels of Force

        1) Define Use of Force and When Can it be Used

        2) Elements of Resistance

        3) Escalation and De-Escalation of Force

        4) Handcuffs/Restraints

        5) Physical Force

        6) Non-Lethal Weapon Use and Company Policies (Tasers, Mace, Capstun, Batons, etc.)

        7) Deadly Physical Force (Choke Holds, Lethal Strikes, Unauthorized Weapons)

5. **Crime Scene Preservation/First Response**

4

Figure 3.22 (Continued) Arizona Department of Public Safety Unarmed Guard training courses syllabus. (*Continued*)

Range:

Principles of marksmanship—six hours

Single action course—six hours

Double action course—six hours

3.4.1.11.3 Basic training course

Within three months of assuming duties, a security officer should complete a 32-hour basic training course. At least four hours should be classroom instruction and up to a maximum of 16 hours may be supervised, on-the-job training.

Classroom:

Prevention in security systems—one hour

Legal aspects and enforcement of rules—one hour

Routine procedures—one hour

Emergency and special procedures—one hour

A.   Responsibilities

B.   Reasons for denial of entry to a crime scene

C.   Procedures for protecting a crime scene

D.   Emergency Response Procedures

E.   Practical Exercise

6.   Ethics

Include a basic ethics policy in regard to good moral character.

1) Guards on Duty

2) Guards off Duty (Incidents Leading to Loss of Guard Card)

3) Driving Courtesy (On Duty in Security Vehicles)

7.   Sexual Harassment

1) Verbal

2) Non-Verbal

3) Innuendos

8.   General Security Guard Procedures (Post or Job Procedures) Specific post responsibilities should be explained at the work location

9.   Close of Training – Sign Training Forms and Submit Applications – **Guards may not work a security post until they are physically in possession of a valid guard card and wearing the DPS approved uniform (as applicable).**

5

Figure 3.22   (Continued) Arizona Department of Public Safety Unarmed Guard training courses syllabus.

3.4.2 Licensing, regulatory, and hiring standards

The licensure and regulatory process impact the nature of professional requirements and educational training for the security industry. Since there is no national standard on education, 50 state jurisdictions create and craft a host of approaches to the knowledge preparation for security professionals. Hence, the state legislative process promulgates varying degrees of requirements for the security professional—some more demanding and some far more lenient. Legislative analysis manifests a trend toward education and training. While some states such as Colorado[119] are constitutionally unable, at least at this juncture, to mandate licensure requirements, and others simply do not require it, more and more states require some level of training for personnel.

---

[119] See Colorado v. Romar, 559 P. 2d 710 (1977).

Some states require applicants to pass an examination covering a broad range of topics. State administrative agencies even provide bibliographic lists to help applicants prepare.[120] Recent statutory amendments in Illinois highlight the trend toward education and training. For the applicant in Illinois, a security training program of at least 20 hours must be documented. Topics include the following:

1. The law regarding arrest and search and as it applies to private security.
2. Civil and criminal liability for acts related to private security.
3. The use of force, including but not limited to the use of nonlethal force (i.e., disabling spray, baton, stungun or similar weapon).
4. Arrest and control techniques.
5. The offenses under the Criminal Code of 2012 that are directly related to the protection of persons and property.
6. The law on private security forces and on reporting to law enforcement agencies.
7. Fire prevention, fire equipment, and fire safety.
8. The procedures for report writing.
9. Civil rights and public relations.
10. The identification of terrorists, acts of terrorism, and terrorist organizations, as defined by federal and State statutes.[121]

Education is the centerpiece of the Illinois legislation. When combined with undergraduate training and experience, the proviso rewards those seeking licensure with such backgrounds. Applicants can substitute certain experience requirements with postsecondary education. Specifically, for private security contractors, the educational provision states that in lieu of experience, the applicants may demonstrate that they have the following:

> An applicant who has a baccalaureate degree or higher in police science or a related field or a business degree from an accredited college or university shall be given credit for 2 of the 3 years of the required experience … An applicant who has an associate degree in police science or in a related field or in business from an accredited college or university shall be given credit for one of the 3 years of the required experience.[122]

Additionally, Georgia insists on certification for all security personnel utilizing weaponry.

> The board shall have the authority to establish limits on type and caliber of such weapons by rule.
> The board shall have the authority to require periodic recertification of proficiency in the use of firearms and to refuse to renew a permit upon failure to comply with such requirement.[123]

Louisiana education and training for an armed security guard includes the following:

1. Legal limitations on use of weapons.
2. Handling of a weapon.
3. Safety and maintenance.
4. Dim light firing.
5. A shoot, don't shoot program.
6. Stress factors.[124]

The level of education and training will also differ when the purpose of the licensure sought is different—such as the armed versus unarmed guard category. Virginia lays out two distinct training curricula for these categories.

---

[120] Some states requiring exams include North Dakota, Montana, Delaware, New York, Ohio, New Mexico, Vermont, Arkansas, and Iowa.
[121] 225 ILCS 447/25-20 (2016).
[122] 225 ILCS 447/25-10.
[123] Ga. Code ANN. § 43-38-10 (2009).
[124] La. Rev. Stat. Ann. § 37:3284 (2016).

3.4.2.1 Unarmed security officer training requirements

18 Hours, Consisting of:

- 01E - Security Officer Core Subjects Entry-Level (18 hours)[125]

3.4.2.2 Armed security officer training requirements

50–53 Hours, Consisting of:

- 01E - Security Officer Core Subjects Entry-Level (18 hours)
- 05E - Armed Security Officer Arrest Authority (8 hours)
- 75E - Security Officer Handgun (24 hours)
- 08E - Shotgun Training Entry-Level (3 hours)—If Applicable[126]

Just because the complexity increases in the license sought, one cannot be sure the content will reflect the added roles and responsibilities. To be sure, there is great variety in the private security industry. Tennessee, for example, requires training for the armed guard consisting of the following topics:

> Training Requirements
>
> Training includes an examination covering subjects in which the individual must have training. All candidates must complete a four hour basic course including one (1) hour each of:
>
> - Orientation.
> - Legal powers and limitations of a security guard/officer.
> - Emergency procedures.
> - General duties.
> - Any additional training for weapons or other devices that are less than lethal he or she will use.
> - An armed guard must complete eight additional hours in the classroom covering:
> - Legal limitations on the use of a firearm:
>   - Handling of a firearm
>   - Safety and maintenance of firearms
>
> In addition, an armed guard applicant must complete an additional four hours of marksmanship training and achieve a minimum of 70% on any silhouette target course approved by the commissioner.[127]

This curriculum seems short on hours and deficient to a fault and leaves a poor impression of industry seriousness about the quality of the officers. In Washington state, an unarmed guard has far more preparation than the armed personnel in Tennessee. Washington's curricular content covers a broad range of topics and relevant knowledge essential to the security professionals.

Basic principles

1. Basic role of the security guard.
2. Washington State licensing laws.
3. Observation.
4. Proper actions, reactions, ethics and diversity.
5. Homeland Security – Terrorism and Surveillance.

Legal powers and limitations

1. Citizen arrest.
2. Authority to detain, question, or search a private citizen.

---

[125] Virginia Department of Criminal Justice Services, Unarmed Security Officer/Courier page https://www.dcjs.virginia.gov/licensure-and-regulatory-affairs/unarmed-security-officercourier.

[126] Virginia Department of Criminal Justice Services, Armed Security Officer https://www.dcjs.virginia.gov/licensure-and-regulatory-affairs/armed-security-officer.

[127] Tennessee Department of Commerce & Insurance, Get a License-Tennessee Private Protective Services https://www.tn.gov/commerce/article/prot-get-a-license.

3. Authority to search or seize private property.

4. Use of force.

5. Building relationships with law enforcement.

6. Avoiding liability.

Emergency Response

1. How to define what is or is not an emergency situation.

2. Response to fires.

3. Response to medical emergencies.

4. Response to criminal acts.

5. Bomb threats.

Safety and accident prevention

1. Hazardous materials including MSDS.

2. Accident reporting.

Report writing. It's a legal document

1. Elements and characteristics of a report.[128]

New York, by way of comparison, adopts a legislative design that combines classroom and actual training by mandating entry-level educational programs of 8 hours, then within 90 days, a 16-hour on-the-job training course. If armed, a 47-hour firearms program must be successfully completed.

§ 89-n. Training requirements. 1. Security guards shall be required to satisfactorily complete training programs given and administered by security guard training schools, schools which provide security guard training programs or security guard companies prescribed, certified and approved by the commissioner pursuant to section eight hundred forty-one-c of the executive law to include:

  a. an eight-hour preassignment training course;
  b. an on-the-job training course to be completed within ninety working days following employment, consisting of a minimum of sixteen hours and a maximum of forty hours, as determined by the council, generally relating to the security guard's specific duties, the nature of the work place and the requirements of the security guard company;
  c. a forty-seven hour firearms training course for issuance of a special armed guard registration card;
  d. an eight-hour annual in-service training course; and
  e. an additional eight-hour annual in-service training course for holders of special armed guard registration cards.[129]

California authors a similar model to New York but with the additional 16-hour training requirement during the first year of service.

40-hour security guard training requirement[130]

Prior to being assigned on post	8 hours
Training required within the first 30 days	16 hours
Training required within the first six months	16 hours
TOTAL HOURS	40 HOURS

Naturally, as the complexity of security work increases, so too the educational and training requirements. Florida sets up a variable system of educational requirements, depending on job classifications. For example,

[128] Washington State Department of Licensing, Preassignment training study guide: Security guards http://www.dol.wa.gov/business/security-guards/sgpreassigntrain.html.

[129] NY Gen Bus L § 89-N (2012).

[130] Security Guard Training HQ website http://www.securityguardtraininghq.com/security-guard-training-california/.

an applicant for a Class "G" license must satisfy minimum training criteria for firearms established by rule of the department, which training criteria includes, but is not limited to, 28 hours of range and classroom training taught and administered by a Class "K" licensee; however, no more than 8 hours of such training shall consist of range training.[131]

The requirements are not staggering by any stretch of the imagination, but a start; a posture emphasizing the role education plays in attaining professionalism.

Delaware has mandatory firearms training for all private detectives and investigators. Delaware's Board of Examiners is the watchdog agency for the security industry and decided effective July 30, 1979, that

> No person duly licensed by the Board shall be permitted to carry a pistol, revolver, or any firearm, prior to the completion of a course of instruction as designed by the Division of State Police. Instruction shall include, but not be limited to, safety, use of deadly force and marksmanship training. Each person shall thereafter be recertified annually.[132]

Legislative coverage, at least in the education and training area, is becoming more specialized. With strong advocacy for specialized training and instruction in computer-based fields,[133] airport and aircraft,[134] and animal handling, both the industry itself and governmental authorities are focusing on training requirements. Virginia, as an example, has promulgated Compulsory Minimum Training Standards for Courthouse and Courtroom Security Officers. The coverage comprises the following:

1. Basic Security Procedures
   a. Security Threats
   b. Search Procedures and Prisoner Movement in Court Environment
   c. Explosives and Bomb Search and Security Procedures
2. Court Security Responsibilities
   a. Duties and Responsibilities of Court Security Personnel
   b. Identification of Personnel, Package Control, and Detection Devices
   c. Sequestered Juries and Witnesses
   d. Recognizing and Handling Abnormal Persons
3. Legal Matters
   a. Constitutional Law and Liabilities
   b. Virginia Court Structure
4. Notebook and Report Writing
5. Skills
   a. Firearms
   b. Moot Problem
   c. Disorders and Proper Techniques of Removing Unruly Prisoners from the Courtroom
   d. Courtroom Demeanor and Appearance[135]

States have utilized the PSAC advisory recommendations in designing their own curricula. Assess the similarities as well as differences in the educational components of the North Dakota plan.

Apprentice Security Officer Training Curriculum Outline (16 Hours)

---

[131] Fla. Stat. Ann. § 493.6105 (2016).

[132] State of Delaware, *Rules for the Board of Examiners for Private Detectives, Mandatory Firearms Training Program* (1979).

[133] J. Lobel, Training: The Missing Line in Computer Security, 17 *Sec. World* 28 (1980); International Association of Chiefs of Police, *Fifth Annual Law Enforcement Data Processing Symposium* (1981).

[134] A. Potter, Security Training: The Airport Operator's Responsibility, 43 *FBI L.E. Bul.* 131 (1974).

[135] Va. Code Ann. § 53–168.1 (1979).

SECTION I. SECURITY ORIENTATION/OVERVIEW:

1. Introduction and overview.
   a. To the course.
   b. To the employing organization.
2. Role of private security.
   a. Brief history of private security.
   b. Overview of organization's security operations.
   c. Role of security in crime prevention and assets.
   d. Protection.
   e. Components of private security services.
   f. Primary functions/activities of security personnel.
3. Ethical standards for security personnel.
   a. Code of ethics for private security personnel.
4. Qualities essential to security personnel.
   a. Attitude/public relations.
   b. Appearance.
   c. Personal hygiene.
   d. Physical fitness.
   e. Personal conduct/deportment.
   f. Discipline.
   g. Knowledge of responsibilities.

SECTION II. CRIMINAL JUSTICE AND SECURITY PERSONNEL:

1. The nature and extent of crime.
   a. Overview.
      i. The criminal law.
2. The criminal justice system.
   a. Overview.
      i. The security person's relationship.
3. Legal powers and limitations.
   a. Rights of a property owner.
   b. Detention/arrest powers (citizen's or statutory).
   c. Search and seizure.
   d. Use of force.

SECTION III. GENERAL DUTIES:

1. Patrol techniques.
   a. Functions of patrol.
   b. Types of patrol.
   c. Preparing for patrol.
   d. Dealing with juveniles.
   e. Personal safety on the job.
   f. Traffic control.

2. Access control.

    a. Why access control.

    b. Types of access control systems.

    c. Controlling an entrance or exit.

3. Note taking/report writing.

    a. Importance of note taking/report preparation.

    b. Daily/shirt reports.

    c. Incident/special reports.

SECTION IV. EMERGENCIES:

1. Fire prevention and control.

    a. What is fire.

    b. Causes of fire.

    c. Classes of fire.

    d. Recognition and identification of fire hazards.

    e. Firefighting, control and detection equipment.

    f. Role in fire prevention.

    g. What to do in case of fire.

2. Handling emergencies.

    a. Bomb threats and explosions.

    b. Natural disasters.

    c. Mentally disturbed persons.

    d. Medical emergencies.

    e. First aid.

Security Officer Training Curriculum Outline (32 Hours)

SECTION I. SECURITY SYSTEMS:

1. Physical security.

    a. Definition.

    b. Purpose.

    c. Locks and key control.

    d. Barriers.

    e. Access control systems.

    f. Alarm systems.

2. Information security.

    a. Definition.

    b. Information classifications.

    c. Information and document control procedures.

3. Personnel security.

    a. Threats to employees.

    b. Employee theft.

SECTION II. EMERGENCY PROCEDURES:

1. Medical emergencies of other emergency procedures.

2. Defensive tactics.

3. Unusual occurrences.

    a.   Strikes, demonstrations, etc.

SECTION III. ROUTINE PROCEDURES:

1. Patrol.

    a.   Prevention.

    b.   Response to calls for service.

    c.   Response to crime-in-progress.

    d.   Crime scene protection.

2. Reporting.

    a.   Information collection.

    b.   Report preparation.

3. Dealing with problems unique to the individual's assignment.

SECTION IV. LEGAL ASPECTS AND ENFORCEMENT OF RULES:

1. Legal authority.

    a.   Authority of security personnel.

    b.   Regulation of security personnel.

2. Observing and reporting infractions of rules and regulations.

    a.   Organizational rules and regulations.

    b.   Security rules and regulations.[136]

Arkansas also provides a formidable program of instruction for prospective security professionals.

17-40-208. Training of personnel.

1. The Arkansas Board of Private Investigators and Private Security Agencies shall establish training programs to be conducted by agencies and institutions approved by the board.

2. The basic training course approved by the board may include the following:

    a.   Legal limitations on the use of firearms and on the powers and authority of the private security officer;

    b.   Familiarity with this chapter;

    c.   Field note taking and report writing;

    d.   Range firing and procedure and handgun safety and maintenance; and

    e.   Any other topics of security officer training curriculum which the board deems necessary.

3. The board shall promulgate all rules necessary to administer the provisions of this section concerning the training requirements of this chapter.

4. When an individual meets the training requirements approved by the board, that individual shall not be required to be trained over again until the private security officer's or commissioned security officer's renewal training is required, which is two (2) years after the private security officer or commissioned security officer is licensed, regardless of the company by which the private security officer or commissioned security officer is employed or trained.[137]

3.4.3 Educational certifications and the private security industry

Certification programs play a critical role in the development of a professional class within the security industry. Certifications take many forms although nearly all of them highlight a specific subject matter that requires unique

---

[136] N. D. Cent. Code § 43-30-05-06 (2010).
[137] Ark. Code Ann. § 17-40-208 (2009).

preparation of a body of specialized knowledge. In addition, certifications are usually the invention of the professional bodies and associations that are inexorably tied that body of knowledge needed for skilled implementation. ASIS International has been on the forefront of certifications for many generations. Its Certified Protection Professional (CPP) programs make a real contribution to substantive professionalism. The CPP program's chief objectives are as follows:

1. To raise the professional standing of the field and to improve the practice of security management by giving special recognition to those security practitioners who, by passing examinations and fulfilling prescribed standards of performance, conduct, and education, have demonstrated a high level of competence and ethical fitness.

2. To identify sources of professional knowledge of the principles and practices of security and loss prevention, related disciplines, and laws governing and affecting the practice of security.

3. To encourage security professionals to carry out a continuing program of professional development.[138]

The CPP Program tests rigorously those wishing the designation. Topics are broken down into distinct domains that include the following:

- Emergency planning
- Legal aspects
- Personnel security
- Protection of sensitive information
- Security management
- Substance abuse
- Loss prevention
- Liaison
- Banking
- Computer security
- Credit card security
- Department of Defense
- Educational institutions
- Manufacturing
- Utilities
- Restaurants and lodging
- Retail security
- Transportation and cargo security
- Telecommunications[139]

Jon C. Paul, Director of Security Services for a major hospital, applauds the CPP designation. "The CPP designation is the hallmark of excellence in our profession—a fact that is recognized in our industry and is becoming more widely recognized by the organizations we serve."[140] To be eligible for the exam, the individual must meet the following requirements.

- Nine years of security work experience, with at least three of those years in responsible charge* of a security function

  or

- A bachelor's degree or higher and seven years of security work experience, with at least three of those years in responsible charge* of a security function[141]

---

[138] Note, Certified Protection Security and Law Enforcement, *Sec. Mgmt.* 75 (1980).

[139] J.T. Smith, Develop Yourself Professionally, 35 *Sec. Mgmt.* 92, 92–93 (1991).

[140] I.C. Paul, Certified Protection Professional Progress Report, 35 *Sec. Mgmt.* 86 (1991).

[141] ASIS International, Certified Protection Professional https://www.asisonline.org/Certification/Board-Certifications/CPP/Pages/default.aspx.

ASIS International awards other certifications as well. "The Physical Security Professional (PSP)® credential provides demonstrable knowledge and experience in threat assessment and risk analysis; integrated physical security systems; and the appropriate identification, implementation, and ongoing evaluation of security measures. Those who earn the PSP are ASIS board certified in physical security."[142] Eligibility requirements include the following:

- High school diploma, GED equivalent, or associate degree and six years of progressive physical security* experience or
- Bachelor's degree or higher and four years of progressive physical security* experience[143]

The emphasis here is obviously dedicated the mechanics, policy, and technology of physical security. The domain area for testing breaks down into these categories.

ASIS also awards a Certification of Professional Certified Investigator (PCI) where the chief emphasis is on the protocols and practices of investigation, evidence collection, and case management and evaluations as well as best practices in surveillance, interrogation, and evidence gathering. The PCI domains of knowledge include the following:

- Case Management (29%)
- Investigative Techniques and Procedures (50%)
- Case Presentation (21%)[144]

Finally, ASIS International delivers a wide array of short-term certificates in a host of topics relevant to the security professional. A few examples offered in 2016 include the following:

- Soft Targets, Active Shooters, Workplace Violence: CPTED Solutions
- Security Leadership & Tools – Prepare Now for Tomorrow
- Successful Security Consulting
- Like Oil & Water, Physical and Cybersecurity Don't Mix. But Can They?
- Principles of Investigation and Interrogation
- Workplace Violence Prevention and Intervention
- Wharton/ASIS Program for Security Executives
- Security Documents and Project Management Process
- Physical Security Master Planning Workshop
- Risk, Threat, and Vulnerability Assessment
- ASIS Assets Protection Course™: Principles of Security (APC I)
- Executive Protection
- Crisis Management: Program Planning and Crisis Plan Development[145]

The American Bankers' Association awards the Certified Financial Services Security Professional (CFSSP) to those passing an exam covering banking practices. The CFSSP certification is designed to

- Establish a recognized standard of knowledge and competence for security professionals working in the financial services industry
- Formally recognize those who meet these standards
- Provide employers with a tool to identify skilled, knowledgeable professionals
- Support the benefits of professional continuing education and development

The International Association of Security Consultants (IAPSC) administers the Certified Security Consultant test for eventual certification. The organization promotes professionalism in the security industry and calls upon its

[142] ASIS International, Physical Security Professional https://www.asisonline.org/Certification/Board-Certifications/PSP/Pages/default.aspx.
[143] ASIS International, Physical Security Professional https://www.asisonline.org/Certification/Board-Certifications/PSP/Pages/default.aspx.
[144] ASIS International, Professional Certified Investigator https://www.asisonline.org/Certification/Board-Certifications/PCI/Pages/default.aspx.
[145] ASIS International, Classroom Programs https://www.asisonline.org/Education-Events/Education-Programs/Classroom/Pages/default.aspx.

Figure 3.23 Certified Security Consultant logo.

members to adhere to the highest standards of ethics in the industry. To become a CSC requires both extensive experience and education but also verification of unimpeachable character as well as having made significant contributions to the industry. See Figure 3.23.

Web Exercise: Find out more about the CSC Exam at https://iapsc.org/about-us/certification/qualifications/.

Other organizations and group devise membership requirements based upon education and experiential backgrounds. While not technically a certification, the membership designation represents proof of high-level preparation. A good illustration of this is the eligibility requirements posed by the International Security Management Association whose requirements are

- The applicant must be actively employed and operate autonomously as the senior security executive of the enterprise.
- The enterprise must have gross revenues exceeding one billion ($1,000,000,000) or equivalent sum in local currency per annum.

The fundamental issue of "one company-one member" shall be determined by the following criteria:

- Does the candidate control the security budget?
- Is the candidate's compensation determined within that company?
- Are security policies and procedures established within that company?
- Is the direct report for the candidate within that company?
- If the identified parent company is an ISMA member, does the CSO for that company sponsor the candidate's membership and confirm his/her autonomy?
- The applicant must be a recipient of a baccalaureate degree or its international equivalent or have as a minimum six years of experience in a policy making role in the security profession in private industry.[146]

Other continuing education programs, training seminars, and other advanced studies are provided by a wide array of professional associations and groups. CPP Chris Hertig advises busy security operatives that even Web-based education is now readily available. These newer programs take "correspondence courses" one step further. "There's the Certified Protection Officer (CPO) and Security Supervisor programs from the International Foundation for Protection Officers (IFPO) Bellingham, Wash., and Calgary, Canada," says Hertig. In addition, the Carrollton, Texas–based Professional Security Television Network offers a videocassette series. The U.S. Department of Defense offers distance learning for its facility security managers. And firms such as Defensive Tactics Institute in Albuquerque, New Mexico offer video training and critiques in areas such as personal protection. Universities offering criminal justice and security degree programs may also have independent distance studies.[147]

3.5 CONCLUSION

As we set out to define the private security industry and its specialists, a cross, comparative analysis with the public police sector is a very worthy method of discerning the nature of the industry. While private and public police

---

[146] International Security Management Association, Membership flyer https://isma.com/cms/wp-content/uploads/2012/04/application-form-REVISED_FILLABLE.pdf.

[147] Note, Distance Education: Learn from Home, 30 *Security* 8 (1993); for a current listing of programs offered, visit the NCES' IPEDsCool search engine at http://nces.ed.gov/ipeds/cool/Search.asp. See if there is an update.

operatives increasingly share roles and duties, while privatization continues unabated and the types of services offered by private security increases with little restriction, there are still many differences between these two worlds. Both recognize the need for cooperation and both discover greater commonality rather than differences. Both also witness a natural interchange of duty and function.

Add to this is our assessment of function and duty as a means to define. Precisely what does private security do—or better said, what does it not do since the latter list is getting very small day by day. The chapter provides a wide array of occupational profiles to discern the definition and nature of the industry. Finally, the chapter looks to how private security seems on an inevitable path to higher standards, higher education, and professionalization by a host of industry groups as large as the ASIS and as narrow as NASLEO, which deals with school safety officers. The complete array of professional bodies and the standards that they promulgate are discussed.

Keywords

alarm services

American Society for Industrial Security

armed couriers

asset protection

campus security

certification

Certified Financial Services Security Professional

Certified Protection Professional

Certified Security Consultant

Community Oriented Policing Services

community policing

contract security officer

core values

crime prevention programs

criminal justice

detectives

fire prevention

guard companies

Hallcrest Report

industry sectors

International Association of Chiefs of Police

licensing

loss prevention specialist

mutual assistance agreement

Physical Security Professional

private investigators

private patrol officers

private security

Private Security Advisory Council

Professional Certified Investigator

professionalism

protection

protective studies

public policing

school security

security agency

security assessment

security firm

security specialists

security studies

specializations

theft prevention

training standards

Discussion Questions

1. Discuss how the nature of a security officer or private operative depends on an understanding of how the private security system compliments the public policing infrastructure.

2. List various areas of conflict between the public and the private sectors and the areas of practice in which they agree.

3. Describe how the historic functions of private policing can help foster a better understanding of their true functions and contradict misconceptions and inaccurate caricatures of private security's value?

4. Outline the various roles and occupations that exist in the private security industry.

5. Summarize how campus security programs are prime illustrations of public/private cooperation.

6. Review increased state and local regulation in importance in promoting the professionalism of the private security industry.

CHAPTER 4

Private security industry, organizational structure, and definition

OBJECTIVES

After completing this chapter, the student will be able to

1. Demonstrate the organizational, managerial, and operational structure of the private security industry lends to fully define the private security industry.
2. Discuss the similarities and differences between individual, contractual, and proprietary security services.
3. List the various rationales for utilizing individualized security services.
4. Outline how proprietary security services reflect the growing institutional, corporate, and agency marketplace, which needs to assure its public of a safe and secure environment.
5. Summarize the various individual security services available in the marketplace.
6. Relate the reason for the continuing growth of contractual security services.
7. Identify the most common positions in contractual security chains of command.
8. Define the major tasks of a corporate security director.

4.1 INTRODUCTION

Arriving at an accurate definition of the private security industry has been a journey on various fronts: first, the historical evolution of policing as presently understood was gauged and evaluated from ancient times to modern-day operations; second, occupational roles and functions of the private security industry were examined closely, especially in light of professional associations and standards of performance; and third, a full comparison of public police and private police was delivered with special attention given to the ongoing merger of functions and duties so prominent since the events of 9/11. Each of these contexts fleshes out the definition of what private security really is and what it really does on a day-to-day basis.[1] In this chapter, we will examine a fourth context—how the organizational, managerial, and operational structure of the private security industry lends to further definition about this dynamic industry. Security services essentially come in three structures—individual, contractual, and proprietary. Figure 4.1 illustrates these common organizational models.

Whether by *individual* delivery, by *proprietary* service, or under a *contractual* agreement for services, private security moves at a frighteningly fast pace. Contractual services, whereby money is paid for specific services, continue unabashed. "The 'private contractual security services' industry encompasses guards, private investigative services, central-station alarm monitoring, armored transport and ATM servicing, security consulting and data security and private correctional facility management services. Niche markets also exist for a wide range of specialized security

---

[1] For a fascinating look at how the City of New Orleans appears to be relying on private sector police more heavily than public police, see D. Amsden, Who Runs the Streets of New Orleans? *The New York Times Magazine* (July 30, 2015) available at http://mobile.nytimes.com/2015/08/02/magazine/who-runs-the-streets-of-new-orleans.html?referrer=&_r=0, last accessed August 27, 2016.

Proprietary Security	Contract Security	Individual Security Services
Delivery of Direct Services as Employees	Delivery of Specified Services as Independent Contractors for another Entity	Sole Proprietorships as Private Detectives, Private Investigators, Security Consultants, Executive and other Specialized Services.

Figure 4.1   Various types of security services.

services, including: bomb sweeps and metal detection; drug testing; preemployment screening; renting of site secure vaults; radon and hazardous gas testing; and guard dog services."[2]

Proprietary security services reflect the growing institutional, corporate, and agency marketplace, which needs to assure its public of a safe and secure environment to carry out its business and responsibilities. Hence, colleges and hospitals, libraries and museums, and businesses and industries invest in "employed" security personnel whose interests perfectly align with the institution served. The proprietary sector offers services directly to the public from property protection to private background checks, from fraud prevention systems to banking security controls. Propriety security reflects the ingenuity and brilliance of its inventors.[3]

Individual services show no signs of stagnation with a surge of private investigators, computer and tech crime specialists, antiterrorism practitioners, and executive protection specialists. No matter what the organizational setting, the private security industry shows no signs of lethargy.

Web Exercise: Allied Universal, one of the premier private security firms, explains its complex hiring process on the company's website at http://www.aus.com/Security-Services/Our-Approach.

4.2 INDIVIDUALIZED SERVICES IN PRIVATE SECURITY

From a structural standpoint, the individual, sole deliverer of security services is the simplest form of organization discovered in the industry. Operating, usually, as a sole proprietor, the security specialist conducts his or her business within a highly specialized subject matter. The rationale for individualized services is by both choice and occupational necessity. In the former instance, the security operatives prefer a singular approach to the corporate or collective delivery of private security services. In the latter instance, the group method could not accomplish the security task at hand. For example, investigations, at least in most circumstances, are better grounded in a designated individual rather than in an entire department. The same could be said for private detective work involving marital discord, background checks, and undercover operation in work and other settings. For these and other reasons, private detectives and private investigators generally deliver services individually rather than collectively. See Figure 4.2.

Private detectives and investigators generally engage in the following activities:

- Write reports or case summaries to document investigations
- Search computer databases, credit reports, public records, tax or legal filings, or other resources to locate persons or to compile information for investigations
- Obtain and analyze information on suspects, crimes, or disturbances to solve cases, to identify criminal activity, or to gather information for court cases
- Conduct background investigations of individuals, such as preemployment checks and to obtain information about an individual's character, financial status, or personal history
- Conduct private investigations on a paid basis
- Testify at hearings or court trials to present evidence
- Question persons to obtain evidence for cases of divorce, child custody, or missing persons or information about individuals' character or financial status

---

[2] P.S. Bailin & S.G. Cort, Industry Corner: Private Contractual Security Services: The U.S. Market and Industry, 31 *Business Economics* (April 1996) at 57.

[3] See Securitas International's website at http://www.securitasinc.com/en/.

Figure 4.2 Police cooperating with a private detective during an investigation.

- Observe and document activities of individuals to detect unlawful acts or to obtain evidence for cases, using binoculars and still or video cameras
- Alert appropriate personnel to suspects' locations
- Perform undercover operations, such as evaluating the performance or honesty of employees by posing as customers or employees
- Investigate companies' financial standings or locate funds stolen by embezzlers, using accounting skills
- Expose fraudulent insurance claims or stolen funds
- Confer with establishment officials, security departments, police, or postal officials to identify problems, provide information, or receive instructions
- Apprehend suspects and release them to law enforcement authorities or security personnel

Private detectives and investigators are part of a larger array of occupational roles and functions witnessed in both the public and private justice systems. Aside from these two main designations, other occupational titles encompass the chief function of the investigator and detective such as

- Asset protection detective
- Field investigator
- Loss prevention agent
- Loss prevention associate
- Loss prevention detective
- Loss prevention investigator
- Loss prevention officer
- Special investigator
- Insurance investigator
- Claims investigator
- Accident investigator
- Fraud investigator
- Benefits investigator

Web Exercise: Many security investigators work for law firms. Visit the National Association of Legal Investigators and find out about their certification program at http://www.nalionline.org/.

The power and influence of the private sector in investigative detective services have resulted in the development of new lobby groups to protect the industry and new associations to promulgate generally accepted forms of performance.

For example, the mission of the National Council of Investigation and Security Services is

- To monitor national legislative and regulatory activities affecting the investigation and security industry
- To develop and encourage the practice of high standards of personal and professional conduct among those persons serving in the investigation and security industry
- To promote the purpose and effectiveness of investigation and security companies by any and all means consistent with the public interest
- To promote the private investigation and security industry and to educate members and the public in the advancement, improvement, and uses of investigation and security services
- To assist local, state, or regional groups of investigation and security companies in the common endeavor to advance and promote the investigation and security industry
- To provide the opportunity for the exchange of experiences and opinions through discussion, study, the Internet, and publications
- To cooperate in courses of study for the benefit of persons desiring to fit themselves for positions in the investigation and security industry, and to hold meetings and conferences for the mutual improvement and education of its members
- To acquire, preserve, and disseminate data and valuable information relative to the functions and accomplishments of investigation and security companies

On another individualized front, security specialists deliver highly sophisticated services on a one-to-one basis. For example, the executive protection business depends on single actors whose skill and acumen in personal protection make them invaluable. Executive protection delivers personal safety to politicians, entertainment personalities, and business leaders as well as rich, entrepreneurial people who might be a target for kidnap and extortion. By nature, this is an individualized service though it is often part of a larger menu of services offered by the typical security firm.[4]

Web Exercise: Find out about the new certification in executive protection offered by ASIS International at https://www.asisonline.org/Education-Events/Certificate-Programs/Pages/default.aspx.

The breadth and depth of security consultants is directly linked to market demand and the uniqueness and sophistication of the services offered. For example, some security consultants possess high-level expertise in cyber matters while others possess expertise in risk assessment and planning. Others might combine a background in military intelligence that companies find useful as these entities protect their vested interests. Other individuals may deliver highly complex services relating to educational safety, background services, and technology issues. Put another way, the extent of consultant services in the security industry has few if any limitations.

Bringing some standardization to security consultant services and assuring ethical and professional practices for those consultants is the chief aim of the International Association of Private Security Consultants (IAPSC). See Figure 4.3.

The IAPSC publishes a series of best practices for the consultant industry and recommendations for use of force in retail and other settings, the avoidance of conflicts in representation and testimony in actual cases, and protocols for detaining shoplift suspects. The IAPSC also administers the Certified Security Consultant (CSC) examination. Aside from traditional education, experience, and character qualifications, the CSC also mandates that the applicant

---

[4] U.S. Security Associates, Consulting, Investigation and International Specialized Services, http://www.ussecurityassociates.com/usa-services/specialized-services/documents/ss_executive_protection_usa.pdf, last accessed July 28, 2016.

Figure 4.3   International Association of Professional Security Consultants logo.

demonstrate three levels of "significant and meaningful contribution" to the security industry at large. The definition of this standard encompasses the following language:

> Each candidate for certification will demonstrate significant and measurable contribution to the security industry. Examples of contributions include, but are not limited to security-related presentations or public speaking; publishing; teaching; serving in a responsible charge position for a security industry association (officer, board member, committee chairperson). Each contribution must be security-related and verifiable. Other contributions may also be accepted at the discretion of the Professional Certification Committee. A minimum of three Significant and Measurable contributions must be demonstrated in the five year period prior to application.

Web Exercise: The IAPSC provides a search engine for finding security specialists acting in the consultant capacity; see https://iapsc.org/find-a-consultant/.

4.3 CONTRACT SECURITY SERVICES

At every level of the private security industry, including contract services, the growth continues its undeniable upward trend. The think tank Freedonia Group graphically charts this upward path for the next decade. See Figure 4.4.[5]

Even governmental entities soon learn of the extraordinary cost benefits of "outsourcing" services, "funerals, directing traffic, responding to burglar alarms, citing parking violations, prisoner transport, watching over buildings found to be unlocked, dispatching police vehicles and others that do not require sworn officers."[6] Providing security and safety for office buildings, parking lots, seaports, public parks, pipelines, railroads, communities, public housing, and even entire neighborhoods corroborates the substantial inroads of the privatized model. Specialized services in corporate investigations for white-collar fraud cases; executive, dignitary, and celebrity protection; and antibomb and explosives tactics and antiterror strategies further edify the shift. Private companies lead the way in labor dispute security, prisoner transport, protection for nuclear power plants, and privately operated prison systems.

When institutionally provided as compared with individual delivery of private security services, there are two primary approaches: In the first approach, those services may be provided by contract, whereby a firm and its employees are directly hired to provide security services under designated contract terms. Under this scenario, the company hiring the contract security firm is distinct and legally separate from the security firm, and as a result, does not have employees in the strict sense of the word, but rather, a firm that has employees who work for the hiring company as independent contractors. Under the second "proprietary" model, the company or entity hires actual employees at its location to carry out the security mission. In this way, under the proprietary protocol, the employees of the company are identical to any other employee of the vested interest and thereby more directly connected to the mission of the company seeking the services. In both circumstances, there are positive and negative arguments. On the contract side, the company or interest needing the security services avoids legal liability for the acts of the independent

[5] J. Griffin, Demand for Private Security Services Projected to Rise in U.S., *SecurityInfoWatch* (November 7, 2012) http://www.securityinfowatch.com/article/10826461/freedonia-group-study-projects-steady-increase-in-demand-for-private-security-services, last accessed August 27, 2016.

[6] Calvert Institute for Policy Research, Calvert Issue Brief Vol. 3 (September 1999).

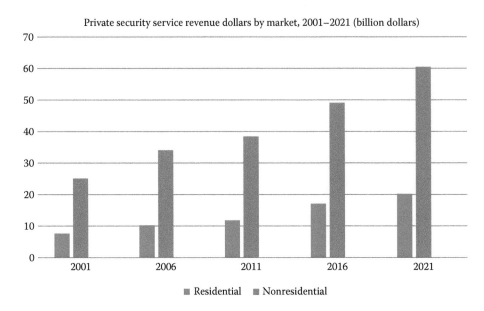

Private security service revenue dollars by market, 2001–2021 (billion dollars)

■ Residential   ■ Nonresidential

Figure 4.4 A new study from projects shows that demand for private contracted security services in the United States will increase by 5.4% annually to $64.5 billion in 2016. (Data source: The Freedonia Group, Inc.)

contractors unless or when the act is so egregious and so known to the company that the immunity or shield falters. From another front, the contract officer is cheaper since he or she will not gain benefits nor be paid under company plans of compensation but instead, those of his or her employer. In essence, the company, institution, or other entity chooses to "outsource" the task of security to a firm with which it contracts. As a result, in the contract scenario, the parties enter into an agreement whereby the rights, duties, and obligations of the respective parties are fully delineated.

Web Exercise: Review the sample agreement between the City of San Jose, California and a private security firm for services at http://sanjoseca.gov/DocumentCenter/View/13311.

And while there are many, many economic advantages to hiring independent contractors, the IRS and other federal agencies are becoming more aggressive about limiting the designation. Independent contractors are not subject to social security taxes or other withholding, nor is the company or entity hiring the contractor responsible for benefits under statutory requirements. For too many years, the IRS has construed the contract designation a route that has natural suspicion. As a result, the decision to move toward this model must be done in a spirit of vigilant compliance with existing rules. The designation of "independent contractor" must mean what it naturally means rather than merely be a pseudodesignation that avoids the rules. To be adherent to the rules, the company or other entity must be mindful of the following requirements:

- The institution's right of supervision and control over the worker would evidence a nonindependent status.
- Determine whether the worker is integrated into the institution's workforce and operations. If the worker is not integrated into the institution's operations and the right of control is not obviously apparent (no training, no work hours, no reports), he or she may not be independent.
- If the worker is integrated into the institution's operations, the institution is at risk for misclassification.
- The decision to hire an independent contractor represents a calculated business risk. Assess the risk of misclassification, including the dollar amount of payment and duration of relationship, probability that worker will voluntarily pay income tax withholding and social security self-employment tax, risk of liability for workplace injury, etc.

For a statutory checklist to provide contract security services in the state of Alabama, see the form in Appendix A.[7]

---

[7] Alabama Security Regulatory Board, Company License Application, available at http://www.asrb.alabama.gov/PDF/forms/CompanyAppl5-6-15.pdf, last accessed July 28, 2016.

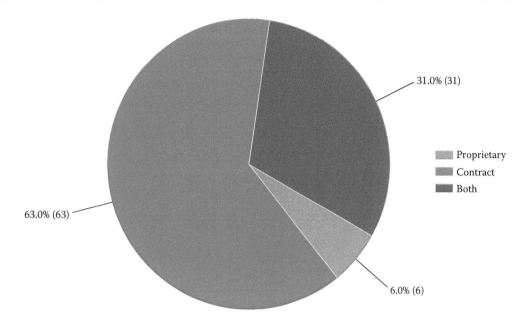

Figure 4.5 Data from a survey of Corporate security officers (CSOs) on whether they use proprietary security personnel, contract personnel, or both. (Data source: ASIS International, CSO roundtable.)

While contract security appears the dominant form of delivery in the private security industry,[8] its support and advocacy depend upon a host of factors. See Figure 4.5.[9]

Long gone is the idea that cheap-labor security forces will suffice and that standards and professional expectations not be part of the operational philosophy.[10] Both contract and proprietary systems "stress the need for quality personnel, continuing training and a constantly expanding business-centric role for security officers beyond typical patrols."[11] Today, quality, professional security operatives are essential to success in the security industry, although contract security personnel—no matter how convincingly one argues—cannot really be identical in vision or approach to the actual employee. The question largely boils down to one major issue: how deeply vested are these personnel? Cutting corners, paying lower wages, denying benefits, failing to promulgate entry or advanced requirements for positions, and refusing to train and develop contract officers is a sure recipe for substandard performance. On the other hand, there is nothing that forces this vision on any contracted security firm. The same entities that choose the "cheaper" way can decide on the most professional model possible. "Not all contract security firms are created equal. It is the responsibility of the buyer to properly research and hire a quality security firm with a solid background."[12] The National Association of Security Companies lays out five challenges for the contract security industry:

- Recruiting, screening, and retaining qualified candidates
- Uniform standards for licensing security companies and registering, screening, and training security officers
- Procure processes that emphasize price over value
- Perceptions and expectations of security officers
- Demonstrating value and differentiating services[13]

---

[8] See J. Griffin, Private Contract Security Services to See Steady Global Demand, *SecurityInfoWatch* (February 1, 2013) available at http://www.securityinfowatch.com/article/10862533/freedonia-group-report-forecasts-global-demand-for-contract-security-services-to-reach-244b-in-2016, last accessed August 27, 2016.

[9] CSO Roundtable Survey, Security Department Organizational Structure (August 20, 2012) available at https://www.asisonline.org/About-ASIS/Documents/CSOOrgSurvey_FINAL.pdf, last accessed July 28, 2016. © (2017) ASIS International, 1625 Prince Street, Alexandria, VA 22314. Reprinted by permission.

[10] See B. Zalud, Enterprise-Wide Alignment Drives Contract or Proprietary Decision, *Sec. Mag.* (February 2007) available at http://www.securitymagazine.com/articles/78349-enterprise-wide-alignment-drives-contract-or-proprietary-decision-1, last accessed August 27, 2016.

[11] Zalud, Enterprise-Wide, at 48.

[12] *Ibid.* at 52.

[13] J. Ricci, Contract Security Community Faces Common Challenges, *Security* (February 2007) at 58.

For NASCO and other professional advocates, the temptation to economic savings can be both a hidden and obvious enemy of quality services. Contracts are, by nature, rooted in compensatory and consideration schemes that make sense to the signatories of the document. No one enters into a contract to intentionally lose money. On the other hand, many enter into contracts to make an inordinate killing—a profit margin that appeals but in the end may undermine and destroy the integrity of present and future services. "Economic pressures are forcing clients to focus on cost reductions,"[14] although these same pressures must not undercut the efficacy and professionalism of the services sought.

Side by side with this analysis, the question of whether to contract for security services is also a business decision, a judgment that companies, institutions, and other entities must reach when considering their overall financial health and station. For some clients, contract may be the only way to go due to the impossibility of absorbing full employee costs. Many entities desirous of security services may be limited economically yet still carry the security imperative. John Rankin poses six foundational questions for the parties:

1. *Costs are not limited to pay rates*: Government payloads, vacation pay, medical benefits, WSIB, training, severance, uniforms, and insurance must be included.

2. *Training*: Who will be the trainer? Will they be competent to train in many security functions? Where will the courses come from? Will they meet government standards?

3. *Human resources*: Who will hire, background check, license, maintain records, schedule, and deal with unionization, discipline, or terminations?

4. *Liability*: Who will take responsibility in a legal action? What has been done in order to not be found negligent, and have all aspects been addressed in relation to personal safety? Have we met minimum standards on training? Do postorders cover all aspects related to the specific job specifications?

5. *Backup*: Who will cover for vacation, illness, last-minute book off, no shows, resignations, and emergencies?

6. *Supervision*: How will you ensure all shifts are supervised? Who can attend the sit after-hours in case of an emergency?[15]

From another vantage point, the company or institution seeing security services may deem that a combination of both contract and proprietary is the perfect mix. For mundane security purposes, such as perimeter and fencing, access, or other issue, the contract security firm may be the complement to a proprietary force that is concentrating on more complex matters.[16] This blending of in-house proprietary and outsourced contract is sometimes referred to as "cooperative security."[17] This sort of arrangement often makes perfect sense when the outside security provider delivers state-of-the-art technology such as surveillance and command operations centers, forensic means and methodologies, and technological capacities that most companies are unable to design or implement.[18] The decision to outsource will depend on the complexity of the subject matter. See Figure 4.6[19] for the most common subject areas outsourced.

Ultimately, the contract security firm is as good or as effective as the investment behind its personnel. The care and feeding, the training and education, and the professional expectations of the hired parties cannot be neglected or minimized. Otherwise, performance issues will abound in the marketplace. Contract security services should never be construed as an excuse to cut corners yet rightfully gauged as an economic alternative to those needing the services. Like anything else, there are ways of assuring a quality, professional experience. Tory Brownyard's "The Do's and Don'ts of Contract Security" lays out a cogent vision for quality assurance:

Do:

- Hire security personnel from the upper level of the candidate pool, such as former/retired law enforcement personnel. They have undergone extensive training and screening, and they provide a very favorable impression to employees and visitors.

---

[14] Ricci at 56.

[15] J. Rankin, Why Go Contract for Security Officers? *Security* (April 2007) at 16.

[16] J.B. Stover, When Security Doesn't Add Up, *Sec. Mgmt* (May 2000) at 80–83.

[17] Cooperative Security, *Sec. Mag.* (August 2006) at 20.

[18] *Ibid.* at 22.

[19] K. Strom et al., The Private Security Industry: A Review of the Definitions, Available Data Sources, and Paths Moving Forward (Washington, DC: NCJRS, 2010) available at https://www.ncjrs.gov/pdffiles1/bjs/grants/232781.pdf, last accessed August 27, 2016.

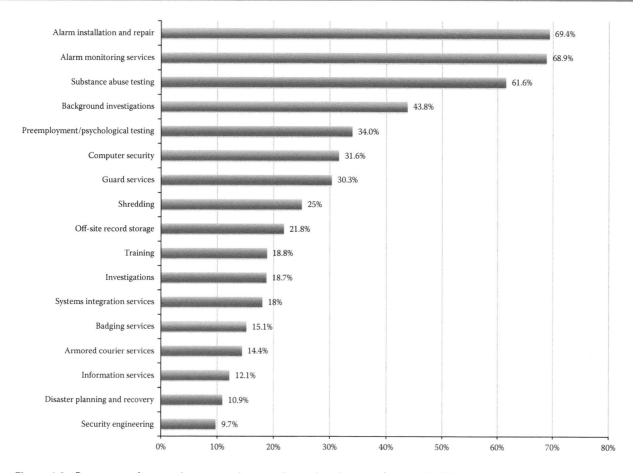

Figure 4.6 Percentage of companies outsourcing security services by type of service (2005).

- Make sure security personnel have situational training specific to the risks of your industry.
- Have periodic meetings with the security personnel's supervisors to point out any issues or concerns to make sure that the security personnel are meeting your requirements.

Don't:

- Pay below industry average. In any instances the security officer at the front desk is the first impression a client gets of your firm and you to make sure they look professional and provide a professional appearance. Prior to 9/11, security professionals were treated more as a commodity, and firms would want to pay as little as possible to get that security officer firm. Since then, however, it became more important to have a well-trained security professional with a professional appearance.
- Try to save money by replacing security personnel with remote video monitoring without carefully analyzing what you are looking to protect and which solution will be most effective.[20]

Finally, the company, institution, or entity in need of security services must do all in its power to integrate the visions of the provider with the party seeking these services. These are not different continents spread apart by legalistic term and operational division but parties dedicated to a common purpose. In this way, says Chris Hertig, both the contract firm and the client need to train and develop personnel with this unified vision in mind.[21] Hertig exhorts security clients to minimize "role confusion" and to mitigate the "inherent level of dissonance due to the

---

[20] T. Brownyard, The Do's and Don'ts of Contract Security, *Sec. Mag.* (January 2015) at 24.
[21] C.A. Hertig, Contract Security Training and Development: Examining Methods of Contract Training, *Sec. Mag.* (April 2001) at 7.

employer–client relationship."[22] This can be accomplished by many strategies, though the below suggestions are worth noting:

- Cooperative efforts in the design of training
- Encourage drills and scenarios at the client setting
- Support the professional memberships of the contract officers to assure best practices

In these and other ways, the contract officer integrates his or her vision more compatibly with that of the client and as a result, the parties operate under an identifiable and agreed-upon mission.

4.4 PROPRIETARY SECURITY SERVICES

According to ASIS International, proprietary security is any organization, or department of that organization, that provides full-time security officers solely for itself.[23] Traditional employer–employee principles are primarily applicable when deciding to use proprietary security service. Under the proprietary design, security personnel are employees like any other in the client—no different than any other category of staff. Following similar benefit and compensation programs as other employees, it is difficult not to recognize the sense of ownership that traditional employees have when compared to the outsourced security officer.[24] Robert McCrie charts the obvious advantages of the proprietary model, especially when compared to the contracted officer. See Table 4.1.[25]

From a contrary viewpoint, the costs of the proprietary model are more significant when compared to the contract service model. Proprietary officers share in the full measure of the employer and this largesse is sometimes the difference between the viability of a security plan and its economic implausibility.

The decision to stay in-house rather than to outsource to a third party is a serious determination. In-house, proprietary security models retain better control over employees and their performance than many outsourced firms. Steve Adler et al. caution security professionals to weigh seriously an array of variables before moving beyond the proprietary model by posing these queries:

- Who should be allowed to bid/what are the criteria?
- What exactly is each party required to do?
- When will each party be providing the goods or services, and over what period of time and when will payment be made?

Table 4.1 Contract or proprietary security: Weighing factors

Factors favoring contract security	Factors favoring proprietary security
Less total cost normally	Personnel retention high
Administrative ease	Perception of greater quality of employee
Criminal records screening	Greater site knowledge
Recruiting and vetting transferred	More flexible controls
Training transferred	Greater loyalty to the employer
Supervision transferred	Reliability of service
Specialized liability insurance	Cost savings in some circumstances
Specialized protective experience	
Personnel scheduling flexibility	
Less likelihood of collusion with proprietary employees	
Emergency staff may be available	

---

[22] *Ibid.*

[23] ASIS International, Security Glossary, available at https://www.asisonline.org/Membership/Library/Security-Glossary/Pages/Security-Glossary-A.aspx, last accessed August 27, 2016.

[24] See R.F. Gordon & C.V. Bartley, Proprietary versus Contract Security in the College Campus Setting (September/October 2001) 1–3(3).

[25] R. McCrie, *Security Operations Management*, 250 (Butterworth Heinemann, 2011).

- Where will the services be performed or where will the goods be delivered?
- How will satisfactory performance or delivery be measured?[26]

Knowing what the performance expectations are is key to the decision, and without clarity in these categories, it is best to stay proprietary.

Web Exercise: For an excellent analysis of contract/proprietary security services, see the survey conducted by the Smithsonian on museums at a national level at http://natconf.si.edu/docs/Museum Security Benchmark Report 140709.pdf.

Even though proprietary security officers and personnel are employed directly by an employer, most jurisdictions still require the necessary licensure. New York State requires that both the firms and the personnel be subject to its regulatory oversight. See Figure 4.7[27] for policy and application.

4.5 CORPORATE SECURITY SERVICES AND SETTINGS

In the corporate and business world, private security has found a permanent and most respectful home. Given the complexities of today's modern world, especially as it relates to the protection of business assets, the care and oversight of business, industrial, and corporate facilities and most importantly, the personal protection of key employees and executives, it is hard to imagine any major business enterprise surviving long without security services. And at the business and industrial level, one witnesses the full array of organizational and operational qualities discussed throughout this chapter since these entities are served by strong proprietary security employees and just as often reliant upon the contract security industry. America's corporations blend and merge both the proprietary and contractual, and encourage partnerships between the private sector police and the public law enforcement of the pertinent jurisdiction.[28]

Corporate security is no longer an afterthought or a begrudging cost on the business balance sheet but an integral part of the business model to assure profits and a healthy environment. Randy Lippert et al. comment on the important role of the corporate security operative:

> If the common representation of corporate security is a skeleton crew housed within private corporations struggling to justify their worth to the organization, it is a mirage. Corporate security's current iterations, locations, constraints and powers suggest these units and corresponding practices represent more than resource starved survivors wandering an organizational desert in search of meaningful purpose.[29]

Just as compellingly, corporate security now sits comfortably, as peers and colleagues, with the movers and shakers in public law enforcement settings. The government may be effective conducting wars and battles, but it has yet to demonstrate the creativity and acumen to develop a full range of security products and services readily invented by the private sector. The public sector knows only too well that its reliance on technology is a reliance on private partners who design, install, and test the technological advance. Corporate security companies are on the front, inventing cutting-edge technology in biometrics and retinal identification, scanners and detection equipment, monitors and access devices incapable of penetration, as well as other innovations. Since 9/11, the growth has accelerated and "been substantial and far-reaching on a global basis."[30] On the technological front, the growth has been as "if the security industry developed 100 years of technology in 10 years."[31] Security at the corporate level engenders respect from both internal and external constituencies. Internally, corporate security is central to the mission and operation of the company and now a member of the C-Suite. Externally, corporate security directors and corporate security officers (CSOs) partner with local, state, and federal law enforcement, serve on boards and fusion centers, and engage the

---

[26] S.I. Adler, P. Robertson, & K.L. Dickson, The Inside Story of Outsource Planning, *Sec. Mgmt* 65 (August 2005).

[27] New York Department of State, Proprietary Security Guard Employer Application, available at https://www.dos.ny.gov/forms/licensing/1628-a.pdf, last accessed August 27, 2016.

[28] R.K. Lippert, K. Walby, & R. Steckle, Multiplicities of Corporate Security: Identifying Emerging Types, Trends and Issues, 26 *Security J.* 213 (2013).

[29] Lippert at 206.

[30] D. Ritchey, Proud to Be Security: How Roles Changed after 9/11, *Sec. Mag.* (September 2011) at 39.

[31] *Ibid.*

New York State
DEPARTMENT OF STATE
Division of Licensing Services
P.O. Box 22001
Albany, NY 12201-2001

Customer Service: (518) 474-4429
www.dos.ny.gov

Proprietary Security Guard Employer

Please take the time to read the instructions in this package carefully before beginning the application form.

When would I be required to submit a Proprietary Security Guard Employer form?

Any private or public entity employing individuals, other than peace and police officers, to perform security services is regulated by the New York State Department of State.

Do Security Guards employed by proprietary entities need to register and complete training?

Yes. Although proprietary employers of security guards are exempt from the business licensing requirement, they are still considered to be Security Guard Companies under the law. As such, they are required to employ registered security guards and provide proof of self-insurance or liability insurance coverage. A proprietary employer must designate a Security Guard Coordinator to provide the Department of State with the necessary information.

What is a Security Guard?

A Security Guard is defined as: Any individual who is employed to principally perform any or all of the following duties, and the person is not performing the functions of a private investigator as defined in Section 71 of Article 7 of the General Business Law.

- *Prevention*, protecting persons and/or property from harm, theft, and/or unlawful activity, including response to a security system alarm; or

- *Deterrence*, such category shall include: deterring, observing, detecting and reporting unlawful or unauthorized activity; or

- *Control*, controlling, by street or other patrol service, access to property, including employee personnel, visitors, vehicles and traffic; or

- *Enforcement*, enforcing security policies, rules, regulations, and procedures; or

- *Any individual* who is employed to perform any or all of the above duties, irrespective of whether such duties constitute a principal part of such individual's employment, with the condition of such employment being that s/he is armed with a weapon.

"Security Guards" do not include doorperson, superintendent, handyperson, porter, elevator operator, private investigator, proprietary investigator, telephone operator, lifeguard, school crossing guard, receptionist, clerical person, resident advisor or assistant, parking lot attendant or assistant, fire safety director or fire inspector, fireguard, environmental safety person, or any other title which shall not require such person, to perform any or all of

the above functions more than 50% of the person's regularly scheduled work hours.

Do I need to have insurance?

Yes. Section 89-g sub. 6 of Article 7A requires the filing of a certificate of insurance evidencing comprehensive general liability coverage in the minimum amount of $100,000 per occurrence and $300,000 in the aggregate.

What are the fees?

No fee is required to file this application. However, the appropriate fee must accompany each security guard application filed with the Department of State.

PRIVACY NOTIFICATION

Do I need to provide my Social Security and Federal ID numbers on the application?

Yes. The Department of State is required to collect the federal Social Security and Employer Identification numbers of all licensees. The authority to request and maintain such personal information is found in §5 of the Tax Law and §3-503 of the General Obligations Law. Disclosure by you is mandatory. The information is collected to enable the Department of Taxation and Finance to identify individuals, businesses and others who have been delinquent in filing tax returns or may have underestimated their tax liabilities and to generally identify persons affected by the taxes administered by the Commissioner of Taxation and Finance. It will be used for tax administration purposes and any other purpose authorized by the Tax Law and may also be used by child support enforcement agencies or their authorized representatives of this or other states established pursuant to Title IV-D of the Social Security Act, to establish, modify or enforce an order of support, but will not be available to the public. A written explanation is required where no number is provided. This information will be maintained in the Licensing Information System by the Director of Administration and Management, at One Commerce Plaza, 99 Washington Avenue, Albany, NY 12231-0001.

Figure 4.7 Proprietary security guard employer application.

(Continued)

Proprietary Security Guard Employer

NYS DEPARTMENT OF STATE
DIVISION OF LICENSING SERVICES
P.O. Box 22001
ALBANY, NY 12201-2001

BUSINESS INFORMATION

License Fee
Exempt

Please PRINT CLEARLY in blue or black INK using ALL CAPITAL LETTERS. Example: `A B C 1 2 3`

Federal Taxpayer ID:
(See instructions - Privacy Notification)

Business Name:

Business Address:

STREET ADDRESS (Required - PO Box may be added below to ensure delivery)

APT/UNIT/PO BOX

CITY

STATE   ZIP-CODE   ZIP + 4

COUNTY

PHONE NUMBER (Including Area Code)   FAX NUMBER - IF ANY (Including Area Code)

( )   -   ( )   -

E-MAIL ADDRESS - IF ANY

	YES	NO
1. I have attached proof of self-insurance or liability insurance coverage	☐	☐
2. I have attached the certificate of insurance evidencing comprehensive general liability coverage in the minimum amount of $100,000 per occurrence and $300,000 in the aggregate	☐	☐

Coordinator's Name:

LAST NAME

FIRST NAME   MIDDLE NAME

NAME SUFFIX

$\left(\text{e.g., Sr / Jr / III} \right)$

Entities exempt from the licensing requirement of Article 7 must comply with all other sections of Article 7A and all rules and regulations promulgated thereof.

X_____
Applicant's Signature   Date Signed

Below: Please enter any Unique Identification Number(s) previously assigned to the business by the Division of Licensing Services:

Applicant please initial in box

DOS 1628-a (Rev. 12/09)   Page 2 of 2

Figure 4.7 (Continued)   Proprietary security guard employer application.

Corporate Security Evolution	
What Was	**What Is**
Reactive	Pro-active
After-the-fact executor	A voice in the strategy
Business preventer	Business enabler
Cost center	Value add
Security-focused skills	Business acumen
Security jargon	Communicator/business language
Silos	Network builder
Security for security's sake	Integrated with the business
Focus on operations, not people	Personnel developer/manager
People just like me	Diversity of thought and skills

Figure 4.8   Evolution of corporate security. (Adapted from *The Conference Board CEO Challenge 2012 Survey.*)

DHS as to private–public partnerships. Insularity has been replaced by active participation and engagement. Since 9/11, Diana Ritchey observes, the culture of acceptance has developed regarding the crucial role of corporate security.

> With all that, corporate security's role was pushed center stage. It was a role that many security executives were more than willing to embrace, because prior to 9/11, many argue that corporate security's mission was largely taken for granted.[32]

Overall, notions of corporate security have undergone a radical evolution in the last decade or so. And while the roots and heritage of the security industry surely rest easy with the protection of business assets, from the time of Pinkerton onward, there is something far larger taking place in early twenty-first century. Aside from the continual transference of once sacrosanct public functions to the private sector, under the unstoppable phenomenon of privatization, there is also a recognition that the skill and expertise of the private sector is something the public system cannot forego—not merely in the sense of technology and innovation but also in the distinct way in which problems are evaluated and resolved. The public system is a lumbering, nonnimble player in a world that needs immediate response and attention. Slow to react and encumbered by everything from work rules and union demands, from bureaucratic mindsets to entrenched interests, the public system of protection cannot compete with the evolutionary capacity of the private security industry. The Conference Board CEO Challenge of 2012 calls this "corporate security's evolution"; the results are charted in Figure 4.8.[33]

Web Exercise: Find out about the International Security Managers Association (ISMA) at https://isma.com/about-isma.

4.5.1 Structure and hierarchy in the corporate security office

As already noted, the nature and structure of a corporate security office will usually be proprietary although that office is more than willing to engage contract security services when necessary. Corporate security executives are now more likely than ever before to be part of the management team rather than be mere outsiders delivering reports when necessary. The designation of a CSO reflects the growing importance of this position in the corporate culture. Business executives see the position in a light just as critically important as the chief financial officer (CFO). Without a secure and safe environment to conduct business, the bottom line would forever be under siege. Security directors and security officers are now properly construed as "business leaders." "Corporate security is a resource to solve business problems, not just security problems."[34] CSOs, like other corporate executives, are attuned to the overall mission of the business enterprise and take seriously the task of getting all security personnel on board with this business culture. The "security strategy and the business plan development"[35] are one and the same. A typical placement of the CSO in the chain of command might be as shown at Figure 4.9.

---

[32] *Ibid.* at 42.

[33] Leveraging Corporate Security for Business Growth and Improved Performance: The Transformative Effect of 9/11 (September 2012) available at https://www.conference-board.org/topics/publicationdetail.cfm?publicationid=2310&topicid=30&subtopicid=250, last accessed August 27, 2016.

[34] M. Lynch, B. Anderson, & C.J. Nebel, The Security Leader, the Business Leader, *Sec. Mag.* (June 2013) at 20.

[35] *Ibid.* at 22.

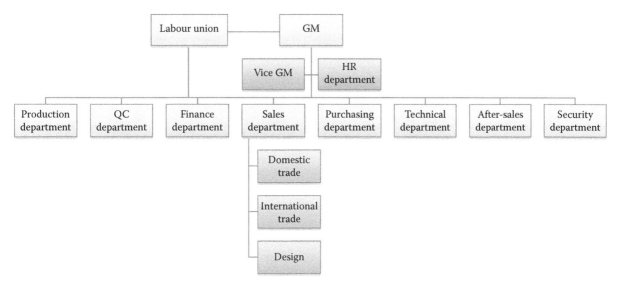

Figure 4.9 Example of corporate chain of command showing the placement of the CSO in the hierarchy.

Additionally, the position is more than mere advisor to the higher-ups in the organization but instead a resource for the entire company. Each unit of the enterprise must see the necessity of what security provides—it must be comfortable weighing and evaluating its particular function in light of security dilemmas and not hesitate to contact the CSO and his or her staff if issues arise or need prevention. Dennis Dalton argues that a CSO and his or her staff are only as good as the services delivered to the larger corporate community since their primary role is "to advise end users, the internal customers regarding benefits to be gained and risks to be avoided by following proven security strategies."[36]

At its center, the CSO and his or her staff are entrusted with risk management in the enterprise. It is not enough to act in a law enforcement mindset, for the corporate and business culture insists on something more narrowly defined— maintenance and protection of the business entity and its assets and people. "While there are common risks that impact organizations, there are also unique risks. Each sector, product line and market will carry its own set of risks that many times change rapidly as emerging or disruptive factors are introduced."[37]

The CSO and his or her team are also part of the community at large—just as corporate citizenship dictates that companies being willing contributors to the common good. Corporate social responsibility (CSR) is something every company should take seriously as inhabitants of the community. A CSR "imposes on the company policies and practices that help create positive social and environmental impacts and that show a commitment to both the stakeholders and the community."[38]

Web Exercise: Visit the Tyco Company's CSR program at http://www.tyco.com/about/corporate-citizenship.

4.5.2 Professional role and duties of the CSO

The range and extent of security services tackled by the corporate office have surely increased over the last decade or so. CSOs and their staffs are laden with many responsibilities. In a recent ASIS survey, CSO personnel were asked to catalog the many duties; the results are portrayed in Figure 4.10.[39]

Corporate security directors are now entrusted with duties far beyond historic expectations since most offices are simultaneously in charge of emergency planning and homeland matters as well as threats arising from public health

---

[36] D.R. Dalton, What Should Security's Function Be? *Sec. Mgmt* (July 2001) 160.
[37] J. Brennan & L. Mattice, Earning a Seat in the C-Suite by Adopting Management Culture, *Sec. Mag.* (February 2013) at 32.
[38] G. Kane, Security's Role in Corporate Social Responsibility, *Sec. Mag.* (March 2001) at 54.
[39] ASIS International, Security Department Organizational Structure: CSO Roundtable Survey, 11 (August 20, 2012) available at https://www.asisonline.org/About-ASIS/Documents/CSOOrgSurvey_FINAL.pdf, last accessed August 27, 2016. © (2017) ASIS International, 1625 Prince Street, Alexandria, VA 22314. Reprinted by permission.

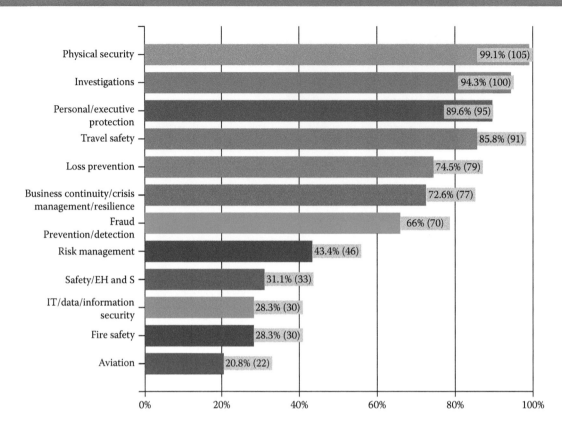

Figure 4.10 Functions of corporate private security. (Data source: ASIS International.)

and catastrophe. In addition, the corporate security office handles abuse and violence complaints, misconduct on the job and sexual harassment, as well as workplace substance abuse. A comprehensive job description for a CSO lists the myriad of functions and responsibilities of the position. See Figure 4.11.

CSO are obliged—in a continuous way—to educate the corporate community on a range of issues relevant to the business purpose. If dealing with supply chains and product delivery, the office must be attuned to breaches in security common to these locales. If handling high-interest products, such as pharmaceuticals or precious metals, the environment needs to be free from threat or risk of theft. In other words, the CSO must gear his or her operational philosophy to the underlying aim of the corporate enterprise and take an active role in assuring a safe and secure setting for employees, visitors, and assets. Issues of compliance, recent crime data, physical security breaches, and regulatory adherence are but a few of the essential topics for the CSO and his staff.[40]

Finally, the CSO and his or her team must see their value as ongoing, even in the event of merger or acquisition. In this circumstance, the incoming owners and investors will properly rely upon the office not only for historical understanding of the security challenges but also for present-day maintenance of day-to-day operations. Great turmoil is common in these changeovers, and the CSO team should be ready, willing, and able to assist during the transition. In this way, whoever the owner or manager might be, corporate reorganizations are really an opportunity to solidify the CSO position, "build its influence, align it with business risks and better reduce risk."[41]

4.6 CONCLUSION

To understand the world of private security requires a close examination of how its services and functions are delivered to a wider world. Variety best describes the structures and methods for that delivery, commencing with the sole proprietor or individual service provider. Next, how security services are provided depends upon whether the

---

[40] See G. Campbell, Building a Corporate Security Dashboard, *Security Technology Executive* (February/March 2014) at 14.

[41] B. Hayes & K. Kotwica, Rebuilding Influence after Corporate Restructuring, *Sec. Mag.* (May 2011) at 28.

Summary/Objective

The director of security position plans, directs and coordinates activities relating to the protection, safeguarding and security of company assets, employees, invitees and others; ensures that established goals and objectives are accomplished with prescribed priorities, time limitations and with fiscal responsibilities; advises, makes recommendations, assists in the formulation of goals and objectives; designs, implements and monitors security policies, procedures and programs; complies with federal, state and local legal regulations; and exercises independent judgment in the course of carrying out overall responsibilities and other activities as assigned.

Essential Functions

Reasonable accommodations may be made to enable individuals with disabilities to perform the essential functions.

1. Plans, examines, analyzes, evaluates and supervises ABC Corporation security operations, inclusive of physical security assets and security personnel.
2. Prepares reports and records for management team.
3. Evaluates current procedures, practices and precedents for accomplishing ABC Corporation activities and functions relative to security.
4. Identifies and resolves security related problems.
5. Develops and implements alternative methods for security operation improvement.
6. Coordinates activities within security area.
7. Prepares periodic budget estimate and reports.
8. Orders supplies and equipment as needed.
9. Reviews financial reports to ensure security operation efficiency and quality control.
10. Develops preventative security programs, including the supervision of security personnel.
11. Performs audits of security related performance and conducts physical surveys of premise security, including security equipment condition.
12. Conducts, supervises and prepares reports relating to internal investigations of any losses or violations of ABC Corporation regulations, policies and procedures; develops, implements and manages security training.
13. Assists in preparation of emergency management and contingency planning.
14. Serves as ABC Corporation's liaison with public law enforcement, fire and other agencies as it relates to security at ABC Corporation and/or ABC Corporation personnel.
15. Performs, arranges and supervises executive protection.
16. Performs other activities as assigned.
17. Directs and coordinates, through subordinate and/or contract personnel, ABC Corporation activities and security functions, utilizing knowledge of established policies, procedures and practices.
18. Initiates personnel actions such as recruitment, selections, transfers, promotions and discipline or dismissal measures.
19. Resolves work grievances or submits unsettled grievances to the Senior Vice President of Human Resources and Administration or other ABC Corporation corporate officer for action.
20. Prepares work schedules; assigns or delegates responsibilities.
21. Provides work directives for subordinates.
22. Sets deadlines to ensure completion of operational security functions.
23. Interprets and disseminates ABC Corporation policy to subordinate personnel; and evaluates employee performance.

Competencies

1. Communication Proficiency.
2. Decision Making.
3. Discretion.
4. Ethical Conduct.
5. Organizational Skills.
6. Problem Solving/Analysis.
7. Results Driven.
8. Stress Management/Composure.
9. Strategic Thinking.

Supervisory Responsibility

This position manages all employees of the department and is responsible for the performance management and hiring of the employees within that department.

Work Environment

This job operates in a clerical office environment, as well as periodical rounds throughout the corporation's grounds and worksite. This role also routinely uses standard office equipment such as computers, phones, photocopiers, filing cabinets and fax machines.

Physical Demands

The employee is occasionally required to sit; climb or balance; and stoop, kneel, crouch or crawl. The employee must frequently lift and/or move up to 10 pounds and occasionally lift and/or move up to 25 pounds. Specific vision abilities required by this job include close vision, distance vision, color vision, peripheral vision, depth perception and ability to adjust focus.

Figure 4.11   Corporate security officer—sample job description.   (*Continued*)

Position Type and Expected Hours of Work

This is a full-time position, and typical work hours and days are Monday through Friday, 8:30 a.m. to 5 p.m. This position regularly requires long hours and frequent weekend work.

Travel

Travel is primarily local during the business day, although some out-of-the-area and overnight travel may be expected.

Required Education and Experience

[Indicate education based on requirements that are job-related and consistent with business necessity. See example below.]

1. Bachelor's degree in business administration, criminal justice, law enforcement, security or a closely related field, or equivalent number of years of experience, and/or 10 years full-time experience performing supervisory responsibilities or highly responsible work relating to tasks assigned to this position, or any combination of education and experience provided the required skill and knowledge for successful performance would be qualifying.

Preferred Education and Experience

[Indicate education based on requirements that are job-related and consistent with business necessity. See example below.]

1. Ph.D., J.D. or master's degree in business administration, criminal justice, law enforcement, security or a closely related field.
2. Law enforcement experience.

Additional Eligibility Qualifications

1. Possession of a valid motor vehicle license and willingness to operate motor vehicles in the course of employment.
2. Certified Protection Professional (CPP) by the American Society for Industrial Security.
3. Certified Fraud Examiner (CFE) by the Association of Certified Fraud Examiners.
4. Any professionally recognized certifications in the security related field.

Work Authorization/Security Clearance

[This section lists visa requirements, H1-B sponsorship, special clearances, etc. If applicable, insert if you have government contracts or special requirements.]

AAP/EEO Statement

[Insert if applicable.]

Other Duties

Please note this job description is not designed to cover or contain a comprehensive listing of activities, duties or responsibilities that are required of the employee for this job. Duties, responsibilities and activities may change at any time with or without notice.

Signatures

This job description has been approved by all levels of management:

Manager_____

HR_____

Employee signature below constitutes employee's understanding of the requirements, essential functions and duties of the position.

Employee_____ Date_____.

Figure 4.11 (Continued)   Corporate security officer—sample job description.

company or consultancy is "contracted" or whether or not employees of the organization are truly employees rather than outside independent contractors delivering the work of private security. In the latter category, security services are designated "proprietary." These distinctions have extraordinary legal ramifications from both a liability and tax perspective. Finally, the chapter correctly addresses the role of the corporate security department, the role of the CSO, a now mainstream player in corporate and business life, and the roles and tasks of these officers and the departments they lead.

Keywords

accident investigator	contract security services	field investigator
asset protection detective	corporate security executives	fraud investigator
benefits investigator	corporate social responsibility	fraud prevention
central-station alarm monitoring	data security	independent contractors
claims investigator	executive protection	individual delivery of security services

insurance investigator	personal protection	security directors
loss prevention officer	proprietary security services	sole proprietor
organizational models	security consulting	special investigator

Discussion questions

1. Discuss the three steps in arriving at an accurate definition of private security.

2. Choose three of the missions of the National Council of Investigation and Security Services and discuss how they foster professionalism in the private security field.

3. Describe how providing safety and security for office buildings, parking lots, seaports, public parks, pipelines, and railroads helps security the homeland.

4. Discuss the two primary distinctions between individual and contract security services.

5. Discuss the primary distinctions between proprietary and contract security services.

6. What are the main requirements of contract security employment?

7. Discuss the technological advances that have assisted in the growth of private security companies.

CHAPTER 5

Private security and the law

5.1 INTRODUCTION: INDUSTRY GROWTH AND THE LEGAL IMPLICATIONS

By all accounts, the past four decades have evidenced phenomenal growth of the private security sector.[1] In 1972, a benchmark study was performed by James S. Kakalik and Sorrel Wildhorn for the RAND Corporation[2] and prophetically indicated the influential role security would play in the protection of people and assets. At the same time, the RAND Report harshly criticized the quality and preparedness of the security industry, observing:

> [T]he vast resources and programs of private security were overshadowed by characterizations of the average security guard—under-screened, under-trained, under-supervised and underpaid and in need of licensing and regulation to upgrade the quality of personnel and services.[3]

This undeniable growth, coupled with a fairly uniform conclusion that private security officers and other personnel in the industry are in need of better preparation and training, highlights why legal liability is a constant concern for the industry at large. On the one hand, the industry continues its "takeover" and "privatization" march over once sacrosanct public enforcement and protection functions, while on the other, trudges slowly to educate and ratchet up requirements for their personnel. This disconnect causes legal liabilities—both civil and criminal—for the industry.[4]

---

[1] E.E. Joh, The Paradox of Private Policing, 95 *J. Crim. L. & Criminology.*

[2] J.S. Kakalik & S. Wildhorn, *The Private Police Industry: Its Nature and Extent* (1972).

[3] W.C. Cunningham & T.H. Taylor, *The Hallcrest Report, Private Security and Police in America* 4 (1985).

[4] T. Frank, Practical Knowledge for the Private Security Officer, *Sec. Mgmt* (August 1994) at 119.

In addition, with new and emerging opportunities come the natural liabilities for industry personnel and its employing agencies. The industry knows how liability impacts the bottom line better than any other constituency. The *Hallcrest Report II* corroborates this picture of escalating liability:

> Perhaps the largest indirect cost of economic crime has been the increase in civil litigation and damage awards over the past 20 years. This litigation usually claims inadequate or improperly used security to protect customers, employees, tenants, and the public from crimes and injuries. Most often these cases involve inadequate security at apartments and condominiums; shopping malls, convenience and other retail stores; hotel, motels and restaurants; health care and educational institutional; office buildings; and the premises of other business or governmental facilities. Frequently, private security companies are named as defendants in such cases because they incur 2 basic types of liability: (1) negligence on the part of the security company or its employees and (2) criminal acts committed by the security company or its employees.[5]

Private sector justice is deep in the mix of things, places, and circumstances where liability problems are most likely to occur. In retail and parking complexes, in government buildings, and in nuclear facilities, the industry is exposed to liability just because of how and where it carries out its responsibilities. Other locales where liability is part of the territory include

- Shopping malls, convenience stores, and other retailers
- Apartments and condominiums
- Hotels, motels, casinos, bars, and restaurants
- Health care and educational institutions
- Security service and equipment companies
- Transportation operators such as common carriers, airports, and rail and bus stations
- Governmental and privately owned office buildings and parking lots
- Sports and special event centers[6]

Add to this striking growth the trend toward privatization itself[8] and it is only logical that accentuated levels of responsibility and legal liability are part of the security industry landscape. With increased functionaries laboring in the private sector, there will be a corresponding increase in legal liability.

Increased functional responsibility begets enhanced legal liability. "Because the effects of liability cases are far reaching, potentially affecting all levels … the more security personnel know about their responsibilities and exposure to liability, the less chance the company will be crippled with lawsuits."[7] Given the range and diversity of services private security implements, including "a whole spectrum of concerns, such as emergency evacuation plans, security procedures, bomb threats, liaisons with law enforcement agencies, electronic security systems, and the selection, training and deployment of personnel within institutions,"[8] liability is an ongoing policy issue. Dennis Walters, in his article *Training—The Key to Avoiding Liability*, notes:

> In the United States, where lawyers occupy a significant portion of the professional class, it is important to keep track of emerging legal trends when you are developing a comprehensive security training program. It is very helpful to know what forms of legal action are appearing that will affect the security industry.[9]

In fact, legal liability concerns are by nature part of the security game since the multidimensional involvement of the industry is now simply part of mainstream American life.

---

[5] Cunningham et al. at 34–35.

[6] *Ibid.* at 37–38.

[7] Chamberlain, Understanding Your Exposure to Liability Increases Your Chance of Avoiding Litigation, 20 *Sec. World* 26 (1983); see also V.E. Kappeler, *Critical Issues in Police Civil Liability* Ch. 1 (2001); V.E. Kappeler, *Police Civil Liability: Supreme Court Cases and Materials* Ch. 1 (2002).

[8] W.O. Dyer, D.S. Murrell, & D. Wright, Training for Hospital Security: An Alternative to Training Negligence Lawsuits, in *Violence in the Medical Care Setting, A Survival Guide* 1 (J.T. Turner, ed., 1984); see also Kappeler, Critical Issues, *supra* note 11, at Ch. 1 (2001); Kappeler, Supreme Court Cases, *supra* note 11, at Ch. 1.

[9] D. Walters, Training—The Key to Avoiding Liability, 29 *Sec. Mgmt.* 79 (1985); see generally D. Carter & A. Sapp, Higher Education as a Policy Alternative to Reduce Police Liability, 2 *Police Liability Review* 1–3 (1990); H.E. Barrineau, *Civil Liability in Criminal Justice* (2nd ed., 1994).

Whether crowd supervision and control or security at defense installations, the industry's growth cannot escape the legal liability of an emerging economic force. With the industry's tentacles around every place imaginable, private sector justice will have to discover how to mitigate and prevent legal liability. Hence, those entrusted with running the security operations—the directors, owners, and managerial class—need a complete understanding of how and why legal liability arises in various contexts, whether civil, criminal, or governed by specialized Civil Rights Acts. Ignorance of these laws will assure a proliferation of problems and the security company owner has to become competent in legal policy analysis and how it impacts the firm.

Legal liability can be costly to the industry's bottom line. Damages determined by a jurist or a jury can be economically devastating. It is difficult to get an exact figure on how many corporate dollars are lost through jury judgments against security personnel and their employers, but the fact that those losses are substantial is indicated by the circumstances of the legal climate as it affects security today. For example, jury awards in the past often amounted to only a few thousand dollars in many cases. Today, awards of $1,000,000.00 or more are becoming increasingly common. Various industry authorities estimate that at least one suit involving security is filed in the United States every day.[10]

Knowing how to avoid legal liability is a mandatory skill set for the security manager and operative in the field and being aware of the various laws and remedies is central to the endgame in this chapter. Yet, the legal analysis here is not all defensive and negative in design and the private security industry also needs to recognize that it has a natural and highly profitable, even highly efficacious, advantage in the constitutional dimension. Since the private security officer is not a public agent or functionary, and since privatized law enforcement is not state supported or governed so heavily to characterize the services as public law enforcement, the U.S. Constitution and its Bill of Rights, especially as to search, seizure, warrants, and general state action, are not applicable to the industry. In a nutshell, the industry is not concerned, nor is there any basis for it to be concerned about Miranda and its long progeny of case law that is severely restrictive to the public sector law enforcement agent. Succinctly, the Bill of Rights has no natural applicability to the security industry, and this has, from various circles, been construed as advantageous to the industry, which does not get bogged down in these constitutional battles. Of course, progressive civil libertarians hope for an eventual expansion to the private sector but in order to do so, the courts would have to disregard the language—expressly so—as to state action. It is essential that the prospective security professional gain a true appreciation for this legal advantage for it has shaped the industry and been an impetus to growth.

From another vantage point, the civil justice system is more naturally compatible with how private security and its industrial and corporate interests conduct business. Private security does not choose, as a matter of first resort, the criminal justice model with its dizzying array of adjudicative steps. Instead, private security has long been a proponent of alternative resolution, arbitration, mediation, and internal forms of informal justice. The private security system does not have to prosecute everyone and everything and shows a general willingness toward civil remedies over criminal penalties. And the industry itself sometimes favors to keep both the investigation and eventual resolution closer to the vest and keep control of the process rather than "giving away its control over the matter in the end."[11]

Hence, this chapter's approach is threefold: first, exactly what is the definition of civil liability and what types of civil liabilities are there and how does the law classify the various types of torts and civil harms? Second, how can the industry and its operatives be culpable for criminal activity and just as critically, what types of defenses are best argued in criminal prosecutions? Third, what is the current state of constitutional applicability and the private security industry at large and what are the various arguments for and against its continued restriction and expansion? In this last category, this chapter questions the seeming advantages of the private sector over the public counterparts.

5.2 CIVIL LIABILITY AND THE PRIVATE SECURITY INDUSTRY

Security agencies and personnel need to become accustomed to the common civil actions that firms and their officers will likely encounter. Internal and external policies of security firms and the defensibility of their practices and procedures need constant evaluation to prevent litigation. At its core, a civil liability arises from an action

---

[10] W. Saiat, The Need for Security and the Limits of Liability, 19 *Sec. World* 23 (1982); see also H.E. Barrineau, *Civil Liability in Criminal Justice* (2nd ed., 1994).

[11] C. Meerts, Corporate Security-Private Justice? (Un)Settling Employer–Employee Troubles, 26 *Sec. J.* 264, 268 (2013).

that causes a particular and demonstrable harm. Civil wrongs harm personally and cause measurable damages. For example, the individual who is victimized by an unsafe driver is personally victimized. While criminal law is chiefly concerned with protection of society and restoration of the public good, the basic policy behind civil law is: "to compensate the victim for his loss, to deter future conduct of a similar nature, and to express society's disapproval of the conduct in question."[12] Civil remedies are more concerned with making injured parties economically and physically whole, while criminal remedies are more preoccupied with just desserts, namely, punishment of the perpetrator either by fines or incarceration. Tort remedies involve damages, while criminal penalties result in incarceration or fines.[13]

Web Exercise: Find out about trends in law and regulation at the University of Denver's Private Security Monitor at http://psm.du.edu/national_regulation/.

Civil actions that are intentionally done are referred to as "torts," which imputes that the actor desires the particular outcome, not with the same intentionality as the criminal actor who premeditates or plans but acts knowing the likely outcome of injury to the party eventually harmed. Civil wrongs or causes of action can be defined in various ways although the central distinction of a civil action rests in its capacity to inflict a personal rather than a public harm. To compare, criminal activity is conceived as an act against the collective, the common good, or the whole society, while on the other hand, civil wrongs or harms are against a particular person. Civil actions are further divided into three main categories:

1. Intentional torts
2. Negligence
3. Strict liability torts[14]

Given the diversity of functions now being assumed by the private security industry, its exposure to civil liability in these forms is now a given in day-to-day operations. A review of common civil wrongs that regularly influence and affect security practice with illustrative case examples follows.

5.2.1 Intentional torts

Intentional torts imply an understanding or willingness to act or cause a specific end. Intentional acts are not driven by carelessness, accident, or mistake, but a clear intentionality. In civil law, the specificity and clarity of mind and intent are less rigid than the criminal counterpart, although proof of intent remains a fundamental element. Criminal law insists on more intentionality with terms like *premeditation*, *willfully*, and *purposely*. In assessing criminal behavior, the law requires that the person choose consciously to perform a certain act, and not be under duress, coercion, or suffering from any other impediment that influences volition.

Civil intent partially mirrors criminal intent. "Evil motive or the desire to cause injury need not be the end goal; intent to cause the actual result is sufficient."[15] In the law of torts, intention can be strictly "without malice or desire to harm but with full knowledge to a substantial certainty that harm would follow."[16]

Consider this factual situation:

> *Mr. X and his fiancée Ms. Z were shopping in a large department store in the State of Missouri. The evidence indicated that Mr. X left the department store without purchasing a tool. Soon after, Mr. X was confronted by a security officer in a hostile fashion. Mr. X was handcuffed after engaging in a physical altercation with the security guard. Mr. X's face was bleeding, his ribs were bruised and he suffered other injuries. Mr. X was eventually acquitted at trial on all charges brought forth by the department store.[17]*

---

[12] A.J. Bilek, J.C. Klotter, & R.K. Federal, *Legal Aspects of Private Security* 158 (1980).

[13] For an overview of the distinctions between crimes and torts, see the Cornell University Legal Information Institute comparison at http://topics.law.cornell.edu/wex/tort, last visited August 27, 2016.

[14] W.L. Prosser, *Handbook of the Law of Torts* (1971); see Kappeler, Supreme Court Cases.

[15] Bilek et al. at 158; J.E. Douglas, *Crime Classification Manual* (1997).

[16] C. Friend, *Police Rights: Civil Remedies for Law Enforcement Officers* 93 (1979); W. Aitchison, *The Rights of Law Enforcement Officers* (4th ed., 2000).

[17] Keenoy v. Sears Roebuck & Zeis, 642 S.W.2d 665 (Mo. App. E.D. 1982).

Who bears the legal responsibility for these physical injuries? Is the liability civil and/or criminal in scope? Has there been an assault or battery? Was the restraint and confinement of the suspected shoplifter reasonable? Has there been a violation of Mr. X's constitutional or civil rights? How are civil actions distinguishable from criminal actions when reflecting on this situation?[18]

Intentional torts most commonly witnessed in the world of private security are:

- Assault
- Battery
- Abuse of process
- Malicious prosecution
- Conversion
- Deceit
- Defamation
- False imprisonment
- Intentional infliction of emotional distress
- Invasion of privacy
- Trespass

Each intentional tort is further defined by the elements that make up that particular tort. Proof of the tort's specific elements are required, for mere allegation lacks legal sufficiency and the party asserting damages or injury from the specific tort must "cover every element of the cause of action," then "the party has stated a *prima facie* case."[19]

In the fact pattern above, a host of intentional torts are quickly evident, including:

1. Assault
   a. An act
   b. Intent to cause harm or apprehension of the said harm
   c. Apprehension that is imminent
   d. Causation
2. Battery
   a. A specific act
   b. Intent to cause harmful or offensive conduct
   c. Actual harmful or offensive conduct
   d. Causation
3. False imprisonment
   a. An act that confines a plaintiff completely within fixed boundaries
   b. Intent to confine plaintiff
   c. Plaintiff was conscious of his own confinement or was harmed by it
   d. Causation
4. Intentional infliction of emotional distress
   a. An act that is extremely outrageous
   b. Intention to cause severe emotional distress
   c. Actual emotional distress is caused
   d. Causation

[18] In fact, this case resulted in a $75,000.00 damage award given to the accosted customer at a large department store.
[19] W.P. Statsky, *Torts: Personal Injury Litigation* 1 (1982).

5. Malicious prosecution
   a. Initiation of legal proceedings
   b. Without probable cause
   c. With malice
   d. Favorable termination of legal proceedings regarding defendant[20]

Similarities and differences exist between the civil law and criminal law. Despite the subtle crossover capacity of these two legal domains, there are parallel remedies to the same injury or harm. Table 5.1 provides a concise overview.

While there is much that distinguishes civil and criminal actions, "the same conduct by a defendant may give rise to both criminal and tort liability."[21] Selection of either remedy does not exclude the other, and in fact, success in the civil arena is generally more plausible since the burden of proof is less rigorous. Remember the evidentiary burden for the proof of a crime requires proof beyond a reasonable doubt. A successful civil action merely mandates proof by a preponderance of the evidence or by clear and convincing evidence.

Web Exercise: Some law firms specialize in suing private security companies. See an example at http://www.bglawyers.com/case-results/private-security-2.

5.2.2 Negligence

In contrast to intentional conduct, civil law encompasses remedies based on negligent conduct—harms caused by errant conduct, carelessness, and mistake. Instead of the intended harm, such as witnessed in assault and battery, defamation, or false imprisonment, the negligent actor causes his or her harm without intentionality and does not necessarily intend the end or result. On the other hand, the party that is alleged to be negligent must bear some occupational oversight, such as in hiring and retention, and reasonably know that injury could occur, a feature known as foreseeability.[22]

In negligence law, the negligent actor acts without the due care owed to another, although the act generally lacks the malevolence and willfulness that intentional torts require. In negligence theory, the security company and its aligned employees fail, err in some aspect of their service, adjudged according to what the ordinary security professional does. In addition, the finding of liability is assessed in light of the reasonableness of conduct taken by the security operative. Bond and Feliton delineate universal factors:

- Degree of certainty that the plaintiff suffered injury
- Closeness of the connection between the defendant's conduct and injury suffered by plaintiff
- The moral blame attached to the defendant's conduct
- The policy of preventing harm
- The extent of the related burden to the defendant
- The availability and cost of insurance for the risk involved[23]

Table 5.1 Comparison of civil and criminal wrongs

Torts or civil wrongs	Crimes
Personal harm	Harm against society
Does not require intentional behavior	Generally requires intentional behavior
Requires proof by a preponderance of evidence	Proof beyond a reasonable doubt
Selection of civil remedy does not exclude a criminal prosecution	Selection of criminal prosecution does not exclude a civil remedy
Results in damage awards generally compensatory and sometimes punitive in nature	Results in fines, imprisonments, and orders of restitution

---

[20] See generally R.T. Weitkamp, Crimes and Offenses, 16 *Ga. St. U. L. Rev.* 72, 73 (1999); G.F. Taft & V.R. Gordon, Criminal Law (Legislative Survey—North Carolina), 21 *Campbell L. Rev.* 353, 353 (1999).

[21] Bilek et al. at 158.

[22] See T. Anderson, U.S. Judicial Decisions, *Sec. Mgmt* 122 (November 2005).

[23] D.B. Owen & J.R. Feliton, Guarding against Liability, 38 *Sec. Mgmt* 125 (1994).

Negligence theory examines the harm that arises from an accident or careless behavior and measures the damages. Negligence is the stuff of everyday life that people fail to do with due care. Forgetting to engage auto turn signals, failing to file documents in a legal appeal, misreading a right of way, or missing an important court date, all illustrate the nature of negligence. To find negligence, the litigant needs to start with what the average person is expected to do depending on the nature of the activity. Negligence evaluates acceptable levels of human conduct by determining what most people do in similar circumstances. Put another way, what would a "reasonable person" do? What should we expect from the average person in his or her dealings with others? The reasonable person is an amalgam of human behavior, a predictable player on the world's stage. While mistakes are part of the human equation, the law of negligence, despite the predictability of human error, holds the negligent actor accountable. The law is even less tolerant of behavior that is either gross or reckless in design. And these expectations will additionally depend on the actor's level of preparation, education, and expertise. We surely expect more from doctors and lawyers than we do from janitors or construction workers. So, in this sense, the average, reasonable person acts reasonably under the circumstances they live and labor under.

How the legal system holds the reasonable person accountable will also depend on the particular industry the actor is employed in. What is certain is that the security industry will be held to its own standard of professional conduct and that resulting injuries will be scrutinized in accordance with these expectations of professional performance and due care owed. Security's reasonable person will have to carry out the industry's diverse responsibilities without harm to others.

In order to prove a case of negligence, the claimant must demonstrate the following elements:

1. A duty
2. A breach of duty
3. Proximate causation

Hence, negligence analysis initially considers human conduct in a global sense and then moves to the particular reality of a specific party whose level of obligation will trigger a corresponding expectation of due care and conduct. Here, the ideas of duty and due care coalesce and the security industry has its expectations of performance as well. To prove the principal elements of negligence, a duty must be demonstrated and a standard expectation of due care delineated; a harm, connected to the breach itself, then must occur due to a breach of the said due care. The harm caused can then result in a finding of proximate causation.

5.2.2.1 Nature of duty

To reach any conclusion on liability, the advocate for the harmed person will have to demonstrate that the party was owed a duty of performance by another. What is duty, and to whom is it owed? When does the duty arise, and what is the standard in which there must be some level of uniformity and conformity? Duty depends not only on station and occupation, level of expertise, and sophistication of field, but also whether that particular duty is relevant in the events and conditions that surround the harm and injury. Security professionals, like other occupations, have a duty to others when carrying out their diverse functions. That duty must be more than a remote association, as was evident in *Armor Elevator v. Hinton*,[24] where a security officer, who had just ridden in an elevator that experienced some malfunction, failed to warn other passengers of the defect. Here, the court did not reach a conclusion of negligence since the scope and extent of the duty owed was unlikely to include warnings about elevators. While a "legal duty can arise not only by operation of law but by a contract between the parties,"[25] in the matter of elevator warnings, the security firm had no significant duty. That same analysis must be tailored to what the average person does or does not do in an occupation. In short, what does the average pediatrician do in these circumstances? Negligence never measures duty by the best and most sophisticated expert, but instead, employs the average practitioner as a guide. For an attorney, the same rule applies, that he or she owes a duty of competent, intelligent, and ethical representation to his or her client, as other attorneys in his or her same situation would offer. It does not require the highest level of advocacy, only a reasonable level of advocacy. Other examples of duty abound, including a parent to a child, teacher to student, and an engineer to a construction company.

---

[24] 443 S.E.2d 670 (Ga. App. 1994).
[25] *Ibid*. at 672–73.

What standards of duty should apply in the assessment of security companies and security personnel in regard to clients or the general public? Is it not reasonable to expect that security personnel be competent in basic legal applications, or that they generally understand what techniques ensure the protection of people and property? And what is a reasonable expectation of duty owed to the consumer when entering a commercial premise? The duty of the premise owner is to provide a safe, secure environment. Even criminal conduct suffered by customers opens the doors to negligence actions.

The results have staggering personal and economic costs for companies and clients. An eight-year study by Liability Consultants, Inc. found the average jury verdict for a rape on a business premises to be $1.8 million. For a death, jurors awarded $2.2 million. The Framingham, Massachusetts, security consulting company compiled the survey results from verdicts voluntarily reported by attorneys to a national group of plaintiffs' lawyers.[26]

5.2.2.2 Duty and foreseeability

Another essential factor in the analysis of duty is whether or not the harm suffered was reasonably foreseeable. By foreseeable, one means: could the actor have predicted the result; was it possible for the actor to have predicted harm and injury that would have resulted from the breach of that duty? In negligence law, the question is not only the defined duty, as well as its corresponding conduct expectation, but also the predictability and foreseeability of the injuries inflicted. In the case of security practice, the issue of duty is bound to its foreseeability. A recent case in a McDonald's restaurant confronts the duty question in light of foreseeability.[27] Restaurant management used security forces to prevent loitering and other problems in the parking lot and surrounding area. Sweeps of the area were dutifully performed every half hour. Despite this attention, trouble festered in the parking lot and a person was shot. The decedent's family called an expert criminologist who testified as to the paucity of protection and the failure of the McDonald's restaurant to provide a safe environment. In order to find negligence, the proof will evaluate the scope and extent of duty owed to the patrons of the McDonald's restaurant, and whether the restaurant chain breached that duty. How much safety and security does the proprietor owe the patron? How foreseeable were the events that led up to the wrongful death? What additional steps could the proprietor have taken to prevent harm? The appellate court analysis could find little evidence of foreseeability in these facts and exonerated McDonald's.

> We are of the opinion that McDonald's was not negligent in either failing to assist Kelly at the time of the encounter by not providing an armed security guard or by the Assistant Manager's failing to interject himself into the fray rather than call the police.[28]

Foreseeability, the ability to project and predict, relates to the duty of the security specialist. Here, the security firm is unable to know, to see, and to predict, and thus, could not be held to a standard of duty and obligation it could not discern or foretell. If the criminal conduct was regular and continuous, or if the proprietor had advance notice, the story would be different. Due diligence, due care, and reasonable precaution cannot take place without some level of knowledge.

Crafting a benchmark of duty and foreseeability is difficult. Some commentators merely suggest that merchants, business and industrial leaders, and other parties take extra preventive precaution to protect against liability.[29] Companies cannot be held to a duty threshold when events are utterly unpredictable.[30] "The Courts have placed a public trust upon store owners, retailers must treat their security measures as public property or risk paying a financial penalty in the event of injury to a member of the public."[31]

The task of the security specialist is avoidance of these and every type of claim based on the theory of negligence. The costs are simply too high.[32] Foresee and foretell, predict and evaluate are professional expectations that security firms

---

[26] Note, Premises-Liability Suits Become Tougher for Business to Defend, *Wall St. J.* (September 1, 1993) at B1.

[27] Kelly v. McDonald's Restaurant, 417 So. 2d 556 (Miss. 1982).

[28] *Ibid.* at 561.

[29] Fontaine v. Ryan, 849 F. Supp. 190 (S.D.N.Y. 1993).

[30] Hunley v. DuPont, 174 F. Supp. 2d 602 (E.D. Mich. 2001).

[31] M.B. Rosen, Limiting Liability, 20 *Sec. World* 47 (1983).

[32] S.R. Perry, Cost–Benefit Analysis and the Negligence Standard, 54 *Vanderbilt L. Rev.* 893 (2001).

and their clients have rightfully come to expect and demand. Consider a third-party criminal conduct carried out in a hotel or motel on an innocent customer. How does the hotel proprietor predict or foresee this event?[33]

Certainly, past regular criminal conduct at the facility puts the owner on notice of this criminal propensity. In an action by a motel patron against a motel to recover for a sexual assault, rape, and robbery that occurred after she opened her motel room door, a judgment in the patron's favor was upheld. The court concluded that motel owners' negligence was the proximate cause of the guest's injuries. The court relied upon a series of evidentiary deductions, including the hotel's highway intersection being a high-crime area, coupled with five armed robberies having occurred in the motel next door.[34]

On the other hand, reasonable minds could differ on this and lack the type of knowledge that leads to foreseeability. In *Satchwell v. LaQuinta Motor Inns, Inc.*,[35] the court retorted the foreseeability claim since there was "no evidence of any significant criminal activity against motel guests within five miles of location of motel. … Appellant called no expert witness, and did not present evidence of reasonable precautions that motel operator … should have taken … nor did appellant establish how the facts and circumstances of this case gave rise to the appellee's actual or constructive knowledge of any danger to motel guest from third party criminal assaults."[36]

Other settings, like apartment complexes and other facilities with public traffic, manifest the foreseeability dynamic for security firms. In *Abraham v. Raso*,[37] the court grants protection based on status. Invitees, that is, consumer/customers, get more security than the unwelcome trespasser, though this principle is not without limitation. "Generally, 'the proprietor of premises to which the public is invited for business purposes of the proprietor owes a duty of reasonable care to those who enter the premises upon that invitation to provide a reasonably safe place to do so that which is within the scope of the invitation.'[38] … 'Whether a duty exists is ultimately a question of fairness. The inquiry involves a weighing of the relationship of the parties, the nature of the risk, and the public interest in the proposed solution.'"[39] [40]

Gate attendants at an apartment complex were held not accountable for criminal conduct by third parties since the security service was strictly defined in the contract between the provider and the owner. In *Whitehead v. USA-One, Inc.*,[41] the court held:

> [I]t is clear both from the contract here as well as from the deposition testimony … that the employees of USA-One were at Sharpsburg Manor for the benefit of [the owner]. We are unpersuaded by the plaintiffs' … that USA-One voluntarily assumed a duty to protect them. Here, the fact that the gate attendants patrolled the grounds of Sharpsburg Manor "more frequently" after the second assault is insufficient to establish that USA-One undertook to protect the residents of the apartment complex.[42]

Another locale of heightened interest to the security industry, at least in matters of duty and foreseeability, is the commercial parking lot. Tortious, as well as criminal, conduct is more commonly witnessed in these facilities. A landowner or commercial property owner has a duty to "take affirmative action to control the wrongful acts of third persons which threaten invitees where the [owner] has reasonable cause to anticipate such acts and the probability of injury resulting therefrom."[43] Such affirmative action would seem to mean that the owner or possessor of a parking facility should take reasonable security measures, such as adequate lighting and the presence of security guards, and, if practical, additional measures, such as strategically placed television cameras or alarm systems, warnings, and the availability of escort services.[44]

[33] Negligence & Foreseeability: Doctrine of Law or Public Policy (1999) at http://www.supremecourt.tas.gov.au/__data/assets/pdf_file/0003/53760/Negligence99.pdf, last accessed August 27, 2016.
[34] Murros v. Daniels, 364 S.E.2d 392 (N.C. 1988).
[35] 532 So. 2d 1348 (Fla. App. 1988).
[36] Satchwell v. LaQuinta Motor Inn. Inc., 532 So. 2d 1348, 1350 (Fla. App. 1988).
[37] 997 F. Supp. 611 (N.J. 1998).
[38] Butler v. Acme Markets, Inc., 445 A.2d 1141, 1143 (N.J. 1982).
[39] Goldberg v. Housing Auth. of the City of Newark, 186 A.2d 291, 293 (N.J. 1962) quoting Butler v. Acme Markets, Inc., 445 A.2d 1141, 1148 (N.J. 1982).
[40] Abraham v. Raso, 997 F. Supp. 611, 613 (N.J. 1998).
[41] 595 So. 2d 867 (Ala. 1992).
[42] *Ibid.* at 871–872.
[43] Taylor v. Centennial Bowl, Inc., 416 P.2d 793 (Cal. 1966).
[44] C.S. Parnell, Tort Liability of Owner or Operator of Public Parking Facility, 46 Am. Jur. Trials 17–18 (1993).

5.2.3 Negligence, personnel, and the security manager/director

The analysis of negligence and its impact on security practice from a managerial point of view is an exercise worth serious energy. Negligent behavior on the part of lower-echelon security personnel can give rise to multiple causes of action, both individually and vicariously.[45] More telling is the negligent behavior of management and policy makers of security companies. Supervision, training, personnel, policy making, and performance standards are the primary responsibility of security managers and the failure to carry out these professional obligations competently is a fertile ground for negligence actions.

The security industry's costs of poor human relations and personnel practices are significant, and in hiring, supervision, and discipline, the industry needs to take its responsibility seriously.[130] "Private security companies or businesses which hire their own security forces should exercise great care in choosing security employees."[46] Hiring an individual without investigation of their background or improper placement of an individual in a position that requires higher levels of expertise than the applicant possesses is a possible negligence case. In *Easly v. Apollo Detective Agency*,[47] the court found a security guard company negligent in the hiring of a security guard entrusted with a pass key for an apartment building. "Such negligence usually consists of hiring, supervising, retaining, or assigning the employee with the knowledge of his unfitness, or failing to use reasonable care to discover the unfitness, and is based upon the negligence of the employer to a third person entirely independent of the liability of the employer under the doctrine of *respondeat superior*."[48] While on duty, the security guard entered, without license or privilege, a tenant's quarters with criminal intent. "The evidence showed that the company did not check any of the prior addresses or personal references listed by the guard on his application, nor did it require the guard to take any intelligence or psychological tests."[49] A company that appoints or hires an individual should be assured not only of competence, but of personal character too.[50] In *Violence in the Medical Care Setting*, hospital administrators are urged to not only carefully select, but also adequately train all security personnel.

Preemployment testing and evaluation, postemployment training and evaluation and adequate supervision corresponding to carefully drafted guidelines and policies are the new protective shields. Failure to take these minimal precautions in the highly explosive medical care environment leaves the employee, the negligent supervisor, and the entity facing liability unnecessarily.[51]

The entire company, its employees, and responsible policy makers must deal with the quality of employees. Employees should be enlisted to assure a safe, secure workplace inhabited by safe and secure personnel. "From the mail room to the executive suite, successful security awareness programs leave their mark. Once a luxury, awareness programs are evolving as a necessity to help curb security's high costs. Changing workplace demographics call for awareness training at all employee ranks."[52]

5.2.3.1 Negligent retention

When security management knows that present employees are professionally inept but willingly chooses to retain despite the employee flaws, the argument of negligent retention has legitimate merit. Case law and common sense dictate that retention of any troubled employee inevitably leads to larger problems for the firm and the client served.

Like negligent hiring, the courts have found liability under a theory of negligent retention when employers know or should have known, in the exercise of ordinary care, that their employees had violent tendencies. Employees with a history of sexual offenses, such as rape and sodomy, prompt strict scrutiny of the negligent retention. In addition, employees with checkered histories that include convictions of theft, larceny, embezzlement, and extortion are all

---

[45] See T. Anderson, Legal Reporter, 43 *Sec. Mgmt.* 115 (1999).

[46] Bilek et al. at 164 (1980); Aitchison, *supra* note 27.

[47] 587 N.E.2d 1241 (Ill. App. 2 Dist. 1979); see also Stein v. Burns International, 430 N.E.2d 334 (Ill. App. 1981).

[48] P. Carter, Employer's Liability for Assault, Theft, or Similar Intentional Wrong Committed by Employee at Home or Business or Customer, 13 A.L.R.5th 217, 230.

[49] Security Guard Company's Liability for Negligent Hiring, Supervision, Retention or Assignment of Guard, 44 A.L.R.4th 620; see also Association News, 19 *Sec. World* 69 (1982).

[50] Dyer, Murrell, & Wright, Training for Hospital Security: An Alternative to Training Negligence Lawsuits, *Violence in the Medical Care Setting, A Survival Guide* 7 (J.T. Turner, ed., 1984); see also Kirschenbaum, Security Companies Are Liable for Their Employees, 24 *Sec. Mgmt* 36 (1984).

[51] Dyer et al. at 9.

[52] B. Moss, Security Awareness at Work 28 Sec. 35 (1991).

prime candidates for a claim of negligent retention when offenses occur at the work location. Any employee with a propensity for violence should not be a candidate for employment without a risk.[53]

Any personnel program must comprehensively examine the background of any prospective employees by the analysis of these variables:

- Identification information
- Records of conviction
- Proof of civil actions and other litigation
- Credit and financial history
- Educational records
- Neighborhood information
- Personal and business references
- Previous and current employment
- Opinions of previous and current employers
- Their financial data[54]

When security employees engage in misconduct, the company should give notice to the employer, specifying the exact nature of the misdeed. See Figure 5.1.[55]

If wrongful behavior persists, a warning formalizing future consequences for the said behavior is warranted. See Figure 5.2.

If all corrective steps are futile, a discipline and/or termination report assures a significant record in the event of a challenge based on wrongful termination. Any legal action asserted by a third party for negligence in the handling of personnel can be rebutted by the due diligence these documents memorialize. See Figure 5.3.

5.2.3.2 Negligent assignment and entrustment

As personnel histories unfold, security firms can err in judgment at various stages: first, at initial hiring; second, at continued retention even when aware of employee problems as severe as criminal backgrounds; and finally, at the assignment and reassignment stage knowing fully well that the assignment may cause difficulties for others. Once put on notice of employee problems, the employer should take remedial steps to assure that the employee is not assigned to any position or delegated tasks likely to create conflicts. With this knowledge, the employer will be negligent since he or she foreseeably knows the nature of the employee and realizes the real injury is likely. In *Williams v. The Brooklyn District Telephone Company*,[56] the security company was held liable for assigning a guard to a sensitive position that allowed easy access to larcenable items. "Rejecting the company's contention that it was not liable for the guard's theft because his act was outside the course and scope of his employment, the court held that the company was bound to exercise reasonable care in the selection of its guards and therefore could not be permitted to say that it had no responsibility for the unlawful acts of its guards."[57]

Allegations of negligence have even greater credibility when the claimant can demonstrate actual knowledge on the part of security management or administration. Assigning security officers who suffer from a bona fide alcohol or drug problem constitutes a negligent assignment or entrustment case.[58] The U.S Court of Appeals, Fifth Circuit, issued a strongly wording ruling in *Aetna v. Pendelton Detectives*,[59] where a company's substandard performance

---

[53] Carter at 231–232.

[54] Nemeth at 307.

[55] E.T. Guy, J.J. Merrigan, Jr., & J.A. Wanat, *Forms for Safety and Security Management* 34 (1981).

[56] 33 N.Y.S. 849 (1895).

[57] Security Guard Company's Liability at 629; Aitchison; V.E. Kappeler, S.F. Kappeler, & R.V. del Carmen, A Content Analysis of Police Civil Liability Cases: Decisions of the Federal District Courts, 1978–1990 (1993).

[58] Walters at 80; J. Maahs & C. Hemmens, Train in Vain: A Statutory Analysis of Security Guard Training Requirements 22 *Internat'l J. Comp. and Applied Crim. J.* 91–101 (1998).

[59] 182 F.3d 376 (5th Cir. 1999).

EMPLOYEE MISCONDUCT NOTICE

DATE:

TO PERSONNEL DEPARTMENT:

Time:

Name of Employee _____ No._____ Dept. _____

    The above-named employee has displayed the following misconduct, and has been warned that this miscon-
duct will be entered on his Personnel Record.

MISCONDUCT (Check where applicable and specify details in section indicated below)

Smoking in Restricted Areas	_____
Leaving Work Without Permission	_____
Violation of Safety Rules or Dept. Rules	_____
Refusal to Carry Out Supervisor's Instructions	_____
Irregular Attendance	_____
(Specify No. of absences to date)	
Violation of Eating Regulations	_____
Breakage	_____
Poor Service	_____
General Inefficiency	_____
a. Quality	_____
b. Quantity	_____
c. Accuracy	_____
Discourtesy Toward Guest	_____
Discourtesy Toward Fellow Employee	_____

_____

(Employee)

_____

(Union Representative)

_____

(Employer)

(Mention other Employee)

Attitude	_____
Carelessness	_____
Other	_____

Specify Misconduct in Detail _____

_____

_____

EMPLOYEE COMMENTS _____

_____

_____

DISCIPLINARY ACTION TAKEN _____

Signature of Supervisor

(Reprimand) (Layoff) (Other)

I acknowledge receipt of this notice

_____

Signature of Employee

Figure 5.1 Employee misconduct notice.

severely impacted a package delivery company. Indeed, the unprofessional security services caused the firm to fail in its core operations. Security was to assure delivery although the lack of it assured failure. The court objectively listed a series of variables that proved the negligent assignment.

Merchants presented the following evidence of Pendleton's negligent security practices: (1) guards slept on the job; (2) guards watched TV on the job; (3) guards drank on the job; (4) guards entertained guests of the opposite sex

WARNING NOTICE

SECURITY DEPARTMENT

Employee: Department: Date:

Rule(s) Violated: _____

_____

Details of Violation: On_____

                     Date(s)

_____

_____

Immediate satisfactory improvement must be shown and maintained of further disciplinary action will be taken.

Action to be Taken: ____Suspension   ____Days   ____Discharge

                 ____Warning   ____Final Warning

Supervisor   Date   Employee   Date

Sign Here   Sign Here

If Employee Refuses to Sign:

"This is to certify that the employee named in this report was warned by his superior in my presence concerning the subject matter contained therein."

If Employee Refuses to Accept Copy of Form:

"Employee refuses to accept his copy of this warning notice."

Witness: _____ Date: _____ Supervisor: _____ Date: _____

Figure 5.2 Security department employee warning notice.

on the job; (5) guards left the gate to the warehouse open; (6) Pendleton's admission of failing to perform sufficient background checks on its guards; (7) the private investigator's conclusion that night shift employees were responsible for the losses; (8) several of Merchants' night shift employees' confessions to stealing large amounts of food; (9) Pendleton's contractual obligation to provide security from 4 p.m. to 8 a.m. and 24 hours a day on weekends; (10) Merchants' repeated reports of suspected employee theft to Pendleton; (11) the report of a person wearing a Pendleton baseball cap selling Merchants' products from the trunk of his car; and (12) Merchants' security expert's testimony that it was more probable than not that Pendleton's lax security practices caused the losses.[60] Few cases as clearly edify the principle of negligent assignment as *Aetna*.

5.2.3.3 Negligent supervision

Once hired and assigned, security managers have a continuing obligation to exercise a duty of due care relative to employee development and performance. A security company is vicariously liable for the actions of its employees,

---

[60] *Ibid.* at 378.

DISCIPLINE AND TERMINATION FORM

1. Are there written rules or guidelines of conduct?   ____Yes   ____No

2. When and how are employees informed of employer rules? _____
_____

3. Who is responsible for enforcing these rules?
_____

4. Do persons responsible for enforcing rules have any power when determining the disciplinary penalty imposed once offense has occurred?   ____Yes ____No

5. Is there progressive discipline procedures?   ____Yes ____No

6. How are managers/supervisors informed of the disciplinary procedure of an employee?
_____

7. How and when are employees made aware of the disciplinary procedure?
_____

8. Are disciplinary decisions made by supervisors reviewed?   ____Yes   ____No

9. How and when are employees informed of a decision of a disciplinary action?
_____

10. Prior to being disciplined, is an employee given an opportunity to present his/her explanation?   ____Yes ____No

11. Are employees given the opportunity to discuss the reasons for disciplinary actions?
          ____Yes   ____No

If yes, please explain.
_____

12. Are employees allowed to appeal disciplinary actions?   ____Yes   ____No

If yes, please explain the appeal procedure.
_____

13. Is an employee who is being investigated, permitted to have a person of his/her choice present at the investigation or negotiation meeting?   ____Yes ____No   If yes, are there exceptions?
_____

14. If an employee receives more than one warnings or negative evaluations, are any of the following measures taken to remedy the problem: ____Yes   ____No

   a. Vertical transfer to place the employee in a position more closely suited to his/her abilities?   ____Yes   ____No

   b. Lateral transfer to reduce personality conflicts between the employee and supervisor or between the employee and workers?   ____Yes   ____No

   c. Additional employee job training?   ____Yes   ____No

   d. Other?   ____Yes   ____No

15. Who is responsible for the termination process?
_____

16. What is the procedure for documenting disciplinary decisions?
_____

17 .Is age or race ever used as a factor in a termination decision?   ____Yes   ____No

If yes, explain its use.
_____

18.Is sex ever used as a factor in a termination decision?   ____Yes   ____ No

If yes, explain its use.
_____

Figure 5.3 Discipline and termination form.   (*Continued*)

19. Is a terminated employee allowed to appeal to a higher-level manager of panel of officials?   ____Yes ____No

If yes, please explain the procedure.

_____

20. Are employees given a written notice of termination?   ____Yes ____No

21. When are terminated employees given a final paycheck?

_____

22. Are terminated employees eligible for severance pay?   ____Yes ____No

23. Are exit interviews conducted?   ____Yes ____No

By whom? _____

24. Are records maintained of all disciplinary actions?   ____Yes ____No

25. If yes, what records maintained and where.

_____

26. Are copies of warnings and terminations placed in the Employee's personnel file?

____Yes ____No

27. Do warnings contain the following:

a. Offense   ____Yes ____No

b. Action necessary for improvement ____Yes ____No

c. Consequences of failure to improve ____Yes ____No

Figure 5.3   (Continued) Discipline and termination form.

and a lack of supervision creates a presumption of negligence. Wayne Saiat, editorial director for *Security World Magazine*,[61] highlights the severe problem caused by a lack of supervision.

> Although security personnel and their employers can be subjected to legal action for a wide variety of causes, the vast majority of cases involve the action or inaction of security guards. But the suits generally do not name only a guard as a defendant; they will often name the guard's supervisor, the guard company, if one is involved, and the ultimate employer of the guard and the guard's company.[62]

Supervision takes on added importance when complicated by the temptations of technology. In *National Labor Relations Board v. J. Weingarten*,[63] the court fluently assessed the need for heightened supervision when security machinery is in use.

> There has been a recent growth of sophisticated techniques—such as closed circuit television, undercover security agents and lie detectors—to monitor and investigate the employees' conduct at their place of work. These techniques increase, not only the employees feeling of apprehension but also their need for experienced assistance in dealing with them.[64]

A failure to supervise or manage can be management's failure to hire sufficient personnel, to insufficiently or improperly train secondary managerial employees, or a failure to allot sufficient time and energy to train employees for appropriate tasks.

5.2.3.4 Negligent training

The final theory under the negligence umbrella is negligent training. Sophisticated training, hopefully, will upgrade the quality and efficacy of security personnel. Critics have long argued that training presently required is superficial

[61] Saiat at 23; Aitchison.
[62] Saiat at 24; Ross at 169–193; Maahs & Hemmens at 91–101.
[63] 420 U.S. 251 (1975).
[64] NLRB v. J. Weingarten, Inc., 420 U.S. 251, 265 at fn. 10 (1975).

rather than substantive and the industry needs greater dedication to training. In *Training, The Key to Avoiding Liability*, the essential nature of training is espoused:

> The bottom line then is this: Your security officers must be adequately trained. Moreover, the training they receive must be sufficiently practical to enable them to demonstrate technical and legal competency commensurate with the duties they perform. Classroom theory is fine, but it isn't enough. Academics should be combined with performance exercises so that officers can try out and become confident with the techniques they may be required to use.[65]

The security industry's response to education and training has been less than enthusiastic and often more rhetoric than substance. While some strides are being made, industry foot dragging and a lack of legislative uniformity or standards influence the rigor and intensity of training. Saiat argues that security malpractice is on the horizon. While negligence implies a duty, malpractice implies reliance on the duty. Negligence implies a failure to perform with reasonable care; malpractice implies a failure to perform to a higher standard of care.[66] And this lack of training is quite evident in the use of arms and dangerous instrumentalities where the degree of care and professionalism rises dramatically in the assessment of negligence. As a result, there is a natural expectation that sufficient training occurs before any security officer becomes armed.[67]

Certain professional groups, such as American Society for Industrial Security (ASIS) International, have called for certification programs, like the Certified Protection Program (CPP) and the Certified Protection Officer (CPO). Security liability has given impetus to a host of educational delivery systems in the private sector, what is referred to as "niche" training. Some examples are:

Orleans Regional Security Institute, New Orleans, Louisiana

- Semiautomatic pistol training
- Basic revolver handgun training
- Security training course
- CCP course
- Basic investigator
- Advanced investigator
- Psychological stress evaluation training

Sandia National Laboratories, Albuquerque, New Mexico

- Physical protection systems training course

Bob Bondurant Security Services Division, Phoenix, Arizona

- Drivers training programs in antiterrorist/executive protection
- Advanced antiterrorist driving course
- Motorcycle training course[68]

ASIS International has also posed standards and guidelines for educational programs, which in turn ensure uniform preparedness and skills acquisition, something crucially necessary when defining acceptable or normative standards of professional conduct.[69]

5.2.4 Strict liability torts

While intentional torts require a mental decision to act, defendants in cases of strict liability are held accountable regardless of their intentions. The act, in and of itself, is deemed serious enough to cause absolute, unconditional

---

[65] Ross at 169–193; Maahs & Hemmens at 91–101.
[66] Saiat at 25; Ross at 169–193; Jeff & Craig.
[67] To Arm or Not to Arm Security Officers: A Complex Issue, 35 *Sec. Mgmt* 77 (1998).
[68] Note, Officer Liability Spurs Niche Training, 29 Sec. 69 (1992).
[69] W.B. Hanewicz, New ASIS Program Guidelines—A Preview, *J. Sec. Admin. & Pri. Police* 37–46 (1978).

liability without mental intent. The burden of proof in strict liability cases is less rigorous than its negligence or intentional tort counterparts since the act alone suffices for liability. Certain types of activities, for public policy reasons, qualify for strict liability coverage. If an action is inherently dangerous, like explosives or wild animals, a tort claim needs no proof of intentionality. In the case of products, there is a body of strict liability case law. The elements of a strict liability case include

1. That there be a seller of a product or service
2. That the product is unreasonably dangerous to person and property
3. That a user or a consumer suffers physical harm
4. That there be causation

Strict liability law is plainly in its infancy stage when applied to the security industry and its practices. Any ultra-hazardous action like the use of ballistics, explosives, underwater gear, and/or injuries caused by wild, undomesticated, and uncontrollable animals would qualify. Outside of the ballistics and explosives area, there has been little litigation in the security industry.[70] One exception to this general rule is that strict liability may be imposed on security interests that operate by a "certificate of authority" issued by the state or other governmental entity.[71] "This means that such a private security company will be held liable for the acts of its employees regardless of whether the employee's acts were negligent or intentional as long as the acts were committed while the employee was actually on the job."[72] Alarm companies and other electronically sophisticated enterprises do have to consider the defensive or hazardous propensities of their products.

5.2.4.1 Negligence and vicarious liability

Depending on the nature of a relationship, certain persons will be responsible or legally accountable for another's specific act or form of behavior even if they have not acted, solicited, or conspired in the action. To be responsible through another is to be vicariously responsible. By vicarious liability, the principal—characteristically an employer, a security supervisor, or a management team—having the right to govern, supervise, manipulate, and control the action of employees or agents, can be held accountable for the agent's actions. This legal relationship has sometimes been characterized as a master–servant relationship governed by the doctrine of *respondeat superior* (let the master answer).[73] Under the doctrine of *respondeat superior*, an employer is liable for injuries to the person or property of third persons resulting from the acts of his employee, which, although not directly authorized or ratified by the employer, are incidental to the class of acts that the employee is hired to perform and are within the scope of his employment. Under the doctrine, the law imputes to the employer that act of the employee. Although employers have been held liable under this doctrine for the intentional and criminal acts of their employees under some circumstances, the viability of the doctrine is somewhat limited because intentional and criminal actions generally are not within an employee's scope of employment and usually are not committed at the request of or with the approval of an employer.[74] "The importance of this determination results from the general rule that a master is liable for the torts of his servants committed within the scope of a servant's employment, whereas the hirer of an independent contractor is ordinarily not liable for the torts of a contractor committed in carrying out work under the contract."[75]

Much of the security industry can be divided into these two classifications: employer/employee and independently contracted services. One might also argue there is a hybrid model, whereby the public police officer moonlights or assumes the role of the private security officer in an off-duty capacity. This brings some special legal challenges.[76]

Contract firms are hired by private companies or corporations to provide security services. The economic and legal advantages in contract services are many, since the company is not responsible for hiring, firing, tax liability, or

---

[70] See generally Annotation, Liability of One Contracting for Private Police of Security Service for Acts of Personnel Supplied, 38 A.L.R.3d 1332; Annotation, Liability of Hiring Private Investigator or Detective for Tortious Acts Committed in Course of Investigation, 75 A.L.R.3d 1175.

[71] *Ill. Rev. Stat.* Ch. 11 §2622 (10).

[72] Products Liability: Modern Cases Determining Whether Product Is Defectively Designed, 96 A.L.R.3d 22.

[73] See generally Principal's Liability for False Arrest or Imprisonment Caused by Agent or Servant, 92 A.L.R.2d 15; Brill, The Liability of an Employer for the Willful Torts of His Servants, 45 *Chic. - Kent. L. Rev.* 1 (1968); Liability of One Hiring Private Detective, 13 A.L.R.3d 1175.

[74] Carter at 229.

[75] Hiring Private Detective at 1178.

[76] J.C. Trimble, The Hazards of Hiring-Duty Police, *Sec. Mgmt* 65 (February 1993).

any other administrative or procedural matters governing the security force. What type of workplace climate that employer provides bears on the question of liability.[77] In other words, the employer is generally only subject to an employee's misconduct when foreseeable and within the scope of the employee's responsibilities. Couple tortious conduct with poor management, and cases of civil liability are assured, but any conclusion as to liability will depend upon reasonableness or unreasonableness of the employer oversight and supervision of the security personnel.[78]

Bruce Harman lays out the types of business climate that indubitably lead to individual and vicarious liability:

- Failure to support elementary security and audit procedures
- Lack of climate for security and control consciousness
- Inept or complacent management without feedback to measure losses
- Inadequate implementation of plans and/or personnel and training procedures
- Dishonest management[79]

The assumption that the independent contractor status will hold harmless the employer from potential liability under either civil or criminal liability may be premature. By hiring independent contractors, employers hope to "convey all potential liability to the contract security company and to protect the security manager against joinder in a civil action that could arise out of a negligent or wrongful act by the security contractor."[80] However, while generally true, there are numerous exceptions to the rule:

1. Independent contractor status will not be upheld if the employer ratifies specific conduct.
2. Independent contractor status will not shield the employer from intentional torts.
3. Independent contractor status will not relieve the employer from strict liability tortious conduct.
4. Independent contractor status will not provide a defense to the employer if the duty is nondelegable.[81]

The doctrine of *respondeat superior*, the basic principles of agency, and the common law standard on master–servant relationship make unlikely an employer's complete insulation and isolation from legal responsibility for the acts of employees or independent contractors. Whether the security operative's actions, tortious or not, are within the scope of his or her employment is a seminal question in the imposition of vicarious liability. In *Sunshine Security & Detective Agency v. Wells Fargo Armored Services Corp.*,[82] a bank security guard robbed his employer. "The employee's tortious actions in conspiring to rob the bank he was hired by the defendant agency to guard, the court said, represented a classic case of an employee acting outside the scope of his employment."[83] Whether the relationship exists "depends on the particular facts of each case."[84]

Case law conservatively construes the definition of an independent contractor. The American Law Institute sought to distinguish an employee from an independent contractor by considering the following factors:

a. The extent of control which, by agreement, the master may exercise over the details of the work;
b. Whether or not the one employed is engaged in a distinct occupation or business;
c. The kind of occupation with reference to whether, in the locality, the work is usually done under the direction of the employer or by a specialist without supervision;
d. The skill required in the particular occupation;
e. Whether the employer or the workman supplies the instrumentalities, tools, and the place for the person doing the work;

---

[77] Howard v. J.H. Harvey Co., Inc., 521 S.E.2d 691 (Ga. App. 1999).

[78] See L.M. Gatdula & T.G. Gattoni, How to Win Vicariously: An Old Legal Theory Offers a New Defense, 46 *Sec. Mgmt* 52 (2002).

[79] J. Chuvala, Boss on Board: Get Your CEO Involved, 28 Sec. 19 (1991).

[80] See generally Ross at 169–193: Maahs & Hemmens.

[81] See generally Liability for Acts of Security Guards, 38 A.L.R.3d 1332; see also as to ratification: Dillon v. Sears-Roebuck Co., 235 N.W. 331 (Neb. 1934).

[82] 496 So. 2d 246 (Fla. App. 1986).

[83] Carter at 272.

[84] Moorehead v. District of Columbia, 747 A.2d 138 (D.C. 2000).

f.   The length of time for which the person is employed;

g.   The method of payment, whether by the time or by the job;

h.   Whether or not work is a part of the regular business of the employer;

i.   Whether or not the parties believe they are creating the relation of master/servant; and

j.   Whether the principal is or is not in business.[85]

In *Safeway Stores v. Kelley*,[86] a supermarket chain denied all liability for an abusive arrest process claiming that its guard service contract could only be characterized as an independent contractor relationship.

Determining whether a security agency is independent largely depends upon who controls the operation. In *Cappo v. Vinson Guard Service Inc.*,[87] a Louisiana court denied independent contractor status in an intentional battery case. Actions by the employer were largely imputed to by the conduct of the restaurant manager who:

1. Periodically checked on parking lot as part of his duties;

2. Told security agent who to admit and exclude from parking lot;

3. Had authority to replace security guard with other personnel; and

4. Had exercised his authority over security agent on night of incident by sending security agent home; in addition, trial court noted that security agent's activities during performance of his duties benefited restaurant as well.[88]

5.3 CRIMINAL LIABILITY AND THE PRIVATE SECURITY INDUSTRY

While civil liability problems are natural risks in the security industry, the panorama of liability extends beyond the civil realm and into the criminal context. While the term "liability" is acceptable in criminal settings, the more accurate term might be culpability. In short, how can and how does the security operative become responsible for and culpable under criminal constructions? Can the security industry, as well as its individual personnel, suffer criminal culpability? Can security personnel, in both a personal and professional capacity, commit crimes? Are security corporations, businesses, and industrial concerns capable of criminal infraction or can these entities be held criminally liable for the conduct of employees? Are there other criminal concerns, either substantive or procedural, that the security industry should be vigilant about?

As the privatization of once historic criminal justice functions continue, corresponding civil and criminal liability questions will remain and even accelerate. Security professionals engage the public in so many settings and circumstances that it is a sure bet that criminal conduct will be witnessed.

5.3.1 Criminal liability under the federal civil rights acts

While security operatives may directly act in a criminal manner, or either aid or abet others, or even neglect duties and responsibilities, resulting in liability based upon omission, their particular actions, under diverse statutory and codified laws may give rise to criminal culpability. In the area of the federal *Civil Rights Act*, the prosecutorial authority has the latitude to charge a criminal action. While the majority of litigation and actions under 42 U.S.C. § 1983 have been, and continue to be, civil in design and scope, Congress has enacted legislation that attaches criminal liability for persons or other legal entities acting under color of state law, ordinance, or regulation who are:

1. Willfully depriving any inhabitant of a state of any right, privilege or immunity protected by the Constitution or the Laws of the United States, or

2. Willfully subjecting any inhabitant to a different punishment or penalty because such an inhabitant is an alien because of his race or color, then as prescribed for the punishment of citizen[89]

---

[85] Restatement 2d of Agency §220 (2) (1958).

[86] 448 A.2d 856 (D.C. 1982).

[87] 400 So. 2d 1148 (La. App. 1981).

[88] *Ibid*.

[89] 18 U.S.C. §242 (2010); see also Center for Criminal Justice, *Private Police Training Manual* (1985); R.V. del Carmen & D.L. Carter, An Overview of Civil and Criminal Liabilities of Police Officers, *Pol. Chief* (August 1985), at 46; see generally M.S. Vaughn & L.F. Coomers, Police Civil Liability under Section 1983: When Do Police Officers Act under Color of Law? 23 *J. Crim. Justice* 395–415 (1995).

While criminal liability can be grounded within the statutory framework, advocates of this liability must still pass the statutory and judicial threshold question, that is, whether or not the processes and functions of private justice can be arguably performed under "color of state law." As discussed previously, either the state action or the color of state law advocacy requires evidential proof of private action metamorphosing into a public duty or function or of governmental authorities depriving a citizen of certain constitutional rights.

Criminal liability can also be imposed under the federal *Civil Rights Act* if, and when, a victim of illegal state action shows that the injurious action was the product of a conspiracy. The relevant provision as to conspiracy states:

1. A conspiracy by two or more persons;
2. For the purposes of injuring, oppressing, threatening or intimidating any citizen in the free exercise or enjoyment or past exercise of any right or privilege secured to him by the Constitution or laws of the United States.[90]

Various factual scenarios illustrate this statutory application:

- Public police and private security personnel are engaged in a joint venture, cooperative effort, or alliance.
- Public police solicit, request, entice, or encourage the activity of private law enforcement interests, knowing fully well their activity is not legally sound.
- State officials, administrative heads, and agency policy makers hire, contract, or otherwise utilize the services of a private entity they know will make possible constitutional violations.

In sum, the pressing crossover question in the world of private security still remains whether or not private justice agents can be held to public scrutiny.

5.3.2 Criminal liability and the regulatory process

Since the private security industry is subject to the regulatory oversight of governmental authorities, there is always a chance that criminal culpability will rest or reside in the failure to adhere to particular guidelines. A repetitive theme originating with the RAND Study,[91] through the National Advisory Committee on Criminal Justice Standards and Goals, to the recent *Hallcrest Report II*, is the need for regulations, standards, education and training, and qualifications criteria for the security industry.[92] The National Advisory Committee further relates:

> Incidents of excessive force, false arrests and detainment, illegal search and seizure, impersonation of a public officer, trespass, invasion of privacy, and dishonest or unethical business practices not only undermine confidence and trust in the private security industry, but also infringe upon individual rights.[93]

In short, the Commission recognizes that part of the security professional's measure has to be the avoidance of every criterion of crime and criminality. The regulatory and administrative processes involving licensure infer a police power to punish infractions of the promulgated standards.

A recent Arizona case, *Landi v. Arkules*,[94] delivers some eloquent thoughts on why licensing and regulation are crucial policy considerations. In declaring a New York security firm's contracts illegal due to a lack of compliance, the court related firmly:

> The statute imposes specific duties on licensees with respect to the confidentiality and accuracy of information and the disclosure of investigative reports to the client.[95] A license may be suspended or revoked for a wide range of misconduct, including acts of dishonesty or fraud, aiding the violation of court order, or soliciting business for an attorney.[96]

---

[90] 18 U.S.C. §241 (2010).

[91] J.S. Kakalik & S. Wildhorn, *Private Police in the United States: Findings and Recommendations* (1971).

[92] Report of The Task Force on Private Security National Advisory Committee on Criminal Justice Standards and Goals (1976). See also W.C. Cunningham, J.J. Strauchs, & C.W. Vanmeter, *Private Security Trends 1970 to 2000: The Hallcrest Report* 322 (1990).

[93] Report of The Task Force at 121; see also H.E. Barrineau, *Civil Liability in Criminal Justice* (2nd ed. 1994); K.K. Russell, *The Color of Crime* (1998).

[94] 835 P.2d 458 (Ariz. App. 1992).

[95] A.R.S. § 32-2425 (2010).

[96] A.R.S. § 32-2427 (2010).

The Legislature's concern for the protection of the public from unscrupulous and unqualified investigators is woven into the legislative or regulatory intent of these controls. This concern for the public's protection precludes enforcement of an unlicensed investigator's fee contract.[97] The courts will not participate in a party's circumvention of the legislative goal by enforcing a fee contract to provide regulated services without a license.[98] Hence, security professionals may incur criminal liability for failure to adhere to regulatory guidelines. States have not been shy about this sort of regulation. A California statute prohibiting the licensure of any investigator or armed guard who has a criminal conviction in the last 10 years was upheld.[99] A Connecticut statute for criminal conviction was deemed overly broad.[100]

As states and other governmental entities legislate standards of conduct and requirements criteria in the field of private security, the industry itself has not been averse to challenging the legitimacy of the regulations. Antagonists to the regulatory process urge a more privatized, free-market view and balk at efforts to impose criminal or civil liability for failure to meet or exceed statutory, administrative, or regulatory rules and guidelines.[101] Given the minimal intrusion inflicted upon the security industry by governmental entities, and the industry's own professional call for improvement of standards, litigation challenging the regulatory process should be used only in exceptional circumstances. The repercussions and ramifications for failure to adhere to the minimal regulatory standards are varied, ranging from fines, revocation, and suspension to actual imprisonment.

In *State v. Guardsmark*,[102] the court rejected the security defendant's contention that denial of licenses tended to be an arbitrary exercise. The court, accepting the statute's stringent licensure requirements and recognizing the need for rigorous investigation of applicants and testing, found no basis to challenge.[103] In *Guardsmark*, the crime cited under Illinois law was "engaging in business as a detective agency without a license."[104] Similarly, *State v. Bennett*[105] held the defendant liable in a prosecution for "acting as a detective without first having obtained a license."[106]

The fact that a security person, business, or industrial concern is initially licensed and granted a certificate of authority to operate does not ensure absolute tenure. Governmental control and administrative review of security personnel and agencies are ongoing processes. Revocation of a license or a certificate to operate has been regularly upheld in appellate reasoning. In *Taylor v. Bureau of Private Investigators and Adjustors*,[107] suspension of legal authority and license to operate as a private detective was upheld since the evidence clearly sustained a finding that the investigators perpetrated an unlawful entry into a domicile. The private detective's assertion that the regulation was constitutionally void because of its vagueness was rejected outright.[108]

In summary, it behooves the security industry to stick to the letter of regulatory process. Failure to do so can result in actual criminal convictions or a temporary or permanent intrusion on the right to operate.

5.3.3 Criminal acts: Felonies and misdemeanors by security professionals

Both corporations and individuals in the security industry may be convicted of actual criminal code violations, though in the former instance, this is an exceedingly rare event. This liability can attach either in an individual or vicarious sense. By *vicarious*, covered previously, we mean that the employer is responsible for the conduct of their employees. Most jurisdictions, however, do impose a higher burden of proof in a case of vicarious liability since "the prosecution must prove that the employer knowingly and intentionally aided, advised or encouraged the employee's

---

[97] Shorten v. Milbank, 11 N.Y.S.2d 387 (N.Y. Sup. 1939), aff'd 12 N.Y.S.2d 583 (1939).

[98] Landi, 835 P.2d at 467.

[99] Schanuel v. Anderson, 546 F. Supp. 519 (S.D. Ill. 1982), aff'd 708 F.2d 316 (C.A.7 Ill.).

[100] Smith v. Fussenich, 440 F. Supp. 1077 (D.C. Conn. 1977).

[101] See generally J.C. Williams, Regulation of Private Detectives, Private Investigations and Security Agencies, 86 A.L.R.3d 691 (2010); J. Maahs & C. Hemmens, Train in Vain: A Statutory Analysis of Security Guard Training Requirements, 22 *Int'l J. Comp. & Applied Crim. Just.* 91–101 (1998); Courses and Seminars, *Int'l Security Rev.*, November–December 1997, at 12.

[102] Guardsmark, 190 N.W.2d.

[103] See Williams.

[104] Guardsmark, 190 N.W.2d, at 399.

[105] 14 S.W. 565 (Mo. 1890).

[106] *Ibid.*

[107] 275 P.2d 579 (Cal. App. 1954).

[108] *Ibid.*; see also Donkin v. Director of Professional and Vocational Standards, 49 *Cal Rptr.* 495 (1966).

criminal conduct."[109] Other legal issues make difficult a prosecution against corporations for criminal behavior. A broad critique corporate criminal intent can be summarized as follows:

How can a corporation formulate specific or general intent, the mens rea necessary for a criminal conviction?

More particularly, in violent acts of criminality such as rape, murder, or robbery, to whom or on whose authority within the corporate structure would the responsibility lie?

Both queries pose difficult legal dilemmas. While it is common to hear a sort of class warfare critique of the corporate heads of state, this type of "them versus us" will simply not do. To be culpable requires knowledge of the crime and its purpose. In the evolving analysis of corporate crime, a trend toward corporate responsibility has emerged.[110] Does a corporate officer and director who has actual knowledge of criminal behavior on the part of subordinates within the corporation bear some level of responsibility? Is a corporation responsible, as principal, for the acts of its agents both civilly and criminally? While "officers may be held criminally responsible on the presumption that it authorized the illegal acts,"[111] that judgment will depend on the facts and circumstances of each case.

There are other rationales for imposing criminal culpability on the corporate officers and directors. Criminal charges are regularly brought forth and eventual liability sometimes imposed for failure to uphold the rules and regulatory standards promulgated by government agencies, such as

- Occupational Health and Safety Act (OSHA)
- The Food and Drug Administration (FDA)
- National Labor Relations Board (NLRB)
- Environmental Protection Act (EPA)
- Homeland Security Administration (HSA)
- National Transportation Safety Board (NTSB)

Government agencies are empowered to charge and assess criminal penalties and fines. OSHA is the classic federal agency with these sweeping powers. Other common corporate areas of criminality in business crime include securities fraud, antitrust activity, bank fraud, tax evasion, violations against the *Racketeer Influenced and Corrupt Organizations Act (RICO)*, and acts involving bribery, international travel, and business practices.[112] Finding corporations criminally responsible for particular actions is not the insurmountable task it once was.

The nature and functions of security practice provides a ripe ground for violations of the criminal law. Evaluate the common scenarios below:

Assault[113]

1. A security officer can easily create an apprehension of bodily harm in a detention case.[114]
2. A security officer, in a crowd control situation, threatens, by a gesture, a private citizen.[115]

---

[109] Schnabalk, The Legal Basis of Liability, Part II, 27 *Sec. Mgmt* 29 (1983). See also L. Friedman, In Defense of Corporate Criminal Liability, 23 *Harv. J. L. & Pub. Pol'y* 833 (2000); W.A. Simpson, Corporate Criminal Intent (August 5, 2009), available at http://ssrn.com/abstract=1444543; County of Santa Clara v Southern Pacific Railroad Company 118 U.S. 394 (1886); Arthur Andersen LLP v United States 544 U.S. 696 (2005); New York Cent. & H.R.R. Co. v. U.S., 212 U.S. 481 (1909); U.S. v. Bank of New England, N.A., 821 F.2d 844 (C.A.1 Mass. 1987).

[110] See W.T. Grant Co. v. Superior, 23 Cap. App. 3d 284 (1972); N.Y. Central & Hudson Railroad v. U.S., 212 U.S. 481 (1908); People v. Canadian Fur Trappers Corp., 161 N.E. 455 (N.Y. 1928); see generally S. Baccus-Lobel, Criminal Law 52 *S.M.U. L. Rev.* 881, 910–911 (1999); R.V. del Carmen, An Overview of Civil and Criminal Liabilities of Police Officers and Departments, 9 *Am. J. Crim. L.* 33 (1981); R.V. del Carmen, Civil and Criminal Liabilities of Police Officers, in *Police Deviance* (T. Barker & D.L. Carter eds., 1994); R.V. del Carmen & V.E. Kappeler, Municipal and Police Agencies as Defendants: Liability for Official Policy and Custom, 10 *Am J. Police* 1–17 (1991).

[111] A.J. Bilek, J.C. Klotter, & R.K. Federal, *Legal Aspects of Private Security* 144 (1980).

[112] Schnabalk, *supra* note 37.

[113] See C.P. Nemeth, *Criminal Law* 183–187 (2004); R.T. Weitkamp, Crimes and Offenses, 16 *Ga. St. U. L. Rev.* 72, 73 (1999); G.F. Taft & V.R. Gordon, Criminal Law (Legislative Survey—North Carolina), 21 *Campbell L. Rev.* 353, 353 (1999); K.D. Harries, *Serious Violence: Patterns of Homicide and Assault in America* (1990).

[114] For a representative statute, see Ga. Code Ann. § 16-5-20(2) (West 2010).

[115] See Model Penal Code § 211.1(c) (Proposed Official Draft 1962).

3. An industrial security agent, protecting the physical perimeter, unjustly accosts a person with license and privilege to be on the premises.[116]

Battery[117]

1. A security officer in a retail detention case offensively touches a suspected shoplifter.[118]

2. A security officer uses excessive force in the restraint of an unruly participant in a demonstration.[119]

3. A security officer utilizes excessive force to affect an arrest in an industrial location.[120]

False arrest or imprisonment[121]

1. A security officer, in a jurisdiction with no merchant's privilege, arrests without probable cause, and motivated by malice toward a particular suspect who is eventually acquitted.

2. A security officer restrains and detains a suspected shoplifter without probable cause.

3. A security officer restrains and detains a suspected intruder on an industrial premises and does so in an abusive and physically harmful manner.

Unlawful use of weapons

1. A security officer is not properly trained in the usage of weapons.

2. A security officer does not possess a license.

3. A security officer inappropriately utilizes weaponry best described as excessive force.

Theft[122]

1. Security personnel steal, take by deception, by fraud, or through simple unlawful acquisition property from their place of employment.

2. Security personnel aid and abet outside individuals in conducting an inside theft.

Manslaughter[123]

1. A security officer negligently drives an auto, which in turn kills either a pursued suspect or an innocent bystander.

2. A security officer handles his or her weaponry in a grossly negligent way, thereby causing a fatality.

3. A security officer reacts with excessive force in a property protection case causing the death of the suspect or an innocent bystander.

4. A security officer in hot pursuit shoots a fleeing felon and injures an innocent bystander.[124]

Murder[125]

1. A security officer kills another without proper investigation and with an extraordinary and wanton disregard of human life.

---

[116] See Ga. Code Ann. § 16-5-20(1) (West 2010); MPC at § 211.1(a).

[117] Also called "assault and battery" or "aggravated assault" in some jurisdictions.

[118] See State v. Humphries, 586 P.2d 130 (Wash. App. 1978).

[119] See MPC at §211.1(2).

[120] See *Ibid.*

[121] See Nemeth, *Criminal Law*, at 178–179. See also *Neb. Rev. Stat.* § 38-314 (2010); MPC, *supra* note 43, at § 212.3; 18 Pa. Cons. Stat. Ann. § 2903 (West 2010); *Colo. Rev. Stat.* § 18-3-303 (2010).

[122] See Nemeth, *Criminal Law*, at 254–263; Weitkamp at 73; Taft & Valeree at 353; J. Gibson, How Much Should Mind Matter? Mens Rea in Theft and Fraud Sentencing, 10 *Fed. Sentencing Rep.* 136, 137 (1997).

[123] See Nemeth, *Criminal Law*, at 128–132; see also P.K. Lattimore & C.A. Nahabedian, *The Nature of Homicide: Trends and Changes* (1997); M.E. Wolfgang, *Patterns in Criminal Homicide* (1975).

[124] J. Horder, Provocation and Responsibility (1992); J. Dressler, Provocation: Partial Justification or Partial Excuse?, 51 *Mod. L. Rev.* 467 (1988); J. Dressler, Rethinking Heat of Passion: A Defense in Search of a Rationale, 73 *J. Crim. L. & Criminology* 421 (1982); F. McAuley, Anticipating the Past: The Defense of Provocation in Irish Law, 50 *Mod. L. Rev.* 133 (1987); A. Von Hirsch & N. Jareborg, *Provocation and Culpability in Responsibility, Character, and the Emotions* 241 (Ferdinand Schoeman ed., 1987).

[125] See Nemeth, *Criminal Law*, at 115–128; see also F. Wharton, *Wharton's Criminal Law*, vol. 2 (C.E. Torcia ed., 15th ed. 1993); Baccus-Lobel, *supra* note 38, at 910–911; J.R. Snowden, Second Degree Murder, Malice, and Manslaughter in Nebraska: New Juice for an Old Cup, 76 *Neb. L. Rev.* 399, 410 (1997).

2. Private military mercenaries kill without justification or right in a war zone.[126]

Misprision

1. A security officer fails to report crimes or take actions necessary to prevent it.
2. Security personnel purposely conceal a major capital offense.

Compounding

1. A security officer makes a deal with a suspect in a theft or other criminal case for an agreement not to pursue the investigation.
2. A security officer decides not to cooperate, for internal or economic reasons, with the prosecutorial staff assigned to the case.

Solicitation[127]

1. Security officers or investigators entice, encourage, or solicit others to perform criminal acts.
2. A security officer or a private investigator encourages, solicits, or induces another to commit an illegal act for the purpose of acquiring a specific piece of evidence.
3. A security investigator devises a plan that will ensnare a criminal; however, such tactics or plan may be construed as a case of entrapment.[128]

Criminal conspiracy[129]

1. A security agent, investigator, or officer enters into an agreement with one or more individuals for the purposes of committing a criminal act such as internal theft.
2. A security officer engages in conduct or in concert with other business entities, which seek to illegally eavesdrop and investigate the personal backgrounds of prospective job applicants.
3. A security company, in concert with other business interests, perform polygraph examination on prospective applicants in direct violation of state law.
4. A security professional performs an overt act toward the commission of any crime that assists the principal perpetrator in effecting a successful criminal plan.[130]

The range and extent of individual security crime is only limited by the roles, tasks, and duties undertaken by the industry's participants.

5.3.3.1 Assault

Aside from theft actions, no other crime is as regularly witnessed by security officers than assault and battery. At common law, assault and battery were separate offenses, the former being a threat to touch or harm and the latter being the actual offensive touching. Most jurisdictions have merged the offenses, at least in a criminal context, though still distinguishing the offenses by severity and degree. The *Model Penal Code* (MPC) poses the following construction:

1. *Simple Assault.* A person is guilty of assault if he:
   a. Attempts to cause or purposely, knowingly or recklessly causes bodily injury to another; or
   b. Negligently causes bodily injury to another with a deadly weapon; or

---

[126] J.S. Thurnher, Drowning in Blackwater: How Weak Accountability over Private Security Contractors Significantly Undermines Counterinsurgency Efforts, 2008 *Army Law.* 64 (2008); C.S. Jordan, Who Will Guard the Guards? The Accountability of Private Military Contractors in Areas of Armed Conflict, 35 *N.E. J. Crim. & Civ. Con.* 309 (2009); O.R. Jones, Implausible Deniability: State Responsibility for the Actions of Private Military Firms, 24 *Conn. J. Int'l. L.* 239 (2009); G.F. Hackman, Lipping through the Cracks: Can We Hold Private Security Contractors Accountable for Their Actions Abroad?, 9 *Loy. J. Pub. Int. L.* 251 (2008).

[127] See Nemeth, *supra* note 41, at 377, 378–379; see also W.L. Clark & W.L. Marshall, *A Treatise on the Law of Crime* (6th ed 1958); People v. Burt, 288 P.2d 503 (Cal. 1955).

[128] Ex parte Moore, 356 U.S. 369 (1952).

[129] See Nemeth, *Criminal Law*, at 377, 385–391; J.F. Mcsorley, *Portable Guide to Federal Conspiracy Law: Developing Strategies for Criminal and Civil Cases* (1996).

[130] See Bilek et al. at 152; Sears v. U.S., 343 F 2d 139 (5th Cir. 1965); State v. St. Christopher, 232 N.W.2d 798 (Minn. 1975).

   c.   Attempts by physical menace to put another in fear of imminent serious bodily harm.

2. *Aggravated Assault.* A person is guilty of aggravated assault if he:

   a.   Attempts to cause serious bodily injury to another, or causes such injury purposely, knowingly or recklessly under circumstances manifesting extreme indifference to the value of human life; or

   b.   Attempts to cause or purposely or knowingly causes bodily injury to another with a deadly weapon.[131]

Most security specialists will encounter the crimes known as assault. Efforts to control crowds, secure buildings and installations, apprehend or detain a disgruntled employee, break up disputants in commercial establishments, and handle unruly and disgruntled shoppers in retail establishments, are ripe settings to encounter assailants.

Assault can be an extremely serious offense, particularly under the "aggravated" provision.[132] In fact, some jurisdictions have adopted reckless endangerment,[133] a new statutory design that describes even more severe conduct. See the example below:

3. A person acts recklessly with respect to a material element of an offense when he consciously disregards a substantial and unjustifiable risk that the material element exists or will result from his conduct.

The risk must be of such a nature and degree that, considering the nature and intent of the actor's conduct and the circumstances known to him, its disregard involves a gross deviation from the standard of conduct that a reasonable person would observe in the actor's situation.[134]

Assaults are now a recurring concern for security officers working in domestic and international terrorism. It behooves security policy makers and planners to educate themselves as well as their staff on these criminal acts and corresponding statutes:

- Terrorist threats
- Use of tear gas or other noxious substances
- Harassment
- Ethnic intimidation[135]

Proof of an assault may or may not require proof of physical injuries.

5.3.3.2 Arson

Industrial and business concerns have a grave interest in the protection of their assets and real property from arsonists.[136] Around-the-clock security systems, surveillance systems, and electronic technology have done much to aid private enterprise in the protection of its interests.[137]

Arson, as defined in the MPC, includes the following provisions:

Arson. A person is guilty of arson, a felony of the second degree, if he starts a fire or causes an explosion with the purpose of:

   a.   Destroying a building or occupied structure of another; or

   b.   Destroying or damaging any property, whether his own or another's, to collect insurance for such loss.[138]

Judicial interpretation of arson statutes has been primarily concerned either with the definition of a "structure" or in the proof an actual burning or physical fire damage. Structure has been broadly defined as any physical plant,

---

[131] Model Penal Code §211.1 (1962).
[132] See Nemeth, *Criminal Law*, at 185.
[133] Model Penal Code §211.2 (1962).
[134] 18 Pa. Cons. Stat. § 302 (2010).
[135] See 18 Pa. Cons. Stat. §§2705-710 (2010).
[136] See Nemeth, *Criminal Law* at 310.
[137] R.A. Neale, Arson: The Overlooked Threat to Homeland Security, *Emergency Management Online Issue*, September 7, 2010, at http://www.emergencymgmt.com/safety/Arson-Homeland-Security.html, last visited August 27, 2016.
[138] Model Penal Code §220.1 (1962).

warehouse, or accommodation that permits the carrying on of business or the temporary residents of persons, a domicile, and even ships, trailers, sleeping cars, airplanes, and other movable vehicles or structures.[139] Any burning, substantial smoke discoloration and damage, charring, the existence of alligator burn patterns, destruction and damage caused as the results of explosives, detonation devices, and ruination by substantial heat meets the arson criteria. Total destruction or annihilation is not required.[140]

Most jurisdictions have also adopted related offenses:

- Reckless burning or exploding
- Causing or risking a catastrophe
- Failure to prevent a catastrophe
- Criminal mischief
- Injuring or tampering with fire apparatus, hydrants, etc.
- Unauthorized use or opening of a fire hydrant
- Institutional vandalism[62]

5.3.3.3 Burglary

Of major interest to the security industry is the crime of burglary, a crime whose felonious intent requires an illegal entry into a domicile or other structure for the purpose of committing any felony therein. Clark and Marshall's *Treatise on Crimes*,[141] provides the common law definition of the crime of burglary:

1. The premises must be the dwelling house of another…
2. There must be a breaking of some part of the house itself. The breaking must be constructive, as well as actual.
3. There must be an entry. The slightest entry of a hand or even an instrument suffices.
4. The breaking and entering must both be at night; but need not be on the same night.
5. There must be an intent to commit a felony in the house and such intent must accompany both the breaking and entry. The intended felony need not be committed.[142]

Statutory modification of these elements has been quite common. A definition of a dwelling house has been liberally construed and includes a chicken coop, a cow stable, a hog house, a barn, a smoke house, a mill house, and any other area or any other building or occupied structure.[143] The term "breaking" does not require an actual destruction of property, merely the breaking of a plane or point of entrance into the occupied structure.[144] Additionally, most jurisdictions have reassessed the nighttime determination and made the requirement nonmandatory, though they make the time of the intrusion applicable to the gradation of the offense.[145] Be aware that burglary is not necessarily motivated by a property offense but rather the intent to commit any felony.[146]

A related act that has applicability to the security environment is criminal trespass.[147]

> *Trespass*
> (1) Buildings and occupied structures. A person commits an offense if, knowing he is not licensed or privileged to do so, he enters or surreptitiously remains in any building or occupied structure or separately secured or occupied portion thereof. An offense under this Subsection is a misdemeanor if it is committed in a dwelling at night. Otherwise, it is a petty misdemeanor.[148]

---

[139] *Ibid.* at §220.1 (1962); see Nemeth, *Criminal Law*, at 315–319.
[140] See G.E. Dix & M.M. Sharlot, *Basic Criminal Law Cases and Materials* §410 (1980).
[141] W.L. Clark & W.L. Marshall, *A Treatise on the Law of Crimes* (1967); 1.
[142] *Ibid.* at 984.
[143] *Ibid.* at 986–987.
[144] See Nemeth, *Criminal Law*, at 298–302.
[145] See *N.Y. Criminal Law* §§140 (McKinney 1980); Nemeth, *Criminal Law*, at 302.
[146] See A. Coates, Criminal Intent in Burglary, 2 *N.C. L. Rev.* 110 (1924); see also Champlin v. State, 267 N.W.2d 295 (Wis. 1978); State v. Ortiz, 584 P.2d 1306 (N.M. 1978).
[147] See Nemeth, *Criminal Law*, at 307–310.
[148] Model Penal Code §221.2 (1) (1962).

5.3.3.4 Robbery

The unlawful acquisition or taking of property by forceful means constitutes a robbery.[149] In retail and commercial establishments, security officers and personnel are frequently endangered by the activities of felons. Robbery is more than a property crime since it is coupled with a violent thrust. The exact provisions of a general robbery statute include those outlined in the MPC provision.

1. Robbery Defined. A person is guilty of robbery if, in the course of committing a theft, he:
   a. Inflicts serious bodily injury upon another; or
   b. Threatens another with or purposely puts him in fear of immediate serious bodily injury; or
   c. Commits or threatens immediately to commit any felony of the first or second degree.

An act shall be deemed "in the course of committing a theft" if it occurs in an attempt to commit theft or in flight after the attempt or commission.[150]

Distinguishing robbery from a larceny or a theft offense is not a difficult task since both judicial interpretation and statutory definitions insist upon a finding of force, violence, or a physical threat of imminent harm. Robbery can be accomplished by threats only if the threats are of death or of great bodily injury to the victim, a member of the victim's family or some other relative of the victim, or someone in the victim's presence.

5.3.3.5 Theft or larceny

No other area of proscribed behavior affects the security practice as much as in the crime of theft or as it was once known at common law, larceny.[151] Shoplifting is a form of larceny and has become retail security's central concern as it seeks to devise loss prevention strategies.[152] Stock pilferage, fraudulent accounting and record-keeping systems, embezzling of corporate funds, and theft of benefits and services are all criminal behaviors that significantly influence the profitable nature of business and industry. In the broadest definitional terms, larceny consists of

- A taking that is unlawful
- A carrying away or movement thereafter of personal property
- Property of which the taker is not in rightful ownership or possession
- With a mens rea that is felonious

Historical argument on what exactly could be the subject of a larceny is quite prolific, from disputes about whether rabbits and fish are larcenable, or whether vegetables, land, or the skins of deer could be the subject of theft.[153] In contemporary legal parlance, literally any type of property is potentially larcenable. Maryland delineates an extensive list of property classifications, including

1. "Property" means anything of value.
2. "Property" includes:
   a. Real estate;
   b. Money;
   c. A commercial instrument;
   d. An admission or transportation ticket;
   e. A written instrument representing or embodying rights concerning anything of value, or services, or anything otherwise of value to the owner;

---

[149] See Nemeth, *Criminal Law*, at 168–172.
[150] Model Penal Code §222.1 (1) (1962).
[151] See Nemeth, *Criminal Law*, at 253.
[152] J. Cleary, *Prosecuting the Shoplifter, A Loss Prevention Strategy* (1986); A.-M.G. Harris, Shopping While Black: Applying 42 U.S.C. § 1981 to Cases of Consumer Racial Profiling, 23 *B.C. Third World L.J.* 1 (2003); see also Center for Retail Research, *The Global Retail Theft Barometer* (10th ed. 2010) available at http://www.globalretailtheftbarometer.com/pdf/grtb-2010-summary.pdf
[153] Clark & Marshall at 804–807.

f. A thing growing on, affixed to, or found on land, or that is part of or affixed to any building;

g. Electricity, gas, and water;

h. A bird, animal, or fish that ordinarily is kept in a state of confinement;

i. Food or drink;

j. A sample, culture, microorganism, or specimen;

k. A record, recording, document, blueprint, drawing, map, or a whole or partial copy, description, photograph, prototype, or model of any of them;

l. An article, material, device, substance, or a whole or partial copy, description, photograph, prototype, or model of any of them that represents evidence of, reflects, or records a secret:

   i. Scientific, technical, merchandising, production, or management information; or

   ii. Designed process, procedure, formula, invention, trade secret, or improvement;

m. A financial instrument; and

n. Information, electronically produced data, and a computer software or program in a form readable by machine or individual.[154]

Aside from the requisite form, the fact finder must then consider the claim or right of a possessor of property, for larceny is an infringement on that right to possess. One need not own property to suffer a larceny but need be its rightful and privileged possessor. Finally, the taking of the said property must not arise from violence or force, for to take in that fashion would call for a robbery charge over that of larceny. The MPC's provision on theft is fairly straightforward:

Theft by Unlawful Taking or Disposition.

1. *Moveable Property.* A person is guilty of theft if he takes, or exercises unlawful control over, moveable property of another with purpose to deprive him thereof.

2. *Immovable Property.* A person is guilty of theft if he unlawfully transfers immovable property of another or any interest therein with the purpose to benefit himself or another not entitled thereto.[155]

As a result, "the general definition of theft consolidates into a single offense a number of heretofore distinct property crimes, including larceny, embezzlement, obtaining by false pretense, cheat, extortion and all other involuntary transfers of wealth except those explicitly excluded by provisions of this article."[156] Therefore, security personnel must be concerned about the closely aligned theft provisions and correctly evaluate the facts to see the applicability of certain offenses. A summary review follows.

5.3.3.6 Theft by deception/false pretenses

Be aware of individuals who are best described as "flim-flam" artists who create false impressions and deceive others[157] into giving up their rightful possession of property.[158] In the case of false pretense, the criminal actor deceptively attains ownership in a deed, a stock certificate, auto title, or other form of property interest evidenced by a legal document.[159]

5.3.3.7 Theft by extortion

Theft's methods may employ threats that are futuristic in design. Future threats of bodily injury or even by words disclosing private matters or secrets that will cause serious injury to a party[160] are common artifices employed by

---

154 Md. Code Ann. Criminal Law § 3-401 (West 2010).
155 Model Penal Code §223.2 (Proposed Official Draft 1962).
156 Model Penal Code 56 (Tentative Draft 1953).
157 Model Penal Code §223.3 (1962).
158 See Nemeth, *Criminal Law*, at 275.
159 R.I. Gen. Laws § 11-41-4 (2009).
160 Model Penal Code §223.4 (1962).

those seeking funds illegally.[161] Public officials, refusing to cooperate in an official capacity, or by their offices causing harm or injury without justification, unless in receipt of sum kickback or other payback, fall under the theft by extortion umbrella.

5.3.3.8 Theft of property lost, mislaid, or delivered by mistake

Security personnel must be particularly concerned about employees in retail establishments or other business concerns who have access to lost and found property departments, or who take advantage of incorrectly delivered warehouse shipments.[162]

5.3.3.9 Receiving stolen property

One often-discovered activity, especially in retail circles, is an internal network of illegal goods and services flowing either from employee to employee or to third-party outsiders.[163]

5.3.3.10 Theft of services

Cable companies, electric utilities, hotel, motel, and other tourist facilities are subject to thieving scams as are rental car companies, entertainment venues, and telephone companies.[164] At common law, theft had to be of a tangible item. Services lacked that corporeal quality. Modern statutes incorporate services for these activities are things of value.

5.3.3.11 Retail theft

Considering the rampant onslaught of shoplifting cases in the judicial system and the need for specialized statutory designs that recognize the many demands that business labors under as it seeks to prevent the activity, retail theft is a major concern for private security policy makers.[165] Modern retail theft statutes are distinctively less draconian in punishment. In addition, most provide some sort of immunity in the form of merchant's privilege or other protection. Some statutes permit and even promote alternative diversion or disposition of the said cases. A typical construction might be:

1. Offense defined—A person is guilty of a retail theft if he:
   a. Takes possession of, carries away, transfers or causes to be carried away or transferred, any merchandise displayed, held, stored or offered for sale by any store or other retail mercantile establishment with the intention of depriving the merchant of the possession, use or benefit of such merchandise without paying the full retail value thereof;
   b. Alters, transfers or removes any label, price tag marking, indicia of value or any other markings which aid in determining value affixed to any merchandise displayed, held, stored or offered for sale in a store or other retail mercantile establishment and attempts to purchase such merchandise personally or in consort with another at less than the full retail value with the intention of depriving the merchant of the full retail value of such merchandise;
   c. Transfers any merchandise displayed, held, stored or offered for sale by any store or other retail mercantile establishment from the container in or on which the same shall be displayed to any other container with intent to deprive the merchant of all or some part of the full retail value thereof; or
   d. Under-rings with the intention of depriving the merchant of the full retail value of the merchandise;
   e. Destroys, removes, renders inoperative or deactivates any inventory control tag, security strip or any other mechanism designed or employed to prevent an offense under this section with the intention of depriving the merchant of the possession, use or benefit of such merchandise without paying the full retail value thereof.[166]

The appearance of shoplifters has given way to some creative programs of civil recovery. The retailer, instead of formally prosecuting the shoplifter, bills him or her to recover the proceeds of the theft. Thirty-eight states now permit civil recovery, according to R. Reed Hayes Jr., president, LP Specialists, Winter Park, Florida. Hayes, a pioneer in civil recovery, has watched the technique blossom after its 1973 Nevada start. Typically, the business gives notice to a

---

[161] See Nemeth, *Criminal Law*, at 270–274.
[162] Model Penal Code §223.5 (1962).
[163] *Ibid.* at §223.6; see Nemeth, *Criminal Law*, at 269–270.
[164] *Ibid.* at §223.7; see Nemeth, *Criminal Law*, at 264–265.
[165] See Nemeth, *Criminal Law*, at 265–267.
[166] 18 Pa. Cons. Stat. § 3929 (2010).

person by mail, asking for payment for money owed. If the person neglects a certain number of notices, civil action is initiated. More often, the person pays the money owed in one lump sum or in a series of payments.[167]

5.3.3.12 Related property offenses: Fraudulent behavior

The illegal acquisition of property may take place under fraudulent or deceptive circumstances. Criminals are inventive creatures who employ devious tactics and techniques to secure property not rightfully theirs to possess. If property cannot be taken outright, then the devious felon will invent a new technique, a new design, to fraudulently acquire some property or interest.[168]

Problems with fraud trickle throughout the entire economic and business system, whether auto, homes, stocks, bonds, and commercial paper, as well as intellectual property. At times, fraud activities seem insurmountable, but some are banding together to do something about it. The National Insurance Crime Bureau is one such entity. "[A] new agency—a merger of the National Automobile Theft Bureau and the Insurance Crime Prevention Institute—employs a national network of 165 investigators who help law enforcement prosecute insurance fraud perpetrators."[169] For more information, call 1-800-TEL-NICB. Another resource center on fraud detection to contact is:

National Fraud Information Center/National Consumers League

Fraud hotline: 1-800-876-7060 or online complaint at www.fraud.org

1701K Street, N.W., Suite 1200

Washington, DC 20006

Phone: 202-835-3323

Fax: 202-835-0747

www.nclnet.org/

In the case of insurance fraud, contact:

Coalition against Insurance Fraud

1012 14th Street, NW, Suite 200

Washington, DC 20005

Phone: 202-393-7330

Fax: 202-393-7329

info@InsuranceFraud.org

www.insurancefraud.org

Fraudulent behavior, aside from its potential criminal behavior, may also trigger various sorts of civil liability.

5.3.3.13 Forgery

Property takings may be by simulation, forgery, or other deception. Individuals who create false documentation, false writings, or forged stamps, seals, trademarks, or other symbols of value, right, privilege, or identification may be subject to charges of forgery.[170] A common example of criminal forgery involves tampering with wills, deeds, contracts, commercial instruments, negotiable bonds, securities, or any other writing, which influences, executes, authenticates, or issues something of monetary value. To constitute forgery, a fraudulent intent is always essential. There must not only be a false making of an instrument, but it must be with the intent to defraud.[171]

715A.2 Forgery.

1. A person is guilty of forgery if, with intent to defraud or injure anyone, or with knowledge that the person is facilitating a fraud or injury to be perpetrated by anyone, the person does any of the following:

---

[167] Bill Zalud, Retail's 7 Greatest Security Hits! 28 Sec. 34, 35 (1991).
[168] See Nemeth, *Criminal Law*, at 275–277.
[169] Note, Insurance Firms Toughen Fraud Fight, 29 Sec. 65 (1992).
[170] See Nemeth, *Criminal Law*, at 277–283.
[171] Clark & Marshall at 954; see *Me. Rev. Stat. Ann. tit.* 17-A §702 (2009); *Or. Rev. Stat.* §165.013 (2009); State v. Tarrence, 985 P.2d 225 (Ore. App. 1999); U.S. v. Sherman, 52 M.J. 856 (U.S. Army Ct. Crim. App. 2000).

a. Alters a writing of another without the other's permission.

b. Makes, completes, executes, authenticates, issues, or transfers a writing so that it purports to be the act of another who did not authorize that act, or so that it purports to have been executed at a time or place or in a numbered sequence other than was in fact the case, or so that it purports to be a copy of an original when no such original existed.

c. Utters a writing which the person knows to be forged in a manner specified in paragraph "a" or "b."

d. Possesses a writing which the person knows to be forged in a manner specified in paragraph "a" or "b."[172]

5.3.3.14 Simulating objects of antiquity or rarity

Security officials given the responsibility of protecting museum collections, art centers, or other nonprofit institutions dedicated to articles of antiquity or rarity should always be aware of possible reproduction or simulation of their employer's collections.

> *Simulating objects of antiquity, rarity, etc.*
> A person commits a misdemeanor of the first degree if, with intent to defraud anyone or with knowledge that he is facilitating a fraud to be perpetrated by anyone, he makes, alters or utters any object so that it appears to have value because of antiquity, rarity, source, or authorship which it does not possess.[173]

5.3.3.15 Fraudulent destruction, removal, or concealment of recordable instruments or their tampering

Internal security, particularly in the area of personnel, payroll, and administrative matters, should give substantial thought to the preventative security measures that are presently in place or should be implemented.

> *§ 4103. Fraudulent destruction, removal or concealment of recordable instruments*
> A person commits a felony of the third degree if, with intent to deceive or injure anyone, he destroys, removes or conceals any will, deed, mortgage, security instrument or other writing for which the law provides public recording.
> *§ 4104. Tampering with records or identification*
> (a) Writings.--A person commits a misdemeanor of the first degree if, knowing that he has no privilege to do so, he falsifies, destroys, removes or conceals any writing or record, or distinguishing mark or brand or other identification with intent to deceive or injure anyone or to conceal any wrongdoing.[174]

5.3.3.16 Bad check and credit card violations

Retail centers are regularly victimized by check and credit card fraud and related violations. Here too, property is acquired without the proper payment of consideration. The seemingly endless stream of fraudulent and bounced checks received by commercial establishments is mind-boggling. The security industry must adopt an aggressive posture against these actors in order to protect pricing and value in the exchange of goods and services. Bad checks and credit card fraud drive up the prices. The language of bad check laws is fairly uniform.

§ 4105. Bad checks

a. OFFENSE DEFINED.—

1. A person commits an offense if he issues or passes a check or similar sight order for the payment of money, knowing that it will not be honored by the drawee.

2. A person commits an offense if he, knowing that it will not be honored by the drawee, issues or passes a check or similar sight order for the payment of money when the drawee is located within this Commonwealth. A violation of this paragraph shall occur without regard to whether the location of the issuance or passing of the check or similar sight order is within or outside of this Commonwealth. It shall be no defense to a violation of this section that some or all of the acts constituting the offense occurred outside of this Commonwealth.[175]

---

[172] Iowa Code § 715A.2 (2008).
[173] 18 Pa. Cons. Stat. § 4102 (2010).
[174] Ibid. at §§4103-4104.
[175] Ibid. at §§4105; see also Md. Code. Ann. Criminal Law §§8-103, 8-214 (West 2010).

5.3.4 Defenses to criminal acts: Protection of self, third parties, and property

The idea of self-help and self-protection is as old as Western tradition itself. Since the time of the Romans and the Greeks, God's chosen people, the Jews, and other early societies, there has always been a recognition that protection of self and property is a matter of right. Roman law, such as the *Code of Justinian* or the *Corpus Juris Civilis*, could not be more unequivocal about the right of individuals to rightfully defend oneself. The *Code* notes, in part:

> We grant to all persons the unrestricted power to defend themselves (*liberam resistendi cunctis tribuimus facultatem*), so that it is proper to subject anyone, whether a private person or a soldier, who trespasses upon fields at night in search of plunder, or lays by busy roads plotting to assault passers-by, to immediate punishment in accordance with the authority granted to all (*permissa cuicumque licentia dignus ilico supplicio subiugetur*). Let him suffer the death which he threatened and incur that which he intended.[176]

Thus, cultural and common law traditions, as well as religious and spiritual standards, provide a strong basis for the defense of person and things.

5.3.4.1 Personal self-defense and the proportionate use of force

Much activity in the security industry is geared toward the protection of the person.[177] As a result of this orientation, security professionals must understand defense tactics and "use it wisely."[178] If one unreasonably responds in a protection situation, allegations of criminal conduct may be in the offing. For the defender of using excessive force, an assault or even a murder or manslaughter may be charged. In protection of person cases, "the obvious human instinct to meet physical aggression with counter force … [must be balanced with] … desirability in a civilized society … of encouraging the resolution of disputes through peaceful means."[179] Since the preservation instinct is strong, conduct delineations regarding reasonable and justifiable force are critical policy questions.

Imperative in security training is the topic of force in the application of self-defense principles, excessive force, and self-protection.[180] Professional bodies and groups, associations, and the internal policies of agencies and organizations, all seek a clear and consistent policy on the defense of self. Think tanks such as the American Law Institute, by and through its MPC, propose a well-respected statutory design for the party acting in self-defense.[181]

1. Use of Force Justifiable for Protection of the Person. Subject to the provision of this Section and of Section 3.09 the use of force upon or toward another person is justifiable when the actor believes that such force is immediately necessary for the purpose of protecting himself against the use of unlawful force by such other person on the present occasion.

2. Limitations on Justifying Necessity for Use of Force.

   a. The use of force is not justifiable under this Section:

      i. to resist an arrest which the actor knows is being made by a peace officer, although the arrest is unlawful ….

   b. The use of deadly force is not justifiable under this Section unless the actor believes that such force is necessary to protect himself against death, serious bodily harm, kidnapping or sexual intercourse compelled by force or threat, nor is it justifiable if:

      i. the actor, with the purpose of causing death or serious bodily harm, provoked the use of force against himself in the same encounter; or

---

[176] Code Just. 3.27.1 (Valentinian, Theodosius, & Arcadius 391). See also W. Tysse, The Roman Legal Treatment of Self Defense and the Private Possession of Weapons in the Code of Justinian, 16 *J. Firearms & Pub. Pol'y*, available at http://secondamendmentlibrary.com/JFPPIndexhtmlpdf.htm.

[177] National Institute of Justice, *Crime and Protection in America, A Study of Private Security and Law Enforcement Resources and Relationships* (1985). See Nemeth, *Criminal Law*, at 389–407; R.L. Christopher, Mistake of Fact in the Objective Theory of Justification: Do Two Rights Make Two Wrongs Make Two Rights … ?, 85 *J. Crim. L. & Criminology* 295 (1994); K. Greenawalt, The Perplexing Borders of Justification and Excuse, 84 *Colum. L. Rev.* 1897 (1984); G.P. Fletcher, The Right and the Reasonable, 98 *Harv. L. Rev.* 949 (1985); 2 P.H. Robinson, *Criminal Law Defenses*, §3-3, Model Codifications, app. A (1984).

[178] L. Jackson, Using Force Wisely, 36 *Sec. Mgmt* 65 (1992).

[179] G.E. Dix & M.M. Sharlot, *Basic Criminal Law Cases and Materials* 527 (1980).

[180] S. Wallerstein, Justifying the Right to Self-Defense: A Theory of Forced Consequences, 91 *Va. L. Rev.* 999 (2005).

[181] MPC at §3.04.

   ii. the actor knows that he can avoid the necessity of using such force with complete safety by retreating or by surrendering possession of a thing to a person asserting a claim of right thereto, or by complying with a demand that he abstain from any action which he has no duty to take, except that:

     1. the actor is not obliged to retreat from his dwelling or his place of work unless he was the initial aggressor…

     2. a public officer justified in using force in the performance of his duties, or a person justified in using force in his assistance or a person justified in using force in making an arrest or preventing an escape is not obliged to desist from efforts to perform such duty, effect such arrest or prevent such escape.[182]

Readily apparent from a first read of the MPC are the explicit restrictions on the use of force,[183] compelling the employer of force to think about its potential ramifications and limitations. First, force is not a permissible activity against law enforcement officers, though a few states accept extraordinary situations. Second, force is only tolerated in environments of heightened necessity or immediate need, when a victim of physical harm can objectively point to real and immediate bodily harm. Third, force is only to be employed in situations where a reasonably prudent person believes that he or she could suffer serious bodily harm, death, kidnapping, or sexual assault. "The requirement that the defendant be operating under the reasonable belief that he is in imminent danger of death, great bodily harm, or some felony, involve two elements: (1) the defendant in fact must have acted out of an honest, bona fide belief that he was in imminent danger and (2) the belief must be reasonable in light of the facts as they appeared to him."[184]

Security professionals, during the typical career, will likely confront the tension between the defense of self and the parameters for the use of force. Some cases will be easier than others. Violent aggression by suspects can be met by some level of proportionate response. Indeed, a slingshot should not be met with a rapid-fire weapon. The potential for abuse and disproportionate reaction is a natural risk in private policing for, as the *Hallcrest Report I* notes, "one inescapable fact is that firearms tend to be used when they are carried."[185] The *Report* further explains that firearms' training, proper care, and usage thereof in the security industry are often abysmal and frighteningly inadequate exercises.

Weigh and evaluate:

- A security investigator catches a thief in the act. The thief reaches into his side pocket. Before he could remove the object, the security official fired a weapon, inflicting a fatal injury. Would this be a case of excessive force in the protection of self?

- Security officer comes upon a crime scene and sees a juvenile, with stolen goods in hand, riding his bike from the scene of a crime. As the juvenile accelerates his bicycle, he directs the path of the bike toward the security officer. The officer, in order to protect his life, even though he has an easy retreat and an opportunity to move in another direction, inflicts a fatal injury on the juvenile. Is this a case of excessive force?

Which of these two cases is contrary to the MPC's demand that the force exerted by a defender be proportionate to that being exhibited by the aggressor? Which case relies upon the objective reality the actor believes to be true when in fact it may or may not be? In these cases, judgment calls are common and gauged by an officer's reasonable belief.

5.3.4.2 Protection of other persons

Another typical task in the security industry is the protection of other persons. Persons of social importance such as entertainers, politicians, business executives, religious leaders, and other highly public and visible individual personalities rely heavily on the expertise of the security industry. Executive protection has become a multimillion-dollar business. What level of protective action is permissible in the protection of other persons?[186] The MPC again provides some general guidance:

1. Subject to the provisions of this Section and of Section 3.09, the use of force upon or toward the person of another is justifiable to protect a third person when:

---

[182] MPC at §3.04 (1 & 2).

[183] For more information on the subject, see Nemeth at 401–407; see also Christopher; Greenawalt; Fletcher; Robinson.

[184] Summary of Pennsylvania Jurisprudence 2D, Criminal Law §7.19.

[185] Cunningham & Taylor, *supra* note 63, at 94.

[186] See Nemeth at 407–408; see Christopher; Greenawalt; Fletcher; Robinson.

a. The actor would be justified under 3.04 in using such force to protect himself against the injury he believes to be threatened to the person whom he seeks to protect;

b. Under the circumstances as the actor believes them to be, the person whom he seeks to protect would be justified in using such protective force; and

c. The actor believes that his intervention is necessary for the protection of the other person.[187]

At its heart, the MPC provides for a transference of authority in the protection of self. In essence, one is permitted to defend another person entrusted to their care or oversight, as if defending oneself. In private sector justice, we witness this reality with great regularity. Indeed, the entire infrastructure of executive protection needs these parameters to know what defense can be exerted. In short, one may exert such force as is proportionate, reasonable, and necessary as the party entrusting this authority would be capable of. What the defender believes is also crucial. However, belief should not be governed by hypersensitivity and delusion, and it must be the product of a reasoned, well-defined justification. There should be "a threat, actual or apparent to the use of deadly force against the defender. The threat must have been unlawful and immediate. The defender must have believed that he was in imminent peril of death or serious bodily harm and that his response was necessary to save himself. These beliefs must not only have been honestly entertained, but also objectively reasonable in light of the surrounding circumstances."[188]

The role of self-defense is further influenced by the evolution of defense technology and occupational hardware. Review the list below as only a partial example of defensive equipment available to public and private police systems:

1. Revolvers
2. Shotguns
3. Rifles
4. Machine guns
5. Flair guns
6. Armored vehicles
7. Helmets
8. Bulletproof vests
9. Combat shields
10. Tear gas
11. Grenade launchers
12. Batons
13. Water cannon
14. Military vehicles

Such an arsenal is bound to generate "defense" questions for industry planners and leaders.

5.3.4.3 Defense of property

The value placed on personal property versus human life is markedly distinguishable. Most American jurisdictions, supported by common law tradition and well-entrenched case law precedent, have always placed a heavy burden on those seeking to employ force in the protection of personal property. The MPC confirms that tradition.

1. Use of force justifiable for the protection of property. Subject to the provisions of this Section and of Section 3.09, the use of force upon or toward the person of another is justifiable when the actor believes that such force is immediately necessary:

   a. To prevent or terminate an unlawful entry or other trespass upon land or a trespass against or the unlawful carrying away of tangible, movable property, provided that such land or movable property is, or is believed by the actor to be, in his possession or in the possession of another person for whose protection he acts; or

---

[187] MPC at §3.05(1).

[188] U.S. v. Peterson, 483 F. 2d 1222, 1223 (1973); see also State v. Goodseal, 183 N.W.2d 258 (Neb. 1971); Commonwealth v. Martin, 341 N.E. 885 (Mass. 1976); Commonwealth v. Monico, 366 N.E.2d 1241 (Mass. 1977).

b. To effect an entry or reentry upon land or to retake tangible movable property, provided that the actor believes that he or the person by whose authority he acts or a person from whom he or such other persons derives title was unlawfully dispossessed provided further, that:

  i. The force is used immediately or on fresh pursuit after such dispossession; or

  ii. The actor believed that the person against whom the force is used has no claim of right to the possession of the property and, in the case of land, the circumstances, as the actor believes them to be, are of such urgency that it would be an exceptional hardship to postpone the entry or reentry until a court order is obtained.[189]

Common sense and legal tradition dictate that the degree of force permissible is dependent on the totality of circumstances. Factual situations that include entry into one's domicile or residence, of course, heighten the right to exert force.[190] Simple thefts or property disputes of tangible property such as a television, a garden tool, or some other item do not justify the exertion of life-threatening force.

The use of deadly force in defense of property is justifiable if there has been an entry into the actor's dwelling, which the actor neither believes nor has reason to believe is lawful, and the actor neither believes nor has reason to believe can be terminated by force less than deadly force. Otherwise, the use of deadly force in defense of property is not justifiable unless the actor believes either that the person against whom the deadly force is used is trying to dispossess him of his dwelling without a claim of right, or that deadly force is necessary to prevent a commission of a felony in the dwelling.[191]

The most confused cases occur when a dwelling place is involved. Numerous jurisdictions have grappled with the crosscurrents that occur in this area. Recent history indicates a movement toward favoring the owner of a domicile in the protection of his own property.[192] In *State v. Miller*,[193] a North Carolina court held:

> When a trespasser enters upon a man's premises, makes an assault upon his dwelling, an attempt to force an entrance into a house in a manner such as would lead a reasonably prudent man to believe that the intruder intends to commit a felony or inflict some serious personal injury upon the inmates, a lawful occupant of the dwelling may legally prevent the entry, even by the taking of the life of the intruder.[194]

5.4 LEGAL CHALLENGES TO PRIVATE SECURITY SAFE HARBOR

As a general rule, the constitutional protections inherent in basic criminal processes, such as arrest, search, warrants, and seizures, simply do not apply to private sector police. Since the inception of the Republic, the idea of governmental action, public action, or state action was intentionally listed and delineated in the Bill of Rights. These early protections were initially framed for federal action alone, but with the elimination of slavery and the adoption of the Fourteenth Amendment, whereby the language that includes "No state shall" explicitly sets boundaries of how and why those rights apply.

Web Exercise: At the law school level of scholarship, there have been persistent cries for expansion of these constitutional principles to the private sector. See an example from the University of Missouri at http://scholarship.law. missouri.edu/cgi/viewcontent.cgi?article=3644&context=mlr.

Considerable protections are provided against governmental action that violates the Bills of Rights. Most applicable is the Fourth Amendment, which provides:

> The right of the people to be secure in their persons, houses, papers, and effects, against unreasonable searches and seizures, shall not be violated and no warrants shall issue upon their probable cause supported by oath, affirmation and particularly describing the place to be searched and the persons or things to be seized.[195]

---

[189] MPC at §3.06 (1).

[190] See Nemeth at 408–409; see Christopher; Greenawalt; Fletcher; Robinson.

[191] Pennsylvania Jurisprudence § 7:36.

[192] The State of New Jersey recently expanded the right of the homeowner to protect his or her interests with deadly force.

[193] 148 S.E. 2d 279, 281–282 (N.C. 1966).

[194] *Ibid.*; see also Law v. State, 318 A.2d 859 (Md. App. 1974); People v. Givens, 186 N.E.2d 255 (Ill. 1962).

[195] U.S. Const. amend. IV.

On its face, and in its express text, the Fourth Amendment is geared toward public functions.[196] The concepts of a "warrant," an "oath," or "affirmation" are definitions that expressly relate to public officialdom and governmental action. Courts have historically been reticent to extend those protections to private sector activities. In *Burdeau v. McDowell*,[197] the Supreme Court held unequivocally that Fourth Amendment protection was not available to litigants and claimants arrested, searched, or seized by private parties. Private action and private entities are never included in the earliest of our founding documents, and the whole history of American jurisprudence has held firmly to this distinction.[198]

The private security industry unreservedly defends the explicit exemption from constitutional oversight and not surprisingly so. However, owing to the abject absence of an industry application, or even a suggested industry standard, the lack of constitutional oversight is a constant irritant for critics of the security industry. Antagonists of the private security industry have vociferously argued that its secondary status or minor league position, when compared to public police, will remain a constant reality until the industry itself adopts well-defined procedural guidelines. The National Advisory Committee on Criminal Justice Standards and Goals calls for research and corresponding guidelines in these procedural areas:

1. General private security functions:
   a. arrests
   b. detentions
   c. use of force (including firearms)
   d. impersonation of and confusion of public law enforcement officers and
   e. directing and controlling traffic

2. Specific investigatory functions:
   a. search and seizure of private property
   b. wiretapping, bugging, and other forms of surveillance
   c. access of private security personnel to public law enforcement information and procedures for the safeguarding of the information
   d. obtaining information from private citizens and the safeguarding of information and
   e. interrogation[199]

The National Advisory Committee and other authoritative bodies see continued resistance to procedural standards somewhat similar to the public model as a negative for the industry. In addition, procedural regularity will bring, allegedly, a substantial reduction in the industry's rate of criminal and civil liability. In time, the argument is that a more enlightened, professional industry will make fewer mistakes, although this claim may be more ambition than a realistic conclusion. The *Hallcrest Report* observes:

> There are some overwhelming public safety issues which justify public concern for adequate controls on private security. The serious consequences of errors in judgment or incompetence demand controls which insure the client and the general public of adequate safeguards. If government is to allow private security a larger role in providing some traditional police services, then it needs to insure that sufficient training and appropriate performance standards exist for the participating security programs—both proprietary and contractual.[200]

---

[196] Note, Seizures by Private Parties: Exclusion in Criminal Cases, 19 *Stan. L. Rev.* 608, 608–609 (1967).

[197] 256 U.S. 465 (1921).

[198] E.W. Machen, Jr., *The Law of Search and Seizure* (1950); J.A. Varon, *Searches, Seizures and Immunities* (1974); Note, The Concept of Privacy and the Fourth Amendment, 6 *U. Mich. J. L. Rev.* 154 (1972); Note, From Private Places to Personal Privacy: A Post-Katz Study of Fourth Amendment Protections, 43 *N.Y.U. L. Rev.* 96 (1968); Blancard, Clark, and Everett, *Uniform Security Guard Power To Arrest, Part II* (1977); F.E. Inbau, *Protective Security Law* (1983); Note, The Legal Basis of Authority, 26 *Sec. Mgmt* 50 (1982); see also R. Sarre, The Legal Basis for the Authority of Private Police and an Examination of Their Relationship with the "Public" Police (1992) available at http://www.aic.gov.au/publications/previous%20series/proceedings/1-27/~/media/publications/proceedings/23/sarre.ashx, last accessed August 27, 2016.

[199] Task Force on Private Security at 127; see also W. Aitchison, *The Rights of Law Enforcement Officer* (4th ed. 2000); R.V. del Carmen, *Criminal Procedure for Law Enforcement Personnel* (5th ed. 2001); del Carmen & Kappeler, at 1–17; S.M. Ryals, *Discovery and Proof in Police Misconduct Cases* (1995).

[200] Cunningham & Taylor, at 264.

Despite this general resistance to expanding the constitutional dynamic to private sector police, legal advocates push hard for such reforms and a variety and steady stream of case law reaches appellate courts across the country each and every year. Some case laws are more significant than others. Few cases have had much success in altering this legal landscape. An appeals decision from California carved out a noticeable precedent for those arguing for the expansion of these constitutional rights.

In *People v. Zelinski*,[201] the California Supreme Court ruled that security officers were thoroughly empowered to institute a search to recover goods that were in plain view, but that any intrusion into the defendant's person or effects was not authorized as incident to a citizen's arrest or protected under the *Merchant's Privilege Statute*. The court concluded that the evidence seized was "obtained by unlawful search and that the constitutional prohibition against unreasonable search and seizure affords protection against the unlawful intrusive conduct of these private security personnel."[202] The decision temporarily shook the status quo. The court fully recognized its own disregard of previous U.S. Supreme Court rulings, stating:

> Although past cases have not applied the constitutional restriction to purely private searches, we have recognized that some minimal official participation or encouragement may bring private action within the constitutional restraints on state action.[203]

Mindful of the facts of this case, the Supreme Court of California could not recite any case including a connection or legal nexus between private and public police activity. Instead, the court simply dismissed previous decisions based upon a variety of rationales, including the security industry's new and dynamic involvement in the administration of justice.[204] The court cited the "increasing reliance placed upon private security personnel by local enforcement of criminal law"[205] particularly as it relates to privacy rights and procedural rights of defendants. In the end, the California Supreme Court relied upon its own Constitution, Article 2, Section 13, which ironically is a mirror image of the federal provision.

Just when the private act transforms into a public one is difficult to tell. The level of public inducement, solicitation, oversight, and joint effect manifests a transformation. In *State of Minnesota v. Beswell*,[206] the court claims to have witnessed the transformation of private security personnel at a racetrack who conducted searches on patrons, into a public persona. When cocaine was discovered, defendants assert that the private security agents had sufficient public connections to trigger a series of constitutional protections. The court qualified its public finding by corroborating the private–public interplay.[207]

Add to this reasoning the adoption of the "public function" test that imputes constitutional remedies when the nature and scope of private police conduct exhibit all the qualities and characteristics of a "public" act.[208] Regardless of direct police involvement, systematic use of random contraband searches serves the general public interest and may reflect pursuit of criminal convictions as well as protection of private interests. Courts in the mold of *Beswell* look to corroborate the advocate's assertions. In short, does the private security officer act like a public police officer?[209]

Wearing police uniforms, and using police restraint processes "(handcuffing appellants to fences, conducting body searches), indicates the similarity of function and role."[210] Function infers a similarity of approaches and thereby awards an identical series of protections—at least in a theoretical sense. Finally, the court weighed the security agency

---

[201] 594 P. 2d 1000 (1979).

[202] *Ibid.*

[203] *Ibid.* at 1002.

[204] *Ibid.* at 1006.

[205] *Ibid.* at 1005.

[206] 449 N.W.2d 471 (Minn. App. 1989).

[207] State of Minnesota v. Beswell, 449 N.W.2d 471, 474 (Minn. App. 1989).

[208] *Private Security, Public Order: The Outsourcing of Public Services and Its Limits* (S. Chesterman & A. Fisher, eds. 2009). See also Marsh v. Alabama, 326 U.S. 501, 66 S.CT. 276, 90 L.ED. 265 (1946); see 1 W. LaFave, § 1.8(d) at 200. See also Feffer, 831 F.2d at 739; State of Minnesota v. Beswell, 449 N.W.2d 471, 474 (Minn. App. 1989).

[209] For an interesting analysis of this transformation from the former Eastern block nation of Estonia, see N. Parrest, Constitutional Boundaries of Transfer of Public Functions to Private Sector in Estonia, 16 *Juridica International* 44 (2009) available at http://www.juridicainternational. eu/public/pdf/ji_2009_1_44.pdf, last accessed August 27, 2016.

[210] State of Minnesota v. Beswell, 449 N.W.2d 471, 474 (Minn. App. 1989).

hiring a full-time public police officer as further evidence of the transformation. Such officers are formally affiliated with the government and usually given authority beyond that of an ordinary citizen. Thus, they may be treated as state agents and subject to the constraints of the Fourth Amendment.[211]

Web Exercise: The National Association of Security Companies (NASCO) is particularly sensitive to how things appear as a basis for liability. Visit http://www.nasco.org/about/nasco-accomplishments.

Zelinski and *Beswell* manifest a voice of discontent and a resulting intellectual demand for change in traditional constitutional applications for the private security industry.[212] In this sense, *Zelinski* and *Beswell* signify a slow and very ineffective evolution. A quick glance at the precedential power of these cases attests to the firmness of the present legal foundation.

5.4.1 Platinum platter doctrine

Challenges to the applicability of the exclusionary rule, whereby evidence is excluded for errant search, seizure, or arrest processes, are continuously witnessed in higher courts. It is not a popular legal principle in more conservative quarters. Initially, the exclusionary rule was held applicable to federal action alone and was not applicable in state cases.[213] Federal agents realized this early on and clandestinely employed the services of state agents who delivered evidence or other treasure while avoiding the constitutional challenges. For state police officers, the delivery of the evidence, despite its procedural impropriety, was figuratively handed over on a "silver platter."[214]

Hence, the use by state and federal officials of private security operatives to arrest, search, or seize, without the usual constitutional oversight, has been labeled the *platinum platter doctrine*. In arguing that the entanglement of private sector/state involvement creates a relationship substantial enough to justify expansion of the Fourth Amendment, B.C. Petroziello, calls for a reexamination of the *Burdeau* doctrine. Referring to special police officers in the state of Ohio as quasi-public figures, he argues that special police should no longer be permitted to hand over elicit evidence on a "platinum platter."[215] His comments provide food for thought:

> The confusion caused by the current state of the law could be obviated by the use of a much simpler and more preferable standard. The substance of this standard encompasses a different view of what is meant by private individual: no one should be considered private under *Burdeau* if he is employed or paid to detect evidence of crime or has delegated any more power possessed by the average citizen. Whenever a person meeting either of these qualifications tramples a defendant's rights the evidence so gathered is to be excluded at trial.[216]

For critics of unbridled private sector power, the more the private sector cooperates with public authority, the more its occupational role metamorphoses from private to public function. In essence, the entanglement and entwining is so complex and complicated that distinct roles have evaporated. As attractive as the theory is, it suffers conceptually. The principles of *Burdeau* should not be inapplicable simply because a person is employed or paid to detect criminality or because that person is chartered by the state or other governmental authority. If such reasoning were followed, then any attorney or licensed individual, including truck drivers, polygraph examiners, forest rangers, or park attendants, who are subject to governmental review, would fall within this scheme.

Despite the difficulties of merging public and private functions to the extent they are one and the same, it is equally undeniable that the private security industry is increasingly engaged in public activity, public protection and safety, and public function. The question of whether this "public" dimension is substantial enough to apply the constitutional regimen is still debatable. What is certain is that in the age of escalating privatization, adoption of a public function theory may be plausible in a host of contexts.

---

[211] *Ibid.*

[212] Note, The Legal Basis of Authority, 26 *Sec. Mgmt.* 54 (1982).

[213] See Weeks v. U.S., 232 U.S. 383 (1914); Wolf v. People of The State of Colo. 338 U.S. 25 (1949).

[214] See Lustig v. U.S., 338 U.S. 74, 79 (1949); Elkins v. U.S., 364 U.S. 200 (1960). See also M. McGuinness, The "Silver Platter" in the Context of State Constitutional Adjudication, *Albany Law Review* (2008) available at http://www.albanylawreview.org/articles/McGuinness.pdf.

[215] Note, The Platinum Platter in Ohio: Are Private Police Really Private? 2 *U. Dayton L. Rev.* 290 (1977).

[216] *Ibid.* at 287–288.

5.4.2 Private action as state action

A second strategy that attempts to apply the Fourth Amendment in private sector arrests, searches, and seizures is to manifest the public nature of the alleged private conduct or action. The traditional method of conducting this analysis is to determine the extent of the government's involvement. If the government's role in the search and seizure is significant enough, as it is in traditional public police settings, the Fourth Amendment applies.[217] State action, that is, the involvement of state and local officials, including police and law enforcement officials, with, by, and through private security operatives, makes the once clear line of demarcation muddled. "It has been argued that despite the *Burdeau* doctrine, private conduct or actions may be subject to some level of constitutional scrutiny if they are sufficiently impregnated with state actions."[218] Expansive judicial reasoning like this was used to justify a plethora of civil rights decisions during the mid-1960s and early 1970s.[219]

Few functions, systems, enterprises, endeavors, or institutions are completely free from some level of governmental involvement or oversight. The tentacles of governmental influence weave their way into literally every facet of modern life. Whether it be business operation or licensing, environment or workplace safety, unions, and work rules, the heavy hand of government is discoverable just about everywhere. The security industry, like any other commercial concern, is subject to an endless series of oversights, including

1. State licensing requirements
2. State and federal taxes
3. State inspections
4. Reporting requirements
5. Statutory grant of authority to merchants, business, or industries to protect their property and interests
6. Immunities and privileges granted by legislatures for certain conducts and behaviors
7. Subcontractor and delegation rules
8. Bonding requirements
9. Regulatory compliance

Some legal advocates and their plaintiffs think any interaction is sufficient to meet the public function theory.[220]

Consider the case of *United States v. Francoeur*.[221] Defendants sought to reverse a conviction by asserting a constitutional violation by private employees. While in a Disneyland amusement park, security personnel detained and emptied the pockets of multiple suspects. Subsequently, counterfeit bills were retrieved and these suspects were eventually found guilty of various offenses. To challenge the admission of the evidence, defendants claimed that since Disneyland was a public place, freely accessible and open to the world, the security officials working within its borders were government officials. To uphold this appellate argument would have had far-reaching ramifications, and the court reminded the defendants that any possible remedy was civil in nature rather than constitutional.[222]

Direct involvement or participation is not proven by inference, but instead, by a defendant's demonstration of direct involvement. In *United States v. Lima*,[223] the D.C. Appellate Court articulately espoused that private individuals can become agents or instruments of the state if the government is sufficiently involved in the development of actual plans or actions carried out by private persons. The *Lima* decision mandates "a significant relationship… between the state and private security employees to find state action; something whereby the state intrudes itself into private entity."[224]

A second rationale for finding state action, outside of direct assistance or participation, is when private security personnel are found not to have acted alone but at the direct suggestion, supervision, or employment of the public police

---

[217] Note, Private Searches and Seizures: An Application of the Public Function Theory, 48 *Geo. Wash. L. Rev.* 185 (1980).
[218] See Coolidge v. New Hampshire, 403 U.S. 443, 487 (1971); U.S. v. Guest, 383 U.S. 745, 771–772 (1966).
[219] See particularly Burton v. Wilmington Parking Authority, 365 U.S. 715 (1961).
[220] Copeland v. City of Topeka Case No. 01-4016-SAC, 2003 U.S. Dist. LEXIS 9367 (Kansas May 23, 2003).
[221] 547 F. 2d 891 (1977).
[222] U.S. v. Francoeur, 547 F. 2d 891 (1977).
[223] U.S. v. Lima, 424 A. 2d 13 (1980).
[224] *Ibid.* at 121.

system.[225] In short, the private security officers act as fronts for the public police. This form of supervision, control, or direction would include instigation, encouragement, direct suggestions as to an operation, or any other strategy illustrating law enforcement involvement.[226] "Whether there has been enough police contact for an agency, the relationship to have existed is a question of fact to be answered by the court."[227]

In *Snyder v. State of Alaska*,[228] a defendant appealed his conviction, asserting that his Fourth Amendment rights were violated. An airline baggage employee had called police on at least 12 previous occasions to report the discovery of drugs and illegal goods. Police informed airline employees that they themselves were not permitted to open packages without a warrant, but that under Civil Aeronautics Board rules, airline employees had a right to open packages if they believed there was something wrong or that the items listed on the bill of lading did not accurately reflect what was in the parcels. The airline employee opened the package, on direction of the Alaskan Police authorities, and the defendant contended that this level of active involvement, encouragement, and investigation transformed private conduct into state action.[229] Governmental action, arising in a private policing context, requires a substantial correlation between public and private behavior.

The third and final situation where state action is arguable in the private security industry is when security personnel act in a quasi-police status as when commissioned as special police officers.[230] Professor Stephen Euller, in his article, "Private Security and the Exclusionary Rule," notes:

> In such cases state action has been recognized when private officers have been formally designated "special police officers." States often commission "special police officers" to patrol retail stores or to perform occasional public law enforcement services such as traffic or crowd control at parties or sports events.[231]

Another case, which manifests the delicate line between public and private function, is *State of Ohio v. McDaniel*.[232] The defendants/appellants sought to demonstrate that the security staff, consisting of about 45 full-time employees at a department store in Franklin County, Ohio, were governmental agents by their commission as special deputy sheriffs. Searches made by security employees resulted in the seizure of various incriminating goods. Defendants sought to overturn the seizures based upon Fourth Amendment protections and argued emphatically the state action theory. The court, recognizing that privacy was important to the defendant appellants, attempted to balance the interest of both parties. It found:

> The right to privacy is not absolute and the Constitution prohibits only unreasonable searches. Shoplifting is a serious problem for merchants. Merchants may utilize reasonable means to detect and prevent shoplifting. Where the merchant or his employee has probable or reasonable cause to believe that an apparent customer is in reality a thief planning to shoplift merchandise, the merchant or his employee may utilize reasonable means of surveillance and observation in order to detect and prevent the crime.[233]

The court further rejected the argument that simply being commissioned as special deputies is a sufficient basis for a finding of state action.[234] Deputization, a special commission, or other status, in and of itself, appears an insufficient basis for finding state action. State action requires meaningful participation, significant involvement, and intentional instigation, a series of conducts rarely witnessed.[235]

---

[225] Note, Developments in the Law: State Action and the Public/Private Distinction, 123 *Harv L. Rev.* 1248 (2010) at http://www.harvardlawreview.org/media/pdf/DEVO_10.pdf.

[226] G.S. Buchanan, A Conceptual History of the State Action Doctrine: The Search for Governmental Responsibility (pt. 1), 34 *Hous. L. Rev.* 333, 336 (1997).

[227] Euller, *supra* note 55, at, 655; see also Tarnef v. State, 512 P. 2d 923, 934 (1973); People v. Agnosepoulous, 77 MISC. 2d 668, 354 N.Y.S. 2d 575, 576 (1974); U.S. v. Clegg, 509 F. 2d 605, 609–611 (1975); People v. Moreno, 64 Cal. App. 3D Supp. 23, 135 *Cal. Rptr.* 340 (1976).

[228] Synder v. State of Alaska, 585 P. 2d 229 (1978).

[229] *Ibid.* at 232. See also Gillett v. State of Texas, 588 S.W. 2d 361 (1979). People v. Horman, 22 N.Y. 2d 378 (1968). State v. Keyser, 369 A 2d 224 (1977).

[230] See generally Griffin v. Maryland 378 U.S. 130 (1964); People v. Diaz, 85 MISC. 2d 41, 376 N.Y.S. 2d 849 (1975); People v. Frank, 52 Misc. 2d 266, 275 N.Y.S. 2d 570 (1966); State v. Bolan, 27 Ohio St. 2d 15, 271 N.W. 2d 839 (1971).

[231] Euller, at 606.

[232] State v. McDaniel, 44 Ohio App. 2d 163, 377 N.W. 2d 173 (1975); see also U.S. v. Miller, 668 F.2d 652 (1982).

[233] *Ibid.* at 180.

[234] *Ibid.*

[235] See State v. Scrotsky, 39 N.J. 410, 189 A. 2d 23 (1963); Moody v. U.S., 163 A.2d 337 (1960); People v. Tarantino, 45 Cal. 2d 590, 290 P.2d 505 (1955); People v. Fierro, 238 Cal. App. 2d 344, 46 *Cal. Rptr.* 132 (1965).

A more provocative argument emerges in *Austin v. Paramount Parks*,[236] where plaintiffs alleged that Kings Dominion Park Police where answerable, in a supervisory sense, to the public office of the local county sheriff. The case is further complicated by an employee manual that designates the necessary interaction of the private force with public authority. The manual listed a chain of commands that undeniably integrates public policing into this private security context.

> The Chain of Command and authority for all Kings Dominion Park Police shall be as follows involving official law enforcement:
>
> a. Sheriff of Hanover County
> b. Lieutenant of Kings Dominion Park Police
> c. Kings Dominion Park Police Sergeant
> d. Kings Dominion Park Police Corporal
> e. Kings Dominion Park Police Officer[237]

Despite this clear entanglement of private/public law enforcement, the Austin majority rejected the plaintiff's allegation of sufficient public assumption to trigger constitutional protections. The court further held that the Park's Manager of Loss Prevention lacked all authority over the operations of the public force and dismissed the argument with scant reservation.

> Put simply, there was no evidence that Hester, despite his title of Manager of Loss Prevention, in practice exercised any control over the decisions of the special police officer regarding detention and/or arrests of park guests suspected of criminal offenses in this case. … In fact, we find no support in the record for any specific policy-making authority given to or exercised by Hester regarding matters of law enforcement.[238]

5.4.3 Public function of private security

Proponents of the public function theory would expand and extend the protections of the Fourth Amendment and other aligned constitutional provisions by alleging the public nature of tasks performed by private security. The theory of public function was first advocated in *Marsh v. Alabama*.[239] The case involved a company town, which was privately owned, though its services and functions mirrored a typical municipality or city. Services undertaken primarily for the benefit of the general public, and exercising functions traditionally associated with a form of sovereignty, can lead to a public function charge. Advocates of the public function doctrine assertively point out that all police functions are inherently public in nature and design. "Policing is one of the most basic functions of the sovereign when security personnel are hired to protect business premises, arrest, question and search for evidence against criminal suspects. They perform public police functions."[240] In the eyes of Professor William J. O'Donnell, in his article, "Private Security, Privacy in the Fourth Amendment,"[241] courts give far too much credence to the legal status of the party performing the public function rather than the function itself. He notes persuasively:

> On the other hand where status does not correspond with function courts have been too quick to rule out state action. Security guards who have not been deputized, specially commissioned, or otherwise formally charged to protect public interest are routinely equated with private persons by courts despite the fact they are hired to survey, apprehend, detain, and interrogate criminal suspects.[242]

Professor O'Donnell proposes a reorientation to function in place of occupational status. State action, therefore, is evaluated in light of what is done, rather than who is doing it.

> This kind of problem exists, of course, largely because legal authorities continue to define state action principally on the basis of status rather than function—a *de jure* as opposed to a de facto orientation. As long as this remains the approach,

[236] 195 F.3d 715 (4th Cir. 1999).
[237] *Ibid.* at 730.
[238] *Ibid.*
[239] Marsh v. Alabama, 326 U.S. 501 (1946).
[240] Euller at 658.
[241] O'Donnell at 11.
[242] *Ibid.* at 12.

however, the threats to individual privacy rights will increase in proportion to the privatization of policing. A functional approach … subject[s] the greater portion of private security industry to Fourth Amendment coverage.[243]

That security performs an enormous array of public functions, which include, but are not limited to, arresting shoplifters, controlling crowds, keeping peace in educational institutions, correctional institutions, providing secure environments in banks, hospitals, and other institutions open to the general public, is not a debatable contention. If this is so, does participation in public functions naturally lead to public status?

The public function analysis is particularly persuasive when applied to cases involving private security protection. The demands of modern commerce have created a need for large numbers of private security forces to assist in the protection of persons and property. Private security companies and their personnel engage in activities that are normally reserved to the police. They often have authority to detain suspects, conduct investigations, and make arrests. Their actions can be as intrusive to individual privacy rights as those carried out by the police. Whether these activities can be construed or defined strictly as governmental functions and thereby as state action subject to the Fourth Amendment may be a breach too difficult to fill.[244] If function becomes the dominating factor, then status becomes irrelevant.

Public function theorists posit that a private citizen's privacy rights are undermined when the unreasonableness of a search is "made to depend on the identity of the searcher rather than the activity itself and its infringement on his privacy."[245] This argument was unconvincingly made in *New Hampshire v. Keyser*.[246] The setting included a department store shopper who switched the contents of a $6.99 cooler with two tape decks worth a total of $150.00. The defendant claimed he had no knowledge of how the tape decks got into the box. Upon conviction, the defendant appealed, asserting that his Fourth Amendment rights were violated, not by the members of the local police department, but instead by the security guards. The court noted the issues:

> The question in this case is whether the Fourth Amendment protections extend to the action of the security guards because of their authority, official appearance and police-type function.[247]

Providing security in a retail store environment is an insufficient basis to invoke the exclusionary rule.[248] Hence, the future of the public function argument appears less likely to expand into the private security domain as other competitive theories.

5.4.4 Color of state law: A legislative remedy

When constitutionalism fails, the appellate strategist considers legal actions based on statutory schema. Instead of a plea rooted in the Bill of Rights, the advocate urges remedial action based on a particular code or section of a particular act. For example, claims based on civil rights infractions and violations are commonly witnessed in the actions against private security personnel. Borrowing from the civil rights theater, plaintiffs assert civil rights violations, infractions, and other wrongs by utilizing the "color of state law" standard discoverable at 42 U.S.C. §1983.[249]

Put another way, the advocate does not claim a harm arising under a particular amendment, but rather an injury to self or property caused by a specific action, which eventually connects to some state action. Proof or demonstration that a state action caused a personal loss, affront, or indignity under the auspices of color of state law, is part and parcel of the *Civil Rights Acts*, and in select portions of the said Acts, these allegations must be grounded in matters that are racially, religiously, or ethnically motivated. Examples might be arbitrary state licensing boards or bodies that

---

[243] W. Clinton Terry, *Policing Society* (1985).

[244] People v. Holloway, 82 Mich. App. 629, 267 N.W. 2d 454 (1978).

[245] State v. Keyser, 369 A 2d 224 (1977).

[246] *Ibid.* at 225.

[247] *Ibid.* at 226.

[248] See Smith v. Brookshire, Inc., 519 F.2d 93 (5th Cir. 1975); cert denied, 424 U.S. 915, 96 S. Ct. 1115, 47 L. Ed. 2d 320 (1976); Duriso v. K-Mart No. 4195, Division of Kresge Co., 559 F.2d 1274 (5th Cir. 1977); El Fundi v. Deroche, 625 F.2d 195 (8th Cir. 1980); White v. Scraner Corp., 594 F.2d 140 (5th Cir. 1979).

[249] See Civil Liability for Acts of Off-Duty Officers—Part I, 9 AELE Mo. L. J. 101 (2007) at http://www.juridicainternational.eu/public/pdf/ji_2009_1_44.pdf, last visited August 27, 2016.

reject applications on racial grounds, or denial or rejection of applicants based on religion or creed. Another claim might be a contrived or intentional plan to single out targeted minority groups in a shoplifting deterrence program.[250]

To claim that security officers or other personnel are acting under color of state law requires objective proof of a racial, religious, or gender motivation, or at least a demonstration that the acts alleged and the injury inflicted were done under the auspices and approval of the state or other governmental authority. The *Civil Rights Acts* have leaned toward a more liberal application in recent years with their emphasis on personal harm arising because of government action by government personnel.[251]

A well-respected Pennsylvania Superior Court decision, *Commonwealth v. Lacey*,[252] assessed an appellant's claim that a statute governing security guard conduct provided a basis for a color of state law declaration. The court, in interpreting a retail theft statute, dealt precisely with the color of state question:

> A peace officer, merchant, or merchant's employee, or an agent under contract with a merchant who has probable cause to believe that retail theft has occurred or is occurring on or about a store or other retail mercantile establishment and has probable cause to believe that a specific person has committed or is committing the retail theft may detain the suspect in a reasonable manner for a reasonable time on or off the premises for all or any of the following purposes: to require the suspect to identify himself, to verify such identification, to determine whether such suspect has in his possession un-purchased merchandise taken from the mercantile establishment, and, if so, to recover such merchandise, to inform a peace officer or to institute criminal proceedings against the suspect, such detention shall not impose civil or criminal liability on the peace officer, merchant, employee or agent so detaining.[253]

The appellant's reasoning concludes that the retail theft statute, in its terms and applicability, inherently bestows police powers on private persons, which the court completely rejected.

A direct relationship between a public official and private security agent is required for proof of color of state law. The evidence must demonstrate significant involvement of the private agent acting under a state law and as a result, causing injury. In *Bouye v. Marshall*,[254] a U.S. District Court held, in the rarest of cases, that an off-duty county police officer crossed the line from private to public since he "wore a police sweatshirt and bullet-proof vest, displayed badge, was performing police function, and used police authority to detain and search visitor."[255]

To prove color of state law cases, the courts have devised a series of tests that seek to quantify the level of state involvement, such as the *significant involvement test*. The test mandates a look at how much state action and state oversight played a role in the harm inflicted while simultaneously looking for participatory schemes between state and federal officials. In *Byars v. United States*,[256] the Supreme Court held that evidence was inadmissible when the unreasonable search and seizure was performed by state officials, concluding that state law enforcement was significant enough to satisfy the term "significant."

Another argument bolstering color of state law theory is the *police security nexus* test. "Under the nexus approach to state action analysis, a court considers the facts of the situation, looks for a contact between the private actor and the government, and makes a qualitative judgment as to whether there is enough involvement in a challenged action to say that it was an action of the state."[257] As in previous attempts to corral in the protection of the Fourth Amendment, liberal constructionists must show either a significant involvement; a private action fostered, authorized, or colored by state authority; or a public–private relationship conspiratorial in design. The natural procedural ties that develop between private security and public policing give further ammunition to those who propose an expansion of the color of state law theory. Since both public and private law enforcement seek similar ends, are hankering for increased cooperation, and are increasing their overall interaction, some critics call for an end to the immune status accorded

---

[250] Davis v. Carson Pirie Scott and Co., 530 F. Supp. 799 (1982).

[251] United States v. McGreevy, 652 F.2d 849 (9th Cir. 1981).

[252] 471 A. 2d 888 (Pa. Super. 1984).

[253] Commonwealth v. Lacey, 471 A. 2d 888 (Pa. Super. 1984).

[254] 102 F.Supp.2d 1357 (N.D.Ga. 2000).

[255] *Ibid*. at 1358.

[256] 273 U.S. 28 (1927). See also Gambino v. U.S. 275 U.S. 310 (1927); see also Stonehill v. U.S., 405 F.2d 738 (9th Cir. 1968); U.S. v. Mekjian, 505 F.2d 1320 (5th Cir. 1975). Note, Private Searches and Seizures at 185.

[257] *Ibid*.

private practice.[258] Not unexpectedly, public law enforcement has long been considered the private security industry feeder system for informants and assistance. There is a pipeline of trained investigators and security administrators moving from public law enforcement agencies into the private sector. These agencies train the personnel in patrol techniques, investigation, interrogation, arrest, search and seizure, and police administration.

5.4.5 Private security and Miranda warnings

Constitutional protections apply to governmental action only. Extending warnings prior to custodial interrogation in private security settings has generally not been required though the climate for change alters according to abuses.[259] There have been cracks in this solid wall of immunity. A series of reports involving Cumberland Farm convenience stores, in Boston, allege an array of abuses by security guards who charged employees with theft. "Almost without exception, employees said they were subjected to the same procedure. Each was taken to a backroom, seated on an overturned milk crate, accused of theft and threatened with public humiliation or prosecution if they did not sign a confession of guilt. This process continued for years, but the accused individuals failed to take significant action because they did not know that other employees were similarly treated."[260] A host of Cumberland employees brought a class action against the employer.[261] So extensive were the alleged abuses that certain legal commentators, like Joan E. Marshall, made impassioned pleas in the *Dickinson Law Review* for extending Miranda protection to the private sector.

> Despite historical reasons for allowing merchants to practice so-called self-help in the protection of their property, the example of employee abuse by Cumberland Farms shows the need for new legislation to prevent the Fifth Amendment from becoming an anachronism. While some civil action may lie for harassment, the employee who is essentially robbed of his cash, his job, and his reputation is unlikely to feel vindicated even if victorious. Allowing evidence obtained in backroom interrogations to be turned over to the State for prosecution directly contradicts the Fifth Amendment guarantee that coerced confessions cannot and will not be used against an individual in a court of law.
>
> Clearly, courts will exclude confessions if they were not, "voluntarily" given following "reasonable" efforts by private security. Not all merchants, however, are interested in prosecuting their employees. Testimony from former Cumberland Farms' employees shows that there is a great deal of money to be gained by threatening employees. Private security guards in uniform carry visible authority. The courts and legislatures must recognize that this authority may be abused, particularly given the minimal restrictions placed in private security guards.[262]

The authority for this plea has limited precedential support. In *Williams v. United States*,[263] the court found that a private detective who held a special police officer's card and badge granted, authorized, and licensed by the state and who was accompanied by a city police officer in obtaining evidence, was acting under color of state law.[264] The decision, though chronologically pre-Miranda, set some persuasive authority for *Tarnef v. State*.[265] In *Tarnef*, a private investigator, working under the direction of local police, was required to advise the defendant of his constitutional rights before eliciting a statement. Cases in which private security are acting in consort with, under the authority of, or at the encouragement or enticement of the public sector forge the nexus necessary for Miranda rights.[266] Cases involving moonlighting police officers and off-duty deputy sheriffs have held that Miranda rights are generally not required.[267] The California Supreme Court in a retail setting, held the Miranda rights inapplicable under the following reasoning:

1. Store detectives do not enjoy the psychological advantage of official authority when they confront a suspected shoplifter.

2. Store detectives believe that they must act with greater circumspection to avoid costly civil suits than do police officers. Thus, the compelling atmosphere inherent in custodial interrogation is diminished.

---

[258] See generally National Institute of Justice, *Crime and Protection in America: A Study of Private Security and Law Enforcement Resources and Relationships* (1985).

[259] People v. Oxnell, 166 N.W. 2d 279 (1968); see also Aitchison; del Carmen, Criminal Procedure; del Carmen & Kappeler at 1–17; Ryals.

[260] J.E. Marshall, The At-Will Employee and Coerced Confessions of Theft: Extending Fifth Amendment Protection to Private Security Guard Abuse, 96 *Dickinson L. Rev.* 37, 40 (1991).

[261] Curly v. Cumberland Farms, Inc., 13 F.R.D. 77 (D. N.J. 1991).

[262] Marshall at 57; see also Aitchison; del Carmen, Criminal Procedure; del Carmen & Kappeler at 1–17; Ryals.

[263] 341 U.S. 97 (1951).

[264] Williams v. U.S., 341 U.S. 97 (1951); City of Grand Rapids v. Impens, 327 N.W.2d 278 (Mich. 1982).

[265] 512 P.2d 923 (Alaska 1973).

[266] See Griffin v. Maryland, 378 U.S. 130 (1964); People v. Jones, 288 N.W.2d 385 (Mich. App. 1979).

[267] See People v. Faulkner, 282 N.W.2d 377 (Mich. App. 1979).

3. Store detectives may only detain those who shoplift in their presence, limiting any motivation they might otherwise have to vigorously seek confessions.

4. If a store detective engages in psychological or physical abuse or provides improper inducements, any resulting statements by a defendant would be involuntary and an exclusionary remedy would be available.[268]

5.4.6 The law of citizen's arrest: The private security standard

The scope of permissible citizen's arrest has remained fairly constant in American jurisprudence. At common law, the private citizenry could make a permissible arrest for the commission of any felony in order to protect the safety of the public.[269] An arrest could also be effected for misdemeanors that constituted a breach of the peace or public order, but only when immediate apprehension and a presence of an arresting officer was demonstrated. Much of our contemporary analysis of reasonable suspicion and probable cause also relates to the citizen's right to subject another individual to the arrest process. "A citizen could perform a valid and lawful arrest on his own authority, if the person arrested committed a misdemeanor in his presence or if there were reasonable grounds to believe that a felony was being or had been committed by the arrestee although not in the presence of the arresting citizen."[270] Private citizens are also permitted to search individuals that they have arrested or detained for safety reasons, and this right is comparable to the incident to arrest or stop and frisk standard applicable in the public jurisdiction. "When an articulable suspicion of danger exists, granting a private policeman or citizen the authority to search for the purpose of finding or seizing weapons of an arrestee is at least equivalent to a pat down approved by Terry, and seems to be a necessary concomitant of the power to arrest."[271]

When compared to public officials' arrest rights, the private citizen has a heavier burden of demonstrating actual knowledge, presence at the events, or other firsthand experience that justifies the apprehension. These added requirements of citizen's arrest reflect caution. In some states, a private citizen can arrest under any of the following scenarios:

1. For the public offense (misdemeanor) committed or attempted in his presence

2. When the person arrested has committed a felony and the private citizen has probable cause to believe so, although not in his presence

3. When the felony has been in fact committed and the private citizen has reasonable cause for believing the person arrested has committed that offense

Statutorily, the scope of citizen's arrest varies according to jurisdiction. Two legislative examples are:

Alaska:

1. A private person or a peace officer without a warrant may arrest a person

   a. For a crime committed or attempted in the presence of the person making the arrest;

   b. When the person has committed a felony, although not in the presence of the person making the arrest;

   c. When a felony has in fact been committed, and the person making the arrest has reasonable cause for believing the person to have committed it.[272]

New York:

§ 140.30. Arrest without a warrant; by any person; when and where authorized

1. Subject to the provisions of subdivision two, any person may arrest another person (a) for a felony when the latter has in fact committed such felony, and (b) for any offense when the latter has in fact committed such offense in his presence.

---

[268] R.K. Federal & J.L. Fogleman, *Avoiding Liability in Retail Security, A Casebook* 168–169 (1986), quoting Metigoruk v. Anchorage, 655 P.2d 1317 (Alaska App. 1982).

[269] Note, The Law of Citizen's Arrest, 65 *Colum. L. Rev.* 502 (1965); see also L. Harrison, Citizen's Arrest or Police Arrest? Defining the Scope of Alaska's Delegated Citizen's Arrest Doctrine, 82 *Wash. L. Rev.* (2007).

[270] National Advisory Committee at 393.

[271] Note, Private Police Forces: Legal Powers and Limitations, 38 *U. Chic. L. Rev.* 565 (1971); see also Pastor, *Security Law*; Pastor, *Privatization of Police*.

[272] Alaska Stat. §12.25.030 (2010).

2. Such an arrest, if for a felony, may be made anywhere in the state. If the arrest is for an offense other than a felony, it may be made only in the county in which such offense was committed.[273]

To thwart and effectively defend against citizen-based challenges to the regularity of the citizen's arrest, the security officer conducting any arrest should complete documentation that justifies the decision making.

Generally, legislation, concerning citizen's arrest, needs to attend to diverse variables and criteria that determine its legality. Types and category of crimes, standards of action, time of day, and alternative retreat potential, are but a few of these. Critics have charged that the codification appears to be "more a product of legislation in discrimination than a logical adaptation of a common law principle to the conditions of modern society."[274] While legislators hope and wish for skilled, trained, and educated individuals to effect as many arrests as possible, the statutes have essentially sought a middle ground permitting arrests only when needed and emphasizing the system of citizen referral to public authority when at all possible. However, the process of citizen's arrest is "filled with legal pitfalls," which "may depend on a number of legal distinctions, such as the nature of the crime being committed, proof of actual presence at the time, and place of the incident."[275] Some analyses of these variables and factors follow.

5.4.6.1 Time of the arrest

Both common law and statutory rationales for the privilege or right of citizen's arrest impose time restrictions on the arresting party. In the case of felonies, the felon's continuous evasion of authorities was considered a substantial and continuing threat against the public order and police. Therefore, an arresting party could complete the process regarding a felon at any time. Persons committing misdemeanors, however, were afforded greater protection from private citizen's arrest actions. Some states require that the person committing a misdemeanor be arrested by a private citizen only when actually engaging in conduct that undermines the public order. However, other states have dramatically expanded the misdemeanor defense category beyond the breach of the public peace typology. More specifically, states have expanded the arrest power to include petty larceny and shoplifting,[276] and have provided a rational barometer of when citizens' arrests are appropriate.

Also relevant to time limitation analysis is "freshness" of the pursuit. A delay or deferral of the arrest process will result in a loss of the arrest privilege. Predictably, freshness in the pursuit may be difficult to measure in precise terms. Timing restrictions "serve to compel reliance on police once the danger of immediate public harm from criminal activity has ceased."[277]

5.4.6.2 Presence and commission

Presence during commission of the offence is a clear requirement in a case involving misdemeanors where firsthand, actual knowledge corroborates the arresting party's decision making. "The purpose of the requirement is presumably to prevent the danger and imposition involved in mistaken arrests based upon uncorroborated or second hand information. Its principal impact is in cases where the citizen learns the commission of a crime and assumes the responsibility of preventing the escape of an offender."[278] If firsthand observation is called for, the arrest is properly based on an eyewitness view. In other cases, especially the full range of felonies, a citizen can arrest another person based on the standard of reasonable grounds, a close companion to the probable cause test. To find probable cause, one must demonstrate that someone has committed, is likely committing, or is about to commit a crime. Being present during an offense plainly meets this standard. But numerous other cases are just as probative despite a lack of immediate presence. Critics have charged that requiring presence as a basis for the privilege to arrest is nonsensical. A note in the *Columbia Law Review* gives an example by analogy:

> It is here that the requirement produces incongruous results. If a citizen hears a scream and turns around to see a bleeding victim on the ground and a fleeing figure, he can arrest the assailant with impunity. Yet if he comes upon the scene but a moment later under identical circumstances, his apprehension of the fugitive would be illegal.[279]

---

[273] N.Y. C.P.L. § 140.30 (2010).
[274] Note, Citizen's Arrest at 504.
[275] National Advisory Committee at 391.
[276] Private Security Advisory Council at 10.
[277] Note, Citizen's Arrest at 505.
[278] *Ibid*. at 506.
[279] *Ibid*. at 506–507.

Table 5.2 Citizen's arrest standards by state

State	Minor offense — Type of minor offense						Minor offense — Type of knowledge required					Major offense — Type of major offense													Certainty of correct arrest		
	Crime	Misdemeanor amounting to a breach of the peace	Breach of the peace	Public offense	Offense	Offense other than an ordinance	Immediate knowledge	Presence	Immediate knowledge	View	Upon reasonable grounds that is being committed	Felony	Larceny	Petit larceny	Crime involving physical injury to another	Crime	Crime involving theft or destruction of property	Committed in presence	Information a felony has been committed	View	Reasonable grounds to believe being committed	That felony has been committed in fact	Is escaping or attempting	Summoned by peace officer to assist in arrest	Is in the act of committing	Reasonable grounds to believe person arrested committed	Probably cause
Alabama				X				X				X														X	
Alaska	X																										
Arizona		X																									
Arkansas																					X	X					
California				X				X														X					
Colorado	X														X				X								
Georgia	X			X								X			X										X	X	
Hawaii	X							X							X				X								
Idaho			X									X										X				X	
Illinois					X						X	X									X					X	
Iowa			X					X				X														X	
Kentucky												X															
Louisiana												X															
Michigan																			X					X			
Minnesota			X				X																			X	
Mississippi			X	X			X																			X	
Montana														X													
Nebraska															X												
Nevada				X	X																						
New York					X	X																					
North Carolina			X													X	X					X					X
North Dakota			X					X													X						
Ohio			X					X				X									X						
Oklahoma	X			X				X				X															
Oregon	X														X		X										X
South Carolina											X	X	X				X										
South Dakota			X					X																		X	
Tennessee		X	X						X								X					X					
Texas		X	X					X								X	X									X	
Utah			X					X				X										X				X	
Wyoming												X	X									X				X	

A few jurisdictions have attempted to reconcile this dilemma by allowing felony arrests to occur without a presence requirement. Presence is simply replaced with reasonable grounds or reasonable cause criteria. A review of citizen's arrest standards on a state-by-state basis is provided in Table 5.2.

Note that Table 5.2 makes a distinction between minor and major offenses, namely, between felonies and misdemeanors. It also outlines the general grounds leading to a finding of probable or reasonable grounds required to effect an arrest. Some general statutory conclusions can be made:

1. Probable cause, the standard utilized for arrest, search, and seizure by public officials is not commonly employed in the citizen's arrest realm.
2. Reasonable grounds is the standard generally employed by statutes outlining a citizen's right to arrest.
3. Presence is generally required in all minor offenses commonly known as misdemeanors.
4. Presence is required in a minority of jurisdictions in felony cases.
5. Before an arrest can be effected in a felony case, the private citizen must have some definitive knowledge that a felony has been committed.

Web Exercise: See the Pennsylvania Code's guidance on citizens' arrest and the appropriate use of force at: http://www.legis.state.pa.us/cfdocs/legis/li/consCheck.cfm?txtType=HTM&ttl=18&div=00.&chpt=005.&sctn=008.&subsctn=000.

Depending upon jurisdiction, another factor to be considered by security personnel in the arrest process is notice, an announcement advising a suspect of one's intention to arrest. The level of force utilized and the detention techniques for a person awaiting formal processing may also be significant factors in any resolution of the propriety of a citizen's arrest.

5.5 CONCLUSION

The private security industry and its managerial class, in particular, need to understand a great deal of law and legal principles in order to properly carry out its many functions. While it is surely true that the industry has a constitutional advantage in relation to its public police counterparts, this advantage does not negate or minimize the various forms of legal liability that the industry needs to prepare for and prevent—for all legal liability eventually impacts the bottom line. In the private security industry, civil liability is the greatest liability challenge, especially from a "negligence" perspective where company and owners, officers, and managers err in their performance and cause significant, measurable harm to identifiable victims of that negligence whether it be in actual performance of duties, training and oversight, and supervision and retention. Negligence undergirds literally every facet of private security industry performance. Just as compellingly, private security operatives may engage in other civil harms such as the traditional intentional torts like assault, wrongful death, infliction of mental distress, false imprisonment, and defamation. This chapter lays out all the fundamental elements of these causes of action and covers strict liability torts too. After this, the reader is exposed to the types of crimes that security specialists often find themselves accused of—from assault and false arrest to theft and burglary. Private security officers can be liable under simultaneous legal theories, both civil and criminal. Finally, this chapter highlights the stark differences in constitutional applications when it comes to the arrest, search, and seizure function, and while the industry has generally maintained its safe harbor from this constitutional scrutiny, recent efforts to erode that protection have been more frequently witnessed, especially when the industry is entangled with public police, where there is active cooperation and partnership between the two entities in order to bypass constitutional protections or when courts accept novel theories like the public function argument, whereby the role of the officer is defined by the public nature of the function carried out. Various, although very rare, case law decisions that undermine the historic inapplicability of the Bill of Rights to private security are featured and analyzed.

Keywords

abuse of process	assault	Bill of Rights
arson	battery	burglary

citizen's arrest

civil justice

civil liability

civil remedies

Civil Rights Act

color of state law

constitution

conversion

criminal law

criminal penalties

deadly force

deceit

defamation

exclusionary rule

false imprisonment

felony

forgery

fraudulent behavior

intentional infliction of emotional distress

intentional torts

invasion of privacy

justifiable force

larceny

legal liability

malicious prosecution

Miranda warnings

misdemeanor

negligence

platinum platter doctrine

police security nexus

premeditation search

prima facie case

private action

purposely

receiving stolen property

respondeat superior

retail theft

robbery

seizure

self-defense

shoplifting

significant involvement test

state action

strict liability torts

theft

theft by deception

theft by extortion

theft of services

tort remedies

trespass

use of force

vicarious liability

warrants

willfully

Discussion questions

1. Discuss the major differences between civil liability and criminal activities as it relates to intentionality and harm.
2. Define intentional torts, negligence, and strict liability torts and give examples of each type of civil harm.
3. Describe three of the types of defenses that can be used in criminal prosecutions against private security operatives.
4. Outline the theory of vicarious liability and respondeat superior as it relates to private security.
5. Compare and contrast the crimes of theft by deception and theft by extortion.
6. Discuss how the platinum platter doctrine applies to the exclusionary rule.

CHAPTER 6

Risk management

OBJECTIVES

After completing this chapter, the student will be able to

1. Describe how private security operates in the world of risk management and provides for a safe and secure environment.
2. Outline which methods for prediction and mitigation of risk are the most suitable.
3. Define a threat, its scope, types, and categories, and then distinguish between the natural and man-made varieties of risk.
4. Summarize how to identify risk, how to assess its impact, and how to track its influence.
5. Relate the most effective means of planning and preparing for risk.
6. Discuss the similarities and differences between threats and hazards.
7. Recognize and identify the four basic categories of weapons of mass destruction.
8. Name the various threats and vulnerabilities that exist to software, hardware, and information technology.

6.1 INTRODUCTION

The fundamental thrust of security, dealing with risks, threats, and hazards, encompasses this chapter. In other words, how does private security operate in the world of risk and threat and provide for a safe and secure environment? What means and methods for prediction and mitigation are the most suitable? What types of plans and planning seem to work best? This chapter delves into standard as well as best practices in the risk management arena. First, it will consider the idea of threat, its scope and definition, its types and categories, and the distinction between the natural and man-made varieties. Second, the coverage will include an analysis of risk theory—that body of thought that teaches operatives how to identify risk, how to assess its impact, and how to track its influence. In addition to risk and threat, the chapter will evaluate the most efficacious means of planning and preparedness. It could be said that an ounce of prevention is worth a pound of cure. How one prepares for tragedy has much to do with its success or failure in response and recovery. How one trains and educates the professional can be just as telling.

In the world of risk managcmcnt, interests cannot simply wait for the government to do it all but must jump into the mix of deterrence and prevention. Infrastructure is largely owned by private enterprise and is in need of a defense plan. "Industries must plan to respond … and undertake recovery under severe conditions where much of the infrastructure of the surrounding area is unavailable and site access is limited."[1] Preparedness is an industrial and

---

[1] N. Santella & L. Steinberg, Accidental Releases of Hazardous Materials and Relevance to Terrorist Threats at Industrial Facilities, 8 *J. Homeland Sec. & Emergency Mgmt.* 11 (2011).

commercial concern. And it is also the private citizen that encompasses the private sector as well. The question of how much more prepared private homes and families can be has yet to be fully measured.[2]

Each facet of the private sector needs to understand

- How communities are impacted by crime and terrorism
- How to create a plan of response consistent with state and federal standards
- How to mitigate loss in the event of catastrophe and disaster
- How to be active partners in the development of policies and procedures
- How to work closely with public agencies
- How to add new programs in traditional Neighborhood Watch programs that focus on terrorism[3]

On a second front, the role of private sector security firms and personnel in relation to risk management can only be described as significant. The private sector portion of criminal justice operations grows at an almost immeasurable clip.[4] According to the Homeland Security Research Corporation, the private sector "will trail only DHS in HLS industry procurement volume. This stems from the forecasted 50% private sector procurement growth from 2007–2011, totaling an accumulated $28.5B."[5] From Iraq to the local water facility, private sector justice operatives are engaged in a host of activities once exclusively reserved for the public sector. This trend, often labeled "privatization," assumes that the private sector, with its usual efficiencies and profit motivations, will carry out its task with greater effectiveness.

In this sense, the private sector is driven by bottom-line considerations more than its governmental counterpart. It is motivated by efficiencies never weighed or evaluated in the public sector.

As the Bureau of Justice Assistance notes in its *Engaging Private Security to Promote Homeland Security*, private sector justice can jump in with feet first. Private security can

- Coordinate plans with the public sector regarding evacuation, transportation, and food services during emergencies
- Gain information from law enforcement regarding threats and crime trends
- Develop relationships so that private practitioners know whom to contact when they need help or want to report information
- Build law enforcement understanding of corporate needs (e.g., confidentiality)
- Boost law enforcement's respect for the security field

Working together, private security and law enforcement can realize impressive benefits:

- Creative problem solving
- Increased training opportunities
- Information, data, and intelligence sharing
- Force multiplier opportunities
- Access to the community through private sector communications technology
- Reduced recovery time following disasters[6]

---

[2] M. Kano et al., Terrorism Preparedness and Exposure Reduction since 9/11: The Status of Public Readiness in the United States, *J. Homeland Sec. & Emergency Mgmt.*, 8 (2011).

[3] J. Fleischman, Engaging the Private Sector in Local Homeland Defense: The Orange County Private Sector Terrorism Response Group, *Sheriff* 33 (September/October 2004).

[4] C.P. Nemeth, *Private Security and the Law* 12 (London: Elsevier, 2008).

[5] Homeland Security Research Corporation, Private Sector to Become 2nd Largest Homeland Security Industry Customer by 2011, News release (April 9, 2008), at http://homelandsecurityresearch.com/2008/03/private-sector-to-become-2nd-largest-hls-industry-customer-by-2011/, last accessed August 27, 2016.

[6] Bureau of Justice Assistance, *Engaging the Private Sector to Promote Homeland Security: Law Enforcement-Private Security Partnerships* 11 (2003).

Position Information:

Plans, directs, and administers a comprehensive city-wide program for risk management, loss prevention, and loss control; develops and implements policies, procedures, and programs; serves as advisor and technical resource for City officials, managers, and employees; and performs other related duties as required.

Additional Job Information:

At time of application, you must be a citizen, national, or permanent resident alien of the United States or a noncitizen eligible under federal law for unrestricted employment.

Salary Negotiable, pending approval and subject to funding availability.

1 Only ONLINE applications will be accepted.
2. Paper applications will NOT be accepted.

There is one vacancy with the Department of Budget & Fiscal Services. Vacancy is located in Honolulu. This list may be used to fill future vacancies in this and/or other departments.

Minimum Qualification Requirements:

EDUCATION REQUIREMENT

Equivalent to graduation from an accredited four-year college or university with a bachelor's degree in public or business administration, the social sciences, or a related field. Work experience may be substituted for a bachelor's degree on a year-for-year basis. Such experience must have provided the knowledge, skills, and analytical ability normally gained from attainment of a bachelor's degree.

Verification Requirement: You must submit evidence of your education in order to be given credit. Please attach an electronic copy of your diploma and/or official transcript which shows the embossed seal to your application. Or mail or drop off a photocopy of your diploma and/or official transcript by the closing date of this recruitment to the following address: *Department of Human Resources, 650 South King Street, 10th Floor, Honolulu, HI 96813.*

Unofficial transcripts will not be accepted. All information on your diploma and/or transcript must be legible in order to receive credit. Copies will not be returned.

EXPERIENCE REQUIREMENT

Three years of responsible administrative experience in risk management or in the management, investigation, and adjustment of insurance claims, including but not limited to workers' compensation, general liability, vehicular bodily injury, and property damage.

Such experience must have demonstrated knowledge of: risk management concepts and techniques; methods of handling risk exposure; claims administration and adjustment services; the various types and purposes of insurance agreements; insurance theories, practices, laws, and regulations; sources of information pertinent to insurance matters; and State and Federal safety laws. Additionally, such experience must have demonstrated the ability to: analyze and evaluate exposure to losses and resolve risk exposure problems; measure the financial impact of various risks; and analyze and interpret insurance policies and problems.

Nonqualifying Experience: Work experience acquired as an insurance salesperson or agent, in processing insurance claims, or in loss prevention or safety, which does not demonstrate knowledge of risk management principles and applications including risk financing and loss control, is not qualifying.

NOTES

Additional Salary Information: EM-05

Figure CP6.1 Career Profile: Risk management director—City of Honolulu.

6.2 RISK MANAGEMENT

The work of private security delves into the nature of risk, whether at airports or busways, public courthouses, or national monuments. Risk constitutes what might happen or what is likely to happen, given a certain set of circumstances. Risk is what can go wrong. Risk is what the stay-behind homeowner takes when he or she fails to get out of the path of a hurricane. Risk is what air travelers are willing to tolerate in an air system that lacks security checkpoints. Risk is what the country will tolerate when no mechanisms exist to check visitors at the border. In a word, risk is something each person lives with each day, from driving in a car to cycling across the hinterlands. Yet some risks are more preventable and less serious than others. In evaluating risk, one must look to not only the nature of any risk, but also its consequences in both an individual and collective sense. Some refer to this formula in an equational sense[7]—as a series of risk constituents. The risk is calculated relative to the harm the hazard causes and the level and magnitude of exposure to the said harm. The formula might look like this:

$$Risk = Hazard \times Exposure$$

Hazard is the mechanism that causes the harm, and exposure the extent, depth, and breadth of the risk as influenced by the nature of the hazard. Thus, if anthrax is plugged into the risk equation, it is a small chore to conclude that anthrax constitutes the type of risk the individual and the collective should avoid. In a policy context, therefore, it makes perfect sense for governments to marshal resources to attack this risk—more so than an avalanche of candy bars from an upended truck. Herein lies the rub—to weigh and factor the risk in light of harm and its scope. Some risks are high, others lower, and some "risks" pose no risk at all. To be sure, terrorism is high up on the list of potential harms that the specialist must prepare for. "Terrorism has many faces and countless are the possibilities of implementing an attack against American interests under the umbrella of terrorism."[8] The risk manager must anticipate every imaginable scenario to properly prepare for it.

Looked at from a different perch, risk relies upon probability analysis.

6.2.1 Nature of risk

Risk is not an easy concept to fully define for it has both actual and anticipatory qualities. On the one hand, all one can do is predict or anticipate what might happen; yet, on the other hand, experience dictates the reality of risk. For example, will the risk injure a human? Is it likely that this risk will be in the form of a weapon? Is there a correlation between some religious practice and an act of terror? Is there a particular day or holiday where events are more apt to occur? If a chemical industry fails to secure a certain substance, what are the health ramifications? One could go on endlessly about the nature of risk and its various types. To be sure, the concept is forever evolving. FEMA makes a valiant effort to quantify the process. FEMA employs probability theory when making judgments about risk. In short, risk is the probability that something will occur with an evaluation of consequence.[9] See Table 6.1.

The Department of Homeland Security (DHS) defines the nature of risk by three principal variables: *threat*, or the likelihood of a type of attack that might be attempted; *vulnerability*, or the likelihood that an attacker would succeed with a particular attack method; and *consequence*, or the potential impact, individually or collectively, of a particular attack. In this context, one deals in generalities rather than specifics. Sound risk reasoning demands that a measure or modality of quantification be employed when making policy about risk. In other words, can risk be quantified in some way? FEMA thinks so by evaluating some specific variable relative to the nature of the risk.[10] See Figure 6.1.

Here, the evaluator of risk moves beyond the definition seeking to formalize the precise nature and attributes of risk. What is this risk worth? How much, in terms of assets, will it destroy? What level, in a global sense, of seriousness does this risk pose? How much is at stake? When, compared to other assets, is it worth our dedication to thwart all

Table 6.1   Definition of risk

Risk is a combination of
- The probability that an event will occur
- The consequences of its occurrence

	Low risk	Medium risk	High risk
Risk factors total	1–60	61–175	≥176

Risk = Asset value × Threat rating × Vulnerability rating

---

[7] J.C. Chicken & T. Posner, *The Philosophy of Risk* (London: Thomas Telford, 1998).

[8] D. Dunai, A Framework of Cardinal Directions: Threats and Challenges to the United States, 10 *AARMS Security* 327–357 (2011), at 331.

[9] Federal Emergency Management Agency, Building Design for Homeland Security (Washington, DC: U.S. Government Printing Office, 2004) V-5.

[10] FEMA, Building Design, V-6.

> *Risk assessment*
>
> Determine asset value
> Determine threat rating value
> Determine vulnerability rating value
> Determine relative risk for each threat against each asset

Figure 6.1   Quantifying risk.

risks? For security professionals, the thrust will be toward quantification—using distinct variables with assigned point values to type the risk. The risk formula should look something like this:

$$\text{Risk} = \text{Asset value} \times \text{Threat rating} \times \text{Vulnerability rating}$$

The severity of a risk will be assessed in light of its value, the nature of the threat itself, and the potential for harm and injury. So, as evident in Table 6.2, infrastructure damage is heavily weighted yet variably dependent upon the method employed to inflict the damage and harm.[11]

So, this leads to the matter of risk assessment in particular terms. How do our private security, homeland professionals, and policy makers decide that this risk is more tolerable than another form of risk? Can they devise a meaningful system of quantification that reliably measures the effect and consequence of a risk gone wrong? Put another way, how can risk be predicted and assessed?

6.2.2 Risk assessment

There are diverse ways in which risk can be measured. The Rand Organization suggests three methodologies of risk assessment:[12]

- *Analytic*: An analytic process must address all three factors that determine terrorism risk—threat, vulnerability, and consequences.
- *Deliberative*: A deliberative process is necessary because the notion of a cold, actuarial terrorism risk assessment is unrealistic. Values and judgment are part and parcel of the process and require transparency and a comprehensive public discussion of outcomes.
- *Practical*: Finally, risk assessment must be practical, which means that data collection and management requirements must be technically and economically feasible.

For example, DHS prefers the analytic, though it would be shortsighted to avoid the other modalities. DHS posits new interesting variables into its risk assessment formula primarily in two ways: the value of asset and the impact on geography. In both instances, the more the value, the more the coverage, and the greater the impact on the populace,

Table 6.2   Critical infrastructure

Infrastructure	Cyber-attack	Armed attack (single gunman)	Vehicle bomb	CBR attack
Site	**48**	**80**	**108**	**72**
Asset value	4	4	4	4
Threat rating	4	4	3	2
Vulnerability rating	3	5	9	9
Structural systems	**48**	**128**	**192**	**144**
Asset value	8	8	8	8
Threat rating	3	4	3	2
Vulnerability rating	2	4	8	9

---

[11] FEMA, Building Design, V-9.
[12] H.R. Willis, *Risk Informed Resource Allocation at the Department of Homeland Security* 3 (Santa Monica: Rand Corporation, 2007).

• Chemical manufacturing facilities	• Natural gas compressor stations
• City road bridges	• Nonpower nuclear reactors
• Colleges and universities	• Nuclear power plants
• Commercial airports	• Nuclear research labs
• Commercial overnight shipping facilities	• Petroleum pumping stations
• Convention centers	• Petroleum refineries
• Dams	• Petroleum storage tanks
• Electricity generation facilities	• Potable water treatment facilities
• Electricity substations	• Primary and secondary schools
• Enclosed shopping malls	• Railroad bridges
• Ferry terminals—buildings	• Railroad passenger stations
• Financial facilities	• Railroad tunnels
• Hospitals	• Road commuter tunnels
• Hotel casinos	• Road interstate bridges
• Levees	• Road interstate tunnels
• Liquefied Natural Gas (LNG) terminals	• Stadiums
• Maritime port facilities	• Tall commercial buildings
• Mass transit commuter rail and subway stations	• Telcomm—telephone hotels
• National health stockpile sites	• Theme parks
• National monuments and icons	• Transoceanic cable landings

Figure 6.2   High-value assets as determined by DHS.

the higher the event will place in tabulations. At first glance, it may seem arbitrary, although nothing in the soft sciences can ever lay claim to the certitude of the hard sciences. What is so strikingly evident is that DHS is willing to place a value on these two things. In a sense, it is about as good as it can be in the imperfect world of risk assessment.

Web Exercise: Find out about the prevent approach to risk assessment at http://www.prevent.se/globalassets/documents/prevent.se/arbetsmiljoarbete/systematiskt-arbetmiljoarbete/checklista/english/checklist_public_places.pdf.

As for value, the DHS and other entities attempt to predict the most notable of the targets a terrorist might choose—chemical plants, stadiums, and commercial airports. DHS then analyzes the vulnerability of each asset type relative to each attack method and plausibility of the chosen attack method. Additionally, DHS computes the consequential costs of a successful attack and its impact on the value of assets, the health of the collective, our economic system, military, and overall psychological impact on the national psyche. This analysis yields a relative risk estimate for each asset type, applied to a given geographic area, and based on the number of each asset type present within that area. DHS lists those assets that carry higher values in its equation in Figure 6.2.[13]

The risk assessment formula is then tested geographically. The geographic-based approach weighs the value of assets in that particular region. Geographic regions are weighted in accordance with their area listings.[14] See Figure 6.3.

• Defense industrial base facilities	• Population
• Federal Bureau of Investigation (FBI) basic and special cases	• Population density
• Gross Domestic Product (GDP)	• Port of entry/border crossings (people from countries of interest and annual throughput)
• I-94 visitors from countries of interest	• Ratio of law enforcement to population
• Intelligence community credible and less credible threat reports	• Special events
• Immigration and Customs Enforcement (ICE) basic and special cases	• State international export trade
	• State total agriculture sales
• Miles of international border	• Sum of population density of urban areas in state
• Military bases	• Sum of population of urban areas in state
• Nuclear Waste Isolation Pilot Plan (WIPP) transportation routes	• Suspicious incidents (credible and less credible)

Figure 6.3   High-value geographic target regions.

---

[13] U.S. Department of Homeland Security, Risk Analysis: Fact Sheet Series (2006).
[14] USDHS, Risk Analysis Sheet.

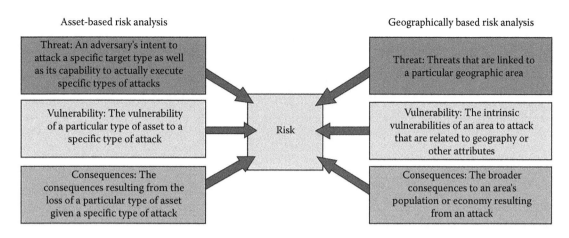

Figure 6.4   Comparison of asset-based risk analysis and geographically based risk analysis methodology.

In light of this valuation, DHS computes the threat level, police and law enforcement activity relative to threats, as well as intelligence from customs and immigration, and other suspicious incident data. Then, DHS considers vulnerability factors for each geographic area, such as the area's proximity to international borders and the potential for international incident. Lastly, DHS estimates the potential consequences of an attack on that area, including human health, size of population, economic conditions, military complex, and overall business and industry. DHS charts its methodology in Figure 6.4.[15]

On a narrower front, the task of risk assessment can be departmentally and programmatically driven. For example, risk for a small business may be distinctively different than the risks of concern to a multinational conglomerate. Each organization must perceive risk in light of its overall structure and mission.

Private security firms present customers with a wide array of risk assessment approaches.[16] As an example, the security firm Securitas tailors and markets its capacity to conduct risk analysis and assessment for business, appealing to bottom-line considerations.

Web Exercise: Learn how Securitas looks at business risk analysis here: http://www.securitasinc.com/en/who-we-are/business-approach/operational-analysis/.

Whatever approach is taken with risk assessment, it is critical to gather information, anticipate events and incidents, understand the value of assets and potential harm, and weigh and contrast the functionality and importance of geographic territory. See the potential incidents and corresponding required information in Table 6.3.

Do not forget to mitigate potential harm. Every event can be influenced in some way, whether it is the movement of people or the protection of property. Every risk can be addressed in some fashion. Hazard mitigation planning is the process of determining how to reduce or eliminate the loss of life and property damage resulting from natural and human-caused hazards. See Figure 6.5, which charts the four-step process of mitigation.[17]

6.3 VARIOUS RISK ASSESSMENT TOOLS

Risk and vulnerability analysis and assessment can be conducted by diverse methodologies, and in order to have any professional credibility, the security firm needs to rely on an accepted, industry-wide tool. A short review of the more pertinent choices follows. How assessments are carried out inexorably depends upon the subject matter.

---

[15] USDHS, Risk Analysis Sheet.

[16] K. Strom et al., The Private Security Industry: A Review of the Definitions, Available Data Sources, and Paths Moving Forward, 4-11-4-13 (2010), at https:// www.ncjrs.gov/pdffiles1/bjs/grants/232781.pdf, last accessed August 27, 2016.

[17] Federal Emergency Management Agency, *Mitigation Planning How-To Guide #3: Developing the Mitigation Plan* 1 (Washington, DC: U.S. Government Printing Office, Apr. 2003).

Table 6.3   Possible hazards and emergencies risk abatement

Possible hazards and emergencies	Risk level (none, low, moderate, or high)	How can I reduce my risk?
Natural hazards		
1. Floods		
2. Hurricanes		
3. Thunderstorms and lightning		
4. Tornadoes		
5. Winter storms and extreme cold		
6. Extreme heat		
7. Earthquakes		
8. Volcanoes		
9. Landslides and debris flow		
10. Tsunamis		
11. Fires		
12. Wildfires		
Technological hazards		
1. Hazardous materials incidents		
2. Nuclear power plants		
Terrorism		
1. Explosions		
2. Biological threats		
3. Chemical threats		
4. Nuclear blasts		
5. Radiological dispersion device (RDD)		

6.3.1 CARVER + Shock assessment tool

In the area of food supply, water, and consumables, risk evaluators have come to depend upon the CARVER + Shock assessment methodology. The CARVER system employs various criteria labeled as CARVER; CARVER is an acronym for the following six attributes used to evaluate the attractiveness of a target for attack:

- Criticality—measure of public health and economic impacts of an attack
- Accessibility—ability to physically access and egress from the target
- Recuperability—ability of the system to recover from an attack
- Vulnerability—ease of accomplishing an attack
- Effect—amount of direct loss from an attack as measured by loss in production
- Recognizability—ease of identifying the target

In addition, the modified CARVER tool evaluates a seventh attribute, the combined health, economic, and psychological impacts of an attack, or the shock attributes of a target.

The CARVER system attempts to quantify risk by the assignment of specific numbers for specific conditions. It looks to products and food, facilities, and manufacturing processes. So valued is its methodology that the U.S. Food and Drug Administration (FDA) has developed and disseminated software that is downloadable on the web. CARVER + Shock software requires the user to build a process flow diagram for the system to be evaluated and answer a series of questions for each of the seven CARVER + Shock attributes for each process flow diagram node. Flow processes can be shaped and designed in a host of applications. The CARVER program employs an icon system that correlates to a particular industry or business application. Table 6.4 is a sample listing of the flow process possibilities.[18]

---

[18] See U.S. Food and Drug Administration, *CARVER + Shock Users' Manual, Version 1.0* (2007) Appendix B.

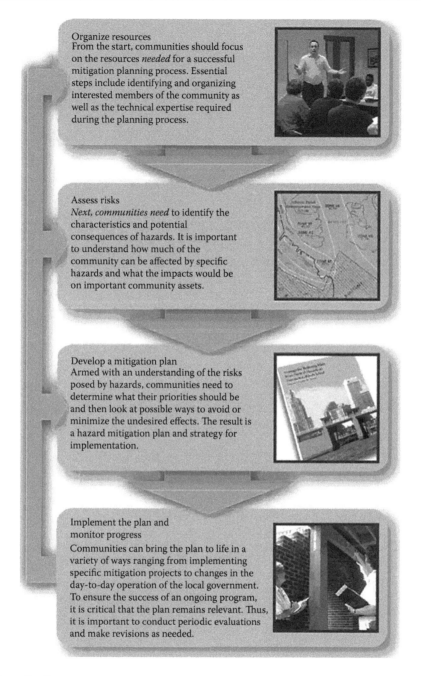

Figure 6.5   Four-step mitigation process.

Each question has an associated score. Based on the answers given, the software calculates a score for each CARVER + Shock attribute and sums them to produce a total score for each node. Analogous to a face-to-face session, total scores range from 1 to 10 for each CARVER + Shock attribute, and therefore from 7 to 70 for each node.

The interview questions seek to corroborate the flow process, as to the variables under the CARVER acronym. Then, once the results are tabulated, a scoring system is linked to each of these variables. Table 6.5 displays the scoring criteria for accessibility.

This process relies upon a comprehensive interview schema in order that calculations have reliability. At Figure 6.6, a sample interview page, published by the software, is provided.

Table 6.4 CARVER + Shock flow process possibilities

Icon	Category	Subcategory	Description
Acid	Materials	Processed ingredients	A water-soluble chemical compound with a pH less than 7 when dissolved. Has a sour taste.
Air dryer	Processing	Drying	Device that dries product by direct contact with heated air.
Aircraft	Transportation/distribution		Using an aircraft for the transportation of materials from one location to another.
Aseptic packager	Packaging		Equipment that places and seals product in a sterile container/package.
Auger tank	Processing	Processing tanks	Enclosure for a large mechanical screw that mixes and moves material/product.
Bags	Packaging	Packaging materials	A container of flexible material (paper, plastic, etc.) used for packaging.
Bakery	Retail food service		Location where products like bread, cake, and pastries are baked.
Balance tank	Processing	Processing tanks	Used to balance the pH of a discharge so it is within certain parameters.
Barge	Transportation/distribution		Transportation of materials along a body of water from one location to another.
Batch tank	Storage	Storage tanks	A mixing/storage tank large enough for a single batch of product.
Batterer	Processing	Other processing	A machine used to mix or beat a material.
Bin/tub	Storage	Other storage	A large open storage vessel.
Blancher	Processing	Cooking	Equipment that uses water or steam to parboil or scald material/product to remove skin or stop enzymatic action.
Blast freezer	Processing	Chilling	Device that quickly freezes materials or products as they move along a conveyor using a controlled stream of cold air. Generally used when small pieces need to be kept separate as they freeze, such as cut-up vegetables.
Blend tank	Processing	Processing tanks	A tank used to blend/mix materials.
Blender	Processing	Mixing	Mechanical mixer for chopping, mixing, or liquefying materials.
Blower	Conveyance		A machine, such as a fan, that produces an air current to move materials.
Bottle cleaner	Cleaning/washing		A process to clean, wash, and sterilize bottles.
Bottle hopper	Packaging		Provides continuous flow of containers to be loaded on a conveyer.
Bottler	Packaging		Automated equipment for filling bottles.
Bottles	Packaging	Packaging materials	Containers with a narrow neck and no handles that can be plugged, corked, or capped.
Boxes	Packaging	Packaging materials	Container with four sides and a lid or cover used for storage or transport.
Breader	Processing	Other processing	Equipment used to coat meat/fish/poultry with a crumb coating.
Briner	Processing	Other processing	Process to preserve food using a concentrated salt solution.
Browner	Processing	Cooking	Equipment used to sear the outside surface of meats.
Bulk storage	Storage	Other storage	Storage for a large amount of ingredient/product in a single container.
Butcher	Processing	Meat processing	To cut up meat or poultry.
Cans	Packaging	Packaging materials	Cylindrical metal container.
Capper	Packaging	Packaging materials	Applies caps to containers.
Car	Storage	Other storage	Storage for a material waiting to be shipped.
Caser	Packaging		Sorts and places product into cases.
Centrifuge	Processing	Separation/extraction	Machine that uses centrifugal force to separate substances with different densities.
Check weigher	Control checks		A scale to check the weight of product.
Chemicals	Materials	Processing materials	Cleaning chemicals.
Chilled distribution	Transportation/distribution		Refrigerated transport of product.

Source: United States Food and Drug Administration, *CARVER + Shock Users' Manual Version 1.0,* 2007, Appendix B: Alphabetical Icons with Descriptions.

Table 6.5   CARVER + shock scoring criteria

Accessibility criteria	Scale
Easily accessible (e.g., target is outside building and no perimeter fence). Limited physical or human barriers or observation. Attacker has relatively unlimited access to the target. Attack can be carried out using medium or large volumes of contaminant without undue concern of detection. Multiple sources of information concerning the facility and the target are easily available.	9–10
Accessible (e.g., target is inside building, but in an unsecured part of the facility). Human observation and physical barriers limited. Attacker has access to the target for an hour or less. Attack can be carried out with moderate to large volumes of contaminant, but requires the use of stealth. Only limited specific information is available on the facility and the target.	7–8
Partially accessible (e.g., inside building, but in a relatively unsecured, but busy, part of facility). Under constant possible human observation. Some physical barriers may be present. Contaminant must be disguised, and time limitations are significant. Only general, nonspecific information is available on the facility and the target.	5–6
Hardly accessible (e.g., inside building in a secured part of facility). Human observation and physical barriers with an established means of detection. Access generally restricted to operators or authorized persons. Contaminant must be disguised and time limitations are extreme. Limited general information available on the facility and the target.	3–4
Not accessible. Physical barriers, alarms, and human observation. Defined means of intervention in place. Attacker can access target for less than five minutes with all equipment carried in pockets. No useful publicly available information concerning the target.	1–2

6.3.2 Threat assessment

The identification of potential and actual criminal activities is called a *threat assessment*. The threat assessment precedes any deployment of manpower, determination of specific protective strategies, and authorship of security measures. A threat assessment attempts to answer the "what," "when," "how," and "where" of criminal activity. "The threat assessment process involves identifying, assessing, and managing individuals who might pose a risk of violence to an identified or identifiable target."[19] See Figure 6.7.

Once the broad picture has been determined from the community profile, the analysis turns to criminological questions. Exactly what drives the criminal element in this community? The assessment raises these fundamental issues:

- Who engages in a criminal lifestyle?
- How are criminal designs carried out?
- Where do criminals reside?
- When will the criminals act?
- What conduct can the community expect from the criminal?

In threat analysis, the world and the community are viewed through the eyes of the enemy. The evaluation assesses the weaknesses and vulnerabilities of the target environment, identifies the root causes that nurtures negative elements, and searches for the common denominators that bind the environment to the threat. Finding out where the community's criminals operate is a good starting point. Threat assessment analysis will be effective if the practitioner adheres to fundamental principles. They are:

- Targeted violence is the end result of an understandable, and oftentimes discernible, process of thinking and behavior.
- Targeted violence stems from an interaction among the person, the situation, the setting, and the target.
- An investigative, skeptical, inquisitive mindset is critical to successful threat assessment.
- Effective threat assessment is based on facts, rather than characteristics or "traits."
- An "integrated systems approach" should guide threat assessment investigations.
- The central question of a threat assessment is whether an individual poses a threat, not whether the individual made a threat.[20]

---

[19] Chapter IV, Implementing a School Treat Assessment Process, 29–30.
[20] Ibid. at 30–33.

Threats will vary in intensity. The U.S. Department of Justice categorizes three levels of threat:

Low level: A threat that has been evaluated as low level poses little threat to public safety and in most cases would not necessitate law enforcement investigation for a possible criminal offense. (However, law enforcement agencies may be asked for information in connection with a threat of any level.)

ABC
Criticality Category Interview Report

What is the serving size for the product? (If the product is used as an ingredient, how much of the product is used in each serving?)

What is the distribution unit (package size sold to the consumer)?

How many retail outlets typically receive units from one batch?
- ○ 1
- ○ 2-3
- ○ 3-10
- ○ >10

What percentage of each batch is sold...

--	Within one day of purchase?
--	Within first 3 days after purchase?
--	Within first week after purchase?
--	Within first two weeks after purchase?
--	Within first month after purchase?
--	During the first two months?

What percentage of the product is typically consumed...

--	Within one day of purchase?
--	Within the first 3 days after purchase?
--	Within the first week after purchase?
--	Within two weeks after purchase?
--	Within first month after purchase?
--	Within first two months after purchase?

On average, how many individuals eat from the same distribution unit?

Does the company have a published support line for end consumers with concerns or questions?
- ○ Yes
- ○ No

Is there a formal company procedure for communicating information on a contamination incident to the public?
- ○ Yes
- ○ No

Does your company or facility have a mechanism in place to effectively implement a recall and withdraw product from the marketplace?
- ○ Yes
- ○ No

Does your company conduct mock product recalls?
- ○ Yes
- ○ No

Figure 6.6   CARVER + Shock sample interview page.   (*Continued*)

How well can you trace your product to the distribution centers (D.C.s) and retail outlets?
○ Cannot trace at all.
○ Can identify independent D.C.s and entire distribution chains to major distributors that may have received units from one batch.
○ Can trace specific pallets to independent D.C.s and entire distribution chains to major distributors such as Wal-Mart.
○ Can identify all retail outlets that received units from a batch.
○ Can trace specific pallets to each retail outlet that received it.

Is this product an uncoded product or uncoded raw ingredient?
○ Yes
○ No

Are you aware of large-scale counterfeiting or diversion for this product?
○ Yes
○ No

Figure 6.6   (Continued) CARVER + Shock sample interview page.

Environmental Threat Assessment &
Residential Property Security Survey Outline

1. Contact Information
2. Property Description
   2.1 Layout & Construction
   2.2 Resident Population
   2.3 Surrounding Environment
3. Criminal Activity
   3.1 General
   3.2 Violent Offenses
   3.3 Nonviolent Offenses
   3.4 Rules Violations
   3.5 Gang Presence & Activity
   3.6 High Activity Areas
   3.7 Surrounding Environment
4. Community Attitudes & Integration
   4.1 Crime Perceptions
   4.2 Community Unity & Trust
   4.3 Community Care & The Environment
   4.4 Perceptions About Law Enforcement & Property Management
   4.5 Resident Interviews
5. Physical Site Survey
   Daytime Survey
   5.1 Grounds & Outdoor Community Areas
   5.2 Apartment Buildings
   5.3 Pools & Clubhouses
   5.4 Parking Lots
   5.5 Surrounding Neighborhood
   Nighttime Survey
   5.6 Lighting
   5.7 After Hours Activity
6. Policies & Management Practices
   6.1 Applicant Screening
   6.2 Community Orientation
   6.3 Resident Problem Resolution & Eviction
   6.4 Trespassing & Outsider Interdiction
7. Local Resources

Figure 6.7   Environmental threat assessment and residential property security survey outline.

Medium level: When a threat is rated as medium level, the response should in most cases include contacting law enforcement agencies, as well as other sources, to obtain additional information (and possibly reclassify the threat into the high or law category).

High level: Almost always, if a threat is evaluated as high level, immediately inform the appropriate law enforcement agency. A response plan, which should have been designed ahead of time and rehearsed by both private security professionals and law enforcement personnel, should be implemented, and law enforcement should be informed and involved in whatever subsequent actions are taken in response to threat.[21]

Case by case, the assessor must systematically weigh circumstances and conditions that qualify the criminal threat. Some predictable method is mandated. "A standardized approach will help security firms construct a database, with information on the types and frequency of threats, which may help evaluate the effectiveness of policies. Consistency in threat response can deter future threats if criminals perceive that any threat will be reported, investigated, and dealt with firmly."[22]

Concentration should then turn to the more immediate problems stemming from quality of life issues, and the "who," "what," "when," and "where" of criminal activity. The real insight is the actual evaluation of ongoing and current problems, situations, and criminal activity. The evaluation of these elements will deliver reliable insight into the casual factors that promote the felonious lifestyle. When conducting a threat assessment in an effort to get answers to the issues just discussed, the practitioner will have to conduct physical inspections of the intervention areas. By surveying the environment, practitioners are able to locate drug paraphernalia such as empty plastic bags, broken glass pipes, and syringes. Organized gang activity can be gleaned from graffiti on buildings and sidewalks, much of which forms the basis for communication between rivals and internal members. Abandoned homes and crack houses filled with vagrants, drug dealers, or gang bangers edify the threat problem and zero in on the suspected criminal players.

Security practitioners need to work cooperatively with police agencies by reviewing data, crime reports, and police activity logs. Using historical data to spot trends and crime patterns can reap solid results. Alleged victimless crimes, such as prostitution and vagrancy, should not be discounted in the threat assessment. If anything, the emphasis on these types of offenses should be heightened. While the past is not always predictive, it is always educational. Interpreters of data must keep in mind its inherent reliability, particularly in high-crime neighborhoods where only a small percentage of crimes committed are actually reported by citizens to the police. The threat assessment team can also review "security threats to facilities, materials, and activities. The team also conducts liaison activities with the community, law enforcement, and other Federal agencies in support of its threat."[23]

Additionally, the types of crimes reported are somewhat disproportionate to the actual rate and incidence of criminal conduct. Naturally, the most commonly reported crimes are those that directly affect the residents themselves (robbery, battery, sexual assault, etc.). Many crimes that "indirectly" affect residents are rarely reported, despite their impact on the overall status of the community. Citizens in high-crime areas, for example, rarely report drug dealing and prostitution, although it may be notorious in the area. The same is true for crimes that do not result in physical harm or loss of property, such as a gang member threatening a resident with a gun (aggravated assault). Fear of reprisal often overtakes the urge to report. While assessors should evaluate crime statistics over long periods of time, gaining a "snapshot" of police and criminal activity; however, the statistics should not be relied upon as an accurate picture of the level of victimization occurring in the community.

During the same physical inspection, the practitioner should interact with residents seeking feedback and input. Find out about the quality of life and the associated threats by those who reside in the neighborhood. The skills and training necessary for threat assessment are varied and demanding. The assessor needs

- A questioning, analytical, and skeptical mindset
- An ability to relate well to members of the community, colleagues, and other professionals

---

[21] National Center for the Analysis of Violent Crime: Critical Response Group, The School Shooter: A Threat Assessment Perspective 27 (U.D. DOJ).

[22] Ibid. at 25.

[23] Nuclear Regulatory Commission, Threat Assessment, at http://www.nrc.gov/what-we-do/safeguards/threat.html, 8/29/02.

- Familiarity with childhood and adolescent growth and development, the school environment, the need for safe schools, and the community
- A reputation within the community for fairness and trustworthiness
- Training in the collection and evaluation of information from multiple sources
- Discretion, and an appreciation for the importance of keeping information confidential, and of the possible harm that may result in the inappropriate release of information
- Cognizance of the difference between harming and helping in an intervention[24]

Residents that live in the "combat zone" may have reliable intelligence on criminal activity, so professionals, both public and private, should seek out the information wisely to build trust in the sources. Threat assessment requires observation, surveillance, and intelligence gathering over extended periods to confirm the information received. Threat assessment examines "traditional crime data, including calls for service and alcohol and drug-related arrests. The evaluation will also measure outcomes important to the practice of community policing, such as changes in citizen participation in reporting crime, the level and extent of problem-solving collaboration between police and community members, and citizen satisfaction with police services."[25]

The Association of Threat Assessment Professionals sets standards for these practices. See their website at http://www.atapworldwide.org.

6.3.2.1 Preincident indicators: A tool for threat assessment

Threat assessments must be conducted on a regular basis to keep up with environmental changes. Threats should be somewhat predictive, that is, the protection specialist becomes adroit in identifying the signals of trouble to come. Factors worth continual evaluation are labeled *preincident indicators*. The indicators fall into two main classifications: *trend* and *individual* indicators. "Trend indicators" target particular social, economic, and cultural factors such as

- Crime incidence rates
- Results of juvenile surveys
- Types of crime
- Levels of gang activity[26]
- Levels of poverty
- Rates of drug activity

Much in the same manner as the state and federal Uniform Crime Reports, the assessment looks at these variables for policy-making purposes and for justification in the implementation of community tactics.[27]

The second type of indicator is "individual." These indicators focus on individuals with known propensities for criminal conduct, whether by drugs or domestic violence, weaponry, or school violence. Individuals are matched to potential situations and circumstances in the target community where these behaviors can occur. The data reveal that a specific individual or situation is developing a potential for victimization.

---

[24] Chapter IV, Implementing a School Treat Assessment Process, 38.

[25] S.E. Curtis & M. Townsend, What Works 2.

[26] See J. Ripley, Deputy Points to Signs a Gang Is Trying to Take Root, *St. Petersburg Times* (April 5, 2002) at http://www.sptimes.com/2002/04/05/Northoftampa/Deputy_points_to_sign.shtml, last accessed August 27, 2016.

[27] The Florida Department of Education, for example, produced a study of youth violence in Florida public schools for the year 1996–1997. The statewide study revealed that there were 227,872 reported incidents of violence for a total student population of 551,456. This would be a very good example of a trend indicator. This type of indicator allows the practitioner to foresee the strong influential trends that are in place. If we continue with the Florida example, the practitioner would then assess if the trends apply to the specific community he/she is responsible to protect. In this case, we will use Hillsborough County. By using the same survey, we find that Hillsborough has the third highest rate of school violence in the state. By looking at the statistics, we can clearly see that the county averages are very similar to the overall state figures. Out of 33,763 students, Hillsborough had 13,694 reported violent crimes in its public schools. By observing this trend indicator, it would be clear to any practitioner that the school violence issue is very applicable to the Hillsborough school environments. In turn, the practitioner can identify the need for prevention planning and adjust the desired techniques to eliminate or minimize the potential for violence and crisis. It also enables the development of tailored contingency planning in the event of an occurrence of violence on a large-scale occurs. Florida Department of Juvenile Justice.

Recent school violence incidents illustrate the utility of preincident indicators. In many instances, the perpetrator foretold intent to commit criminal acts. Letters, notes, and e-mails to innocent and conspiratorial parties announce intentions. These same individuals may have substantial criminal or juvenile histories that make recidivism a sure bet. Weapons, previous altercations, threats, and sociopathic behavior can be targeted in individual cases.

Workplace security specialists must be on the lookout for preindication signs. Larry Moore's *Preventing Homicide and Act of Violence in the Workplace* highlights three phases that trace the evolution of violent behavior:

> Trigger Phase.… can be triggered by other people, events, situations … Responses may be as unique as the individuals themselves; however, in many instances, triggers can be identified and managed.
>   Escalation Phase.… first clear warning sign … is a noticeable change in behavior.… triggers begin to accumulate … Recognizing this stage facilitates … an appropriate response.
> Crisis Phase.… The individual has lost the ability to cope. The key is to keep the agitated person talking … Law enforcement research shows that an armed person seldom pulls the trigger while talking …[28]

Once individual indicators are identified, the practitioner has the ability to develop a rapid response to the potential situation and effectively intervene prior to acts of violence. Hindsight, unfortunately, is always more intelligent than the assessment of what could happen. Human beings cannot always be predictive.

In order to be able to develop a clear picture using multiple preincident indicators, an effective communication network must be established between many entities (parents, teachers, other students, as examples). A proactive effort must be implemented to encourage communication between parents, students, school staff, and community leaders. Unfortunately, the larger the school or community, the harder this analysis becomes. The U.S. Department of Education offers what it terms "attack-related behaviors" to ferret out dangerous individuals roaming the schools. Violence is predictive if the student exhibits

- Ideas or plans about injuring him/herself or attaching a school or persons at school
- Communications or writings that suggest that the student has an unusual or worrisome interest in school attacks
- Comments that express or imply the student is considering mounting an attack at school
- Recent weapon-seeking behavior, especially if weapon-seeking is linked to ideas about attack or expressions about interest in attack
- Communications or writings suggesting the student condones or is considering violence to redress a grievance or solve a problem
- Rehearsals of attacks or ambushes[29]

What private security offers is a more aggressive approach to preincident prevention than can possibly be exhibited by its colleagues in the public sector. Security officers are not besieged and overwhelmed with the imaginable demands that public officers now experience. Security officers, looking to the principles of efficiency and economy, and driven by the underlying quest for success in the marketplace, can focus on these trends a little more. Security officers are the pivot points for information and the interpretation of information in communal settings.

By knowing the collective, that body of individuals that comprise the common social order, the security officer dwells on individual conducts in both a positive and negative way. Foretelling violent situations, zeroing in on troubled settings where violence reoccurs, and realizing that reaction will be too late and that intervention in advance is the better response, security officers can often tackle threats before germination.

These practitioners must be aware of all constituencies in the community, the stable and dependable, as well as the "outsiders," the "loners," and the "misfits." By getting to know people with issues and problems, and being able to assess the potential for violent behavior, practitioners can gauge these preincident indicators. Being familiar with common motives for adult and juvenile violence, the officer can predict when events may occur. There is nothing all that magical about this skill. Those entrusted with community protection should be mindful of these preincident indicators:

---

[28] Chapter V: Conducting a School Threat Assessment, 50.
[29] See D.L. Beyer, *Industrial Security* 255 (Butterworth-Heinemann, 1999).

- Gang conflicts, both within gangs and between rival gangs
- Neighborhood and ethnic conflicts, often over "turf"
- Contributing feuds between individuals over perceived insults or disrespect
- Disputes over girlfriends or boyfriends
- Acquisitive violence, such as extortion or robbery
- Preemptive or strategic violence, that is, "I'm going to get him before he gets me"
- Dating violence
- Ritualized violence, for example, gang initiations

6.4 THREATS AND HAZARDS

6.4.1 Evolutionary concept of threat and hazard

Threats come in many forms, and if anything is true about the last decade, it would be the evolution in the definition of threat. Some might argue that threats are those things emanating from military sources alone—in the form of armies or weaponry. Of even more compelling recent interest has been the emergence of the homegrown, domestic terrorist threat where our enemies reside among the populace, waiting to carry out the deed. This is part of what Secretary Janet Napolitano calls the "new threat picture."[30] Others might claim that a threat is driven by natural disaster or events that are unpredictable, such as a typhoon or hurricane. And still another conception deals with the threats of nuclear, chemical, and biological incidents. Threats and hazards are often distinguished by their motive and purpose. Hazards are generally construed as acts of nature, unintentional events without political motive or purpose. Threats, on the other hand, are usually bound to some improper aim or end, such as the political destruction of a government or the radical altering of leadership. Hurricanes and floods are events lacking any animus and, as such, are relegated to the hazard category. What is undeniable is that the private security industry is actively engaged in the risk and threat assessment culture.[31]

Web Exercise: Conduct your own online risk and safety assessment at your workplace using the following interactive tool: https://client.oiraproject.eu/eu/eu-private-security/private-security-eu.

What cannot be accepted is that the United States daily remains subject to a host of threats and hazards from every imaginable direction. Professor Daniel Dunai, of Hungary's National Defence University, graphically charts the onslaught at Figure 6.8.[32]

Natural hazards fall into these categories:

- Hurricanes
- Tornadoes
- Floods
- Winter storms
- Heat-related emergencies
- Droughts
- Wildfires
- Thunderstorms
- Geologic events

---

[30] Prepared Remarks by Secretary Napolitano at Harvard University's John F. Kennedy Jr. Forum (April 15, 2010), at http://www.dhs.gov/ynews/speeches/sp_1271366935471.shtm, last accessed August 27, 2016.
[31] D.J. Landoll, *The Security Risk Assessment Handbook* (Auerbach Publications, 2005); Kroll website: http://www.kroll.com/en-us/security-risk-management, last accessed August 27, 2016.
[32] D. Dunai, A Framework, at 330.

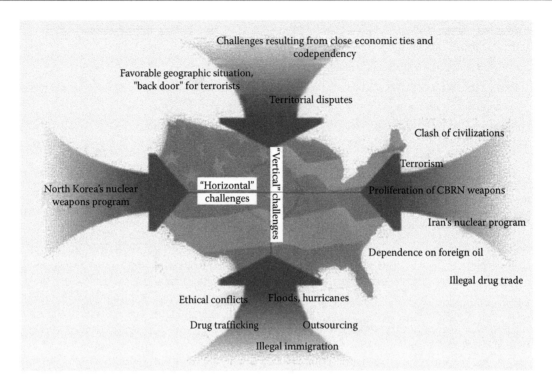

Figure 6.8   A convenient scheme for categorizing different threats and challenges.

Law enforcement and security personnel frequently misread the full impact of these natural disasters, at least as to the homeland defense mindset.[33] These events wreak extraordinary havoc. The death toll alone is a distressingly impressive count. See Figure 6.9.[34]

More than 26 million people have been negatively impacted by natural disasters in the last century—a statistic that lays out a permanent obligation for homeland personnel. See Figure 6.10.[35]

Threats fall into these typologies:

- Crimes
- Terrorism
- Unintentional events
- Blackouts
- Radiological events
- Hazmat incidents
- Fires

Threats arising from terrorism signify a malicious intent to cause widespread harm. Terrorism and civil hazards include actions that people intentionally do to threaten lives and property. These acts may range from a single person on a shooting rampage, to a cyber-attack that harms computer systems, to the organized use of weapons of mass

---

[33] N.E. Busch & A.D. Givens. Public–Private Partnerships in Homeland Security: Opportunities and Challenges. *Homeland Security Affairs* 8, Article 18 (October 2012), at https://www.hsaj.org/articles/233.

[34] EM-DAT: The OFDA/CRED International Disaster Database, www.emdat.be—Université catholique de Louvain–Brussels–Belgium. Events recorded in the CRED EM-DAT. First Event: Sep/1900, Last Entry: Mar/2012. Epidemics include: Viral Infectious Diseases (Encephalitis), Parasitic Infectious Diseases (Cryptosporidiosis), Viral Infectious Diseases (West Nile Fever), Viral Infectious Diseases (Acute Respiratory Syndrome (SARS)).

[35] Ibid.

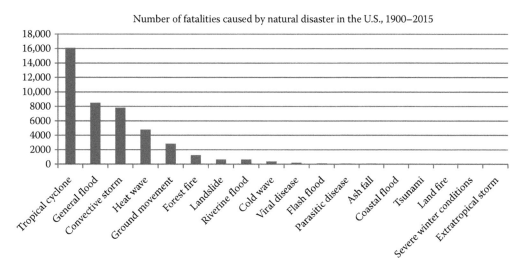

Figure 6.9 Deaths from natural disasters in the United States from September 1900 to March 2012.

destruction (WMD). WMD events could involve chemical, biological, explosive, or radioactive weapons. Acts of terrorism include threats of terrorism, assassinations, kidnappings, hijackings, bomb scares, and bombings. High-risk targets for acts of terrorism include military and civilian government facilities, international airports, large cities, and high-profile landmarks. Terrorists might also target large public gatherings, water and food supplies, utilities, and corporate centers. Infrastructure of every variety needs constant vigilance in the matter of threat, from its original construction phase to its maintenance. Building design must anticipate threat even in the materials side so that the structure might withstand natural disasters, blast, projectiles, and fire.[36]

Identifying, anticipating, and defending against such a broad band of threats can only be described as daunting. If security and homeland policy makers have learned anything over the last decade, it is that these concepts, like threat and disaster, have an evolutionary quality. In short, both the ideas and the means of execution change whether we

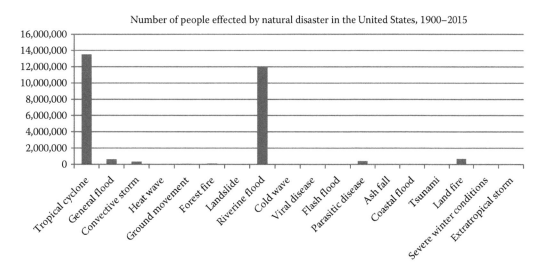

Figure 6.10 People affected by natural disasters in the United States from September 1900 to March 2012.

---

[36] See Department of Homeland Security, Science and Technology Directorate, at https:// www.dhs.gov/science-and-technology, last accessed August 27, 2016.

Table 6.6 Local threats and hazards

Type of hazard	Likelihood of occurrence	Potentially devastating impact on people	Potentially devastating impact on structures
Natural hazards			
Floods			
Winter storms			
Tornadoes			
Thunderstorm			
Hurricanes			
Extreme heat/cold			
Viral epidemics			
Human-induced hazards			
Hazardous materials incidents			
Transportation accidents			
Infrastructure disruptions			
Workplace violence			
Civil disorder/disobedience			
Terrorist hazards			
Conventional weapons			
Incendiary devices			
Biological and chemical agents			
Radiological			
Cyber-terrorism			
Weapons of mass destruction			

Source: Hazard Analysis and Vulnerability Study, done under contract to DC Emergency Management Agency (May 2002).

admit it or not. Those entrusted must stay "in the box" as well as be capable of jumping "out of the box." In other words, past history tells us much about these events, although these same events may not evolve in just the way predicted. Alain Bauer's insights on this dilemma are most helpful for he urges the policy maker to find the commonality in all forms of terror. No matter what the group, what the religious sect, or what the purpose or aim, he argues that all terrorists

- Have common harmonies
- Frequent common lands and territories
- Have a common (submerged) economy
- Offer real opportunities for symbiosis[37]

Agencies and communities can chart potential threats by the use of the checklist in Table 6.6.

Of course, hazards can arise by human negligence and carelessness, which gives rise to a man-made catastrophe.

6.4.2 Weapons of mass destruction

No ambition is more glorifying for the terrorist than the successful delivery of a WMD. The terror associated with WMD is well founded and not to be addressed cavalierly. The stuff of WMD can only be described as frightful and has the capacity to inflict global injury. There are four generally accepted categories of WMD, covered in the following subsections.

---

[37] A. Bauer, War on Terror or Policing Terrorism? Radicalization and Expansion of the Threats, *Police Chief* 46–52, 52 (January 2011).

Figure 6.11   Nuclear power plant.

6.4.2.1 Nuclear

Some terrorist organizations, such as Al Qaeda and ISIS,[38] openly declare their desire to acquire and use nuclear weapons. Even the complexities of devising a nuclear delivery mechanism are amply documented. The complete production of a nuclear weapon largely depends on the terrorist group's access to nuclear material and a high level of scientific expertise. Black market materials can be utilized, though the crudeness of the enterprise is dangerous in and of itself (Figure 6.11).

The DHS, by and through its office of Domestic Nuclear Detection, is entrusted with the detection and prevention of nuclear terrorist threats. The basic objectives of the office are:

- Develop the global nuclear detection and reporting architecture
- Develop, acquire, and support the domestic nuclear detection and reporting system
- Fully characterize detector system performance before deployment
- Establish situational awareness through information sharing and analysis
- Establish operation protocols to ensure detection leads to effective response
- Conduct a transformational research and development program
- Establish the National Technical Nuclear Forensics Center to provide planning, integration, and improvements to USG nuclear forensics capabilities

The demands and complexities of nuclear threat call for constant and continuous assessment. Aside from perimeter concerns and access issues, the typical nuclear power facility not only utilizes physical materials capable of mass destruction but also must find ways to store and treat the by-products of nuclear power and production. As a result, the industry itself, and government overseers have regularized practices regarding data storage and collection, physical security plans, and disposal.[39] The organization chart of the office of the Domestic Nuclear Detection is presented in Figure 6.12.

Physical security at nuclear power plants is provided by well-armed and well-trained security personnel who remain ready to respond to an attack 24 hours a day, seven days a week. The sites are protected by sensitive intrusion detection

---

[38] B. Cole, War on ISIS: Threat of Nuclear Terror Attack "Highest since the Cold War" says Think Tank, *International Business Times Online* (June 7, 2016), at http://www.ibtimes.co.uk/war-isis-threat-jihadi-nuclear-terror-attack-highest-since-cold-war-says-think-tank-1564192, last accessed August 27, 2016.

[39] See Department of Homeland Security, Nuclear Reactors, Materials, and Waste Sector-Specific Plan: An Annex to the National Infrastructure Protection Plan (2010).

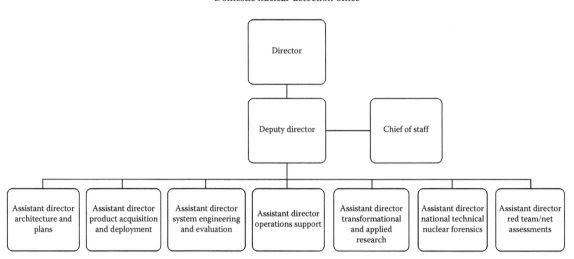

Figure 6.12   Organization chart of the office of Domestic Nuclear Detection.

equipment, fences, and barriers, and are monitored by cameras and security patrols. And this protective function needs to be coordinated among many players, assuring an interagency cooperation. "Federal, state, local and private sector partners regularly and actively assess the risk environment in the Nuclear Sector in light of changes or potential changes to threats, vulnerabilities and consequences."[40]

In 2002, the Nuclear Regulatory Commission (NRC) announced the creation of the Office of Nuclear Security and Incident Response (NSIR) to improve the effectiveness of NRC in ensuring protection of public health and safety from security threats at licensed facilities. On January 20, 2004, the commission announced the creation of the Emergency Preparedness Project Office (EPPO) to improve NRC's effectiveness. On June 13, 2004, EPPO was integrated within NSIR, creating the Emergency Preparedness Directorate (EPD), and aligned the NRC's preparedness, security, and incident response missions.

Nuclear terrorism can also be carried out at nuclear facilities. Each nuclear facility has high-level security responsibilities and must take seriously its charge to thwart any attempts on the facility. Nuclear facilities are required to have layers of security systems in place to prevent intrusion, contamination, or release of materials, or loss or theft of radioactive and plutonium materials. In the most general terms, a security program for nuclear facilities minimally includes

- A well-trained security force
- Robust physical barriers
- Intrusion detection systems
- Surveillance systems
- Plant access controls

In addition, nuclear facilities are required to conduct threat assessments regularly and are subject to regular and continuous security visitations by the NRC.

Training is rigorous and continuous. So concerned are the operators of nuclear reactors that extensive training, labeled Force on Force (FOF) training, anticipates an assault on the facility itself. Two sets of security officers—the first for maintenance of the actual facility and the second for the attack force—will engage one another in mock battle. The FOF exercise is highly realistic and essential to a preventive security program.

---

[40] Department of Homeland Security, Nuclear Sector—Specific Plan 47 (2010).

Physical Security Specialist

OFFICE OF DISASTER MANAGEMENT AND NATIONAL SECURITY

Work Schedule is Career/Career Conditional—Full-time

- *Salary Range*
  $64,650.00 to $84,044.00/Per Year

- *Series & Grade*
  GS-0080-11/11

- *Promotion Potential*
  12

- *Supervisory Status*
  No

- *Who May Apply*
  U.S. citizens; no prior Federal experience is required.

  This opportunity is also open to Status eligibles under Announcement 16-HUD-997. Please refer to that announcement for details on open period, eligibility, and how to apply.

- *Control Number*
  446780600

- *Job Announcement Number*
  16-HUD-998-P

Job Overview

Summary

About the Agency

This position is located in the Office of Administration (OA), The Office of Disaster Management and National Security, Protective Services Division (PSD). The Office of Administration (OA) is comprised of five offices and is responsible for a wide range of administrative services that support HUD's mission, personnel and HUD offices throughout the country. The Office of Disaster Management and National Security is responsible for planning and managing HUD's Continuity of Operations Program and other national security programs, development and coordination of disaster management programs, and providing protective services for the HUD Secretary and Deputy Secretary.

****Amended to extend the closing date; correct Security Clearance Required; add Medical Requirements; correct FLSA; and add additional statements under Conditions of Employment.****

Duties

The following are the duties of this position at the GS-12. If you are selected at a lower grade level, you will have the opportunity to learn to perform all these duties, and will receive training to help you grow in this position.

- Participate and/or lead efforts required to plan and perform protective service operations. These operations include conducting advance security surveys of sites to be used or visited; conducting intelligence collection on the area to be visited; coordinating with local, state, and federal law enforcement agencies for support; and assigning duties and responsibilities to the supporting local law enforcement officers.
- Serve as the investigative liaison for the department to assist and/or conduct internal department investigations involving security-related employee misconduct or allegations of employee misconduct, and make sure the correct department or agency has the required information to actually carry out full investigations.
- Advise and provide recommendations to the Director, PSD on appropriate courses of action relating to the conduct of security-related administrative inquiries and investigations of incidents involving potential infractions and violations of security policies and possible criminal activity.
- Advise and brief senior management and officials within the Departmental Offices regarding results of administrative inquiries and investigations, as appropriate.

Travel Required

- 50% or Greater
- Excessive travel can be expected.

Figure CP6.2   Career Profile: Security specialist in disaster management.   (*Continued*)

Job Requirements

Key Requirements

- Click "Print Preview" to review the entire announcement before applying.
- Please refer to "Conditions of Employment."

Qualifications

You must meet the following requirements by the closing date of this announcement.

Age Restriction: The date immediately preceding an individual's 37th birthday is the maximum entry age for original appointment to a law enforcement officer position.

This requirement does not apply to a) Preference-eligible veterans; OR b) Individuals who are 37 years of age or older and have previously served in law enforcement officer positions that were covered by a special law enforcement retirement plan.

Medical Requirements

The duties of positions in this series require moderate to arduous physical exertion involving walking, prolonged periods of standing, use of firearms, impact weapons, and exposure to inclement weather. Manual dexterity with comparatively free motion of finger, wrist, elbow, shoulder, hip, and knee joints is required. Arms, hands, legs, and feet must be sufficiently intact and functioning in order that applicants may perform the duties satisfactorily. Sufficiently good distance vision in each eye, correction permitted, to 20/20 is mandatory. Near vision, corrective lenses permitted, must be sufficient to read printed material the size of typewritten characters. Hearing loss, as measured by an audiometer, must not exceed 35 decibels at 1000, 2000, and 3000 Hz levels. Since the duties of these positions are exacting and responsible, and involve activities under trying conditions, applicant must possess emotional and mental stability. Any physical condition that would cause the applicant to be a hazard to him/herself, or others is disqualifying.

Specialized experience For the GS-11, you must have one year of specialized experience at a level of difficulty and responsibility equivalent to the GS-09 grade level in the Federal service. Specialized experience for this position includes:

- Applying risk assessment methods, threat assessment principles and physical security practices in order to make recommendations, plan, evaluate and develop physical security program components for the protection of resources and high-value assets.

OR

You may substitute education for specialized experience as follows:

- A Ph.D. or equivalent doctoral degree or 3 full years of progressively higher level graduate education leading to such a degree or LL.M., if related.

OR

A you may qualify by a combination of experience and education. Options for qualifying based on a combination will be identified in the online questions.

Selective Factor: This position requires that you have prior law enforcement certification. Based on this requirement, at the time of appointment you will be required to have completed a certified basic police academy, Federal law enforcement training program, or have been previously deputized as a U.S. Marshall, through the U.S. Marshall Service.

The experience may have been gained in either the public, private sector or volunteer service. One year of experience refers to full-time work; part-time work is considered on a prorated basis. To ensure full credit for your work experience, please indicate dates of employment by month/day/year, and indicate number of hours worked per week on your resume.

Security Clearance

Top Secret/SCI

Figure CP6.2   (Continued) Career Profile: Security specialist in disaster management.

The NRC requires nuclear power plant operators to defend the plant against attackers seeking to cause damage to the reactor core or spent fuel to prevent the release of radiation. Postassessment highlights any deficiencies in training and security protocol and is an important part of the day-to-day security plan at the facility.

As in all aspects of nuclear security, there must be clear lines of authority and agency cooperation at every level of government. In the event of a nuclear breach, the line between the NRC and the DHS is precisely drawn, as shown in Figure 6.13.[41]

Finally, in terms of response and advance mitigation, FEMA is entrusted with dealing with the effects and aftereffects of a nuclear blast. The extent of that participation will depend on a host of variables, including the size of the nuclear

---

[41] U.S. Nuclear Regulatory Commission, Office of Nuclear, Security and Incident Response 44 (Washington, DC: U.S. Government Printing Office, April 2005).

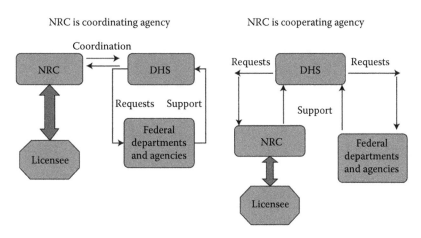

Figure 6.13 NRC interface with Department of Homeland Security.

device, its detonation height, the nature of the ground surface, and existing meteorological conditions. Not only will FEMA encounter the damage resulting from the blast and explosion, but also the long-term influences of fallout.

Practitioners are now lucky enough to conduct measurements for present and future harm regarding nuclear and radiological threats and consequences by modeling and software programs. The Radiological Assessment System for Consequence Analysis (RASCAL) is considered the industry's best example of this sort of measuring tool.

6.4.2.2 Radiological

Some terrorists seek to acquire radioactive materials for use in a radiological dispersal device (RDD) or "dirty bomb." In conjunction with the NRC, the office of the Domestic Nuclear Detection is always on the hunt for individuals or groups intent on delivering nuclear WMD.

The most referenced threat in this sector is the use of a dirty bomb. The dirty bomb combines a conventional explosive, such as dynamite, with radioactive material. Upon detonation, aside from the immediate injuries inflicted, there will be severe collateral damage from the nuclear material itself.

The extent of local contamination will depend on a number of factors, including the size of the explosive, the amount and type of radioactive material used, means of dispersal, and weather conditions. The effects of radiation exposure would be determined by

- Amount of radiation absorbed by the body
- Type of radiation (gamma, beta, or alpha)
- Distance from the radiation to an individual
- Means of exposure—external or internal (absorbed by the skin, inhaled, or ingested)
- Length of time exposed

See the graphic from the NRC in Figure 6.14 representing the various modes of exposure.

Most radioactive materials lack sufficient strength to present a significant public health risk once dispersed, and the materials posing the greatest hazard would likely infect the terrorists themselves. The secondary and cultural effects of a dirty bomb would be quite acute since fear and panic would naturally be expected. The availability of radiological source material is more extensive than most know since this product is used widely in industrial, medical, and research applications, cancer therapy, food and blood irradiation techniques, and radiography.

Law enforcement takes the dirty bomb seriously, and agencies throughout the country regularly engage in tabletop or field exercises anticipating the dynamics of the event. In May 2003, the DHS hosted a large, multiagency, and international exercise dealing with a dirty bomb in Seattle and a covert biological attack in Chicago. In all, 25 federal agencies, as well as the American Red Cross, were involved in the five-day exercise, as well as partner agencies from

Armed Nuclear Security Officer

Summary

Title: Armed Nuclear Security Officer

ID: 1027332

Job Classification: Security Officer

Job Type: Full Time

Hourly Rate: $14.00

Locations: Baxley, GA

Description

U. S. Security is hiring armed contract Security Officers for Plant Hatch

Baxley, Georgia immediately.

You must meet the following requirements for this position:

- Must be a U. S. citizen or have a valid passport
- Must be at least 21 years of age
- Possess High School Diploma or GED equivalent
- Must have valid driver's license
- No felony or prior convictions, or pending dispositions
- Must meet U.S. Nuclear Regulatory Commission (NRC) background screening and Fitness for Duty requirements
- Successful completion of onsite medical physical examination, physical argillites test and must be able to see, hear, speak, stand, walk, run, climb, perform heavy lifting, push, pull, bend, stoop and squat
- Must meet and maintain NRC requirements for physical fitness to include normal weight based on Body Mass Index ratio/waist circumference
- Must be able to work rotating shifts, including weekends, holidays and other days as scheduled when required, and be able to work in inclement weather and temperature extremes
- Must meet all training requirements, which include written tests and practical exercises
- Have good oral and written communication skills, problem solving skills, basic computer skills
- Must be able to work alone or as a team
- Selection process may require up to 5 separate visits to the facility and other local locations to complete all employment criteria.
- Must meet the state and company guidelines for armed work

U.S. Security Associates is an Equal Opportunity Employer (Minorities/Females/Vets/Disabled)

Discrimination and all unlawful harassment (including sexual harassment) in employment is not tolerated. We encourage success based on our individual merits and abilities without regard to race, color, religion, national origin, gender, sexual orientation, gender identity, age, disability, marital status, citizenship status, military status, protected veteran status or employment status. We support and obey laws that prohibit discrimination everywhere we do business. U.S. Security Associates fully considers all qualified applicants including those with a criminal history. Click here to learn more.

Figure CP6.3 Career Profile: Nuclear security officer—USAA Security Associates.

the Canadian Government. The trend continues with regularly scheduled dirty bomb and disaster drills on the federal, state, and local levels (Figure 6.15).

6.4.2.3 Biological

Bioterrorism, another deadly threat, and discussed widely throughout this text, is the deliberate dispersal of pathogens through food, air, water, or living organisms in order to launch disease and other harms to the public. Biological agents can kill on a massive scale and have the potential to move quickly through large populations, leaving high rates of mortality.[42] Biological agents are, for the most part, tasteless, odorless, and invisible. The havoc occurs quickly and without much warning. Biological agents can be introduced by air, by water, or in the food supply. FEMA categorizes agents by application, duration, extent of effects, and mitigation at Figure 6.16.

The DHS has played an increasing role in this sort of detection. Through its Science and Technology Directorate, a series of programs that identify and detect biological agents have been implemented. Of recent interest is BioWatch—a program that measures air samples in 30 urban areas across the United States. Using BioWatch sensors, the technology

---

[42] House introduces new biological weapons legislation, *Homeland Security News Wire* (June 27, 2011), at http://homelandsecuritynewswire.net/.

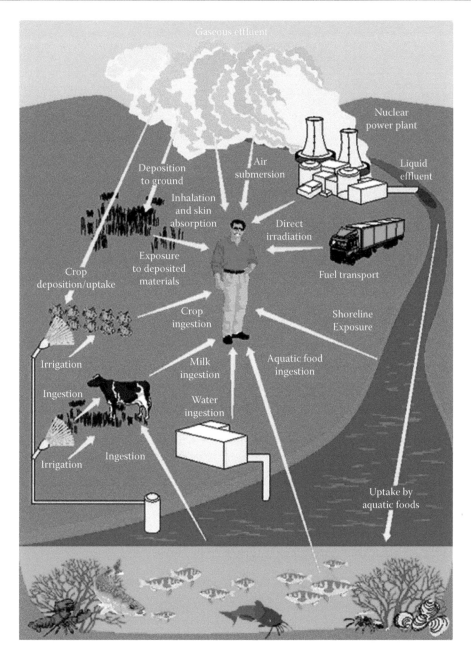

Figure 6.14 Some of the pathways that may lead to exposure. Radiation released in the environment will result in the exposure of general members of the public.

monitors specific locations as well as events of national significance such as the Olympics or Super Bowl.[43] Figure 6.17 illustrates the latest generation in BioWatch technology.

When compared to nuclear risks, biological threats are a much easier scientific row to hoe, and anyone with some level of biological training and access to common laboratory equipment can develop terror tools that emerge from biological products. Biological agents, as the anthrax cases of the last decade demonstrate, foment high rates of fear in the general public.

---

[43] Testimony of Tara O'Toole before the House Subcommittee on Homeland Security Appropriations, on Biosurveillance, April 16, 2010, Washington, DC.

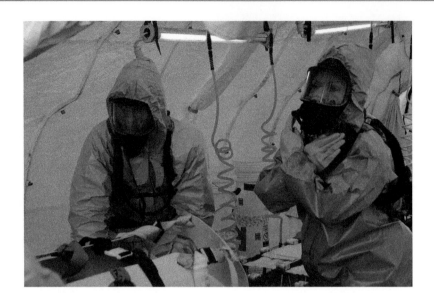

Figure 6.15 Soldiers from the 222nd Chemical Company in full hazardous material gear assist civilian participants during the decontamination phase of a joint force first responders exercise in reaction to a radioactive attack. New York National Army and Airmen Guardsmen collaborate with local authorities to help train for the response to a radioactive terrorist attack, November 6, 2011. (Photo credit: Spc. Brian Godette, New York Army National Guard, 138th PAD.)

The Centers for Disease Control and Prevention (CDC) assumes the preeminent position when it comes to the identification, mitigation, response, and recovery from a biological attack. It classifies biological agents into three major categories:

Category A diseases/agents: The U.S. public health system and primary health care providers must be prepared to address various biological agents, including pathogens that are rarely seen in the United States. High-priority agents include organisms that pose a risk to national security because they

- Can be easily disseminated or transmitted from person to person
- Result in high mortality rates and have the potential for major public health impact
- Might cause public panic and social disruption
- Require special action for public health preparedness

Category B diseases/agents: Second highest-priority agents include those that

- Are moderately easy to disseminate
- Result in moderate morbidity rates and low mortality rates
- Require specific enhancements of the CDC's diagnostic capacity and enhanced disease surveillance

Category C diseases/agents: Third highest-priority agents include emerging pathogens that could be engineered for mass dissemination in the future because of

- Availability
- Ease of production and dissemination
- Potential for high morbidity and mortality rates and major health issues

The CDC types all known biological agents into these three categories. As of 2008, the list of biological agents consisted of

Category A

- Anthrax (*Bacillus anthracis*)
- Botulism (*Clostridium botulinum* toxin)

SELECTED BIOLOGICAL AGENT CHARACTERISTICS

Agent Type	Disease/Condition Causative Agent/ Pathogen	Description of Agent	Transmissible Person to Person	Infectivity/ Lethality	Incubation Period	Duration of Illness	Persistence/ Stability	Vaccination/ Toxoids	Rate of Action	Symptoms	Treatment	Possible Means of Delivery
BACTERIA	Anthrax (inhalation) *Bacillus anthracis*	Rod-shaped, gram-positive, aerobic sporulating micro-organism, individual spores ~(1–1.2)x(3–5)μ	No	Moderate/ High	1–7 days	3–5 days	Spores are highly stable	Yes	Symptoms in 2–3 days; Shock and death occurs with 24–36 hrs after symptoms	Fever, malaise, fatigue, cough and mild chest discomfort, followed by severe respiratory distress with dyspnea, diaphoresis, stridor, and cyanosis	Usually not effective after symptoms are present, high dose antibiotic treatment with penicillin, ciprofloxacin, or doxycycline should be undertaken. Supportive therapy may be necessary.	Aerosol.
	Brucellosis *Brucella suis, melitensis & abortus*	All non-motile, non-sporulating, gram negative, aerobic bacterium; ~(0.5-1)x(1-2)μ	No	High/Low	Days to months	Weeks to months	Organisms are stable for several weeks in wet soil and food.	Yes	Highly variable, usually 8-60 days.	Chills, sweats, headache, fatigue, myalgias, arthralgias, and anorexia. Cough may occur. Complications include sacroiliitis, arthritis, vertebral osteomyelitis, epididymoorchitis, and rarely endocarditis.	Recommended treatment is doxycycline (200 mg/day) plus rifampin (900 mg/day) for 6 weeks.	Aerosol. Expected to mimic a natural disease.
	Cholera *Vibrio cholerae*	Short, curved, motile, gram-negative, non-sporulating rod. Strongly anaerobic, these organisms prefer alkaline and high salt environments.	Negl.	Low/Moderate-High	1-5 days	1 or more weeks	Unstable in aerosols and pure water, more so in polluted water.	Yes	Sudden onset after 1-5 day incubation period.	Initial vomiting and abdominal distension with little or no fever or abdominal pain. Followed rapidly by diarrhea, which may be either mild or profuse and watery, with fluid losses exceeding 5 to 10 liters or more per day. Without treatment, death may result from severe dehydration, hypovolemia, and shock.	Therapy consists of fluid and electrolyte replacement. Antibiotics will shorten the duration of diarrhea and thereby reduce fluid losses. Tetracycline, ampicillin, or trimethoprim-sulfamethoxazole are most commonly used.	1. Sabotage (food/water supply) 2. Aerosol
	Glanders *Burkholderia mallei*	Gram-negative bacillus primarily noted for producing disease in horses, mules, and donkeys	Negl.	/Moderate-High	10-14 days	N/A	N/A	No	N/A	Inhalational exposure produces fever, rigors, sweats, myalgia, headache, pleuritic chest pain, cervical adenopathy, splenomegaly, and generalized papular/pustular eruptions. Almost always fatal without treatment.	Few antibiotics have been evaluated *in vivo*. Sulfadiazine may be effective in some cases. Ciprofloxacin, doxycycline, and rifampin have *in vitro* efficacy. Extrapolating from melioidosis guidelines, a combination of TMP-SMX + ceftazidime ± gentamicin might be considered.	Aerosol.
	Plague (pneumonic, bubonic) *Yersinia pestis*	Rod-shaped, non-motile, non-sporulating, gram-negative, aerobic bacterium; ~(0.5-1)x(1-2)μ	High	High/Very High in untreated personnel, the mortality is 100%	2 to 6 days for bubonic and 3 to 4 days for pneumonic	1-2 days	Less important because of high transmissibility.	Yes	Two to three days	High fever, chills, headache, hemoptysis, and toxemia, progressing rapidly to dyspnea, sturdier, and cyanosis. Death results from respiratory failure, circulatory collapse, and a bleeding diathesis.	Early administration of antibiotics is very effective. Supportive therapy for pneumonic and septicemic forms is required.	May be delivered via contaminated vectors (fleas) causing bubonic type, or, more likely, via aerosol causing pneumonic type.
	Shigellosis *Shigella Dysenteriae*	Rod-shaped, gram-negative, non-motile, non-sporulating bacterium	Negl.	High/Low	1-7 days (usually 2-3)	N/A	Unstable in aerosols and pure water, more so in polluted water.	No	Symptoms usually within 2-3 days, however, known to demonstrate in as little as 12 hours or as long as 7 days.	Fever, nausea, vomiting, abdominal cramps, watery diarrhea, and occasionally, traces of blood in the feces. Symptoms range from mild to severe with some infected individuals not experiencing any symptoms.	The antibiotics commonly used for treatment are ampicillin, trimethoprim/sulfamethoxazole (also known as Bactrim® or Septra®), nalidixic acid, or ciprofloxacin. Persons with mild infections will usually recover quickly without antibiotic treatment. Antidiarrheal agents such as loperamide (Imodium®) or diphenoxylate with atropine (Lomotil®) are likely to make the illness worse and should be avoided.	Contaminated food or water
	Tularemia *Francisella tularensis*	Small, aerobic, non-sporulating, non-motile, gram-negative *cocco-bacillus* ~0.2x(0.2-0.7)μ	No	High/ Moderate if untreated	1-10 days	2 or more weeks	Not very stable	Yes	Three to five days	Ulceroglandular tularemia with local ulcer and regional lymphadenopathy, fever, chills, headache, and malaise. Typhoidal or septicemic tularemia presents with fever, headache, malaise, substernal discomfort, prostration, weight loss, and non-productive cough.	Administration of antibiotics with early treatment is very effective. Streptomycin – 1 gm I. M. q. 12 hrs x 10 10-14 d. Gentamicin – 3-5 mg/kg/day x 10-14 d.	Aerosol.
	Typhoid *Salmonella typhi*	Rod-shaped, motile, non-sporulating gram-negative bacterium	Negl.	Moderate/ Moderate if untreated	6-21 days	Several weeks	Stable	Yes	One to three days	Sustained fever, severe headache, malaise, anorexia, a relative bradycardia, splenomegaly, nonproductive cough in the early stage of the illness, and constipation more commonly than diarrhea.	Chloramphenicol amoxicillin or TMP-SMX. Quilone derivatives and third generation cephalusporins and supportive therapy.	Sabotage of food and water supplies.
RICKETTSIAE	Q-Fever *Coxiella burneti*	Bacterium-like, gram-negative organism, pleomorphic 300-700 nm	No	High/Very low	10-20	2 days to 2 weeks	Stable	Yes	Onset may be sudden	Chills, retrobulbar headache, weakness, malaise and severe sweats.	Tetracycline or doxycycline are the treatment of choice and are given orally for 5 to 7 days.	May be a dust cloud either from a line source or a point source (downwind one-half mile or more).
	Typhus (classic) *Rickettsia prowazeki*	Non-motile, minute, coccoid or rod shaped rickettsiae, in pairs or chains, 300 nm	No	High/High	6-15 days	Weeks to months	Not very stable	No	Variable onset, often sudden. Terminates by rapid lysis after about 2 weeks of fever	Headache, chills, prostration, fever, and general pain. A macular eruption appears on the fifth to sixth day, initially on the upper trunk, followed by spread to the entire body, but usually not the face, palms, or soles.	Tetracyclines or chlormphenical orally in a loading dose of 2-3 g, followed by daily doses of 1-2 g/day in 4 divided doses until ind. becomes afelorite (usually 2 days) plus 1 day.	May be delivered via contaminated vectors (lice or fleas).
VIRUSES	Encephalitis	Lipid-enveloped virions of 50-60 nm dia., icosohedral nucleocapsid w. 2 glycoproteins										
	-Eastern/Western Equine Encephalitis (EEE, WEE)		Negl.	High/High	5-15 days	1-3 weeks	Relatively unstable	Yes		Inflammation of the mengies of the brain, headache, fever, dizziness, drowsiness or stupor, tremors or convulsions, muscular incoordination.	No specific treatment; supportive treatment is essential	Airborne spread possible.
	-Venezuelan Equine Encephalitis		Low	High/Low	1-5 days	Days to weeks	Relatively unstable	Yes	Sudden	Inflammation of the mengies of the brain, headache, fever, dizziness, drowsiness or stupor, tremors or convulsions, muscular incoordination.	No specific treatment; supportive treatment is essential	Airborne spread possible.
	Hemorrhagic Fever									Malaise, myalgias, headache, vomiting, and diarrhea may occur with any of the hemorrhagic fevers	No specific treatment; intensive supportive treatment is essential	Airborne spread possible.
	-Ebola Fever	Filovirus	Moderate	High/High	7-9 days	5-16 days	Relatively unstable	No		May also include a macular dermatologic eruption.		
	-Marburg	Filovirus	Moderate					No		May also include a macular dermatologic eruption.		
	-Yellow Fever	Flavivirus. Isosahedral nucleocapsid 37-50 nm diam., lipoprotein env. w/ short surface spikes	Negl.	High/High	3-6 days	1-2 weeks	Relatively unstable	Yes	Sudden			
	Variola Virus (Smallpox)	Asymmetric, brick-shaped, rounded corners; DNA virus	High	High/High	7-17 days	1-2 weeks	Stable	Yes	2-4 days	Malaise, fever, rigors, vomiting, headache, and backache. 2-3 days later lesions appear which quickly progress from macules to papules, and eventually to pustular vesicles. They are more abundant on the extremities and face, and develop synchronously.	No specific treatment; supportive treatment is essential	Airborne spread possible.
TOXIN	Botulinum Toxin	any of the seven distinct neurotoxins produced by the bacillus, *Clostridium botulinum*	No	NA/High	Variable (hours to days)	24-72 hours/Months if lethal	Stable	Yes	12-72 hours	Initial signs and symptoms include ptosis, generalized weakness, lassitude, and dizziness. Diminished salivation with extreme dryness of the mouth and throat may cause complaints of a sore throat. Urinary retention or ileus may also occur. Motor symptoms usually are present early in the disease; cranial nerves are affected first with blurred vision, diplopia, ptosis, and photophobia. Bulbar nerve dysfunction causes dysarthria, dysphonia, and dysphagia. This is followed by a symmetrical, descending, progressive weakness of the extremities along with weakness of the respiratory muscles. Development of respiratory failure may be abrupt.	(1) Respiratory failure—tracheostomy and ventilatory assistance, fatalities should be <5%. Intensive and prolonged nursing care may be required for recovery (which may take several weeks or even months). (2) Food-borne botulism and aerosol exposure—equine antitoxin is probably helpful, sometimes even after onset of signs of intoxication. Administration of antitoxin is reasonable if disease has not progressed to a stable state. Use requires pretesting for sensitivity to horse serum (and desensitization for those allergic). Disadvantages include rapid clearance by immune elimination, as well as a theoretical risk of serum sickness.	1. Sabotage (food/water supply) 2. Aerosol
	Ricin	Glycoprotein toxin (66,000 daltons) from the seed of the castor plant	No	NA/High	Hours	Days	Stable	Not effective	6-72 hours	Rapid onset of nausea, vomiting, abdominal cramps and severe diarrhea with vascular collapse; death has occurred on the third day or later. Following inhalation, one might expect nonspecific symptoms of weakness, fever, cough, and hypothermia followed by hypotension and cardiovascular collapse.	Management is supportive and should include maintenance of intravascular volume. Standard management for poison ingestion should be employed if intoxication is by the oral route.	Aerosol
	Staphylococcal enterotoxin B	One of several exotoxins produced by *Staphylococcus aureus*	No	NA/Low	Days to weeks	Days to weeks	Stable	Not effective	30 min-6 hours	Fever, chills, headache, myalgia, and nonproductive cough. In more severe cases, dyspnea and retrosternal chest pain may also be present. In many patients nausea, vomiting, and diarrhea will also occur.	Treatment is limited to supportive care. No specific antitoxin for human use is available.	1. Sabotage (food/water supply) 2. Aerosol
	Trichothecene (T-2) Mycotoxins	A diverse group of more than 40 compounds produced by fungi.	No	NA/High	Hours	Hours	Stable	Not effective	Sudden	Victims are reported to have suffered painful skin lesions, lightheadedness, dyspnea, and a rapid onset of hemorrhage, incapacitation and death. Survivors developed a radiation-like sickness including fever, nausea, vomiting, diarrhea, leukopenia, bleeding, and sepsis.	General supportive measures are used to alleviate acute T-2 toxicoses. Prompt (within 5-60 min of exposure) soap and water wash significantly reduces the development of the localized destructive, cutaneous effects of the toxin. After oral exposure management should include standard therapy for poison ingestion.	1. Sabotage 2. Aerosol

Figure 6.16 Biological agent characteristics.

Figure 6.17 BioWatch: Generation 3 Monitoring Station, Department of Homeland Security.

- Plague (*Yersinia pestis*)
- Smallpox (*Variola major*)
- Tularemia (*Francisella tularensis*)
- Viral hemorrhagic fevers (filoviruses [e.g., Ebola, Marburg] and arenaviruses [e.g., Lassa, Machupo])

Category B

- Brucellosis (*Brucella* species)
- Epsilon toxin of *Clostridium perfringens*
- Food safety threats (e.g., *Salmonella* species, *Escherichia coli* O157:H7, *Shigella*)
- Glanders (*Burkholderia mallei*)
- Melioidosis (*Burkholderia pseudomallei*)
- Psittacosis (*Chlamydia psittaci*)
- Q fever (*Coxiella burnetii*)
- Ricin toxin from *Ricinus communis* (castor beans)
- Staphylococcal enterotoxin B
- Typhus fever (*Rickettsia prowazekii*)
- Viral encephalitis (alphaviruses [e.g., Venezuelan equine encephalitis, eastern equine encephalitis, western equine encephalitis])
- Water safety threats (e.g., *Vibrio cholerae, Cryptosporidium parvum*)

Category C

- Emerging infectious diseases, such as Nipah virus and hantavirus

6.4.2.4 Chemical

Chemical weapons represent another form of WMD for terrorists. Chemical weapons have seen usage in both accidental and intentional terms. For example, the release of chemical toxins in an industrial accident can wreak havoc on the public health. More maliciously, the intentional infliction of chemical toxins by a terrorist manifests the mindset and a complete and utter disregard for human life. In World War I, soldiers on the trench fronts experienced the ferocity and terminal quality of various chemical gases. Chemical weapons can cause high levels of mortality. Often referred to as the chemist's war, the range, depth, and breadth of usage shocks even today's hardened soldier. Today's terrorist threat is just as real and dangerous. As recently as 1995, the Tokyo subway was flooded with Sarin gas, delivered via plastic bottles; it is miraculous that more injuries and deaths did not occur.

More recently, terrorists have concentrated on acquiring and employing chemical materials with dual uses, such as pesticides, poisons, and industrial chemicals. Chemical threats come in a variety of forms and delivery systems. These agents are far more common and much easier to develop and distribute than the biological and nuclear counterparts. Many household products, farm fertilizers, and other agricultural and industrial products contain the elements necessary to shape the chemical terror.

The general typology of chemical agents includes

- Biotoxins—poisons that come from plants or animals
- Blister agents/vesicants—chemicals that severely blister the eyes, respiratory tract, and skin on contact
- Blood agents—poisons that affect the body by being absorbed into the blood
- Caustics (acids)—chemicals that burn or corrode people's skin, eyes, and mucus membranes
- Choking/lung/pulmonary agents—chemicals that cause severe irritation or swelling of the respiratory tract
- Incapacitating agents—agents that can affect consciousness
- Long-acting anticoagulants—poisons that prevent blood from clotting properly
- Metals—agents that consist of metallic poisons
- Nerve agents—highly poisonous chemicals that work by preventing the nervous system from working properly
- Organic solvents—agents that damage the tissues of living things by dissolving fats and oils
- Riot control agents/tear gas—highly irritating agents normally used by law enforcement for crowd control
- Toxic alcohols—poisonous alcohols that can damage the heart, kidneys, and nervous system
- Vomiting agents—chemicals that cause nausea and vomiting

6.4.2.5 Improvised explosive devices

In addition to WMD and potential weapons of mass effect, there is the threat of terrorist attack by means of improvised explosive device (IED). IED weapons are explosive devices fashioned and deployed by means other than through conventional military operations, thus the term "improvised." They can be created from traditional explosive devices such as bombs, warheads, grenades, and land mines, or otherwise fashioned from explosive raw materials. Ball bearings, nails, metal filings, and other materials can be utilized as damage-causing projectiles.[44] The Boston Marathon bombing devices, consisting of pressure cookers packed with nails and other projectiles, were devastating devices. See Figure 6.18.

Detonation can be accomplished by wired means or remotely through a rigged cell phone, handheld device, or other wireless technology. The fuel to ignite the IED can be common products such as "drain openers, sulfuric acid and car batteries."[45] The FBI disseminates an IED threat card, which categorizes the various products, compounds, and chemicals common to IEDs. See Figure 6.19.

The methods of IED delivery will vary depending on the target as well as the IED design. The Consortium of National Academies including Science, Engineering, Medicine and the National Research Council charts the variety at Figure 6.20.

An inordinately high number of incidents of IED attack globally over the last several years have occurred in Iraq and Afghanistan, in addition to attacks in a number of other countries that have begun to experience increased terrorist attacks firsthand. Unfortunately, there exist numerous online terrorist organization websites and sources that provide detailed instructions, including videos, on how to construct and deploy bombs. Often, new sites crop up as

---

[44] H. Hogan, Identifying Explosives, After the Fact, *Homeland Security Today Magazine* 18–19 (September 2011).
[45] K. Yeager, What Law Enforcement Needs to Know about Improvised Explosives, *Police Chief* 52–55 (September 2011).

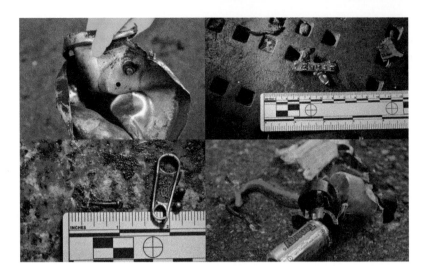

Figure 6.18 Photographs of the suspected bombing device fragments taken in the immediate aftermath of the Boston Marathon investigation.

quickly as sites can be discovered and deactivated by authorities. In August 2016, federal and local officials investigating a possible explosive attack on the DC Metro Subway systems apparently prevented a large-scale event.[46]

IED attacks have given rise to other means and related classifications of attack. Multiple IEDs can be strung together to create a "daisy chain" whereupon multiple devices can be discharged, either at once or concurrently, with a single signal. Other means of attack include VBIED (vehicle-borne improvised explosive device), SVBIED (suicide vehicle-borne improvised explosive device), and SPBIED (suicide pedestrian-borne improvised explosive device).

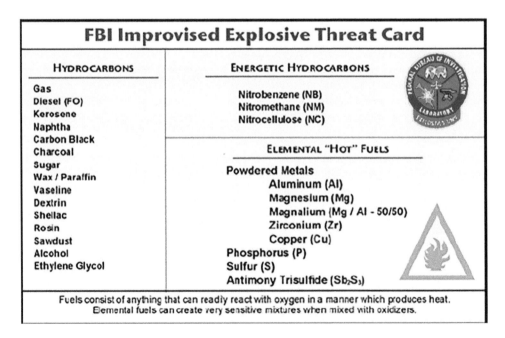

Figure 6.19   IED threat card.

[46] See A. Noble, D.C. Transit Police Officer Accused of Trying to Support Islamic State, *The Washington Times* (August 3, 2016), at http://www.washingtontimes.com/news/2016/aug/3/dc-area-police-officer-charged-trying-help-isis, last accessed August 27, 2016.

BOMB THREAT STAND-OFF CHART

Threat Description Improvised Explosive Device (IED)	Explosives Capacity[1] (TNT Equivalent)	Building Evacuation Distance[2]	Outdoor Evacuation Distance[3]
Pipe Bomb	5 LBS	70 FT	1200 FT
Suicide Bomber	20 LBS	110 FT	1700 FT
Briefcase/Suitcase	50 LBS	150 FT	1850 FT
Car	500 LBS	320 FT	1500 FT
SUV/Van	1,000 LBS	400 FT	2400 FT
Small Moving Van/ Delivery Truck	4,000 LBS	640 FT	3800 FT
Moving Van/ Water Truck	10,000 LBS	860 FT	5100 FT
Semi-Trailer	60,000 LBS	1570 FT	9300 FT

1. These capacities are based on the maximum weight of explosive material that could reasonably fit in a container of similar size.
2. Personnel in buildings are provided a high degree of protection from death or serious injury; however, glass breakage and building debris may still cause some injuries. Unstrengthened buildings can be expected to sustain damage that approximates five percent of their replacement cost.
3. If personnel cannot enter a building to seek shelter they must evacuate to the minimum distance recommended by Outdoor Evacuation Distance. These distance is governed by the greater hazard of fragmentation distance, glass breakage or threshold for ear drum rupture.

Figure 6.20 Bomb threat stand off chart showing evacuation distances for various types of threats. (Courtesy U.S. Technical Support Working Group [TSWG].)

Either way, the results are often physically devastating. Health impacts are immediate when in proximity to an IED and include

- Overpressure damage to the lungs, ears, abdomen, and other pressure-sensitive organs. Blast lung injury, a condition caused by the extreme pressure of an explosion, is the leading cause of illness and death for initial survivors of an explosion.
- Fragmentation injuries caused by projectiles thrown by the blast—material from the bomb, shrapnel, or flying debris that penetrates the body and causes damage.
- Impact injuries caused when the blast throws a victim into another object, that is, fractures, amputation, and trauma to the head and neck.
- Thermal injuries caused by burns to the skin, mouth, sinus, and lungs.
- Other injuries including exposure to toxic substances, crush injuries, and aggravation of preexisting conditions (asthma, congestive heart failure, etc.).[47]

Timothy McVeigh carried out a VBIED attack in the case of the Oklahoma City bombing in 1995. A waterborne SVBIED attack method was utilized in the bombing of the USS Cole in 2000. It can be argued that the 9/11 attacks were the largest-ever SVBIED attack carried out, with the jet fuel on board the planes serving as the explosive material. A series of SVBIED attacks were carried out in perpetrating the July 7, 2005 London bombings.

While generally smaller in scale than WMD attacks, the various IED attack methods pose an increasingly real and challenging threat in the United States and particularly to interests globally. In addition, the acquisition of bomb-making materials and delivery and discharge of the weapon are generally far easier than with WMD weapons, and the effects are certainly just as deadly.

---

[47] National Academies and Department of Homeland Security, News & Terrorism, Communicating in a Crisis, Fact Sheet: IED Attack Improvised Explosive Devices, at https:// www.dhs.gov/sites/default/files/publications/prep_ied_fact_sheet.pdf, last accessed August 27, 2016.

The level of harm caused by IED attacks will also depend on its delivery location. A deserted road is a very different setting than a mass transit station. Terrorists are always looking for the maximum effect possible.

6.5 COMPUTER SECURITY AND RISKS TO THE INFORMATION INFRASTRUCTURE

The cyber world presents its own array of security challenges, and not to be forgotten is that the terrorists know that damage to the national cyber system can be devastating. Cyberspace has been defined as "the independent network of information technology infrastructures, and includes the Internet, telecommunications networks, computer systems, and embedded processors and controllers in critical industries."[48]

From a terrorist perspective, the virtual world provides a host of avenues of attack. From their vantage point, terrorists see a world of opportunity—the disruption of essential systems, the ruination of data and protection systems, the destruction of finance and banking, and the chance to destroy and disrupt on a major scale. Security in the virtual world should not be taken lightly. In essence, the computer system is nothing less than information infrastructure—as legitimate and likely a target for the terrorist as a bridge or water treatment center. The information infrastructure, including government, educational institutions, and research centers, as well as business and industry, is rich in potential damage. Terrorists will target U.S. corporations, facilities, personnel, information, or computer, cable, satellite, or telecommunications systems—all of which are part of the information infrastructure. The possibilities are limitless and can include

- Denial or disruption of computer, cable, satellite, or telecommunications services
- Unauthorized monitoring of computer, cable, satellite, or telecommunications systems
- Unauthorized disclosure of proprietary or classified information stored within or communicated through computer, cable, satellite, or telecommunications systems
- Unauthorized modification or destruction of computer programming codes, computer network databases, stored information, or computer capabilities
- Manipulation of computer, cable, satellite, or telecommunications services resulting in fraud, financial loss, or other federal criminal violations[49]

So serious and continuous are the threats to our cyber security structure that in the early days of the formation of DHS, there was a keen recognition that a unit dedicated to this protection would be necessary. US-CERT (U.S. Computer Emergency Readiness Team) was designated as that unit. US-CERT is responsible for the management, defense, and mitigation of cyber-attacks for the federal government. To get some sense of just how extensive and continuous these threats are to the cyber world, review the reportable, high-level threats, by top five threats and category from the US-CERT in Figure 6.21. Threats can be categorized as shown in Table 6.7.[50]

The US-CERT program is expected to advance information sharing among all agencies dedicated to the defense of the homeland. Its overall mission can be summarized as follows:

- Support to national and international public and private sectors
- Event monitoring, predictive analysis, and aligned reporting tools
- Advance warnings regarding emerging threats
- Incident response for national agencies, malware analysis, and recovery support
- Involvement in national and international exercises

Threats of every sort and variety are vulnerabilities to both software and hardware. US-CERT defines cyber threats by using six distinct categories:

---

[48] National Security Presidential Directive 54, *Cyber Security and Monitoring* (January 8, 2008).

[49] The National Counterintelligence and Security Center, at https:// www.ncsc.gov/publications/archives/index.html, last accessed August 27, 2016.

[50] Government Accountability Office (GAO) Department of Homeland Security's (DHS's) Role in Critical Infrastructure Protection (CIP) Cybersecurity, GAO-05-434 (Washington, DC: May 2005), http://www.gao.gov/htext/d05434.html, last accessed August 27, 2016.

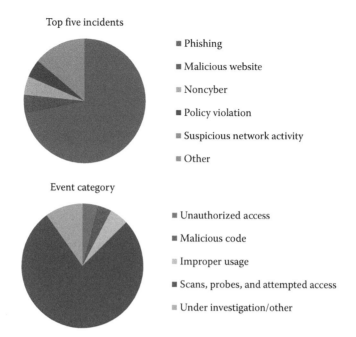

Top five incidents

- Phishing
- Malicious website
- Noncyber
- Policy violation
- Suspicious network activity
- Other

Event category

- Unauthorized access
- Malicious code
- Improper usage
- Scans, probes, and attempted access
- Under investigation/other

Figure 6.21 National cyber alert system cyber security bulletin.

Category 1 (CAT 1)—Unauthorized access

In this category an individual gains logical or physical access without permission to a federal agency network, system, application, data, or other resource.

Category 2 (CAT 2)—Denial of service (DoS)

An attack that successfully prevents or impairs the normal authorized functionality of networks, systems, or applications by exhausting resources. This activity includes being the victim or participating in the DoS.

Category 3 (CAT 3)—Malicious code

Successful installation of malicious software (e.g., virus, worm, spyware, bot, Trojan horse, or other code-based malicious entity that infects or affects an operating system or application). Agencies are not required to report malicious logic that has been successfully quarantined by antivirus (AV) software.

Category 4 (CAT 4)—Improper usage

A person violates acceptable computing use policies.

Category 5 (CAT 5)—Scans, probes, or attempted access

Any activity that seeks to access or identify a federal agency computer, open ports, protocols, service, or any combination for later exploit. This activity does not directly result in a compromise or DoS.

Category 6 (CAT 6)—Investigation

Unconfirmed incidents of potentially malicious or anomalous activity deemed by the reporting entity to warrant further review.

The National Strategy to Secure Cyberspace delineates the challenges of the cyber world in the world of terrorism. Security will depend on mastery of the following tasks:

- Establish a public–private architecture for responding to national-level cyber incidents
- Provide for the development of tactical and strategic analysis of cyber-attacks and vulnerability assessments
- Encourage the development of a private sector capability to share a synoptic view of the health of cyberspace
- Expand the Cyber Warning and Information Network to support the role of DHS in coordinating crisis management for cyberspace security

Table 6.7 Cyber security threats

Threat	Description
Bot-network operators	Bot-network operators are hackers; however, instead of breaking into systems for the challenge or bragging rights, they take over multiple systems in order to coordinate attacks and to distribute phishing schemes, spam, and malware attacks. The services of these networks are sometimes made available in underground markets (e.g., purchasing a denial-of-service attack, servers to relay spam, and phishing attacks).
Criminal groups	Criminal groups seek to attack systems for monetary gain. Specifically, organized crime groups are using spam, phishing, and spyware/malware to commit identity theft and online fraud. International corporate spies and organized crime organizations also pose a threat to the United States through their ability to conduct industrial espionage and large-scale monetary theft and to hire or develop hacker talent.
Foreign intelligence services	Foreign intelligence services use cyber tools as part of their information-gathering and espionage activities. In addition, several nations are aggressively working to develop information warfare doctrine, programs, and capabilities. Such capabilities enable a single entity to have a significant and serious impact by disrupting the supply, communications, and economic infrastructures that support military power—impacts that could affect the daily lives of U.S. citizens across the country.
Hackers	Hackers break into networks for the thrill of the challenge or for bragging rights in the hacker community. While remote cracking once required a fair amount of skill or computer knowledge, hackers can now download attack scripts and protocols from the Internet and launch them against victim sites. Thus, while attack tools have become more sophisticated, they have also become easier to use. According to the Central Intelligence Agency, the large majority of hackers do not have the requisite expertise to threaten difficult targets such as critical U.S. networks. Nevertheless, the worldwide population of hackers poses a relatively high threat of an isolated or brief disruption causing serious damage.
Insiders	The disgruntled organization insider is a principal source of computer crime. Insiders may not need a great deal of knowledge about computer intrusions because their knowledge of a target system often allows them to gain unrestricted access to cause damage to the system or to steal system data. The insider threat also includes outsourcing vendors as well as employees who accidentally introduce malware into systems.
Phishers	Individuals, or small groups, who execute phishing schemes in an attempt to steal identities or information for monetary gain. Phishers may also use spam and spyware/malware to accomplish their objectives.
Spammers	Individuals or organizations that distribute unsolicited e-mail with hidden or false information in order to sell products, conduct phishing schemes, distribute spyware/malware, or attack organizations (i.e., denial of service).
Spyware/malware authors	Individuals or organizations with malicious intent carry out attacks against users by producing and distributing spyware and malware. Several destructive computer viruses and worms have harmed files and hard drives, including the Melissa macro virus, the Explore.Zip worm, the CIH (Chernobyl) virus, Nimda, Code Red, Slammer, and Blaster.
Terrorists	Terrorists seek to destroy, incapacitate, or exploit critical infrastructures in order to threaten national security, cause mass casualties, weaken the U.S. economy, and damage public morale and confidence. Terrorists may use phishing schemes or spyware/malware in order to generate funds or gather sensitive information.

- Improve National Incident Management Systems (NIMS)
- Coordinate processes for voluntary participation in the development of national public–private continuity and contingency plans
- Exercise cyber security continuity plans for federal systems
- Improve and enhance public–private information sharing involving cyber-attacks, threats, and vulnerabilities[51]

The author of these threats is not always discernible. What is clear has been the dramatic increase in every type of vulnerability that attacks systems and software. Carnegie Mellon University operates a computer emergency readiness team (CERT), and its statistics tracking vulnerabilities show a steady and dramatic rise of these intrusions. From 1995 to 2002, the increase has been quite marked, from 1,090 to over 4,100.[52] See Figure 6.22.

---

[51] Office of the President, The National Strategy to Secure Cyberspacex (February 2003), at https:// www.us-cert.gov/sites/default/files/publications/cyberspace_strategy.pdf, last accessed August 27, 2016.

[52] See Carnegie Mellon University, Computer Emergency Readiness Team: Vulnerability Statistics, at http://www.cert.org/vulnerability-analysis/, last accessed August 27, 2016. See also President, Strategy to Secure Cyberspace, 10.

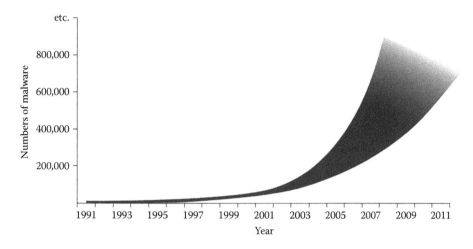

Figure 6.22   CERT vulnerabilities reported and incidents handled.

6.6 CONCLUSION

Any operational notion of security must include a look at traditional aspects of security, such as risk and threat, as well as new and emerging hazards. This chapter surveys the likely and even unlikely events that will challenge those laboring in private and public policing position—those entrusted with the prevention and minimization of threats, the identification and elimination of vulnerabilities and the implementation of policies that mitigate all harms and hazards. First, how does the security professional define and measure risk? What criteria and variables need to be considered when assessing risk? Are some risks worth taking and others never tolerable? Are some locations more vulnerable to risk than others? And how do we weigh and assess in a community context? What types of communal settings are more prone to risk and harm than others? Are the costs of the risk, relative to its potential harm, worth the investment? In short, risk cannot be assessed in a vacuum but must be weighed in light of likelihood of occurrence, costs of prevention, and the nature of the harm to be inflicted. Various systems of measurement relative to risk are also provided, including CARVER + Shock methodology.

Next, the chapter's coverage turns to the typology of threat and hazard. From natural to terrorist in design, threats and hazards must be evaluated in light of the perpetrator's motivation. In the natural world, there is no malice. In the world of terrorism, the security professional must anticipate to what extent the actor will go to achieve a particular end. Hijackings, bombs, and WMD manifest a direct intentionality, while hurricane and flood do not.

Nothing is more pressing or compelling than the world of WMD. WMD are unique in many senses, especially when one considers the nature of the harm inflicted and the potentiality for widespread destruction.[53]

The fear and dread of a nuclear event is probably the most pronounced of any form of WMD. In particular, the chapter looks at the relative ease of delivery of various WMD by a dirty bomb mechanism. The world of bioterrorism is just as frightening, and the accessibility and general availability of bioagents should give any security professional cause for concern.

Keywords

accessibility

asset value

biological agents

bioterrorism

biotoxins

BioWatch

blister agents

blood agents

CARVER + Shock assessment tool

caustics

chemical weapons

---

[53] This is why efforts at threat reduction as to nuclear arsenals are a sensible part of the homeland plan. See A.F. Woolf, Department of Defense Cooperative Threat Reduction Program, Nonproliferation and Threat Reduction Assistance: U.S. Programs in the Former Soviet Union (Congressional Research Service, March 6, 2012).

consequence

crisis phase

criticality

cyber threats

deterrence

dirty bomb

effect

escalation phase

exposure

fragmentation injuries

hazard mitigation

hazards

impact injuries

improvised explosive device (IED)

incapacitating agents

information technology infrastructures

long-acting anticoagulants

mitigation

natural hazards

nuclear terrorism

nerve agents

nuclear weapons

organic solvents

planning

preincident indicators

preparedness

pulmonary agents

Radiological Assessment System for Consequence Analysis (RASCAL)

radiological dispersal device

recognizability

recuperability

risk

risk assessment

risk management

suicide pedestrian-borne improvised explosive device

suicide vehicle-borne improvised explosive device

tear gas

thermal injuries

threat assessment

threat rating

threats

toxic alcohols

trigger phase

vehicle-borne improvised explosive device

vesicants

vomiting agents

vulnerability

vulnerability analysis

vulnerability rating

weapons of mass destruction

Discussion questions

1. Outline the three methodologies of risk assessment proposed by Rand Corporation.

2. Discuss the six categories of cyber threats defined by US-CERT and how private security operatives can defend against them.

3. Describe the challenges that the National Strategy to Secure Cyberspace states exist in the world of cyber terrorism and identify some practices strategies to overcome them.

4. Relay the two equations used to determine risk and discuss the similarities and differences of each one. Discuss how they are used in practical applications.

5. Outline the CARVER + Shock methodology and discuss how it is applied in practical assessments.

6. Illustrate the usefulness of a community profile in threat assessment.

7. Discuss the four categories of weapons of mass destruction and how threat assessments can help in the prevention of attacks.

CHAPTER 7

Physical security

OBJECTIVES

After completing this chapter, the student will be able to

1. Outline the two levels of physical security, both interior and exterior.
2. Define physical security and perimeter protection and list common crime risks in the physical environment.
3. List the various types of interior security applications from doors to access control.
4. Recall the many purposes for video surveillance.
5. State the steps to successful surveillance and summarize the importance of surveillance.
6. Identify the equipment used in video surveillance and identify the best equipment for each circumstance.
7. Discuss the theory of crime prevention through environmental design (CPTED) and how it is implemented in crime prevention.
8. Evaluate the usefulness of both natural and structural barriers in crime prevention and illustrate their appropriate uses.

7.1 INTRODUCTION: THE PHYSICAL NATURE OF SECURITY

The average citizen encounters the private security industry on a very mechanical level—at the surface where security equipment can be readily identified. Whether it be the surveillance camera at the mall, the CCTV monitors witnessed in control centers, or the plethora of locks and access controls, most people recognize the security industry at the street level. Common, ordinary events are regulated by the controls that the security industry provides, from scanning and detection equipment at courthouses and airports, to swipe cards and other identification measures at controlled access locations, to barriers and fencing that contain a safe zone—all of these comprise the "physical" world of security. The American Society for Industrial Security (ASIS) provides an exceptionally precise definition of what "physical security" really means:

> That part of security concerned with physical measures designed to safeguard people; to prevent unauthorized access to equipment, facilities, material, and documents; and to safeguard them against a security incident.[1]

That "physicality" so to speak is grounded in two levels: first, the spatial-geographic reality in need of protection, whether it be the cattle ranch or the high-rise urban apartment; and second, the actual, physical measures employed, whether these be man-made or natural, technological, or architecturally designed. In physical security, the operative

---

[1] ASIS International, Security Glossary—P, at https://www.asisonline.org/Membership/Library/Security-Glossary/Pages/Security-Glossary-P.aspx.

worries about the physical world and the physical means to protect its assets and inhabitants. P.J. Ortmeier correctly labels physical security "a first line of defense against potential threat."[2] For others, the idea of physical security primarily relates to the technology, the software, and the hardware that provide this protection, as Purpura labels a process "increasingly automated" and "smart."[3] But this vision fails to fully incorporate the full dimensions of the physical world that security encounters. Barriers, by way of example, need not be anything shaped or crafted by technological man—and can be nothing more than the natural contour of a river bed and adjoining rock formation—this too surely physical. Or, lighting the landscape need not only rely upon the placement of lighting fixtures to detect criminality but also must sensibly expect the designer or architect of physical space to account for how natural light and placement of facilities complement one another. The entire crime prevention through environmental design (CPTED) movement, highlighted in the last portion of this chapter, edifies this argument. Hence, it seems prudent to argue that physical security is about both tools and artifices in place, whether high technological or a planted fence, as well as about the space in need of that defensive posture, whether it be a stretch of land or a sports stadium.

This chapter exposes both sides of the definition of physical security with its dual emphasis on physical means and methods, which protect assets and individuals as well as the place or locale where this precious cargo, both tangible and human, find themselves stationed.

7.2 PHYSICAL SECURITY: EXTERIOR APPLICATIONS

The analysis and typing of physical security can be further broken down into two major camps: exterior and interior. In the former, the emphasis is, for lack of a better way of describing it, on the outside world, the physical world externally. Physical security is the interplay between the physical environment and the rate or opportunity for crime, where crime is evaluated in light of a larger "ecosystem."[4] Physical design encompasses many elements; roads, parks, building architecture, street lighting, and signs are all elements. The environment can be planned to most effectively thwart criminal activity. Physical security and its design either enhances or restricts the opportunity for crime in a community. Historically, "physical security is defined as a system of barriers, entry and search controls, intrusion detection, alarm assessment, and testing and maintenance. Collectively this system, along with practices and procedures specific to each site, is intended to deter, delay, detect, assess and appropriately respond to an unauthorized activity."[5] Physical security can also be about larger environments and collective living space. Residents keenly realize the places worth visiting and those to avoid. Citizens are well aware of danger zones in the environment. Common crime risks in a physical environment include:

1. Inadequate lighting
2. Inadequate perimeter security
3. Places of concealment for attackers such as vacant structures, dense shrubbery, trash accumulations, isolated parking areas, bus stations, public rest rooms, alleys, etc.
4. Situations that create potential access difficulties for police

Oscar Newman refers to the integration of environmental and crime prevention as a question of "defensible space." He relates:

> Defensible space is a model for residential environments which inhibits crime by creating the physical expression of a social fabric that defends itself. All the different elements which combine to make a defensible space have a common goal—an environment in which latent territoriality and sense of community in the inhabitants can be translated into responsibility for ensuring a safe, productive, and well-maintained living space.[6]

An effective physical security plan sets up overlapping barriers to crime, which thwarts the criminal element. That process commences with a global view of the location to be protected. For example, in a recent security study at the Marine Base at Camp Lejeune, North Carolina, the process begins regionally—looking at the Base from the

---

[2] P.J. Ortmeier, *Introduction to Security* 94 (3rd ed., Prentice Hall, 2009).

[3] P.P. Purpura, *Security: An Introduction* 262 (CRC Press, 2011).

[4] M. Felson, Crime Prevention, Apartments, and the Larger Ecosystem, 22 *Sec. J.* 61 (1998).

[5] IOPA website, Physical Security Systems, at http://www.oa.doc.gov/sase/physical-sec.html, last accessed August 29, 2002.

[6] O. Newman, *Defensible Space* 3 (Macmillan, 1972).

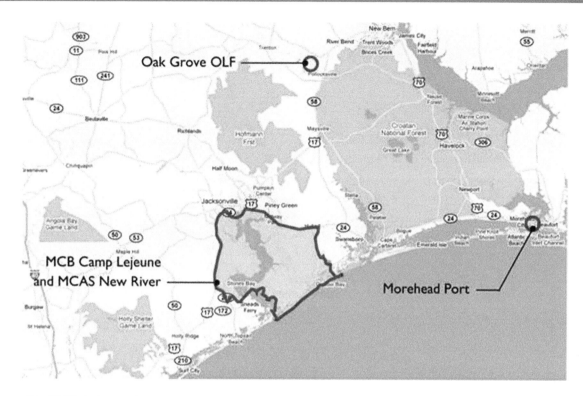

Figure 7.1 BEAP study area.

largest possible perspective in order to determine natural defenses and obvious and not-so-obvious vulnerabilities. See Figure 7.1.[7]

In this scenario, the physical security specialist notes the points of ingress and egress, the natural water dimensions of the Base, the ease of threat taking place in select portions of the space, and the need and necessity of anticipating how this physical reality impacts the larger security question. And that physical analysis continues downward to the micro level of particular buildings and installations, and decision making as to where and how to place particular activities in order to assure a safe and secure setting. As it moves closer to a designated building or other structure, the security specialist begins the focus on that setting by setting a broad perimeter first and accounting for the facility after authoring several layers of protective defense. Figure 7.2[8] graphically portrays this next stage in exterior physical security.

Barriers may be of two general types, natural and structural. Natural barriers include mountains, cliffs, canyons, rivers, or other terrain difficult to traverse. Structural barriers are man-made devices such as fences, walls, floors, roofs, grills, bars, or other structures that deter penetration. If a natural barrier forms one side or any part of the perimeter, it in itself should not automatically be considered an adequate perimeter barrier, since it may be overcome by a determined intruder. Structural barriers should be provided for that portion of the perimeter, if required. See Figure 7.3.[9]

The physical security assessment will be guided by the purpose of the facility itself such as a hospital or educational institution, an industrial office and a corporate conference center, or sports venue or transportation hub. Each of these exterior facilities has unique demands for security. Consider mass transit and public rail centers—a place where terrorism seems always drawn too—and most because of its capacity to inflict great harm with minimal effort or

[7] U.S. Marine Corp, Marine Corps Base Camp Lejeune, Base Exterior Architectural Plan, Section Es-2.3 Study Area, at http://www.lejeune.marines.mil/OfficesStaff/InstallationDevelopmentDivision/BEAP_web.aspx.

[8] Infosec Institute, Physical Security: Managing the Intruder, at http://resources.infosecinstitute.com/physical-security-managing-intruder, last accessed August 27, 2016.

[9] U.S. Marine Corp, Marine Corps Base Camp Lejeune, Base Exterior Architectural Plan, at http://www.lejeune.marines.mil/OfficesStaff/InstallationDevelopmentDivision/BEAP_web.aspx at 3.1.4 Anti-Terrorism and Force Protection, last accessed August 27, 2016.

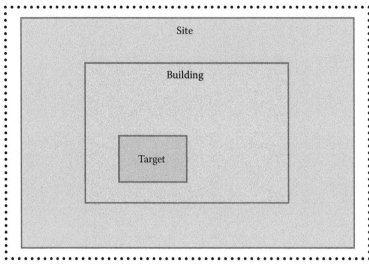

Figure 7.2   Layered barriers.

Figure 7.3   Vehicle control barrier.

sophistication of weaponry. On top of this, subway systems, by way of illustration, are complex, subterranean places difficult to defend. Larger systems of public transit like New York, Chicago, and London are ripe locations for a terror plot. As a result, physical security specialists have to be the best and brightest in fashioning defensive postures that thwart harm. Consider and weigh the many relevant issues in the physical security assessment directed at public transit found in Appendix F.[10]

But exactly how that physical security should take shape in a specified exterior setting is the subject of much discussion and from many viewpoints and perspectives.[11] Crime and harm will not be prevented by adopting the "armed" camp or lockdown image of an entity in fear as a main long-term strategy. Effective physical security must blend with

---

[10] Federal Transit Administration, Physical Security Survey Checklist, at https://transit-safety.fta.dot.gov/training/Archived/EPSSeminarReg/CD/documents/OHIO_DOT/PhysicalSECURITY.doc, last accessed August 27, 2016.

[11] S. Ludwig, Property Management Security: A Swirl of CPTED, Challenges and Balance, *Sec. Mag.* (February 2015) at 48.

the life of a community, entity, or facility that it is protecting—giving off the appearance of safety and security alongside an air of confidence in the quality of life that residents and owners have. Painting a picture of sheer defensive survival will not safeguard or insure the long-term safety and security of any exterior place whether it be a neighborhood, business, or institution. Kevin Marier argues that every physical security plan must be mindful of what he terms the 5 Ds of physical security, namely,

- Deter
- Detect
- Deny
- Delay
- Defend[12]

Smart and intelligent physical security makes the integration of security measures almost second nature to the client served—otherwise, the steps of physical security proclaim the danger rather than the confidence to defend. The Heritage Foundation keenly describes this awful cycle:

> Another cost of crime is that employers are reluctant to expand or relocate in high-crime neighborhoods even if given economic development incentives. When an office, store, or factory is said to be in a dangerous neighborhood, employers have difficulties finding and retaining a work force ... Local residents, fearing crime, are unwilling to patronize neighborhood businesses during evening hours. Business owners may be willing to bear the risk of crime in order to attract evening customers, but if residents are too frightened to shop, many of the businesses will not survive ... When fear of crime drives out or cuts back the hours of neighborhood enterprises, employment opportunities shrink. This is especially harmful to teenagers seeking their first jobs. If they are to enjoy productive lives as adults, avoiding the welfare dependency trap, they must develop marketable skills before they enter adulthood.[13]

Therefore, physical security is the compatible combination of residence and business and the protection needed for safety and security without sacrificing the aesthetic quality of life issues. A program of physical security should not appear to be the product of fear and intimidation but rather of community and business confidence that the neighborhood is not only worth defending but also inhabiting. Here again, the "art" of the security profession instructs better than its science and an overreliance on technology and equipment. Even so, design for physical security calls for a mix of the two philosophies. The mix of art and science is quite evident in the dual purpose of this stone sitting area, which also serves as a deterrent perimeter device. See Figure 7.4.[14]

In the exterior context, the physical security plan will often employ a series of barriers that limit or thoroughly make implausible criminal conduct. Community, spatially based approaches should assertively erect or use barriers to increase the quality of life, such as:

1. Fences and other barriers
2. Lights
3. Locks
4. Alarms
5. Turnstiles, gates, and so on
6. Video surveillance and CCTV
7. Special construction

Web Exercise: See how the Department of Defense recommends protection from threat with physical security measures in the webinar at http://www.cdse.edu/catalog/webinars/physical-security/physical-security-postures.html.

---

[12] K. Marier, The 5 D's of Outdoor Perimeter Security, at http://www.securitymagazine.com/articles/82833-the-5-d-s-of-outdoor-perimeter-security, last accessed August 27, 2016.

[13] C.F. Horowitz, An Empowerment Strategy for Eliminating Neighborhood Crime, The Heritage Foundation, Backgrounder #814 (March 25, 1991), at http://www.heritage.org/research/reports/1991/03/an-empowerment-strategy-for-eliminating-neighborhood-crime, last accessed August 27, 2016.

[14] FEMA 430, Site and Urban Design for Security: Guidance against Potential Terrorist Attacks on 4-37 (2007).

Figure 7.4   Concrete and marble benches can be aesthetically pleasing while serving a practical function.

A combination of natural and man-made designs will be the best tactic when blended with enhanced technology. For example, berms and undulations in the land mass serve as extraordinary, exterior defense mechanisms as do trees, water barriers, rock formations, and other natural designs. See Figure 7.5.[15,16]

Physical security not only prevents injury to the community, but it also anticipates the possibility of it. The physical environment must warn those who wish to engage in criminal conduct.[17] The environment must send a message to possible malefactors that they have something to fear, something to be concerned about. Without an effective physical infrastructure, in addition to the social, political, and moral framework under which communities thrive, crime runs rampant. A community, like a building, needs access control. "Physical barriers are used to control, impede, or deny access, and effectively direct the flow of personnel and vehicles through designated portals."[18]

Flexibility, ingenuity, understanding, and careful consideration of the physical environment are necessary components in the protection design. Each environment and the people and purpose within are diverse and multifaceted. Any reasoned plan of crime prevention will be tailored to the specific needs of the environment and its residents. Office buildings, gated communities, subsidized housing, government facilities, retail establishments, inner city blocks, and suburbia have distinct environmental and security demands. In the environment, the only plan worth preserving is that "which can be employed by inhabitants for the enhancement of their lives, while providing security for their families, neighbors, and friends."[19]

As already noted, the task of the security specialist is to gauge the targeted area from a macro perspective—as to geography and space and then descend to a more particularized target like a building or institution that might be on the receiving end of terror or harm. The World Trade Center buildings, despite their massive size, fit this descending order, for terrorist starts his or her perverse trip focusing first on the United States and then its financial capital

[15] FEMA 430, Site and Urban Design for Security: Guidance against Potential Terrorist Attacks (2007), at http://www.fema.gov/media-library-data/20130726-1624-20490-0371/430_ch4.pdf, last accessed August 27, 2016.

[16] Electronic Physical Security Toolbox, Deterrents-Barriers, at http://www.fs.fed.us/t-d/phys_sec/deter/index.htm, last accessed August 27, 2016.

[17] The displacement of the criminal offender/terrorist alters the physical in and of itself.

[18] U.S. Department of Energy, Physical Security Systems Inspectors Guide 5-1 (2000).

[19] Newman at 3.

Figure 7.5 Trees on a perimeter line.

New York; moving to its financial district where Wall Street resides and then targets the two largest building representing industry and commerce in the city. At each step of the way, the security specialist must develop a physical security plan to deter and deny these opportunities. While no one can be absolutely perfect in the world of terror prevention, physical security plans anticipate and often foretell the path of the terrorist or other malefactors. Thus, planning for exterior physical security looks to the outskirts—the "perimeter" of the building location.

7.2.1 Perimeter security measures

Perimeter protection is the first line of defense in providing physical security for a facility. The perimeter is an outward zone, sufficiently distant to afford a reaction time by security officers who are entrusted with assuring a safe environment. See Figure 7.6.

This can be accomplished by installing fences or other physical barriers, natural assets converted into defense lines, lighting, lockable gates, intrusion detectors, or a guard force. Perimeters can also be further delineated into various sectors, or portions of the facility to be secured may include designated walls, doors and windows, bars and grills, and fire escapes.

Aside from controlling access to a facility, the perimeter barrier creates a physical and psychological deterrent to unauthorized entry; aids in detection and apprehension; and provides a method for controlling the flow of persons

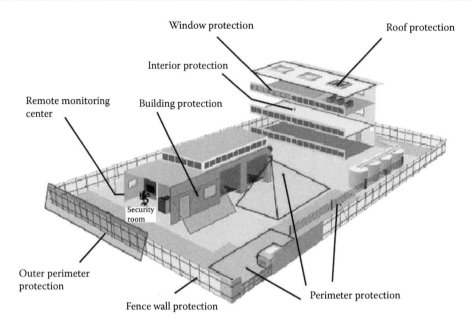

Figure 7.6   Perimeter zones.

into a designated area.[20] The extent of perimeter controls is largely determined by the facility itself and the already-known or predictable challenges to its integrity.

Web Exercise: Find out about the many ways in which breach of the perimeter can be measured by visiting Senstar, a provider of perimeter products and services at http://senstar.com/.

The means and methods of perimeter protection are quite diverse and private security is the leader in the development of a very vigorous product line to protect that perimeter line.[21] The array of options for perimeter protection includes

Wedge and plate barriers

- Shallow mount
- Surface mount
- Portable

Barrier arms

- Drop arms
- Swing arm
- Sliding beam barriers
- Vertical pivot beam barrier
- Rising beam barriers

Fabricated engineered structures

- Guard booth
- Gatehouse
- Overwatch booth

---

[20] C. Meyer, Building Perimeter Security to Increase Service, Safety, *Sec. Mag.* (October 2013) at 50.
[21] M. Khairallah, Identifying Control Perimeters, *Sec. Mag.* (April 2007); see also Get Creative with Outdoor Perimeter, *Sec. Mag.* (November 2006) at 36.

- Quick ship guard booths
- Elevated guard booths
- Trailer-mounted guard booths
- Canopies
- Bus shelters

Fencing systems

- Commercial
- High security
- Crash rated

Bollards

- Automatic
- Manual/retractable/semiautomatic
- Removable
- Fixed

Architectural precast concrete

- Bollards
- Planters
- Spheres
- Walls

Controls

- Overspeed detection
- Overheight detection
- Wrong-way detection
- Touch screens
- Push button panels
- Traffic lights
- Traffic arms
- Signage and lighting

Cable systems

- Post and rail cable system
- Post and cable system

Perimeter gates

- Swing gates
- Sliding gates
- Cantilever gates
- Vertical pivot gates
- Turnstiles[22]

---

[22] Concentric Security, Perimeter Security Products, at http://www.concentricsecurity.com/downloads/PerimeterSecurityProductsS.pdf, last accessed August 27, 2016.

7.2.2 Perimeter design and planning

In general, the design of a perimeter security plan largely depends on the target to be protected.[23] With so many government buildings and installations in congested urban areas, planners have learned to blend the urban city fixtures into the line of defense itself. What seems innocuous and for other purposes may really be serving primarily as a means to protect the public.[24] That street fence may be more than ornamental or the rock garden using boulder may really be for protecting a particular asset. The point is that perimeter protection seeks to blend the expected into the unexpected world of criminality and terrorism. Figure 7.7[25] portrays the many methods of blending common street scenes into a world of defensive security.[26]

7.2.2.1 Bollards

Bollards are increasingly employed by security professions and can be decoratively covered to match the facility design. See Figure 7.8.

A bollard is a deep-rooted piling, or a collapsible or retractable design, that is usually a blended, almost ornamental barrier that sets off the perimeter from the entry zone of a building or other protected area. Bollards come in every shape and size but the key to their success, aside from their capacity to thwart off the physical intrusion, is how naturally these artifices are to the surrounding landscape.[27]

PRACTICAL EXERCISE 7.1 MULTIBUILDING PHYSICAL SECURITY CHECKLIST

Use this checklist to assess the readiness of a building, commencing with its perimeter to provide safe shelter to employees and visitors.

Visible security

- ❏ Is the facility visible from the street during both the day and night so that roving patrols can conduct external security checks?
- ❏ Are all entrances and exits visible from a distance and well lit in the evening?
  Such visibility provides a deterrent to crime and assists employees in the event of an evacuation.
- ❏ Are shrubs cut to midpoint of window or lower?
  Low shrubbery discourages crime and provides a safer work environment.
- ❏ Are tree limbs cut at least 6 feet from ground level?
  This policy increases visibility and helps deter crime.
- ❏ If the property incorporates fences into to its security, are they in good condition?
- ❏ Have you installed motion-activated lights around entrances and exits?
  This type of lighting has been shown to deter criminal activity.
- ❏ Are all pathways and parking areas well lit?
- ❏ Are pathways and parking lots patrolled?
- ❏ Are pathways and parking lots equipped with emergency communication equipment that links to a centrally monitored or police system?

Location security

- ❏ Are details on the business' location listed on an outside directory?
- ❏ Does the organization's website provide detailed information on the building's location?
- ❏ Does the organization's website provide detailed information on the location of the management team?

---

[23] R. Smith, Set-Back Then Sit Back, *Sec. Mag.* (July 2006) at 44.

[24] R. Kessinger, From Jericho to Jersey Barrier, 48 *Sec. Mgmt* 57 (2004).

[25] FEMA, Perimeter Security Design, 4-34, at http://www.fema.gov/media-library-data/20130726-1624-20490-0371/430_ch4.pdf, last accessed August 27, 2016.

[26] R. Nason, Crash Course in Perimeter Security Technology, *Security Technology & Design* (February 2008) at 28.

[27] FEMA, Perimeter Security.

Lockdown security

- ❏ Are all doorways and exits easily accessible and clear of blockage?
- ❏ Do all doors and windows close completely?
- ❏ Do all doors and windows have working locks?
- ❏ Are doors and windows alarmed and monitored?
- ❏ Do all sliding windows have antislide locks?
- ❏ Are curtains, blinds, or other privacy-providing covers installed on all windows?

Access security

- ❏ Is outgoing mail accessible only to the U.S. Postal Service or other designated carriers?
- ❏ Are all deliveries and delivery personnel monitored when inside the facility?
- ❏ Are all incoming deliveries inspected before being delivered to the designated recipient?
- ❏ Are all visitors asked to sign in on any visit to the facility?
- ❏ Are visitors assigned a temporary security badge?
- ❏ Are employees instructed to visibly display security badges?
- ❏ Are employees instructed to challenge anyone not wearing a security or visitors badge?
- ❏ Can windows, heating-ventilating air conditioning (HVAC) equipment, and doors be secured in the event of the release of hazardous material?

7.2.2.2 Fencing

Fences provide efficient and effective perimeter barrier or control.[28] The most common fencing used are chain link and barbed wire, although the technology of fencing has changed dramatically over the last few decades and aesthetically pleasing designs of fencing are now much more common, although economically costlier. See Figure 7.9 for a stone design fence.

7.2.2.2.1 Chain link

Chain link fencing should be laid out in straight lines to permit unhampered observation. It should be constructed of number 11 gauge or heavier wire mesh (two-inch square) and should be not less than seven feet high and have a top guard. It should extend to within two inches of firm ground. It should be taut and securely fastened to rigid metal posts set in concrete. Antierosion measures like surface priming may be necessary. See Figure 7.10.

Where the fence traverses culverts, troughs, or other openings larger than 96 square inches in area, the openings should be protected by fencing, iron grills, or other barriers to prevent the passage of intruders. Chain link fencing has low maintenance cost, a minimal safety hazard, and openings small enough to discourage the passage of pilfered articles.

7.2.2.2.2 Barbed wire

Standard barbed wire is twisted, double-strand, 12-gauge wire, with four-point barbs spaced four inches apart. Barbed wire fencing, including gates intended to prevent trespassing, should be no less than seven feet in height plus a top guard, tightly stretched, and firmly affixed to posts not more than six feet apart. Distances between strands should not exceed six inches. The pattern and placement of barbed wire shall vary based on product design, including both circular and straight line patterns. The height of the fencing will also vary depending on the area to be secured and the physical layout of the area to be protected.

Web Exercise: Find out about the difference between concertina and razor wire used on barbed fences at https://www.youtube.com/watch?v=nj7pjKz8IKc.

---

[28] S.M. Poremba, Putting Up Barriers, *Sec. Mag.* (April 2001) at 54; see also Intrusion Detection for Aluminum Protection, *Security Technology Executive* (November/December 2010) at 48.

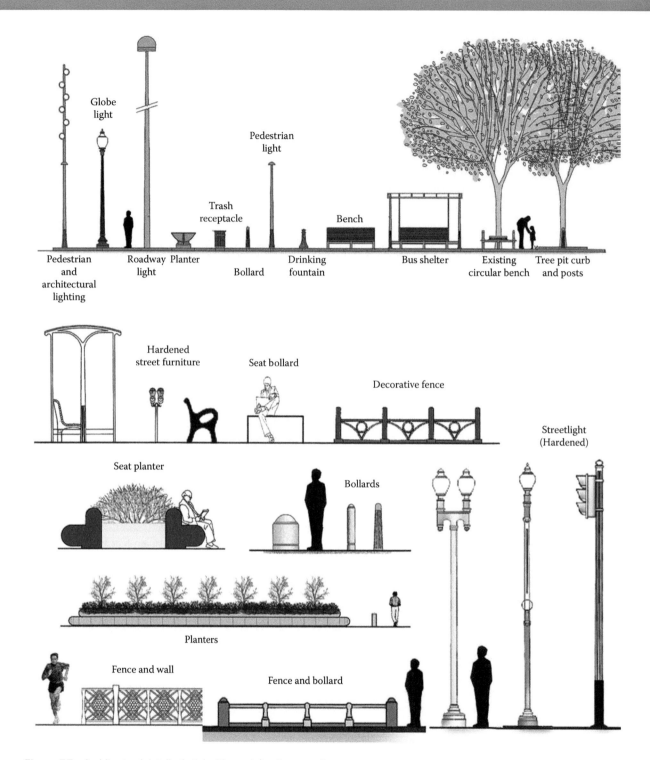

Figure 7.7 Architectural details that double as defensive security.

7.2.2.2.3 Top guard fencing

A top guard is an overhang of barbed wire, in circular concertina style or pulled straight and perpendicular to the other portions of the fence sitting along the top of a fence, facing outward and upward at an angle of 45°. Supporting arms should be affixed to the top of the fence posts and be of sufficient height to increase the overall height of the fence by at least 1 foot. The design of the fence makes entry and exit difficult due to the overhang. See Figure 7.11a and b.

Figure 7.8   (a) Antiram bollard indicating the structure required below grade. (b) Bollards can add a decorative character to a building or landscape.

7.2.2.2.4 Wedges

Part of the rationale for perimeter protection has always been access control to both pedestrians and vehicular traffic. In some respects, this has caused increased interest in bollards, since these are difficult barriers for vehicular passage. In fact, traditional means of obstructing vehicular confrontation are pretty much tried and true. See the standard methods and means to halt a vehicular attack in Figure 7.12.[29]

Web Exercise: Discover how effective the wedge is by watching the crash tests at http://www.ameristarsecurity.com/entry-barriers/sentinel.

Figure 7.9   Stone fencing.

---

[29] Department of the Army, Physical Security Field Manual No. 3-19.30, Active Vehicle Barriers at page 3.7 (2001).

Figure 7.10   Chain link fencing.

Wedges are even more challenging and under most circumstances cannot be breached. Wedges come in varying designs—some rising from a flat surface by mechanical means. Others are fixed station and serve as barriers impossible to drive through. See Figure 7.13.

7.2.2.2.5 Gates

Gates are another effective perimeter control technique before arrival at a targeted location. Guards serve as guard centers, crowd and access control points, and as locals for CCTV and alarms. The type and style of a gate depend largely on the overall purpose of its manufacture and end to be achieved such as traffic control or integrity review of those seeking access. The number of gates and perimeter entrances should be limited so that the bulk of the locale remains less accessible than the gate system permits. See Figure 7.14.

Gates should be adequately lighted and be fully or partially automated. Gates may also be fully hand operated, or triggered by card keys, detection devices, push button combination locks, or other technology.

Figure 7.11   (a), (b) Top guard fencing is possibly the most difficult obstacle to overcome.

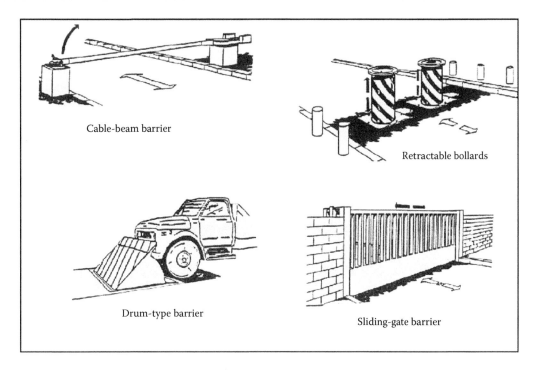

Figure 7.12 Various vehicle barriers.

It may be prudent to install intrusion detection devices when the gate is used intermittently or when a higher level of protection is desired. Devices might include motion, sensor, or sound wave technology. Gates have become decoratively appealing in order that installation complements rather than detracts from the landscape.

7.2.2.2.6 Protective lighting

Protective lighting around the perimeter setting is a crucial component to a solid and effective security strategy.[30] If the perimeter is a major access point for vehicular access or personal access, lighting is mandatory. If the access

Figure 7.13 A mechanical wedge barrier.

---

[30] B. Zalud, Lots of Parking Bumps: IP, Lighting and Terrorism, *Sec. Mag.* (January 2006) at 28.

Figure 7.14   Access gate.

location needs 24-hour coverage, the installation of lighting in the perimeter setting becomes mandatory. Verifying identity, checking credentials, and matching people with those same documents cannot occur without sufficient lighting. In addition to halting the onslaught of illegal persons and vehicles, the protective lighting program serves as a valuable and inexpensive deterrent to crime. Determining whether or not protective lighting is an essential part of the security plan, consider the queries in Figure 7.15.

Web Exercise: Find out about how security lighting works at http://www.securityinfowatch.com/article/12103875/video-surveillance-lighting-101.

Place protective lighting where it will illuminate shadowed areas and be directed at potential intrusion points. Lights may be fixed or movable depending on perimeter needs. Lights need to illuminate not only the targeted area but also those areas that are physically adjoined that may prove a security challenge. Effective lighting concentrates its beam and illumination on ground areas rather than the dispersal into space or air. See Figure 7.16.

- Cost of replacing lamps and cleaning fixtures, as well as the cost of providing the required equipment (such as ladders and mechanical buckets) to perform this maintenance.
- Provision of manual-override capability during a blackout, including photoelectric controls.
- Effects of local weather conditions on lighting systems.
- Fluctuating or erratic voltages in the primary power source.
- Grounding requirements.
- Provisions for rapid lamp replacement.
- Use of lighting to support a CCTV system.
- Limited and exclusion areas.
- Lighting in these areas must be under the control of the guard force.
- For critical areas, instantaneous lighting with a backup source is required.
- Security-lighting systems are operated continuously during hours of darkness.
- Protective lights should be used so that the failure of one or more lights will not affect the operation of the remaining lights.
- Lighting requirements for adjoining properties and activities.
- Restrike time (the time required before the light will function properly after a brief power interruption).
- Color accuracy.
- Other facilities requiring lighting, such as parking areas.

Figure 7.15   Protective lighting checklist.

Figure 7.16   Many low-cost lighting solutions still provide ample lighting on the ground with minimal dispersal.

7.3 PHYSICAL SECURITY: INTERIOR APPLICATIONS

Once the perimeter area is secured, the attention turns to the security, safety, and integrity of the targeted building or other structure. These facilities may or may not have all the accoutrements of physical security and choose to adopt only a few of the tools.[31] Most of this depends upon design and architectural features. For example, a building with few windows and access points will require less security than one dramatically more open and transparent. Upon entry to the structure, the "interior" now formally breached, the question of security tools will again depend on security needs.

Access control strategy depends on a host of factors, including proprietary interests, sensitivity of the information or product, inherent danger involved in production or movement of the said product, as well as other issues. How much one secures the interior largely depends on the functionality and purpose of the facility in the first place. A box factory, by way of example, will call for less interior security than a plutonium processing plant as would a personal residence over the state residence of a Governor. Security needs are dictated by security demands. The most common interior methods of securing the locale follow.

7.3.1 Doors

A door is a vulnerable point of the security of any building precisely because it is an access point. Every facility must recognize that vulnerabilities naturally emerge at points of egress or exit. Doors, the type chosen, will largely depend

---

[31] Industry Innovations, *Sec. Mag.* (June 2013) at 62.

Device Security Program Manager
Security Industry Specialists, INC.

Location: Sunnyvale, California

Salary: Up to 79,040.00
Type: Full Time - Experienced
Categories: Asset Protection, Physical Security, Warehouse/Distribution

Security Industry Specialists (SIS) provides security solutions to some of the most recognized companies and brands in the world. We deliver services that consistently exceed those of our peers. We accomplish this through innovation, constant process improvement, and through an uncompromising commitment to hiring, retaining and rewarding the best talent available.

General Statement of Job

The Device Security Program Manager is responsible for reducing risk, limiting exposure to liability/losses, within the client's Global Safety & Security operations team. This position will focus on client prototypes/devices and creating a security program covering each step in the life cycle. The Device Security Program Manager will partner with the clients Global Corporate Security team to develop, implement and manage all physical safety and security programs that align with the client's culture, values and policies regarding prototype/device storage and destruction. This includes development of the program, coordination with local security workforce and third party vendors, budget management, and project management. The Device Security Program Manager reports directly to the Account Manager.

Specific Duties and Responsibilities

Essential Job Functions

- Design, develop, and implement standards, policies and procedures for prototype device location- management, storage, and destruction
- Maintain close coordination, planning, communication and regular direct liaison with the client's Global Corporate Security management team and SIS team around all aspects of product/prototype life cycle (idea inception through finished product/prototype) security initiatives
- Manage and build the security operations at local client campus for secure storage and destruction efforts of pre-released products and prototypes in conjunction with client representative
- Create and deploy new product security awareness campaigns
- Responsible for identifying areas of program improvement, expansions of service, customer service improvements and other evolutionary changes
- Create measurable reporting process to determine the impact of the program with different client groups and teams
- Oversee contractual obligations and manage billing within the client's budget or purchase order authority
- Work closely with any investigators to assist in preliminary investigations and write reports on any and all incidents that take place in secure storage and destruction areas, as needed
- Maintain relationships with Federal, State and Local law enforcement and other government agencies in support of private-public partnership initiatives
- Assess existing training and implement new training procedures and processes for staff members at all levels of the Operation for any and all facilities in the scope of the program
- Benchmark prototype processes and policies across similar industry peers

Additional Job Functions

- Perform other related duties as required.

Minimum Qualifications and Requirements

- Bachelor's Degree in Criminal Justice, Emergency Management, Business Management or related discipline preferred OR any equivalent combination of education, specialized training and/or experience which provides the requisite knowledge, skills and abilities required
- Minimum 5 years of experience in safety and security management, law enforcement and/or military with an emphasis in manufacturing environments highly preferred
- Must complete and maintain state guard certification as prescribed by presiding state law, as well as client requested certifications; all documentation and fees are the responsibility of the employee unless otherwise noted
- Demonstrated understanding of best practices in physical security strategies, principles, standards, policies and procedures
- Must have effective time management, communication, technical writing, presentation development, facilitation, and organizational skills
- Must have strong verbal and written communication skills
- Must have impeccable work ethic and high degree of integrity
- Must be technically proficient with common PC/MAC based software and applications

What we can offer:

- $79–85k Salary
- Health, Dental and Vision benefits, plus access to dependent coverage and a variety of other benefits
- Eligibility to contribute to a 401k Plan after the first year of employment
- Paid Time Off
- A dynamic and challenging work environment

Figure CP7.1   Career Profile: Physical security—device control.

Figure 7.17   High-level security steel door.

on the depth and breadth of security needed and the desire to either facilitate or impede traffic for designated reasons. See Figure 7.17.

A door should be installed so the hinges are on the inside to preclude removal of the screws or the use of chisels or cutting devices. Pins in exterior hinges should be welded, flanged, or otherwise secured, or hinge dowels should be used to preclude the door's removal. Stanley produces a wide array of security hinges that preclude easy removal or destruction. See Figure 7.18.

A truly secure door should be metal or solid wood, not plastic or fiberboard, which are readily hacked into. Remember that locks, doors, doorframes, and accessory builder's hardware are inseparable when evaluating barrier value. Be consistent by buying strong materials for the door, its frame, and the lock hardware. Bars and dead bolt sliding functionality further adds to the safety and security that the door provides. Doors may be highly secure yet aesthetically pleasing, which adds to the effectiveness of the door choice. Choices of colors, decorative styles, and artistic form make the modern security door vastly different than the historically drab products long in use.

"Overhead roll" provides solid security in commercial settings where goods and products flow regularly from the facility such as in manufacturing or assembly line–based buildings. Overhead doors that are not controlled or locked by electric power should be secured by slide bolts on the bottom bar. See Figure 7.19.

Doors may also have side or top "transoms" as part of the door design. A transom is usually an additional side or top window slot in the makeup of the door. Good design assures these transom portion are just as impenetrable as the main door frame and locking system.

Pin design

- Nonrising pin construction features an easily seated pin that will not rise
- Hole in bottom tip provides for easy pin removal on button and flush tip hinges
- Pin is removed by inserting a punch or a thin rod through bottom hole of tip and tapping upward
- Helps prevent marring of the hinge or hinge finish
- Standard feature on size 3" × 3" (76 mm × 76 mm) and larger hinges

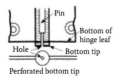

Nonremovable pins

NRP—Set screw in barrel intercepts groove in loose pin as shown. Set screw is not accessible when door is closed. Not available on size 3" (76 mm) and smaller. Specify "NRP" (nonremovable pin) when ordering

Security stud

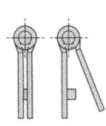

- Full mortise hinges are available with security studs for added safety
- With the door in its closed position, a stud attached to one leaf of the hinge projects into a hole in the matching leaf
- Hinged side of door cannot be moved, even with hinge pins removed, because the stud prevents the leaves from being slid apart

Shear-resistant stud

- Optional feature for prison hinges
- Withstands 200-foot pound (271.2-J) ram test
- Dimensionally consistent
- Keeps hinge in position even if all the screws break under attack
- Studs engage into door and frame

Figure 7.18   Various types of door hinges. (Courtesy of Stanley.)

Figure 7.19   Overhead rolling door.

7.3.2 Access control

Policy concerning access to any building or facility begins, as discussed above, at the perimeter.[32] Gates and vehicular stalls, either manned or unmanned, control the flow of traffic and inhibit unbridled access to those intent on doing harm.[33] Hence, many of the technologies of access are already incorporated in the outer perimeter that controls access.[34] Upon entry into the interior of a building or facility, these same protocols may apply. Access policy is a matter that is both traditional and technologically innovative.

7.3.2.1 Keys

Most facilities limit access by key, although the array and typology of keys is more than most people know about. From the common key, cut mechanically, which mimics a preordained pattern for lock placement to newer contemporary wireless systems and keys, the security specialist has many options in design and placement. See Figure 7.20.

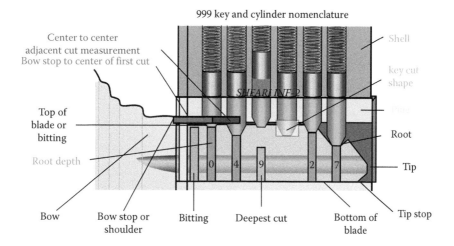

Figure 7.20   How key cuts release mechanism.

---

[32] R. Pearson, Access Control Best Practices, *Security Technology Executive* (September 2012) at 68.

[33] B. Scaglione, Determining and Implementing Successful Access Control Solutions, *Sec. Mag.* (January 2009) at 42; see also C. Meyer, Compounding Technologies for More Accurate Intruder Detection, *Sec. Mag.* (February 2015) at 45.

[34] J. Friedrick, Access Control Opens Up to Offer More, *Security Systems News* (May 2006) at 29.

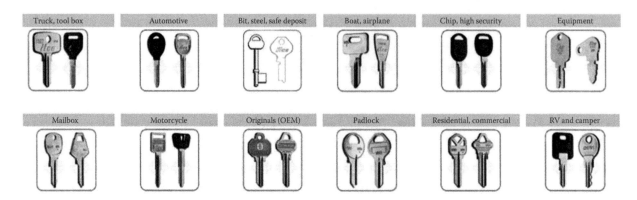

Figure 7.21 Key type/function can be determined by the design. (Courtesy of Sandy Spring Locksmiths at https://sandyspring-slocksmith.com/keys-locks-doors.)

When relying on a common key design for an entire facility, the security team will have to deal with recuts and retooling in the event of change or alteration, and recutting often leads to higher costs. The design of keys correlates to its intended purpose. Figure 7.21 lays out the general designs based on targeted usage.

The engineering of keys is just as multidimensional and reflects new and better ways to assure security.

Web Exercise: Find out about keys and locks and their engineering at http://wonderopolis.org/wonder/how-do-locks-work.

When dealing with dead bolt or latch–type locking systems, the key triggers movement by rotating, in conjunction with the movement of the doorknob, the actual latch or sliding dead bolt in order to enter. The same would also be true of spring-loaded versions of a door lock—it is the key that releases the spring, which in turn makes all parts move. See Figure 7.22a through c.

More contemporary keys are engineered with specified programming tied to a particular locking system. Keys like this are referred to as "chip" or "transponder" keys because a chip has in fact been embedded in the key itself. These types of keys are commonly employed on auto vehicles but the same technology is now being used on access keys. Electromechanical or E-cylinders combine electronic data encryption and are only operated by the usage of smart keys, which send a signal proving access rights. This type of system is capable of communicating remotely in the event a party forgets to secure their location.

Web Exercise: Read up on the latest E-cylinders and smart keys technology from Mul-T-Lock at http://areasafe.com/products/category/e-cylinders-smart-keys/.

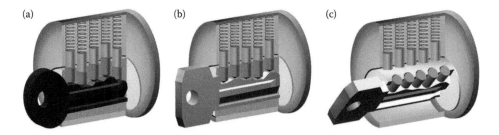

Figure 7.22 Spring-based pin-tumbler key system. (a) When an incorrect key is inserted into the lock, the key pins (red) and driver pins (blue) do not align with the shear line; therefore, it does not allow the plug (yellow) to rotate. (b) When the correct key is inserted, the gaps between the key pins (red) and driver pins (blue) align with the edge of the plug (yellow). (c) With the gaps between the pins aligned with the shear line, the plug (yellow) can rotate freely. (From Wikipedia, fair use per Creative Commons 3.0; Derivative images works by user Pbroks13; originals by user Wapcaplet. Image not altered.)

Figure 7.23   Keypad system model without traditional key lock.

7.3.2.2 Keypad entry

Access can also be controlled by some form of restrictive coding that needs to be punched in a keypad. This type of keyless system is very popular for a host of reasons: first, it removes the need for costly key programs, from original installation to constant refit; second, the keypad coding can be instantaneously changed without much difficulty; and third, the keypad hardware is sufficiently complex to stave off the traditional lock picker. The key receptacle can also remain in some cases, depending on the manufacturer and locking system, as a secondary, backup system or as a part of the primary access requirement of using a keypad and a key at the same time. See Figure 7.23.

7.3.2.3 Access control by alternative keyless systems

There are a host of other methods providing physical security at access control points.[35] Already alluded to are the increased usage of "electronic locks," which negate the need for a key protocol. Electronic locks are triggered or prompted in or at a centralized center of some type whether the security station or by designated offices.[36] Another version of this method is by "card-operated lock mechanism" where the party seeking access swipes his or her card into some type of scanning, reading device, or simply allows a reader to display, and then have data read from that card, for eventual access. This type of technology is frequently witnessed in ID technology, personal identification cards that verify the employee's permitted regular access. See Figure 7.24.

---

[35] A. Canfield, One Source Security and Automation Keen on Keyless Locks, *Security Systems News* (February 2016) at 34; see also S.E. Ludwig, Trading in Keys for Cards, Codes, Apps or Prints, *Sec. Mag.* (October 2014) at 40.

[36] See B. Kozak, Online Wireless Locks Gaining Market Share, *Security Systems News* (June 2014) at 30.

Figure 7.24   RFID electronic key and locking systems can use smart cards or similar key tags.

Personnel identification cards usually contain sensitive information about a company employee—unique to that individual, which subsequently opens access if properly vetted. These types of cards usually have employer logo or other imagery on the card as well as designate what the role or position of the employee is within the facility.

Of all the alternative means of reliable identification for access control, biometrics appears an unstoppable phenomenon—facial, palm, fingerprint, voice patterns, and retina patterns are now being measured with scientific certitude.[37] See Figure 7.25.

Biometric identification primarily rests on two main tenets: first, the physiological reaction or measure, and second, the behavioral reaction the person seeking access.[38] Figure 7.26[39] provides a broad overview of the methods of biometric identification.

Web Exercise: Visit the FBI's Library of Source Material on Biometrics at https://www.fbi.gov/about-us/cjis/fingerprints_biometrics/biometric-center-of-excellence/resources/online-library#decade.

Hand Geometry Recognition	The use of the geometric features of the hand such as the lengths of fingers and the width of the hand to identify an individual.
Odor	The use of an individual's odor to determine identity.
Signature Recognition	The authentication of an individual by the analysis of handwriting style, in particular the signature.
Typing Recognition	The use of the unique characteristics of a person's typing for establishing identity.
Vein Recognition	Vein recognition is a type of biometrics that can be used to identify individuals based on the vein patterns in the human finger or palm.
Speaker Verification / Authentication	The use of the voice as a method of determining the identity of a speaker for access control.
Speaker Identification	The task of determining an unknown speaker's identity.
Figure 7.37	

Figure 7.25   Types of biometric identification.

---

[37] Banks are more heavily relying upon biometrics to halt the onslaught of fraud and chicanery, see B. Zalud, Transition Times for Bank and Financial Services Security (June 2015) at 50; see also J. Dingle, Locks to Fingerprints: Access Basics, *Sec. Mag.* (November 2008) at 88.

[38] M. Lepley et al., *State of the Art Biometrics Excellence Roadmap* (Mitre Corp., 2008), at https://www.fbi.gov/about-us/cjis/fingerprints_biometrics/biometric-center-of-excellence/files/cpl-20-nov.pdf, last accessed August 27, 2016.

[39] National Science & Technology Council, Biometrics Overview (2006), at http://www.biometrics.gov/Documents/BioOverview.pdf, last accessed August 27, 2016.

"Biometrics" is a general term used alternatively to describe a characteristic or a process.

As a characteristic:

1. A measurable biological (anatomical and physiological) and behavioral characteristic that can be used for automated recognition.

As a process:

2. Automated methods of recognizing an individual based on measurable biological (anatomical and physiological) and behavioral characteristics.

Biometric systems have been researched and tested for a few decades, but have only recently entered into the public consciousness because of high profile applications, usage in entertainment media (though often not realistically) and increased usage by the public in day-to-day activities. Example deployments within the United States Government include the FBI's Integrated Automated Fingerprint Identification System (IAFIS), the US-VISIT program, the Transportation Workers Identification Credentials (TWIC) program, and the Registered Traveler (RT) program. Many companies are also implementing biometric technologies to secure areas, maintain time records, and enhance user convenience. For example, for many years Disney World has employed biometric devices for season ticket holders to expedite and simplify the process of entering its parks, while ensuring that the ticket is used only by the individual to whom it was issued.

A typical biometric system is comprised of five integrated components: A sensor is used to collect the data and convert the information to a digital format. Signal processing algorithms perform quality control activities and develop the biometric template. A data storage component keeps information that new biometric templates will be compared to. A matching algorithm compares the new biometric template to one or more templates kept in data storage. Finally, a decision process (either automated or human-assisted) uses the results from the matching component to make a system-level decision.

Figure 7.26   Methods of biometric identification. (From National Science and Technology Council [NSTC], Committee on Homeland and National Security, Subcommittee on Biometrics.)

Both retinal scans and fingerprint analysis by digital means are available to the agency. Biometric fingerprint machines are becoming a common experience for both residential and international travelers (Figure 7.27).

Machines that trace and match retinal patterns are sure to grow just as quickly.

7.3.2.3.1 Biometric application: The registered traveler program

Biometric applications are becoming very common in the travel and transportation industries. The FBI has taken the lead on the various modalities relating to biometric applications by and through its biometric center of excellence.[40] See Figure 7.28.

Figure 7.27   Biometric fingerprint scanner.

---

[40] FBI, About the Biometric Center of Excellence, at https://www.fbi.gov/about-us/cjis/fingerprints_biometrics/biometric-center-of-excellence/about/about-the-biometric-center-of-excellence, last accessed January 24, 2016.

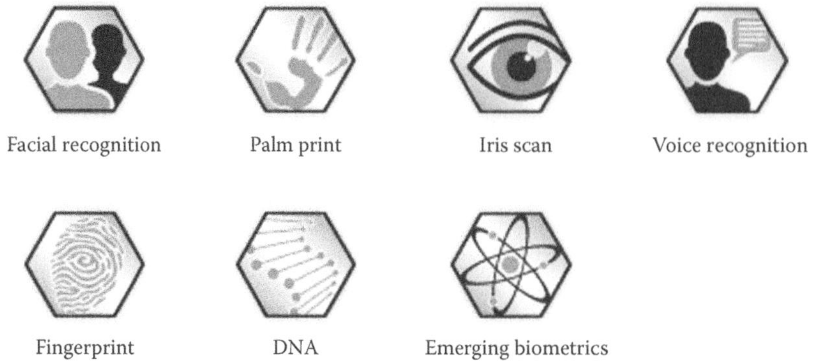

Figure 7.28 Various biometric modalities.

All of these new technologies hope to speed up the travel process and may or may not use biometric applications. Early on, the TSA created the Registered Traveler (RT) program in an effort to speed up the traveling process for business and repeat travelers. In order to participate, passengers undergo a TSA-conducted security threat assessment (STA). It was a voluntary program with both corporate entities and individuals participating. Biometrics plays a key role in this program. To enroll, applicants voluntarily provide RT sponsoring entities (participating airports/air carriers) and service providers with biographic and biometric data needed for TSA to conduct the STA and determine eligibility. To date, the following agencies participate in the RT program:

- Air France (operating out of Terminal 1 at JFK)
- AirTran Airways (operating out of the Central Terminal at LGA)
- Albany International Airport (ALB)
- British Airways (operating out of Terminal 7 at JFK)
- Cincinnati/Northern Kentucky International Airport (CVG)
- Denver International Airport (DEN)
- Gulfport-Biloxi International Airport (GPT)
- Indianapolis International Airport (IND)
- Jacksonville International Airport (JAX)
- Little Rock National Airport (LIT)
- Norman Mineta San Jose International Airport (SJC)
- Oakland International Airport (OAK)
- Orlando International Airport (MCO)
- Reno/Tahoe International Airport (RNO)
- Ronald Reagan Washington National Airport (DCA)
- Salt Lake City International Airport (SLC)
- San Francisco International Airport (SFO)
- Virgin Atlantic (operating out of Terminal B at EWR)
- Virgin Atlantic (operating out of Terminal 4 at JFK)
- Washington Dulles International Airport (IAD)
- Westchester County Airport (HPN)

The RT program has largely been replaced with the Trusted Traveler programs of the TSA, which are TSA Pre-Check, and in conjunction with Customs and Border Protection, Global Entry, NEXUS, and SENTRI programs. A comparison chart of these four expedited programs is reproduced in Table 7.1.

Table 7.1   Trusted traveler programs offered by the Department of Homeland Security

Agency	Transportation Security Administration		Customs and Border Protection	
Program	TSA Pre✓®	Global Entry	NEXUS	SENTRI
Website	www.tsa.gov/ tsa-precheck	www.globalentry.gov	NEXUS	SENTRI
Eligibility required	U.S. citizens and U.S. lawful permanent residents	U.S. citizens, U.S. lawful permanent residents, and citizens of certain other countries[1]	U.S. citizens, lawful permanent residents, Canadian citizens, and lawful permanent residents of Canada	Proof of citizenship and admissibility documentation
Application fee	$85.00 (5-year membership)	$100.00 (5-year membership)	$50.00 (5-year membership)	$122.25 (5-year membership)
Passport required	No	Yes; or lawful permanent resident card	No	No
Application process	Preenroll online, visit an enrollment center; provide fingerprints and verify ID	Preenroll online, visit an enrollment center for an interview; provide fingerprints and verify ID	Preenroll online, visit an enrollment center for an interview; provide fingerprints and verify ID	Preenroll online, visit an enrollment center for an interview; provide fingerprints and verify ID
Program experience	TSA Pre✓™ expedited screening at participating airports	Expedited processing through CBP at airports and land borders upon arrival in the United States Includes the TSA Pre✓™ experience	Expedited processing at airports and land borders when entering the United States and Canada Includes Global Entry benefits Includes the TSA Pre✓™ benefits for U.S. citizens, U.S. lawful permanent residents, and Canadian citizens	Expedited processing through CBP at land borders Includes Global Entry and TSA Pre✓™ benefits for U.S. citizens and U.S. lawful permanent residents

Web Resource: The Department of the Army has produced an excellent overview of biometric applications at http://www.eis.army.mil/programs/biometrics.

7.3.2.3.2 TSA: Paperless boarding pass

In an effort to streamline the security processes and to assure a free flow of traffic in congested airports, TSA has implemented the "paperless boarding pass" program. Here, the passenger downloads the boarding pass to the cell phone or other device and scans it at a designated station. Currently, 69 airports have adopted the program. Using a scan code, the TSA agent verifies the pass by a mere swipe (Figure 7.29).

Figure 7.29   An example of a paperless boarding pass as it appears on a smartphone.

The program has been favorably received by the general public though there are the usual caveats about privacy issues and the sharing of this personal information. TSA has issued strict guidelines on privacy requirements and reigned in technology to prevent unauthorized disclosure.[41]

There is much more that could be written concerning the activities of TSA. Throughout the remainder of this chapter, the role of TSA in other aspects involving the transportation industry will be highlighted. In fact, our coverage turns to two key areas in the transportation arena: maritime and rail.

7.3.2.4 Access control by sensor detection

Detection of intrusion can be accomplished by a host of technologies. Aside from personal observation on CCTV designs and actual detection by uniformed officers and traditional "tripped" alarm systems, there are a host of new methods that detect intrusion into the interior of a structure. A summary list follows:

- Photoelectric detectors: Relies on a beam of light falling upon a photosensitive detector. If the beam is broken, the camera operates.
- Audio detectors: Relies on a microphone detector that triggers the camera when noises are made.
- Vibration detectors: Triggers camera operation with any sensitive detection of movement.
- Capacitance detectors: A capacitance field is established surrounding an area. A person who breaks the field triggers the camera.
- Ultrasonic detectors: Sound wave patterns that generate camera operation.
- Passive infrared (PIR): Detects body heat (infrared energy).
- Microwave (MW): By use of microwave pulses and measures, the technology identifies moving objects. Reflection off a moving object.
- Dual technology motion sensors: Incorporates both PIR and MW.
- Area reflective type: Emits infrared rays from an LED. Using the reflection of those rays, the sensor measures the distance to the person or object and detects if the object is within the designated area.
- Wireless motion sensors: Wireless motion sensors use wireless technology and thereby make drilling and complex hardware installation a thing of the past.
- Contact motion sensors (door/window): When a door or window is opened while the system is armed.

See Figure 7.30.

Web Exercise: Take this tutorial on the PIR sensor at https://www.youtube.com/watch?v=56HClX8EWOs.

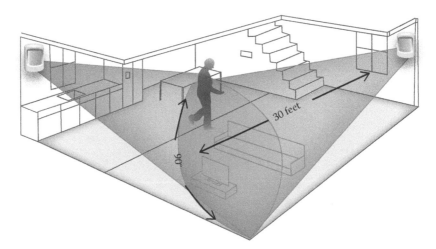

Figure 7.30   Motion detector coverage area illustrated.

---

[41] U.S. Department of Homeland Security, Privacy impact assessment update for the credential authentication technology/boarding pass scanning system (August 11, 2009), at http://www.dhs.gov/xlibrary/assets/privacy/privacy_pia_tsa_catbpss.pdf, last accessed August 27, 2016.

7.4 VIDEO SURVEILLANCE

Another crucial form of access control and general security practice for employees, visitors, and intruders into the interior of any building or facility is video surveillance. That surveillance, as in other forms of access and identification control, usually commences outside the interior at the perimeter. See Figure 7.31 for a Customs and Border Protection surveillance tower.

Presented thus far are the lighting and surveillance equipment that goes hand in hand with fencing and barrier—ferreting out unwanted parties before ever getting to the main compound. However, that process of visually identifying these sorts of unwanted parties, or even tracking day-to-day activity to memorialize improper behavior, criminal conduct, or other unacceptable behavior, could not be fully possible without the benefits of surveillance.

To surveill is to watch another, whether by personal observation or technological means. Surveillance is an integral component for the security of any site, but its object, that is, the person surveilled, and the activities under scrutiny, are unknowing subjects. To have any effectiveness, surveillance needs to take place without notice or public awareness. The use of surveillance should be a blend of the aggressive and the cautious, aggressive in the sense that it is one of the more remarkable tools in the security professional's toolbox while simultaneously recognizing the privacy implications of its usage.

Surveillance complements traditional methods of security. The techniques complement direct observation. Surveillance or covert observation is not only risky, but also difficult. Its purposes are multifaceted:

- To protect undercover officers or to corroborate their testimony
- To obtain evidence of a crime
- To obtain evidence of a civil wrong
- To locate persons
- To check on the reliability of informants, witnesses, and other parties
- To locate hidden property or contraband
- To obtain probable cause for search warrant processes
- To prevent the commission of an act or to apprehend a suspect in the commission of an act
- To obtain information for later use in interrogation
- To develop leads and information received from other sources

Figure 7.31   Customs and Border patrol: Video surveillance station.

- To know at all times the whereabouts of an individual
- To obtain admissible legal evidence for use in court

The ASIS defines surveillance practice as

> Broadly stated, a surveillance may serve to detect or prevent questionable or illicit acts, to obtain evidence of such acts, to help in identifying persons, or to collect general intelligence information. Often a surveillance may be conducted only in the hope of developing leads in a case if other efforts have been unproductive.[42]

The uses of surveillance for private security specialist are myriad.[43] Aside from detecting criminality and misbehavior, surveillance will vary according to the exact objective of the practice either in place for individual conduct or to assure a safe and secure environment. In other words, the aim of the surveillance will be as varied as the diverse subject of its end or purpose.[44] When planning or implementing surveillance policy for employees, visitors, and those not warranted on the premises, some sound questions must be posed and resolved.

Planning and preparation are key elements in surveillance practice.

7.4.1 What are the steps of surveillance?

Successful surveillance requires four basic steps:

1. Planning
2. Organizing
3. Directing
4. Controlling[45]

Preparation, planning, and organization are fundamental to best practices in surveillance.[46] Preliminary assessment of the physical construction of the site as well as the needs of the firm will lead to intelligent decision making regarding the use of surveillance. Consider these issues:

- Is there any alternative to surveillance?
- Do you know what information is needed from the surveillance?
- Have you decided what type of surveillance is needed?
- Do you know enough about the area of surveillance to determine equipment and manpower needs?
- Do you have the required equipment and manpower?
- Are proper forms available to record necessary information during the surveillance?
- Are all signals preestablished?[47]

Be attuned to the legal and ethical dynamics of surveillance. Perennially tied to the constitutional protection of privacy, and heavily regulated by legislation, the surveillance must not commence without legal inquiry. Always keep in mind the "Who–What–When–Where–How–Why" analysis. Because surveillance is a costly undertaking, the client, as well as the firm, must justify this form of expenditure.

7.4.2 What is the exact objective of surveillance?

Effective surveillance sets goals and parameters. Solid surveillance practice keeps the endgame in view by laying out specific objectives for the action. It must have an initial purpose in mind with full awareness that the purpose may be subject to change. At a minimum, the objective should correlate to the purpose of the surveillance. The ends of the surveillance will be as varied as the subject matter of that surveillance.

---

[42] American Society for Industrial Security, *Basic Guidelines for Security Investigations* 41 (1981).

[43] M.A. Gips, Image Is Everything in Stopping Crime, *Sec. Mgmt* (February 2004) at 12; Public Cameras Yet to Be Real-Time Intelligence for Security, *Corporate Sec.* (January 31, 2007) at 6.

[44] B. Zalud, Technology's WOW Factor, 23, *Security* (2003).

[45] Pinkerton's, Inc., *Surveillance Manual* 2 (1990).

[46] K.C. Scott-Brown & P.D.J. Cronin, Detect the Unexpected: A Science for Surveillance, 31 *Policing* 395 (2008).

[47] W. Bennett & K. Hess, *Criminal Investigation* 235 (1981).

7.4.3 Where is the location of surveillance?

Professional surveillance requires a full understanding of not only the subject but also his or her surrounding environment. In a phrase, know your territory and be aware of entry and exit points at your location.[48] Be sure to do your research about the culture of the firm where surveillance is taking place.

7.4.4 When will surveillance occur?

The decision to commence surveillance activities is both organizational and tactical. The surveillance decision should also be based upon tactical considerations, such as the following:

- How the time of day affects the ability of video surveillance to be effective.
- Difficulties with visibility caused by angle of observation, or clarity of direction.
- Any specialized equipment needed to conduct surveillance.
- Budgetary considerations of the client.
- The sophistication of the firm, causing greater sensitivity and patience in the surveillance process.

7.4.5 Who or what will be surveilled?

The surveillance subject can be either a person or a nonhuman entity, such as a plant, business, industry, or other installation. No matter who or what is under surveillance, that person or entity is labeled the "subject." "It can be a person, place, property, vehicle, group of persons, organization, or object."[49] The target of surveillance will impact the comprehensiveness of that surveillance. In other words, the drug dealer selling on a neighborhood street has less of an expectation of privacy than a citizen praying at the local church. The level of intrusion will depend on many factors, although the extent of the intrusion will be guided by constitutional expectations of privacy. A highly intrusive, technologically entranced surveillance of a home is a trickier proposition than the lobby of a high-rise building in a busy city.

7.4.6 Surveillance equipment

Having the right equipment to conduct video surveillance is critical to success. Regular equipment checks are central to the planner. Review the checklist:

- Are all radio or electronic monitoring equipment, cameras, or remote receivers functioning properly?
- Are there additional types of specialized equipment that could be of use to the firm?
- Are radio communications equipment functioning properly?
- Can photographic equipment add to the effectiveness of the regular surveillance program?
- Are there any new legal restrictions that may affect the firm's current surveillance program?

The complexity of the surveillance process has triggered a multimillion-dollar industry that produces surveillance materials and equipment. This reliance on equipment is sometimes labeled "enhanced surveillance." See Figure 7.32.

For further research, Ross Engineering of Adamstown, Maryland, has recently begun the publication of a journal titled *Surveillance*.[50] *Physical Security: Practices and Technology* by Charles Schnabolk provides a comprehensive examination of technology employed in security practice with excellent insight into the electronic aspect of surveillance.[51]

7.4.6.1 CCTV equipment

A number of manufacturers produce high-resolution and high-sensitivity closed-circuit television systems for the purposes of ongoing surveillance. With CCTV systems, each camera is wired directly into individual monitors. In situations where the CCTV is connected into a conventional home unit, the CCTV camera has to "'feed' the picture

---

[48] National Institute of Justice, Video Surveillance of Public Places, COPS (February 2006).
[49] W. Bennett & K. Hess, at 225.
[50] J. Ross, Ross Engineering, Inc., 7906 Hope Valley Court, Adamstown, MD 21710.
[51] C. Schnabolk, Physical Security: Practices and Technology 324 (1984). For an interesting website that features the intricacies of casino surveillance, visit http://www.casinosurveillancenews.com

Title	Director, Global Security Operations
Requisition Number	17724BR
Job Function	General Management
Business Unit Group	Alcoa Corporate
Primary Location	PA-Pittsburgh
Job Status	Full-Time
Minimum Education Required	Bachelors
Minimum Years of Experience	10+
Minimum Travel Required	25–50%
Position Description	*Major activities*

Major activities

- Provides ongoing support to the regions and locations in supporting the objectives of the global security program
  - Security Operations
  - Investigations
  - Incident response including crisis management programs
  - Security Technology and systems
  - Deployment of specific security programs and standards
  - Global Threats and Intelligence
- Ensures compliance to Alcoa's Global Security architecture and processes and all supporting tools, technology and organization components
- Provides help chain to regions/locations on the execution of their security requirements regulations, tools, programs, and risk management
- Provides site assessments and threat analyses for Alcoa locations; consults to regional and location security personnel in performing the same
- Provides ongoing coaching/consulting to regional/location security professionals
- Enables security and risk management knowledge transfer across location and across regions
- Along with and in support of Alcoa's Chief Security Officer, continue efforts in the transformation of Alcoa's current security program to the new target state vision:
  - Center-led global security program for personnel and asset protection, intelligence and threat analysis, risk and incident management, investigations, and compliance coordination
  - Optimize program that balances risk, compliance, and cost to better align with Alcoa business goals
  - Establish standards and governance for employees, assets, information and process protection
  - Develop methods to measure, track, analyze and report on department metrics
  - Facilitate awareness, communication, and education for Alcoa locations and employees
  - Process for sharing security best practices
  - Collaboration with Alcoa, Audit, EH&S, Legal, Ethics and Compliance, Business Units, Human Resources, IT, and other internal and external stakeholders

Responsibilities

- Directs the development and implementation of Alcoa's global security policies and programs.
- Provides guidance to the global security staff (regional security managers, location security teams) in identifying, developing, implementing and maintaining security processes across Alcoa to reduce risks, respond to incidents, and limit exposure to liability in order to reduce financial loss to the organization.
- Mitigate significant security risks, designs and implements strategies and programs to prevent and reduce loss of the organization's assets while reducing costs.
- Prioritize Global Security Initiatives
- Provide guidance, oversight and support to Alcoa location security operations and activities to ensure the protection of employees, information and physical assets, while ensuring optimal use of personnel and equipment.
- Develops and delivers preventative programs and services to protect against criminal financial loss, crime against persons, sabotage, threats, emergencies, illegal acts, and property.
- Researches and deploys state-of-the-art technology solutions and innovative security management techniques to safeguard assets and increase cost savings.

Figure CP7.2   Career Profile: Director, global security operations—Alcoa.   (*Continued*)

	• Directs and conducts a wide range of investigations, in conjunction with other internal and external resources.
	• Acts as the subject matter expert on security technology systems and provides strategic direction for their integration in conjunction with current established internal standards.
	• Serves as the subject matter expert for state, federal, international security regulated programs such as CFATS, ISPS.
	• Develops close relationships with high-level law enforcement and international counterparts to include in-country security and International Security agencies, intelligence and private sector counterparts worldwide.
	• Briefs executive management on status of security issues.
	• Leads and maintains travel security and threat intelligence programs.
Basic Qualifications	• Bachelor's degree in Criminal justice, Law enforcement, or related field from an accredited institution
	• Minimum of 5 years of experience in corporate security management and leadership
	• Minimum of 15 years of experience in security management, law enforcement or intelligence agency
	• Employees must be legally authorized to work in the United States. Verification of employment eligibility will be required at the time of hire. Visa sponsorship is not available for this position.
Preferred Qualifications	• Experience with a major corporation or global Fortune 500 industries.
	• Proficiency in the international security arena
	• Certified Protection Professional (CPP) and Certified Fraud Examiner (CFE) certifications preferred
Job Type	Experienced

Figure CP7.2   (Continued) Career Profile: Director, global security operations—Alcoa.

Figure 7.32   Surveillance equipment comes in various models.

image through a device called a modulator into the master antenna, where it is tuned along with the channels that transmit radio frequency signals."[52]

While CCTV is touted as an indispensable tool in security technology, overreliance may be unwise. C.A. Roper points out the specific disadvantages:

1. The monitoring screen does not provide as faithful a reproduction of the scene as does direct vision. For this reason, small details are not discernible or are vague to the eye.

2. Dividing the guard's attention between several monitoring screens may not provide the continuity of coverage desired.

3. The resulting eye strain and the boredom of watching a monitor may cause a lack of attention on the part of the security guard.

4. The area viewed may contain so many obstructions that even several CCTV cameras could not give proper coverage; a roving guard or guard patrol would be a better choice in this case.

5. The camera is incapable of taking corrective actions in response to an event that is taking place. The time required to move a security guard or guards to the area may be too great.[53]

Many security companies have an impressive array of surveillance cameras, many of which are creatively disguised in components such as

- Garbage cans
- Fence posts
- Clocks
- Exit signs
- Cameras
- Sprinkler system

Covering both perimeter and the interior of a facility can be a sophisticated CCTV system, which is perpetually searching out for the intruder and the act of intrusion. CCTV typically is set up from a command center with adjoining software and hardware installed in the main computers.[54] The technology that connects various fields has been rapidly changing from the surveillance product quality benefiting from digital technology as well as the implementation of wireless setup as well.[55] Others predict that analog CCTV will soon be a thing of the past with computer-based IP cameras capable of extraordinary amounts of storage and interpretation.[56] The physical locale, externally and internally, are tracked by actual monitors tied to the central command. Those in central command have visual access to all portions of the facility in need of security protection. Incidents are recorded through the monitoring system. A common CCTV engineering design may be as shown in Figure 7.33.[57]

Also trending is the integration of private security surveillance systems, placed in diverse environments such as businesses, schools, and gated neighborhoods, to be fully integrated with local public police systems. The City of Atlanta, by and through its program Operation Shield, has succeeded in this ambition.[58]

7.4.6.2 Photographic/video equipment

Employing the photograph as an aid is wise; however, the agent will have the added pressure of operating photographic equipment correctly. "Good surveillance photographs require good police work plus good photographic techniques. Such techniques include the use of telephoto lenses, the use of infrared flashes or lamps, the processing of film for maximum film speed, and the use of motion picture and time lapse cameras."[59]

---

[52] *Ibid.* at 327.
[53] C.A. Roper, *Physical Security and the Inspection Process* 165 (1997).
[54] C. Freschi, A Smart Future for Video Surveillance, *Sec. Mag.* (June 2008) at 74.
[55] S. Walin, What's Hot, What's Not in Video Surveillance, *Sec. Mag.* (April 2009) at 50.
[56] F. Nilsson, Video Surveillance Is Living on the Edge, *Security Executive Technology* (June/July 2013) at 16.
[57] U.S. Army, Physical Security at page 6–46.
[58] Case Study, Integration of Video Surveillance Systems Enhances Public Safety, *Sec. Mag.* (March 2015) at 56.
[59] Eastman Kodak Co., Photographic Surveillance Techniques for Law Enforcement Agencies (1972).

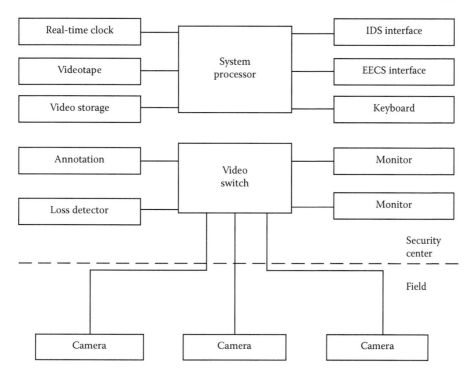

Figure 7.33 Typical CCTV system.

Photographic surveillance can be either active or passive in nature. In the active category, the investigator is making a conscious decision to be on the scene with the correct equipment. The investigator must be attuned to the difficulties of normal light photography, taking into consideration distances, light, exposure, and climatic factors, and whether or not telephoto shutter speeds, depth of field, and other accessories are needed to take acceptable pictures. Telephoto lenses are also a necessity. It is becoming even more common for the private security industry to employ video recording devices as they become more economical for firms to own and operate.

Passive surveillance is activated by the suspect himself or herself. Video technology has obviously impacted the industry's surveillance practices in a positive way.

ASIS International concurs in the importance of photography in surveillance methods:

> Photographic equipment of every sort should be considered. Concealed cameras or videotape equipment may be adroitly placed, not requiring the presence of an investigator except to check on its operation periodically. Time lapse cameras, which can shoot scenes over a long period of time, are often helpful to develop evidence; arrangements should be made for quick film development if information is needed for subsequent surveillance. Hand-held cameras can be disguised in various ways (by being placed inside a briefcase or by being made to resemble a book).[60]

Finally, surveillance results, especially those related to unwarranted visitors and unauthorized parties, must be formally memorialized in report documentation. The examples in Figures 7.34 and 7.35 accomplish this purpose.

7.5 PHYSICAL SECURITY AND CPTED

Environmental design of buildings, facilities, parks, and entertainment complexes are perpetual concerns for the security specialist.[61] In a way, the environment completely represents the physical reality the security operatives

---

[60] American Society for Industrial Security, American Society for Industrial Security, Basic Guidelines for Security Investigations (1981) at 42.

[61] Security Designed into New and Remodeled Facilities, *Sec. Mag.* (August 2008) at 32; see also M.A. Gips, CPTED Still the Exception, 47 *Sec. Mgmt* 12 (2003); M. Blades, Knowledge of CPTED Useful in Meeting Public and Private Security Industry Standards, *Security Technology & Design* (April 2008) at 46.

Surveillance Log Cover Sheet

Subject _____   Conducted by (Investigators) _____

Address _____   _____

Telephone _____   Case No. _____

Social Security # _____   Case Name _____

Date of Birth _____

Description _____

_____

Type of Injury _____

_____

Vehicles _____

_____   Date _____

Persons Observed   Times Observed

Synopsis:

☐ Subject Observed   ☐ Contact Observed   ☐ Photos Attempted
☐ Subject not Observed   ☐ Unusual Activity   ☐ Assessment Data Obtained

_____ Hours   _____ Minutes = Total Time on Subject

Administrative Data:

Equipment:

Van: _____   Starting Mileage: _____ Finish Mileage: _____

Photos   Yes _____   No _____
Video   Yes _____   No _____

_____

_____

_____

_____

_____

Figure 7.34 Surveillance log cover sheet.

must labor in—the locale where their security services are delivered and what those services are widely dependent on how the environment unfolds before them. In another way, the environment is both natural and man-made. Noted already is how rivers, streams, rock faces, and the earth's own undulations are natural security barriers—a reality that every security specialist be cognizant of. As to the building of facility, building, and other edifice, its architecture in the fullest sense of the word, the environment can be altered or adjusted to reflect security needs. In fact, most contemporary builders already cost or factor in the idea of security in the planning and blueprint stage.

CPTED should be integrated into all planning for safety and security. Security specialists need to adopt proactive approaches, which create "defensible space" within those environments. Transit systems across the United States,

```
┌─────────────────────────────────────────────────────────────────────────┐
│                          Daily Surveillance Report                        │
│                                                                           │
│   To:                                                                     │
│   From:                                                                   │
│   RE:        Surveillance of                                              │
│   On:        [Date]                                                       │
│                                                                           │
│              (Paragraph 1)                                                │
│                     Summary of debriefing to include date, time, information received from supervisor │
│                                                                           │
│              (Paragraph 2)                                                │
│                     Proposed method of surveillance.                      │
│                                                                           │
│              (Paragraph 3)                                                │
│                     Any deviation from plan and reason for such.          │
│                                                                           │
│              (Paragraph 4)                                                │
│                     Activity Log                                          │
│                                                                           │
└─────────────────────────────────────────────────────────────────────────┘
```

Figure 7.35 Daily surveillance report.

by way of example, have paid serious attention to CPTED and the results have been dramatically beneficial. In the present age of terrorism, communities and the buildings that compose it must be mindful of how design inhibits and advances the criminal plotter. Richard Healy's *Design for Security* foretells the interplay between the environment and the opportunity for crime. "Better lighting, emergency phone systems, more and better directional signs, and the closing off of dead-end passageways in which riders could become lost or trapped by assailants are built-in features today of new systems and receive high priority when old systems undertake station renovations. The importance of landscaping for safety is well known."[62]

Herein lies the physicality of security in the largest possible sense—the entire area and at the same time the particular buildings and facilities that make it up. CPTED creatively mixes criminology with architecture and seeks ways to negate or inhibit the activity. "A comprehensive CPTED analysis attempts to identify central problems and craft changes in the physical and social environment that will reinforce positive behavior. Posted rules and theme-oriented artwork to reinforce pro-social curriculum, greater use of windows to enhance visibility and reduce isolation, student art displays to build a sense of pride, altered seating arrangements to encourage supportive group interactions, or changes in scheduling the use of space to avoid conflict are all potential CPTED measures that could be implemented."[63] When the environment integrates and installs a physical protection system, those that live and work in that environment are active players in its defense. CPTED forges and shapes mindsets and conceptions about safety and security. In other words, people are intensely influenced—whether in a good or bad way, by the environment experienced.

For example, picture the different states of mind between shoppers in a mall and the person experiencing the rigors of the new and improved airport security.[64] The corresponding environments offer attitudes that vary because the security applied to those environments are so markedly different. Physical barriers and controls impact the citizen's psyche and foster personal well-being. The same is certainly true for citizens living and laboring in high-crime

---

[62] D.M. Schulz, Private Security Comes on Board, *Sec. Mgmt* (April 1997) at 255.

[63] T. Schneider, Safe School through Environmental Design, ERIC Digest Number 144.

[64] For an interesting analysis as to how to create the proper environment for retail settings, see R. Atlas, How May We Help You: 15 Ways to Secure Quick Service Retail Environments, *Security Technology Executive* (October 2012) at 30.

regions, whose outlook radically varies from the affluent community member. To be effective, physical security must reflect the needs and characteristics of the community.[65]

Governments have often been the antagonists to the CPTED approach. In a sort of perverse elitism, planners and community designers at the public and private level have assumed less concern about safety and security in low-income areas. The entire infrastructure of 1960–1980 public housing designs, with its penchant for high rises and cement block compaction, was arrogantly built on this disregard for quality of life questions. Oscar Newman cuts cogently to the issue:

> Defensive space, it may be charged, is middle-class thinking. The poor have their own culture. They don't want the peaceful, secure, dull life of middle class. They don't want property. They don't want the value middle-class society wishes to foist upon them. Violence, it is contended, is part of their culture. So, apparently, is communality. They don't want walls, whether real ones, or the ones you place in their minds by the design of space.
>
> The romantic view of the poor is without foundation. Interviews with hundreds of low-income housing residents reveal that most hold the goals and aspirations of the middle class. The desire for security is not limited to the middle class.[66]

CPTED critically illustrates the interplay between design and safety. "That insight has been incorporated into the literature on design against crime, and is also covered under at least three other keywords: environmental criminology, defensible space, and crime prevention through environmental design or CPTED. An underlying concern of design is to enhance individual responsibility to look after places."[67] Crime prevention, applied to specified locales, addresses the interaction between social and physical environment by changing the design, management, and use of a particular place. Here, the specialists implement crime prevention tactics that transform an area beleaguered by crime.[68] CPTED philosophy incorporates a wide array of input and data sources, and goes well beyond the architectural engine. The U.S. Department of Justice advocates the widest possible level of participation.

> Architects included landscape architects; general architects; architects with railroads, developers, hospitals, government, schools, universities, medical school, and hotels; and parking consultants or designers. School administrators, security specialists, and facility planners were supplemented with their university counterparts, including university housing directors. We interviewed parks and recreation officials at several levels. Additional interviews included management consultants, plant protection specialists, drug prevention specialists, theater managers, air transport and aviation crime prevention specialists, insurance security specialists, and professors with special expertise in crime prevention. Due to strong cooperation from professional societies, we supplemented our samples of architects and hospital security personnel, as well as park officials.[69]

Any effective CPTED approach will stress:

- Planning and execution of a well-conceived set of *physical redesign* elements, based on close analysis of the ways the built environment was being used
- Implementation of wide-ranging *changes in the management of private and public property* in each community, with the involvement of private owners and managers, public agencies, and residents
- Expansion or reorientation of *security efforts*, involving a shift to community policing and (in some cases) the coordinated use of private security forces
- Strengthening of the *role of residents* in addressing community conditions, through the development of communication and cooperation with law enforcement officials, private owners and managers, and other local players

---

[65] The National Institute of Justice's recent Research in Brief that studies Baltimore neighborhoods produced surprising result. In part, the study argued that "[p]hysical conditions had deteriorated significantly on the street blocks assessed in 1981 and 1994. Graffiti and abandoned houses occurred more frequently. Despite the worsening physical conditions, resident did not report that local physical or social problems in the neighborhood were significantly worse." R.B. Taylor, Crime, Grime, Fear and Decline: A Longitudinal Look—Research in Brief—NCJ 177603, 7 (1999).

[66] Newman at 19.

[67] Felson at 1; see also Poyner, 1983; Brantingham and Brantingham, 1991; Newman, 1996; Jeffrey, 1971; and Crowe and Zahm, 1994.

[68] J.D. Feins et al. *Solving Crime Problems in Residential Neighborhoods: Comprehensive Changes in Design, Management, and Use* 3 (Washington, DC, 1997).

[69] M. Felson, *Designing Crime Free Environments: Broadening the Crime Prevention Repertoire* (Washington, DC: U.S. Department of Justice, 2000).

- Reduction in crime and other *improvements in the quality of life* in the community, as indicated by police data and by observers and participants in the local programs[70]

For CPTED to be effective, one must analyze the physical layout of the community and developing recommendations for environmental improvement. Both development and redevelopment plans should be fully reviewed and recommendations regarding environmental design relative to crime prevention fully incorporated. The community crime problem is scrutinized in the broadest environmental categories, yet at the same time, microscopically dissected building by building, store by store, and home by home. See Figure 7.36.[71]

Place-Specific Crime Prevention Components and Sources Components

Physical design changes

- Target-hardening
- Controlling access
- Increasing opportunities for surveillance
- Targeting crime "hot spots"
- Improving image

Management changes

- Revamping security (including policing)
- Altering property ownership and/or management
- Expanding the role of residents

Use changes

- Increasing use at different times of the day and night
- Increasing the variety of business uses
- Increasing use by residents and others for leisure activities

Sources (Theories and Practices)

Physical crime prevention

- Defensible space
- Symbolic barriers (delineating public vs. private space)
- Crime prevention through environmental design (CPTED)

Understanding criminal behavior

- Rational choice theory
- Routine activity theory

Recent developments in crime prevention theory

- Situational crime prevention (combines physical and other means of reducing crime opportunities)

Developments in local crime prevention practice

- Community crime prevention
- Neighborhood crime prevention

Recent developments in local law enforcement practice

- Community-oriented policing (COP)
- Problem-oriented policing (POP)
- Call management/police response analysis (MIS/GIS)
- Expansion of law enforcement role (better coordination with other agencies)
- Neighborhood-based planning and service approaches

Figure 7.36   Place-specific crime prevention components and sources components.

---

[70] J.D. Feins et al. *Solving Crime Problems in Residential Neighborhoods: Comprehensive Changes in Design, Management, and Use* 67 (Washington, DC, 1997).

[71] J.D. Feins et al. *Solving Crime Problems in Residential Neighborhoods: Comprehensive Changes in Design, Management, and Use* 4 (Washington, DC, 1997).

Summary of CPTED Strategies and Tactics		
Target hardening <ul><li>Strong doors (magnetic locking, foam-core steel)</li><li>Locks (dead bolt)</li><li>Window screens</li><li>Reinforced glass (marine glazing)</li><li>Alarms</li></ul>	**Access control** <ul><li>Doors and gates locked</li><li>Interior areas fenced off</li><li>Visitor check-in booths</li><li>Guard houses</li><li>Number of entrances and exits reduced</li><li>Pass-card system in use</li><li>Key access to laundry rooms and elevators</li><li>Indoor and outdoor spaces divided into smaller, easily identifiable areas</li><li>Resident IDs checked</li><li>Buzzer and intercom systems</li><li>[Metal] detectors</li><li>Assigned parking places</li><li>Parking stickers</li></ul>	**Deflecting offenders** <ul><li>Traffic patterns changed</li><li>Streets and alleys closed</li><li>"No Parking" or "No Standing"</li><li>zones created</li></ul>
Closing crack houses and repairing "broken windows" <ul><li>Garbage-strewn lots cleaned up</li><li>Abandoned cars towed</li><li>Abandoned houses boarded up</li><li>24-hour graffiti removal</li></ul>	**Cameras and other formal surveillance** <ul><li>Closed-circuit television</li><li>Portable camera systems</li><li>Police call boxes</li><li>Trained resident patrols</li><li>Police substations</li><li>On-site security offices</li><li>Kobans (mini-stations)</li></ul>	**Surveillance by employees** <ul><li>Housing authority staff</li><li>Bus drivers</li><li>Crossing guards</li><li>Mail handlers</li><li>Utility company workers</li><li>Social services staff</li></ul>
Improving natural surveillance <ul><li>Improved street and interior lighting</li><li>Non-see-through fencing and barriers removed</li><li>Trees and hedges pruned</li><li>Alcoves and other interior blind spots removed</li><li>Vulnerable areas redesigned or relocated</li></ul>	**Removing inducements to crime** <ul><li>Vacant apartments rented</li><li>Overnight street parking banned</li></ul>	**Signage and bans on use** <ul><li>"Drug-Free Zones"</li><li>Posted guest and visitor policies</li><li>"No Trespassing" signs</li></ul>

Figure 7.37   Summary of CPTED strategies and tactics.

A full survey of CPTED strategies and tactics for healthy communities is reproduced in Figure 7.37.[72]

Physical barriers may be of two general types, natural and structural. Natural barriers include mountains, cliffs, canyons, rivers, or other terrain difficult to traverse. Structural barriers are man-made devices such as fences, walls, floors, roofs, grills, bars, or other structures that deter penetration. If a natural barrier forms one side or any part of the perimeter, it in itself should not automatically be considered an adequate perimeter barrier, since it may be overcome by a determined intruder. Structural barriers should be provided for that portion of the perimeter, if required.

7.6 CONCLUSION

The idea of physical security can be summarized as the space, the asset, and the person's safe station in relation the surrounding environment. In other words, physical security encompasses the geography and architecture as well as the protected assets, human or otherwise. Physical security secures us within the reality we live and work. Hence, the entity to be protected is analyzed from both an interior and exterior perspective; it is studied from a technological perspective, such as cameras and lighting, barriers and access points, natural as well as man-made devices and

---

[72] Adapted from R.V. Clarke, S.L. Sorensen, & J. Fagan, Situational CPTED Matrix for Public and Indian Housing. The matrix appears in S.L. Sorensen & E. Walsh, *Crime Prevention through Environmental Design and Situational Crime Prevention in Public Housing: Workshop Curriculum, HUD Crime Prevention and Security Division, Technical Assistance Workshop(s)* (Bethesda, MD: Prevention Agency RTA Consulting Corporation, March 1995), 13; J.D. Feins et al. *Solving Crime Problems in Residential Neighborhoods: Comprehensive Changes in Design, Management, and Use* 28 (Washington, DC, 1997).

designs, and from a hardware and software program that tracks human behavior and motion. Physical security is a massive undertaking applied in literally thousands of settings. Career opportunities and consulting services relative to physical security are a fast-growing sector of the private security industry.

Keywords

access security	guard booth	Registered Traveler (RT) program
alarms	intrusion detection	sensor detection
barbed wire	keyless systems	smart card technology
barrier arms	keypad entry	structural barriers
biometric identification	location security	surveillance
bollards	lockdown security	top guard fencing
CCTV	natural barriers	turnstiles
crime prevention through environ- mental design (CPTED)	paperless boarding pass	vehicle control barrier
	passive surveillance	video surveillance
defensible space	perimeter security	visible security
fences	physical security	wedges
gates	physical security assessment	

Discussion questions

1. Review the definition of physical security provided by the American Society for Industrial Security and appraise its completeness. Discuss how the definition can be improved upon.
2. Outline the various exterior applications to physical security and describe which methods are best suited for specific applications.
3. Review interior access control strategies, list which vulnerabilities they address, and indicate when specific types of access control are appropriate.
4. Many types of keyless, sensor, and biometric systems exist. What are some of the downfalls to relying solely on technological security systems?
5. Two biometric applications are currently in use by the TSA: the Registered Traveler program and the paperless boarding pass. What privacy issues exist with the use of these programs?
6. What specific questions must be posed when implementing video surveillance programs?

CHAPTER 8

Security
Human resources and personnel

OBJECTIVES

After completing this chapter, the student will be able to

1. Assess the role private security plays in the personnel side of any business and industry.
2. Demonstrate the importance of background checks in private security and relate the various procedures used to conduct the investigation.
3. Outline specific programs such as active shooter and workplace violence mitigation programs and discuss how they promote safety in the community.
4. Identify special requirements for highly placed employees and managerial personnel in private security in need of executive or celebrity protection.
5. Appraise why hate crimes are so specialized and differentiated from traditional assault offenses.
6. Describe specific recommendations on how to be safe in travel nationally and internationally.
7. Discuss the various offenses common in workplace violence, such as harassment and stalking, and relay specific measures to mitigate these incidents.
8. Explain the elements that should exist in an active shooter mitigation plan.

8.1 PRIVATE SECURITY INDUSTRY: PROTECTION OF PEOPLE

Too often, the private security industry is typed as an exclusive protector of "assets" and within particular settings such as business and corporate interests. To be fair, much of this caricature is actually a realistic portion and portrayal of the industry since the days of the Molly Maguires and the Homestead Steel Strike because the essence of the industry was then and is now grounded in commercial protection.

What is just as obvious is how the industry has so dramatically evolved, and while its heart and soul may belong to assets, facilities, and places in need of protection, the shift toward protecting the personnel within these business, governmental, and industrial entities has become just as central to its overall aim and purpose. People, employees, visitors, and partners are not faceless commodities but precious human beings in need of care and secured protection. In fact, security professionals need to understand the workings, the structural organization, and the personnel process in a typical enterprise to do their jobs correctly. Natalie Runyon properly asserts that to be an expert in business and personnel assures an expertise in the "business of security."[1] People are what make up the asset-driven corporation or governmental courthouse or airport installation. People are more crucial than any given thing and the private security industry assures a viable and secure environment for these players.

---

[1] N. Runyon, Skills for a Successful Executive in the Business of Security, *Sec. Mag.* (August 2011) at 54.

Figure 8.1   Workplace incidents between 2000 and 2013.

In addition, business, industry, and government cannot always trust their people and personnel to do the right thing and in fact suffer at their criminality and diverse chicanery at participation rates mostly never imagined. People harm one another in violent confrontations at these settings, from the deranged shooter who was terminated from a job, to the vengeance-filled former employee returning to express his anger against management. See Figures 8.1 and 8.2.[2]

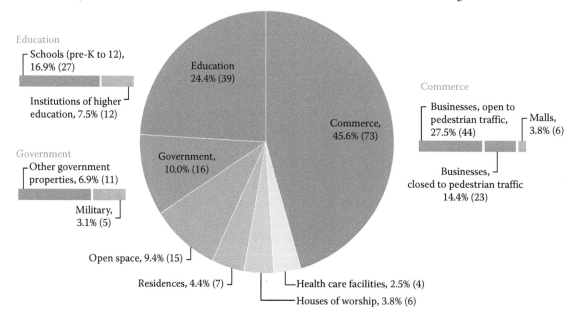

Figure 8.2   Active shooter incidents in the United States, 2000–2013.

---

[2] FBI, A Study of Active Shooter Incidents in the United States between 2000 and 2013 (2013), at https://www.fbi.gov/about-us/office-of-partner-engagement/active-shooter-incidents/a-study-of-active-shooter-incidents-in-the-u.s.-2000-2013, last accessed August 28, 2016.

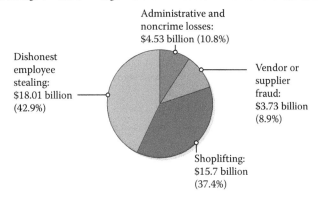

Percentage of retail shrinkage in the United States due to each of these factors:

Figure 8.3 Losses caused by workers. (Data source: Global Retail Theft Barometer.)

Hence, the private security industry expends a great deal of its energy and resources on the protection as well as investigation and control of people. Aside from violence, active shooter syndrome, and a host of other warped motivations, the security industry confronts employees who steal and thieve like there is no tomorrow—and not just in simple retail settings but from every business model conceivable. The costs of employee theft are becoming the difference between staying afloat and pricing a product out of its attractiveness.[3] Losses are now calculated in the billions according to the Society of Human Resource Managers. See Figure 8.3.[4]

On top of thievery, the contemporary employee has mastered the art and science of identity theft, cyber-crime, and a full array of employee frauds that undermine the integrity of any economic operation. Making sure that the company hires and oversees the right people, from preemployment screening to postemployment scrutiny, is a never-ending private security function. Here, people consume a great many resources because people and personnel can cause a plethora of problems.[5]

But the challenges are not strictly economic for personnel and people bring a great deal of personal challenges and moral baggage to the marketplace, whether it be mental and emotional disorders, drug and alcohol addictions, obsessive stalking behaviors, or problems with supervision. This is even relevant in questions of promotion or transfer within an enterprise for assuring longevity to a troublemaker is a recipe for all sorts of problems.[6] Those entrusted with a safe and secure work environment must be endlessly vigilant for the many nuances of employee behavior.[7]

For but one example of transportation, the addictive culture shapes an industry in distress to combat the rising rates of abuse. See the U.S. Department of Transportation figures in Figure 8.4.[8]

Because of all these forces, the private security industry has become a major player in preemployment screening of potential employees, as well as monitoring on a day-to-day basis of negative behaviors, whether it be drug and alcohol related, rooted in violent tendencies or other unpredictable, yet highly consequential behavior, or to the protection of others laboring side by side with those so troubled.[9]

This chapter assesses the role private security plays in the personnel side of any business and industry; focuses on specific programs such as active shooter and workplace violence mitigation programs as well as the special requirements

[3] R. Maurer, Employee Theft Costs Retailers Billions (July 29, 2015) Society for Human Resource Management, at https://www.shrm.org/hrdisciplines/safetysecurity/articles/pages/employee-theft-costs-retailers-billions.aspx, last accessed August 28, 2016.

[4] Global Retail Theft Barometer 2015, at http://www.globalretailtheftbarometer.com/index.html, last accessed August 28, 2016.

[5] *Ibid.*

[6] R. Cormican, Interview Tips for Promotions and Transfers, *Law and Order* (September 2005) at 151.

[7] The CBHSQ Report, Substance Use and Substance Use Disorder by Industry, at http://www.samhsa.gov/data/sites/default/files/report_1959/ShortReport-1959.html, last accessed August 28, 2016; see also NCADD, Drugs and Alcohol in the Workplace, at https://www.ncadd.org/about-addiction/addiction-update/drugs-and-alcohol-in-the-workplace, last accessed August 28, 2016.

[8] U.S. Department of Transportation, 2016 DOT Random Testing Rates, at https://www.transportation.gov/odapc/random-testing-rates?prog=, last accessed August 28, 2016.

[9] See L. Klein, Tips on Workplace Investigations, *The American City & County* (July 2010) at 34; see also C. Hale, The Employee Interview Exercise, *Law and Order* (August 2005) at 33.

2016 DOT random testing rates

The following chart outlines the annual minimum drug and alcohol random testing rates established within DOT Agencies and the USCG for 2016:

DOT agency	2016 random drug testing rate	2016 random alcohol testing rate
Federal Motor Carrier Safety Administration (FMCSA)	25%	10%
Federal Aviation Administration (FAA)	25%	10%
Federal Railroad Administration (FRA)	25%	10%
Federal Transit Administration (FTA)	25%	10%
Pipeline and Hazardous Materials Safety Administration (PHMSA)	25%	N/A
United States Coast Guard (USCG) *(now with the Dept. of Homeland Security)*	25%	N/A

Figure 8.4   U.S. Department of Transportation drug testing results.

for highly placed employees and managerial personnel in need of executive or celebrity protection as well as guidance on how to be safe in travel nationally and internationally.

8.2 PREEMPLOYMENT SCREENING AND BACKGROUND CHECKS

One of this nation's largest security firms, G4S, is under heavy scrutiny for its failure to conduct due diligence on Omar Mateen, the vicious Islamic radical, who executed 50 people and injured many more in the recent Orlando, Florida rampage (Figure 8.5). With Mateen under multiple FBI queries and other intelligence services, how could regulatory authorities in Florida so readily grant a security license to this terrorist? On top of this, how could G4S conduct such a poor inquiry into the background of this individual? It is simply astonishing that a state and a company that pride themselves on rigorous standards could be so lax.

If the results are as devastating for G4S, with the acumen to ferret out the worst characters imaginable, how can an ordinary business be expected to do much better? Indeed, the Orlando case magnifies the costs of poor screening to a level never envisioned by the security industry, which has lead the way with its own excellence in background checks and employment screening.[10]

8.2.1 General recommendations on background and employment investigations

Like every investigative regimen, the investigator must adopt and implement practices, procedures, and protocols that successfully reach the aim or goal of the investigation. In background investigations, the investigator seeks to complete the most accurate possible profile of the targeted person under this type of scrutiny.

Web Exercise: Find out about some of the more favored companies in the area of background investigation at http://www.businessnewsdaily.com/7638-best-background-check-services.html.

---

[10] S. Ludwig, How Federal Background Checks Are Changing, *Sec. Mag.* (August 2014), at http://www.securitymagazine.com/articles/85673-how-federal-background-checks-are-changing, last accessed August 28, 2016.

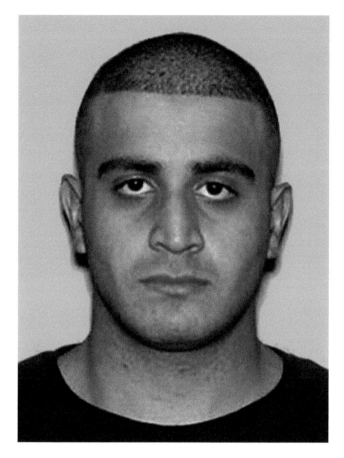

Figure 8.5   Omar Mateen: Islamic radical and jihadist—the Orlando shooter.

Precisely what constitutes the various measures of one's background often differs by occupation, type of client making the requests, legal restrictions, and finally, the persons to be evaluated. Nevertheless, there are some uniform and consistent measures that lead to an accurate profile of the individual.

A large portion of private security assignments consist of background investigation.

Owing to rising concerns about alcohol and drug addiction; the ease of document forgery, transcript alteration, assumption of false names and backgrounds; and the threat of espionage and terrorist activities, background investigations are increasingly important to businesses, institutions, and individuals.

Within corporate settings, personnel departments greatly rely upon background reviews. According to William Cunningham and Todd Taylor, authors of the first *Hallcrest Report*:

> It is essential that a person hired for a specific position possesses the background, training, and skills stated in his or her résumé and employment application. Certain positions have special requirements for trust, deportment, confidentiality, and other character traits. For these positions, the organization must be able to verify that there have been no previous adverse reflections on the candidate's character and that there are no tendencies toward inappropriate conduct.[11]

Business' natural hesitancy in believing an applicant's stated background is intelligent discretion, especially when one considers the civil actions that can be brought against an employer who negligently retains and fails to terminate an employee.[12] As J. Kirk Barefoot remarked:

---

[11] W. Cunningham & T. Taylor, The Hallcrest Report: Private Security and Police in America 43 (1985); see also P. Psarouthakis, Business Background Investigations: Tools and Techniques for Solution Driven Due Diligence, *Sec. Mgmt* (June 2008) at 120.

[12] See C.P. Nemeth, *Private Security and the Law*, 4th ed. (2012).

Position:
Background Investigator
Company:
OMNIPLEX World Services Corporation
Job Location(s):
Springfield, VA
Start Date:
As soon as possible

Employment Term:
Regular
Employment Type:
Full Time
Starting Salary Range:
Not Provided

Required Education:
High School or Equivalent
Required Experience:
3 years
Required Security Clearance:
None
Related Categories:
Employment and Staffing Services, HR - Recruiting

Position Description

OMNIPLEX is seeking talented individuals committed to excellence, honesty, and integrity to join our team. We are a trusted provider of high quality background investigations programs to Department of Homeland Security (DHS) and the intelligence community at locations throughout the United States. If you have investigations experience, OMNIPLEX is where you want to be for the future.

Geographic Location: Northern Virginia, Springfield, Fairfax, Chantilly

$2500 Signing Bonus!

Job Description: As an *OMNIPLEX* Background Investigator (BI), you work cases throughout the geographic area of responsibility and travel to various places of employment, residence and education institutions. Your flexible schedule gives you the freedom to plan your appointments, interviews, and administrative work in a way that works best for you. Our diverse portfolio supporting Intelligence Community and Department of Homeland Security (DHS) contracts means that you can perform work for different customers each day. You work independently but this job is full of interaction with different and new people every day. You can also take full advantage of the experienced management and support staff that are available to answer questions and provide guidance whenever you need it.

We equip you for success with a state-of-the-art case management tool and ongoing training. We make it easy and convenient for you to get the information you need as quickly as possible. At OMNIPLEX you have a supportive, stable work environment with many avenues for communication with other investigators, support staff, and management.

OMNIPLEX Background Investigators conduct federal background investigations for the Intelligence and the DHS Community and prepare reports of investigations in compliance with ICD 704 standards, all laws, and other required federal agency regulations. Additional duties may be assigned.

Geographic Location - Northern Virginia, Springfield, Fairfax, Manassas, Chantilly

Requirements:

- U.S. Citizenship.
- H.S. Diploma or equivalent.
- Minimum of three (3) years within the last ten (10) years of investigations experience at the federal, state, or local level of government Intelligence Community/ICD 704.1 Investigations trained and experienced.
- Successful completion an approved National Training Standards program/course.
- Experience conducting one-on-one subject interviews.
- Reliable personal vehicle, valid driver's license, and satisfactory driving record.
- Willing to travel on temporary duty assignments as needed (by car or plane).
- Successfully pass background checks and all required training.
- Current (within the last 2 years) Single Scope Background Investigation (SSBI) or active Secret level security clearance based on an SSBI and able to obtain required clearance.

Preferred Experience and Education:

- Bachelor's Degree in Criminal Justice, National Strategic/Intelligence Studies or a related field.
- Three (3) years within the last ten (10) years of experience conducting background investigations for U.S. Government Security Clearances.
- Completion of an approved OPM investigator training program.
- Active Top Secret clearance.

OMNIPLEX rewards it employees through an incentive program for excellent quality and efficiency of work. We will provide laptop, cell phone, printer/internet allowance, and mileage reimbursement. We also offer a comprehensive benefits package to include health, dental, vision, life & AD&D insurance, 401(k), paid time off, holiday pay, and tuition reimbursement.

OMNIPLEX is committed to a drug-free workplace. As such, the Company conducts pre-employment, reasonable cause, random and contract-mandated testing in accordance with federal and state law.

EOE Minority/Female/Disabled/Veteran

Figure CP8.1   Career Profile: Background investigations.

It is absolutely essential in building a healthy company to begin with the selection of persons who are inherently honest, or at least basically honest if the proper controls and procedures are in effect. Hiring persons who have a history of consistent employee theft only insures that security problems will continue to develop and that there will be always be plenty of work to occupy the investigation section of the security department.[13]

In this framework, background investigation serves a major function in employee screening. The philosophy extends not only to the initial date of hire but the ongoing evaluation and assessment of an employee. Background assessment can take many forms, including, but not limited to, personal and community interview, polygraph tests, and psychological examinations designed to measure various personality characteristics. "Screening procedures used should be based on the nature of the business, its resources for carrying out the procedures, and the security needs of the business."[14]

The ability to determine the background of an individual in employment settings, surveillance operations, skip/trace analysis, or other matter depends upon the access to the following types of records:

- Educational and school materials
- Employment information
- Neighborhood information
- Criminal background and court records
- Civil litigation and court records
- Credit and financial resources
- Personal references

Many security firms solely focus on this aspect of practice.

This chapter's focus is a generic discussion of the investigative sequence used in establishing background history with specialized suggestions, forms, documents, and checklists of practical use to the private investigator. Figure 8.6 reviews the areas of a background investigation and can help the investigator refine the search process. An investigator's checklist, guiding the security professional through the facets of background check, is shown in Figure 8.7. The investigator must adhere to federal, state, and local legislation bearing on background investigation practices and access to background information.

8.2.2 Background issues

Exactly what constitutes the idea and concept of a background is the first order of business for the investigator. Background encompasses a history of identity, or residence and employment, or military background and economic ownership. A summary review follows.

8.2.2.1 Establishing identity

The task of checking individual backgrounds, as in all facets of investigation, requires an orderly process of thinking and action. Figure 8.8 lists the appropriate investigation sequence.

Access to records and information will vary by the locality but access, in every circumstance, is essential to success in the background investigation process. States and counties are somewhat more liberal than federal agencies in granting access to records. According to Bottom and Kostanoski:

Many public records are available to personnel directors and to security and loss control personnel. Each state has its own repository for workers' compensation claims. Each state has a central driver's license records center. Criminal records are available at the county level (over 3,000 in the United States) and at all state levels (with the exception of Nevada). Rules of access to these records vary from state to state. The vast majority of counties and/or state agencies will provide some information by telephone or letter. Computerized access to these records is expanding every year. All states and the District of Columbia will make driving records available to the public.[15]

---

[13] J.K. Barefoot, *Employee Theft Investigation* 190 (1979).

[14] R. O'Block, *Security and Crime Prevention* 191 (1981).

[15] N. Bottom & J. Kostanoski, *Introduction to Security and Loss Control* 158 (1990); see also The National Employment Screening Services, *The Guide to Background Investigations* (1990).

```
┌─────────────────────────────────────────────────────────────────────┐
│                      Request for Investigation                        │
│                                                                       │
│   To:            _____                            │
│   From:          _____                            │
│                  _____                            │
│                  _____                            │
│   Phone Number: _____                       │
│   SUBJECTS TO BE SEARCHED:                                            │
│   NAME _____      NAME _____  │
│   DOB _____ SSN _____    DOB _____ SSN _____  │
│   LAST KNOWN ADDRESS _____     LAST KNOWN ADDRESS _____    │
│   _____        _____      │
│   NAME _____      NAME _____  │
│   DOB _____ SSN _____    DOB _____ SSN _____  │
│   LAST KNOWN ADDRESS _____     LAST KNOWN ADDRESS _____    │
│   _____        _____      │
│   COMPANIES _____      COMPANIES _____   │
│   _____        _____      │
│   _____        _____      │
└─────────────────────────────────────────────────────────────────────┘
```

Request for Investigation

To: _____
From: _____
_____
_____
Phone Number: _____
SUBJECTS TO BE SEARCHED:
NAME _____   NAME _____
DOB _____ SSN _____   DOB _____ SSN _____
LAST KNOWN ADDRESS _____   LAST KNOWN ADDRESS _____
_____   _____

NAME _____   NAME _____
DOB _____ SSN _____   DOB _____ SSN _____
LAST KNOWN ADDRESS _____   LAST KNOWN ADDRESS _____
_____   _____

COMPANIES _____   COMPANIES _____
_____   _____
_____   _____

COUNTIES TO BE   1)_____   3)_____   5)_____
SEARCHED   2)_____   4)_____   6)_____

TYPE OF SEARCH REQUESTED:
_____ UCC's (County and Secretary of States)   COPIES ☐YES ☐NO
_____ Property (Real & Personal)   COPIES ☐YES ☐NO
_____ Judgments/Liens   COPIES ☐YES ☐NO
_____ Bankruptcy (specify County _____)   COPIES ☐YES ☐NO
_____ Federal Civil Actions   COPIES ☐YES ☐NO
_____ Motor Vehicles (including boats/planes)   COPIES ☐YES ☐NO
_____ Assumed Names   COPIES ☐YES ☐NO
_____ Incorporation Info. Ltd. Partnerships   COPIES ☐YES ☐NO
_____ All of the Above   COPIES ☐YES ☐NO

Figure 8.6 Request for investigation.

Policies of access will depend on the type of institution as well. For example, educational institutions are guided by a host of privacy and data rules that make easy access an impossibility. While colleges and universities will allow confirmation of attendance or a degree granted, access to a transcript without the party's consent is nothing more than a pipe dream. Federal agencies are more aggressively guided by "sunshine" or "right to know" policies than their state counterparts. As a result, federal records, such as criminal convictions, civil litigation records, federal tax liens, and bankruptcy filings, are not difficult to acquire. Statutory designs and even internal agency and entity policies will have much to do with how much information can be garnered with or without the permission of the target.

8.2.2.2 Employment history

From the first day of application to the date of resignation, retirement, or termination, employment history manifests a great deal about the investigative subject. In employment settings, the application form serves as a significant tool in screening applicants and verifying the identities and conduct of present employees. The form should be a detailed document that is sensitive to legal issues. To accomplish its divergent purposes, an application should address these topical concerns:

- Request an applicant to write his/her name and address on an application.
- Ask an applicant if a complaint has been placed against him/her or if he/she has been indicted or convicted of a crime and under what name.

Investigator's Checklist

Subject: _____ Date received: _____

Position applied for:

Application review

1. Handwriting: Note any areas requiring further attention:
2. Area number-social security number:
3. Address and telephone number: note any discrepancies:

Previous employers

1. Verify dates of employment, job responsibility, etc.
2. Employers' comments:

Schools and/or colleges

1. Correspondence-response received?
2. Results of personal visit, if required:

Licenses held

1. DMV check
2. Department of State-Division of Licensing
3. County, town, and/or city clerk
4. Police Department
5. Education Department
6. Coast Guard
7. Insurance Department
8. Health Department
9. Other

County clerk (town or city registrar's) office

1. Criminal Index
2. Civil Index
3. Judgment & Liens Index
4. Mortgage Index
5. Filings under UCC

District Court

1. Criminal Clerk's Index
2. Civil Clerk's Index

U.S. District Court

1. Criminal Index

Summary of interview with references: Verify how long reference has known subject, and how reference came to know the subject:

Police Department

1. Any field interrogations
2. Other information given by police sources

Results of neighborhood investigation

1. Indicate who was interviewed, and where they live in relation to the subject
2. Substance of the interview:

Attach consumer report (if needed).

Figure 8.7 Investigator's checklist.

- Ask an applicant's age (only if the information is an occupational qualification).
- Explain to an applicant the hours and days he/she will be required to work.
- Ask if applicant is a U.S. citizen, or if he/she has the intent to become one.
- Ask about schooling, both academic and vocational.
- Inquire about relevant work experience.
- Inquire into his/her character and background.

1. Name Verification
   a. Telephone directory (either print or online)
   b. Credit records
   c. Pretext
2. Address Verification
   a. Telephone directory (either print or online)
   b. Credit records, etc.
   c. Pretext
   d. Utility Bills
3. Voter Registration
   Check principals to identify full name, confirm address, place and date of birth, social security number (if available), spouse, and other residents of household.
4. Assumed/Fictitious Business Names
   In some states, this may be referred to as Fictitious Name, DBA (doing business as), or Fictitious Business Name.
5. Secretary of State
   Check Secretary of State records to confirm ownership of corporations and limited partnerships.
6. Property Tax Records
   Identify all properties, real and personal, owned by the individuals or companies at the time of the last tax roll, and obtain copies, if necessary.
7. County Clerk Records
   a. Pull all documents identified in the Appraisal/Assessor's Office.
   b. Obtain copies of all Warranty Deeds and Deeds of Trust for those properties identified.
   c. Check the Indexes for any property transactions since the last tax roll up to the present date.
   d. Check Indexes for properties sold in the last two years and obtain copies of the documents.
   e. Check Indexes for liens and abstracts of judgments, to include re¬leases, for the past five years, and obtain copies. Make note of any other information identifiable with principals.
   f. Check for oil and gas information.
8. Filings
   Check Uniform Commercial Code filings (financing statements) at County and State levels, to identify assets other than real property.
9. Divorce Records
   Check divorce records at county level to obtain list of property (assets) awarded in proceedings.
10. Bankruptcy
    Check bankruptcy records at servicing Federal courts to obtain list of assets and creditors, and statement of filings.
11. Federal Civil Cases
    Check Federal civil records for judgments, pending cases, etc.

Figure 8.8 Investigation sequence.

- Ask for name, address, and relationship of person to be notified in case of an accident or emergency.
- Inquire into applicant's military experience in the U.S. Armed Forces. After hiring, ask to see discharge papers.
- Ask an applicant about memberships in organizations that may indicate race, religion, or national origin.
- Ask an applicant if he/she belongs to an organization advocating the overthrow of the U.S. government.
- Ask the sex of the applicant only where it constitutes a qualification for the job.[16]

Employers who design their own application forms need to be conscious of issues that raise red flags—particularly legal ones. Under some state and federal legislation, certain types of questions from prospective employers are inappropriate, such as

- Asking an applicant whose name has been changed to disclose the original name.
- Inquiring as to the birthplace of an applicant or applicant's family if outside the United States.
- Requiring an applicant to produce discharge papers from the U.S. Armed Forces (before employment).
- Inquiring into foreign military experience.
- Asking an applicant's age when it is not an occupational qualification or is not needed for state or federal minimum age laws.
- Asking about an applicant's race or color.

---

[16] T. Ricks, B. Tillett, & C. Van Meter, *Principles of Security* 204–205 2nd ed. (1988).

- Requiring an applicant to provide a photograph with the application.
- Asking an applicant to disclose membership in organizations that may indicate race, religion, or national origin.
- Asking a male applicant to provide the maiden name of his spouse or his mother.
- Asking the place of residence of an applicant's spouse, parents, or relatives.
- Inquiring whether an applicant's spouse or parents are naturalized or native citizens.
- Asking an applicant his religion.[17]

Similarly, federal consumer legislation has restrictive guidelines regarding information on these matters:

- Records of arrests, indictments, or conviction of crimes where the disposition of the case, release, or parole has been more than seven years prior to the date of application.
- Any bankruptcies that have been more than fourteen years before the application.
- Any paid tax liens, legal suits or judgments, or other such information that has a harmful effect.[18]

From the outset, it is important to determine the breadth of the background investigative request. In Figure 8.9, the client, referred to as subscriber, has placed an order regarding a certain applicant. The items in the lower section of

Personnel Investigation Request

Client _____ Date _____

Address _____

Report to _____ Tel. # _____

Applicant's Name _____ Tel. # _____

Home Address _____

Previous Addresses _____

_____

DOB _____ Driver's License # _____

Sex _____ Nationality _____ Ht _____ Wt _____ SS# _____

Marital Status _____ Spouse _____ Maiden Name _____

Dependants _____

Education (High School, College, Trade School, etc.)

_____

_____

_____

Employment (past & present)

Name & Address	Position & Supervisor	Date

Services Ordered (please check)

☐ Credit	☐ Education	☐ Present Employment
	☐ Neighborhood	
☐ Court	☐ (present) ☐ (previous)	☐ Previous Employment
☐ Criminal	☐ Motor Vehicle Record	☐ Industrial Accident Record

Figure 8.9 Personnel investigation request.

[17] *Ibid.* at 205–206.
[18] *Ibid.* at 206.

Request for Employment Information

Dear

The above name applicant applied to use for a position of considerable responsibility. The applicant has stated you can verify the following information:

[insert data]

Is the above information correct? _____. If not please provide correct information.

From your personal knowledge or available records, would you recommend the applicant for employment with us? _____. If no, please explain on reverse side.

Do you consider the applicant to be of good character? _____. If no, please explain on reverse side.

If the applicant was employed by you, please indicate:

Reason for termination _____			
Eligible for re-employment	Yes	No	
Quality of Work	Good	Satisfactory	Poor
Attendance Record	Good	Satisfactory	Poor
To your knowledge, does the applicant use illegal drugs?		Yes	No
Or associate with anyone involved with illegal drugs?		Yes	No

Please use the reverse side of this letter to inform us of any additional comments concerning this applicant. If you prefer, you may contact me personally at the phone number below.

This applicant is aware of this inquiry and has voluntarily authorized us to conduct a background investigation. Your reply will be kept confidential.

Figure 8.10   Request for employment information.

the document, where the subscriber is asked to choose from a menu of services—credit, court, criminal, education, neighborhood, motor vehicle, present employment, previous employment, and industrial accident records—indicate the range of choices the investigator has in deciding the breadth of investigation.

Oral assertions about the applicant's reputation are hearsay (second- or third-hand remarks) and are therefore of little value. Quality and professionalism of a background investigation depend on written documentation. Information regarding the applicant's use of drugs, attendance record, and overall quality of labor can be requested from the applicant's previous employer (Figure 8.10) and is a mandatory attachment to a finalized report on the applicant's employment background.

8.2.2.3 Credit history

Some security professionals hold that a subject's credit history, whether good or bad, is a reflection of character. Individuals who properly handle financial affairs, who intelligently weigh assets and liabilities, who do not take undue risk, or who do not show a history of impulsive buying, are usually considered reliable. Regulatory acts, such as the Fair Credit Reporting Act, limit inspection. However, documents such as the authorization permit shown in Figure 8.11 allow access.

Unless consent is given or there are statutory exemptions in federal and state law, investigators have restricted access to credit reports. Typically, the reverse side of a credit report explains the terms, conditions, and rules of construction for the interpretation of the credit report. The investigator should check local telephone directories for address and phone numbers of companies that specialize in tracking and reporting credit histories. Some of the more prominent companies engaged in the business are:

- Equifax
- Experian
- Trans Union Credit Information Co.

Name and Address or Guarantor

Full name of Guarantor (1): _____

Signature: _____

Date: _____

Address: _____

Full name of Guarantor (2): _____

Signature: _____

Date: _____

Address: _____

Figure 8.11   Credit investigation inquiry form.

- Dun & Bradstreet
- National Association of Credit Management

At a minimum, a credit report makes an honest, though not perfect, attempt to reflect the overall credit history of an individual. Although the report deals mostly with forms of public credit, such as that reported by banks, investment companies, credit card companies, or other personal grant of credit, the results are not all-encompassing. Investigators should realize some of the more obvious omissions:

- Credit acquired under an assumed or changed name
- Credit not publicly reported, such as a loan between parent and child
- Mortgages/personal loans provided by owners of property in a land transaction
- Temporary lines of credit or corporate loans for key executives

Weighing credit-worthiness calls for an examination of many other sources and documents. Access to a courthouse is essential for an investigator reviewing an individual's credit background and financial stability. According to the American Society for Industrial Security:

> Information on real estate transactions or occupational or business licenses applied for by the subject or his spouse are a matter of public record. Information on divorces, civil litigation, suits, judgments, and other pertinent matters may be found in the files of the county. Both the subject and his spouse may be checked.[19]

Direct or inferential evidence regarding financial data and credit-worthiness can be collected from numerous sources:

- Credit bureaus
- Banks and financial institutions
- Employment records
- Local sources
- Public records
- Collection agencies
- Directories
- Key informants
- Newspapers
- Investment manuals
- Landlords

---

[19] American Society for Industrial Security, *Basic Guidelines for Security Investigations* 71 (1981).

- State authorities
- Collection services
- Federal government
- Post offices
- Stock exchanges
- Company or person being investigated
- Investment firms
- Creditors
- Insurance companies
- Trade references[20]

To determine the exact scope of the financial investigation, the investigator should rely upon a document such as that shown in Figure 8.12. The assignment form has a "confirm/verify" section and a courthouse record search section to pinpoint the types of activities the client wishes to undertake.

Often, the search for credit-worthiness deals with the subject's assets and overall net worth. The investigator requests a review of the applicant's credit, businesses or corporations owned, real property, security interests, and other

Assignment Form

To _____ From _____ Date Assigned _____	
Assigned to _____ Requested by _____	
Cost Limitation _____ Completion date _____	

Request is made for your office to conduct an asset search, or other specified investigation on the following individuals and/or businesses

Name   Address
_____
_____
_____
_____

Please search the following areas covering a period of at least five years unless requested otherwise. Provide telephone numbers for each subject and/or business assigned and verify all possible information through pretext calling. Obtain copies of all complete documents pertinent to this investigation.

Please direct your research to the following counties and include the following search areas for each of the subjects and/or businesses assigned.

Counties: _____
_____

CONFIRM/VERIFY

Resident address – resident telephone number – present ownership of residence –
Market value – marital status – business status – business telephone number

COURTHOUSE RECORDS SEARCH

Deed records – UCC filings – assumed names – tax assessor – tax liens –
Criminal and civil records – bankruptcy – divorce – probate – voter registration – motor vehicles

Other _____
Special instructions _____

Figure 8.12 Assignment form.

---

[20] Pinkerton's Inc., *Investigations Department Training Manual* 97 (1990).

Asset Investigation Authorization

Date Rec'd _____ Due Date _____

Subject _____ Investigator _____

Address _____ Completed _____

_____ Date Mailed _____

SS# _____ Auth. Hrs. _____

SS# _____ Auth. Rate _____

Employer _____ Mileage _____

_____ County _____ State _____

Summary of report _____

_____

_____

_____

_____

Daily Progress of investigation

Date	Description	Hrs	Exp
	Credit		
	Corp.		
	CPF		
	Real Property		
	UCC		
	SS# Trace		
	Address Update		
	Neighborhood Search		

Figure 8.13   Asset investigation authorization.

personal information. The hours, expenditures, and authorization rates for fees and expenses are also calculated. See Figure 8.13 for a sample form.

Information on real property can be found in a courthouse. The review of real property can also determine the liens and liabilities currently attached against the property, such as mortgages, promissory notes, judgments, and other secured or liened interests.[21] Figure 8.14 has the necessary language and clauses to thoroughly document the current state of liabilities against specific real property.

The investigator must also be aware of personal property information recorded at the offices of tax assessors, recorder of deeds, or register of wills. In some jurisdictions, personal property tax forms listing stocks, bonds, other negotiable instruments, and even jewelry and other delineated personal property must be filed annually. An excellent worksheet for recording this information is included in Figure 8.15.

A search of motor vehicle records through the Division of Highway and Public Safety or other governmental authority provides another insight into the asset and liability quotient of a subject. Primary and secondary liens on the title of a vehicle suggest overextended credit or larger-than-normal liabilities. Boats and aircraft are also reportable in a central registry such as the Department of Marine Resources or the Federal Aviation Administration. This type of information can be recorded on a form such as that shown in Figure 8.16.

At the Secretary of State's office or other office of corporate and consumer business filings, Uniform Commercial Code filings or financing statements, evidencing a secured interest in another person's property, are centrally stored.

[21] See C.P. Nemeth, *The Reality of Real Estate* (2007).

Date Searched   Subject   County, State

Real Property

Our investigation in _____ County, _____ (State) revealed

The following information pertaining to _____

Type of Deed: _____

Date Filed: _____

Volume & Page No. _____

Grantor: _____

Grantee: _____

Property Location: _____

Property Description: _____

_____

A promissory note dated _____ in the amount of _____

is payable to _____ (Lender & City).

The current assessed value of property if _____

Type of Deed: _____

Date Filed: _____

Volume & page No. _____

Grantor: _____

Grantee: _____

Property Location: _____

Property Description: _____

_____

A promissory note dated _____ in the amount of _____

is payable to _____ (Lender & City).

The current assessed value of the property is _____

_____
Initials

Figure 8.14   Real property investigation form.

Owners who have property and tangible assets that have sizable or inordinate financing statements on record often evidence a troubled financial situation. According to O'Block:

> Serious indications of financial instability, which could lead to employee dishonesty, include a history of declared bankruptcies, defaults, and repossessions. Financial strains of this type may induce an employee to steal from the employer as a means of getting additional income or could force the employee to take a second job, which could cause decreased proficiency in the first job.[22]

The party who owes money is the debtor and the party who has extended credit is the secured party. Collateral is the property pledged as security during the life of the loan.[23] Figure 8.17 is a sample of a form that can be used to record UCC filings.

Figures 8.18 through 8.20 are useful to record information related to judgments, liens, and bankruptcies. A variety of security enterprises exclusively emphasize these types of service.

---

[22] R. O'Block at 193.

[23] See C.P. Nemeth, *The Paralegal Resource Manual* 226 3rd ed. (2007).

Date Searched _____   Subject _____   County, State _____

Personal Property

Year of Tax Roll: _____

Obtained from: _____ Tax Assessor's Office

_____ Tax Appraisal District

Owner _____

Property Location: _____

Property Description: _____

_____

Valuation _____

Volume & page No. _____

Owner _____

Property Location: _____

Property Description: _____

_____

Valuation _____

Volume & page No. _____

Owner _____

Property Location: _____

Property Description: _____

_____

Valuation _____

Volume & page No. _____

_____

Initials

Figure 8.15   Personal property investigation sheet.

Because private individuals often funnel assets through corporate and partnership enterprises, the investigator cannot acquire a true and accurate representation of overall net worth or credit-worthiness without consideration of other business entities. Through various legal maneuverings and other corporate machinations, a subject may have transferred personal assets into corporate entities to render them untouchable. With this in mind, the investigator must always undertake an assessment of the subject's companies or corporate interests. The information regarding a company's officers, shareholders, and the like are accessible through the Secretary of State or other delegated agency. A sample of a form to record this type of data is shown in Figure 8.21.

8.2.3 Additional methods of background investigation

In an age of electronically accessible information, there has been an unfortunate tendency to skip some of the more traditional methods of assessing personal backgrounds, personal character, and reputation in the community. Mechanical and computer-based models of personal review are good to be sure but the polished and professional investigator need not forget some of the tried-and-true methods, such as "References" in oral interview or written form; testing systems that measure personality traits and value orientation; as well as voluntary polygraph tests to confirm or corroborate background. A summary of each follows.

8.2.3.1 References for character, competency, and reputation

Background investigators should cherish what others think of a candidate under review, for any assertion made, confirmed, and corroborated by another party is worth a close look. References provide that window to another and deliver a perspective that fleshes out a more accurate picture of the party under assessment.

Date Searched _____   Subject _____   County, State _____

Vehicles

Owner _____

Year, Model, Make: _____

License #, State: _____

Vehicle ID Number: _____

Lien Date: _____

Lien Holder & Address: _____

_____

Value (Approx): _____

Remarks: _____

Owner _____

Year, Model, Make: _____

License #, State: _____

Vehicle ID Number: _____

Lien Date: _____

Lien Holder & Address: _____

_____

Value (Approx): _____

Remarks: _____

_____

Initials

Figure 8.16   Vehicle ownership investigation form.

References were once the chief means of personal evaluation and assessment, but as a result of the rise of technology, information sharing, and the polygraph machine, references have taken a backseat.[24] Nevertheless, reference documents, such as that at Figure 8.22, are still one of the most reliable methods for assessing a person's character.

The reference system has come to be viewed as a cumbersome, difficult, and unreliable process for many reasons: (1) the investigator had to track down the author of the reference to assess the integrity of the information, (2) the content and quality of the references is never uniform, and (3) the fear of lawsuits for falsehoods or misinformation, even when innocently made, make an honest evaluation unlikely. "Consequently, employers have come to put little faith in the traditional reference letters because they themselves refuse to be candid in responding when such questionnaires reach their own desks."[25]

Investigators who have read enough of these documents to understand their language and the implications that come forth recognize a good evaluation at once—the author is unequivocal in commendation. Mediocre or even negative assessments often are presented in a bland or neutral commendation, such as: "The applicant really tries hard," or "It's a shame the applicant has to leave, but he feels there are better opportunities elsewhere." Experienced investigators can differentiate the language of commendation versus the language of mediocrity.

References have long been part of the employment process even in the age of technical methods in background review. From the very beginning of most search processes, the reference creates a history of the applicant that is fully

---

[24] P. Mirfield, Character and Credibility, *Crim. L. Rev.* (March 2009) at 135.

[25] J. Barefoot, at 191.

Date Searched	Subject	County, State

Uniform Commercial Code Filings
(Financing Statement)

Instrument Number: _____

Date Filed: _____

Debtor: _____

Secured Party: _____

_____

Collateral: _____

_____

_____

This UCC is also filed with the: _____
                              (Secretary of State/County)

under number _____ dated _____

Instrument Number: _____

Date Filed: _____

Debtor: _____

Secured Party: _____

_____

Collateral: _____

_____

_____

This UCC is also filed with the: _____
                              (Secretary of State/County)

under number _____ dated _____

_____
Initials

Figure 8.17   UCC filings.

available to all human resource professionals as well as other offices in the enterprise. References become part of the systematic decision making for those entrusted with assuring a verifiable background. A recent innovation in the area of reference review verifies previous positions, but goes deeper, evaluating critical traits of success and matching competency needs with candidate backgrounds—it is reflected in Proforma Screening Solutions's Tru-View reference management solution, as well as other such companies providing screening services.

Web Exercise: Find out more about Proforma's Tru-View Reference management product at http://tru-view.com/solutions.cfm.

In the final analysis, reference letters tell us much about personal and professional backgrounds, although there is both an art and science to proper interpretation of the content.[26] However, reliance on electronic records alone seems shortsighted for those tasked with painting an accurate profile of a candidate.

---

[26] C. White, The Pros and Cons of Writing Letters of Recommendation, *The Chronicle of Higher Education* (October 11, 2012), at http://chronicle.com/article/The-ProsCons-of-Writing/134926, last accessed August 28, 2016.

Date Searched   Subject   County, State

Judgments

Case Number: _____

Court of Record: _____

Volume & Page Number: _____

Date Filed: _____

Petitioner vs. Defendant: _____

Amount of Judgment: _____

Case Number: _____

Court of Record: _____

Volume & Page Number: _____

Date Filed: _____

Petitioner vs. Defendant: _____

Amount of Judgment: _____

Initials _____

Figure 8.18 Judgments.

Date Searched   Subject   County, State

Liens
(Tax, Mechanics, or Materialman's)

Document Number: _____

Date Filed: _____

Amount of Lien: _____

Petitioner vs. Defendant: _____

Document Number: _____

Date Filed: _____

Amount of Lien: _____

Petitioner vs. Defendant: _____

Document Number: _____

Date Filed: _____

Amount of Lien: _____

Petitioner vs. Defendant: _____

Initials _____

Figure 8.19 Liens.

```
_____       _____       _____
Date Searched                   Subject                         County, State

                                    Bankruptcy
                                (Financing Statement)

Name of Bankrupt: _____

Case Number: _____

Date Filed: _____

Type of Bankruptcy: _____
                    (Voluntary/Involuntary – Chapter 7, 11, or 13)


U.S. Bankruptcy Court: _____      _____
                              (District)                              (Location)


Status (Choose One):        □ Pending        □ Closed

If closed, disposition: _____

List or provide copies of assets, debts and creditors.

                                                          _____
                                                          Initials
```

Figure 8.20 Bankruptcy.

8.2.3.2 Testing and consultative services

Character and reputation as well as basic behavioral dispositions are often measured by quantitative means—by testing and personality assessment. Police departments and other government agencies have long relied upon and continuously search for accurate, objective methods of assessing applicants for both staff and line officers. In the world of policing, how do we know that the applicant's overall disposition fits the traits necessary to be a successful officer? Private security companies are increasingly dealing with this issue and the terrorist Omar Mateen, who worked and was licensed in the security industry, was obviously poorly screened and scrutinized. Coming up with objective tools to measure character traits and personality has long been the province of social and behavioral scientists.

Web Exercise: Try a personality self-assessment at https://www.testpartnership.com/personality.html.

Social and behavioral scientists are increasing their visibility in background investigations by creating tests and other evaluative methodologies for the workplace. Tests of various forms and construction have been devised in the following areas:

- Personality
- Minnesota Multiphasic Personality Inventory
- The Glueck Predictability Table
- The Kvaraceus Delinquency Scale and Checklist
- The Rorschach Test
- Honesty or integrity
- Drug or alcohol usage
- Productivity and efficiency
- Work history
- Service capacity and relations
- Conduct and personal habits

Date Searched

Subject

County, State

Companies/Corporations
Incorporation

Our search of the records of the _____ Secretary of State Office revealed the following
(State)

information pertaining to

Corporation Name: _____

Address: _____

Charter Number: _____

Date of Incorporation: _____

Registered agent: _____

Officers: _____ Title: _____

Officers: _____ Title: _____

Officers: _____ Title: _____

Status: _____

Corporation Name: _____

Address: _____

Charter Number: _____

Date of Incorporation: _____

Registered agent: _____

Officers: _____ Title: _____

Officers: _____ Title: _____

Officers: _____ Title: _____

Status: _____

_____

Initials

Figure 8.21 Business investigation form.

One of the leaders in consultative background screenings and evaluations is Vangent Human Capital Management, formerly Reid Psychological Services, established in 1947, and located at 200 South Michigan Avenue, Chicago, Illinois 60604. Through a series of surveys and testing instruments—mainly in a yes-and-no format—multiple areas of character and personality development can be measured, like integrity or honesty. In the service test, a party's desire to establish effective and helpful relationships with customers, peers, and supervisors are the measurable factors. Specifically, the Reid Report Assessment helps identify job applicants with high levels of integrity who are likely to become productive employees by assessing and measuring the following dimensions:

- Integrity
- Social behavior
- Substance
- Work background[27]

Personality and character traits run the gamut and are hard to fully quantify; however, most fall in what is commonly labeled the "Big Five," namely,

---

[27] See Creative Organizational Design website at http://www.creativeorgdesign.com/tests_page.php?id=204, last accessed August 28, 2016.

To Whom It May Concern

I have known _____ for approximately two years. As the Director of the Criminal Justice Program, I am responsible for the evaluation of all faculty teaching within the program. In fulfilling this responsibility I am able to develop an awareness of the abilities demonstrated with the classroom. I have found _____ to be a mentally mature, emotionally intelligent, and highly sensitive professional person who works very well with people. He represents his ideas articulately and with enthusiasm. He certainly has had a profound effect upon my perception of the role of educator; he is able to combine research, intellectual concern, and communication arts into a very practical and understandable reality for the student.

Over the past year _____ has developed a sustained record of academic excellence in teaching, professional development, and service to the college. His consistently positive student evaluations reflect a unique ability to relate complex abstract material to the daily experiences of students' lives and a capacity to maximize the motivation of the students with diverse needs and varying histories of academic anxiety. As such, _____ has scheduled classes at times inconvenient to himself so as to accommodate the needs of shift workers who must change schedules from day to evening classes over the course of a semester. He has successfully instilled a love for learning in housewives, police officers, plant workers, and younger students with a history of academic failure.

_____ has an excellent basic understanding of the nuances of everyday living which gives him a rather remarkable ability to work effectively with the more difficult pragmatic realities of life. In addition, he works well within our social system and confronts issues and problems rationally and intelligently within a professional framework.

_____ is a superior member of the teaching profession and a dedicated force to the professionalism of our criminal justice system. I recommend him with the highest respect I can hold for an individual.

Figure 8.22   Reference letter.

1. Extroversion
2. Emotional stability
3. Agreeableness
4. Conscientiousness
5. Openness to experience

Testing instruments tend to be objective by design, the bulk being yes–no formats or sliding scales of opinion. A sample page is shown in Figure 8.23.

8.2.3.3 Polygraph and lie detector technology

Before the passage of the Polygraph Protection Act of 1980, the provisions of which became effective in the latter part of 1988,[28] the polygraph was considered by many American businesses as the instrumental means of background investigation and review. Thus, before 1989, there were "tens of thousands of companies…that utilize[d] polygraph screening for job applicants."[29] State and other federal laws have placed extensive limitations on preemployment screening. As a result, individual internal investigations are encumbered, which causes employers and security vendors to be uncertain about the future role of the polygraph.[30] Even so, public employees still engage security firms to conduct such tests. For example, the polygraph is still regularly utilized in police applicant screening since consent must be given by that applicant.[31]

In addition, the polygraph is a tool for the prosecutor's office as it seeks to screen and test the veracity of the defendant's claim of innocence. Here too the defendant must consent. The admissibility of the polygraph results, except in the restrictive case of stipulation of the parties, has yet to be witnessed in the American legal system.

Polygraphs are freely usable with consent and many sensitive occupations still employ the machinery and others have employed the technology as a sort of negotiator—for those who proclaim innocence, by way of example, may willingly submit to prove their claims. Even so, the public and intellectual community still have extraordinary suspicions about the mechanical capacity to deal with truth or falsity.[32] See Figure 8.24.

---

[28] See Congressional Record, Vol. 131, No. 148, S. 1815 (1988).

[29] J. Barefoot, at 192.

[30] C.P. Nemeth, Erosion of Privacy Right and Polygraphs, 21 *Forensic Sci. Int'l* 103 (1984).

[31] M. Handler et al., A Focused Polygraph Technique for PCSOT and Law Enforcement Screening Programs, 38 *Polygraph* 77 (2009); A.-M. Leach et al., The Reliability of Lie Detection Performance, *L. & Human Behav.* (February 2009) at 96.

[32] See the American Psychological Association's general distrust at: The Truth about Lie Detectors, at http://www.apa.org/research/action/polygraph.aspx.

Please read each statement carefully and then mark the appropriate response below. Use the following scale to record your responses:

1	2	3	4	5
Strongly disagree	slightly disagree	neutral or cannot decide	slightly agree	strongly agree

----- 1. I get upset easily.

----- 2. I enjoy being part of a group.

----- 3. I like to solve complex problems.

----- 4. I believe that others have good intentions.

----- 5. I am always prepared.

----- 6. I have a low opinion of myself.

----- 7. I have a natural talent for influencing people.

----- 8. I enjoy the beauty of nature.

----- 9. I try to anticipate the needs of others.

----- 10. I can be trusted to keep my promises.

----- 11. I get irritated easily.

----- 12. I have a lot of fun.

----- 13. I like to visit new places.

----- 14. I love to help others.

----- 15. I set high standards for myself and others.

Sum up the following items to see how you score on five general personality traits. The numbers below indicate which questions correspond to each trait. A high score indicates a stronger level of that trait:

1	6	11	Neuroticism
2	7	12	Extraversion
3	8	13	Openness/Intellect
4	9	14	Agreeableness
5	10	15	Conscientiousness

Figure 8.23 Personality testing instrument. Modified versions of items included in the International Personality Item Pool (IPIP),* which is a rich source of personality-related content in the public domain. For more information about IPIP, go to http://ipip.ori.org. *Note*: *L.R. Goldberg, J.A. Johnson, H.W. Eber, R. Hogan, M.C. Ashton, C.R. Cloninger, & H.C. Gouth, The International Personality Item Pool and the Future of Public-Domain Personality Measures 40, *Journal of Research in Personality* 84–96 (2006).

The legal and ethical restrictions concerning the use of polygraphs have never succeeded in ending this method of evaluation and while there may be many constraints in its usage, the proliferation of groups, associations, and professional bodies that engage the polygraph has never been larger. See Figure 8.25 for the full sweep of polygraph organizations and their respective web locations.

Web Exercise: Learn about the American Polygraph Association at www.polygraph.org.

8.3 EXECUTIVE PROTECTION

In both personal and personnel security, the need to protect a body from harm remains the central task of the security specialists. Whether it is the President or a celebrity, these protected parties are in deep need of highly sophisticated and learned security services. Corporate executives, wealthy families, dignitaries, celebrities, politicians, and military leaders, by way of illustration, are enhanced targets for those seeking to do harm. It is the very nature of a public figure to be in someone's crosshairs at one point or another.

Exactly how these figures operate under safe cover depends on a host of issues although there are some predictable and mandatory steps that weave their way into effective techniques of executive protection. First, there has to be an effective operational philosophy in place for assuring protection of the targeted person—and both the person

Figure 8.24   Subject taking a polygraph test. (Courtesy of Manchester Police Department, Manchester, New Hampshire at www. manchesterpolice.org.)

protected and the protector must be on the same page. Second, every executive protection program must understand the law of the land in order that protection be feasible, given geopolitics, geography and environmental factors, present state of security where the protected principal or party might be, and other factors that give context to the operational plan. "Advance" planning may be the most crucial step for the overall strategy, knowing where and in what conditions the principal might find himself or herself. Some call this planning a program of "protective intelligence" that anticipates what may happen along the executive's route.[33] The need for "intelligence-led operations" is particularly crucial in overseas and international travel, especially in the present age of terrorist instability.[34] Long before any transport or movement of the principal, the security professionals must be completely familiar with the space encountered, totally anticipatory of potential threats and pitfalls, and prepared to both protect and extract the protected party in the event of difficulty. The executive protection professional must predict even the unpredictable in order to mitigate harms in the care and protection of a client. Some of the more common issues in the "advance" planning stage consider these factors:

Predeparture preparations	Preliminary telephone contacts
Biographical data and risk survey	Threat assessment
Intelligence reports	Arrival sites at the city of visit
Airport arrivals and departures surveys	Private and corporate aircraft
Hotels	Vehicles and vehicle equipment
Chauffeur responsibilities and guidelines	Setting up a 24/7 command center
Route surveys	Travel contact information
International travel plans	Building surveys
Restaurant surveys	Maritime survey public appearances
Bomb threats and procedures	Handling mail and packages
Weapons of mass destruction response	Technical countermeasures sweep
Hospital survey	Medical and police response
First aid	

[33] R.D. Bond, One-on-One Protection, *Sec. Mgmt.* (October 2005) at 85.
[34] C. Meyer, Never Too Vigilant, Using Executive Protection Services Overseas, *Sec. Mag.* (February 2015) at 30.

National Polygraph Organizations
American Association of Police Polygraphists - http://www.policepolygraph.org/
American Polygraph Association - http://www.polygraph.org/
National Polygraph Association - http://www.nationalpolygraph.org/

Regional Polygraph Associations
Midwest Regional Polygraph - http://www.midwestregionalpolygraph.org/
Northwest Polygraph Examiners Association - http://www.nwpea.net/

State Polygraph Associations
Arizona Polygraph Association - http://www.azpa4truth.org/
California Polygraph Association - http://www.californiapolygraph.com/
Colorado Association of Polygraph Examiners - http://www.coloradopolygraph.org/
Florida Polygraph Association - http://www.floridapolygraph.org/
Georgia Polygraph Association - http://www.georgiapolygraph.org/
Indiana Polygraph Association - http://www.indianapolygraphassociation.com/
Kansas Polygraph Association - http://www.kansaspolygraph.org/
Kentucky Polygraph Association - http://www.kypolygraph.org/
Maryland Polygraph Association - http://www.mdpolygraph.org/
Michigan Association of Polygraph Examiners - http://www.michiganpolygraph.org/
Missouri Polygraph Association - http://www.missouripolygraph.com/
Nebraska Association of Polygraph Examiners - http://www.nebraskapolygraph.com/
New York State Polygraph Examiners Association - http://www.nyspea.com/
North Carolina Polygraph Association - http://www.northcarolinapolygraphassociation.org
Ohio Association of Polygraph Examiners - http://www.ohiopolygraph.org/
Texas Association of Law Enforcement Polygraph Investigators - http://www.talepi.com/
Texas Association of Polygraph Examiners - http://www.texaspolygraph.org/
Utah Polygraph Association - http://www.utahpolygraph.org/
Virginia Polygraph Association - http://www.vapolygraph.com/

APA Certified Polygraph Schools
Academy for Scientific Investigative Training - http://www.polygraph-training.com/
American International Institute of Polygraph - http://www.polygraphschool.com/
Backster School of Lie Detection - http://www.backster.net/
Department of Defense Polygraph Institute - http://www.ncca.mil/
International Academy of Polygraph - http://www.deception.com/polygraph_school.html
Maryland Institute of Criminal Justice - http://www.micj.com/
Pennsylvania State Police/Harrisburg Area Community College Polygraph Institute - http://www.virginiaschoolofpolygraph.com/
Virginia School of Polygraph - http://www.virginiaschoolofpolygraph.com/

International Polygraph Associations
British & European Polygraph Association - http://www.europeanpolygraph.org/
Israel Polygraph Examiners Association - http://www.polygraph.org.il/
Latin American Polygraph Association - http://www.alponline.org/

Polygraph Examiner Listings
Global Polygraph Network - http://www.polytest.org/
The Polygraph Place - http://www.polygraphplace.com/

Research & General Information
Crime Beat Gazette - http://www.thecrimebeatgazette.com/
CrimeLynx - http://www.crimelynx.com/forensic.html
Dr. Charles Honts Research Site - http://truth.boisestate.edu/
Emerald Journals - http://www.emeraldinsight.com/info/journals/pijpsm/pijpsm.jsp
National Polygraph Consultants - http://www.nationalpolygraphconsultants.com/
The Polygraph Place - http://www.polygraphplace.com/

Polygraph Insurance
Complete Equity Markets - http://www.cemins.com/additional/poly.html

State Licensing Information
Virginia Polygraph Examiners Advisory - http://www.state.va.us/dpor/pol_main.htm

Polygraph Law
Americans for Effective Law Enforcement, Inc. - http://www.aele.org/
Policing.com - http://www.policing.com/

State Regulatory Agencies
Arkansas - http://www.state.ar.us/directory/detail2.cgi?ID=1083
Texas - http://www.txdps.state.tx.us/polygraph/index.htm

International Associations
Vidocq Society - http://www.vidocq.org/

Current Books & CD's for Polygraph
J.A.M. Publications - http://www.mattepolygraph.com/

Equipment Sales & Service
Lafayette Instrument Company - http://www.lafayettepolygraph.com/

Figure 8.25   Polygraph organizations.

Most companies that deploy executive professionals plan by an advance committee where the parties brainstorm the potential for harm and insecure settings. Others suggest that, especially in corporate settings, a "crisis management team" be established and be already in place in the event of actual threat.[35]

Third, aside from planning, produce a working document that guides the protection of the principal such as an advance security survey or threat assessment. In this way, the parties memorialize and educate one another on the various issues that could be encountered. An example of such a survey is given in Figure 8.26.[36]

Fourth, effective executive protection, once it has amassed all needed intelligence, needs to engineer a plan that draws in all the players and the various locations where this protection will occur. Some refer to this oversight as a sort of "choreography," being sure, by way of example, that transportation needs are fully interconnected and conducive to safe passage. Depending on the complexity of the protection, this task can be logistically challenging. Make sure that the plan of protection works in the real world of personal residence, of typical commutes by air, train, or car, and even on foot. In addition, be certain that across this time, space, and methods of mobility, that communication capacity is always functional as well as secure from cyber-attack. Check that the methods of transport can withstand a terror attack in select cases or that the protected persons have sufficient personal protection from armed assault. Finally, implement effective countersurveillance techniques that target and prospectively identify potential enemies. In sum, the task of executive protection is no minor matter but one that blends sophisticated business, intelligence, and security protocols.[37]

The growth and dynamism of executive protection services are undeniable so much so that ASIS has established a council fully dedicated to its research and best practices. Public police are simply incapable of providing these high-level and very labor-intensive services. In addition, the protection of executives and celebrities calls for cutting-edge technology, vehicles, and equipment, a luxury most public departments simply cannot afford.

Every aspect of executive protection takes on added meaning, even simple transport, by auto or other method. In the case of auto travel, the executive is particularly prone to possible capture or injury. Since executive protection specialists are hired to ensure safety as the celebrity or executive moves from locale to locale, the industry expects the safest and most reliable techniques to assure safety. See Figure 8.27.

Bill Zalud delineates common errors in this responsibility:

1. Improper vehicle distance from other vehicles
2. Too rural a geographic destination
3. Excessive red light and other stopping
4. Poor maintenance on the vehicle
5. Gaudy, loud vehicles bringing attention to the movement
6. Lack of safety equipment
7. Parking in dark areas
8. Failure to check vehicle—inside and out
9. Driving alone
10. Failure to notify others in the event of threat[38]

Web Exercise: Visit the ASIS Council on Executive Protection at https://www.asisonline.org/Membership/Member-Center/Councils/Executive-Protection-Council/Pages/default.aspx.

ASIS recently launched a Certification in Executive Protection whose content coverage includes

- Threat assessment
- Advance procedures

[35] Purpura, *Security: An Introduction* 248 (CRC, 2011).
[36] Independent Security Advisors, Site Survey, at http://dignitaryprotection.us/isa/wp-content/themes/revolution-20/pdf/ISA_enhanced_Site_Survey.pdf, last accessed August 28, 2016.
[37] B. Zalud, Executive Protection Grows, 94 *Sec. Mag.* (August 2008) 94.
[38] B. Zalud, C-Suites at Home and on the Road, *Sec. Mag.* (June 2009) at 70–71.

SITE SURVEY

Survey NCOIC:	SURVEY DATE:
PRINCIPAL #:	MISSION DATE:

GENERAL INFORMATION

NAME OF LOCATION / SITE:

NAME OF HOST:	PHONE:
PRIMARY POC:	PHONE:
SITE SECURITY POC:	PHONE:

Site Security Information

Outer Cordon:
- ☐ Police
- ☐ Site Security
- ☐ Other

POC
PHONE
Radio Freq:

- ☐ Exterior security check points
- ☐ Traffic control points
- ☐ Vehicle Gate entry
- ☐ Pedestrian gate entry
- ☐ Outer Roving patrol
- ☐ Lateral routes and roads secured
- ☐ Air space controlled
- ☐ Waterway security
- ☐ Other

Middle Cordon:
- ☐ Police
- ☐ Site Security
- ☐ Other

Venue/Building/Site Security:
- ☐ Police
- ☐ Site Security
- ☐ Other

Site security staff
- ☐ Uniformed
- ☐ Plain clothes
- ☐ Armed
- ☐ Speak English
- ☐ Vetted

    Number on duty   **DAY**   **NIGHT**

POC
PHONE
Freq:

- ☐ Interior Roving patrol
- ☐ Exterior roving patrol
- ☐ Security check points
- ☐ Access control to each floor
- ☐ Access control to elevator
- ☐ Access control to stairs
- ☐ Access control to parking area

SECURITY OR PROTOCOL AT CHECKPOINTS:
- ☐ X-Ray of handbags
- ☐ Magnetometer
- ☐ Check of Invitation or Tickets
- ☐ Hand screen/search
- ☐ Check IDs

How long has building been secured

- ☐ Is there an access roster to the site
- ☐ Badge requirements for approved access

Will the site be cleared prior to arrival   Y   N

How far in advance will the building be cleared or swept

- ☐ EOD or dog search teams available

OFFICIAL USE ONLY

Figure 8.26   Site survey form.

(Continued)

SITE SURVEY

Event associated with visit

☐ **Meal**	☐ **Menu**
☐ **Meeting**	☐ **Guest or attendee list**
☐ **Tour**	☐ **Seating chart**
☐ **Press conference**	☐ **Tour route map**
☐ **Graduation/Ribbon cutting**	☐ **Floor plan**
☐ **Other**	☐ **Copy host site security plan**

Event site sweeps ☐ **EOD** ☐ **K-9** ☐ **X-RAY**	**POC** **PHONE** **POC** **PHONE**

IS THERE A RECEIVING LINE? ☐ No ☐ Yes Location:	**WILL A GIFT BE PRESENTED TO THE PRINCIPAL?** ☐ No ☐ Yes Presenter:

DESCRIBE THE WALKING ROUTE FROM THE DROP OFF POINT TO THE FUNCTION:

WILL ELEVATOR(S) BE USED AT THIS SITE? ☐ Yes ☐ No ☐ N/A	**WHAT IS THE CAPACITY OF THE ELEVATOR(S)?** Weight:_____ Max Occupants:_____
WILL ELEVATOR(S) BE LOCKED-DOWN? ☐ No ☐ Yes POC for Keys:	**WHAT FLOOR IS THE FUNCTION ON?**
IF PRINCIPAL WILL USE STAIRS, HOW MANY FLIGHTS?	**LOCATION OF SAFE HAVEN:**

DESCRIBE THE WALKING ROUTE FROM FUNCTION TO SAFE HAVEN:

DESCRIBE THE EVACUATION ROUTE FROM FUNCTION TO THE MOTORCADE:

Nearest Medical facility and trauma level:
POC:
PHONE:
Freq:

LOCATION OF NEAREST RESTROOM TO FUNCTION SITE:

WERE BACKGROUND CHECKS CONDUCTED OF STAFF THAT WILL BE CLOSE TO THE PRINCIPAL?
☐ Yes
☐ No
☐ N/A

OFFICIAL USE ONLY

ISA Advance Form 1	Page 2 of 7	Encl #

Figure 8.26   (Continued) Site survey form.   (*Continued*)

SITE SURVEY

HOLDING ROOM WHERE PRINCIPAL CAN HAVE A PRIVATE

CONVERSATION:_____

OBTAINED KEYS TO PRINCIPAL S HOLDING ROOM:
- ❑ Yes   POC:_____
- ❑ No   Phone # _____
- ❑ N/A

LOCATION OF HOLDING ROOM FOR STAFF IF SEPARATED FROM

PRINCIPAL:_____
_____

OBTAINED KEYS TO STAFF HOLDING ROOM:
- ❑ Yes
- ❑ No
- ❑ N/A

Other PSDs on site during visit/event
- ❑ YES
- ❑ NO
- ❑ N/A

Organization or agencies
POC
PHONE
Freq

POC
PHONE
Freq

Are there other events that may impact visit
- ❑ Yes
- ❑ No
- ❑ n/a

Are there protests, demonstrations planned due to this visit/event
- ❑ Yes
- ❑ No
- ❑ n/a

ARRIVAL INFORMATION

LOCATION WHERE HOST WILL GREET PRINCIPAL:
- ❑ Curbside, in front of main entrance
- ❑ Inside main entrance
- ❑ N/A (No Host)
- ❑ Other:

COPY OF FLOOR PLAN ATTACHED:
- ❑ Yes
- ❑ No
- ❑ N/A

ARRIVAL TIME:

DEPARTURE TIME:

ARRIVAL / DEPARTURE AREA OF MOTORCADE:
- ❑ Curbside, in front of main entrance
- ❑ N/A (Walking)
- ❑ Other:_____

PARKING AREA FOR MOTORCADE / PARTY VEHICLES:
- ❑ Vehicles will remain curbside
- ❑ Parking lot adjacent to function site
- ❑ Parking Garage adjacent to function site
- ❑ N/A (Walking)
- ❑ Other:

NEAREST SECURE TELEPHONE/RADIO WHERE PRINCIPAL CAN PLACE A CALL: PHONE NUMBER:

PRESS/PAO

WILL THERE BE PRESS COVERAGE AT THIS SITE?
- ❑ No
- ❑ Yes   How Many?_____

POC FOR PRESS:

WHERE WILL THE PRESS BE LOCATED:
- ❑ Throughout function site
- ❑ Upon arrival (curbside)
- ❑ Upon departure (curbside)
- ❑ Organized, indoor press conference
- ❑ Other:

OFFICIAL USE ONLY

ISA Advance Form 1   Page 3 of 7   Encl #

Figure 8.26   (Continued) Site survey form.   (Continued)

SITE SURVEY

WERE PRESS CREDENTIALS VERIFIED BY HOST OR POC?	TYPE OF PRESS COVERAGE:
☐ Yes ☐ No ☐ N/A	☐ National News / Television / Video ☐ Magazine / Newspaper / Photographers ☐ Still pictures or Video only (no questions) ☐ Armed Forces Radio/TV (US or Host)

PAO Requests;

Airfield

Location:

BASE OPNS / FLIGHT OPNS POC:	PHONE:
SECURITY POC:	**PHONE:**
DV LOUNGE / HOLDING ROOM POC:	**PHONE:**

TYPE OF AIRPORT:	AIRPORT HOURS OF OPERATION:	TARMAC IS ACCESSIBLE:
☐ US International ☐ US Civilian/Commercial ☐ Private ☐ Military	☐ 24 Hours ☐ Other: _____	☐ 24 Hours ☐ Other: _____

ARRIVAL INFORMATION

TYPE OF AIRCRAFT:	CIVILIAN AIRCRAFT EQUIVALENT:
TAIL NUMBER:	**CALL SIGN:**

MOTORCADE STAGING AREA:	WILL THERE BE AN HONOR CEREMONY?
☐ Adjacent to aircraft, on tarmac ☐ Adjacent to DV Lounge; principal will enter DV Lounge prior to motorcade movement ☐ Other:	☐ No ☐ Yes How Many?

WHO WILL GREET THE PRINCIPAL?

WILL THE AIRCRAFT REQUIRE A STAIRCASE?	POC:	PHONE:
☐ No, stairs are self contained ☐ Yes How Many?		

CONVEYOR BELT FOR BAGGAGE?	POC:	PHONE:
☐ No ☐ Yes How Many?		

LUGGAGE / BAGGAGE UNLOADING PROCEDURE:	DOES THE AIRPORT ASSIST/PROVIDE BAGGAGE HANDLERS?
☐ Plane-side; baggage truck will go directly to rear of aircraft after plane stops ☐ Other:	☐ Yes ☐ No

OFFICIAL USE ONLY

Figure 8.26   (Continued) Site survey form.   (Continued)

SITE SURVEY

WILL THERE BE PRESS COVERAGE? ❏ No ❏ Yes How Many?_____ POC FOR PRESS:	LOCATION OF PRESS: ❏ Throughout function site ❏ Upon arrival (curbside) ❏ Upon departure (curbside) ❏ Organized, indoor press conference ❏ Other:	TYPE OF PRESS COVERAGE: ❏ National News / Television / Video ❏ Magazine / Newspaper / Photographers ❏ Still pictures or Video only (no questions) ❏ Armed Forces Radio/TV (US or Host) ❏ Other:

DEPARTURE INFORMATION

MOTORCADE ARRIVAL AREA: ❏ Adjacent to aircraft, on tarmac ❏ Adjacent to DV / Departure Lounge ❏ Other:	HONOR CORDON / DEPARTURE CEREMONY? ❏ No ❏ Yes How Many? _____

WHO WILL FAREWELL THE PRINCIPAL?

WILL THE AIRCRAFT REQUIRE A STAIRCASE? ❏ No, stairs are self contained ❏ Yes How Many?	POC:	PHONE:
CONVEYOR BELT FOR BAGGAGE? ❏ No ❏ Yes How Many?	POC:	PHONE:

LUGGAGE / BAGGAGE LOADING PROCEDURE: ❏ Plane-side; baggage truck will go directly to rear of aircraft ❏ Other:	DOES THE AIRPORT ASSIST / PROVIDE BAGGAGE HANDLERS? ❏ Yes ❏ No

WHERE WILL BAGGAGE SWEEP TAKE PLACE?
❏ Airport; plane-side
❏ Other – Explain:

TYPE OF BAGGAGE SWEEP: ❏ K-9	POC:	PHONE:
❏ X-Ray	POC:	PHONE:
❏ Magnetometer	POC:	PHONE:

WILL THERE BE PRESS COVERAGE? ❏ No ❏ Yes How Many?_____ POC FOR PRESS:	LOCATION OF PRESS: ❏ Throughout function site ❏ Upon arrival (curbside) ❏ Upon departure (curbside) ❏ Organized, indoor press conference ❏ Other:	TYPE OF PRESS COVERAGE: ❏ National News / Television / Video ❏ Magazine / Newspaper / Photographers ❏ Still pictures or Video only (no questions) ❏ Armed Forces Radio/TV (US or Host) ❏ Other:

Closest Medical Facility

Location Grid Street Map Imagery FOB PB	Type ❏ Aid station ❏ Cache ❏ Hospital	POC Phone Freq

TYPE OF FACILITY

❏ CIVILIAN ❏ MILITARY	❏ INPATIENT WITH EMERGENCY ROOM	❏ INPATIENT W/O EMERGENCY ROOM	❏ OUTPATIENT WITH EMERGENCY ROOM	❏ OUTPATIENT WITHOUT ER

OFFICIAL USE ONLY

ISA Advance Form 1   Page 5 of 7   Encl #

Figure 8.26   (Continued) Site survey form.   (*Continued*)

SITE SURVEY

EMERGENCY ROOM INFORMATION	
EMERGENCY ROOM PRIMARY POC:	**PHONE: (Direct Line)**
EMERGENCY ROOM ALTERNATE POC:	**PHONE:**
AMBULANCE SERVICE:	**PHONE:**
MED-EVAC POC:	**PHONE:**

DESCRIBE FACILITY'S MED-EVAC PROCEDURE:

DURING MED-EVAC, WOULD PSO BE ABLE TO STAY WITH PRINCIPAL?
❑ Yes
❑ No   Explain:

IS THIS FACILITY CAPABLE OF STABILIZING AND EVACUATING ANY INJURY OR MEDICAL CONDITION?
❑ Yes
❑ No   Explain:

IS THE EMERGENCY ROOM EASY TO LOCATE BY VEHICLE?
❑ Yes
❑ No   Explain:

IS THE EMERGENCY ROOM OPEN 24 HOURS?
❑ Yes
❑ No   Explain:

IS AN ENGLISH SPEAKING INTERPRETER ON-DUTY 24 HOUR A DAY?
❑ Yes
❑ No
❑ N/A

❑ **Emergency Room**	❑ **X-Ray**	❑ **Cardiologist**	❑ **Neurosurgeon**	❑ **Whole Blood**
❑ **Trauma Unit**	❑ **Burn Unit**	❑ **Operating Team**	❑ **Heliport**	❑ **MED-EVAC**

The agencies identified below were each asked to provide the undersigned with any information that may adversely impact this visit or event.

	❑ Yes [Critical / High / Medium / Low / Negligible] (circle one)		
Venue security /Local Police	❑ Yes (See Telephone Contact Sheet)	❑ No	❑ N/A
State Police	❑ Yes (See Telephone Contact Sheet)	❑ No	❑ N/A
Federal law enforcement	❑ Yes (See Telephone Contact Sheet)	❑ No	❑ N/A
Federal Intelligence Agency	❑ Yes (See Telephone Contact Sheet)	❑ No	❑ N/A
Other	❑ Yes (See Telephone Contact Sheet)	❑ No	❑ N/A

OFFICIAL USE ONLY

ISA Advance Form 1	Page 6 of 7	Encl #

Figure 8.26   (Continued) Site survey form.

(Continued)

SITE SURVEY

❏ **No, there was no adverse or threat information developed or identified.**

❏ **Yes, threat information was developed (see attached report).**

MOVEMENT #:	SCHEDULED DEPARTURE TIME / DATE:
FROM:	TO:
DISTANCE (MILES/KILOMETERS):	TRAVEL TIME (MINUTES):
SAFE HAVEN DURING MOVEMENT:	PHONE NUMBER:
HOSPITAL DURING MOVEMENT:	PHONE NUMBER:
PRIMARY ROUTE MAP ATTACHED: ❏ Yes ❏ No Reason:	ALTERNATE ROUTE MAP ATTACHED: ❏ Yes ❏ No Reason:
Comments:	

Lead Vehicle	License # / Model
Dvr:	

Limo	License # / Model
Dvr:	

Chase	License # / Model
Dvr:	

Chase	License # / Model
Dvr:	

OFFICIAL USE ONLY

Figure 8.26   (Continued) Site survey form.

SECURITY GUARD/EXECUTIVE PROTECTION AGENT QUALIFICATIONS

Minimum qualifications for all security positions:

US citizenship required.

Must be at least 19 years of age at time of application for Entry Level Security Guard; 21 years of age for Executive Protection Agent.

Must have 2 years verifiable prior Executive Protection experience (applies only to Executive Protection position).

(1) Minimum: High school diploma or GED equivalent; (2) Preferred: Bachelor's degree from an accredited college or university; or (3) and equivalent combination of education and related experience.

Vision: Must be correctable to at least 20/30 (either eyeglasses or contact lenses).

Excellent physical health with no disabling physical or mental condition.

Interview: In-depth interview to determine an applicant's suitability for security and/or high-level public figure protection, which includes, but is not limited to, the person's appearance, personality, maturity, temperament, background, and ability to communicate.

Must not have a history of criminal or improper personal conduct that may affect suitability for security and/or hig-level public figure protection. (Complete and thorough background investigation.)

Reading and Writing Ability. Be able to read and write fluent English at the levels necessary to perform the job.

Valid California Class C driver's license.

Valid U.S. Passport and International Certificates of Vaccination. (Required only for Executive Protection Agents on international travel assignments.)

Valid certification in Adult, Infant, and Child CPR / First Aid

Visible Tattoos and Branding: An Agent, while on-duty, shall not display any tattoos and/or branding. Agents shall cover all tattoos/branding by wearing an authorized long-sleeved uniform shirt if in uniform; if in business attire, the business attire shall cover all tattoos. However, if an Agent has only one tattooed/branded area of a three-inch square or less to cover, the Agent may, instead of wearing a long-sleeved shirt, cover that area with only one patch, of a color as close to the wearer's skin color as is reasonably available, up to a three-inch square. If the tattoo/branding area is more than can be covered by a three-inch square skin patch, the Agent shall wear the long-sleeved uniform shirt or business attire, as appropriate for the assignment. The intent is that no tattoos/branding shall be visible and that no more than one three-inch square skin patch shall be visible.

California Bureau of Security and Investigative Services (BSIS) guard registration for Entry Level Security, and exposed firearms permit (for Executive Protection position only). *Applicants must be qualified for .40 caliber. Applicants who do not yet have these licenses may still apply but must demonstrate submission of license application to the State.*

For more information on California licensing, click the State of California Department of Consumer Affairs logo below.

Figure CP8.2   Career Profile: Executive protection.

Figure 8.27   Executive protection professionals must remain vigilant on behalf of their clients at all times.

- Choreography of protection
- Countersurveillance
- Emergency extraction of the principal
- Working with foreign security providers
- Detecting armed adversaries
- Transportation security
- The lone gunman
- Managing and directing an EP program

Web Exercise: Find out about the new certification exam for executive protection offered by the American Board for Certification for Dignitary and Executive Protection at http://www.abchs.com/pdf/cdep%20candidate%20hand-book.pdf.

8.4 SPECIAL SECURITY PROBLEMS IN THE WORKPLACE ENVIRONMENT

Aside from the many preliminary phases that review backgrounds, character, and reputation as well as personality traits, the security team and HR need to remain constantly vigilant concerning behavior in the workplace. David Hyle asserts that "workplace violence has grown into perhaps the most significant risk issue facing corporate security departments today."[39]

Great tragedies are now unfolding with regularity in the workplace environment. See Figure 8.28.[40]

From mass shootings and retaliation violence from former employees, from harassment to sexual criminality inflicted on employees, and from spilling over domestic violence to unstable employees inflicting harm on innocent employees, the safety and security of the workplace environment is not what it once was. Workplace violence is now a permanent fixture across the American economy and something that security professionals need to prepare for and defend, and the rates of violent acts vary by industry and vocation. For example, health care professionals, medical personnel, and social workers are under a stronger threat than comparable occupations.[41]

Despite this unfortunate advantage, every industry, business, vocation, and institutional entity is now laboring under the perpetual threat of workplace violence in some form. The Bureau of Labor Statistics (BLS) tracks fatalities, among

Violent crimes against victims working or on duty, 2008*

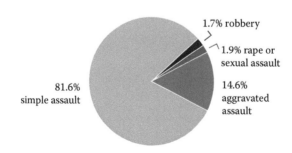

1.7% robbery

1.9% rape or sexual assault

14.6% aggravated assault

81.6% simple assault

* Percentage do not add up to 100 due to rounding.

Figure 8.28 Violent crimes against workers. (Data source: http://www.victimsofcrime.org.)

---

[39] D. Hyde, Workplace Violence: What Role for Corporate Security? *Sec. Mag.* (July 2011) at 56.

[40] Victims of Crime, *Workplace Violence*, at http://victimsofcrime.org/docs/default-source/ncvrw2014/workplace-violence-statistics-2014.pdf?sfvrsn=2, last accessed August 28, 2016.

[41] See OSHA, *Guidelines for Preventing Workplace Violence*, at https://www.osha.gov/Publications/osha3148.pdf, last accessed August 28, 2016.

Workplace homicide by type of crime

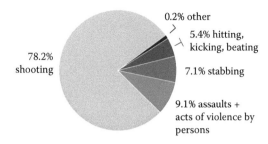

0.2% other

5.4% hitting, kicking, beating

78.2% shooting

7.1% stabbing

9.1% assaults + acts of violence by persons

Figure 8.29   Workplace homicide. (Data source: http://www.victimsofcrime.org.)

other injuries, in the workplace, and incredibly violent crime is now one of the chief reasons for death in the workplace. See Figure 8.29.[42]

Homicide is now the fourth leading cause of fatalities in the workplace. See Figure 8.30.[43]

The security plan should also not only educate the employees and management about how to deal with workplace violence but should also maintain strong public law enforcement contacts in the event of crime at the enterprise. On top of this, the security team should prepare the facilities, in a physical security sense, to prevent, detect, and provide sufficient means to subsequently investigate workplace violence incidents. Helpful physical security protocols include but are not limited to closed circuit cameras, silent alarms, metal detectors, two-way mirrors, electronic access systems, barriers to prevent cars from driving too close to the building, emergency internal code words, extra lighting in the parking lots, and escorts to and from parking lots after dark. Planning groups should review security measures and procedures and make recommendations for modifications and improvements as necessary.

Both federal and state laws now mandate preventative measures, educational programs, and other requirements to monitor violence in the workplace—especially as it regards "sexual" harassment and aligned criminality. Security departments make sure the business, industry, or other entity is compliant with these requirements for most security professional would argue that "prevention" is key to deterrence in the matter of workplace violence. Some facilities, such as behavioral or mental health facilities, offer very challenging security challenges.[44] Other facilities are far less challenging, although every security department of a workplace environment needs to visit what its terrain, its layout, and its condition presently are in order that violent acts be prevented.[45]

Every entity and institution needs to be cognizant and prepared for the unfortunate rise in sexual offenses. For example, the U.S. Coast Guard has just published its action plan to deal with these offenses.[46] The primary goal and aim of the Sexual Assault Prevention and Response program is to create an environment where victims can freely report violent action and the system remains objective and detached from a biased or prejudgment perspective. SAPR's overall mission is

> The Coast Guard's Sexual Assault Prevention and Response (SAPR) Program seeks to eliminate sexual assault by implementing and sustaining comprehensive SAPR strategies that focus on prevention, including awareness and cultural change, and response, including victim support, intimidation-free reporting, fair and impartial investigations, and accountability to protect the safety and well-being of all our Active Duty, Reserve, Civilian, and Auxiliary shipmates and their families.[47]

See Figure 8.31.

---

[42] See Victims of Crime, *Workplace Violence*.

[43] Bureau of Labor Statistics, Economic News Release, Table 1 (2016), at http://www.bls.gov/news.release/cfoi.t01.htm, last accessed August 28, 2016.

[44] A. Notaroberta, Workplace Violence Prevention: Team Collaboration is the Key, *Sec. Mag.* (March 2012) at 100.

[45] B. Scaglione, Workplace Violence Prevention Revisited, *Sec. Mag.* (June 2011) at 54.

[46] USMC, Sexual Assault Prevention & Response Strategic Plan 2013–2017, at http://www.uscg.mil/SAPR/docs/pdf/SAPR_strat_plan.pdf, last accessed August 28, 2016.

[47] *Ibid.*

Fatal occupational injuries by event or exposure, 2013-2014

Event or exposure(1)	2013(2) (revised)	2014p	
		Number	Percent
Total....................................	4,585	4,679	100
Violence and other injuries by persons or animals....................................	773	749	16
Homicides—intentional injury by other person....................................	404	403	9
Shooting by other person—intentional...	322	307	7
Stabbing, cutting, slashing, piercing....	38	39	1
Self-inflicted injury—intentional........	282	271	6
Transportation incidents....................	1,865	1,891	40
Roadway incidents involving motorized land vehicle................................	1,099	1,075	23
Roadway collision with other vehicle.....	564	566	12
Roadway collision—moving in same direction.........................	144	135	3
Roadway collision—moving in opposite directions, oncoming................	192	211	5
Roadway collision—moving perpendicularly.....................	136	120	3
Roadway collision with object other than vehicle.............................	332	294	6
Vehicle struck object or animal on side of roadway....................	311	269	6
Roadway noncollision incident...........	201	211	5
Jack-knifed or overturned, roadway.....	171	178	4
Nonroadway incidents involving motorized land vehicles.........................	227	246	5
Nonroadway noncollision incident.........	181	191	4
Jack-knifed or overturned, nonroadway..	118	127	3
Pedestrian vehicular incident..............	294	313	7
Pedestrian struck by vehicle in work zone	48	53	1
Rail vehicle incidents.....................	41	55	1
Water vehicle incidents....................	60	53	1
Aircraft incidents.........................	136	135	3
Fires and explosions........................	149	137	3
Falls, slips, trips.........................	724	793	17
Falls to lower level......................	595	647	14
Fall from collapsing structure or equipment............................	45	42	1
Fall through surface or existing opening	68	82	2
Fall on same level........................	110	129	3
Exposure to harmful substances or environments................................	335	390	8
Exposure to electricity....................	141	156	3
Exposure to temperature extremes...........	38	26	1
Exposure to other harmful substances.......	124	180	4
Inhalation of harmful substance..........	39	59	1

Figure 8.30   Fatal occupational injuries by event or exposure, 2013–2014.

(Continued)

Contact with objects and equipment...........	721	708	15
Struck by object or equipment..............	509	498	11
Struck by falling object or equipment— other than powered vehicle............	245	240	5
Struck by discharged or flying object....	29	21	(3)
Caught in or compressed by equipment or objects................................	131	131	3
Caught in running equipment or machinery	105	104	2
Struck, caught, or crushed in collapsing structure, equipment, or material.......	78	74	2

(1) Based on the BLS Occupational Injury and Illness Classification System (OIICS) 2.01 implemented for 2011 data forward.

(2) Totals for 2013 are revised and final. The BLS news release issued September 11, 2014, reported a total of 4,405 fatal work injuries for calendar year 2013. Since then, an additional 180 job-related fatal injuries were identified, bringing the total job-related fatal injury count for 2013 to 4,585.

(3) Less than or equal to 0.5 percent.

p Data for 2014 are preliminary. Revised and final 2014 data are scheduled to be released in spring 2016.

Note: Totals for major categories may include subcategories not shown separately. Percentages may not add to totals because of rounding. CFOI fatality counts exclude illness-related deaths unless precipitated by an injury event.

Source: U.S. Bureau of Labor Statistics, in cooperation with state, New York City, District of Columbia, and federal agencies, Census of Fatal Occupational Injuries.

Figure 8.30   (Continued) Fatal occupational injuries by event or exposure, 2013–2014.

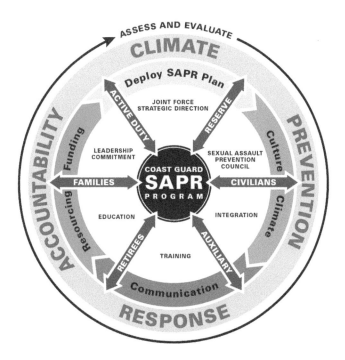

Figure 8.31   Coast Guard's SAPR program.

The Coast Guard's program is a model of human understanding, evidence preservation and investigative integrity, and most importantly, a cultural milieu that ultimately leads to prevention and cooperation among all interested parties. The C-suite high-level management must take seriously the impact of workplace violence on the bottom line both as to personnel and their health and happiness but also to an economic outlook of profitability. Nothing positive ever comes from a culture laden with violence in any form. Management should not treat workplace violence as a sideshow and instead see it as a major threat to institutional continuity. Felix P. Nater concludes that every nook and cranny of a business must be considered as a safe harbor for violence, from "threats posed by employee on employee, vendors, contractors, external threats away from the workplace, domestic violence spill-over and active shooter protocols."[48] And every company, business, and institutional entity has the capacity to cut back on violence by employing so many of the tried-and-tested strategies for personnel assessment and background checks. The C-suite cannot forget basic screening protocols to identify those ready to inflict violence. Human resources security, in steps and stages, goes a long way to preventing these horrid events. Those steps that edify the possibilities of violence include

- Background screening
- Hiring, retention, terminations
- Selection, training, assignments, and staffing
- Performance appraisals and promotions
- New employee orientations
- EAP counseling
- Employee relations
- Safety and injury prevention
- Workplace violence response planning and coordination
- Domestic violence and partner relationships[49]

Every company or entity must deal openly and professionally with the problems that can no longer be denied in the workplace.[50]

Security professionals always need to be on the lookout for signs and warning lights of those who may inflict workplace violence. W. Barry Nixon, founder and director of the National Institute for the Prevention of Workplace Violence, lists the "Unlucky 13 Signs" that trouble is around the bend, which are:

1. Threats: Person makes direct, veiled or conditional threats of harm.
2. Unreasonable: Person is never happy with what is going on. He or she is consistently unreasonable and overreacts to feedback or criticism. He or she has a tendency to take comments personally and turns it into a grudge.
3. Intimidation and Control-Oriented: Person feels a need to constantly force their opinion on other and/or has a compulsive need to control others.
4. Paranoid: Person thinks other people are out to get them. He or she thinks there is a conspiracy to all functions of society.
5. Irresponsible: Person doesn't take responsibility for any of their behaviors or faults or mistakes; it's always someone else's fault.
6. Angry, Argumentative & Confrontational: Person has many hate and anger issues with co-workers, family, friends or the government. He or she is frequently involved in confrontations and arguments and has low impulse control.
7. Violence Fascination and Acceptance: Person applauds certain violent acts portrayed in the media such as racial incidences, domestic violence, shooting sprees, executions, etc. and is fascinated with the killing power of weapons.
8. Vindictive: She or he often verbalizes hope for something to happen to the person against whom the employee has a grudge.
9. Bizarre Behavior: Person is quirky, strange; considered weird and behaves in unusual manner, their presence makes others feel uneasy and uncomfortable.

---

[48] F.P. Nater, Workplace Violence Prevention a Training Management Commitment, *Sec. Mag.* (October 2010) at 10.

[49] *Ibid* at 106.

[50] T. Scherwin & C. Calvert, Romancing the Workplace, *Security Management Online* (August 2012), at https://sm.asisonline.org/Pages/Romancing-the-Workplace.aspx, last accessed August 28, 2016.

10. Desperation: Person expresses extreme desperation over recent family, financial or personal problems.
11. Obsessions: Person has obsessive involvement with the job, particularly when no apparent outside interests exist.
12. Substance Abuse: Person has signs of alcohol and/or drug abuse.
13. Chronic Depression: Person displays chronic signs of depression, loss of interest and confident in life or work, is lethargic, lacks energy, particularly when this is a significant change in behavior.[51]

Web Exercise: For a case of a security firm, namely, Securitas, not having appropriate processes and procedures in place, and thereby suffering the legal remedies posed by the EEOC, see https://www.eeoc.gov/eeoc/newsroom/release/9-30-10l.cfm.

This section reviews the more typical challenges discovered in the workplace such as harassment and stalking, violent actions, as well as the brave new and very disturbing reality of the active shooter.

8.4.1 Harassment in its various forms

The gradations and stages of harassment are difficult to fully catalog. Harassment can surely start small with mere words as a foundation for eventual physical altercation. Harassment might be at first a misjudged remark, a sexual innuendo, or the result of escalating tension between workers.

Educating the workforce on how to react will surely assist in the overall handling of tension-filled events. The Federal Protective Service provides handy note cards to all its employees on what to do in these traumatic circumstances. See Figure 8.32.[52]

To be sure, not all contentiousness is the stuff of harassment and criminality but instead a reflection of predictable difficulties between employees and even management. Friction is a natural event in all workplaces and being overly legalistic is not helpful to the bottom line. What is certain is that harassment starts in smaller situations and evolves into a more complicated one. ASIS refers to this as a "continuum" of possible scenarios that may start out small and get big in scope and level of harm or stay put and never escalate beyond its initial confrontation. See Figure 8.33.[53]

Coping With Threats and Violence

For an angry or hostile customer or coworker

- Stay calm. Listen attentively.
- Maintain eye contact.
- Be courteous. Be patient.
- Keep the situation in your control.

For a person shouting, swearing, and threatening

- Signal a coworker, or supervisor, that you need help. (Use a duress alarm system or prearranged code words.)
- Do not make any calls yourself.
- Have someone call the FPS, contract guard, or local police.

For someone threatening you with a gun, knife, or other weapon

- Stay calm. Quietly signal for help. (Use a duress alarm or code words.)
- Maintain eye contact.
- Stall for time.
- Keep talking—but follow instructions from the person who has the weapon.
- Don't risk harm to yourself or others.
- Never try to grab a weapon.
- Watch for a safe chance to escape to a safe area.

Figure 8.32   Coping with threats and violence tips.

---

[51] C. Meyer, Building Workforce Protection on Awareness, Communication, *Sec. Mag.* (October 2013) at 46.
[52] Federal Protective Service, U.S. General Services Administration, at https://archive.opm.gov/Employment_and_Benefits/WorkLife/OfficialDocuments/handbooksguides/WorkplaceViolence/p3-s5.asp#security, last accessed August 28, 2016.
[53] ASIS International, *Workplace Violence Prevention and Response Guideline* 9 (Alexandria, VA: ASIS International, 2005).

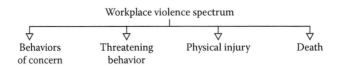

Figure 8.33 Workplace violence spectrum.

Harassment, like other forms of crime, has to start at the start, but given its predictability to evolve and escalate, it is a problem perpetually on the private security industry's radar screen.

An overview of common harassment contexts follows. Security specialists handling harassment and threat cases need to memorialize their investigations of these allegations since many of these actions are part of an escalating pattern of behavior. See Figure 8.34.

A great deal of human activity can be classified as abusive while there is a complete lack of physical aggression. People can be harassed in grotesque and frightening ways without any offensive contact. The crime of harassment attempts to fill the void and is also instructive about motive and past association with those suffering an even greater criminality. New York's first-degree harassment fits like a glove corralling these criminals.

> A person is guilty of harassment in the first degree when he or she intentionally and repeatedly harasses another person by following such person in or about a public place or places or by engaging in a course of conduct or by repeatedly committing acts which places such person in reasonable fear of physical injury.[54]

The key term "repeatedly" says much about the statute's direction. Repetitive conduct means numerous rather than few events.[55]

Harassment calls for more than bickering and disagreement but proof of a systematic pattern of behavior that truly offends the ordinary sensibilities of the average person. In the first-degree case, the accused parameters may involve some type of physical injury. In lower degrees of harassment, the intent is annoyance and actual or real threats of less severity.

When telephones or other communication devices are utilized as the instrument of harassment, legislatures have crafted menacing or aggravated harassment statutes, which mete out some severe penalties.[56] Without a pattern of communication, one that is continual and repetitive, the aggravated charge of menacing or harassment will not hold up.[57] If the conversations are infrequent and erratic, the charge is insufficient.[58]

Obscene phone calls have been the setting for a harassment charge when the content of the communications is demonstrably offensive to the average person.[59] Those who have been at the receiving end of obscene telephone calls understand the unsettling nature of the behavior. Defendants counter with free speech claims, though the First Amendment does not protect speech that is "lewd, lascivious, threatening or obscene words, language, drawings or caricatures,"[60] intended expressly to harass.[61]

---

[54] N.Y. Penal Law § 240.25 (McKinney 2010).

[55] In the area of sexual harassment, based on workplace behavior and in violation of employment and civil rights, laws are increasingly considering non-workplace harassment behavior as pattern evidence. A.M. Patterson, None of Your Business: Barring Evidence of Non-Workplace Harassment for Title VII Hostile Environment Claims, 10 *U. C. Davis Bus. L. J.* 237 (2010).

[56] N.Y. Penal Law § 240.30 (McKinney 2010).

[57] See People v. Rusciano, 171 Misc. 2d 908, 656 N.Y.S. 2d 822 (Town of Eastchester Justice Ct., Westchester Co. 1997), where court emphasized the telephone as central to the aggravated case. The gravamen of the crime of aggravated harassment is the use of the telephone, but for which the accompanying offending conduct would constitute, other elements being present, simple harassment. *Id.* at 913.

[58] See N.Y. v. Price, 178 Misc. 2d 778, 683 N.Y.S.2d 417 (City of New York Criminal Court, New York County, 1998).

[59] Harassment also has a civil remedy grounded in traditional torts in Civil Rights Acts depending upon the basis for the harassment. See Employment Law—Title VII—Third Circuit Issues Split Decision in Case Involving Gay Man's Harassment, 123 *Harv. L. Rev.* 1027 (2010); see also Prowel v. Wise Business Forms, 579 F.3d 285 (3d Cir. 2009).

[60] 18 Pa. Cons. Stat. § 1312(1) (2010).

[61] See Delaware v. Horowitz, 1998 Del. Super. 227 (1998).

Threat Report

Name of person(s) making threat _____

Relationship to company _____

Relationship to recipient of threat, if any _____

Name(s) of the recipients or victims _____
_____

Date and location of incident _____

What happened immediately prior to the incident _____
_____
_____
_____

The specific language of the threat _____
_____
_____

Any physical conduct that would substantiate an intention to follow through with the threat _____
_____

How the threat-maker appeared, both physically and emotionally _____
_____

Names of others who were directly involved, and any actions they took _____
_____
_____
_____

How the incident ended _____
_____
_____

Names of witnesses _____
_____
_____

What happened to the treat-maker after the incident _____
_____

What happened to other employees directly involved in the incident, if any _____
_____
_____

Names of any supervisory staff involved and how they responded _____
_____

What event(s) triggered the incident _____

Any history leading up to the incident _____

The steps that have been taken to assure the threat will not be carried out _____
_____
_____

Suggestions for preventing this type of incident from occurring again _____
_____
_____

Figure 8.34 Threat report.

In the area of sexual harassment on the job, the proponent typically takes advantage of civil remedies rather than criminal prosecutions. State and federal remedies for sexual harassment, particularly in employment settings, are extensive and are based on gender discrimination or the maintenance of a hostile work environment. EEOC remedies are not usually a criminal law matter, although cases can degenerate into subsequent liability.[62]

8.4.2 Stalking

Increasingly, workplace situations witness employees, for whatever reason—estranged love affairs, obsessive compulsive behaviors, and retaliatory behavior for discipline or denial of promotion or salary increase—who stalk another employee. The aim here is to frighten and intimidate the other employee. This type of behavior is typically witnessed in the celebrity and executive protection world where stalkers thrive. Stalking has a wide array of legal definitions and conceptual parameters but generally fall into the following sort of language:

> Stalking. (2003)
>   (a) OFFENSE DEFINED.-- A person commits the crime of stalking when the person either:
>   (1) engages in a course of conduct or repeatedly commits acts toward another person, including following the person without proper authority, under circumstances which demonstrate either an intent to place such other person in reasonable fear of bodily injury or to cause substantial emotional distress to such other person; or
>   (2) engages in a course of conduct or repeatedly communicates to another person under circumstances which demonstrate or communicate either an intent to place such other person in reasonable fear of bodily injury or to cause substantial emotional distress to such other person.[63]

In each stalking law, there are uniform expectations that the behavior be continuous or pattern driven; that creates fear and intimidation in the victim; and that lacks a legitimate purpose and causes mental and emotional anguish. All stalking laws call for more than simple inconvenience but adjudge the behavior by how a reasonable person would interpret the pervasive following and contacts.

Web Exercise: For a full list of stalking laws in all 50 jurisdictions, see https://victimsofcrime.org/our-programs/stalking-resource-center/stalking-laws/criminal-stalking-laws-by-state.

The extent of stalking victimization is difficult to fully compute, but it is clear that security professionals entrusted with personal protection and a safe work environment encounter the behavior with regularity. Some data on the breadth of stalking activity include these conclusions:

- 7.5 million people are stalked in one year in the United States.
- Over 85% of stalking victims are stalked by someone they know.
- 61% of female victims and 44% of male victims of stalking are stalked by a current or former intimate partner.
- 25% of female victims and 32% of male victims of stalking are stalked by an acquaintance.
- About 1 in 5 of stalking victims are stalked by a stranger.
- Persons aged 18–24 years experience the highest rate of stalking.
- 11% of stalking victims have been stalked for 5 years or more.
- 46% of stalking victims experience at least one unwanted contact per week.[64]

8.4.3 Protection from abuse/domestic/spousal abuse

The workplace frequently suffers from domestic violence spillage, meaning it is not uncommon for problems in the home to spill over into the work environment. Domestic violence encompasses "one person's use of emotional, physical, or sexual violence, or threat of violence to obtain control of another family member or intimate partner. Domestic violence may occur in the context of marriage, common-law relationships, or dating relationships and does

---

[62] For close calls that might allow the victim to avail of either civil or criminal remedies, see Fowler v. Kootenai County, 918 P.2d 1185 (Id. Sup. Ct., 1996) and Norris v. Hathaway, 1999 Neb. App. 4 (No. A-97-916) (1999).

[63] 18 Pa. C.S. § 2709.1.

[64] Victims of Crime, Stalking Resource Center, at https://victimsofcrime.org/our-programs/stalking-resource-center/stalking-information#vic, last accessed August 28, 2016.

not discriminate; it affects people from all walks of life, regardless of age, race, religious beliefs, educational background, income, or sexual preference."[65]

The fundamental dilemma for prosecution, under the historical offenses of assault, is the difficulty of proving a level of intentionality sufficient above and beyond the misdemeanor assault. Spousal abuse is far more complicated than a bar room brawl. On top of this, there is a general unwillingness on the part of the judicial system to invade the domestic province too aggressively. Courts do many things well but guarding the internal affairs of family is not their forte. Arguments and sometimes very heated exchanges between partners are natural over the life of any relationship. The fine and intricate lines between abuse and normal bickering are sometimes murky. Add to this the usual reticence witnessed in spouses that fight vigorously yet still hope to achieve a successful relationship, and the emotional crosscurrents can buffet the parties to positions that may not work in the world of common-law assault. Any experienced law enforcement officer will tell amazing and befuddling stories of how complicated these affairs can be, of how today's verbal and physical confrontations become forgiven before the first witness takes the stand.

So significant are domestic violence issues to the American workplace that business and industry have coalesced to end or inhibit their presence and very negative influences in the workplace. The Corporate Alliance to End Partner Violence is just one such group, and you can read about their mission and initiatives at www.caepv.org.

Governmental responses regarding the scourge of domestic violence have been vigorous to say the least. With these types of cases reaching the public domain and their corresponding increase, the federal government has passed a host of laws to protect its employees from the impact of domestic violence.[66]

Legislatures have been frantically trying to halt the tide of domestic violence but the patterns are not being significantly altered, and if there are signs of improvement, it is because the raw data are impacted by less formal, intimate partner relationship other than traditional family structure. This skews data because the tendency is to categorize the data by marriage or partners rather than live-in or changeable relationships. In essence, one side sees assault, while the other sees assault and spousal abuse. This is not a small matter statistically.

Web Exercise: To see the full extent of the domestic violence problem, visit http://www.census.gov/newsroom/cspan/2014/dom_violence.html.

The Domestic Violence Resource Center paints a picture of extraordinary victimization to individuals that eventually impacts the workplace. In its recent report,[67] it states:

- Nearly 33% of women killed in U.S. workplaces between 2003 and 2008 were killed by a current or former intimate partner.[68]

- Nearly one in four large private industry establishments reported at least one incidence of domestic violence, including threats and assaults, in 2005.[69]

- A survey of American employees found that 44% of full-time employed adults personally experienced domestic violence's effect in their workplaces, and 21% identified themselves as victims of intimate partner violence.[70]

- 64% of the respondents in a 2005 survey who identified themselves as victims of domestic violence indicated that their ability to work was affected by the violence. More than half of domestic violence victims (57%) said they were distracted, almost half (45%) feared getting discovered, and two in five were afraid of their intimate partner's unexpected visit (either by phone or in person).[71]

---

[65] R.T. Weitkamp, Crimes and Offenses, 16 *Ga. St. U. L. Rev.* 72, 73 (1999).

[66] U.S. Department of Labor, Workplace Violence Resources, at https://www.dol.gov/oasam/hrc/policies/dol-workplace-violence-program-appendices.htm#federallaws, last accessed August 28, 2016.

[67] Domestic Violence Resource Center, at http://www.dvrc-or.org/dv-facts-stats, last accessed August 28, 2016.

[68] H.M. Tiesman et al., Workplace Homicides among U.S. Women: The Role of Intimate Partner Violence, 22 *Annals of Epidemiology* 277 (2012), at http://www.annalsofepidemiology.org/article/S1047-2797(12)00024-5/abstract, last accessed August 28, 2016.

[69] U.S. Department of Labor News, Survey of Workplace Violence Prevention (2005), at http://www.bls.gov/iif/oshwc/osnr0026.pdf, last accessed August 28, 2016.

[70] Corporate Alliance to End Partner Violence, Workplace Violence, at http://www.caepv.org/getinfo/facts_stats.php?factsec=3, last accessed August 28, 2016.

[71] *Ibid.*

- Nearly two in three corporate executives (63%) say that domestic violence is a major problem in our society and more than half (55%) cite its harmful impact on productivity in their companies.[72]

- Nine in ten employees (91%) say that domestic violence has a negative impact on their company's bottom line. Just 43% of corporate executives agree. Seven in ten corporate executives (71%) do not perceive domestic violence as a major issue at their company.[73]

- More than 70% of U.S. workplaces do not have a formal program or policy that addresses workplace violence.[74]

- Nearly 8 million days of paid work each year is lost due to domestic violence issues—the equivalent of more than 32,000 full-time jobs.[75]

- 96% of domestic violence victims who are employed experience problems at work due to abuse.[76]

Many aspects of domestic violence in the workplace can be mitigated by training and preparation of security staff in order that these professionals understand the offense's extraordinary complexity. To be sure, the problems of the home will never be completely separate from the workplace, but trained security professionals will be able to spot problems before harm has been caused; to mediate and remedy specific conflicts; and to devise a plan or strategy that anticipates the employee laboring under severe emotional stress caused by domestic violence. The American Society for Industrial Security urges training in these distinct areas:

> *Background screening* for job applicants to uncover information such as criminal records, frequent job changes or the falsification of data in the resume or job application. While there might be valid explanations for frequent job changes, it's recommended that organizations adopt a zero-tolerance policy toward falsified or unexplained data.
>
> *Uniform policies and procedures for reporting and disciplining employees* who exhibit threatening behavior or engage in harassment, stalking, verbal abuse, theft, etc. To foster a fair and harmonious work environment, written policies and procedures must be universally applied and disseminated to all staff on the day they join the organization, so that no one can later claim he or she wasn't aware of the policies.
>
> *Conflict resolution training* for both supervisors and employees. Staff should learn how to help defuse potential violence rather than exacerbate it.
>
> *Zero-tolerance policies and procedures* regarding harassment and violence. These policies should be periodically reviewed to determine their effectiveness, and updated whenever necessary.
>
> *An employee grievance system.* Employees who aren't given the chance to formally air complaints may silently stew in their resentments until a "trigger" unleashes suppressed anger. An effective grievance system involves transparency, communication and followup with those who come forward. If employees believe that nothing has been done to address their complaints, they might assume that management has swept the issues under the rug, which can fuel simmering resentment.
>
> *Job counseling for laid-off workers.* Though job loss is a leading cause of workplace violence, few companies provide extended job counseling and outplacement services for terminated workers. Companies may reduce the risk of violence by demonstrating that they care enough about former employees to help them find new employment.
>
> *An effective crisis management plan.* This plan should be communicated company-wide and periodically rehearsed—like a fire drill. Preparing for a crisis is an essential step, but if you fail to thoroughly educate, communicate and train the staff—and then follow-up with "after-action reports"—the plan's shortcomings may not be apparent until the worst possible moment.[77]

8.4.4 Hate crimes and the workplace

Recent cases involving death or assaults based on racial, gender, or sexual motivation have certainly caught the public eye. Dragged from the rear of a pickup truck in Texas, or lynched unmercifully from a tree, these types of offenses

---

[72] Corporate Alliance to End Partner Violence, CEO & Employee Survey 2007, http://www.caepv.org/about/program_detail.php?refID=34, last accessed August 28, 2016.

[73] *Ibid.*

[74] *Ibid.*

[75] CDC, Intimate Partner Violence: Consequences, http://www.cdc.gov/ViolencePrevention/intimatepartnerviolence/consequences.html, last accessed August 28, 2016.

[76] Click to Empower, Domestic Violence Facts, http://www.clicktoempower.org/domestic-violence-facts.aspx, last accessed August 28, 2016.

[77] K. Carter, J. Lawrence, & R. Pohl, Workplace Violence: Prevention and Response 2–3 (Securitas, 2014), at http://www.securitasinc.com/global-assets/us/files/knowledge-center/whitepapers/workplace-violence---prevention-and-response_whitepaper.pdf, last accessed August 28, 2016.

Figure 8.35   President Barack Obama walks away from the lectern with Vice President Joe Biden after making a statement about the mass shooting in Orlando, Florida, June 16, 2016. (Official White House photo by Pete Souza.)

strike a most disconcerting chord in the American conscience.[78] Witnessed as national tragedy, they have triggered a host of legislative responses at both the state and federal level.[79] The same can be said about the Orlando mass murder in a targeted lesbian and gay bar, where the motivation seems at least partially driven by intense religious objections to homosexuality. For all those who work or labor in these settings, hate crime may directly impact life and limb. See Figure 8.35.

Yet, why are these offenses so specialized and differentiated from traditional assault offenses? Is not the beaten man the same as the beaten black youth? How does a person of one sexual orientation suffer any differently than the heterosexual whose face was smashed in or arms broken in a vicious attack? Objectively, the results are identical. Subjectively, does the assaulter who fights and attacks with rage, anger, jealousy, and envy appear slightly less malevolent than the predator waiting for a person of the Jewish faith or a gay man leaving work? Certainly, motivators vary, but the physical injury remains similar. If this be so, why craft "hate" crimes? The popular legislative consensus has been to enact competing versions of hate crime legislation.[80] Commencing with "ethnic intimidation" statutes, our political process sought to identify criminal acts that were reserved and motivated on account of ethnic or racial hatred. The act addresses criminal agents that possess more than the usual level of animus in the commission of the felony or misdemeanor since the object of the offense is grounded in racial, ethnic, or other motivation and by a "malicious intention."[81] See the statute from California below:

(a) No person, whether or not acting under color of law, shall by force or threat of force, willfully injure, intimidate, interfere with, oppress, or threaten any other person in the free exercise or enjoyment of any right or privilege secured to him or her by the Constitution or laws of this state or by the Constitution or laws of the United States in whole or in part because of one or more of the actual or perceived characteristics of the victim listed in subdivision (a) of Section 422.55.[82]

---

[78] M. Shepard & J. Byrd, Jr. Hate Crimes Prevention Act, Pub. L. No 111-84, §§ 4701-13, 123 Stat. 2190, 2835-44 (2009); D. Jackson, Obama Signs Hate-Crimes Law Rooted in Crimes of 1998, usatoday.com (October 28, 2009), at http://content.usatoday.com/communities/theoval/post/2009/10/6200000629/1; see also A.L. Bessel, Preventing Hate Crimes without Restricting Constitutionally Protected Speech: Evaluating the Impact of the Matthew Shepard and James Byrd, Jr. Hate Crimes Prevention on First Amendment Free Speech Rights, 31 *Hamline J. Publ. L. & Pol'y* 735 (2010).

[79] Matthew Shepard Act, §4704(a)(1); J.B. Woods, Ensuring a Right of Access to the Court for Bias Crime Victims: A Section 5 Defense of the Matthew Shepard Act, 12 *Chap. L. Rev.* 389 (2008).

[80] For an in-depth discussion, see J.M. Fernandez, Bringing Hate Crime into Focus, 26 *Harv. Cr-Cl L. Rev.* 261 (1991).

[81] 18 Pa. Cons. Stat. § 2710(c) (2010).

[82] Cal. Penal Code § 422.6(a) (West 2001). See also Md. Code, Public Safety, § 2-307 (West 2010); Fla. Stat. § 877.19 (2010); Idaho Code Ann. §18-7902 (2010); see also Fernandez, *supra* note 72, at 267 n.32.

The federal system has adopted a sophisticated civil rights labyrinth for victims to avail when suffering from this offense. Either by money damages or criminal sanction, the United States Code addresses the issue of hate motivated criminality in various quarters.[83] The FBI, especially as a result of fringe groups and historical terrorists like the KKK, has long been adept at strategies for ferreting out those inclined to such activities. In the FBI's *Training Guide*, the following recommendations are posed for law enforcement:

The types of factors to be considered by the Reporting Officer in making a determination of whether the incident is a Suspected Bias Incident are:

- Is the motivation of the alleged offender known?
- Was the incident known to have been motivated by racial, religious, disability, ethnic, or sexual-orientation bias?
- Does the victim perceive the action of the offender to have been motivated by bias?
- Is there no clear other motivation for the incident?
- Were any racial, religious, disability, ethnic, or sexual-orientation bias remarks made by the offender?
- Were there any offensive symbols, words, or acts which are known to represent a hate group or other evidence of bias against the victim's group?
- Did the incident occur on a holiday or other day of significance to the victim's or offender's group?
- What do the demographics of the area tell you about the incident?[84]

Federal law now requires hate crime statistics to be included in the Uniform Crime Report (UCR).[85] See the FBI Hate Crime Incident Report form in Figure 8.36.

8.4.5 Terroristic threats

Recent events surely highlight how the workplace becomes intensely victimized by those wishing to inflict terror on specific employer locations. While all traditional felonies apply in these cases of murder and mayhem, there are specialized crimes that highlight the employee seeking to make his or her mark by using terror as a tool. The San Bernardino case surely manifests how a simple holiday party can turn into the worst of possible nightmares. Whatever the place or location, security personnel need to be on the lookout for those motivated by terror purposes. After the fact, as is usually the case, the warning signs were there in great number and a failure to act by either private sector officers or the public system itself led the way to carnage. In terroristic threats, the action is anticipatory more than actual and it is where the actor uses the potentiality of terror to impress fear into his coworkers. Special legislative designs have been implemented to address situations in which touching or injury does not occur. As experience tells us, much can be coerced or extorted from people by threat, by the subtle manipulation of words, and by the play on emotion. The Russian KGB's victims often remarked that being killed was less troubling than anticipation of where and when one confrontation would occur. It is the threat that manipulates the psyche. It is the threat that leaves open the question of potential or actual injury. In this world of indecision and fear, the party who threatens knows the true story of the threat—the victim can only surmise and remain on edge.

If the threatening party denies the sincerity of the threat, the charge will still stick since it is the victim's reasonable perspective that drives the analysis. We cannot know what the defendant intends internally but we can discern what the words of the threat represent. In the *United States v. Myers*,[86] the First Circuit of the Court of Appeals evaluated the meaning of threat in the mind of both the speaker and the recipient. For it to be a threat, it must have the capacity to "create apprehension that its originator will act according to its tenor."[87] To constitute threat, the trier assesses how the recipient of the message could be expected to react under the "factual context in which the statement was made."[88]

Public buildings and places of assembly where threats force their evacuation are prime locales for this criminal act. Schools receiving bomb threats may rely on the language of the terroristic threat statute. Threatening actions that involve felonious conduct certainly fit the requirements of this important statute.

---

[83] See 18 U.S.C. §241 (2011). Victims of hate-motivated violence can sue for damages and injunctive relief under 42 U.S.C. §§ 1981–1982, passed as part of the Civil Rights Act of 1866.

[84] Federal Bureau of Investigation, Training Guide for Hate Crime Data Collection, Uniform Crime Reporting 21 (1996).

[85] The Hate Crime Statistics Act of 1990, P.L. N. 101-275 (Apr. 23, 1990).

[86] 104 F.3d 76 (5th Cir. 1997).

[87] U.S. v. Bozeman, 495 F.2d 508, 510 (5th Cir. 1974).

[88] U.S. v. Fulmer, 108 F.3d 1486, 1491 (1st Cir. 1997).

1-699 (Rev. 1-20-06)

OMB No. 1110-0015
Expires 10-31-10

HATE CRIME INCIDENT REPORT

Initial ☐ Adjustment ☐ ORI ☐☐☐☐☐☐☐☐☐ Date of Incident ___/___/___ (Month Day Year)

Incident No. ☐☐☐☐☐☐☐☐☐☐☐☐ **Page** ☐ **of** ☐ **of Same Incident**

Offense *(Enter an offense code and number of victims for each bias-motivated offense.)*

	Offense	# of victims		Offense	# of victims
#1	☐☐	☐☐☐	#3	☐☐	☐☐☐
#2	☐☐	☐☐☐	#4	☐☐	☐☐☐

01 Murder
02 Forcible Rape
03 Robbery
04 Aggravated Assault
05 Burglary
06 Larceny-Theft
07 Motor Vehicle Theft
08 Arson
09 Simple Assault
10 Intimidation
11 Destruction/Damage/Vandalism

Location *(Check one for Offense #1.)*

01 ☐ Air/Bus/Train Terminal
02 ☐ Bank/Savings and Loan
03 ☐ Bar/Night Club
04 ☐ Church/Synagogue/Temple
05 ☐ Commercial/Office Building
06 ☐ Construction Site
07 ☐ Convenience Store
08 ☐ Department/Discount Store
09 ☐ Drug Store/Dr.'s Office/Hospital
10 ☐ Field/Woods
11 ☐ Government/Public Building
12 ☐ Grocery/Supermarket
13 ☐ Highway/Road/Alley/Street
14 ☐ Hotel/Motel/etc.
15 ☐ Jail/Prison
16 ☐ Lake/Waterway
17 ☐ Liquor Store
18 ☐ Parking Lot/Garage
19 ☐ Rental Storage Facility
20 ☐ Residence/Home
21 ☐ Restaurant
22 ☐ School/College
23 ☐ Service/Gas Station
24 ☐ Specialty Store (TV, Fur, etc.)
25 ☐ Other/Unknown

Enter a Location for each offense having a different location than Offense #1:
#2 ☐☐
#3 ☐☐
#4 ☐☐

Bias Motivation *(Check one for Offense #1.)*

Race
11 ☐ Anti-White
12 ☐ Anti-Black
13 ☐ Anti-American Indian/Alaskan Native
14 ☐ Anti-Asian/Pacific Islander
15 ☐ Anti-Multiple Races, Group

Ethnicity/National Origin
32 ☐ Anti-Hispanic
33 ☐ Anti-Other Ethnicity/National Origin

Religion
21 ☐ Anti-Jewish
22 ☐ Anti-Catholic
23 ☐ Anti-Protestant
24 ☐ Anti-Islamic (Muslim)
25 ☐ Anti-Other Religion
26 ☐ Anti-Multiple Religions, Group
27 ☐ Anti-Atheism/Agnosticism

Sexual Orientation
41 ☐ Anti-Male Homosexual (Gay)
42 ☐ Anti-Female Homosexual (Lesbian)
43 ☐ Anti-Homosexual (Gay & Lesbian)
44 ☐ Anti-Heterosexual
45 ☐ Anti-Bisexual

Disability
51 ☐ Anti-Physical Disability
52 ☐ Anti-Mental Disability

Enter a Bias Motivation for each offense having a different bias motivation than Offense #1:
#2 ☐☐
#3 ☐☐
#4 ☐☐

Victim Type *(Check all applicable victim types for each offense listed above.)*

	Offense #1	Offense #2	Offense #3	Offense #4
1 Individual*	☐	☐	☐	☐
2 Business	☐	☐	☐	☐
3 Financial Institution	☐	☐	☐	☐
4 Government	☐	☐	☐	☐
5 Religious Organization	☐	☐	☐	☐
6 Society/Public	■	■	■	■
7 Other	☐	☐	☐	☐
8 Unknown	☐	☐	☐	☐

*Indicate the total number of individuals (persons) who were victims in the incident. Total # of Victims ☐☐☐

Number of Offenders ☐☐ *(Use "00" for Unknown Offender.)*

Race of Offender(s) as an individual or group *(Check one.)*

1 ☐ White
2 ☐ Black
3 ☐ American Indian/Alaskan Native
4 ☐ Asian/Pacific Islander
5 ☐ Multiple Races (group only)
6 ☐ Unknown

Figure 8.36 FBI hate crime incident report form. *(Continued)*

Finally, do not confuse the nature of a criminal threat with pranks and the act of hazing. To those on the receiving end of hazing, oft-times, university pledges and sorority/fraternity members or military trainees in elite units, the practices of hazing can prompt dire and deadly circumstances. Binge drinking, pranks that risk health and limb, and retaliatory action out of control can no longer be tolerated. University liability for failure to supervise has already caused extraordinary damage claims in the civil courts.

INSTRUCTIONS FOR PREPARING *QUARTERLY HATE CRIME REPORT* AND *HATE CRIME INCIDENT REPORT*

This report is authorized by Title 28, Section 534, U.S. Code, and the Hate Crime Statistics Act of 1990. Even though you are not required to respond, your cooperation in using this form to report hate crimes known to law enforcement during the quarter will assist the FBI in compiling timely, comprehensive, and accurate data regarding the incidence and prevalence of hate crime throughout the Nation. Please submit this report quarterly, by the 15th day after the close of the quarter, and any questions to the FBI, Criminal Justice Information Services Division, Attention: Uniform Crime Reports/Module E-3, 1000 Custer Hollow Road, Clarksburg, West Virginia 26306; telephone 304-625-4830, facsimile 304-625-3566. Under the Paperwork Reduction Act, you are not required to complete this form unless it contains a valid OMB control number. The form takes approximately 7 minutes to complete. Instructions for preparing the form appear below.

GENERAL

This report is separate from and in addition to the routine Summary UCR submission. In hate crime reporting, there is no Hierarchy Rule. Offense data (not just arrest data) for Intimidation and Destruction/Damage/Vandalism of Property should be reported. On this form, all reportable bias-motivated offenses should be included regardless of whether arrests have taken place. Please refer to the publication *Hate Crime Data Collection Guidelines* for additional information.

QUARTERLY HATE CRIME REPORT

At the end of each calendar quarter, each reporting agency should submit a single *Quarterly Hate Crime Report*, together with an individual *Incident Report* for each bias-motivated incident identified during the quarter (if any). If no hate crimes occurred during the quarter, the agency should submit only the *Quarterly Hate Crime Report*.

The *Quarterly Hate Crime Report* should be used to identify your agency, to state the number of bias-motivated incidents being reported for the calendar quarter, and to delete any incidents previously reported that have been determined during the reporting period not to have been motivated by bias.

HATE CRIME INCIDENT REPORT

The *Incident Report* should be used to report a bias-motivated incident or to adjust information in a previously reported incident. Include additional information on separate paper if you feel it will add clarity to the report.

Indicate the type of report as Initial or Adjustment. Provide the Originating Agency Identifier (ORI) and Date of Incident.

INCIDENT NUMBER: Provide an identifying incident number, preferably your case or file number.

UCR OFFENSE: Provide codes for all offenses within the incident determined to be bias motivated and the number of victims for each offense. In multiple offense incidents, report only those offenses determined to be bias motivated. Should more than four bias-motivated offenses be involved in one incident, use additional *Incident Reports* and make an appropriate entry in the Page □ of □ portion of each form.

LOCATION: Provide the most appropriate location of each bias-motivated offense.

BIAS MOTIVATION: Provide the nature of the bias motivation for each bias-motivated offense.

VICTIM TYPE: Provide the type of victim(s) identified within the incident. Where the type of victim is Individual, indicate the total number of individuals (persons) who were victims in the incident. Society/Public is applicable only in the National Incident-Based Reporting System (NIBRS).

NUMBER OF OFFENDERS: Provide the number of offenders. Incidents involving multiple offenders must not be coded as Unknown Offender. Indicate an Unknown Offender when nothing is known about the offender including the offender's race. When the Race of Offender(s) has been identified, indicate at least one offender.

RACE OF OFFENDER(S): Provide the race of the offender(s), if known. If there was more than one offender, provide the race of the group as a whole. If the number of offenders is entered as Unknown Offender, then the offender's race must also be indicated as Unknown.

Figure 8.36 (Continued) FBI hate crime incident report form.

States recognize the injury that can result from these activities that are unchecked and unregulated. Colorado has passed a hazing law that states:

(2) As used in this section, unless the context otherwise requires:
   (a) "Hazing" means any activity by which a person recklessly endangers the health or safety of or causes a risk of bodily injury to an individual for purposes of initiation or admission into or affiliation with any student organization; except that "hazing" does not include customary athletic events or other similar contests or competitions, or authorized training activities conducted by members of the armed forces of the state of Colorado or the United States.[89]

[89] Colo. Rev. Stat. § 18-9-124 (2)(a) (2010).

8.4.6 Assault: From simple to aggravated

Actual physical confrontation and offensive touching with accompanying physical harm encompass the assault category of crime. Workplace violence includes every imaginable type of assault from its threat to inflict bodily harm and injury to aggravated forms using weapons and instruments as well as the harsh injuries resulting from brutal sexual activity. The range of the assault category varies widely and depends on specific factual accounts.

8.4.6.1 Assault

The threat or the actual commission of serious bodily injury to another person has long been criminalized in Western jurisprudence. Assault forbids another from inflicting any type of injury on the person of another and it is graded on its level of severity by the means and method used. Fist fights and barroom altercations are usually placed in lower-grade assault while assault using weaponry or other instruments is placed in the higher grade. At common law, assault was distinguished from battery since the latter occurred when the touching or contact actually took place, while in assault, the injury by threat was one of expectancy. Naturally, battery was deemed a more serious offense because the criminal agent carried out the threat to its physical fruition while the assaulter merely threatened to do so. Nearly every state has merged the two offenses under the assault umbrella, leaving open the possibility of either imminent threat or actual physical touching. Hence, the distinction is primarily academic.

Assault cases all contain core elements, from simple to aggravated. First, the harm threatened or done must be of a serious nature, not the petty trifles and insults that civil damages cover. By serious, we mean substantive. One cannot assault another with a feather or spaghetti noodle, nor can a two-day-old baby inflict injury on another. The type of injury warranted in assault has pathological and medical substance—the smash to the face, the broken bone, the tear or laceration, and the bruise or contusion. The substantiality of the injury directly correlates to its severity and the law of assault requires something measurable.[90]

Second, the reaction of the injured party must be one of reasonableness. Threats of imminent harm and injury should be kept in some rational perspective, according to how the average and most reasonable person might react. Thus, if a mafia enforcer tells you, "I am going to break your face if your payment is not here tomorrow!," the average Mary and Joe Blow appreciate the sincerity of the threat. On the other hand, if a seven-year-old screams at an adult that "I am going to break every bone in your body," the threat is illusory and without reasonable potential. To be a threat in any sense, the harm offered must have a bona fide possibility of being inflicted, and the party communicating the threat needs to have the capacity to carry it out.

Third, the person accused must possess the requisite intent set out in the statute. In the graver versions of assault, the actor wills and intends specifically, while in the lower varieties, the actor knows or should know that injury is an inevitable outcome of the confrontation. Accidental touching does not qualify for criminal responsibility, though mistaken contact can be remedied by damages in the civil courts.[91]

Fourth, for a high-grade assault, such as aggravated injury, the prosecution team may have to produce a weapon or other instrument capable of inflicting harm. Weapons in the form of firearms and knives will always qualify but so do blunt instruments like tire irons and tools, wooden planks and baseball bats, and chains and steel bars. Aggravated cases may also involve the commission of a concurrent felony like rape or kidnapping, which generates a greater degree of culpability because of the forcible actions.

In general, the law of assault should not pose many problems for the justice professional as long as the facts fit nicely into the statutory definition.

8.4.6.2 Simple assault

Lowest in criminal gravity, simple assault covers a lot of territory in human interaction. While every form of assault can be deemed harmful, the simple version wreaks the least amount of personal havoc. Simple assault is applicable in the most usual of cases law enforcement deals with on a day-to-day basis. In the bulk of American jurisdictions,

---

[90] M.S. Scott & K. Dedel, Assaults in and around Bars, NCJ 215877 (2nd ed., 2006).

[91] To the dismay of many, assaultive behavior frequently targets pregnant women. See H.B. Weiss et al., Pregnancy-Associated Assault Hospitalizations: Prevalence and Risk of Hospitalized Assaults against Women during Pregnancy, NCJ 199706 (2004); Violence against Women and Family Violence: Developments in Research, Practice, and Policy, NCJ-199701 (Bonnie Fisher ed., 2004).

the offense is a misdemeanor and usually results in some type of diversion or alternative disposition due to its commonality. A typical statute might be as follows:

> (a) A person commits the offense of simple assault when he or she either:
> (1) Attempts to commit a violent injury to the person of another; or
> (2) Commits an act which places another in reasonable apprehension of immediately receiving a violent injury.[92]

The coverage of these types of laws becomes fairly comprehensive by labeling the unacceptable conduct as negligent, reckless, careless, and even intentional. The statute has often been labeled a "catch all" since it affords so much prosecutorial discretion. Within any series of facts where an altercation occurs, the statute predictably has some applicability. To the consternation of defense teams, assault at its most basic level is almost impossible to defend against if other qualifying elements for higher grades of assault are available. Thus, one who brandishes a weapon while assaulting another surely falls under the generic coverage of assault. The question of aggravation will not be guaranteed.

Precisely what serious bodily injury is has been the subject of endless legal and academic debate. Lower forms of assault display a liberal leaning to apparently small injury. The contact need not produce a medical diagnosis or resulting damages.

8.4.6.3 Aggravated assault

At the upper echelons of assault resides the aggravated form. "Aggravated" means that the infliction is more than the garden variety of push and shove and results in significant injury. To find aggravation, one must evaluate both the mind of the actor, who specifically intends the outcome, and the means or instrumentality utilized to reach the desired end. A major felony with extraordinary penalties attached, aggravated assault inhabits territory closely aligned to felonious homicide since the means to kill accompany the assaulter. The means do not necessarily translate into the specific intent to kill, but can impute a lower form of homicidal intent if death occurs. This is why the offense is viewed as seriously as it is.

The Model Penal Code delivers a crystal-clear picture of how this offense differs from assault:

> A person is guilty of aggravated assault if he:
> (a) attempts to cause serious bodily injury to another, or causes such injury purposely, knowingly or recklessly under circumstances manifesting extreme indifference to the value of human life; or
> (b) attempts to cause or purposely or knowingly causes bodily injury to another with a deadly weapon.[93]

The crux of the offense is its pure and unadulterated intentionality. There is no mistaking the mindset of the accused for he or she cannot offer alternative explanations for why they precariously placed the victim in harm's way. When a criminal actor directs the path of a vehicle toward an intended victim, when the perpetrator fires weapons into a crowd, or when the actor concentrates on one member of the body hoping to impair its usage, aggravated assault exists.

8.4.6.4 Mayhem

The common-law offense of mayhem has largely been incorporated in the provisions of aggravated assault. For those states that maintain the distinction, it is largely an artificial one. The essence of aggravated assault, as mayhem, is the infliction of serious bodily injury that can potentially kill or maim the individual. As noted already, this type of offense is far more than the rough and tumble argument with clenched fists. Mayhem represents a special category of aggravated assault since the act focuses primarily on the "members" of the human physique. Arms, legs, ears, nose, eyes, and genitalia are the appendages that the mayhem artist cuts away. At common law, the motivation had to be malicious in design, though one would be hard pressed to explain the hacking away under some other guise. In our time, terrorists often employ the tools of mayhem—such as the beheading of Christians, the hacking off of limbs in Munich train platform or cars, and other too numerous to mention. Mayhem connotes a high degree of terror and when used effectively forever impacts a place of worship, a place of work, or commuter setting, and given the brutality of the crime, it is worth giving it a special place in the extreme felony category.

---

[92] Ga. Code Ann. § 16-5-20 (2010); see also 18 Pa. Cons. Stat. § 2701 (2010).
[93] Model Penal Code § 211.1(2) (Proposed Official Draft 1962).

While there are a host of other criminal offenses that might be mentioned and analyzed here in detail, the bulk of workplace violence falls into these detailed offenses. One could rightfully expend further effort assessing the aggravated assault as applied to sexual attack, and discussed throughout this text is how homicide remains a perpetual concern for private security operatives, especially those entrusted with executive protection or those working in terror target facilities. The chances to kill or be killed in the world of private security are growing as fast as every other element in the private security industry. And with the gravity of the potential harm, the increase in being fully sacrificed for a particular installation or person, the security office must take his or her charge very, very seriously. This is not the world of caricature—the donut-eating guard sleeping at the wheel while the mayhem around occurs. The world of private security has become and will increasingly become a very dangerous world where not only are property and assets on the line, but life itself. Private security is no longer the domain of the unqualified and instead where the industry better start to focus on the best and the brightest people it can find, train, and retain.

8.5 ACTIVE SHOOTER PROGRAMS FOR THE PRIVATE SECURITY INDUSTRY

The ongoing slaughter caused by active shooters is being witnessed nationally and internationally.[94] Just when one thinks the problem is under control, another event, such as Brussels, San Bernardino, Paris or Orlando, Wurzberg or Munich, smacks us back into this horrid reality.[95] Many reasons can explain this unpredictability and ineffectual response by authorities. First, the world is undeniably consumed by political correctness—so much so that civil authorities are incapable of defining the threat and its agents. Instead, we hear of workplace violence, homophobia, gun control issues, poverty and a lack of jobs, discrimination, and the perennial favorite known as the "lone wolf." None of these explanations target the terrorist's motivation and none can lead the way out of this dilemma. The first step in any strategic plan to eliminate a problem is to "know thy enemy" and that many of our political class seem incapable of. Other reasons are political where national police and justice agencies control what happens at the street level—where officers and agents know who the threats are but like soldiers in a politically correct war, have both hands tied behind their backs as they seek to protect us. In addition, there is little recognition in our present political culture that is in fact a "war" and not a matter of criminal justice. That distinction is so crucial because when the emphasis remains on the latter, it becomes all about rights and processes rather than enemies in wartime. Enemies in wartime have very few rights and are rightfully treated differently in both a legal and military sense. Couple this with a multicultural tolerance meter off the chart, whereby any law, including Sharia, is as good as any other law, and you have a recipe for tolerance that fosters violence whether it be the alleged "honor killing" of women accused of adultery in the Islamic world operating under these principles or the need for that same women to produce three to four eyewitnesses in any allegation of rape. To be sure, many would argue that our Western values that include tolerance have been undermined by a mentality that all differences are equally good, when clearly for women, for gay people, for political dissidents and critics, and even for Christians and other religious minorities, the tolerance levels are minimal. In essence, there is a cultural war as well going on in America, and all of this nurtures violence and a proliferation of active shooters, driven by the jihadist mindset, which never has been part of our landscape.[96]

However, the jihadi motivation is not the sole rationale for the active shooter since these maniacal players are regular visitors to K–12 schools in the mold of Newtown, Connecticut or the estranged and emotionally disturbed killers—the alleged victims of bullying and jilted love, who victimize community colleges in Washington and Oregon state, or Virginia Tech or other institutions of higher learning. Some active shooters kill because they do not like the grades, the professor, or the fact that their dissertations are not approved.[97] There are some other conclusions that are permissibly reached such as the shooter usually has a relational quality with the victims, whether by work or association;

---

[94] See E.T. Winn, Emergency Management/Disaster Preparedness: Active Shooters: Plan Today to Mitigate Future Tragedies, *Homeland Security Today* (April 29, 2015), at http://www.hstoday.us/focused-topics/emergency-managementdisaster-preparedness/single-article-page/active-shooters-plan-today-to-mitigate-future-tragedies.html, last accessed August 28, 2016.

[95] S. Lee & R. McCrie, Mass Homicides by Employees in the American Workplace, at https://foundation.asisonline.org/FoundationResearch/CRISP-Reports/CRISP-Report-Library/Pages/Mass-Homicides-by-Employees-in-the-American-Workplace.aspx?cart=1f17902eec6b49b4a0c4145cc1edeef3, last accessed August 28, 2016.

[96] See C.R. Hamilton, Active Shooters and Workplace Violence Incidents around the World, *Sec. Mag.* (April 2014) at 54.

[97] See M. Maximino, Active Shooters: U.S. Trends and Perpetrators' Characteristics (Feb. 11, 2015), at http://journalistsresource.org/studies/government/criminal-justice/active-shooters-u-s-mass-killing-trends-perpetrators-characteristics, last accessed August 28, 2016.

A study of 160 active shooter incidents in the United States between 2000 and 2013:
Incidents annually

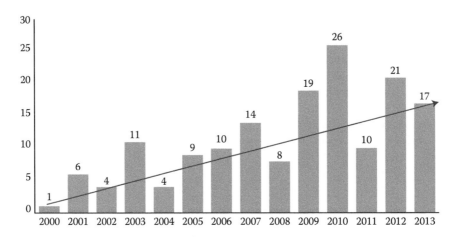

Figure 8.37   Annual active shoot casualties. (Adapted from Federal Bureau of Investigation, 2014.)

the shooters become familiar with security restrictions at the targets they wish to strike; and they control the event in terms of time and space.[98]

The locales and locations for the active shooter continue their undeniable spread into zones once held sacrosanct such as churches and houses of worship, cultural centers, and community centers, and to be sure, the range of targets shows no sign of restriction. Like rats in the sewer, these troubled and mentally disturbed characters now roam the landscape with impunity—hiding behind HIPPA laws and other privacy protections when professional people already know the "devil" is on the loose. The data on the rise of the active shooter can only be described as disturbingly upward. See Figures 8.37[99] and 8.38.[100]

Unfortunately, it is certain that the active shooter is now part of our permanent landscape and efforts to thwart and end this siege under our current leadership has been feckless and ineffective.

What we also know is that the role of the private security industry can be termed crucially relevant to the perverse world of the active shooter. Since so many installations and facilities are under the direct control of private sector law enforcement, it is imperative that security firms be on the cutting edge of deterrence, response, and mitigation in active shooter events. Today, the private sector security is an active player in the defense of military installations, courthouses, government buildings, entertainment facilities, colleges and universities, hospitals and health settings, and schools and religious settings.[101] In each of these setting, the private security industry must be prepared for the active shooter.[102]

Web Exercise: Download and watch the DHS webinar on active shooters and its call for an active role for the private security industry at https://share.dhs.gov/asaware2011.

---

[98] M. Finkelstein, Striking a Balance: Design Basis Threats and Active Shooter Threats, *Sec. Mag.* (April 2015) at 62; see also The Active Shooter—New Solutions Suggested to Manage Incidents, *Sec. Mag.* (September 2012) at 12.

[99] See FBI, *A Study of Active Shooter Incidents in the United States between 2000 and 2013*, 9 (Washington, DC, 2013), at https://www.fbi.gov/about-us/office-of-partner-engagement/active-shooter-incidents/a-study-of-active-shooter-incidents-in-the-u.s.-2000-2013, last accessed August 28, 2016.

[100] US DHS, Active Shooter Event Quick Reference Guide, at https://www.dhs.gov/sites/default/files/publications/active_shooter_pamphlet_508.pdf, last accessed August 28, 2016.

[101] FBI, *Active Shooter Planning and Response in a Healthcare Setting* (Washington, DC, 2015), at https://www.fbi.gov/file-repository/active_shooter_planning_and_response_in_a_healthcare_setting_2015.pdf/view, last accessed August 28, 2016.

[102] D. Ritchey, Proud to Be Security: How Roles Changed after 9/11, *Sec. Mag.* (September 2011), at http://www.securitymagazine.com/articles/82306-proud-to-be-security-how-roles-changedafter-911, last accessed August 28, 2016; see also U.S. Security Associates Coordinate Active Shooter Training Events (Jun. 4, 2015), at https://securitytoday.com/articles/2015/06/04/us-security-associates-coordinate-active-shooter-training-events.aspx, last accessed August 28, 2016.

When law enforcement arrives:
- Remain calm and follow instructions
- Drop items in your hands (e.g., bags, jackets)
- Raise hands and spread fingers
- Keep hands visible at all times
- Avoid quick movements toward officers, such as holding on to them for safety
- Avoid pointing, screaming or yelling
- Do not ask questions when evacuating

Information to provide to 911 operations:
- Location of the active shooter
- Number of shooters
- Physical description of shooters
- Number and type of weapons shooter has
- Number of potential victims at location

For questions or additional assistance contact:
Your local law enforcement authorities or FBI Field office :

Department of Homeland Security
3801 Nebraska Ave, NW
Washington, DC 20528

ACTIVE SHOOTER EVENT
QUICK REFERENCE GUIDE

An "active shooter" is an individual who is engaged in killing or attempting to kill people in a confined and populated area; in most cases, active shooters use firearms(s) and there is no pattern or method to their selection of victims.

☐
☐ *Victims are selected at random*
☐ *Event is unpredictable and evolves quickly*
  Knowing what to do can save lives

Figure 8.38   U.S. DHS active shooter event guide.   (*Continued*)

DHS also publishes a pocket card that summarizes best reactive strategies when active shooter events are unfolding. See Figure 8.39.[103]

The security industry is also encouraged to see the active shooter in similar ways to other emergencies, such as bomb threats, earthquakes, and other natural disasters, although the intensity and bloodletting of the unbridled active shooter intent on mass casualties is a distinctively different dynamic. However, there are similar protocols on how to handle the crisis. An emergency preparedness plan should anticipate the active shooter in the facility under protection. See Appendix B for a sample plan that can be tailored to each and every catastrophic event.

Web Exercise: For a highly instructive powerpoint on how to handle an active shooter situation, review the powerpoint program prepared by the National Tactical Officers Association at www.muni.ri.net/middletown/vendor/ag1.ppt.

---

[103] U.S. DHS, Active Shooter Pocket Card, at https://www.dhs.gov/xlibrary/assets/active_shooter_pocket_card.pdf, last accessed August 28, 2016.

ACTIVE SHOOTER EVENTS

When an Active Shooter is in your vicinity, you must be prepared both mentally and physically to deal with the situation.

You have three options:

1 | RUN

- Have an escape route and plan in mind
- Leave your belongings behind
- Evacuate regardless of whether others agree to follow
- Help others escape, if possible
- Do not attempt to move the wounded
- Prevent others from entering an area where the active shooter may be
- Keep your hands visible
- Call 911 when you are safe

2 | HIDE

- Hide in an area out of the shooter's view
- Lock door or block entry to your hiding place
- Silence your cell phone (including vibrate mode) and remain quiet

3 | FIGHT

- Fight as a last resort and only when your life is in imminent danger
- Attempt to Incapacitate the shooter
- Act with as much physical aggression as possible
- Improvise weapons or throw items at the active shooter
- Commit to your actions . . . your life depends on it

The first officers to arrive on scene will not stop to help the injured. Expect rescue teams to follow initial officers. These rescue teams will treat and remove injured.

Once you have reached a safe location, you will likely be held in that area by law enforcement until the situation is under control, and all witnesses have been identified and questioned. Do not leave the area until law enforcement authorities have instructed you to do so.

Figure 8.38   (Continued) U.S. DHS active shooter event guide.

Critics of the security industry claim that its lack of professionalism, training, and overall standards for licensure make it a woefully inadequate force to handle the active shooter. Some security specialists are trying to change that picture by high-level training and expectations for performance. The Advanced Law Enforcement Rapid Response Training (ALERRT) at Texas State University (http://alert.org), San Marcos, is an established program that has trained thousands of law enforcement professionals, and more private companies are offering such training for the private sector. As privatization of once-public functions continues its unstoppable trend, the sophistication and professional education of the security operative will have to continue its upward trek.

The industry itself is dramatically stepping up the training and awareness for the active shooter. The International Foundation for Protective Officers publishes a handbook on active shooter protocol.[104] ASIS holds regular training sessions on the complexities of security in active shooter situations.[105] While there are many suggested techniques

---

[104] See International Foundation for Protection Officers, *Active Shooter: A Handbook on Prevention*, 2nd ed., at http://www.ifpo.org/news/second-edition-active-shooter-handbook-prevention-released/, last accessed August 28, 2016.

[105] ASIS International, Resource Guide on Active Shooter Situations (2013), at https://www.asisonline.org/About-ASIS/Who-We-Are/Whats-New/Documents/Active-Shooter.pdf, last accessed August 28, 2016.

COPING
WITH AN ACTIVE SHOOTER SITUATION

- Be aware of your environment and any possible dangers
- Take note of the two nearest exits in any facility you visit
- If you are in an office, stay there and secure the door
- Attempt to take the active shooter down as a last resort

Contact your building management or human resources department for more information and training on active shooter response in your workplace.

PROFILE
OF AN ACTIVE SHOOTER

An active shooter is an individual actively engaged in killing or attempting to kill people in a confined and populated area, typically through the use of firearms.

CHARACTERISTICS
OF AN ACTIVE SHOOTER SITUATION

- Victims are selected at random
- The event is unpredictable and evolves quickly
- Law enforcement is usually required to end an active shooter situation

CALL 911 WHEN IT IS SAFE TO DO SO

HOW TO RESPOND
WHEN AN ACTIVE SHOOTER IS IN YOUR VICINITY

1. Evacuate
- Have an escape route and plan in mind
- Leave your belongings behind
- Keep your hands visible

2. Hide Out
- Hide in an area out of the shooter's view
- Block entry to your hiding place and lock the doors
- Silence your cell phone and/or pager

3. Take Action
- As a last resort and only when your life is in imminent danger
- Attempt to incapacitate the shooter
- Act with physical aggression and throw items at the active shooter

CALL 911 WHEN IT IS SAFE TO DO SO

HOW TO RESPOND
WHEN LAW ENFORCEMENT ARRIVES

- Remain calm and follow instructions
- Put down any items in your hands (i.e., bags, jackets)
- Raise hands and spread fingers
- Keep hands visible at all times
- Avoid quick movements toward officers such as holding on to them for safety
- Avoid pointing, screaming or yelling
- Do not stop to ask officers for help or direction when evacuating

INFORMATION
YOU SHOULD PROVIDE TO LAW ENFORCEMENT OR 911 OPERATOR

- Location of the active shooter
- Number of shooters
- Physical description of shooters
- Number and type of weapons held by shooters
- Number of potential victims at the location

Figure 8.39   DHS active shooter pocket card.

for dealing with active shooters, potential victims must engage in a sort of natural self-preservation by avoiding the casualty list.[106] DHS, to most security firms, has a simple protocol for employees caught in the midst of the active shooter, summarized in Figure 8.40.

---

[106] New York City Police Department, Active Shooter Recommendations and Analysis for Risk Mitigation (2012), at http://www.nccpsafety.org/assets/files/library/Active_Shooter_Recommendations_and_Analysis.pdf, last accessed August 28, 2016.

Figure 8.40 DHS active shooter protocol.

While seemingly simplistic, the suggestions are all about surviving rather than confronting an impossible situation. In general, security firms must prepare for this terrible event long before it occurs. Preparation naturally mitigates the damage since the company, the firm, and its employees are fully educated on the dynamics of an active shooter. Anticipate the worst by preparing for the possibility of an active shooter.[107]

Every plan to defend against the active shooter should contain certain elements, namely,

1. *Risk assessment:* The risks inherent in the facility where the event might take place have to be fully scrutinized, especially as to points of ingress and egress with special emphasis on evacuation procedures.

2. *Access control:* Identifying potential threats before they enter the building decreases the likelihood of a shooting incident. Access cannot be free form.

3. *Surveillance:* If there is an active shooter in the building, seconds matter and early detection is essential. If a possible threat is identified on the premises, remote surveillance may allow security personnel to locate and respond more quickly.

4. *Mass notification/communication:* Notifying personnel in the building may help in the safe evacuation or lockdown of a facility. This should also include communication within security teams, local law enforcement, and other emergency services.

5. *Trained personnel:* Security should have active shooter training; however, they are not the only entity that should be trained. Administrators, personnel, and other frequent visitors (e.g., students) should be trained on what to do in the incident of an active shooter.

6. *Delegated authority figures:* A delegated line of authority or leaders can help contain chaos in many emergency situations.

The above are just a few useful elements in active shooter response.

What is unequivocally clear is that private sector police and personnel must take ownership of both the location and its potential victims. Being purely reactive will lack the muscle to control events and circumstances and give no assurances that anyone has a real chance of survival. Best practices in active shooter prevention and reaction demand that the security company be proactive, fully prepared, and aware of its surroundings in order to minimize loss of life. To gain control early is to assure the least damage possible in a terrible setting. A recent study at the University of North Florida labels early action a series of "imperatives"—things that must be done to minimize the damage from an early shooter. If implemented, the active shooter impact will be keenly minimized. See Figure 8.41.[108]

Each active shooter event is also a teachable moment—something in which justice personnel can learn from both success and mistake, and security firms can fine tune their protocol and approaches. Over time, the professionals entrusted with safety and security will learn the best strategies for success. After-action reports summarize the event

[107] Police Executive Research Forum, PERF Report Details Changes in Police Response to Active Shooter Incidents, at http://www.policeforum. org/active-shooter-report, last accessed August 28, 2016.

[108] C3 Pathways, Active Shooter Incident Management, 5 (2013), at http://www.c3pathways.com/whitepaper/White_Paper_4_Best_Practices_ Active_Shooter.pdf, last accessed August 28, 2016.

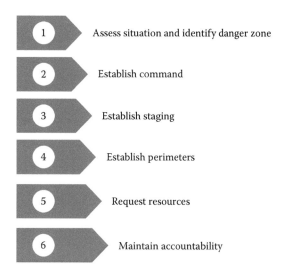

Figure 8.41   Active shooter recommended actions per C-3 pathways.

Managing the Consequences of An Active Shooter Situation

After the active shooter has been incapacitated and is no longer a threat, human resources and/or management should engage in post-event assessments and activities, including:

- An accounting of all individuals at a designated assembly point to determine who, if anyone, is missing and potentially injured
- Determining a method for notifying families of individuals affected by the active shooter, including notification of any casualties
- Assessing the psychological state of individuals at the scene, and referring them to health care specialists accordingly
- Identifying and filling any critical personnel or operational gaps left in the organization as a result of the active shooter

Lessons Learned

To facilitate effective planning for future emergencies, it is important to analyze the recent active shooter situation and create an after action report. The analysis and reporting contained in this report is useful for:

- Serving as documentation for response activities
- Identifying successes and failures that occurred during the event
- Providing an analysis of the effectiveness of the existing EAP
- Describing and defining a plan for making improvements to the EAP

Figure 8.42   After-action report.

and issue a series of critiques and recommendations on how to react to the event and even more importantly, steps to prevent, deter, or mitigate the damages. An example of an after-action report on an active shooter case is given in Figure 8.42.

8.6 CONCLUSION

Any notion that the workplace is safe and secure from the violence and harm so prevalent across the culture is both naïve and ill-prepared. From the entry-level stage to terminal situations in which murder occurs, the workplace is visited by every sort of harm imaginable. Domestic violence now occurs with regularity; offices must anticipate both terror potential and reactive steps to active shooters; crime is now a common occurrence, especially between employees in areas of assault, stalking, and sexual offenses, and most other forms of criminality now inhabit the workplace environment. And it starts before the employee ever commences his or her association with the company or firm. Background checks, employee vetting, and other screening techniques from polygraphs to psychological evaluation are now part of the employment landscape, and the private security industry is a major player in the delivery and oversight of the said activities. It is an area of major growth for private security specialists and one likely to continue an upward demand for its skilled services.

Keywords

access control

active shooter

advance security survey

after-action reports

aggravated assault

assault

asset investigation

background checks

credit history

domestic violence

employment history

employment investigations

executive protection

harassment

hate crimes

mayhem

partner violence

personal property investigation

polygraph tests

preemployment screening

protection from abuse

psychological examinations

radical Islamic jihadism

real property investigation

risk assessment

sexual assault prevention and response program

simple assault

site survey

spousal abuse

stalking

surveillance

terroristic threats

threat assessment

workplace violence

Discussion questions

1. Discuss the various procedures used to conduct a background investigation and relay the pitfalls of each method.

2. Review the steps that exist to ensure an effective executive protection program.

3. Discuss how to avoid Bill Zalud's common errors in executive protection and develop recommendations to eliminate these errors.

4. Analyze the recommendations of the ASIS for training of security professionals in the areas of domestic violence. Relate any shortcomings and make suggestions for improvement.

5. Describe the factors that are considered in deciding whether an incident is considered a suspected bias incident.

6. Explain the elements in an active shooter mitigation plan and discuss the various security measures that can be integrated into the plan.

CHAPTER 9

Investigations and investigative reporting for the security professional

OBJECTIVES

After completing this chapter, the student will be able to

1. Recognize the proper mindset necessary for successful investigations.
2. Recall the basic questions that must be asked in every investigation by private security personnel.
3. Demonstrate how to apply the general investigatory principles, in particular, security settings.
4. Write complete and succinct reports that accurately memorialize the investigative record.
5. Relate the characteristics that make up a good investigator.
6. Compare and contrast private police practice to public police investigations.
7. Describe and apply the uniform practices in any investigation.
8. Outline the purposes of the investigative process in the civil and criminal justice systems.

9.1 INTRODUCTION

It is difficult to envision any security professional functioning without strong investigative skills. The security industry's very worth is tied to its many investigative functions and capacities. Whether a background investigation, a theft or shoplifting incident, or a workplace or governmental benefits claim, the security professional must know the key steps of the investigative process as well as the particular protocols applicable to specific cases. See Figure 9.1.[1]

This chapter lays out the general and particular parameters of the investigative process by commencing with a review of the mindset necessary for successful investigations; it then reviews the most basic questions needed to be asked in every investigation and then applies these general principles to particular security settings such as property offenses in the retail and commercial setting, internal fraud and insurance crime, and negative workplace incidents. This chapter also delivers useful suggestions on how to memorialize the investigative record by its emphasis on reports and their composition.

9.2 ESSENTIAL INVESTIGATIVE CHARACTERISTICS FOR THE SECURITY PROFESSIONAL

In the investigative realm, as in any other occupation, certain skills, qualities, and competencies are essential to success. While differing personalities, styles of operation, and skill levels exist, there are common traits that constitute the professional investigator. While there is variation in how to accomplish the investigative task, there

---

[1] Bureau of Labor Statistics, U.S. Department of Labor, *Occupational Outlook Handbook, 2016–17 Edition, Private Detectives and Investigators*, at http://www.bls.gov/ooh/protective-service/private-detectives-and-investigators.htm, last accessed August 28, 2016.

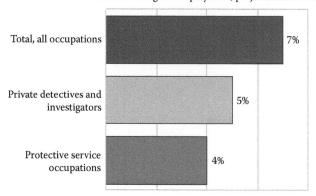

Note: All occupations includes all occupations in the U.S. Economy.

Figure 9.1   Employment outlook. (Adapted from U.S. Bureau of Labor Statistics, Employment Projections program.)

is a sort of "investigative DNA." Russell Colling, in his text *Hospital Security*, portrays the solid investigator as a "natural."

> The really good investigator has a natural aptitude and is intrigued by the investigative process coupled with the human relations involved. An investigation offers a challenge and will often succeed or fail in direct relation to the degree of competence and enthusiasm displayed.[2]

Colling further indicates that adept investigators must possess these attributes:

- Energy and alertness
- Knowledge of the law
- Ability to set realistic objectives
- Methodical approach
- Knowledge of human nature
- Observation and deduction abilities
- Ability to maintain meaningful notes[3]

Undoubtedly, the competent investigator, whether public or private, encompasses all these traits and more. This chapter highlights the types of traits and skill levels needed to succeed in the world of investigative practice.

9.2.1 Objectivity and investigative practice

Good investigators are driven by facts rather than by emotions, preconceptions, biases, or opinions that lack a factual basis. "Once an investigator loses sight of the facts and commences to be led by opinions, he no longer maintains the necessary objectivity."[4] Investigators who commence the process of fact-gathering and assimilation with preconceptions and preconceived conclusions are destined to produce a faulty result. Therefore, the investigator's strongest suit is an open-minded, hypothesis-driven, scientific approach to the case. Only when an investigator purges personal feelings and preconceptions will the investigative process have integrity, for facts are what drive the investigator and comprise the subject matter of the investigation itself.

Fact-gathering must become the hallmark of the security operative's investigative process. If so, the investigator's actions inspire others to believe in the integrity of the process and that judgments are reliable and credible. A recent job description for an investigator stresses these capacities:

---

[2] R. Colling, *Hospital Security* 221 (Butterworth Publishers, 1982).

[3] *Ibid.*; see also the historic role investigative services have played in the world of private security and private protection at C.P. Nemeth & K.C. Poulin, *Private Security and Public Safety: A Community Based Approach* 22 (Pearson–Prentice Hall, 2005).

[4] A. Markle, *Criminal Investigation and Presentation of Evidence* 1 (West Publishing Co., 1976).

- Analyze problems to identify significant factors, gather pertinent data, and recognize solutions
- Plan and organize work
- Communicate effectively orally and in writing

These skills develop a professional approach in the investigator and assure a "confident, business-like"[5] investigator working in the field. This allegiance to objective fact-gathering is not always easy. Security investigators are often placed in situations that are emotional by design. Domestic disputes, labor unrest, and public protest, to name a few settings, represent the types of cases involving heightened emotions.[6] Keeping your head in these scenarios is professionally demanding. Adhering to the objective method, remaining emotionally detached, and carrying out the assigned task without animus is a tall order. Norman Bottom and John Kostanoski's *Introduction to Security and Loss Control* emphasizes the role objectivity plays in the investigative method.

> Few private investigators rely overmuch on technology. Their primary trade is extracting information from the willing and unwilling, and locating records and documents. Some investigators have good technical skills in one or more of the following categories: photography, computer usage, eavesdropping equipment (technical intelligence-gathering), accident investigation, lighting measurements, marine transportation, and so on.[7]

In the final analysis, the effective investigator searches for objective reality and records it.[8]

9.2.2 Logic and investigative practice

Aside from the emotional control just discussed, the competent investigator must depend upon a logical method and protocol. Fact-gathering and deductive reasoning about the facts, conditions, and circumstances of a given case demand a logical mind. Logic can best be described as the orderly and sensible review of facts, conditions, and events in a consistent and sequential order. To do so, the investigator must devise appropriate inquiry techniques. Simply, *ask the right questions in the right order*! Since logic is an exercise of pure reason, facts can be evaluated by direct, deductive, inferential, or reverse forms of reasoning. Queries in a general sense will be:

- *Who* was responsible for this information?
- *What* does the information mean?
- *Where* was this information gathered?
- *When* was this information collected?
- *How* was this information acquired?
- *What* other parties or individuals might be responsible for this information?
- *Why* was this information found in this location?

In this way, the investigator looks for correlations. "All possible cause and effect relations must be examined, links found, and conclusions drawn, but only after thoroughly exploring all alternatives."[9]

As an illustration, consider a claim of food poisoning alleged against a restaurant and hotel establishment. Assume that you are a security officer assigned to investigate the claim. What types of logical inquiries should be made? Walter J. Buzby and David Paine, in *Hotel and Motel Security Management*, suggest these various lines of inquiry:

1. When did the victim become ill? (date and hour)
2. What was the nature of the illness? (pains, vomiting, dizziness, etc.)
3. How long did the illness continue?
4. Was a doctor consulted or any medicine taken? If a doctor was consulted, a copy of his findings should be secured.

---

[5] Art Buckwalter, *Investigative Methods* 36 (1984).

[6] K. Ask & P. Anders Granhag, Hot Cognition in Investigative Judgments: The Differential Influence of Anger and Sadness, 31 *Law Hum. Behav.* 537–551 (2007).

[7] N.R. Bottom & J. Kostanoski, *Introduction to Security and Loss Control* 26 (1990).

[8] R. Sarre, Book Review, 34 *Crim. J. Rev.*, 142 (2009) (reviewing F. MacHovec, *Private Investigation and Security Science: A Scientific Approach*, 3rd ed. (2006).

[9] W.W. Bennett & K.M. Hess, *Criminal Investigation* 11 (West Publishing Co., 1976).

5. What food or foods does the victim claim caused his illness?

6. Why does he feel that these foods caused the illness? Did they have a particular odor, taste, or appearance that caused suspicion?

7. What activities did the victim engage in prior to eating the suspected foods? Had he been to any parties, consumed any alcohol, medicine? Had he been in the company of any other persons? If so, get names and addresses so they may be contacted for statements.

8. Had the victim sustained any traumatic experience prior to eating? If so, get full details.

9. If the victim is unable to pinpoint any particular item of food that is suspicious, secure a complete list of all food eaten.

10. Check hotel records (restaurant records) as to number of servings of each item consumed by the victim that were served that day.

11. Check records for any other reports of illnesses on that particular day.[10]

This type of logical processing is often described as the *Who*, *What*, *Where*, *When*, *How*, and *Why* questioning sequence. Adept investigators, who ask the right questions, in the right order, will find the facts that are essential to successful case resolution. In a criminal or civil context, the standard 5W and H lines of questioning look like this:

Who questions

- Who discovered the incident or crime?
- Who reported the incident or crime?
- Who saw or heard anything of importance?
- Who had a motive or other reason for participation?
- Who was responsible for the incident or crime?
- Who can be considered an aider, abetter, coconspirator, codefendant, or coplaintiff?
- With whom did the defendant associate?
- Who are the witnesses?

What questions

- What occurred during this incident or crime?
- What are the incidents or crimes in question?
- What are the elements of these causes of action or crimes?
- What are the facts and actions committed by the defendant or suspect?
- What do the witnesses know?
- What evidence has been obtained?
- What was done with the evidence?
- What tools and other instruments were employed?
- What weapons or other real evidence exists?
- What means of transportation was used in the incident or commission of the crime?
- What was the modus operandi (method of operation)?

Where questions

- Where was the incident or crime discovered?
- Where was the incident or crime committed?
- Where were the suspects or defendants seen?
- Where were the witnesses during the event?
- Where was the victim found?

---

[10] W.J. Buzby & D. Paine, *Hotel & Motel Security Management* 122–123 (Butterworth Publishers, 1976).

- Where were the tools and other instruments obtained?
- Where does the suspect or defendant live?
- Where does/did the victim live?
- Where is the suspect or defendant now?
- Where is the suspect or defendant likely to frequent?
- Where was the suspect or defendant tracked down?

When questions

- When did the incident or crime take place?
- When was the incident or crime discovered?
- When were appropriate parties notified of the incident or crime?
- When did the police arrive at the scene?
- When was the victim last seen?
- When was the suspect apprehended?

How questions

- How did the incident or crime take place?
- How did the suspect or defendant get to the scene?
- How did the suspect or defendant depart from the scene?
- How did the suspect or defendant get the necessary information to commit the wrongful act?
- How much damage was done?
- How much property was stolen?
- How much skill, knowledge, and personal expertise were necessary for this incident or crime to take place?

Why questions

- Why did the incident or crime take place?
- Why were particular tools or instruments utilized?
- Why was there a particular method employed?
- Why did the witnesses talk?
- Why did the witnesses show reluctance in talking?

Investigative documentation like the *security department incident report* in Figure 9.2[11] mirrors this logical penchant necessary for effective investigation.

Any investigative report should be objective and logical—in most cases, a standardized report form will aid the investigator in collecting the "who, what, where, when, how, and why." In investigative practice, the search for truth, through the reconstruction of events and conditions, requires that the facts be carefully collected and studied.

Investigative logic is an exercise of both the intellect and the imagination. However, it is not fabrication or some type of delusion. Instead, it is the capacity and ability to draw natural inferences based on logic and reality from well-grounded facts. The investigator must be able to distinguish, compare, and contrast the reliable from the conjectural, and just as importantly, be willing to change, modify, and adjust one's basic theory as the facts, and therefore, as the case evolves. E. Smith, in his book *A Practical Guide for Investigators*, concurs with the view of logical flexibility.

> The theory must be abandoned as soon as proof shows it is inconsistent with facts uncovered. Every theory should be investigated to an end. Nothing should be taken for granted. When discarding a theory, it should not be entirely eliminated from the mind. The ability to judge when a theory should be abandoned is a valuable asset to the investigator.[12]

---

[11] J.J. Merrigan & J.S. Wanat, *Forms for Safety and Security Management* 128 (Butterworth Publishers, 1981).
[12] E. Smith, *Practical Guide for Investigators* 34 (Paladin Press, 1982).

SECURITY DEPARTMENT INCIDENT REPORT					
OFFENSE CATEGORY	DATE-TIME RECEIVED	DAY OF WEEK	DATE MO DAY YR	TIME AM. PM.	INVESTIGATION NO.

FORCED ENTRY | COMPLAINANT'S NAME | HOME PHONE

THEFT	PERS.PROP.	
	COMPANY PROP.	ADDRESS
	COIN MACHINE	
	AUTO	STATUS

BUSINESS PHONE

□VISITOR □EMPLOYEE □OTHER (SPECIFY)

ROBBERY				
ASSAULT	DATE-TIME OF OFFENSE	DAY OF WEEK	DATE MO. DAY. YR.	TIME AM. PM.
RAPE				

MANSLAUGHTER	PLACE	WEAPON USED
DISTURBANCE		
VANDALISM		
TRAFFIC	TRADEMARK	

OTHER (SPECIFY)

VICTIM'S NAME   ADDRESS

SEX   AGE   RACE | STATUS
□M □F

□VISITOR □EMPLOYEE □OTHER (SPECIFY)

MEDICAL TREATMENT □YES (EXPLAIN) □NO	DESCRIPTION OF LOST PROPERTY	VALUE

DESCRIPTION OF OFFENDERS

NO.1	SEX □M □F	RACE	HEIGHT	BUILD	EYES	HAIR	GLASSES □Y □N	COMPLEXION
	MARKS				AGE	HAT	COAT	SHIRT
NO.2	SEX □M □F	RACE	HEIGHT	BUILD	EYES	HAIR	GLASSES □Y □N	COMPLEXION
	MARKS				AGE	HAT	COAT	SHIRT

WITNESS NAME	ADDRESS	TELEPHONE
WITNESS NAME	ADDRESS	TELEPHONE

LAW ENFORCEMENT AGENCY NOTIFIED	TIME	PERSON
1.	□AM □PM	
2.	□AM □PM	

NAME OF PERSON ARRESTED 1.	ADDRESS
NAME OF PERSON ARRESTED 2.	ADDRESS

CHARGES

1.   2.

WAS PHYSICAL FORCE USED?   □ YES   □NO

SIGNATURE OF REPORTING OFFICER	DATE	FOR SECURITY OFFICE USE ONLY APPROVED_____ DATE NAME CARD COMPLETED_____

Figure 9.2 Security department incident report.   (*Continued*)

9.2.3 Perseverance, diligence, and investigative practice

"Stick-to-itiveness," a professional and personal obsession with getting the facts right, and a corresponding desire to discern the proper resolution of a case are mandatory attributes of a good investigator. Cases are rarely resolved by chance but rather by hard work. The investigator must be not only a collector and assimilator of information and facts, who subjects those facts to deductive and inferential analysis, but also a person of enormous perseverance. Since most investigations do not move forward in a straight line, and are very likely to have impediments placed in the path of resolution, an intense desire to reach proper conclusions can only aid the investigator. The security specialist must be able to handle adversity, dead ends, frustrations, and setbacks, and a wide array of unexpected and

NARRATIVE – BE SPECIFIC IN WRITRING OF THIS REPORT. BE SURE TO TUSE THE GUIDELINES: WHO, WHAT, WHEN, WHY, WHERE AND HOW. DESCRIPBE OFFENSE IN DETAIL, INCLUDE INITIAL STATEMENTS UTTERED BY VICTIM, WITNESSES AND SUSPECTS. EXAMPLE: IN CAR THEFT, WHAT WAS VICTIM'S RESPONSE TO DIRECT QUESTION, "WAS CAR LOCKED?" DESCRIBE SCENE OF OFFENSE AND CONTRIBUTORY CONDITIONS SUCH AS POOR LIGHTING, EXTREME ISOLATION, ETC. LIST EVIDENCE FOUND AT SCENE AND ALL OTHER RELEVANT INFORMATION SUCH AS SOBRIETY OF VICTIM, WITNESSES AND SUSPECTS. SAFEGUARD REPORT FOR REFERENCE.

FOR SECURITY DEPARTMENT USE ONLY

THIS OFFENSE IS DECLARED:
UNFOUNDED
CLEARED BY ARREST
EXCEPTIONALLY CLEARED   SIGNED_____DATE_____
INACTIVE (NOT CLEARED)   SECURITY DIRECTOR

Figure 9.2 (Continued)   Security department incident report.

even surprising contingencies. Perseverance can be described as a deliberateness that withstands excuse or mitigating factors. Perseverance can also take the form of mental and physical endurance that is not readily swayed. These qualities are particularly essential when the private security operative is involved in cases of terrorism, hostage negotiation, and the design and implementation of executive protection systems.

Perseverance generates a steady stream of leads during the investigative process, such as witnesses. "Occasionally, the investigator may be able to produce an unknown or unsuspected witness, but the discovery of such a witness cannot usually be credited to chance."[13] Instead, the witness will be discovered because the investigator has followed a lead

[13] 1 Am. Jur. Trials 357, 365 (1987).

with persistence. In every aspect of the investigative process, this dedication to task and result reaps fruit in the long run. Despite the tediousness of much investigative work, the security specialist must stay resolved and attuned to the overreaching goal. The practices of surveillance, inventory, and warehouse searches; auditing techniques; records analysis; and title, tax, and record abstraction are hardly exciting activities, yet each and every one of these practices may yield remarkable results. The investigator must remain steadfast in the mission and fully recognize that while the investigative process is slow and deliberate, in time, it will generate laudable leads.

For example, in building a case for divorce based upon infidelity, adultery, cruelty, or abuse, the investigator must find and evaluate the circumstances, events, and conditions supporting the client's position. The investigator must also accord the opposing party an objective view and not simply believe the allegations and affirmations of any client, but confirm the claims. In short, the investigative perspective requires looking at the whole picture—all parties and evidence that bear upon a case. To do so requires a persevering and diligent personality. "Investigation often involves hours, or even days, of waiting and watching, of performing tedious, boring assignments that may or may not yield information or evidence helpful to the case. Nonetheless, patience and perseverance are often the key to successful investigation."[14] Be mindful, however, that perseverance and diligence are not equated with stubbornness and intractability. Perseverance must be tempered with and complemented by an intellectual and personal flexibility.

9.2.4 Human relations skills and investigative practice

Because so much of an investigator's success depends upon the ability to collect information, one's capacity for human interaction adds to this competency. Investigators, who cannot relate to clients, witnesses, agency heads, government employees, police system and social service personnel, and insurance and claims adjusters will be less than proficient. Interpersonal skills promote the acquisition of information and provide a steady stream of intelligence worthy of collection.

An investigator that alienates a witness loses valuable information. If an investigator cannot express or communicate in clear, understandable terms, questions will not be answered. In this sense, being an educated person is crucial to the operation—having the capacity to express ideas and doing so while engendering ease in the party interviewed.[15] If an investigator makes people feel ill at ease, offended, or defensive, the ability to collect information will be substantially impaired. Ideally, private investigators must have personal characteristics that attract and motivate the opposition. "The investigator's career is totally people oriented. Investigation is concerned, directly and indirectly, with and

---

Private Investigator Job Description:

[Are you an experienced private investigator? We are looking to employ investigators in all experience types for our high growth company.]

This job offer is not restricted. We offer many types of employment, travel, and relocation options.

Must be able to conduct personal interviews with subjects (in covert and overt manners), interview neighbors, coworkers, friends and family. Perform record searches with police departments, courthouses, education facilities, financial institutions, medical providers, and mental health facilities. Conduct surveillance for long periods of time. Work with other highly motivated investigators. Be supervised by ICS selected senior investigators and case managers. Work with a consultant in the recommendation of case planning.

Qualifications:

- Previous investigative experience in law enforcement, military, fraud prevention, or current investigations.
- Excellent written and verbal communication skills.
- Strong analytical skills are a must. Strong PC skills required.

Requires a detail oriented, independent thinker with multi-tasking skills.

Desired Skills:

Knowledge of the UCC and criminal code. A bachelor's degree preferred or the equivalent law enforcement experience.

Figure CP9.1 Career Profile: Security investigator.

---

[14] Bennett & Hess at 13.

[15] Questions regarding the value of education in human interaction have been long analyzed in the criminal justice sector—in both public and private settings. See P. Carlan, Do Officers Value Their Degrees? *Law & Order* (December 2006) at 59.

about people. Thus, private investigators need to feel at home with them, understand, motivate, and communicate with them."[16] Without sufficient human relations skills, security specialists operate at a continuous disadvantage. At a minimum, an investigator must be able to accomplish the following:

1. To express positive attitudes toward others
2. To be able to manifest interest in others
3. To be able to build good human relations
4. To be able to express empathy and concern for others
5. To be able to establish a good rapport with others
6. To be able to adapt to different personalities and circumstances
7. To be able to communicate effectively with others
8. To be a believable personality
9. To be clear and accurate in communications with others
10. To be able to persuade and motivate other people
11. To be able to effectively manage conversations and to elicit information
12. To understand the emotional strengths and weaknesses of others
13. To exercise control of one's emotions
14. To be able to make friends rather than enemies[17]

Another measure of human relations skills is the art of communication itself. Most people think of communication as verbal or written; however, nonverbal communication plays a role in investigative practice. Nonverbal communication includes body language and an awareness of sensory perceptions, such as sight, smell, taste, hearing, and touch. Investigators must be attuned to human and environmental conditions. "'Why' people instinctively like or dislike others; trust or fear them; are attracted to or repelled by others is too complex for us to study definitively. [Investigators] must be aware that their total communication effort is affected by the impression they give others, whether in the form of body odors (good or bad), facial expressions, 'body language', voice tone, phrasing, and vocabulary, or writing style and technique."[18]

Common sense dictates that information-gathering and fact assimilation and collection will be easier for those who can skillfully interact with others. From another perspective, certain personality traits plainly benefit an investigator. A partial listing of those personality traits and characteristics and part of a solid investigator has been posed by Art Buckwalter, in his very worthy work, *Investigative Methods*:

Alert—ready and quick to understand or act; aware

Believable—one whom other persons can believe and trust

Calm—able to control emotions; free from agitation and excitement

Common sense—down-to-earth, good judgment

Dependable—worthy of being depended on; reliable and trustworthy

Determined—resolute; able to see an investigation through to its finish

Honest—truthful, frank, honorable, and straightforward in conduct or speech

Impartial—unbiased, equitable, free from favoritism, fair

Ingenious—possessed of inventive ingenuity, shrewd, capable of creating a clever and effective solution to an investigative problem

Law-abiding—conforms to or lives in accordance with the law

Level-headed—has sound judgment, balanced reasoning

Objective—able to concentrate on facts and external aspects of investigation without focusing on subjective feelings

---

[16] Buckwalter at 36.
[17] *Id.* at 35–47.
[18] National Association of Legal Assistants, *Manual for Legal Assistants* 10 (West Publishing Co., 1979).

Requisition Number	16-0736
Post Date	8/17/2016
Title	Senior Investigator
City	Fargo
State	ND
Description	PRIMARY OBJECTIVE OF POSITION

Position is responsible for independently investigating allegations of fraud, waste, and abuse perpetrated by healthcare providers, facilities, members, and/or groups. Investigator will proactively identify areas of concern through the use of software, tips, interviews, and other means to initiate, develop, complete and resolve investigations of mid to high level complexity. Resolution may include financial recovery through internal processes, and/or administrative, civil, and/or criminal prosecution. Individual will make recommendations when internal processes deficiencies are identified to prevent future occurrences of fraud, waste, or abuse. Additional responsibilities include assisting the Manager of the SIU with reviewing case files, training SIU staff and developing and providing fraud, waste, and abuse awareness training to internal departments and external contacts.

ESSENTIAL FUNCTIONS
1. Independently conduct investigations of fraud, waste and abuse by healthcare providers, facilities, members, and/or groups of mid to high level complexity.
   a. Determine the most effective and efficient method of investigation for each case.
   b. Gather and analyze data from internal and external resources including claims data, medical records, contracts, and public record information.
   c. Collect and preserve detailed evidence in a manner that protects its integrity in the event of prosecution.
   d. Conduct interviews of witnesses, accomplices and suspects.
   e. Thoroughly document all steps of investigations.
   f. Perform investigative field work such as onsite audits, surveillance and undercover operations.
   g. Collaborate with appropriate resources as the needed such as FWA Coding Analyst, other SIU Staff, Medical Management, etc.
   h. Collaborate with other Blue Plans, FBI, and others to be the main SIU contact on multi-jurisdictional cases.
   i. Develop detailed formal case reports in conjunction with each investigation.
   j. Manage a full case load by performing multiple high quality investigations concurrently.
   k. Use professional judgment and discretion in case development and prioritization.
2. Resolve cases
   a. Submit claims for adjustment in accordance with established processes.
   b. Communicate Quality of Care findings to Medical Management.
   c. Collaborate with the SIU Manager to determine case adjudication: unsubstantiated, education and follow up, administrative, civil, or criminal prosecution and submit through established processes.
   d. Report cases of suspected fraud to required parties incompliance with state and federal laws.
   e. Testify and give depositions on behalf of BCBSND in conjunction with conducted investigations.
   f. Submit any recommendations for internal process improvement to prevent future fraud, waste, or abuse occurrences to the SIU Manager.
3. Use software and other resources to proactively identify aberrant and/or suspect fraud, waste, or abuse practices
   a. Ability to interpret and analyze complex data.
   b. Ability to quickly identify and eliminate false positive data from an analysis.
   c. High level of ability to analyze BCBSND's exposure level (current and future) to help determine case prioritization.
4. Support SIU staff in case development and assist with training needs
   a. Assist SIU Manager in case review to ensure thorough case investigation and development.
   b. Act as a mentor and provide guidance and direction to SIU staff when requested or need is observed.
   c. Assist in the development of fraud, waste, and abuse training for companywide internal staff.
   d. Assist in the development of fraud, waste, and abuse awareness education for external contacts (members, facilities, providers, and the public).
   e. Deliver internal and external training as requested.

Figure CP9.2 Career Profile: Senior investigator.   (*Continued*)

5. Professional Development
   a. Successfully complete the training required for this position and retain information.
   b. Participate in company committees as a resource and for self-education.
   c. Seek opportunities to increase knowledge and skills for both current position and future development.
   d. Attain continuing education credits for professional certification(s).
6. Contribute positively to a team based work environment.
   a. Actively practice and apply Leadership Skills.
   b. Actively practice, apply and support the Noridian Values.
   c. Provide and seek constructive feedback.
   d. Participate in meeting and in the development of Team/Divisional goals.
   e. Participate in process improvement initiatives.
   f. Cross train others and be cross trained, helping to answer co- workers questions and to train new co-workers.
   g. Be dependable, flexible and adaptable, supporting decisions made.
   h. Promote professional behavior in work, actions and attitude.
   i. Demonstrate self-initiative and persistence in completing projects.
   j. Accept responsibility for job performance in both quality and quantity, realizing extra effort may be necessary.

Requirements   KNOWLEDGE

- Expert level knowledge of investigative theories, techniques, and practices
- Expert level knowledge of data analytics/informatics
- Expert level knowledge of local, state and federal laws
- In-Depth knowledge of fraud, waste, and abuse schemes
- Knowledge of healthcare and claims processing desired
- Familiarity with medical coding helpful

ABILITIES/SKILLS

1. High level of capacity to conduct complex investigations that will include the ability to apply law, medical policy and various contracts to investigations and subsequent outcomes.
2. High level of written and oral communication abilities to develop detailed case reports, to communicate process improvement recommendations, to work with outside agencies, to prepare cases for possible prosecution, to testify in court, to perform witness and subject interviews, and able to professionally respond to decisions that are routinely challenged.
3. High level of organizational abilities to manage multiple, ongoing investigations, and meet deadlines. Projects may include concurrent investigations, case evaluations, training staff, and working with outside agencies.
4. High level of computer experience that includes Excel, Word, and Access programs.
5. Ability to quickly analyze data utilizing problem solving skills and creativity. Identify aberrant practice patterns and proactively investigate to determine cause of aberrancy and need for further investigation.
6. Ability to maintain professionalism and confidentiality.
7. Ability to prioritize tasks and meet deadlines.

EDUCATION/EXPERIENCE

- Bachelor Degree in Criminal Justice, Health Care Administration, Business Management, Accounting, or other relevant field
- Minimum of 5 years of investigation experience in insurance fraud, law enforcement, fraud and abuse auditing or equivalent
- Certified Fraud Examiner (CFE) or equivalent (AHFI, CIA, CFI, etc.) required

OTHER INFORMATION

Job Posting Policy 6.05

New employees with Blue Cross Blue Shield of North Dakota will be eligible to apply for positions within their assigned department after successfully completing a 90-day review. For positions outside your department, you must attain a minimum of six months of service before you can apply.

EQUAL OPPORTUNITY EMPLOYMENT

Equal Opportunity Employer of Minorities, Females, Protected Veterans and Individual with Disabilities, as well as Sexual Orientation or Gender Identity.

For questions, please email careers@bcbsnd.com. This job posting will be closed 08/31/2016 at 8:00AM CST. No further applications will be considered.

Figure CP9.2 (Continued)   Career Profile: Senior investigator.

Observant—takes careful notice; with keen powers of observation

Patient—capable of calm waiting and forbearance under provocation; undaunted by obstacles and delays

Perceptive—discerning, aware; has alert senses

Persistent—tenacious, dogged, able to see the problem through

Prudent—capable of directing and conducting oneself wisely and judiciously; discreet, sensible, reasonable, and skillful in the application of capabilities

Remembers well—capable of recollection and recall

Responsible—accountable, reliable; able to answer for own conduct and obligations and to assume trust

Resourceful—able to fall back on other sources or strategies when the usual means are not effective; has reserve abilities and alternative resources

Thorough—able to carry things through to completion; painstaking, exact, and careful about details

Versatile—has many aptitudes, circumstances, and situations that require change in tactics or positions[19]

9.3 PRIVATE POLICE INVESTIGATIVE PRACTICE AS COMPARED TO PUBLIC POLICE

While the cross-over between how private security personnel conduct investigations and how public police carry out the same function is undeniable, there are differing visions and ends in mind. Surely, the qualities of a competent investigator apply equally in both settings. And that the subject matter of investigations may mirror one another is equally concluded. Indeed, the level of partnership between the public and private systems is exponentially increasing at every level of the investigative process—a reality made even clearer as the privatization transference continues without much restriction. Private police are increasingly carrying out once-entrenched public functions. Russell Colling, in his work *Hospital Security*, concludes that the differences between the investigative protocol of the public officer from the private officer are really one of form and mission, and indeed the missions are very complementary.

> It is techniques and varying purposes that differentiate the security investigation from that of a law enforcement agency. This is not to say that the security investigation always has a different focus. A police investigation is conducted basically for the purpose of apprehending the perpetrator of a crime and locating evidence for the successful prosecution of a case. Security investigations, on the other hand, may involve, in addition to crimes, the gathering of information in regards to the violation of organizational rules and regulations; a job applicant's background, for conditions that may lead to criminal violations; the need for new security controls and procedures; liability claims or potential claims; unsafe conditions; or evidence needed to prove or disprove certain allegations.[20]

The investigative process itself inherently serves the justice system—both the criminal and civil systems that depend upon hard facts and evidentiary quality to prove the case at hand.[21] Whether conducted by private or public police, the criminal and civil systems depend upon an investigative process that is able

1. To determine if there is sufficient factual evidence to support or defeat each element of a cause of action

2. To accumulate the necessary factual evidence to prove or defeat a case at trial or to form the basis for a settlement

3. To locate leads to additional evidence

4. To locate persons or property

5. To find evidence that might be used to discredit (impeach) a witness or the opponent[22]

The question of what to investigate largely correlates to the mission and goals of the entity undertaking the investigation.[23] While similarities abound between the public and private systems, the difference and distinction between these systems are undeniable. Public policing must, by nature, be more concerned about criminal felonies than any private security firm. Homicide is not as critical a concern for private security forces as it is for the investigator

---

[19] Buckwalter at 47–49.

[20] Russell Colling, *Hospital Security* 211 (Butterworth Publishers, 1982).

[21] IACP, National Policy Summit (2004) http://www.theiacp.org/Portals/0/pdfs/Publications/ACFAB5D.pdf.

[22] J. Mccord, *The Litigation Paralegal* 69 (West Publishing Co., 1988).

[23] See L. Perry, How Private Security Can Help Law Enforcement (May 31, 2012) http://www.policemag.com/blog/patrol-tactics/story/2012/05/how-private-security-can-help-law-enforcement.aspx.

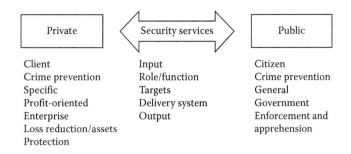

Figure 9.3 Comparison between public and private police functions.

laboring in Chicago or New York City. Other felonies may be better suited to shared practice such as burglary, grand theft, and other forms of larceny, fraud and corrupt practice, and assault and battery, all of which touch upon the day-to-day grind common to both systems.[24] The Hallcrest Report II surveyed both public and private security professionals as to their overall impressions of what the ultimate goals of these systems are. Both agree that "security services" are part of the overall mission. See Figure 9.3.[25]

The differences are quite obvious with the private model more concerned with profit, asset protection, and more targeted activities. The public system, comparatively, displays a broader vision with little if any entrepreneurial spirit since it is governmentally housed. Hallcrest II also assessed how security administrators, the higher echelon of the industry, in proprietary and contractual settings, rank ordered their proper ends and goals. The comparison between these two security sectors is pretty uniform.[26]

However, the similarities dissipate a bit when public law enforcement executives prioritize functions.[27]

Public officers are clearly more concerned with arrest and prosecution than their private counterparts. This conclusion is further buttressed by the "general public" concerns within the same list of priorities. This prioritization, in and of itself, is a telling distinction, though it should not be viewed as justification for a sharp division. If anything, both public and private law enforcement share a generic goal, namely, the general enforcement of laws. As Bill Strudal points out in his article, *Giving the Police a Sense of Security*,

> Our goal, usually not shared by police and security is law enforcement … if we accept the premise that police and security have the same goals, then why don't we work together on a regular basis? There are differences; nobody can deny that … there are many other gaps between the two forces, but none is insurmountable with good training and dialogue.[28]

The similarities between function, duty, and obligation are very apparent when the tasks of investigation are considered. The skills of the private sector are essentially identical to the public. Review Figure 9.4 to see the diverse opportunities shared and borne by both the private and public sectors.

Web Exercise: As more and more public law enforcement services are taken up by private security, the investigative differences melt away. See the content of the upcoming sexual offense investigations for campus police sponsored by the State of Virginia at http://dcjs.virginia.gov/vcscs/training/sexualAssaultInvestigator/2015/.

Private security investigators differ in other ways because of its clientele. For instance, the task of locating people, conducting accurate and dependable background information and vital record checks, and conducting due diligence for corporate and business purposes take on far greater importance than the public police model. LexisNexis, among a growing number of consulting and subscription services, provides state-of-the-art data services, information publicly available on individuals for background checks and investigative purposes.[29]

---

[24] See COPS website, Private Security and Public Law Enforcement, http://www.cops.usdoj.gov/Default.asp?Item=2034.

[25] W.C. Cunningham, J.J. Strauchs & C.W. VanMeter, *Private Security Trends 1970 to 2000: The Hallcrest Report II*, 116 (1990).

[26] Cunningham et al. at 120; see also Operation Cooperation.

[27] Cunningham et al. at 118.

[28] B. Strudel, The Private Security Connection: Giving the Police a Sense of Security, *Police Chief* (February 1982) at 28–29; Law Commission of Canada, In *Search of Security: The Roles of Public Police and Private Agencies* (2002); G.S. Rigakos, *The New Parapolice* (2002).

[29] LexisNexis Accurint for Private Investigations, http://www.lexisnexis.com/risk/downloads/literature/accurint-private-investigations.pdf.

- Public Prosecutors and Law Enforcement Agencies
- Tort Investigation
- Publisher Actions
- Bank Investigations and Security
- Insurance Companies and Self-Insurer Investigations
- Railway, Bus and Airlines Companies Security
- Motor Freight, Warehouse and Freight Terminal Security
- Manufacturing, Wholesale Distributing and Retail Security
- Hotel Security
- Character Investigations
- Surveillance
- Plant and Store Surveillance
- Undercover Investigations

Figure 9.4   Private and public sector opportunities.

Despite the differences, the private–public alignment continues to be tighter, so much so that state regulators are now attempting to set up more dependable and uniform standards for the designation of a "private investigator." The International Association of Security and Investigative Regulators (IASIR) was founded in 2001 for this very purpose. See Figure 9.5.

The IASIR mission includes

- Enhancing applicant processing and records management
- Advocating for expedient background investigation and fingerprint processing
- Disseminating information on insurance/bonds
- Keeping abreast of and sharing information about new licensing technology
- Promoting effective state regulation and enforcement
- Assisting in education and training standards
- Eliminating unlicensed activity
- Developing harmony between law enforcement and the regulated industries
- Influencing federal legislation
- Formulating model laws and regulations
- Assisting states in developing and enforcing laws and regulations
- Encouraging reciprocity between states
- Providing training and education opportunities for state regulators

Web Exercise: For an excellent overview of the world of private investigation, visit the Detective Training Institute's summary at http://www.detectivetraining.com/lesson1html/.

Figure 9.5   International Association of Security and Investigative Regulators logo.

9.3.1 Investigative practice and protocols for private security: Distinct legal dimensions

Investigative practice has long been subject to intense legal scrutiny in the American legal and police system. Guided by the constitutional framework outlined in the Bill of Rights, state action or governmental action by police agents has delineated boundaries of acceptable, lawful action. While any public police officer may investigate events and conditions arising out of criminal conduct, that investigation must be mindful of constitutional considerations such as personal privacy, expectation of privacy in home or domicile, need or necessity for judicial approval by warrant, stage of police investigation, and whether the targeted defendant has been or is about to be arrested. At the center are the provisions of the Fourth Amendment, which states in part:

> The right of the people to be secure in their persons, houses, papers, and effects, against unreasonable searches and sei-zures, shall not be violated and no warrants shall issue upon their probable cause supported by oath, affirmation and particularly describing the place to be searched and the persons or things to be seized.[30]

Responding to the clamor for individual rights, calls for a reduction in arbitrary police behavior, and a general recognition that the rights of the individual are sometimes more important than the rights of the whole, judicial reasoning, public opinion, and academic theory for the last 20 years have suggested and formulated an expansive interpretation of the Fourth Amendment.[31] When and where police can be constrained and criminal defendants liberated appears to be the trend.

On its face, and in its express text, the Fourth Amendment is geared toward public functions.[32] The concepts of a "warrant," an "oath," or "affirmation" are definitions that expressly relate to public officialdom and governmental action. Courts have historically been reticent to extend those protections to private sector activities. In *Burdeau v. McDowell*,[33] the Supreme Court held unequivocally that Fourth Amendment protection was not available to litigants and claimants arrested, searched, or seized by private parties. The court explicitly remarked,

> The Fourth Amendment gives protection against unlawful searches and seizures…. Its protection applies to governmental actions. Its origin and history clearly shows that it was intended as a restraint upon the activity of sovereign authority and was not intended to be a limitation upon other than governmental agencies.[34]

The court's ruling is certainly not surprising, given the historical tug-of-war between federal and states' rights in the application of constitutional law. Over the long history of constitutional interpretation, courts have been hesitant to expand constitutional protections to cover the actions of private individuals rather than governmental actions. *Burdeau* has been continuously upheld in a long sequence of cases and is considered an extremely formidable precedent.[35] The *Burdeau* decision and its progeny enforce the general principle that the Fourth Amendment is applicable only to arrests, searches, and seizures conducted by governmental authorities. The private police and private security system have historically been able to avoid the constrictions placed upon the public police in the detection and apprehension of criminals.[36]

If constitutional protections do not inure to defendants and litigants processed by private sector justice, then what protections do exist? Could it be argued that the line between private and public justice has become indistinguishable or at least so muddled that the roles blur? Are private citizens, subjected to arrest, search, and seizure actions by private police, entitled to some level of criminal due process that is fundamentally fair and not overly intrusive? Does the Fourth Amendment's strict adherence to the protection of rights solely in the public and governmental realm blindly

---

[30] U.S. Constitution. Amend. IV.

[31] E.W. Machen, Jr., *The Law of Search and Seizure* (1950); J.A. Varon, *Searches, Seizures and Immunities* (1974); Note, The Concept of Privacy and the Fourth Amendment, 6 *U. Mich. J. L. Rev.* 154 (1972); Note, From Private Places to Personal Privacy: A Post-Katz Study of Fourth Amendment Protections, 43 *N.Y.U. L. Rev.* 96 (1968); Blancard, Clark, and Everett, *Uniform Security Guard Power to Arrest, Part II* (1977); F.E. Inbau, *Protective Security Law* (1983).

[32] Note, Seizures by Private Parties: Exclusion in Criminal Cases, 19 *Stan. L. Rev.* 608, 608–609 (1967).

[33] 256 U.S. 465 (1921).

[34] *Burdeau v. McDowell*, 256 U.S. 465, 475 (1921).

[35] See generally *Smith v. Maryland*, 59 U.S. (18 How.) 71, 76 (1855); *Barron v. Baltimore*, 32 U.S. (7 Pet.) 243, 250 (1833).

[36] See *U.S. v. Janis*, 428 U.S. 433, 456 n. 31 (1976); *Coolidge v. New Hampshire*, 403 U.S. 443, 487 (1971); *Walter v. U.S.* 48 U.S. L.W. 4807 (1980); see contra *People v. Eastway*, 241 N.W. 2nd 249 (1976).

disregard the reality of public policing? Is this an accurate assessment of what the general citizenry experiences? Or should the constitution be more generously applied to encompass the actions of private police and security operatives? All of these dilemmas are, at first glance, easy to answer, when assessing case law. Even despite the continuous resistance to the said applications, the advocates for such arguments are perpetually persistent.

The unique and preferred legal status of private security has had much to do with its extraordinary growth and attractiveness, for as the public system has been bogged down and manipulated by excessive judicial oversight, the private system conducts most of its affairs without similar legal oversight.[37]

To be sure, there is no completely safe harbor, for the errant actions of private security operatives can trigger a host of legal responses, from the regulatory to the administrative, from the civil to the criminal. Indeed, the private sector officer needs to be always legally aware of his or her potential liability based on multiple theories and because of this, a serious series of protocols and safeguards must be adhered to when conducting investigations.[38]

Private security is not immune to legal consequences, although it possesses a constitutional edge when compared to the public police model.[39] No legal case has been more emphatic about this legal reality than *Burdeau v. McDowell*, which can be found in Appendix E.[40]

Web Exercise: Visit the University of Denver's "Private Security Monitor," which tracks legal and regulatory developments in the private security industry at http://psm.du.edu/national_regulation/united_states/laws_regulations/.

While it is not the aim of this section to cover the full array of legal issues, suffice it to say that investigation does trigger potential legal liability. Harmed parties might allege that privacy laws were violated or that unlawful investigative practices may lead to a claim of trespass, assault, battery, or other civil or criminal action. Nothing the security operative does, in an unlawful investigative tactic, precludes legal actions for nuisance, defamation, intentional infliction of mental distress, or arguments concerning false light. Nothing the security operative carries out, in an unlawful investigative tactic, will shield him or her from consequences of damages or costs resulting from the illegal action. And this same conclusion can be reached as to criminal charges—for an investigation that seriously injures a targeted person, causes harm from a firearm, or specialized restraint method may result in the initiation of a criminal complaint.

However, nothing, at least presently, will provide a foundational basis for a traditional constitutional claim based on the Fourth Amendment of the U.S. Constitution.[41] The problem becomes particularly acute for these critics of the status quo when public and private parties share the results or fruits of the investigations. The NCJRS lays out the potential dilemmas in Figure 9.6.[42]

9.4 INVESTIGATIONS AND INVESTIGATIVE PROCEDURE

Investigation is the process of factual assimilation and the systematic collection of evidence; of observation, inspection, and analysis, involving continuous and regular inquiry into a specific subject. It requires balancing the theories of investigative practice and the information in policy manuals and textbooks with experience and "street smarts." Investigative practice depends on facts and hard information. A successful investigation must uncover the information necessary to support or refute a claim, cause of action, or criminal prosecution. Solid investigative practice operates under an investigative plan, creates a theoretical framework that underlines the investigative process, and proposes a cause or case in law that relates to the investigative regimen.

The investigative process must reconstruct events, conditions, or the "truth" itself. Finding the truth can be a challenge for even the most seasoned investigators as objective, fully reliable, and verifiable information can be hard to come by. The investigator will seek out many sources of information, including witnesses, both lay and expert,

---

[37] See M.K. Sparrow, Managing the Boundary between Public and Private Policing (September 2014) https://www.ncjrs.gov/pdffiles1/nij/247182.pdf.

[38] See L. Klein, Tips on Workplace Investigations at 34.

[39] See C. Goldberg, A Training Triumph at 12.

[40] *Burdeau v. McDowell*, 256 U.S. 465, 475 (1921).

[41] Certainly in the academic sectors, there is an ongoing demand for the extension of the constitution, yet the arguments lack precedent and legal logic. See: M. Rhead Enion, Constitutional Limits on Private Policing and the State's Allocation of Force, 59 *Duke L.J.* 519 (2009) http://scholarship.law.duke.edu/cgi/viewcontent.cgi?article=1445&context=dlj.

[42] Sparrow, Managing the Boundary at 9.

Potential Benefits and Risks of Public/Private Police Partnerships

Grounds for Support and Engagement (the Benefits)	Grounds for Skepticism and Concern (the Risks)
1. Increased Effectiveness Through Public/Private Partnerships. Collaboration between the public and private sectors enhances performance by sharing complementary skills, knowledge and resources. Partnerships facilitate information exchange and provide access to broader networks. All parties can benefit from properly functioning partnership arrangements.	**1. Lack of Accountability.** Private police are not subject to the same formal and legal systems of accountability that govern public police agencies. Nevertheless, they may carry weapons, use force, detain suspects and intrude on the privacy and rights of individuals. They may discover crimes and choose not to inform public authorities. The exercise of policing powers without commensurate accountability is inherently dangerous to society.
2. Alignment With the Ideals of Community Policing. Community policing is essentially collaborative and involves sacrificing a purely "professional agenda" in favor of one negotiated with the community. The community, which includes businesses, should be able to participate in setting the crime-control agenda and should be encouraged to participate in carrying it out.	**2. Threats to Civil Liberties.** Many restrictions on the conduct of public police do not apply to private police (unless formally deputized by public agencies). For example, confessions extracted by private police without Miranda warnings and evidence obtained through unlawful searches conducted by private agents are not subject to exclusionary rules.
3. Greater Equality in Protection. The ability of the better off to protect themselves by purchasing private protection at their own expense allows the public police to concentrate their efforts on poorer and more vulnerable segments of the community. The overall effect, therefore, is to raise the floor in terms of levels of protection for the most vulnerable.	**3. Loss of "Stateness."** Policing services and security operations require judicious balancing of the multiple and often conflicting rights of different groups or individuals. Therefore, only state ("civic") institutions can be trusted to reflect the broad societal values required to carry out such functions. The particular interests of private clients and the for-profit motivations of commercial providers will inevitably distort the public agenda to some extent.*
4. Access to Specialized Skills and Technical Resources. The private sector can provide the public police with highly skilled and technical specialists that the public sector could not routinely employ. Collaboration with the private sector thus makes highly skilled and specialist resources available for public purposes.	**4. Threats to Public Safety.** Private police, who are not as well-trained as public police, may display poor judgment or overreact to situations, thus endangering public safety. Citizens may be confused about the status or rights of uniformed security personnel and may therefore act in ways that create danger for themselves or others.
5. Efficiencies Through Contracting Out. Government operations should seek to exploit the efficiencies of private-sector competitive markets by contracting out any components of their operations that can be clearly specified and carved out, and for which competitive markets exist.	**5. Greater Inequality in Protection.** The growth of private security exacerbates inequality regarding citizens' access to protection. Citizens will get the level of protection they can pay for. Those who are better off, and are able to purchase or enhance their own security, will reduce their commitment to public policing. Funding and support for public policing will suffer, which will ultimately result in lower levels of protection for the poorer and more vulnerable segments of society.
	6. Reputational Concerns. Inadequate performance or improper conduct by private security personnel may produce reputational or litigation risk for public police if the public police have formally recognized, qualified, trained, contracted, or in some other way recognized or validated the operations of private operators. Such operators should therefore be kept at arm's length.
	7. Threats to Police Jobs. Increased availability of lower skilled and lower paid security jobs, coupled with the contracting out of some police tasks to the private sector, may undermine job security and limit career prospects for public police. Competition from the private sector is inherently unfair because of their tolerance for lower training standards and access to cheaper labor.

*The term "stateness" has been used by other commentators as an umbrella term to cover a broader range of public-interest concerns. Several of these concerns, including loss of equity in public security and loss of public accountability, appear as separate items on this list. This paper will hereafter use the "stateness" term to focus more narrowly on the importance of judicious balancing of competing interests and values.

Figure 9.6   Potential benefits and risks of public–private police partnerships.

physical, real, documentary, and demonstrative evidence and forensics. In a sense, the investigator reconstructs the history of a past event for the present. James Davidson and Mark Lytle's *After the Fact* suggests that the investigative process is really a journey into the historical past:

> "History is what happened in the past." That statement is the everyday view of the matter…The everyday view recognizes that this task is often difficult. But historians are said to succeed if they bring back the facts without distorting them or forcing a new perspective on them. In effect, historians are seen as couriers between the past and present. Like all good messengers, they are expected simply to deliver their information without adding to it.[43]

---

[43] J. Davidson & M. Lytle, *After the Fact: The Art of Historical Detection* xv (5th ed., McGraw-Hill: Boston, 2005).

Job Search

Close

Close Application limit reached.
Close You have already applied for this job. Check application status

Investigator

387588BR

Job Description

At Disney, we're storytellers. We make the impossible, possible. We do this through utilizing and developing cutting-edge technology and pushing the envelope to bring stories to life through our movies, products, interactive games, parks and resorts, and media networks. Now is your chance to join our talented team that delivers unparalleled creative content to audiences around the world.

The Global Security Investigations team is responsible for a variety of investigative activities within The Walt Disney Company (TWDC) and affiliated companies, to include:

- Conducting investigations on matters including: intellectual property loss and theft; personal information loss and theft; employee misconduct; physical property theft; workplace violence issues; and cybercrimes.
- Leading threat assessments and developing threat mitigation plans.
- Partnering with other business units, within and outside of Global Security, to develop protocols, response, and investigative plans for workplace safety and security incidents.
- Collaborating with business units to develop proactive measures to capture and maintain incident reports and prevent security incidents.
- Teaming with various units with TWDC, affiliated companies, other corporate security investigations teams, and law enforcement representatives at the local, federal, and international levels, to facilitate investigations and collaborate to promote and practice preventative initiatives.

Responsibilities

- Independently conduct complex investigations into unlawful activity and into violations of company policies and procedures in an efficient, thorough and professional manner.
- Prioritize multiple tasks and responsibilities in a fast-paced environment, while maintaining positive customer/client relations.
- Conduct threat assessments and provide options for threat management strategies.
- Author detailed professional reports and maintain well-organized and accurate Incident/Case files.
- Conduct professional investigative interviews of employees and others, often involving sensitive subjects.
- Ability to be flexible with work-hours in order to respond to urgent issues and to the situational needs and requirements of the workload.
- Maintain strict discretion and confidentiality.
- Independently conduct complex investigations into unlawful activity and into violations of company policies and procedures in an efficient, thorough and professional manner.
- Prioritize multiple tasks and responsibilities in a fast-paced environment, while maintaining positive customer/client relations.
- Conduct threat assessments and provide options for threat management strategies.
- Author detailed professional reports and maintain well-organized and accurate Incident/Case files.
- Conduct professional investigative interviews of employees and others, often involving sensitive subjects.
- Ability to be flexible with work-hours in order to respond to urgent issues and to the situational needs and requirements of the workload.
- Maintain strict discretion and confidentiality.
- Collaborate with other investigators to conduct investigations. Work both independently and with other investigators on initiatives for security and investigative enhancements and process improvements.
- Interface, as necessary, with executives on security and investigative matters.
- Build and maintain effective working relationships with law enforcement agencies and with counterparts in the industry.
- Partner with other business units to develop and deliver employee training to maintain awareness and minimize incidents.
- Travel may be required.

Basic Qualifications

- 5 years of experience in positions of increasing responsibility within the security field
  Proven investigative experience to include: conducting interviews; locating, reviewing and analyzing data; conducting investigative research in physical security systems (CCTV, alarms, access control); preserving evidence; and producing cohesive and thorough written reports.
- Experience with a standard case management systems, including entering and maintaining case documents and evidence.
- Excellent written and interpersonal communication skills.

Figure CP9.3   Career Profile: Private security investigator. (Continued)

- Proficiency in internet and open source/social media research.
- Experience interfacing with leadership on security and investigative matters.
- Experience in fundamental business skills (working with a budget, etc.) and proficiency in standard office software programs, such as word processing and spreadsheets.

Preferred Qualifications

- Prior corporate security or law enforcement experience.
- Experience in behavioral threat assessments.
- Cyber security awareness and experience in conducting computer related investigations.
- Experience with producing basic statistics and producing case analysis data in a standard case management system.
- Experience interfacing with local, state or federal law enforcement agencies.
- Experience in corporate structure and culture.
- Security related memberships and certifications.

Required Education

- Bachelor's degree

Company Overview

At Corporate, you'll team with the best in the business to build one of the most innovative global businesses in any industry. Uniquely positioned at the center of an exciting, multi-faceted Company, the forward-thinkers at Disney Corporate constantly pursue new ideas and technologies to help the Company's many businesses drive value, all the while gaining something valuable from the experience themselves. Come see the most interesting Company from the most interesting point of view.

Additional Information

This position is a legal entity of The Walt Disney Company, an equal opportunity employer.

Job Posting Company
Corporate/Shared Services
Job Posting Industries
Corporate
Employment Type
Full Time
Primary Location-City
Glendale
Primary Location-State
CA
Primary Location-Postal Code
91201
Primary Location-Country
US

Figure CP9.3   Career Profile: Private security investigator.

With these thoughts in mind, there are certain universal characteristics and traits necessary in the investigative process. First, the hallmark of any investigation is the ability to gather facts. *The Association of Trial Lawyers of America* makes this point abundantly clear:

> The principles of investigation are the same for the professional investigator or the attorney.... It is common knowledge among experienced lawyers that the case may be won or lost in the investigation. It is therefore essential that the investigator be both well trained in the art of conducting an investigation and carefully briefed in the specific objectives of his investigation of a particular case.[44]

Continuing this line of reasoning, Art Buckwalter, in his amply documented work, *Investigative Methods*, comments on this reality:

---

[44] The Association of Trial Lawyers of America, *The Anatomy of a Personal Injury Lawsuit, A Handbook of Basic Trial Advocacy*, 14–15 (2nd ed., 1981).

No list can possibly cover all potentialities. Constantly new situations and complexities develop, calling for special investigative assignments. One of the realities for investigators is the persistence of variable factors that make every case and every career different. These variables of personalities and situations can never be standardized. They spring from the nature of the human heart and mind and from the conflicts and complexities of our modern life.[45]

No matter what the case or subject matter, security professionals who hope to attain a high level of professional standing must be competent investigators. Business, industry, attorneys, agencies at the federal, state, and local levels, and other employers look to the security investigator to collect information and to resolve factual disputes and confusing data. In a general sense, the security investigator lays a foundation, a conceptual framework, upon which cases can be evaluated, decisions can be made, or eventual action and policy making can be formulated.

Investigation is the process of fact assimilation. Investigation is the systematic collection of evidence necessary to support or refute a claim, whether civil or criminal in nature. Investigation is the process of observation, close inspection and analysis, and continuous and regular inquiry into a specific subject matter.[46] Investigation is the search and journey toward the reconstruction of events and conditions pertinent to a client's needs and interests:

> Successful investigation involves a balance between the scientific knowledge of the investigative process acquired by study and experience and the skills acquired by the artful application of learned techniques.[47]

In sum, without obtaining facts, data, and real evidence, the investigator has not performed effectively. The security professional wishing to be considered successful must provide the information requested, rather than operate by conjecture or hunch. Sound investigative practice cannot rely upon the assertions and allegations of a client, but a corroboration of same.

Therefore, astute investigative practice must include these uniform practices:

1. A logical sequence must be followed.
2. Real, physical evidence must be legally obtained.
3. Real, physical evidence must be properly stored and preserved.
4. Witnesses must be identified, interviewed, and prepared for any potential or actual litigation.
5. Leads must be developed.
6. Reports and documentation must be collected.
7. Information must be accurately and completely recorded.
8. Evidence collected must correlate to the claim, cause of action, or offense charged.[48]

The investigative process must comprehensively reconstruct events, conditions, or, as is often stated, the truth itself. Finding the truth is often an elusive undertaking. In the process of finding truth, investigators must evaluate, gauge, and assess witnesses, physical and real evidence, documents, testimony, and the entire array of evidentiary considerations in the formulation of a case. *Simply put, the process of investigation requires the conversion of alleged acts into real and useful evidence.*[49] In sum, the process of investigation requires the conversion of alleged acts into real and useful evidence.

And investigators must work hard in the virtual world as well, for more and more information and data are being kept and housed in the virtual domain. As the recent travails of Hillary Clinton illustrate, once the information has entered into the virtual world, it appears always retrievable. Data of every sort are stored virtually and are just as illuminating as the handwritten document. Data must not be neglected and come from a host of sources, including but not limited to

---

[45] A. Buckwalter, *Investigative Methods* 22 (Butterworth Publishers, 1984).

[46] See B. Tuskan, The Corporate Investigations Discipline, Pinkerton Blog (November 11, 2014) https://www.pinkerton.com/blog/the-corporate-investigations-discipline/.

[47] W. Bennett & K. Hess, *Criminal Investigation* 9 (West Publishing Co., 1981).

[48] *Ibid.* at 9.

[49] Kittredge, Guideposts for the Investigation of a Negligence Case, 90 *Prac. Law* 55 (1973); Baker, Reconstruction of Accidents, 17 *Traffic Dig. & Rev.* 9 (1969); 1 Am. Jur. Trials 357 (1987).

- Access control
- PBX
- Digital phone recordings
- Blogs
- ID systems
- Report writing systems
- Internet logs
- E-mail
- Calendars
- Video
- Delivery logs
- PeopleSoft
- SAP
- Travel and expense records
- Point of sales data
- Time clocks
- Wireless networks
- Webcams
- Bluetooth personal area networks (PANs)[50]

In fact, the computer—which is central to every business entity—is now considered a primary source of evidence during common investigative regimens. John Mallery urges security practitioners to see "cyberforensics" are routine rather than extraordinary when developing investigative strategies when he notes:

> Everyone is starting to recognize that investigations are incomplete unless they consider digital evidence. In many cases there is evidence that exists only in digital form… The ultimate goal of cyberforensics is to recover evidence so it can be used in a court proceeding.[51]

9.4.1 Types of investigations in the security industry

The role of private security in the investigative process is also determined by the subject matter of the investigation. The investigative process serves many purposes in both the criminal and civil justice systems, including

1. To determine if there is sufficient factual evidence to support or defeat each element of a cause of action
2. To accumulate the necessary factual evidence to prove or defeat a case at trial or to form the basis for a settlement
3. To locate leads to additional evidence
4. To locate persons or property
5. To find evidence that might be used to discredit (impeach) a witness or the opponent[52]

The role of private security in the investigative process is also determined by the subject matter of the investigation. Professor Thomas Eimermann affirms how the subject matter of an investigation, and its corresponding methodology, will depend upon the subject matter of that investigation.

> The nature of the investigation will, of course, vary considerably with the area of law involved, as well as with the particular facts of the case at hand. Negligence cases require a great deal of investigative work. Damaged cars, broken machines, and injured persons all have to be examined. Witnesses have to be interviewed at length in order to determine the existence of

---

[50] C. Harold, The Detective and the Database at 66 Security Management (March 2006) available at https://sm.asisonline.org/Pages/The-Detective-and-the-Database.aspx.

[51] Page 46 Cyberforensics; see also The Do's and Don'ts of Digital Evidence by Dave Lang.

[52] J. Mccord, The Litigation Paralegal 69 (West Publishing Co., 1988).

negligence on the part of one or more parties to the accident. In work[ers'] compensation cases, negligence is not an issue, but the extent of damage is. Likewise, the extent to which an injury was work-related becomes an important aspect of the investigation. In probate, an investigation could involve either locating missing heirs or attempting to determine what the mental state of the deceased was at the time the will was written. The underlying skills in all areas are basically the same.[53]

The range and scope of investigative practice are as varied as the multiplicity of subject matters. A representative list might include

- Claims investigation
- Divorce investigation
- Location of missing persons
- Location of heirs and assigns
- Civil investigation
- Criminal investigation
- Credit investigation
- Background investigation
- Undercover investigation
- Insurance investigation
- Personal injury investigation
- Traffic accident investigation
- Property loss investigation
- Medical malpractice investigation
- Government agency investigation
- Fire, safety, and OSHA investigations
- Domestic relations investigation
- Patent and trademark investigations
- Organized crime investigation
- Fraud and white-collar crime investigations
- Employee investigation
- Polygraph investigation
- Housing code investigation
- Building trades investigation
- Surveillance activities
- Witness location
- Workers' compensation cases
- Corporate investigation
- Judgment investigation
- Product liability and consumer claims
- Public record searches
- Title searches
- Marine investigation
- Construction accident investigation
- Toxic tort investigation

[53] T. Eimermann, *Fundamentals of Paralegalism* 102–103 (Little, Brown, 1980).

- Psychological and psychiatric investigation
- Questioned document investigation

The above list is a partial attempt to cover investigative strategy, since the nature and extent of investigative work and practice in the security industry are impossible to categorize fully. As technological, scientific, and other advances occur, for example, in the areas of forensic science, DNA or computer forensics, the need for skilled investigators will mirror the emerging fields. Both investigation method and the investigators that carry out the said investigation will come to depend not only on expertise but also a recognizable field. In this sense, investigative practice is forever changing. Security firms reflect this multifaceted approach to investigating.

9.5 PRIVATE SECURITY AND INVESTIGATIVE APPLICATIONS

While many techniques of investigative practice apply across the spectrum of crime and criminality, some activity catches the eye of the security industry more than others. Since asset protection is a perennial security function, retail theft, burglary, and related property offenses are perpetual concerns for the private security sector as are the problems of fraud, cyber-crime, and insurance and benefits verification and integrity corroboration. These are issues that each security professional encounters on a day-to-day basis.

9.5.1 Theft by shoplifting

Theft, retail shoplifting, corporate fraud, and other forms of white-collar crime attack not only the profit potential in the commercial marketplace, but also undermine institutional and employer trust and, unfortunately, cause an indirect escalation of prices inevitably passed on to consumers.[54] While there may be considerable disagreement as to the exact amounts of economic losses due to theft and other property offenses, it is a certainty that "[c]rimes victimize all businesses, small or large, retail, wholesale, manufacturing, or service."[55]

Property offenses have a monumental impact on both personal and business environments. The impact of economic crime and its related costs is difficult to fully define and appreciate because criminal conduct takes on many forms and directions.[56]

> In an annual study of waste and abuse of on-the-job time, it was estimated that in 1981 employees cost the American economy "a staggering $120 billion" resulting from employee "time theft"—excessive socializing, conducting personal business on employer time, late arrivals, abuse of sick leave, etc. An interesting example of fraud is the estimated $73.2 million a year lost by the Bell Telephone operating companies through fraudulent billings, that is, telephone calls charged to a number that is not the caller's own. About $48 million of the loss is from pay phones.[57]

Those numbers have continued unabated until the present.[58]

Theft, retail shoplifting, corporate fraud, and other forms of white-collar crime attack not only the profit potential in the commercial marketplace, but also undermine institutional and employer trust and, unfortunately, cause an indirect escalation of prices inevitably passed on to consumers. Economic crime impacts society in many indirect ways, such as

1. *Business effects*
   a. Increased costs of insurance and security protection
   b. Costs of internal audit activities to detect crime
   c. Cost of investigation and prosecution of suspects measured in terms of lost time of security and management personnel

---

[54] See C. Hertig, *Investigation Next Training Goal.*

[55] R. O'Block, *Security and Crime Prevention* 156 (1981).

[56] R.D. McCrie, Shoplifting: Managing the Problem, *Security Letter* (July 2006) at 4; R. Hayes & K. Rogers, Catch Them If You Can, *Sec. Mgmt* (October 2003) at 80.

[57] Cunningham & T. Taylor, *The Hallcrest Report: Private Security and Police in America* 18 (1985).

[58] A.F. Greggo, Attention Shoplifters, *Sec. Mgmt* (December 2008) at 56.

    d. Reduced profits

    e. Increased selling prices and weakened competitive standing

    f. Loss of productivity

    g. Loss of business reputation

    h. Deterioration in quality of service

    i. Threats to the survival of small business

2. *Local government effects*

    a. Costs of investigation and prosecution of suspects

    b. Increased costs of prosecuting sophisticated (e.g., embezzlement) and technology-related (e.g., computer) crime

    c. Costs of correctional programs to deal with economic crime offenders

    d. Cost of crime prevention programs

    e. Cost of crime reporting and mandated security programs

    f. Loss of tax revenue (e.g., loss of sales tax, untaxed income of perpetrator, and tax deductions allowed business for crime-related losses)

3. *Public effects*

    a. Increased costs of consumer goods and services to offset crime losses

    b. Loss of investor equity

    c. Increased taxes

    d. Reduced employment due to business failures[59]

Although there may be considerable disagreement as to the exact amounts of economic losses due to theft and other property offenses, it is a certainty that "[c]rimes victimize all businesses, small or large, retail, wholesale, manufacturing, or service."[60] Cunningham and Taylor concur:

> Even using similar crime index and inflationary adjusting techniques, the direct cost of economic crime which was at least $67 billion in 1980, and other estimates, though not substantiated, would place economic crime at $200–300 billion. The cumulative direct and indirect costs are much greater, and valid estimates are necessary if public and private organizations are to allocate their resources cost-effectively.[61]

Case clearance rates—the rates at which cases are closed through a resolution and identification of the perpetrator—are low in property crime categorizations. Police resources and energies are more likely to be allotted for major personal crimes such as murder, rape, and robbery. Our culture has become so inundated with personal, felonious conduct that property offenses tend to take a back seat in the investigative scheme of things. There have even been efforts to "decriminalize" offenses such as shoplifting.[62]

Instead of referring to it as a traditional larceny, that is, the unlawful taking of another's property, legislators have constructed and designed a new statute for shoplifting that is less felonious than an actual larceny. Prosecution clearance rates, a measure of successful convictions, are even less impressive.

Web Exercise: The International Foundation for Protection Officers (IFPO) has developed a distance loss prevention educational program. Discover its approach at http://www.ifpo.org/resource-links/retail-loss-prevention/.

9.5.1.1 Rationalizations and justifications for shoplifting

Business planners and other entrepreneurs take for granted a certain level of internal and external pilferage and shoplifting. Shoplifting has reached epidemic proportions due to a host of factors, including but not limited to cultural tolerance, sheer volume, a lack of remedy and corresponding consequence, and a legal system

---

[59] Hallcrest at 19.

[60] R. O'Block, *Security and Crime Prevention* 156 (1981).

[61] Hallcrest at 25.

[62] There has been a trend to decriminalization. See Charles P. Nemeth, *Criminal Law* (2004).

incapable of handling the rush of cases. In addition to these explanations, the perpetrators have rationalized away the criminality of shoplifting—urging a tolerant view that does not reach the traditional threshold of crime and punishment.[63] The act of shoplifting or retail theft has become so common that in many circles there is a cry for decriminalization.

Web Exercise: The National Association of Shoplifting Prevention gives keen insight into the motivation of shoplifters at http://www.shopliftingprevention.org/WhatNASPOffers/NRC/UnderstandingTheRootCauses.htm.

Its perpetrators are skilled at posing rationalizations that seek to excuse this illegal conduct. The rationalizations can be categorized as follows:

1. That shoplifting is not stealing but simply borrowing
2. That shoplifting is a sign of the times
3. That shoplifting is a correct, moral act
4. That shoplifting is an indirect benefit or reward of the job
5. That shoplifting is not a crime but instead a political act in a class struggle

What is clear and irrefutable is that shoplifters have diverse motivations for the act and just as many rationalizations that explain it as something more in the province of nuisance rather than crime. And some are more experienced than others. Robert O'Block, in his book *Security and Crime Prevention*, distinguishes between amateur and professional shoplifters:

> Shoplifting occurs for a variety of reasons, including desperation, impulse, peer pressure, revenge, or (rarely) kleptomania. Persons who shoplift for these reasons are generally amateurs and represent a majority over professional shoplifters, amateurs comprising about 85 percent of all shoplifters.[64]

Whatever rationalization is conveyed, the act of shoplifting or retail theft has become so common that in many circles it is synonymous with decriminalized conduct.

Aside from motivations, shoplifters can be classified according to type. They can be categorized as follows:

1. The amateur adult shoplifter
2. The juvenile shoplifter
3. The professional shoplifter
4. The kleptomaniac
5. The shoplifter-addict
6. Vagrant and the alcoholic shoplifter[65]

In *Corporate Fraud: The Basics of Prevention and Detection*, thieves and shoplifters are categorized according to motivation rather than personality. The standard rationalizations are referred to as "personal inducements," with the following synopsis indicating the motivations:

1. Economic—To fulfill actual or perceived economic needs
2. Ideological—To take revenge against those with ideological differences
3. Egocentric—To prove that they are clever and knowledgeable or because they have an extravagant sense of self-importance
4. Psychotic—Out of a distorted sense of reality, for example, delusions[66]

Whatever the type or the motivation, it is a glaring difficulty for contemporary business.

---

[63] R. McCrie, Retail Mgmt.: Center Helps Lp Dirs. & Aids Shoplifters to Break Habits, *Security Letter* (November 3, 2008).
[64] O'Block, *supra* note 7, at 158.
[65] Pinkerton's, Inc., *Investigations Department Training Manual* 127 (1990).
[66] J. Bologna, *Corporate Fraud: The Basics of Prevention and Detection* 82 (1984).

9.5.1.2 Shoplifting methods

Every investigator should become familiar with the techniques and methods of shoplifting and its related deceptions. As a rule, shoplifters must rely upon their hands to commit acts of thievery. Shoplifters are keenly attuned and aware of their environment and, in scanning territory, they have a tendency to look quickly from side to side before committing the theft act. Because the shoplifter is performing an illegal act and is under the strain of trying to do so without getting caught, the physical movements and motions of the shoplifter tend to be less fluid and are instead quick, jerky, and sporadic. Body language speaks loudly.

Web Exercise: Eugene, Oregon published an excellent guide for merchants and security officers on how to deter and identify shoplifters at http://www.eugene-or.gov/DocumentCenter/Home/View/6136.

Shoplifters also use diversions, decoys, and disturbances that distract the eyes of salesclerks and other responsible personnel. Shoplifters may engage in some of these deceptive tactics:

1. Palming is the simplest and most common method for theft.
2. Purses and pockets are common concealing places for shoplifted items.
3. A loose coat or full skirt can conceal items.
4. Rubber bands can be snapped around bundles of ties, stockings, or socks.
5. Hats, gloves, scarves, coats, sweaters, and purses can be worn out of the store.
6. Coats or sweaters may be thrown down over merchandise desired, and then picked up with the merchandise concealed inside.
7. Jewelry and other accessories can be dropped into clothing or inserted into the hair.
8. In fitting rooms, tight or closely fitting garments can be put on under street clothes. Packages and purses can be rearranged to conceal the addition of a dress or blouse.
9. Intentional confusion with merchandise: Handling so much clothing or products that sales personnel lose track; using accomplices or other party to distract sales personnel.
10. Price switching: Taking a price from one product with a higher price and relabeling with a lower price label.
11. Stepping around the end of the counter, using the excuse of wanting to see something, in order to steal expensive articles from the unlocked side of a showcase.
12. Distracting sales personnel by persistent bell ringing while accomplice steals merchandise.
13. Removing small items from a display case and hiding them in another portion of the store for later retrieval by an accomplice.[67]

To identify and catch shoplifters, keen senses and developed skills of human observation are necessary.[68] See Figure 9.7.[69]

By both direct and inferential conduct, the investigator can make reasonable, probable-cause judgments relative as to suspected parties if he or she watches closely.[70] In addition to the initial observations, security personnel should watch for other conditions, circumstances, and behavioral characteristics of suspects:

- Watching out for customers who ask to be shown more articles than a clerk can keep track of
- Repeatedly sending a clerk away for more merchandise
- Two or more customers shuffling articles at the same time and at the same counter
- Two or three persons grouped together around a counter, thereby restricting the view of the salesclerk
- Examining articles in corners and odd locations
- Continuously dropping articles on the floor
- Holding identical pieces of merchandise for comparison

---

[67] Pinkerton's, Inc., *Investigations Department Training Manual* 131–132 (1990).
[68] See J. Petrocelli, Shoplifting, *Police* (December 2008) at 16.
[69] Rutgers, Common Shoplifting Techniques, http://crimeprevention.rutgers.edu/crime/shoplifting/techniques.htm.
[70] C.P. Nemeth, *Private Security and the Investigative Process*, 3rd ed. 234 (CRC Press, 2010).

Common shoplifting techniques

Hiding the Merchandise

Favorite Shoplifter Devices

A large open bag is a common shoplifter tool. It is placed at the thief's feet, and objects are casually dropped into it. Be on the lookout for the "bad bag" -- a paper bag that is dirty and wrinkled. Also keep an eye out for shopping bags that are not from local stores. Preventing this is why many stores staple bags shut. Other stores require customers to leave their bags by the front door when they come in.

Women sometimes use purses to hide stolen items. There is little you can do to stop women from carrying purses and handbags. The best prevention in these cases is to watch the customers very carefully.

The baby carriage or stroller is a great tool for shoplifters. There are always blankets, toys, and other things in strollers (including the baby) that merchandise can be hidden under. Some thieves have even built false bottoms in baby carriages.

A newspaper can be used to hide small objects.

Umbrellas with handles are handy for shoplifters trying to steal small items. A common tactic is to keep a closed (but not snapped) umbrella hanging on one's elbow or leaning against a counter, and then to drop items into it.

Favorite Shoplifter Clothing

"Crotch-walking" is a technique used by women wearing full skirts and dresses. They simply place the merchandise between their thighs and walk away. Thieves who are good at this have been known to steal hams, typewriters, and other large objects.

Baggy clothes in general are good places to hide stolen items. Some people have extra pockets or hooks sewn into coats and jackets.

Beware of the customer with a large coat who keeps his hand in a coat pocket. Some shoplifters have cut slits in the pocket lining, so they can reach for items without being seen. They may make a big deal out of inspecting an item while the other hand slips out and grabs something.

A More Brazen Approach

Some shoplifters just grab stuff and walk out with it. They rely on the gullibility and slow response time of sales clerks.

Some shoplifters grab garments from racks close to the door and run off. This can be prevented very easily by alternating the directions of hangers. This makes the hangers "lock up" when someone tries to remove many at once.

The really brazen thieves simply walk out with large items that are not ordinarily put in bags. Prevent this by making it unusual for legitimate customers to carry out their large purchases, with a policy that all large items must be picked up at a location physically separate from the sales floor, or that employees take all large items out to customer's cars. Or you could put big bright stickers on purchased large items. This at least makes it easy for employees to tell if the merchandise is being stolen.

A common technique, especially if your fitting rooms aren't well monitored, is for the thief to steal garments by putting them on under her own clothes and wearing them out of the store. Others will just put the clothing on and walk out. It's tricky to catch one of these people, because if they haven't concealed the item, they technically haven't stolen it until they exit the store without paying. (Click here for more on preventing shoplifting in fitting rooms.)

Tricks to Distract You

Most shoplifters cannot succeed unless they get some privacy. This is why one of the best ways to stop shoplifting is to greet customers as soon as they walk in, then be attentive to them the rest of the time. But skilled shoplifters can distract sales associates using the following tricks:

They enter the store in groups, then separate, so there is no way the employees can watch all of them.

A pair of shoppers comes in, and while one distracts you with questions, the other steals.

A single shopper sends the only employee in the store into the back room to find something, and then steals stuff and leaves before the employee comes back.

Figure 9.7 Common shoplifting techniques and tricks.

- Holding or crumbling merchandise
- Hesitation or sudden decisions at elevators
- Making exits via back stairways
- Movement throughout the store but constantly reappearing at one counter
- Large groups of teenagers entering and splitting into smaller groups
- Removing tags from merchandise
- Nervous actions such as moistening dry lips or perspiring excessively
- Startled looks[71]

---

[71] Pinkerton's, Inc. at 136–137.

The deception and the acts selected will vary by the establishment victimized. Store security personnel need to recognize the unique clues that signal impending shoplifting at a grocery store or any other mercantile operation. Watch out for the following:

1. Customer who enters the market with an empty paper bag in her purse, fills the bag with merchandise, and walks through an unused check-out line. If questioned, suspect assures the clerk that he or she has already been checked out.

2. Boxed items that are easily opened and reclosed may have more valuable items placed inside.

3. Produce bags are an easy mark for the shoplifter who brings his or her own crayon or stapler. This is called "price marking" and could occur on almost any product, but is very popular on meat items. (Today, many stores use computerized pricing.)

4. Supermarket shoplifters have been known to open an expensive package of tea and pour the contents into a pocketbook where it settles at the bottom.

5. A customer places an item in her purse and at the check-out counter asks for credit, explaining that another member of the family bought the item by mistake. If the clerk refuses the refund because of no receipt, the shoplifter wins. The shoplifter, of course, also wins if the store grants a refund.

6. Another variation of price switching is "cap switching." With prices frequently stamped on the caps, a shopper with a desire to steal will simply exchange the cap on a large size container for that on a small container.[72]

Security investigators will note differences in shoplifting not only by establishment but also by department. The attractiveness and expense of goods directly correlate to the level and intensity of shoplifting.

To identify and catch shoplifters, keen senses and developed skills of human observation are necessary.[73] By both direct and inferential conduct, the investigator can make reasonable, probable-cause judgments relative as to suspected parties if he or she watches closely. Examples that tip off the observer are:

- Persons entering stores with heavy overcoats, out of season.
- Persons wearing baggy pants, full or pleated skirts (when current styles do not dictate the wearing of such apparel).
- Persons demonstrating darting eye movement and who conspicuously stretch their neck in all directions. Many professional shoplifters often do not give any clues other than eye movement.
- Persons who exit the store with undue hurriedness.
- Customers who do not seem interested in merchandise about which they have asked.
- Customers who do not seem to know what they want and change their mind frequently about merchandise.
- Individuals who leave the store with an unusual gait or who tie their shoes or pull up their socks frequently, or make any other unusual body movements that might assist them in concealing articles.
- Customers who walk behind or reach into display counters.
- A disinterested customer who waits for a friend or spouse to shop.
- Customers who constantly keep one hand in an outer coat pocket.
- Customers who make a scene to distract clerks, so that an accomplice can remove property without paying for it.[74]

A highly skilled investigator, in the retail theft arena, possesses extraordinary observational powers about human behavior and just as keenly understands the territory to which he or she has been assigned. To identify a shoplifter calls for more than catching the act itself but anticipating and identifying the common behaviors that manifest this illicit purpose. Thus, a private security investigator enlisted by a retail establishment to determine how goods are being pilfered should have a comprehensive understanding of the establishment. Prospective suspects will be numerous; before proceeding on wild goose chases or professional conjecture, become familiar with the assigned area. As always, use common sense when formulating your investigative strategy and practice.

---

[72] *Ibid.* at 134–135.
[73] See Joseph Petrocelli, Shoplifting, *Police* (December 2008) at 16.
[74] O'Block at 160–161; see also Nemeth, Investigative Process at 236–238.

Security Department
REPORT OF THEFT OR
LOSS OF PROPERTY

File #

1. Complainant's Name	2. Location and Tele. Ext.		3. Date Reported
4. Description of Item			Company Property ☐ Personal Property ☐

5. Model #	6. Serial #	7. Company Inventory No.	8. Value

9. Estimated Time of Theft

10. Last Known Location (Bldg., Floor, Office)	11. Property Assigned to or Owned by

12. Describe Precautions Taken to Protect Property

13. Furnish Additional Details

14. Details Concerning Police Report

	15. Report Prepared by	16. Date

17. Recommended Action

Figure 9.8   Report of theft.

9.5.1.3 Practice suggestions: Forms to detect and report shoplifting

If a case of missing personal property leads to the allegation of theft or shoplifting, most security departments will have a "report of theft" document. Figure 9.8 not only contains space for comments about the theft, but also solicits recommendations for response.

Tracking the location of property that was seized by private security operatives assures a proper chain of custody. Figure 9.9 is a sample of a property control receipt used to trace the movement of property.

Security firms operating within larger corporations, educational institutions, hotels and motels, and transport companies generally have more than one incident to report in a typical workday. The use of a special form to report losses is an outstanding way to track complicated and voluminous information. Figure 9.10 shows one style of this type of report.

Web Exercise: Consider the many useful suggestions concerning shoplifting posed by the Sacramento Sheriff's Department at http://www.sacsheriff.com/pages/crimeprevention/JuvenileCrimes02.aspx.

PROPERTY CONTROL RECEIPT				
NAME	TITLE		SIGNATURE	
LOCATION			TELEPHONE EXTENSION	
PROPERTY SURRENDER AUTHORITY				
NAME	TITLE		SIGNATURE	
REMOVAL TYPE: ☐ PERMANENT ☐ TEMPORARY ☐ OTHER				
ITEM	COUNT	DESCRIPTION	ISSUE DATE	RECOVER DATE

Figure 9.9   Property control receipt.

Finally, the best possible defense against shoplifting, aside from skilled officers tasked with apprehension and detection, is preventative steps the establishment can easily implement. A combination of video surveillance, access control, and technology controls, both high and low in design, provide a deterrence culture that is "always less expensive than attempting to catch thieves in the act and prosecuting them later."[75] Security officers should aggressively advise the merchant about ways to deter shoplifting, including these lines of defense:

- Train employees in the methods of shoplifting.
- Maximize visibility by raising cash register area; use convex mirrors; one-way mirrors are closed circuit television cameras.
- Use an electronic article surveillance system (EAS).
- Post signs in plain view stating that all shoplifters will be prosecuted.
- Keep cash registers locked and monitored at all times.
- Use cable tie-downs.
- Watch for price switching.
- Monitor all delivery men.
- Cashiers should check every item sold that might hide other merchandise.[76]

Finally, technology continues to play a crucial role in theft prevention in every corner of the commercial and retail marketplace. For example, GPS systems that track property movements, locations, and relocations are now considered

---

[75] J. Matthew Ladd, Helping Retailers Fight Crime at 58.
[76] M. Gleckman, Crime Prevention/Community Relations, in *The Security Supervisor Training Manual* (Sandi J. Davies & Ronald R. Minion, eds., 1995).

SECURITY DEPARTMENT		REPORT OF LOSSES			MONTH OF_____20_____			
DATE OF REPORT	DATE OF LOSS	NAME	STATUS	NATURE OF LOSS	VALUE	LOSS OR THEFT	RECOVERED	

Figure 9.10 Report of losses.

essential to security professionals tracing the history of product and its corresponding integrity.[77] New and innovative surveillance systems at location and off-site are finding permanent homes in the security arsenal too.[78] Access control and more sophisticated ID systems assure that facilities are being visited by only authorized personnel rather than intruders bent on theft and other criminality. Most commercial interests assume the critical role of technology in access and identification.[79]

9.5.2 Theft by employees

Internal theft, waste, and fraud by employees account for the largest part of shrinkage in many companies.[80]

How employee theft is consummated depends largely on positions, opportunities, and levels of access. In sum, people find a way to commit thievery and fraudulent acts depending on individual circumstances and conditions. Investigators, especially those working in institutional settings, should have a feel for the organizational and

---

[77] A New Vision for Theft Prevention at 86.
[78] *Security Magazine* (April 2013) at 14.
[79] See B. Scaglione, Grabbing the Access Control; and Joel Jensen, Access Control and Remote Control at 76.
[80] Hallcrest at 26.

administrative makeup of their clients. Companies that are loosely organized and have administrative problems will be more likely to have serious problems with internal theft and pilferage. The entire corporate or institutional environment influences an investigator's judgment. To perform the job properly, the investigator must know how management operates, how it intends to pursue parties that are apprehended, and how it oversees the scheme of things. The company that invests resources in the detection and prevention of criminality will most likely be rewarded with lower theft rates. Know thy employees before hire makes perfect sense.[81] The American Society for Industrial Security warns investigators that even a company's most trusted employees must not be overlooked in the process of investigating an action.

> [T]he investigator must consider all possible suspects, not eliminating anyone because they seem honest. In a pre-employment interview, all the signs may indicate that an employee can be trusted. However, people change, and negative attitudes toward the company can develop for many reasons. An updated background investigation may reveal that the employee has become a victim of alcohol or drug abuse, is in a financial bind, or is being strongly influenced by unsavory associates.[82]

Internal theft, waste, and fraud by employees account for the largest part of shrinkage in many companies. Within the retail setting, internal theft rates are astronomical. The National Institute of Justice's Executive Summary, *Theft by Employees in Work Organizations* reports:

> In each of the three industry sectors surveyed, roughly one-third of the employees reported some involvement in the taking of company property (e.g., merchandise, supplies, tools, and equipment) during the prior year. Additionally, over two-thirds of the sample reported counter-productive behavior such as long lunches and breaks, slow or sloppy workmanship, sick leave abuse, and the use of alcohol or drugs at work... The highest levels of property theft were reported by the younger (16 to mid-20s), unmarried, and male employees. In each type of industry those employees with the greatest unrestricted access to and knowledge about the property stolen (i.e., sales clerks in retail stores, engineers in manufacturing plants, and registered nurses and technicians in hospitals) were the occupational groups reporting the highest levels of theft. In addition, both property theft and particularly counterproductive behavior was more likely among those employees expressing dissatisfaction with their employment—especially dissatisfaction with their immediate supervisors and the company's attitude toward the workforce.[83]

Security firms must anticipate and plan for internal theft.[84]

9.5.2.1 Reasons and rationales for employee theft

Considerable differences of opinion exist as to why internal pilferage and other forms of employee thievery have risen so markedly. Some theorists hold that employees and, for that matter, employers, have lost all sense of loyalty to one another and to the company. As Barefoot remarks:

> Unlike Japanese firms, which generally enjoy a high degree of loyalty on the part of their employees, the typical American employer has seen employee loyalty dwindle to a point where it can no longer be considered a viable factor in any well-balanced security program.[85]

How do employees rationalize their illegal conduct? A survey of 100 certified public accountants and 90 data processing specialists revealed the following reasons that employees steal or embezzle from their employers:

1. They think stealing a little from a big company won't hurt.

2. Most employees are caught by accident rather than by audit or design, thus fear of being caught is not a deterrent

3. Employees steal for any reason the human mind and imagination can conjure up.[86]

---

[81] Fuss et al., The Importance of Background Investigation at 58; see also Charles Hale, The Employee Interview Exercise; and Russell Cormican, Interview Tips for Promotions and Transfer.

[82] ASIS International, *Basic Guidelines for Security Investigations* 91 (1981). See John H. Christman & Charles A. Sennewald, *Shoplifting: Managing the Problem* (2006).

[83] U.S. Department of Justice, National Institute of Justice, *Theft by Employees in Work Organizations* iii (1983).

[84] See Retailer Security Chief Pushes Proactive Approach, *Corporate Security* (January 31, 2008) at 8.

[85] Barefoot at 8.

[86] Hallcrest at 26.

Barefoot offers some other explanations:

- Population shifts
- Organized crime
- Limitation of reference checking
- Drugs
- Restrictions on screening
- Gambling
- Lack of security expertise[87]

Many public and private law enforcement officials note that the employee's rationale is often "Everybody does it. Why shouldn't I?" Private security investigators have to understand and contend with this type of reasoning since it permeates the thief's moral decision making.

9.5.2.2 Employee theft tactics

How employee theft is consummated depends largely on positions, opportunities, and levels of access. In sum, people find a way to commit thievery and fraudulent acts depending on individual circumstances and conditions. Some of the crimes might involve

- Merchandise swindles
- Embezzlement
- Organized crime schemes
- Commercial bribery and kickbacks
- Credit card fraud
- Receiving stolen goods
- Expense account fraud
- Price switching
- Medical and health care frauds
- Shoplifting
- Charitable and religious frauds
- Mortgage milking
- Insurance fraud
- Forgery and other document tampering
- False security fraud

Employee theft strategies and tactics are multidimensional, including

- Passing merchandise across the counter to an accomplice
- Putting merchandise in concealed places
- Under-ringing cash registers
- Overcharging a customer and pocketing the difference
- Theft of merchandise through unsupervised exits
- Failure to register sales
- Writing false refunds
- Collusion with delivery men and drivers
- Stealing from the warehouse or stockroom

---

[87] Barefoot at 7–9.

- Stealing from returned goods and layaway
- Voiding a sales check and then pocketing the money
- Cashing fraudulent checks for accomplices
- Giving fraudulent refunds to accomplices
- Failing to record returned purchases and stealing an equal amount of cash
- Falsifying sales records to take cash
- Concealing thefts by falsifying store records
- Taking money from cash registers
- Giving employee discounts to unauthorized parties
- Concealing stolen goods in trash or other containers
- Shipping clerks mailing goods to their own address
- Wearing store clothing and accessories home at the end of a shift
- Intentionally damaging goods in order to buy them at discount
- Buying damaged merchandise at discount prices and later substituting damaged goods for first quality merchandise
- Stealing checks made payable to cash
- Picking up receipts discarded by customers and using them for refunds
- Stealing during early or late store hours
- Stealing from the dock or other exit areas
- Forging checks
- Keeping collections on uncollectible accounts
- Receiving kickbacks from suppliers[88]

9.5.2.3 Investigating internal theft

The American Society for Industrial Security warns investigators that even a company's most trusted employees must not be overlooked in the process of investigating an action.

> [T]he investigator must consider all possible suspects, not eliminating anyone because they seem honest. In a pre-employment interview, all the signs may indicate that an employee can be trusted. However, people change, and negative attitudes toward the company can develop for many reasons. An updated background investigation may reveal that the employee has become a victim of alcohol or drug abuse, is in a financial bind, or is being strongly influenced by unsavory associates.[89]

When conducting an investigation of internal theft among retail store clerks, one should consider the following questions:

1. Are the clerks waiting on the customers promptly and courteously?
2. Are all sales being rung up and the monies deposited in the cash register?
3. Is the cash register kept closed at all times other than when a transaction takes place?
4. Are the clerks giving the employee discount privileges to nonstore employees?
5. Are the employee purchase procedures being followed?
6. Are employees taking extended breaks and lunch periods?
7. Is there an unusually close relationship between clerks in different departments, and do they handle each other's employee purchases?
8. Do certain customers insist on being serviced by a specific clerk even though other clerks are available?
9. Are the clerks following the store procedures on refunds and exchanges?

---

[88] O'Block at 184–185.

[89] ASIS International, *Basic Guidelines for Security Investigations* 91 (1981). See John H. Christman & Charles A. Sennewald, *Shoplifting: Managing the Problem* (2006).

10. Are the clerks familiar with pricing within their department, thereby limiting the possibility of "price switching" by customers?

11. Are the proper taxes being charged?

12. Do clerks know where to find in-stock items that are not on display?

13. Are the clerks wearing store merchandise, such as jewelry, and "forgetting" to return it?

14. Are clerks placing store merchandise under the counter to be purchased by them at some later date?

15. Is there a specific clerk who is extremely proficient in her duties and adherence to store policies?[90]

Web Exercise: Read Charles Sennewald's reflection on why shoplifting rates have yet to meaningfully drop at http://www.shoplifting.com/flawedstrategies.pdf.

The investigator should also observe the conduct of the suspected employee. Look for behavior that sends up a red lag:

- Salesperson wears clothes with large, exterior pockets.
- Salesperson has a purse, bag, or other item behind the counter.
- Salesperson works alone at a register in a high-volume, low-cash sales department.
- Salesperson asks you if you want to put the item in another bag you are carrying.
- Salesperson writes figures on a scrap of paper near the register.
- Salesperson throws register receipts on the floor instead of giving them to you.[91]

Certain evidence may directly implicate a suspect:

- High shortage departments
- Below-average cash sales
- Consistent overages and shortages
- Excessive "No Sales"
- Maladjusted employee
- Store policy violators
- Temporary personnel
- Cash register consistently open[92]

Prevention strategies for mitigating internal theft are summarized in Figure 9.11.[93]

9.5.2.4 Employee theft tests and protocols

Investigators, especially those working in institutional settings, should have a feel for the organizational and administrative makeup of their clients. Companies that are loosely organized and have administrative problems will be more likely to have serious problems with internal theft and pilferage. The National Institute of Justice urges:

> [T]he control of employee taking of property seems to be a problem that the business organization must keep visible on its list of priorities and objectives. It cannot be ignored or relegated to a topic of temporary or minimal importance, nor should it be assigned as a task for a specialized portion of the organization's management team. This research suggests that only by exhibiting a conspicuous and consistent climate of concern about the control of internal theft at all occupational levels can an organization hope to have a significant effect on the behavior of its employees[94].

The entire corporate or institutional environment influences an investigator's judgment. To perform the job properly, the investigator must know how management operates, how it intends to pursue parties that are apprehended, and

---

[90] Pinkerton's, Inc. at 155–156.

[91] *Ibid*. at 161.

[92] *Ibid*. at 160.

[93] Beverly Police Department, Internal Theft Prevention, http://www.beverlypd.org/pdf/PRIVATE%20BUSINESS%20SAFETY%20TOPICS/INTERNAL%20THEFT%20PREVENTION.pdf

[94] U.S. Department of Justice, National Institute of Justice, Theft by Employees in Work Organizations 2 (1983).

Internal Theft Prevention

Virtually all companies suffer losses due to internal theft. It is estimated that 75 - 80% of inventory shrinkage is due to employee theft, while shoplifting accounts for the remainder.

Methods of Theft

- Employees may hide merchandise or goods either on their person or in a handbag, lunch box, backpack or briefcase and take it out at lunch break, smoke break or at the end of their shift.
- Employees may remove equipment or merchandise from the building in the trash and retrieve it later.
- Customers may be overcharged and the employee may pocket the money later on.
- Employees may take incoming cash (bill payments) and fail to credit the customer's account.
- Employees may give employee discounts to friends or family members.
- Employees may consume goods in a store.
- They may provide items free or at a reduced price to co-workers, family members or friends.
- Employees may under ring a sale, collect the full amount from the customer and pocket the difference.
- The employee may overcharge customers and pocket the extra money later on.
- The employee may prepare a fraudulent refund voucher and pocket the money.
- The employee may give a fraudulent refund to an accomplice.
- Employees may ring "no sale" on a cash register, accept cash from a customer for payment and keep the money.
- Payroll and/or personnel employees may falsify records by the use of nonexistent employees or by retaining terminated employees on the payroll.
- Contract maintenance or cleaning personnel may steal goods, materials or office equipment.
- Delivery persons and receiving clerks may falsify records and convert unaccounted merchandise.
- Purchasing agents in collusion with vendors may falsify purchase and payment records.
- Accounts payable personnel may pay fraudulent bills to an account established for their own use.
- Checks may be issued and cashed for returned merchandise not actually returned.
- An employee may take money from a cash register assigned to another employee.
- Employees may intentionally damage goods in order to purchase them at discount prices.
- Employees may duplicate keys and enter the business during closed hours.
- An employee may receive kickbacks from suppliers for invoicing goods above the established price.

Prevention Strategies

- Develop a purchase policy that specifies how employee purchases are to be processed. Employees should not be allowed to process their own sales.

Figure 9.11   Strategies for mitigating employee theft.   (*Continued*)

how it oversees the scheme of things. Companies that treat their employees poorly, that provide little or no feedback on performance, and that do not restrict or restrain conduct or behavior risk far greater losses due to employee misconduct. In essence, a lack of control results in an almost chaotic environment. As a rule of thumb, if employees feel the scrutiny of management, that there are repercussions to illegal and immoral conduct, and that the company has invested significant time and energy in assuring the protection of its assets, it is less likely that criminal conduct will occur. There are many factors that enhance the potentiality for criminal conduct, especially internal theft, fraud, and embezzlement within the business entity, including

- Inadequate pay, benefits, job security, and promotional opportunities
- Ambiguity in job roles, relationships, responsibilities, and areas of accountability
- Lack of recognition for good work, loyalty, longevity, and effort

- Provide lockers for employees, and develop a policy stating that employees may not take personal articles such as purses, backpacks, lunch boxes and briefcases into merchandise areas.
- Restrict employees to a single monitored exit, if possible.
- Number refunds and keep control over refund books.
- Develop a policy regarding trash removal. It should indicate when trash should be removed from the building and what is to be done with empty boxes. Transparent trash bags should be used.
- If a contract cleaning company is used, the following questions should be asked:

  How long have the custodians worked for the company?
  Do they have references from other locations?
  Are the custodians bonded?
  Do the custodians work alone or with someone else?
  Is a supervisor present while custodians are cleaning?

- Perform random checks of employees who arrive early or stay late when there is no need to do so.
- Flatten all trash cartons and boxes and spot check trash containers.
- Do not permit truck drivers to load their own vehicles without inspection.
- Have supervisory personnel conduct periodic truck checks before the vehicle leaves.
- Develop strong audit controls and inventory all supplies, equipment and merchandise regularly.
- Have an effective access management policy:

  Have a written and distributed access management and key control policy.
  The only basis for the issuance of a key or access card should be job necessity.
  An accurate record of issued keys must be maintained and a periodic audit of keys conducted.
  Unauthorized loaning or duplicating of keys should be strictly forbidden.
  There should be an effective mechanism (holding last paycheck, for example) for retrieving keys from employees who resign, retire or are terminated.

- Have returned merchandise inspected by someone other than the person who made the sale.
- All employees should have identification cards.
- Limit the amount of cash allowed to accumulate in a cash register —— make unannounced counts on registers.
- Bookkeepers should not be responsible for shipping and receiving merchandise. Purchasing should not be involved in any aspect of accounts receivable or the receipt of merchandise.
- Managers or supervisors should periodically open and inspect incoming mail.
- All employees should be required to take periodic vacations. This could reveal a trend or practice of employee thefts.
- Companies should have periodic audits by outside auditors.
- All cash book entries should be checked against cash on hand at the end of each day.
- Companies should have strict accountability and routine audit of blank checks, order forms, payment authorizations, vouchers, receipt forms and all other forms which authorize or verify transactions.

Figure 9.11 (Continued)   Strategies for mitigating employee theft.   (*Continued*)

- Lack of periodic audits and inspections
- Ambiguous corporate social values and ethical norms
- Tolerance or indifference toward antisocial behavior
- Bias or unfairness in selection, promotion, compensation, or appraisal
- Inadequate training on security matters and company policies with respect to sanctions for security breaches
- Failure to screen applicants thoroughly for sensitive positions before appointment
- General job-related stress or anxiety

The company that invests resources in the detection and prevention of criminality will most likely be rewarded with lower internal theft rates. The measures in Figure 9.12 should provide obstacles to internal theft.

- Whenever possible or practical, competitive bids should be sought for the acquisition of goods and services.
- Persons responsible for preparing payroll should not be involved in its distribution.
- The payroll should be periodically audited for irregularities by external auditors.
- In accounts payable, periodic audits should be conducted by external auditors to examine records for any sign of nonexistent vendors, irregularities in receipts or payment authorizations, forgeries, fraud or procedures that could lead to embezzlement.
- Require the giving of register receipts to each customer.
- Receiving, warehousing, and shipping of materials or products should be the responsibility of three different areas.
- Both criminal and prior employment background checks should be conducted for prospective employees.
- All inventory shortages should be immediately and aggressively investigated.

Symptoms of Persons Involved in Internal Theft

There are certain symptoms or characteristics of persons involved in internal theft. They include the following:

- A significant change in spending habits.
- A noticeable increase in the employee's standard of living.
- An unusual devotion to a job or work function.
- An employee with financial responsibilities who does not take earned vacations.
- Employees who object to procedural changes that could lead to closer supervision.
- An employee with financial responsibilities who refuses a promotion or transfer that would alter their current job function.

Figure 9.11 (Continued)   Strategies for mitigating employee theft.

Efforts to reduce internal theft in the retail, business, and corporate settings need constant vigilance and a resilient approach. Passivity will not assure success but a combination of protocols that target potential as well as actual employees will mitigate the damage. That culture begins long before the employee ever arrives in a prospective status. Dave Sawyer zeroes in on the importance of prescreening when he remarks:

> Gone are the days when the hiring process was based on a "gut" feeling and firm handshake, yet there remain a fair number of otherwise very savvy business people who take the self- service approach to background screening.[95]

Companies must maintain "constant skepticism, brainstorm to identify fraud risks, cultivate a vigorous 'whistle-blower' program and adopt other measures."[96] David McCoy refers to this as a "culture of compliance"—an aura essential to minimizing internal theft and fraud.[97]

A highly skilled investigator possesses two fundamental traits: first, the investigator knows the territory to which he or she is assigned, its personalities, its geographic location, its layout, and its overall operation; and second, the investigator is able to apply theory in practical situations. Thus, a private security investigator enlisted by a retail establishment to determine how goods are being pilfered should have a comprehensive understanding of the establishment. Prospective suspects will be numerous; before proceeding on wild goose chases or professional conjecture, become familiar with the assigned area. As always, use common sense when formulating your investigative strategy and practice.

Testing for internal and external shoplifting and pilferage falls into two major categories: honesty and service tests. When conducting an honesty test, the investigator determines whether employees are stealing cash during customer purchase transactions. In service testing, the investigator reports to management how he or she was treated during a specific transaction while observations were made.

Web Exercise: Visit Jack Hayes International—a firm that specializes in assisting business with inventory shrinkage and retail theft controls at http://hayesinternational.com/lp-services/loss-preventionshrinkage-control-analysis/.

---

[95] Pre-Employment Background Screening at 112; see also John O'Gara, Corporate Fraud: Case Studies in Detection and Prevention (Wiley, 2004).

[96] M. Gips, Tips for Tightening Fraud Controls, 18.

[97] Executive Roadmap at 110.

1. Prevention measures
   a. Internal accounting controls
      i. Separation of duties
      ii. Rotation of duties
      iii. Periodic internal audits and surprise inspections
      iv. Development and documentation of policies, procedures, systems, programs, and program modifications
      v. Establishment of dual signature authorities, dollar authorization limits per signatory, expiration date, and check amount limits
      vi. Off-line entry controls and limits
      vii. Batch totals, hash totals
   b. Computer access controls
      i. Identification defenses
         A. Key or card inserts
         B. Passwords and code numbers
         C. Exclusion—repeated error lockout
         D. Time activator/deactivator
         E. Periodic code and password changes
      ii. Authentication defenses
         A. Random personal data
         B. Voice, fingerprint, or palm geometry recognition
         C. Callbacks
      iii. Establishment of authorizations by levels of authority or levels of security (compartmentalization and "need to know")
2. Detection measures
   a. Exceptions in logging systems
      i. Out of sequence, out of priority, and aborted runs and entries
      ii. Out-of-pattern transactions: too high, too low, too many, too often, too few, unusual file access (odd times and places)
      iii. Attempted access beyond authorization level
      iv. Repeated attempts to gain access improperly—wrong password, entry code, etc.
      v. Parity and redundancy checks
   b. Management information system
      i. Monitoring operational performance levels for
         A. the variations from plans and standards
         B. deviations from accepted or mandated policies, procedures, and practices
         C. deviations from past quantitative relationships, i.e., ratios, proportions, percentages, trends, past performance levels, indices, etc.
   c. Intelligence gathering
      i. Monitoring employee attitudes, values, and job satisfaction level
      ii. Soliciting random feedback from or surveying customers, vendors, and suppliers for evidence of dissatisfaction, inefficiency, inconsistency with policies, corruption, or dishonesty by employees

Figure 9.12   Internal theft prevention measures.

9.5.2.4.1 Honesty testing

To detect theft, deception, fraud, pilferage, or other illegal conduct on the part of employees, investigators conduct honesty testing. In this type of test, the investigator simultaneously buys two of the same item. Prices can be the same or different. The investigator notes the register reading for the previous sale. The investigator then selects two of the same item and pays the employee the exact amount for the entire purchase. The investigator should then observe whether or not the cash register drawer was opened or closed before, after, or at the time of the purchase. In addition, the investigator should check whether or not the employee issued a receipt. The investigator should formally document these facts, the subsequent items purchased, and their related costs. Other notations worthy of mention include

- Whether the purchase was wrapped or payment was received from the investigator.
- Did the clerk call back the amount of the purchase or the amount of money tendered?
- Did you receive correct change?
- Was the amount of the sale correctly recorded on the register?

Troubling or suspicious conduct should be reflected in the report. An example of a document recording honesty testing is shown in Figure 9.13.

Shopping investigation report

Firm_____   Store No._____   Case No._____

Address_____   City_____   State_____

Date_____   Time_____ Opr._____   Report No._____

NAME

NUMBER   Reg loc.no: _____

LETTER_____   Reg read: _____

Sex_____ Age_____   Other cust/oprs/salespeople: _____

Height_____ Weight _____

Build_____

Eyes_____ Nose_____

Teeth_____

Complexion_____

Hair Color_____

Style_____

Glasses_____

Jewelry_____

Other_____

PAYMENT MADE

	$20	$10	$5	$1	50¢	25¢	10¢	5¢	1¢	
1. Pur										Trans #_____
2. Pur										Trans #_____

DESCRIPTION OF TRANSACTION

SALESPERSON'S APPEARANCE

_____ Well Groomed

_____ Passable

_____ Average

_____ Unimpressive

_____ Unkempt

_____ Other

SALESPERSON'S ATTITUDE

_____ Enthusiastic

_____ Pleasant

_____ Routine

_____ Indifferent

_____ Antagonistic

_____ Served Promptly

_____ Suggested other items

_____ Offered a "thank you"

_____ Other

PURCHASES MADE

Total

Figure 9.13 Shopping investigation report.

Barefoot comments on arranging this type of testing:

It is normally up to the agency supervisor or the retail security manager to make arrangements with the crew chief for storing the purchases while the target stores are being shopped. Ultimately, all merchandise is normally returned to the company for full credit, and this is usually handled through a high-ranking member of the store accounting staff. In this way, the rank-and-file sales personnel do not become aware that the merchandise has been returned for credit.[98]

[98] J.K. Barefoot, *Undercover Investigation* 3rd ed., 117 (1995).

The combination buy. In a combination buy, the investigator buys two or more different items at the same time and pays the employee the exact amount for the entire purchase. Observe and record whether or not the employee rings up all, part, or none of the transaction. The investigator records whether a receipt was received for the purchase. In a follow-up report, the investigator inserts findings regarding the exact time of the purchase and the reading on the register before the clerk rings up the transaction. (This is helpful if the employee fails to give you a receipt.) By knowing the amount on the register prior to your purchase, it will be easy to check the sale for which no receipt was received.

The double buy. In effecting a double buy, the investigator buys one or more items. The transaction should result in paying an uneven amount of money, more than the price of the goods in total, resulting in change. Because an overage of funds exists, the cash register tabulates the difference, and a receipt is remitted to the investigator. In this scenario, the investigator receives a receipt to identify either the cash register used or reference to its employee operator. This serves the first purpose of the double-buy process, namely, identification.

The second phase of the double-buy investigation tests the honesty of the employee. After the employee has returned the change, the investigator purchases an additional item. In buying the second item, the exact purchase price should be paid. The investigator should request that the employee put the second purchase in the same bag used for the first purchase. (The employee may even suggest this.) The investigator should be alert at this point to record whether a second receipt was received.

Pinkerton's, Inc. relates other sensible information regarding the double-buy process:

> Use common sense when making a double buy. It would not be normal, for example, to spend 39 cents on the first buy and ten dollars on your second buy…. Plan your approach and articles to be purchased prior to making your first buy. In this way you can control the type of goods in the first part so the bag will be large enough to hold the goods bought on the second part…. In picking items for your second buy in a double buy, try to locate goods as far away as possible from the register…. It is also possible to wear out or take out an unwrapped item which you have purchased on the second part of a double-buy test. This could be the case when buying at a jewelry department.[99]

As one final caution, in a double-buy test, the second purchase must occur immediately after the first purchase so that the factual chain and monetary sequence are not interrupted by other purchasers. The investigator should not act in a contrived or awkward manner; they should appear completely disinterested and aloof. Upon the second buy, the investigator should immediately leave the retail area without waiting for a receipt (but if the employee harkens you to accept it, do so).

The exchange buy. When customers have difficulty in choosing between multiple products, dishonest employees succumb to temptation. In the exchange buy, the investigator has two or more items to consider. In the investigator's original decision, the choice is to purchase the less costly item. The investigator then pays the employee with an uneven amount of money. Upon receipt of change, package, and sales receipt, the investigator, acting as a bewildered customer, changes heart and decides to take the higher-priced item. The purchaser (investigator) then must pay the difference between the lower-priced item and the higher-priced item. At this juncture, the investigator should watch carefully to see whether or not the employee records, registers, or makes notation of the difference between the two prices or simply pockets the difference.

The refund buy. Investigators who perform the refund test return an item to the selling department. After receipt of the cash or credit refund, the money is then used to make an even-money purchase. The objective of the refund buy is to test the store's system by attempting to get a refund without a receipt. If the employee will not grant the refund without the receipt, the investigator can then "discover" the receipt and complete the transaction.

Web Exercise: Review the power points on honesty testing produced by the University of West Florida at uwf.edu/svodanov/psa/Honesty-testing.ppt.

---

[99] Pinkerton's, Inc., *supra* note 14, at 165.

9.5.2.4.2 Service testing

In service testing, the scrutinized employee is assessed on diverse issues:

- Approach
- Suggested purchase
- Appearance
- Service effect
- Courtesy
- Product knowledge
- Salesmanship
- Closing of the sale

Service testing should take the following questions into account:

- How much of a product was purchased?
- What is the description of the merchandise?
- What is the price of the merchandise?
- What is the tax or other special assessment on the merchandise?
- What was the total amount paid?
- What money denominations were used as payment?
- Was the money handled at the register in compliance with the store's system?
- Was a receipt issued and what were its contents?
- Did the clerk charge the correct price and give the correct change?
- Was the clerk busy? Orderly? Clean?
- How did the employee act? Careless? Complaining? Professional?

Testing an employee's service level is a circumstantial tool for management, targeting employees who are weak in customer service, or who are disgruntled, difficult, and likely to cause problems for the business enterprise.

Web Exercise: Some suggest that the best defense against employee theft is employee screening. Review the ERI test at https://www.youtube.com/watch?v=tlS4Ey03xRY.

Coupled with theft, commercial and retail establishments need to be constantly vigilant about check fraud, forged and counterfeit funds, as well as fraudulent bank drafts and other negotiable instruments. Here too, technology plays a crucial role in identifying false currency and forged papers, or in providing a video history memorialized by surveillance technology. This is particularly true when repeat, professional offenders are targeted. "Using technology similar to what made millions of Internet pages searchable, these systems make thousands of hours of video from geographically distributed locations searchable in minutes. Underlying analytics like face recognition and motion analytics help investigators find information about a specific case, link fraudsters to other cases and ferret out links between accomplices to build cases against fraud rings."[100]

Web Exercise: Find out about emerging software programs that trace and track habitual offenders, such as Crimedex at https://www.crimedex.com.

9.5.3 Theft by burglary

Of major interest to the security industry is the crime of burglary, a crime whose felonious intent may be oriented toward property, but always requires illegal entry into a domicile or other structure. Private security operatives with residential contract responsibilities have a heavy burden in identifying and apprehending residential burglars. Aside

---

[100] J. Hudson, Searchable Video Surveillance Nabs Fraudsters and Robbers, *Law Enforcement Technology* (September 2007) at 112. See also J. Ratley, *Top Five Ways*.

Asset Protection Manager: Sam's Club 6410 - Pearl City, HI
PEARL CITY, HI

Position Description

- Coordinates, completes, and oversees job-related activities and assignments
- Detects, deters, investigates, and resolves violations of company policies and criminal activities
- Drives the execution of operational procedures to minimize shrink, damages, and/or variances
- Ensures compliance with company policies and procedures and supports company mission, values, and standards of ethics and integrity
- Leads safety team to ensure a safe shopping and working environment for associates and members
- Manages compliance procedures to adhere to standards of Federal, State and Local regulatory agencies (for example, Environmental Protection Agency, Occupational Safety and Health Administration (OSHA), Alcohol/Tobacco/Firearm (ATF), United States Department of Agriculture, Weights and Measures, Department of Transportation, Federal Drug Administration, as well as government agencies that address Privacy, Financial, and Fuel)
- Manages facility operations and security resources within the clubs
- Models, enforces, and provides direction and guidance to associates on proper member service approaches and techniques to ensure member needs, complaints, and issues are successfully resolved within company guidelines and standards.
- Provides supervision and development opportunities for associates
- Secures and safeguards the assets of the facility and surrounding areas
- Works as part of the management team to ensure all opening and closing procedures are followed, including communicating with opening and closing managers to ensure a smooth transition from day to night operations, discussing merchandising opportunities and directions, scheduling concerns, associate issues, any issues needing to be escalated, additional resources needed, and any special opening or closing instructions or information.

Minimum Qualifications

- 1 year supervisory experience in a multi-department retail environment, OR 1 year experience in one of the following areas: Claims, Invoicing, Human Resources or Asset Protection in a multi-department retail environment, OR completion of two or more years of college.

Additional Preferred Qualifications

- 2 or more years of general work experience supervising 5 or more direct reports to include the responsibility of performance management, mentoring, hiring, and firing.
- 2 or more years of experience working in a safety/regulatory compliance field.
- 2 or more years of investigative experience.

Employment Type: Full Time
Position Type: Salary
Shift: 0
Req ID: 705992BR

Figure CP9.4   Career Profile: Retail Asset Manager.

from apprehension and identification, the security officer is also obliged to assist the client in the recovery of lost property. In an overwhelming number of cases, property lost in burglary cases (particularly those that involve little use of force) is rarely recovered. From varied perspectives, the costs of crime from both personal and business viewpoints are immeasurably negative.

> The impact of the many crimes against business cannot be ignored, since losses or shrinkages of the magnitude described cannot be tolerated. Crime against business has reached such proportions that it has been recognized as a major contributing factor in some business closings and corporate bankruptcies. The business community must begin to emphasize aggressive policies and procedures that anticipate and fight criminal opportunities that are particularly common to the business world.[101]

The investigation of burglary requires the same general investigative approach as all other offenses. Proof of the felony's elements is tied to the objective facts collected. Be concerned with these steps:

1. Carefully check the scene of the burglary for latent fingerprints.
2. If fingerprints are obtained, fingerprint all employees for the purpose of elimination.
3. Check polished floor surfaces or any papers on the floor, for any trace of footprints.

---

[101] O'Block at 157.

4. Check the area surrounding the burglarized building for tire marks or footprints that may be connected with the burglary.

5. Obtain an accurate, detailed description of all missing property or monies.

6. Check the loss-payable clauses of any insurance carried.

7. Interview all persons having access to the premises. This step should include the night watchman, the patrolman, or trooper working the area, the last person to leave the premises prior to the burglary, and the person who discovered and reported the burglary.

8. Attempt to trace any tools recovered.

9. If explosives are recovered, do not attempt to transport them. Contact the laboratory.

10. Take scale photographs of the attacked safe (if applicable).

11. If possible, obtain the make, serial number, size, and weight of the safe (if applicable).

12. If a suspect is arrested and charged with burglary at or near the scene of the crime, immediately obtain all the clothing he is wearing. Clothing may contain safe insulation, paint fragments, or metal particles.

13. If the suspect is in an automobile when apprehended, mark any recovered tools for identification and forward with all other evidence.[102]

In surveying the area subject to the burglary, be on the lookout for tools, instruments, and mechanical means and aids used to accomplish the breaking and entry. Private security plays a critical role in the reduction of business theft and burglary.[103] The former Law Enforcement Assistance Administration admonishes business, industry, and individuals, stating that their own negligence fosters an opportunity for burglary and other property offenses:

> Many experts also believe that no-force burglaries are frequently the work of individuals, many of them children, who simply cannot resist an easy opportunity to steal. If this is so, we could reduce the burglary rate and the size of the offender population by limiting the opportunities available to commit "easy" offenses. If failure to adequately protect personal and household property is directly related to the commission of the crime, can we say the victims are in some way responsible? This is a difficult question to answer.[104]

The best approach is to establish a theft/burglary deterrence program. In facility or perimeter protection, the security specialist takes on a wide array of responsibilities. Ralph F. Brislin's well-crafted text, *The Effective Security Officer's Training Manual* suggests these preventive measures:

> [A] security officer must know what doors and windows are normally open/closed, locked and unlocked...Often, while patrolling a security officer will notice that there are several other persons in the facility... It is essential that prior to patrolling a security officer obtain as much information as possible as to what employees/visitors are in the facility. When are these persons scheduled to depart? Once all of this information has been obtained, a security officer should not be startled to find other persons in the facility... Much of this information should be known by the security officer who is going off duty. A final part of theft prevention when patrolling will occasionally require a security officer to inspect equipment begin removed from the facility. The security officer must know what material can be removed from the facility with proper paperwork and authorization... If no paperwork is required, the security officer should note in their shift log the identity and description of the person removing the material and what material is being removed.[105]

9.5.4 Theft by fraud in insurance cases

The insurance industry has an ongoing need for the services of private security professionals. Admirable performance records are prerequisites to a contractual relationship, because the insurance industry—in commercial, casualty, auto, and workers' compensation settings—can basically pick and choose in a competitive market. Private security's contribution to insurance practice and procedure is quite substantial and includes

---

[102] Pennsylvania State Police, Bureau of Training and Education, *Investigation of Safe Burglaries* 1–2 (1972).

[103] See C.P. Nemeth & K.C. Poulin, *Private Security and Public Safety: A Community-Based Approach* 71–72 (2005).

[104] U.S. Department of Justice, Law Enforcement Assistance Administration, *The Costs of Negligence: Losses from Preventable Household Burglaries* 9 (1979).

[105] R.F. Brislin, *The Effective Security Officer's Training Manual* 59 (1995).

- Interviewing claimants and witnesses
- Record searches
- Securing statements
- Credit bureaus
- Securing medical and autopsy reports
- Courts
- Subpoena service
- Motor vehicle records
- Locating witnesses
- Activity checks
- Establishing criminal histories
- Background investigations

Investigative practice in the insurance industry generally involves four basic types of insurance: life, fire, marine, and casualty. In general terms, investigators analyze tragedy (in insurance parlance, "casualty"). Insurance claims usually comprise these four areas of casualty coverage:

- Death
- Property damage
- Personal/bodily injury
- Illness and disability

An insured and insurer are contractual parties to an explicit, well-defined agreement, the insurance policy. As a result, when a claim occurs, the insurance company needs verification of the status, credibility, and authenticity of the claim in order to determine whether or not there is legal liability. Private security firms are frequently asked to perform these authoritative reviews.

Whatever the type of insurance claim, the underlying investigation determines the truth by obtaining the facts and recording the information. See Figure 9.14.

Insurance companies are primarily concerned with clear and accurate factual representations, which in turn permit their legal counsel to make judgments, develop tactical strategies, or formulate settlement positions. However, there is, Cynthia Mango tells us, a "convergence" of fraud in both a civil and criminal context in most insurance cases.[106] In essence, the fraudulent conduct, regarding the particular policy, has criminal connotations as well and these two paths are likely to "intersect."[107] Hence, the investigator must weigh and evaluate in light of this two sorts of intentionality—civil and criminal.

9.5.4.1 Fraudulent property claims in arson

In fire casualty and property policies, a frequent inquiry involves whether or not damaged property, goods, or other collateral is a compensable claim and whether or not the claim for property is fraudulent by design. Arson can be a means, albeit an illegal one, to gain access to cash proceeds in a fire case. The crime of arson is often committed by the insured. Arson is a multimillion-dollar drain on businesses, governmental entities, and individuals. When investigators review fire-damaged structures, owners' names appear on the initial suspect list. Burning to defraud the insurer is particularly likely in economically depressed areas or when an owner is under extraordinary financial pressure. The investigator should consider these possible motives:

- Fraud
- Juvenile theft

---

[106] Where Crimes Converge Investigations Merge.
[107] *Ibid.* at 91.

```
                    Insurance Claim Investigation Form

                                                    Date:_____

Company _____        Address  _____

Report to _____      Telephone _____

Assured  _____

Claim No _____

Claimant _____

Address  _____

Description:   Sex _____ Marital Status _____ Age _____ Race _____

               Height _____ Weight_____Occupation_____

               Last Employer _____

               Automobile _____        License No._____

Date of Accident   _____

Description of Accident_____
_____
_____
_____

Nature of alleged disability   _____

Extent of Injury Claimed   (  ) Partial          (  ) Continuing          (  ) Permanent

Desired:   (  )   Activities checked (Through personal inquiry:  Yes___; No ___)

           (  )   Dependency Status

           (  )   Investigation of accident, including statements

           (  )   Activities through observation. (Specific authorization will be requested beyond 2 days)

           (  )   Video, if active.

           (  )   Previous medical history.

Rate:   _____     (  ) Flat Rate          (  ) Hourly Rate _____

Remarks   _____
_____
_____
```

Figure 9.14   Insurance claim investigation report.

- Effort to hide other crimes
- Riot
- Jealousy
- Vandalism
- Revenge
- Thrill (pyromania)
- Terrorism[108]

Establishing motive is a priority of the investigator.[109] The checklist at Figure 9.15 suggests motives or mitigating factors might point to a fire set by the insured. A more comprehensive document regarding motivation and other issues relative to the proof of an arson insurance investigation case is given in Figure 9.16.

---

[108] National Institute of Justice, *Sourcebook of Justice Statistics* (1988).

[109] R.N. Kocsis, Arson: Exploring Motives and Possible Solutions, *Trends & Issues in Crime and Crim. Jus.* (August 2002) at 1.

---

1. Is there a need for cash?
2. Is there a reason to terminate the lease?
3. Is there cause to relocate a business?
4. Is there an unprofitable contract?
5. What is the profit picture?
6. What are people saying?
7. What type of neighborhood is the building located in?
8. Is the fire advantageous to anyone?
9. What other crimes might have been perpetrated?
10. Is there other trouble or difficulty in the neighborhood?
11. Is arson a common crime in the neighborhood?
12. Was insurance recently increased?

Figure 9.15   Arson motivations.

Proof of arson is difficult without credible, forensic physical evidence.[110] Private investigators are often requested to perform a thorough fire inspection report on a burned vehicle. By answering questions such as those listed in Figure 9.17, the investigator can be assured of making a comprehensive analysis and coverage.

9.5.4.2 Theft by fraud in workers' compensation

Injuries in the workplace are often feigned for purposes of illegally collecting worker compensation benefits. The workers' compensation program is a strict liability program whereby lost wages, compensatory damages for specified loss of limb, or reduced usability are factored into a legislatively determined formula. Fault is irrelevant in worker compensation cases, the idea simply being to make the worker whole again and reduce the amount of workplace litigation. Unfortunately, most states have experienced big increases in fraudulent behavior regarding these benefits. Workers' compensation replaces the common law principles of negligence and intentional torts with a strict liability, no-fault, statutory remedy. Employees who are injured on the job must be able to demonstrate that their injuries were work-related, were within the scope of employment. As in disability cases, it is easy enough to feign injury and the resulting costs for these frauds are higher employer premiums.[111] A worksheet collecting information regarding the compensability of a claim is given in Figure 9.18.[112]

Prior to the enactment of workers' compensation legislation, American law was more concerned with assessing or analyzing the negligent or intentional conduct of the employer, such as an employer who provided unsafe tools or equipment, fostered a dangerous work environment, or failed to warn of dangers in the work environment. These lines of advocacy have been legislatively swept away, and injuries are now adjudged on a strict liability basis, that is, an injury in the workplace will be compensable regardless of who is at fault. The following examples illustrating situations that indicate the basis of liability are taken from the Michigan State Code:

1. An employee who receives a personal injury arising out of and in the course of employment by an employer who is subject to this act at the time of the injury, shall be paid compensation as provided in the Act. In a case of death resulting from personal injury to the employee, compensation shall be paid to the employee's dependents as provided in this Act. Time of injury or date of injury as used in this act in the case of a disease or in the case of an injury not attributable to a single event shall be the last day of work in the employment of which the employee was last subjected to the conditions that resulted in the employee's disability or death.

2. Mental disabilities and conditions of the aging process, including but not limited to the heart and cardiovascular conditions, shall be compensable if contributed to or aggravated or accelerated by the employment in a significant manner.

3. An employee going to and from his work, while on the premises where the employee's work is to be performed, and within a reasonable time before and after his working hours is presumed to be in the course of his or her employment.[113]

---

[110] M.R. Williams & M. Sigman, Performance Testing of Commercial Containers for Collection and Storage of Fire Debris Evidence, 52 *J. Forensic Sci.*, 579 (2007).

[111] "Loss" from Employer's Fraud on Insurers Is Unpaid Workers' Compensation Premiums, 83 *Crim. L. Rep.*, 752 (2008).

[112] North Carolina Bar Foundation, VI Practical Skills Course, Workers' Compensation 36 (1988).

[113] See Mich. Stat. Ann. § 17.237.301.

Sources of Interview Information

The following is a list of some of the possible witnesses to acts committed in connection with an arson-for-profit scheme and the types of questions they should be asked:

1. Interview of Witnesses at Scene of Fire
   a. Possible Witnesses:
      i. Tenants of building
      ii. Tenants of surrounding buildings
      iii. Businessmen in building
      iv. Businessmen in surrounding buildings
      v. Customers in businesses in building
      vi. Customers in businesses in surrounding buildings
      vii. Passersby including: bus route drivers, taxi drivers, deliverymen, garbage collectors, police patrol, people waiting for buses and taxis.
   b. Questions to be Asked:
      i. Did you observe the fire?
      ii. At what time did you first observe the fire?
      iii. In what part of building did you observe the fire?
      iv. What called your attention to the building?
      v. Did you see anyone entering or leaving the building prior to the fire?
      vi. Did you recognize them?
      vii. Can you describe them?
      viii. Did you observe any vehicles in the area of the fire?
      ix. Can you describe them?
      x. Can you describe the smoke and the color of the flame?
      xi. How quickly did the fire spread?
      xii. Was the building burning in more than one place?
      xiii. Did you detect any unusual odors?
      xiv. Did you observe anything else?
      xv. What else did you observe?
2. Interview of Fire Officers and/or Firefighters at Scene
   a. Questions to be Asked:
      i. What time was alarm received?
      ii. What time did you arrive at scene of fire?
      iii. Was your route to the scene blocked?
      iv. What was the extent of burning when you arrived?
      v. Were doors and windows locked?
      vi. Was the entrance and/or passageways blocked?
      vii. What kind of fire was it?
      viii. What was the spread speed of the fire?
      ix. In what area(s) did the fire start?
      x. What was the proximity of the fire to the roof?
      xi. Was there evidence of the use of an accelerant?
      xii. Was there any evidence of arson recovered?
      xiii. Did the building have a fire alarm system?
      xiv. Was it operating?
      xv. Was there any evidence of tampering with the alarm system?
      xvi. Did the building have a sprinkler system?
      xvii. Did it operate?
      xviii. Was there any evidence of tampering with the sprinkler system?
      xix. Was there anyone present in the building when you arrived?
      xx. Who was that person in the building?
      xxi. Did he or she say anything to you?
      xxii. Were there any people present at the scene when you arrived?
      xxiii. Who were they?
      xxiv. Did you observe any vehicles at the scene or leaving when you arrived?
      xxv. Can you describe them?
      xxvi. Were there contents in the building?
      xxvii. Was there evidence of contents removed?
      xxviii. Was the owner present?
      xxix. Did the owner make a statement?
      xxx. What did the owner say?
      xxxi. What is the prior fire history of the building?
      xxxii. What is the prior fire history of the area?
3. Interview of Insurance Personnel
   The profit in many arson-for-profit cases is the payment from an insurance policy or policies. There are three classes of people who may be interviewed in order to determine if the profit centers around an insurance claim. They are the insurance agent/broker, the insurance adjuster, and the insurance investigator.

Figure 9.16   Sources of information in an arson investigation.   (*Continued*)

a. Questions to Ask the Agent or Broker:
   i. Who is the insured?
   ii. Is there more than one insured?
   iii. Is the insured the beneficiary?
   iv. What type of policy was issued?
   v. What is the amount of the policy?
   vi. When was it issued?
   vii. When does it expire?
   viii. What is the premium cost?
   ix. Are payments up-to-date?
   x. Have there been any increases in the amount of coverage?
   xi. What amount?
   xii. When did increase take effect?
   xiii. What was the reason for the increase?
   xiv. Are there any special provisions in the policy (e.g., interruption of business or rental income)?
   xv. What are they, and when did they take effect?
   xvi. Has the insured ever received a cancellation notice on this property? If so, when? Why?
   xvii. Does the insured have any other policies?
   xviii. Were there previous losses at the location of the fire?
   xix. Were there losses at other locations owned by the insured?
b. Questions to Ask the Insurance Claims Adjustor:
   i. Did you take a sworn statement from the insured?
   ii. Did the insured submit documents regarding proof of loss, value of contents, bills of lading, value of building, etc.?
   iii. Did you inspect the fire scene?
   iv. Did you inspect the fire scene with a public insurance adjustor?
   v. Did you and the public adjuster agree on the cost figure in the loss?
   vi. Have you dealt with this public adjuster before?
   vii. Has the adjuster represented this owner before?
   viii. Has the insured had any other losses with this company? If so, provide details.
c. Questions to Ask the Insurance Adjuster:
   i. Were you able to determine the cause of the fire?
   ii. Did you collect any evidence?
   iii. Who analyzed the evidence?
   iv. What were the results of the analysis?
   v. Was the cause of the fire inconsistent with state of building as known through underwriting examination?
   vi. Have you investigated past fires involving the location?
   vii. Have you investigated past fires involving the insured?
   viii. What were the results of the investigations?
   ix. Have you had prior investigations involving the public adjuster?
   x. Have you had prior investigations involving buildings handled by the same insurance agent/broker?
   xi. What were the results of these investigations?
   xii. Does this fire fit into a pattern of fires of recent origin in the area?
   xiii. What are the similarities?
   xiv. What are the differences?
   xv. Have you taken any statements in connection with this burning?
   xvi. Whose statements did you take?
   xvii. What do they reveal?

There may be restrictions on the amount of information insurance personnel can turn over without a subpoena, but the investigator should be able to determine enough to indicate whether the issuance of a subpoena or search warrant would prove fruitful.

4. Other Witnesses Concerning Finances of Insured
   There are a number of other people who may have information relating to the finances of the owner which may indicate how they stood to profit from the burning. These witnesses would include business associates, creditors, and competitors. Following are the types of questions these witnesses may be able to answer:
   a. How long have you known the owner/insured?
   b. What is the nature of your relationship with the owner?
   c. Do you have any information on the financial position of the business?
   d. Is the owner competitive with similar businesses?
   e. Have there been recent technological advances which would threaten the business's position?
   f. Has there been a recent increase in competition which would affect the business's position?
   g. Have changes in the economy affected the business's position?
   h. Has the owner experienced recent difficulty in paying creditors?
   i. Has the owner's amount of debt increased recently?
   j. Has the business lost any key employees recently?
   k. Has the location of the business changed for the worse recently?
   l. Has the owner increased the mortgage or taken out a second or third mortgage?
   m. Has the owner had difficulty making mortgage payments?
   n. Do you have any other information about the owner's financial position?

Figure 9.16 (Continued)   Sources of information in an arson investigation.

TOTAL FIRE INSPECTION REPORT

NAME OF INSURED _____ INSPECTION DATE _____

ADDRESS _____ LOSS DATE _____

INSURANCE COMPANY _____ POLICY NUMBER _____

SALVAGE EXAMINED AT (Location) _____

YR. & MAKE OF VEHICLE _____ VIN _____

EXTERIOR

Body metal sagged or warped? _____ Where? _____

Glass melted or fused? _____ Where? _____

Any evidence of collision? _____ Where? _____

Have tires/wheels been changed? _____ Which ones? _____

Tires burned? _____ Which ones? _____

Condition _____

Spare in trunk? _____ Condition _____

Exterior mirrors or other accessories missing? _____

Which ones? _____

Excessive wear in suspension linkage? _____

Any additional observations? _____

INTERIOR

Doors open? _____ Which ones? _____

Windows down? _____ Which ones? _____

Upholstery and trim burned? _____ Extent? _____

Floor mats burned? _____ Extent? _____

Any evidence of an accelerant? _____

Any accelerant container? _____

Any tension left in seat springs? _____

Any evidence of personal property burning? _____

What? _____

Vehicle equipped with radio? _____ Missing? _____

Air conditioning? _____ Missing? _____

Any other accessories? _____ Missing? _____

Tools? _____ Missing? _____

Ignition key anywhere in evidence? _____

Any additional observations? _____

MECHANICAL CONDITION

Hood up or down during the fire? _____

Condition of drive belts? _____

Wiring? _____

Motor mounts? _____

Radiator melted? _____ Full? _____

Engine grease deposits? _____ Evidence of burning? _____

Start motor if possible. Run for 5 or 10 minutes.

Are there any cracks or breaks on block or head? _____

Any unusual noises? _____

If not possible to start motor, secure the services of a reliable mechanic. Remove oil pan and head. Check all parts for wear or breaks. When serious mechanical defects are discovered, obtain a brief statement from mechanic and have it witnessed, incorporating a description of defects and if, in the mechanic's opinion, they occurred prior to the fire.

Clutch, transmission, drive shaft, rear axle assembly: Jack up rear of car with motor running or, if not running, test running gear.

Evidence of wear or breakage? Clutch? _____ Transmission? _____

Drive shaft split or bent? _____ Rear axle & housing worn? _____

Broken? _____

Any additional observations? _____

Figure 9.17 Fire inspection report.

(*Continued*)

```
FUEL SYSTEM
Where was gas cap during fire? _____
Drain plug: Tampered with? _____    If in tank, is it right? _____
Gasoline: Burned from tank? _____    If not, how much in tank? _____
Fuel lines & connections: (trace to pump and carburetor)
Evidence of tampering? _____    Where? _____
How? _____    Before or after fire? _____
Fuel pump: Gasoline in sediment bowl? _____    Bowl broken? _____
Removed? _____    Melted? _____
Air filter in place? _____    Missing? _____
Any additional observations? _____

ELECTRICAL SYSTEM
Battery: In place? _____
If damaged, where burned? _____    Clamp tight? _____
Cable shorted out? _____    How? _____
Wiring: Any shorts? _____    Disconnections? _____
Switches: (on or off) Ignition? _____    Lights? _____
Spark plugs: Condition? _____    Any wires disconnected? _____
Distributor: In working condition? _____    Burned or melted? _____
Any additional observations? _____

GENERAL REMARKS:
```

Figure 9.17 (Continued)   Fire inspection report.

As a result of this statutory construction, injuries on the job, from broken bones to lung disease, are subject to the provisions of the Workers' Compensation Act. In most jurisdictions, a schedule of benefits is published (see Figure 9.19[114]).

Upon initial interview and case assessment, the investigator's most pressing concern must be whether or not an injury exists and whether or not the injury is related to or arose from the work environment. To confirm the legitimacy of the claim, the investigator should consider using the techniques and tactics of surveillance—the most often used strategy to assure the credibility of a claim. Workers' compensation, disability, and proof of contested injuries should rely heavily on the use of photographic or video surveillance. The end result of this type of surveillance should, by visual means, verify or refute the authenticity of the claimant's condition. The best approach is to consider the injury from the claimant's point of view to determine exactly how the injury affects the ability to function. The more extreme the claimant's movements are and the more they conflict with those of a truly disabled person, the more important it is to record the claimant's action visually. The investigator should also document whether the claimant is able to perform activities that bear on the alleged injury.

Types of actions to look for include

1. Back injury
   a. Subject is carrying bundles (such as groceries) in a normal fashion.
   b. Subject is carrying anything of moderate weight in an awkward position (such as a large container of water in front of him with both hands).
   c. Subject is leaning in an awkward position (such as out a window to clean an upper pane of glass).
   d. Subject is using his body to hold a heavy object in place or to apply pressure (such as applying pressure to an electric drill to bore a hole at the level of one's head or above).

---

[114] *Ibid.*

CLIENT DATA SHEET – WORKER'S COMPENSATION CASE

IN RE: _____   Date Of Injury: _____

INS. CO: _____   Hearing Commissioner: _____

Hearing Date: _____

I.C. Docket No. _____

1.   Full Name _____ S.S. No. _____ Age _____

2.   Address _____ Telephone No _____

3.   Name of Spouse or Nearest Kin and Address: _____

_____

Number of children: _____

4.   Employer and Address: _____

Job Held: _____

5.   Hired In: _____ Length of Employment: _____

6.   Work Week: _____ Hours per day: _____ Days per Week: _____

7.   Wage Rate: _____Per hour/day/week _____ For overtime: _____

8.   Average Weekly Wage: _____ Extras Furnished: _____

9.   Date of Accident: _____ Hour: _____

10. Paid for Date of Injury? _____ Started Losing Time: _____

11. Now receiving comp. _____ Weeks paid at _____ per week _____

12. Place of accident _____ County _____

13. Description of Accident and Injury: _____

_____

_____

Accident Details: _____

_____

_____

14. Any Part of Body Amputated? _____ Member and Point of Amputation: _____

15. Notice of Accident: Who: _____ Title: _____

When: _____

16. Witnesses: _____

_____

17. Doctors: _____

Sent by: _____

18. Hospital: _____ From: _____ To: _____

19. Travel: _____

20. Returned to Work? _____ Date: _____ Rate of Pay: _____

21. Any statements or Recorded interviews given? _____To Whom: _____

22. Other Attorneys Consulted? _____ Who: _____

23. Third Party Liability: _____

24. All Other Injuries and Claims: _____

_____

_____

25. Prior Health: _____

26. Date of Contract: _____ Referred by: _____

27. Additional Information: _____

_____

_____

Figure 9.18   Workers' compensation data sheet.

WORKER'S DISABILITY COMPENSATION ACT OF 1969 (EXCERPT)
Act 317 of 1969

418.361 Partial incapacity for work; amount and duration of compensation; effect of imprisonment or commission of crime; scheduled disabilities; meaning of total and permanent disability; limitations; payment for loss of second member.

Sec. 361. (1) While the incapacity for work resulting from a personal injury is partial, the employer shall pay, or cause to be paid to the injured employee weekly compensation equal to 80% of the difference between the injured employee's after-tax average weekly wage before the personal injury and the after-tax average weekly wage which the injured employee is able to earn after the personal injury, but not more than the maximum weekly rate of compensation, as determined under section 355. Compensation shall be paid for the duration of the disability. However, an employer shall not be liable for compensation under section 351, 371(1), or this subsection for such periods of time that the employee is unable to obtain or perform work because of imprisonment or commission of a crime.

(2) In cases included in the following schedule, the disability in each case shall be considered to continue for the period specified, and the compensation paid for the personal injury shall be 80% of the after-tax average weekly wage subject to the maximum and minimum rates of compensation under this act for the loss of the following:

(a) Thumb, 65 weeks.

(b) First finger, 38 weeks.

(c) Second finger, 33 weeks.

(d) Third finger, 22 weeks.

(e) Fourth finger, 16 weeks.

The loss of the first phalange of the thumb, or of any finger, shall be considered to be equal to the loss of 1/2 of that thumb or finger, and compensation shall be 1/2 of the amount above specified.

The loss of more than 1 phalange shall be considered as the loss of the entire finger or thumb. The amount received for more than 1 finger shall not exceed the amount provided in this schedule for the loss of a hand.

(f) Great toe, 33 weeks.

(g) A toe other than the great toe, 11 weeks.

The loss of the first phalange of any toe shall be considered to be equal to the loss of 1/2 of that toe, and compensation shall be 1/2 of the amount above specified.

The loss of more than 1 phalange shall be considered as the loss of the entire toe.

(h) Hand, 215 weeks.

(i) Arm, 269 weeks.

An amputation between the elbow and wrist that is 6 or more inches below the elbow shall be considered a hand, and an amputation above that point shall be considered an arm.

(j) Foot, 162 weeks.

(k) Leg, 215 weeks.

An amputation between the knee and foot 7 or more inches below the tibial table (plateau) shall be considered a foot, and an amputation above that point shall be considered a leg.

(*l*) Eye, 162 weeks.

Eighty percent loss of vision of 1 eye shall constitute the total loss of that eye.

(3) Total and permanent disability, compensation for which is provided in section 351 means:

(a) Total and permanent loss of sight of both eyes.

(b) Loss of both legs or both feet at or above the ankle.

(c) Loss of both arms or both hands at or above the wrist.

(d) Loss of any 2 of the members or faculties in subdivisions (a), (b), or (c).

(e) Permanent and complete paralysis of both legs or both arms or of 1 leg and 1 arm.

(f) Incurable insanity or imbecility.

(g) Permanent and total loss of industrial use of both legs or both hands or both arms or 1 leg and 1 arm; for the purpose of this subdivision such permanency shall be determined not less than 30 days before the expiration of 500 weeks from the date of injury.

(4) The amounts specified in this clause are all subject to the same limitations as to maximum and minimum as above stated. In case of the loss of 1 member while compensation is being paid for the loss of another member, compensation shall be paid for the loss of the second member for the period provided in this section. Payments for the loss of a second member shall begin at the conclusion of the payments for the first member.

History: 1969, Act 317, Eff. Dec. 31, 1969;—Am. 1980, Act 357, Eff. Jan. 1, 1982;—Am. 1985, Act 103, Imd. Eff. July 30, 1985.

Constitutionality: The statutory limitation in subsection (2)(g) of this section is not unconstitutional. Johnson v Harnischfeger Corp, 414 Mich 102; 323 NW2d 912 (1982).

Compiler's note: For legislative intent as to severability, see Compiler's note to MCL 418.213.

Popular name: Act 317

Popular name: Heart and Lung Act

Figure 9.19   Worker's Disability Compensation Act of 1969 (excerpt).

Title	Strategic Case Investigator
Country	United States
State/Region/Province	Florida
City	Orlando Tampa
Job Category	Claim
Target Openings	1
Position Type	Experienced/Professional
Company Information	Solid reputation, passionate people and endless opportunities. That's Travelers. Our superior financial strength and consistent record of strong operating returns mean security for our customers - and opportunities for our employees. You will find Travelers to be full of energy and a workplace in which you truly can make a difference.
Job Summary	Under general supervision, this position is responsible for analyzing data to determine fraud schemes, trends and conducting major case investigations concerning non-medical systemic and organized fraud investigations in all lines of business, including: Auto, Property, General Liability and Workers Compensation. Provides investigative expertise to detect fraud, limit exposure and protect company assets. Focus is directed towards multiple complex case investigations with regional and national implications. This job does not manage staff.
Primary Job Duties & Responsibilities	Analyzes and summarizes highly technical information related to multiple complex case investigations with regional and national implications. Makes key decisions regarding the structuring and conduction of major case investigations involving multiple claims and/or organized fraud ring activity with regional and national impact. Proactively uses analytical skills to identify potential areas of organized fraud activity or identify areas of vulnerability to fraud to develop investigative plans and/or solutions. Assists in forecasting needs from emerging trends in the major case and/or organized fraud arena in local area. (e.g., NICB and industry alerts, leads from lines of business, etc.) May conduct missed opportunity reviews of claim files as needed (e.g., by line of business, by emerging trends, etc.). Conducts thorough insurance field investigations while managing resources with a focus on uncovering all potentially fraudulent aspects of claims Conducts technical training for investigative staff to build knowledge base in major case and/or fraud ring identification & Investigative techniques. Applies the techniques of critical thinking to prioritizes and develop investigations that have complex allegations and/or significantly financial impact to multiple claims and/or organized ring activity spanning across multiple lines of business and potentially across several states Applies Local, State and Federal statutes to ensure investigations are carried out within the requirements of applicable law and local office expectations Provides exceptional customer service by maintaining contact with business partners, customers and external resources throughout the life of each investigation. Acts as a liaison with local/state/federal law enforcement personnel, industry advocates and other companies. Serves as the subject matter expert (liaison) on fraud to business and industry partners. Applies rules of evidence; recognizes evidence and determines its value to specific claim, evidence collection and interpretation. Establishes and maintains liaison network with public officials, law enforcement officers and others to obtain assistance in conducting investigations. Identifies cases for potential insurance fraud prosecution and submits questionable claims to the National Insurance Crime Bureau Reviews, understands and applies all applicable statutes: local, state and federal to ensure duties and assignments are carried out within the requirements of applicable law and local office expectations. Identifies and addresses investigative priorities through strategic partnerships. Prepares and conducts technical training in detecting and applying techniques to multiple complex cases. Testifies to findings Other duties as assigned.
Education, Work Experience & Knowledge	Bachelor's degree preferred. A minimum of five years of investigative experience; or a minimum of five years insurance claim related experience required. Journeymen level tradesmen experience a plus.

Figure CP9.5   Career Profile: Strategic case investigator.   (*Continued*)

2. Head injury
   a. Subject is extremely active, physically, in extreme heat (such as working on a roof laying shingles).
   b. Subject continuously moves his head in a quick, jerky fashion (such as one does in some strenuous dances).
   c. Subject is involved in strenuous running.

Job Specific & Technical Skills & Competencies	Analytical skills and ability to make deductions; logical and sequential thinker. - Advanced Analytical and problem solving skills to use and interpret information and facts as well as apply critical techniques to investigative process - Advanced Effective business communication skills (Written & Verbal) - Advanced Computer literate; database, Internet and social media proficient - Advanced Interviewing skills - Advanced Computer literate; database and internet emerging social media use/search proficiency. - Advanced Conflict management skills to deal with crisis situations, hostile witnesses, etc. -Advanced Must be a self-motivated individual - Intermediate Excels at working independently, while making decisions to successfully pursue non-medical insurance fraud through establishing significant facts while preserving material that leads to the resolution of the investigation. - Intermediate Knowledge of available resources (internal and external) to assist in investigations- Advance Working level knowledge of insurance and claim operations, Commercial Lines, Personal Lines, and Workers Compensation insurance products. - Intermediate Time management and accurate record keeping - Intermediate Effective business communication skills (Written & Verbal) - Advanced -Strong case management skills and the ability to manage your own work independently. - Intermediate Adapt to changes in process and shifting priorities - Intermediate Must take ownership/initiative; significant planning and goal setting skills required - Intermediate Presentation and training skills. Intermediate Understanding of claim best practices - Intermediate Leadership, including delegation and ability to get work done through others- Intermediate Influence and conflict management skills - Intermediate
Environmental/Work Schedules/Other	Environmental Exposure to Excess Noise - Occasionally Exposure to Dirt, Dust, Fumes, Smoke, Gases, or Other Irritating Substances - Occasionally Exposure to Variable Weather Conditions - Occasionally Operate or work around moving machinery - Frequently Work Schedules Weekend work hours - Occasionally Overnight work hours - Occasionally Holiday work hours (Federal and religious) - Occasionally Other Travel - Frequently
Physical Requirements	Operates standard office equipment - Frequently Sitting (can stand at will) - Continuously Standing - Occasionally Lifting items up to 20 pounds - Occasionally Climbing unprotected heights (ladder, rooftop, stairs, loading dock) - Occasionally Use of Keyboards, Sporadic 10-Key - Frequently Working in a confined or restricted area - Occasionally Driving ? Frequently

Figure CP9.5 (Continued)   Career Profile: Strategic case investigator.

3. Leg injury
   a. Subject is walking in a quick, carefree manner (such as skipping or quickly crossing the street).
   b. Subject is running.
   c. Subject is freely and quickly climbing stairs without the assistance of a railing or cane.
   d. Subject is found carrying a heavy object upstairs.
   e. Subject gets up from an extended crouching position (such as one is in when washing a car or weeding a garden).
   f. Subject remains in a crouching position for some time.
4. Arm injury
   a. Subject carrying something heavy at arm's length (such as a car tire).
   b. Subject is seen grasping or pulling something (such as a large rock or root from the ground).
   c. Subject is propping something of weight up (such as an extension ladder).
   d. Subject is twisting something (such as wringing out a wet towel).
   e. Subject is lifting something above the belt (such as loading luggage, groceries, or boxes into a vehicle).
5. Whiplash
   a. Basically the same activities shown under back injury and head injury with the addition of unusual movement of the neck.[115]

Figure 9.20 includes detailed data on types of information to gather, pertinent medical information to find, and surveillance to report, as well as a summary of the investigator's findings.

---

[115] Pinkerton's Inc., *supra* note 1, at Using Your Camera on an Insurance Investigation.

Worker's Compensation Investigation
FINAL REPORT

Client: [Name]   File No:
          [Title]   Date:
          [Company Name]   Report by:
          [Address]

Report of Investigation
Re: [Subject's name or other pertinent information]

Synopsis:

As requested by [client and address], a [type of investigation] was conducted on [subject's name] to determine.... The [investigation] and/or [activity] included [photographs or videos]. These efforts revealed....

Details

A.   Personal Information:
     Name of subject and any aliases
     Address of Subject
     Telephone Number
     Date of Birth
     Social Security Number
     Height/Weight
     Hair/Eye color

B.   Intelligence Information
     A check of the [state] Department of Motor Vehicle Records revealed that the subject has a [current/expired/suspended] [state] driver's license, OLN [number], expiration [date].
     Subject owns and/or uses the following vehicles:
     [year/make/model/color of car]
     [registration]

C.   Interview Results (if any)
     On [date] [name of interviewee] was interviewed. [name] is the [relationship] of the subject. The interview took place at [location]. The Agent learned that [results of interview].
                                        or
     Interviews were not conducted [reason].

D.   Medical Information
     According to [source: include name, title and address], the subject's medical condition is [explain].

E.   Surveillance Results
     July 8, 2009
     7:00 am – 10:00 am
     7:35 am   On Wednesday, July 8, 2009, at 7:35 am Agents arrived at 456 East Main Street, West Hills, PA and
                          initiated a surveillance on subject. Agents observed a 1999 black Buick (PA registration ABC-1234)
                          parked in front of the residence. Agents observed the residence to be a side-by-side duplex, orange
                          brick, subject residing in the left side facing the house. The right side is unoccupied.
     9:35 am   Agents unsuccessfully attempted to contact the subject by telephone. Agents listened to a recorded mes-
                          sage indicating that subject was not at home. Agents terminated surveillance at approximately 10:00 am.
     July 9, 2009
     6:00 am – 12:00 pm
     6:00 am   On Thursday, July 9, 2009 at 6:00 am Agents arrived at 456 East Main Street, West Hills, PA and initi-
                          ated a surveillance on subject. Subject's vehicle (1999 Black Buick, PA registration ABC-1234) was
                          parked on the street in front of the residence.
                          At approximately 9:00 am, a pretext telephone call was placed to subject to verify her presence at the
                          residence with positive results. Agents maintained surveillance until 12:00 pm and observed no move-
                          ment. Surveillance was terminated at approximately 12:00 pm.

     July 10, 2009
     2:30 pm – 6:00 pm
     2:30 pm   On Friday, July 10, 2009 at 2:30 pm Agents arrived at 456 East Main Street, West Hills, PA and initiated
                          a surveillance on subject. Agents observed subject enter vehicle (1999 Black Buick, PA registration
                          ABC-1234) and proceed to the West Hills Shopping Center where the subject entered the deli.

Figure 9.20   Final report of investigation.   (*Continued*)

2:45 pm		At 2:45 pm the subject exited the deli with an unidentified white female, entered her vehicle and proceeded to the Richmond Shopping Center located at 123 East Main Street, Mars, PA. Subject parked in front of a MAC Banking Machine and made what appeared to be several transactions.
3:10 pm		At 3:10 pm the subject and companion returned to the West Hills Shopping Center and entered the Food King Supermarket.
3:55 pm		At 3:55 pm the subject exited the supermarket with one bag of groceries and proceeded to her vehicle and placed the groceries in the trunk of the car (Photograph #1) Subject then proceeded into the ice cream store.
4:05 pm		At 4:05 pm the subject exited the ice cream store, eating an ice cream cone, entered her vehicle and finished eating the cone. (Photograph #2)
4:10 pm		At approximately 4:10 pm subject proceeded to a MAC Banking Machine located at 456 East Main Street. Subject made a transaction on the machine and proceeded home. Surveillance was terminated at approximately 5:45 pm.

F. Summary
Agents observed no apparent physical disability that would impair movement.

or

Agents observed....

<u>End of Report</u>

Figure 9.20 (Continued)   Final report of investigation.

9.5.4.3 Theft and fraud in disability claims

Insurance companies that issue disability policies have a recurring need for verification on the legitimacy of disability claims. Private security firms and investigators provide these services. The following elements are crucial to determine whether the claimant is really disabled:

1. Was claimant hospitalized?
   a. Where, when, and for how long?
   b. Name of attending physician.
2. Is claimant confined to his house?
   a. For what period of time is claimant bedridden?
3. Is claimant wearing any braces, aided by orthopedic equipment or other medical accoutrements as a result of the injury? Give description and names of medical aids, if possible.
4. What injuries can be documented?
5. Is the claimant restricted in his activities?
   a. Is the claimant working? Confirm status.
6. Has there been any time lost from work due to the accident?
   a. Give confirmation and facts.
7. Are there any previous accidents?
   a. Does the claimant have a significant past medical history?
8. Does the claimant drive?
9. In what activities is the claimant presently engaged?[116]

In addition to standard security surveillance techniques discussed throughout this text, a disability claim investigation relies heavily upon an on-site claimant interview. The investigator need not fear personal confrontation or discussion with the claimant unless the insurance company has a strong certainty of subterfuge and fraud. A pretext of some kind is advisable, and a neighborhood investigation is likely to be the most informative.

> With very few exceptions, the neighborhood investigation is performed under a pretext. A pretext means we do not identify ourselves as a representative of the client or of our own company, and we do not state the actual purpose of our inquiries.[117]

---

[116] *Ibid.* at 4.
[117] *Ibid.*

NEIGHBORHOOD INVESTIGATION CHECKLIST

1. How long have they known the subject?
2. Does a family relationship exist between the subject and neighbors (or reference)?
3. Present address (how long there); previous address.
   How frequently is subject seen?
4. Age, race and marital status (spouse's name).
5. Dependency status (include relationship, names, and approximate ages of dependents).
6. Is the subject employed? If so, where? If place of employment is not known, what time does he leave for work and what is his mode of travel? (Also, if employment status is unknown, does the subject leave his residence at about the same time every day?)
7. If unemployed, when and where did he last work; what were his duties and why did he leave this employment? Does he appear able to work? What I his source of income? His normal occupation?
8. Are neighbors aware of any injuries or hospitalization? (Details, where, when, how long ago, etc.)
9. Health and prior to and subsequent to the injury in question.
10. Did the injury in question affect his normal activities? (yard work, house repairs, car repairs, etc.)
11. Present activities (golf, bowling, dancing, etc.).
12. Is spouse or are children employed? If so, where, how long, etc.
13. Property owned (residence, automobile, boat, truck, machinery, etc.).
14. Desirability as a neighbor and reputation (does subject drink alcohol, fight, gamble, use drugs, file suits, etc.)
15. Names and addresses of personal references, friends, and relatives.

Figure 9.21   Investigation checklist.

When questioning people, the investigator should be thoroughly prepared, orderly in presentation, and not appear intense or driven to a given end. The information elicited should come forth naturally from these third parties. Use of a checklist, such as that shown at Figure 9.21, will ensure that the investigator focuses on appropriate lines of questioning.

9.5.4.4 Theft and fraud in auto liability claims

Owing to escalating rates of auto litigation, the services of the private security industry are in high demand to develop a reliable record. Some insurance companies have adopted hardball strategies in contesting the claims and losses filed by lawyers. The typical automobile case arises from the auto insurance contract, that is, the agreement entered into between an insurer (the insurance company) and an insured (the claimant).

9.5.4.4.1 Policy declaration

The economic basis of the contractual obligation between the insured and the insurer is listed on a policy declaration page. Most policy declaration pages are uniform in content and comprise these categories:

- Bodily injury liability
- Collision protection
- Property damage liability
- Towing and labor costs
- Medical payments and benefits
- Funeral expenses
- Comprehensive coverage regarding personal effects
- Fire and theft
- Uninsured and underinsured motorist

Although dollar amounts influence the parameters of a potential lawsuit, the policy itself includes contractual provisions, which guide the obligations of the insured and the insurer. Three initial components are described in the insurance contract:

1. Specific agreements and coverages
2. Exclusions to coverage
3. Covenants and other contingencies

The investigator may have many functions within auto liability claims investigation, but the primary function is to determine the facts by obtaining an unbiased, factual recitation of what occurred. Decisions regarding liability, claims damages, and litigation are matters beyond the scope of investigative practice. Pinkerton's, Inc. emphasizes this fact in their handbook, *Investigation-Insurance Claims*:

> We are not experts in determining liability, but we are experts in investigation, in obtaining the facts. Once we have the facts, it is up to the client to take it from there.[118]

SUSPICIOUS MOTOR VEHICLE CLAIMS

- Cash purchase of late model or new vehicle
- Behind in payment to lien holder
- Out-of-state purchase
- Individual named as lien holder
- Insured has no bill of sale or the bill of sale is out of line with the car's value
- Vehicle is totally burned
- Vehicle Identification Number (VIN) of the damaged car does not match the VIN of the insured car or match the model shown in appraisal photographs
- NICB cannot match VIN
- VIN plate is different than VIN on the title
- Vehicle was rebuilt
- Prior loss or salvage on vehicle
- Prior owner cannot be located
- All vehicles in accident taken to the same body shop
- Recently duplicated or assigned title
- Counterfeit title documentation
- Insured claims expensive equipment and items
- Vehicle has poor reputation (defects, recalls, performance, etc.)
- Neighbors, friends and relative have no knowledge of vehicle
- Car has not been seen for some time prior to theft
- Insured is unemployed
- Insured wants to retain title to salvage
- Loss takes place between insurance of binder and state-mandated pre-inspection (where applicable)
- Premium paid in cash
- Comprehensive coverage only
- Duplicate coverage
- Repair shop estimates include repairs that body shop is not equipped to make (painting, straightening)
- Body shop has history of high damage claims
- Appraiser/adjuster is threatened or offered a bribe for quick settlement
- There is heavy property damage to the vehicles indicating a major collision but no bodily injuries are reported
- Salvage or repair shop takes active interest in claim

---

[118] *Ibid.* at 7.

- Repair or installation bills are numbered consecutively or dates show work done on Sundays or Holidays
- Two vehicles are involved with heavy damage to struck vehicle and relatively light damage to striking vehicle
- The striking vehicle is a rented car
- Accounts of the accident by drivers, passengers and witnesses appear rehearsed or are conversely inconsistent
- Appraisal photography show only close-ups of the damage, but not enough of the car to identify make and model
- Vehicle is recovered and ….
- No ignition or steering column damage
- Carefully stripped lug bolts and washers put back
- Extensive body damage and no towing charges; vehicle remains drivable
- Car shows signs of previous damage
- Damage does not match type of accident claimed

GENERAL INDICATORS OF SUSPICIOUS CLAIMS

- History of claims activity
- Familiar with insurance claim terms and procedures
- Refrains from using the mail of fax; conducts business in person
- No police report or on-scene report
- Aggressive demands for a quick settlement, sometimes for less than full value of claim
- Threatens to contact higher company authority to push demands
- Temporary address used – post office box or motel
- Recent policy or walk-in business
- Photocopied support documentation or computer generated invoices
- Insured's employer address is a post office box
- Unreasonable delay in reporting loss
- Refuses to give recorded or written statement
- Self-employed in vague occupation; reluctant to produce tax records
- First notice of claim and/or immediate attorney representation
- Recent changes in coverage/inquiries to agent
- Loss occurs immediately before or after policy renewal/inception dates
- Claimant experiencing financial problems
- Discrepancies between official reports of incident and statements made by insured/claimant
- Lifestyle inconsistent with observation and facts
- Insured/Claimant wants a friend or relative to pick up check
- Over documentation of loss
- Insured/Claimant has no phone
- Claimant is transient or out-of-towner[119]

Investigators assist the insurance company in the compilation of facts that lead to strategic policy relative to litigation. In an automobile accident case, multiple remedies and causes of action may exist. The negligence action is not mutually exclusive but is predictably the cause of action first pled. Traditional negligence law asserts that certain careless acts, a breach of due care, result in actual injury and damage. The person who runs a stop sign or a red light, falls asleep at the wheel, or has his or her eyes distracted from the roadway, thereby causing injury, will be deemed to

---

[119] Beau Dietl & Associates, Fraud Indicators, http://www.investigations.com/insurance/fraud-indicators/.

have breached the standard of care and conduct owed to others in the operation of an automobile. Beyond negligence, other remedies must not be overlooked, such as

1. First-party benefits—Under contemporary no-fault provisions, an insured in a contractual capacity with his insurance company may collect benefits for injuries arising out of the ownership, operation, or utilization of a motor vehicle.

2. Intentional torts—Individuals who are not simply careless but intentional in their conduct, who inflict bodily injury, or who destroy property, can be sued on intentional tort theories such as assault, battery, trespass, or intentional infliction of mental distress.

3. Underinsured or uninsured benefits—If the tortfeasor's policy limits do not adequately compensate for injury, or the tortfeasor has no insurance (this is labeled "uninsured"), the insured's own policy may make up the inadequacy through its underinsurance or uninsured coverages. Frequently, competing carriers will insist on a right to consent to any settlement before payment of any underinsurance.

Web Exercise: Visit one of the many firms that operates in the auto claims portion of the insurance industry at http://www.theeyewitness.com/auto-liability-investigations.html.

9.5.4.4.2 Processing the auto liability case

Governing investigative action in auto accident and liability cases is the need to discover the sequence, the chain of events, and the flow of conditions that led to the collision or other injury. The chain of events leading to the accident consists of

1. Principal event, the time, the place, and type of accident—for example, running off the road, collision on the road with a pedestrian

2. Perception of a hazard—the seeing, sensing, or hearing the unusual or unexpected movement or condition that could be taken as a sign of an accident about to happen

3. The point of perception—the time and place at which the unusual or unexpected movement or condition could have been perceived by a normal person

4. The point of no escape—the time and place beyond which the accident can no longer be prevented by the person who is watching

5. Maximum engagement—the time and position in which the objects in a collision are pushed together as far as they will be

6. The final position—the time and place when objects involved finally come to rest; this is the position before anything is moved[120]

Auto accident investigators must do all they can to maintain the final position of the persons or objects involved in the accident. Except for lifesaving issues and the minimization of property destruction, objects should remain in their final position to provide the most untainted picture of the accident scene. Insurance companies realize profits based on their capacity to analyze and reconstruct accident cases. Investigators, working on behalf of either the insured or the insurer, must possess the same level of dedication and proficiency. Where contributory negligence operates as a pure defense, reconstruction of the accident scene becomes an even more critical step in the investigative process.

Investigators need to document and complete memoranda outlining accident fact patterns because police reports and diagrams, as discussed in earlier sections of this text, serve as foundational pieces of evidence in the investigation of accident cases. Two types of forms regularly used to gather data are medical information sheets and accident data sheets. Samples of these types of forms are shown in Figures 9.22 and 9.23.

9.5.4.4.3 Scene sketch

Ask the client to diagram the accident as he or she remembers it. This type of active, graphic participation will help the client get the facts straight, and the investigator can verify and authenticate a client's story.

9.5.4.4.4 Photographing the accident scene

Although reports and documentation are necessary parts of investigative technique, photographs of the accident scene are vital pieces of evidence. Investigators should become proficient photographers or develop strong relationships

---

[120] W. Strobl, *The Investigator's Handbook* 90 (1984).

```
                              MEDICAL DATA

   Please summarize the following items:
   Description of Injuries: _____
   _____
   _____

   History of Accident: _____
   _____
   _____

   Progress: _____
   _____
   _____

   Past Medical History: _____
   _____
   _____

   Present Complaints:
         Date                    Nature                Permanency
   _____      _____      _____
   _____      _____      _____
   _____      _____      _____
```

Figure 9.22   Medical data.

with police photographers, or private photographers who work as independent contractors. Photographic coverage of an accident scene should include

1. *Approach to the scene* from the viewpoint of the driver or drivers involved. It may be necessary to make several photographs of the scene at different distances. Make these from the driver's eye level as he or she would be seated in the vehicle. Remember that the high cab of a tractor-trailer rig may place the driver as much as eight feet from the ground. Climb on a tow truck or station wagon tailgate to get the needed height.

2. *Eyewitness' viewpoint.* To corroborate eyewitness statements, make pictures of the scene from the eyewitness' position and eye level.

3. *Position of the vehicles.* Try to get shots of the final position of vehicles before they are moved. If they must be moved before they can be photographed, mark their positions with chalk or tape.

4. *Position of victims.* Where victims are thrown clear of the vehicles, get photographs of the position of a body or mark the position of an injured victim who is being removed for treatment.

5. *Point of impact.* If it is possible, determine and photograph the point of impact of the vehicle or vehicles involved in the accident. This may correspond to the final position of the vehicles, or it may be some distance from that point. Relate the two in a photograph if possible.

6. *Overall view of scene.* One or several pictures that relate the overall scene elements can be useful to the accident investigator. One viewpoint for such photographs is a high position overlooking the scene; a rooftop, an embankment, a bridge, or even a truck can provide a commanding position. Other overall shots can be made with the camera at eye level in the direction of vehicle travel and then by looking back through the scene from the opposite direction to show the area of approach.

7. *Close-ups of accident details.* Details of vehicle damage, skid marks, tire marks, worn or damaged tires, registration plates, oil–water–gasoline spills, and broken parts provide key information to aid the accident investigator. Photograph questionable items within the car such as wine, beer, and liquor bottles; narcotics; or firearms.[121]

---

[121] Eastman Kodak Co., *Photography in Traffic Accident Investigation* 4 (1979).

Accident Data Form

Your name _____

Accident date _____ Time _____ am/pm

Address_____ City _____ State _____ Zip _____

Police Dept. _____ Case # _____ Tickets Issued? ☐Yes ☐No

If yes, to whom? _____ Charges _____

Other Vehicle:

Year _____ Make _____ Model _____

Color _____ License Plate # _____ State _____

Driver of Other Vehicle:

Name _____ Apparent injuries? ☐Yes ☐No

Home Address _____ City _____ State _____ Zip _____

Home Phone _____ _____ Business Phone _____

Drivers License # _____ State _____ Insurance Carrier _____

Age _____ Sex _____ Ht _____ Wt _____

Injury type _____

Registered Owner of Other Vehicle:

Name _____ Apparent injuries? ☐Yes ☐No

Home Address _____ City _____ State _____ Zip _____

Drivers License # _____ State _____ Insurance Carrier _____

Passengers in Other Vehicle:

Name _____ Apparent injuries? ☐Yes ☐No

Home Address _____ City _____ State _____ Zip _____

Home phone _____ Business phone _____

Drivers License # _____ State _____ Insurance Carrier _____

Age _____ Sex _____ Ht _____ Wt _____

Injury type _____

Position in vehicle at time of accident _____

Name _____ Apparent injuries? ☐Yes ☐No

Home Address _____ City _____ State _____ Zip _____

Home phone _____ Business phone _____

Drivers License # _____ State _____ Insurance Carrier _____

Age _____ Sex _____ Ht _____ Wt _____

Injury type _____

Position in vehicle at time of accident _____

Witnesses:

Name _____ Apparent injuries? ☐Yes ☐No

Home Address _____ City _____ State _____ Zip _____

Home phone _____ Business phone _____

Name _____ Apparent injuries? ☐Yes ☐No

Home Address _____ City _____ State _____ Zip _____

Home phone _____ Business phone _____

Figure 9.23   Accident data form.

The Center for Public Safety at Northwestern University has the following suggestions on accident scene photography:

What to photograph

1. Vehicle identification
   a. Vehicle license plate
   b. Vehicle identification plate
   c. Vehicle's make and model

2. Contact damage area

    a. Overlap

    b. Collapse

    c. Direction of thrust

3. Induced damage area

4. Undamaged area

5. Interior—when needed

6. Vehicle lamps (if there is a question regarding #6 and #7, take picture)

7. Vehicle tires

8. Close-up photographs[122]

The Traffic Institute also recommends that each picture be charted as to shutter speed, focal point, distance, and depth of field.

9.5.4.4.5 Auto accident reconstruction

Investigators involved in traffic accident investigation will be confronted with problems from the simple to the complex. "Like many other specialized activities, traffic accident investigation may be done at various levels or degrees of technology depending on the needs and the resources available."[123] Northwestern University's Traffic Institute,[124] now known as the Center for Public Safety, a private, nonprofit organization founded in 1936, has provided accident reconstruction services to law enforcement, criminal justice, private security, and highway transportation agencies. Private investigators wishing to enhance professional standing in accident reconstruction may wish to participate in one of the Traffic Institute's many educational programs. The webpage regarding their Accident Reconstruction Course is given in Figure 9.24.[125]

The Center distinguishes five levels of traffic accident investigation:

1. Reporting

2. Supplementary data collection

3. Technical preparation

4. Professional reconstruction

5. Cause analysis

At the first level, the investigator *identifies* and *classifies* the accident conditions, persons, and property involved. Reports and other documents discussed throughout this text are filled out indicating time of day, location, environment, damage to vehicles and drivers, pedestrians, passengers, witnesses, and officials on the scene. At the second level, the *supplementary data* phase, the initial accident report is supplemented by the following:

- Measurements to locate final positions of vehicles and bodies of persons killed or injured
- Measurements to locate tire marks, gouges, debris left on the road
- Photos of final positions of vehicles
- Photos of tire marks, gouges, and debris left on the road
- Descriptions of damage to vehicles and measurements of collapse
- Photos of damage to vehicles
- Blood samples for alcohol tests
- Informal statements of people involved and other witnesses

---

[122] The Traffic Institute, *Vehicle Damage Photography* 2–3 (SN 7717).

[123] The Traffic Institute, *Level of Traffic Accident Investigation* 1 (SN 8000).

[124] Northwestern University, The Center for Public Safety 555 Clark St., Evanston, IL 60204.

[125] Northwestern University, The Center for Public Safety, http://sps.northwestern.edu/program-areas/public-safety/programs/crash-investigation.asp.

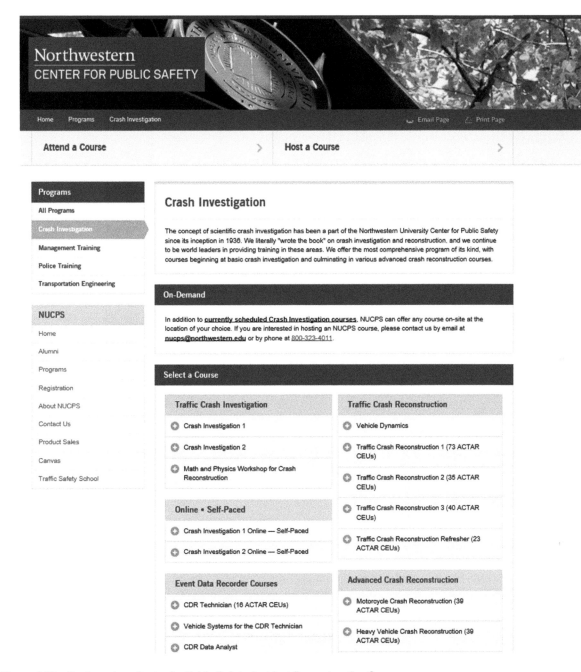

Figure 9.24 Northwestern Center for Public Safety Accident Reconstruction Courses.

- Preliminary matching of contact damage between vehicles and between vehicles and road surface or fixed objects
- Descriptions and photos of damage to such equipment as lamps, tires, batteries, safety belts, and obtaining these for test if possible
- Samples of paint and glass for examination
- Chemical tests for intoxication
- Autopsies to determine cause of death
- Medical descriptions of injuries[126]

---

[126] Traffic Institute, Traffic Accident at 4.

Proceeding to the third level, *technical preparation*, the investigator begins to map out or graphically portray the incident. It may involve activities such as

- Elementary ground photogrammetry
- Mapping from perspective template photos
- Matching vehicle damage areas and preparing maximum engagement, first contact, and disengagement diagrams
- Preparation of after-accident situation map
- Simple speed estimates from skid marks, yaw marks, and falls
- Determination of design speed and critical speed of curves and turns[127]

Yaw marks and other reference points can be photographically examined.

As discussed earlier, the investigator's comprehension of the accident site will be fostered by a scene sketch or other descriptive means. To construct an accident map, the investigator should follow the step-by-step instructions below:

1. Decide detail needed based on how map will be used:
   a. for *working* (reconstruction) *purposes*, minimum detail;
   b. for *display* (court) *purposes*, additional detail for realism.
2. Determine layout of roadways by inspection.
   a. Single roadway:
      i. straight or curved;
      ii. number of lanes.
   b. Junction of two or more roadways:
      i. number of legs;
      ii. number of lanes in each leg;
      iii. which roadway edges align without offset or angle;
      iv. what angles between roadways are not right angles.
3. Draw on field sketch basic layout of roadways. Use light lines. Show approximate widths, angles, and curves (freehand).
4. Connect all edges which align by dashed line on field sketch.
5. If any leg is not square with the others, project one edge of it until it intercepts the edge of another leg to form an intercept.
6. Select RP (Reference Point or Points). Mark it on field sketch. Write description of RP on field sketch.
7. Mark accident RPs on field sketch if they are known.
8. Draw in edge returns (curves between edges of roadways), shoulders, sidewalks, etc., which may be needed.
9. Draw roadside objects which may be needed (fixed objects, etc.)
10. Draw in other things (buildings, fences, etc.) needed for display.
11. Indicate measurements to be made by dimension lines from coordinates or RPs to Items 3, 5, 7, 8, 9, and 10 above. Show measurements in series as much as possible (a series of measures from one point along a line).
12. Show additional measurements for curves and angles.
13. Add check measurements between important points.
14. Mark road surface (RP, etc.) if needed. Use yellow crayon.
15. Make measurements indicated. Record on field sketch.
16. Note grades, elevations, and character of surface. Record if needed.
17. Show north by arrow. (Add accident identifiers.)

---

[127] *Ibid.* at 5.

18. Identify location by road name and, if needed, distance and direction to recognizable landmark. Give city or county and state.

19. Sign and date field sketch.[128]

At the fourth level of accident scene investigation, *professional reconstruction*, the investigator—after gathering all information and graphically reproducing it—attempts to define the accident in order to pose an explanation. While not arriving at a specific cause or amassing enough evidence to deduce legal causation, the fourth level of accident analysis seeks "opinions, deductions, and inferences…usually in the form of estimates of speed, position on the road, and visibility; descriptions of driving tactics (evasive action), strategy, communications, and how injuries were received; or proof of law violations and who was driving."[129]

In the final stage of accident reconstruction, *cause analysis*, a conclusion as to the actual cause is determined. Conceptually, the accident reconstruction now defines circumstances and events, relays why the accident occurred, and gives direct or conditional explanations. The investigator's position can include, but is not limited to, the following findings:

- Probable contribution of road or vehicle design deficiencies to accident, injury, and damage occurrence
- Probable contribution of [derelicts] to accident and injury occurrence
- Probable contribution of temporary road or vehicle conditions, accident and injury, and damage occurrence
- Probable contribution of temporary driver conditions (such as intoxication) to accident and injury occurrence
- Complete combination of probable and possible factors contributing to tactical (evasive action) failures in the highway transport system
- Complete combination of probable and possible factors contributing to strategy (precautionary measures) that prevented successful tactics or otherwise influenced the outcome of events
- Recommendations for prevention of future accidents with some of the same factors as the one under study[130]

Even a lifetime of field experience will not enable the investigator to claim perfection in auto accident analysis and reconstruction. As insurance companies seek ways of defending the onslaught of accident litigation, private security serves as the objective third party that provides information without bias or prejudice.

9.5.4.4.6 Special problems: Auto theft, fraud, and parts pilferage

Crime statistics point to a staggering rate of auto theft, illegal trafficking in auto parts, and the establishment of chop shops, underground operations that steal cars, strip them, and sell individual parts. The National Crime Insurance Bureau was formed in 1992 from a merger between the National Automobile Theft Bureau (NATB) and the Insurance Crime Prevention Institute (ICPI), both of which were not-for-profit organizations. The NATB—which managed vehicle theft investigations and developed vehicle theft databases for use by the insurance industry—dates to the early twentieth century, while the ICPI investigated insurance fraud for approximately 20 years before joining with the NATB. The primary purpose of the NCIB is to lead a united effort of insurers, law enforcement agencies, and representatives of the public to prevent and combat insurance fraud and crime through data analytics, investigations, training, legislative advocacy, and public awareness.

Web Exercise: See the NCIB poster at https://www.nicb.org/newsroom/psas.

To combat this plague of fraud, collusion, and thievery, the insurance industry, auto dealers, manufacturers, and legislative agencies have called upon the services of private investigators to pinpoint the location and identification of suspect motor vehicle practices. Investigators should cautiously evaluate an affidavit of vehicle theft, filed at either the local police department or the insurance company for the purpose of claim reimbursement. Figure 9.25 shows one such form.

Investigators must be wary of many claims and allegations, especially when certain insured profiles and other mitigating factors appear. Be skeptical of an insured, a claimant, who

- Gives address and phone number of a bar, hotel, or motel as a place where he can be contacted
- Is unavailable or difficult to contact

---

[128] The Traffic Institute, *Measuring for Maps 2* (SN 1097).
[129] Traffic Institute, *Maps*, at 6.
[130] *Ibid.* at 7.

Received	
Dispatched	
Arrived	

Police Department
Property Crimes Bureau
Auto Theft Detail
Stolen Vehicle Agreement & Affidavit

Case/Report number:_____

Name of registered owner of stolen vehicle (printed): _____
Name of reporting person (printed): _____
ID type: _____ ID #:_____ DOB: _____

Description of stolen vehicle:

MAKE_____ MODEL_____ YEAR_____
STYLE_____ COLOR_____ VIN _____
LICENSE_____ STATE_____ LIEN HOLDER _____
INSURANCE COMPANY_____ POLICY#_____
FURTHER VEHICLE DESCRIPTION:_____

I _____ certify that the above-described vehicle was taken without my
knowledge or permission from_____ between the time span of
_____.

Due to the number of stolen vehicle reports the Police Department receives, it is necessary that:

- I immediately notify the P.D. if I become aware of the location of the stolen vehicle. _____(INITIAL)

- I agree to assist in the prosecution of the theft of my vehicle._____(INITIAL)

It is unlawful for a person to knowingly make to a law enforcement agency of either this state or a political subdivision of this state a false, fraudulent or unfounded report or statement or to knowingly misrepresent a fact for the purpose of interfering with the orderly operation of a law enforcement agency or misleading a peace officer. False Reporting to a law enforcement agency is a **class 1 misdemeanor** punishable up to six months in jail, $2,500 fine and three years probation. Furthermore, under state law, it is unlawful for a person to knowingly destroy, remove, conceal, encumber, convert, sell, transfer, control, or otherwise deal with property subject to a security interest with the intent to hinder or prevent the enforcement of that interest. Defrauding Secured Creditors is a **class 6 felony** punishable up to 1.5 years in jail, and up to a $150,000 fine.

IF THE AFFIDAVIT IS NOT TAKEN IN PERSON BY A LAW ENFORCEMENT OFFICER OR AGENCY, THE PERSON WHO ALLEGES THAT A THEFT OF MEANS OF TRANSPORTATION HAS OCCURRED SHALL MAIL OR DELIVER THE SIGNED AND NOTARIZED AFFIDAVIT TO THE APPROPRIATE LOCAL LAW ENFORCEMENT AGENCY WITHIN SEVEN (7) DAYS AFTER REPORTING THE THEFT. IF THE APPROPRIATE LAW ENFORCEMENT AGENCY DOES NOT RECEIVE THE SIGNED AND NOTARIZED AFFIDAVIT WITHIN THIRTY (30) DAYS AFTER THE INITIAL REPORT, THE VEHICLE INFORMATION SHALL BE REMOVED FROM THE DATABASES OF THE NATIONAL CRIME INFORMATION CENTER AND THE STATE CRIMINAL JUSTICE INFORMATION SYSTEM.

Signature of Reporting Person   Date/Time

Complete Address

Home Phone   Cell Phone   Work Phone

Officer Signature   Serial #   Date/Time

Subscribed and sworn to me on this_____day of _____, 20____.
Notary Public_____

My Commission Expires:_____

Figure 9.25 Auto theft detail.

- Has family members or household who know nothing about the loss
- Avoids the use of the U.S. Mail
- Has income incompatible with the amount of the car payment
- Is a single male under 28 years of age
- Is unemployed
- Is in arrears with lienholder
- Has no prior business with the insurer
- Is in an extreme hurry to settle the claim
- Has made recent inquiry into policy coverages
- Wishes to retain title on a total loss

The type of vehicle is also instructive regarding potential fraud, theft, or collusion. Consider these queries:

- Is it a late model, expensive auto?
- Is the vehicle expensively customized?
- Are there expensive extras and accessories?
- Has the vehicle been rebuilt from a prior major collision claim?
- Is the vehicle inefficient on fuel?
- Is the VIN suspect?
- Does the recovered vehicle have no collision damage?
- Has the vehicle been stolen, subsequently recovered, and then shortly thereafter been burned?

The whole essence of effective auto theft, fraud, and collusion investigation involves the search for patterns, trends, special characteristics, and factors, such as

- Type of car
- Time of the theft
- Day of the week
- Location of vehicle when stolen
- Suspects or vehicles seen
- Location of vehicle when recovered
- Condition of vehicle when recovered

Use the auto theft fraud indicator checklist in Figure 9.26 as a guide to this type of investigation.

Aside from auto theft, auto fraud—which involves deceit, trickery, and intentional perversion of the truth—is another rampant activity. Simple frauds include reporting a stolen vehicle to accomplish these ends:

1. To cover up a hit-and-run accident
2. To cover up a one-car accident to beat the deductible
3. To cover an accident in which operators are under the influence of alcohol or drugs
4. To cover the need for extensive repairs such as new transmission, new motor, new paint job
5. Has large vehicle with large gasoline consumption
6. To purchase a good vehicle, export it by selling to foreign country, then report as stolen
7. Import fraud—to allege purchase of a vehicle from outside the United States, obtain the vehicle, then report as stolen
8. Strip fraud—to purchase a vehicle, strip unit of most of its parts, return it, and claim it was recovered in stripped condition

---

AUTO THEFT FRAUD INDICATORS

1. Policy in effect ninety (90) days or less, or recent vehicle purchase.
2. Auto stolen while not in possession of insured.
3. In arrears with lienholder.
4. The vehicle was a previously recovered theft or the subject of a prior major collision claim.
5. Insured furnished address and phone number of a bar, hotel or motel as a place to be contacted by the claims adjuster.
6. The insured has failed to report the theft to the police.
7. The insured is unable to identify himself (i.e., does not know his own social security or driver's license number)
8. Late notice of theft to insurance company or police.
9. Any discrepancy in VIN or license plate numbers.
10. Cash purchase from an individual rather than a dealer.
11. The vehicle was alleged to have been stolen prior to titling and registration.
12. The previous owner cannot be located or is unknown to the insured.
13. Mail address differs from garaging address on policy.
14. Date of coverage and date of claim are closely related.
15. Title or proof of ownership is a duplicate issue or from a distant state.
16. The insured has just recently titled the vehicle in his name.
17. The insured presents an assigned title, still in the name of the previous owner, as proof of his ownership.
18. The insured is unable to produce title or proof of ownership.
19. Time and location of loss are suspicious – usually away from insured's premises and in the evening.
20. The vehicle is reported to be expensively customized or a show model.
21. The vehicle has become unpopular for any reason (i.e., inefficient to operate, difficult to find repair parts, has received unfavorable press coverage concerning safety, etc.)
22. Members of the insured's family or household know nothing about the loss.
23. Insured has little or no liability coverage.
24. Insured quickly pressures for claim settlement including threats of complaints to Insurance Commissioner.
25. Demands car settlement in lieu of replacement.

Figure 9.26 Auto theft fraud indicator checklist.

At a minimum, the investigator should always be dubious of auto theft claims when these factual scenarios exist:

- Ownership of the vehicle is very recent.
- Vehicle was purchased from a private individual.
- Vehicle was purchased out of state.
- The insured presents an assigned title with the previous owner's name still on it.
- Previous owner cannot be located.
- Payment for vehicle is made in cash.
- Duplicate title or no title is available.
- The loss occurred shortly after obtaining an insurance policy.
- Fire loss occurred at night in an out-of-the-way location.
- Notice of loss was not timely.
- Recovered vehicle had heavy collision damage.
- Reported to police rather than through insurance agency.
- Not reported to police at all.
- Loss occurred prior to final title and registration.

9.5.4.4.6.1 VIN systems

Automobiles are identified by several methods, including insurance identification number, title, registration, and other motor vehicle documentation. Identification of a vehicle at its point of manufacturing origin is accomplished through the vehicle identification numbering (VIN) system. The VIN method of vehicle marking and identification is an impressive defense mechanism because foreign and domestic automakers make a concerted effort to inscribe, without chance of alteration or obliteration, identification numbers at selected points on a vehicle. These identification numbers are stamped and registered at the factory. The engine and vehicle identification numbers are used on legal documents and recorded upon transfer.

Under rules established by the National Highway Traffic Safety Administration, specifically Federal Motor Vehicle Safety Standard 115, commencing in 1981, all motor vehicles must adopt a vehicle identification numbering system. The VIN is a series of 17 alphanumeric characters. For vehicles with a gross vehicle weight of 10,000 pounds or less, the VIN must be located inside the passenger compartment adjacent to the left windshield pillar and readable from the outside of the vehicle. For vehicles with a gross vehicle weight rating of more than 10,000 pounds, location and visibility requirements are not specified. All VINs shall appear clearly and indelibly upon either a part of the vehicle, other than the glazing, that is not designed to be removed except for repair or upon a separate label or plate, which is permanently affixed to such a part. Figure 9.27 illustrates the basis of the VIN system.

Auto manufacturers designate specific areas on each model for identification number placement. See Figure 9.28.

9.5.4.4.6.2 Parts

Identification numbers are also placed on certain parts of a vehicle. Because of the high cost of parts replacement, the crude practices of chop shops and the ease with which engines, transmissions, and other selected parts can be sold, manufacturers have inscribed identification numbers on engines and transmissions. As a rule, the number is derivatively based upon the VIN.

As the price of replacement parts has risen, automobile manufacturers have embarked on parts identification programs. Probably the most advanced contribution is from General Motors Corporation, which, in 1980, established a special parts marking program by which parts such as luggage lids, fenders, doors, and other body panels are labeled. The labels consist of a special brand of security film, approximately 2.25 inches wide and 6.25 inches high. The label is designed so that once it is affixed to the surface, any attempt to remove it will result in the border pulling away from the window, which will destroy the integrity of the label. Under ordinary light, the label will appear light blue in color. It can be authenticated by examination under retroreflective light. This is accomplished by using an inexpensive retroreflective viewer, available from several commercial sources, or by holding a flashlight parallel to and at the same

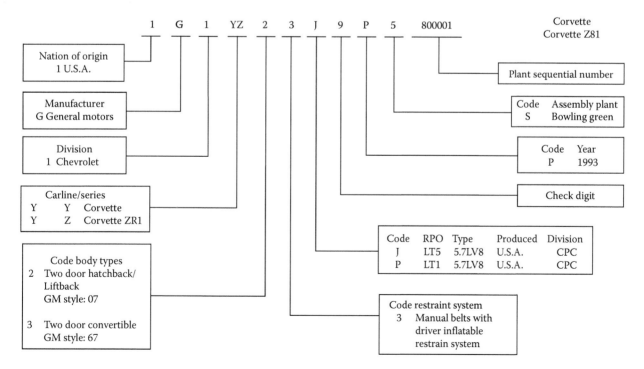

Figure 9.27   VIN numbering diagram.

Common locations for your VIN number

Driver side interior dash

1969 and newer cars will have the VIN on the driver's side dash viewable through the windshield.

Additional possibilities:
Trunk (under spare)
Driver door jam (open door)
Back wheel well

Front of engine block

Raise hood and look at front of engine.

Stamped on front end of frame

You can see it by looking down between your front carb and your windshield washer unit. Most likely older cars.

Figure 9.28 VIN number locations.

level as the viewer's eye. Under retroreflective light, an authentic label will display a pattern of GM logos across the entire face of the label. The lack of such a pattern or discontinuity in the pattern will indicate counterfeit products.

To stay on the cutting edge of this complex field, private investigators should strongly consider membership in the International Association of Auto Theft Investigators.

Web Exercise: Visit the Web location of the IAATI at http://www.iaati.org/about.

9.6 REPORTING AND MEMORIALIZING THE INVESTIGATIVE METHOD

Despite its drudgery, report writing is a core and mandatory function throughout the investigative process and serves as the formal record of investigative steps and practices. Reports are crucial to historical accuracy and assure an objective appraisal of events and conditions surrounding the case at hand. Reports also promote professional best practices for the security industry.

Reports and record keeping also promotes productivity and efficiency in a typical security agency's operation. "There is a direct relationship between the efficiency of a security operation and the quality of its records and record procedures. The simple task of performing security in health care facilities only a few years ago is in sharp contrast to the exceedingly complex and difficult problems and demands of today's facilities. In meeting these demands, the security operation must function according to plans that provide for detailed records regarding each phase of its operational responsibility."[131] Reports cause two things: first, initial steps are memorialized; second, subsequent investigative actions are not a rehash of the first steps taken. As case investigations progress, it is difficult to remember it all and

---

[131] R. Colling, *Hospital Security* 2nd ed., 235 (1982); see how the rise of technology has influenced report writing in Bryan Roberts, The Keyboard Is Mightier than the Sword, 41 *J. Calif. L. Enforcement* 14 (2007).

report documents keep the investigator on an efficient path. Without reports, the case and its personnel are likely to falter or at least proceed in a less efficient way.

Both short-term and long-term memories are subject to a variety of forces that can affect clarity and recall. Note-taking at the scene and creation of the report as soon as possible after an event reduces the risk of inaccuracy. Case documentation, fully accepting the fallibility of human memory, provides a permanent locale for later reference. "The need to retrieve information contained in a report may occur within hours or days after it is written or perhaps even years later. A quick and effective technique for evaluating a security system is to determine how many questions concerning past activity are answered by personal memory as opposed to answers supplied according to documented facts."[132] The passage of time, the fading of capacity to remember, and the diversity of external influences, such as varied opinions, all undermine the quality of memory alone and the urgent need for a documentary record.

Reports force the investigator to evaluate a case in a formal sense rather than in an exclusively extemporaneous method. Reports themselves engender a stronger organizational method. While oral communication tends to be spontaneous, communicating thoughts in written form requires a more formal organizational approach. The investigator must keep in mind the "who, what, when, where, and how" of the case and author language that reflects these fundamental queries of the skilled investigator. From an administrative perspective, reports and documentation organize the functions of a security firm.

The report demonstrates, to new and long-term clients, exactly what has been undertaken thus far. Reports not only cover the professional tracks of the investigator but also provide clients with a formal proof of work done so far. Sophisticated clients, especially those with business and industrial concerns, are investing a sizeable chunk of money in the world of security services and have a rightful expectation of a documentary record of the said activities. Permanent records reflect the firm's efforts. Records and reports can secure a company's goodwill as well as educate the client on the nature of investigative results. Thus, the report is not only a tool of investigation, but also a critical communicative aid between the client and the investigator.

Accuracy is a perpetual concern to the security professional in two contexts: first, whether or not the information included in the report is factually and legally correct; and second, whether or not the information contained in the report is technically correct. Notes that are filled with chronological or sequential gaps will provide little aid in recall, and are dubious factually. In fact, if incomplete notes are relied upon to refresh memory during the testimonial phase of trial litigation, attorneys easily poke holes in the accuracy and credibility of such notes; thus, thoroughness is imperative. The final report comprehensively portrays the major results of the investigation. Stylistic attention is just as important as factual content. Cox and Brown use common sense and a bit of humor to drive home the stylistic aspect of report writing:

1. *Accuracy is important in word use as well as in information.* Poor word choice will get you into trouble. One officer wound up in court on three occasions trying to explain what he meant when he said that the suspect "crowded" him. Was he pushed, shoved up against the wall, verbally intimidated, or what? *Value judgments must be avoided, and brief details should be given instead.* For example, don't say, "The child seemed afraid of his father." Instead, give the facts that led you to this assumption: "When the father came into the room, the boy stopped talking and began to cry. The father smiled and offered the boy candy, but the son backed up to his mother and clung to her, crying harder."

2. *Brevity is important, as long as it is not used at the cost of accuracy or completeness.* This applies to words, too. Never use a complicated word when a simple one will do. The active form is shorter and generally more accurate than the passive form.

3. *Completeness is essential.* One of the stories used recently on this point is that of the young lawyer Abraham Lincoln, who won a case because he proved that the moon was not shining on a night that the presumed suspect was supposedly identified by the full light of the moon. Do not assume anything, even the obvious. A recent case in Australia made the front page of a newspaper for its rather humorous point: A man was alleged to be drunk, and the report stated that the officer observed the man's eyes to be bloodshot. "Both of them?" asked the defense attorney. Looking at the now clear-eyed defendant the officer said firmly, "Yes, both of them." Whereupon the defendant removed his clear, artificial eye and rolled it on the table. Case dismissed.[133]

---

[132] R. Colling at 234.
[133] C. Cox & J. Brown, *Report Writing for Criminal Justice Professionals* 14–15 (1992).

Grammatical rigor is central to professional report writing. Conciseness, brevity of thought and idea, and an objective presentation do much to insure the authenticity and usefulness of a report. The investigator has the professional obligation to ensure that spelling is correct, that sentences are grammatically sound, and that the presentation provided is logical and comprehensive. Opinions and emotional responses without factual justification are to be avoided at all costs. Before submitting a report to a client or supervisor, the investigator should take the time to read and review its contents thoroughly. In making the final assessment, the investigator should make sure the report is

- Factual
- Clear
- Accurate
- Mechanically correct
- Objective
- Written in Standard English
- Complete
- Legible
- Concise

Effective report writing also requires familiarity with the basic styles and formats of report design. The checklist format, the most abbreviated and least narrative of all report systems, simply calls upon the author to check by mark, asterisk, or initial, the information requested. Numerous examples of the checklist format are included throughout this text.

Some reports are intentionally designed to call upon the investigator to make a deduction, a finding, or a conclusion regarding certain matters. Sometimes, a list of alternative explanations or descriptions might be requested. Interpretative questionnaires can call for deductive or inferential conclusions regarding a suspect description, motive, or *modus operandi* (method of operation or MO).

9.7 CONCLUSION

The depth and breadth of investigative practice reaches its full and complete glory in the private security industry and the coverage just presented in this chapter edifies just how many investigative pursuits exist in this industry. This chapter commences with a close look at the qualities and attributes of the effective investigator, poses basic conceptual questions as to how an investigator should proceed in every investigation, and highlights traits that are conducive to effective investigation. The coverage then turns to specific investigative applications and expends considerable energy on the world of theft, shoplifting, and other asset integrity issues. Private security made its bones in the world of theft and it is right to highlight the many ways in which the industry seeks to prevent continuing losses whether it be by direct shoplifting, fraud in insurance, disability and workers' compensation, auto theft and parts chopping, false and fraudulent claims in arson, and residential housing and accident cases. The full array of investigative steps and procedures are considered within this chapter as well as suggestions for forms and other methods of documentation.

Keywords

arson	human relations skills	real evidence
background investigation	incident report	reports
burglary	insurance fraud	security services
cause of action	investigative characteristics	shoplifting
claim	investigative methods	systematic collection of evidence
fact-gathering	investigative process	theft by employees
factual assimilation	offense	witnesses
fraud	physical evidence	

Discussion Questions

1. List the characteristics that are essential for an investigator and explain why each is necessary.
2. Compare and contrast the private security investigations and police investigations.
3. Outline the purposes of investigation in the criminal and civil justice systems.
4. Discuss the various motivations for shoplifting and make recommendations to guard against them.
5. Relay the tactics used for theft by employees and discuss methods to investigate them.
6. List the four difference areas of insurance claims and identify the most effective methods of investigating each claim.
7. Discuss the most important aspects of report writing.

CHAPTER 10

Crisis planning and prevention of accidents, emergencies, and disasters

OBJECTIVES

After completing this chapter, the student will be able to

1. Discuss security industry's role in the prevention of accidents, and compliance and adherence to regulatory requirements regarding workplace safety and hazards encountered on the job.
2. Summarize the security professional's role in planning and preparation in the advance of natural disasters, medical emergencies, pandemics, and fire and safety protocols.
3. Identify various OSHA standards for hazardous materials or conditions in the work environment and plan for on-site investigations and inspections at work locations.
4. Evaluate a site's potential accidents and emergencies and make recommendations for the mitigation of the said incidents.
5. Assess a building's vulnerabilities where fire and life safety are concerned and make recommendations for preventative action and detection equipment.
6. Develop a hazmat security plan that accounts for and screens personnel, access points, security of facility and the perimeter, and the many dynamics of WMD delivery.
7. Describe the various pandemic threats that a security professional may encounter, how to generally guard against pandemic threats in a general sense, and understand the basic response procedures.
8. Explain the four basic operational levels in emergency and crisis planning and be able to apply them in any given situation.

10.1 INTRODUCTION

The private security industry comprises a wide array of duties and obligations and has been historically caricatured as primarily a replace- or rent-a-cop business. Nothing could be further from either past or present reality, for the industry's tentacles weave their way into every imaginable corner. To be sure, the security officer business, which primarily protects assets and people, continues unabated; however, the varied functions of security professional grow without much restriction. One area where growth seems unlimited is on the safety and emergency side, where security companies now deliver services relating to accident prevention, safety protocols, hazmat policy, preparation and preparedness for natural disaster and emergency, and workplace safety and compliance, to name just a few. Gone are the days when security directors were asset protectors alone. Today, the private security industry has ventured into diverse worlds, although none seems as evident as on the safety and emergency side. Security directors are expected to know the security business in esoteric ways but are also expected to be cognizant of safety and emergency protocols.

University Health System Job Description: MANAGER, SECURITY/SAFETY

Job Title: MANAGER, SECURITY/SAFETY
FLSA: E
Date: 06/13/2005

Job Code: 50XX
Pay Target: G2
Supervisory Responsibility: Yes

General Description of the Job Class

Perform a variety of management functions in planning and implementing security, loss prevention and traffic/parking policies and procedures, coordinating the activities of the security staff in the safeguarding of hospital property.

Manage and oversee all assigned areas in order to maintain a safe environment for patients, visitors and personnel.

Duties and Responsibilities of this Level

Plan, coordinate and direct activities such as: staff assistance with patient restraint and intervention in disruptions by patients, visitors and staff; traffic control; guard and patrol physical property; escort service for visitors and staff; monitor systems response; orient and monitor personnel working in high risk areas; and investigation of accidents and criminal acts.

Develop and implement security procedures and compliance with hospital policies and procedures and applicable state and federal laws.

Review and evaluate reports prepared by security staff regarding investigations of reports of criminal activities.

Conduct follow-up investigation of reports of criminal activity

Analyze traffic and parking problems and make recommendations for new or revised programs, policies and procedures.

Supervise security personnel, participate in the interviewing and selection of applicants for employment, review employee performance and recommend promotion and salary adjustment, and apply hospital and personnel policy to daily operations.

Supervise and/or conduct security awareness programs for the hospital staff including new employee orientation, department in-service, as well as the security staff continuing education.

Confer with representatives of management to formulate policies, determine need for programs and coordinate programs with hospital activities. Confer with representatives of local government to ensure cooperation and coordination of hospital activities with law enforcement and fire fighting agencies.

Intervene whenever conditions exist that pose an immediate threat to life or health, or poses a threat to equipment or the facility.

Develop and recommend new procedures and approaches to safety and loss prevention based on reports of incidents, accidents, and other relevant information.

Figure 10.1   Job description: Security Manager.   *(Continued)*

Michael A. Gips refers to these connections as "synergies among the various functions,"[1] which now prompt continuous emergence of safety and security responsibilities. The designation of the chief security officer (CSO) now assumes this interplay of task and function.[2]

In other words, safety and security now appear natural handmaidens in the corporate and institutional world. Consider the director position previously advertised by the University Health System in Figure 10.1.[3]

---

[1] M.A. Gips, Safe and Secure, *Sec. Mag.* 83 (February 2005).
[2] See Special Report on Executive Protection, It Starts with a Profile, *Sec. Mag.* (June 2009) at 64.
[3] Duke University.

Disseminate information to department heads and others regarding toxic and hazardous waste and materials, safe medical devices and supplies, emergency preparedness, and safety information

Assist department managers/directors and administrators in enforcing safety regulations and codes.

Measure and evaluate effectiveness of safety program, using established goals.

May be assigned as member and/or chair of entity safety/security related committees on findings, recommendations, actions and monitoring. Support safety/security committee meetings by collecting and formulating relevant information in such a way that decision making is facilitated. Conduct building and grounds hazard surveillance surveys on a periodic and regular basis to detect code violations, hazard, and incorrect work practices and procedures.

Ensure that all infection control risk assessments are conducted for all construction or remodel projects.

Develop, review and participate in safety training for hospital staff.

Maintain administrative control of records related to safety and health programs.

Required Qualifications at this Level

Education:	Background in criminal justice, business administration, safety education or related discipline.
Experience:	Four years experience in law enforcement or security field including two years supervisory experience or a combination of education and experience as a director or assistant director of security and safety in a healthcare facility for a minimum of three years, or an equivalent combination of education and experience.
Degrees, Licensure, and/or Certification:	Must have valid North Carolina driver's license and good driving record.
	Must successfully pass an extensive background investigation.
Knowledge, Skills, and Abilities:	Thorough knowledge of law enforcement procedures, state law and corporate/hospital rules and regulations.
	Working knowledge of interpretive application of federal and state occupational safety and health standards and regulations.
	General knowledge of budgetary and personnel policies and ability to administer these effectively at the department level. General knowledge of public relations.
	Ability to develop and execute departmental policies and procedures regarding security, safety and traffic/parking.

Figure 10.1   (Continued) Job description: Security Manager.   (Continued)

The industry itself sees that this movement toward safety and emergency has a significant growth area. The American Society of Industrial Security (ASIS) list of core elements for the private security industry makes this tendency toward safety and emergency a full-blown reality. Among the list are clear safety and emergency responsibilities:

1. Physical security
2. Personnel security
3. Information systems security

Ability to read, analyze and interpret general business periodicals, professional journals, technical procedures or governmental regulations. Ability to write reports, business correspondence and procedures manuals. Ability to effectively present information and respond to questions from groups of managers, clients, customers and the general public. Must become familiar with applicable federal, state and local regulations. Ability to define problems, collect data, establish facts, and draw valid conclusions. Ability to interpret a variety of technical instructions in mathematical or diagram form.

Ability to meet the physical demands of this position. Reasonable accommodations may be made to enable individuals with disabilities to perform the essential functions.

Distinguishing Characteristics of this Level

N/A

The intent of this job description is to provide a representative and level of the types of duties and responsibilities that will be required of positions given this title and shall not be construed as a declaration of the total of the specific duties and responsibilities of any particular position. Employees may be directed to perform job-related tasks other than those specifically presented in this description.

Figure 10.1   (Continued) Job description: Security Manager.

4. Investigations

5. Loss prevention

6. Risk management

7. Legal aspects

8. Emergency and contingency planning

9. Fire protection

10. Crisis management

11. Disaster management

12. Counterterrorism

13. Competitive intelligence

14. Executive protection

15. Violence in the workplace

16. Crime prevention

17. Crime prevention through environmental design (CPTED)

18. Security architecture and engineering[4]

Hence, the private security industry has increasingly merged the functions of security and safety with traditional protection protocols for asset protection.[5] As a result, security directors are often entrusted with safety and emergency functions such as

---

[4] See ASIS Foundation (2009). Compendium of the ASIS Academic/Practitioner Symposium, 1997–2008. Retrieved July 30, 2010, at http://www.asisonline.org/foundation/noframe/1997- 2008_CompendiumofProceedings.pdf ASIS International (2009a). International Glossary of Security.

[5] D. Raths, Private-Sector Organizations Earn a Seat in the Emergency Operations Center, *Emergency Management* (May 17, 2010), at http://www.emergencymgmt.com/disaster/Private-Sector-Organizations-Emergency-Operations-Center.html; see also D. Ritchey, Why You Need Tactical Medical Training, *Sec. Mag.* 114 (September 2014).

- Emergency plans
- Evacuation plans
- Hazmat policy
- Business continuity plans
- Mitigation strategies
- Medical emergency policy
- OSHA compliance

Thus, the chapter's overall focus targets security industry's role in the prevention of accidents, and compliance and adherence to regulatory requirements regarding workplace safety and hazards encountered on the job. Despite this natural inclination to merge and meld functions, be aware that these knowledge centers are not natural in every sense of the word, for safety considerations are often vastly different than a security mindset. In the former instance, the safety practitioner is constantly operating in a preventive mode, and anticipating what might occur. In the latter instance, the security professional reacts as law enforcement does—charging in to protect people and assets. In the mix of safety and security, there must be two operational philosophies, especially in regard to hazmat conditions where a rush to protect may result in a series of needless injuries. At the top of the list of injured parties are often the police and security sectors. As such, practitioners should "approach with caution."[6] Finally, the chapter emphasizes the role of planning and preparation in the advance of natural disasters, medical emergencies, pandemics, and fire and safety protocols.

10.2 PRIVATE SECURITY INDUSTRY: OCCUPATIONAL SAFETY AND HEALTH—OSHA

Occupational and workplace safety has become an area of expertise for the security professional, especially in manufacturing and corporate settings where injury and exposure problems are common. In this way, the harms inflicted are not the result of a natural disaster or terroristic or criminal act, but a hazard or condition that causes injury in a specific setting.[7]

For example, those working in shipyards over the last 50 years were often exposed to asbestosis, which led to significant diseases. This hazardous material, once identified as harmful, was listed as a material that was then prohibited by governmental authorities. And in fact, the emergence of the U.S. Department of Labor's Occupational Safety and Health Administration (OSHA) was a reaction to an overall lack of safety at various workplace settings. OSHA became the enforcement agency to assure safe workplace environments. OSHA primarily issues standards for hazardous materials or conditions in the work environment; conducts on-site investigations and inspections at work locations; and has enforcement and penalty power as applied to OSHA infractions. In this way, OSHA promulgates workplace safety rights for the employee.[8]

OSHA itself declares that each employee should have

Working conditions that do not pose a risk of serious harm.
Receive information and training (in a language workers can understand) about chemical and other hazards, methods to prevent harm, and OSHA standards that apply to their workplace.
Review records of work-related injuries and illnesses.
Get copies of test results done to find and measure hazards in the workplace.
File a complaint asking OSHA to inspect their workplace if they believe there is a serious hazard or that their employer is not following OSHA rules. When requested, OSHA will keep all identities confidential.

---

[6] See E.G. Vendrell, Hazmat Pressures Life Safety Training, *Sec. Mag.* 90 (October 2007).
[7] There are legal and human costs for a failure to account for these potential harms. See J.B. Stover, Putting a Premium on Risk Reduction, 50 *Sec. Mgmt* 71 (2006).
[8] See Global News and Analysis, Employees Uniformed about Workplace Safety Issues, *Sec. Mag.* 12 (October 2012).

Figure 10.2   OSHA logo.

Use their rights under the law without retaliation. If an employee is fired, demoted, transferred or retaliated against in any way for using their rights under the law, they can file a complaint with OSHA. This complaint must be filed within 30 days of the alleged retaliation.[9]

See Figure 10.2.

Injuries in the workplace vary by the industry itself. The Bureau of Labor Statistics charts workplace injuries by industry type. See Figure 10.3.[10]

Promoting a safer workplace environment depends not only upon adherence to OSHA and other regulatory standards, but also compliance with any state or local requirements as to particular occupations and hazards. OSHA does not preempt entirely the right of a state to make the standards more stringent nor does its jurisdiction prohibit other federal agencies, such as the EPA and Commerce, from issuing their own standards regarding certain workplace conditions. While the hazards greatly vary from job location to job location, the security team needs be concerned about OSHA's most common list of infractions and violations.

OSHA's 2015 top 10 most frequently cited violations:

1. 1926.501—Fall protection (C)
2. 1910.1200—Hazard communication
3. 1926.451—Scaffolding (C)
4. 1910.134—Respiratory protection
5. 1910.147—Lockout/tagout
6. 1910.178—Powered industrial trucks
7. 1926.1053—Ladders (C)
8. 1910.305—Electrical, wiring methods
9. 1910.212—Machine guarding
10. 1910.303—Electrical, general requirements

Note: (C) = construction standard.

---

[9] OSHA at a Glance, at https://www.osha.gov/Publications/3439at-a-glance.pdf
[10] See Bureau of Labor Statistics, 2014 Survey of Occupational Injuries & Illnesses (2015), at http://www.bls.gov/iif/oshwc/osh/os/osch0054.pdf

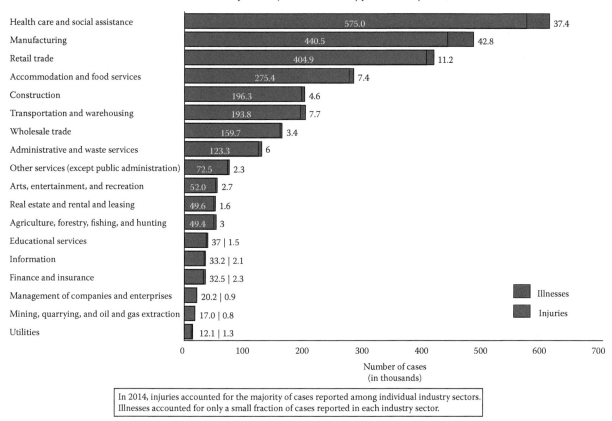

Distribution of nonfatal occupational injuries and illnesses by private industry sector, 2014

Figure 10.3   Occupational injuries by sector.

OSHA lays out particular guidance on each of these common violations.[11] For example, in chemical and hazardous substances, OSHA promulgates rules regarding usage and safety protocols, a portion of which is given in in Figure 10.4.

Thus, a security officer in a chemical plant, a petrochemical facility, or other energy distribution center is likely to encounter and be prepared to identify and correct these violations.[12]

Web Exercise: OSHA has produced an interactive training tool on identifying specified hazards in the workplace at https://www.osha.gov/hazfinder/.

OSHA, working closely with security firms, also provides training at the introductory and advanced levels that educate those responsible for safety in the workplace with the fundamentals of hazard and harm in the workplace. Courses are quite varied and result in basic and advanced certifications.[13]

With various outreach programs, OSHA expends enormous energy on four specific industries: manufacturing, maritime, disaster, and general industry. The curriculum for each program reflects the unique safety challenges for that particular industry. See Figure 10.5.

For example, the general industry course covers the topics shown in Figure 10.6.[14]

---

[11] See Global News and Analysis, Oops—Companies Slipping When It Comes to OSHA Fall Protection Requirement, *Sec. Mag.* 12 (February 2013).

[12] OSHA, Outreach Training Program Requirements (2013), at https://www.osha.gov/dte/outreach/program_requirements.pdf

[13] *Ibid.*

[14] OSHA, General Industry Procedures (2011), at https://www.osha.gov/dte/outreach/generalindustry/generalindustry_procedures.html#4

1910.1200(a)(1)

The purpose of this section is to ensure that the hazards of all chemicals produced or imported are classified, and that information concerning the classified hazards is transmitted to employers and employees. The requirements of this section are intended to be consistent with the provisions of the United Nations Globally Harmonized System of Classification and Labelling of Chemicals (GHS), Revision 3. The transmittal of information is to be accomplished by means of comprehensive hazard communication programs, which are to include container labeling and other forms of warning, safety data sheets and employee training.

1910.1200(a)(2)

This occupational safety and health standard is intended to address comprehensively the issue of classifying the potential hazards of chemicals, and communicating information concerning hazards and appropriate protective measures to employees, and to preempt any legislative or regulatory enactments of a state, or political subdivision of a state, pertaining to this subject. Classifying the potential hazards of chemicals and communicating information concerning hazards and appropriate protective measures to employees, may include, for example, but is not limited to, provisions for: developing and maintaining a written hazard communication program for the workplace, including lists of hazardous chemicals present; labeling of containers of chemicals in the workplace, as well as of containers of chemicals being shipped to other workplaces; preparation and distribution of safety data sheets to employees and downstream employers; and development and implementation of employee training programs regarding hazards of chemicals and protective measures. Under section 18 of the Act, no state or political subdivision of a state may adopt or enforce any requirement relating to the issue addressed by this Federal standard, except pursuant to a Federally-approved state plan.

1910.1200(b)

Scope and application.

1910.1200(b)(1)

This section requires chemical manufacturers or importers to classify the hazards of chemicals which they produce or import, and all employers to provide information to their employees about the hazardous chemicals to which they are exposed, by means of a hazard communication program, labels and other forms of warning, safety data sheets, and information and training. In addition, this section requires distributors to transmit the required information to employers. (Employers who do not produce or import chemicals need only focus on those parts of this rule that deal with establishing a workplace program and communicating information to their workers.)

1910.1200(b)(2)

This section applies to any chemical which is known to be present in the workplace in such a manner that employees may be exposed under normal conditions of use or in a foreseeable emergency.

1910.1200(b)(3)

This section applies to laboratories only as follows:

1910.1200(b)(3)(i)

Employers shall ensure that labels on incoming containers of hazardous chemicals are not removed or defaced;

1910.1200(b)(3)(ii)

Employers shall maintain any safety data sheets that are received with incoming shipments of hazardous chemicals, and ensure that they are readily accessible during each workshift to laboratory employees when they are in their work areas;

1910.1200(b)(3)(iii)

Employers shall ensure that laboratory employees are provided information and training in accordance with paragraph (h) of this section, except for the location and availability of the written hazard communication program under paragraph (h)(2)(iii) of this section; and,

1910.1200(b)(3)(iv)

Laboratory employers that ship hazardous chemicals are considered to be either a chemical manufacturer or a distributor under this rule, and thus must ensure that any containers of hazardous chemicals leaving the laboratory are labeled in accordance with paragraph (f) of this section, and that a safety data sheet is provided to distributors and other employers in accordance with paragraphs (g)(6) and (g)(7) of this section.

1910.1200(b)(4)

In work operations where employees only handle chemicals in sealed containers which are not opened under normal conditions of use (such as are found in marine cargo handling, warehousing, or retail sales), this section applies to these operations only as follows:

1910.1200(b)(4)(i)

Employers shall ensure that labels on incoming containers of hazardous chemicals are not removed or defaced;

1910.1200(b)(4)(ii)

Employers shall maintain copies of any safety data sheets that are received with incoming shipments of the sealed containers of hazardous chemicals, shall obtain a safety data sheet as soon as possible for sealed containers of hazardous chemicals received without a safety data sheet if an employee requests the safety data sheet, and shall ensure that the safety data sheets are readily accessible during each work shift to employees when they are in their work area(s);

Figure 10.4 OSHA regulation.

Outreach training program

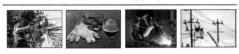

General industry procedures

Figure 10.5   OSHA's general industry training program.

OSHA tailors its instruction to larger- as well as smaller-scale business side by offering a diversity of educational programs to prepare security and safety specialists to handle its legal and regulatory coverage.[15] Compliance with OSHA standards helps minimize legal problems and goes a long way to showing good faith efforts to providing a safe work environment. This in turn mitigates damage claims in lawsuits and essentially undermines claims for punitive damages in injury cases. Overall, the security industry is a significant player in assuring a safe and secure work environment.

OSHA issues hazard alerts on particular substances and equipment. Of recent interest was the OSHA finding on silica clouds resulting from hydraulic fracking in the energy industry. See Figure 10.7.[16]

The security industry is also heavily involved in providing on-location training, which reflects the OSHA standards as to equipment and materials. Courses are commonly offered to companies that seek to be in constant OSHA compliance, such as

- Scaffold competent person/erector
- Trenching and excavation competent person
- Hoistering and rigging competent person
- Confined space entry and rescue
- Fork lift operator certification
- Boom lift operator certification
- Scissor list operator certification
- Skid loader operator certification
- Heavy equipment operator certification
- Personal fall arrest certification
- Lock-out/tag-out

For a career profile of an occupational health and safety specialist from the U.S. Department of Labor, see Figure 10.8.[17]

10.3 PRIVATE SECURITY INDUSTRY: ACCIDENTS AND EMERGENCIES

Security professionals tasked with risk evaluate a multitude of settings at their location—always, always on the lookout for potential harm and injury that might arise in a diversity of settings—office building, factory and manufacturing facilities, government buildings and public properties, commercial centers and districts, corporate headquarters, and related campuses. Risk avoidance, harm minimization, and hazard mitigation have to be at the forefront of security and safety planning. Those risks, if not corrected, lead to accidents and by implication, open the door to legal liability. Security firms sell many services but accident prevention is worth every penny expended.

---

[15] C.P. Howes, Are Your Guards Secure in Complying with OSHA? *Industrial Safety & Hygiene News* (October 11, 2010), at http://www.ishn.com/articles/90064-are-your-guards-secure-in-complying-with-osha

[16] See OSHA, Hydraulic Fracturing Publications, at https://www.osha.gov/dts/hazardalerts/hydraulic_frac_hazard_alert.pdf

[17] Bureau of Labor Statistics, U.S. Department of Labor, Occupational Outlook Handbook, 2016–17 Edition, Occupational Health and Safety Specialists, at http://www.bls.gov/ooh/healthcare/occupational-health-and-safety-specialists.htm, last accessed August 13, 2016.

A. 10-Hour General Industry - Designated Training Topics. This training program is intended to provide entry level general industry workers information about their rights, employer responsibilities, and how to file a complaint as well as how to identify, abate, avoid and prevent job related hazards on a job site. The training covers a variety of general industry safety and health hazards which a worker may encounter. Training should emphasize hazard identification, avoidance, control and prevention, not OSHA standards. Learning objectives on some of these topics are on the CD which is distributed in all OSHA General Industry trainer classes, and available for download at the Outreach Training Program website (www.osha.gov/dte/index.html). Instructional time must be a minimum of 10 hours. The minimum topic requirements are as follows:

1. Mandatory - 7 hours
   a. Introduction to OSHA - 2 hours.
      i. OSHA has required training content for this module.
      ii. Covers workers' rights, employer responsibilities and how to file a complaint. It includes helpful worker safety and health resources. It also provides samples of a weekly fatality and 3 catastrophe report, material data safety sheet and the OSHA Log of Work-Related Injuries and Illnesses.
      iii. Materials include an Instructor Guide, PowerPoint slides, student handouts, and participatory activities.
   b. Walking and Working Surfaces, including fall protection - 1 hour.
   c. Exit Routes, Emergency Action Plans, Fire Prevention Plans, and Fire Protection - 1 hour.
   d. Electrical - 1 hour.
   e. Personal Protective Equipment - 1 hour.
   f. Hazard Communication - 1 hour.
2. Elective - 2 hours. Must present at least two hours of training on the following topics. At least two topics must be presented. The minimum length of any topic is one-half hour.
   a. Hazardous Materials
   b. Materials Handling
   c. Machine Guarding
   d. Introduction to Industrial Hygiene
   e. Bloodborne Pathogens
   f. Ergonomics
   g. Safety and Health Program
   h. Fall Protection
3. Optional - 1 hours. Teach other general industry hazards or policies and/or expand on the mandatory or elective topics. The minimum length of any topic is one-half hour.

B. 30-Hour General Industry Outreach Training Program - Designated Training Topics. The 30-hour General Industry Outreach Training Program is intended to provide a variety of training to workers with some safety responsibility. Training should emphasize hazard identification, avoidance, control and prevention, not OSHA standards. Instructional time must be a minimum of 30 hours. The topic requirements are as follows:

1. Mandatory - 13 hours
   a. Introduction to OSHA - 2 Hours. See above 10-hour section for additional information.
   b. Managing Safety and Health - 2 hours. May include Injury and Illness Prevention Programs, job site inspections, accident prevention programs, management commitment and employee involvement, worksite analysis, hazard prevention and control, accident 4 investigations, how to conduct safety meetings, and supervisory communication.
   c. Walking and Working Surfaces, including fall protection - 1 hour.
   d. Exit Routes, Emergency Action Plans, Fire Prevention Plans, and Fire Protection - 2 hours.
   e. Electrical - 2 hours.
   f. Personal Protective Equipment (PPE) - 1 hour.
   g. Materials Handling - 2 hours.
   h. Hazard Communication - 1 hour.
2. Elective - 10 hours. Must present at least 10 hours of training on the following topics. At least 5 of the following topics must be presented. The minimum length of any topic is one-half hour.
   a. Hazardous Materials (Flammable and Combustible Liquids, Spray Finishing, Compressed Gases, Dipping and Coating Operations)
   b. Permit-Required Confined Spaces
   c. Lockout / Tagout
   d. Machine Guarding
   e. Welding, Cutting, and Brazing
   f. Introduction to Industrial Hygiene
   g. Bloodborne Pathogens
   h. Ergonomics
   i. Fall Protection
   j. Safety and Health Programs
   k. Powered Industrial Vehicles
3. Optional - 7 hours. Teach other general industry hazards or policies and/or expand on the mandatory or elective topics. The minimum length of any topic is one-half hour.

Figure 10.6 Topics covered in OSHA's general industry training program.

OSHA•NIOSH

HAZARD ALERT

Worker Exposure to Silica during Hydraulic Fracturing

> The National Institute for Occupational Safety and Health (NIOSH) identified exposure to airborne silica as a health hazard to workers conducting some hydraulic fracturing operations during recent field studies.

Introduction

Hydraulic fracturing or "fracking" is a process used to "stimulate" well production in the oil and gas industry. It is not a new process, but its use has increased significantly in the last 10 years because of new horizontal drilling and multi-stage fracking (or "completions") technologies that improve access to natural gas and oil deposits. It involves pumping large volumes of water and sand into a well at high pressure to fracture shale and other tight formations, allowing oil and gas to flow into the well.

NIOSH's recent field studies show that workers may be exposed to dust with high levels of **respirable crystalline silica** (called "silica" in this Hazard Alert) during hydraulic fracturing.

This Hazard Alert discusses the health hazards associated with hydraulic fracturing and focuses on worker exposures to silica in the air. It covers the health effects of breathing silica, recommends ways to protect workers, and describes how OSHA and NIOSH can help. Workers and employers need to be aware of the hazard that silica dust poses. Employers must ensure that workers are properly protected from exposure to silica. This Hazard Alert also provides a brief summary of other health and safety hazards to workers conducting hydraulic fracturing activities.

> Crystalline silica is a common mineral found in the earth's crust. It occurs primarily as quartz and is a major component of the sand, clay and stone materials used to make every day products such as concrete, brick and glass.
>
> *Respirable crystalline silica* is the portion of crystalline silica that is small enough to enter the gas-exchange regions of the lungs if inhaled; this includes particles with aerodynamic diameters less than approximately 10 micrometers (μm).

Photo credit: NIOSH

Silica dust cloud by worker delivering sand from sand mover to transfer belt.

> **OSHA** and **NIOSH** have been investigating worker safety and health hazards in oil and gas extraction, including chemical exposures during hydraulic fracturing operations.
>
> **OSHA** has jurisdiction over the safety and health of workers, including workers involved in upstream oil and gas operations. The General Duty Clause of the Occupational Safety and Health (OSH) Act and OSHA's General Industry Standards (29 CFR 1910) apply to the upstream industry. As part of the enforcement of these regulations, five OSHA regions located in areas of significant upstream activities use national, regional, and local emphasis programs to inspect oilfield worksites, including those that may have ongoing hydraulic fracturing operations.
>
> **NIOSH** made safety and health in the oil and gas extraction industry a priority focus area in 2005 by creating the National Occupational Research Agenda (NORA) Oil and Gas Extraction Council, which includes OSHA and industry leaders in a cooperative effort to address occupational safety and health issues. To address an existing lack of information on occupational dust and chemical exposures associated with hydraulic fracturing, NIOSH established specific industry partnerships and initiated the NIOSH Field Effort to Assess Chemical Exposures to Oil and Gas Extraction Workers (http://www.cdc.gov/niosh/docs/2010-130/pdfs/2010-130.pdf). Exposure to silica during hydraulic fracturing has been the focus of the NIOSH study to date.

Figure 10.7   OSHA-NIOSH hazard alert.

Occupational Health and Safety Specialists

EN ESPAÑOL | PRINTER-FRIENDLY 🖨

| Summary | What They Do | Work Environment | How to Become One | Pay | Job Outlook | State & Area Data | Similar Occupations | More Info |

Summary

Quick Facts: Occupational Health and Safety Specialists	
2015 Median Pay ❓	$70,210 per year $33.75 per hour
Typical Entry-Level Education ❓	Bachelor's degree
Work Experience in a Related Occupation ❓	None
On-the-job Training ❓	None
Number of Jobs, 2014 ❓	70,300
Job Outlook, 2014-24 ❓	4% (Slower than average)
Employment Change, 2014-24 ❓	2,800

Occupational health and safety specialists examine the workplace for environmental or physical factors that could affect employee health, safety, comfort, and performance.

What Occupational Health and Safety Specialists Do

Occupational health and safety specialists analyze many types of work environments and work procedures. Specialists inspect workplaces for adherence to regulations on safety, health, and the environment. They also design programs to prevent disease or injury to workers and damage to the environment.

Work Environment

Occupational health and safety specialists work in a variety of settings, such as offices, factories, and mines. Their jobs often involve fieldwork and travel. Most specialists work full time.

How to Become an Occupational Health and Safety Specialist

Occupational health and safety specialists typically need a bachelor's degree in occupational health and safety or in a related scientific or technical field.

Pay

The median annual wage for occupational health and safety specialists was $70,210 in May 2015.

Job Outlook

Employment of occupational health and safety specialists is projected to grow 4 percent from 2014 to 2024, slower than the average for all occupations. Specialists will be needed to work in a wide variety of industries to ensure that employers are adhering to both existing and new regulations.

State & Area Data

Explore resources for employment and wages by state and area for occupational health and safety specialists.

Similar Occupations

Compare the job duties, education, job growth, and pay of occupational health and safety specialists with similar occupations.

More Information, Including Links to O*NET

Learn more about occupational health and safety specialists by visiting additional resources, including O*NET, a source on key characteristics of workers and occupations.

Figure 10.8   Career profile.

There are many ways to catalog or categorize these potential risks but Figure 10.9[18] delineates the more common settings where accidents and emergencies emerge.

From physical hazards to possible chemical contamination, from dangerous design conditions causing slip and fall incidents or head injuries due to height, by way of example, the security team needs to look at the environment in a holistic way, identifying, preventing, and mitigating potential accident situations. In the academic sector, security management programs and research centers increasingly laud the symbiotic connection of safety and security. John

---

[18] European Commission, Preventing Occupation Hazards in the Private Security Sector (2004), at http://www.eesc.europa.eu/resources/docs/140-private-act.pdf

■ **RISKS AND RISK FACTORS IN PRIVATE SECURITY**

1. RISKS RESULTING FROM THE GENERAL SITUATION
   Security company operations within the client company

2. SPECIFIC RISKS RELATED TO SECURITY ACTIVITIES
   A. Violence at work (physical attack, bullying, and sexual harassment)
   B. Risks posed by dogs
   C. Handling weapons
   D. Risks related to exposure to radiation
   E. Risk factors related to work organization
   F. The physical workload
   G. The psychosocial workload
   H. Specific risks facing female security personnel

3. RISKS RELATED TO THE POST HELD
   A. Safety risks
      1. Risk of falls, slips, and trips
      2. Risk of collisions, bumps, and jamming
      3. Risk of road accidents
      4. Risk of electrical accidents
      5. Risk of fire
   B. Risks related to the working environment
      1. Physical hazards
         Noise
         Unsuitable levels of ventilation, humidity, and temperature
         Insufficient or unsuitable lighting
      2. Biological hazards
      3. Chemical hazards

Figure 10.9   Risks and risk factors for private security.

Jay College's Center for Private Security and Safety has, since its inception, melded these two worlds—just as its academic programs have done. See Figure 10.10.[19]

Web Exercise: Security officers are often at the receiving end of accident and harm when carrying out their duties. Read the advice provided by G4S to employees on how to prevent accidents at http://www.g4s.us/~/media/files/usa/pdf-safety%20matters/safety%20matters%20september%202013%20-%20risk(1).pdf.

The National Safety Council has computed the 10 most common accident situations that occur in the marketplace. See Figure 10.11.[20]

Web Exercise: Find out about the common accident challenges in the chemical industry at https://www.solano-county.com/civicax/filebank/blobdload.aspx?BlobID=6359.

In the final analysis, a security professional must provide his or her clients with safety and accident prevention advice and guidance. It is not enough that the security firm protects assets and prevents theft and pilferage from taking place on the facility. Much more is required and expected since these assets need people to oversee and produce and in an environment where injury is common and predictable, the company's most treasured resource—their personnel—are always under threat of harm and injury. In fact, there are those who argue that this movement to emergency services elevates the security profession to a higher vocation since it sheds the exclusive "asset protection" image that security labors under.[21] Accidents, while these events may be utterly benign, still have the capacity to undermine the enterprise, the business, and the mission of a client. In order to maintain continuity of operations or to be resilient in the event of accident or disaster, the firm and client must prepare for these eventualities.

Security firms usually adopt a survey or plan to track the common scenarios that lead to accident and harm. See Figure 10.12[22] for a representative example of a facility inspection report.

---

[19] See John Jay College of Criminal Justice, The Center for Private Security and Safety, at http://www.jjay.cuny.edu/center-private-security-and-safety
[20] National Safety Council Nebraska, Safety by the Numbers (2013), at http://www.safenebraska.org/files/8113/8444/8700/National_Safety_Council_Top_10_Preventable_Workplace_Injuries.pdf
[21] International Foundation for Protection Officers, Improving the Image and Reputation of the Security Profession (2013), at http://www.ifpo.org/wp-content/uploads/2013/08/Tancredi_Reputation.pdf
[22] Texas Department of Insurance, Sample Accident Prevention Plan, 17 (n.d.), at http://www.tdi.texas.gov/pubs/videoresource/wsapp.pdf

Figure 10.10   John Jay College's Center for Private Security and Safety.

10.4 EMERGENCIES IN THE WORKPLACE

Just as with accidents, the security team given the physical responsibility for the facility, its assets, and people needs to advance and develop plans and procedures for emergencies in the client's location. Of course, the type of emergency will vary by client since security providers work in so many settings. Hence, an emergency at a nuclear power plant connotes more harmful implications than perimeter protection in a 4,000-acre livestock farm. Both places have the likelihood of emergencies, although the harm levels differ greatly.

Ready.gov lays out a 10-step plan to begin the initial process of emergency planning.

10 Steps for Developing the Emergency Response Plan

1. Review performance objectives for the program.
2. Review hazard or threat scenarios identified during the risk assessment.

Figure 10.11   National Safety Council top 10 preventable workplace incidents.

Appendix A
Self-Inspection Forms

Inspection Date:_____

Location or Department Inspected:_____

Signature:_____

		YES	NO	N/A
1.	**Housekeeping** - Is the work area clean and orderly?	☐	☐	☐
2.	**Floors** - Are floors in good condition (smooth, clear surfaces without holes, cracks, or humps)?	☐	☐	☐
3.	**Aisles** - Are aisles and passageways clear, dry, and free of tripping hazards?	☐	☐	☐
4.	**Stairways** - Are stairs in good condition, with handrails, and adequate lighting?	☐	☐	☐
5.	**Storage** - Are materials, products, or supplies properly and safely stacked to a workable height?	☐	☐	☐
6.	**Ladders** - Are ladders provided where needed, of standard construction, and in good physical condition?	☐	☐	☐
7.	**Machines & Equipment** - Are machines and equipment in safe operating condition? Are the necessary guards provided and used?	☐	☐	☐
8.	**Hand Tools** - Are the right tools for the job being used? Are they in good condition?	☐ ☐	☐ ☐	☐ ☐
9.	**Electrical** - Are all required grounds provided on power tools and extension cords? Is electrical equipment in good operating condition?	☐ ☐	☐ ☐	☐ ☐
10.	**Lighting** - Is adequate lighting provided in all work areas?	☐	☐	☐
11.	**Eye Protection** - Are all employees provided with suitable eye protection when around operations that produce flying particles?	☐	☐	☐
12.	**First Aid** - Are first aid supplies provided and accessible?	☐	☐	☐
13.	**Fire Extinguishers** - Are fire extinguishers easily accessible and properly serviced?	☐	☐	☐
14.	**Entrances** - Are entrances kept dry or provided with nonskid mats?	☐	☐	☐
15.	**Exits** - Are emergency exits marked, clear, and easily accessible? Are exit doors unlocked and do they swing toward the outside?	☐ ☐	☐ ☐	☐ ☐
16.	**Exterior** - (sidewalks, parking lots, etc.) -Are sidewalks and parking lots smooth and free of cracks, holes, and tripping hazards?	☐	☐	☐
17.	**Training** - Are all employees trained in proper lifting techniques and material handling?	☐	☐	☐
18.	**Signs** - Are safety instructions and warning signs posted where needed?	☐	☐	☐

17

Figure 10.12 Facility self-inspection form.

3. Assess the availability and capabilities of resources for incident stabilization including people, systems and equipment available within your business and from external sources.

4. Talk with public emergency services (e.g., fire, police and emergency medical services) to determine their response time to your facility, knowledge of your facility and its hazards and their capabilities to stabilize an emergency at your facility.

5. Determine if there are any regulations pertaining to emergency planning at your facility; address applicable regulations in the plan.

6. Develop protective actions for life safety (evacuation, shelter, shelter-in-place, lockdown).

7. Develop hazard and threat-specific emergency procedures using guidance from the resource links on this page. Write your emergency response plan using this template.

8. Coordinate emergency planning with public emergency services to stabilize incidents involving the hazards at your facility.

9. Train personnel so they can fulfill their roles and responsibilities.

10. Facilitate exercises to practice your plan.[23]

The common emergencies in work settings are

- Natural hazards: flood, hurricane, tornado, earthquake, or widespread serious illness in pandemic form
- Human-caused hazards: accidents, acts of violence, and acts of terrorism
- Technology-related hazards: malfunction of mechanical or computer systems, equipment, software, or other cyber vulnerability

The prevention of emergencies calls for a six-step process of review:

- Means of reporting fires and other emergencies
- Evacuation procedures and emergency escape route assignments
- Procedures for employees who remain to operate critical plant operations before they evacuate
- Accounting for all employees after an emergency evacuation has been completed
- Rescue and medical duties for employees performing them
- Names or job titles of persons who can be contacted[24]

OSHA publishes a solid checklist for the authorship of an emergency action plan, a tool every security firm likely employs and business and industry should readily adopt. See Figure 10.13.[25]

The security industry pursues this line of service without much hesitation since business, industry, and institutions so heavily rely upon the expertise of those predicting and reacting to emergencies.[26]

U.S. Security Associates delivers not only consulting and specialized services in the world of emergency planning and response, but just as critically trains clients and other security specialists in this far-reaching expertise. Through its U.S. Security Associates Training Academy, clients and employees of competing firms take advantage of all sorts of training. Of particular interest here is the company's Disaster and Emergency Response Team (DERT), which delivers emergency expertise to institutional clients within hours of an emergency event.

Web Exercise: Read up on U.S. Security Associates Disaster and Emergency Response Team here: http://www.ussecurityassociates.com/usa-services/specialized-services/disaster-emergency-response.php.

Finally, after all of this preparation and survey, the security firm, in constant consultation with the client, is not prepared to author an emergency action plan. The EAP has certain base components, including

- Means of reporting fires and other emergencies
- Evacuation procedures and emergency escape route assignments
- Procedures for employees who remain to operate critical plant operations before they evacuate
- Accounting for all employees after an emergency evacuation has been completed
- Rescue and medical duties for employees performing them
- Names or job titles of persons who can be contacted

Web Exercise: For full details on these and other pieces essential to the EAP, visit https://www.osha.gov/SLTC/etools/evacuation/min_requirements.html.

Finally, review Appendix C,[27] which contains a sample emergency action plan.

---

[23] See Ready.gov, Emergency Response Plan, at https://www.ready.gov/business/implementation/emergency

[24] OSHA, Evacuation Plans and Procedures eTool, at https://www.osha.gov/SLTC/etools/evacuation/min_requirements.html

[25] OSHA, Evacuation Plans and Procedures eTool EAP Checklist, at https://www.osha.gov/SLTC/etools/evacuation/checklists/eap.html

[26] E. Wolff & G. Koenig, The Role of the Private Sector in Emergency Preparedness, Planning, and Response, Chapter 6 in *Homeland Security and Emergency Management: A Legal Guide for State and Local Governments*, Ed. E.B. Abbott & O.J. Hetzel (2010), at http://www.atlanta-businesslitigation.com/The-Role-of-the-Provate-Sector-Article.pdf

[27] University of Missouri, Environmental Health & Safety, Emergency Action Template, ehs.missouri.edu/work/forms/eap-template.doc

Figure 10.13   OSHA evacuation plan etool.

(Continued)

10.5 FIRE PROTECTION AND LIFE SAFETY

That security and safety professionals are increasingly assuming leadership roles in the fire safety side of business and institutional operations is now common knowledge. As in the emergency function, CSOs and their teams have assumed a very active role in the prevention, control, and recovery from fires.[28] And for understandable reasons: first, the private security industry continues its lead role in technology for security and safety purposes and by extension,

---

[28] See Fire Protection, Life Safety Get Higher Priority, *Sec. Mag.* 8 (March 2004).

8. Does the plan identify how or where personal information on employees ☐ can be obtained in an emergency?

In the event of an emergency, it could be important to have ready access to important personal information about your employees. This includes their home telephone numbers, the names and telephone numbers of their next of kin, and medical information.

EVACUATION POLICY AND PROCEDURES

1. Does the plan identify the conditions under which an evacuation would ☐ be necessary?

The plan should identify the different types of situations that will require an evacuation of the workplace. This might include a fire, earthquake, or chemical spill. The extent of evacuation may be different for different types of hazards.

2. Does the plan identify a clear chain of command and designate a person ☐ authorized to order an evacuation or shutdown of operations?

It is common practice to select a responsible individual to lead and coordinate your emergency plan and evacuation. It is critical that employees know who the coordinator is and understand that this person has the authority to make decisions during emergencies. The coordinator should be responsible for assessing the situation to determine whether an emergency exists requiring activation of the emergency procedures, overseeing emergency procedures, notifying and coordinating with outside emergency services, and directing shutdown of utilities or plant operations if necessary.

3. Does the plan address the types of actions expected of different ☐ employees for the various types of potential emergencies?

The plan may specify different actions for employees depending on the emergency. For example, employers may want to have employees assemble in one area of the workplace if it is threatened by a tornado or earthquake but evacuate to an exterior location during a fire.

4. Does the plan designate who, if anyone, will stay to shut down critical ☐ operations during an evacuation?

You may want to include in your plan locations where utilities (such as electrical and gas utilities) can be shut down for all or part of the facility. All individuals remaining behind to shut down critical systems or utilities must be capable of recognizing when to abandon the operation or task and evacuate themselves.

5. Does the plan outline specific evacuation routes and exits and are these ☐ posted in the workplace where they are easily accessible to all employees?

Most employers create maps from floor diagrams with arrows that designate the exit route assignments. These maps should include locations of exits, assembly points and equipment (such as fire extinguishers, first aid kits, spill kits) that may be needed in an emergency. Exit routes should be clearly marked and well lit, wide enough to accommodate the number of evacuating personnel, unobstructed and clear of debris at all times, and unlikely to expose evacuating personnel to additional hazards.

6. Does the plan address how rescue operations will be performed? ☐

Unless you are a large employer handling hazardous materials and processes or have employees regularly working in hazardous situations, you will probably choose to rely on local public resources, such as the fire department, who are trained, equipped, and certified to conduct rescues. Make sure any external department or agency identified in your plan is prepared to respond as outlined in your plan. Untrained individuals may endanger themselves and those they are trying to rescue.

7. Does the plan address how medical assistance will be provided? ☐

Most small employers do not have a formal internal medical program and make arrangements with medical clinics or facilities close by to handle emergency cases and provide medical and first-aid services to their employees. If an infirmary, clinic, or hospital is not close to your workplace, ensure that onsite person(s) have adequate training in first aid. The American Red Cross, some insurance providers, local safety councils, fire departments, or other resources may be able to provide this training. Treatment of a serious injury should begin within 3 to 4 minutes of the accident. Consult with a physician to order appropriate first-aid supplies for emergencies. Establish a relationship with a local ambulance service so transportation is readily available for emergencies.

8. Does the plan identify how or where personal information on employees ☐ can be obtained in an emergency?

In the event of an emergency, it could be important to have ready access to important personal information about your employees. This includes their home telephone numbers, the names and telephone numbers of their next of kin, and medical information.

EVACUATION POLICY AND PROCEDURES

1. Does the plan identify the conditions under which an evacuation would ☐ be necessary?

The plan should identify the different types of situations that will require an evacuation of the workplace. This might include a fire, earthquake, or chemical spill. The extent of evacuation may be different for different types of hazards.

2. Does the plan identify a clear chain of command and designate a person ☐ authorized to order an evacuation or shutdown of operations?

It is common practice to select a responsible individual to lead and coordinate your emergency plan and evacuation. It is critical that employees know who the coordinator is and understand that this person has the authority to make decisions during emergencies. The coordinator should be responsible for assessing the situation to determine whether an emergency exists requiring activation of the emergency procedures, overseeing emergency procedures, notifying and coordinating with outside emergency services, and directing shutdown of utilities or plant operations if necessary.

Figure 10.13   (Continued) OSHA evacuation plan etool.   (*Continued*)

these same firms develop and apply technology across the globe relative to fire safety. For example, Tyco Industries, a technology specialty company, has aggressively delivered state-of-the-art technology to the security industry in the matter of fire prevention and protection.[29]

Tyco, like other technology components, delivers crucial components to detect and monitor the fire protection program and installs equipment that has advanced preventive efforts across the nation. From sprinkler systems to

[29] Tyco Security Industries, at https://www.tycois.com/solutions-by-need/protect-my-business/fire-and-life-safety/fire-detection

3. Does the plan address the types of actions expected of different employees for the various types of potential emergencies? ☐	The plan may specify different actions for employees depending on the emergency. For example, employers may want to have employees assemble in one area of the workplace if it is threatened by a tornado or earthquake but evacuate to an exterior location during a fire.
4. Does the plan designate who, if anyone, will stay to shut down critical operations during an evacuation? ☐	You may want to include in your plan locations where utilities (such as electrical and gas utilities) can be shut down for all or part of the facility. All individuals remaining behind to shut down critical systems or utilities must be capable of recognizing when to abandon the operation or task and evacuate themselves.
5. Does the plan outline specific evacuation routes and exits and are these posted in the workplace where they are easily accessible to all employees? ☐	Most employers create maps from floor diagrams with arrows that designate the exit route assignments. These maps should include locations of exits, assembly points and equipment (such as fire extinguishers, first aid kits, spill kits) that may be needed in an emergency. Exit routes should be clearly marked and well lit, wide enough to accommodate the number of evacuating personnel, unobstructed and clear of debris at all times, and unlikely to expose evacuating personnel to additional hazards.
6. Does the plan address procedures for assisting people during evacuations, particularly those with disabilities or who do not speak English? ☐	Many employers designate individuals as evacuation wardens to help move employees from danger to safe areas during an emergency. Generally, one warden for every 20 employees should be adequate, and the appropriate number of wardens should be available at all times during working hours. Wardens may be responsible for checking offices and bathrooms before being the last person to exit an area as well as ensuring that fire doors are closed when exiting. Employees designated to assist in emergency evacuation procedures should be trained in the complete workplace layout and various alternative escape routes. Employees designated to assist in emergencies should be made aware of employees with special needs (who may require extra assistance during an evacuation), how to use the buddy system, and any hazardous areas to avoid during an emergency evacuation.
7. Does the plan identify one or more assembly areas (as necessary for different types of emergencies) where employees will gather and a method for accounting for all employees? ☐	Accounting for all employees following an evacuation is critical. Confusion in the assembly areas can lead to delays in rescuing anyone trapped in the building, or unnecessary and dangerous search-and-rescue operations. To ensure the fastest, most accurate accounting of your employees, consider taking a head count after the evacuation. The names and last known locations of anyone not accounted for should be passed on to the official in charge.
8. Does the plan address how visitors will be assisted in evacuation and accounted for? ☐	Some employers have all visitors and contractors sign in when entering the workplace. The hosts and/or area wardens, if established, are often tasked with assisting these individuals evacuate safely.

REPORTING EMERGENCIES AND ALERTING EMPLOYEES IN AN EMERGENCY

1. Does the plan identify a preferred method for reporting fires and other emergencies? ☐	Dialing 911 is a common method for reporting emergencies if external responders are utilized. Internal numbers may be used. Internal numbers are sometimes connected to intercom systems so that coded announcements may be made. In some cases employees are requested to activate manual pull stations or other alarm systems.
2. Does the plan describe the method to be used to alert employees, including disabled workers, to evacuate or take other action? ☐	Make sure alarms are distinctive and recognized by all employees as a signal to evacuate the work area or perform other actions identified in your plan. Sequences of horn blows or different types of alarms (bells, horns, etc.) can be used to signal different responses or actions from employees. Consider making available an emergency communications system, such as a public address system, for broadcasting emergency information to employees. Ideally alarms will be able to be heard, seen, or otherwise perceived by everyone in the workplace including those that may be blind or deaf. Otherwise floor wardens or others must be tasked with ensuring all employees are notified. You might want to consider providing an auxiliary power supply in the event of an electrical failure.

EMPLOYEE TRAINING AND DRILLS

1. Does the plan identify how and when employees will be trained so that they understand the types of emergencies that may occur, their responsibilities and actions as outlined in the plan? ☐	Training should be offered employees when you develop your initial plan and when new employees are hired. Employees should be retrained when your plan changes due to a change in the layout or design of the facility, when new equipment, hazardous materials, or processes are introduced that affect evacuation routes, or when new types of hazards are introduced that require special actions. General training for your employees should address the following: ▪ Individual roles and responsibilities. ▪ Threats, hazards, and protective actions. ▪ Notification, warning, and communications procedures. ▪ Emergency response procedures. ▪ Evacuation, shelter, and accountability procedures. ▪ Location and use of common emergency equipment. ▪ Emergency shutdown procedures. You may also need to provide additional training to your employees (i.e. first-aid procedures, portable fire extinguisher use, etc.) depending on the responsibilities allocated employees in your plan.

Figure 10.13   (Continued) OSHA evacuation plan etool.   (*Continued*)

monitor panels, from check valves to heat sensors, Tyco technology goes hand in hand with an aggressive fire and security protocol.[30,31]

Web Exercise: Research Tyco's latest fire protection products and industry-leading fire detection solutions at http://www.tycofsbp.com/index.php?P=new-product.

---
[30] Advanced Fire Tech Integrates into the Business, *Sec. Mag.* 74 (September 2008).
[31] Tyco Fire Protection Products, at http://www.tyco-fire.com/index.php?P=new-product

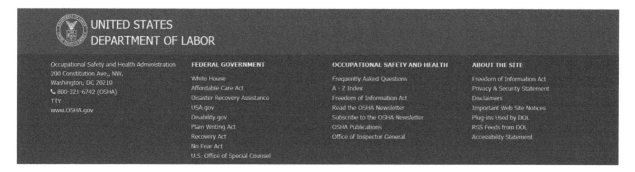

2. Does the plan address how and when retraining will be conducted? ☐   If training is not reinforced it will be forgotten. Consider retaining employees annually.

3. Does the plan address if and how often drills will be conducted? ☐   Once you have reviewed your emergency action plan with your employees and everyone has had the proper training, it is a good idea to hold practice drills as often as necessary to keep employees prepared. Include outside resources such as fire and police departments when possible. After each drill, gather management and employees to evaluate the effectiveness of the drill. Identify the strengths and weaknesses of your plan and work to improve it.

Print Checklist   Clear Form

*Accessibility Assistance: Contact OSHA's Directorate of Technical Support and Emergency Management at (202) 693-2300 for assistance accessing PDF materials.

All other documents, that are not PDF materials or formatted for the web, are available as Microsoft Office® formats and videos and are noted accordingly. If additional assistance is needed with reading, reviewing or accessing these documents or any figures and illustrations, please also contact OSHA's Directorate of Technical Support and Emergency Management at (202) 693-2300.

**eBooks - EPUB is the most common format for e-Books. If you use a Sony Reader, a Nook, or an iPad you can download the EPUB file format. If you use a Kindle, you can download the MOBI file format.

Home | Emergency Action Plan | Emergency Standards | Expert Systems | Additional Assistance
Site Map | Credits

UNITED STATES
DEPARTMENT OF LABOR

Occupational Safety and Health Administration 200 Constitution Ave., NW, Washington, DC 20210 📞 800-321-6742 (OSHA) TTY www.OSHA.gov	**FEDERAL GOVERNMENT** White House Affordable Care Act Disaster Recovery Assistance USA.gov Disability.gov Plain Writing Act Recovery Act No Fear Act U.S. Office of Special Counsel	**OCCUPATIONAL SAFETY AND HEALTH** Frequently Asked Questions A - Z Index Freedom of Information Act Read the OSHA Newsletter Subscribe to the OSHA Newsletter OSHA Publications Office of Inspector General	**ABOUT THE SITE** Freedom of Information Act Privacy & Security Statement Disclaimers Important Web Site Notices Plug-ins Used by DOL RSS Feeds from DOL Accessibility Statement

Figure 10.13   (Continued) OSHA evacuation plan etool.

Technology alone does not suffice on the fire safety side of the security business, especially when one considers the rising regulatory environment on architectural designs and fire prevention, Life Safety Codes promulgated across the United States, and the National Fire Protection Association Standards and Codes proliferating in every jurisdiction. Everything from extinguishers to sprinkler design is now fully regulated by some governmental authority, and compliance alone is a full-time job.[32] Figure 10.14[33] is a sample page of NFPA codes.

Web Exercise: Visit the National Fire Protection Association's standards for free online at http://www.nfpa.org/freeaccess.

Fire and life safety concerns are natural companions to the security team that hopes to protect both people and assets, for the impact of fire on American business is quite substantial. See Figure 10.15.[34]

The causes of fires and resulting casualties, injuries, and economic losses are quite varied, although a close scrutiny of the data shows that smaller, preventable things usually cause fires more than larger catastrophic events. Bolts of lightning and wind-spread fireballs are far less likely to be the culprit than the cook stove left on or dormitory heat plate left unattended. The amount of damage caused by the smallest and most insignificant item is simply incomprehensible, though these items are regular workplace accoutrements that need to be stored and checked by security officials. The U.S. Fire Administration tracks and traces nonresidential causes of fire and the results, outlined in Figure 10.16,[35] are quite illuminating.

---

[32] See R. Bielen, Fire and Life Safety and Security's Role, *Sec. Mag.* 26 (July 2011).
[33] NFPA, Codes and Standards, at http://www.nfpa.org/codes-and-standards/all-codes-and-standards/list-of-codes-and-standards
[34] NFPA, News & Research, at http://www.nfpa.org/news-and-research/fire-statistics-and-reports/fire-statistics
[35] Source: U.S. Fire Administration, at https://www.usfa.fema.gov/data/statistics/

Code No.	Code Name
NFPA 2	Hydrogen Technologies Code
NFPA 3	Recommended Practice for Commissioning of Fire Protection and Life Safety Systems
NFPA 4	Standard for Integrated Fire Protection and Life Safety System Testing
NFPA 10	Standard for Portable Fire Extinguishers
NFPA 11	Standard for Low-, Medium-, and High-Expansion Foam
NFPA 11A	Standard for Medium- and High-Expansion Foam Systems
NFPA 11C	Standard for Mobile Foam Apparatus
NFPA 12	Standard on Carbon Dioxide Extinguishing Systems
NFPA 12A	Standard on Halon 1301 Fire Extinguishing Systems
NFPA 13	Standard for the Installation of Sprinkler Systems
NFPA 13E	Recommended Practice for Fire Department Operations in Properties Protected by Sprinkler and Standpipe Systems
NFPA 13R	Standard for the Installation of Sprinkler Systems in Low-Rise Residential Occupancies
NFPA 14	Standard for the Installation of Standpipe and Hose Systems
NFPA 15	Standard for Water Spray Fixed Systems for Fire Protection
NFPA 16	Standard for the Installation of Foam-Water Sprinkler and Foam-Water Spray Systems
NFPA 20	Standard for the Installation of Stationary Pumps for Fire Protection
NFPA 30	Flammable and Combustible Liquids Code

Figure 10.14 NFPA standards.

Estimates of 2014 fires, civilian deaths, civilian injuries, and property loss in the United States

	Estimate	Range	Percent change from 2013
Number of fires	1,298,000	1,286,500–1,309,500	+4.7
Number of civilian deaths	3,275	3,115–3,435	+1.1
Number of civilian injuries	15,775	15,225–16,325	+0.9
Property loss	$11,605,000,000	$11,421,000,000–12,067,000,000	+1.0

The estimates are based on data reported to the NFPA by fire departments that responded to the 2014 National Fire Experience Survey.

Figure 10.15 Estimates of 2014 fires, deaths, and injuries, and property loss in the United States.

The picture, as surprising as it is, demonstrates that fire safety is a very achievable goal when one considers causes. At the same time, the costs, both in economic and human terms, are simply too staggering to tolerate. As a result, every investment in fire protection and safety certainly helps the bottom line of the typical business or institutional client.[36]

[36] See C. Meyer, Small Fires Mean Big Damage without Fire Suppression, *Sec. Mag.* 88 (November 2013).

Cooking	29.1%
Unintentional, careless	10.0%
Heating	9.0%
Intentional	8.9%
Electrical malfunction	8.1%
Open flame	6.1%
Other heat	5.1%
Appliances	4.9%
Other equipment	4.7%
Exposure	4.4%
Natural	3.4%
Equipment malfunction	2.5%
Smoking	2.1%
Cause under investigation	1.6%
Playing with heat source	0.4%

Figure 10.16   U.S. Fire Administration tabulation of causes of fire.

In high-rise environments, such as Chicago and New York City, the security professional needs to become or align him or herself with a building's fire safety director (FSD), whose training and expertise are crucial in these complex facilities.

Web Exercise: Find out about NYC's Fire Safety Directors Association at http://fsdagreaterny.org/the-mission.

Security now regularly coordinates fire safety and its demanding protocols into the overall security plan for any facility and educates the inhabitants of these buildings with safety measures and evacuation routes. Shared video and surveillance monitors is now a common partnership between police and fire and private security operatives working the same building.[37] Traditional technologies such as alarms and extinguishers, coupled with new emerging technologies, are now the province of the security director and manager.[38] Fire safety inspections should be a regular practice for the security firm charged with assuring a safe environment. Governmental authorities frequently author forms for educational and compliance reasons, some being highly complicated, while others are less complicated, such as the City of Omaha producing an easy-to-undertake inspection. See Figure 10.17.[39]

Most security firms provide fire protection and fire safety services. For example, Securitas delivers a wide range of fire and safety services, including:

- Evacuation assistance
- Workplace safety
- Traffic safety
- School safety
- Safety consulting
- Firefighting training
- Safety compliance audits

---

[37] See T. Maddry, Emergency Planning Get Stronger, *Sec. Mag.* 80 (April 2009).
[38] See R. Elliott, Extinguishing Fire Safety Problems, 50 *Sec. Mgmt* 40 (2006).
[39] See Omaha Public Schools, at http://district.ops.org/Portals/0/Business%20Services/Risk%20Management/Fire%20Inspection%20Checklist. pdf

FIRE INSPECTION CHECKLIST
RISK SAFETY DEPARTMENT

BUILDING_____ DATE_____ INSPECTOR_____

ITEM

Daily Checks	Yes	No	Corrective Action You Took i.e. Work Order or other Repair
1. Are stairways and exit doors inside the building kept clear, unblocked and in proper working condition?			
2. Are hallway doors kept closed and not blocked or propped open?			
3. Are outside exit doors, stairs, and sidewalks kept unblocked at all times?			
4. Are all exit doors kept unlocked, unbolted, and unchained so people can exit to the outside in case of a fire emergency?			
5. Are all exit lights working properly? Missing or burned out bulbs must be replaced ASAP.			
6. Are all emergency lights in interior corridors working properly? Missing or burned out bulbs must be replaced promptly.			
7. Are hallways clear of accumulating flammable materials such as clothing, piles of paper, and personal effects?			
8. Are student drawings and other artwork hung in properly designated spaces? Note: Paper/artwork cannot be suspended from classroom ceilings or aligned from the top to the bottom of wall areas. Only in portions of the walls designated for that purpose.			
9. Check the location and condition of the Siamese – Y hose connect on building for sprinkler system. Are the hose connections intact? Are there any missing caps?			
10. Are all portable fire extinguishers checked to be in good working order and initialed on their tag?			
11. Are fire lanes around the building kept clear and unblocked by parked cars or any other vehicles?			
12. Are fire panels in an operational state? If trouble lights are present, contact your Building Engineer.			
Monthly Checks	**Yes**	**No**	**Corrective Action You Took** i.e. Work Order or other Repair
1. Are all portable fire extinguishers checked to be in good working order and initialed on their tag?			
2. Are fire drills being conducted and documented routinely?			
Annual Checks	**Yes**	**No**	**Corrective Action You Took** i.e. Work Order or other Repair
1. Are portable fire extinguishers removed from service annually? If you see any that are overdue for an exchange, contact your Building Engineer to initiate the replacement sequence.			

Figure 10.17   Fire inspection checklist.

CIVIL SERVICE COMMISSION

JOB SPECIFICATION

FIRE AND SAFETY OFFICER

JOB DESCRIPTION

Employees in this job are responsible for safeguarding people and property in state occupied buildings, facilities, and grounds.

There are three classifications in this job.

Position Code Title – Fire and Safety Officer-E

Fire and Safety Officer 6
This is the intermediate level. The employee, in an intermediate capacity, performs fire and safety officer assignments while learning the policies, procedures, practices, and methods necessary to perform the work. Work is performed under close supervision.

Fire and Safety Officer E7
This is the experienced level. The employee performs a full range of fire and safety officer assignments associated with safeguarding people and property in or on state occupied buildings, facilities, and grounds. The employee uses judgment in making decisions where alternatives are determined by established policies and procedures. The work is performed under general supervision.

Position Title – Fire Safety Officer-A

Fire and Safety Officer 8
This is the advanced level. The employee performs advanced fire and safety officer assignments in one of two capacities. The employee may serve as a lead worker overseeing other Fire and Safety Officers while participating in the work. The lead worker typically has responsibility for all fire and safety officer activities for an assigned shift or the employee may serve as a senior-level Fire and Safety Officer. Typically, a senior-level Fire and Safety Officer has the sole responsibility for all safety officer activities of the facility.

NOTE: Employees generally progress through this series to the experienced level based on satisfactory performance and possession of the required experience.

JOB DUTIES

NOTE: The job duties listed are typical examples of the work performed by positions in this job classification.   Not all duties assigned to every position are included, nor is it expected that all positions will be assigned every duty.

Figure 10.18   Career Profile: Security and fire safety.   (*Continued*)

- Emergency planning
- Crisis management
- Evacuation exercises[40]

See Figure 10.18.[41]

---

[40] See Securitas International, Security Services, at http://www.securitas.com/en/our-offering/security-services/safety-services/

[41] Michigan Civil Service Commission, Fire and Safety Officer Job Specification, at http://www.michigan.gov/documents/FireandSafety Officer_12666_7.pdf

FIRE AND SAFETY OFFICER
PAGE NO. 2

Patrols building and grounds on foot or in a vehicle in order to protect state occupied buildings and grounds against trespassing, theft, and vandalism.

Identifies potential safety or fire hazards; takes action or makes recommendations to eliminate hazard.

Determines the identity and business of visitors; gives directions to or escorts authorized visitors to the proper destination.

Assures that fire extinguishers, smoke detectors, fire alarms, sprinkler system and fire hydrants are in operating condition; conducts fire drills and participates in fire prevention programs.

Performs traffic control work such as the patrolling of parking facilities and the directing of traffic.

Transports residents of state facilities or visitors and makes deliveries.

Conducts or participates in employee safety and accident prevention programs; conducts a preliminary investigation of employee accidents.

Apprehends persons suspected of theft, vandalism, or trespassing; contacts police and detains suspect until police arrive.

Renders first aid to employees, residents, and visitors in cases of injury or illness.

Responds to all fire alarms; determines whether a fire exists; attempts to extinguish fire and contacts fire department.

Answers telephone calls and/or operates a telephone switchboard when the facility or building is closed.

Writes incident and accident reports and maintains a record of activities.

Performs related work as assigned.

Additional Job Duties

Fire and Safety Officer 8 (Lead Worker)
Assures safety coverage for an assigned shift by scheduling assignments and overseeing the work of other Fire and Safety Officers.

Provides training and explains work instructions to subordinate Fire and Safety Officers.

Fire and Safety Officer 8 (Senior Worker)
Provides all safety coverage for a state facility.

Figure 10.18   (Continued) Career Profile: Security and fire safety.   (*Continued*)

10.6 PRIVATE SECURITY INDUSTRY: HAZMAT AND WMD

Hazardous materials are a constant concern charged with insuring a safe and secure environment whether in business or public facilities. In some locales, such as factories and production lines, to name a few, hazardous materials sit side by side with the worker in his or her daily life. Chemical factories are inherently locations where hazmat concerns never really dissipate and continually weigh on the minds of corporate officers and decision makers.[42] Insert Figure 10.19.[43]

---

[42] See M.A. Gips, Plants Find Right Chemistry, 50 *Sec. Mgmt* 26 (2006); M.A. Gips, Chemical Facilities Get Help, 47 *Sec. Mgmt* 18 (2003).

[43] U.S. Department of Transportation, Hazardous Materials Transportation Enhanced Security Requirements, 1, at https://hazmatonline.phmsa.dot.gov/services/publication_documents/esrequirements.pdf

FIRE AND SAFETY OFFICER
PAGE NO. 3

Plans, develops and conducts employee safety, fire prevention and accident prevention programs.

Regularly performs safety and security activities recognized as the most complex and difficult.

JOB QUALIFICATIONS

Knowledge, Skills, and Abilities

NOTE: Developing knowledge is required at the intermediate level, considerable knowledge is required at the experienced level, and thorough knowledge is required at the advanced level.

Knowledge of state laws related to the safety of people and property.

Knowledge of the principles of safety, accident, and fire prevention.

Knowledge of first aid methods and techniques.

Knowledge of departmental policies, procedures, rules and regulations related to the safety and security of people and property.

Skill in the proper use of firearms.

Ability to maintain composure and respond properly during emergencies.

Ability to learn and apply written laws, rules, and regulations related to the work.

Ability to concentrate on a designated area for extended periods.

Ability to walk for long periods.

Ability to communicate effectively.

Additional Knowledge, Skills, and Abilities

Fire and Safety Officer 8 (Lead Worker)
Ability to train, guide and evaluate the work of other Fire and Safety Officers.

Ability to determine work priorities and allocate work to other Fire and Safety Officers.

Fire and Safety Officer 8 (Senior Worker)
Ability to work independently.

Ability to plan, develop and conduct employee safety, fire prevention and accident prevention programs.

Figure 10.18   (Continued) Career Profile: Security and fire safety.   (Continued)

In essence, "hazmat" may be the product manufactured itself or may be subject to delivery and containment.[44] For example, with the explosion of the "fracking industry," there has been a natural growth in corresponding hazardous situations and placements of materials. In fact, the use of rail cars to deliver the end product has resulted in some serious industrial accidents. While not a common event, it is the flammability of the product and its interactions with both environmental and usage factors that give rise to a hazardous event. Fracking, like many other industries, has a supply chain dilemma each and every day it brings its product to the market, and those entrusted with the security and safety function must always be on the lookout for "three key areas: recognition, evaluation and control of emerging threats."[45]

---

[44] International Foundation for Protection Officers, Responding to a Hazardous Materials Incident, at http://www.ifpo.org/resource-links/articles-and-reports/safety-fire-protection-and-emergency-management/responding-to-a-hazardous-materials-incident
[45] B. Anderson, Supply Chain Security Innovations to Adapt to Emerging Threats, *Sec. Mag.* 28 (June 2011).

FIRE AND SAFETY OFFICER
PAGE NO. 4

Ability to determine work priorities.

Working Conditions

Some jobs require skill in the proper use of firearms as employees may be required to carry a firearm.

Some jobs require an employee to work any shift or any day of the week.

Some jobs require an employee to work in adversarial situations.

Some jobs require direct contact with prisoners and patients.

Some jobs are located in a correctional or mental health facility.

Some jobs require an employee to walk for long periods.

Some jobs require an employee to concentrate on a designated area for extended periods.

Physical Requirements

The job duties require an employee to be absent of any physical limitation, which would impair effective performance in the Departments of Corrections, Military and Veterans' Affairs, and Community Health.

Education

Educational level typically acquired through completion of high school.

Experience

Fire and Safety Officer 6
One year of experience in a security guard or public safety occupation.

Fire and Safety Officer E7
One year of experience equivalent to a Fire and Safety Officer 6.

Fire and Safety Officer 8
Two years of experience equivalent to a Fire and Safety Officer, including one year equivalent to a Fire and Safety Officer E7.

Special Requirements, Licenses, and Certifications

Absence of a criminal record of felony convictions which would prohibit the applicant from receiving, possessing, and carrying a firearm.

FIRE AND SAFETY OFFICER
PAGE NO. 5

NOTE: Equivalent combinations of education and experience that provide the required knowledge, skills, and abilities will be evaluated on an individual basis.

JOB CODE, POSITION TITLES AND CODES, AND COMPENSATION INFORMATION

Job Code	Job Code Description
FIRSFYOFR	Fire Safety Officer

Position Title	Position Code	Pay Schedule
Fire Safety Officer-E	FRSFOFRE	A02-002
Fire Safety Officer-A	FRSFOFRA	A02-015

ECP Group 1
Revised 6/1/06
TeamLeaders

Figure 10.18   (Continued) Career Profile: Security and fire safety.

(Continued)

Figure 10.19 Tagged materials in tanker trucks.

And without a security and safety outlook, the employer awaits some form of legal liability when injury and harm occur. A well-run enterprise has to factor in security at every level and make it part of the institutional fabric.[46] Of course, being potentially injurious to a larger product does not inherently preclude or forbid production, for an advanced economy works with dangerous materials on a day-to-day basis.[47]

From start to finish, the fracking process, despite its numerous economic benefits, has to potential to wreak havoc on our water supply and aligned communities. See Figure 10.20.[48]

The danger alone should not prohibit production, for the benefits outweigh the risks; however, this is assuming that such companies give more than lip service to safety and security issues. In this sense, hazmat can, if not properly managed, be a deal-breaker for the business hoping to thrive and prosper in the contemporary economy. See Figure 10.21.[49]

The term "hazmat" encompasses many things, nicely memorialized in the hazmat team logo in Figure 10.22.

Anything with the potential to inflict individual or collective harm falls into the designation as long as it is a material, a substance, or content that harms another—whether biological, chemical, nuclear/radiological, or fire and explosives.[50]

Web Exercise: For a complete listing of all substances within the realm of hazmat, see the 308-page listing at http://www.phmsa.dot.gov/staticfiles/PHMSA/DownloadableFiles/Files/Hazmat/Alpha_Hazmat_Table.pdf.

At a minimum, every firm, transportation business, manufacturer, or other business needs a hazmat security plan. In general, the plan must account and screen personnel, access points, security of facility and the perimeter, and the many dynamics of route delivery. The plan should include

- An assessment of transportation security risks for shipments of hazmat, including site- or location-specific risks associated with facilities where hazmat is prepared for transportation, stored, or unloaded
- Measures to address the assessed risks

---

[46] For an interesting analysis of the Clorox Bleach facility and how it elevated security and safety concerns, see M. Arata Jr, Clorox Cleans up Site Security, *Sec. Mgmt.* 39 (December 1995).

[47] See R. Gold & C. Dawson, North Dakota Fracking: Behind the Oil-Train Explosions, *The Wall Street Journal Online* (July 7, 2014), at http://www.wsj.com/articles/north-dakota-fracking-behind-the-oil-train-explosions-1404761720; see also D. Ritchey, The Chemical Safety Train 68 (August 2010).

[48] EPA, Assessment of the Potential Impacts of Hydraulic Fracturing for Oil and Gas on Drinking Water Resource (2015), at https://www.epa.gov/sites/production/files/2015-07/documents/hf_es_erd_jun2015.pdf

[49] U.S. DOT, Hazardous Materials Transportation.

[50] See the formal listing at the CFR at Title 49 CFR 172.101 Table (List of Hazardous Materials Descriptions), at http://www.phmsa.dot.gov/portal/site/PHMSA/menuitem.6f23687cf7b00b0f22e4c6962d9c8789/?vgnextoid=d84ddf479bd7d110VgnVCM1000009ed07898RCRD&

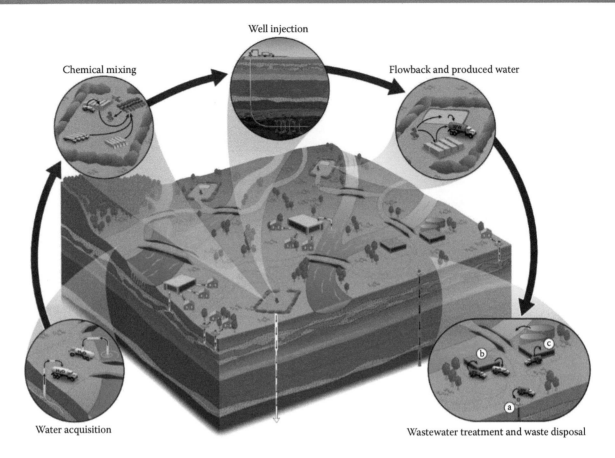

Figure 10.20 Stages of the hydraulic fracturing water cycle. Shown here is a generalized landscape depicting the activities of the hydraulic fracturing water cycle and their relationship to each other, as well as their relationship to drinking water resources. Arrows depict the movement of water and chemicals. Specific activities in the "wastewater treatment and waste disposal" inset are (a) underground injection control (UIC) well disposal, (b) wastewater treatment and reuse, and (c) wastewater treatment and discharge at a centralized waste treatment (CWT) facility. Note: Figure not to scale.

Figure 10.21 Hazardous materials being transported by rail.

Figure 10.22 Hazmat logo.

- Name/job title of senior official responsible for developing/implementing the security plan
- Specific security duties for each position/department responsible for implementing the plan
- A plan for training hazmat employees

The security plan, including the facility and transportation security risk assessment, should be in writing and regularly reviewed and revised as warranted. Finally, to have any meaningful impact requires that each employee be familiar with the security plan and be aware of the risks it seeks to avoid.[51]

At all cost, involve personnel actively throughout the hazmat process. Employees are the preventive eyes and ears to hazmat injury and harm. Employees, working at the various stages of production and transport, have a sixth sense of where problems will emerge and happen. Hence, security planning for hazmat must include a vigorous dose of employee participation, especially in the following forms:

- Encourage employees to report suspicious incidents or events
- Implement routine security inspections
- Convene regular employee/management meetings on security measures
- Communicate with staff using an internal communication system to provide information on facts, trends, and other security issues[52]

Web Exercise: To evaluate a team's response to a hazmat situation, consider the content of the State of Texas Evaluation Response document at http://www.tdi.texas.gov/pubs/videoresource/stperplan.pdf.

See Figure 10.23.[53]

---

[51] U.S. DOT, Hazardous Materials Transportation.
[52] *Ibid.* at 8.
[53] ASIS International Career Center Job Listings, at http://careercenter.asisonline.org/jobs/8241853/supply-chain-security-c-tpat-manager

Supply Chain Security C-TPAT Manager, Employment

Employers? Sign In and More

Home   **Jobs**   Your Profile   Resources

Job Seekers Sign In

Your Account ▾

☐ Help

☐ **Search**   ☐ Browse   ☐ Explore   ☐ Your Job Alerts   ☐ Your Saved Jobs

◀ Return to Search Results

Supply Chain Security C-TPAT Manager

Toy Company ABC

☒ f ⊻ in + ☒ 🖶

The Supply Chain Security Manager position will oversee the successful implementation of global supply chain security compliance measures, including C-TPAT, AEO and related supply chain security initiatives. This position will report to the Director Security Compliance and will ensure that industry best practices are implemented in conjunction with established *Toy Company ABC* supply chain security standards.

Responsibilities include the implementation of supply chain security compliance programs, and managing ABC's supply chain security compliance program to ensure on-going compliance to supply chain security requirements as set forth by ABC, U.S. Customs and other foreign Customs agencies as well as managing the C-TPAT program at ABC.

Responsibilities include:
• Prepare and execute global SCS audit plan.
• Ensure SCS audits are conducted per SCS compliance standards.
• Maintain SCS data in audit portal.
• Review and provide timely feedback and approval for all global supply chain security audit reports and follow-up audits for approximately 80 manufacturing facilities, 50 transportation carriers and 4 distribution centers comprising approximately 135 audits annually.
• Compile a detailed summary of audit results for carriers, manufacturing facilities and domestic warehouses biannually to include roll-up of results by Tier 1 suppliers and identification of

Apply Now

APPLY NOW

By using this feature you agree to our Terms and Conditions and Privacy Policy.

Details

Posted:
June 22, 2016

Location:
Providence, RI/Boston, MA

Figure 10.23   Career Profile: Supply chain security C-TPAT manager.   (*Continued*)

10.6.1 Weapons of mass destruction

The terror associated with WMD is well founded and not to be addressed cavalierly and contemporary reality paints a global picture of bombs and explosives being used with now normative regularity. Today, there appears no safe place in the civilized and uncivilized worlds and with irrationally fueled hatemongers, jihadists, supremacists, government haters, and environmental and animal extremists, the picture is unlikely to improve in the next few decades. It is all the more reason why the private security industry grows so feverishly since the public system is incapable of handling this onslaught, this plague of violence and terror. WMD is part of the arsenal relied upon by the enemies of culture

Supply Chain Security C-TPAT Manager, Employment

key issues and recommendations.

• Conduct a supply chain security risk assessment for all supply chains annually. This includes compiling all supplier data, documenting all supply chains and conducting a threat assessment.

• Conduct an internal assessment annually.

• Ensure standardization and consistent execution of supply chain security policies, standards and audit protocols.

• Update Supply Chain Security Standards, audit criteria and guidance material as needed based on changes to supply chain security programs as implemented by U.S. Customs or foreign Customs agencies.

• Update ABC's C-TPAT Security Profile annually.

• Assist in the investigation of supply chain security breaches.

• Conduct SCS audits as needed.

Reporting and status updates - Responsible for all activity reporting related to supply chain security compliance programs.

• Provide program and project updates and budget status reports monthly.

• Manage global audit plans and provide monthly updates with regards to schedules, audit costs and preliminary and final audit and CAP results.

• Update and conduct quarterly Global Security presentation for SCS.

• Compile and archive all audit records and related documents.

• Manage current and historical compilation of audit data.

• Manage supplier self-assessment schedule.

• Monitor SVI status of ABC's current C-TPAT certified business partners.

• Maintain and report ABC supplier data to include location and contact information, shipping volume and C-TPAT status biannually.

• Assist in the preparation for C-TPAT revalidations.

Contractor Management - Provide day-to-day direction for third party auditing resources.

• Train contract auditors and staff as needed.

• Ensure audits are conducted in accordance with ABC's current audit protocols.

• Review audit travel expenses and invoices and submit to Director Security Compliance for approval monthly.

• Ensure third party consulting performance standards and pricing are met according to contractual requirements.

Training - Assist in the development and implementation of training programs.

• Prepare global auditor training material and conduct auditor training and training audits as needed.

• Manage supply chain security supplier on-line training program and schedule.

• Obtain lists of training participants and facilitate communication between facilities and training provider.

• Review training test results and make recommendations for

Salary:
Open

Type:
Full Time - Experienced

Categories:
Anti-Terrorism, Audits (Security-Related), Computer Security

Preferred Education:
4 Year Degree

Figure 10.23   (Continued) Career Profile: Supply chain security C-TPAT manager.   (Continued)

and cooperation. The private security industry needs to know about WMD dynamics, for their expertise, their technological sophistication, and freedom of investigative protocols, when compared to public sector policing, have never been more critical. Indeed, many in the practitioner and academic community are fully aware that a heavy private sector involvement is essential to nonproliferation of WMD.[54]

---

[54] I.J. Stewart et al., Partnerships with the Private Sector to Prevent Proliferation, University of Georgia, Center for International Trade & Security, at http://cits.uga.edu/1540compass/article/partnerships-with-the-private-sector-to-prevent-proliferation

Supply Chain Security C-TPAT Manager, Employment

changes to on-line training content based on results.

Qualifications
• Bachelor's degree in criminal justice, business administration or
related discipline (preferred).
• Minimum five years' experience in managing supply chain
security audit programs and C-TPAT compliance programs
• Strong knowledge of distribution center, manufacturing,
transportation and physical auditing practices and procedures.
• Excellent (oral and written) communication skills.
• Intermediate to advanced proficiency in Microsoft Excel.
• Intermediate proficiency in Microsoft Word, PowerPoint and Visio.
• Must be willing to travel internationally.

Internal Number: 10XX

Figure 10.23   (Continued) Career Profile: Supply chain security C-TPAT manager.

Private security contractors and soldiers, serving in Iraq and Afghanistan, are already well aware of the devastating impact of WMD and improvised explosive device (IED)—both dying and being injured by these weapons and at the same time, becoming technologically wise about the nefarious usages of these terror tools.[55] There are four generally accepted categories of WMD, covered in the following subsections.

10.6.1.1 Nuclear

The complexities of devising a nuclear delivery mechanism are amply documented. The complete production of a nuclear weapon largely depends on access to nuclear material and a high level of scientific expertise. Black market materials can be utilized, though the crudeness of the enterprise is dangerous in and of itself.

The demands and complexities of nuclear threat call for constant and continuous assessment. Aside from perimeter concerns and access issues, the typical nuclear power facility (refer to Figure 6.11) not only utilizes physical materials capable of mass destruction but also must find ways to store and treat the by-products of nuclear power and production.

Physical security at nuclear power plants is provided by well-armed and well-trained security personnel who remain ready to respond to an attack 24 hours a day, 7 days a week. The sites are protected by sensitive intrusion detection equipment, fences, and barriers and are monitored by cameras and security patrols (Figure 10.24).

10.6.1.2 Radiological

Some threats involve procuring and using radioactive materials in a radiological dispersal device (RDD) or "dirty bomb." The dirty bomb combines a conventional explosive, such as dynamite, with radioactive material. Upon detonation, aside from the immediate injuries inflicted, there will be severe collateral damage from the nuclear material itself. The discovery and tracking of dirty bomb devices and such radioactive material is an ongoing private–public sector concern due to the potential for human harm.[56] See Figure 10.25.

Thus far, the United States has been successful at prevention in this horrid tactic, and through technology, human observation, and solid equipment to scan and detect, the security industry has played a critical role in the constraint on this tactic.[57,58]

[55] J.L. Gomez del Prado, The Privatization of War: Mercenaries, Private Military and Security Companies (PMSC) (November 2010), at http://www.globalresearch.ca/the-privatization-of-war-mercenaries-private-military-and-security-companies-pmsc/21826

[56] B. Zalud, Exercises, Arrests, Technology Aim at Dirty Bomb Worries, Sec. Mag. 124 (November 2012).

[57] See Bomb Detection Includes Human Element, Integration, Sec. Mag. 35 (February 2000); see also B. Zalud, Plane Talk on Metal, Bomb Detection, Sec. Mag. 66 (May 2004); see also S. Detienne, Blast and Ballistic Door Selection Criteria, Sec. Mag. 22 (May 2006).

[58] Secintel Security and Defense Technologies, Dirty Bomb Detector, at http://www.secintel.com/ecom-prodshow/dirty_bomb_detector.html

Figure 10.24 Protection officer at a nuclear facility.

The extent of local contamination will depend on a number of factors, including the size of the explosive, the amount and type of radioactive material used, means of dispersal, and weather conditions. The effects of radiation exposure would be determined by

- Amount of radiation absorbed by the body
- Type of radiation (gamma, beta, or alpha)
- Distance from the radiation to an individual
- Means of exposure—external or internal (absorbed by the skin, inhaled, or ingested)
- Length of time exposed

Figure 10.25 U.S. Nuclear Regulatory Commission: Yellowcake—the by-product of uranium processing in demand for terrorist activity.

The graphic from the Nuclear Regulatory Commission represents the various modes of exposure (refer to Figure 6.14).

Most radioactive materials lack sufficient strength to present a significant public health risk once dispersed, and the materials posing the greatest hazard would likely infect the criminals themselves.[59] Others argue that dirty bombs are really not as catastrophically capable of inflicting damage as appears at first glance with most damage being "psychological" rather than physical.[60]

The secondary and cultural effects of a dirty bomb would be quite acute since fear and panic would naturally ensue. The availability of radiological source material is more extensive than most known since this product is used widely in industrial, medical, and research applications, cancer therapy, food and blood irradiation techniques, and radiography.

Web Exercise: For an NRC fact sheet on dirty bombs, see http://www.nrc.gov/reading-rm/doc-collections/fact-sheets/fs-dirty-bombs.html.

Finally, most security specialists rely just as heavily on behavioral observations as upon the technological screening systems, for human agents carrying such devices are likely to act in identifiable behavioral ways that give notice of the improper purpose or aim.[61]

10.6.1.3 Biological

Bioterrorism is the deliberate dispersal of pathogens through food, air, water, or living organisms in order to launch disease and other harms to the public. Biological agents can kill on a massive scale and have the potential to move quickly through large populations, leaving high rates of mortality.[62] Biological agents are, for the most part, tasteless, odorless, and invisible. The havoc occurs quickly and without much warning. Biological agents can be introduced by air, by water, or in the food supply. Federal Emergency Management Agency (FEMA) categorizes agents by application, duration, extent of effects, and mitigation (refer to Figure 6.16).

The Centers for Disease Control and Prevention (CDC) assumes the preeminent position when it comes to the identification, mitigation, response, and recovery from a biological attack. The CDC types of all known biological agents are listed into these three categories.[63] As of 2015,[64] the list of biological agents comprised of

- Anthrax (*Bacillus anthracis*)
- Arenaviruses
- *Bacillus anthracis* (anthrax)
- Botulism (*Clostridium botulinum* toxin)
- *Brucella* species (brucellosis)
- Brucellosis (*Brucella* species)
- *Burkholderia mallei* (glanders)
- *Burkholderia pseudomallei* (melioidosis)
- *Chlamydia psittaci* (psittacosis)
- Cholera (*Vibrio cholerae*)
- *Clostridium botulinum* toxin (botulism)

---

[59] D.G. Arce & K. Siqueira, Motivating Operatives for Suicide Missions and Conventional Terrorist Attacks, 26 *J. Theoretical Politics* 677 (2014); R. Braun & M. Genkin, Cultural Resonance and the Diffusion of Suicide Bombings: The Role of Collectivism, *J. Conflict Res.* (August 2013).

[60] J. Dingle, Dirty Bombs: Real Threats, *Sec. Mag.* 48 (April 2005).

[61] See R. Elliott, Assessing Threats from Passengers, 50 *Sec. Mgmt* 32 (2006).

[62] White House Office of the Press Secretary, President Obama Releases National Strategy for Countering Biological Threats, (December 9, 2009), at https://www.whitehouse.gov/the-press-office/president-obama-releases-national-strategy-countering-biological-threats.

[63] See the National Institute of Health's List of Pathogens and Infectious Materials, at https://www.niaid.nih.gov/topics/biodefenserelated/biodefense/pages/cata.aspx

[64] Centers for Disease Control and Prevention, Bioterrorism Agents/Diseases list, at http://emergency.cdc.gov/agent/agentlist.asp

- *Clostridium perfringens* (Epsilon toxin)
- *Coxiella burnetii* (Q fever)
- Ebola virus hemorrhagic fever
- E. coli O157:H7 (*Escherichia coli*)
- Emerging infectious diseases such as Nipah virus and hantavirus
- Epsilon toxin of *Clostridium perfringens*
- *Escherichia coli* O157:H7 (*E. coli*)
- Food safety threats (e.g., *Salmonella* species, *Escherichia coli* O157:H7, *Shigella*)
- *Francisella tularensis* (tularemia)
- Glanders (*Burkholderia mallei*)
- Lassa fever
- Marburg virus hemorrhagic fever
- Melioidosis (*Burkholderia pseudomallei*)
- Plague (*Yersinia pestis*)
- Psittacosis (*Chlamydia psittaci*)
- Q fever (*Coxiella burnetii*)
- Ricin toxin from *Ricinus communis* (castor beans)
- *Rickettsia prowazekii* (typhus fever)
- *Salmonella* species (salmonellosis)
- *Salmonella* Typhi (typhoid fever)
- Salmonellosis (*Salmonella* species)
- *Shigella* (shigellosis)
- Shigellosis (*Shigella*)
- Smallpox (variola major)
- Staphylococcal enterotoxin B
- Tularemia (*Francisella tularensis*)
- Typhoid fever (*Salmonella* Typhi)
- Typhus fever (*Rickettsia prowazekii*)
- Variola major (smallpox)
- *Vibrio cholerae* (cholera)
- Viral encephalitis (alphaviruses [e.g., Venezuelan equine encephalitis, eastern equine encephalitis, western equine encephalitis])
- Viral hemorrhagic fevers (filoviruses [e.g., Ebola, Marburg] and arenaviruses [e.g., Lassa, Machupo])
- Water safety threats (e.g., *Vibrio cholerae*, *Cryptosporidium parvum*)

For the present, the bulk of attention has been on four to five biological agents with the potential for severe harm. A summary analysis of these follows.

10.6.1.3.1 Anthrax

Anthrax is caused by *Bacillus anthracis*, a disease-causing bacterium that forms spores. A spore is a cell that is dormant (asleep), but over time may arise from its slumber. Anthrax can be broken down anatomically:

- Skin (cutaneous)
- Lungs (inhalation)
- Digestive (gastrointestinal)

The diagnosis of anthrax will be evidenced by certain warning signs in the infected party and where the disease has found a home:

Cutaneous: Initial symptoms are blisters that eventually turn black.

Gastrointestinal: Symptoms are nausea, loss of appetite, bloody diarrhea, fever, and significant stomach pain.

Inhalation: Cold or flu symptoms, including a sore throat, mild fever, and muscle aches. Later symptoms include cough, chest discomfort, shortness of breath, tiredness, and muscle aches.

The effects of anthrax on the human body are both painful and extreme (Figure 10.26). Without care, death is the ultimate end of the infected party.

Remediation of anthrax will be dependent on its stage and the party's resistance to antibiotics. The sooner the medical attention is sought, the better the cure.

10.6.1.3.2 Plague

Just as in centuries past, plague is an infectious bacteria carried by rats, flies, and fleas. Plague is an infectious airborne disease that affects others who come into contact with its strain of bacteria. Plague is normally transmitted from an infected rodent to man by infected fleas. Bioterrorism-related outbreaks are likely to be transmitted through dispersion of an aerosol. Person-to-person transmission of pneumonic plague is possible by a large dose of aerosol droplets. There are three kinds of plague:

- Pneumonic plague can spread from person to person through the air. Transmission can take place if someone breathes in aerosolized bacteria, which could happen in a bioterrorist attack.
- Bubonic plague is the most common form of plague. This occurs when an infected flea bites a person or when materials contaminated with *Y. pestis* enter through a break in a person's skin.
- Septicemic plague occurs when plague bacteria multiply in the blood. It can be a complication of pneumonic or bubonic plague, or it can occur by itself.

Plague could be used in an aerosol that would cause the pneumonic version. Once the disease is contracted, the bacteria can spread to others by close contact. Bubonic plague could be generated by releasing plague-infected fleas or animals. The *Y. pestis* bacterium occurs in nature and also is widely available in microbiology laboratories around the world. Thousands of scientists are working with plague organisms on a daily basis. See Figure 10.27.[65]

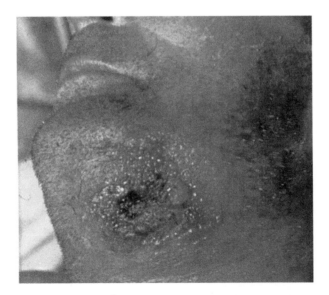

Figure 10.26 Anthrax infection. (Anthrax Vaccine Immunization Program for Combined Services.)

---

[65] Centers for Disease Control and Prevention, Division of Vector-Borne Diseases, Plague Symptoms, at http://www.cdc.gov/plague/symptoms/index.html, last updated September 14, 2015.

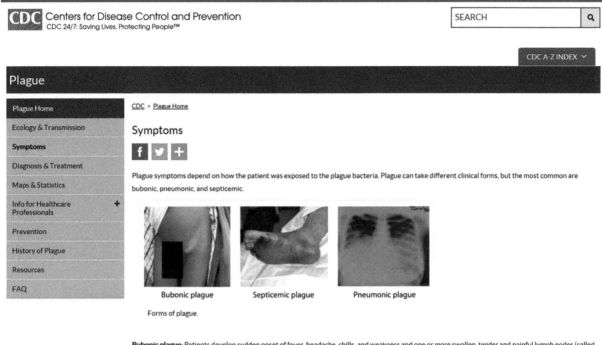

Figure 10.27   CDC's webpage on plague symptoms.

If detected early enough, antibiotics can be effective. A vaccine has yet to be developed.

Web Resource: Watch the CDC training video on the preparation and management of plague at http://emergency. cdc.gov/agent/plague/trainingmodule/powerpoint.asp.

10.6.1.3.3 Smallpox

Smallpox has been referred to as the king of bioterrorism due to its ease of transmission and simplicity of delivery. It was the scourge of many a nation until its almost complete eradication in the 1970s. Unfortunately, the world has seen a return of this virulent disease and, just as distressingly, heard of its potential to be a WMD. Smallpox is a serious, contagious, and sometimes fatal infectious disease. Smallpox comes in two varieties: *Variola major*, the most severe and most common form of smallpox, and *Variola minor*, a less common presentation of smallpox with medical effects.

There is no specific treatment for smallpox, and the only prevention is vaccination. Generally, direct and fairly prolonged face-to-face contact is required to spread smallpox, usually by saliva, from one person to another. Smallpox can also be spread through direct contact with infected bodily fluids or contaminated objects (Figure 10.28).

Smallpox has the capacity to inflict horrid damage. Containment and isolation are urgent requirements. Calming the public, the victims' families, and loved ones is another essential task. The CDC publishes protocols on how to handle the smallpox case—from the initial communications chain, to isolation, to vaccination, to subsequent media demands. Use the checklist in Table 10.1 to organize that sort of operation.[66]

---

[66] Centers for Disease Control, *Smallpox Response Plan and Guidelines* (Washington, DC: U.S. Government Printing Office, November 2002), Annex 8.

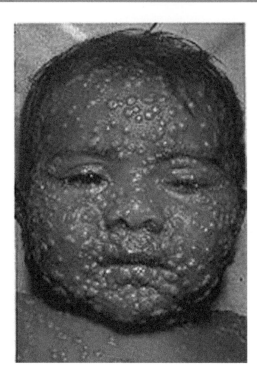

Figure 10.28 The rash and body lesions that result from smallpox are intense and unrivaled in epidemiology. Less than a week after an infection, the results are plain enough.

10.6.1.4 Chemical

Chemical weapons have seen usage in both accidental and intentional terms. For example, the release of chemical toxins in an industrial accident can wreak havoc on the public health. More maliciously, the intentional infliction of chemical toxins by a terrorist manifests the mindset and a complete and utter disregard for human life. Chemical weapons can cause high levels of mortality.

Chemical threats come in a variety of forms and delivery systems. These agents are far more common and much easier to develop and distribute than the biological and nuclear counterparts. Many household products, farm fertilizers, and other agricultural and industrial products contain the elements necessary to shape the chemical threat.

The general typology of chemical agents includes

- Biotoxins—Poisons that come from plants or animals
- Blister agents/vesicants—Chemicals that severely blister the eyes, respiratory tract, and skin on contact
- Blood agents—Poisons that affect the body by being absorbed into the blood
- Caustics (acids)—Chemicals that burn or corrode people's skin, eyes, and mucus membranes
- Choking/lung/pulmonary agents—Chemicals that cause severe irritation or swelling of the respiratory tract
- Incapacitating agents—Agents that can affect consciousness
- Long-acting anticoagulants—Poisons that prevent blood from clotting properly
- Metals—Agents that consist of metallic poisons
- Nerve agents—Highly poisonous chemicals that work by preventing the nervous system from working properly
- Organic solvents—Agents that damage the tissues of living things by dissolving fats and oils
- Riot control agents/tear gas—Highly irritating agents normally used by law enforcement for crowd control
- Toxic alcohols—Poisonous alcohols that can damage the heart, kidneys, and nervous system
- Vomiting agents—Chemicals that cause nausea and vomiting

Table 10.1   Team leader's list of actions and decisions to be considered

Action or decision	Lead person— state or local HD	Lead person— CDC team
Identify key decision makers and infrastructure at state and local HD		
Identify with above officials the counterparts for CDC team members		
Identify and review existing state/local emergency or BT plans		
Identify state/local chains of command for action and decisions and communications and agree on access points		
Negotiate roles of CDC team in collaboration with state/local officials		
Identify office space, transport, and facilities for team members		
Identify and clarify roles of press spokespersons		
Review smallpox response plan and priority task lists and establish plan for implementation		
Identify other state/local/federal agencies involved and their roles		
Identify serious issues (isolation policy, quality of medical care vs. isolation) for which immediate, high-level discussions and decisions are needed—note eight areas below:		
• Immediate need to determine number, composition, and identify personnel for state/local first response team and facilities such as vaccination clinics and isolation/hospitals, assure training, vaccination, transport, and other support needs		
• Surveillance—provider and public health alert system. Laboratory alert system; active/passive rash illness reporting networks; ER alert; case response plan in place; source of exposure; data compiling support		
• Contact and contacts of contact identification, tracing, vaccination, and surveillance for fever/rash. Vaccine site and severe adverse events; risk prioritization for contact tracing		
• Vaccination policy(s); who, where, when, and by whom; containment or containment and mass; fixed vaccination clinics, household/neighborhood vaccination, mobile teams; separate vaccination sites for contacts, response teams, and essential services (police, water, power, fireman, other security groups, child health services, etc.). Smallpox vaccine storage, distribution, and security		
• Decide on isolation policy(s) home, hospital, smallpox isolation facility; transport of cases; security; enforcement and maintenance issues; level of medical care to be provided		
• Status of state quarantine rules/laws and who and how would they be implemented		
• Training and educational plans; supplies of educational and training materials; facilities, trainers, schedules needed; various curricula; identifying personnel to be trained; web-based and other alternatives for training and education		
• Security arrangements for all team members; plans for controlling the population and enforcement of vaccination and isolation		
• Supplies on hand; such as bifurcated needles, multiple forms. Spox disease identification cards, vaccine take cards. VIS (languages), etc.		
Delegate assignments reflecting above needs and begin implementation with written notes of persons responsible and deadlines		
Identify political officials needed (e.g., governor, mayor) to reach decision quickly		
Reach consensus and schedule daily (or more frequent) meetings with key officials		
Schedule phone briefings and meetings with team members daily		
Arrange conference calls with CDC "smallpox central" in Atlanta		

Web Exercise: Find out more about chemical threats by visiting the National Institute of Occupational Safety and Health pocket guide on chemical threats at http://www.cdc.gov/niosh/npg.

10.6.1.4.1 Ricin

Ricin is a poison found naturally in castor beans. Ricin can be made from the waste material left over from processing castor beans (Figure 10.29).

Figure 10.29   Castor beans. (Minnesota Department of Health.)

Ricin may be produced in various forms, including powder, mist, or pellet. It can also be dissolved in water or weak acid. Castor beans are processed throughout the world to make castor oil, and its by-product, the "mash," provides the source material for the dangerous chemical.

The production is not a natural by-product but an intentional manufacture, which indicates malevolence on the part of the maker of the ricin. Ricin can be delivered in various ways, including

- *Indoor air*: Ricin can be released into indoor air as fine particles (aerosol).
- *Water*: Ricin can be used to contaminate water.
- *Food*: Ricin can be used to contaminate food.
- *Outdoor air*: Ricin can be released into outdoor air as fine particles.
- *Agricultural*: If ricin is released into the air as fine particles, it can damage and contaminate agricultural products.

Ricin can be absorbed into the body through ingestion, inhalation, or eye contact. Ricin can be absorbed through open skin or wounds, but most likely not through intact skin, unless aided by a solvent. Ricin causes acute respiratory problems, impacts central organs in the human body, and can negatively affect eyes and ears. It can cause death in less than 24 hours.

Clues that indicate the presence or release of ricin include but are not limited to

- An unusual increase in the number of patients seeking care for potential chemical-release-related illness
- Unexplained deaths among young or healthy persons
- Emission of unexplained odors by patients
- Clusters of illness in persons who have common characteristics, such as drinking water from the same source
- Rapid onset of symptoms after an exposure to a potentially contaminated medium
- Unexplained death of plants, fish, or animals (domestic or wild)
- A syndrome suggesting a disease associated commonly with a known chemical exposure (e.g., neurologic signs or pinpoint pupils in eyes of patients with a gastroenteritis-like syndrome or acidosis in patients with altered mental status)[67]

---

[67] M. Patel et al., Recognition of Illness Associated with Exposure to Chemical Agents—United States, 2003, *Morbidity and Mortality Weekly Report* 52 (October 3, 2003) 938–940, at http://www.cdc.gov/mmwr/preview/mmwrhtml/mm5239a3.htm#tab.

Web Exercise: For a recent case of ricin contamination at a South Carolina postal facility, see http://www.cdc.gov/nceh/hsb/chemicals/pdfs/mmwr5246p1129.pdf.

10.6.1.4.2 Nerve agents

Chemicals can also influence, in an extremely negative way, the central nervous system of the human body. Chemical nerve agents and gases have been around for more than a century. There are four main nerve agents: nerve agents GA (tabun), GB (sarin), GD (soman), and VX are manufactured compounds. The G-type agents are clear, colorless, tasteless liquids miscible in water and most organic solvents. Sarin is odorless and is the most volatile nerve agent. Tabun has a slightly fruity odor, and soman has a slight camphor-like odor. VX is a clear, amber-colored, odorless, oily liquid. It is miscible with water and dissolves in all solvents. VX is the least volatile nerve agent. Most of the nerve agents were originally produced in a search for insecticides, but because of their toxicity, they were evaluated for military use.

Sarin was produced before the commencement of World War II and was primarily used as a pesticide. However, the gas was quickly valued for its capacity for chemical weaponry and was tested, though not used, during World War II. It has been alleged that Saddam Hussein used sarin against the Iranians in the long and very costly war between Iraq and Iran in the 1980s and early 1990s.[68] Sarin was delivered into a Tokyo subway by the radical terrorist cult Aum Shinrikyo, a cell that intended to install Shoko Asahara as its new savior. Asahara, who strove "to take over Japan and then the world," according to the State Department, was arrested in May 1995 for his role in the subway attack. His trial took eight years, from 1996 until 2004, when he was sentenced to death.

Sarin gas is a preferred method for the terrorist due to its ease of delivery. Aerosol or vapor forms are the most effective for dissemination, which can be carried by sprayers or an explosive device.

Web Exercise: Chemical facilities, due to their stockpiles and ready availability of chemical substances, need to conduct vulnerability assessments of their facilities. The U.S. Department of Homeland Security has published a vulnerability assessment guide at https://www.dhs.gov/csat-sva-ssp.

As in all other forms of nerve agents and other threats, the CDC disseminates educational literature to the professional community. Known as cards, these informational pieces lay out symptoms and response regarding a particular agent. See the complete description of tabun in Table 10.2.

VX is another recent nerve agent originally developed for industrial purposes but then construed to be an effective tool in chemical warfare. VX was originally developed in the United Kingdom in the early 1950s. VX is tasteless and slow to evaporate. Following release of VX into the air, people can be exposed through skin or eye contact or inhalation. It can also be ingested through contaminated water or food (Figure 10.30).

VX, like other nerve gases, generally causes death by asphyxiation.

Soman also qualifies under the definition of nerve agent. Soman was originally developed as an insecticide in Germany in 1944. Soman is commonly referred to as GD. It will become a vapor if heated. Soman is not found naturally in the environment. Soman, like other nerve agents, can be exposed by air, touch, or contaminated food or water. The most likely method of transmission is for people to breathe air containing soman gas or droplets, or when the liquid form of soman comes into contact with the skin or eyes. Because soman mixes easily with water, it has the potential to be used as a poison for food and water supplies. Clothing from a contaminated person can release vapors for about 30 minutes after exposure, thus endangering people who were not in an original area of release.

Exposure to soman can be treated with specific antidotes—atropine and pralidoxime chloride (2-PAM)—along with supportive medical care in a hospital. These nerve agent antidotes are most effective when given within minutes of exposure.

10.6.1.5 Bomb threats

In addition to WMD and potential weapons of mass effect, there is a threat of attack by means of IED or other explosive designs. IED weapons are explosive devices fashioned and deployed by means other than through conventional

---

[68] The Arms Control Association makes this claim at M. Nguyen, Report Confirms Iraq Used Sarin in 1991, *Arms Control Today*, 36 (January/February 2006), at http://www.armscontrol.org/act/2006_01-02/JANFEB-IraqSarin.

Table 10.2 Tabun card

Nerve agent
CAS # 77-81-6
RTECS #
Counterterrorism card 0002

Tabun (GA)
Dimethylphosphoramidocyanidic acid, ethyl ester ethyl N,N-dimethylphosphoramidocyanidate
Chemical formula $C_5H_{11}N_2O_2P$
Molecular mass: 162.12

Types of hazard/exposure	Acute hazards/symptoms	Prevention	First aid/firefighting
Fire	React with steam or water to produce toxic and corrosive vapors	Contain to prevent contamination to uncontrolled areas	Water mist, fog, and foam, CO_2. Avoid methods that will cause splashing or spreading
Explosion			
Exposure	May result in the formation of hydrogen cyanide	Do not breathe fumes. Skin contact must be avoided at all times	Seek medical attention Immediately
	• Liquid or vapors can be fatal • Clothing releases agent for about 30 min after contact with vapor • Contaminated surfaces present long-term contact hazard		
Inhalation	Inhalation can cause symptoms in 2–5 min Same sequence of symptoms despite the route of exposure: *Mild* • Runny nose • Tightness of the chest and breathing difficulty • Eye pain, dimness of vision, and pin pointing of pupils (miosis) • Difficulty in breathing and cough *Moderate* • Increased eye symptoms with blurred vision • Drooling and excessive sweating • Severe nasal congestion • Increased tightness of the chest and breathing difficulty • Nausea, vomiting, diarrhea, and cramps • Generalized weakness, twitching of large muscle groups • Headache, confusion, and drowsiness *Severe* • Involuntary defecation and urination • Very copious secretions • Twitching, jerking, staggering, and convulsions • Cessation of breathing, loss of consciousness, coma, and death	Hold breath until respiratory protective mask is donned Firefighting personnel should wear full protective clothing and respiratory protection during firefighting and rescue Positive pressure, full face piece, NIOSH-approved self-contained breathing apparatus (SCBA) will be worn	• If severe signs, immediately administer, in rapid succession, all three nerve agent antidote kit(s), Mark I injectors (or atropine if directed by a physician) • If signs and symptoms are progressing, use injectors at 5–20-min intervals. (No more than three injections unless directed by medical personnel) • Maintain record of all injections given • Give artificial respiration if breathing has stopped. Use mouth-to-mouth when mask-bag or oxygen delivery systems not available. Do not use mouth-to-mouth if face is contaminated • Administer oxygen if breathing is difficult

(Continued)

Table 10.2 (*Continued*) Tabun card

Nerve agent
CAS # 77-81-6
RTECS #
Counterterrorism card 0002

Tabun (GA)
Dimethylphosphoramidocyanidic acid, ethyl ester ethyl *N*,*N*-dimethylphosphoramidocyanidate
Chemical formula $C_5H_{11}N_2O_2P$
Molecular mass: 162.12

Types of hazard/ exposure	Acute hazards/symptoms	Prevention	First aid/firefighting
Skin	See Inhalation Lethal doses can kill in 1–2 hours. Pupil size may range from normal to moderately reduced	Protective gloves: Butyl rubber glove M3 and M4 Norton, chemical protective glove set	The primary mode for decontamination of chemical agents is soap and water. A 0.5% hypochlorite solution can be used. There are differing guidelines for decontamination and more research is needed to identify the optimal decontamination method. See "Personal Decontamination" and Appendix D in Treatment of Chemical Agent Casualties and Conventional Military Chemical Injuries (from the U.S. Navy Counterproliferation Office). See also the *Medical Management of Chemical Casualties Handbook* (from the U.S. Army Medical Research Institute of Chemical Defense [USAMRICD]) for a general review of the issues and more on the military decontamination powder approach
Eyes	See Inhalation Very rapid onset of symptoms (less than 2–3 min)	Chemical goggles and face shield	Immediately flush eyes with water for 10–15 min, then don respiratory protective mask
Ingestion	See Inhalation Pupil size may range from normal to moderately reduced		Do not induce vomiting. First symptoms are likely to be gastrointestinal. Immediately administer nerve agent antidote kit, Mark I

Figure 10.30 VX was used as the murder weapon in the February 13, 2017 assassination of Kim Jong-nam, estranged half-brother of North Korean dictator Kim Jong Un.

military operations, thus the term "improvised." They can be created from traditional explosive devices such as bombs, warheads, grenades, land mines, or otherwise fashioned from explosive raw materials. Ball bearings, nails, metal filings, and other materials can be utilized as damage-causing projectiles.[69] Detonation can be accomplished by wired means or remotely through a rigged cell phone, handheld device, or other wireless technology. The fuel to ignite the IED can be common products such as "drain openers, sulfuric acid, and car batteries."[70] The FBI disseminates an IED threat card, which categorizes the various products, compounds, and chemicals common to IEDs. See Figure 10.31a, b, c, and d.[71]

The methods of IED delivery will vary depending on the target as well as the IED design. The U.S. Department of Homeland Security charts the variety as referenced previously in Figure 6.20.[72]

An inordinately high number of incidents of IED attack globally over the last several years have occurred in Iraq and Afghanistan, in addition to attacks in a number of other countries that have begun to experience increased attacks

(a)   (b)

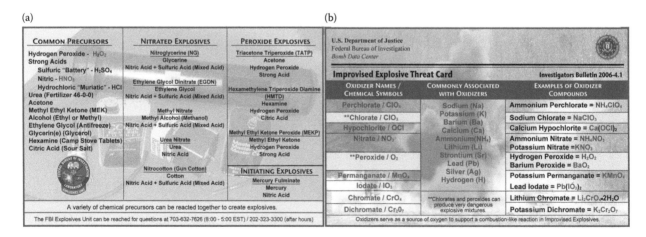

Figure 10.31   (a), (b), (c), and (d) IED fuels.   (*Continued*)

[69] H. Hogan, Identifying Explosives, After the Fact, *Homeland Security Today Magazine* 18–19 (September, 2011).

[70] K. Yeager, What Law Enforcement Needs to Know about Improvised Explosives, *Police Chief* 52–55 (September, 2011).

[71] National Academies & Department of Homeland Security, *Fact Sheet: IED Attack Improvised Explosive Devices, News & Terrorism, Communicating in a Crisis.*

[72] U.S. DHS, VBIED Search Procedures Student Guide, at https://www.eiseverywhere.com/file_uploads/12062e24d2fd637ca8ba1c5f6c5c73fd_ VBIEDStudentGuide.pdf

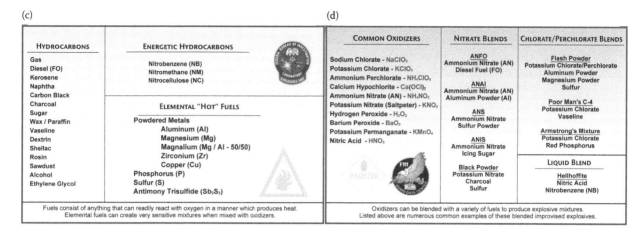

(c)

HYDROCARBONS	ENERGETIC HYDROCARBONS
Gas Diesel (FO) Kerosene Naphtha Carbon Black Charcoal Sugar Wax / Paraffin Vaseline Dextrin Shellac Rosin Sawdust Alcohol Ethylene Glycol	Nitrobenzene (NB) Nitromethane (NM) Nitrocellulose (NC) ELEMENTAL "HOT" FUELS Powdered Metals Aluminum (Al) Magnesium (Mg) Magnalium (Mg / Al - 50/50) Zirconium (Zr) Copper (Cu) Phosphorus (P) Sulfur (S) Antimony Trisulfide (Sb$_2$S$_3$)

Fuels consist of anything that can readily react with oxygen in a manner which produces heat.
Elemental fuels can create very sensitive mixtures when mixed with oxidizers.

(d)

COMMON OXIDIZERS	NITRATE BLENDS	CHLORATE/PERCHLORATE BLENDS
Sodium Chlorate - NaClO$_3$ Potassium Chlorate - KClO$_3$ Ammonium Perchlorate - NH$_4$ClO$_4$ Calcium Hypochlorite - Ca(OCl)$_2$ Ammonium Nitrate (AN) - NH$_4$NO$_3$ Potassium Nitrate (Saltpeter) - KNO$_3$ Hydrogen Peroxide - H$_2$O$_2$ Barium Peroxide - BaO$_2$ Potassium Permanganate - KMnO$_4$ Nitric Acid - HNO$_3$	**ANFO** Ammonium Nitrate (AN) Diesel Fuel (FO) **ANAl** Ammonium Nitrate (AN) Aluminum Powder (Al) **ANS** Ammonium Nitrate Sulfur Powder **ANIS** Ammonium Nitrate Icing Sugar **Black Powder** Potassium Nitrate Charcoal Sulfur	**Flash Powder** Potassium Chlorate/Perchlorate Aluminum Powder Magnesium Powder Sulfur **Poor Man's C-4** Potassium Chlorate Vaseline **Armstrong's Mixture** Potassium Chlorate Red Phosphorus **LIQUID BLEND** **Hellhoffite** Nitric Acid Nitrobenzene (NB)

Oxidizers can be blended with a variety of fuels to produce explosive mixtures.
Listed above are numerous common examples of these blended improvised explosives.

Figure 10.31   (Continued) (a), (b), (c), and (d) IED fuels.

firsthand. Unfortunately, there exist numerous websites and sources that provide detailed instructions, including videos, on how to construct and deploy bombs. Often, new sites crop up as quickly as sites can be discovered and deactivated by authorities.

10.7 NATURAL DISASTERS

Natural hazards fall into these categories:

- Hurricanes
- Tornadoes
- Floods
- Winter storms
- Heat-related emergencies
- Droughts
- Wildfires
- Thunderstorms
- Geologic events

Business owners and security professionals frequently underestimate the full impact of these natural disasters. These events wreak extraordinary havoc. The death toll alone is a distressingly impressive count as was previously mentioned in the listing of deaths from natural disasters in the United States from 1900 to 2015 (refer to Figure 6.9).[73] More than 7 billion people worldwide have been negatively impacted by natural disasters in the last century (refer to Figure 6.10).[74]

Floods and hurricanes are very different animals than nuclear leaks or sarin gas inhalation. The types of emergencies that occur on a daily basis, such as car accidents, road spills, or house fires, are routine events. Catastrophic events, such as tornadoes, terrorist attacks, superstorms like Hurricane Sandy or floods, tend to cover a larger area, impact a greater number of citizens, cost more to recover from, and occur less frequently.[75] See the table in Figure 10.32[76] for event duration estimates.

---

[73] Data from the Centre for Research on the Epidemiology of Disasters (2015), at www.cred.be.

[74] Data from the Centre for Research on the Epidemiology of Disasters, (2015), at www.cred.be.

[75] Department of Homeland Security, *Safe Rooms and Shelters—Protecting People against Terrorist Attacks National Geospatial Preparedness Needs Assessment* (May 2006) Figure 4.3.

[76] Department of Homeland Security, *Safe Rooms and Shelters*, Figure 4.1.

| Classification | Routine | | | Catastrophic |
	Local	Regional	State	National
Examples	• Minor traffic Incidents • Minor load spills • Vehicle fires • Minor train/bus accidents • Accidents with injuries but no fatalities	• Train derailment • Major bus/rail transit accidents • Major truck accidents • Multivehicle crashes • Hazmat spills • Accidents with injuries and fatalities	• Train crashes • Airplane crashes • Hazmat incidents • Multivehicle accidents • Tunnel fires • Multiple injuries and fatalities • Port/airport incidents • Large building fire or explosion • Industrial incidents • Major tunnel/bridge closure	• Terrorist attack/WMD • Floods, blizzards, tornadoes • Transportation infrastructure collapse • Extended power/water outages • Riots • Mass casualties
Expected event duration	0–2 Hours	2–24 Hours	Days	Weeks

Preparedness versus scale of event.

Source: DHS national geospatial preparedness needs.

Figure 10.32   Duration estimates for catastrophic and routine emergency events.

The security specialist must first identify the risk and then take the necessary steps compatible with that risk. Some of the usual events are:

• Dam failure
• Fire or wildfire
• Wildfire
• Hurricane
• Nuclear explosion
• Hazardous material
• Tornado
• Volcano
• Thunderstorm
• Earthquake
• Flood
• Winter storm
• Landslide
• Terrorism
• Heat
• Tsunami

How one goes about preparatory functions largely depends on the type of threat, natural disaster, or hazard under review.[77] Any effective response, recovery, or other answer to a threat or catastrophe heavily depends upon preparedness. By preparedness, one means that the agency, community, and constituency affected, and public and private partners stand ready to deal with the threat in an effective manner. Our own experience teaches us that well-prepared

---

[77] For a general series of considerations on planning and preparation, see R.W. Perry & M.K. Lindell, Preparedness for Emergency Response: Guideline for the Emergency Planning Process, 27 *Disasters* 336–350 (2003).

agencies of government generally do a better job of handling the natural disaster than ill-prepared agencies. The Hurricane Katrina experience edifies this conclusion—while most would agree the Coast Guard knew what and how to do, FEMA struggled in the dark the entire event. In every natural disaster, those that respond must know what can happen but just as critically, how to prepare for its impact and soften its overall blow.

Preparedness encompasses a whole range of operational and policy concerns for the security professional. Preparedness models envelop the capacity to plan, organize, train, equip, exercise, evaluate, and improve. FEMA, after undergoing severe and relentless criticism in the Katrina affair, developed a cycle of preparedness as shown in Figure 10.33.[78]

Hence, preparedness steps depend upon the disaster type itself but also on the best practices collated on similar events.

Once the threat has been identified and the inventory or potential costs calculated, the security professional seeks ways to mitigate these harms. The term *mitigation* implies an intervention before the threat or catastrophe takes place. Mitigation is the effort to reduce loss of life and property by lessening the impact of disasters. Effective mitigation measures can break the cycle of disaster damage, reconstruction, and repeated damage. While it cannot identically work in all threats, the idea of mitigation works particularly well in the case of natural disasters, fire, and other catastrophes. For example, in the event of a hurricane or flood, or even a nuclear error, there are mitigation steps that may prevent the level of expected destruction. Building design, for instance, goes a long way in mitigating the impact of either the earthquake or the flood.[79] Hence, particular attention is provided for the mitigation of buildings against natural and manmade threats, and the security and safety of schools, hospitals, and government installations. See Figure 10.34.[80]

In natural disaster scenarios, the premitigation analysis must consider evacuation as a legitimate part of the mitigation program. If one does not account for the means, the method, or the alternatives in evacuation, aside from being caught flat-footed, the expense of failing to plan will surely be higher than the expense of being organized. Drs. Olornilua and Ibitaya surprisingly conclude that this lack of uniformity directly undermines our planned efficiencies and that every mitigation plan must prepare for "multihazard" situations. The lack of uniformity is portrayed a "dismal."[81]

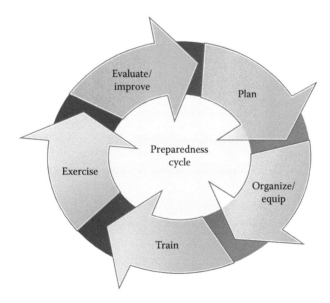

Figure 10.33   Cycle of preparedness.

[78] Department of Homeland Security, *National Response Framework* 27 (January, 2008).
[79] P. Gilbert, Defending by Design, *Sec. Mag.* 68 (April 2014).
[80] FEMA, Risk Management Series at www.fema.gov/plan/prevent/RMS/, last accessed August 30, 2009.
[81] O.O. Olonilua & O. Ibitayo, Toward Multihazard Mitigation: An Evaluation of FEMA-Approved Hazard Mitigation Plans under the Disaster Mitigation Act of 2000, 9 *Journal of Emergency Management* 37–49, 48 (January/February 2011).

What is the Risk Management Series?

The Risk Management Series (RMS) is a new FEMA series directed at providing design guidance for mitigating multihazard events. The objective of the series is to reduce physical damage to structural and nonstructural components of buildings and related infrastructure, and to reduce resultant casualties during natural and manmade disasters.

The RMS is intended to minimize conflicts that may arise from a multihazard design approach. A multihazard approach requires a complex series of tradeoffs. Security concerns need to be balanced with requirements in terms of earthquakes, floods, high speed winds, accessibility, fire protection, and aesthetics, among others. Designing to mitigate natural hazards should avoid considering manmade hazards as an afterthought, but rather as a critical concern to be studied early during the project cycle. Natural hazards are the largest single contributor to catastrophic or repetitive damage to communities nationwide. Manmade hazards can be categorized as rare events with a potential high impact and very difficult to predict.

Risk Management Series

Minimizing the Effects of Natural Disasters and Potential Terrorist Attacks on Large Buildings

FEMA

Figure 10.34 FEMA's risk management series.

In earthquake design, a building must be capable of withstanding the move and sway caused by the earthquake. The recent completion of the Paramount, a high-rise office complex in San Francisco, an earthquake-prone area, manifests the role of engineering design in building plans. In the Paramount, precast concrete is utilized as well as the Precast Hybrid Movement Resistant Frame (PHMRF) system (Figure 10.35).

Web Exercise: Review the construction of Donald J. Trump's tower in Chicago, which captures this sort of earthquake anticipation. https://www.youtube.com/watch?v=pXM1UdmULPk.

The preparedness and mitigation stress continues into the world of flooding and hurricanes. The last decade has witnessed a wave of flood events caused by anything from heavy rains to hurricanes. This includes areas that are regularly prone to reoccurrences of disaster-level flooding. So important is the minimization of flood damage before the flood occurs that FEMA has erected a subagency—the Federal Insurance and Mitigation Administration (FIMA), solely dedicated to its mitigation.

FIMA deals with

- Complying with or exceeding NFIP floodplain management regulations
- Enforcing stringent building codes, flood-proofing requirements, seismic design standards, and wind-bracing requirements for new construction or repairing existing buildings

Figure 10.35   The Paramount in San Francisco. (Wikipedia image used per CC 3.0, image posted by user Minesweeper. No edits made.)

- Adopting zoning ordinances that steer development away from areas subject to flooding, storm surge or coastal erosion
- Retrofitting public buildings to withstand hurricane-strength winds or ground shaking
- Acquiring damaged homes or businesses in flood-prone areas, relocating the structures, and returning the property to open space, wetlands, or recreational uses
- Building community shelters and tornado-safe rooms to help protect people in their homes, public buildings, and schools in hurricane- and tornado-prone areas

FEMA has made its greatest contribution to assisting both public and private flood planning with the FEMA Map Center, where professionals can scan and assess just about every geographic area prone to flooding. FEMA's new MAP MOD program is an ambitious attempt to draw the flood-prone areas. Using the latest mapping technology, including but not limited to geographic information system (GIS)-based format, flood maps are now digitally produced. FEMA promotes a host of other risk reductions, including its National Flood Insurance Program, its Flood Map Center, and its software programs for both individual and commercial interests.

Just as compellingly, FEMA serves as a depository for best practices in the world of catastrophic mitigation. By best practices, we mean a collection of what in fact works in the event of flood or other hazard or threat. FEMA labels the most effective mitigation practices as either superior or commendable. FEMA publishes a compendium of exemplary or best practices in the area of mitigation and preparedness. It asks practitioners in the field to submit programs that they consider not only workable but on the cutting edge of innovation in mitigation.

Finally, FEMA relies on postassessment reports after the hurricane has passed. Postassessment reports are essential for FEMA's future operations since these documents provide lessons learned from past storms; measures of hurricane and coastal flooding preparedness; the need for reform in public policy, building performance, and hurricane mitigation; the assessment of growth and the efficacy of evacuation shelter selection guidelines; and other contingency planning. In the age of smartphones and mobile communications, the agency must incorporate more innovative technology when communicating with its constituencies.[82] As a result, FEMA must aggressively employ all forms of social media to get the warning and alerts communicated across many strata. Mobile apps are an economical and highly efficient method of communication (Figure 10.36).

Mitigation teams play a crucial role in this stage of the natural or catastrophic event. At postassessment, the team can determine the efficacy of risk reduction methods and simultaneously recommend protocols for improvement. Postassessment is central to sound policy making since it looks to

- Assess factors that contributed to disaster effects
- Identify risk reduction opportunities
- Educate the public and local government officials in methods to reduce future risks
- Promote hazard mitigation community planning and project development that will result in sustainable community development
- Provide grants to fund hazard mitigation projects
- Assist communities in marketing the National Flood Insurance Program (NFIP)
- Provide technical assistance to state, tribal, and local governments to utilize rebuilding as an opportunity for enhanced local codes and ordinances

While government entities set the stage for the larger natural disaster policy making, this role does not negate the partnerships and relationships that flourish between the private and public sectors on disaster management and response. Most major private security firms engage in this sort of actual consultancy or management thereto for a particular disaster.

Web Exercise: Watch the disaster preparedness video produced by Wells Fargo Security Services at https://wellsfargoworks.com/run/disaster-preparedness.

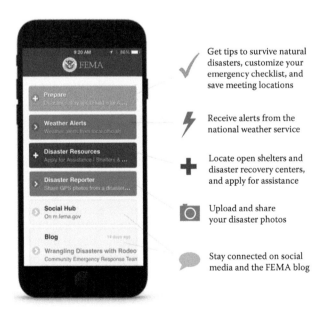

Figure 10.36   FEMA mobile app. http://www.fema.gov/mobile-app.

[82] Congressional Research Service, *Social Media and Disasters: Current Uses, Future Options, and Policy Considerations* (2011).

10.8 PANDEMIC THREATS

The term *pandemic* connotes many things and generally conjures up images of fear and trepidation. Some pandemics are more serious than others. A flu outbreak, the nonlethal variety, is a pandemic of sorts. And then there are those outbreaks that are more serious and that cause death on a global scale, such as the bird flu—caused by H1N1 virus where nearly 300 people died worldwide. See Figure 10.37 for various strains of the flu virus.[83]

At other levels of potential destruction, the fears are well founded, for pandemic instances are global in scope and have the capacity to injure and kill on a widespread basis.[84] Ebola surely ranks higher up in the echelon of threats on the African continent. While the spread appears in check, the reemergence is very likely in the years ahead (Figure 10.38[85]).

Pandemics are not a new phenomenon but have long been tracked globally. Pandemics fall into these basic categories:

- Bird flu is commonly used to refer to AI (see below). Bird flu viruses infect birds, including chickens, other poultry, and wild birds such as ducks.

- AI is caused by influenza viruses that occur naturally among wild birds. Low pathogenic AI is common in birds and causes few problems. Highly pathogenic H5N1 is deadly to domestic fowl, can be transmitted from birds to humans, and is deadly to humans. There is virtually no human immunity and human vaccine availability is very limited.

- Pandemic flu is a virulent human flu that causes a global outbreak, or pandemic, of serious illness. Because there is little natural immunity, the disease can spread easily from person to person. Currently, there is no pandemic flu.

- Seasonal (or common) flu is a respiratory illness that can be transmitted from person to person. Most people have some immunity, and a vaccine is available.[86]

To compare and contrast the pandemic from other types of flu or influenza, see Figure 10.39.[87]

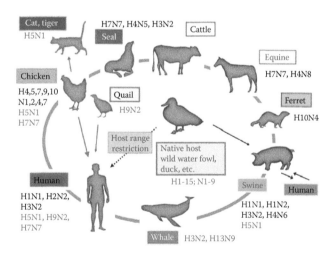

Figure 10.37   Flu virus strains, including hosts and transmitters.

---

[83] World Health Organization, *Timeline of Influenza A (H1N1) Cases: Laboratory Confirmed Cases and Deaths as Reported to WHO*, at http://www.who.int/csr/disease/swineflu/history_map/InfluenzaAH1N1_maps.html.

[84] There are even more legal issues and potential liabilities associated with pandemics when compared to other natural disasters. See B. Courtney, Five legal preparedness challenges for responding to future public health emergencies, *Journal of Law, Medicine & Ethics* 60 (Spring 2011).

[85] World Health Organization Ebola Situation Report (January 6, 2016) available at http://www.who.int/csr/disease/ebola/situation-reports/archive/en/, last accessed February 7, 2016.

[86] U.S. Department of Health and Human Services, PandemicFlu.gov, at http://pandemicflu.gov/general/index.html, last accessed February 27, 2009.

[87] Flu.gov, *About Pandemics, Seasonal Flu versus Pandemic Flu*, www.pandemicflu.gov/individualfamily/about/pandemic/index.html.

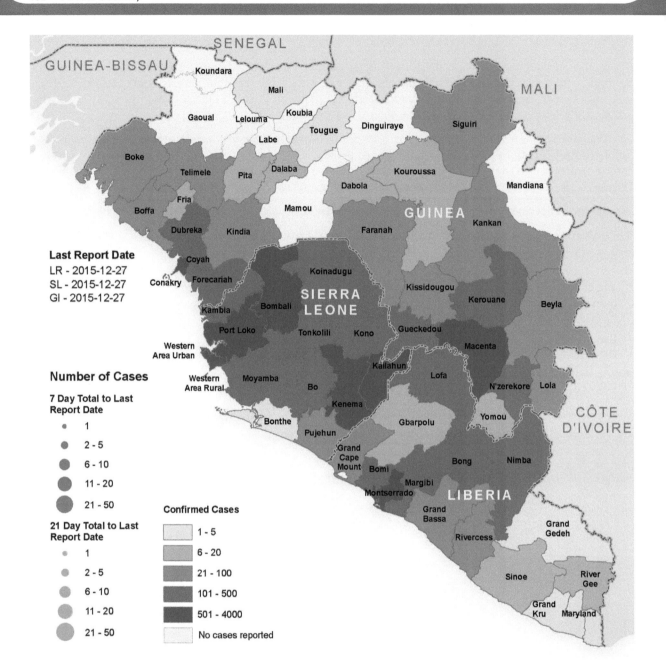

Figure 10.38   Geographical distribution of new and total confirmed cases in Guinea, Liberia, and Sierra Leone, January 6, 2016.

Pandemics are largely the by-product of influenzas (Figure 10.40[88]).

Influenza viruses have mutated and caused pandemics or global epidemics. In the United States, the most severe outbreaks occurred in 1918 (Figures 10.41 and 10.42).

Web Exercise: For a history of flu epidemics, visit http://www.flu.gov/pandemic/history/1918/index.html.

The very definition of pandemic implies a broad impact, a disease or infection with the capacity to cover a large swath of geography. The World Health Organization (WHO) gauges the severity of influenza outbreak by phases—with the

---

[88] Centers for Disease Control and Prevention, Influenza (Flu), at http://www.cdc.gov/flu/images.htm, last accessed February 7, 2016.

Seasonal Flu versus Pandemic Flu	
Pandemic Flu	Seasonal Flu
Rarely happens (three times in 20th century)	Happens annually and usually peaks in January or February
People have little or no immunity because they have no previous exposure to the virus	Usually some immunity built up from previous exposure
Healthy people may be at increased risk for serious complications	Usually only people at high risk, not healthy adults, are at risk of serious complications
Health care providers and hospitals may be overwhelmed	Health care providers and hospitals can usually meet public and patient needs
Vaccine probably would not be available in the early stages of a pandemic	Vaccine available for annual flu season
Effective antivirals may be in limited supply	Adequate supplies of antivirals are usually available
Number of deaths could be high (The U.S. death toll during the 1918 pandemic was approximately 675,000)	Seasonal flu-associated deaths in the United States over 30 years ending in 2007 have ranged from about 3,000 per season to about 49,000 per season.
Symptoms may be more severe	Symptoms include fever, cough, runny nose, and muscle pain
May cause major impact on the general public, such as widespread travel restrictions and school or business closings	Usually causes minor impact on the general public, some schools may close and sick people are encouraged to stay home
Potential for severe impact on domestic and world economy	Manageable impact on domestic and world economy

Figure 10.39   Seasonal flu versus pandemic flu.

infection commencing in lower animal forms, progressing to various levels of human infection to eventual reductions.[89] It is difficult to predict when the next influenza pandemic will occur or how severe it will be.

Responding to pandemic threats and infectious diseases is just as important for the security professional.[90] Globally, the WHO has a system of alerts and notice as to potential or actual pandemics. Each day, the WHO publishes existing or developing threats; an example is shown in Figure 10.43.[91]

At the federal level, a prevention and response program has been formalized. The National Strategy for Pandemic Influenza guides the country's preparedness and response to an influenza pandemic, with the intent of (1) stopping, slowing, or otherwise limiting the spread of a pandemic to the United States; (2) limiting the domestic spread of a pandemic, and mitigating disease, suffering, and death; and (3) sustaining infrastructure and mitigating impact to the economy and the functioning of society.[92] The strategy charges the U.S. Department of Health and Human Services with leading the federal pandemic preparedness. Working with the WHO, federal officials seek to mitigate and contain as well as prevent future events from taking place. See Figure 10.44.[93]

[89] The World Health Organization, *Pandemic Influenza Preparedness and Response: A WHO Guidance Document* (Washington, DC: U.S. Government Printing Office, 2009).

[90] For general advice on the preparedness model, see World Health Organization, Pandemic Influenza Preparedness: Sharing of Influenza Viruses and Access to Vaccines and Other Benefits, 63rd World Health Assembly (April 2010), at http://apps.who.int/gb/ebwha/pdf_files/WHA63/A63_4-en.pdf; see also World Health Organization, Regional Pandemic Influenza Preparedness and Response Plan, 2009–2010 (May 2009), at http://www.afro.who.int/index.php?option=com_docman&task=doc_download&gid=3762; J.R. Langabeer II and J.L. DelliFraine, Incorporating Strategic Management into Public Health Emergency Preparedness, 9 *Journal of Emergency Management* 17 (March/April 2011).

[91] CDC Newsroom, Zika Virus, at https://www.cdc.gov/media/dpk/diseases-and-conditions/zika-virus/dpk-zika-virus.html, last accessed February 7, 2016.

[92] U.S. Department of Homeland Security, *Pandemic Influenza: Preparedness, Response and Recovery Guide for Critical Infrastructure and Key Resources,* 2006, at http://www.flu.gov/planning-preparedness/business/cikrpandemicinfluenzaguide.pdf.

[93] FEMA, Pandemic Influenza Continuity of Operations Annex Template Instructions, 13, at http://www.fema.gov/media-library-data/1396880633531-35405f61d483668155492a7cccd1600b/Pandemic+Influenza+Template.pdf.

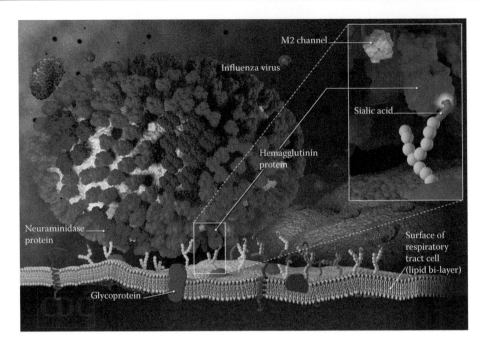

Figure 10.40   Illustration of the very beginning stages of an influenza (flu) infection. Most experts think that influenza viruses spread mainly through small droplets containing influenza virus. These droplets are expelled into the air when people infected with the flu cough, sneeze, or talk. Once in the air, these small infectious droplets can land in the mouths or noses of people who are nearby.

Figure 10.41   In July, an American soldier said that while influenza caused a heavy fever, it "usually only confines the patient to bed for a few days." The mutation of the virus changed all that. (http://www.flu.gov/pandemic/history/1918/the_pandemic/influenza/index.html; National Library of Medicine.)

Pandemic planning also incorporates the resources of state and local law enforcement agencies that are on the frontlines throughout this public health threat.[94] See Figure 10.45.[95]

For business owners and their respective security teams, the pandemic cannot be discounted, for its impact on existing workforces can be utterly devastating, sweeping aside whole labor forces with its pan-global reach.[96] The stark

---

[94] G. Waight et al., The Role of Medical Students in Influenza Pandemic Response, 9 *Journal of Emergency Management* (March/April 2011) 60.

[95] U.S. Department of Health and Human Services, *Law Enforcement Pandemic Influenza Planning Checklist*, www.flu.gov/planning-preparedness/business/lawenforcement.pdf.

[96] See M.A. Gips, Pandemic Resources for Business, 50 *Sec. Mgmt* 32 (2006); see also M.A. Gips, A Dose of Flu Preparedness, 50 *Sec. Mgmt* 20 (2006).

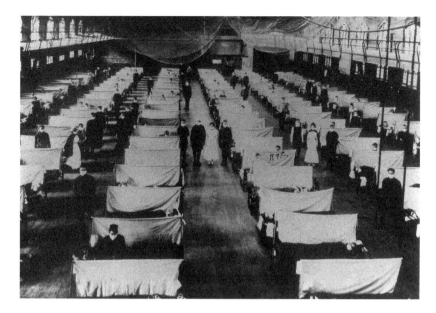

Figure 10.42   When it came to treating influenza, patients, doctors, nurses, and druggists were at a loss. (From http://www.flu.gov/pandemic/history/1918/the_pandemic/iowa_flu2.jpg; Credit: Office of the Public Health Service Historian.)

reality is that everyone is at risk in a global pandemic and whatever steps can be taken by security and safety professionals, to thwart its influence, is wise strategy.[97]

10.8.1 Infectious diseases

The idea that disease can be a threat is not new.[98] In World War I, mustard gas and other virulent gases were used in the battlefield. In Saddam Hussein's Iraq, he thought so little of the Kurds that he used biological agents on them. Anthrax cases have been in the headlines in the last decade. The release of dangerous pathogens and disease-borne agents has allegedly occurred in the battlefield in certain nations, though we have yet to see a full-scale terrorist attack using these agents.[99] See Figure 10.46.

The list of communicable diseases contains a full range of conditions that need reporting to local, state, and federal health authorities. DHS, HHS, and other agencies mandate the reporting of any case that makes the list of diseases. See Table 10.3.[100]

For those entrusted with security, the problem of disease generally comes in the form of biological agents used in terror attacks. Hence, the term "bioterrorism" has become part of the security vocabulary.[101] The CDC tracks and publishes data on the more pressing agents, such as anthrax[102] (Figure 10.47).

Web Exercise: For the Department of Health and Human Services (HHS)-recommended protocol for countermeasures for bioterrorism, see http://emergency.cdc.gov/bioterrorism/prep.asp.

---

[97] Avian Flu and Enterprise Security Preparations, *Sec. Mag.* 8 (July 2006).

[98] See Congressional Research Service, *Federal Efforts to Address the Threat of Bioterrorism: Selected Issues and Options for Congress* (February 8, 2011), at http://www.fas.org/sgp/crs/terror/R41123.pdf; for examples of experts who downplay the threat posed by bioterrorism, see M. Leitenberg, *Assessing the Biological Weapons and Bioterrorism Threat*, Strategic Studies Institute, U.S. Army War College; *Scientists Working Group on Biological and Chemical Weapons, Center for Arms Control and Non-Proliferation, Biological Threats: A Matter of Balance (January 26, 2010)*; Scientists Working Group on Biological and Chemical Weapons, Biological Threats: A Matter of Balance, *Bulletin of the Atomic Scientists* (February 2, 2010).

[99] See Congressional Research Service, *Federal Efforts to Address the Threat of Bioterrorism: Selected Issues and Options for Congress* 8–9 (February 8, 2011).

[100] Centers for Disease Control and Prevention, Nationally Notifiable Infectious Diseases (2013), at http://wwwn.cdc.gov/nndss/conditions/notifiable/2013/infectious-diseases, last accessed February 7, 2016.

[101] See J. Tropper, C. Adamski, C. Vionion, & S. Sapkota, Tracking Antimicrobials Dispensed during an Anthrax Attack: A Case Study from the New Hampshire Anthrax Exercise, 9 *Journal of Emergency Management* 65 (January/February 2011).

[102] Centers for Disease Control and Prevention, at http://www.cdc.gov/anthrax/images/anthrax-timeline.jpg.

CDC Centers for Disease Control and Prevention
CDC 24/7: Saving Lives, Protecting People™

SEARCH ⬜ 🔍

CDC A-Z INDEX ⌄

CDC Newsroom

Newsroom Home

Press Materials —

CDC Newsroom Releases +

Digital Press Kit —

Alcohol

Antibiotic Resistance

Cancer

Cardiovascular Disease

CDC Works for you 24/7

Child Development

Disease & Conditions —

Zika Virus

Food Safety

Healthcare Associated Infection

Healthy Living

HIV-AIDS

Injury, Violence & Safety

Motor Vehicle Safety

Obesity

Prescription Drug Overdose

Teen Pregnancy

Tobacco

Other

Features +

Journal Summaries +

Newsroom Image Library +

Audio/Video +

CDC Spokesperson +

Contact Media Relations +

Connect with CDC Media

📶 Subscribe to Media RSS Feeds

Subscribe to CDC Media

CDC > Newsroom Home > Press Materials > Digital Press Kit > Disease & Conditions

Zika Virus

f 𝕏 +

Zika virus spreads to people primarily through the bite of an infected *Aedes* species mosquito (*Ae. aegypti* and *Ae. albopictus*), but can also be spread during sex by a person infected with Zika to his or her sex partners. Many people infected with Zika won't have symptoms, but for those who do, the illness is usually mild with symptoms lasting from several days to a week. The most common symptoms of Zika are fever, rash, joint pain, and conjunctivitis (red eyes). Severe disease requiring hospitalization is uncommon. However, Zika infection during pregnancy can cause a serious birth defect of the brain called microcephaly and other severe fetal brain defects. Until more is known, CDC recommends that pregnant women avoid traveling to areas with Zika.

Outbreaks of Zika are occurring in many countries and territories, and because the mosquitoes that spread Zika virus are found throughout the world, it is likely that outbreaks will spread to new countries. On Feb. 1, 2016 the World Health Organization (WHO) declared a Public Health Emergency of International Concern because of clusters of microcephaly and other neurological disorders in some areas affected by Zika. Lab tests have confirmed Zika virus in travelers returning to the United States and in some non-travelers who got Zika through sex with a traveler. Local transmission of Zika virus has been reported in the United States (https://www.cdc.gov/zika/intheus/florida-update.html). Additionally, local transmission of Zika has been reported in US territories, including the Commonwealth of Puerto Rico, the US Virgin Islands, and American Samoa.

What CDC is doing

CDC's Emergency Operations Center is activated at Level 1, its highest level, to respond to the Zika outbreak. CDC is working with public health partners and with state, local, and territorial health departments to alert healthcare providers and the public about Zika; post travel notices and other travel-related guidance; provide state health laboratories with diagnostic tests; monitor and report cases of Zika; publish guidelines to inform testing and treatment of people with suspected or confirmed Zika; study what might be responsible for the reported rise in microcephaly; and working with partners around the world to develop a better understanding of Zika virus.

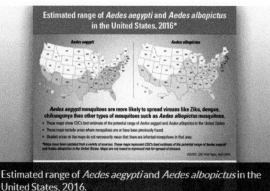

Estimated range of *Aedes aegypti* and *Aedes albopictus* in the United States, 2016.

Language: English ⌄

Contact Information

CDC Media Relations
(404) 639-3286
media@cdc.gov

Vital Signs Issue: Zika and Pregnancy

Factsheet:
English 📄 [1.5MB]
Spanish 📄 [1.55MB]

Zika Summit, April 1, 2016

Zika Action Plan Summit
ZAP Summit Follow-up Teleconferences

Spokespersons

⌄ **Lyle R. Petersen, MD, MPH**

Biography 📄

"We are working with the Ministry of Health in Brazil and other international public health partners to investigate an unexpected increase in the number of babies being born with microcephaly to mothers who were infected with Zika virus during their pregnancy."

Lyle R. Petersen, MD, MPH - Director, Division of Vector-Borne Diseases, NCEZID

❯ **Cindy Moore, MD, PhD**

Figure 10.43   CDC outbreak news on the Zika virus.

Phase 1	No animal influenza virus circulating among animals has been reported to cause infection in humans.
Phase 2	An animal influenza virus circulating in domesticated or wild animals is known to have caused infection in humans and is therefore considered a specific potential pandemic threat.
Phase 3	An animal or human–animal influenza reassortant virus has caused sporadic cases or small clusters of disease in people, but has not resulted in human-to-human transmission sufficient to sustain community-level outbreaks.
Phase 4	Human-to-human transmission (H2H) of an animal or human–animal influenza reassortant virus able to sustain community-level outbreaks has been verified.
Phase 5	The same identified virus has caused sustained community-level outbreaks in two or more countries in one WHO region.
Phase 6	In addition to the criteria defined in Phase 5, the same virus has caused sustained community-level outbreaks in at least one other country in another WHO region.
Postpeak period	Levels of pandemic influenza in most countries with adequate surveillance have dropped below peak levels.
Possible new wave	Level of pandemic influenza activity in most countries with adequate surveillance rising again.
Postpandemic period	Levels of influenza activity have returned to the levels seen for seasonal influenza in most countries with adequate surveillance.

Figure 10.44   Global pandemic phases and the stages for federal government response.

Hospitals, outpatient facilities, health centers, poison control centers, EMS, and other health care partners work with the appropriate state or local health department to acquire funding and develop health care system preparedness through this program. Most hospitals now have designated officers and offices, usually at the CSO level and below, that are responsible for these issues and the training of staff and administration in emergency response.

As for response capacity, hospitals and other medical facilities should have interoperable communications systems, task forces and advisory boards, and a steady stream of communication protocols that interconnect state, local, and federal authorities. Response also implies the capacity to react in the event of a threat. In biological and chemical situations, the medical facility needs adequate stockpiles of vaccine. Medical facilities need to be assured that suitable vendors and companies can supply basic medical goods.

The CDC also plays a major role in any bioterrorism event. Their most important task in the event of bioterrorism is the maintenance and oversight of the National Pharmaceutical Stockpile (NPS). The stockpile is a repository for lifesaving pharmaceuticals, antibiotics, chemical interventions, as well as medical, surgical, and patient support supplies, and equipment for prompt delivery to the site of a disaster, including a possible biological or chemical terrorist event anywhere in the United States. The NPS serves in a support role to local and state emergency, medical, and public health personnel.

A primary purpose of the NPS is to provide critical drugs and medical material that would otherwise be unavailable to local communities. The CDC prioritizes the stockpile based on seriousness of the threat and the availability of both the agent and the antidote. The stockpile targets biological agents: smallpox, anthrax, pneumonic plague, tularemia, botulinum toxin, and viral hemorrhagic fevers (Figure 10.48).

Internet Exercise: Find out about the many activities of the stockpile at http://www.cdc.gov/phpr/stockpile/stockpile. htm#sns1.

10.9 EMERGENCY CRISIS MANAGEMENT AND RESPONSE

It is not enough to catalog the broad-spectrum emergency and crisis situations encountered by security and safety professionals but more pressingly the planning and various protocols to deal with these disasters, threats, and emergencies. Planning is crucial at every stage. From its earliest stages, the emergency and crisis manager must "empower the protectors," meaning those charged with providing emergency and safety protection. Arm them with significant levels of knowledge.[103] John Rendiero calls this preparation and professionalism part of security's "sacred responsibility to provide for the safety of people who fall within their areas of responsibility."[104]

---

[103] K. Lennartsonn, Emergency Memo: Collaborate in a Crisis, *Sec. Mag.* 44 (January 2006).
[104] J. Rendiero, Threat Analysis and Ratings for the Security Manager: The Broad View, *Security* 22 (January 2013).

LAW ENFORCEMENT PANDEMIC INFLUENZA PLANNING CHECKLIST

In the event of pandemic influenza, law enforcement agencies (e.g., State, local, and tribal Police Departments, Sheriff's Offices, Federal law enforcement officers, special jurisdiction police personnel) will play a critical role in maintaining the rule of law as well as protecting the health and safety of citizens in their respective jurisdictions. Planning for pandemic influenza is critical.

To assist you in your efforts, the Department of Health and Human Services (HHS) has developed the following checklist for law enforcement agencies. This checklist provides a general framework for developing a pandemic influenza plan. Each agency or organization will need to adapt this checklist according to its unique needs and circumstances. The key planning activities in this checklist are meant to complement and enhance your existing all-hazards emergency and operational continuity plans. Many of the activities identified in this checklist will also help you to prepare for other kinds of public health emergencies.

Information specific to public safety organizations and pandemic flu preparedness and response can be found at http://www.ojp.usdoj.gov/BJA/pandemic/resources.html. For further information on general emergency planning and continuity of operations, see www.ready.gov. Further information on pandemic influenza can be found at www.pandemicflu.gov.

Develop a pandemic influenza preparedness and response plan for your agency or organization.

Completed	In Progress	Not Started	
☐	☐	☐	Assign primary responsibility for coordinating law enforcement pandemic influenza preparedness planning to a single person (identify back-ups for that person as well) with appropriate training and authority (insert name, title, and contact information here).
☐	☐	☐	Form a multidisciplinary law enforcement/security planning committee to address pandemic influenza preparedness specifically. The planning team should include at a minimum: human resources, health and wellness, computer support personnel, legal system representatives, partner organizations, and local public health resources. Alternatively, pandemic influenza preparedness can be addressed by an existing committee with appropriate skills and knowledge and relevant mission (list committee members and contact information here). This Committee needs to have the plan approved by the Agency Head.
☐	☐	☐	Review Federal, State, and local public health and emergency management agencies' pandemic plans in areas where you operate or have jurisdictional responsibilities. Ensure that your plan is NIMS (National Incident Management System) compliant and align your plan with the local Incident Command System (ICS) and local pandemic influenza plans to achieve a unified approach to incident management. See "State and Local Governments," www.pandemicflu.gov/plan/states/index.html and http://www.fema.gov/emergency/nims/index.shtm.
☐	☐	☐	Verify Command and Control areas of responsibility and authority during a pandemic. Identify alternative individuals in case primary official becomes incapacitated.
☐	☐	☐	Set up chain of command and procedures to signal activation of the agency's response plan, altering operations (e.g., shutting down non-critical operations or operations in affected areas or concentrating resources on critical activities), as well as returning to normal operations.
☐	☐	☐	Determine the potential impact of a pandemic on the agency or organization by using multiple possible scenarios of varying severity relative to illness, absenteeism, supplies, availability of resources, access to legal system representatives, etc. Incorporate pandemic influenza into agency emergency management planning and exercise.
☐	☐	☐	Identify current activities (by location and function) that will be critical to maintain during a pandemic. These essential functions might include 911 systems in communities where law enforcement is responsible for this activity, other communications infrastructures, community policing, information systems, vehicle maintenance, etc. Identify critical resources and inputs (e.g., employees, supplies, subcontractor services/products, and logistics) that are necessary to support these crucial activities.

September 4, 2007
Version 1

Figure 10.45   Law enforcement pandemic influenza planning checklist from the CDC.   (*Continued*)

Develop a pandemic influenza preparedness and response plan for your agency or organization *(continued)*

Completed	In Progress	Not Started	
☐	☐	☐	Develop, review, and approve an official law enforcement/security pandemic influenza preparedness and response plan. This plan represents the output of many or all of the activities contained in this checklist. This plan can be an extension of your current emergency or business continuity plans with a special focus on pandemic influenza and should identify the organizational structure to be used to implement the plan. Include procedures to implement the plan in stages based upon appropriate triggering events.
☐	☐	☐	Develop a pandemic-specific emergency communications plan as part of the pandemic influenza preparedness and response plan, and revise it periodically. The communications plan should identify a communication point of contact, key contacts and back-ups, and chain of communications and clearance. Plan may also include potential collaboration with media representatives on the development of scripts based on likely scenarios guided by the public information officer(s). Coordinate with partners in emergency government and public health in advance.
☐	☐	☐	Designate an individual to monitor pandemic status and collect, organize, and integrate related information to update operations as necessary. Develop a plan for back-up if that person becomes ill during a pandemic. Develop a situational awareness capability that leadership can use to monitor the pandemic situation, support agency decisions, and facilitate monitoring of impact.
☐	☐	☐	Distribute pandemic plan throughout the agency or organization and develop means to document employees/staff received and read the plan.
☐	☐	☐	Allocate resources through the budgeting process as needed to support critical components of preparedness and response identified in your plan.
☐	☐	☐	Periodically test both the preparedness and response plan and the communications plan through drills and exercises; incorporate lessons learned into the plans.

Plan for the impact of a pandemic on your employees

Completed	In Progress	Not Started	
☐	☐	☐	Develop contingency plans for 30 – 40% employee absences. Keep in mind that absences may occur due to personal illness, family member illness, community mitigation measures, quarantines, school, childcare, or business closures, public transportation disruptions, or fear of exposure to ill individuals, as well as first responder, National Guard, or military reserve obligations.
☐	☐	☐	As necessary, plan for cross-training employees, use of auxiliary personnel and recent retirees, recruiting temporary personnel during a crisis, or establishing flexible worksite options (e.g., telecommuting) and flexible work hours (e.g. staggered shifts) when appropriate.
☐	☐	☐	Develop a reporting mechanism for employees to immediately report their own possible influenza illness during a pandemic (24/7).
☐	☐	☐	Establish compensation and leave policies that strongly encourage ill workers to stay home until they are no longer contagious. During a pandemic, employees with influenza-like symptoms (such as fever accompanied by sore throat, muscle aches and cough) should not enter the worksite to keep from infecting other workers. Employees who have been exposed to someone with influenza, particularly ill members of their household, may also be asked to stay home and monitor their symptoms.
☐	☐	☐	Employees who develop influenza-like symptoms while at the worksite should leave as soon as possible. Consult with State and local public health authorities regarding appropriate treatment for ill employees. Prepare policies that will address needed actions when an ill employee refuses to stay away from work. Federal agencies can consult guidance provided by the Office of Personnel Management (OPM) at www.opm.gov/pandemic.
☐	☐	☐	Identify employees who may need to stay home if schools dismiss students and childcare programs close for a prolonged period of time (up to 12 weeks) during a severe pandemic. Advise employees not to bring their children to the workplace if childcare cannot be arranged. Plan for alternative staffing or staffing schedules on the basis of your identification of employees who may need to stay home.
☐	☐	☐	Identify critical job functions and plan now for cross-training employees to cover those functions in case of prolonged absenteeism during a pandemic. Develop succession plans for each critical agency position to ensure the continued effective performance of your organization by identifying and training replacements for key people when necessary. These replacements should be integrated into employee development activities, and should include critical contracted services as well.
☐	☐	☐	Develop policies that focus on preventing the spread of respiratory infections in the workplace. This policy might include social distancing practices, the promotion of respiratory hygiene/cough etiquette, the creation of screening mechanisms for use during a pandemic to examine employees for fever or influenza symptoms, using the full range of available leave policies to facilitate staying home when ill or when a household member is ill, and appropriate attention to environmental hygiene and cleaning. (For more information see the www.pandemicflu.gov and http://www.pandemicflu.gov/plan/community/mitigation.html as well as OPM's guidance at www.opm.gov/pandemic.)

2

Figure 10.45   (Continued) Law enforcement pandemic influenza planning checklist from the CDC.   *(Continued)*

Plan for the impact of a pandemic on your employees *(continued)*

Completed	In Progress	Not Started	
☐	☐	☐	Provide educational programs and materials (language, culture, and reading-level appropriate) to personnel on: • pandemic fundamentals (e.g., signs and symptoms of influenza, modes of transmission, medical care), • personal and family protection and response strategies (e.g., hand hygiene, coughing/sneezing etiquette, etc.). Post instructional signs that illustrate correct infection control procedures in all appropriate locations, including offices, restrooms, waiting rooms, processing rooms, detention facilities, vehicles, etc. and, • community mitigation interventions (e.g., social distancing, etc.). See www.pandemicflu.gov, www.cdc.gov/flu/protect/stopgerms.htm, http://www.cdc.gov/flu/protect/covercough.htm, www.cdc.gov/flu/professionals/infectioncontrol/resphygiene.htm, and http://www.pandemicflu.gov/plan/community/mitigation.html.
☐	☐	☐	Provide training for law enforcement officers, office managers, medical or nursing personnel, and others as needed for performance of assigned emergency response roles. Identify a training coordinator and maintain training records. Ensure all staff are familiar with the local Incident Command System (ICS) and understand the roles and persons assigned within that structure. See http://www.fema.gov/emergency/nims/index.shtm for more information
☐	☐	☐	Stock recommended personal protective equipment (PPE) and environmental infection control supplies and make plans to distribute to employees, contractors, and others (including detainees) as needed. These supplies should include tissues, waste receptacles, single-use disinfection wipes, and alcohol-based hand cleaner (containing at least 60% alcohol). EPA registered disinfectants labeled for human influenza A virus may be used for cleaning offices, waiting rooms, bathrooms, examination rooms, and detention facilities. PPE may include gloves, surgical masks and respirators (disposable N95s or higher respirators or reusable respirators), eye protection, pocket masks (for respiratory resuscitation) and protective cover wear (e.g., impervious aprons). The specific uses for the above supplies will be advised by State and local health officials during a pandemic. Further information can be found at www.pandemicflu.gov. and at http://www.osha.gov/Publications/OSHA3327pandemic.pdf.
☐	☐	☐	Provide information to employees to help them and their families prepare and plan for a pandemic. See www.pandemicflu.gov/plan/individual/index.html.
☐	☐	☐	Work with State and/or local public health to develop a plan for distribution of pandemic influenza vaccine and antiviral medications to law enforcement personnel. See current HHS recommendations for pandemic influenza vaccine and antiviral use at http://www.hhs.gov/pandemicflu/plan/sup6.html and http://www.hhs.gov/pandemicflu/plan/sup7.html.
☐	☐	☐	Encourage and track seasonal influenza vaccination for employees every year. See www.cdc.gov/flu/protect/preventing.htm. Encourage all employees and their families to be up-to-date on all adult and child vaccinations recommended by the Advisory Committee on Immunization Practices. See www.cdc.gov/nip/recs/adult-schedule.htm and www.cdc.gov/nip/recs/child-schedule.htm.
☐	☐	☐	Evaluate employee access to and availability of health care, mental health, social services, community, and faith-based resources during a pandemic, and improve services as needed. See www.hhs.gov/pandemicflu/plan/sup11.html.

Plan for providing services to the public during a pandemic

Completed	In Progress	Not Started	
☐	☐	☐	Identify community–based scenarios and needs likely to occur in a pandemic emergency, and plan how to respond. These might include security of health care and/or vaccine distribution sites, sites that store antiviral medications or vaccines, first-responder activities, protection of critical infrastructure, management of panic and/or public fear, crowd/riot control, enforcement of public health orders, etc.
☐	☐	☐	Develop traffic flow plans to deal with standard traffic management and traffic flow around health-care delivery sites, including vaccine and antiviral distribution sites
☐	☐	☐	Anticipate community vulnerabilities (vulnerable populations, crimes of opportunity, fraudulent schemes, etc.) and specifically train employees to respond.
☐	☐	☐	Develop guidance for managing/assisting special populations (e.g., persons who are homeless, substance abusers, elderly, and individuals with disabilities, etc.) during a pandemic. This will require coordination with public health agencies, social services, correctional facilities, legal system representatives, and community-based organizations serving these populations.
☐	☐	☐	Work with local and/or State health departments or other relevant resources to ensure health protection and care for detainees or other individuals for whom the agency has responsibility.
☐	☐	☐	Establish policies on post-arrest management of an ill or exposed individual, including what to do should a care facility, precinct, and/or other law enforcement facility refuse entry to an ill or exposed individual.

3

Figure 10.45   (Continued) Law enforcement pandemic influenza planning checklist from the CDC.   *(Continued)*

Plan for coordination with external organizations and help your community

Completed	In Progress	Not Started	
☐	☐	☐	Review your pandemic influenza preparedness and response plan with key stakeholders inside and outside the agency, including employee representatives, and determine opportunities for collaboration, modification of the plan, and the development of complementary responsibilities.
☐	☐	☐	Share preparedness and response plans with other law enforcement agencies and law enforcement support agencies in your region or State (to include the National Guard) in order to share resources, identify collaboration strategies, and improve community response efforts. Develop, review, and modify local and State mutual aid agreements, if necessary. Mutual aid during an influenza pandemic can not be counted on as multiple jurisdictions in a given region may be affected simultaneously and have limited aid to offer. Availability of one State's National Guard to support another States plans under an existing compact (e.g., Emergency Management Assistance Compact) may be limited due to competing demands in their home State.
☐	☐	☐	Coordinate all requests for assistance with the next higher level governmental entity (e.g., local officials coordinate with State officials, State officials coordinate with Federal officials). Coordination is essential to ensure the assets: (1) can be provided in accordance with existing laws, (2) the requested resources are available. During a pandemic influenza, assistance from the next higher level of government may be limited due to competing higher priority demands and the effects of the influenza pandemic on these assets.
☐	☐	☐	Integrate planning with emergency service and criminal justice organizations such as courts, corrections, probation and parole, social services, multi-jurisdictional entities, public works, and other emergency management providers (fire, EMS, mutual aid, etc.).
☐	☐	☐	States should plan on utilizing their National Guard to perform law enforcement and security functions during a pandemic influenza. The National Guard under the command and control of the respective State's Governor is not subject to Posse Comitatus Act restrictions as are Federal military forces. Availability of one State's National Guard to support another States plans under an existing compact (e.g., Emergency Management Assistance Compact) may be limited due to competing demands in their home State.
☐	☐	☐	Security functions are essential during a pandemic influenza. Through your city or county attorney, corporation counsel or other appropriate authority, collaborate with the Office of the State Attorney General to clarify and review the authorities granted to law enforcement to include the National Guard. Suggest clarifications and work arounds as needed, and integrate into agency policy, training, and communications activities.
☐	☐	☐	Identify local or regional entities, such as health-care agencies, community organizations, businesses, or critical infrastructure sites, to determine potential collaboration opportunities. This collaboration might involve situational awareness, exercises or drills, or public safety training.
☐	☐	☐	Collaborate with local and/or State public health agencies to assist with the possible investigation of contacts within a suspected outbreak, the enforcement of public health orders, as well as the provision of security, protection, and possibly, critical supplies to quarantined persons. Each law enforcement agency will need to interact with local, State, county, and tribal public health officials to define the extent of the authorities provided from State legislation, develop procedures for the local initiation, implementation, and use of those authorities, as well as define protections from liability for law enforcement that may arise from quarantine and isolation enforcement. Operational planning must be flexible enough to address all scenarios in an all hazards environment, and in light of emerging infectious diseases.

CS113326

Figure 10.45   (Continued) Law enforcement pandemic influenza planning checklist from the CDC.

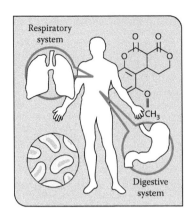

1. A biological attack is the release of germs or other biological substances. Many agents must be inhaled, enter through a cut in the skin, or be eaten to make you sick. Some biological agents can cause contagious diseases, others do not.

Figure 10.46   Biological attack effects on the major systems of the human body.

A failure to plan for emergency and crisis can only be described as a severe dereliction of duty on the part of the security and safety specialist. Risk, one security specialist argues, "never sleeps" and surely those given the responsibility of emergency and crisis management cannot sleep either.[105]

Planning must be integrated at every step of the process when dealing with every sort of disaster and hazard. Ignoring the grim reality of what is in store from disaster and threat will not cut it in the business and corporate world. Security managers and directors must remain in a heightened state of preparedness so that the recovery will be easier to come by.[106] While there are varying approaches to emergency and crisis planning, most experts concur that there are four basic operational levels:

1. *Preparedness: The planning and preparations required to handle an emergency or disaster.* Preparedness entails written plans and procedures to ensure continuity in operations. Preparedness identifies essential supplies and actions, critical positions, specific roles, responsibilities, orders of succession and delegation of specific authorities, and communication, and lays out a plan of evacuation and alternative safety for staff and employees. In the preparedness cycle, the parties train and get ready for what may occur.

2. *Mitigation: The steps and activities related to preventing future emergencies or minimizing their effects.* Once the problem is anticipated and prepared for, mitigation focuses on ways of minimizing the harm or injury from the threat or disaster. In other words, how can the amount of harm be minimized by proper planning. Examples include, but are not limited to, maintenance of electrical power by generator to power critical equipment, secure storage area for food and potables, portable heaters or air conditioners, flood control, and cyber-protection for sensitive records.

3. *Response: The actual activation of the emergency plan.* The term *response* connotes many things, including immediate actions to save lives, protect property and the environment, and meet basic human needs.[107] Response also includes the execution of emergency plans and actions to support short-term recovery. The level of response will

---

[105] B. Mitchell, Protecting Your People, Property and Posterior: The Top 11 Errors in Emergency Planning, *Sec. Mag.* 38 (May 2013).

[106] J. Pekich, What Happens When Prevention Fails, *Sec. Mag.* 84 (November 2013).

[107] R. McCreight, Establishing a National Emergency Response and Disaster Assistance Corps, *Homeland Defense Journal* 10 (September 2007); C. Hines, Disaster Management, 58 *Law & Order* 54 (August 2006).

Table 10.3   List of diseases that must be reported

Anthrax	Arboviral diseases, neuroinvasive, and non-neuroinvasive	Babesiosis
Botulism/*Clostridium botulinum*	Brucellosis	Chancroid
Chlamydia trachomatis infection	Cholera	Coccidioidomycosis/valley fever
Cryptosporidiosis	Cyclosporiasis	Dengue virus infections
Diphtheria	Ehrlichiosis and anaplasmosis	Giardiasis
Gonorrhea	*Haemophilus influenzae*, invasive disease	Hansen's disease/leprosy
Hantavirus pulmonary syndrome (HPS)	Hemolytic uremic syndrome, postdiarrheal (HUS)	Hepatitis A, acute
Hepatitis B, acute	Hepatitis B, chronic	Hepatitis B, perinatal infection
Hepatitis C, acute	Hepatitis C, past or present	HIV infection (AIDS has been reclassified as HIV Stage III) (AIDS/HIV)
Influenza-associated pediatric mortality	Invasive pneumococcal disease (IPD)/*Streptococcus pneumoniae*, invasive disease	Legionellosis/Legionnaires' disease or Pontiac fever
Listeriosis	Lyme disease	Malaria
Measles/rubeola	Meningococcal disease	Mumps
Novel influenza A virus infections	Pertussis/whooping cough	Plague
Poliomyelitis, paralytic	Poliovirus infection, nonparalytic	Psittacosis/ornithosis
Q fever	Rabies, animal	Rabies, human
Rubella/German measles	Rubella, congenital syndrome (CRS)	Salmonellosis
Severe acute respiratory syndrome-associated coronavirus disease (SARS)	Shiga toxin-producing *Escherichia coli* (STEC)	Shigellosis
Smallpox/variola	Spotted fever rickettsiosis	Streptococcal toxic shock syndrome (STSS)
Syphilis	Tetanus/*Clostridium tetani*	Toxic shock syndrome (other than streptococcal) (TSS)
Trichinellosis/trichinosis	Tuberculosis (TB)	Tularemia
Typhoid fever	Vancomycin-intermediate *Staphylococcus aureus* and vancomycin-resistant *Staphylococcus aureus* (VISA/VRSA)	Varicella/chickenpox
Varicella deaths	Vibriosis	Viral hemorrhagic fever (VHF)
Yellow fever		

depend upon the circumstances and conditions at specific locations.[108] In the preparedness and mitigation phase, the planners have already authored an emergency action plan and conducted various risk and vulnerability assessments. When disaster and threat strike, the emergency and security team launches and implements these strategies to secure the facility and personnel.

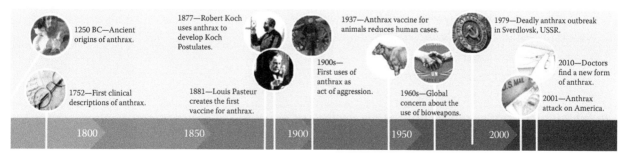

Figure 10.47   Anthrax timeline.

---

[108] For an example of distinctly and very differently FEMA would act in the case of a Dirty Bomb, see Congressional Research Service, "Dirty Bombs": Technical Background, Attack Prevention and Response, Issues for Congress (2011), at http://www.fas.org/sgp/crs/nuke/R41890.pdf.

Figure 10.48   CDC stockpiles.

4. *Recovery: The actions needed to restore normal operations—sometimes labeled business continuity.* Planning for aftereffects from disaster and threat demands not only adherence to an EAP but a workable command and control structure. After the event, medical intervention, damage assessment, emergency repairs, dealing with ongoing hazards, as well as contact with insurance contractors and necessary vendors next take place in the planning cycle.

At center of the emergency planning is how to assure the continuation or minimization of business or individual harm—how do we ensure that life can go on as "usual" despite the difficult challenges caused by the disaster or threat?[109]

Web Exercise: Find out the many FEMA careers in emergency services at https://service.govdelivery.com/accounts/USDHSFEMA/subscriber/new?topic_id=USDHSFEMA_114.

To know how to plan, prepare, mitigate, respond, and recover calls for a full and comprehensive understanding of the entity we seek to protect. Accordingly, security professionals urge a series of questions and concerns that must be asked to give any guarantees of continuity, namely,

1. Have all business partners been included in the plan?
2. What is the entity's precise headcount?
3. What is the chain of command and command structure?
4. What backup systems exist for cell phones and IT?
5. Has sufficient training, in compliance with law, taken place?
6. What is the status of fire extinguishers and equipment?
7. Is there an approved evacuation map?
8. What is the medical emergency plan?
9. What is the first aid and blood plan?
10. What is the evacuation plan for disabled and special needs people?
11. Is there an EAP?[110]

See Figure 10.49.

---

[109] J. Schmidt, How to Prepare for "Business Not as Usual," *Sec. Mag.* 30 (April 2012).
[110] *Ibid.*

IAEM Find a Job

Please note that State/Province, Country and Language selection boxes are populated based on current job listings. Therefore, only current job listings with State/Prov, Country or Language specified will show up in the drop down menus for each category. To expand your search, leave these boxes blank.

Search Options

Search Text [ ]	Category [All Categories ▾]	Type [All ▾] State/Province [Any ▾]
Education [Any Level ▾]	Language [Any/All ▾]	Salary [Any ▾] Country [Any/All ▾]

[clear all] [search]

Currently sorting by **Job posted date descending**. Alternating colors represent a change of **Job posted date**.

Details	Job Title	Organization	Category	Type	State/Prov	Country	Posted	Expires
view	Emergency Management Specialist	Coconino County Department of Emergency Management	Emergency Management		AZ	UNITED STATES	08/27/2016	09/09/2016
view	IT Specialist - Programmer	FEMA	Emergency Management		DC	UNITED STATES	08/25/2016	09/14/2016
view	American Sign Language Interpreter-2 Positions	FEMA	Emergency Management		DC	UNITED STATES	08/25/2016	11/23/2016
view	Emergency Management Specialist II, Grade 26	Montgomery County Office of Emergency Management and Homeland Security	Emergency Management	Full time	MD	UNITED STATES	08/25/2016	09/15/2016
view	Emergency Management Division Chief	Durham County Fire Marshal/Emergency Management	Emergency Management	Full time	NC	UNITED STATES	08/25/2016	09/02/2016
view	*Closing Date Extended* EM Division Chief	Durham County Fire Marshal/Emergency Management	Emergency Management	Full time	NC	UNITED STATES	08/25/2016	09/10/2016
view	*Closing Date Extended* Senior Emergency Management Coordinator	Durham County Fire Marshal/Emergency Management	Emergency Management		NC	UNITED STATES	08/25/2016	09/10/2016
view	Deputy Emergency Management Coordinator	Portage County Wisconsin	Emergency Management	Full time	WI	UNITED STATES	08/25/2016	09/08/2016
view	Emergency Management Coordinator (Planning Section Chief)	Cape Coral Fire Department Division of Emergency Management	Emergency Management	Full time	FL	UNITED STATES	08/25/2016	09/10/2016
view	OES Incident Management Coordinator	City of San José Office of Emergency Services (OES)	Emergency Management	Full time	CA	UNITED STATES	08/25/2016	09/25/2016
view	IUPUI Emergency Management Coordinator	Indiana University Emergency Management and Continuity	Emergency Management	Full time	IN	UNITED STATES	08/24/2016	09/05/2016
view	IUPUI Emergency Management Coordinator	Indiana University Emergency Management and Continuity	Emergency Management		IN	UNITED STATES	08/24/2016	09/05/2016
view	Emergency Management Coordinator	City of Hermosa Beach	Emergency Management		CA	UNITED STATES	08/24/2016	11/22/2016
view	Section Head, Operations	Ministry of Environment	Emergency Management	Full time	BC	CANADA	08/24/2016	09/09/2016

Figure CP10.1 Career Profile: Career list from International Association of Emergency Managers.

Given the horrid results of governmental reaction to disaster and threat, and the overall incompetence of leaders in time of disaster, a great deal of pain and suffering occurred needlessly. Who could forget the detached flyover of President George Bush with his flyover during Katrina when effective leadership calls for a confrontation with this reality? This is not something that is to be avoided, rather something to be dealt with directly and intimately. Crisis management during disasters calls for a straight look and a straight shooter who softens the blow rather than festers the worry.[111]

Too often, our leaders, including CSOs and their teams, fail to fully appreciate the emotional costs and toll of the crisis. It was painfully obvious that a response and recovery protocol had completely escaped those entrusted with the disaster. One thing that is surely certain, a prominent CSO argues, is that "there will be ever less time to plan and control fast-moving and unpredictable events; furthermore, there will be even greater penalties and burdens for failing to react effectively."[112] At the governmental level, some uniformity of plan and action were taken up by

---

[111] See Delivery Calm in Crisis Times, *Sec. Mag.* 10 (January 2000).
[112] R. Hall, Detecting Early Signs of Trouble, 50 *Sec. Mag.* 50 (2006).

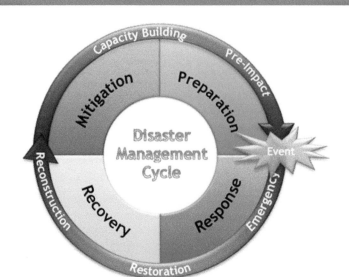

Figure 10.49 Disaster management cycle.

DHS and FEMA, by the creation and implementation of national homeland security model—the National Response Framework.[113]

10.9.1 National Response Framework

The Framework is a guide for a national, all-hazards response—from the smallest incident to the largest catastrophe.[114] The Framework identifies the key response principles, as well as the roles and structures that organize national response. How communities, states, the federal government, the private sector, and nongovernmental partners apply these principles for a coordinated, effective national response is the chief aim of the National Response Framework.[115]

Web Exercise: Familiarize yourself with the many resources relevant to a response plan by visiting the National Response Framework resource center at http://www.fema.gov/national-response-framework.

The Framework systematically incorporates public sector agencies at all levels, the private sector, and nongovernmental organizations. The Framework also emphasizes the importance of personal preparedness by individuals and households. FEMA lays out the key principles of a functional and effective response plan in Figure 10.50.

The Framework operates from very distinct and enlightened premises. Its ideology is primarily one of decentralization. Local, decentralized response is usually more responsive than waiting in line for the federals to show up. Here again, we saw clearly how New Orleans acted without decisiveness since it had been, at least in some ways, trained to await the federal invasion before taking action itself. The response must be first and foremost be local. As even FEMA points out:

> Incidents begin and end locally, and most are wholly managed at the local level. Many incidents require unified response from local agencies, NGOs, and the private sector, and some require additional support from neighboring jurisdictions or the State. A small number require Federal support.[116]

---

[113] For a list of authorities that permit federal, state, and local authorities to engage in homeland defense and intervention, see http://www.fema.gov/pdf/emergency/nrf/nrf-authorities.pdf.

[114] See Department of Homeland Security, *National Response Framework Fact Sheet*, at http://www.fema.gov/pdf/emergency/nrf/NRFOnePageFactSheet.pdf.

[115] A. Bitto, Say What? Who? Me? Right Here in the Trenches? Collaborate or What? Seeking Common Ground in Regional All-Hazards Preparedness Training, 69 *Journal of Environmental Health* 28–33 (January/February 2007).

[116] Department of Homeland Security, *National Response Framework* 9 (January 2008). Despite this preference, national exercises are still in vogue at FEMA. DHS still sponsors National Level Exercise programs. See E. Pitman, National Response, *Emergency Management* 30 (March/April, 2011).

Engaged Partnership with the Whole Community

Engaging the whole community is critical to successfully achieving a secure and resilient Nation, and individual and community preparedness is a key component. An effective partnership relies on engaging all elements of the whole community and, when appropriate, international partners. Engaged partnership and coalition building includes clear, consistent, effective, and culturally appropriate communication and shared situational awareness. Participation within these partnerships should include advocates for all elements of the whole community. The most effective partnerships within a community capitalize on all available resources—identifying, developing, fostering, and strengthening new and existing coordinating structures to create a unity of effort.

Scalability, Flexibility, and Adaptability in Implementation

Core capabilities should be scalable, flexible, and adaptable and executed as needed to address the full range of threats and hazards as they evolve. Scalable, flexible, and adaptable coordinating structures are essential in aligning the key roles and responsibilities to deliver the core capabilities. The flexibility of such structures helps ensure that communities across the country can organize efforts to address a variety of risks based on their unique needs, capabilities, demographics, governing structures, and nontraditional partners.

Integration Among the Frameworks

The five mission areas aid in organizing national preparedness activities. Core capabilities are highly interdependent and applicable to any threat or hazard. All five mission areas integrate with each other through interdependencies, shared assets, and overlapping objectives.

Three core capabilities span all five mission areas: Planning; Public Information and Warning; and Operational Coordination. The common core capabilities serve to unify the mission areas, promote unity of effort, and are essential foundations for the success of the remaining core capabilities.

In addition to the three common core capabilities, a number of other core capabilities involve more than one mission area (e.g., Protection and Prevention share a number of common elements and rely on many of the same core capabilities). Integration among mission area resources and processes is important to maximize core capabilities and minimize risk. Many of the core capabilities can be linked across mission areas through shared assets and services. For example, functionality provided through geospatial services that build situational awareness can be applied across multiple Response core capabilities, as well as core capabilities in the other four mission areas.

Figure 10.50 Response doctrine key themes.

The National Response Framework advances a partner-based model—fully recognizing that the locality can and will do a better job in response. Incidents must be managed at the lowest possible jurisdictional level and supported by additional capabilities at a higher level if and when needed.

On the other hand, it is crucial that a chain of command and leadership be part of any response and recovery program. Another feature of the National Response Framework is its inherent flexibility. Instead of a one-size-fits-all mentality, the Framework urges emergency professionals to apply a response that fits the event. Incidents come in many shapes and sizes, and their complexity or simplicity will affect the nature of the response. As the Framework recommends:

> As incidents change in size, scope, and complexity, the response must adapt to meet requirements. The number, type, and sources of resources must be able to expand rapidly to meet needs associated with a given incident. The Framework's disciplined and coordinated process can provide for a rapid surge of resources from all levels of government, appropriately scaled to need. Execution must be flexible and adapted to fit each individual incident. For the duration of a response, and as needs grow and change, responders must remain nimble and adaptable. Equally, the overall response should be flexible as it transitions from the response effort to recovery.[117]

Finally, the Framework advances the perpetual concept of readiness in the design of any response plan. Private and public partners must be prepared and ready to carry out the response mission, must understand the dilemma, have mastered the problem, and present themselves as being capable of a prepared and ready response.[118] Responders must not victimize those harmed by delay in their operations or responsibilities and must move quickly in response and avoid the cumbersome delays that always emerge from a lack of preparation and readiness.[119] Not only must emer-

---

[117] Department of Homeland Security, *The National Response Framework* (Washington, DC: U.S. Government Printing Office, January 2008) 10, at http://www.fema.gov/pdf/emergency/nrf/nrf-core.pdf.

[118] Department of Homeland Security, *National Response Framework*, 27.

[119] See R. Humphress, Building an Emergency Response Competency System: Optimizing Emergency Personnel Mobilization, 1 *Journal of Homeland Security and Emergency Management* 4 (2007); D. Philpott, Emergency Preparedness Communications, *Homeland Defense Journal* 44 (June 2007).

gency and justice professionals know the risk is to be dealt with, but just as compellingly, they need to place a high priority on the timeliness of response:

> Acting swiftly and effectively requires clear, focused communication and the processes to support it. Without effective communication, a bias toward action will be ineffectual at best, likely perilous. An effective national response relies on disciplined processes, procedures, and systems to communicate timely, accurate, and accessible information on the incident's cause, size, and current situation to the public, responders, and others. Well-developed public information, education strategies, and communication plans help to ensure that lifesaving measures, evacuation routes, threat and alert systems, and other public safety information are coordinated and communicated to numerous diverse audiences in a consistent, accessible, and timely manner.[120]

Web Exercise: Visit the National Incident Management System website at https://www.fema.gov/national-incident-management-system.

Depending upon the subject matter, the critical infrastructure in question, and the event itself, any response will need to be tailored to it. For example, the National Response Framework resource location provides response protocols for industries and business, critical infrastructure, and other likely targets in need of response.

10.9.2 Continuity and resiliency and the security industry

The desire to keep business and industry in operational mode during times of disaster and threat is a foremost policy consideration in the boardroom and in the CSO and his security team's overall design. Keeping things up and running represents the best about preparedness, for here the security professionals anticipate the harm to be inflicted and take preventative steps and remedial actions to insure the consequences are not worse than they should be. Disasters can devastate entire industries and injure large populations of workers and residents. It is crucial to envision not only the harm that shall be inflicted but more essentially the steps to soften this negative impact. Security directors and managers are on the frontline of assuring a resilient reaction—not being flattened or destroyed by the event and doing all possible to rebound and recover from it. Continuity assumes longevity, not mere survival, and all of the systems that make business or institutions continually capable of operations need to be considered—from communications to marketing, from storage to dispersal of product, from transport of persons and assets to safer ground, from prevention from injury to treatment of inevitable damages that occur in large-scale disasters. CSOs must engage all the interested parties in the continuity plan by consulting with "legal, human resources, marketing communications and IT to create a holistic plan and response program for their enterprise."[121]

Just as importantly, the security team must train employees on the many nuances of a continuity plan and set up exercises, educational sessions, and table-top exercises that provide a realistic audition into the disaster.[122] Information should be readily shared with all interested parties and stakeholders. The day of the disaster is not the day to educate the constituencies essential to success in continuity planning.[123]

Continuity and crisis planning can be reduced to a five-step process as is clear in Figure 10.51.

The cycle here stresses information gathering in the form of risk assessment and continuity self-assessment as well the full integration of the entire staff of the business or institution in question. Continuity planning demands an active, fully engaged population, not a disinterested group of employees waiting to be told what to do. The stress also includes the development of a clear-cut chain of command and control and an ongoing dedication to training, testing, and simulation. Do not forget the basic of IT, communications, a broad rather than narrow view of mission and well documented processes for dealing with infrastructure issues that provide a real chance for continuance and assure a resilient reaction to the disaster.[124] CSOs should never minimize the potentiality for harm such as the severe potential for damages emerging from weather patterns, flooding, and loss of utilities. All of these factors have the potential to disrupt the continuity of business operations.[125]

---

[120] Department of Homeland Security, *National Response Framework*, 10–11.
[121] M. McCort, Enterprise Resilience Means Business, *Sec. Mag.* 10 (July 2013).
[122] See Business Continuity Put to the Test, *Sec. Mag.* 12 (March 2011).
[123] I. Walks, Emergency Response Outside the Envelope, 47 *Sec. Mgmt* 52 (2003).
[124] K. Howells, Ten Ways to Improve Your Business Continuity Plan, *Sec. Mag.* 16 (January 2013).
[125] M. McCort, Everybody Talks about the Weather, but…, *Sec. Mag.* 10 (January 2014).

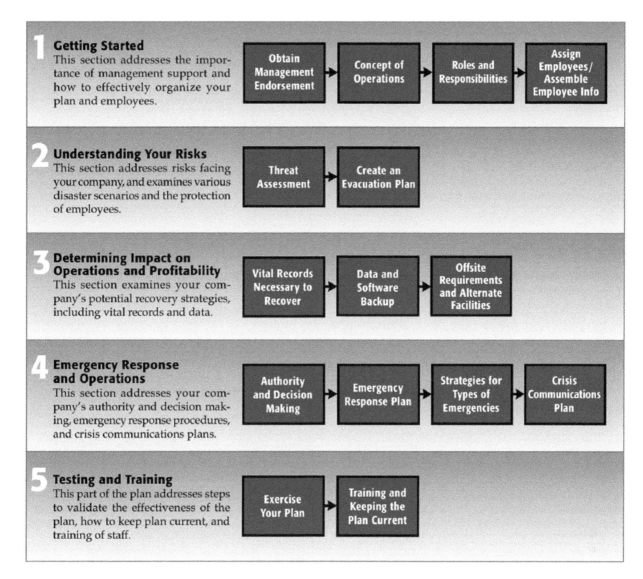

Figure 10.51   Continuity and crisis planning process flowchart.

To not plan for continuity assures another inevitability, the rising insurance premium, an economic damage that can be minimized by a vigorous and robust program of continuity planning.[126] Some businesses designate a specified business continuity specialist, or a committee that engages the entire hierarchy of the company or institutions. See Figure 10.52.

In the final analysis, the private security industry plays a crucial role in the continuous operation of business and industry at times of disaster and threat. It is crucial that security managers and directors create a climate, a "culture of preparedness," throughout the enterprise that assures "responsibility, compliance and prudence" in business operations.[127]

To assure business continuity and resiliency, certain steps are essential for the security director or manager. First, a risk assessment plan, covered in other sections of this text, should be fully completed—a document that shall lay out

[126] Global News and Analysis, Catastrophes of 2011 Force Businesses to Reassess Insurance Needs, *Sec. Mag.* 14 (2012).

[127] See C. Haase, Leading with Resiliency during a Natural Disaster, *Sec. Mag.* 48 (March 2011).

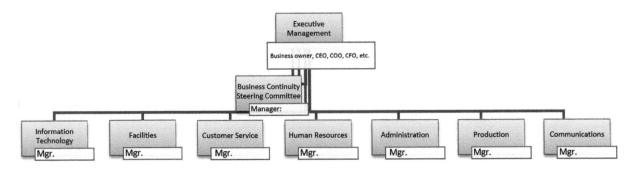

Figure 10.52   Crisis management hierarchy.

the most likely vulnerabilities to plan for. Second, a continuity self-assessment study goes a long way to anticipating those factors that influence the lifeblood of operations at any firm or business.[128]

The self-assessment looks at people, technology, premises, product, vendors, and customers, which are just a few of the variables the business continuity model seeks to measure. The United Kingdom has produced an unrivaled tool-kit for conducting this type of assessment. The chief criteria of review are charted in Figure 10.53.[129] Also useful is the business continuity plan checklist shown in Figure 10.54.[130]

10.9.3 Evacuation plan

All businesses and institutional clients need an evacuation plan that assures the safety of employees in times of disaster or threat. The CSO and safety committee are generally charged with the development of the said plan. See Figure 10.56 for a sample template.

PEOPLE
- Inventory of staff skills not utilised within their existing roles - to enable redeployment
- Process mapping and documentation - to allow staff to undertake roles with which they are unfamiliar
- Multi-skill training of each individual
- Cross-training of skills across a number of individuals
- Succession planning
- Use of third party support, backed by contractual agreements
- Geographical separation of individuals or groups with core skills can reduce the likelihood of losing all those capable of undertaking a specific role

PREMISES
- Relocation of staff to other accommodation owned by your organisation such as training facilities
- Displacement of staff performing less urgent business processes with staff performing a higher priority activity. Care must be taken when using this option that backlogs of the less urgent work do not become unmanageable.
- Remote working – this can be working from home or working from other locations
- Use premises provided by other organisations, including those provided by third-party specialists
- Alternative sources of plant, machinery and other equipment

TECHNOLOGY
- Maintaining the same technology at different locations that will not be affected by the same business disruption
- Holding older equipment as emergency replacement or spares

INFORMATION
- Ensure data is backed-up and it is kept off site
- Essential documentation is stored securely (e.g. fire proof safe)
- Copies of essential documentation are kept elsewhere

SUPPLIERS AND PARTNERS
- Storage of additional supplies at another location
- Dual or multi-sourcing of materials
- Identification of alternative suppliers
- Encouraging or requiring suppliers/partners to have a validated business continuity capability
- Significant penalty clauses on supply contracts

STAKEHOLDERS
- Mechanisms in place to provide information to stakeholders
- Arrangement to ensure vulnerable groups are accommodated

Previous view

Previous Next

Contents

Figure 10.53   Self-assessment criteria.

---

[128] NFPA, Standard on Disaster/Emergency Management and Business Continuity Programs (2013), at http://www.nfpa.org/assets/files/AboutTheCodes/1600/1600-13-PDF.pdf

[129] Her Majesty's Government, How Prepared Are You? Business Continuity Management Toolkit, at https://www.gov.uk/government/uploads/system/uploads/attachment_data/file/137994/Business_Continuity_Managment_Toolkit.pdf

[130] Business Development Bank of Canada, Business Continuity Plan Checklist, at https://www.bdc.ca/en/documents/businesscontinuityplanning/checklist.pdf

Business Continuity Plan Checklist

Please note: some of these items listed below are pandemic-specific.

1. Plan for the impact of an emergency on your business:

Tasks	Not Started	In Progress	Completed
1. Identify an emergency coordinator and/or team with defined roles and responsibilities for preparedness and response planning. The planning process should include input from labour representatives.	☐	☐	☐
2. Identify essential employees and other critical inputs (e.g. raw materials, suppliers, sub-contractor services/ products, and logistics) required to maintain business operations by location and function during an emergency .	☐	☐	☐
3. Train and prepare ancillary workforce (e.g. contractors, employees in other job titles/descriptions, retirees).	☐	☐	☐
4. Develop and plan for scenarios likely to result in an increase or decrease in demand for your products and/or services during an emergency (e.g. effect of restriction on mass gatherings, need for hygiene supplies, disruptions to telecommunications or transport infrastructure).	☐	☐	☐
5. Determine potential impact of an emergency on company business financials using multiple possible scenarios that affect different product lines and/or production sites.	☐	☐	☐
6. Determine potential impact of an emergency on business-related domestic and international travel (e.g. quarantines, border closures).	☐	☐	☐
7. Find up-to-date, reliable information on emergencies from community public health, emergency management, and other sources and make sustainable links.	☐	☐	☐
8. Establish an emergency communications plan and revise periodically. This plan includes identification of key contacts (with back-ups), chain of communications (including suppliers and customers), and processes for tracking and communicating business and employee status.	☐	☐	☐

Figure 10.54   Business continuity plan checklist.   (*Continued*)

10.10 CONCLUSION

The world of crisis and emergency is naturally aligned to the private security industry. Since the industry is tasked with assuring the safety and security of assets and people, it cannot reserve its dedicated service based on crime and criminality alone but instead must inevitably branch out into a brave new world of threats and hazards. Natural disasters in the form of storm and flood, hurricane and tornado, fire, and drought all have extraordinary capacity to destroy assets, whether fixed or agricultural. In fact, a full-fledged natural disaster can do more harm than any terrorist would ever be capable of and because of this potentiality, the private security industry has taken on a pre-eminent role in preparedness regarding natural risks, in the assessment of specific vulnerabilities relative to those natural events that might cause heavy damages, and in the design and authorship of response, mitigation, and recovery mechanisms that minimize the destruction and enable continuity in operations.

Tasks	Not Started	In Progress	Completed
9. Implement an exercise/drill to test your plan, and revise periodically.	☐	☐	☐

2. Plan for the impact of an emergency on your employees and customers:

Tasks	Not Started	In Progress	Completed
1. Forecast and allow for employee absences during an emergency due to factors such as personal illness, family member illness, community containment measures and quarantines, school and/or business closures, and public transportation closures.	☐	☐	☐
2. In the event of a pandemic, implement guidelines to modify the frequency and type of face-to-face contact (e.g. hand-shaking, seating in meetings, office layout, shared workstations) among employees and between employees and customers.	☐	☐	☐
3. Encourage/ track annual employee flu vaccination.	☐	☐	☐
4. Evaluate employee access to and availability of healthcare services during an emergency, and improve services as needed.	☐	☐	☐
5. Evaluate employee access to and availability of mental health and social services during an emergency including corporate, community, and faith-based resources, and improve services as needed.	☐	☐	☐
6. Identify employees and key customers with special needs, and incorporate the requirements of such persons into your preparedness plan.	☐	☐	☐

3. Establish policies to be implemented during an emergency:

Tasks	Not Started	In Progress	Completed
1. Establish policies for employee compensation and sick-leave absences unique to an emergency (e.g. non-punitive, liberal leave). Include policies applicable to a pandemic, to state when a previously ill person is no longer infectious and can return to work after illness.	☐	☐	☐
2. Establish flexible policies re: worksite (e.g. tele-commuting) and work hours (e.g.	☐	☐	☐

Figure 10.54   (Continued) Business continuity plan checklist.   (*Continued*)

On the man-made side, the challenges are just as daunting with terrorism, WMD, biological warfare, and pandemic release of toxins or other harmful material with the potential to destroy assets and persons at incalculable rates. Hence, the chapter correctly targets chemical, biological, radiological, and other toxic threats capable of mass destruction. Private security must also evaluate the human actor bent on this sort of devastation whether he or she be a terrorist or a madman. Either way, the private security industry must adopt methods and protocols that prevent crisis and whole-scale harm from occurring and be just as nimble in returning to our former safety and security. The chapter addition-ally provides a host of practice tools, forms, checklists, and practical recommendations on how to achieve these goals.

Keywords

accident prevention	business continuity plans	continuity planning
asset protection	compliance	crisis planning

staggered shifts).

Tasks	Not Started	In Progress	Completed
3. In the case of a pandemic, establish policies to prevent influenza spread at the worksite (e.g. respiratory hygiene/cough etiquette, and prompt exclusion of people with influenza symptoms).	☐	☐	☐
4. In the case of a widespread pandemic, establish policies for employees who have been exposed to pandemic influenza, are suspected to be ill, or become ill at the worksite (e.g. infection control response, immediate mandatory sick leave).	☐	☐	☐
5. Establish policies for restricting travel to affected geographic areas (consider both domestic and international sites), evacuating employees working in or near an affected area when an emergency occurs, and guidance for employees returning from affected areas.	☐	☐	☐
6. Set up authorities, triggers, and procedures for activating and terminating the company's response plan, altering business operations (e.g. shutting down operations in affected areas), and transferring business knowledge to key employees.	☐	☐	☐

4. Allocate resources to protect your employees and customers during an emergency:

Tasks	Not Started	In Progress	Completed
1. Provide sufficient and accessible emergency supplies (e.g. safety equipment, hand-hygiene products, tissues and receptacles for their disposal) in all business locations.	☐	☐	☐
2. Enhance communications and information technology infrastructures as needed to support employee telecommuting and remote customer access.	☐	☐	☐
3. Ensure availability of medical consultation and advice for emergency response.	☐	☐	☐

Figure 10.54   (Continued) Business continuity plan checklist.   (Continued)

5. Communicate to and educate your employees:

Tasks	Not Started	In Progress	Completed
1. Develop and disseminate programs and materials covering emergency fundamentals (e.g. safety procedures, evacuation, signs and symptoms of influenza, modes of transmission, etc.)	☐	☐	☐
2. Anticipate employee fear and anxiety, rumours and misinformation and plan communications accordingly.	☐	☐	☐
3. Ensure that communications are culturally and linguistically appropriate.	☐	☐	☐
4. Disseminate information to employees about your emergency preparedness and response plan.	☐	☐	☐
5. Provide information for the at-home care of ill employees and family members.	☐	☐	☐
6. Develop platforms (e.g. hotlines, dedicated Websites) for communicating emergency status and actions to employees, vendors, suppliers, and customers inside and outside the worksite in a consistent and timely way, including redundancies in the emergency contact system.	☐	☐	☐
7. Identify community sources for timely and accurate emergency information (domestic and international) and resources for obtaining counter-measures (e.g. specialized safety equipment, vaccines and antivirals).	☐	☐	☐

6. Coordinate with external organizations and help your community:

Tasks	Not Started	In Progress	Completed
1. Collaborate with insurers, health plans, and major local healthcare facilities to share your emergency plans and understand their capabilities and plans.	☐	☐	☐
2. Collaborate with federal, provincial, and local public health agencies and/or emergency responders to participate in their planning processes, share your emergency plans, and understand their capabilities and plans.	☐	☐	☐
3. Communicate with local or provincial public health agencies and/or emergency responders about the assets and/or services your business could contribute to the community.			
4. Share best practices with other businesses in your communities, chambers of commerce, and associations to improve community response efforts.			

Figure 10.54   (Continued) Business continuity plan checklist.

Newark, NJ - Business Continuity Management Specialist

Thursday, 14 April 2016 05:00

Job Summary:

To provide professional, specialized skills including project management, problem analysis and resolution related to Business Continuity, Disaster Recovery as it relates to Information Technology and Incident/Emergency Management process.

Responsibilities:
- Contribute to the development of Business Continuity Management best practices suitable for Horizon Blue Cross Blue Shield of NJ to sustain viable operations during disruption.
- Partner with various internal department to assist & coordinate the annual Business Continuity Management plan maintenance.
- Lead the annual Business Impact Analysis process.
- Assist in the development of recovery strategies in collaboration with the Disaster Recovery and IT teams.
- Provide maintenance and reporting of the BCM plans status to Senior Management.
- Coordinate BCM training and awareness for areas of coverage change to coordinate and conduct.
- Assist in coordination and documentation of BCM plan exercises.
- Provide expertise and support to management and business functional areas, as requested, when a business disruption occurs.
- Other related duties as appropriate, with responsibilities growing over time.

Knowledge:
- Strong knowledge and application of the Business Continuity Management professional practices
- Strong analytical, organizational, and decision-making skills
- Strong verbal / written communications. Must be able to interface and coordinate work efficiently and effectively with business partners in remote locations
- Strong administrative skills, with effectiveness in developing tasks and managing resources to achieve target dates
- Ability to present to various business areas regarding BCM practices and plans
- Strong PC skills (Microsoft Office, Word, Excel, PowerPoint, etc.), Sharepoint and Infopath a plus
- Must be available to assist with disaster recovery, building emergencies, etc.

Education/Experience:
- Four year degree is required
- Minimum 5-7 years direct experience in business continuity planning or related fields required (Business Continuity, Incident Management or Disaster Recovery field as it relates to Information Technology
- CBCP certification a plus
- Travel and off-hour on-call support required

Figure 10.55   Career Profile: Business continuity specialist.

preparedness	risk assessment plan	security risk assessment
recovery	risk avoidance	technology-related hazards
resiliency	risk management	weapons of mass destruction
response	safety protocols	workplace safety

Discussion questions

1. Discuss the safety and emergency responsibilities as put forth by the American Society of Industrial Security and discuss what measures security professionals can take to carry out their duties professionally and responsibly.

2. OSHA has promulgated workplace safety rights for the American worker. How can the private security operative help ensure that workers are notified of these rights?

3. Evaluate the six-step process of review for emergency prevention and suggest where the necessary information to complete the report may be obtained. What difficulties may you encounter during the planning phase? How does this information help the firm complete an emergency action plan?

4. How does planning for fire and life safety emergencies compare to planning for natural disasters and man-made threats?

Evacuation Plan for (▨▨▨▨)

Roles and Functions:

To help prevent loss of life and minimize injury, we recommend you assign staff to the following roles: evacuation coordinator, manager, and monitor. Your staff assignments may vary depending on the size and structure of your organization.

The evacuation coordinator is responsible for:

1. Ensuring a safe evacuation of the entire building and directing the medical attention needed to injured personnel.
2. Giving direction and assistance to emergency medical technicians (EMTs) if needed.
3. Reporting head count of evacuated personnel to emergency officials and to emergency coordinator.
4. Seeing that security is established after tending to injured personnel.

The following evacuation coordinator(s) are assigned at the following facilities:

Location	Title/position held	Name
Site A		
Site B		

Managers are responsible for:

1. During an evacuation, managers direct their staff out of the building through the nearest exit and to the designated safe area.
2. Reporting a head count of their team members to the evacuation coordinator.
3. If conditions allow, performing a general damage assessment of their department area and issuing an assessment.

Monitors are responsible for:

1. Guarding all exterior doors to the facility if the building is not secure due to power loss or other concern (after confirmation that all staff and visitors have evacuated the building).
2. Overseeing that all employees needing special assistance are tended to.

In the event of an emergency situation that warrants an evacuation, the evacuation coordinator and all emergency officials are in charge and will need complete cooperation from everyone. Depending on the level of urgency, the notification to evacuate may be presented verbally by the evacuation coordinator.

Designated Safe Areas for All Staff in the Event of an Evacuation:

Business location	Designated safe area (exterior)
Site A	
Site B	

Evacuation Procedures

X	Emergency evacuation procedures	Responsible party
☐	Note: If the fire alarm sounds without acknowledgement of a practice drill or system test, do not question whether it's real or false alarm. Leave the building immediately.	
☐	Upon call for evacuation, employees remain calm and proceed to evacuate using designated exits in their area of the building. Employees stay to the right in the hallway and use walls to guide them if vision is limited.	
☐	Evacuation coordinator: • Takes the visitor log with him/her. • Verifies that any handicapped individuals are assisted. • Directs the evacuation of any visitors from the building. • Checks for people in restrooms, storage rooms, and other areas. • Checks assigned areas to ensure everyone has evacuated and provides assistance as needed. • Reports medical issues and safety concerns to arriving emergency officials.	

Figure 10.56 Evacuation plan template.

(Continued)

☐ Report the emergency by dialing 9-1-1. Provide the 9-1-1 dispatcher with the following information:
  – Your name
  – Building address
  – Location
  – Type of emergency

☐ Once outside, everyone proceeds to the designated evacuation safe area. Do not leave safe area until head count takes place. Wait for further instructions from evacuation coordinator.

☐ Secure all doors.

☐ Secure all department records and equipment. Department managers make sure sensitive files have not been carried out.

☐ Receive reports of status of building and any missing persons.

☐ Report the conditions of the building and personnel head count to evacuation coordinator.

X	Evacuation Preparation and Emergency Preparedness	Responsible party

☐ Maintain the following:
  • First-aid kits
  • Battery-powered emergency lighting
  • Exit markings/floor plans posted throughout the building
  • Building safety code compliance
  • Flood protection: Covering for computer equipment
  • Fire protection: Fire extinguishers available and tested on a regular basis
  • Hazardous material storage: Hazardous materials stored on the floor or lowest shelf away from electrical devices and heaters
  • Tool kits: Hammer, nails, saw, wrenches, wire cutter, rope and pliers are on site

☐ Make sure all staff are aware of evacuation procedures.
  • Identify individuals who will serve as monitors and make sure they are aware of their responsibilities.
  • Rehearse evacuation yearly.

Figure 10.56   (Continued) Evacuation plan template.

5. Hazmat and WMD threats have special issues that must be considered that do not exist in other types of emergencies. What are these special issues? How can their resulting harm be planned for and mitigated?

6. Discuss the methods the security professional can use to remain up to date on any pandemic threats and how the information can be communicated in the firm's prevention and response plan.

7. When implementing the five step process of continuity and crisis planning, who must be consulted and involved in the process?

CHAPTER 11

Critical infrastructure security

OBJECTIVES

After completing this chapter, the student will be able to

1. Evaluate the various governmental programs in place that promote security in the cargo and port security critical infrastructure sector.
2. Identify the scope of operations of the Transportation Security Agency and give examples of when private security operatives will work in concert with these professionals.
3. State the various security concerns of rail and mass transit and outline the industry initiatives that exist to secure the sector.
4. Recognize the various methods that may be used to attack food and water supplies and outline corresponding methods of protection.
5. Discuss how the Strategic Partnership Program on Agroterrorism (SPPA) makes a noble effort to unify diverse perspectives into one framework of food safety.
6. Summarize the importance of protecting the energy sector and discuss how its interlocking nature makes it an even more crucial sector than most other sectors.
7. Explain why the nuclear critical infrastructure sector is such a unique sector and the specific measures that can be taken to protect against threats, both natural and man-made.
8. Prepare vulnerability assessments and site security plans for all critical infrastructure sectors that address all known vulnerabilities and satisfy identified risk-based performance standards.

11.1 THE CRITICAL INFRASTRUCTURE AND THE PRIVATE SECURITY INDUSTRY

The term "critical infrastructure" connotes many things in the modern marketplace and mindset of security—most of the opinions generally relating to a place, a facility, access point such as a bridge, tunnel, or other transportation structure. This vision is all correct although a bit myopic for critical infrastructure subsumes much more. Aside from the rightful conclusion that infrastructure is about public works, public facilities, the idea of criticality in place extends well beyond this definition.[1] Critical infrastructure includes a host of critical, key assets in the national, regional, and local marketplace and community. An appropriate definition would encompass:

> [A]ssets, systems, and networks, whether physical or virtual, … considered so vital to the United States that their incapacitation or destruction would have a debilitating effect on security, national economic security, national public health or safety, or any combination thereof.[2]

---

[1] Presidential Policy Directive/PPD-21, *Presidential Policy Directive—Critical Infrastructure Security and Resilience* (February 21, 2013), at https://www.whitehouse.gov/the-press-office/2013/02/12/presidential-policy-directive-critical-infrastructure-security-and-resil.

[2] DHS, Critical Infrastructure Sectors, at https://www.dhs.gov/critical-infrastructure-sectors.

Hence, critical infrastructure may surely be a bridge, a tunnel, or a nuclear power plant, and additionally, an airport, mass transit hub, or government installation, and just as readily an information network, a cyber-security center which houses intelligence and top secret data. Indeed, the DHS delineates 16 distinct sectors that fully encompass the various angles of what is termed critical infrastructure:

Critical Infrastructure Sectors

- Chemical Sector
- Commercial Facilities Sector
- Communications Sector
- Critical Manufacturing Sector
- Dams Sector
- Defense Industrial Base Sector
- Emergency Services Sector
- Energy Sector
- Financial Services Sector
- Food and Agriculture Sector
- Government Facilities Sector
- Healthcare and Public Health Sector
- Information Technology Sector
- Nuclear Reactors, Materials, and Waste Sector
- Sector-Specific Agencies
- Transportation Systems Sector
- Water and Wastewater Systems Sector[3]

See Figure 11.1.

U.S. Critical Infrastructure Sectors

Homeland Security Presidential Directive 7 (HSPD-7) along with the National Infrastructure Protection Plan (NIPP) identified and categorized U.S. critical infrastructure into the following 18 CIKR sectors

- Agriculture and Food
- Banking and Finance
- Chemical
- Commercial Facilities
- Critical Manufacturing
- Dams
- Defense Industrial Base
- Emergency Services
- Energy
- Government Facilities
- Information Technology
- National Monuments and Icons
- Nuclear Reactors, Materials and Waste
- Postal and Shipping
- Public Health and Healthcare
- Telecommunications
- Transportation
- Water and Water Treatment

Many of the processes controlled by computerized control systems have advanced to the point that they can no longer be operated without the control system.

Homeland
Security

Figure 11.1   Critical infrastructures.

---

[3] *Ibid.*

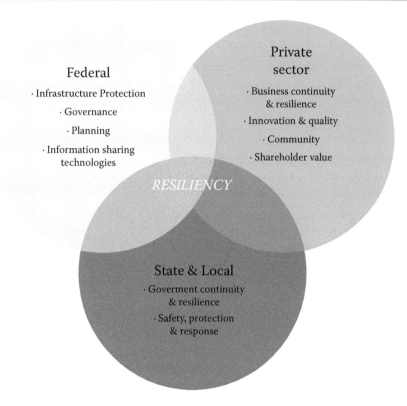

Figure 11.2 Overlap of infrastructure responsibility and protection.

The idea of infrastructure and its protection cannot be separate from public and private participation.[4] Today so much of our infrastructure is defended by private security operatives. ASIS has a working group exclusively dedicated to its protection and analysis, and the professional group produces a host of reports on the subject matter.[5] As DHS charts in Figure 11.2,[6] the private sector is an indispensable player in the process of civilian protection. Instead of an afterthought, the private security officer is now regularly entrusted with the protection of infrastructure as the following pages will make abundantly clear.

Governmental authorities fully recognize their own natural incapacity to cover the nation's legion of critical infrastructure and as a result, encourage partnerships with the private sector at nearly every level and category of critical infrastructure.[7] The security of the nation's critical infrastructure requires an effective partnership framework between public and private sector partners and does so through a host of initiatives, including the Critical Infrastructure Sector Partnership program. Each of the sectors has its own council.

Web Exercise: Review the Sector Coordinating Council for Energy at https://www.dhs.gov/sites/default/files/publications/nipp-ssp-energy-2015-508.pdf.

Private security firms are equally engaging in solidifying their respective stations within the world of critical infrastructure. This opportunity produces vast amounts of revenue for private security firms and displays another privatization opportunity in the defense of a nation. Securitas has developed a division exclusively dedicated to various infrastructure services including energy, aviation, and the petrochemical industry.

---

[4] See U.S. Government Accountability Office, *Critical Infrastructure Protection: Sector-Specific Agencies Need to Better Measure Cybersecurity Progress* (2015), at http://www.gao.gov/assets/680/673779.pdf.

[5] ASIS Critical Infrastructure Working Group, *Critical Infrastructure Resource Guide 2011* (ASIS, 2011).

[6] See Homeland Security Advisory Council, *Report of the Critical Infrastructure Task Force* 11 (2006), at https://www.dhs.gov/xlibrary/assets/HSAC_CITF_Report_v2.pdf.

[7] N.E. Busch & A.D. Givens, Public-Private Partnerships in Homeland Security: Opportunities and Challenges, *Homeland Sec. Aff.* (October 2012), at https://www.hsaj.org/articles/233; see also U.S. DOJ, *Engaging the Private Sector to Promote Homeland Security: Law Enforcement-Private Security Partnerships* (2005), at https://www.ncjrs.gov/pdffiles1/bja/210678.pdf.

Web Exercise: Learn more about the vital role the private sector can play in securing critical infrastructure from Securitas Critical Infrastructure Services page here: https://www.scisusa.com/.

The future of private security inside critical infrastructure appears very bright given the limited resources of government. As long as the infrastructure has the potentiality of widespread or mass impact in either an economic, social, or cultural or political and communal sense, that need is likely to increase.

11.2 CRITICAL INFRASTRUCTURE: TRANSPORTATION

Probably no other area offers present as well as the future promise of private security services in critical infrastructure than the transportation sector. In a word, the sector is a massive one and includes not only the movement of people but also the delivery of commercial goods and services across a global economy.[8]

In rail and air, ports and harbors, transportation centers and hubs, and access and egress points, the world of private security has made an indelible mark. There are a host of reasons for this. First, the infrastructure is simply too large to rely on government alone for its protection; second, the sector is frequently driven by private enterprise and private economic interests; and third, the government is conceptually incapable of fully appreciating or even understanding how it all operated. Hence, it has been a long-standing area of partnerships requiring "coordinated action on the part of government (federal, state, and local) and the private sector. New forms of public-private partnerships are essential to meet the challenges posed by new technologies and non-traditional threats."[9]

In addition, the interplay and intertwining of a "secure" critical infrastructure assures a profitable picture while the converse certainly insures a shaky outlook for business continuity. Safety and security in the critical infrastructure environment provides the foundational framework for a solid business outlook. In this way, the private security industry assures a "dual benefit"[10] for itself as an industry and the critical infrastructure industry it serves.

11.2.1 Cargo and port security

Control and oversight of trade into the American economy—across land, sea, and air—is not always an easy task for one must balance safety and security with the swift and efficient movement of goods. "This becomes a growing challenge in a global economy where consumers, just-in-time processes, and integrated supply chains demand reliability, accuracy and speed."[11] And that challenge has much to do with the sheer volume of materials moving in and out of our nation' ports. Some estimates calculate that as much as "$1.3 trillion in cargo enters the country by sea annually, and approximately 90% of the goods consumed in the United States come by vessel."[12]

Web Exercise: Find out about this nation's many ports by using the referenced interactive map at http://www.cbp.gov/trade.

The security challenges in cargo and ports are multifaceted—some more dangerous some far less concerning. For example, the mass of containers that cross our seas and waterways is a very predictable venue for contraband, for illegal drugs and counterfeit or copycat drugs and even for weaponry and explosives used by terrorists. From the facility itself to an ever- expanding perimeter, the security challenges multiply. With a mix of human intelligence and technological wizardry, cargo and seaports can be safe locations.[13] Container screening and radiation services is already programmed for discerning the ultimate threat—the nuclear dirty bomb or related device. Once inside the port terminal the problems do not disappear for theft of goods remains a constant concern for companies engaged in commerce and these locations, due to their geographical settings and remoteness, make prime target for organized fencing and illegal trade activities once those goods arrive in port. "Securing freight requires air-tight processes."[14]

---

[8] Even the movement of people on Ferries is a matter of security. See L. Spadanuta, Improving Ferry Security, *Sec. Mgmt* (March 2011).

[9] S. Eckert, *Protecting Critical Infrastructure: The Role of the Private Sector* 1, at https://www.ridgway.pitt.edu/Portals/1/pdfs/Publications/Eckert.pdf.

[10] L. Ritter, What Ails Transportation Security? 49 *Sec. Mgmt* 132 (2005).

[11] U.S. Customs and Border Protection, *CBP Trade Strategy 2009–2013* 24 (2009).

[12] L. Chapa, Port Protection, 59 *Sec. Mgmt* 20 (2015).

[13] C. Meyer, Building Perimeter Security to Increase Service, Safety, *Sec. Mag.* (October 2013), at 50.

[14] S. Heyn, Cargo Security: Protecting the Supply Chain, *Inbound Logistics* (January 2014), at 52.

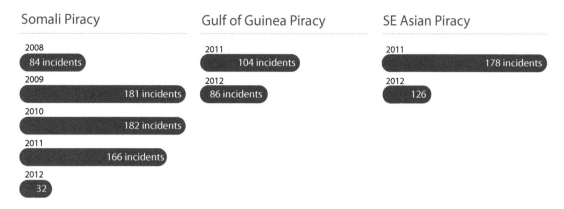

Figure 11.3 Piracy has created a cottage industry in securing vessels; statistics from the U.S. Navy. (From Rear Adm. Joseph Kuzmick's testimony to Congress on counter-piracy operations, April 2013.)

Even before those goods arrive, the security challenges are real and often dangerous, for during the Somalian piracy stage of recent years (Figure 11.3), vessel owners began to heavily rely upon private security specialists—privately contracted armed security personnel (PCASP)—to assure safe passage of these goods. Such companies have been formed and stepped forward in the wake of the rise in piracy to employ specially trained professionals in support of private vessel security. Cargo companies are fully aware of the need to keep the vessel safe from theft, piracy, and political intrigue and terror threats and have accordingly developed a new γtrack for security professionals.

In a global economy, it is critical that goods and services move expeditiously while at the same time safely and securely. With billions of tons of cargo, and nearly 52,000 foreign ships visiting the United States, the job can be daunting.[15] "Protecting the people and freight that move through seaports and the surrounding communities is a crucial, complex and shared responsibility …"[16] Balance this with the entrepreneurial bent of the shipping and cargo industry and you have a delicate problem. To illustrate, the Virginia Port Authority employs 343,000 people and accounts for 41 billion dollars of goods and services in its harbor facilities—no slouch in economic growth to be sure.[17] On the one hand, the safety and security issue runs front and center, yet on the other hand, policy must be sensitive to the question of productivity and finance. Some have argued that the costs of maritime security may be too high and not worth the investment.[18] Even afar, the costs associated with ensuring security are staggering and sometimes demonstrate the subservience of the maritime industry, which is "at the beck and call of a government whose legal initiatives, understandably, are more in tune with security than economy."[19] Security measures in a free economy requires keen balancing act. Implementing "new security policies with economic and trade objective is a complicated task given the potential risks to human life should the United States under-protect its borders."[20]

Port facilities are subject to a wide array of safety and security standards. Each facility is required under the Maritime Security Act of 2002 to develop and implement a security plan.[21] By 2011, the Coast Guard had confirmed the following:

- Reviewed and approved over 11,000 domestic vessel security plans and 3,100 domestic facility security plans;
- Oversaw the development of 43 Area Maritime Security Plans and Committees;
- Completed domestic port security assessments for all U.S. ports using the Maritime Security Risk Analysis Model;
- Visited almost 160 foreign countries to assess the effectiveness of port security measures and implementation of ISPS Code requirements; and

---

[15] D. Philpott, Improving the Security of U.S. Harbors and Seaports, *Homeland Defense J.* (November, 2007), at 31.

[16] K.R. Nagle, Investments, Interactions Help Ensure Seaport Security, *Sec. Mgmt* (September 2010), at 58.

[17] D. Ritchey, Tracking and Compliance at a Seaside Port, *Sec. Mgmt* (April 2010), at 62.

[18] K.L. Walters III, Industry on Alert: Legal and Economic Ramifications of Homeland Security Act on Maritime Commerce, 30 *Tul. Mar. L. J.* 311 (2006).

[19] *Id.* at 334–335.

[20] M. Florestal, Terror on the High Seas: The Trade and Development Implications of the U.S. National Security Measures, 72 *Brook. L. Rev.* 441 (2007) ; see also On the Potential Use of Underwater Robots; see Global News and Analysis, *Sec. Mgmt* (November 2014), at 18.

[21] See 46 U.S. Code § 70103.

- Oversaw the continuing development of the National Maritime Security Plan, which is one of eight supporting implementation plans of the National Strategy for Maritime.[22]

The U.S. Coast Guard takes a lead role in the implementation and assessment of cargo and port security measures and works closely with industry, private sector security specialists, and governmental entities and agencies to highlight vulnerabilities and work with these parties to adjust and correct deficiencies. Coast Guard inspectors enter the facility to determine the consistency of the plan with the reality of that facility. Breaches in facilities are noted as well as deficiencies relating to record keeping and access control.

Web Exercise: For the federal regulations regarding the content of the security plan, see http://edocket.access.gpo.gov/cfr_2003/julqtr/pdf/33cfr105.305.pdf.

Upon the completed inspection, the Coast Guard issues a vulnerability report that the carrier will concur with or appeal. See Figures 11.4 and 11.5.

In addition, the CBP (Customs and Border Protection), in conjunction with DHS and private sector partners, has implemented some innovative programs relative to cargo.

11.2.1.1 Secure Freight Initiative

The Secure Freight Initiative (SFI) evaluates capabilities for large-scale radiation scanning of cargo before it ever reaches the United States. Presently, the SFI program is operating at less than a dozen foreign ports with a goal to fully scan all inbound cargo.[23] The stress of SFI is the nuclear and radiological material that might be employed as WMD. Port security relies upon a multilayered approach to security best illustrated by Figure 11.6.[24]

Relying on radiographic equipment, funded by the Department of Energy's National Nuclear Security Administration (NNSA) the SFI uses both active and passive detection systems; SFI scans cargo in large quantities. Passive radiation detection technology used includes radiation portal monitors. As the cargo and its hold pass through the system, the equipment generates various images by spectrograph, bar graph, infrared or thermograph reading, and traditional x-ray imagery. Radiography uses x-rays or gamma rays to penetrate a container (Figure 11.7).

SFI tends to favor what are known as megaports, that is, locations with huge volumes of cargo. This first phase of the SFI partners with Pakistan, Honduras, the United Kingdom, Oman, Singapore, and Korea, and it will provide these governments with a greater window into potentially dangerous shipments moving across their territory. In Port Qasim, Puerto Cortes, and Southampton, the deployed scanning equipment will capture data on all containers bound to the United States, fulfilling the pilot requirements set out by Congress in the SAFE Ports Act[25] (Figure 11.8).

The SFI program also operates in selected foreign ports to scan outgoing cargo before leaving port. At the same time, Secure Freight integrates new data into U.S. government screening and targeting systems, including the proposed new U.S. CBP security filing, as well as the creation of a proposed private sector–operated Global Trade Exchange (GTX). The SFI is testing the feasibility of scanning 100% of U.S. bound cargo.

11.2.1.2 Container Security Initiative

Beginning in January 2002, CBP proposed the Container Security Initiative (CSI). CSI inspects cargo units rather than the entire freight load and pushes U.S. port security back into the supply chain at its port of origin. CSI pre-screens and evaluates containers before they are shipped. Under the CSI program, high-risk containers receive security inspections by both x-ray and radiation scan. Containers, before being loaded on board vessels destined for the United States, are inspected at CSI ports. Upon arrival, these same containers are exempt from further inspection,

---

[22] See Written testimony of U.S. Coast Guard Assistant Commandant for Prevention Policy Rear Admiral Joseph Servidio for a House Committee on Transportation and Infrastructure, Subcommittee on Coast Guard and Maritime Transportation hearing titled, Tenth Anniversary of the Maritime Transportation Security Act: Are We Safer? (September 11, 2012), at https://www.dhs.gov/news/2012/09/11/written-testimony-us-coast-guard-house-transportation-and-infrastructure.

[23] For a recent assessment of America's ports and their relative safety and security, see H.H. Willis, Ten Years after the Safe Port Act, Are America's Ports Secure? *Rand Corporation* (April 6, 2016), at http://www.rand.org/blog/2016/04/attractive-targets.html.

[24] National Nuclear Security Administration, Megaports Initiative (September 2010), at http://nnsa.energy.gov/sites/default/files/nnsa/inline-files/singlepages_9-15-2010.pdf, last accessed January 23, 2016.

[25] Security and Accountability for Every Port Act of 2006, P.L. 109-347, 120 *U.S. Statutes at Large* 1884 (2006).

U.S. DEPARTMENT OF HOMELAND SECURITY U.S. COAST GUARD CG-6025 (05/03)	FACILITY VULNERABILITY AND SECURITY MEASURES SUMMARY	OMB APPROVAL NO. 1625-0077

An agency may not conduct or sponsor, and a person is not required to respond to a collection of information unless it displays a valid OMB control number.

The Coast Guard estimates that the average burden for this report is 60 minutes. You may submit any comments concerning the accuracy of this burden estimate or any suggestions for reducing the burden to: Commandant (G-MP), U.S. Coast Guard, 2100 2nd St, SW, Washington D.C. 20593-0001 or Office of Management and Budget, Paperwork Reduction Project (1625-0077), Washington, DC 20503.

FACILITY IDENTIFICATION

1. Name of Facility

2. Address of Facility

3. Latitude

4. Longitude

5. Captain of the Port Zone

6. Type of Operation (check all that apply)

- [ ] Break Bulk
- [ ] Dry Bulk
- [ ] Container
- [ ] RO-RO
- [ ] Petroleum
- [ ] Chemical
- [ ] LHG/LNG
- [ ] Explosives and other dangerous cargo
- [ ] Certain Dangerous Cargo
- [ ] Barge Fleeting
- [ ] Offshore Support
- [ ] Passengers (Subchapter H)
- [ ] Passengers (Ferries)
- [ ] Passengers (Subchapter K)
- [ ] Military Supply
- [ ] If other, explain below:

VULNERABILITY AND SECURITY MEASURES

7a. Vulnerability

7b. Vulnerability Category

[ ] If other, explain

8a. Selected Security Measures (MARSEC Level 1)

8b. Security Measures Category

[ ] If other, explain

9a. Selected Security Measures (MARSEC Level 2)

9b. Security Measures Category

[ ] If other, explain

10a. Selected Security Measures (MARSEC Level 3)

10b. Security Measures Category

[ ] If other, explain

VULNERABILITY AND SECURITY MEASURES

7a. Vulnerability

7b. Vulnerability Category

[ ] If other, explain

8a. Selected Security Measures (MARSEC Level 1)

8b. Security Measures Category

[ ] If other, explain

9a. Selected Security Measures (MARSEC Level 2)

9b. Security Measures Category

[ ] If other, explain

10a. Selected Security Measures (MARSEC Level 3)

10b. Security Measures Category

[ ] If other, explain

Figure 11.4 Facility security and vulnerability measures summary form.

and as a result, goods move through our port system with greater efficiency. CSI is operational in 58 foreign ports, as shown in Figure 11.9.

A total of 35 customs administrations from other jurisdictions have committed to join the CSI program. CSI now covers 80%[26] of all maritime containerized cargo destined to the United States.

---

[26] U.S. Customs and Border Protection, CSI: Container Security Initiative, at http://www.cbp.gov/border-security/ports-entry/cargo-security/csi/csi-brief, last accessed January 23, 2016.

Figure 11.5 Coast Guard on the sea.

11.2.1.3 Container inspection

Container integrity and security is a primary concern for all shippers, commerce traders, and those entrusted with assuring safe passage of the contents. The intent of recent governmental initiatives is to assure 100% screening for containers, but most recent reports show this ambition a pipe dream.[27] ASIS in a 2012 study on port security showed

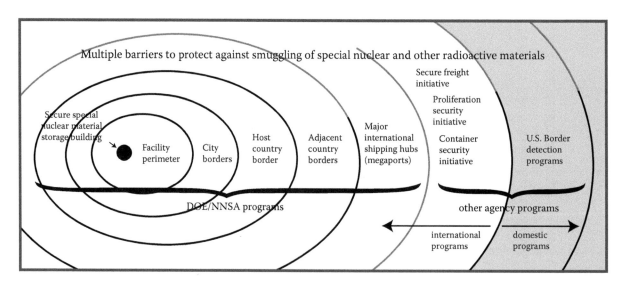

Figure 11.6 DOE/NNSA program combine with Department of Homeland Security and other U.S. and inter-governmental efforts to protect the U.S. homeland against threats from illicit movement of special nuclear and other radioactive materials.

---

[27] J. Weiss & M. Davis, Cargo Security and the Terrorist Threat, *Law and Order* (May 2006), at 72.

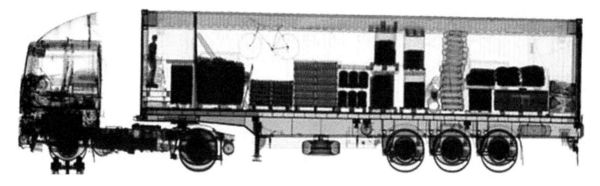

Figure 11.7 X-ray image at SFI location.

a 4.1% container compliance—an unacceptable result.[28] Along a wide array of locales, the container is readily capable of being breached.[29] Figure 11.10[30] tracks the history and flow of the typical container—a journey with a myriad opportunity for theft, inclusion of contraband and illegal materials, as well as delivery agent for a terrorist. These various steps in the genealogy of any container must be accounted for by security professionals.

The range and extent of cargo theft mirrors market demands, a sort of perverted correlation between the types of cargo stolen and the current demands for the product. "Thefts of pharmaceuticals, food/drink loads ... stolen loads of nuts, seafood, candy, cookies, snacks, dairy, eggs, meat were all more than doubled since 2012."[31] Other hot products include "computers, entertainment equipment, name-brand clothing and footwear, perfume, jewelry, cigarettes and prescription drugs."[32]

The CBP requires all sea carriers to develop written plans and protocols for security relating to their containers both on and off ship.[33] From initial labeling, sealing, and record keeping, the company must follow a specified seven-point protocol for each container.[34] See Figure 11.11.

Figure 11.8 SFI scan.

---

[28] Rx-360 Supply Chain Security, White Paper: Cargo Risk Assessment (May 2012).

[29] See Transportation and Cargo Security, *Security* (September 2006), at 62; see also B. Zalud, Don't Unchain that Supply Chain Melody, *Sec. Mag.* (September 2011), at 52.

[30] Testimony before the Subcommittee on Border and Maritime Security, Committee on Homeland Security, House of Representatives, Supply Chain Security: Container Security Programs Have Matured, but Uncertainty Persists over the Future of 100 Percent Scanning, Statement of Stephen L. Caldwell, Director Homeland Security and Justice, 8 (February 7, 2012), at http://www.gao.gov/assets/590/588253.pdf.

[31] Threat of Cargo Theft Remains High in 2024, *Sec. Mag.* (April 2014), at 16.

[32] See C. Mayhew, The Detection and Prevention of Cargo Theft, *Australian Institute of Criminology: Trends and Issues* (September 2001), at 1.

[33] See U.S. Customs & Border Protection, Security Profile, at https://www.cbp.gov/sites/default/files/documents/sc_security_profile_overview_3.pdf.

[34] See E. Rundle, Port Security Improves with Nonintrusive Cargo Inspection and Security Port Access, *Emerg. Mgmt* (July 28, 2009), at http://www.emergencymgmt.com/infrastructure/Port-Security-Improves-With.html; see also USCBP, Security Profile.

Container Security Initiative
Office of Field Operations

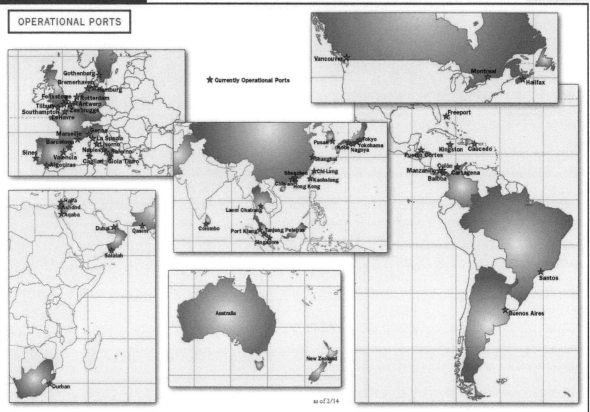

Figure 11.9 CSI partner ports.

In addition, the Coast Guard deploys teams to moving and stationary vessels for inspection of cargo and containers. The Coast Guard has developed and deployed Container Inspection Training and Assistance Teams (CITATs) to conduct container inspections at harbors and ports.

11.2.1.4 Vessel inspection

On the high seas and waterways, the Coast Guard has jurisdictional authority to board vessels for inspection purposes. This practice is one of its most crucial missions. Section 89 of Title 14 of the U.S. Code authorizes the Coast Guard to board vessels subject to the jurisdiction of the United States, anytime upon the high seas and upon waters over which the United States has jurisdiction, to make inquiries, examinations, inspections, searches, seizures, and arrests. Even despite the statutory authority, there are multiple reasons why boarding programs exist.

First, the Coast Guard tracks and issues certificates of operation to vessel owners.

Web Exercise: Download the certification form at http://www.uscg.mil/nvdc/nvdcforms.asp.

Second, the Coast Guard maintains a central depository of vessel records at its National Vessel Documentation Center. Records of registered vessels are fully cataloged and documented and serve as an information center in the event of accident or other calamity. Third, the Coast Guard boards ships to conduct inspections or to carry out interdiction or intervention actions in the event of criminal activities. In the first instance, the Coast Guard may simply board under a voluntary request for ship inspection. To commence the voluntary inspection program, the applicant need only fill out the request as outlined in Figure 11.12. See Figure 11.13.

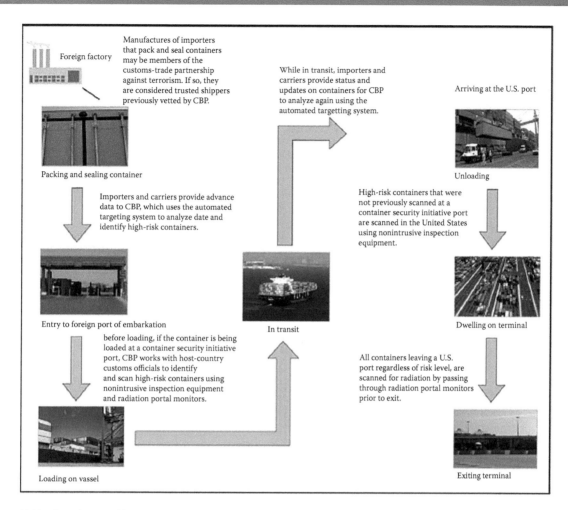

Figure 11.10   Container tracking.

Figure 11.11   Cargo containers at U.S. seaport awaiting processing. (Courtesy of US Customs and Border Protection.)

U.S. DEPARTMENT OF HOMELAND SECURITY U.S. COAST GUARD CG-3752 (Rev. 6-04)	APPLICATION FOR INSPECTION OF U.S. VESSEL	FORM APPROVED OMB NO. 1625-0002

An agency may not conduct or sponsor, and a person is not required to respond to, a collection of information unless it displays a valid OMB control number.

The Coast Guard estimates that the average burden for this report is 15 mins. You may submit any comments concerning the accuracy of this burden estimate or any suggestion reducing the burden to: Commandant (G-MOC), U.S. Coast Guard, Washington, DC 20593-0001 or Office of Management and Budget, Paperwork Reduction Project (1625-0002), Washington, DC 20503.

Address to reply to:

TELEPHONE NUMBER:

DATE:

TO: Officer in Charge, Marine Inspection

Marine Inspection Zone ______

The undersigned applies to have the ☐ Steam Vessel ☐ Motor Vessel

☐ Motorboat ☐ Barge ☐ Other *(Indicate)* ______

named ______ Official or Award No. ______

inspected under the laws of the United States; to be employed as a ☐ Passenger Vessel *(No. of Passengers ______)*

☐ Cargo Vessel ☐ Tank Vessel ☐ MODU ☐ Other *(Indicate)* ______

on the following route: *(Waters, Geographical limits)* ______

______

Liquid cargo in bulk ☐ will ☐ will not be carried as follows:

☐ Flammable or Combustible *(Indicate grade)* ______

☐ Chemicals *(Indicate)* ______

Length of vessel ______ ft.

Hull material: ☐ Steel ☐ Other *(Indicate)* ______

Vessel will be at *(Port, Pier, etc.)* ______

The current Certificate of Inspection expires on ______.

Inspection is desired on ______.

Cargo Ship Safety Construction Certificate to be issued by ☐ ABS ☐ USCG.

Vessel ☐ is ☐ is not to be classed.

If classed, indicate Classification Society: ☐ ABS ☐ Other *(Indicate)* ______

I CERTIFY that previous application for this inspection ☐ has ☐ has not been made. I further certify that I have instructed the master to present the vessel ready in all respects for the above requested inspection on the date specified. I understand that if this inspection is to be conducted at foreign port or place the vessel owners will be billed for the costs incurred in accordance with 46 USC 385b-1.

(Signature) ______

(Title) ______

Figure 11.12 Application for inspection of a U.S. vessel by the Coast Guard.

11.2.1.5 Customs Trade Partnership against Terrorism

As noted previously, the scope and magnitude of cargo commerce makes it impossible for government alone to monitor safety and security issues. Global trade and commerce demands a partnership mentality where the sea carriers, and their security forces and personnel work closely with the Coast Guard, CBP, and DHS. In fact, the bulk of sea going commerce relies on self-reporting and the integrity of shippers and maritime operators. To foster this partnership mentality, the CBP adopted the Customs Trade Partnership against Terrorism (C-TPAT) program. C-TPAT recognizes the essential role that private cargo carriers play in the safety and security of goods flowing through ports and harbors. C-TPAT is a voluntary government-business initiative that works closely with the prime players in international cargo, namely, importers, carriers, consolidators, licensed customs brokers, and manufacturers. C-TPAT asks business to ensure the integrity of their security practices and communicate and verify the security guidelines of their business partners within the supply chain.[35]

[35] See Busch & Givens, *supra* note 7.

Figure 11.13   Coast Guard boarding a vessel for inspection.

The general theme of C-TPAT is to promote efficiency in the cargo processes and to provide a forum for private–public cooperation in matters of cargo movement.[36] More than 10,000 American companies are ready participants in the C-TPAT program.[37]

Web Exercise: For an application regarding C-TPAT membership, see http://www.cbp.gov/border-security/ports-entry/cargo-security/c-tpat-customs-trade-partnership-against-terrorism/apply. Also find out more about the program by reading the C-TPAT brochure at https://www.cbp.gov/sites/default/files/documents/ctpat_brochure.pdf.

Private security firms are ready players in the C-TPAT program by providing training, compliance services, software packages and designs, and regulatory expertise to firms throughout the world. Firms such as Pinkerton's and Allied Barton promote their business model by exceeding the compliance requirements, so potential clients never worry or fear about staying within the program's boundaries. Under the general theme of "supply chain" protection, firms such as Pinkerton's deliver a host of services that include C-TPAT but many other aligned functions (https://www.pinkerton.com/security-risk-management/global-supply-chain-security/).

11.2.1.6 Automated Commercial Environment

Modernizing the free flow of goods takes much more than mere personnel and novel policies. The sheer volume of material flowing in and out of the global marketplace demands the highest systems of technology. The CBP, and its many public and private partners, is upgrading and electronically manifesting the flow of goods through its Automated Commercial Environment (ACE) program. ACE is part of a multiyear modernization effort that is not yet fully operational and is being deployed in phases though the overall compliance rates manifest close to completion results (Figure 11.14).[38]

By the end of 2016, the ACE will become the "single window," the primary system through which the trade community will report imports and exports and the government will determine admissibility. Through ACE as the single window, manual processes will be streamlined and automated, paper will be eliminated, and compliance will be a much more dependable process.[39] See Figure 11.15.

The ACE seeks to

- Allow trade participants access to and management of their trade information via reports
- Expedite legitimate trade by providing CBP with tools to efficiently process imports/exports and move goods quickly across the border

---

[36] See Heyn, *supra* note 14.

[37] J.B. Rice & D. Purtell, Assessing Cargo Supply Risk, 50 *Sec. Mgmt* 78 (2006).

[38] U.S. Customs & Border Protection, *ACE Adoption Rate Monthly* (May 2016), at https://www.cbp.gov/sites/default/files/assets/documents/2016-Jun/External_May_ACE%20Adoption%20Rate_Final.pdf.

[39] See U.S. Customs and Border Protection, ACE and Automated Systems, at https://www.cbp.gov/trade/automated.

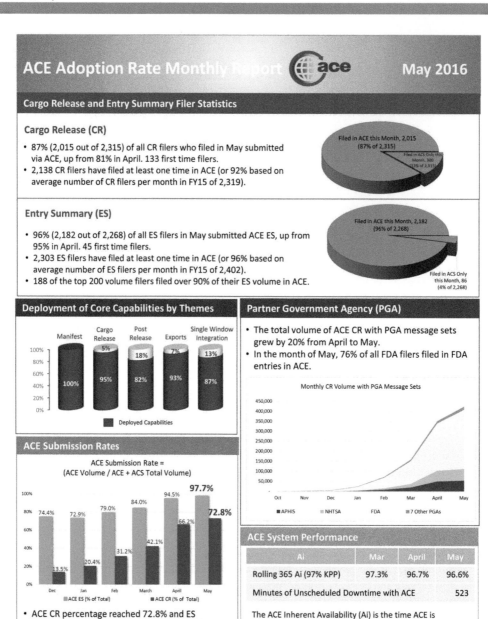

Figure 11.14   ACE adoption rate monthly.

Figure 11.15   ACE program logo.

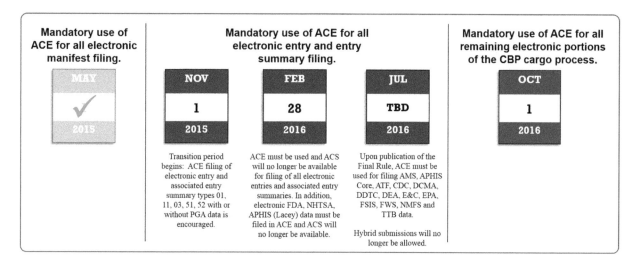

Figure 11.16   Mandatory use of ACE for all electronic manifest filings.

- Improve communication, collaboration, and compliance efforts between CBP and the trade community
- Facilitate efficient collection, processing, and analysis of commercial import and export data
- Provide an information-sharing platform for trade data throughout government agencies

For example, in trucking, relative to cargo and container, the ACE electronic truck manifest capabilities are now available at all 99 U.S. land border ports of entry. Truckers electronically author E-manifests, which provide CBP with cargo information, such as crew, conveyance, equipment as applicable, and shipment details. In ports of entry, there are now mechanisms to file reports and paperwork electronically. In 2015–2016, the ACE program shall impose mandatory usage and participation dates for the program. By the end of the 2016 cargo season, nearly all cargo moving through the American marketplace shall be subject to the ACE electronic requirements. See the timelines charted in Figure 11.16.[40]

The benefits to the ACE program are well documented and include the following:

Financial savings with the periodic monthly payment capability

- Reduced processing time at the border with features like electronic truck manifest
- Ability to view shipment status and store data via the ACE secure data portal
- Capabilities to develop over 100 customized reports

See Figure 11.17[41] for a graphic explanation on the ACE basics.

In each aspect of the supply chain and coupling this protocol with assuring safe and secure passage, complex problems can be overcome only with exceptional planning. The private security industry has taken a lead in providing guidance and oversight to many layers of the maritime industry, making sure that assets are protected, that terror is mitigated, and that the free flow of commerce can be guaranteed. Cargo and port security require a

> multi-layered approach to a secure, end-to-end chain of custody that includes well-defined and enforced protocols, an understanding of worldwide regulations, employee training, physical security measures, thorough carrier vetting and driver identification, video surveillance of warehouses, loading docks and gate areas as well as the use of secure facilities, lots and drop yards.[42]

---

[40] U.S. Customs and Border Protection, ACE Mandatory Use Dates, at http://www.cbp.gov/trade/automated/ace-mandatory-use-dates, last accessed January 23, 2016.

[41] U.S. Customs and Border Protection, The ACE Basics, at http://www.cbp.gov/sites/default/files/documents/ACE%20Basics_Update_FINAL.pdf, last accessed January 23, 2016.

[42] See B. Zalud, The Daily Challenges of Supply Chain Security, Sec. Mag. (April 1, 2016), at http://www.securitymagazine.com/articles/87010-the-daily-challenges-of-supply-chain-security.

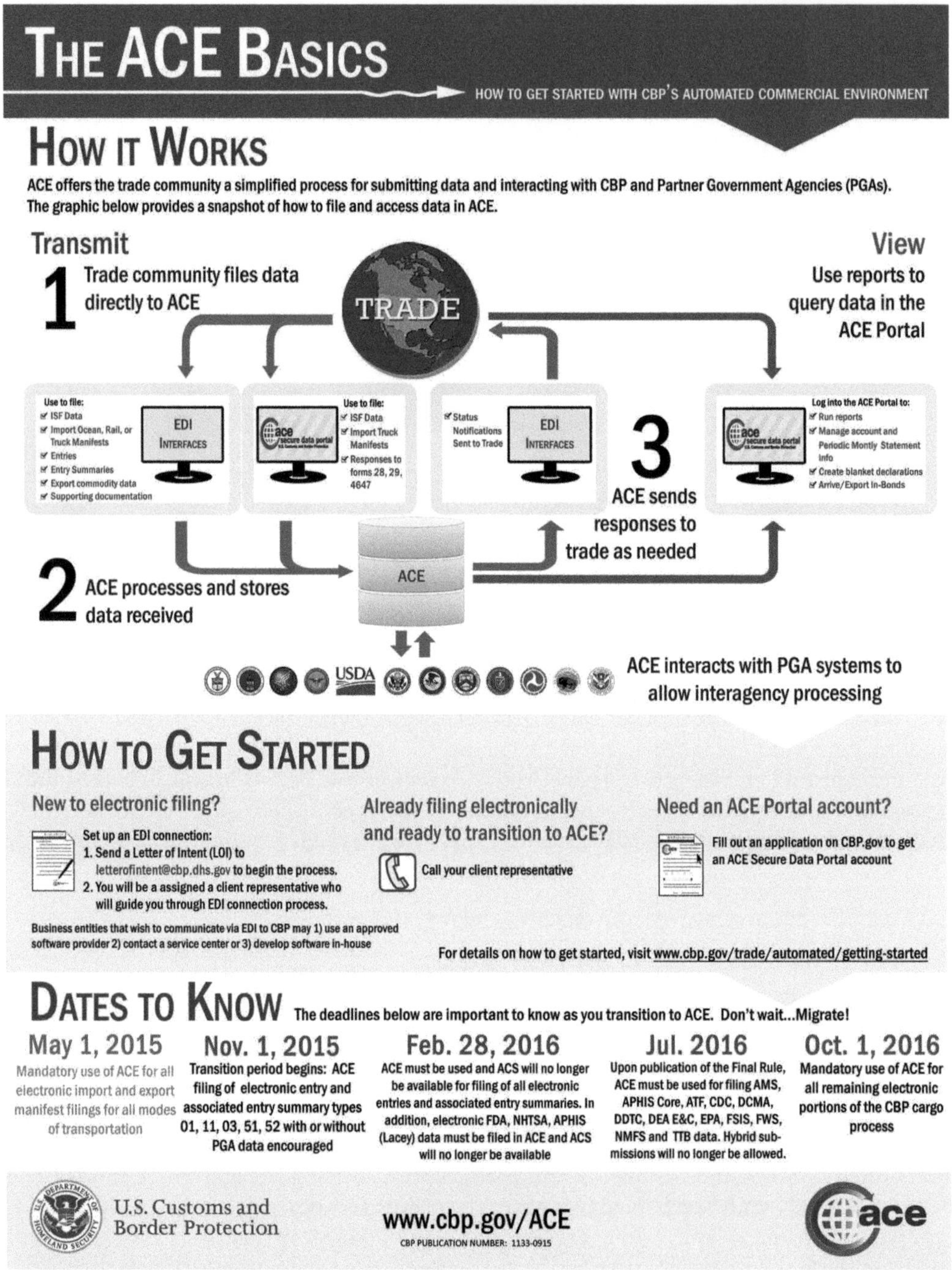

Figure 11.17   ACE basics: how to get started with CBP's ACE.

11.2.2 Airline transportation: A short history

The responsibility for security and safety in America's airline facilities, airplanes, and commercial hubs manifests an interesting and very changeable history.[43] For a time, the airport facilities remained the province of state and local

---

[43] Note that Airport Control Towers operate under the aegis of the Department of Transportation's Federal Aviation Administration (FAA)—places that have been hacked by outside enemies of our way of life. See M. Harwood, Dept. of Transportation: Air Traffic Control Systems Have Been Hacked, *Sec. Mgmt* (May 8, 2009), at https://sm.asisonline.org/Pages/Dept.-of-Transportation-Air-Traffic-Control-Systems-Have-Been-Hacked.aspx.

police authorities, and indeed this reality is still even true today in many American facilities. State and county police authorities are often entrusted with the perimeter of the airport or even the prescreened side of the facility—while post screening gate portions are now the exclusive province of the TSA—the vaunted Transportation Security Agency. At other times and other facilities, the bulk of the responsibility, especially in the pre-9/11 world, was entrusted to private contractors in the form of private security firms who manned screening stations or provided the technology to detect weaponry and explosives. Previous to 9/11, this was a major growth industry for the private sector. Post 9/11, the private security firm almost disappeared from the marketplace with TSA operatives the sole means of passenger screening and airplane safety sweeps. In fact, it is fair to conclude that the erection and imposition of the TSA was almost an over-reaction to this horrid event and at the same time a certain amount of scapegoating commonly accused the industry of substandard practices that made this sort of event possible.[44] Of course, neither assertion really all that accurate, for on the one hand, the air safety mindset never really envisioned the possibility of this sort of destruction and on the other hand, looking to the federal government for its expertise in these matters was and is equally ludicrous. To be frank, the birth of the TSA is the direct result of the tragedy and not the result of any perceived private security failure.

11.2.2.1 Transportation Security Agency

The entire infrastructure of the TSA is built upon a series of faulty assumptions, too many to delineate in this text but a few are worth mentioning, namely,

1. All passengers are equally suspicious and should receive the same scrutiny, and
2. The principal purpose of airport security is to keep dangerous objects (e.g., knives, guns, and bombs) off of airplanes.[45]

As a result of just these two faulty assumptions, the entire known world is subjected to an endless pursuit of Assumption 2 while Assumption 1 is adhered to with ferocious zeal. Everyone must be subjected to the inane invasion of the TSA. And as the agency presses these assumptions to the point of obsession, it mass insults so many sectors of the general population that it is difficult to catalog the offenses. Some examples include the following:

- Rousted children with Barbie backpacks
- Veterans forces to remove prosthetic devices, artificial limbs and steel plates
- Cancer patients with certain devices forces to expose
- Children hidden from parents when searched
- Groping sexual organs of both men and women
- Reaching down into clothing and fondling
- Filming, taping, and photographing by technical means—then selling imagery on Internet
- Abusing passengers with hip replacements
- Regular abuse of the elderly by forcing stand-up searches when in wheelchairs

These are but representative examples of the abusive, one- size- fits-all mentality that permeates the TSA. There is nothing surprising here for government could care less about the customer it allegedly serves—nor does it really care about the end result. If it did, the results would simply do the agency in. Random testing of the TSA methodology displays shockingly bad success rates at rooting out the weaponry and dangerous artifices.

Web Exercise: See the ABC News Report on the 95% failure rate of the TSA at:

http://abcnews.go.com/US/exclusive-undercover-dhs-tests-find-widespread-security-failures/story?id=31434881.

In the summer of 2016, the agency's performance had become legendarily bad with government- inclined and union-preferred jurisdictions, like New York City, threatening to throw the TSA out for the long lines and thousands of

---

[44] See A.B. Taylor, The Evolution of Airline Security Since 9/11, (December 2003), at http://www.ifpo.org/resource-links/articles-and-reports/protection-of-specific-environments/the-evolution-of-airline-security-since-911/.
[45] R.W. Poole Jr. & J.J. Carafano, Time to Rethink Airport Security, Backgrounder #1955 on Dept. of Homeland Security (July 26, 2006), at http://www.heritage.org/research/reports/2006/07/time-to-rethink-airport-security.

frustrated passengers. When New York City's Mass Transit Authority makes such a threat toward the TSA, and then follows that threat with a replacement service provided by the private security industry, the agency is seriously dysfunctional.

Web Exercise: See the New York CBS station analysis of this treat at http://newyork.cbslocal.com/2016/05/09/tsa-port-authority-airports/.

Hence, by any reasonable measure, this is an agency that falters miserably in providing an essential service to the American people and just as crucially fails to protect effectively the critical infrastructure the airline industry must rely upon. In a way, the airline industry is complicit in this abuse for it acquiesced far too quickly to a government bent on control and authority and a business model more concerned about profits than real and meaningful security. For in the final analysis, the industry itself should be the guarantor that its fleet and its facilities are safe and secure. And in this sense, it should vociferously argue for a return to the pre-9/11 model, which was largely a world controlled and overseen by the private security industry. Only the private security industry understands customer relations, consumers, accountability, and effectiveness, the government merely pays lip service to these notions. From another vantage point, it may be the government's monopoly that does most of the damage for it always makes better sense for government to partner with the industry it serves and to give consideration to other voices of expertise in these matters. If government moves toward a coordinating role than an operational role, the results would likely be very different. For government, in its natural function to protect and serve, is a better player when it combines that mentality with efficacy, satisfaction rates and policies that work.

For the moment, the TSA maintains its prominent perch in the world of air transportation but those heights are under severe critique and even more compellingly, governmental authorities, at the congressional level, have turned their eyes to the world of private security as a remedy for the present malaise. Slowly but surely, the private security industry weaves its way back into the fabric of airlines and the airports. More on that shall follow.

In the world of transit security, private professionals will undoubtedly come into contact, and work frequently, with TSA employees, the visible arm of safety in our terminals. Passenger and baggage screening are the prime tasks of TSA. Despite these responsibilities, TSA engages in a broad range of other activities. TSA is a component of DHS and not only is responsible for the security of the country's airline transportation systems, but also, with state, local, and regional partners, oversees security for the highways, railroads, buses, mass transit systems, ports, and the 450 U.S. airports. TSA employs approximately 60,000 people. TSA is a mammoth bureaucracy that has yet to fully find its way nor has it been capable of capturing significant public support in how it carries out its mission.

The bulk of what TSA does relates to airline safety. TSA's primary mission is transportation—all forms and all locales. TSA deals with a staggering array of travelers, personnel, and issues. From airports to bus stations, rail terminals to pipelines, TSA is entrusted with extraordinary responsibilities. TSA has shown little hesitation in expanding its reach into all forms of transportation.[46] For example, recent implementation of the VIPR (Visible Intermodal Prevention and Response) program—including teams of local and federal law enforcement officers, along with TSA specialists combing the subways, the ferries, and all forms of public transportation—signifies TSA's reach over the entire national transportation system (Figure 11.18).

Whatever system is reviewed, TSA's mission includes the development of various layers of security protection at the facilities it is entrusted with. TSA works to identify questionable passengers long before the security checkpoint including intelligence analysis, watch lists and passenger manifests, random canine searches, and insertion of federal air marshals and flight deck officers and crew. TSA charts these layers in Figure 11.19.

11.2.2.1.1 Risk management programs

TSA has played an integral role in the development of risk assessment protocols and tools for the transportation system, though not without regular criticism.[47] Opponents of TSA argue that there is not much thinking going on when it comes to new and innovative protocols. Some have said that the agency agrees too quickly to adopting new

---

[46] C.J. Ciaramella, *Abolish the TSA*, *The Washington Post* (April 16, 2015), at https://www.washingtonpost.com/posteverything/wp/2015/04/16/abolish-the-tsa/.

[47] U.S. Government Accountability Office, *Aviation Security: TSA Has Made Progress, but Additional Efforts Are Needed to Improve Security*, GAO Highlights (2011).

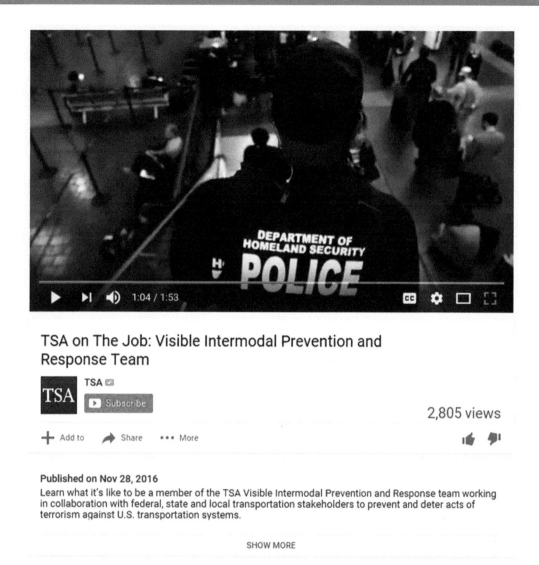

Figure 11.18 Screen capture of a YouTube™ video from TSA for VIPR team roles and responsibilities.

technology. Even the General Accounting Office (GAO) found that TSA "does not routinely consider costs and benefits when acquiring new technologies."[48]

Despite this, TSA completely appreciates the interrelationship between a risk or series of risks and the critical infrastructure and assets it protects. To understand the risk is to comprehend the landscape to be protected. To comprehend the landscape to be protected surely leads to the identification and mitigation of risk. TSA also recognizes that transportation assets, such as airplanes and tunnels, are part of larger systems, such as the national aviation system or a mass transit system. Taken together, all the individual transportation systems form the national transportation system. Essentially, TSA discerns systems within systems. The behavior of transportation systems cannot be fully explained by confining observations to individual cars, vessels, and aircraft or fixed infrastructure. As a result, TSA has developed self-assessment tools for maritime, transportation, and mass transit systems.

---

[48] A. Sternstein, *Experts Chide TSA for Poor Risk Assessment of Security Measures*, NextGov.com (September 30, 2011), at http://www.nextgov.com/technology-news/2011/09/experts-chide-tsa-for-poor-risk-assessment-of-security-measures/49866; see also U.S. Government Accountability Office, *Aviation Security: A National Strategy and Other Actions would Strengthen TSA's Efforts to Secure Commercial Airport Perimeters and Access Controls* (September 30, 2009).

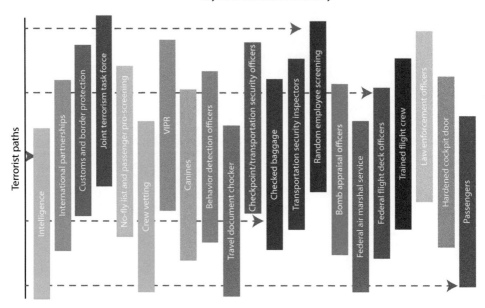

Figure 11.19   Layers of U.S. aviation security.

In 2014, TSA modified its approach to risk management by adopting a new methodology—enterprise risk management (ERM). See Figure 11.20.

ERM tries to target appropriate targets rather than attempting to screen the entire universe for threats and harm. The primary goals of ERM are the following:

- Provide a structured, disciplined, and consistent approach to assessing risk aligned with U.S. Department of Homeland Security guidance.
- Identify strategic risks that threaten TSA's achievement of our long-term objectives and goals, and manage those risks at the enterprise level through the ERSC.

Figure 11.20   ERM protocol.

- Ensure that risks are managed in a manner that maximizes the value TSA provides to the nation consistent with defined risk appetite and risk tolerance levels.

- Align our strategy, process, people, technology, and information to support agile risk management.

- Provide greater transparency into risk by improving our understanding of interactions and relationships between risks in support of improved risk-based decision making.

- Establish clear accountability and ownership of risk.[49]

Web Exercise: For a full analysis of the ERM methodology, visit https://www.aferm.org/wp-content/uploads/2015/10/TSA-ERM-Policy-Manual-August-2014.pdf.

11.2.2.1.2 TSA's Canine Explosive Detection Unit

Given the broadening responsibilities of TSA, moving beyond the airports and venturing into seaports and harbors, train and municipal transit facilities, TSA has had to get creative in how it carries out its task.[50] The use of canines has long been a beneficial and very economical police practice. TSA uses canines to detect explosives in various quarters (Figure 11.21).

Canines are particularly effective in ports and harbor areas where the sheer volume of coverage area can be daunting for law enforcement. TSA has developed certification standards for canine units for purposes of uniformity and quality in practice. TSA is aggressively developing units and teams throughout the United States. The agency will train and certify more than 400 explosives detection canine teams, composed of one dog and one handler, during the next two years. Eighty-five of these teams will be TSA employee led and will primarily search cargo bound for passenger-carrying aircraft. TSA handlers will be nonlaw enforcement employees and will complement the 496 TSA-certified state and local law enforcement teams currently deployed to 70 airports and 14 mass transit systems. Currently, there are now 800 various canine teams throughout the United States (Figure 11.22).

Web Exercise: Find out about the crucial role canines play in the defense of our nation at https://www.youtube.com/watch?v=AV4I7XNSph0.

Finally, the air transport industry deals with a great deal of international and national cargo—a security concern that is sometimes an afterthought given the stress of passenger traffic. "With 7.6 billion pounds of cargo transported by

Law enforcement officer team patrolling mass transit terminal

Transportation security inspector team screening air cargo

Passenger screening canine team searching airport terminal

Figure 11.21   LEO, TSI, and PSC teams performing searches in different environments.

---

[49] Transportation Security Administration, *Enterprise Risk Management ERM Policy Manual* 8 (August 2014), at https://www.aferm.org/wp-content/uploads/2015/10/TSA-ERM-Policy-Manual-August-2014.pdf.

[50] Statement of Jennifer Grover, Acting Director, Homeland Security and Justice, Testimony Before the Subcommittee on Transportation Security, Committee on Homeland Security, House of Representatives, Explosives Detection Canines: TSA Has Taken Steps to Analyze Canine Team Data and Assess the Effectiveness of Passenger Screening Canines, GAO-14-695T (June 24, 2014), at http://www.gao.gov/assets/670/664331.pdf, last accessed January 24, 2016.

Figure 11.22   TSA canine searching for contraband in a shipment.

U.S. carriers each day, roughly 20% of which is carried on passenger aircraft,"[51] the 2007 congressional demand for 100% screening appears quite unrealistic. See Figure 11.23.

11.2.2.2 Private security industry and the Screening Partnership Program

As previously commented upon, the TSA dissatisfaction rate and negative public sentiment have opened up a world of opportunity for the private security industry. With customer concern and its inherent results orientation, the private sector appears ready for a fully and unbridled return to its former home—the airport. Pre-9/11 reality is being replayed, albeit in a modified way as public outcries over the performance of TSA continue unabated. Congressional hearings in the summer of 2016 further solidified these negative perceptions, with the operational head of the TSA Melvin Carraway being asked to step down. This termination event is a major rarity in the world of government, which often fails to hold people accountable for performance. But TSA, in order to survive, must be customer driven whether it likes it or not since its service is front line with millions of people on a month-to-month basis.[52]

Figure 11.23   Cargo being screened before flight.

---

[51] J. B. MacNeil, Air Cargo Security: How to Keep Americans Secure Without Harming the Economy, *Backgrounder: Heritage Foundation* (June 2010), at 1.

[52] P. Seidenstat, Terrorism, Airport Security, and the Private Sector, 21 *Rev. Pol'y Res.* 275 (2004).

> **SPP Airports**
>
> - Bozeman Yellowstone International Airport
> - Charles M. Schulz–Sonoma County Airport
> - Dawson Community Airport
> - Glacier Park International Airport
> - Greater Rochester International Airport
> - Havre City-County Airport
> - Jackson Hole Airport
> - Kansas City International Airport
> - Key West International Airport
> - L. M. Clayton Airport
> - Orlando Sanford International Airport
> - Portsmouth International Airport
> - Punta Gorda Airport
> - Roswell International Air Center
> - San Francisco International Airport
> - Sarasota-Bradenton International Airport
> - Sidney-Richland Municipal Airport
> - Sioux Falls Regional Airport
> - Tupelo Regional Airport
> - Wokal Field/Glasgow International Airport
> - Yellowstone Airport

Figure 11.24   Airport authorities that have opted out for private security services.

These same hearings prompted even more calls for legislation allowing the easier and more free- flowing return of private sector interests to the TSA function, such as the opt-out program for airport authorities choosing to switch from TSA to contracted private security services.[53]

Known as the Screening Partnership Program, and orchestrated under the direction of the TSA, nearly two dozen airport authorities have opted out for private security services. See Figure 11.24.

Web Exercise: Read and research the SPP legislation and the various processes required at https://www.law.cornell.edu/uscode/text/49/44920.

11.2.3 Rail and mass transit

The task of securing the country's rail and mass transit system is just as critical as the air industry protections. Mass transit systems carry nearly 10 billion passengers per year and the mass transportation fleet is nearly 150,000 vehicles, and the trend toward mass transit is both short term and longitudinally upwards. See Figure 11.25.[54]

Amtrak carries nearly 31 million passengers on its national network.[55] The country's rail system, a series of weaving lines for both freight and passenger traffic, constitutes a major part of this country's economic life. In the world of commerce, trains deliver more cargo mile per mile, and more efficiently than any on-land trucking company is capable of doing. "Every day, more than one million shipments of hazardous chemicals are transported throughout the nation's infrastructure; a large percentage of these chemicals are transported by rail and are prone to becoming airborne."[56]

The security of this commercial flow is critical to the U.S. economic health. The potential for both human and infrastructure destruction is easy to project and anticipate. Both rail and mass transit systems are part of the family of critical infrastructure essential to a secure America. While there are a host of laws governing hazmat transport and

---

[53] 49 U.S. Code § 44920.

[54] American Public Transportation Association, *2013 Public Transportation Fact Book* 11 (2013), at http://www.apta.com/resources/statistics/Documents/FactBook/2013-APTA-Fact-Book.pdf, last accessed January 24, 2016.

[55] Amtrak, *National Fact Sheet: FY 2014*, at https://www.amtrak.com/ccurl/101/724/Amtrak-National-Fact-Sheet-FY2014,0.pdf, last accessed January 24, 2016.

[56] R.C. Paolino, All Aboard: Making the Case for a Comprehensive Rerouting Policy to Reduce the Vulnerability of Hazardous Rail-Cargoes to Terrorist Attack, *193 Mil. L. Rev.* 144 (2007).

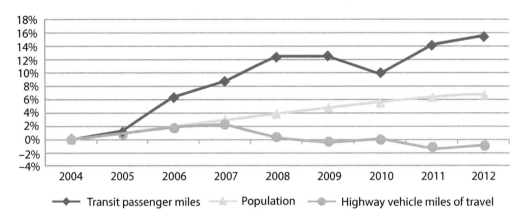

Figure 11.25 Since 2004, transit use has grown more than population or highway travel. (From Transit Passenger Miles from *APTA Public Transportation Fact Book* for 2004 through 2011 and estimated from *APTA Public Transportation Ridership Report* unlinked trip data for 2012, Population from U.S. Census Bureau, Highway Vehicle Miles of Travel from Federal Highway Administration *Travel Volume Trends*.)

other regulatory requirements for the movement of goods, the rail industry and government itself are trying to play catch- up with all possible harms and threats. The current emphasis by TSA and other governmental authorities is to engage industry partners that aid in tracking and the security of freight.[57]

Web Exercise: To assess the vulnerabilities of a mass transit system and discover proper steps to prevent, visit http://www.apta.com/resources/standards/Documents/APTA-SS-SIS-RP-012-13.pdf.

In rail and mass transit, the demands of risk assessment are more global and less contained than the security checkpoint at an airport. TSA, working closely with state, federal, and local law enforcement and private security forces, must see vulnerability, threat, and risk in a much larger framework. Instead of the targeted emphasis of passenger at a point of entry, the risk analysis in transit and rail must be conducted at various headquarters and stations, as well as in the whole field of operation. The tracks are the path to follow so to speak. Strengthening the security of the country's freight and passenger rail systems, and reducing the risk associated with the transportation of security-sensitive materials, such as poisonous by inhalation hazard materials, certain explosive materials, and certain high-level radioactive material shipments, is a constant challenge for security professionals. At the federal level, DHS has also formally codified the right of the TSA to inspect rail facilities and equipment for these purposes.[58] DHS also works closely with a wide array of other federal agencies to carry out this purpose, including the Department of Transportation, the Federal Railroad Administration, and federal law enforcement agencies concerned about interstate crime and terrorism.[59]

In the private corporate sector, DHS depends upon the cooperation of the country's numerous freight carriers, such as CSX, Norfolk Southern, BNSF, Union Pacific, and others, to ensure safety on the rails. DHS created a public–private partnership committee of both public and private entities to consult on rail policy. Its members include the following:

- Association of American Railroads
- American Short Line and Regional Railroad Association
- Amtrak
- Anacostia and Pacific
- BNSF Railway Company
- Canadian National
- Canadian Pacific Railway

---

[57] J. Straw, Report: Federal Freight Security Must Go Beyond Hazmat, *Sec. Mgmt* (May 2009).

[58] See M.A. Gips, Rail Security in Transition, *Sec. Mag.* (July 2006), at 29.

[59] Congressional Research Service, *Transportation Security: Issues for the 112th Congress* 12 (February 1, 2011), at http://www.fas.org/sgp/crs/homesec/RL33512.pdf.

- CSX Transportation
- Genesee & Wyoming
- Iowa Interstate Railroad Ltd.
- Kansas City Southern Railway Company
- Metra
- Norfolk Southern
- RailAmerica
- Union Pacific Railroad Company
- Wheeling & Lake Erie Railway

Both the public and the private sector are stakeholders in ensuring a safe and secure rail and mass transit system. More than 6,000 transit service providers, commuter railroads, and long-distance trains travel daily. Nearly 600 transit systems operate in urban areas, while Amtrak provides passenger service on nearly 22,000 miles of track. The story for freight is even more positive. See Figure 11.26.[60]

Rail companies provide both internal and external security for their valuable assets, trackage, buildings, and facilities as well as store houses and warehouses for capital equipment.

Major rail firms have long-established security offices with tested protocols to protect these assets.[61] CSX, a major northeastern freight carrier, funds its own police department whose mission is

Just like the other departments within CSX, the CSX Police know that our Core Values are more than a catchy phrase or slogan – they are the values we live by. We are a professional, highly trained and fully accredited law enforcement agency dedicated to protecting CSX employees, our customers' freight and the communities we serve.

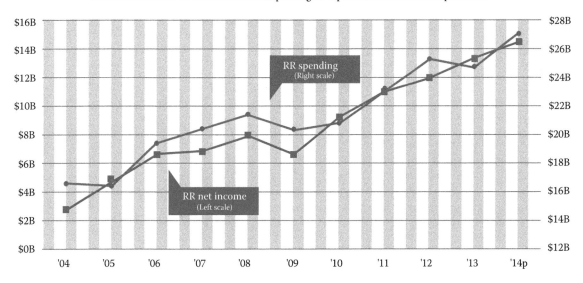

RAILROAD PROFITABILITY ENABLES INCREASED SPENDING
Railroad net income correlates to railroad spending on capital and maintenance expenditures

Figure 11.26 Net railroad income correlates to railroad spending on capital and maintenance expenditures. (From Association of American Railroads.)

[60] Association of American Railroads, *2015 Outlook* (2015), at https://www.aar.org/Documents/Outlook%202015/2015OutlookReport.pdf, last accessed January 24, 2016.

[61] See P. Luica, Public-Private Partnerships Are a Security Must, *Railway Pro* (November 24, 2011) , at http://www.railwaypro.com/wp/public-private-partnerships-are-a-security-must/.

It Starts with the Customer

We believe everyone is our customer: the communities in which CSX operates, our business partners, and our employees. From education and awareness programs to partnership development, and from emergency response to training exercises, the CSX Police Department is committed to the safety and security of all of our customers.

People Make the Difference

We believe in the professional and personal development of all members of the Police Department. More importantly, we expect that CSX Special Agents treat everyone they encounter with dignity and respect. CSX Special Agents are assigned throughout the 23-state CSX operating network and work closely with local, state and federal law enforcement agencies to amplify the efforts of all agencies in their territories.

Safety is a Way of Life

We believe in maintaining a safe environment and protecting the community, our employees, and our property from potential threats, and our commitment is unwavering. Our special agents and other CSX employees are woven into the fabric of the communities throughout our operating network.

Fact Based – Right Results, Right Way

No speculation. No bias. No shortcuts. We believe in making fact-based decisions and doing things the right way, regardless of how much time and effort it takes. Our reputation as solid partners in the community needs to be earned each and every day.[62]

Web Exercise: Find out about the CSX police force and various careers in rail security at https://www.csx.com/index.cfm/about-us/company-overview/csx-police-department/.

Other rail freight companies such as Burlington Northern Sante Fe Rail and Norfolk Southern Railway have similar police and security frameworks.

Web Exercise: Find out about the diverse career opportunities for safety and security professionals by visiting the American Association of Railroads at https://www.aar.org/Pages/Careers.aspx.

Private security firms are actively engaged in rail, both freight and passenger, and mass transit security at every level of protection. Mass transit security is perceived as the most aggressive growth area for private security firms with projections of 1.57 billion in revenue during 2016.[63] As an industry example, Securitas delivers three levels of rail security and safety by directing traffic at rail facilities, overseeing parking facilities and providing direct track security services in designated areas. In commuter services, Securitas has taken an aggressive posture providing wholesale security services such as Sound Transit, located in Western Washington State.

Web Exercise: Read how the company delivers a full menu of rail security services at http://www.securitasinc.com/globalassets/us/files/case-studies/updated-case-studies/case-study---sound-transit.pdf.[64]

Allied Barton delivers a similar series of services in Santa Clara Valley Transit Authority (VTA) in California. The company rightfully is proud of its cutting-edge services but also its healthy and efficient partnership with local law enforcement. Each needs one another to carry out security oversight in this large system.

Security for the VTA operates under the Protected Services Division and consists of two parts: law enforcement duties provided by the Santa Clara County Sheriff's Department and private security. "Local law enforcement and the private security provider work together to create a complete security program for the VTA," said Mark Mahaffey, Operations Manager Facilities Maintenance and Security for the VTA. "It is important that our public transportation system is safe, and that rules and regulations are enforced."[65,66]

The private security industry has been particularly successful in moving into once- sacrosanct areas of public policing, especially in public transportation and commuter hubs. Privatization in this area appears not to be temporary,

---

[62] CSX, CSX Police Department, at https://www.csx.com/index.cfm/about-us/company-overview/csx-police-department/.

[63] D. Gelinas, Securing Mass Transit a Growing Area of Opportunity for Security Integrators, *Security Systems News* (March 2011), at 2; see also S. Ives, Mass Transit Security Market on Track for Big Growth, *Security Systems News* (January 2015), at 2.

[64] Securitas International, Case Study: Sound Transit, Western Washington State, at http://www.securitasinc.com/globalassets/us/files/case-studies/updated-case-studies/case-study---sound-transit.pdf.

[65] See Allied Barton, Security Strengthens Public Transportation Safety Message, at http://www.alliedbarton.com/Resources-for-You/Case-Studies/View-Case-Study/ArticleId/210/Security-Program-Strengthens-Message-that-Public-Transportation-is-Safe.

[66] *Ibid.*

and when you couple this undeniable trend with rising passenger rates, it is a niche the industry can look forward to.[67] As a result of this growth, the security dynamics are intensifying. The same can also be said of freight rail where the economics of goods movement is undeniably efficient and environmentally unrivaled. Indeed, the entire rail industry often touts its lack of an environmental footprint when compared to other methods of passage.[68]

In November 2008, DHS promulgated rules that ensure a safer system, which include the following:

- *Secure chain of custody*: Shippers will physically inspect security-sensitive materials rail cars prior to shipment. The rule is applicable to 46 key urban areas.

- *Communication*: The rule requires freight and passenger railroad carriers, rail transit systems, and certain rail hazardous materials facilities to designate a rail security coordinator (RSC). The RSC will serve as the liaison to DHS for intelligence information, security-related activities, and ongoing communications with TSA.

- *Reporting security concerns*: The rule requires freight and passenger railroads to immediately report incidents, potential threats, and significant security concerns to TSA.

- *Location tracking*: The rule requires freight railroad carriers and certain rail hazardous materials shippers and receivers, at the request of TSA, to report the location of individual rail cars containing security-sensitive materials within 5 minutes, and the locations of all cars containing security-sensitive materials within 30 minutes.

- *Inspection authority*: TSA is authorized to inspect freight and passenger railroad carriers, rail transit systems, and certain facilities that ship or receive specified hazardous materials by rail.

TSA, in conjunction with the Federal Transit Administration, has published specific protective measures for mass transit systems. Review this comprehensive list of recommendations in Appendix E.

11.2.3.1 Private security for rail and transit

Whether for freight or passenger, whether operated by public or private entities, the demand for security protocols has never been greater than at the present. Indeed, DHS concluded in 2007 that rail and mass transit operations were woefully inadequate in various areas, including information sharing, research and development, public education, training and exercises, tunnels, and underwater passages.[69]

The sheer geographic volume of critical infrastructure makes the task of security and safety a daunting task and requires high-level professionalism to carry it out. For example, Norfolk Southern's "system" captures nearly half of the United States. See Figure 11.27.[70]

Despite some predictable shortcomings, most rail and transit systems have made enormous strides in the world of security. The GAO concluded that slow but sure improvements to rail security were being made but further improvements were critical to its future as an industry.[71] The GAO also concluded that the rail industry failed to share information as seamlessly as need be in matters of security and called upon the industry to make improvements in this direction.[72,73]

Web Exercise: Take a virtual train tour aboard the Burlington Northerner Santa Fe Line at http://www.bnsf.com/tour/.

---

[67] M. Roberts, Keeping Mass Transit Ahead of the Curve, *Sec. Mgmt* (November 2005), at https://sm.asisonline.org/Pages/Keeping-Mass-Transit-Ahead-of-the-Curve.aspx.

[68] See California High Speed Rail Authority, High-Speed Rail Environmental Benefits, at http://www.hsr.ca.gov/Programs/Green_Practices/environmental_benefits.html.

[69] Department of Homeland Security, Transportation Systems: Critical Infrastructure and Key Resources Sector Specific Plan as Input to the National Infrastructure Protection Plan A81-81 (2007), at http://www.cfr.org/us-strategy-and-politics/transportation-systems-critical-infrastructure-key-resources-sector-specific-plan-input-national-infrastructure-protection-plan/p14638.

[70] Norfolk Southern, System Overview, at http://www.nscorp.com/content/nscorp/en/system-overview.html.

[71] U.S. Government Accountability Office, *Rail Security: TSA Improved Risk Assessment but Could Further Improve Training and Information Sharing* (June 14, 2011), at http://www.gao.gov/assets/130/126419.html.

[72] U.S. Government Accountability Office, *Transit Security Information Sharing: DHS Could Improve Information Sharing through Streamlining and Increased Outreach* (September 2010), at http://www.gao.gov/new.items/d10895.pdf; see also *U.S. Government Accountability Office, Rail Security: TSA Improved Risk Assessment But Could Further Improve Training and Information Sharing* (June 14, 2011), at http://www.gao.gov/assets/130/126419.html.

[73] BNSF Railway, Rail Bridge Safety, at http://www.bnsf.com/communities/pdf/BNSF-Rail-Bridge-Safety.pdf.

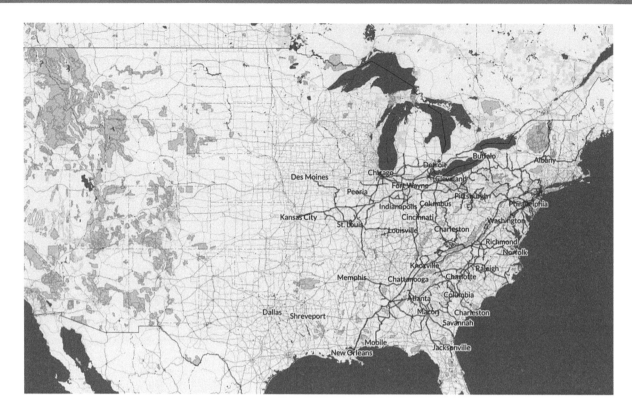

Figure 11.27   Norfolk Southern's route map.

Figure 11.28   London Underground Bombing in 2005.

The array of new initiatives in rail and mass transit is beginning to make its mark.[74] Aside from inculcating a general theory of risk assessment and mitigation, the industry sees itself as a partner with public officials. A good deal of debate exists on how to provide strong security protocols for mass transit given the events in London Underground and Munich Ax Attacks and others. The capacity for destruction at mass transit is unfathomable. See Figure 11.28.

---

[74] U.S. Government Accountability Office, *Positive Train Control: Additional Oversight Needed as Most Railroads Do Not Expect to Meet 2015 Implementation Deadline*, GAO-15-739 (September 2015), at http://www.gao.gov/assets/680/672320.pdf, last accessed January 24, 2016; U.S. Government Accountability Office, *Passenger Rail Security: Consistent Incident Reporting and Analysis Needed to Achieve Program Objectives*, GAO-13-20 (December 2012), at http://www.gao.gov/assets/660/650995.pdf, last accessed January 24, 2016.

To beef up security, some specialists argue that mass transit need adopt the TSA air security protocols. Others find the suggestion impractical due to the sheer volume of traffic. Other methods of automated intelligence and behavioral assessment may make better sense.[75] Just as evident has been the technological investment of mass transit carriers seeking to provide a safe environment for their passengers. Hence, mass transit is heavily invested in "video surveillance, access control, bollards, gates, chemical sensors and tunnel intrusion detection."[76] Technology crucially provides that layer of security that human beings cannot fully deliver for in effective technologies "creates value for millions of consumers every day."[77] Technology comprises more than software and data programs but unfailing dedication to proper design, environmental architecture that comports with safety and security, and lighting systems that eliminate "dark shadows on the rail platforms and stairwells."[78] The clamor for technological and security improvements shall simply increase as federal authorities continue to see the transit location as a real and bona fide target for the terrorist. A great deal of grants and related funding drives this emphasis in operational boards that oversee transit for these funds make physical security improvements a reality.[79]

11.2.3.2 Amtrak: The National Passenger Rail Corporation

Amtrak carries out both behind-the-scenes and front-line security measures aimed at improving passenger rail security. While it has its own police force, it relies on private security partners in various locales and works collaboratively with the many freight lines it shares track with. Depending upon the locale and other factors, the security practices may be uniform or random in design. Some of the common Amtrak security protocols are the following:

- Uniformed police officers and mobile security teams
- Random passenger and carry-on baggage screening
- K-9 units
- Checked baggage screening
- Onboard security checks
- Identification checks

Amtrak has also received generous funding for the safety and security of its complex infrastructure. In the Northeast corridor, Amtrak operates in diverse environments with dramatic challenges for the security operative. In 2008, DHS awarded $25 million to Amtrak to begin the process of securing bridges, tunnels, overhangs, and other locations with target potential. That sum has either been renewed or increased until the present.[80] Preparedness grants have been regularly awarded Amtrak and other intercity passenger rail programs since that time. In 2015, DHS provided more than $10 million to protect critical surface transportation infrastructure and the traveling public from acts of terrorism and increase the resilience of the Amtrak rail system.[81]

Amtrak now deploys specialized mobile tactical units that conduct random baggage searches and other security responsibility. The mobile security team's squads take on many forms, including armed specialized Amtrak police, explosives-detecting K-9 units, and armed counterterrorism special agents in tactical uniforms. The mobile units were developed in conjunction with the federal, state, and private industry sectors to improve security practices. The mobile security team's procedures will not impact train schedules (Figure 11.29).

The new procedures are an enhancement to strategic security measures already in place, such as

- Uniformed police and plainclothes officers on trains and in stations
- Security cameras

---

[75] See L. Fiondella, S. Gokhale, N. Lownes & M. Accorsi, Security and Performance Analysis of Passenger Screening Checkpoint for Mass-Transit Systems, *Homeland Sec. Aff.*, Supplement 6, Article 3 (April 2013).

[76] See B. Zalud, Mass Transit's Fast Track to Better Security, *Sec. Mag.* (April 2015), at 34–35.

[77] S. Hunt, The Heartland of Security Innovation, *Sec. Mag.* (February 2007), at 16.

[78] T. Anderson, A Site for Safe Transit, *Sec. Mgmt* (March 2008).

[79] D. Erikson, Ensuring a Robust Level of Federal Funding for Transit Security, *Sec. Mgmt* (June 2009), at 56.

[80] U.S. Dept. of Homeland Security, Office of Inspector General, DHS Grants Used for Mitigating Risk to Amtrak Rail Stations, at http://www.documentcloud.org/documents/240714-dhs-grants-used-for-mitigating-risks-to-amtrak.html, last accessed January 24, 2016.

[81] U.S. Dept. of Homeland Security, DHS Announces Grant Guidance for Fiscal Year (FY) 2015 Preparedness Grants, at http://www.dhs.gov/news/2015/04/02/dhs-announces-grant-guidance-fiscal-year-fy-2015-preparedness-grants, last accessed January 24, 2016.

Figure 11.29   Amtrak's Mobile Tactical Unit helps secure the railways.

- Random identification checks
- "See Something, Say Something" passenger education program to promote involvement and raise vigilance
- Investments in state-of-the-art security technology
- Security awareness training for the entire Amtrak workforce
- Behind-the-scenes activities that remain undisclosed

Amtrak is also investing in cutting-edge technologies to improve its security efforts and presently testing intrusion detection technologies, employing explosive detection and vapor K-9 teams, conducting more passenger screenings, and actively participating in the Joint Terrorism Task Force in its various regions. Finally, Amtrak is calling upon its customer base to be active players in the security effort. Through its Partners for Amtrak Safety and Security (PASS) program, customers are asked to be active participants in the who, what, where, when, and how of criminal conduct.

Web Exercise: Learn about the PASS program at: https://pass.amtrak.com/.

In addition, Amtrak launched in 2010, Operation Railsafe targets rail line infrastructure and partners with local, state, and federal law enforcement and corporate and private security interests to assure safe and secure operation (Figure 11.30).

The program has three primary goals, most of which relate to training and awareness:

- Provide participating agencies, first responders, and other Amtrak stakeholders with situational awareness and a better understanding of how to protect Amtrak's passengers, employees, and critical infrastructure from acts of terrorism
- Decrease Amtrak's risk from and vulnerability to a potential attack by enhancing situational awareness of critical assets, establishing interoperability, sharing resources, providing an overview of rail safety, and promoting partnership opportunities with like agencies
- Aid antiterrorism efforts designed to protect the Amtrak employees, passengers, trains, and infrastructure and maximize resource planning and allocation, as well as establish and maintain critical relationships with partner agencies.

11.2.3.3 CSX: The freight line

Just as the public rail entities have core responsibilities, so too do the private rail companies. CSX is an excellent example of a progressive freight shipper with a massive route network in the eastern half of the United States. Shipment

Figure 11.30   Operation railsafe logo.

of hazardous and security-sensitive materials is subject to a host of regulations and other requirements.[82] Railroads also must

- Compile security data based on commodity and route type
- Identify security vulnerabilities
- Identify alternative routes
- Develop programs of safety and security
- Revisit route selections
- Communicate with state and federal officials
- Design tracking systems for sensitive material
- Work in unity with the motor carriers whose cargo the rail transports

See Figure 11.31 for a map of CSX's rail system.

CSX, just as its sister carriers, abides by a host of regulations. Of recent interest are the TSA requirements that shipments to designated urban areas be processed according to new protocols, and additionally, that the chain of custody of these shipments be tracked. The materials subject to the rules include explosives, toxic by inhalation materials (TIH), poisonous by inhalation materials (PIH), and bulk amounts of radioactive materials, all of which are now designated rail security-sensitive materials.

TSA now insists that certain rail secure areas be the exclusive points of shipping or receiving facilities in these designated areas. As of February 15, 2009, rail companies, such as CSX, are only able to accept shipments of rail security-sensitive materials from rail secure areas. In areas designated high-threat urban areas (HTUAs), delivery will be possible only to a rail secure area.

Internally, CSX has established a sophisticated and impressive security and safety program. Aside from its materials training, emphasis on employee safety, and other industrial applications, CSX fully comprehends the mix of the public and private interests in its rail operation. The line shares information with governmental entities and partners with myriad agencies dedicated to safety and security. Examples of these efforts are what follow:

- *CSX Transportation's (CSXT) Network Operations Workstation*: A cornerstone of this partnership is CSXT's sharing of its highly specialized secure Network Operations Workstation (NOW) system. Key highlights of the NOW system include
- *Enhanced monitoring*: Provides state homeland security and law enforcement officials with a tool to identify the status of CSXT trains and rail cars in each state. Before, officials needed to call CSXT to access this information.
- *Information sharing*: Helps security officials prepare for and, if needed, respond to emergency situations.
- *Targeted security*: With additional information about what is carried on rails, state officials can more efficiently allocate law enforcement resources, coordinate with CSXT security officials, and integrate rail security into ongoing law enforcement operations.
- *Joint law enforcement and emergency responder training*: Law enforcement officials train with the CSXT Police Rapid Response Team—a group of highly skilled police officers specifically trained to respond to security incidents. Additionally, state and community emergency first responders train alongside CSXT's experts in hazardous materials and emergency response.
- *Sharing of hazardous materials density studies*: These data help emergency response organizations plan their resources and identify the types of emergency response training applicable to their jurisdiction.
- *Closer coordination of law enforcement operations in and around CSXT yards*: CSXT can provide its partners with an around-the-clock access to its rail security professionals.
- *Developing better rail security policies*: States and CSXT continue to work with policy makers to identify important public policy issues that can impact and improve rail security.

---

[82] J.B. Reed, Securing Dangerous Rail Shipments, *State Legislatures* 38 (October/November 2007).

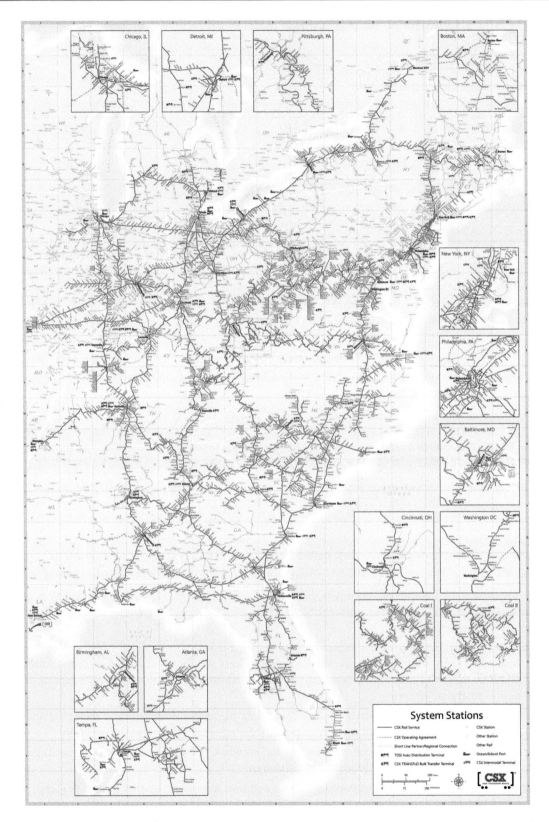

Figure 11.31   CSX's rail system map.

The industry works closely with local, state, and federal authorities to secure the nation's railroads. Freight railroads remain in constant communication with the U.S. Department of Transportation security personnel, the FBI, the National Security Council, and state and local law enforcement officers.

11.2.3.4 Southeastern Pennsylvania Transit Authority: Rail mass transit

The Southeastern Pennsylvania Transit Authority (SEPTA) is one of the nation's largest rail commuter systems. It also connects and collaborates with other carriers and is part and parcel of a very large collective of mass transit providers, including New Jersey Transit, Delaware Area Transit, and Amtrak. The system can readily and very easily hook up the rider to New York, Baltimore, and Washington, DC. In this extreme congestion, SEPTA needs always be mindful of the security threat (Figure 11.32).

SEPTA takes security threats very seriously so that passengers are afforded maximum security and protection. Increased presence of transit police officers on the system's cars and stations has been a high priority for SEPTA management. Also present throughout the transit system, although obviously less visible, is a trained team of undercover, plainclothes SEPTA police officers who are working to ensure the security of our passengers.

Web Exercise: Learn about careers in law enforcement on SEPTA at http://autohire.careershop.com/septajobs/default.asp?ContentID=7.

Yet when one considers the sheer volume of passengers on this system day to day, are these general recommendations enough? Does a transit police force have the capability to trace and track every imaginable threat? Is the geography alone too much to cover? Most observers of mass transit indicate there are simply too many holes in the dike to be confident about thwarting the all threats—and just as frustratingly, too many players in the overall mix. To be successful, mass transit systems will have to be better organized. Here are some suggestions:

TSA's 17 Security and Emergency Preparedness Action Items

1. Establish written System Security Programs and Emergency Management Plans.
2. Define roles and responsibilities for security and emergency management.

Figure 11.32   SEPTA's Wilmington Delaware station.

3. Ensure that operations and maintenance supervisors, forepersons, and managers are held accountable for security issues under their control.

4. Coordinate Security and Emergency Management Plan(s) with local and regional agencies.

5. Establish and maintain a security and emergency training program.

6. Establish plans and protocols to respond to the DHS Homeland Security Advisory System threat levels.

7. Implement and reinforce a public security and emergency awareness program.

8. Conduct Table Top and Functional drills.

9. Establish and use a risk management process to assess and manage threats, vulnerabilities, and consequences.

10. Participate in an information-sharing process for threat and intelligence information.

11. Establish and use a reporting process for suspicious activity (internal and external).

12. Control access to security-critical facilities with identification badges for all visitors, employees, and contractors.

13. Conduct physical security inspections.

14. Conduct background investigations of employees and contractors.

15. Control access to documents of security-critical systems and facilities.

16. Implement a process for handling and access to sensitive security information.

17. Conduct security program audits.[83]

While all of the recommendations are poignant, the training side of the security and risk plan cannot be forgotten or neglected. In every facet of mass transit, the risk to passengers and employees is high. Those entrusted with transit operation must be sure to train the employees to the highest level. TSA has devised an excellent matrix of learning to assure that the essential subject matter is covered and that costs are contained. See Figure 11.33.

Web Exercise: Enjoy SEPTA's interactive instructional tool, "Respect the Train," which highlights safety and security issues in transit stations at http://www.septa.org/safety/safety-interactive-2015/index.html.

11.3 CRITICAL INFRASTRUCTURE: FOOD, AGRICULTURE, AND WATER

Just as water contamination has enormous impacts on the public health of the nation, so too does the integrity of its food supply. Here again, there exists a widespread potential for harm to a significant portion of the population.[84] Agriculture and food systems are vulnerable to disease, pests, or poisonous agents that occur naturally, are unintentionally introduced, or are intentionally delivered by acts of terrorism. Food can be attacked on many fronts, including

- Biological and chemical agents
- Naturally occurring, antibiotic-resistant, and genetically engineered substances
- Deadly agents and those tending to cause gastrointestinal discomfort
- Highly infectious agents and those that are not communicable
- Substances readily available to any individual and those that are more difficult to acquire
- Agents that must be weaponized and those that are accessible in a useable form[85]

America's agriculture and food system is an extensive, open, interconnected, diverse, and complex structure.

---

[83] TSA, *TSA's Preparedness for Mass Transit and Passenger Rail Emergencies* 32 (March 2010), at https://www.oig.dhs.gov/assets/Mgmt/OIG_10-68_Mar10.pdf.

[84] See Congressional Research Service, *The Federal Food Safety System: A Primer* (January 11, 2011), at http://www.fas.org/sgp/crs/misc/RS22600.pdf.

[85] U.S. Food and Drug Administration, *Risk Assessment for Food Terrorism and Other Food Safety Concerns* (2003), at http://seafood.oregonstate.edu/.pdf%20Links/Risk%20Assessment%20for%20Food%20Terrorism%20and%20Other%20Food%20Safety%20Concerns.pdf, last accessed February 7, 2016.

BASIC MASS TRANSIT SECURITY TRAINING PROGRAM

Training Description	Focus	Standard	Categories of Employees to Receive									Federal Course Availability	
			Front-Line Employees	Station Managers	Administrative and Support Staff	Maintenance Workers	Mid-Level Management	Senior Management	Operations Control Center Staff	Security Guards	Law Enforcement	Title	Duration
Security Awareness	Enhance capability to identify, report, and react to suspicious activity and security incidents	2 Hours Annually (minimum) Recurring	X	X	X	X	X	X	X	X	X	System Security Awareness for Transportation Employees	4 Hours Classroom 6 Hours Train the Trainer
Behavior Recognition	Recognize behaviors associated with terrorists' reconnaissance and planning activities, including the conduct of surveillance. Applies lessons learned from the Israeli security meeting.	2 Hours Annually (minimum) Recurring	X	X		X	X	X	X	X	X	Terrorist Awareness Recognition and Reaction (TARR)	4 Hours Classroom 6 Hours Train the Trainer
Immediate Emergency Response	Prepare passenger rail train operators to deal with explosive detonations, incendiaries, released chemical hazards, and similar threats in the confines of trains and system infrastructure.	4 Hours Annually (minimum) Recurring	X	X					X		X	Incident Management for Transit Employees and Passenger Management (courses in development by NTI) Transit agencies do conduct local programs on this subject	TBD
National Incident Management System (NIMS)	Ensure transit agency emergency preparedness and response personnel gain and retain the knowledge and skills necessary to operate under NIMS in accordance with the National Response Plan (NRP).	Train on NIMS once; reinforce in drills and exercises		X				X	X		X	National Incident Management System (NIMS) for Transit	1 to 3 Days
Operations Control Center Readiness	Identify security vulnerabilities. Understand and exercise role of OCC personnel in preventing terrorist attacks. Distinguish characteristics of improvised explosive devices (IEDs) and weapons of mass destruction. Specify priorities during a terrorist attack and manage incident response. Apply transit agency's operational plans for response to IED and WMD scenarios, directing and coordinating activities in the system.	Train for OCC readiness once; reinforce in drills and exercises							X			Rail Operations Control Center Response to WMD Incidents	6 Hours

Figure 11.33 Basic Mass Transit Security Training Program.

(Continued)

MASS TRANSIT SECURITY FOLLOW-ON COURSES

Training Description	Focus	Standard	Front-Line Employees	Station Managers	Administrative and Support Staff	Maintenance Workers	Mid-Level Management	Senior Management	Operations Control Center Staff	Security Guards	Law Enforcement	Federal Course Title	Duration
Management of Transit Emergencies I (4-day course)	Ensure employees throughout the transit agency understand individual roles in emergency response and the transit system's role in emergencies or disasters in the system and the broader community.		X	x	X	X	X	X	X	X	X	1) Effectively Managing Transit Emergencies	1) 4 Days
Management of Transit Emergencies II (1-day course)	Ensure employees throughout the transit agency understand individual roles in emergency response and the transit system's role in emergencies or disasters in the system and the broader community.		X	x	X	X	X	X	X	X	X	2) Managing Terrorist Incidents in Rail Tunnels	2) 6 Hours
Coordinated Interagency Emergency Response	Advance interoperability of the transit agency with multiple responding entities in emergency response.		X	x		X				X	X	Connecting Communities Emergency Response and Preparedness Forum	2 Days
Managing Counterterrorism Programs	Enable transit agency management officials to develop and manage a counterterrorism program in a transit system.						X	X	X			Strategic Counterterrorism for Transit Managers	2 Days
Prevention and Mitigation - IEDS and WMD: T4 3-day course	Enhance capabilities to identify threats from improvised explosive devices and weapons of mass destruction (chemical, biological, radiological, nuclear) to identify, report, and react to suspicious activity and security incidents		X	X	X	X				X	X	1) Transit Terrorist Tools & Tactics (T4)	1) T4 - 3 days
Prevention and Mitigation - IEDS and WMD: CBRNE Incident Management 1-day course	Enhance capabilities to identify threats from improvised explosive devices and weapons of mass destruction (chemical, biological, radiological, nuclear) to identify, report, and react to suspicious activity and security incidents		X	X	X	X				X	X	2) Transit Explosives (CBRNE) Incident Management Seminar	2) CBRNE Incident Management - 5 hours

(Continued)

Figure 11.33 (Continued) Basic Mass Transit Security Training Program.

Training Description	Focus	Standard	Front-Line Employees	Station Managers	Administrative and Support Staff	Maintenance Workers	Mid-Level Management	Senior Management	Operations Control Center Staff	Security Guards	Law Enforcement	Federal Course Availability — Title	Duration
Transit Vehicle Hijacking Prevention and Response	Enable employees to develop and implement plans and procedures to respond to transit vehicle hijackings and workplace violence		X	X		X			X	X	X	Threat Management and Emergency Response to Bus and Rail Hijackings	1 Day
Integrated Anti-Terrorism Security Program	Enhance capabilities of transit agency security officials, law enforcement personnel, and others with interaction with passengers to detect, deter, and prevent acts of terrorism.						X	X		X	X	Land Transportation Anti-Terrorism Training Program (FLETC)	5 Days
Transit System Security Design	Expand integration of security considerations into designs of new transit systems and improvements of existing systems.						X	X				Transit System Security Design Review	3 days
TRAIN-THE-TRAINER COURSES													
Security Awareness	Enhance capability to identify, report, and react to suspicious activity and security incidents		X	X	X	X	X	X	X	X	X	System Security Awareness for Transportation Employees	4 Hours Classroom 6 Hours Train the Trainer
Behavior Recognition	Recognize behaviors associated with terrorists' reconnaissance and planning activities, including the conduct of surveillance. Applies lessons learned from the Israeli security meeting.		X	X		X	X	X	X	X	X	Terrorist Awareness Recognition and Reaction (TARR)	4 Hours Classroom 6 Hours Train the Trainer

Figure 11.33 (Continued) Basic Mass Transit Security Training Program.

> *Vision and Purpose of DHS: Food and Agricultural Section*
>
> The FA Sector comprises complex production, processing, and delivery systems. The mission of the FA Sector is to protect against a disruption in the food supply that would pose a serious threat to public health, safety, welfare, or to the national economy. These food and agriculture systems are almost entirely under private ownership, and they operate in highly competitive global markets, strive to operate in harmony with the environment, and provide economic opportunities and an improved quality of life for U.S. citizens and others worldwide.
>
> Differences in commodity type, farm size, operator, and household characteristics complicate prevention and protection efforts for individual operations and, ultimately, the sector as a whole. In recent years, changes in the rules of trade, shifts in domestic policy, and new developments in technology have altered the competitive landscape of global agriculture and challenges facing American farmers.
>
> Securing this sector presents unique challenges because food and agriculture systems in the United States are extensive, open, interconnected, and diverse, and they have complex structures. Food products move rapidly in commerce to consumers, but the time required for detection and identification of attacks and contaminations, such as animal or plant disease introduction or food contamination, can be lengthy and complex. Therefore, attacks and contaminations on the FA Sector could result in severe animal, plant, public health, and economic consequences.

Figure 11.34   Vision statement for the food and agriculture sector.

Responsibility for the food supply, in addition to the private security operative, resides in three government agencies: the U.S. Department of Agriculture (USDA), EPA, and DHS. In a recent report, these agencies set out a vision statement on the food supply.[86] See Figure 11.34.[87]

However, given the industrial and commercial nature of the farming industry, foodstuffs and food production, and agri-conglomerates, there is a free market, commercial and corporate aspect to the protection of these assets. For example, the behemoth food conglomerate Cargill, with 150,000 employees in 70 countries, readily takes an active role in assuring the safety and security of its product and its people. Cargill, like any other major corporation and business enterprise, has precious assets and people to protect, and with its worldwide presence in the agri-business, it needs skilled and highly educated professionals to staff and coordinate its offices throughout both the civilized and the developed world.

See Figure 11.35.

The agricultural industry is well aware of the security implications that food and water naturally bring to the fore—and why security systems and protocols are essential to success in this marketplace. This holds especially true in the undeveloped world where poverty and starvation make food a weapon for the unprincipled. Cargill, like other agri-businesses, delivers goods throughout the world by vessel and even aircraft to both rich environments and those bordering on the edge of malnutrition.[88] While there are at least a dozen major agricultural providers in the United States, each takes the challenge of security very seriously, mostly because the stakes are so high and the losses are so potentially significant.[89]

As appropriate, the role of government takes central stage in food supply protection with the USDA taking the lead role. The USDA, as part of its overall mission, holds thus: "The protection and integrity of America's agricultural production and food supply are essential to the health and welfare of both the domestic population and the global community."[90]

Web Exercise: The list of food recalls due to safety and health questions is quite surprising. Visit http://www.fsis.usda.gov/FSIS_Recalls/Recall_Case_Archive/index.asp.

---

[86] Department of Agriculture, Department of Homeland Security, and the Food and Drug Administration, *Critical Infrastructure and Key Resources for Sector Specific Plan as Input to the National Infrastructure Protection Plan* 2 (Washington, DC: U.S. Government Printing Office, 2007).

[87] Food and Agriculture DHS, *Sector-Specific Plan: An Annex to the National Infrastructure Protection Plan* (2010).

[88] Cargill, at http://www.cargill.com/wcm/groups/public/@ccom/documents/document/na3074109.pdf.

[89] No free Lunch: Agribusiness and Risks to Food Security, at http://www.preventionweb.net/english/hyogo/gar/2013/en/gar-pdf/chap10.pdf.

[90] U.S. Department of Agriculture, *Pre-Harvest Security Guidelines and Checklist 2006* 3 (Washington, DC: U.S. Government Printing Office, 2006), at http://www.usda.gov/documents/PreHarvestSecurity_final.pdf.

Security Manager (SM) will, under general supervision by the Russia Business Leaders and the Global Security Department, implement and manage country specific security strategic planning and coordination. The SM will align the security function (asset security, investigations, security intelligence, executive protection and crisis management) with the organization's overall objectives and the Global Security requirements and guidelines; track security and investigative trends while providing written metrics regarding the efficiency/effectiveness of security operations; provide requested data/projections during the annual budgeting process; and develop internal relationships with local business unit/function management and external relationships with local and federal law enforcement/intelligence agencies.

Key Responsibilities

+ Provides asset security leadership and support to businesses by developing and implementing local security plans, policies, procedures, standards and training for protecting personnel, property, product, and confidential information - 30%
+ Identify the largest potential risk areas (before allegations are made) and determine where we have gaps — a proactive approach.
+ Provides investigative leadership and at the direction of Global Security and country management, the SM will provide direct investigative support to resolve allegations of serious criminal activity, significant violations of corporate/local policy as well as alleged violations of Cargill's Guiding Principles - 30%
+ Responsible for the development of internal relationships with local business unit management, law, audit, information security, human resources and procurement. Additionally, responsible for external relationships with local and federal law enforcement and intelligence agencies - 13%
+ Provides security intelligence support to country management and the business units to keep them informed of issues that are, or could potentially impact, our businesses throughout the country including crime, terrorism, protests, civil unrest, weather, etc. - 8%
+ Following the Global Security guidelines, conducts threat assessments, gathers intelligence and develops the plans to protect local company executives and any visiting company executives - 4%
+ Tracks trends and measures the efficiency and effectiveness of security operations and provides written metrics - 4%
+ In support of Global Security, provides crisis management leadership, planning and support for the businesses to ensure the security/safety of our personnel during crises impacting our businesses - 4%
+ Implement and manage country specific fire safety and emergency politics, practices and results - 7%

Qualifications

Requirements

+ Master's Degree in criminal justice, security management or relevant subject matter
+ Certified Protection Professional (CPP) certified through ASIS
+ Minimum of 5 years of corporate security management experience
+ Experience managing security at several industrial sites across Russia
+ Experience conducting security risk assessments and implementing security best practices and procedures
+ Experience investigating criminal activity at a public or corporate level
+ Experience with executive protection and personal security
+ Crisis management and security intelligence experience
+ Strong multi-tasking capabilities
+ Ability to work within deadlines and time pressures
+ Excellent interpersonal and customer service skills
+ Strong problem solving skills and the ability to work independently/develop solutions independently.
+ Fluent in both the Russian and English languages (includes speaking, writing and reading)
+ Knowledge of Microsoft Office programs (Word, Excel, Powerpoint, Outlook, etc.)
+ Working knowledge and experience with security equipment such as card access, intrusion alarms and security cameras

Job Safety/Environmental Health

Primary Location: Russia-MOW-Moscow

Other Locations: Russia-TUL-Efremov, Russia-Leningrad Region, Russia-ROS-Rostov-on-Don, Russia-VOR-Voronezh

Figure 11.35   Career profile: security manager—Cargill.

DHS plays a critical role in the protection of our food supply and pays particular attention to the risk of large-scale food contamination. DHS poses seven criteria that measure the impact of agricultural contamination.

Criticality: What will be the public health impacts and economic costs associated with the attack?

Accessibility: How easy will it be for a terrorist to gain access and egress from the location of the food and agricultural product?

Recuperability: How readily will the food supply system recover from an attack?

Vulnerability: How easy or difficult will the attack be?

Effect: What calculable losses will there be directly resulting from the attack?

Recognizability: Are targets easy to discover and identify?

Shock: In a cumulative sense, how significant are the health, economic, and psychological impacts that result from the attack?

Those entrusted with production must be mindful of their product's safety and security as well. Whether it is grain or cattle, soybeans or chicken, the agricultural entrepreneur must tend to questions of security on a daily basis. Determining exactly how to ensure security in the agricultural sphere is no simple undertaking. Aside from the broad range of products and services, there is the added dilemma of multiple agency responsibility. While the USDA may be at the forefront, its policy making on food and its safety is influenced by myriad other agencies, such as the FDA and EPA, and its own internal history has protocols and programs that have historically dealt with food safety. In a sense, the question of food security, as evaluated in light of terroristic acts or mass scale contamination, is less on the forefront than natural spoilage or losses. Put another way, food safety and security must be evaluated in light of other risks previously not considered. The USDA urges its constituency to conduct risk assessments, to realize that security questions are central to farm operation, and to accept some level of personal responsibility for the integrity of facility and product. In fact, the USDA fully integrates the functions of security into its very makeup, as evidenced by its organizational chart in Figure 11.36.[91]

The USDA calls upon all owners in the agricultural sector to view security in both general and specific product terms. In the more general arena, it recommends the following assessment protocol:

- Procedures are in place for notifying appropriate law enforcement when a security threat is received, or when evidence of actual product tampering is observed.

- Procedures are in place for heightened awareness (especially when the DHS terrorism threat level is elevated) for unusual activities around the farm and increased disease symptoms among animals or crops.

- A current local, state, and federal government Homeland Security contact is maintained.

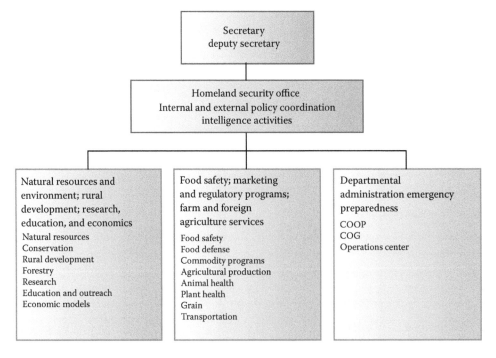

Figure 11.36   USDA structure for homeland protection and food safety.

[91] Agriculture, *supra* note 86 , at 36.

- All employees are encouraged to report any sign of product tampering.
- Facility boundaries are secured to prevent unauthorized entry.
- "No Trespassing" and "Restricted Entry" signs are posted appropriately.
- Alarms, motion detection lights, cameras, and other appropriate security equipment are used in key areas, as needed.
- Facility perimeter is regularly monitored for signs of suspicious activity or unauthorized entry.
- Doors, windows, gates, roof openings, vent openings, trailer bodies, railcars, and bulk storage tanks are secured at all times.
- Outside lighting is sufficient to allow detection of unusual activities.
- Fire, smoke, and heat detection devices are operable throughout the farm.
- Storage tanks for hazardous materials and potable water supply are protected from, and monitored for, unauthorized access.
- Wells and other water supplies are secured and routine testing is performed.
- Truck deliveries are verified against a roster of scheduled deliveries.
- Unscheduled deliveries are held away from facility premises pending verification of shipper and cargo.
- Records are maintained for all vehicles and equipment: make, model, serial number, service date, and so on.
- Vehicles and equipment are secured or immobilized when not in use; keys are never left in unattended vehicles.
- Machinery is removed from fields and stored appropriately; valuable equipment and tools are locked in a secure building.
- Entry into facility is controlled by requiring positive identification (i.e., picture ID).
- New employees are screened and references are checked.
- Visitors and guests are restricted to nonproduction areas unless accompanied by a facility employee.
- Where required by biosecurity procedures, visitors wear clean boots or coveralls (disposable boots and coveralls are provided for visitors).
- Areas are designated for check-in and check-out for visitors/deliveries (with a sign-in sheet for name, address, phone number, reason for visit).
- An inspection for signs of tampering or unauthorized entry is performed for all storage facilities regularly.
- Hazardous materials are purchased only from licensed dealers.
- A current inventory of hazardous or flammable chemicals (including drugs, chemicals, pesticides, and fertilizers) or other products (including chemical trade names, product type, EPA numbers, quantity, and usage) is maintained, and discrepancies are investigated immediately.
- A current inventory of stored fuel (diesel, gasoline, fuel oil, propane, oxygen, acetylene, kerosene, etc.) is maintained.
- A disease surveillance plan is available.
- Risk management plans have been developed or updated and shared with employees, family, visitors, customers, and local law enforcement.
- Plans include awareness of animal and plant health, as well as signs of tampering with crops, livestock, supplies, vehicles, equipment, and facilities.
- Orientation/training on security procedures is given to all facility employees at least annually.
- Passwords for USDA systems and programs are protected to prevent unauthorized user entry.[92]

11.3.1 Strategic Partnership Program on Agroterrorism

Attacks against the agricultural system would be an effective and frightful way of inflicting a terrorist act and law enforcement needs to anticipate the possibility. "Agroterrorism has been defined as the deliberate introduction of an

---

[92] USDA, *supra* note 90, at 10–11.

animal or plant disease with the goal of generating fear, causing economic losses or undermining social stability."[93] Knowledge about food supply resides in a bevy of private and public entities and will require a major collaboration. Blending diverse agencies with distinct approaches to security has been a challenge for those protecting the food supply. Put another way, private security, law enforcement officials, such as the FBI or Customs, will see the food problem through a prism of enforcement, while food safety specialists at the USDA or FDA may see things from a different perspective. The Strategic Partnership Program on Agroterrorism (SPPA) makes a noble effort to meld these various visions and to unify these diverse perspectives into one framework—that of food safety. Just as critically, the SPPA will enlist private industry concerns, from farmers to grain processors, from stockyard owners to fertilizer companies. The objectives of the SPPA are

- Validate or identify sector-wide vulnerabilities by conducting critical infrastructure/key resources (CI/KR) assessments in order to:
  - Identify gaps;
  - Inform Centers of Excellence and Sector Specific Agencies (SSA) of identified research needs; and
  - Catalog lessons-learned.
- Identify indicators and warnings that could signify planning for an attack.
- Develop mitigation strategies to reduce the threat/prevent an attack. Strategies may include actions that either industry or government may take to reduce vulnerabilities.
- Validate assessments conducted by the United States Government (USG) for food and agriculture sectors.
- Gather information to enhance existing tools that both USG and industry employ.
- Provide the USG and the industry with comprehensive reports including warnings and indicators, key vulnerabilities, and potential mitigation strategies.
- Provide sub-sector reports for the USG that combines assessment results to determine national critical infrastructure vulnerability points to support the National Infrastructure Protection Plan (NIPP) and national preparedness goals.
- Establish and/or strengthen relationships between Federal, State, and local law enforcement and the food and agriculture industry along with the critical food/agriculture sites visited.[94]

SPPA relies upon industry visitations to reach its conclusions about safety and security in the agricultural sector. This is why private industry, namely, farmers and food suppliers, is so integral to the SPPA process. SPPA assessments are conducted on a voluntary basis between one or more industry representatives for a particular product or commodity. As recommended by DHS and the USDA, industry production processes are evaluated in light of law enforcement officials. Together, they conduct a vulnerability assessment using the seven criteria noted above: *criticality, accessibility, recuperability, vulnerability, effect, recognizability*, and *shock*.

As a result of each assessment, participants identify weaknesses in the production cycle as well as recommendations on protective measures and mitigation steps that may reduce the vulnerability. By 2008, the assessments shown in Table 11.1 had been conducted under the SPPA program.[95]

Proposed future inspections, conducted by the USDA and the FDA, will tackle a host of foodstuffs and agricultural products including those shown in Table 11.2.[96]

Web Exercise: For full instructions on how to devise a food safety program, see http://www.fsis.usda.gov/PDF/Food_Defense_Plan.pdf.

---

[93] D. K. Stocker, P. M. Griffin, C.J. Kocher & T. M. Raquet, Agroterrorism: Risk Assessment and Proactive Responses, 5 *Homeland Sec. Rev.* 17 (2011) ; see also K. Govern, Agroterrorism and Ecoterrorism: A Survey of Indo-American Approaches under Law and Policy to Prevent and Defend against These Potential Threats Ahead, 10 *Fla. Coastal L. Rev.* 223 (2009).

[94] U.S. Food and Drug Administration, Strategic Partnership Agroterrorism (SPPA) Initiative, at http://www.fda.gov/Food/FoodDefense/FoodDefensePrograms/ucm080836.htm, last accessed February 7, 2016.

[95] U.S. Food and Drug Administration, *Strategic Partnership Program Agroterrorism (SPPA) Initiative: Final Summary Report September 2005–September 2008* (2008), Appendix A, at http://www.fda.gov/downloads/Food/FoodDefense/UCM181069.pdf, last accessed February 7, 2016.

[96] U.S. Food & Drug Admin., *U.S. Dept. of Homeland Security, U.S. Dept. of Agriculture, Federal Bureau of Investigation, Strategic Partnership Program Agroterrorism (SPPA) Initiative*—Second Year Status Report July 2006–September 2007, at http://www.fda.gov/Food/FoodDefense/FoodDefensePrograms/ucm08992.htm.

Table 11.1   Assessments conducted

Industry	SPPA assessments, trade associations, and subsectors					
	Food/commodity assessed	Date	States	Trade associations	SSA	Subsector(s)
Yogurt	Yogurt	Nov-05	TN, MN	International Dairy Foods Assn., National Yogurt Assn.	FDA	Processors/ manufacturers
Grain export elevator	Corn	Dec-05	LA	National Grain and Feed Assn.	FDA/ USDA	Producers/ plants
Bottled water	Bottled water	Jan-06	NJ	International Bottled Water Assn.	FDA	Processors/manufacturers
Baby food	Baby food (jarred)	Feb-06	MI	Food Products Assn.	FDA	Processors/manufacturers
School kitchens	Spaghetti sauce with meat	Feb-06	NC	None	USDA	Restaurant/food service
Frozen food	Frozen pizza varieties	Mar-06	WI, FL	American Frozen Food Institute	FDA/ USDA	Processors/manufacturers
Swine production	Swine	Mar-06	IA	Multiple host farms	USDA	Producers/animals
Apple juice	Apple juice	Apr-06	NH	Food Products Assn.	FDA	Processors/manufacturers
Fresh produce	Lettuce (bagged)	May-06	CA	United Fresh Fruit and Vegetable Assn., Produce Marketing Assn., International Fresh-cut Produce Assn., Western Growers Assn.	FDA	Processors/manufacturers, producers/ plants
Infant formula	Infant formula (powdered)	Jun-06	AZ	International Formula Council	FDA	Processors/manufacturers
Ready-to-eat chicken products	Chicken strips	Jun-06	AR	American Meat Institute	USDA	Processors/manufacturers
Beef cattle feedlot	Cattle	Jul-06	NE	National Cattlemen's Beef Assn.	USDA	Producers/animals
Dairy processing	Milk	Jul-06	NY	International Dairy Foods Assn.	FDA	Processors/manufacturers
Ground beef	Ground beef	Aug-06	KS	American Meat Institute	USDA	Processors/manufacturers
Livestock auction markets (cattle sale barn)	Cattle	Aug-06	MO	Livestock Marketing Assn., Missouri Cattlemen's Assn., National Cattlemen's Beef Assn.	USDA	Producers/animals
Dairy cattle farm	Dairy cattle	Sep-06	ID	Idaho Dairymen's Assn., Idaho Department of Agriculture	USDA	Producers/animals
Soybean farm	Soybean	Oct-06	IL	Illinois Crop Improvement Assn., National Corn Growers Assn.	USDA	Producers/plants
Corn/grain	Corn	Nov-06	IL	National Corn Growers Assn.	USDA	Producers/plants
Retail-fluid milk	Milk (one-gallon containers)	Jan-07	TX	International Dairy Foods Assn.	FDA	Processors/manufacturers, Retail

(Continued)

Table 11.1 (Continued) Assessments conducted

Industry	Food/commodity assessed	SPPA assessments, trade associations, and subsectors				
		Date	States	Trade associations	SSA	Subsector(s)
Link sausage processing	Sausage	Mar-07	WI	American Meat Institute	USDA	Processors/manufacturers
Stadium retail food service	Hot dogs, ketchup	Mar-07	KS	Kansas State University	FDA	Restaurant/ food service
Correctional institution food processing	Ground beef patties	Apr-07	OH	Ohio Department of Rehabilitation and Correction	USDA	Processors/manufacturers
Egg products	Eggs (liquid)	Apr-07	PA	United Egg Assn.	USDA	Processors/manufacturers
Commercial feed mill	Animal feed	Jun-07	IA	National Grain and Feed Assn.	FDA	Processors/manufacturers
Hot dogs	Hot dogs	Jun-07	PA	American Meat Institute	USDA	Processors/manufacturers
Breakfast cereal	Frosted flakes	Jul-07	MN	Grocery Manufacturers/Food Products Assn.	FDA	Processors/manufacturers
Domestic grain cooperative	Grain (all)	Jul-07	NE, IA	National Grain and Feed Assn.	USDA	Producers/plants
Grocery stores	Rotisserie chicken	Aug-07	PA	Food Marketing Institute	FDA	Retail
High fructose corn syrup	High fructose corn syrup	Sep-07	AL	Corn Refiners Assn.	FDA	Processors/manufacturers
USDA commodity warehouse	Beef trimmings	Sep-07	MO	None	USDA	Warehousing and logistics
Distribution centers	Lettuce	Nov-07	VA	International Foodservice Distributors Assn.	FDA/USDA	Warehousing and logistics
Import re-inspection facility	Beef trimmings	Nov-07	MD	International Assn. of Refrigerated Warehouses, Global Cold Chain Alliance	USDA	Warehousing and logistics
Poultry broilers	Poultry	Nov-07	GA	Georgia Poultry Federation	USDA	Producers/animals
Flour	Flour	Feb-08	OK	North American Millers' Assn.	FDA	Processors/manufacturers
Beet sugar	Beet sugar	Mar-08	MN	US Beet Sugar Assn.	USDA	Processors/manufacturers
Transportation (livestock hauling)	Cattle	May-08	CO	Agricultural and Food Transporters Conference—American Trucking Assn.	USDA	Producers/animals, warehousing and logistics

Table 11.2   USDA and FDA site visits initially proposed

USDA proposed site visits	FDA proposed site visits
Production agriculture	• Animal by-products
	• Animal foods/feeds
• Aquaculture production facility	• Baby food
• Beef cattle feedlot	• Breaded food, frozen, raw
• Cattle stockyard/auction barn	• Canned food, low acid
• Citrus production facility	• Cereal, whole-grain, not heat treated
• Corn farm	• Deli salads
• Dairy farm	• Dietary supplement, botanical, tablets
• Grain elevator and storage facility	• Entrees, fully cooked
• Grain export handling facility	• Flour
• Poultry farm	• Frozen packaged entrees
• Rice mill	• Fruit juice
• Seed production facility	• Gum arabic (ingredient)
• Soybean farm	• High fructose corn syrup (ingredient)
• Swine production facility	• Honey
• Veterinary biologics firm	• Ice cream
	• Infant formula
Food Processing and Distribution	• Milk, fluid
	• Peanut butter
• Deli meats processing	• Produce, fresh-cut, and modified atmosphere packaged
• Ground beef processing facility	• Retail setting
• Hot dog processing	• Seafood, cooked, refrigerated, ready-to-eat
• Import reinspection facilities	• Soft drink, carbonated
• Liquid eggs processing	• Spices
• Poultry processing	• Vitamin/micro-ingredient premixes/flavors
• Retailers (further processing on-site)	• Vitamins, capsules
• School food service central kitchens	• Water, bottled
• Transportation companies	• Yogurt
• Warehouses	

The USDA's Food Safety and Inspection Service (FSIS) has developed a surveillance program to randomly screen and check food facilities as well as be stationed at ports of entry. Food safety officers are a sought-after career track due to the excellent working conditions and challenging work. FSIS continues to hire import surveillance liaison officers who are responsible for the agency's oversight of food defense issues relating to imported food products at ports of entry, border entries, and in-commerce around the country. In particular, they have expanded their liaison activities with DHS's CBP.

Web Exercise: To learn about jobs in food safety, see www.fsis.usda.gov/Factsheets/FSIS_Workforce_Introduction_of_CSO/index.asp.

11.3.2 Water

As part of our critical infrastructure , water, water plants, and reservoirs are favored targets for the terrorist, mostly because of the potentiality for widespread and wide-scale harm their destruction or contamination would cause. In response to the September 11, 2001 attacks, the EPA formed the Water Security Division (WSD) in the Office of Ground Water and Drinking Water. WSD oversees all drinking water and wastewater homeland security matters. The Office of Homeland Security (OHS) was created in the EPA Office of the Administrator to oversee all EPA matters related to homeland security. See Figure 11.37.[97]

The WSD tackled a host of issues relating to security and the water supply, and these tasks can be broken down into the following:

• Sector profile and goals

• Identifying assets, systems, networks, and functions

---

[97] U.S. Environmental Protection Agency, Information about Public Water Systems, at http://www.epa.gov/dwreginfo/information-about-public-water-systems, last accessed February 7, 2016.

- The public drinking water systems regulated by EPA and delegated states and tribes provide drinking water to 90 percent of Americans.
- A public water system provides water for human consumption through pipes or other constructed conveyances to at least 15 service connections or serves an average of at least 25 people for at least 60 days a year.
- A public water system may be publicly or privately owned.
- There are approximately 155,000 public water systems in the United States.
- EPA classifies these water systems according to the number of people they serve, the source of their water, and whether they serve the same customers year-round or on an occasional basis.

EPA has defined three types of public water systems:

Community Water System (CWS): A public water system that supplies water to the same population year-round.

Non-Transient Non-Community Water System (NTNCWS): A public water system that regularly supplies water to at least 25 of the same people at least six months per year. Some examples are schools, factories, office buildings, and hospitals which have their own water systems.

Transient Non-Community Water System (TNCWS): A public water system that provides water in a place such as a gas station or campground where people do not remain for long periods of time.

Figure 11.37   Information about public water systems in the United States.

- Assessing risks
- Prioritizing infrastructure
- Developing and implementing protective programs
- Measuring progress
- Protection research and development (R&D)
- Managing and coordinating responsibilities

The infection of a water supply due to a natural or man-made incident would be a major health risk and likely cause more casualties than any aircraft flying into a building.[98] The EPA views threat analysis broadly, encompassing natural events, criminal acts, insider threats, and foreign and domestic terrorism. Natural catastrophic events are typically addressed as part of emergency response and business continuity planning, yet the same skill sets necessary for the planning and mitigation of the terrorist attack on the water supply are needed.

To analyze and prepare for threats and attacks, one needs to perform an assessment with foresight. The oft-cited methodology regarding water facilities usually includes

- Chemical, biological, or radiological (CBR) contamination attacks on drinking water assets, especially distribution systems
- Vehicle-borne improvised explosive devices and improvised explosive device attacks on infrastructure, especially single points of failure and chemical storage sites
- Cyber-attacks on industrial control systems
- Chemical attacks, which may include introduction of a combustible contaminant into a wastewater collection system, affecting infrastructure or the treatment process

Hence, risk assessment is a mandatory exercise for every water facility, and this task must be carried out by more than managers but an integrated team at every level of the personnel hierarchy and in cooperation with local, state, federal, and private security entities.[99]

And that assessment follows the lifeblood of water from collection to processing, a complicated series of steps and processes where risk remains ever present. The EPA charts these many stages and steps in water risk analysis. See Figure 11.38.[100]

---

[98] U.S. Environmental Protection Agency, *Planning for an Emergency Drinking Water Supply* (June 2011), at http://www.epa.gov/sites/production/files/2015-03/documents/planning_for_an_emergency_drinking_water_supply.pdf, last accessed February 7, 2016.

[99] *AWWA G430-14 Security Practices for Operation and Management* (American Water Works Assoc., 2015).

[100] EPA, *Water Safety Plans*, http://www.epa.ie/water/dw/drinkingwatersafetyplans/.

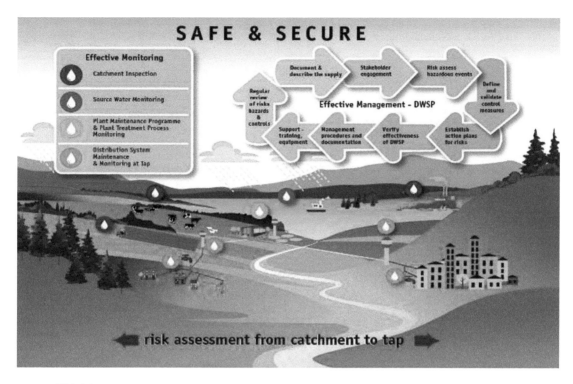

Figure 11.38 EPA risk assessment management.

Security professionals working at the facility or provider need to ask the right questions and coordinate with all interested parties.[101] At most water facilities, the threats are encompassed in these queries:

- What are the most plausible threats, contaminants, and threat scenarios facing the drinking water industry?
- How does this information compare with intelligence information on possible threats?
- What types of biological and chemical contaminants could be introduced into water systems, and what are their physical, chemical, and biological properties?
- What are the potential health impacts of these contaminants?
- What are the most effective means to destroy contaminants in water?
- How can this information be combined with reporting, analysis, and decision- making to arrive at a reliable system?
- Can effective methods be developed to ensure that a sufficient number of qualified laboratories exist to perform rapid analysis of water contaminants in the event of an attack?
- If contaminants are introduced into a water system, where will they travel?
- How quickly will they travel?
- What will be their concentration at various points along their path?
- Can human exposures and the health impacts of these contaminants be effectively minimized?
- How can water that has been contaminated be effectively treated so that it can be released to wastewater systems or otherwise disposed of?
- Are alternative water supplies available in the event of an attack?
- How would water utilities or governments most effectively select a cost-effective early warning system?

---

[101] Risk management and Assessment of Wastewater Treatment Plants (WWTPs) Using a Fuzzy Multi Attribute Decision - Making (FMADM) Approach,athttp://www.academia.edu/5649069/Risk_management_and_Assessment_of_Wastewater_Treatment_Plants_WWTPs_Using_a_Fuzzy_Multi_Attribute_Decision_-_Making_FMADM_Approach; see also J. M. P. Vieira, Water Safety Plans: Methodologies for Risk Assessment and Risk Management in Drinking-Water Systems, at http://www.aprh.pt/celtico/PAPERS/RT2P3.PDF.

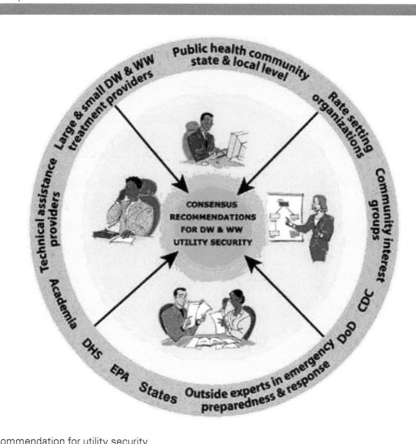

Figure 11.39   Recommendation for utility security.

Any meaningful security plan will anticipate these questions and will prompt the security professional to devise a strategy that mitigates the damage and redirects the water facility to positive productivity after this event. Most water facilities need to rely upon both internal and external constituencies to fully comprehend the dynamics of their location. The interplay between state and federal regulators alone gives some sense of this necessary interconnection. See Figure 11.39.

Web Exercise: Find out about the WaterISAC professional association of water providers and the security tool made available by this group at http://www.dhs.gov/critical-infrastructure-sectors.

Not to be forgotten is the central role of the general public that can watch for irregularities and potential threats. Given the size and scope of the watershed itself, reliance on the general citizenry and the encouragement to actively monitor the waters encountered is sound policy.

Web Exercise: Find out about the "Waterwatchers" program at https://www.epa.gov/sites/production/files/2015-10/documents/waterwatchers_revised2.pdf.

Most water facilities engage in a serious self-assessment program that looks to these 14 variables, as published by the EPA:

- Explicit commitment to security
- Promote security awareness
- Defined security roles and employee expectations
- Vulnerability assessment (VA) up-to-date
- Security resources and implementation priorities
- Contamination detection
- Threat-level-based protocols

- Emergency Response Plan (ERP) tested and up-to-date
- Utility-specific measures and self-assessment
- Intrusion detection and access control
- Information protection and continuity
- Design and construction standards
- Communications
- Partnerships

To ensure basic compliance with these criteria, the water facility should conduct its own vulnerability analysis (VA). The EPA, as well as a host of software companies, makes available VA programs. The EPA publishes vulnerability guidelines, which are reproduced in the following section. See Table 11.3.[102]

Web Exercise: Learn how to prepare for flooding's impact on the water supply at http://www.epa.gov/sites/production/files/2015-06/documents/flooding.pdf.

The private security industry plays a pivotal role in the protection of water plants and related water assets especially since these systems can be too large for any one entity to fully monitor.[103]

In addition to providing security at the Hoover Dam,[104] G4S was engaged by the Denver Water Commissioners to monitor its massive and extensive water facilities in 2014. Figure 11.40[105] is the actual memorandum of agreement between the parties.

11.4 CRITICAL INFRASTRUCTURE: ENERGY

Energy is vital to the lifeblood of the American economy, and threats, man-made or natural by design, cause great serious interruptions in the economic system. Terrorists surely appreciate the significance of these facilities, whether these be oil and petroleum, nuclear or natural gas installations. In each of these settings, the possibility of large, sweeping destruction is continuous cause of concern for security professionals. Surely, the governmental experts at DHS, Energy, and other governmental sectors are continuously providing guidance on how to secure these installations and utility centers. The DHS has designated the energy as one of its 21 sectors and concludes thus:

> The energy infrastructure is divided into three interrelated segments: electricity, oil, and natural gas. The U.S. electricity segment contains more than 6,413 power plants (this includes 3,273 traditional electric utilities and 1,738 nonutility power producers) with approximately 1,075 gigawatts of installed generation. Approximately 48% of electricity is produced by combusting coal (primarily transported by rail), 20% in nuclear power plants, and 22% by combusting natural gas. The remaining generation is provided by hydroelectric plants (6%), oil (1%), and renewable sources (solar, wind, and geothermal) (3%). The heavy reliance on pipelines to distribute products across the nation highlights the interdependencies between the Energy and Transportation Systems Sector.[106]

Since the sector is so heavily weighted with critical infrastructure, it is all the more imperative that precise and workable solutions for security and safety be in place in the event of some disaster or terror event.[107] Just as crucially, the energy sector interconnects with a multiplicity of other security sectors that its interlocking nature makes it an even

---

[102] Environmental Protection Agency, *Vulnerability Assessment Fact Sheet* (Washington, DC: U.S. Government Printing Office, 2002), EPA 816-F-02-025, at http://nepis.epa.gov/Simple.html by searching "816-F-02-025," last accessed February 7, 2016.

[103] Oregon Health Authority, *Physical Security for Drinking Water Facilities* (2009), at https://public.health.oregon.gov/HealthyEnvironments/DrinkingWater/Preparedness/Documents/PhysicalSecurity-Oregon.pdf.

[104] G4S, Case Study: Hoover Dam, at http://www.g4s.us/~/media/Files/4pg%20PDF%20Case%20Studies/g4s_case_HooverDam1_200310%20FINAL.pdf.

[105] Denver Board of Water Commissioners, *Agreement for Armed Security Guard Services at Denver Water Facilities* (April 9, 2014), at http://www.denverwater.org/docs/assets/CF9D67A3-AAE5-1B28-92C82953B0D8C0A5/IIc.pdf.

[106] DHS, Energy Sector, at https://www.dhs.gov/energy-sector.

[107] Addressing Cyber and Physical Risks in Modern Utility Security, *Sec. Mag.* (March 2014), at http://www.securitymagazine.com/articles/85275-addressing-cyber-and-physical-risks-in-modern-utility-security.

Table 11.3   EPA vulnerability assessment guidelines

Vulnerability assessment factsheet

What is the purpose of vulnerability assessments?

Vulnerability assessments help water systems evaluate susceptibility to potential threats and identify corrective actions that can reduce or mitigate the risk of serious consequences from adversarial actions (e.g., vandalism, insider sabotage, terrorist attack, etc.). Such an assessment for a water system takes into account the vulnerability of the water supply (both ground and surface water), transmission, treatment, and distribution systems. It also considers risks posed to the surrounding community related to attacks on the water system. An effective vulnerability assessment serves as a guide to the water utility by providing a prioritized plan for security upgrades, modifications of operational procedures, and/or policy changes to mitigate the risks and vulnerabilities to the utility's critical assets. The vulnerability assessment provides a framework for developing risk reduction options and associated costs. Water systems should review their vulnerability assessments periodically to account for changing threats or additions to the system to ensure that security objectives are being met. Preferably, a vulnerability assessment is "performance-based," meaning that it evaluates the risk to the water system based on the effectiveness (performance) of existing and planned measures to counteract adversarial actions.

What are the basic elements of vulnerability assessments?

The following are *common elements of vulnerability assessments*. These elements are conceptual in nature and not intended to serve as a detailed methodology:

1. Characterization of the water system, including its mission and objectives
2. Identification and prioritization of adverse consequences to avoid
3. Determination of critical assets that might be subject to malevolent acts that could result in undesired consequences
4. Assessment of the likelihood (qualitative probability) of such malevolent acts from adversaries
5. Evaluation of existing countermeasures
6. Analysis of current risk and development of a prioritized plan for risk reduction

The vulnerability assessment process will range in complexity based on the design and operation of the water system itself. The nature and extent of the vulnerability assessment will differ among systems based on a number of factors, including system size, potential population affected, source water, treatment complexity, system infrastructure, and other factors. Security and safety evaluations also vary based on knowledge and types of threats, available security technologies, and applicable local, state, and federal regulations.

What are some points to consider in a vulnerability assessments?

Some points to consider related to the six basic elements are included in the following tables. The manner in which the vulnerability assessment is performed is determined by each individual water utility. It will be helpful to throughout the assessment process that the ultimate goal is twofold: *to safeguard public health and safety, and to reduce the potential for disruption of a reliable supply of pressurized water.*

Basic element	Points to consider

1. Characterization of the water system, including its mission and objectives. (Answers to system-specific questions may be helpful in characterizing the water system.)	• What are the important missions of the system to be assessed? Define the highest priority services provided by the utility. Identify the utility's customers:
	   • General public
	   • Government
	   • Military
	   • Industrial
	   • Critical care
	   • Retail operations
	   • Firefighting
	• What are the most important facilities, processes, and assets of the system for achieving the mission objectives and avoiding undesired consequences? Describe the
	   • Utility facilities
	   • Operating procedures
	   • Management practices that are necessary to achieve the mission objectives
	   • How the utility operates (e.g., water source including ground and surface water)
	   • Treatment processes
	   • Storage methods and capacity
	   • Chemical use and storage
	   • Distribution system
	   In assessing those assets that are critical, consider critical customers, dependence on other infrastructures (e.g., electricity, transportation, other water utilities), contractual obligations, single points of failure (e.g., critical aqueducts, transmission systems, aquifers etc.), chemical hazards and other aspects of the utility's operations, or availability of other utility capabilities that may increase or decrease the criticality of specific facilities, processes, and assets.

(Continued)

Table 11.3 (*Continued*)   EPA vulnerability assessment guidelines

Basic element	Points to consider

2. Identification and prioritization of adverse consequences to avoid	• Take into account the impacts that could substantially disrupt the ability of the system to provide a safe and reliable supply of drinking water or otherwise present significant public health concerns to the surrounding community. Water systems should use the vulnerability assessment process to determine how to reduce risks associated with the consequences of significant concern.
	• Ranges of consequences or impacts for each of these events should be identified and defined. Factors to be considered in assessing the consequences may include
	  • Magnitude of service disruption
	  • Economic impact (such as replacement and installation costs for damaged critical assets or loss of revenue due to service outage)
	  • Number of illnesses or deaths resulting from an event
	  • Impact on public confidence in the water supply
	  • Chronic problems arising from specific events
	  • Other indicators of the impact of each event as determined by the water utility
	    Risk reduction recommendations at the conclusion of the vulnerability assessment should strive to prevent or reduce each of these consequences.

3. Determination of critical assets that might be subject to malevolent acts that could result in undesired consequences	• What are the malevolent acts that could reasonably cause undesired consequences? Consider the operation of critical facilities, assets, and/or processes and assess what an adversary could do to disrupt these operations. Such acts may include physical damage to or destruction of critical assets, contamination of water, intentional release of stored chemicals, interruption of electricity, or other infrastructure interdependencies.
	• The "Public Health Security and Bioterrorism Preparedness and Response Act of 2002" (PL 107-188) states that a community water system which serves a population of greater than 3300 people must review the vulnerability of its system to a terrorist attack or other intentional acts intended to substantially disrupt the ability of the system to provide a safe and reliable supply of drinking water. The vulnerability assessment shall include, but not be limited to, a review of
	  • Pipes and constructed conveyances
	  • Physical barriers
	  • Water collection, pretreatment and treatment facilities
	  • Storage and distribution facilities
	  • Electronic, computer or other automated systems which are utilized by the public water system (e.g., Supervisory Control and Data Acquisition [SCADA])
	  • The use, storage, or handling of various chemicals
	  • The operation and maintenance of such systems

4. Assessment of the likelihood (qualitative probability) of such malevolent acts from adversaries (e.g., terrorists, vandals)	• Determine the possible modes of attack that might result in consequences of significant concern based on the critical assets of the water system. The objective of this step of the assessment is to move beyond what is merely possible and determine the likelihood of a particular attack scenario. This is a very difficult task as there is often insufficient information to determine the likelihood of a particular event with any degree of certainty. • The threats (the kind of adversary and the mode of attack) selected for consideration during a vulnerability assessment will dictate, to a great extent, the risk reduction measures that should be designed to counter the threat(s). Some vulnerability assessment methodologies refer to this as a "Design Basis Threat" (DBT) where the threat serves as the basis for the design of countermeasures, as well as the benchmark against which vulnerabilities are assessed. It should be noted that there is no single DBT or threat profile for all water systems in the United States. Differences in geographic location, size of the utility, previous attacks in the local area and many other factors will influence the threat(s) that water systems should consider in their assessments. Water systems should consult with the local FBI and/or other law enforcement agencies, public officials, and others to determine the threats upon which their risk reduction measures should be based. Water systems should also refer to EPA's "Baseline Threat Information for Vulnerability Assessments of Community Water Systems" to help assess the most likely threats to their system. This document is available to community water systems serving populations greater than 3300 people. If your system has not yet received instructions on how to receive a copy of this document, then contact your Regional EPA Office immediately. You will be sent instructions on how to securely access the document via the Water Information Sharing and Analysis Center (ISAC) website or obtain a hardcopy that can be mailed directly to you. Water systems may also want to review their incident reports to better understand past breaches of security.

(Continued)

Table 11.3 (*Continued*) EPA vulnerability assessment guidelines

Basic element	Points to consider

5. Evaluation of existing countermeasures. (Depending on countermeasures already in place, some critical assets may already be sufficiently protected. This step will aid in identification of the areas of greatest concern, and help to focus priorities for risk reduction.)	• *What capabilities does the system currently employ for detection, delay, and response?*
	  • Identify and evaluate current detection capabilities such as intrusion detection systems, water quality monitoring, operational alarms, guard post orders, and employee security awareness programs.
	  • Identify current delay mechanisms such as locks and key control, fencing, structure integrity of critical assets, and vehicle access checkpoints.
	  • Identify existing policies and procedures for evaluation and response to intrusion and system malfunction alarms, adverse water quality indicators, and cyber system intrusions.
	It is important to determine the performance characteristics. Poorly operated and maintained security technologies provide little or no protection.
	• *What cyber protection system features does the utility have in place?* Assess what protective measures are in-place for the SCADA and business-related computer information systems such as
	  • Firewalls
	  • Modem access
	  • Internet and other external connections, including wireless data and voice communications
	  • Security policies and protocols
	It is important to identify whether vendors have access rights and/or "backdoors" to conduct system diagnostics remotely.
	• *What security policies and procedures exist, and what is the compliance record for them?* Identify existing policies and procedures concerning
	  • Personnel security
	  • Physical security
	  • Key and access badge control
	  • Control of system configuration and operational data
	  • Chemical and other vendor deliveries
	  • Security training and exercise records

6. Analysis of current risk and development of a prioritized plan for risk reduction	• Information gathered on threat, critical assets, water utility operations, consequences, and existing countermeasures should be analyzed to determine the current level of risk. The utility should then determine whether current risks are acceptable or risk reduction measures should be pursued.
	• Recommended actions should measurably reduce risks by reducing vulnerabilities and/or consequences through improved deterrence, delay, detection, and/or response capabilities or by improving operational policies or procedures. Selection of specific risk reduction actions should be completed prior to considering the cost of the recommended action(s). Utilities should carefully consider both short- and long-term solutions. An analysis of the cost of short- and long-term risk reduction actions may impact which actions the utility chooses to achieve its security goals.
	• Utilities may also want to consider security improvements in light of other planned or needed improvements. Security and general infrastructure may provide significant multiple benefits. For example, improved treatment processes or system redundancies can both reduce vulnerabilities and enhance day-to-day operation.
	• Generally, strategies for reducing vulnerabilities fall into three broad categories:
	  • Sound business practices—affect policies, procedures, and training to improve the overall security-related culture at the drinking water facility. For example, it is important to ensure rapid communication capabilities exist between public health authorities and local law enforcement and emergency responders.
	  • System upgrades—include changes in operations, equipment, processes, or infrastructure itself that make the system fundamentally safer.
	  • Security upgrades—improve capabilities for detection, delay, or response.

more crucial sector than most other sectors. Hence, when the energy sector suffers from its natural service point, other sectors are severely impacted by this lack of service. DHS charts this interlocking influence in Figure 11.41.[108]

Add to this the volatile nature of some fuel supplies, the transport mechanisms and infrastructure for delivery of the product and the volatility of the product, and one has a select mix of challenges for the security professional. For example, securing the oil storage terminal and processing facility calls for vastly different protocols than securing

---

[108] See U.S. DHS, *Energy Sector-Specific Plan* (2015), at https://www.dhs.gov/sites/default/files/publications/nipp-ssp-energy-2015-508.pdf.

DENVER BOARD OF WATER COMMISSIONERS

Meeting Date: April 9, 2014

Board Item: II-C

Agreement for Armed Security Guard Services
at Denver Water Facilities
Contract # 15328A

☐ Action by Consent	☒ Action	☐ Information

Denver Water requires armed security guard services to protect its Critical Infrastructure and Key Resources located in the Denver Metropolitan Area as well as those located in the mountain areas. The primary objective is to provide the necessary level of physical security to protect Denver Water facilities, staff, the community, and the drinking water supply.

A Request for Proposal (RFP) was solicited through the Rocky Mountain E-Purchasing System (Bid-net) with a mandatory pre-bid meeting held on February 20, 2014 at Denver Water. Eleven proposals were submitted. The responses were evaluated based on a number of criteria including experience, staffing plan and qualifications, understanding of the work, training curriculum, and price. From that list, the four top proposers were selected for further consideration: U.S. Security Associates, Securitas, G4S Secure Solutions (USA) Inc. and Pro Security. G4S Secure Solutions (USA) Inc. was selected as the most responsive security firm.

Twenty-one Minority and Women Business Enterprise (MWBE) were solicited and none provided a proposal.

Funds for armed security guard services are included in the Operations and Maintenance 2014 Budget and ten-year operating plan.

Recommendation:

It is recommended that the Board authorize the award of Agreement No. 15328A to G4S Secure Solutions (USA) Inc. to provide armed security guard services for the period May 1, 2014 through April 30, 2016 for a total amount not to exceed $2,800,446.00.

Approvals:

Respectfully submitted,

_____
Thomas J. Roode
Director of Operations & Maintenance

_____
James S. Lochhead
CEO/Manager

_____
Terri Bryant
Controller

| March 27, 2014March 26, 2014
Revised by CEO's Office 8/19/2011

Figure 11.40   Memorandum of agreement.

fuel rods and plutonium waste at the local nuclear plant. And it is best to see the facility in the fullest of contexts. For oil, one could start at the Strategic Petroleum Reserve and move to the specific refinery. See Figure 11.42.[109]

Along the way to the refinery are pipelines of enormous dimensions and scale as well as various delivery points where rail and trucks arrive with the product. Each of these settings is ripe for potential disaster, and each setting must be

---

[109] See Energy.gov, Office of Fossil Energy, SPR Storage Sites, at http://energy.gov/fe/services/petroleum-reserves/strategic-petroleum-reserve/spr-storage-sites.

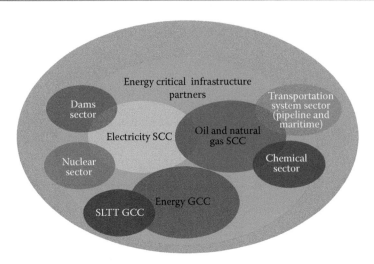

Figure 11.41 Critical infrastructure stakeholders.

gauged for the safest possible outcomes.[110] With more than 190,000 miles of pipeline, the potential for actual threat and risk is quite predictable. And pipelines carry natural gas in great volume too and as the "fracking" revolution continues, that energy sector will continue to witness dramatic growth and critical infrastructure design. At every corner of the delivery system, a security challenge naturally sits side by side. See Figure 11.43a and b.

The volatility of natural gas should be an inbred concern for the security professionals keeping watch over critical infrastructure. See Figure 11.44.[111]

Refineries are continuously looking for specialized personnel to secure a highly complex and equally dangerous environment where oil and gas products are produced and packaged for delivery purposes. At the refinery level, the opportunities for natural and man-made disasters are clearly evident. Most companies invest heavily in the protective divisions that keep a close eye on unauthorized activity and employees that appear to be acting with improper or suspicious motives. On top of this, refinery installations need to be shut down in all natural disasters because of their environmental impacts alone. See Figure 11.45.[112]

Figure 11.42 Petroleum reserve sites.

---

[110] American Petroleum Institute, *Security Guidelines for the Petroleum Industry* (3rd ed., 2005), at http://www.nj.gov/dep/enforcement/security/downloads/API%20Security%20Guidance%203rd%20Edition.pdf.

[111] G. Shambaugh & A. Zlotnick, Cave Hic Dragones: Transit Countries and the Geopolitical Consequences of Energy, *Geo J . Int'l Aff.* (November 2014), at http://journal.georgetown.edu/cave-hic-dragones-transit-countries-and-the-geopolitical-consequences-of-energy/.

[112] Rida Security, at http://www.ridasecurity.com.

U.S. Energy Mapping System

Welcome to the U.S. Energy Mapping System. Please explore all of the options available to you within the map above. There are many features and options available through the "Layers/Legend" menu including our recommended map views on a variety of subjects as well as the ability to customize mapping layer options that may better suit your energy needs.

Figure 11.43   (a) U.S. Energy Mapping System for the United States at the U.S. Energy Information Administration (ww.eia.gov) and (b) an example of a close-up from the interactive map.   (*Continued*)

G4S delivers a bevy of services to the energy sector including but not limited to

- Corporate Risk Services that combat internal and external threats to your workplace, operations and research and development programs
- Security Technology Integration solutions that include incident reporting platforms, access control, facility management and remote guarding systems, alarm monitoring, and response capabilities
- Symmetry™ Security Management System solutions that deliver access control, identity, visitor and video management, alarm handling, mobile applications, and policy based solutions for compliance reporting
- Consulting Services that assist with government regulation requirements, including Security Vulnerability Assessments, Site Security Plans
- Security Personnel consistently ranked the best in the security business who are specifically selected and trained to work in the energy, chemical, and petrochemical environment[113]

See Figure 11.46.

---

[113] See G4S, Energy and Chemical Security, at http://www.g4s.us/en-US/Industries/Energy%20and%20Chemical/.

U.S. Energy Mapping System

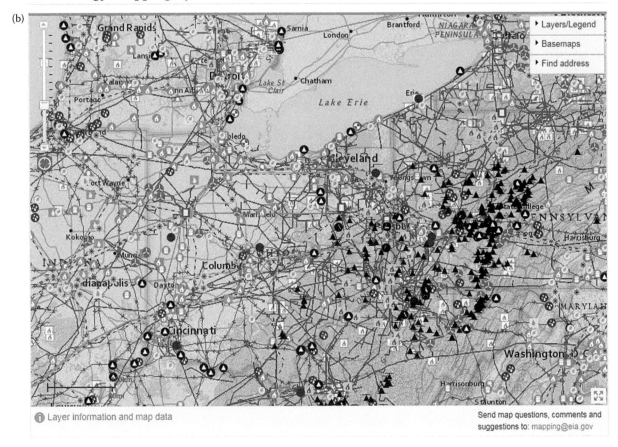

Figure 11.43 (Continued) (a) U.S. Energy Mapping System for the United States at the U.S. Energy Information Administration (ww.eia.gov) and (b) an example of a close-up from the interactive map.

Figure 11.44 Communities, safety, and security professionals must plan for the security implications in both the processing and transport of natural gas.

Figure 11.45   Aerial view of oil refinery.

11.5 CRITICAL INFRASTRUCTURE: NUCLEAR

While energy is a specific sector of concern for governmental planners, nuclear has been assigned its unique sector designation and rightfully so. Nuclear is a dangerous enterprise that a zealous and completely irrational terrorist would favor against all other destruction. Even human accidents and natural forces have extraordinary consequences for damage and human illness. The recent Fukushima plant in Japan, powerless because of a tsunami, was a near complete meltdown with long-term health consequences for the region. See Figure 11.47a and b.[114]

The consequences resulting from the human failure and weather alone should give nuclear planners pause over how to maintain constant continuity of operations. Given this potential reality, nuclear operators go to mind-numbing lengths to assure a safe and secure environment and for the most part, data tell us that accidents and intrusions are very rare. However, the finality of the harm is what makes this caution a necessity. Coal fired generators and natural gas facilities lack the capacity to inflict harm at this global geographical level, and at the same time, their harm is not measured in half-lives or generations of injury. Nuclear security must be multilayered and utterly duplicative to assure one failure is saved by another system. Given this inevitability, most nuclear plants have sophisticated security protocols including

- Physical barriers, electronic detection and assessment systems, and illuminated detection zones
- Electronic surveillance and physical patrols of the plant perimeter and interior structures
- Bullet-resisting protected positions throughout the plant
- Robust barriers to critical areas
- Background checks and access control for employees
- Highly trained, well-armed security officers

Physical security measures are critical in nuclear facilities, and the more redundant the layers of protection, the better the protection.[115] Plants are broken down into three basic sections or zones:

Owner-controlled area. The outer perimeter, called the "owner-controlled area," is sufficiently distant from the reactor that only minimal security is deemed necessary. Explosives, firearms and alcohol are prohibited in this area.

Protected area. The level of security increases dramatically at the boundary of the "protected area," which is fenced, protected by sophisticated security systems and guarded by armed security officers. Individuals who are granted unescorted access to the protected area must first undergo a background check, psychological evaluation and fitness-for-duty testing (drug testing).

Vital area. The innermost circle is called the "vital area," which contains equipment needed to safely shut down the reactor and keep it in a safe condition. The control room, used fuel pool and main security alarm stations are in this area as well as the reactor and safety equipment. Access is technologically limited.[116]

---

[114] See Nearly All Fuel in Fukushima Reactor Has Melted, Says TEPCO, *Phys.org* (March 19, 2015), at http://phys.org/news/2015-03-fuel-fukushima-reactor-tepco.html.

[115] See M. Harwood, NRC Strengthening Security and Nuclear Plants, *Sec. Mgmt* (December 2008).

[116] See Nuclear Energy Institute, Fact Sheets—Nuclear Power Plant Security, at http://www.nei.org/master-document-folder/backgrounders/fact-sheets/nuclear-power-plant-security.

Full-Time Security Officer/Refinery Facility/TWIC Required in Corpus Christi, Texas

Overview

Essential Details:

- Work Environment—Refinery Facility, position is subject to outdoor foot/vehicle patrol.
- Requires a TWIC (Transportation Workers Identification Credential) card, or the ability to obtain one.
- Must be at least 21 years of age by hire date.
- Intermediate knowledge of various computer programs or the ability to train.
- Previous contract security experience is highly preferred, or experience in a similar field.
- Must have a valid driver license with at least one year of driving experience.
- Schedule: Typically a non-rotating schedule, must be able to days, evenings or graveyards as assigned upon completion of Allied-Barton's Orientation program.

Job Description

Essential Functions:

Security Officers are the cornerstone of AlliedBarton Security Services. Our officers allow us to accomplish our company's core purpose which is "to serve and secure the people and business of our community". They are responsible for the safety and security of the facilities they protect. Our security officers act as a visible deterrent to crime and client rule infractions; they detect and report suspicious, unsafe or criminal acts at or near their assigned posts which may be a threat to the property, clients, guests or employees at the site. Although essential activities may differ based on the facility at which they work, below are some of the standards.

- Ensure the facility is provided with high quality security services to protect people and property.
- Report safety concerns, security breaches and unusual circumstances both verbally and in writing.
- Build, improve and maintain effective relationships with both client employees and guests.
- Answer questions and assist guests and employees.
- Remain flexible to ever changing environments; adapt well to different situations.
- Patrol the facility on foot or vehicle.
- Answer phones or greet guests/employees in a professional, welcoming manner.
- Monitor closed circuit television systems and alarms.

Additional Responsibilities:

- Fully embrace security / safety training programs to enhance performance and ability to advance. These may be specific to the security industry or specific to the industry associated with the client you are assigned to secure.
- Be aware of and familiar with the site-specific operations performance manual and post orders.
- Take additional certification training (as required by some positions) to carry OC sprays, drive bicycles, operate Segways, etc.

Qualifications:

- Previous contract security, military or law enforcement experience is beneficial (and sometimes required);
- Ability to work in a team-oriented environment with the ability to work independently;
- Must be at least 18 years of age or older as required by applicable law or contractual requirements;
- Must have a high school diploma or GED, or at least 5 years of verifiable employment history;
- Must have at least one verifiable employer;
- Ability to communicate effectively in English, both orally and in writing, for the purpose of public interaction and report writing;
- Strong interpersonal skills are important as most of our positions require regular interaction with the public;
- Successful completion of AlliedBarton's Master Security Officer Basic (Level 1) Course;
- Ability to maintain satisfactory attendance and punctuality standard;
- Neat and professional appearance;
- Ability to provide quality customer service;
- Ability to handle both common and crisis situations at the client site, calmly and efficiently.

Closing:

AlliedBarton Security Services is the industry's premier provider of security personnel to many industries including commercial real estate, higher education, healthcare, chemical/petrochemical, government, manufacturing and distribution, financial institutions, shopping centers and residential communities. More than 60,000 employees and 120 offices serve thousands of clients with levels of protection that anticipate needs and build enduring relationships. AlliedBarton is known as the most responsive security services provider and it is our people that differentiates AlliedBarton. Recognized as a training leader, AlliedBarton offers on-the-job, web-based and ongoing training programs for all personnel from security officers through executive level management. Our focus on learning and development and our leadership culture help our employees grow personally and professionally.

Dare to be GREAT! Be daring, be GREAT, be one of us! For additional information, please visit our website at http://jobs.alliedbarton.com/.

AlliedBarton is proud to be an Equal Opportunity Employer M/F/Disabled/Veteran.

Figure 11.46 Career profile: Security officer at refinery.

Figure 11.47 (a) The Fukushima I Nuclear Power Plant after the 2011 Tohoku earthquake and tsunami. Reactors 1 –4 from right to left. (Wikipedia image used per CC 3.0 license. Image is unedited.) (b) IAEA experts depart Unit 4 of TEPCO's Fukushima Daiichi Nuclear Power Station on April 17, 2013 as part of a mission to review Japan's plans to decommission the facility. (Photo credit: Greg Webb / IAEA. Wikipedia image used per CC 2.0 license. Image is unedited.)

Security technology is another central element in the defense of nuclear facilities, and aside from specially trained security officers, the security plan must use video, motion, heat, and infrared detection systems throughout the facility and just as intelligently place that technology at various points of egress and exit and the perimeter at large. See Figure 11.48.

Security personnel are also trained to use deadly force in the event of an encroachment and when power plant integrity is at stake. The Nuclear Regulatory Commission authorized Force on Force, even if deadly when the reactor core appears the target. A detailed discussion of Force on Force training has already been laid out in Chapter 6. See Figure 11.49; its policy is unequivocally clear:

- The NRC requires nuclear power plant operators to defend the plant against attackers seeking to damage the reactor core or spent fuel and cause a radiation release.

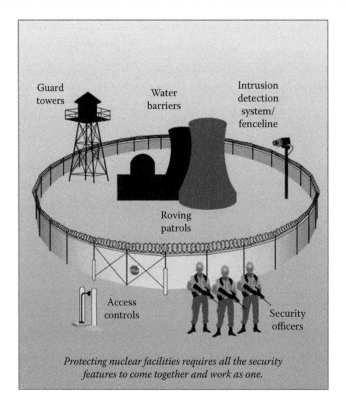

Protecting nuclear facilities requires all the security
features to come together and work as one.

Figure 11.48 Security components.

Figure 11.49 Warning sign at a nuclear facility sends a clear message as to how unauthorized trespassers could be dealt with.

- During each FOF inspection, a number of commando-style attack exercises are carried out against a plant's security forces to test the plant operator's protective strategy.
- Any significant problems are promptly addressed.
- Each nuclear power plant site has at least one FOF inspection every three years.[117]

See Figure 11.50.

---

[117] See U.S. Nuclear Regulatory Commission, Backgrounder on Force-on-Force Security Inspections, at http://www.nrc.gov/reading-rm/doc-collections/fact-sheets/force-on-force-bg.html.

Job Title: Armed Nuclear Security Officer Trainee

Job Post ID: 11235

Posted Until: 12/14/2012

Salary: $18.85/hr.

Location: Braceville

Hours: Other Shift

WorkType: Full Time

Job Description:

Exelon Nuclear is currently looking to add a class of Armed Security Officers at the Braidwood Station in Braceville, IL (Southwest of Chicago, IL). Start date 1/29/2013 or 2/5/2013. The pay rate is $18.85 per hour.

PRIMARY PURPOSE OF POSITION

Protect the health and welfare of the public by defending the station against any act of radiological sabotage, attack, or theft of special nuclear material. As specified by procedure and the site security plan, maintain a secure perimeter for site access and egress and employee, contractor and visitor entry.

MAJOR ACCOUNTABILITIES:

Item Accountability

1. Maintain qualifications for position
2. Conduct patrols and inspections
3. Monitor access to security areas
4. Perform search activities
5. Respond to threats and contingency events
6. Perform equipment testing

POSITION SPECIFICATIONS:

The successful candidate will be responsible for the following:

Provide physical protection of Exelon nuclear generating facilities against intrusion and acts of sabotage. Conduct armed stationary, foot and/or vehicle patrol (interior and/or exterior). Control access and/or egress of personnel, materials and vehicles. Monitor CCTV, plant surveillance equipment and alarm systems. Deter criminal activity, misconduct, and safety violations. Perform other duties as specified in Nuclear training and qualification plan and post orders.

Job Requirements:

Candidates must meet the follow basic qualifications for this position:

Pass Any State-required training or other qualifications for licensing

Be at least 21 years of age

Have a High School diploma or GED

Have access to reliable transportation

You must be able to pass a drug test with negative results (except when undergoing documented medical treatment)

Be able to pass extensive background check, including criminal history, personal references, employment and educational verifications, and Department of Motor Vehicle and Credit Check

Pass a State licensing test as you will be driving a company-owned vehicle

Be able to operate a radio or telephone equipment and/or console monitors and surveillance equipment

Be able to successfully complete all training required for the position

Demonstrate an ability to interact cordially and communicate with the public

Pass the following, post-offer in accordance with code of federal regulations for armed nuclear security assignment: MMPI ' Psychological testing Physical Exams, including vision and hearing, in accordance with nuclear regulatory requirements and site training and qualification plan

Physical fitness (agilities) test in accordance with site training and qualification plan

Firearms qualification with handgun, shotgun and rifle per client site training and qualification plan

Nuclear site specific training and testing providing general knowledge of nuclear power generation science and principles, this training and testing will include radiation worker principles including respirator training, fit and dress out

Figure 11.50   Career profile: Armed security officer—nuclear facility.   (*Continued*)

Benefits:

Will discuss if interviewed

Company Information

At Exelon, we've got a place for you. Exelon is developing sustainable energy to provide for the communities of today and planning for a brighter tomorrow. Exelon knows the future of energy is you.

Exelon Corporation is one of the nation's largest electric utilities, with more than $32 billion in annual revenues. The company has one of the industry's largest portfolios of electricity generation capacity, with a nationwide reach and strong positions in the Midwest and Mid-Atlantic. Exelon distributes electricity to approximately 6.6 million customers in northern Illinois, central Maryland and southeastern Pennsylvania and natural gas to more than 1.1 million customers in the Baltimore and Philadelphia areas. Exelon is headquartered in Chicago and trades on the NYSE under the ticker EXC.

We know that before we can generate more than 34,000 megawatts of electricity and deliver electric and gas service safely to millions of families and businesses, we need to recognize that each of our employees plays an integral part in the process. Join Exelon and you can share your ideas at a forward-thinking company and the next big idea could be yours. You've just found Exelon, a place where you can truly shine.

Figure 11.50   (Continued) Career profile: Armed security officer—nuclear facility.

Securitas delivers highly trained security specialists to work in the nuclear sector.[118]

Key offerings to their clients, per their website, include the following:

- Adherence to the stringent federal regulatory environment
- Industry leading human performance and safety program
- Largest ISFSI (Independent Spent Fuel Storage Installation) contract security provider in the US
- Specialized management experience securing facilities throughout the decommissioning process
- Proactive planning for force-on-force and other regulatory inspections
- Best practice model for contingency preparation and planning
- Committed to delivering on the Nuclear Promise[119]

11.6 CRITICAL INFRASTRUCTURE: CHEMICAL PLANTS

DHS has been actively involved in the oversight of chemical facilities due to their capacity to inflict widespread damage. Antiterrorism standards must be integrated in the design, plan, and operational security of designated chemical facilities. Congress, in passage of the 2007 Homeland Security reauthorization,[120] applies these standards because of the inherent risk to these facilities. DHS defines the risk as

- The consequence of a successful attack on a facility (consequence)
- The likelihood that an attack on a facility will be successful (vulnerability)
- The intent and capability of an adversary in respect to attacking a facility (threat)

DHS establishes risk-based performance standards for the security of the country's chemical facilities. Covered chemical facilities are required to

- Prepare security vulnerability assessments, which identify facility security vulnerabilities
- Develop and implement site security plans, which include measures that satisfy the identified risk-based performance standards

Web Exercise: Review the antiterrorism standards for chemical plants at http://www.dhs.gov/cfats-risk-based-performance-standards.

---

[118] See Securitas International, Energy, at http://www.scisusa.com/energy/.
[119] *Ibid.*
[120] Homeland Security Appropriations Act of 2007, P.L. 109-295, Section 550, 120 *U.S. Statutes at Large* 1355 (2006).

Figure 11.51   Chemical plant.

DHS publishes both a list of chemical products of significant interest to the country and a list of assessment tools to ensure compliance.[121] Chemical facilities are construed as infrastructure.

Web Exercise: Watch the critical infrastructure video on chemical plants at https://www.dhs.gov/video/chemical-sector-critical-infrastructure.

That chemical plants and facilities are another of the DHS 21 sectors of concern is not surprising since these setting often deal with caustic materials that have widespread potential for injury and harm.[122] Chemicals in the production or storage phase can be released into the air or water supply or stolen and used for nefarious purposes or due to accidental human behavior become major health risks for the workforce. Chemical plants and facilities are often severely impacted by storms, hurricanes, and earthquakes. See Figure 11.51.

Just as concerning is the capacity for cyber-attacks and cyber-crime to cause a plant to fail or to redirect a safety system to a contrary result, for chemical plants are highly mechanized and computerized and cannot function without high-level technology.[123] For a host of reasons, security specialists need to anticipate the multiplicity of harms that can arise from a breached chemical plant.[124]

Web Exercise: Find out about the chronology of this nation's more notorious chemical disasters at https://preventchemicaldisasters.org/resources/158971-2/.

Partnerships are essential to chemical plant security too since chemical plants are privately owned and operated. As a result, the government depends on corporate partners for effective countermeasures. The chemical sector has a coordinating council that pairs government agencies such as DHS, EPA, etc. with specific industry and corporate partners. The chemical sector coordinating council includes the following members:

- Agricultural Retailers Association
- American Chemistry Council

---

[121] For a complete list of chemicals subject to the administrative regulations, see Code of Federal Regulations, title 6, part 27 (2007), at https://www.dhs.gov/xlibrary/assets/chemsec_appendixafinalrule.pdf.

[122] M. Lawrence, A Clear Shot at Chemical Plant Security, *Sec. Mgmt* (July 2006), at 36; see also S.R. Gane, Security Compliance at Chemical Facilities, *Sec. Mag.* (July 2007), at 32.

[123] See E. Stoye, Security Experts Warn Chemical Plants Are Vulnerable to Cyber-Attacks, *Chemistry World* (June 10, 2015), at http://www.rsc.org/chemistryworld/2015/06/chemical-plants-vulnerable-cyber-attacks.

[124] Training Is Key in Chemical Plant Security. See The DHS Guide at https://www.dhs.gov/video/chemical-sector-critical-infrastructure.

- American Coatings Association
- American Fuel and Petrochemical Manufacturers
- American Petroleum Institute
- The Chlorine Institute
- Compressed Gas Association
- Council of Producers & Distributors of Agrotechnology
- CropLife America
- Dow Chemical Company
- The Fertilizer Institute
- International Institute of Ammonia Refrigeration
- International Liquid Terminals Association
- Institute of Makers of Explosives
- LSB Chemical Corp.
- National Association of Chemical Distributor
- Praxair, Inc.
- Society of Chemical Manufacturers & Affiliates

These firms bring a special expertise to governmental authorities at every level of the security process, from the preventive side to the mitigation and remediation side when disaster occurs. Government alone cannot resolve these often complex and highly dangerous situations in which chemicals are released beyond their normal boundaries. In these same companies and enterprises are teams of security specialists whose expertise is both prevention and containment. When these security forces work collaboratively with governmental authority, all interested parties benefit. Here, as in other sectors discussed throughout this chapter, are career tracks for private security professionals whose primary task is safety and security in the industrialized, chemical environment. A host of major security firms announce their expertise in the chemical domain —although there is room for improvement.[125]

U.S. Security Associates delivers a myriad of differing services for the chemical industry per their informative fact sheet[126]:

> Oil, gas, and energy companies are key players in critical infrastructure development and thus in our nation's economy and security. The global scope of the petrochemical industry, operating safety hazards, and terrorist threats, as well as social responsibility and public image perceptions, present a unique risk profile with security challenges that go beyond traditional facilities protection.
>
> U.S. Security Associates (USA) provides security solutions for organizations that own or operate business components engaged in the exploration, development, and production of crude oil and natural gas, refining and manufacturing of petroleum products, transportation of crude and finished products, and product sales.
>
> The Petrochemical Division offers a benchmark program featuring hybrid security and safety professionals called National Security Safety Officers (NSSOs), who not only meet rigorous experience and background standards but also complete extensive training in safety, government regulations, and petrochemical operational security protocols. The NSSO force is complemented by a team of petrochemical experts and safety professionals, who provide client specific interpretation and case management and support development and execution of customized safety and training programs.
>
> We bring to our energy and infrastructure clients an integrated approach to security that provides a range of services and a proven level of reliability, which meets both the conventional and extended security needs of the industry. Our approach to enterprise security focuses on threat assessments, situation analysis, and proactive planning to identify and mitigate potential risks.
>
> We provide key services that meet the specific needs of the industry.
>
> - Facilities protection
> - Contraband canine inspection and education programs

---

[125] Editorial, A Failure to Police Chemical Plants, *The New York Times* (June 1, 2013), at http://www.nytimes.com/2013/06/02/opinion/sunday/a-failure-to-police-chemical-plants.html?_r=0.

[126] U.S. Security Associates, Petrochemical Flyer, at http://www.ussecurityassociates.com/markets-served/vertical-market-sheets/petrochemical.pdf.

- Environmental health and safety
- Emergency/storm/unusual event response
- Oil spill response
- Executive protection
- Armed and unarmed security officers
- Workplace violence response
- Threat assessments

Our rigorous selection process involves thorough testing, background checks, past performance analysis, personality/integrity profiles, and other qualifying procedures. Our comprehensive training program assures that security personnel master security fundamentals and site specifics, while strong benefits, incentive awards, and career advancement opportunities keep personnel retention well above the industry norm.

Allied Barton has launched a specialized certification dedicated to the chemical industry, namely, the Certified Petrochemical Security Officer (CPSO) program, the training including four levels of expertise.

1. Upon completion of AlliedBarton's MSO 1, officers receive classroom instruction on the Chemical Facility Antiterrorism Standards (CFATS) or the Maritime Transportation Security Act/(MARSEC) depending on the facility of assignment, plus a series of nine CPSO essential courses to ensure they have basic knowledge required for them to perform their duties.
2. Next is on-the-job training (OJT). As part of their OJT program, officers receive instruction and testing of on-site policies and procedures, FTO- guided post- training, and client site– specific safety and security training.
3. Upon successful completion of CPSO essentials and OJT, officers will move on to advanced training that includes Master Security Officer Program courses and our monthly CPSO safety and security refresher training program.
4. The final level consists of any specialized training that may be required for officers assigned to your facility(s). This training will be given in accordance with the security services agreement.

Upon successful completion of all the required courses/sections and passing a comprehensive final exam, officers will earn the designation of AlliedBarton Certified CPSO.

11.7 CONCLUSION

The term critical infrastructure connotes a very heavy security responsibility for when security professionals are entrusted with airport protection, bridges, tunnels, dams, and power plants, all of these structures play a central role in the social, economic, and military defense of this country. All of these and other structures, whether chemical or nuclear in design, electrical assets or pipelines, have extraordinary damage potential. The role of private security that assures safety and unfettered operations cannot be denied in the current climate. Nearly all the major security enterprises offer up critical infrastructure services.

Keywords

Automated Commercial Environment (ACE)
Canine Explosive Detection Unit
cargo
critical infrastructure
chemical sector
commercial facilities sector
communications sector
Container Security Initiative
critical manufacturing sector

Customs Trade Partnership against Terrorism (C-TPAT)
dams sector
defense industrial base sector
emergency services sector
energy sector
enterprise risk management (ERM)
financial services sector
food and agriculture sector

global marketplace
government facilities sector
healthcare and public health sector
information technology sector
megaports
memorandum of agreement
National Vessel Documentation Center
nuclear reactors, materials, and waste sector
partner ports

port security

Secure Freight Initiative

transportation systems sector

Screening Partnership Program

Strategic Partnership Program on
Agroterrorism

vulnerability analysis

sector-specific agencies

water and wastewater systems sector

Discussion questions

1. Discuss the three reasons why the private security sector has made an indelible mark on the critical infrastructure sector.

2. Explain how the SFI and the CSI could work hand in hand to assure safe cargo. Check the list of SFI ports against CSI ports to see if both initiatives exist at the same location.

3. Summarize the short comings of the TSA as it relates to airline security. How could private security offer better options to the airline transportation industry? What would the outcome likely be?

4. Compare and contrast Amtrak's, CSX's, and SEPTA's efforts to provide secure passenger and cargo transportation.

5. Using a facility chosen by your instructor and the DHS criteria for impact evaluation, analyze the impact of a large-scale food contamination by at least two methods. How would you protect against these threats?

6. The WSD of the EPA broke down the tasks that must be tackled relating to security and the water supply. Take three of the tasks and state, acting as a security manager, what specific steps could be taken to accomplish the overall task.

CHAPTER 12

Private security and art and cultural, educational, religious, and medical institutions

OBJECTIVES

After completing this chapter, the student will be able to

1. Recognize that while many of the protocols and practices of the private security industry have universal applicability, each domain presents its own unique set of challenges for the security professional.
2. Discuss how the world of art and cultural institutions represents a dynamic environment with large numbers of public citizens and high value assets, which requires sophisticated techniques of theft and damage protection and prevention.
3. Evaluate the unique situation of educational security as it relates to myriad threats that must be protected against from theft and assault to natural disasters, active shooters, and terrorist threats.
4. Compare and contrast the Community Oriented Policing Services (COPS) program and the Congressional Research Service programs for school security and discuss their viability.
5. Recognize the unique challenges encountered in the safety and security of religious centers and devise prevention and detection recommendations for each unique setting.
6. Compose a risk assessment for religious centers.
7. Describe the interplay of security and emergency in the hospital setting, and recognize the maze of regulatory processes that need navigated, as well as the bureaucratic nightmare that must be navigated.
8. Develop a hospital survey or assessment, planning for continuity of service, taking a diversity of variables into account.

12.1 INTRODUCTION

The role of the private security industry in the protection of institutions, their personnel and assets, is one of the industry's earliest and most notable functions. From its days of origin, the industry has been a major player in the protection of places, whether for business and industry to event settings and sports facilities and to educational settings where safety for students is and has been an ongoing priority. Institutional security might also be delivered at a prison facility, a courthouse, or a college campus, or it could be at a large convention hall or exhibitor center. The fact of the matter is that there are simply too many institutions of varying sorts for any public system to fully cover. In this chapter, the stress is fourfold:

- Private security and cultural institutions: art, museums, and libraries
- Private security and educational institutions: K–12 and colleges and universities
- Private security and religious institutions
- Private security and healthcare institutions

While many of the protocols and practices of the private security industry have universal applicability as well as technological universality, each domain presents its own unique set of challenges for the security professional. The multifaceted task of securing the typical college or university setting is a complimentary yet vastly different environment from a local house of worship. Throughout this chapter, there will be the crossover and the chasm in how to get things done in the world of security and safety—the end results merely reflecting the best practices for these unique institutional settings.

12.2 PRIVATE SECURITY AND CULTURAL INSTITUTIONS: ART, MUSEUMS, AND LIBRARIES

Most people would own a general caricature about museum and cultural institution security, such as, is it really necessary? How exciting and demanding could it be? Are there really any challenges associated with cultural venues and spaces? Most people would never fully appreciate the depth and breadth of cultural institutional security and how much is really at stake in this world of art, artifacts, collection, and antiquities. Put another way, this institutional treasure trove is worth billions to those caring, owning, and displaying art or exhibitions, special collections of texts and monographs, or any artifact worthy of public display. It is also an institutional setting where visitors come by the multimillions throughout the civilized world and an entire infrastructure of employees and staff working among these works must be verified and properly vetted. It is not a quiet, tranquil environment where security plays second fiddle but no "better place to steal high-priced assets than museums."[1]

Securing art is securing "pricelessness" and cultural, iconic treasures that simply cannot be replaced readily.[2,3]

Web Exercise: See the American Museum Association security recommendations at http://www.aam-us.org/docs/professional-resources/suggested-practices-for-museum-security.pdf.

The trick to securing cultural, museum, and artistic environments relates to their inherent openness to a larger public. Given that the prime aim of these institutions is public consumption and enjoyment, the proper balance of security and accessibility is not always easy to achieve. The environment must be welcoming, yet at the same time highly protective.[4] This balancing act applies to special collections of texts and books of antiquity that are generally housed in special collection rooms. For those works, previous to 1,500, often works of art at the same time, like "illuminated incunabula" or other rare books, the challenges of security include not just the asset's protection from theft but just as critically prevention of environmental damage and destruction.

Rare books and all antiquities are worth extraordinary amounts of money and are frequently targeted by thieves for their obvious value and given the draconian cuts that libraries are currently operating under throughout the Western world, these collections are under security pressures that make viability a challenge.[5] Hence, the world of art and cultural institutions represents a dynamic environment where large public visitation occurs and the value of the assets on display sits near the top of the value chain. It is a very serious business that requires sophisticated techniques of theft and damage protection and prevention.

Career Profile: Security Manager: Whitney Museum of American Art

See Figure 12.1.

Aside from the valued assets, the facility which houses the collections need be designed for preservation purposes and present an aura of accessibility and impenetrability at the same time.[6]

---

[1] B. Zalud, The Art of Theft, *Sec. Mag.* (December 2008), at 70; see also G. Shirar, Art Indiscretions, *Sec. Mag.* (November 2006), at 43.

[2] See S. Berinato, Museum Security: The Art of Securing Pricelessness, *CSO* (September 1, 2004), at http://www.csoonline.com/article/2122573/physical-security/museum-security--the-art-of-securing-pricelessness.html, last accessed August 31, 2016; see also S. Keller, Museum Security: The Arts of Alarms (1994), at http://www.architectssecuritygroup.com/Consulting/Architect_Support_files/TheArtofAlarms.PDF, last accessed August 31, 2016.

[3] ArtGuard website, at http://www.artguard.net, last accessed August 31, 2016.

[4] D. Ritchey, It's Priceless: The Art of Securing Museums and Libraries, *Sec. Mag.* (September 2010), at 80; for an analysis on special book collections and their limited access, see M.A. Gips, Library Security Guidelines Revised, 45 *Sec. Mgmt* 18 (2001).

[5] M.A. Gips, Special Collections Not Always Special, 49 *Sec. Mgmt* 16 (2005).

[6] Intrusion detection systems are extremely important in this area, see R. Elliott, Military Museum Guards Against Fire, 50 *Sec. Mgmt* 40 (2006).

Security Manager

Reporting to the Director of Security, the Manager has general responsibility for the security of the Museum, the art, the staff and visitors.

Responsibilities:

- Oversee scheduling and supervise the Security staff on a daily basis and for special events; this will require the ability to work flexible hours, including regular evenings and weekends (and will also cover management duties for special events)
- Train the Security forces for NYS license and in security procedures
- Maintain all security records and logs
- Act as Fire Safety Director and maintain all fire related equipment and records necessary to the city or insurance requirements
- Help to develop, manage and administer all security-based systems, ensuring compliance and functionality at all times; work with facilities managers to ensure public safety systems are properly tested and maintained
- Act as a contact for Health and Safety, and Fire Safety inquiries (investigating accidents and recommending solutions), and work with other operational managers to ensure best practice and compliance relating to Health and Safety and Fire Safety legislation
- Manage the contract for agency security provisions to ensure that the service provided is in line with the standards and requirements set out in the service level agreement
- Collaborate with other museum staff to ensure artwork protection
- Other duties and project assignments as required

Requirements:

- B.A.; 10 years of managerial experience in the Security field preferred
- A background in law enforcement or the military is a plus
- Other requirements include: NYS Training and Security licenses; Fire Safety Director license preferred
- Excellent communication skills (written and verbal)
- Ability to work collaboratively with all staff at a premier NYC cultural institution

Figure 12.1   Career profile: security manager—Whitney Museum of American Art.

Web Exercise: Since 1996, the Museum Security Network compiles a current and updated list of security challenges to collections throughout the world. See www.museum-security.org.

It is not thievery alone that remains a constant security concern for forgery and fraudulent duplication with subsequent sales consumes the time and energy of private security operatives as well as public law enforcement such as the FBI, which has created a special division dedicated to art forgery and related shenanigans. See Figure 12.2.

Crimes and destructive actions taking place in art, cultural, and special collection libraries are no very commonplace. Technology has advanced a host of legitimate technologies to conduct illegal and illegitimate activity. To illustrate, forgeries and reproductions are now so commonplace that it often takes years to ferret out the original from the con artist. See Figure 12.3.

The Museum Security Network tracks and traces all levels of crime dealing with art and culture. For a representative sampling of illegality in art alone and how security must anticipate its multilayered attack on the integrity of art, see Figure 12.4.[7]

In every imaginable context, the thief, the forger, the con artist, and other villain keep a careful eye on the world of art, special collections, and museum antiquities. Skyrocketing valuations assure that the problem is not going away anytime soon and the private security industry must remain at the forefront of protection. Pinkerton's delivers specialized security protocols for the art and cultural world and provides keen insight into how multilayered and tiered the protection system must be—far more than mere protection at the display location. Security professionals here must factor in the art and museum security issues at various stages in the life of an antiquity, which include but are not limited to the following:

- Type of artwork: painting, photo, sculpture
- Materials used

---

[7] Museum Security Network website, at www.museum-security.org, last accessed August 31, 2016.

Figure 12.2   Counterfeit Picasso print of "Francoise Gilot." (Courtesy of FBI at https://archives.fbi.gov/archives/news/stories/2008/march/artscam_032108.)

Figure 12.3   Forged Renoir. (From http://www.museum-security.org/2016/07/fake-monet-renoir-paintings-cost-dealer-31m-and-his-reputation.)

> Vietnam museum says all paintings fake in high-profile exhibition - July 20, 2016
> These Four Technologies May Finally Put an End to Art Forgery - July 19, 2016
> A Forger Confessed to Faking Millions in Lee Ufan Works—Now the Artist Says They're Real - July 8, 2016
> Fake Monet, Renoir paintings cost dealer $31M and his reputation - July 8, 2016
> CNS – Investor Fears Her Warhols May Be Rip Offs - July 5, 2016
> Why is Korean art market vulnerable to forgery? - June 23, 2016
> A house full of stolen antiques - June 23, 2016
> Connoisseur & Smuggler:The 84-year-old art dealer and his collection of 'stolen' idols in Chennai - June 21, 2016
> 13 of Lee U-fan's paintings confirmed to be forged - June 4, 2016
> Insider theft – Jail for woman who plundered famous photo prints - June 3, 2016
> 'Imagine how easy Keith Haring is to fake' - June 3, 2016
> Ukranian art buyer hands back stolen Dutch masterpiece - May 31, 2016
> Inside the great Brett Whiteley art fraud - May 13, 2016
> Brett Whiteley fake art: Dealer and conservator guilty of Australia's biggest art fraud - May 12, 2016
> Art forger goes straight selling £5,000 fakes - May 8, 2016
> Committing Crime Is Just Another Way To Use A City - May 2, 2016
> Terrorisme een dreiging voor musea? – Museum Security Network - April 29, 2016
> Protected: The rise of fakes and false attributions in the art world - April 19, 2016

Figure 12.4   Posts on the Museum Security Network website regarding forgery, theft, and security. (From www.museum-security.org.)

- Insurance policies
- Artist's requests
- Loan agreements
- Environmental conditions and concerns
- Storage procedures
- Transportation[8]

Web Exercise: Find out about careers and responsibilities for security directors at cultural facilities at http://www.ifcpp.org/.

See Figure 12.5.[9]

The International Foundation for Cultural Property Protection delivers four distinct programs for individuals and directors working in the art and cultural world. These programs include the following:

Certification Options for the Certified Institutional Security Supervisor (CISS)
The International Foundation for Cultural Property Protection offers quality training and certification for security supervisors working in cultural, educational, or public institutions. Our Certified Institutional Security Supervisor (CISS) certification program will be available soon (April 2015) in live and online formats.
IFCPP's requirements for CISS supervisor certification include active membership, institutional protection experience, evidence of a clear criminal history, final approval by the IFCPP Certification Team, and completion of live or correspondence coursework and examination, and required reading (Safeguarding Cultural Properties).
Certification Options for the Certified Institutional Protection Specialist (CIPS)
The International Foundation for Cultural Property Protection offers quality basic training and certification for officers and other front-line staff. Our Certified Institutional Protection Specialist (CIPS) certification program is now available in live, DVD, and online formats.
IFCPP's requirements for CIPS basic certification include active membership, institutional protection experience, evidence of a clear criminal history, final approval by the IFCPP Certification Team, and completion of live or correspondence coursework and examination.

---

[8]   See J. Bechmann, Museum Security: Preserving the Art Experience, *Pinkerton Blog* (August 28, 2014), at https://www.pinkerton.com/blog/museum-security-preserving-the-art-experience, last accessed August 31, 2016.
[9]   International Foundation for Cultural Property Protection website, at http://www.ifcpp.org, last accessed August 31, 2016.

Figure 12.5   IFCPP logo.

Certification Options for the Certified Institutional Protection Manager (CIPM I and CIPM II)

The International Foundation for Cultural Property Protection offers quality advanced training and certification for managers, supervisors, executives and administrators. The Certified Institutional Protection Manager (CIPM) certification program is now available in live and online formats.

The CIPM and CIPM II programs designate those managers, directors, administrators, or others responsible for the protection of a cultural, educational, or public institution. Candidates in this category include contract or proprietary security managers, security directors, law enforcement officers, facility managers, administrators, or those ultimately responsible for protection of the institution.

The CIPM II program offers the advance level of management certification, and requires completion of the CIPM level one program as a prerequisite.

CIPM II certification is the next step in IFCPP's industry recognized CIPM program, offering qualified managers the opportunity to further advance their cultural property protection knowledge. Graduates attain the highest designation in the field, joining the ranks of leading professionals across the globe.[10]

Career Profile: Security Shift Supervisor: Philadelphia Museum of Art

See Figure 12.6.

12.2.1 Security tactics and protocols in the protection of art, museum, and special collections

The task of security in any installation that houses art, artifacts, museum content, and special collections encompasses a great deal more than the placement of security officers and guards at point of ingress and egress. The level of sophistication of criminals seeking illegal gain from these locales calls for more than ID checks but an awareness that art and museum criminals display no boundaries as typical felons do. In some ways, these sorts of criminal actors

---

[10] *Ibid.*

Philadelphia Museum of Art

Security Shift Supervisor

The Philadelphia Museum of Art is seeking a Security Shift Supervisor for the first shift working from 12am-8am, two days per week. Working under limited supervision, the Security Shift Supervisor ensures the safety and security of the Philadelphia Museum of Art's campus from staff to the precious art collections. The Shift Supervisor will monitor building access, CCTV, and emergency response systems. The Shift Supervisor is also responsible for the timely and accurate reporting and completion of documentation related to reportable incidents.

The successful candidate will demonstrate the ability to work independently as well as with a team of support staff. The preferred candidate will have at least 5 years of supervisory experience with a track record of success with analysis, problem solving, and decision making in a cooperative and coordinated planning environment. Strong written and verbal communication skills are also essential for the job.

This position requires a high school diploma or GED. Computer proficiency is a must. Possessing a working knowledge of emergency response and building security systems including access control, CCTV, and intrusion detection is also a plus.

To apply, please attach a cover letter and resume to submit with your application.

Figure 12.6 Career profile: security shift supervisor—Philadelphia Museum of Art.

are even more esoteric and technical in their approach than the cybercriminal. In this world, we witness simulation, forgery, copycats, and digital reproduction so advanced to fool even the best art and collection critics, and their zeal to visit and take these valuable assets never sleeps. These domains must be protected for 365/24 hours a day and 7 days a week. Even jihadi terrorists—whose warped perception demands that ancient artifacts be obliterated from the world's stage—become a major security concern for the industry.[11] Diane Ritchey, in *It's Priceless: The Art of Securing Museums and Libraries*, appreciates the complexity of the security plan needed to protect these treasures:

> But it's much more, as most security staff are expected to keep up with new technologies, respond to emergencies, maintain public order and crowd control and ensure that a large visiting public complies with museum regulations. Security in museums and libraries has increasingly taken on a more important role, to developing and implementing a comprehensive security response for every aspect of the business.[12]

As a result, the security team must have excellent observational and behavioral skills as to employees, visitors, and the identification of those parties who appear out of place.[13]

Other simple, yet profoundly important suggestions include the following:

- Combine and blend security consideration with facility and exhibit design
- Train all facility personnel so a common core of security exists at every level of the institution
- Maintain good flow of the visiting audience and avoid bottlenecks and crowd confusion—the perfect environment for something to go missing
- Develop and maintain strong communication systems across all levels of employees needing security cooperation
- Use technology wisely and aggressively to track human activity

Figure 12.7, developed by Museum Security Expert, Steve Keller, graphically portrays the diverse systems of security that a museum needs to protect its assets.

Vibration sensors are crucial to any museum setting for these are set off by movement and a change in environment. 1–3 represent strategically placed sensors to notify security personnel that movement is occurring in the setting that is presently closed. Artwork is often protected by encased glazing or other cover. A plastic encasement makes pilferage far more difficult. See 4.

---

[11] B. Zalud, The Art of Museum Protection, *Sec. Mag.* (June 2005), at 18.
[12] Ritchey, *supra* note 4, at 80.
[13] V. Contavespi, The Art of Security, *Security Today.com* (May 1, 2014), at https://securitytoday.com/Articles/2014/05/01/The-Art-of-Security.aspx, last accessed August 31, 2016.

Figure 12.7 Museum security systems.

Changes in temperature can be measured by environmental sensors that would detect a human agent in close proximity to a painting or other artifact. See 5. Additional railings or other barriers, which mark out the line of accessibility, are mainly of a warning nature that distinguishes ground readily open to the visitor and closed beyond. See 6.

Motion detection equipment, as installed at 7, covers a field where any intruder would be targeted and captured as he or she moved to take the artwork. For each item protected, the strategy remains the same. Additionally, placed motion detectors always make sense in the museum for in the event that one system is disabled of dysfunctioned, another system steps in. Placement in hard to detect or unlikely places is wise. See 8. Once in the zone of motion, the detector picks up the actor within a targeted area. Multiple motion detectors trap the actor from various angles (refer to Figure 7.30).

Unobtrusive CCTV cameras, close to the prized art in question are also essential to any museum security plan. The cameras should be strategically placed as is clear at 9.

Fire alarms and temperature controls will also highlight potential damaging effects of fire or disaster about to happen. In this sense, the equipment serves in both an emergency and security capacity. See 10. Security officers, when open to the public, need to be strategically positioned as evident in 12.

All of these tactics are effective measures in the protection of artwork and other museum assets and when combined with a command and control center, armed with a plethora of surveillance points and coupled with strong, professional human intelligence, the security place for the museum can only be effective.[14]

12.3 PRIVATE SECURITY AND EDUCATIONAL INSTITUTIONS

That schools, colleges, and universities have been transformed by crime and mass casualties is an undeniable and very grim reality in the modern world. No longer are these institutions safe havens without security concerns and those security concerns continue to be graver and graver each passing year.[15]

Teenagers stealing hubcaps or other hooliganism have been replaced by mass shooters, goth killers, and mentally disturbed and emotionally distressed players trying to make a mark in the world, all of which have catastrophically changed the environment of educational security. And this plague starts at Pre-K and never ceases even to the highest levels where disgruntled PhD candidates kill their advisors and instructors. The pace and volume of crime in educational settings inclines upward without much hesitation. And understanding your facility and audience is a seminal

[14] A. Farren-Bradley, What Makes a Museum Secure? *Apollo* (March 1, 2016), at http://www.apollo-magazine.com/what-makes-a-museum-secure/.
[15] D. Richey, Protecting the Ever-Expanding Perimeter, *Sec. Mag.* (May 2014), at 54.

step in any security plan. Do not assume things are rosy and safe—be wary of all possible threats. As in all other settings, be attentive to an Emergency Operations Plan (EOP), which provides the planning and reaction context to respond. Something as simple as Figure 12.8[16] would be suitable.

Early on, security professionals couple the EOP with a school risk assessment, which cannot predict all that can go wrong, but can provide a series of risk parameters. Figure 12.9[17] contains a simplified risk and hazard analysis.

Web Exercise: Engage the Risk Assessment Toolkit for Higher Education at https://www.youtube.com/watch?v=I11 QWfvz75w&list=PLELhYPOXzeUenl9QKqPHRc3gm3z52VI3j.

See Figure 12.10.

The Bureau of Justice Statistics paints a miserable picture in its most recent release on crime and school data; the highlights include the following:

- In 2014, among students ages 12–18, there were about 850,100 nonfatal victimizations at school, which included 363,700 theft victimizations and 486,400 violent victimizations (simple assault and serious violent victimizations).
- In 2014, students ages 12–18 experienced 33 nonfatal victimizations per 1,000 students at school and 24 per 1,000 students away from school.
- Between 1992 and 2014, the total victimization rate at school declined 82 percent, from 181 victimizations per 1,000 students in 1992 to 33 victimizations per 1,000 students in 2014. The total victimization rate away from school declined 86 percent, from 173 victimizations per 1,000 students in 1992 to 24 victimizations per 1,000 students in 2014.
- In 2014, students residing in rural areas had higher rates of total victimization at school (53 victimizations per 1,000 students) than students residing in suburban areas (28 victimizations per 1,000 students).[18]

In homicide and suicidal activity, the primary and secondary schools are dealing with casualty rates that can only be termed devastating. The National Center for Education Statistics charts the recent decades, in the 5–18 age brackets, as shown in Figure 12.11.[19]

Even teachers laboring in school environments are the ever increasing target of criminal activity with numbers escalating each year that passes. The National Center's most recent data show that growing, escalating violence has become a way of life in primary and secondary schools. See Figure 12.12.[20]

Much to the misfortune of our children, active shooter activity targets school settings at rates once imaginable. The FBI's analysis of active shooter activity demonstrates that nearly a quarter of all active shooter incidents occur in educational settings. See Figure 12.13.[21]

The picture never improves at the college and university level, with mass killings and criminality of every sort now almost normative in the modern collegiate setting.[22] See Figure 12.14.[23]

With an average of 100,000 arrests per year over the last decade or so, college campuses are in severe need of security. See Figure 12.15.[24]

---

[16] State of Colorado, School Safety Resource Center, School EOP Exercise Checklists, at http://cdpsdocs.state.co.us/safeschools/CSSRC%20 Documents/Colorado%20School%20Emergency%20Operations%20Plan%20Exercise%20Toolkit/Tab%2011_Checklists%20School%20 EOP%20TTX,1.pdf, last accessed August 31, 2016.

[17] University of Edinburgh, Health and Safety Department, General Risk Assessment, at http://www.docs.csg.ed.ac.uk/Safety/ra/RA1.pdf, last accessed August 31, 2016.

[18] See A. Zhang et al., *Indicators of School Crime and Safety: 2015*, NCJ 249758 (Bureau of Justice Statistics, 2016), at http://www.bjs.gov/index. cfm?ty=pbdetail&iid=5599, last accessed August 31, 2016.

[19] National Center for Education Statistics, Digest of Education Statistics, Table 228.10, at http://nces.ed.gov/programs/digest/d15/tables/ dt15_228.10.asp, last accessed August 31, 2016.

[20] National Center for Education Statistics, Digest of Education Statistics, Table 228.70, at http://nces.ed.gov/programs/digest/d15/tables/ dt15_228.70.asp, last accessed August 31, 2016.

[21] FBI, *A Study of Active Shooter Incidents in the United States Between 2000 and 2013* 13 (Washington, DC: FBI, 2013), at https://www.fbi.gov/ file-repository/active-shooter-study-2000-2013-1.pdf, last accessed August 31, 2016.

[22] See FBI Report: Frequency of Active Shooter Events Has Increased, *Campus Safety* (January 27, 2014), at http://www.campussafetymagazine. com/article/fbi-report-frequency-of-active-shooter-events-has-increased#, last accessed August 31, 2016.

[23] Official: Man Who Opened Fire at Oregon College Was Chris Harper Mercer, 26, *Times Free Press* (October 1, 2015), at http://www.timesfree- press.com/news/breakingnews/story/2015/oct/01/officials-report-active-shooter-oregon-college/328184/, last accessed August 31, 2016.

[24] U.S. Department of Education, Campus Safety and Security, Trend Data, at http://ope.ed.gov/campussafety/Trend/public/#/answer/4/401/ trend/-1/-1/-1/-1, last accessed August 31, 2016.

School EOP Exercise Checklists

Participant Checklist

- ✓ Personnel from participant schools have created a school emergency operations plan.
- ✓ Participant schools agree to update hazard analysis to identify natural and man-made hazards or other credible threats that could present a risk to students and staff.
- ✓ Participant schools agree to upgrade/revise school emergency operations plan.
- ✓ Participant schools agree to update emergency contact list and to coordinate with local emergency management and public safety personnel.
- ✓ Participant agencies agree to conduct facility drill or full-scale exercise to improve capabilities for evacuating and/or sheltering in place.

Player Briefing Checklist

- ✓ Review exercise purpose, concept and scope
- ✓ Summarize importance of emergency preparedness planning and highlight illustrative examples based on actual school emergency situations.
- ✓ Review exercise objectives.
- ✓ Review exercise scenario.
- ✓ Review exercise design and explain exercise ground rules.
- ✓ Review player rules of conduct.
- ✓ Emphasize importance of utilizing actual plans and resources available to players (as opposed to assets that are not operational or not currently available to player agencies).
- ✓ Review exercise safety procedures and security measures.
- ✓ Review administrative requirements (sign-in sheets, evaluation forms).
- ✓ Review logistics issues (parking, restrooms, refreshments, lunch).
- ✓ Review participant feedback form and emphasize the importance of player input for improving future exercises.
- ✓ Review format and purpose of player hot wash.

Controller/Evaluator Briefing Checklist

- ✓ Review exercise purpose, scope and objectives.
- ✓ Review Master Sequence of Events List (MSEL).
- ✓ Review exercise ground rules and player rules of conduct.
- ✓ Review setup and layout of exercise facility/training room.
- ✓ Review the role and responsibilities of the Exercise Director (overall responsibility for exercise planning, control of exercise, and direction of controller/evaluator team).
- ✓ Review controller responsibilities (monitor play; implement MSEL; inject exercise events; explain/clarify exercise assumptions and artificialities; simulate actions of agencies not in attendance).
- ✓ Review evaluator responsibilities (cooperation with controllers; record events and assist with documentation for after-action report and improvement plan; avoid interaction with players).
- ✓ Distribute forms for controller notes and evaluator feedback.
- ✓ Assign evaluators to monitor specific functional areas based on expertise of the evaluator.

Figure 12.8   School EOP exercise checklists.   (Continued)

✓ Identify communication procedures for controller/evaluator team.
✓ Review safety and security procedures, including measures for terminating the exercise prematurely due to an actual emergency or other unanticipated event.
✓ Review evaluation plan and related forms.
✓ Review the format and purpose of the player hot wash.

De-Briefing Checklist

✓ Discuss exercise objectives and evaluate effectiveness of exercise in achieving objectives.
✓ Evaluate exercise design and identify improvements for future exercise delivery.
✓ Review and summarize comments from hot wash.
✓ Review/discuss exercise activities by functional area (e.g., notification, facility-response agency communications, media relations).
✓ Obtain input from controllers and evaluators for preparation of After-Action Report and Improvement Plan.
✓ Identify player/responder strengths and weaknesses, with respect to exercise events and the scenario, and identify future training needs.

Figure 12.8 (Continued) School EOP exercise checklists.

Web Exercise: Watch the Bureau of Justice educational video on campuses crime at http://nces.ed.gov/blogs/nces/post/crime-and-safety-on-college-campuses.

Unfortunately, college and university security officers and chiefs must now develop protocols for the active shooter possibility. Students must now be oriented toward this eventuality as the pace and rate of shooting incidents continues. Figure 12.16[25] contains a suggested student reaction protocol in the event of an active shooter.

The rise in crime on college and university campuses has been so significant that Congress has mandated the collection and publication of campus crime rates—covering most major felonies. Known as the Clery Act that tabulates crime, this annual report is always the responsibility of security staff and command.[26] For an example of the reporting template that each college and university has to complete, see Figure 12.17.[27]

12.3.1 How the security industry serves educational institutions

Observers of college and university security systems would agree that this domain is dynamic and subject to innovative change and modification. Security practice in K–12 as well as the collegiate environment is forever subject to change due to evolving crime pressures. This capacity to alter operations and to modify the status quo is a natural companion to the private security industry given its customer- and client-based mentality. Public, civil service positions are locked in a series of roles and functions and the difficult to change job description. Private security delivers a malleable functionality that the public system cannot.[28]

Sometimes, it is private security that critiques public practices by either demonstrating by study and analysis the effectual practice or by recommending a better alternative. For example, the industry has concluded the 2012 DHS recommendation that one "run, hide, fight" protocol during an active shooter situation, may be mis-prioritized. Paul Timm holds that "hide" may be a better first step especially since children are habituated to follow the lead

---

[25] Auburn University at Montgomery, Active Shooter webpage, at http://www.aum.edu/active-shooter.

[26] See Campus Security Act, the Jeanne Clery Disclosure of Campus Security Policy and Campus Crime Statistics Act (20 USC § 1092(f)).

[27] U.S. Department of Education, *The Handbook for Campus Safety and Security Reporting* (2016 Edition, Washington DC: U.S. Department of Education, 2016); University of California, Riverside, 2016 Annual Security Report (Clery Act) Crime Statistics Collection Form, at http://police.ucr.edu/clery2016form.pdf, last accessed August 31, 2016.

[28] C. Meyer, Addressing the Human Side of School Security, *Sec. Mag.* (January 2014), at 28; see also Private Security Turns Big Business, *Deccan Chronicle* (September 1, 2016), at http://www.deccanchronicle.com/150505/nation-current-affairs/article/private-security-turns-big-business, last accessed August 31, 2016.

General Risk Assessment

Form RA1

(Refer to Notes for Guidance before completing this form)

School Assessment No:	
Title of Activity:	
Location(s) of Work:	
Brief Description of Work:	

Hazard Identification: Identify all the hazards; evaluate the risks (low / medium / high); describe all existing control measures and identify any further measures required. Specific hazards should be assessed on a separate risk assessment form and cross-referenced with this document. Specific assessments are available for hazardous substances, biological agents, display screen equipment, manual handling operations and fieldwork.

Hazard(s)	Present Risk Evaluation L/M/H	Control Measures (i.e., alternative work methods / mechanical aids / engineering controls, etc.)	Risk Evaluation after control L/M/H

Continue on separate sheet if necessary

Figure 12.9   General risk assessment.

(Continued)

Engineering Controls: *Tick relevant boxes*

Guarding		Extraction (LEV)		Interlocks		Enclosure	
Other relevant information (incl. testing frequency if appropriate):							

Personal Protective Equipment (PPE): Identify all necessary PPE.

Eye / Face		Hand /Arm		Feet / Legs		Respiratory	
Body (clothing)		Hearing		Other (Specify)			
Specify the grade(s) of PPE to be worn:							
Specify when during the activity the item(s) of PPE must be worn:							

Non-disposable items of PPE must be inspected regularly and records retained for inspection

Persons at Risk: Identify all those who may be at risk.

Academic staff		Technical staff		P'Grad students		U'Grad students	
Maintenance staff		Office staff		Cleaning staff		Emergency personnel	
Contractors		Visitors		Others			

Additional Information: Identify any additional information relevant to the activity, including supervision, training requirements, special emergency procedures, requirement for health surveillance etc.

Assessment carried out by:

Name:		Date:	
Signature:		Review Date:	

Figure 12.9 (Continued)   General risk assessment.

Figure 12.10 Investigators shown on scene in the wake of the Newtown School shooting.

School-associated violent deaths of all persons, homicides and suicides of youth ages 5-18 at school, and total homicides and suicides of youth ages 5-18, by type of violent death: 1992-93 to 2012-13

Year	School-associated violent deaths[1] of all persons (includes students, staff, and other nonstudents)					Homicides of youth ages 5-18		Suicides of youth ages 5-18	
	Total	Homicides	Suicides	Legal interventions	Unintentional firearm-related deaths	Homicides at school[2]	Total homicides	Suicides at school[2]	Total suicides[3]
1	2	3	4	5	6	7	8	9	10
1992-93	57	47	10	0	0	34	2,721	6	1,680
1993-94	48	38	10	0	0	29	2,932	7	1,723
1994-95	48	39	8	0	1	28	2,696	7	1,767
1995-96	53	46	6	1	0	32	2,545	6	1,725
1996-97	48	45	2	1	0	28	2,221	1	1,633
1997-98	57	47	9	1	0	34	2,100	6	1,626
1998-99	47	38	6	2	1	33	1,777	4	1,597
1999-2000	37[4]	26[4]	11[4]	0[4]	0[4]	14[4]	1,567	8[4]	1,415
2000-01	34[4]	26[4]	7[4]	1[4]	0[4]	14[4]	1,509	6[4]	1,493
2001-02	36[4]	27[4]	8[4]	1[4]	0[4]	16[4]	1,498	5[4]	1,400
2002-03	36[4]	25[4]	11[4]	0[4]	0[4]	18[4]	1,553	10[4]	1,331
2003-04	45[4]	37[4]	7[4]	1[4]	0[4]	23[4]	1,474	5[4]	1,285
2004-05	52[4]	40[4]	10[4]	2[4]	0[4]	22[4]	1,554	8[4]	1,471
2005-06	44[4]	37[4]	6[4]	1[4]	0[4]	21[4]	1,697	3[4]	1,408
2006-07	63[4]	48[4]	13[4]	2[4]	0[4]	32[4]	1,801	9[4]	1,296
2007-08	48[4]	39[4]	7[4]	2[4]	0[4]	21[4]	1,744	5[4]	1,231
2008-09	44[4]	29[4]	15[4]	0[4]	0[4]	18[4]	1,605	7[4]	1,344
2009-10	35[4]	27[4]	5[4]	3[4]	0[4]	19[4]	1,410	2[4]	1,467
2010-11	32[4]	26[4]	6[4]	0[4]	0[4]	11[4]	1,339	3[4]	1,456
2011-12	45[4]	26[4]	14[4]	5[4]	0[4]	15[4]	1,201	5[4]	1,568
2012-13	53[4]	41[4]	11[4]	1[4]	0[4]	31[4]	1,186	6[4]	1,590

[1] A school-associated violent death is defined as "a homicide, suicide, or legal intervention (involving a law enforcement officer), in which the fatal injury occurred on the campus of a functioning elementary or secondary school in the United States," while the victim was on the way to or from regular sessions at school, or while the victim was attending or traveling to or from an official school-sponsored event.

[2] "At school" includes on school property, on the way to or from regular sessions at school, and while attending or traveling to or from a school-sponsored event.

[3] Total youth suicides are reported for calendar years 1992 through 2012 (instead of school years 1992-93 through 2012-13).

[4] Data from 1999-2000 onward are subject to change until interviews with school and law enforcement officials have been completed. The details learned during the interviews can occasionally change the classification of a case.

NOTE: Unless otherwise noted, data are reported for the school year, defined as July 1 through June 30. Some data have been revised from previously published figures.

SOURCE: Centers for Disease Control and Prevention (CDC), 1992-2013 School-Associated Violent Deaths Surveillance Study (SAVD) (partially funded by the U.S. Department of Education, Office of Safe and Healthy Students), previously unpublished tabulation (December 2015); CDC, National Center for Injury Prevention and Control, Web-based Injury Statistics Query and Reporting System Fatal (WISQARS™ Fatal), 1999-2012, retrieved September 2015 from http://www.cdc.gov/injury/wisqars/index.html; and Federal Bureau of Investigation and Bureau of Justice Statistics, Supplementary Homicide Reports (SHR), preliminary data (November 2015). (This table was prepared December 2015.)

Figure 12.11 School-associated violent deaths.

Number and percentage of public and private school teachers who reported that they were threatened with injury or physically attacked by a student from school during the previous 12 months, by selected teacher and school characteristics: Selected years, 1993-94 through 2011-12

[Standard errors appear in parentheses]

Year	Total	Sex		Race/ethnicity				Instructional level[1]		Control of school	
		Male	Female	White	Black	Hispanic	Other[2]	Elementary	Secondary	Public[3]	Private
1	2	3	4	5	6	7	8	9	10	11	12
Threatened with injury				*Number of teachers*							
1993-94	342,700 (7,140)	115,900 (3,870)	226,800 (5,570)	295,700 (6,320)	23,900 (1,380)	15,900 (1,850)	7,300 (680)	135,200 (4,520)	207,500 (5,380)	326,800 (7,040)	15,900 (1,130)
1999-2000	304,900 (7,090)	95,100 (3,610)	209,800 (5,490)	252,500 (5,670)	28,300 (2,150)	17,200 (1,980)	7,000 (850)	148,100 (5,560)	156,900 (4,360)	287,400 (7,060)	17,500 (1,700)
2003-04	252,800 (8,750)	78,400 (3,930)	174,400 (7,260)	198,900 (6,980)	32,500 (3,050)	12,400 (1,810)	9,000 (1,250)	113,600 (7,240)	139,200 (5,280)	242,100 (7,840)	10,700 (1,780)
2007-08	289,900 (10,660)	88,300 (5,970)	201,600 (8,140)	234,700 (8,850)	28,700 (3,080)	17,900 (3,230)	8,600 (1,630)	130,000 (7,720)	160,000 (7,220)	276,600 (10,570)	13,300 (1,460)
2011-12	352,900 (17,080)	84,500 (5,220)	268,400 (15,450)	279,900 (13,300)	34,200 (4,380)	27,100 (4,660)	11,800 (2,200)	189,800 (13,430)	163,200 (7,520)	338,400 (17,290)	14,500 (1,450)
Physically attacked											
1993-94	121,100 (3,950)	30,800 (1,770)	90,300 (3,900)	104,300 (4,020)	7,700 (860)	6,200 (1,290)	2,800 (450)	77,300 (3,240)	43,800 (1,980)	112,400 (3,730)	8,700 (860)
1999-2000	134,800 (4,820)	30,600 (1,990)	104,200 (4,390)	111,700 (3,810)	11,600 (1,540)	8,800 (1,660)	2,600 (460)	102,200 (4,360)	32,600 (2,270)	125,000 (4,630)	9,800 (1,070)
2003-04	129,200 (7,810)	23,600 (2,610)	105,700 (6,460)	102,200 (5,920)	15,100 (2,300)	7,000 (1,860)	5,000 (1,110)	89,800 (6,680)	39,400 (3,410)	121,400 (7,180)	7,800 (1,450)
2007-08	156,000 (8,090)	34,900 (4,760)	121,100 (6,120)	132,300 (6,860)	12,300 (2,350)	8,200 (2,040)	3,200 (1,250)	114,700 (7,220)	41,300 (3,220)	146,400 (8,200)	9,600 (1,170)
2011-12	209,800 (11,880)	32,500 (3,330)	177,300 (11,310)	171,300 (10,950)	18,800 (3,580)	11,800 (2,890)	7,900 (1,990)	160,700 (10,210)	49,100 (4,310)	197,400 (11,730)	12,400 (1,490)
Threatened with injury				*Percent of teachers*							
1993-94	11.7 (0.23)	14.7 (0.40)	10.5 (0.25)	11.5 (0.24)	11.9 (0.61)	13.1 (1.32)	13.4 (1.08)	8.7 (0.30)	15.0 (0.28)	12.8 (0.26)	4.2 (0.29)
1999-2000	8.8 (0.20)	11.0 (0.38)	8.1 (0.20)	8.6 (0.19)	11.6 (0.84)	9.1 (1.01)	8.3 (0.98)	8.0 (0.29)	9.9 (0.26)	9.6 (0.22)	3.9 (0.35)
2003-04	6.8 (0.24)	8.5 (0.39)	6.2 (0.27)	6.4 (0.24)	11.8 (0.96)	5.5 (0.82)	8.7 (1.25)	5.7 (0.37)	8.0 (0.27)	7.4 (0.24)	2.3 (0.40)
2007-08	7.4 (0.26)	9.3 (0.59)	6.8 (0.27)	7.2 (0.26)	11.1 (0.93)	6.7 (1.19)	7.6 (1.36)	6.6 (0.38)	8.4 (0.36)	8.1 (0.30)	2.7 (0.30)
2011-12	9.2 (0.42)	9.2 (0.49)	9.2 (0.50)	8.8 (0.40)	13.8 (1.72)	9.4 (1.54)	9.1 (1.54)	9.6 (0.67)	8.7 (0.34)	10.0 (0.48)	3.1 (0.32)
Physically attacked											
1993-94	4.1 (0.13)	3.9 (0.21)	4.2 (0.18)	4.1 (0.16)	3.9 (0.40)	5.2 (0.99)	5.2 (0.76)	5.0 (0.20)	3.2 (0.14)	4.4 (0.14)	2.3 (0.23)
1999-2000	3.9 (0.14)	3.5 (0.22)	4.0 (0.17)	3.8 (0.13)	4.8 (0.59)	4.6 (0.83)	3.1 (0.54)	5.5 (0.23)	2.1 (0.14)	4.2 (0.15)	2.2 (0.22)
2003-04	3.5 (0.21)	2.6 (0.27)	3.8 (0.24)	3.3 (0.20)	5.5 (0.78)	3.1 (0.85)	4.8 (1.10)	4.5 (0.35)	2.3 (0.19)	3.7 (0.22)	1.7 (0.32)
2007-08	4.0 (0.21)	3.7 (0.49)	4.1 (0.21)	4.1 (0.22)	4.7 (0.89)	3.1 (0.73)	2.8 ! (0.97)	5.8 (0.38)	2.2 (0.16)	4.3 (0.24)	2.0 (0.24)
2011-12	5.4 (0.30)	3.5 (0.35)	6.0 (0.37)	5.4 (0.33)	7.6 (1.41)	4.1 (0.96)	6.1 (1.43)	8.2 (0.50)	2.6 (0.21)	5.8 (0.33)	2.7 (0.33)

! Interpret data with caution. The coefficient of variation (CV) for this estimate is between 30 and 50 percent.

[1] Teachers were classified as elementary or secondary on the basis of the grades they taught, rather than on the level of the school in which they taught. In general, elementary teachers include those teaching prekindergarten through grade 5 and those teaching multiple grades, with a preponderance of grades taught being kindergarten through grade 6. In general, secondary teachers include those teaching any of grades 7 through 12 and those teaching multiple grades, with a preponderance of grades taught being grades 7 through 12 and usually with no grade taught being lower than grade 5.

[2] Includes American Indians/Alaska Natives, Asians, and Pacific Islanders; for 2003–04 and later years, also includes persons of Two or more races.

[3] Includes traditional public and public charter schools.

NOTE: Teachers who taught only prekindergarten students are excluded. Instructional level divides teachers into elementary or secondary based on a combination of the grades taught, main teaching assignment, and the structure of the teachers' class(es). Race categories exclude persons of Hispanic ethnicity. Detail may not sum to totals because of rounding. Some data have been revised from previously published figures.

SOURCE: U.S. Department of Education, National Center for Education Statistics, Schools and Staffing Survey (SASS), "Public School Teacher Data File" and "Private School Teacher Data File," 1993-94, 1999-2000, 2003-04, 2007-08, and 2011-12; and "Charter School Teacher Data File," 1999-2000. (This table was prepared October 2013.)

Figure 12.12   Teacher reports of threats and violence.

A study of 160 active shooter incidents in the United States between 2000 and 2013: Location categories

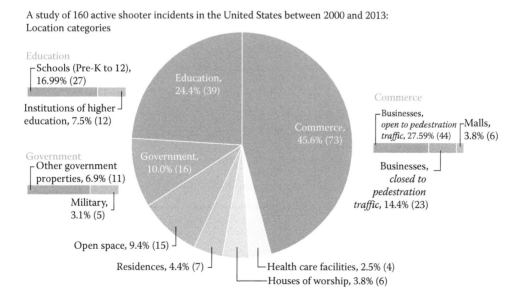

Figure 12.13   Active shooter incidents.

Date	School	Shooter	Dead	Injured
April 16, 2017	Virginia Tech, VA	Seung-Hui Cho	32	
October 1, 2015	Umpqua Comm College, OR	Chris Harper Mercer	9	3
April 2, 2012	Oikos University, CA	One Goh	7	3
May 23, 2014	University of Santa Barbara Santa Barbara Campus, CA	Elliot Rodger	6	13
June 7, 2014	Santa Monica College, CA	John Zawahri	5	Several
October 28, 2002	University of Arizona, AZ	Robert Flores, Jr.	3	
January 16, 2002	Appalachian School of Law, VA	Peter Odighizuwa	3	
August 15, 1996	San Diego University, CA	Frederick Martin Davidson	3	
February 14, 2008	Northern Illinois University, IL	Steven Kazmierczak	2	18
February 8, 2008	Louisiana Technical College, LA	Latina Williams	2	
September 2, 2008	Shepherd University, WV	Douglas W. Pennington	2	
June 5, 2014	Seattle Pacific University, WA	Aaron Rey Ybarra	1	2

Figure 12.14   Recent history of U.S. college and university shootings.

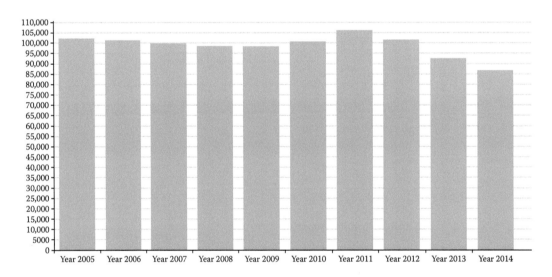

Figure 12.15   Reported arrests annually on collect campuses from 2005 to 2014. (From U.S. Department of Education, Office of Postsecondary Education, Campus Safety and Security (CSS) Survey.)

of their teachers.[29] The same could be said on the technological side where public entities so heavily rely on the expertise of the security industry. Nothing gets invented or tested in the public domain as heavily as the private sector. Hence in access control, there is no better evaluator of such systems than the private security technology firm, which invented it.[30]

Most of what schools, colleges, and universities hope to accomplish in creating a safe and secure environment can be achieved by the wise implementation of technology and human services. Security firms understand the centrality of technology more than their public counterparts. Every comprehensive security plan for a school setting demands the installation of state-of-the-art technology.

---

[29] See P. Timm, Addressing Mistakes in Three Security Trends, *Sec. Mag.* (April 2015), at 85.
[30] See Global News and Analysis, School Security Rising, *Sec. Mag.* (April 2012), at 20; see also Security Solutions to Protect Schools, *Sec. Mag.* (October 2006), at 19.

How will our university react to an active shooter situation on campus?

Make a decision, trusting your instincts, to take action to protect yourself to survive the situation. You generally will have three options:

Run: Can you safely escape?
Hide: Is there a good place to hide?
Fight: Will you take out the shooter?

Run For Safety

- If you can and you deem it safe, get out and get to a safe place.
- You will have to rely partially on instinct.
- Leave belongings behind, but take your cell phone if it is handy.

Hiding In A Safe Place

- Find a hidden location.
- Find protection behind furniture if possible.
- Find a room that locks if you can.
- If possible, close and lock the outside door to the room. Blockade the door with furniture or other heavy objects.
- Close the blinds, turn off the lights, remain quiet, silence cell phones, spread out away from other individuals, and move behind available cover.
- Stay on the floor, away from doors or windows, and do not peek out to see what may be happening.
- Make a plan with others in the room about what you will do if the shooter enters. Make a total commitment to action and act as a team with others.
- Do whatever is necessary to survive the situation.
- If possible and safe to do so, report the location of the assailant.

If Outside When A Shooting Occurs

- Drop to the ground immediately, face down as flat as possible. If within 15-20 feet of a safe place or cover, duck and run to it.
- Move or crawl away from gunfire, trying to utilize any obstructions between you and the gunfire. Remember that many objects of cover may conceal you from sight, but may not be bulletproof.
- When you reach a place of relative safety, stay down and do not move. Do not peek or raise your head in an effort to see what may be happening.
- Wait and listen for directions from Public Safety and/law enforcement personnel.

If Suspect Is In Close Proximity

- An individual must use his/her own discretion about when he or she must engage a shooter for survival.
- Make a plan as to how you will survive the situation.
- Make a total commitment to action and act as a team with others if possible.
- Do whatever is necessary to survive the situation.

Help Out

- Warn others.
- Help others escape.
- Keep others away from the danger area.
- Help the injured.
- Help others stay calm.

Calling For Help

- Call 9-1-1 or Campus Police to report the appropriate authorities. Do not assume that someone else has reported the incident. Be persistent; phones may be jammed.
- Calmly identify yourself and your exact location. Remain calm and answer the dispatcher's questions. The dispatcher is trained to obtain the necessary and required information for an appropriate emergency response.
- If safe to do so, stop and take time to get a good description of the criminal. Note height, weight, sex, race, approximate age, clothing, method and direction of travel, and his/her name, if known.
- If the suspect is entering a vehicle, note the license plate number, make and model, color, and outstanding characteristics. All of this takes only a few seconds and is of the utmost help to the responding officers.

Figure 12.16 Suggested student reaction protocol. *(Continued)*

When Law Enforcement Arrives

- When law enforcement reaches you, do not run at them or make sudden movements.
- The priority of the first responders will be to identify the shooter. Law enforcement will need to ensure that you are not the shooter.
- Do not scream, yell, point, or wave your arms.
- Do not hold anything in your hands that could be mistaken for a weapon (including cell phones).
- Be quiet and compliant.
- Show the officers your empty hands and follow their instructions.
- Give the number of shooters.
- Give the location and physical description of the shooter.
- Give the number and types of weapons.
- When it is safe to do so, you will be given instructions as to how to safely exit your location.

Figure 12.16 (Continued)   Suggested student reaction protocol.

2016 Annual Security Report (Clery Act) Crime Statistics Collection Form

Department:_____ Extension:_____

Contact Name (Please Print): _____

Please Sign Form (Here):_____ Date:____/
____/_____ Date Range: January 01, 2016 through December 31, 2016

MAIL COMPLETED FORM TO:
Federal Clery Act Compliance Officer
Attention: University Police Dept.
<Address>
<City><State><Zip>

OR   XXX-XXX-XXXX FAX

NO INCIDENTS TO REPORT PLEASE CHECK THIS BOX AND RETURN [ ]

INCIDENT TYPE (see back for types)	INCIDENT DATE	INCIDENT DETAILS (location, participant information, other distinguishing information)
	Month ___ Day ___ 2016	Reported to Police Department [ ] Y [ ] (Case # 16-___) [ ] N [ ]
HATE CRIME?	[ ]Yes [ ] No	If YES mark - HATE Crime: Race [ ] Ethnicity [ ] Gender Identity [ ] Religion [ ] Gender [ ] National Origin [ ] Disability [ ] Sexual Orientation [ ]
	Month ___ Day ___ 2016	Reported to Police Department [ ] Y [ ] (Case # 16-___) [ ] N [ ]
HATE CRIME?	[ ]Yes [ ] No	If YES mark - HATE Crime: Race [ ] Ethnicity [ ] Gender Identity [ ] Religion [ ] Gender [ ] National Origin [ ] Disability [ ] Sexual Orientation [ ]
	Month ___ Day ___ 2016	Reported to Police Department [ ] Y [ ] (Case # 16-___) [ ] N [ ]
HATE CRIME?	[ ]Yes [ ] No	If YES mark - HATE Crime: Race [ ] Ethnicity [ ] Gender Identity [ ] Religion [ ] Gender [ ] National Origin [ ] Disability [ ] Sexual Orientation [ ]
	Month ___ Day ___ 2016	Reported to Police Department [ ] Y [ ] (Case # 16-___) [ ] N [ ]
HATE CRIME?	[ ]Yes [ ] No	If YES mark - HATE Crime: Race [ ] Ethnicity [ ] Gender Identity [ ] Religion [ ] Gender [ ] National Origin [ ] Disability [ ] Sexual Orientation [ ]
	Month ___ Day ___ 2016	Reported to Police Department [ ] Y [ ] (Case # 16-___) [ ] N [ ]
HATE CRIME?	[ ]Yes [ ] No	If YES mark - HATE Crime: Race [ ] Ethnicity [ ] Gender Identity [ ] Religion [ ] Gender [ ] National Origin [ ] Disability [ ] Sexual Orientation [ ]
	Month ___ Day ___ 2016	Reported to Police Department [ ] Y [ ] (Case # 16-___) [ ] N [ ]
HATE CRIME?	[ ]Yes [ ] No	If YES mark - HATE Crime: Race [ ] Ethnicity [ ] Gender Identity [ ] Religion [ ] Gender [ ] National Origin [ ] Disability [ ] Sexual Orientation [ ]
	Month ___ Day ___ 2016	Reported to Police Department [ ] Y [ ] (Case # 16-___) [ ] N [ ]
HATE CRIME?	[ ]Yes [ ] No	If YES mark - HATE Crime: Race [ ] Ethnicity [ ] Gender Identity [ ] Religion [ ] Gender [ ] National Origin [ ] Disability [ ] Sexual Orientation [ ]

Figure 12.17   Clery Act form.   (Continued)

Reporting Requirements

WHO MUST REPORT INCIDENTS: The Jeanne Clery Act requires the "Campus Security Authority" and anyone with significant responsibility for student, campus activities, staff and faculty to report crime incidents. Examples: Individuals involved with student housing, student centers, extracurricular activities and human resources; Director of Athletics; team coaches; faculty advisors to student groups; and student judicial affairs staff. Does not include "pastoral" and "professional" mental health counselors.

LOCATIONS THAT MUST BE REPORTED: PLEASE NOTE EXACT LOCATION UNDER "INCIDENT DETAILS"

• On campus not in student housing • On campus in student housing • Off-campus affiliated property (owned, controlled, or affiliated with campus; like - leased property, fraternity, student co-op) • Off-campus public property immediately adjacent to campus (streets, sidewalks and parking facilities)

Incident Types

Compliance with Federal law requires the use of the following definitions for reporting crime incidents:

MURDER – The willful (non-negligent) killing of one human being by another.

SEX OFFENSE, FORCIBLE – Rape, forcible sodomy, sexual assault with an object and forcible fondling.

SEX OFFENSE, NON-FORCIBLE – Incest and statutory rape.

ROBBERY – The taking or attempting to take anything of value from the care, custody, or control of a person or persons by force or threat of force or violence and/or by putting the victim in fear.

AGGRAVATED ASSAULT – An unlawful attack by one person upon another for the purpose of inflicting severe or aggravated bodily injury. This type of assault usually is accompanied by the use of a weapon or by means likely to produce death or great bodily harm.

BURGLARY – The unlawful entry of a structure to commit a felony or theft.

MOTOR VEHICLE THEFT – The theft or attempted theft of a motor vehicle.

MANSLAUGHTER – The negligent killing of a human being by another.

ARSON – The unlawful damage of property by setting fire.

HATE CRIME – Any bias-motivated crime (crimes listed above or other crime involving bodily injury) against any persons based on race; religion; sexual orientation; ethnicity; gender; gender identity; national origin or physical/mental disabilities. Indicate category of prejudice in the INCIDENT DETAILS. Also include any bias-motivated crimes for larceny/theft; simple assault; intimidation & destruction/damage/vandalism of property.

Practical guidance: Report any arrests and/or disciplinary referrals for any violation of a law: regulating weapons / regulating drugs, regardless of the type of drug / the liquor laws listed in the definitions. Do not report arrests or referrals for liquor offenses that violate "University policy" but do not break the law. For ex; do not report a referral of a student who is of drinking age but has violated a University policy against drinking in a specific location.

WEAPON LAW VIOLATION – The violation of laws or ordinances dealing with weapon offenses, regulatory in nature, such as: manufacture, sale or possession of deadly weapons.

DRUG ABUSE VIOLATION – Violations of state and local laws relating to the unlawful possession of sale, use, growing, manufacturing, and making of controlled substances.

LIQUOR LAW VIOLATION – The violation of laws or ordinances prohibiting; the manufacture, sale, transporting, furnishing, possessing of intoxicating liquor; maintaining unlawful drinking places; furnishing liquor to a minor or public intoxication.

DATING VIOLENCE— The term "dating violence" means violence committed by a person.

(A) who is or has been in a social relationship of a romantic or intimate nature with the victim; and

(B) where the existence of such a relationship shall be determined based on a consideration of the following factors:

> • (i) The length of the relationship.
> • (ii) The type of relationship.
> • (iii) The frequency of interaction between the persons involved in the relationship.

Dating violence includes sexual or physical abuse, or the threat of such abuse. Dating violence does not include acts covered under the act of domestic violence.

DOMESTIC VIOLENCE — The term "domestic violence" includes felony or misdemeanor crimes of violence committed by a current or former spouse of the victim, by a person with whom the victim shares a child in common, by a person who is cohabitating with or has cohabitated with the victim as a spouse, by a person similarly situated to a spouse of the victim under the domestic or family violence laws of the jurisdiction receiving grant monies, or by any other person against an adult or youth victim who is protected from that person's acts under the domestic or family violence laws of the jurisdiction.

STALKING — The term "stalking" means engaging in a course of conduct directed at a specific person that would cause a reasonable person to— (A) fear for his or her safety or the safety of others; or (B) suffer substantial emotional distress.

Figure 12.17 (Continued)   Clery Act form.

School security requires a comprehensive approach, from prevention to coordination with local entities during and after incidents, and from physical threats to cyber security. A "layered security" approach addresses every level and phase of security needs, according to LearnSafe.

1. District wide risk assessment
2. Multilevel background checks
3. Behavioral intervention programs
4. Emergency management planning
5. Crisis communications training
6. Complete security monitoring and maintenance
7. Actionable video surveillance
8. Integrated access control and school lockdown
9. Visitor and vendor management
10. Coordination with state and local authorities[31]

As a result, a variety of paradigms of delivery exist in the educational marketplace, the gist of which can be summed up in these three ways:

1. Educational security is solely delivered by public police officers stationed at the educational campuses.

2. Educational security is primarily delivered by one former, and now retired public police officers.

3. Educational security is delivered by contractually hired security firms, by educational institution employees hired as security officer.

What is readily apparent is that educational security becomes the province of all three options with each category being possible by jurisdiction or leadership decision. Nationally, the variations in how security services are delivered vary greatly. Despite the variety, the private security industry remains a major player in a host of educational institutions. See Figure 12.18.[32]

In some educational settings, public police deliver oversight and command over hired college officers who are private or firms contracted to deal with the varied security issues natural to college campuses. When tragedy occurs, and high crime incidents grab the news in hyperventilated ways, there is a tendency to think that the public police professional has the answers and the depth and breadth of training to deter and prevent future events. This reaction is naïve and neglects the unique placement of people and personnel have in the collegiate or school environment. Schools are not war zones nor are these locales best controlled by a military ideology. The debate on what makes for the better if not best security officer in the educational environment has been vigorous, and rightfully so, for the complexities of the educational environment cannot be overemphasized. Thus, it is crucial to ask how best the private security industry can serve the educational marketplace, how effective will security measures be under a client–customer-driven mentality over a simple enforcement outlook, and how best served children, teachers, and staff be by these various models? The crucial player here is the front-line security officer and that description and characterization is a task well worth undertaking.

12.3.2 Security officers in the educational marketplace: Searching for the best model

Precisely what defines a school security or safety specialist has been the subject of intense and constant debate.[33] In the simplest terms, it has been argued that a school officer is nothing more or nothing less than a police officer stationed within a school setting. Hence, the training and background of the officer provides him or her with the universal knowledge to operate in any setting. Others have argued that the school officer is akin to a juvenile officer who operates with a special care and understanding of youth crime and corresponding pressures.[34] Other research appears to

---

[31] B. Zalud, School Bell Rings for Security, *Sec. Mag.* (October 2010), at 98; see also Security School Bells Ring, *Sec. Mag.* (March 2005), at 54.

[32] B.A. Reaves, Campus Law Enforcement, 2011–12, Bureau of Justice Statistics Special Report NCJ 248028 (January 2015), at http://www.bjs.gov/content/pub/pdf/cle1112.pdf, last accessed August 31, 2016.

[33] See, for example, B. Raymond, (2010). *Assigning Police Officers to Schools, Problem-Oriented Guides for Police Response* (Center for Problem-Oriented Policing, Inc., The U.S. Department of Justice, 2010); N. James & G. McCallion, *School Resource Officers: Law Enforcement Officers in Schools*, CRS Report for Congress: Prepared for Members and Committees of Congress (Congressional Research Service, 2013).

[34] See J.C. Alderson, Police and Education, 6 *Oxford Rev. Educ.* 227–230 (1980).

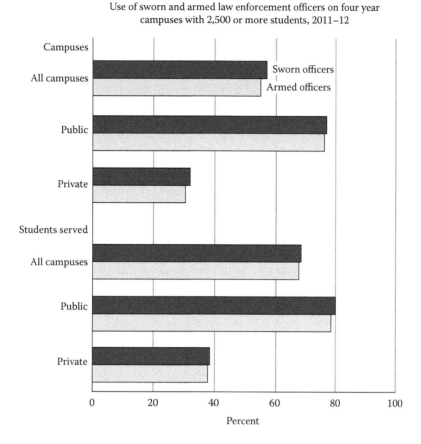

Figure 12.18 Sworn law enforcement officers on campus. (From Bureau of Justice Statistics, Survey of Campus Law Enforcement Agencies, 2011–2012.)

favor the COPS (Community Oriented Policing Services) comparison, for a school is but a mini-community with all the demands and challenges that any community has and therefore, this model of community integration fits best.[35]

12.3.2.1 COPS program

As eventually codified, the COPS program, federally mandated and funded,[36] designates an officer assigned to a school as a "school resource officer" (SRO). The formal definition for the SRO is thus:

> a "school resource officer" is defined as "a career law enforcement officer, with sworn authority, deployed in community-oriented policing, and assigned by the employing police department or agency to work in collaboration with schools and community based organizations—
> (A) to address crime and disorder problems, gangs, and drug activities affecting or occurring in or around an elementary or secondary school; (B) to develop or expand crime prevention efforts for students; (C) to educate likely school-age victims in crime prevention and safety; (D) to develop or expand community justice initiatives for students; (E) to train students in conflict resolution, restorative justice, and crime awareness; (F) to assist in the identification of physical changes in the environment that may reduce crime in or around the school; and (G) to assist in developing school policy that addresses crime and to recommend procedural changes.[37]

By implication, the officer becomes a resource among all other available resources to provide safety and security in the school environment. Thus, the designation, "school resource office" takes on its own life and becomes synonymous

---

[35] Raymond, *supra* note 33; James & McCallion, *supra* note 33.
[36] Authorizing Legislation for the Community Oriented Policing Services (COPS) program (42 U.S.C. § 3796dd-8).
[37] 42 U.S.C. § 3796DD-8; see also Raymond, *supra* note 33.

with public law enforcement placed in school buildings whose mission and outlook lacks universality and uniformity. Exactly how that safety and security is provided has become a subject of extensive debate. For some, the officer must become more the educator than anything, so that he or she might "fit" the locale. So it was common in earlier analysis, for commentators to call upon the officer to become a teacher of "law-related classes."[38] This educational component seemed the distinguishing characteristic for the SRO who is "law enforcement officer, a counselor on law-related matters and a classroom teacher of law-related education."[39] It is equally clear that earlier considerations of this type of officer lacked a cohesive view of how the officer fits into the entire superstructure of school and its environment. Officers were "inside" the school but by training and preparation, role and function, self-image and perception, apart or detached from normal school operations. Historic definitions fail to integrate officers into the reality of their own placements.

While each of these definitions has conceptual value, none in total encompasses the complete nature of the SRO. For said officer cannot work detached from the structural bureaucracy of any given school nor can that officer build the necessary intelligence in isolation from others that know other sources of information. Over the last decade or so, the movement to define the concept of an SRO now includes a holistic vision of the entire school community—a movement to team building and information sharing.

12.3.2.2 Congressional Research Service

A recent Congressional Research Service study, School Resource Officers: Law Enforcement Officers in Schools (2013) delivers a tripartite division of what constitutes the officer, namely,

1. Safety Expert and Law Enforcer
2. Problem Solver and Liaison to Community Resources
3. Educator[40]

Using this model, the United States Department of Justice and its Office of Community Oriented Policing Services specifically delineate the various roles and functions cataloged under this three-part design a

1. Safety Expert and Law Enforcer
   - Assuming primary responsibility for handling calls for service from the school and in coordinating the response of other police resources
   - Addressing crime and disorder problems, gangs, and drug activities occurring in or around the school
   - Making arrests and issuing citations on campus
   - Providing leads and information to the appropriate investigative units
   - Taking action against unauthorized persons on school property
   - Serving as hall monitors, truancy enforcers, crossing guards, and operators of metal detectors and other security devices
   - Responding to off-campus criminal mischief that involves students
   - Serving as liaisons between the school and the police and providing information to students and school personnel about law enforcement matters
   - Developing incident response systems
   - Developing and coordinating emergency response plans (in conjunction with other emergency responders)
   - Incorporating law enforcement onto school crisis management teams
   - Developing protocols for handling specific types of emergencies
   - Rehearsing such protocols using tabletop exercises, drills, and mock evacuations and lockdowns.
2. Problem Solver and Liaison to Community Resources
   - Developing and expanding crime prevention efforts for students
   - Developing and expanding community justice initiatives for students
   - Assisting in identifying environmental changes that can reduce crime in or around schools
   - Assisting in developing school policies that address crime and recommending procedural changes to implement those policies

---

[38] Brown concluded that an SRO was a hybrid of educational, correctional, and law enforcement oriented community policing. Such a person requires a multifaceted responsibility of "acting as a liaison officer between the school, community, and law enforcement while teaching law related education classes, counseling students, and performing law enforcement duties" (Brown 2006); Huffman similarly defines an SRO as someone who is responsible for "teaching law related education classes, counseling students, and performing law enforcement duties are commonly known as a "triad approach." Such an approach focuses on establishing a positive bond with students, preventing school violence, and addressing legal questions (Huffman, 1995). Both in E. Gulen, School Resource Officer Programs, Texas Law Enforcement Management and Administrative Statistics Program, 17 *TELEMASP Bull.* (2010).

[39] See R. Lambert & D. McGinty, Law Enforcement Officers in Schools: Setting Priorities, 40 *J. Educ. Admin.* 257–273 (2002).

[40] James & McCallion, *supra* note 33.

3. Educator
  - Policing as a career
  - Criminal investigation
  - Alcohol and drug awareness
  - Gang and stranger awareness and resistance
  - General crime prevention
  - Conflict resolution
  - Restorative justice
  - Babysitting safety
  - Bicycling, pedestrian, and motor vehicle safety
  - Special crimes in which students are especially likely to be offenders or victims, such as vandalism, shoplifting, and sexual assault by acquaintances[41]

Few would argue that each definition has merit and that the process of full definition is still evolving. On the other hand, there is nothing in these definitions which represents a complete separation or a highly distinguished role from traditional law enforcement. Glaringly apparent is the lack of a "privatized" view of the occupation, a definition that does not depend on the public law enforcement model or background. Equally lacking is the centrality of the unique intelligence methods to be employed in the school environment. Other observations are possible but suffice to say, none of these definitions fully encapsulates the complexity of the SRO. Put another way, the SRO model erects a two-dimensional prototype for the officer who walks the halls or staffs the entry technology, who need not integrate his or her role into the school in totality, and may even be applauded for maintaining the systematic independence from other school functions.

See Figure 12.19.

Given this analysis, it seems a safe bet that the private security industry will continue its aggressive entry into the educational marketplace yet at the same time collaborating and partnering with public police entities. Neither can do the job alone and the examples of these sorts of cooperative arrangements grow day by day.[42] Cooperative alliances exist all over the United States, especially between public departments and private security departments.[43]

The cooperation exhibited between city or municipal police and college and university security forces is a long-standing example of how these two worlds can effectively cooperate. William Bess, Director of Campus Safety at Bowling Green State University, and Galen Ash, Director at the Bowling Green Police Department, feel confident that they have mastered the art of interaction by identifying the essential elements in the recipe for successful cooperation:

1. Mutual assistance agreement
2. Support from the courts
3. Shared training programs
4. Efficient communications (technical)
5. Ongoing administrative working relations
6. Police/advisory committee participation
7. Shared crime prevention programs
8. Cooperative investigations and sharing of information
9. College educational programs
10. Informal daily contacts[44]

At Bowling Green, the private and public police model overcomes the preconceptions and caricatures so often applied to each model. Both parties indicate that rhetoric is easy, but activities that are planned and concerted are the elixirs that smooth over the distrustful state of affairs. The interaction between public and private security, especially between college and university departments and the city or municipalities in which they are located, is an ongoing

---

[41] Raymond, *supra* note 33.

[42] D.J. Maurrasse, *Beyond the Campus: How Colleges and Universities Form Partnerships with Their Communities* (Routledge, 2002).

[43] See generally Police Executive Research Forum et al., *Future Trends in Policing* (2014), at http://www.policeforum.org/assets/docs/Free_Online_Documents/Leadership/future%20trends%20in%20policing%202014.pdf, last accessed August 31, 2016.

[44] W.R. Bess & G.L. Ash, City/University Cooperation, *Police Chief* (1982), at 42; see also Ronso, The U.S. Air Force Security Police: Is There a Civilian Counterpart? *Police Chief* (1982), at 32.

JOB DESCRIPTION
X County Schools

School Resource Officer

Reports to: Principal and Sherriff   Status: Non-Exempt

SUMMARY:

To foster more positive relationships between the police and youth and to increase student knowledge of law enforcement, the judicial and courts systems.

ESSENTIAL DUTIES AND RESPONSIBILITIES:

- Abide by the policies, rules and regulations of the school division;
- Provide law enforcement for the County;
- Be a representative of the Sheriff;
- Perform all duties and responsibilities of a field deputy;
- Protect lives and property for the citizens and public school students;
- Enforce Federal, State, and Local criminal laws and ordinances;
- Assist school officials with Administrative regulations regarding student conduct;
- Investigate criminal activity committed on or adjacent to school property;
- Be a law related educator;
- Attends in-service training to improve skills and knowledge of job expertise;
- Be a community liaison and role model;
- Counsel public school students in special situations;
- Answer questions students might have about state Criminal and Juvenile law;
- Assist other law enforcement officer's investigations concerning students;
- Provide security for special school events or functions;
- Provide traffic control during the arrival and departure of students as needed;
- Prevent juvenile delinquency through close contact with students/school personnel;
- Establish liaison with school principals, faculty, and staff;
- Inform students of their rights and responsibilities as lawful citizens;
- Be a resource to the principal in investigating criminal law violations at school;
- Assist administration and faculty in formulating criminal justice programs;
- Formulate crime prevention programs;
- Coordinate all law enforcement response/service at their school;
- Prevent duplication of effort and provide coordination of law related services;
- Ensure the investigation and enforcement of criminal law violations;
- Provide necessary follow-up investigation as required;
- Remain abreast of investigations involving students at their school;
- Be aware of demographics and distinctive characteristics of the student body;

Figure 12.19   Career profile: school resource officer.   (*Continued*)

- Provide visible deterrence to crime;
- Present a positive impression of a uniformed law enforcement officer at the school;
- Performs duties away from assigned school as agreed upon by the school principal and/or law enforcement officials.

KNOWLEDGE, SKILLS, AND ABILITIES

- Knowledge of applicable Federal, State, and Local codes used in pursuing and convicting perpetrators in the appropriate court.
- Knowledge of administrative and operational policies and procedures.
- Knowledge and skill of laws of arrest, probable cause and search and seizure issues used in the enforcement of laws and in the school setting.
- Knowledge of law enforcement operations, duties, and responsibilities.
- Knowledge of roads and addresses of the county.

EDUCATION AND/OR EXPERIENCE:

High School Graduation or GED and Resource Officer training required.

PHYSICAL DEMANDS:

The physical demands described here are representative of those that must be met by an employee to successfully perform the essential functions of this job. Reasonable accommodations may be made to enable individuals with disabilities to perform the essential functions.

While performing the duties of this job, the employee is regularly required to stand, talk, and hear. The employee frequently is required to walk and use hands to finger, handle, or feel. The employee is occasionally required to sit; climb or balance, reach with hands and arms; and stoop, kneel, crouch, or crawl. The employee must frequently lift and/or move up to 10 pounds, and occasionally lift and/or move up to 50 pounds. Specific vision abilities required by this job include close vision, distance vision, peripheral vision, depth perception, and ability to adjust focus.

EVALUATION:

Performance on this job will be evaluated in accordance with school board policy and administrative regulations on evaluation of personnel.

Figure 12.19 (Continued)   Career profile: school resource officer.

departmental obligation. The National Association of College and University Business Officers affirm the need for continuing interplay.

> The security department must be largely self-sufficient, but able to work harmoniously with other institutional departments. It should also maintain effective liaison with other law enforcement agencies, the courts, the prosecuting agencies and the press. It is also advisable that the local chief of police be informed of public functions to be held at the institution, so that he may be prepared to assist if necessary.[45]

Not all relationships are borne from good will. For example, at both the University of Pennsylvania and Temple University, the cost cutting of once public police forces erected a newer private sector model, which has resulted in efforts to unionize the private guard force. Allied Barton, the replacement company, has been met with severe labor organizing activities that reflect disgruntlement. On October 10, 2010, the private force voted to unionize.[46]

The influence of private sector policing on college campuses is multidimensional. With the implementation of new federal legislation on the reporting of the campus crime rate, under *The Crime Awareness and Campus Security Act of 1990*,[47] private sector justice computes the crime data. Campuses are required to collect and publish the following data:

(A)   A statement of current campus policies regarding procedures and facilities for students and others to report criminal actions or other emergencies occurring on campus and policies concerning the institution's response to such reports.

(B)   A statement of current policies concerning security and access to campus facilities, including campus residences, and security considerations used in the maintenance of campus facilities.

(C)   A statement of current policies concerning campus law enforcement, including
   (i)   the law enforcement authority of campus security personnel;
   (ii)   the working relationship of campus security personnel with State and local law enforcement agencies, including whether the institution has agreements with such agencies, such as written memoranda of understanding, for the investigation of alleged criminal offenses; and
   (iii) policies which encourage accurate and prompt reporting of all crimes to the campus police and the appropriate law enforcement agencies.

(D)   A description of the type and frequency of programs designed to inform students and employees about campus security procedures and practices and to encourage students and employees to be responsible for their own security and the security of others.

(E)   A description of programs designed to inform students and employees about the prevention of crimes.

(F)   Statistics concerning the occurrence on campus, in or on noncampus buildings or property, and on public property during the most recent calendar year, and during the 2 preceding calendar years for which data are available.
   (i)   of the following criminal offenses reported to campus security authorities or local police agencies:
       (I)   murder;
       (II)   sex offenses, forcible or nonforcible;
       (III)   robbery;
       (IV)   aggravated assault;
       (V)   burglary;
       (VI)   motor vehicle theft;
       (VII)   manslaughter;
       (VIII) arson; and
       (IX)   arrests or persons referred for campus disciplinary action for liquor law violations, drug-related violations, and weapons possession; and
   (ii)   of the crimes described in sub clauses (I) through (VIII) of clause (i), of larceny-theft, simple assault, intimidation, and destruction, damage, or vandalism of property, and of other crimes involving bodily injury to any person, in which the victim is intentionally selected because of the actual or perceived race, gender, religion, sexual orientation, ethnicity, or disability of the victim that are reported to campus security authorities or local police agencies, which data shall be collected and reported according to category of prejudice.

(G)   A statement of policy concerning the monitoring and recording through local police agencies of criminal activity at off-campus student organizations which are recognized by the institution and that are engaged in by students attending the institution, including those student organizations with off-campus housing facilities.

---

[45] Bess & Ash, *supra* note 44.

[46] F. Rodriguea, Philadelphia Security Officer Union, *Soc. Pol'y* 4, 6 (Winter 2010).

[47] 20 U.S.C.A. § 1092 (West 2010).

(H) A statement of policy regarding the possession, use, and sale of alcoholic beverages and enforcement of State under-age drinking laws and a statement of policy regarding the possession, use, and sale of illegal drugs and enforcement of Federal and State drug laws and a description of any drug or alcohol abuse education programs as required under section 1011i of this title.

(I) A statement advising the campus community where law enforcement agency information provided by a State under section 14071(j) of Title 42, concerning registered sex offenders may be obtained, such as the law enforcement office of the institution, a local law enforcement agency with jurisdiction for the campus, or a computer network address.

(J) A statement of current campus policies regarding immediate emergency response and evacuation procedures, including the use of electronic and cellular communication (if appropriate), which policies shall include procedures to

    (i) immediately notify the campus community upon the confirmation of a significant emergency or dangerous situation involving an immediate threat to the health or safety of students or staff occurring on the campus, as defined in paragraph (6), unless issuing a notification will compromise efforts to contain the emergency;

    (ii) publicize emergency response and evacuation procedures on an annual basis in a manner designed to reach students and staff; and

    (iii) test emergency response and evacuation procedures on an annual basis.[48]

The International Association of Campus Law Enforcement Administration (IACLEA) has been a major implementer of the new policy. While the reporting requirements are administratively cumbersome, the

> law has, however, delivered some good. Besides placating many victims' rights groups, it directs attention toward campus security with real and positive impact. As prospective students focus more on crime statistics as criteria for choosing a college, campuses will tend to beef up on-site security programs, by specifying integrated access control, communications and monitoring systems in dormitories, classrooms, parking lots and other facilities.[49]

Local police departments, as well as state entities, increasingly rely on this information.

Crime is a growing reality on college campuses as is the paucity of funds to control and eradicate it. Universities and colleges are increasingly looking to the private sector to deliver safety and security on campus. Allied Barton is entrusted with the University of Pennsylvania and works closely with the Philadelphia Police Department and delivers a wide array of services to the educational community including

- Campus fire safety
- Evacuation planning
- Drug and alcohol abuse
- Domestic abuse
- High risk/confrontational situation management
- Clery Act
- Access control
- Lock-outs and vehicle assists
- Campus escort services
- Residential life security
- Campus emergency preparedness

Other companies are major players in the delivery of law enforcement services, and all of these entities work closely and cooperatively with public law enforcement. All of these collaborations need careful planning and proper role delegation so competing jurisdictions do not step on one another province. It is crucial to author a partnership agreement, which

- Defines how the university will interact with its city and county.
- Specifies that university and local police will be operating within each other's jurisdiction.
- Identifies a protocol for when campus police officers need backup from the local police department.

---

[48] 20 U.S.C.A. § 1092(f) (West 2010).
[49] Note, Federal Guidance Lacking as Colleges Report Crime Statistics, 30 *Security* 12 (1993).

- Spells out a system for sharing information about actions that campus police have taken while patrolling off-campus.

- Aside from all these opportunities, it is common knowledge that former police chiefs find the college setting a very attractive second career upon retirement from the first public experience. While this fit may be smooth and without consequence, colleges and universities are distinctly different environments than most places. Academic faculty, for the most part, display extraordinary umbrage at the imposition of a military style of enforcement. Most who encounter this sense of outrage quickly realize that faculties are a "liberal" lot who take exception to police tactics. This is why security directors and managers over traditional policing types appear to be an exceptional fit for college constituencies since private sector chiefs are more consumer and customer driven—and take that extra step to understand the audience served. It is another reason why the future of private security in the educational marketplace is so bright.

See Figure 12.20.

12.3.3 Professional associations and groups in school security

Web Exercise: Find out about the IACP's University and College Committee and its emphasis on partnerships between university and college police with public departments at http://www.iacp.org/portals/0/pdfs/UCSectionApp.pdf.

See Figure 12.21.

Another professional association dedicated to the furtherance of professionalism and best practices in security at colleges and university is the College and University Police and Investigators which holds an annual conference for the major security chiefs at colleges every August at the campus of George Mason University. See Figure 12.22.

The College and University Police and Investigators conference (CUPIC) stresses new and innovative approaches to the daunting task of ensuring a safe collegiate environment. The stress at the 2016 conference was on

- Terrorism on college campuses
- Active shooter response
- Event protection
- Lessons from San Bernardino
- Critical incident protocol update
- Title IX updates

At the primary and secondary level, security forces are active participants in a host of associations and groups. NASSLEO (the National Association of School Safety and Law Enforcement Officials) has been a professional entity dedicated to the advancement of the school safety officer. It tends to look at school safety issues through the lens of the entry-level officer. See Figure 12.23.[50]

NASSLEO membership includes educators, and law enforcement and security directors and officers, operating with the common goal of protecting our students, staff, and physical assets. The National Association of School Resource Officers (NASRO) delivers a highly professional mission, which seeks out best practices for secondary and primary schools.[51] Its mission consists of these elements:

> The National Association of School Resource Officers (NASRO) is dedicated to making schools and children safer by providing the highest quality training to school-based law enforcement officers.
>
> NASRO, the world's leader in school-based policing, is a not-for-profit organization founded in 1991 for school-based law enforcement officers, school administrators and school security and/or safety professionals who work as partners to protect schools and their students, faculty and staff members.[52]

---

[50] National Association of School Safety & Law Enforcement Officers website, at http://www.nassleo.org/, last accessed August 31, 2016.

[51] See the NSRO Study on School Safety and Its Officers, at https://nasro.org/cms/wp-content/uploads/2013/11/NASRO-To-Protect-and-Educate-nosecurity.pdf, last accessed August 31, 2016.

[52] National Association of School Resource Officers website, at https://nasro.org/about/, last accessed August 31, 2016.

Director of Public Safety and Chief of Police

Posting Details

Position Information

Business Title	Director of Public Safety and Chief of Police
Position Number	
Home Department	Public Safety
Employment Type	Regular (Continuous)
Full-Time/Part-Time	Full-Time
Appointment	Staff (12-Month)
Time Limited?	No
Time-Limited Appointment Length	Not Applicable
Work Schedule	Monday-Friday; 8 am to 5 pm; on call as needed
Work Hours per week	40
Travel Required?	N
Primary Function of Organizational Unit	Provides the university and immediate surrounding community a safe environment that is conducive to education for all individuals that study, work and visit the college. Serves the university community with integrity, judicious and appropriate use of discretion, expedient response and in a manner that is fair, proper and thorough.
Primary Purpose of Position	The Director of Public Safety has overall responsibility for directing and overseeing the Public Safety Department and for providing a safe and secure environment for the university community. This includes providing a community oriented policing environment and developing safety programs. The Director plans, directs, and evaluates all aspects of the integrated police, security, and emergency management operations and ensures the enforcement of all local, State, and Federal laws and relevant University policies and procedures.

Key Functions and Related Job Duties

Key Function	Management
Job duties performed for the above function	Oversees the hiring, interviewing, staffing, training, and disciplining of employees in the University Public Safety department. Designs, establishes, and maintains an organizational structure and staffing to effectively accomplish the organization's goals and objectives; oversees recruitment, training, supervision, and evaluation of unit staff. Supervises approximately 23 full-time employees.
Key Function	Liaison
Job duties performed for the above function	Acts as a liaison for the university with local, state, and federal law enforcement agents.

Figure 12.20 Career profile: security chief at college or university.   (*Continued*)

Key Function	Strategic Planning
Job duties performed for the above function	Establishes and implements short- and long-range organizational goals, objectives, strategic plans, policies, and operating procedures; monitors and evaluates programmatic and operational effectiveness, and effects changes required for improvement.

Key Function	Liaison
Job duties performed for the above function	Interacts with various campus and community constituencies. Represents the University to various institutional divisions as well as externally to governmental agencies, vendors, students and their parents, and/or the general public.

Key Function	Supervision
Job duties performed for the above function	Oversees all major criminal investigation, internal and administrative investigations.

Other Duties and Responsibilities

Other Duties and Responsibilities	GC is an Affirmative Action/Equal Opportunity Institution committed to cultural, racial, and ethnic communities. We promote equal employment opportunities regardless of race, religion, color, gender, marital status, genetic information, national origin, disability, sexual orientation, and gender identity. It is expected that successful candidates share these commitments.

Minimum Requirements

Proposed Minimum Experience/Education	Bachelor's degree in Criminal Justice or related field of study from an accredited institution; AND at least five years of experience of campus police field with accelerating supervisor responsibility or eight years of combined municipal, county, state, federal, or campus experience.
Department Required Skills	
List any other requirements	

Other Job Requirements

Describe other job related requirements necessary to effectively perform the job's key functions such as license/certifications, required trainings, etc. Click here for requirement examples listed by occupation titles.

Select Type	License/Certifications
Description of Requirement	Must possess or be able to possess and maintain Georgia P.O.S.T certification as a peace officer within one year of employment; drivers license.

Preferences

Preferred Years Experience, Skills, Training, Education	

Posting Detail Information

Figure 12.20 (Continued)   Career profile: security chief at college or university.   (*Continued*)

Posting Number	SXX
Desired Start Date	
Position End Date (if temporary)	
Open Date	07/08/2016
Close Date	08/08/2016
Open Until Filled	No
Minimum Pay Rate- Annually	$67,800
Special Instructions Summary	

Reference Letters

Reference Letters	
Accept References	No
Minimum Requests	
Last Day a Reference Provider Can Submit Reference	
Applicant Special Instructions	

Supplemental Questions

Required fields are indicated with an asterisk (*).

1. * Do you have a Bachelor's degree in Criminal Justice or a related field of study from an accredited institution?

   - Yes
   - No

2. * Do you have at least five years of experience of college policing with accelerated supervisor responsibility OR eight years of combined municipal, county, state, federal, or campus experience?

   - Yes
   - No

3. * Are you P.O.S.T certified in Georgia or another state?

   - Yes
   - No

4. * Do you have campus law enforcement experience?

   - Yes
   - No

Figure 12.20 (Continued)   Career profile: security chief at college or university.   (*Continued*)

Applicant Documents

Required Documents

1. Resume
2. Cover Letter/Letter of Application

Optional Documents

1. Relevant Certifications/Training Certificates

Figure 12.20 (Continued)   Career profile: security chief at college or university.

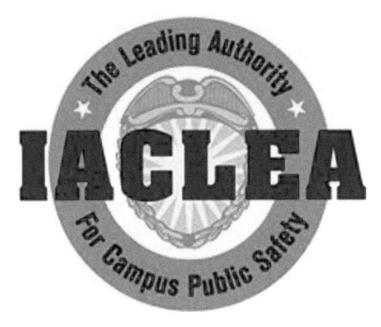

Figure 12.21   International Association of Campus Law Enforcement Association logo.

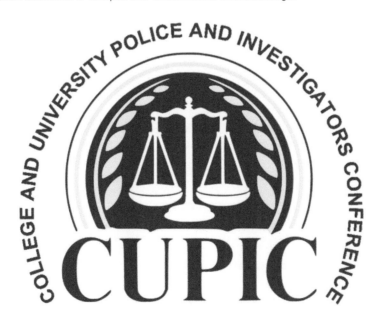

Figure 12.22   CUPIC logo.

Figure 12.23   NASSLEO logo.

NASRO's training schedule and dedication to officer advancement is an enviable mix of traditional policing and innovative private security techniques, stressing a customer service mentality, a client-based approach and a human services philosophy. Some examples include the following:

> Basic SRO Course
> Advanced SRO
> School CPTED
> School Security Officer Course
> SRO Supervisors and Management
> Effective Internet Safety Presentations
> School Law Update
> Risk Management for Interscholastic Athletics and After-School Activities[53]

NASRO also maintains an electronic database for school laws and how these enactments impact security practices at educational institutions. See Figure 12.24.
See Figure 12.25.

12.4 PRIVATE SECURITY AND RELIGIOUS CENTERS

12.4.1 State of the problem: Worship, violence, and terror

It is difficult to envision as unlikely a target of terrorism than a church, a synagogue, or a mosque—yet all three of these settings have been frequent targets of the terrorist or deranged racist or other warped mentality. Worshiping God and violence is a curious mix but to the jihadi, the insane ideologue or other extremist, it is just the place to make a point.[54] Politically correct or not, the bulk of religiously driven terrorism occurs in countries dominated by Islamic theology, interpreted correctly or not. The data succinctly but miserably relate that "70% of the atrocities took place in Muslim countries."[55]

---

[53] *Ibid.* at https://nasro.org/training/nasro-training-courses/, last accessed August 31, 2016.
[54] See K. Krause, Religion, Violence and Terrorism, 20 *Skeptic* 48 (2015).
[55] *Ibid.* at 54.

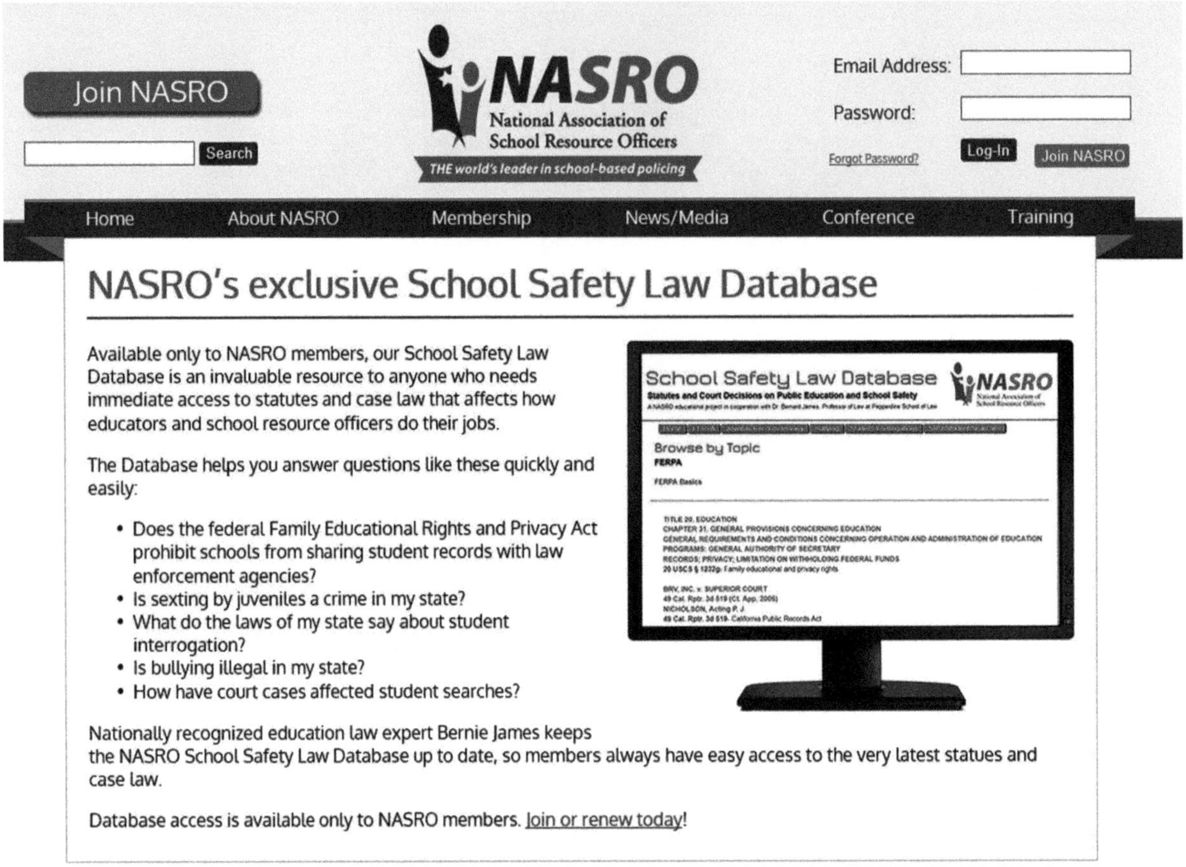

Figure 12.24   NASRO's school safety law database. (From https://nasro.org/nasros-exclusive-school-safety-law-database.)

Jewish synagogues have been on the receiving end of damage and violence due to anti-Semitism, Neo-Nazi movements, and virulent hatred of the Jewish people by certain Islamic jihadis. Christians are systematically being exterminated and destroyed in ancient locations in the Middle East with bombings of churches, execution of members who refuse to convert to Islam becoming a tragic and poorly responded to genocide based on religion. Nearly 20% of all hate crimes, according to the FBI, are motivated by religious intent. See Figure 12.26.

Anti-Islamic hate groups have targeted mosque settings while at the same time, extremist, radical groups within Islam have used the mosque as a planning center for terrorist motivation and implementation. In just the last year

The Paris Police Department has an immediate opening for a School Resource Officer. The SRO is responsible for working directly with the youth in our schools, developing and implementing community orientated programs, and being an overall liaison between school administrators, the student body, and law enforcement.

Candidates must be at least 21 years of age (or 20 years of age with 60 college credits), have a minimum of a high school diploma or equivalent, have a valid Maine driver's license, and must by certified as a full-time officer by the Maine Criminal Justice Academy or its equivalent with at least 5 years of full-time experience. Applicants who are already certified as an SRO and/or D.A.R.E, and who have had experience working in a school environment, will have preference. All candidates will be required to successfully pass an in-depth background investigation to include a polygraph examination, and may be subjected to physical and psychological examinations at the town's discretion.

Please submit an application, resume, and cover letter to the Paris Police Department at 35 Market Sq So Paris, ME 04281 by 4 pm Friday, July 15, 2016. Applications are available at the Paris Police Department during normal business hours or they can be found at www.parismaine.org/documents/forms/. POSTED 6/25/16

Figure 12.25   Career profile: school resource officer.

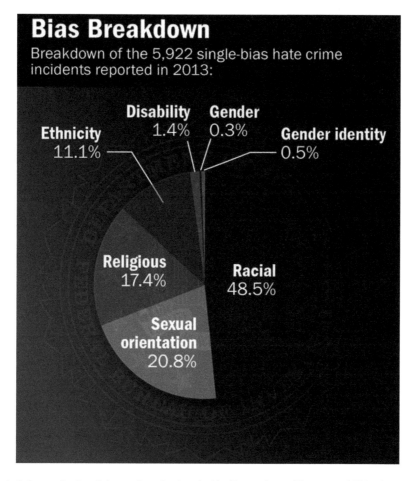

Figure 12.26 2013 statistics on the breakdown of motivations behind hate crimes. (Courtesy of FBI at https://www.fbi.gov/image-repository/hate_crime.jpg/view.)

alone, the World Watch Monitor has tracked attacks on Christian churches across the world and attributed over 7100 deaths to religious hate crimes. See Figure 12.27.

For the racist actor, the American Black church has been a favorite target—killing adherents of the Christian philosophy of love and charity, because of race becomes an irrational, indefensible way of thinking. Most recently in 2015, a bevy of people were cut down at the Mother Emanuel AME church in Charleston, South Carolina where Dylann Roof was driven by extreme hate and racial animus. See Figure 12.28.

Web Exercise: The FBI has been compiling data on this particular form of criminality—the hate crime at https://www.fbi.gov/video-repository/newss-seeking-information-church-hate-crimes/view.

12.4.2 Private security tactics and strategies in worship locations

This grim reality makes clear the need for traditional private security protocols to protect worshipers to the facility. Aside from hiring security staff at religious facilities, there are quite a few recommendations that would surprise most people. Since these locations are houses of God, there has always been a natural resistance to any weaponry on the premises. Hence, nearly all religious facilities are "gun-free" zones although the murdering jihadi, the mindless, violent racist or extreme hater is hardly controlled by such policies. When the count of events alone takes place, it is patently obvious that these policies are ineffectual. "The point is that a "no-gun" policy is not going to keep out these shooters who mean harm from coming into the church."[56] In fact, there are instances when having armed parishioners has actually prevented the shooter from inflicting even more harm and as a result, worship locations

---

[56] B. Donnelly, Church Shooting Incidents—Can They Be Prevented? *Sheriff* (September/October 2009), at 56.

Country	How many Christians have been killed for faith-related reasons (including state sanctioned executions)?	How many churches have been attacked, damaged, bombed, looted, destroyed, burned down, closed or confiscated for faith-related reasons?
Nigeria	4028	198
CAR	1269	131
Chad	750	10
DRC	467	13
Kenya	225	0
Cameroon	114	10
Libya	58	2
Pakistan	39	17
Syria	33	24
Myanmar	13	11

Figure 12.27 Top 10 countries for deaths of Christians due to hate crimes. (From World Watch Monitor at https://www.worldwatchmonitor.org/news/4195287/4195294/4227325.)

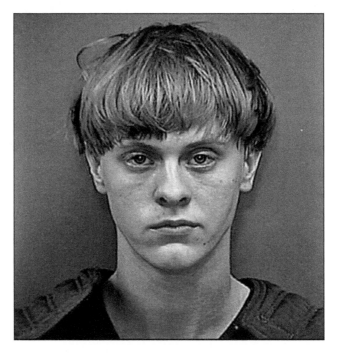

Figure 12.28 Dylann Roof—Charleston Mass Murderer at Mother Emanuel AME.

are reconsidering the general ban.[57] Others urge churches to strongly consider armed access points, especially at the lobby point of entry and to strategically place armed officers whose task is to assure no harm for the parishioners.[58] And while every worship location wants to be open, warm and welcoming to its members as well as visitors, gone are the days when unbridled access is permissible. Churches and synagogues need to place security and emergency preparedness on the same level of importance of other institutional functions and designate a team of people to "first evaluate their specific risks."[59] The image of deployment should be less military and more a blending into the

---

[57] C. Thomas, Lives Saved by Having a Gun at Church, *Human Events* (December 2007), at 17.
[58] Donnelly, *supra* note 56, at 58.
[59] L. Stelter, To Churches 'Look Within' to Enhance Security, *Security Systems News* (March 2010), at 13.

Figure 12.29 NOCSSM logo.

population of worshipers. In addition, the security staff should employ all available behavioral assessment tools to identify potential threats.[60]

Web Exercise: Find out about a new program in a Certified Church Security Specialist at http://www.privateofficer. com/CCSS.html.

At the volunteer level, there has been a growing interest in a church patrol program similar to a neighborhood watch.[61] Some not-for-profit entities have devised whole programs to be used a model template, such as the Gatekeepers Project where the chief stress is providing safe and secure church security either by volunteer patrol or by the hiring of security professionals. See Figure 12.29.

Aside from crime and terror, sacred places of worship are largely under severe stress as to fire, hazards and architectural decline, and those entrusted with the maintenance and preservation of these glorious houses of worship have to be forever mindful of older building challenges.[62] Other recommendations concerning security in church settings include the following:

- Create a Security Team
- Designate a point person on security issues
- Conduct a security and risk assessment to identify your church's vulnerabilities
- Develop a church security and emergency plan and guidelines with defined roles for all staff
- Establish a Communications Plan
- Establish a no tolerance policy for fights, altercations, and other disruptions.
- Work and Partner with local law enforcement agency[63]

Web Exercise: Watch the Power Point Presentation on the unique security problems of religious facilities at https:// www.santarosa.fl.gov/coad/documents/ChurchCrimePreventionVSept2008.pdf. In addition, follow these links to research a collection of recent incidents, with associated timelines, in the former, and a comprehensive list of resources in this area in the latter: https://www.hsdl.org/?view&did=790107 and https://www.illinois.gov/ready/ plan/Documents/DHS_Houses_of_Worship_Security_Practices_Guide.pdf.

Private security firms have cropped up in this space to provide the much needed services for religious institutions no far less about security than about theology and matters of faith.[64]

The challenges for securing a place of worship will vary from venue to venue. For example, Pope Francis's recent visitation to the Shrine of the Immaculate Conception in the District of Columbia brings to the fore all the typical security and emergency concerns that any event or governmental visit would entail.[65] See Figure 12.30.

Web Exercise: Consider the host of security considerations for a papal visit as posed by the Secret Service at http:// www.secretservice.gov/data/press/releases/GPA11-15-Papal-Visit-DC.pdf.

See Figure 12.31.

---

[60] See B. Martin, Church Safety and Security: The Use and Effectiveness of Applying Behavioral Analysis, *Law Officer* (March 30, 2016), at http:// lawofficer.com/2016/03/church-safety-and-security/, last accessed August 31, 2016.

[61] See D. Dykes, More Upstate Churches Increasing Security Measures, *The Layman Online* (June 19, 2015), at http://www.layman.org/ more-upstate-churches-increasing-security-measures/.

[62] D. Cohen & A. Robert Jaeger, *Sacred Places at Risk* (Partners for Sacred Places, 1998), at http://www.sacredplaces.org/uploads/ files/395429189155295863-spar.pdf, last accessed August 31, 2016.

[63] See W.S. Carcara, Advising Houses of Worship on a Comprehensive and Balances Security Plan, *The Police Chief* (July 2009), at http://www. policechiefmagazine.org/magazine/index.cfm?fuseaction=display_arch&article_id=1845&issue_id=72009, last accessed August 31, 2016.

[64] Cambridge Security, Houses of Worship webpage, at http://www.cambridgesecurityservices.com/houses-worship/.

[65] See A. Giambrone, District Braces for Pope's Visit, with Major Road Closures and Detours Planned, *Washington City Paper* (September 10, 2015), at http://www.washingtoncitypaper.com/news/city-desk/blog/13069914/district-braces-for-popes-visit-with-major-road-closures-and-detours-planned, last accessed August 31, 2016.

Figure 12.30   Pope Francis visits Washington DC. (From U.S. Secret Service.)

Safety & Security Director

Summary

Title: Safety & Security Director
ID: XXXX
Department: Campus Operations
Location: Central Support

Description

We are always on the lookout for people who are passionate about using their talents for God's purposes to join our team. As you know, working at our Church is not just a job, it's a calling!

Our Central Support Team is looking for a full-time Safety and Security Director to manage all aspects of the Church's efforts to help ensure that all visitors and staff are safe and secure while on the Church's premises.

Primary Responsibilities include:

- Develop, implement and periodically update a comprehensive safety and security plan including but not limited to: Weekend worship services, special events, children and student programs, staff members, facilities, emergency response planning, medical readiness, and physical property.
- Initiate security response to any suspicious activity on property.
- Oversee all contract police officers providing personal security for teachers, staff, etc.
- Manage access control system and monitor surveillance.
- Coordinate and direct police officer duties during church functions.
- Oversee background check process for volunteers.

Still interested? If you have the following skill set, we'd love for you to apply!

- Good working knowledge of safety and security operations and familiarity with law enforcement systems and procedures.
- Knowledge of relevant equipment, policies, and procedures to promote effective security operations for the protection of people, data and property.
- Excellent verbal and written communication skills.
- Strong people and organizational skills.
- Ability to train and motivate staff and volunteers.

The schedule will vary with 40 hours/week including nights and weekends.

Figure 12.31   Career profile: church safety and security manager.

12.4.3 Special templates and protocols for churches

Churches, synagogues and other religious entities should conduct risk and vulnerability analysis as any other facility.[66] There are obviously some special requirements that have to be tailored and shaped to the spiritual dimensions of the setting.

12.4.3.1 Risk assessment template for churches

The facility's overall condition and state of security should be measured in a global and architectural context first. A more sophistical risk and vulnerability analysis should be carried out once the building's inherent security policies are cataloged and evaluated.[67] See Figure 12.32 for a usable template for spiritual settings.

12.4.3.2 Fire prevention checklist

Fire destroys a house of worship like any other facility and it is crucial to plan and prepare for fire eventualities and prevention. See Figure 12.33.[68]

12.5 PRIVATE SECURITY INDUSTRY, HOSPITAL AND OTHER MEDICAL INSTITUTIONS

12.5.1 Background and context

A long-standing area of private security's institutional participation has been the medical and hospital setting. For the bulk of these installations and facilities, private security, emergency, and fire services are either delivered by institutional employees assigned to these responsibilities or by contractual companies that provide either all or the bulk of these services at the facility.[69] At play in most medical facilities is the undeniable need for a security professional that understands the interplay of security and emergency together for in the hospital setting "security has evolved"… being "more focused today on preparedness and emergency management, as most major security operations around the country."[70] Just as pressing are the maze of regulatory processes that govern hospital and medical facility operations in regards to safety and security, a place the governmental authorities show little resistance to meddling in. Hospitals can be bureaucratic nightmares in regard to safety and security protocols—from disposal of hazardous biomedical materials to safe operation of equipment with potentially dangerous environmental influences—all of these things often fall within the province of a hospital security and safety director.[71]

When one considers the complexities of security and vulnerability in the typical hospital, the untrained, uneducated, and unprofessional guard is a thing of the past. Contemporary security personnel and managers have a great deal to worry about although recent surveys tend to highlight special areas of concern. For the CSO, the main headaches and worries relate to the content of Figure 12.34.[72]

Today's medical installations need top-flight people to handle a bundle of responsibilities both human and hazardous. Add to these challenges, the healthcare security specialists encounter hazardous materials, potential pathogens that could cause widespread harm, nuclear materials as by-products, a drug and pharmacological access unrivaled, and potential for black market activity. Hospital and medical security is no sleepy business. That hospital security is clearly not "child's play" is a massive understatement with the array of challenges and concerns too numerous to mention.[73]

---

[66] For an excellent template on risk analysis in churches, see Ecclesiastical, Self-Assessment Form, at http://www.ecclesiastical.com/churchmatters/images/health%20and%20safety%20self-assessment%20form.pdf, last accessed August 31, 2016.

[67] See T.L. Rowe, *How to Assess the Safety and Security of Your Place of Worship* (2009), at https://www.santarosa.fl.gov/coad/documents/SafetyinChurch.pdf, last accessed August 31, 2016.

[68] See National Church Arson Task Force, *Threat Assessment Guide for Houses of Worship* 13 (2000), at https://www.oodaloop.com/documents/Legacy/asis/threat.pdf, last accessed August 31, 2016.

[69] For an interesting analysis of the arguments and counterarguments involving contract security services in hospitals, see K. Bukowski, Debunking Contract Healthcare Security Myths, *Sec. Mgmt* (April 2015), at 66.

[70] R. Chicarello, Creating a Hospital of Choice, *Sec. Mag.* (November 2009), at 60.

[71] See D. Ritchey, Best Security Systems Mean Better Healthcare, *Sec. Mag.* (July 2009), at 50.

[72] See Safety and Compliance Top Concerns for Hospital C-Suites, *Sec. Mgmt* (March 1, 2015), at http://www.securitymagazine.com/articles/86138-safety-and-compliance-top-concerns-for-hospital-c-suites, last accessed August 31, 2016.

[73] See M.A. Gips, Hospital Safety Is Not Child's Play, 50 *Sec. Mgmt* 70 (2006).

RISK ASSESSMENT FACILITY CHECKLIST				
Windows	Yes	No	N/A	Notes
Note: All windows should be secured no matter how small or remote they are.				Including Sky Lights
Are basement windows clear of shrubbery and other obstructions?				
Are basement and grade level windows protected by:				
Bars?				
Wire Mesh?				
Window Locks?				
Wire Mesh?				
Plexiglas?				
Lexan?				
Other? (Explain)				
Are all windows, including those above ground level:				
Properly fitted with a locking device?				
Checked each night to make sure each window is closed ands securely locked?				
Lights	Yes	No	N/A	Notes
Are exterior lights installed to illuminate the exterior of buildings and their alley ways?				
Are interior lights left on at night?				
Are entrance lights left burning at night so intruders will be clearly visible when forcibly attempting to enter premises?				
Are lights left burning in strategic locations to allow people passing by and/or police to see easily into the premises from foot or vehicle?				
Are timing devices used to turn lights on and off at preset times to give the impression the premises are occupied?				
Locks/Doors	Yes	No	N/A	Notes
Are all exterior doors equipped with proper locks?				
Are exterior doors of solid core construction?				
Are hinges, which are exposed on a door's exterior, equipped with non-removal able hinge pins?				
Are doors to adjoining building locked at night?				
Are all exterior doors kept locked to prevent entry?				
Is there a routine check each night to make sure all doors are locked?				

Figure 12.32 Building/property checklist.

(Continued)

Intrusion Devices	Yes	No	N/A	Notes
Do you have a security alarm?				
If you have a system, is it approved by Underwriters Laboratories, Inc.?				
Was it properly installed by licensed workers?				
Is your security alarm system checked regularly?				
Does your system cover your hazardous points fully?				
Is your Alarm System:				
Connected to a central alarm station?				
Connected to an automatic dialing attachment?				
Local Alarms?				

Closed Circuit TV System	Yes	No	N/A	Notes
Do you have a security camera system?				
Does the system record 7 days or more? Tape or Digital Recorder				
Does the CCTV have motion detection?				
Does the motion detection tie into the alarm system?				
Does the camera placement cover all entry/exit points and vital areas?				
Does the system cover the parking lot? If yes, are low light cameras required?				
Can your system print photos or make video of critical incidents?				

Fire Suppression	Yes	No	N/A	Notes
Are all fire extinguishers in a accessible position?				
Are all fire extinguishers tested and up to date?				
Is there a sprinkler system?				
Has it been tested recently?				
Is Emergency lighting in place and tested every month?				
Are smoke detection devices in place and tested every month?				
Are all fire exits properly marked?				
Are all appliances of in break/kitchen areas?				

Children's Area / Day Care	Yes	No	N/A	Notes
Does the Children's area have a restricted entry point?				
Are there windows in all children's classroom areas?				
Is the diaper changing area in a secure location?				
Are there restroom facilities in the				

Figure 12.32 (Continued) Building/property checklist.   (*Continued*)

children's area?				
Do the doors for the storage area lock to keep toddlers out?				
Is the children's outside area protected by a chain linked fence and gate?				
General Security Measures	**Yes**	**No**	**N/A**	**Notes**
Do you maintain a written or photographic inventory of all valuables and records on the premises?				
Are personnel assigned to check exits, entrances, and windows to make sure they are secure before leaving at night?				
Are precious objects, vessels and other valuables kept in a safe, vault or locked cabinet when not being used?				
When staff or volunteers with access to keys or safe combinations terminate their status, are locks and/or combinations changed?				
Do you have a security guard?				
If so, did you investigate this guard before hiring him/her?				
Are ladders, boxes and other equipment put away after use so that they are not left for use by anyone intent on criminal behavior?				
Are premises used in the evening for meetings and other activities? (Evening activities generally reduce the possibility of burglaries/theft)				
Have you arranged for a regular police patrol or a security force check at night?				
Are the premises available for use 24-hours a-day?				
Entire building?				
Partial Section of building (Explain)				
If a section of the building is open for use 27 hrs a day, is movement from this section to other sections of the building restricted?				
Describe security measures taken if answer to above is yes.				

Completed By _____ Date _____

<Alarm companies
<Locks/Doors/Windows companies
<Camera suppliers

Figure 12.32 (Continued)   Building/property checklist.

ACCIDENTAL FIRE PREVENTION

OK	Needs Work	CHECKLIST
✓	☐	TAKING ACTION TO PREVENT FIRES FROM STARTING IS THE BEST PROTECTION YOU CAN PROVIDE YOUR FACILITY.
☐	☐	Ensure exit doors provide easy escape from inside the building (no locks or fasteners).
☐	☐	Keep exits free of obstruction at all times.
☐	☐	All exits clearly marked with lighted signs.
☐	☐	Make sure electrical system complies with fire code.
☐	☐	Furnace and air conditioner inspected for proper working condition.
☐	☐	Walls and ceiling of furnace room lined with fire-resistant material.
☐	☐	Combustible materials and flammable liquids stored properly.
☐	☐	Draperies, upholstery and furnishings made of fire-retardant materials.
☐	☐	Furnace room free of combustibles.
☐	☐	Use and disposal of incense and candles supervised by an adult.
☐	☐	Electrical system inspected for safe functioning.
☐	☐	Electrical and extension cords inspected for safe operation.
☐	☐	Face plates on all electrical outlets.
☐	☐	Smoke detectors installed and tested regularly.
☐	☐	Test fire alarms and sprinkler system periodically, if applicable.
☐	☐	At least one fire extinguisher every 2,500 square feet.
☐	☐	All personnel trained in fire extinguisher use.

Figure 12.33 Accidental fire prevention checklist.

See Figure 12.35.

On top of the operational aspects that generate safety and security concerns, the security specialist is also concerned about potential terror acts against the facility. While not a common event in the United States, the chance of a hospital being a terror target greatly increases in other parts of the world. Dr. Jamie Johnson and Professor Dean Alexander have cataloged recent terrorist ambitions carried out in the hospital arena, which include the following:

- 1995 hostage-taking incident in Budennovsk, Russia, which killed nearly 130 and injured more than 400.
- 2003 suicide attack in Mozdok, Russia, which killed 50 people and wounded more than 80.
- 2008 suicide bomber in Deta Ismail Khan, Pakistan, who killed 32 and injured 55.
- 2008 gunfire and grenade attack in Mumbai, India, which killed five and injured two.
- 2010 explosion at an emergency room in Karachi, Pakistan, that killed 10.
- 2011 suicide attack at the main military hospital in Kabul, Afghanistan, that killed six and wounded 23.
- 2011 suicide attack in Tikrit, Iraq, which killed 11 and injured more than 80.
- 2013 suicide bombing in Farah, Afghanistan, that killed two.[74]

---

[74] J. Johnson & D. Alexander, Hospital Incident Command Systems and Their Importance, *Sec. Mag.* (March 2014), at 98.

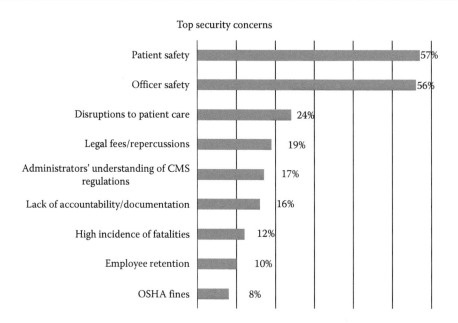

Figure 12.34   Top security concerns among hospitals. (From Guardian8 survey of 379 hospital decision-makers.)

Director, Safety, Security and Emergency Management

Posted 30 days ago

Job description

Department: Security, Safety & Emergency Management

A Life-Changing Career

Responsibilities: Strategic planning, development of policy and procedures and keeping leadership informed on programs, program impacts and issues. The director leads effective safety and security programs compliant with federal and state safety regulations and The Joint Commission standards. Analyzes and assesses environmental safety plans, security plans and hospital disaster plans and evaluates effectiveness and provides solutions and appropriate resources to supervisors and staff in areas of oversight. Serves on committees, work groups and maintains confidentiality of information.

Qualifications: Bachelor's degree and 5 years of leadership experience in safety, security, emergency management or related field; project management and business processes, finance and budgeting skills essential. Demonstrated experience and understanding of healthcare security operations, occupational safety and health and emergency management required.

Additional Qualifications: Experience in medical/healthcare setting is preferred; adaptable to a changing environment and updated laws and standards; Experience and proficiency in report writing, grammar, presentations to groups, writing policies and procedures. Occupational safety experience and knowledge of Occupational and Heatlh Administration (OSHA), Environmental Protection Agency (EPA), Department of Transportation (DOT), Centers for Medicare STrategies (CMS), National Fire Protection Agency (NFPA), and The Joint Commission (TJC) standards helpful, leadership role in healthcare security operation or other security operation and oversight of security systems, fire alarms, access control and investigative processes.

License or Certification: CHSP or higher level safety related certification within 3 years of hire.

Benefit Eligible: Yes
Exemption Status: Exempt
Compensation Detail: Education, experience and tenure may be considered along with internal equity when job offers are extended.
Hours/Pay Period: 80
Schedule Details: Monday- Friday 8:00 a.m. to 4:30 p.m. and available for calls after hours; may require after hours for emergencies, incidents or projects.
Weekend Schedule: May be required to be in house during emergencies, incidents and projects during weekends.

Figure 12.35   Career profile: hospital director security and emergency.

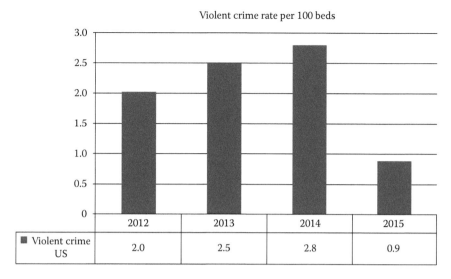

Violent crime rate per 100 beds

	2012	2013	2014	2015
■ Violent crime US	2.0	2.5	2.8	0.9

Figure 12.36   Violent crimes survey. (From The International Association for Healthcare Security and Safety Foundation [IAHSS Foundation].)

Even the facility itself faces many human challenges from emotionally disturbed patients to a rise of violence spilling over from gang and gun wars, overstressed and taxed emergency centers trying to save the victims and the perpetrators of crime, and an unfortunate rise of the drug culture's by-products of violence and human tumult. Most hospital administrators now report significant concerns about violence in the hospital facility itself.[75]

With a corresponding investment in security professionalism in the hospital staff, it appears that the upward trend of violent crime in hospital facilities has finally ended. The 2016 International Association for Healthcare Security and Safety Foundation (IAHSS Foundation) survey on medical facility crime paints a more positive picture as regards a once unceasing escalation in violent crime. See Figure 12.36.

See Figure 12.37.

12.5.2 Career projections and professional associations

Employment prospects for hospital and medical security personnel continue to be very positive. The U.S. Department of Labor Statistics job projections to 2020 deliver a growth-oriented picture of the protective services industry, which includes all aspects of security, but at the same time, the healthcare and medical industry show similar upward promise. When these two sectors of the economy are combined, the level of opportunity is pretty difficult to deny. See Figure 12.38.[76]

When one considers the bureaucratic and structural complexity of the typical hospital facility, the occupational demands for upper management and human resource personnel who oversee day-to-day operations make it a very ripe place for advancement. In the typical career path, sold to our prospective employees in the private security industry, it is this chance at upward mobility that makes these careers more attractive than commonly known.

Opportunity opens up from the entry level to the advanced levels in this model, so the security officer may in fact achieve a high-level management position if performance justifies it. The entire opportunity infrastructure of the security industry rests on this premise of personal advancement. This occupational reality is further buttressed by economic investments by the hospital industry for security purposes. ASIS has been tracking this heavily increasing budgetary allotment, which in turn opens even more opportunities up for the security professional. See Figure 12.39.[77]

---

[75] See H. Schwartz, Hospitals Report Rise in Violence and Assaults, *Facility Executive* (n.d.), at http://facilityexecutive.com/2015/03/hospitals-report-rise-in-violence-and-assaults/, last accessed August 31, 2016.

[76] See C. Brett Lockard & M. Wolf, Occupational Employment Projections to 2020, *Monthly Labor Rev.* 84 (January 2012), at http://www.bls.gov/opub/mlr/2012/01/art5full.pdf, last accessed August 31, 2016.

[77] M. Moran, Security Market Growth Continues, *Sec. Mgmt* (May 15, 2015), at https://sm.asisonline.org/Pages/Security-Market-Growth-Continues.aspx, last accessed August 31, 2016.

DISTINGUISHING FEATURES OF THE CLASS: Under the supervision of the Director of Security - Hospital, this position is responsible for assisting in establishing and administering systems and procedures to provide the comprehensive security and safety of all property, buildings, equipment, personnel and visitors at the Medical Center. Supervision is exercised over a large number of security personnel. Does related work as required.

EXAMPLES OF WORK: (Illustrative Only)

Recommends revisions to the manpower time schedule to provide twenty-four hour a day, seven days a week, security coverage as operational needs change;

Monitors and recommends revisions to the access control system for all buildings of the Medical Center;

Administers and maintains the photo identification system at the Medical Center;

Administers and maintains a system for key control for all Medical Center Buildings;

Continually monitors a system for theft control both internally, and externally and recommends appropriate changes;

Conducts in-service education programs for security division personnel;

Gathers and compiles data for the preparation of budget and personnel requests for Security Division and formulates appropriate justifications;

Assists in administratively maintaining surveillance of parking areas to assure the employees and visitors are parked in designated areas and prevent vandalism;

May attend meetings, training conferences and similar seminars on safety;

Assists in reviewing and analyzing the safety and security programs and makes proposals for necessary revisions and innovations;

Submits security reports and other required reports as requested;

Assists in the development of contingency plans to deal with various types of emergency situations;

Conducts unscheduled tours of the Medical Center to assure that safety and security measures are being carried out;

Figure 12.37   Career profile: hospital: assistant security director.   (*Continued*)

REQUIRED KNOWLEDGE, SKILLS, ABILITIES AND ATTRIBUTES: Good knowledge of the principles, practices and techniques employed in establishing and maintaining institutional and building safety and security; good knowledge of the techniques and methods of safety and security analysis; good knowledge of safety and security laws, rules and regulations; ability to formulate, develop, implement and supervise a multi-scale safety and security program; ability to plan, direct, and evaluate the performance of assigned personnel; ability to establish effective working relationships with key management personnel, associates, subordinates and the general public; ability to identify staff training needs and to obtain those necessary resources in order to satisfy those needs; ability to maintain records and make reports; initiative; sound professional judgment; good health.

MINIMUM ACCEPTABLE TRAINING AND EXPERIENCE: Graduation from an accredited high school and either (a) graduation from college* and three years of experience in safety and security work for a public law enforcement or private security agency, one year of which must have been in a supervisory or administrative capacity; or (b) seven years of the experience listed in (a) including the one year of specialized experience; or (c) a satisfactory equivalent combination of the foregoing training and experience.

Figure 12.37 (Continued)   Career profile: hospital: assistant security director.

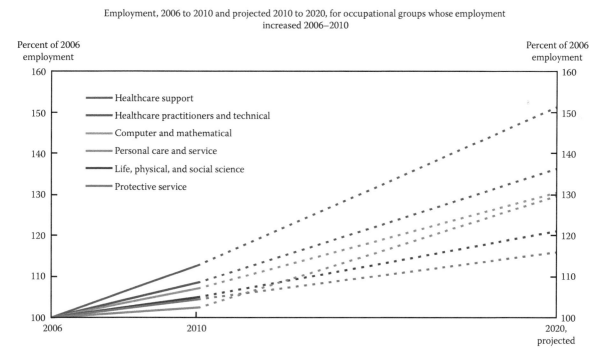

Figure 12.38   Employment projections for the security industry. *Note*: BLS does not project specific data for each of the years between 2010 and 2020. Interim years to the 2020 projection point are expressed by a dashed straight line only. (From U.S. Bureau of Labor Statistics.)

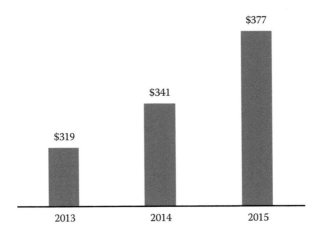

Figure 12.39   Private sector security spending in 2013–2015 (dollars in billion). (From ASIS International.)

Figure 12.40   IAHSS logo.

This investment mentality has also been driven by the need for information and cyber security requirements, and with the paperwork, the billing, and the entwining of government benefits with patient payment, all of these forces drive up cyber security costs.[78]

Professional associations and groups make significant contributions to future growth in the industry, especially when those associations elevate the professional expectations of performance and qualification. The International Association of Healthcare Security and Safety (IAHSS) goes a long way toward that goal by administering a host of certifications. See Figure 12.40.

Current certifications for hospital security specialists include the following:

CHPA Certification: The Certified Healthcare Protection Administrator designation is available to management level healthcare security professionals who meet the qualifying criteria. Once approved, each candidate has twelve months to successfully pass the CHPA certification exam.

CHSO Certification: The Certified Healthcare Security Officer (CHSO) certification is an introductory program in healthcare security and safety. Some of the topics included in the Basic Training Manual are an introduction to healthcare security, fundamental security skills, the role of security in healthcare organizations, protective measures, healthcare safety and emergency management security.

CAHSO Certification: The Certified Advanced Healthcare Security Officer (CAHSO) certification builds upon the knowledge gained in the Basic certification to more advanced topics. The study materials address the special needs of security in healthcare institutions including: investigative techniques, workplace violence prevention, patient risk groups, electronic security technologies and professionalism.

CHSSO Certification: The Certified Healthcare Security Supervisor Officer (CHSSO) builds upon the knowledge gained in both the Basic and Advanced programs and is intended for healthcare security professionals with some level of supervisory responsibilities. The study materials address the special needs of security in healthcare institutions including: crime prevention programs, training plans, security operations, emergency procedures and supervisor development.

---

[78] See J. White, Active Shooter Guide for Healthcare Security, *Prot. Mgmt* (December 15, 2014), at http://protectionmanagementllc.com/active-shooter-guide-healthcare-security/, last accessed August 31, 2016.

Figure 12.41 MHSDA logo.

Healthcare Safety Certificate Program: The Healthcare Safety Certificate Program is an introductory program designed to provide individuals with the basics for healthcare safety. The study CD provides information including the fundamentals of healthcare safety, patient safety, fire safety, hazardous materials, physical hazards and emergency management.[79]

The Metropolitan Healthcare Directors Association (MHDA) is a collective of security directors who work in hospitals and who wish to advance best practices in healthcare settings and afford networking and shared information opportunities for its members. Its membership currently rests at 100 hospital facilities. See Figure 12.41.

Various broader-based membership groups such as ASIS and the International Association of Professional Security Consultants either train the managerial class that oversees hospital security or provide for specialized certifications that may have sub-sections or specialties. The International Board for Certification of Safety Managers[80] administers the Certified Healthcare Safety Professional (CHSP) test, which consists of the following goals.

The CHSP credential was established to focus on the importance of using management principles to improve the safety performance of healthcare organizations. The broad scope of the CHSP Exam attracts applicants from various healthcare backgrounds including, but not limited to, safety, security, infection prevention, employee health, nursing, quality improvement, administration, risk management, facility management, plant operations, hazardous materials management, emergency management, life safety, biomedical services, environmental services, laboratory operations, nursing homes, surgery centers, insurance loss control, and safety consulting.[81]

Exam content and competency measured by the CHSP certification are charted in Figure 12.42.

In general, the world of hospital security is a burgeoning area filled with challenges and professional levels of expertise. While in the hierarchy of careers, the entry level is at the security officer level, a quick perusal of the industry displays a wide array of paths to extraordinary advancement.

---

[79] International Association of Healthcare Security & Safety, certifications webpage, at http://www.iahss.org/?page=certifications, last accessed August 31, 2016.

[80] 173 Tucker Road, Suite 202, Helena, Alabama 35080.

[81] See International Board for Certification of Safety Managers, CHSP Certification, at http://ibfcsm.org/chsp.php, last accessed August 31, 2016.

1. **Safety Management (25% of Questions)**
   a. Hazard Control Techniques and Safety Management Principles
   b. Accident Definitions, Accident Myths, Accident Costs, and Accident Generation Cycle
   c. Accident, Injury, and Illness Prevention and Accident Costing
   d. Inspections, Audits, Surveys, Investigations, and Root Cause Analysis
   e. Safety Policies, Safety Plans, Work Rules, and Reporting Procedures
   f. Safety Cultures, Safety Committees, Safety Slogans, and Safety Perceptions
   g. Industrial Hygiene and Occupational Health
   h. System Safety Methods and High Reliability Organizations
   i. Safety Responsibilities (Leaders, Managers, and Supervisors)
   j. Hazard Controls and Personal Protective Equipment (PPE)
   k. Hazard Categories (Physical, Biological, Chemical, Ergonomics, Psychosocial)
   l. General Management
   m. Management and Leadership Concepts, and Principles
   n. Human Relations and Understanding Organizational Cultures
   o. Written and Oral Communications
   p. Managerial Techniques (Management by Exception, Migrating Decision Making, etc.)
2. **Government Agencies and Standards (22% of Questions)**
   a. Occupational Safety and Health Administration (OSHA)
      i. OSH Act and General Duty Clause (Dangerous Drugs, TB, Lasers, Workplace Violence)
   b. General Industry Standards (29 CFR 1910) and Construction Standards (29 CFR 1926)
      i. Injury/Illness Reporting and Recording (29 CFR 1904)
      ii. Healthcare Related Standards
         A. Hazard Communication (29 CFR 1910.1200)
         B. Respiratory Standard (29 CFR 1910.134)
         C. Controlling Hazardous Energy (29 CFR 1910.147)
         D. Permit Confined Spaces (29 CFR 1910.146)
         E. HazWoper (29 CFR 1910.120)
         F. Air Contaminants (29 CFR 1910, Subpart Z)
         G. Electrical Standards (29 CFR 1910.303)
      iii. Healthcare E-Tools (OSHA Website)B. Environmental Protection Agency (40 CFR)
      iv. Resource Conservation and Recovery Act (RCRA)
      v. Clean Water Act (CWA)
      vi. Clean Air Act (CAA)
      vii. Federal Insecticide, Fungicide, and Rodentcide Act (FIFRA)
      viii. Universal Waste
   c. Nuclear Regulatory Commission (10 CFR)
      i. Nuclear Waste Management
      ii. License/Isotope Management
   d. Food and Drug Administration (21 CFR)
      i. Recalls, Drugs Alerts, and Medical Equipment Error Reporting (SMDA)
      ii. Food Safety Act (FSA)
   e. Department of Transportation (49 CFR)
      i. Federal Motor Carrier Safety Administration (FMCSA)
      ii. Hazardous and Infectious Substance Regulations
   f. Department of Health and Human Services (42 CFR)
      i. National Institute for Occupational Safety and Health (NIOSH)
      ii. Centers for Disease Control and Prevention (CDC)
      iii. Agency for Toxic Substances and Disease Registry (ATSDR)
      iv. Centers for Medicare and Medicaid Services (CMS)
      v. Agency for Healthcare Research and Quality (AHRQ)
      vi. Institute of Medicine (IOM) and National Institutes of Health (NIH)
      vii. Federal Emergency Management Agency (FEMA)
4. **Healthcare Hazard Identification, Evaluation, and Control (20% of Questions)**
   a. Physical Hazards (Electrical, machine, equipment, tools, noise, radiation, etc.)
   b. Chemical Hazards (Disinfectants, pesticides, solvents, dangerous drugs, gases, etc.)
   c. Ergonomic/Environmental Hazards (Repetitive tasks, falls, musculoskeletal disorders, etc.)
   d Biohazards (Legionella, waste handling, sharps exposures, construction risks, etc.)
   e. Psycho-Social Hazards (Workplace violence, security, substance abuse, stress, shift work, etc.)
   f. Healthcare Clinical and Support Department Safety

Figure 12.42 CHSP exam content.

(Continued)

4. **Voluntary and Standards Organizations (13% of Questions)**
   a. National Fire Protection Association (NFPA)
   b. American National Standards Institute (ANSI)
   c. American Society of Testing Materials (ASTM)
   d. American Society of Heating, Refrigerating, & Air Conditioning Engineers (ASHRAE)
   e. Underwriters Laboratory (UL) and Factory Mutual (FM)
   f. American Conference of Government Industrial Hygienists (ACGIH)
   g. American Industrial Hygiene Association (AIHA)
5. **Accrediting Organizations (8% of Questions)**
   a. Joint Commission (EOC, Life Safety, and Emergency Standards)
   b. American Osteopathic Association (AOA), Det Norske Veritas (DNV), and CMS (Nursing Homes and Hospitals)
6. **Fire Safety (6% of Questions)**
   a. Life Safety (NFPA 101) and Healthcare Facilities (NFPA 99)
   b. Fire Safety Management and Other Relevant NFPA Publications
   c. Fire Prevention and Flammable Materials
7. **Infection Control and Prevention (6% of Questions)**
   a. CDC Infection Control Guidelines and OSHA Bloodborne Pathogens Standard
   b. CDC Standard and Isolation Precautions
   c. Pandemic Planning and Infection Related Medical Surge Issues
   d. Healthcare Acquired Infections and Opportunistic Infections (Aspergillus and Pseudomonas)

Figure 12.42 (Continued) CHSP exam content.

12.5.3 Special forms and templates for hospital security

Hospitals will employ traditional means and methods of security analysis, assessment, and practices, so much of what has already been covered can be applied to this specific setting. Even though there are additional human questions in regards to illness and emotional disturbances, as well as some esoteric regulatory requirements in hazmat materials and disposal by-products, the hospital needs all the security regimens as other institutional settings. This section stresses some unique features of the medical facility.

12.5.3.1 Risk assessment template for hospitals

While all risk assessment forms will be helpful when conducting this type of analysis, those developed by the hospital industry itself tend to assess the specialized criteria most relevant to industry-specific standards and requirements.[82]

Web Exercise: Download and review the Kaiser Permanente Vulnerability Assessment Tool at http://www.calhospitalprepare.org/hazard-vulnerability-analysis.

Only by a thorough risk assessment will the security professionals be able to define the institutional risks for vulnerabilities.

12.5.3.2 Hospital planning and continuity

Hospitals must be forever vigilant about their continued operations and resiliency, especially when considering the consumer served. In life and death situations, a reality part of the natural makeup of any medical setting, the planning must be significant because the stakes are so higher.[83] To do an effective survey or assessment, the hospital facility must account for a diversity of variables including but not limited to

1. Planning Framework
2. Command and Control
3. Authorized Personnel
4. Notification Systems
5. Activating the Plan

---

[82] NJHA, *Hospital Security Readiness Assessment Tool* (2004), at https://www.gnyha.org/ResourceCenter/NewDownload/?id=353&type=1, last accessed August 31, 2016.

[83] See J. Snider, *Hospital Resilience Business Continuity Planning for Disasters* (Henry Ford Hospital and Health Network), at https://www.henryford.com/documents/ER/Hospital%20Resilience%20John%20Snider.pdf, last accessed August 31, 2016; see also FEMA, *Continuity Assistance Tool* (2009), at http://www.cchn.org/pdf/clinical_quality/ep/Continuity_Assistance_Tool.pdf, last accessed August 31, 2016.

6. Response Protocols
7. Communication Systems
8. Staffing Considerations
9. Security and Access
10. Internal Traffic
11. External Traffic
12. Patient Reception
13. Evacuating Horizontally and Vertically
14. Sheltering-in-Place
15. Isolated or Out of Communication
16. Visitors
17. Communication and Media
18. Resources
19. Allocating Pharmaceuticals
20. Surveillance
21. Infection Control
22. Staff Education and Training
23. Post Mortem Care
24. Recovery Protocols
25. Exercising the Plan
26. Infrastructure[84]

12.5.3.3 Hospital hazard planning

Hospitals can be very dangerous places, both for patient and employee. With the rise of infectious bacteria, the increased death rate resulting from new pathogens and other illness can result in extraordinary liability for the hospital. A major portion of the security and emergency professional's task is the minimization and mitigation of these sorts of harms. The Workplace Inspection Checklist of Hospitals tackles some new territory and tries to lay out all the possible ways in which injury can occur in these facilities. Insert Figure 12.43.[85]

12.6 CONCLUSION

Private security is an industry that has spread its institutional influences in dramatic and very concrete ways. Whether at local colleges or universities, hospitals or facilities for the emotionally handicapped, houses of worship or art and cultural institutions, the industry provides direct security services to all of these locations. And there are good reasons for this—first, the industry is oriented toward the consumers and attendees of these locales, delivering a customer-based and customer satisfaction orientation that makes security a friendlier and more compatible offering than when compared with traditional police services. Secondly, the industry has mastered the art of protecting these facilities by their long-standing participation. Who better to protect the assets of art and cultural exhibitions than those who have been doing so for generations? Who is capable of blending in with the house of worship or college, the state trooper, or the security specialist? Thirdly, who has the flexibility to adapt and adjust in its service approach, a public bureaucracy, or a company hoping to please a client? There are other reasons too but suffice it say, that private security owns these territories for good cause.

The chapter not only gives advice on the best practices in each of these institutional settings but also provides forms, checklist, documents, and templates for said tasks. It delivers comprehensive advice on the various levels of certification and the professional associations and groups that guide industry development.

---

[84] U.S. Department of Health & Human Services, *Hospital All-Hazards Self-Assessment* (n.d.), at https://www.cdc.gov/phpr/healthcare/documents/hah_508_compliant_final.pdf, last accessed August 31, 2016.

[85] Victorian Council Trades Hall, Workplace Inspection Checklist for Hospitals, http://www.ohsrep.org.au/__data/assets/word_doc/0016/50434/chkhospitals.doc, last accessed August 31, 2016.

Workplace Inspection Checklist for Hospitals

Key:

1	2	3	4	5
Poor		Satisfactory	Good	

Stairways

1. Free of obstacles
2. Step surfaces slippery
3. Carpet intact
4. Stairs and grab rails in good condition
5. Fire doors are closed

1	2	3	4	5

Aisles and floors

6. Free of obstruction
7. Carpet intact
8. In good repair
9. Slippery
10. Smoke doors free from obstacles
11. Appropriate footwear worn by staff

1	2	3	4	5

Lighting

12. Adequate illumination
13. Good natural lighting
14. No direct or reflected glare
15. Light fittings clean and in good repair
16. No single fluorescent tubes
17. Exit signs laminated
18. Night lights fitted

1	2	3	4	5

Windows

19. Lockable
20. Controlled opening height
21. In good condition
22. Fly screens are in good condition

1	2	3	4	5

Storage

23. Adequate
24. Materials/equipment stacked
25. Obstructing access
26. Safety steps provided for high storage
27. Designed to minimise manual handling
    a. light plant/substance/goods stored at higher level than heavy plant/substance goods
    b. in frequently used plant/substances/goods stored at ground level or over shoulder height
28. Shelves are free of dust and rubbish

1	2	3	4	5

Figure 12.43 Workplace inspection checklist for hospitals.

(Continued)

Equipment

General

	1	2	3	4	5
29. Adequate work space to use					
30. Fitted with brakes					
31. Adjustable					
32. In good repair					
33. Regular ongoing maintenance attended (check dates)					
Beds All beds are:					
34. Height adjustable					
35. Fitted with brakes					
36. Cotsides fitted					
37. Accommodates all lifting machines					

Office areas

	1	2	3	4	5
38. The office chairs are adjustable					
39. There is sufficient leg room for the worker					
40. There is foot support for the worker if required					
41. The chair controls are within easy reach					
42. Arms are provided where necessary					
43. There is adequate space to work in					
44. If the chair has castors is it on carpet?					
45. Shelving for manuals and folders					

Screen based equipment

There is:

	1	2	3	4	5
46. Sufficient contrast					
47. Glare (screen)					
48. Glare (external)					
49. Variation from keyboard duties					
50. Work station is adjustable to meet individual needs: • monitor • desk • keyboard • document holder provided • sufficient room to work in					

Waste disposal

	1	2	3	4	5
51. Correct bins provided for:					
a. General – paper, etc.					
b. Sharps					
c. Food					
d. Other: infected / cytotoxic / glass (indicate which)					
52. Appropriate color-coded bags being used					
53. Bins are vermin proof					

Figure 12.43 (Continued)   Workplace inspection checklist for hospitals.   (*Continued*)

Oxygen cylinders

	1	2	3	4	5
54. Trolley provided and used					
55. Cylinder stabilisation – straps / chains - provided					
- used					
56. Empty cylinders stored separately and labelled					
57. Stores advised a replacement is required					
58. Replacement is prompt					
59. Warning signs displayed					
60. There is sufficient oxygen in the cylinder					
61. Frequency checked when not used. Specify					

Hazardous substances

	1	2	3	4	5
62. A material safety data sheet fore each chemical used (including cleaning agent)					
63. Containment materials available for spills					
64. Personal protective equipment:					
• available					
• used correctly					
• suitable					
65. Disposal procedure satisfactory					
66. Flammable agents in a flameproof cupboard					
67. Storage of minimal quantities in the workplace					
68. Ventilation with extraction available at source					
69. Sufficient room to use product					

Physical hazards

	1	2	3	4	5
70. Are cleaning signs used appropriately?					
71. Are all exits clear?					
72. Are all verandahs clear?					

Electrical

	1	2	3	4	5
73. Power cords frayed / damaged					
74. Power cords in the way					
75. Double adaptors used					
76. Unchecked equipment being used					
77. Equipment not in use properly stored					
78. Is equipment checked regularly (check dates)					

Staff amenities

	1	2	3	4	5
79. Washrooms clean					
80. Toilet clean					

Figure 12.43 (Continued)   Workplace inspection checklist for hospitals.   (*Continued*)

Fire and evacuation

Ask staff member:

	1	2	3	4	5
82. Have all staff attended Emergency Procedure lectures/ training?					
83. Do staff know fire procedure?					
84. What is the procedure if you find or suspect a fire?					
a. activate break glass alarm					
b. the hose reel: when last checked? (check dates)					
85. Do staff know evacuation procedure?					
86. Identify lateral evacuation points if fire was located (specify area)					
87. Do the staff know:					
a. the different fire extinguishers and hose reels?					
b. how to use them?					
88. The evacuation kit is available and complete					
89. Do the staff know where the floor plan is for their area?					

Environment

Ask staff:

	1	2	3	4	5
90. Is the area:					
a. too hot?					
b. too cold?					
91. Taps are drip free when turned off					
92. Wet areas:					
• nonslip surface					
• water contained within the area					
93. Drug storage areas are locked:					
• - drug cupboards					
• - drug fridge					
• - drug trolley					
• - drug keys are being carried by a Registered Nurse					
94. Medical Emergency Staff know:					
• where equipment is stored					
• drugs					
• resus equipment					
• suction					

Lifting machine/equipment

	1	2	3	4	5
95. Brakes fitted					
96. Wheels in good order					
97. Free of oil leaks					
98. Slings in good condition					
99. Correct slings available					

Bed bath

	1	2	3	4	5
100. Brakes working					
101. Hydraulics working					
102. Vinyl in good state					
103 Trolley corners have fittings					

Suction machine

	1	2	3	4	5
103. Wheels working					
104. Clean bottle					
105. Oil half way in site glass					
106. Suction working					
107. Pressure <50mHg					
108. Dilly bag: - Gloves Suction Catheters					

Figure 12.43 (Continued)   Workplace inspection checklist for hospitals.

Keywords

accessibility

active shooter

Clery Act

command and control center

Community Oriented Policing Services

continuity

cultural institutions

educational settings

Emergency Operations Plan

environmental sensors

hate crimes

institutional security

motion detection equipment

professional associations

risk assessment

risk management

school resource officer

school risk assessment

security

special collections

vulnerability analysis

Discussion questions

1. Review the museum security systems diagram in Figure 12.7, and then select a local facility to profile. Discuss if the systems in the diagram are utilized, if evident. Also discuss further recommendations that could be implemented to security the facility.

2. Two theories of security officers in the educational setting are popular—COPS program and the Congressional Research Service. Compare and contrast these programs and discuss when one may be more appropriate than the other.

3. Discuss the contributing factors to violence and attack on religious centers and propose measures to alleviate the threat by consulting the risk assessment template, the hazardous materials template, and the fire prevention checklist.

4. Choose five of the variables that must be accounted for in continuity planning for a hospital and discuss recommendations for inclusion in the hospital risk assessment.

5. Discuss how memberships in a professional organization or professional certifications can assist the security officer in special security settings.

CHAPTER 13

Private security
Hospitality, gaming, event, and mall property

OBJECTIVES

After completing this chapter, the student will be able to

1. Recognize that hotels have become favored targets for terrorists due to the widespread impact the destruction causes and list recommendations to protect these facilities.
2. Recall the key vulnerabilities of U.S. lodging industry and apply them as necessary.
3. Review the various educational certifications available in the hospitality sector.
4. Discuss how security firms take the lead in the day-to-day operations event security, operating under the direction of team leadership, and in coordination and partnership with public police entities.
5. Demonstrate an understanding of the complex security challenges commonly faced in event security and applied in a global, massive customer-based setting.
6. Identify the unique security challenges faced by malls and other retail establishments, and address recommendations for the safety and security of these environments.
7. Outline the various occupational opportunities for gaming surveillance officers and general security officers in the expanding casino and gaming industry.
8. Describe how best practices in day-to-day operations have prompted calls for higher levels of professionalism, research, and continuing education and have expanded educational certifications for the gaming industry.

13.1 INTRODUCTION

The private security industry plays in integral role in the prevention, deterrence, and detection of theft and property offenses in a host of institutional settings, so much so that few sectors of the American economy do not encounter the many services offered. Throughout this text, we have discovered how many contexts the industry fits and in this chapter, our analysis turns to another class of institutional settings, all of which are highly entrepreneurial locales where risk takers and investors have much at stake. For example, the hospitality industry, comprising mostly hotels and lodgings, is a fast-moving, fast growth industry desperate for best practices to secure the vast assets the industry owns and cares for. The sheer volume of installations in need of protection, from so many chains and brands, makes this a constant area of opportunity for the private security industry. Hospitality connotes more than lodging but includes food service, restaurant, and bar/liquor industry, and in each of these specific genres, similar patterns of growth and corresponding security concerns rest side by side. In the case of liquor establishments, combined with entertainment, the challenges of security can be daunting. See Figure 13.1.

In the bar and tavern sector, the private security industry continues its traditional asset protection function though its emphasis today is equally geared to the safety and care of its customer base, the prevention of felonies on the

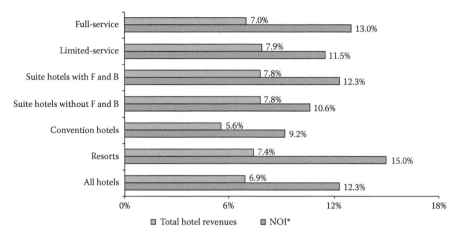

(*)-Before deductions for capital reserves, rent, interest, income taxes, depreciation, and amortization.

Figure 13.1 2014 U.S. hotel revenues and profits. (From PKF Hospitality Research, CBRE Company; 2015 Trends in the Hotel Industry Report.)

premises and preparedness for attacks from jihadis who find these locales fitting for messaging their warped ideology. See Figure 13.2.

Gaming and casino institutions have seen rapid growth well beyond the traditional placements in Atlantic City, New Jersey and Last Vegas, Nevada.[1] The Center for Gaming Research and the University of Nevada at Las Vegas (UNLV) paint a pretty rosy picture of growth and corresponding opportunity for the security industry. See Figure 13.3.[2]

Figure 13.2 Orlando Pulse Nightclub; Secretary of Homeland Security Jeh Johnson visits Pulse Nightclub on the three-month anniversary of the shooting that left 49 people dead in Orlando, September 12, 2016. Secretary Johnson viewed the inside of the nightclub before laying flowers at a makeshift memorial outside of the club where he spoke to a chaplain there who had assisted those impacted by the shooting. (Official DHS photo by Jetta Disco.)

---

[1] See D.G. Schwartz, *United States Commercial Casino Revenues* (Las Vegas, NV: Center for Gaming Research, University Libraries, University of Nevada Las Vegas, 2016).

[2] *Ibid.*

	2006	2007	2008	2009	2010	2011	2012	2013	2014	2015
Colorado	782,099	816,130	715,880	734,591	759,610	750,109	766,254	748,707	745,898	794,761
Delaware	651,734	612,407	588,923	564,239	571,376	547,872	549,643	471,544	408,206	400,854
Florida	10,300	201,132	225,290	216,747	329,127	381,122	427,889	467,587	507,454	530,662
Illinois	1,923,528	1,983,387	1,568,727	1,428,923	1,373,422	1,477,601	1,638,168	1,551,312	1,465,353	2,352,427
Indiana	2,576,192	2,623,939	2,665,663	2,798,195	2,796,005	2,732,773	2,685,503	2,434,284	2,156,766	2,132,889
Iowa	1,253,710	1,363,055	1,419,545	1,380,744	1,368,074	1,423,998	1,467,165	1,416,717	1,396,000	1,424,352
Kansas	–	–	–	1,990	37,788	44,729	341,146	365,079	353,539	367,783
Louisiana	2,567,415	2,566,271	2,583,834	2,455,526	2,373,930	2,374,244	2,388,767	2,442,900	2,472,502	3,242,009
Maine	37,517	43,252	50,515	59,198	61,667	59,453	82,994	126,274	540,483	516,615
Maryland	–	–	–	–	27,596	155,709	377,814	746,914	931,092	1,098,426
Michigan	1,303,303	1,335,016	1,359,585	1,339,479	1,377,929	1,424,445	1,416,734	1,349,504	1,332,783	1,376,408
Mississippi	2,570,884	2,891,546	2,721,139	2,464,662	2,388,997	2,239,084	2,251,090	2,136,624	2,070,157	2,097,066
Missouri	1,592,000	1,592,000	1,682,000	1,735,000	1,795,000	1,815,000	1,775,000	1,706,738	1,660,097	1,701,896
Nevada	12,622,044	12,849,137	11,599,124	10,392,675	10,404,731	10,700,994	10,860,715	11,142,915	11,009,684	11,113,830
New Jersey	5,217,613	4,920,786	4,544,961	3,943,171	3,565,047	3,317,720	3,051,435	2,862,069	2,742,128	2,536,729
New Mexico	238,310	244,780	258,080	243,940	247,350	248,920	241,480	241,300	257,660	265,960
New York	426,305	828,205	947,275	1,019,279	1,087,749	1,259,813	1,802,212	1,925,565	1,898,336	1,950,964
Ohio	–	–	–	–	–	–	429,826	1,070,662	1,457,634	1,642,903
Oklahoma	73,675	78,698	92,477	94,130	99,881	106,229	113,055	112,853	113,370	111,370
Pennsylvania	31,568	1,039,031	1,615,566	1,964,570	2,486,408	3,025,048	3,158,318	3,113,929	3,069,078	3,173,789
Rhode Island	406,504	447,998	475,040	461,169	477,050	512,865	527,959	516,742	550,912	551,923
South Dakota	89,828	98,223	102,264	101,898	106,187	100,898	107,384	103,019	100,509	101,680
West Virginia	975,990	932,210	951,210	905,590	877,650	958,700	948,810	796,589	704,947	722,170
Total	35,350,519	37,467,203	36,167,098	34,305,716	34,612,574	35,657,326	37,409,361	37,849,827	37,944,585	40,207,466

Figure 13.3 U.S. annual commercial casino gaming revenues, 2006–2015.

Figure 13.4   Training exercise on evidence collection at mall facility. (Courtesy of FBI.)

It is now rare to encounter a state without a casino operation and there are also claims of "glut" and overbuilding.[3] The same conclusion can be reached concerning event installations, such as stadiums and sports facilities, entertainment venues, and large-scale meeting centers. Event security has become a complex business due to the potentiality of large-scale harm, especially that desired by the terrorist. Other risks need to be planned and prepared for as well.

At other places in this text, considerable attention has been paid to retail establishments where crime prevention is a primary concern for the security industry, and office buildings and complexes have been already closely examined from a host of applications including but not limited to workplace violence, internal crime, employee and personnel background and screening, and just as critically the many demands these locales have in relation to physical security requirements. At this juncture, our analysis turns to larger retail facilities such as the mall and mega-retail complex where we have unfortunately witnessed far too much tragedy in the last decade. See Figure 13.4.

Web Exercise: Read the transcript that captures the terrorist motivation at the mass shooting and killing at the PULSE nightclub in Orlando, Florida at https://www.fbi.gov/contact-us/field-offices/tampa/news/press-releases/investigative-update-regarding-pulse-nightclub-shooting.

13.2 PRIVATE SECURITY AND THE HOSPITALITY INDUSTRY

The hotel and lodging industry is an area of vibrant growth in the international economy, and with the rise of international travel, especially by corporate and business leaders, entertainers and sports figures, and politicians and world leaders, the significance of delivering a safe and secure place to lodge has never been as important. The American Society for Industrial Security (ASIS) has designated hospitality as one of its councils—*hospitality, entertainment, and tourism security*—its mission being

> Champions the continuous improvement of security and safety through increased professionalism, constant improvement in training programs, certifications, and establishment of best practices for the discipline. The council works with soft targets, including hotels, vacation and time share rentals, congregate residential centers, amusement parks and open air venues, and tourism officials for positive effect on guests, employees, and assets.[4]

---

[3] See D. Holmes, US Gaming Industry Surpasses $70 Billion in Annual Revenue as Organic Growth Returns in 2015, *Casino J.* (March 2, 2016), at http://www.casinojournal.com/articles/90379-us-gaming-growth?v=preview, last accessed September 1, 2016.

[4] ASIS International, Hospitality, Entertainment and Tourism Security webpage, at https://www.asisonline.org/Membership/Member-Center/Councils/lodg/Pages/default.aspx.

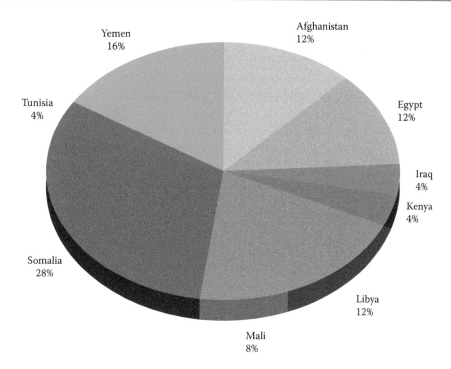

Figure 13.5 Top countries for terrorist attacks at hotels in 2015. (From IntelCenter Database at http://intelcenter.com/reports/charts/hotel-location-country-2015/#gs.cupsTBc.)

Hotels are not immune to the ravages of crime and terror with kidnapping, murders, abductions, and sexual assaults of every level now common place. The "risks are wide-ranging…from petty theft to murderers who lure women to hotels."[5] Hoteliers must provide a reasonably safe place to stay and have a general expectation that the lodging offered will not result in harm or loss to the customer. "Hotels are meant to be welcoming homes away from home, luxury getaways, or ports in the storm."[6] Hotels have also become as noted earlier favored targets for terrorists due to the widespread impact the destruction causes. It is no coincidence that the bulk of hotel terror targets are in the world's most unstable countries. See Figure 13.5.

The Department of Homeland Security (DHS) and the American Hotel and Lodging Association (AHLA) have cataloged the more predictable security and safety challenges that the hospitality industry faces day to day. Security firms and consultants will be kept very, very busy by all of these possibilities where injury and harm can occur.

Among the key vulnerabilities of the U.S. lodging industry are the following:

- *Resistance to a fortress mentality*: Many hotel companies must balance the need for enhanced security screening with positive customer perception. At the same time, increased security at hotels overseas is accepted and, in some locations, expected as a safety measure. There are many instances where U.S. hotels increase security and screening but this is usually done for an event or at the request of a special guest or client that is either staying at the hotel or participating in some function on hotel grounds.

- *Unrestricted public access*: Openness to the public is a feature common to hotels, and it contributes to their vulnerability. In general, hotels may have no security to screen guests for explosives or other weapons before they enter the facility.

- *Differentiating between suspicious activity and tourist activity*: Hotels are expected to have strangers flowing in and out of their properties daily. Tourists and terrorists are similar in that they both are inquisitive about the surroundings and they like to take photographs.

---

[5] L. Spadanuta, Always Room for Improvement, *Sec. Mgmt* (February 2011), at https://sm.asisonline.org/Pages/Always-Room-for-Improvement.aspx.

[6] *Ibid.*

- *Unrestricted access to service areas*: In some hotels, because of fire exit requirements, some doors connecting service areas to public areas must remain unlocked at all times, allowing anyone access to the hotel's back of the house operations, which may include areas such as food storage, food preparation, utilities, chemical storage, etc.

- *Unrestricted access to peripheral areas*: Hotels can be vulnerable within their own parking lots or parking garages where guests and vehicles have access with little or no screening.

- *Unrestricted access to areas adjacent to buildings*: Most hotels have guest drop-off and pick-up points that are close to buildings. These points are generally not distant enough to prevent blasts from explosives packed in vehicles from inflicting significant damage to the buildings and guests. Generally, security personnel do not inspect vehicles stopped at these points for weapons or explosives.

- *Access by suppliers, vendors, and maintenance workers to nonpublic areas*: Many people other than hotel employees are given access to areas of the facility that are not open to the public. Such individuals include construction crews, maintenance personnel, and cleaning crews. In general, hotel security does not screen these individuals. These individuals and their vehicles often enter through loading docks, mailrooms, or service entrances that may not be secured or monitored.

- *Staff turnover*: There is a high turnover rate in housekeeping, wait staff, and security personnel at hotel and motels. This necessitates maintaining regular training for staff. Security is not the sole responsibility of the security staff; all hotel employees should emphasize and practice established security procedures and processes. Staff members that are not as familiar with their hotel's facilities and operations may be less likely to be aware of an unusual situation or individual.

- *Limited employee background checks*: Many hotels, especially smaller ones, may conduct minimal or no background checks when hiring staff.

- *Limited security staff*: Many hotels have only a small security staff and rely mostly on local law enforcement to handle incidents. Larger hotels may have a larger security staff, sometimes under a contract arrangement with a private security firm. The extent to which these personnel are trained and equipped to deal with terrorist incidents varies widely.

- *Lack of exercises for emergency plans*: While some hotels, particularly the larger ones, have documented emergency operations plans, exercises of the plans are limited. It is difficult to interrupt normal business activities to conduct an emergency exercise. Coordination of hotel emergency efforts with those of local emergency responders may be lacking.

- *Multiuse facilities*: Hotels may be integrated with other facilities, such as malls, casinos, convention centers, universities, marinas, and airports. Each of these situations has its own site- and situation-specific vulnerabilities.

- *Unprotected heating ventilating and air conditioning (HVAC) systems*: In some hotels, access to the HVAC systems is not controlled or monitored; air intakes may be in publicly accessible areas. Additionally, HVAC equipment may not be in secured rooms equipped with intrusion-detection equipment. In some cases, it may be necessary to shut down these systems to prevent outdoor-borne contaminants from entering the building as a terrorist may quickly contaminate a building with a biological or chemical agent by releasing it through the hotel's ventilation system.

- *Unprotected utility services*: Some hotels have not secured and do not monitor the utility services (e.g., electric power, natural gas, telecommunications, emergency generator and water supply) for intrusion.

- *Structural configurations*: Key configurations include atrium, tower, slab, and dispersed facility design. Building configurations with guest rooms clustered around a central core or around a multistory atrium may be more vulnerable to several types of threats than those facilities with individual units or low-rise clusters of rooms.

- *Building height*: Low-rise structures (one to two stories) are less vulnerable than high-rise structures. In structures with more than five stories, guest evacuation issues may be of greater concern in situations when elevators are unusable.

- *Building designs are not security oriented*: Many hotel buildings, particularly older ones, may not have been designed with security considerations in mind. Examples of such designs are those that include large areas of glass that is not shatter or blast resistant, structural supports that cannot handle large overpressures from explosives, and doors and windows that are not tamper-resistant.

- *Multiple locations to place explosives or hazardous agents*: Hotels have numerous locations where an explosives package (e.g., a backpack) or a container with hazardous agents can be left without being immediately noticed. These include trash containers, planters, counters, and decorative fixtures.[7]

Given all these potential negatives, the private security industry serves a critical function, both in terms of human intelligence and physical security in assuring a safe location. The industry itself sees extraordinary growth in the sector, but to do so will require a generous investment in both technology and exceptional personnel.

In addition, the industry has amassed and installed the most sophisticated technology in these very complex facilities and uses not only traditional CCTV technology, cameras, and other recording monitors but also access control system to the larger facility and the room itself. See Figure 13.6.

"Electronic locks, specifically offer hotels numerous benefits" none more useful than the "record of key use creating a database of who passed through a door and when the activity occurred."[8]

What further complicates matters is that both internal and external actors become perpetrators. Hence, a hotel's need for background employee screening is more dramatic than many other sectors of the economy. Front-office personnel have access to sensitive cyber information for credit purposes; cleaning and maintenance staff regular access to the personal property within each room and a special class of criminal entrepreneurs "stays" at hotels for nefarious reasons, to carry out criminality.[9] To not check these potential avenues of crime guarantees a hotel's limited lifespan for guests rightfully expect that their inner sanctums in room accommodations and safety to their personal beings and financial data be protected. To fail in these areas spells economic disaster for the hotel enterprise[10]—"inadequate security repercussions" beyond hotel guests losing property, but suffering some high-level victimization including rape and murder, and opening the hotel up to "criminal acts of third parties" and "civil litigation against property owners."[11] Security considerations encompass more than crime and terror since large facilities have extraordinary capacity for mass casualties caused by natural disasters, fires and earthquakes, and catastrophic weather events. Hotels must gauge safety from the date of architectural inception. See Figure 13.7.

Figure 13.6 CCTV room at hotel installation. (Courtesy of DHS.)

[7] U.S. Department of Homeland Security & American Hotel & Lodging Association, Protective Measures Guide for the US Lodging Industry, 2-2 (n.d.), at https://info.publicintelligence.net/DHS-HotelProtection.pdf.

[8] M. Beaudry & H. Skip Brandt, Suite Security, 42 *Sec. Mgmt* 73–74 (1998).

[9] *Ibid.* at 73.

[10] D. Donaldson, 12 Ways to Increase Hotel Security, *Smart Strategy* (November 12, 2013).

[11] *Ibid.*

Figure 13.7 Older buildings often require retrofitting of physical and other security measures. (From DHS, https://info.publicintelligence.net/DHS-HotelProtection.pdf.)

Security companies provide much of the technology to assure a safe environment, such as sprinkler and smoke detection systems, motion and infrared detectors, and communications systems that give proper warning. "The age of the property has a strong influence on its safety and security scores. In general, the newer the hotel the more effective its safety measures are."[12]

The AHLA publishes a *Guest Safety Tip Card,* which becomes central to any solid security plan—which outlines the following recommendations:

1. Don't answer the door to your guestroom without verifying who it is. If a person claims to be an employee, call the front desk and ask if someone from their staff is supposed to have access to your room and for what purpose.

2. Keep your room key with you at all times and don't needlessly display it in public. Should you misplace it, please notify the front desk immediately.

---

[12] C.A. Enz & M.K. Taylor, The Safety and Security of U.S. Hotels: A Post-September-11 Report [Electronic version], 43 *Cornell Hotel & Restaur. Admin. Q.* 119–136 (2002), at http://scholarship.sha.cornell.edu/articles/364/, last accessed September 1, 2016.

3. Close the door securely whenever you are in your room and use all of the locking devices provided.

4. Check to see that any sliding glass doors or windows and any connecting room doors are locked.

5. Don't invite strangers to your room.

6. Be aware of potential phone scams and prank calls to your guestroom. Hotel employees will never request credit card or personal information over the phone, nor will they advise a guest to damage hotel property.

7. Place all valuables in the hotel or motel's safe deposit box.

8. When returning to your hotel or motel late in the evening, be aware of your surroundings, stay in well-lighted areas, and use the main entrance.

9. Take a few moments and locate the nearest exit that may be used in the event of an emergency.

10. If you see any suspicious activity, notify the hotel operator or a staff member.

As can be gleaned thus far, hotels have varying levels of defense when it comes to crime and safety matters. From the perimeter of the facility to the guest room, from the hallways and stairwells to the evacuation routes, the hotel security team engages at a variety of places throughout the complex. Any large-scale hotel will have security officers on staff, although their presence will be the front line as supervisory personnel oversee the operation, cyber personnel assure the integrity of financial transactions, and safety consultants monitor equipment to insure functioning systems as well as technology experts assuring the workability of access control and video and CCTV systems. Even the front door may be staffed with a "doorman" serving in a security and safety capacity. The typical hierarchical chart of a hotel security force might be as shown in Figure 13.8.

See Figure 13.9.

Web Exercise: Discover the job listings for hotel security managers at the Institute of Hotel Security Management at http://www.hotelsecuritymanagement.org/job-listings/view-submission/1350.

13.2.1 Special protocols for hotel and hospitality security

While coverage of every imaginable context for hotel and hospitality security would drive this text beyond ordinary capacity, a few special protocols are worth adding to the mix of this topic—especially as we consider recent terrorist events in hotels, nightclubs, and other hospitality venues. The recent terrorist activities in France and Orlando give security experts great pause on the possibilities of human tragedy.

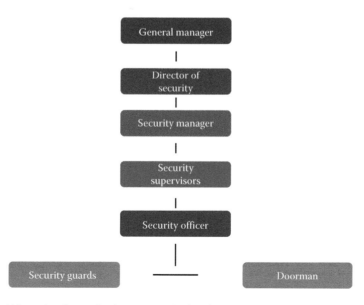

Figure 13.8 Organizational hierarchy of security department at a hotel.

Chief Security Officer / Security Manager

Work Locations: Bali Airport Jalan Airport Ngurah Rai, Kuta Bali 80361

This position is for INDONESIAN PASSPORT HOLDERS ONLY
Please do not apply unless you are an Indonesian National
There are NO opportunities for Work Permits and NO Sponsorship for foreigners

A Chief Security Officer / Security Manager with us manages the security team, policies, systems and procedures that keep Guests, Team Members, and others safe while on and around the hotel property.

What will it be like to work for us?

We are an award-winning, upscale, yet affordable, hotel brand. We continually strive to ensure today's busy travelers have everything they need to be the most productive on the road, no matter the occasion. With high levels of service and amenities usually only found in pricier hotels, guests count on us to help them be successful when they're on the road.

If you know what it feels like to succeed and you can perform on an award-winning team, you may be just the person we are looking for to work as a Team Member.

What will I be doing?

As a Chief Security Officer / Security Manager, you are responsible for the safety and security of all Guests, Team Members and contractors, and visitors while at the hotel. A Chief Security Officer / Security Manager is also responsible for the safety and security of the hotel premises. Specifically, the Chief Security Officer / Security Manager will perform the following tasks at the highest level of service

- Oversee all security related matters in the hotel
- Advise Hotel Management on all security related issues
- Lead Security Team and development of Team Members
- Review, regularly, all policies, systems, and procedures, including emergency drills and bomb procedures
- Drive continual improvement and enhancements to security standards
- Communicate effectively and efficiently with external agencies including police, fire authorities, and other related services

What are we looking for?

A Chief Security Officer / Security Manager are always working on behalf of our Guests and working with other Team Members. To successfully fill this role, you should maintain the attitude, behaviors, skills, and values that follow

- Previous security experience, preferably working within an industry which monitored large volumes of people movement
- Previous experience leading and managing a Security / law enforcement team
- In-depth knowledge of security related systems, practices, legislation, and latest technologies
- Excellent inter-personal skills and personal presentation

What benefits will I receive?

Your benefits will include a competitive starting salary and holiday entitlement. As an employee you will become a member of our Club which provides reduced hotel room rates in our hotels worldwide, plus discounts on products and services offered by our hotel and its global partners. We look forward to explaining in detail the range of excellent benefits that you would expect from a global hotel organization like our.

EOE/AA/Disabled/Veterans
Schedule: Full-time
Shift: Full Availability
Job Level: Manager
Job: Security and Loss Prevention

Figure 13.9   Career profile: Chief security officer—hotel chain.

An active customer base is crucial to safety and security in any large venue, hotel facility or aligned building or locale, such as a bar or nightclub, a common reality in entertainment hotels. Customers using the hotel can be expected to be active participants in warning the authorities about bizarre and notorious behavior.[13] DHS produced an advisory to this effect after a series of bombings at hotel installations. See Figure 13.10.

Web Exercise: Take the short course in hotel security produced by the Commercial Facility Sector of the DHS at https://share.dhs.gov/p23934518/.

13.2.1.1 Risk assessment in hotels and hospitality

Hotels, lodging, and other hospitality vendors need to conduct risk assessments of their facilities to detect vulnerabilities. Hotels are not always designed with security as the highest or upper-tier priority and that is why this sort of analysis is so critical. The Hotel Assessment Template, crafted by the AHLA, covers not only the basic themes of risk and vulnerability analysis but also highly specialized facility questions that are solely applicable to the hotel industry. Appendix D[14] contains the Hotel Assessment Form.

13.2.1.2 Bomb assessment in hotel and hospitality facilities

In all of the settings discussed thus far, though a rare event, bombs and other destructive devices have been unfortunately encountered. Hotel and entertainment staff must be vigilant from every imaginable entry point. Even the mail and packages have to be closely scrutinized. See Figure 13.11.[15]

Delivery trucks, unauthorized personnel, and suspicious looking characters out of the usual ebb and flow of hotel and hospitality life must be watched and checked. These various tasks are not only watched by the installed technology of the facility but also the layers of personnel starting at the door to the front desk to the hotel housekeeping staff. In nightclubs, that scrutiny continues unabated. See Figure 13.12[16] for a bomb assessment report.

13.2.1.3 Special training and licensure for nightclub operators and licensees

That nightclubs are now targets for terrorists is a self-evident conclusion, and even if we do not accept this deduction, nightclubs have always presented challenging security dilemmas. The mix of alcohol, the prevalence of drugs in some circles, and the progressive, all night mentality are bound to produce social and individual quarrels. As a result, governmental entities have increasing security requirements for those seeking a license to operate nightclub facilities. For example, the District of Columbia now requires a fully developed security plan and comprehensive proof of staff training at the facility. Licensees now must achieve the following level of preparation and planning:

1. Training provided to the establishment's personnel, including conflict resolution training, procedures for handling violent incidents and emergencies, as well as the establishment's procedures for contacting the Metropolitan Police Department (MPD);
2. Procedures for crowd control and preventing overcrowding;
3. Procedures for permitting patrons to enter;
4. Locations both inside and outside the establishment where security personnel will be stationed;
5. Number and location of security cameras both inside and outside the establishment;
6. Procedures for preventing patron intoxication;
7. Procedures for preventing persons under the age of 21 from receiving or consuming alcohol;
8. Procedures for maintaining an incident log; and
9. Procedures for preserving a crime scene.[17]

---

[13] See M. Blades, Hotel Security after Mumbai: Resources and Guidelines for Security, *Sec. Tech. Executive* (February 2009), at 32.

[14] AHLA, Hotel Security and Safety Assessment Form (n.d.), at http://www.ahla.com/uploadedfiles/ahlaosachotelassessmentform2014.pdf.

[15] New York City Police Department & New York Nightlife Association, *Best Practices for Nightlife Establishments* 22 (2nd ed., 2011), at http://www.nyc.gov/html/nypd/downloads/pdf/crime_prevention/Best-Practices-Nightlife-2d-Ed-2011.pdf.

[16] *Ibid.*

[17] See Alcoholic Beverage Regulation Administration, *Quick Guide: Security Plans* (2013), at http://abra.dc.gov/sites/default/files/dc/sites/abra/publication/attachments/Quick_Guide_Security_Plan_1_0.pdf.

DHS
Hotel & Lodging Advisory

Are You Aware of
Suspicious Activity?

Hotels and lodging facilities can be venues for criminal or terrorist activities. Be alert to any persons who behave suspiciously or engage in unusual actions; these may be indications of criminal or terrorist activity.

Suspicious Behavior:

- Nervous or evasive guest or visitor attitudes, overly concerned with privacy.
- Denial of access to room or refusal of room cleaning for extended stay.
- Insistence on cash payment.
- Attempts to gain access to restricted areas.
- Individuals taking notes, pictures, or videos of hotel.

Suspicious Items:

- Large amounts of unusual substances (acetone, peroxide, drain cleaner)
- Luggage emanating fumes/odors
- Disassembled electrical components (wires, circuit boards, batteries)
- Plans, drawings, schematics, maps

What Can You Do?

 Understand how criminals or terrorists could use your facility for their own purposes.

 Promptly alert your management and appropriate authorities when you see suspicious behavior or items, or unusual activity.

 Report something if it looks or feels wrong – security is everyone's responsibility.

Concerned? Report your concerns to your supervisor, Security Manager, or Hotel General Manager.

Figure 13.10   DHS: hotel and lodging advisory.

The District of Columbia, as in other jurisdictions, now requires a filed security plan that details compliance and proper preparation. The plan must address these areas of concern:

a. Conflict resolution training

b. Procedures for handling violent incidents, emergencies, and calling the police

c. Procedures for crowd control and preventing overcrowding

SUSPICIOUS MAIL OR PACKAGES

- Leave the mail or package where it was found. Do not disturb. Do not try to clean the substance.

- Immediately call *911*

- Clear the immediate area of all persons and keep others away.

- Cordon off the immediate area.

- Instruct people in the immediate area to wash hands and other exposed skin with soap and water.

- Isolate exposed persons to a designated area away from the substance and await further instruction.

- List the names of the persons in the immediate area of the mail or package.

- Shut down all HVAC (heating, ventilation, air conditioning) systems.

- Document the location of mail or package.

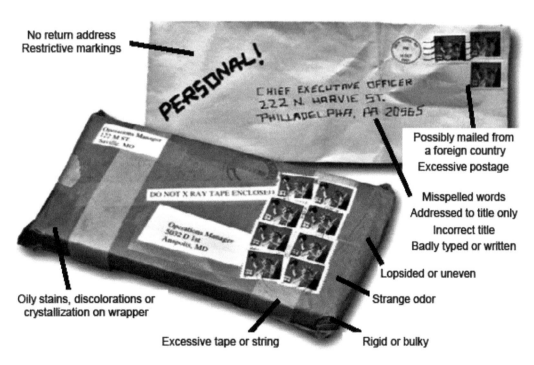

Figure 13.11 Suspicious mail and packaging. (From New York City Police Department.)

d. Procedures for permitting patrons to enter

e. Description of how security personnel are stationed inside and outside the establishment

f. Number and location of security cameras

g. Procedures to prevent patron intoxication

h. Procedures to prevent underage drinking

BOMB THREAT CHECKLIST

CALL 911   Remain calm and try to keep caller on the line.   **CALL** 911

EXACT WORDS OF CALLER:

_____

_____

_____

_____

Questions to ask the caller:

1. When is the bomb going to explode? _____
2. Where is the bomb right now? _____
3. What does the bomb look like? _____
4. What kind of bomb is it? _____
5. What will cause the bomb to explode? _____
6. Did you place the bomb? _____ Why? _____
7. Where are you? _____
8. What is your name? _____
9. What organization do you represent? _____

VOICE		MANNER		BACKGROUND NOISE	
Loud	☐	Calm	☐	Street	☐
Soft	☐	Coherent	☐	Bar/Restaurant	☐
Intoxicated	☐	Angry	☐	Factory	☐
High Pitched	☐	Emotional	☐	Subway	☐
Deep	☐	Laughing	☐	Office	☐
Accent	☐	Other	☐	Other	☐

Was caller male or female? _____
Was caller's voice familiar? _____
Did caller read a prepared statement? _____
Was caller well spoken? _____
What was approximate age of caller? _____
Telephone number where call was received? _____
Time call received: _____ Date call received: _____
Your name: _____ Your position: _____
Your telephone number: _____

Figure 13.12 Bomb assessment report. (From New York City Police Department.)

    i.   Procedures for maintaining an incident log

    j.   Procedures for preserving a crime scene

For the official reporting form, see Figure 13.13.[18]

In addition to all these requirements, there is a general recognition that the age of the "bouncer" is long over and that professionals in the security industry who apply brains more than muscle have become the new norm. Security professionals need apply a host of tactics that blend intelligence, crowd control, and crime prevention and yet still deal with the unruly and intoxicated patron.[19]

---

[18] Alcoholic Beverage Regulation Administration, Security Plan Submission Form, at http://abra.dc.gov/sites/default/files/dc/sites/abra/publication/attachments/Security_Plan_Submission_Form_0.pdf.

[19] See R. Witherspoon, *Security for Bars, Taverns, Lounges and Nightclubs* (2013), at http://www.security-expert.org/nightclubs.htm.

GOVERNMENT OF THE DISTRICT OF COLUMBIA
ALCOHOLIC BEVERAGE REGULATION ADMINISTRATION

SECURITY PLAN SUBMISSION FORM

IMPORTANT: You must answer either 'Yes' or 'Not Applicable' to all questions to ensure your compliance with the law. If you answer 'No' to any question, your security plan will likely be rejected and you will be asked to submit another security plan that complies with the law.

OFFICIAL USE ONLY	
Date Accepted:	Accepted by:

TO BE COMPLETED BY APPLICANT			

1. Licensee Name (Last, First, Middle):			2. Trade Name:	

3. Current License Class:			4. License Number:	

5. Address	City		State	Zip Code

6. Telephone Number:		7. Email	

8. I have attached a complete version of my security plan to this form, which contains my establishment's trade name, license number, and the date the plan was written.
   □ YES   □ NO

9. The attached security plan shall replace and supersede all prior security plans that may be found in ABRA's records.   □ YES   □ NO

10. The attached security plan describes the conflict resolution training provided to employees.   □ YES   □ NO

Provide the page number and section where this information may be found:

11. The attached security plan describes the establishment's procedures for handling violent incidents and emergencies and contacting the Metropolitan Police Department.   □ YES   □ NO

Provide the page number and section where this information may be found:

12. The attached security plan describes the establishment's procedures for controlling crowds and preventing overcrowding.   □ YES   □ NO

Provide the page number and section where this information may be found:

13. The attached security plan describes the establishment's procedures for permitting patrons to enter.   □ YES   □ NO

Provide the page number and section where this information may be found:

14. The attached security plan describes how your establishment stations security personnel both inside and outside the establishment.   □ YES   □ NO

Please attach a diagram of the establishment showing this information. Provide the page number and/or section where this information may be found:

15. Does your establishment contain security cameras?   □ YES   □ NO

16. How many security cameras may be found both inside and outside the establishment?

17. Does your camera system have the capability to save footage for at least thirty (30) days?
□ YES   □ NO   □ Not Applicable

Figure 13.13   Security plan submission form.   (*Continued*)

The International Nightlife Association has promulgated a 10-point plan that every security professional working in the industry must adhere to. By and through its Secure Nightlife Venue, and its Nightlight Secure Seal (see Figure 13.14) program, the industry group urges membership to address the following areas of concern:

1. *Legal*: Has a current business license and approved occupancy permit.
2. *Insurance*: Has a civil liability insurance with an insured capital based on its capacity.
3. *Certifications*: Security and control staff must be certified in security, food and drink safety training. Have written security procedures, protection and evacuation plans. Fire Equipment inspected regularly.
4. *Security*: Venue uses radio communication, metal detectors to forbid weapons & prevent terrorism attacks. Premium venue has an ID scanner and CCTV surveillance system in operation.

18. Does your establishment have the capability to provide a copy of your establishment's security footage to ABRA or the Metropolitan Police Department within 48 hours of receiving such a request. ☐ YES   ☐ NO   ☐ Not Applicable
19. The attached security plan describes where the establishment's indoor and outdoor security cameras are located. ☐ YES   ☐ NO   ☐ Not Applicable **Attach a diagram of the establishment showing this information to this application. Provide the page number and/or section where this information is located:**
20. REQUIRED AFFIRMATIONS I acknowledge, understand, and agree that if my establishment utilizes cameras, either now or at some point in the future, under D.C. Official Code § 25-402: (1) the establishment is obligated to ensure that all security cameras are operational; (2) the establishment is obligated to preserve the establishment's security footage for a minimum of thirty (30) days if the footage is related to the commission of a crime of violence or the presence of a firearm; and (3) the establishment is obligated to surrender any and all security footage requested by ABRA or the Metropolitan Police Department within 48 hours of the request. ☐ YES
21. The attached security plan describes your establishment's procedures for preventing patron intoxication.   ☐ YES   ☐ NO Provide the page number and section where this information may be found:
22. The attached security plan describes your establishment's procedures for ensuring that only patrons 21 years or older are served alcohol. ☐ YES   ☐ NO Provide the page number and section where this information may be found:
23. The attached security plan describes your establishment's procedures for maintaining an incident log.   ☐ YES   ☐ NO Provide the page number and section where this information may be found:
24. The attached security plan describes your establishment's procedures for preserving a crime scene.   ☐ YES   ☐ NO Provide the page number and section where this information may be found:
If applicant is a Sole proprietor, the individual must sign, if Partnership, each partner must sign, if Corporation, President or Vice President must sign, if LLC, managing member must sign the below certification. 25. "Certification: I hereby certify that the information in this application is true and correct. I also certify that the above licensee is the true and actual owner of the business." Please print your name, sign, and date the form on the lines provided below. Printed name:_____ _____   _____ Signature   Date Printed name:_____ _____   _____ Signature   Date Printed name:_____ _____   _____ Signature   Date
26. In what language do you need vital documents translated?

SPECIAL NOTICE

The District of Columbia will provide the appropriate services and auxiliary aids, including sign language interpreters, whenever necessary to ensure effective communication with members of the public who are deaf, hearing impaired or who have other disabilities affecting communications. Requests for services and auxiliary aids should be made at least ten (10) days prior to any scheduled hearing. Please notify the ADA Coordinator at (202) 442-4423.

Figure 13.13   (Continued) Security plan submission form.

5. *Safety*: Must have unobstructed Exits/Evacuation routes indicated with lighted signage. Emergency exit doors must have anti-panic bars and exit outward; to an evacuation area with 120 minutes' minimum stability or fire safe zone.
6. *Health*: Have a First-Aid Kit available. Provide water stations to help prevent heat stroke. Have clean and sanitary cooking and serving areas.
7. *Production*: Construction, decorative and structural elements must be low-flammability. Pyrotechnics and fire must be approved by a fire safety pro. If 10,000 + people are at one stage, you need video screens and speaker towers, but avoid ear damaging sound.
8. *Amenities*: Seating areas, shaded areas, well-stocked and clean toilets, eTickets and set-times schedule.

Figure 13.14 Security Nightlife Venue designation.

9. *Community*: Get creative and crowd source for every opportunity to showcase community art programs and artists anywhere and everywhere.
10. *Recycling*: Should offer something that benefits attendees, not trash that will end up on the ground or in a landfill. Sponsors can reward attendees for supporting recycling.[20]

Web Exercise: Read an interesting legal case that outlines standard-of-care issues that security is to provide in the nightclub setting and whether the security provided was in fact negligent in design at http://caselaw.findlaw.com/dc-court-of-appeals/1681422.html.

13.2.2 Certifications for security specialist in hospitality

The hotel industry has long known of the importance of trained professionals overseeing their vital industry. Special industry domains call for highly specialized professionals tackling the varied layers of security protections. While most of the protocols posed by the industry, in a general sense, are fully applicable to the hotel and hospitality settings, it is clear that narrowly tailored knowledge must be acquired. The AHLA has played a lead role in the development of certifications across the entire industry. Figure 13.15[21] lays out the wide array of certification levels and demonstrates the continuum and continuity of this knowledge at various gradations.

Security and safety is no different than the other content areas. Commencing with the security officer, progressing through the supervisor level, the final certification for the security director reaches a professional and content apex.

---

[20] International Nightlife Association, Nightlife Security Seal webpage, at http://nciaa.com/content.aspx?page_id=22&club_id=160641&module_id=195616.

[21] American Hotel & Lodging Educational Institute, Certification Career Path, at https://www.ahlei.org/uploadedFiles/Content/Certifications/ahleiCertificationCareerPath.pdf.

Certification Career Path

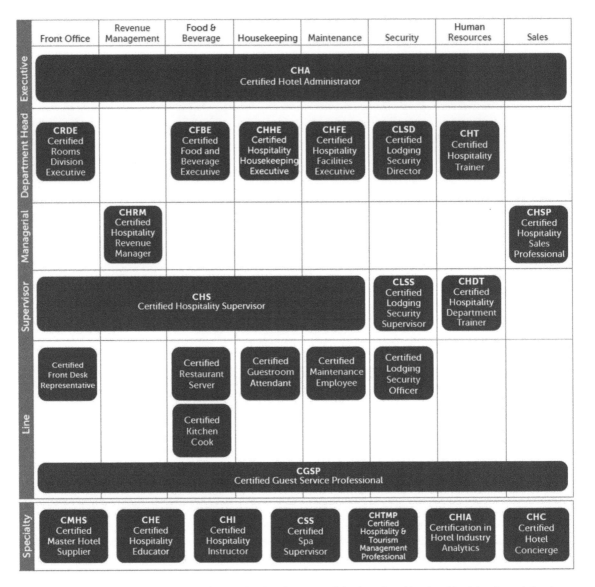

Figure 13.15   Hotel and lodging industry certification levels. (Courtesy of the American Hotel and Lodging Association.)

The Certified Lodging Security Supervisor Exam provides recognition for "effective human resources and emergency management expertise as well as sound judgment and practical skills. [Supervisors] must keep pace with change, improve their knowledge, and share their experience with others."[22]

See Figure 13.16.

13.2.2.1 Certification: National Host Security Training

Large hotels and entertainment venues need skilled security professionals to assure a safe and secure environment for patrons. Hence, while it is still an occupational direction in its infancy, the industry is increasingly calling for more training and a certification process. Being a bouncer is at most a caricature and instead the term "host security"

---

[22] American Hotel & Lodging Educational Institute, Certified Lodging Security Supervisor webpage, at https://www.ahlei.org/CLSS/.

Company

We are one of the leading hotel and leisure companies in the world with more than 1,300 properties in over 100 countries and over 180,000 employees at its owned and managed properties.

Location

Escape to a spectacular mountain getaway in Park City, Utah, where breathtaking landscapes, endless outdoor adventure, unique experiences for children and timeless style captivate your spirit.

Department

Security / Loss Prevention

Job Description

Responsible for the safeguarding of hotel property, assets, guests, visitors and employees. Security officers and supervisor are held to an extremely high level of integrity as they received confidential information. - Patrol hotel property to ensure the safety of guests and employees and to protect all hotel assets. - Answer house calls, assist guests and employees with respect to safety, security and hotel operations. - Initiate and follow-up all investigations of crimes committed against property and persons. - Assist sick and injured guests and employees, ensuring documentation and disposition of reports. - Initiate investigations, write incident and accident reports, monitor investigations to their timely conclusion and ensure appropriate follow-up with guests, visitors and employees, documenting all contacts. - Maintain accurate records while performing basic office duties including, but not limited to, camera monitoring, shift activity log, codebook, and employee and guest binder interaction. Other: Regular attendance in conformance with the standards, which may be established from time to time, is essential to the successful performance of this position. Due to the cyclical nature of the hospitality industry, employees may be required to work varying schedules to reflect the business needs of the hotel. In addition, attendance at all scheduled training sessions and meetings is required. Upon employment, all employees are required to fully comply with chain rules and regulations for the safe and effective operation of the hotel's facilities.

Supportive Functions In addition to performance of the essential functions, this position may be required to perform a combination of the following supportive functions, with the percentage of time performing each function to be solely determined by the manager based upon the particular requirements of the hotel:

- Assist supervisor in checking alarm systems, safety and fire equipment systems and closely monitoring security of building doors, service areas and delivery areas.

Requirements

The individual must possess the following knowledge, skills and abilities and be able to explain and demonstrate that he or she can perform the essential functions of the job, with or without reasonable accommodation, using some other combination of knowledge, skills, and abilities:

- Previous Security/Loss Prevention experience preferred. Luxury oriented a plus.
- Must be able to speak, read, write and understand the primary language(s) used in the workplace.
- Must be able to read and write to facilitate the communication process.
- Excellent communication skills, both verbal and written required.
- Must possess basic computational ability.
- Must possess basic computer skills.
- Knowledge of hotel policy and fire-safety procedures.
- Ability to operate hand held two-way radio and knowledge of ten codes.
- Most work tasks are performed indoors. Temperature is moderate and controlled by hotel environmental systems.
- Must be able to stand and exert well-paced mobility for up to 4 hours in length.
- Must be able to lift up to 15 lbs. on a regular and continuing basis.
- Must be able to push and pull carts and equipment weighing up to 250 lbs. in an emergency.
- Must be able to exert well-paced ability in limited space and to reach other departments and locations of the hotel and outside the hotel on hotel grounds on a timely basis.
- Requires grasping, writing, standing, sitting, walking, repetitive motions, bending, climbing, listening and hearing ability and visual acuity.
- Talking and hearing occur continuously in the process of communicating with guests, supervisors and other employees.
- Vision occurs continuously with the most common visual functions being those of near vision and depth perception.
- Requires manual dexterity to use and operate all necessary equipment.
- Must have finger dexterity to be able to operate office equipment such as computers, printers, 10-key adding machine, electric typewriter, multi-line touch tone phone, filing cabinets, FAX machines, photocopiers, dolly and other office equipment as needed.

Qualification Standards Education: High school or equivalent education preferred. Experience: Minimum of one to two-year security related background required. Flexible schedule to include working weekend, holidays and other shifts as needed. Licenses or Certificates: Ability to obtain and/or maintain any government required licenses, certificates or permits. Current CPR certification and First Aid, Heart Saver A.E.D trainings required. Grooming: All employees must maintain a neat, clean and well-groomed appearance per corporate standards.

Figure 13.16   Career profile: hotel security officer.

appears taking hold. A certification labeled "National Host Security" is a successful attempt to give substance to these complicated roles. The certificate covers the following areas:

- Guard duties and responsibilities
- Powers to arrest and citizen's detention
- Conflict resolution and legal limits to using force
- Criminal, civil, and administrative liabilities
- Alcohol service rules and regulations
- Recognition of fake and false identification
- Recognition of club drug and narcotics usage
- Disaster and terrorism awareness

13.2.3 Professional associations in hospitality, hotel, and lodging industry

Every industry sector, in order to achieve professional, academic, and research respectability, needs professional associations that set the bar high to ensure that best practices are discerned and even more importantly to provide a forum for a professional class seeking to improve its method of security delivery.

13.2.3.1 American Hotel and Lodging Association

As already covered, the AHLA takes the lead association role within the hospitality industry. Long a provider of certification programs, industry research and analysis, and continuing education, the AHLA delivers significant input and guidance as to issues of security and safety. The association has been serving the hospitality industry for more than a century; the AHLA is the sole national association representing all segments of the 1.9 million-employee U.S. lodging industry, including hotel owners, REITs, chains, franchisees, management companies, independent properties, state hotel associations, and industry suppliers. Headquartered in Washington, DC, AHLA provides focused advocacy, communications support, and educational resources for an industry of more than 53,000 properties generating $176 billion in annual sales from 5 million guestrooms.[23] See Figure 13.17.

13.2.3.2 The International Lodging Safety and Security Association

The International Lodging Safety and Security Association (ILSSA) works to improve and professionalize safety and security in the hospitality sector through the exchange of information and experiences among hotel security and safety executives. It promotes cooperation among its members and provides hotel safety and security executives

Figure 13.17   AHLA logo. (From www.ahla.com.)

---

[23] See American Hotel & Lodging Association webpage, at http://www.ahla.com/.

Figure 13.18   ILSSA patch.

with current information through collaboration and intelligence sharing designed to meet the challenges and complexities of protecting modern lodging facilities. A public–private law enforcement partnership founded in Boston, Massachusetts in 1972 where it remains located today although there are branch chapters in other major cities. See Figure 13.18.

13.2.3.3 International Tourism Safety Association

Another professional group dedicated to imparting the best safety and security practices to those laboring the security industry is the International Tourism Safety Association (ITSA). The emphasis, when compared to other groups, involves tourism in a larger framework, which certainly includes hotels and hospitality venues but the many secondary activities that are natural to a tourist experience where security and safety issues are of paramount importance. Based in Las Vegas, Nevada and supported by its tourist industry, ITSA's mission is to provide a forum for tourism security professionals to learn, grow, and develop professionally.[24]

Web Exercise: Find out about the Nightclub and Bar Convention and Trade Show held in Las Vegas annually at http://www.ncbshow.com/.

See Figure 13.19.

13.3 EVENT SECURITY

The security profession's involvement in large-scale events, such as sports arena and entertainment venues, is both broad and sweeping. Gone are the days when National Football League events were exclusively the security province of the local or state police, although that involvement continues in some fashion in nearly every locality. However, for

---

[24] International Tourism Safety Association, Who We Are, at http://www.touristsafety.org/#!about1/c1rm8.

Nightclub Security Manager

Description:

The Nightclub Security Manager is an integral part of the development and promotion of the exciting changes at our Hotel/Casino Las Vegas.

Responsibilities include:

- Responsible for the overall training and management of the Security staff.
- Assists the Director of Security with the development of Security budgets, and addresses all payroll issues.
- Assists in the development, monitoring, and achievement of long term and short term departmental goals.
- Ensures all Security personnel are in compliance with Security Department and Company policies and procedures, and all local, state and federal laws and regulations.
- Oversees and directs the activities of the Security Hosts to ensure the smooth flow of the Security operations. Creates and maintains a sense of urgency.
- Plans and implements the schedules of all Nightclub/Beach Club Security personnel and work activities to ensure uninterrupted service.
- Ensures optimum guest satisfaction through the delivery of excellent customer service.
- Provides appropriate assistance/accommodations for guests (i.e wheelchair, canes, etc.).
- Maintains and promotes a friendly atmosphere for customers and staff.
- Works cooperatively with all other departments to ensure efficient Security support services are provided as needed.
- Investigates accidents, injuries, lost property, property damage, etc. Sees to it that the required reports are completed to document the incident.
- Reviews and approves Security reports.
- Enforces company policies as they pertain to guests and Team Members conduct on the premises. Documents infractions and advises management where appropriate.
- Reports to all emergencies such as fire, injuries, property damage etc. Directs and/or assists with evacuations if required. Investigates and completes reports concerning the same.
- Maintains custody of Security supplies and reports. Makes requisition to replenish all needed supplies. Maintains an up-to-date inventory of property and equipment assigned to the Security Department.
- Supervises the collection and documentation of all lost and found articles.
- Establishes and maintains a progressive and empowered work force. Trains, counsels, and coaches assigned personnel in the performance of their duties.
- Assists the Director of Security in the continual evaluation and development of personnel staffing goals.
- Evaluates and documents the performance of all Security Team Members assigned to the venue.
- Recommends personnel changes in the department, including hiring, promotion, demotion and termination.
- Analyzes and assists the Director of Security in developing and implementing new plans, policies, programs and/or procedures deemed necessary to comply with Company and departmental standards.
- Monitors the implementation of plans, policies, programs and procedures to ensure consistent performance.
- Assists in developing and implementing training programs.
- Actively participates in all training programs.
- Verifies and approves all arrests. Apprehends (where appropriate) individuals who are observed to be engaged in criminal activity and detains these individuals until they can be turned over to law enforcement authorities. Acts as company representative to law enforcement authorities.
- Responds to verbal and/or physical altercations and applies or directs the appropriate measures to resolve the situation. For physical altercations, applies and/or directs the minimum amount of force necessary to restrain any and all involved.
- Initiates formal evictions of disorderly persons.
- Responds to and/or directs the company response to requests for medical assistance. Provides assistance consistent with company policy and the skill level and certifications of available personnel.
- Ensures that the Department Director is advised of all significant events and issues.
- Coordinates and supervises crowd control for special events.
- Assists with cash transports within the venue.
- Attends scheduled departmental training programs (CPR, AED, etc.) and maintains current certifications.
- Performs other duties that may be assigned.

Requirements:

Successful candidates will possess the following qualifications:

- Able to be observant and quick to respond to various situations.
- Must be flexible with shifts and days off.
- Must be fluent in both written and spoken English.
- Has excellent verbal communication skills.
- Minimum of 21 years of age.
- Must be able to present a neat and clean appearance and be physically fit to perform duties required.
- Must be able to stand or walk for a minimum of eight hours.
- Must be able to twist, tow (push or pull), reach, bend, climb and carry as necessary. Must be able to lift at least 50 pounds.
- Must be pleasant, patient, friendly, courteous and respectful.
- Must be able to multi-task, able to handle stressful situations, and must be able to handle a high volume of customers.
- Able to maintain confidentiality.

Figure 13.19   Career profile: private security nightclub security director—Tropicana Las Vegas.

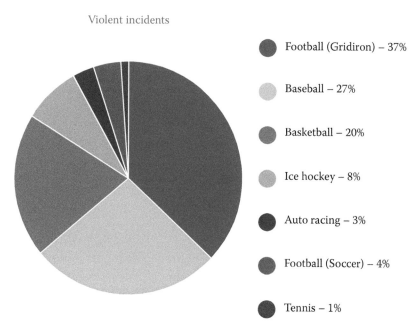

Violent incidents

- Football (Gridiron) – 37%
- Baseball – 27%
- Basketball – 20%
- Ice hockey – 8%
- Auto racing – 3%
- Football (Soccer) – 4%
- Tennis – 1%

Figure 13.20 U.S. data on violence at various sport venues. (From Institute for the Study of Sports Incidents.)

the most part, security firms are taking the lead in the day-to-day operations of providing security at stadiums and arenas and usually operate under the direction of team leadership and in coordination and partnership with public police entities. Stadium fans do not encounter public police in the facility itself, but rather security professionals dealing with access, unruly patrons, quelling altercations from intoxicated fans, and even taking into custody those parties committing crimes and misdemeanors with the facility.[25]

Large-scale event planning requires a holistic understanding of the security challenges commonly faced yet applied in a global, massive customer-based setting—a formula not always easy to calculate. On the one hand, security professionals hope and pray for uneventful events so to speak by applying effective and rigorous security protocols while on the other hand finding a balance of security and entertainment that leaves the customer base happy and healthy. See Figure 13.20.[26]

From another vantage point, security cannot replace the joy of the event but need rests comfortably within the event.[27] The International Association of Chiefs of Police lays out some guiding principles for security services in large-scale events:

- Plan for worst-case scenarios—extraordinary crimes, violence by protestors, a possible terrorist attack, natural disasters—but also be thoroughly prepared to deal with ordinary crimes and incidents (pickpockets, thefts from autos, disorderly conduct, etc.)
- Weigh the security measures that conceivably could be taken (for example, street closures, searches, highly visible tactical units) against the jurisdiction's desire to produce events that are enjoyable, well attended, and profitable
- Establish new and effective—but temporary—organizational arrangements, management structures, and methods of communication
- Ensure that the event continues safely while respecting constitutional rights, including freedom of speech and assembly
- Anticipate unplanned activities and spurof-the-moment gatherings—for example, on the eve of a major event

---

[25] Contemporary Services Corporation website, at http://www.csc-usa.com/.

[26] National Center for Spectator Sports Safety and Security, Researching Spectator Violence at the Institute, at https://www.ncs4.com/sites/default/files/attachments/researching_spectator_violence_at_the_institute.pdf.

[27] K. Bickel & E. Connors, Planning and Managing Security for Major Special Events: Best Practices for Law Enforcement Administrators, *Police Chief* (September 2016), at http://www.policechiefmagazine.org/magazine/index.cfm?fuseaction=display_arch&article_id=1347&issue_id=122007.

- Ensure that the rest of the jurisdiction receives essential law enforcement services, regardless of the size or importance of the event
- Ensure that appropriate federal officials, such as DHS state homeland security advisers, are informed in advance about events with national or international significance to guarantee federal awareness and possible support
- Develop an effective interoperable communications capability if multiple agencies are involved in the field
- Involve citizens and the business community in planning efforts
- Consider building event security training into basic and in-service training, if the jurisdiction routinely handles special events[28]

See Figure 13.21.

Like all other security venues, the sports stadium or large-scale entertainment complex needs full analysis and inspection before any security plan should be developed or implemented. First, know and identify the infrastructure to be secured. Second, identify its critical/key assets and components, that which needs the highest and even lowest levels of protection. Third, collect asset data that fully delineates the size and scope of the facility in need of protection. What is the capacity and how will certain events stress or strain that capacity, to name a few factors? Fourth, do all assessments necessary to prepare, plan, mitigate, and assume continuity in the facility? Hence, threat and vulnerability analysis is central to any serious security plan as well as full-fledged risk assessment document that sets out priorities and involves all the major players of that facility, from management, to the security team, and local, state, and federal partners. Partnerships will be central to any meaningful event security operational plan because the size and scope of the crowd as well as the infrastructure make other players integral to the mission. Some examples of those in need of alliance and cooperation are

- Event Promoters/Sponsors;
- Emergency services agencies (e.g., law enforcement, fire/rescue, emergency medical services, public health and safety) and neighboring Emergency Managers and agency representatives (to coordinate mutual aid needs);
- Local planning agencies and individuals (e.g., community development agencies, city planners, and hazard-mitigation planner);

Figure 13.21   Members of the NYPD patrol the route on West 72nd Street for athletes running the 10-Kilometer part of the NYC Triathlon Race. The race is the only international distance triathlon in New York City. (From Glynnis Jones/Shutterstock.com.)

---

[28] *Ibid.*; see also ASIS International, Special Events Security Resources webpage, at https://www.asisonline.org/Education-Events/Pages/Special-Events-Security-Resources.aspx.

- Local emergency planning committees for hazardous materials information;
- Public works agencies and utility companies;
- State supporting entities, including the State Emergency Management Agency or National Guard;
- Social service agencies and volunteer organizations (e.g., the American Red Cross and Salvation Army), including animal care and control organizations;
- Medical community representatives (e.g., area hospitals, EMS agencies, medical examiner, coroner, mortician);
- Communications representatives (e.g., Public Information Officer, local media, radio);
- Aviation and coastal authorities (e.g., state aviation authority, other air support representatives, port authorities, U.S. Coast Guard station);
- Chief Financial Officer, auditor, and heads of any centralized procurement and resource support agencies;
- Business and retail communities that are directly impacted by the event;
- The jurisdiction's legal counsel and leaders from labor and professional organizations;
- Leaders of area facilities, including industrial and military installations, schools, and universities.[29]

Finally, after amassing all of this information, issue and make recommendations concerning countermeasures to any potential or actual threats or risks. As in all stages of security, planning and preparing for the potential harm is more than half the battle to defend.[30]

Success in event security heavily depends on lessons learned and the best practices gleaned from similar circumstances. It is crucial to rely on historical experiences to plan for the next event. The Bureau of Justice Assistance lays out a helpful template to assist the security planner that integrates past practices into the present challenge. See Figure 13.22.

Just as importantly as the Lessons Learned philosophy, major event planning calls for massive coordination of a host of agencies whose responsibilities differ yet must comfortably intertwine with the entire plan. Noted already are the

Initiating Internal Department - Planning Checklist		
	Key Steps	**Completed** ☑
●	Review Lessons Learned from Previous Large-Scale Events	☐
▲	Begin Planning Immediately; Do Not Wait for Federal Guidance	☐
●	Develop a Strategic Vision	☐
●	Identify a Lead Planner for the Department	☐
●	Determine Authorities of Participating Agencies	☐
●	Establish a Local Core Planning Team	☐
●	Understand that Operational Plans will Remain in Flux	☐
KEY: ● Large-Scale Security Events and NSSEs ▲ NSSEs		

● *Review Lessons Learned from Previous Large-Scale Events*

Figure 13.22 Initiating internal department planning checklist.

---

[29] See CNA, *Managing Large-Scale Security Events: A Planning Primer for Local Law Enforcement Agencies* (2013), at https://www.bja.gov/Publications/LSSE-planning-Primer.pdf.

[30] *Ibid.*

	County Agency	Emergency Medical	Emergency Management	Federal Aviation Administration	Federal Bureau of Investigation	Fire	Law Enforcement	Public Health	Public Works	State Agency	U.S. Secret Service	Utilities	Promoter/ Sponsor
Abandoned Vehicles													
Airspace Encroachment													
Suspicious Package													
Bomb Threat													
Civil Disturbance													
Communications													
Credentials													
Crowd Control													
Demonstrations													
Dignitary Protection													
Emergency Medical Services													
First Aid Stations													
Food Handling													
Hazardous Materials													

U.S. Department of Homeland Security/ Federal Emergency Management Agency, *IS-15: Special Events Contingency Planning Job Aids Manual*, 2005.

Figure 13.23   Pre-event planning matrix. (From U.S. Department of Homeland Security/Federal Emergency Management Agency, *IS-15: Special Events Contingency Planning Job Aids Manual*, 2005.)

many partners and players that a security force must depend upon, but a clear line delegation and demarcation of duties and responsibilities during major events is equally necessary. The adage that there are "too many cooks in the kitchen" could not be more apt in major event security plans. This tendency can be alleviated if roles and tasks are cohesively assigned and jurisdictional authority and subject matter expertise be fully respected. Figure 13.23 provides an exceptionally useful Preplan Matrix to accomplish just that.

Planning and preparation for large-scale events must take into account a multiplicity of factors from geography to the nature of the event, the size and purpose of the crowd gathering, the clientele served, and the level of hostility or entertainment at the center of the event. In other words, the protest gathering or the heavy metal concern is a vastly different crowd from the football attendee or religious revival spiritualist. Events and crowds reflect one another and private security teams need never forget the audience in need of protection. Crowd motivation and typology must be at the center of any overall security and safety strategy, for without a complete comprehension of the audience, decision-making regarding resources and placement will be less dependable. The Bureau of Justice Assistance (BJA) has crafted a very useful crowd planning tool in Figure 13.24.[31]

Geography plays a crucial role in the event security plan too. Every venue must be gauged and evaluated in light of a larger to a more targeted geography. In essence, where is the venue; what is the neighborhood like; how can traffic be controlled as to ingress and egress; and how conducive is the venue to evacuation in the event of disaster or terror? Geography by way of example must be evaluated from the far to the close to get a full picture of the facility for security purposes. For example, the entire neighborhood that surrounds the facility should be inspected. Then, the inspection need move to the facility itself, its design and construction, and its compatibility with any plan for security, safety, and emergency purposes. Mass casualties have occurred simply because of poor architectural design in select venues.[32]

From the neighborhood, the security team moves to the layers of perimeter protection anticipating ways to prevent and defend against every sort of harm, including the mass hysteria and crowd mania that has developed in a host of sporting events, especially in world soccer matches where death and crowd crush is not uncommon. To be effective, various lines and zones of defense need be established as is evident in Figure 13.25.

While myriad other issues arise in large-scale events, preparation and planning for most scenarios involving natural and man-made disasters is time intelligently invested. Understanding the event itself, the crowd psyche and persona,

---

[31] *Ibid.*
[32] J.S. Delaney & R. Drummond, Mass Casualties and Triage at a Sporting Event, 36 *Br. J. Sports* 85 (2002).

Crowd Management - Planning Checklist		
	Key Steps	Completed ☑
●	Anticipate Crowd Behaviors and Actions	☐
●	Use Data to Support the Development of Crowd Control Deployment	☐
●	Develop a Policing Strategy that is Focused on Non-Confrontational Tactics Centered on Team Policing	☐
●	Identify the Most Appropriate Resources for the Mission	☐
●	Determine Officer Dress	☐
●	Control Demonstrator Activities	☐
●	Collaborate with Other Organizations	☐
●	Train Officers on the Policing Strategy	☐
●	Inform the Public of Response Tactics	☐
●	Create Mobile Response Teams	☐
●	Position Commanders in the Field	☐

KEY: ● Large-Scale Security Events and NSSEs ▲ NSSEs

Figure 13.24 BJA crowd planning tool.

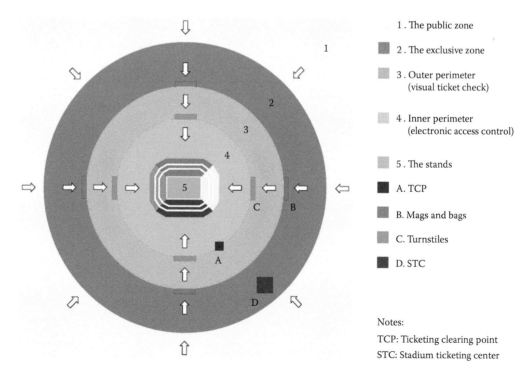

1. The public zone
2. The exclusive zone
3. Outer perimeter (visual ticket check)
4. Inner perimeter (electronic access control)
5. The stands
A. TCP
B. Mags and bags
C. Turnstiles
D. STC

Notes:
TCP: Ticketing clearing point
STC: Stadium ticketing center

Figure 13.25 Levels of defense around the perimeter of a facility.

and its aim and ambition, establishing and maintaining healthy partnerships with a host of official and private entities, and fully assessing the nature of the venue and facility where the event takes place are certainly primordial responsibilities for the security team.

One final central suggestion relates to evacuation, for all of the efforts enunciated throughout this chapter have little meaning if the audience is incapable of escaping a tragedy. Evacuation plays a loftier role in the larger venue because the stakes are so high in terms of human capital and potential loss of life and limb. Hence, a solid evacuation plan that is readily understandable by the public and fully communicated to all staff and employees of the venue must be authored and disseminated. That plan starts with assuring that exits are free and clear as FEMA dictates.

- Ensure that exit doors are not locked. If personnel are concerned about illegal entry, then doors could be fitted with alarms.
- Ensure that exit doors open in the direction of escape and are confirmed as operational.
- Check the placement, function, and signposting of exits.
- Ensure that doors that do not lead to an exit are so marked, preventing "dead end" entrapment and the potential for panic.
- Ensure that all exit corridors are free of all impediments to crowd movement.
- Ensure that turnstiles are freewheeling or can operate in reverse.
- Ensure that cords, which can create trip hazards, do not cross exit corridors. (If this precaution is unavoidable, the cord should be marked, insulated, and secured to the floor to prevent damage and potential electrical risks.)[33]

Stadium and venue security specialists are increasingly relying on software programs that highlight and emphasize the best means for evacuation such as SPORTEVAC, a program supported by the DHS and the National Center for Sports Safety and Security.[34] The program provides an interactive package to anticipate how evacuation could occur depending upon a host of variables.

See Figure 13.26.

13.3.1 Professional certifications in event security

Since there are varied levels of responsibilities in large venues, an increasing array of certifications have emerged. The typical mass crowd facility will tier its personnel based on function. Hierarchically, the security team ascends from managerial to the delegated field operations as represented by Figure 13.27.

For example, since crowd control represents a key responsibility, the industry and academia have attempted to provide a certification schema for crowd control specialists.[35] The Commonwealth of Massachusetts now requires crowd managers to be certified in the subject matter.[36]

A crowd control officer would be responsible for a host of tasks including

- Traffic and crowd management
- Communication protocol for crowd control
- Implement crowd management plan
- Incorporate control devices into crowd plan
- Implement crowd control policies based on need and events
- Author a traffic management plan

---

[33] FEMA, *Special Events Contingency Planning* (2005), at https://training.fema.gov/emiweb/downloads/is15aspecialeventsplanning-jamanual.pdf.

[34] See U.S. Department of Homeland Security, SportEvac: Choreographing a Stadium Stampede, at https://www.dhs.gov/sportevac-choreographing-stadium-stampede.

[35] California Commission on Peace Officer Standards and Training, *POST Guidelines: Crowd Management, Intervention, and Control* (2012), at http://lib.post.ca.gov/Publications/CrowdMgtGuidelines.pdf.

[36] See Massachusetts Executive Office of Public Safety and Security, Crowd Manager Regulations and Training Program, at http://www.mass.gov/eopss/agencies/dfs/crowd-manager-regulations-and-training-prog-.html.

Security supervisor

Division: Security & Public Safety Group
Status: Contractual Part-Time (non-benefitted)
Salary: $15.00/hour
Location: Oriole Park at Camden Yards, Camden Yards Sports Complex
Closing Date: Friday, July 29, 2016

The Maryland Stadium Authority (MSA) is seeking qualified candidates for the position of Security Supervisors.

Responsibilities and Duties:
This is a part-time position responsible for performing 24/7 physical security duties at the Camden Yards Sports Complex. Selected applicants will work to maintain a safe and secure environment for visitors, tenants and employees of the Camden Yards Sports Complex and will be expected to provide unparalleled security services related to emergency response, protection of life and property, and loss prevention.
Duties include supervising and managing security officers assigned to fixed and mobile security patrols, monitoring building life safety, access control, camera surveillance and alarm systems, and reporting suspicious activity and unusual incidents to the security manager.
Work hours vary and may include evenings, weekends and holidays.

Minimum Qualifications Required:
Education: Graduation from an accredited high school or possession of a high school equivalency certificate.
Experience: Minimum of five (5) years of experience in a law enforcement, corrections, military or physical security position, with at least two 2 of the 5 years being in a supervisory or officer-in-charge role.
Licensure: Must possess a valid driver's license.
Supplemental Requirements: Candidates must successfully complete a background screening, including fingerprinting, criminal record checks (local, State, and Federal), and interview. Must have the ability to stand for long periods of time and conduct mobile patrols. Good verbal and written communication skills.

How to Apply
Interested candidates must submit a Maryland Stadium Authority Application.

Figure 13.26   Career profile: event security: security supervisor—Maryland Stadium Authority.

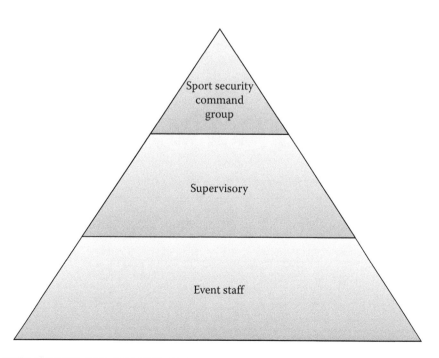

Figure 13.27   Hierarchy of security team in a sports venue.

The University of Southern Mississippi's National Center for Spectator Sports Safety and Security (NCS4) strongly advocates for certification programs at all levels of large venue sport facilities. Its Certified Sport Security Professionals (CSSP) certification program promotes standardized competencies, the most current techniques, and strategies relating to safety and security risks inherent to spectator sport venues. The course consists of six modules that cover the core competencies of sport security professionals tested on the CSSP exam.

- Business and facility management
- Emergency planning
- Emergency management
- Legal and regulatory
- Crowd management
- Security principles and practices

See Figure 13.28.

NCS4 also certifies venue staff at points of entry and customer interaction, a common role for the security officer and security supervisor. The Certified Sport Venue Staff (CSVS) certification accomplishes its chief purpose by credentialing and checking the applicant, which assures not only prepared officers but ones with sterling backgrounds. The NCS4 runs a clearinghouse and information center that tracks the whereabouts of its graduates and serves as control point that verifies competency.

See Figure 13.29.

Figure 13.28   CSSP patch.

Security Manager AT&T Stadium

Industry:	Sports
	Security / Surveillance
	Cool Jobs
Job Type:	Full Time
Degree Level:	Bachelor's Degree
Country:	United States
State/Province:	Texas
City:	Arlington
Salary:	Inquire
Post Date:	08/13/2016 03:35 AM

The Security Manager creates and manages a Security program that fosters a safe and enjoyable experience for all guests. The Security Manager is responsible for event security and the day-to-day security operations at AT&T Stadium. The Security Manager should have a broad spectrum background in facility and event operations. The Security Manager reports to the Senior Director of Event Operations.

Job Duties:
- Manage security services contract
- Oversee daily security operations
- Develop policies and procedures for security operations
- Oversee security operations for events
- Maintain relationships with public safety liaisons
- Manage incident reporting for operations
- Assist in the preparation of budgets relative to staffing daily operations
- Oversee staffing plans for security operations
- Interface with other stadium constituents regarding security issues
- Perform other functions and activities as directed by the Senior Director of Event Operations
- Manage security licenses for Access Management staff

Qualifications:
- Bachelor's Degree in Business, Sports Management or a related area of study required
- 5+ years of experience supervising event and/or security staff (stadium, arena, convention center, performing arts facility) required
- 5+ years of experience managing facility and event operations required
- Experience managing security technology systems including CCTV, electronic access control, and ISS 24/7 Incident Management System required
- Able to be licensed by the Texas Department of Public Safety Private Security Bureau as a Qualified Manager
- Previous attendance at Venue Management School, Academy for Venue Safety and Security or similar programs preferred
- Certified Sport Safety & Security Professional (CSSP) preferred
- Advanced skills in the use of Microsoft Office (Outlook, Word, Excel, PowerPoint, Visio) required
- Excellent interpersonal, verbal and written communication skills; ability to communicate effectively at all levels both internally and externally
- Able to simultaneously manage a high level of detail across multiple projects
- Able to work in high stress situations in a calm manner
- Able to demonstrate flexibility and quickly adapt to changes while maintaining high levels of productivity and effectiveness under pressure
- Able to work well within a team environment, offering assistance and support to team members whenever necessary
- Able to work flexible hours, including nights and weekends

Figure 13.29   Career profile: security director for AT&T Stadium.

13.4 PRIVATE SECURITY INDUSTRY AND MALLS

Just as schools, hospitals, and other community sectors possess environmental qualities, so the retail establishment. With the dawn of mega-malls and super stores, the demands on the private sector have been rapidly rising. Nearly all major security firms deliver security services to malls and other large-scale retail settings.

With the rising challenges faced by malls and other retail establishments, it seems folly to paint the inaccurate picture of the bloated and ineffectual mall guard. To be sure, there are varying levels of staffing from entry level to command, but the rash of contemporary slaughters occurring in malls across American alone makes this an important and increasingly dangerous business.[37] Mall security comprises a mix of high tech and professional observational and investigative techniques.[38] The economic investment alone makes mall safety and security not an afterthought but a front burner issue for investors and owners of these real estate entities.[39] Additionally, the DHS and other governmental entities see the mall as a likely target, a place where harm and injury is not unlikely. It is a sector worth protecting for a host of reasons. Malls fall into the eight subsectors of the Commercial Facilities Sector for DHS purposes. Those sectors include the following:

1. Public Assembly (e.g., arenas, stadiums, aquariums, zoos, museums, convention centers)
2. Sports Leagues (e.g., professional sports leagues and federations)
3. Gaming (e.g., casinos)
4. Lodging (e.g., hotels, motels, conference centers)
5. Outdoor Events (e.g., theme and amusement parks, fairs, campgrounds, parades)
6. Entertainment and Media (e.g., motion picture studios, broadcast media)
7. Real Estate (e.g., office and apartment buildings, condominiums, mixed use facilities,
8. Retail (e.g., retail centers and districts, shopping malls).[40]

Web Exercise: Learn about Mall of America's dedication to security: http://www.mallofamerica.com/guests/security.

Malls have been labeled self-sustaining cities with a full-fledged environment.[41] When a retail environment loses its reputation for safety and security, it is on a sure road to economic decline. University Square Mall of Tampa, Florida was under siege by gangs and turf battles. The Mall, approximately 20 years old, contained a 16-screen theatre with a food court, housed 162 stores over 1,300,000 square feet of lease space spread out over three quarters of a mile, and was utilized by 14,000,000 customers a year. With the arrivals of gangs, the mall lost both its profit base and its reputation with the community as a safe haven. The general manager of the mall, Tom Loch, authored a bold approach in dealing with the growing problem of juveniles out of control.

The first issue that Mr. Loch addressed was the institution of a code of conduct for the mall. At all doors, the mall posted its new rules and regulations. Security personnel were ordered to enforce the new policies to ensure compliance. The rules struck at the heart of the gang culture and sought to undermine the status symbols and other signs of authority in gang activity. For example, dressing left or right, which is common within gang groups, was prohibited within the mall facility. This meant that wearing watches, hats, belt buckles, and shoe laces *all* to the right or *all* to the left was not allowed for any patron of the mall. Juveniles had to make sure that pant legs were down and not rolled up, as many juveniles like to keep one pant leg up to identify them as part of a particular gang. All bandanas or "colors" that gang members are known to wear were prohibited from being worn in the mall. The mall rules went even as far as not allowing jockey shorts to be hanging out, which is a common style among many juveniles today. Other rules were enforced on a broader scale: no personal radios; any weapons; and security personnel tolerated no abusive or foul language of any kind.

To ensure that the new policies were communicated with the target audience, the mall's rules and regulations and a code of conduct were printed on business cards and given out to juveniles encountering security personnel. The good kids that the security interacted with were also awarded with movie passes. Little children were given stickers and security badges, just to name a few of the proactive methods used by the security department.

The program initiated at the Tampa Mall represents a significant alteration of an environment. Once roamed by gangs, the aggressive intervention in what conduct was acceptable within the environment mirrored a differing

---

[37] P. Bradley, No Laughing Matter, *Stores* (June 2015), at http://www.nxtbook.com/nxtbooks/nrfe/STORES0615/#/60.

[38] M. Oteng-Ababio & I.K. Arthur, (Dis)continuities in Scale, Scope and Complexities of the Space Economy: The Shopping Mall Experience in Ghana, 26 *Urban Forum* 151 (2015), at http://link.springer.com/article/10.1007/s12132-014-9249-x.

[39] E. Misonzhnik, Sophisticated Security Drills Help Some Mall Owners and Managers Prepare for the Worst, *Nat'l Real Estate Investor* (April 7, 2011), at http://nreionline.com/property-management/sophisticated-security-drills-help-some-mall-owners-and-managers-prepare-worst.

[40] U.S. Department of Homeland Security, National Infrastructure Protection Plan, Commercial Facilities Sector, at https://www.dhs.gov/xlibrary/assets/nipp_snapshot_commercialfacilities.pdf.

[41] G. Lee, R.C. Hollinger & D.A. Dabney, The Relationship Between Crime and Private Security and U.S. Shopping Centers, 23 *Am. J. Crim. Just.* 2 (1999); L. Sherman, P.R. Gartin & M.E. Buerger, Hot Spots of Predatory Crime: Routine Activities and the Criminology of Place, 27 *Criminology* 27–55 (1989).

culture. In the previous setting, the gang types found a home worth visiting. In the adjusted environment, the attraction was lost. Here, the proactive approach paves the way for success in any environment. In short, gang behavior and imagery were vanquished from the environment. As a result, the customer base lost the negative participation of those who undermine safety and security and gained the law-abiding citizen whose business is always welcome. By changing the environment and the conduct of the juvenile patrons, a large facility that was exposed to serious criminal activities and problems reclaimed its rightful sense of ownership.

See Figure 13.30.

Mall Security Director

Summary

Title:	Mall Security Director
ID:	12XXX
Job Classification:	Security Officer
Job Type:	Full Time
Hourly Rate:	$DOE
Locations:	FAIRLAWN, OH

Description

Job Summary:
The SECURITY DIRECTOR position manages all daily operations at the branch office. Additional responsibilities include:

- Supervise all full-time and part-time security personnel.
- Hire, train, and evaluate security personnel.
- Initiate disciplinary actions and terminations as required.
- Prepare weekly work schedules for full-time and part-time Security Guards, including positing of schedules.
- Provide security staffing for other functions as may be required.
- Enforce and make recommendations regarding building security plans and schedules.
- Account for all Security Guards hours, including sick/vacation, etc; review payroll for submission to accounting.
- Approve time off for Security Guards and submit request to the Branch Manager for final approval.
- Maintain records and files as required for all full-time and part-time security personnel.
- Implement security measures improvements as they are developed.
- Review all daily Security Guard reports, incident reports and log entries; take necessary action; make follow-up reports to the Branch Manager.
- Verify and review Post Positive Reports.
- Maintain all necessary forms.
- Make recommendations to management on staffing needs, budgeting data, and purchase recommendations.
- Establish building security plans and schedules for special events.
- Assist and advise on duty Security Guards around the clock.
- Investigate all Security Guard injuries and prepare necessary reports.
- Participate in day-to-day and special facility functions including service on various committees, task forces, and programs.

Monitors the Security Officer training programs

Job Skills and Responsibilities:

- High School Diploma or equivalent required. Bachelor's Degree preferred.
- Minimum of 1-3 years of experience in the military or security industry.
- Must have working knowledge of Windows XP and Office. AS400 knowledge is a plus.
- The ability to travel to visit current and prospective client sites is required.
- Must be skilled in developing and maintaining customer and employee relationships.

Must be able to work in a fast-paced working environment.

Required Competencies:
- The successful candidate will have the ability to lead and develop an effective team.
- He/she must be customer service oriented.
- He/she must effective decisions in a timely manner under changing conditions.
- The successful candidate will be emotionally stable and remain thoughtful and calm under pressure.

Environment:
Position based at branch office. Requires the ability to work in a fast-paced, multi-faceted environment.

Figure 13.30   Career profile: security director—Summit Mall in Ohio.

WebExercise: Rising crime rates in American malls is a shocking reality for many. See the example from Memphis, Tennessee at http://www.wmcactionnews5.com/story/29576201/police-reveal-surprising-crime-statistics-for-memphis-area-malls.

13.4.1 Special protocols in mall security

In general, mall and large retail establishments depend upon a blend of people and strategically employed technology. Some of the tried and true methods include but are not limited to the following techniques:

- Security Patrol
- Escorts
- Community Policing Substation
- Exterior Lighting
- Placement of Public
- CCTV Cameras
- Convex mirrors at corridor intersection and corners
- Bicycle and Mounted Patrol
- Rooftop Patrol
- Shoplifting Awareness Training
- Exercise Walkers[42]

See Figure 13.31.

Figure 13.31   Mall decorated for the holidays. (From Victor Maschek/Shutterstock.com.)

---

[42] District of Columbia Homeland Security & Emergency Management Agency, *Security Guidance for Commercial Buildings* (2012), at http://hsema.dc.gov/sites/default/files/dc/sites/hsema/publication/attachments/Security%20Guidance%20FINAL_0.PDF.

Types of actions, characteristics profiled by security staff

Characteristic	Responses (n=94)	Percentage
Suspicious behavior (in general)	18	19.5
Taking photographs/videos/notes	16	17.0
Unusual/suspicious clothing	16	17.0
Carrying large/suspicious packages	11	11.7
Loitering	7	7.5
Unusual interest/curiosity	5	5.3
Suspicious appearance (in general)	4	4.2
Suspicious vehicles	3	3.2
Foreigners acting suspicious	3	3.2
Large groups/gangs	2	2.1
Younger adults	2	2.1
Abandoned packages	2	2.1
Other	5	5.5

Figure 13.32 Suspicious behaviors that security staff look for.

Security professionals heavily rely on behavioral and observational skill sets to keep assets and persons safe in the mall and retail environment. Watching, observing, and keeping tabs on what looks and is suspicious is never a talent to neglect in this business.[43]

Security directors, as well as their staff, need to focus on the human element—how people act; how they appear; how their body language delivers particular messages—all of which is often actionable intelligence. For example, a recent study conducted under the auspices of the National Criminal Justice Reference Service surveyed mall security directors to see what their officers and staff were tagging as something worthy of suspicion. The results are charted in Figure 13.32.

Suspicious behavior, carrying large packages that appear out of place, odd or strange clothing, and photograph and note takers all topped the list of behavior that triggers suspicion.[44]

Security firms now need constant vigilance as to terrorist activity in the mall or retail settings. Over the last decade, a significant spike in death and destruction, caused by terrorists, has been quite evident. Review the various factors in Figure 13.33,[45] which targets behavioral indicators from a possible terrorist at a mall setting.

Indicators of potential surveillance by terrorists include:
- Persons using or carrying video/camera/observation equipment over an extended period
- Persons discovered with shopping mall maps, photos, or diagrams with facilities highlighted
- Persons parking, standing, or loitering in the same area over a multiple-day period with no apparent reasonable explanation
- Mall personnel being questioned off-site about practices pertaining to the mall
- Employees changing working behavior or working more irregular hours
- Persons observed or reported to be observing mall receipts or deliveries
- A noted pattern or series of false alarms requiring a response by law enforcement or emergency services
- Unfamiliar cleaning crews or other contract workers
- An increase in buildings being left unsecured
- An increase in threats from unidentified sources
- Unusual or unannounced maintenance activities in the vicinity of the mall
- Sudden losses or thefts of guard force equipment

Figure 13.33 Indicators of surveillance by terrorists.

---

[43] L. Martinez, Mall Security and LP—Communication Is the Watchword, *LPM Insider* (March 1, 2009), at http://losspreventionmedia.com/insider/retail-security/mall-security-and-lp-communication-is-the-watchword-2.

[44] See R.C. Davis et al., *An Assessment of the Preparedness of Large Retail Malls to Prevent and Respond to Terrorist Attack* (December 2006), at https://www.ncjrs.gov/pdffiles1/nij/grants/216641.pdf.

[45] DC Homeland Security, *supra* note 42, at 17.

Security firms and companies constantly engage new techniques and advanced technologies to attract this client base, which clearly wants effective and efficient security protocols.

Other forms of technology are making extensive inroads in the mall and retail culture. Even the mall owners have used technology to keep customers safe, in the right place and direction, warned of potential harms by apps, and available in case of distress by the push of a button.[46] Smartphone technology, hidden and visible camera and video technology, immediate communication capacity with public law enforcement, and the shared data and technology in strong partnerships are but a few of these initiatives. Malls are fully aware that the security is not part of the design and substance of their operation and not a peripheral activity.

Web Exercise: Watch the training video on active shooters produced by the International Council of Shopping Centers (ICSC) at http://www.icsc.org/shopping-center-security.

The ICSC, an industry group, has recently taken a prominent role in the advancement of security and safety across its entire membership. The ICSC has actively developed educational programs and policy guidelines that address the many challenges of mall and retail mega centers. Organized crime in the retail sector is one of the many innovations of the ICSC as well as handling tragedy and emergency situations.

Web Exercise: Watch the video instruction on how organized retail crime (ORC) theft works and the steps to prevent it at http://www.icsc.org/organized-retail-crime-prevention.

Of even more compelling interest has been the Council's keen interest in disseminating an online program in terrorism awareness for shopping malls. The program is a joint production of DHS, the council, and Louisiana State University. See Figure 13.34.

Finally, the rise of organized crime retail theft is a matter of serious and ongoing concern for security professionals and mall owners. This type of organized crime should not be equated with the historic types and methods of organized crime, as if mimicking the Sicilian mafia prototype or Russian mob methods. ORC is a systematic assault on merchants in large-scale quantities by groups organized to not only steal the merchandise but then to resell. Organized groups of professional shoplifters, or "boosters," steal or fraudulently obtain merchandise, then "fence" to individuals and retailers by any means available including actual delivery or online sale. Losses from ORC are estimated in the $15 billion to $37 billion range.[47] See Figure 13.35.[48]

Anywhere in the chain of supply and demand, these roving bands of thieves can apply their methods, from the factory production line to cargo holds, from delivery points to warehouses for storage, from store floors to delivery trucks. What makes the process so organized is that it depends on so many players, including employees who collude for profit. Contrasted with a shoplifter, this is property theft on a mass scale and with gargantuan economic implications.

The National Retail Federation is clearly aware and stunned by the rapid and escalating growth of this form of crime. The methodologies employed are quite sinister, especially coupled with gangs and corresponding violence. The problem, assessed in the NRF survey of retailers, signifies a growing fear in how systematically and aggressively this type of criminality has become. So serious is the threat that an overwhelming majority of mall and retail establishment owners surveyed—78%, or nearly four out of five—think a federal law need to be passed to address this scourge, this according to the 2015 NRF Organized Retail Crime Study.

The question whether legal innovations will stem the tide is another issue worth debating because laws do not work well when utter chaos undermines the traditional shopping experience. This may be a prime opportunity for the private security industry to apply its innovative and creative approaches to this very complex problem.

13.5 PRIVATE SECURITY INDUSTRY: CASINO AND GAMING

Less than a few decades ago, casinos and gaming were not universally received in the American experience. The industry was a mix of both moral and criminal critique, entrepreneurial opportunity and growth, a means to employ

---

[46] See E. Fung, Mall Landlords Embrace High-Tech to Entice Shoppers, *Wall Street J.* (June 8, 2016), at http://www.wsj.com/articles/mall-landlords-embrace-high-tech-to-entice-shoppers-1465291802.
[47] K.M. Finklea, *Organize Retail Crime* (Congressional Research Service, December 11, 2012), at https://fas.org/sgp/crs/misc/R41118.pdf.
[48] *Ibid.* at 11.

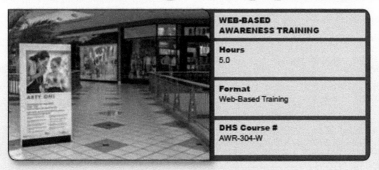

Figure 13.34 Shopping Center Security Terrorism Awareness Training Program information.

while at the same time either elevate or destroy surrounding neighborhoods and a pro–con analysis that seemed never resolved. See Figure 13.36.[49]

To be sure, attitudes of the once only in "Vegas" and Atlantic City have long dissipated. It is safe to say that the public's reception of gaming and casinos is much more tolerant than 30 years ago. But to claim that all is rosy and without

---

[49] K.J. Peak, Policing in the Casino Gaming Environment: Methods, Risks, and Challenges, *FBI L. Enforcement Bull.* (May 5, 2015), at https://leb. fbi.gov/2015/may/policing-in-the-casino-gaming-environment-methods-risks-and-challenges.

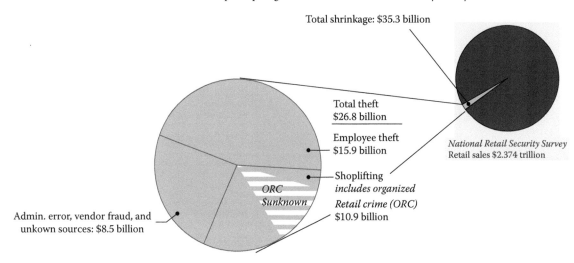

Costs to retailers participating in the 2010 National Retail Security Survey

Total shrinkage: $35.3 billion

Total theft
$26.8 billion

Employee theft
$15.9 billion

Shoplifting
includes organized
Retail crime (ORC)
$10.9 billion

ORC
$unknown

Admin. error, vendor fraud, and
unkown sources: $8.5 billion

National Retail Security Survey
Retail sales $2.374 trillion

Figure 13.35   Retail shrinkage costs. (From 2010 National Retail Security Survey Final Report.)

reservation is a very faulty conclusion too.[50] Ambivalence and condemnation, and approval and tolerance are just a few descriptors regarding the industry.[51]

What is clear are that the industry's and government's promises regarding the positive effects and benefits have never occurred. In Pennsylvania, by way of example, the former Governor Ed Rendell sold the public on gambling by arguing that the revenue would be so substantial that it would significantly or completely eliminate the state's property taxes. This hyperbole was just hyperbole. Other politicos argue that jobs, good paying ones, would greatly reduce

Figure 13.36   Gaming establishments have been expanding, are big business, and have multiple levels of security challenges. (From FBI.)

---

[50] By way of example the comprehensive study by the University of Massachusetts: R.J. Williams, J. Rehm & R.M.G. Stevens, *The Social and Economic Impacts of Gambling. Final Report Prepared for the Canadian Consortium for Gambling Research* (March 11, 2011), at https://www.umass.edu/seigma/sites/default/files/SEIG%20Report-Williams%20Rehm%20%20Stevens%202011.pdf.

[51] J. Orford et al., Negative Public Attitudes towards Gambling: Findings from the 2007 British Gambling Prevalence Survey Using a New Attitude Scale, 9 *Int'l Gambling Stud.* 39 (2009), at http://www.tandfonline.com/doi/abs/10.1080/14459790802652217.

Figure 13.37 The closed out Trump Taj Mahal resort and casino, an entrance from the boardwalk. (From Roman Tiraspolsky/Shutterstock.com.)

unemployment, or elevate distressed neighborhoods or fund social needs while triggering enormous social costs—all of which are a blend of reality and delusion.[52]

Gaming and casinos can never really deliver what its backers hype nor its detractors prophesy about. Certainly, there are moral and religious objections although the majority of American states now have legalized casinos, a far cry from the two-state monopoly of less than 20 years ago.[53] And what is equally demonstrable is that gaming and casinos are not economic saviors—as these facilities are often advertised to be—the prime example being the continued decline of Atlantic City, New Jersey, whose reputation for crime and social ills have never been solved by this industry.[54] See Figure 13.37.

While pictures of Atlantic City may be idyllic, the fact that four major casinos have closed in as many years, that crime rates remain significant, that social ills such as drugs, prostitution, and child neglect remain higher than average, and that an overall quality of life perception remains stubbornly negative confirms the complexity of this industry on the culture and the community. On the other hand, depending on location and the existence or prevalence of social disorder or lack thereof, the industry has made significant contributions to its surrounding communities, especially in economic ways. There are secondary industries that often flourish because of the casino, such as hotels, food services, and aligned technology industries. Communities often benefit from upgraded public services and roads.[55] It is, as they say, a "mixed bag."[56]

[52] See R. Room, N.E. Turner & A. Ialomiteanu, Community Effects of the Opening of the Niagara Casino, 94 *Addiction* 1449 (1999).

[53] D. Chinni, What Happens in Vegas…Happens Everywhere, *PBS Newshour, The Rundown* (July 12, 2010), at http://www.pbs.org/newshour/rundown/what-happens-in-vegas-happens-everywhere/.

[54] G. Gurley, Atlantic City: The Fall of the Boardwalk Empire, *Am. Prospect* (April 8, 2016), at http://prospect.org/article/atlantic-city-fall-boardwalk-empire.

[55] See Global Gaming Revenues Set to Reach US182.8 Billion by 2015, *Pricewaterhouse Coopers*, at http://press.pwc.com/GLOBAL/2011-News-releases/global-gaming-revenues-set-to-reach-us182.8-billion-by-2015/s/7d0dff3b-5b93-4239-8571-1f27092eef6e, last accessed January 14, 2015.

[56] A. Strickhouser, The Unique Challenges of Casino Security, *Int'l Foundation for Protection Officers* (May 14, 2004), at http://www.ifpo.org/resource-links/articles-and-reports/protection-of-specific-environments/the-unique-challenges-of-casino-security/.

13.5.1 Private security industry, gaming and occupational outlook

For the private security industry, the industry on balance has been very lucrative and beneficial to its growth.[57] With the spread of gaming across the bulk of the five states, occupational opportunities continue to grow for gaming surveillance officers and general security officers. See Figure 13.38.[58]

In general terms, the outlook for job prospects is strong even though some observers indicate a "glut" of casino facilities may result in a winnowing-out period. The Bureau of Labor Statistics' *Occupational Outlook Handbook* charts both the gaming security officer and gaming surveillance officer in Figure 13.39.[59]

The projected decline of 7% for gaming surveillance officers can be explained in three ways: first, as already mentioned, the glut of facilities and not enough opportunities; second, the rise of technological means and methods, which replace human intelligence with mechanical assessments; and lastly, when casinos are under economic pressures, these institutions adapt, cut back, and trim where they must.[60]

Web Exercise: Find out more on the gaming and casino opportunities and job prospects at http://www.bls.gov/ooh/protective-service/security-guards.htm.

See Figure 13.40.

The industry has been an aggressive marketer of both its human and technological capacities in this arena. While some firms sell contractual services to the gaming industry, a good many employment opportunities are in-house, reflecting the regulatory demands of the Control Boards and Gaming Commissions that seek to root out corruption from the outside and inside of the facility. Employees can be vetted more aggressively and be held strictly accountable under direct supervision. Hence, there are many direct opportunities for hire at casino facilities.

See Figure 13.41.

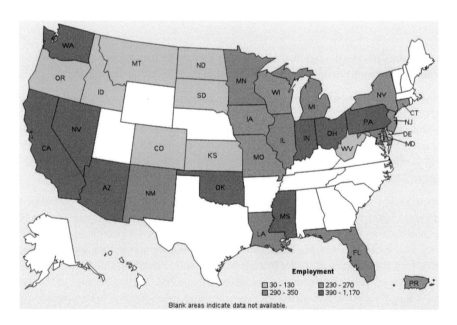

Figure 13.38 Employment of gaming surveillance officers and gaming investigators by state, May 2015. (Courtesy of Bureau of Labor Statistics.)

[57] A. Rodriguez, Security Customer Service to Improve Casino Reputation, *Sec. Mag.* (August 1, 2015), at http://www.securitymagazine.com/articles/86536-security-customer-service-to-improve-casino-reputation.

[58] Bureau of Labor Statistics, Occupational Employment and Wages, May 2016: 33-9031 Gaming Surveillance Officers and Gaming Investigators, http://www.bls.gov/oes/current/oes339031.htm#st.

[59] Bureau of Labor Statistics, U.S. Department of Labor, *Occupational Outlook Handbook* (2016–2017 Edition, Security Guards and Gaming Surveillance Officers), at http://www.bls.gov/ooh/protective-service/security-guards.htm, last accessed August 31, 2016.

[60] J. Edulbehram, All In: Placing Bets on Casino Video Surveillance, *Sec. Mag.* (March 8, 2016), at http://www.securitymagazine.com/articles/86975-all-in-placing-bets-on-casino-video-surveillance.

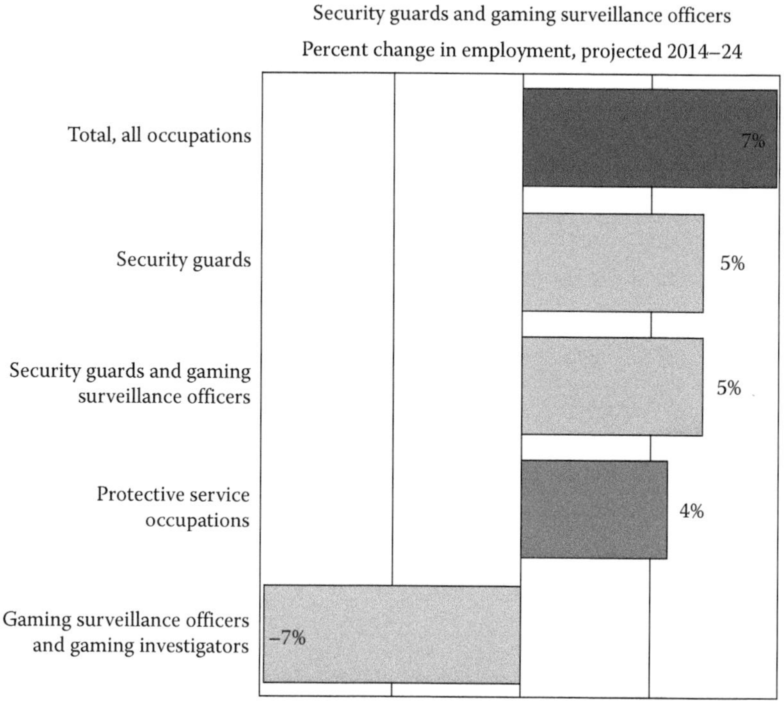

Security guards and gaming surveillance officers

Percent change in employment, projected 2014–24

Figure 13.39 Increase in security guards and gaming officer through 2024. *Note*: All occupations includes all occupations in the U.S. economy. (From U.S. Bureau of Labor Statistics, Employment Projections Program.)

Career opportunities at casino and gaming facilities vary by location and the design of the venue. For those with sweeping parking authorities, the venue will strategically place officers to assure the safety of its customers. For those placed on large geographic complexes, mobile patrols, by car, bike, or other transport, will be needed. Already described are the base line officer positions that interact throughout the complex, deal with front-line issues, control access, and respond to calls. Surveillance and technology specialists are sprinkled everywhere in the facility managing and tracking the many cameras and recording equipment and ferreting out the fraudulent customer. Security managers and directors oversee all of these personnel and interact with state, local, and board authorities or partner closely with assigned state and local officers assigned to the location. For example, in Pennsylvania, the corruption and control oversight is assumed by the Pennsylvania State Police who are always somewhere on location.

13.5.2 Oversight and control boards and commissions

Casinos and gaming facilities are subject to intense regulatory oversight, primarily driven by two fundamental realities: first, that without oversight vice and crime tend to gravitate toward these facilities; and second, the deterrent impact on organized crime activities. It is no secret that both Las Vegas and Atlantic City were under the screws of organized crime syndicates and over time, as the war on organized crime succeeded, for the most part, the casinos never wanted to put into that economic extortion again. See Figure 13.42.

Hence, control boards, with legal, regulatory, and enforcement powers, commencing with licensure review and approval, background vetting of proposed owners and investors, coupled with intensely open and transparent reporting requirements, have done a pretty decent job of keeping the business largely clean. It would be naïve to argue that corruption does not exist in the gaming environment but on balance state and local authorities have been doing a pretty good job of controlling this menace. Nevada, surely the most experienced and sophisticated of all the review commissions, fully charts its diverse functions as to oversight, investigation, compliance, enforcement, criminal referral, and other duties in Figure 13.43.[61]

---

[61] *Nevada Gaming Commission, Nevada State Gaming Control Board* (2014), at https://www.leg.state.nv.us/Division/Research/LegInfo/Orientation/2014-15/Handouts/03-JudHandouts_Gaming.pdf.

Security Manager

Location:	Suquamish, WA
Salary Range:	DOE
Exempt/Non-Exempt:	Exempt
Benefits:	See Benefits Page
Employment Type:	Full Time
Department:	Security
Description:	Under the direction of the Security Director, oversees security operations to ensure a safe, secure and comfortable environment for guests and personnel as well as safeguarding the assets of the company. Assists the Security Director with all responsibilities with the operation of the Security Department with special emphasis on employee relations, training and development, daily operations and guest relations, training of Security Officers, and in the general safety of employees and guests. Assists the Security Director in the development, recommendation and implementation of security and safety programs to fit the changing needs of the property.
	Supervisory Responsibilities:
	Responsible for the supervision of officers and in the absence of the Security Director, assumes responsibility for the department's operation.
Duties:	Assist the Security Director with compliance matters relative to the Tribal-State Compact and departmental procedure manuals
	Makes recommendations and develops an implementation plan for security and safety programs consistent with the changing needs of the property
	Assists the Security Director in the candidate selection process to include potential promotions
	Reviews schedules for consistency, fairness and needs to the business level
	Conducts timely performance management tasks to include evaluations, coaching and corrective action
	Assists the Security Director in conducting security team meetings and department specific training to meet regulatory and compliance standards
	Ensures the facilities are safe and secure from fire, theft, burglary, assault and other such dangers
	Works in conjunction with Tribal Gaming Agency personnel, State Gaming Commission and enforcement agencies (Tribal and local) while complying with NIGC, company policies and procedures (as applicable) and all gaming regulations and ordinances (Gaming Compact, MICS, etc)
	Oversees Port Madison Enterprises Safety Committee and conducts regular inspections
	Stays current with OSHA regulations and serves as company liaison during inspections
	Tests and implements emergency procedures, evacuation plans, security and safety of door access and other related duties
Qualifications:	High school diploma or GED equivalent required. Some college course learning in law enforcement, security or related field helpful. Security Casino Management/Supervisory experience preferred.

Figure 13.40   Career profile: security manager—Casino Resort.

As can be deduced from the chart itself, the control boards and commissions are part and parcel of the gaming and casino industry experience and provide a variety of occupational opportunities as well. For example, the board is in need of hearing officers and investigators, as well as field officer and agents to conduct business. To take action, the board or commission must rely upon persons trained in law enforcement, security and its critical technology, and evidence gathering and analysis. As an example, the Pennsylvania Gaming Control Board publishes a hearing calendar monthly (http://gamingcontrolboard.pa.gov/?p=281) listing appeals and hearings relating to exclusion list of persons, denial of permits, and recovery of winnings allegedly denied, to name just a few.[62]

Each of these adjudications requires personnel knowledgeable of rules, regulations, and laws applicable to the gaming industry but will consider similar talents to deliver adequate due process. All of these processes are publically announced.

---

[62] Pennsylvania Gaming Control Board, Hearings & Appeals Calendar, at http://gamingcontrolboard.pa.gov/?p=281.

Description

Job Summary

Protect Tribal assets in the Casino and provide general security for customers and Team Members. Provide armed escorts when required.

Duties & Responsibilities include the following. Other duties may be assigned.

- Protect Tribal assets from theft, provide armed escorts.
- Stand assigned security post throughout the Casino.
- Provide security during the daily pull.
- Conduct the drop from the various gaming tables.
- Deliver chip fills from the main cashier's cage to a table when requested.
- Provide cash vouchers to video personnel for problem machine payouts.
- Provide general armed security for casino patrons and customers.
- Participate and qualify in various training sessions, including bi-annual firearm training.
- May be responsible for security via exterior and/or bike patrol.

Requirements

Qualifications

To perform this job successfully, an individual must have the ability to maintain strict confidentiality of classified/sensitive information. Must be competent with various PC based software programs and standard office equipment. Must be able to establish and maintain productive working relationship with co-workers and management and prioritize multiple tasks in a fast-paced environment.

Education and/or Experience

High school diploma or GED required. Knowledge of National Indian Gaming Commission licensing and compliance regulations preferred. One year experience in a law enforcement or security position required. Firearms and Guard Card required.

Work Environment

The duties of this position are performed both within the Casino Resort, and outside the Casino Resort. Employees may be exposed to moderate noise. Employees may be exposed to tobacco smoke, and when assigned outside, to direct sun, wind, dust and both very high, and very low temperatures.

Additional Information

Type of Position: Full Time

Category: Security

Figure 13.41   Career profile: security officer at Gaming Facility.

See Figure 13.44.

Most control boards or commissions seek to maintain integrity in the industry and given that money and power often corrupt both people and places, the industry has to be forever mindful of how easily it can slide into criminality. Most control boards are designed with similar organizational structures. See Figure 13.45 for the State of Michigan's model.

13.5.3 Professional associations and certifications

The dramatic rise of the industry and the call for best practices in day-to-day operations have prompted calls for higher levels of professionalism, research, and continuing education.[63] Even major research universities, such as the

---

[63] D.J. Boxx & A. Zajic, *Casino Security & Gaming Surveillance* (CRC Press, 2010).

Figure 13.42   Gaming Control Board officer badge.

UNLV, engage in systematic, quantitative, and qualitative research on the gaming industry as well as offer academic programs that prepare people for mid-level and senior leadership positions. The UNLV offers an undergraduate degree in gaming management, and in its promotional literature, ties the academic offering to the following career possibilities:

- Slot Analyst
- Slot Floorperson
- Casino Financial Analyst
- Casino Marketing Analyst
- Casino Marketing Coordinator
- Poker Room Supervisor
- Race and Sports Supervisor
- ShuffleMaster Management Trainee
- VIP Services Supervisor
- Casino Management Trainee (Table Games and Slots)
- Casino Cage Supervisor
- Pit Clerk Supervisor
- Surveillance Operator
- Credit Administrator
- Title 31 Coordinator
- Technology Sales Representative
- Technology Account Manager[64]

Certificates in gaming management and casino operations are offered by a host of colleges and universities, both online and residentially.

---

[64] UNLV, Gaming Management Brochure, at https://www.unlv.edu/sites/default/files/24/GamingCareers.pdf.

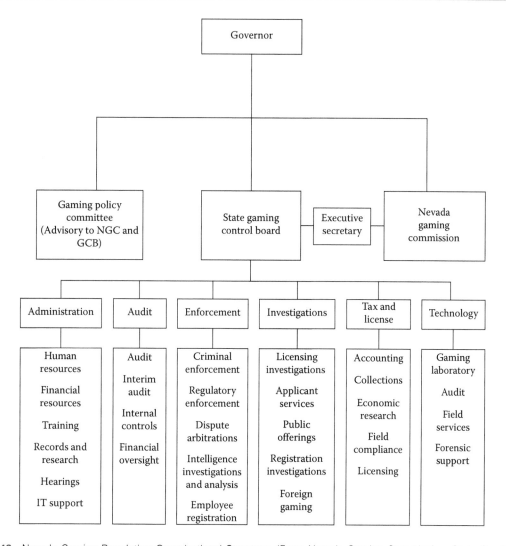

Figure 13.43 Nevada Gaming Regulation Organizational Structure. (From Nevada Gaming Commission, State Gaming Control Board.)

13.5.3.1 Certificate in casino management

Whether you are new to the industry or trying to upgrade your skills to advance into supervisory and managerial positions, the Isenberg Casino Management Certificate provides students with an opportunity to learn the industry, review legal and regulatory aspects of gaming, and understand the relationship of the casino industry to the overall tourism environment.

The certificate in casino management is part of the Isenberg Hospitality and Tourism Management (HTM) program, ranked #1 nationally Best Online Bachelor of Science in HTM and accredited by the Accreditation Commission for Programs in Hospitality Administration (ACPHA).

The certificate in casino management requires completion of five courses. Students may also take courses without pursuing the certificate.

- HT-MGT 260 Personnel Management
- HT-MGT 317 Casino Management
- HT-MGT 356 Beverage Management
- HT-MGT 419 Gaming and Social Policy

Enforcement Investigator

Purpose

- To serve as Investigator in the Enforcement Section ("Section") of the Investigations and Enforcement Division ("Division") of the Indiana Gaming Commission ("Commission"), reporting directly to the Assistant Director of Enforcement. The Investigator is responsible for conducting all investigatory activities on the assigned riverboats.

Responsibilities and Duties

- Work directly under the supervision of the Assistant Director of Enforcement.
- Ensure strict compliance with all applicable Commission policies, directives, administrative rules and regulations.
- Maintain a close relationship with the Assistant Director of Enforcement, coordinating investigatory and enforcement activities.
- Obtain thorough knowledge of the internal controls of the assigned riverboats.
- Remain apprised of current and emerging issues at the assigned riverboats.
- Develop and maintain detailed and current knowledge of gaming enforcement activities.
- Develop and maintain positive working relationships with federal, state and local law enforcement officers as necessary to conduct and assist in investigations and activities effectively.
- Develop and maintain close relationship with all applicable law enforcement and regulatory agencies.
- Obtain working knowledge of riverboat personnel responsibilities and maintain professional working relationships with those individuals.
- Complete all enforcement work and reports with the maximum amount of proficiency, effort and accuracy in accordance with the Case Management System and Standard Operating Procedures.
  - Comply with the Case Management System.
  - Comply with the goals and activities established in conjunction with performance metrics, where applicable.
- Comply with all enforcement schedules, practices and deadlines.
- Comply with performance appraisal activities.
- Conduct gaming enforcement operations on the assigned riverboats.
- Understand, monitor and utilize security and surveillance systems at the assigned riverboats.
- Obtain proficiency in the utilization of the Commission's Electronic Gaming Device System.
- Investigate public and industry complaints, grievances and disputes as assigned.
- Advise the Assistant Director of Enforcement of all matters impacting the Commission.
- Perform general police duties when required.
- Perform daily administrative functions.
- Answer internal and external inquiries as needed or directed.
- Address government and public gatherings as required.
- Facilitate coordination among all federal, state and local law enforcement entities when necessary.
- Maintain optimum level of integrity and professionalism.
- Perform other duties as directed.

Job Requirements and Difficulty of Work

- Bachelor's degree or four years of relevant professional experience. Both education and experience can be substituted on a year for year basis.
- Ability to conduct criminal investigations.
- Ability to conduct investigative interviews effectively.
- Ability to objectively and promptly analyze issues.
- Ability to develop thorough knowledge of the application of criminal law.
- Strong administrative and communication skills.
- Ability to learn and monitor the essential functions of the electronic gaming device tracking system utilized at the assigned riverboats.
- Ability to develop thorough knowledge of Commission rules, regulations and procedures.
- Ability to develop knowledge of intelligence gathering, rules of evidence and court proceedings.
- Ability to develop familiarity with the application of statutes, administrative rules and policies.
- Ability to maintain strict confidentiality.
- Knowledge of covert and overt investigations.
- Be a United States citizen.
- Be a resident of the State of Indiana.
- Possess and maintain a valid driver's license.
- Be a minimum of 21 years of age.
- No felony convictions.
- Successfully pass a background investigation.
- Successfully pass any written and/or physical test required by the Commission.
- Successfully pass the Indiana Gaming Agent's Academy.

Figure 13.44 Career profile: casino enforcement agent—State of Indiana.

(Continued)

- Successfully pass drug testing as required by the Commission.
- Ability to operate state vehicles in compliance with Commission Policy.
- Adhere to the Commission policy prohibiting Commission employees from gambling or playing any licensed game or gaming device under the jurisdiction of the Commission in the State of Indiana.
- Comply with the Indiana Office of Technology's Information Security Policies and Minimum Compliance Requirements.

Personal Work Relationships
- Work with and coordinate activities with the Administrative Division and the Background and Financial Investigations Section.
- Work with and coordinate activities with Supervisors and Enforcement Agents.
  - Maintain positive working relationships with local law enforcement entities in the riverboat communities.
- Work with and facilitate productive relationships with federal, state and local law enforcement agencies.
- Work with and facilitate productive relationships with applicable regulatory agencies sharing oversight responsibilities of the gaming industry.
- Work in a professional and courteous manner with all patrons, applicants and persons related to the riverboat operations and also all persons involved in investigations.

Physical Effort and Work Environment
- Job tasks are primarily accomplished in the riverboat environment.
- Working hours are normally ten (10) hours per day, four calendar days per week, but could be subject to flexible scheduling or be extended by the workload and emergency situations.
- Work is often performed in an accelerated environment and under stressful conditions.
- Overtime and compensatory time must be approved as directed by the Superintendent of Gaming Agents.

Figure 13.44   (Continued) Career profile: casino enforcement agent—State of Indiana.

- HT-MGT 334 Special Events Management or HT-MGT 337 Meeting, Convention & Exposition Management

Other schools such as State University of New York at Morrisville and the University of Southern Mississippi offer similar courses of study and prepare students for managerial careers in the gaming industry. Just as important to the professionalism of the casino setting has been the development of academic journals dedicated to the study and analysis of the gaming setting. A few examples worth reading are *Casino Journal* and UNLV's *Gaming Research and Review Journal*.

Professional certifications from various industry groups are widely available to security professionals in the gaming sector, though colleges and universities appear the lead players. The ASIS lists Gaming and Wagering Protection as one of its essential council components, its mission being

> Promotes the practices, processes, and procedures of security and surveillance management to professionals in venues where gaming and wagering are legalized and regulated.[65]

The International Association of Certified Surveillance Professionals (IACSP) (see Figure 13.46) prepares technologists for the gaming industry and its many locales for placement. The industry's eye is probably the broadest of any context or setting outside of the prison setting. The IACSP targets those areas the casino is most concerned about including

- Blackjack
- Roulette
- Pai Gow
- Poker
- Baccarat
- Internal Theft and Fraud
- Internal Audits
- Players Club
- Food and Beverage
- Retail

---

[65] ASIS International, Gaming and Wagering Protection webpage, at https://www.asisonline.org/Membership/Member-Center/Councils/gw/Pages/default.aspx.

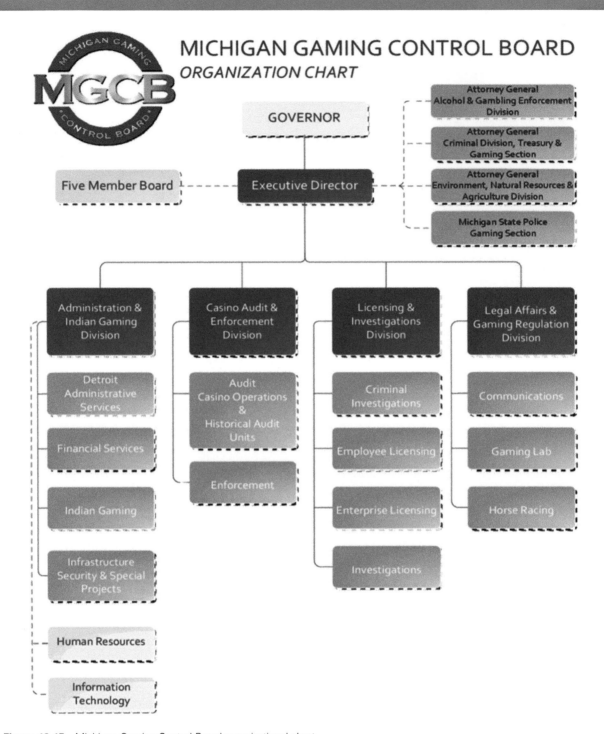

Figure 13.45   Michigan Gaming Control Board organizational chart.

- Camera Skills and Techniques
- Card Counting
- Basic Strategy
- Game Protection
- Investigations
- Surveillance Responsibilities[66]

---

[66] IACSP website, Certification webpage, at http://www.iacsp.org/certification.

Figure 13.46 IACSP logo.

The Institute of Internal Auditors (see Figure 13.47) tracks the money flow at gaming facilities and hopes to prevent or deter money mishandling and misreporting and at the same time ferrets out the fraudulent activity that often goes hand in hand with large money supplies. The certification's overall mission is to

- Provide a forum for gaming audit practitioners working in casinos, lotteries, racetracks, other gaming enterprises, and government regulatory commissions or agencies.
- Foster the development of guidance and educational products regarding the industry.
- Communicate new techniques and best practices to practitioners.
- Provide training for all levels of auditors through on-site seminars and conferences.
- Grow and serve the profession.

When compared to other sectors of the security industry, the gaming and casino sector has a way to go relative to professional bodies or organizations that lay out best practices for security. Certainly, larger organizations such as the American Gaming Association have an interest in the security of their assets and installations, yet even despite this broad coverage, the industry need establish a more vigorous professional membership class. With its many layers of responsibility and increasing levels of technological sophistication, the field is no longer exclusively access guards. Instead, the security gaming side of things gets more complicated by the moment.[67]

States, such as Indiana, are starting to see the advanced nature of security function at a casino facility and are presently considering a new, novel academy for Casino Police—trained to specialize in the often obtuse operations of the casino. The legislature is rightfully considering whether the simple plant of an Indiana State Trooper to oversee the gaming venture is a satisfactory policy. From a knowledge base alone, that program is woefully insufficient.[68]

Finally, if we accept the growing complexity of the industry, understanding that its technology and hardware requirements are only getting more esoteric and that ferreting out the sham gambler and trickster becoming more challenging by the moment, expending time and energy on training, education, certification, and the professional workings of associations and groups makes imminent sent. The industry cannot rest on the present level of expectations, but instead ratchet up to a far higher level.[69]

Figure 13.47 The Institute of Internal Auditors logo.

---

[67] See S. Collen, Leading the Way to the Future of Gambling, *Sec. Tech. Executive* (March 2010), at 36.
[68] See Casino Police Would Get Specialized Training, *Organized Crime Digest* (March 2003), at 3.
[69] See P. Rothman, Lessons Learned from the Casino Floor, *Sec. Tech. Executive* (March 2011), at 50.

13.6 CONCLUSION

Institutional coverage of the private security industry and the many services it provides continues in this chapter. The emphasis here has been on how the industry protects hotels, motels, nightclubs, and aligned entertainment venues, the demands of safety and security in large-scale events and venues, and the unique and complex challenges presented by the world of gaming and casinos. In each of these settings, we witness the preeminent role that the security industry has taken since public policing resources are incapable of handling this massive infrastructure. To be certain, private security is out front in all of these institutional frameworks. In each of these settings, the chapter has provided a broad overview of opportunities in light of career growth, economic expansion, and a very bright participatory future. In each of these settings, the reader has been exposed to the "best practices" that protect both assets and people as well as a special emphasis on professionalization and certification opportunities. The chapter covers the various constituency groups that shape and mold the protocols for security and safety. Finally, the chapter lays out the many unique demands these locales provide: the need to be aligned closely with public entities and the wisdom of working closely with staff, management, and the community leaders where these institutions reside.

Keywords

asset protection	food service	mega-malls
bomb assessment	Gaming Control Board	nightclub operators
boosters	gaming industry	organized retail crime
casino facilities	gaming management	professional shoplifters
Commercial Facilities Sector	gaming surveillance officers	property theft
crime prevention	growth industry	retail establishments
crowd control	hospitality industry	retail theft
crowd managers	hoteliers	shopping mall
crowd motivation	hotels	sports arena
event security	internal crime	super stores
event promoters/sponsors	lodging	traffic management
facility management	mass casualties	workplace violence

Discussion questions

1. Outline the key vulnerabilities in the U.S. lodging industry and discuss how they can be overcome.
2. Discuss the special protocols for hotel and hospitality security and when they may be of use to the security specialist.
3. Review and discuss the guiding principles for security services at large-scale events.
4. What items must be identified and discussed before a security plan for a large-scale event can be developed or implemented?
5. Outline the special protocols in mall security. Discuss any shortcomings or improvements.
6. Discuss the rise of organized retail crime and methods to detect and prevent it.
7. What two realities drive the regulatory oversight of the gaming industry? Why?
8. How do professional certifications assist the security officer in their chosen field?

CHAPTER 14

Information, IT, and computer security

OBJECTIVES

After completing this chapter, the student will be able to

1. Discuss how risk assessments and analyses take into account the potential political, social, and financial losses that could be suffered in the event that information is accessed, modified, and obtained without authorization.
2. Identify the physical security measures used to protect a facility where sensitive data are stored.
3. Describe how and why operations security (or OPSEC) views operations from the perspective of a perpetrator in order to identify vulnerabilities.
4. Explain the methods used by communications security (COMSEC) to deny competitors, criminals, and adversaries information derived from telecommunications and to ensure the authentication of communications.
5. Outline how computer security seeks to protect systems against vulnerabilities, threats, and attacks by seeking not only system security, but also network and data security.
6. Assess the approach known as defense in depth, a combination of physical security, personnel security, and cybersecurity, and discuss its usefulness.

14.1 INTRODUCTION

Information and computer technologies are used to record, store, analyze, and transfer data. The information that is recorded, stored, analyzed, and transferred within these technologies is considered one of the most important and valuable assets of public and private sector organizations. Public sector organizations (e.g., government agencies) seek to protect information, which could harm national security (e.g., state secrets) and national economic security if exposed to a foreign government, foreign agent,[1] or foreign instrumentality.[2] Private sector organizations (e.g., businesses) try to protect trade secrets[3] because this information could harm businesses if disclosed to a third party (e.g., individual, business, or foreign government) without authorization. The unauthorized disclosure of trade secrets can also harm national economic security. Public and private organizations also seek to protect other proprietary information (e.g., financial data) and employee, customer, and operations data. This chapter examines information and

---

[1] Under 18 U.S.C. § 1839(2), a foreign agent is "any officer, employee, proxy, servant, delegate, or representative of a foreign government."

[2] Under 18 U.S.C. § 1839(1), foreign instrumentality refers to "any agency, bureau, ministry, component, institution, association, or any legal, commercial, or business organization, corporation, firm, or entity that is substantially owned, controlled, sponsored, commanded, managed, or dominated by a foreign government."

[3] Trade secrets are defined under 18 U.S.C. § 1839(3) as "all forms and types of financial, business, scientific, technical, economic, or engineering information, including patterns, plans, compilations, program devices, formulas, designs, prototypes, methods, techniques, processes, procedures, programs, or codes, whether tangible or intangible, and whether or how stored, compiled, or memorialized physically, electronically, graphically, photographically, or in writing."

computer security measures, looking in particular at the policies, practices, and procedures used by private organizations to protect information.

14.2 INFOSEC

Information security (INFOSEC) seeks to protect information from accidental or intentional unauthorized disclosure, access, alternation, deletion, copying, or other use. INFOSEC risk assessments and analyses provide insights into the probability (i.e., likelihood), criticality (i.e., impact), and vulnerability (i.e., exposure) of information to a potential threat. These risk assessments and analyses take into account the potential political, social, and financial losses that could be suffered in the event that information is accessed, modified, and obtained without authorization, such as liabilities, abuse of information, and the cost of replacement. INFOSEC includes a combination of physical security, operations security (OPSEC), communications security (COMSEC), and computer security (COMPUSEC) measures, each of which is explored further in Figure 14.1.

14.2.1 Physical security

Organizations implement protective measures designed to deny criminals and adversaries access and proximity to information. To protect information, both the physical security of the facility where data are stored and the security of systems that store this information are required. Physical security measures should include access control systems, which enable an authority to control individual access to computer systems, servers, and the areas within which these are located, alarm systems, surveillance systems, and security personnel (e.g., security guards).[4]

Strong authentication measures are needed to prevent access to areas where computer systems and servers are located and the data within them. These measures should include those that prove "what you know" (e.g., passwords), "what you have" (e.g., tokens and badges), and "what you are" (e.g., biometrics).[5] Effective physical security requires multifactor authentication, which includes a combination of the measures designed to prove "what you know," "what you have," and "what you are."

BOX 14.1   INFORMATION VERSUS INTELLIGENCE

All information is not intelligence. Information becomes intelligence when it is contextually analyzed in relation to other information in order to determine its substantive value. Intelligence can be thought of as a product that results from the gathering, processing, assimilating, examining, evaluating, and interpreting of information about entities gleaned from open source and/or confidential methods and sources.[1] It is collected and analyzed in order to better comprehend an entity whose actions may affect an organization's interests.[2] This intelligence gathering and analysis also enables an organization to forecast an entity's actions[3]; thereby, enabling preemptive action to be taken.

[1] M. Lowenthal, *Intelligence: From Secrets to Policy* (3rd ed., Washington DC: CQ Press, 2006).
[2] A. Breakspear, A New Definition of Intelligence, 28(5) *Intelligence and National Security* 678–693 (2013).
[3] *Ibid.*

14.2.2 OPSEC

An often-overlooked fact is that an essential element of information security is operational security. Operations security (or OPSEC) identifies, controls, and protects an organization's information in order to deny its access to competitors, criminals, and potential adversaries (hereafter perpetrators). To determine which potential information perpetrators might seek and gain access to, a risk assessment is conducted. With OPSEC, operations are viewed from the perspective of a perpetrator in order to identify vulnerabilities. This process assists in anticipating areas within and practices of an organization that a perpetrator might exploit for their own gain. A common tactic used by perpetrators is trash trawling. To prevent anything of value from being obtained in the event that this does occur, documents with employee, customer, operations, and proprietary data should not be disposed of in the regular trash.

---

[4] See Chapter 7 of this book for further information about physical security.
[5] R. Lehtinen, D. Russell, & G.T. Gangemi Sr, *Computer Security Basics* 51 (Sebastopol, California: O'Reilly, 2006).

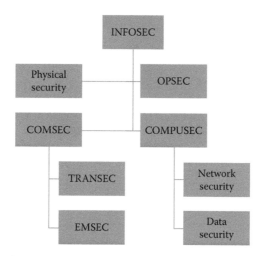

Figure 14.1 Components of INFOSEC.

Policies and procedures must be in place to ensure that information is protected from those who should not have access to them. Personnel should be trained on these procedures as well. Overall, the OPSEC process is designed to assist organizations in applying the countermeasures needed to deny perpetrators access to information.

Web Exercise: Go to http://www.dodea.edu/offices/safety/opsec.cfm and review the information provided about OPSEC. Search online to find a case where a perpetrator (or perpetrators) obtained information from a business/company in the U.S. commercial sector. Provide background information about the case and how OPSEC could have denied the perpetrators access to the information.

14.2.2.1 Social engineering

Social engineering, the practice "of manipulating, deceiving, influencing, or tricking individuals into divulging confidential information or performing acts that will benefit the social engineer in some way,"[6] is not a new phenomenon. For years, individuals have tried to sway, mislead, or con others for their benefit. Those engaging in social engineering first gather information about the target. This information can be obtained through dumpster diving (i.e., checking garbage for documents thrown out without shredding) because organizations have carelessly discarded information in the garbage; information that could be used to target the organization and/or its employees. A case in point is Crest Food, a grocery store in Oklahoma City, Oklahoma. In January 2016, the private information (e.g., social security numbers, bank routing numbers, and direct deposit information) of employees from Crest Food was found in a dumpster. Those engaging in social engineering will also go to the organization's website and social media websites of employees and the organization, and obtain information about the company and its employees from these websites.

The information gathered from these sources is then used to elicit further information from individuals within an organization. Social engineers elicit information from employees by pretending to be technical support or another employee that works for the organization who requires the target's assistance. This assistance is, for example, requested through letters and emails designed to trick employees into revealing information about the organization and/or themselves (e.g., phishing).[7] One such incident occurred in March 2016, where a phishing attack led to the disclosure of employee W-2 information at Sprouts Farmers Market.[8] The ultimate goal of social engineers is to obtain data about a target's vulnerabilities and exploit these vulnerabilities for the benefit of the perpetrator.

---

[6] M.-H. Maras, *Computer Forensics: Cybercriminals, Laws and Evidence* 141 (2nd ed., Burlington, Massachusetts: Jones and Bartlett, 2014).

[7] Phishing is "a type of cybercrime in which individuals deceive others by posing as legitimately established enterprises so as to steal communication users' valuable personal information, such as account data and credit card information." *Ibid., at* 15.

[8] State of California, Office of Attorney General. Submitted Breach Notification Sample—Sprouts Farmers Market. U.S. Department of Justice (2016), at http://oag.ca.gov/ecrime/databreach/reports/sb24-60739

BOX 14.2   BUSINESS COUNTERINTELLIGENCE

Business counterintelligence aims at preventing a competitor from obtaining knowledge that would provide them with an advantage. Businesses also seek to protect information that would have detrimental effects on the organization if it were obtained and/or used by a competitor and/or made available to the public. This information includes confidential data that they are required to protect, such as customer and employee data, which, if compromised, could have adverse consequences on the business. Business counterintelligence protects an organization from the intelligence collection efforts of competitors, criminals, and potential adversaries.

14.2.3   COMSEC

Communications security (COMSEC) seeks to deny competitors, criminals, and adversaries information derived from telecommunications and to ensure the authentication of communications. Transmission security (TRANSEC) and emissions security (EMSEC) are part of COMSEC efforts. TRANSEC seeks to protect transmissions from interception or interference, whereas EMSEC prevents an adversary from using compromising emanations to obtain information. Encryption, which physically blocks third-party access to communications, can be used to protect communications and is part of COMSEC efforts (Figure 14.2).

14.2.4   COMPUSEC

Computer security (or COMPUSEC) seeks to protect systems against vulnerabilities (e.g., unpatched/misconfigured systems and devices), threats (e.g., potential unauthorized access to systems), and attacks (e.g., phishing). Network security and data security are a part of COMPUSEC. Network security includes proactive measures designed to deal with a variety of threats and attacks, and prevents them from accessing, spreading, modifying, damaging, and/or otherwise adversely impacting the network in any way. In its most basic sense, network security involves the policies, procedures, and practices that ensure the validity, reliability, and usability of a network and protection of the network. The purpose of network security is to provide secure connections between senders and receivers and to ensure the integrity (i.e., the data are what they purport to be and have not been modified or otherwise altered in any

---

The Bureau of Labor Statistics of the U.S. Department of Labor lists the summary of duties, requirements, pay, and job outlook for computer security analysts as follows:[1]

What Computer Systems Analysts Do

"Computer systems analysts study an organization's current computer systems and procedures and design information systems solutions to help the organization operate more efficiently and effectively. They bring business and information technology (IT) together by understanding the needs and limitations of both."

How to Become a Computer Systems Analyst

"A bachelor's degree in a computer or information science field is common, although not always a requirement. Some firms hire analysts with business or liberal arts degrees who have skills in information technology or computer programming."

Pay

"The median annual wage for computer systems analysts was $85,800 in May 2015."

Job Outlook

"Employment of computer systems analysts is projected to grow 21 percent from 2014 to 2024, much faster than the average for all occupations. Growth in cloud computing, cybersecurity, and mobile networks will increase demand for these workers."

---

[1] Bureau of Labor Statistics, U.S. Department of Labor. (2016). Computer Systems Analysts. http://www.bls.gov/ooh/computer-and-information-technology/computer-systems-analysts.htm

Figure 14.2   Career Profile: Computer systems analysts.

way), confidentiality (i.e., protection of private, proprietary, and sensitive data), and availability of data transmitted over a network. In a similar fashion, data security seeks to prevent unauthorized access to and intentional or unintentional modification, corruption, or deletion of data. Data security policies provide information on what data are collected, the manner in which they should be stored and secured, and the manner in which they will be deleted. COMPUSEC measures seek not only system security, but also network and data security. Before examining organizations' COMPUSEC measures, the threats to organizations are identified.

14.2.4.1 Cybercrime

Organizations need to be protected from insider and outsider threats. Insider threats are initiated by someone inside of the organization and include the misuse and abuse of systems and networks, and the modification, deletion, and theft of data by employees or contractors. The insider has access to the system, network, and data, but uses it in an unauthorized way that exceeds his or her authorization and privileges. Outsider threats are initiated by someone outside of the organization and include competitors, nation-states, criminals, and cybercriminals. Outsiders are unauthorized users of the system, network, and data. One of the greatest insider and outsider threats to U.S. businesses is cybercrime, which involves the commission of an illicit act that uses and/or targets Internet-enabled computers and related digital technology.[9] It is considered one the greatest threats to U.S. businesses because it has the ability to reach and adversely affect organizations around the globe.[10] Because cybercrime transcends traditional borders, it also poses distinct challenges to organizations worldwide.

Insider and outsider threats are those capable of exploiting system vulnerabilities and harming assets of an organization (i.e., people, property, and proprietary information). Systems are vulnerable to unauthorized access, theft, manipulation, and destruction. Indeed, organizations have experienced breaches of their computer systems, networks, and data. Particularly, cybercriminals have gained unauthorized access to systems, infected systems, and viewed, altered, damaged, and/or stolen information from them. A cybercriminal who gains unauthorized access to a system is known as a hacker. A cybercriminal may also seek to adversely impact the availability of the system to legitimate users by disrupting services through denial of service (DoS)[11] and distributed denial of service (DDoS) attacks.[12] These cyberattacks are designed to "overwhelm...the resources of the target...causing them to deny server access to other computers making legitimate requests."[13]

Cybercriminals may further seek to infect organizations' systems with malicious software (i.e., malware), which causes some form of harm to their targets. One form of malware is a computer virus, which piggybacks on legitimate programs (e.g., Microsoft Office documents, executable files, and zip files) and executes when an action is taken by a user.[14] A common misperception is that users need to do something, such as click on an attachment or website links, to download malware. This is not necessarily true for all forms of malware. In fact, there are certain types of malware that do not require any user activity to spread; namely, computer worms, which are self-propagating and do not require user activity to spread.[15] A Trojan horse is another form of malware, which masquerades as a legitimate program, but includes malware designed to monitor user activity, steal information, or cause some other form of harm to the user whose device is infected with this malicious software. A type of Trojan horse that is currently targeting organizations is cryptoransomware. Cryptoransomware encrypts data on a target's system in an effort to extort money from the target in order to decrypt the information. A hospital in Los Angeles, California was the target of cryptoransomware (Locky), which took systems offline for over a week until the ransom in Bitcoin[16] (the equivalent of $17,000) was paid.[17]

---

[9] Maras, *supra note 6*; M.-H. Maras, *Transnational Security* 137 (Boca Raton, Florida: CRC Press, 2014).

[10] M.-H. Maras, *Cybercriminology* (New York: Oxford University Press, 2016).

[11] A DoS attack involves the use of a single computer to launch cyberattacks against a computer system (or computer systems). Maras, *supra note 6, at 7*.

[12] A DDoS attack involves the use of multiple computers to launch—often simultaneous—DoS attacks against a computer system (or computer systems). *Ibid., at 8*.

[13] *Ibid., at 7*.

[14] *Ibid., at 8*.

[15] *Ibid., at 9*.

[16] M.-H. Maras, Inside Darknet: The Takedown of Silk Road, 98(1) *Criminal Justice Matters* 22 (2014).

[17] K. Zetter. Why Hospitals Are the Perfect Targets for Ransomware, *Wired* (March 30, 2016), at https://www.wired.com/2016/03/ransomware-why-hospitals-are-the-perfect-targets/

A further form of malware is spyware, which, if downloaded to a user's device, monitors user activity and relays this activity to the person who created and/or distributed the malware. This form of malware can also spy on targets by activating their webcams and in some cases, their microphones. Antivirus and antispyware programs have been developed to protect users' digital devices from these forms of malware. Nevertheless, even fake antivirus and anti-spyware programs have been created, which are installed on a user's system and notify the user of purported threats found on the user's machine. Such threats have not actually been found. These programs offer to deal with the ficti-tious malware for a fee.

Cybercriminals who target organizations can be lone actors, groups, businesses, and nation-states. Those who target organizations may or may not have the technical knowledge, skills, and abilities to conduct cybercrime. Those with-out the necessary knowledge, skills, and abilities can purchase goods and services online to enable them to commit cybercrime.[18] Cybercriminals sell hacking and malware services that are "made to order"; that is, a buyer can, for example, request the type of malware they desire and the cybercriminal will create it and provide it to the buyer for distribution.[19] Cybercriminals who target organizations may also purchase exploit kits, which seek to take advantage of systems and software vulnerabilities.

In addition to cyberattacks, cybercriminals targeting an organization may seek to view, steal, or otherwise obtain data for subsequent sale or personal use. The types of information that could be stolen are trade secrets, propri-etary information (e.g., financial data) and employee, customer, and operations data. This information is then used to engage in, for example, economic espionage and fraudulent activity. For instance, in 2012, Derek Wai Hung Tam Sing stole and distributed the trade secrets of an aircraft avionics company, Pasadena-based Rogerson Kratos (RK), to competitors both inside and outside of the United States.[20] In regard to fraudulent activity, in 2016, several hotels that are part of the Trump Hotel Collection reported a pattern of credit card fraud targeting customers.[21] That same year, the credit card system at Wendy's was breached, resulting in the theft and use of debit and credit card data of customers (i.e., names, credit card numbers, and expiration dates) used in over 1000 restaurant locations.[22] The number of affected users has not been released, only the locations where cards were used that were compromised.

Cybercriminals can impersonate an organization to obtain money, credit, goods, or services or can impersonate employees within the company for espionage and fraudulent purposes. A common social engineering tactic used to engage in impersonation fraud is a spearphishing attack. Spearphishing involves the sending of emails from what looks like higher-level officials within an organization, making it more likely that employees will fall victim to this scam.[23] To engage in this type of attack, the perpetrator may have spoofed the email address or hacked into the company executive's or manager's email account to send the messages. In 2016, several spearphishing attacks were reported by U.S. companies. One such incident involved Lamps Plus. In this incident, a perpetrator posing as a company executive was able to obtain employee W-2 information at Lamps Plus through a spearphishing attack.[24] The following month, in April 2016, Bristol Farms reported a breach that involved social engineering. Particularly, the perpetrator posed as a company executive in order to elicit information from employees for subsequent use. The perpetrator compromised current and former employees' names, addresses, social security numbers, and information about employee compensation and deductions. The information obtained from the organization could be used by cybercriminals to engage in identity theft. Identity theft occurs when a perpetrator assumes the identity of the target or utilizes identity data in some way in order to obtain money, credit, goods, or services.

---

[18] See Chapter 11, Maras, *Cybercriminology supra note* 10.

[19] *Ibid.*

[20] U.S. Attorney's Office, Central District of California. Glendale Man Who Stole and Distributed Trade Secrets Belonging to Former Employer Sentenced to One Year in Federal Prison. Department of Justice (2016), at https://www.justice.gov/usao-cdca/pr/glendale-man-who-stole-and-distributed-trade-secrets-belonging-former-employer

[21] B. Krebs, Trump Hotels Breached Again, *Krebs on Security* (April 4, 2016), at http://krebsonsecurity.com/2016/04/sources-trump-hotels-breached-again/#more-34378

[22] C. Isidore, Wendy's Credit Card Hack Hit 1,000 Restaurants, *CNN Money* (July 8, 2016), at http://money.cnn.com/2016/07/08/news/companies/wendys-hack/

[23] Maras, *Transnational supra note 9, at* 305.

[24] State of California, Office of Attorney General. Submitted Breach Notification Sample—Lamps Plus and Pacific Coast Lighting. U.S. Department of Justice (2016), at http://oag.ca.gov/ecrime/databreach/reports/sb24-60670

14.2.4.2 Cybersecurity measures

Cybersecurity seeks to "deter, detect, protect, and defend against threats"[25] and includes policies, procedures, guidelines, practices, and software tools that are designed to protect computer systems. In addition to these, cybersecurity requires that the hardware of computer systems be designed with security in mind. Consider Aldrich Ames, a CIA agent charged with spying for Russia,[26] who was able to download classified material from his work terminal to floppy disks.[27] The case of Ames brought home the lesson that attention needed to be paid to the hardware of computer systems. Because of Ames' actions, disk drives were removed from government computer systems to prevent the copying of information. Additionally, desktops were used that contained no disk drives and USB ports were disabled.[28] Even after the Ames case and the changes made to computer systems, it was revealed that the copying of information was still occurring within the intelligence community. Particularly, Chelsea Manning (formerly Bradley Manning) copied classified information to a CD and later provided this information to WikiLeaks, which subsequently published it.[29] Despite the fact that at the time of the breach, a general ban existed on all removable media, Manning was able to download data to the CD because the policy was inconsistently enforced.[30] This incident illustrates the dangers associated with BYODs (bring your own devices), personal portable digital and storage devices such as smartphones, iPods, USBs, and CDs, among other items, to the workplace. Manning was also able to download a vast amount of information without alerting information technology personnel.[31] Here, the personnel failed to appropriately monitor the network for such abnormal activity and programs were not in place to detect such activities. The Ames and Manning cases brought home the lesson that greater control and monitoring of data, and document accountability were required.

Cybersecurity measures should be implemented in organizations to protect systems, as well as the network and data from cybercrime and other forms of illicit activity. These security measures include access control, data access control, encryption, firewalls, and information security and computer-use monitoring policies.

14.2.4.2.1 Access control

A key cybersecurity measure is access control, which prevents unauthorized users from accessing systems, networks, and data, and monitors access to and actions within systems and networks. Access control systems determine privileges of users; that is, who is authorized to login to the system and network, and what data they are authorized to access once access to the system is granted. Access control, therefore, focuses on authorization and ensuring that users access only the information they have the authority to access by setting limits and monitoring users' access to systems and networks. As a general rule, access control must not impede normal daily operations and place too many burdens on employees of an organization. The policies of an organization will ultimately dictate access control.

Examples of system access controls are login/password controls. Such controls could be implemented to limit the login attempts of users. After a few incorrect attempts to input a username and password combination, the user can be locked out of the system. Other system access controls may delay the user from logging in to the system for a specific period of time (e.g., hours, and depending on the number of attempts, even days) after unsuccessful attempts to input their username and password combination. This control seeks to protect users against the use of a password cracker, which is a program used to recover unknown passwords. Passwords can be cracked through a *brute-force attack*, whereby a program automatically enters passwords utilizing every combination of letters, numbers, or symbols, one password at a time, or *dictionary attack*, a program that utilizes "text files containing words in a dictionary or passwords that specifically relate to the…target."[32]

---

[25] Maras, *Transnational supra note 9*, at 137.

[26] T. Weiner, Why I Spied; Aldrich Ames, *New York Times* (July 31, 1994), at http://www.nytimes.com/1994/07/31/magazine/why-i-spied-aldrich-ames.html?pagewanted=all

[27] Senate Select Committee on Intelligence, An Assessment of the Aldrich H. Ames Espionage Case and Its Implications for U.S. Intelligence—Part 1 (1994), at http://fas.org/irp/congress/1994_rpt/ssci_ames.htm

[28] FBI, Aldrich Ames (n.d.), at https://www.fbi.gov/history/famous-cases/aldrich-ames

[29] P. Lewis, Bradley Manning Given 35-Year Prison Term for Passing Files to WikiLeaks, *The Guardian* (August 21, 2013), at https://www.theguardian.com/world/2013/aug/21/bradley-manning-35-years-prison-wikileaks-sentence; D. Leigh, How 250,000 US Embassy Cables Were Leaked, *The Guardian* (November 28, 2010), at https://www.theguardian.com/world/2010/nov/28/how-us-embassy-cables-leaked

[30] J. Perlow, Wikileaks: How Our Government IT Failed Us. *ZDNet* (December 1, 2010), at http://www.zdnet.com/article/wikileaks-how-our-government-it-failed-us/

[31] L. Greenemeier & C.Q. Choi, WikiLeaks Breach Highlights Insider Security Threat. *Scientific American* (December 1, 2010), at http://www.scientificamerican.com/article/wikileaks-insider-threat/

[32] Maras *supra note 6*, at 109.

Figure 14.3   CAPTCHA systems add another layer and level of security for gaining access or online transactions.

Certain organizations also utilize the Completely Automated Public Turing test to tell Computers and Humans Apart (or CAPTCHA) to prevent the use of password crackers. Nevertheless, research has shown that CAPTCHA images can be bypassed.[33] The reality is that many of the security measures implemented are not designed to prevent system access; instead, they are designed to either slow the perpetrator down long enough for their illicit behavior to be detected or frustrate the offenders' attempts in an effort to deter them from seeking to gain access to the system (a form of situational crime prevention).[34] See Figure 14.3.

Another system access control involves limiting user login access to specific times and days during the week—during normal business hours. These controls enable system access when security and system administrators are present during normal business hours to monitor access to systems and data. Moreover, usernames and passwords that have not been used for an extended period are locked. Furthermore, passwords are set to expire after a specific short period of time, requiring users to frequently change their passwords. The passwords usually must be of a specific length (at least eight characters long) and include a combination of letters, numbers, and symbols. A common restriction is to prevent users from using the same passwords. Within organizations, passwords are stored in encrypted password files that can only be accessed by limited authorized users (e.g., security administrator). The overall goal of the combination of login/password access controls is to make it extremely difficult for perpetrators to bypass them.

According to Swanson and Guttman (1996), there are two accepted standards of practice for access control—separation of duties and least privilege.[35] The former, separation of duties, involves the division of "roles and responsibilities so that a single individual cannot subvert a critical process."[36] As such, the purpose of separation of duties is to prevent the concentration of power—due to privileges and access to all data—to prevent fraud, theft, abuse, errors, sabotage, circumvention of security controls, and other security breaches that could be detrimental to an

---

[33] For example, see E. Bursztein, J. Aigrain, A. Moscicki, & J.C. Mitchell, The End Is Nigh: Generic Solving of Text-Based CAPTCHAs. In *Proceedings of the 8th USENIX Workshop on Offensive Technologies* (2014); S. Sivakorn, I. Polakis, & A.D. Keromytis, I Am Robot: (Deep) Learning to Break Semantic Image CAPTCHAs. In *Proceedings of the 1st IEEE European Symposium on Security and Privacy*, Saarbrucken, Germany (21–24 March 2016), 388–403; S. Gao, M. Mohamed, N. Saxena, & C. Zhang, Gaming the Game: Defeating a Game CAPTCHA with Efficient and Robust Hybrid Attacks. *2014 IEEE International Conference on Multimedia and Expo* (2014), 1–6; A. Hindle, M.W. Godfrey, & R.C. Holt, Reverse Engineering CAPTCHAs. *15th Working Conference on Reverse Engineering*. IEEE. Antwerp (15–18 October 2008), 59–68.

[34] For more information on situational crime prevention, see R.V. Clarke (Ed.), *Situational Crime Prevention: Successful Case Studies* (2nd ed., New York: Harrow and Heston, 1997).

[35] M. Swanson & B. Guttman Generally Accepted Principles and Practices for Securing Information Technology Systems. NIST Special Publication 800-14. U.S. Department of Commerce, 27 (1996), at http://csrc.nist.gov/publications/nistpubs/800-14/800-14.pdf

[36] *Ibid.*

The Bureau of Labor Statistics of the U.S. Department of Labor lists the summary of duties, requirements, pay, and job outlook for network and computer security administrators as follows:[1]

What Network and Computer Systems Administrators Do

"Computer networks are critical parts of almost every organization. Network and computer systems administrators are responsible for the day-to-day operation of these networks."

How to Become a Network and Computer Systems Administrator

"Most employers require network and computer systems administrators to have a bachelor's degree in a field related to computer or information science. Others may require only a postsecondary certificate."

Pay

"The median annual wage for network and computer systems administrators was $77,810 in May 2015."

Job Outlook

"Employment of network and computer systems administrators is projected to grow 8 percent from 2014 to 2024, about as fast as the average for all occupations. Demand for information technology workers is high and should continue to grow as firms invest in newer, faster technology and mobile networks."

---

[1] Bureau of Labor Statistics, U.S. Department of Labor. (2016). Network and Computer Systems Administrators. http://www.bls.gov/ooh/computer-and-information-technology/network-and-computer-systems-administrators.htm#tab-1

Figure 14.4   Career Profile: Network and computer systems administrators.

organization.[37] Separation of duties thus ensures that the necessary checks and balances are in place and that individuals do not have conflicting responsibilities. One person should not have complete control of the design of the security system, the implementation of security, monitoring security, and reporting on the security of the system. The separation of duties, therefore, prevents one person from having the privileges needed to compromise security controls on their own. The latter, the least privilege, grants "users only…[the access] they need to perform their official duties."[38] This principle dictates that users should have the least number of privileges needed to conduct their work. Accordingly, the duties previously assigned to one user (e.g., system or security administrator) should be divided to others, each with their own distinct roles. See Figure 14.4 for a career profile for a network or computer systems administrator.

14.2.4.2.2 Data access control

Data access controls help protect the system and its data. Particularly, these controls monitor individuals' access to data and ensure that the users are authorized to access the data. There are three types of data access control methods that are primarily used to secure a computer system and network: role-based, discretionary, and mandatory access control. Role-based access control limits network access to users based on their position/role within an organization. Discretionary access controls can limit user access to systems, networks, and data to specific dates and times of the day. Mandatory access controls prevent anyone within an organization from granting access to a resource that a user is forbidden from accessing due to the sensitivity label assigned to it. Mandatory access control assigns sensitivity labels to all users and objects within a system and access to data is determined based on the sensitivity level of the user. These policies contain, among other things, sensitivity labels associated with information; these labels indicate what security level is needed for an entity within an organization to access, view, and modify this information.

Sensitivity labels can be nonhierarchical or hierarchical. Nonhierachical sensitivity labels for public sector organizations include caveats (that concern the nationality of authorized viewers) and compartments (which concern the subject matter of the information). In private sector organizations, the compartments (or categories) often correspond to departments within the organizations (e.g., accounting). Hierarchical sensitivity labels for public sector organizations are those of the classification system of government information: *top secret, secret, confidential,* and *for official use only.* Unauthorized disclosure of information within the *top secret* classification could have grave consequences

---

[37] K. Coleman, Separation of Duties and IT Security. CSO (August 26, 2008), at http://www.csoonline.com/article/2123120/it-audit/separation-of-duties-and-it-security.html

[38] *Ibid.*

Top secret

Secret

Confidential

For official use only

Figure 14.5 Classifications serve to safeguard information and help ensure they are viewed and accessed only by those who are authorized to.

for the United States. Unauthorized disclosure of information within the *secret* classification could be damaging to the United States. Unauthorized disclosure of information within the *confidential* classification could have a prejudicial impact on U.S. interests. Finally, unauthorized disclosure of information within the *for official use only* classification could compromise trade secrets, give an unfair advantage to a competitor, or violate the Privacy Act of 1974.[39] By contrast, hierarchical sensitivity labels for private sector organizations are determined by the hierarchy in a company (e.g., corporate) or the level of trust (e.g., restricted, confidential, and public). Ultimately, these classifications and categorizations seek to safeguard information. See Figure 14.5.

Organizations tend to adopt either the Bell–LaPadula or Biba model when regulating access to data. The model chosen will depend on whether the organizations prioritize the confidentiality or integrity of data in its systems. Government organizations adopt models that prioritize the confidentiality of data (Bell–LaPadula), whereas businesses adopt models that prioritize the integrity of data (Biba). The model developed by David Bell and Leonard LaPadula in 1973 (Bell–LaPadula model) explained the levels of security of documents and users' access to these documents.[40] Specifically, users with access to a particular security level have access to all documents at or below that security level (i.e., "no read up" rule). These users cannot share information with those belonging to a lower security level (i.e., property; a.k.a., "no write down" rule). For example, those with top secret clearance can access top secret documents as well as secret and confidential documents. By contrast, the model created by Kenneth J. Biba (Biba model) seeks to prevent the unauthorized modification of data by preventing individuals from a particular level from modifying information at a higher level; that is, users at a particular integrity level can only modify data at or below their level.[41]

14.2.4.2.3 Encryption

Those who gain unauthorized access, exceed authorized access, or even have authorized access but engage in illicit activity can review, transfer, obtain, delete, alter, or otherwise use the data. One way to protect against such access is to utilize encryption. Encryption physically blocks third-party access to data. It does this by rendering a file unusable by scrambling the data and making it unreadable. The data can only be read with a decryption key, which transforms the unreadable data (*ciphertext*) into readable data (*plaintext*). Encryption programs often contain key escrows that enable the recovery of data in the event the decryption key is lost, forgotten, or unknown to those that need to access it in the interests of national security. This practice has existed in countries such as the United Kingdom, France, and the United States for some time.[42]

14.2.4.2.4 Firewalls

A firewall seeks to prevent unauthorized access to a private network by examining and blocking traffic. Fundamentally, the purpose of a firewall is to grant or reject traffic access to a private network based on predetermined security

---

[39] This law requires government agencies to safeguard personal data, restricts the sharing of this information, enables citizens to seek civil remedies, and provides criminal penalties for violations of this law (5 U.S.C. § 552a).

[40] D. Gollman, *Computer Security* (3rd ed., Chichester, United Kingdom: Wiley, 2011).

[41] A. Estes, Biba Integrity Model. In H.C.A. van Tilborg & S. Jajodia (Eds.). *Encyclopedia of Cryptography and Security* 81 (Springer, 2011).

[42] UK Regulation of Investigatory Powers Act (RIPA) 2000, Daily Safety Law (Loi sur la sécurité quotidienne), and missing U.S. citation. Maras, *supra note 6, at* 205.

criteria defined in firewall policies. Firewalls can block all traffic and allow users and network administrators to determine what traffic can gain access to the network. Ultimately, firewalls should be carefully configured to meet the operational and security needs of an organization.

14.2.4.2.5 *Information security and computer-use monitoring policies*

In addition to access control, encryption, and firewalls, other security controls that can be implemented to protect systems, networks, and data include information security policies. These policies must include information about the security expectations of employees within an organization according to their work functions and roles. Employees should be educated on these policies as well. Moreover, policies must exist that cover unauthorized access, theft, manipulation, and destruction of data by employees. These policies should be communicated to employees, along with the consequences of violating these policies. Furthermore, computer misuse policies should exist that govern employees' use of Internet-enabled computers and other digital technologies. Computer misuse involves the use of an organization's computers, networks, data, email, and Internet access privileges (hereafter computer-use) for reasons other than business purposes (e.g., shop online, watch TV shows, send personal emails, and view pornography).[43] The misuse of these privileges is costly to an organization and may result in financial losses and disruption in productivity and operations. Computer-use policies are implemented in organizations to inform employees about acceptable computer-use behavior and about the monitoring practices of organizations. Computer-use can be observed through monitoring software, which can, for example, observe and record Internet activity, block access to particular websites, limit the type of software that can be downloaded to users' machines,[44] track emails and instant messages sent and received, and even record employees' keystrokes. The reports produced by this monitoring software should be reviewed. Those who violate the organizations' computer-use policies should be contacted and reminders should be sent to all employees about the organization's policies. Furthermore, INFOSEC personnel can proactively monitor employee computer-use. Nevertheless, this not a common practice as it is time consuming and requires a great investment in financial and human resources.

14.2.5 Defense in depth

The best INFOSEC approach involves what is known as defense in depth—a combination of physical security, personnel security and cybersecurity (Figure 14.6). Defense in depth includes physical security guards, alarm systems, surveillance systems, rigorous background checks on employees, stringent recruitment, selection, and hiring practices, information security policies, access control systems, encryption, intrusion detection and intrusion protection systems, antivirus and antispyware programs, and firewalls. In addition to these measures, employees should be educated on insider and outsider threats to the organization, and be trained on cybersecurity best practices.

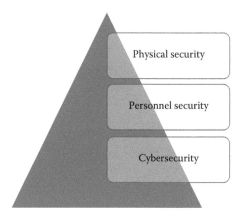

Figure 14.6 A current trend illustration of the long-standing principle of defense in depth.

---

[43] Maras, *Ibid, at* 266–267.

[44] Usually, individuals who can download software to workplace computers and other digital devices are those with administrative privileges. This restricts the majority of employees within the organization from downloading software onto their workplace computers in an effort to minimize the risk of malware infection from software programs. Whitelisting applications are also utilized to ensure that only trusted software is downloaded onto systems.

Two current trends in organizations threaten INFOSEC; namely, allowing employees to bring their own devices (BYOD) to the workplace and the rapid deployment of Internet of Things (IoT) devices. BYOD policies enable employees to bring and use personal digital devices at work for both personal and professional reasons (e.g., a user can connect his or her digital device to the organization's WiFi and use the device for both official and unofficial purposes). BYOD poses a cybersecurity threat because the employees' behavior and any existing protective measures on employee's digital devices can potentially affect the security of the organizations' systems, networks, and data.

Another trend that has been observed is the rapid deployment of IoT devices in public and private sectors. The IoT connects property, people, plants, and animals to the Internet, enabling their real-time and remote monitoring and the mass collection, storage, analysis, and sharing of data about them in order to provide users with a service.[45] The IoT poses a cybersecurity threat because these devices were not built with cybersecurity in mind and the security and privacy standards for these devices have not been adequately identified.[46] IoT devices are vulnerable to hacking and malware infections because they are Internet-enabled and lack protective measures against cybersecurity attacks (e.g., antivirus and antispyware programs, intrusion detection systems, and firewalls). These vulnerabilities may lead to the theft of information about the users of the IoT devices that can subsequently be used by perpetrators to commit fraud or other illicit activities; the surreptitious monitoring of the user through his or her IoT devices; and/or the unauthorized changing of settings and/or remote control of IoT devices.[47]

Web Exercise: Search online for an IoT product. Describe what it does. What are the privacy and security implications of using this product?

14.2.5.1 NIST Cybersecurity Framework

In the United States, private sector organizations are not required to implement cybersecurity measures unless their operations are covered by existing sectoral data protection legislation (e.g., Family Educational Rights and Privacy Act of 1974, Health Insurance Portability and Accountability Act of 1996, and Financial Services Modernization Act of 1999). What is more, U.S. private sector organizations promote self-regulation and believe that they are capable of determining which cybersecurity measures are needed to protect them and do not need nor want government intervention.[48] The private sector resists government mandates for cybersecurity, arguing that such requirements would hamper innovation and impede cybersecurity efforts of the sector.[49] The problem with these arguments is that self-regulation does not work and has not worked for quite some time. Despite this, any attempts to legislate have been met with resistance and ultimately have failed to pass mandatory cybersecurity standards in the private sector. Instead, a voluntary approach to cybersecurity exists. In 2013, Executive Order 13636 was passed, which directed the National Institute of Standards and Technology (NIST) to develop cybersecurity guidelines, standards, and practices. As a result, in 2014, NIST developed a Cybersecurity Framework, which included these guidelines, standards, and practices, and sought to help organizations improve their cybersecurity posture.

The NIST Cybersecurity Framework includes five essential cybersecurity functions[50]:

1. *Identify.* The identify function highlights the need to create a risk management culture within the organization and identifies the assets of an organization, risks, information security policies, cybersecurity laws and regulations, and the roles in the workforce with a cybersecurity function.

2. *Protect.* The protect function safeguards assets of the organization by implementing measures designed to protect people, property, and the confidentiality, integrity, and availability of data and systems (e.g., access control).

3. *Detect.* The detect function develops and implements measures designed to detect cybersecurity threats through the monitoring of assets and systems (e.g., intrusion detection systems).

---

[45] M.-H. Maras, A Look at the 'Internet of Things.' OUPBlog (2015), at http://blog.oup.com/2015/07/internet-of-things-law/

[46] *Ibid*; M.-H. Maras, The Internet of Things: Security and Privacy Implications, 5(2) *International Data Privacy Law* 100 (2015).

[47] Maras, Security and Privacy *Ibid.*, at 5(2).

[48] A. Etzioni, The Private Sector: A Reluctant Partner in Cybersecurity. Institute for Communitarian Policy Studies (George Washington University, 2014), at https://icps.gwu.edu/private-sector-reluctant-partner-cybersecurity

[49] *Ibid.*

[50] NIST, Cybersecurity Framework, 8–9 and 20–35 (2014), at http://www.nist.gov/cyberframework/upload/cybersecurity-framework-021214.pdf

4. *Respond.* The respond function includes the measures that are implemented once a cybersecurity incident occurs. This function also includes the measures needed to mitigate and prevent comparable cybersecurity incidents in the future. This function further includes the measures needed to investigate the cybersecurity incident. This involves utilizing individuals that are well versed in digital forensics to conduct the investigation. Digital forensics "is a branch of forensic science that focuses on criminal procedure law and evidence as applied to computers and related devices."[51] This branch of forensic science delineates the manner in which electronic evidence is collected, identified, evaluated, and presented for subsequent use in legal proceedings.

5. *Recovery.* The recovery function includes the measures needed to restore operations and services to a preincident state. This function also includes the measures needed to evaluate recovery processes and identify lessons learned from the cybersecurity incident.

An essential element in the NIST Cybersecurity Framework is the business continuity plan. Business continuity plans are essential to minimizing the damage or harm caused by the cybersecurity event, quickly and effectively responding to the incident, and recovering from the incident. Preparedness for a cybersecurity event is thus critical. To maintain preparedness, security controls must be reviewed, evaluated, and tested for efficacy, and simulated threats and attacks on systems must be conducted. The latter entails the conducting of drills and exercises to ensure that the business continuity plan is viable and any weaknesses identified are dealt with prior to a cybersecurity incident.

In the past, preparedness was normally sought after the fact. In fact, history is replete with examples where local, state, and federal agencies only started preparing for certain threats after they had already occurred. In other cases, preparedness plans existed but were not up to date, lacked critical information, or otherwise needed to be modified. Lessons can be learned from the way in which other security threats (e.g., natural disasters) were handled or mishandled. Consider the 2004 U.S. preparedness exercise known as Hurricane Pam. In the aftermath of Hurricane Katrina, it was discovered that a disaster exercise that had been conducted, "Hurricane Pam" (that was of the magnitude of Katrina), had identified deficiencies in existing emergency management plans. Following the completion of the exercise, corrective actions that were required were noted; however, these actions were never taken because the funds that would be allocated for these changes went to another national security threat instead.[52] The problem areas identified in the Hurricane Pam exercise were similar to those identified after Hurricane Katrina. Hurricane Pam brought home the lesson that attention needed to be paid to implementing corrective actions after preparedness exercises have been conducted. The plans also have to be reevaluated and further exercises need to be conducted to ensure that the modifications to the plan are effective.

The NIST Cybersecurity Framework also includes a tool that helps organizations understand how their current cybersecurity capabilities measure up to the characteristics included in the NIST Cybersecurity Framework. This tool includes four tiers (Tiers 1–4) describing the cybersecurity posture of organizations (see Figure 14.7). NIST recommends that organizations reach a Tier 3 or Tier 4 cybersecurity posture.[53]

Web Exercise: Review the NIST Cybersecurity Framework. Search online and find a case about a cybercrime that adversely impacted an organization in 2016. Utilizing the NIST Cybersecurity Framework, how would you enhance the cybersecurity posture of the organization to prevent or at the very least mitigate future similar cybersecurity incidents?

14.3 CHAPTER SUMMARY

Security measures need to constantly adapt to the rapid growth and evolution of information and computer technologies. These technologies enable the recording, storing, use, and transfer of data. As such, organizations need to develop and implement security measures that can protect the information obtained, contained, utilized, and shared from these devices. INFOSEC includes physical security, OPSEC, COMSEC, and COMPUSEC. INFOSEC measures must protect computer systems from both internal (e.g., employees, contractors, and vendors) and external threats (e.g., hackers), as well as networks and data from cybercrime and other forms of illicit activity. To

---

[51] Maras, *supra note 6, at* 29.

[52] M.-H. Maras, *Counterterrorism* (Burlington, Massachusetts: Jones and Bartlett, 2012).

[53] PricewaterhouseCoopers, Why You Should Adopt the NIST Cybersecurity Framework, 2 (2014), at https://www.pwc.com/us/en/increasing-it-effectiveness/publications/assets/adopt-the-nist.pdf

NIST Cybersecurity Framework Tiers

Tier 1: Partial

Risk Management Process: "Organizational cybersecurity risk management practices are not formalized, and risk is managed in an ad hoc and sometimes reactive manner...Prioritization of cybersecurity activities may not be directly informed by organizational risk objectives, the threat environment, or business/mission requirements."

Integrated Risk Management Program: "There is limited awareness of cybersecurity risk at the organizational level and an organization-wide approach to managing cybersecurity risk has not been established. The organization implements cybersecurity risk management on an irregular, case-by-case basis due to varied experience or information gained from outside sources. The organization may not have processes that enable cybersecurity information to be shared within the organization."

External Participation: "An organization may not have the processes in place to participate in coordination or collaboration with other entities."

Tier 2: Risk Informed

Risk Management Process: "Risk management practices are approved by management but may not be established as organizational-wide policy. Prioritization of cybersecurity activities is directly informed by organizational risk objectives, the threat environment, or business/mission requirements."

Integrated Risk Management Program: "There is an awareness of cybersecurity risk at the organizational level but an organization-wide approach to managing cybersecurity risk has not been established. Risk-informed, management-approved processes and procedures are defined and implemented, and staff has adequate resources to perform their cybersecurity duties. Cybersecurity information is shared within the organization on an informal basis."

External Participation: "The organization knows its role in the larger ecosystem, but has not formalized its capabilities to interact and share information externally."

Tier 3: Repeatable

Risk Management Process: "The organization's risk management practices are formally approved and expressed as policy. Organizational cybersecurity practices are regularly updated based on the application of risk management processes to changes in business/mission requirements and a changing threat and technology landscape."

Integrated Risk Management Program: "There is an organization-wide approach to manage cybersecurity risk. Risk-informed policies, processes, and procedures are defined, implemented as intended, and reviewed. Consistent methods are in place to respond effectively to changes in risk. Personnel possess the knowledge and skills to perform their appointed roles and responsibilities."

External Participation: "The organization understands its dependencies and partners and receives information from these partners that enables collaboration and risk-based management decisions within the organization in response to events."

Tier 4: Adaptive

Risk Management Process: "The organization adapts its cybersecurity practices based on lessons learned and predictive indicators derived from previous and current cybersecurity activities. Through a process of continuous improvement incorporating advanced cybersecurity technologies and practices, the organization actively adapts to a changing cybersecurity landscape and responds to evolving and sophisticated threats in a timely manner."

Integrated Risk Management Program: "There is an organization-wide approach to managing cybersecurity risk that uses risk-informed policies, processes, and procedures to address potential cybersecurity events. Cybersecurity risk management is part of the organizational culture and evolves from an awareness of previous activities, information shared by other sources, and continuous awareness of activities on their systems and networks."

External Participation: "The organization manages risk and actively shares information with partners to ensure that accurate, current information is being distributed and consumed to improve cybersecurity before a cybersecurity event occurs."

Figure 14.7 NIST Cybersecurity Framework implementation tiers. (From information obtained from NIST Cybersecurity Framework, 10–11.)

adequately protect systems, networks, and data, multiple layers of defense are required that can isolate and protect the assets of an organization, data within systems, and/or network access points and perimeters from internal and external threats. In addition to security controls, organizations must be prepared in the event that a cybersecurity incident occurs. An incident response strategy is needed to ensure that security personnel and employees within an organization will know how to respond to the incident. The NIST Cybersecurity Framework provides guidance to the private sector on how to enhance their cybersecurity posture and what measures are needed to adequately safeguard information.

Keywords

access control

antispyware programs

antivirus programs

authentication measures

badges

biometrics

brute-force attack

business counterintelligence

BYODs (bring your own devices)

communications security (COMSEC)

Completely Automated Public Turing test to tell Computers and Humans Apart (or CAPTCHA)

computer security (COMPUSEC)

computer systems

computer-use monitoring policies

cryptoransomware

cybercrime

cybersecurity

data access control

defense in depth

denial of service (DoS)

dictionary attack

distributed denial of service (DDoS)

emissions security (EMSEC)

encryption

executable files

firewalls

hierarchical sensitivity labels

information

information security (INFOSEC)

insider threats

intelligence

Internet-enabled computers

Internet of Things (IoT) devices

malicious software

malware

nonhierachical sensitivity labels

passwords

phishing

physical security

proprietary information

operations security (OPSEC)

outsider threats

servers

social engineering

spearphishing

theft of data

tokens

transmission security (TRANSEC)

WiFi

zip files

Discussion questions

1. What are the core components of INFOSEC?

2. Is OPSEC relevant to cybersecurity? Why or why not?

3. What is access control? Name and describe two measures that would be considered as a form of access control.

4. What are the three types of data access control methods? Name and describe each one.

5. What models do organizations tend to adopt when regulating access to data? Does the choice of model differ between public or private sector organization? Why do you think so?

6. What is defense in depth and how can it be applied to private sector organizations?

7. What is the NIST Cybersecurity Framework? What are its five cybersecurity functions? Describe each function in your response.

CHAPTER 15

The future of the private security industry
A philosophical outlook

15.1 INTRODUCTION

When I first encountered the field of private security, some 35 years ago, I thought it to be a fledgling undertaking without too much power or wings to elevate itself into higher levels. At the end of the 1970s to the early 1980s, the industry was a guard show at best, an enterprise in its infancy teething away at the margins of a powerful, indomitable public system. Public justice, with its various apparatus in courts, cops, and corrections, stood atop as a king that could never be toppled. Who would have ever envisioned that this mighty force of public employees in public justice and police functions would ever "partner" with private sector justice, would ever delegate its once sacrosanct tasks and duties to private forces, and would ever concede that certain things the private system does are actually far better than the public operational philosophy, and most importantly, who would have ever considered that these two entities are more like colleagues now than an overseer handing out select crumbs to an underling force. No one could have ever imagined any of this, nor the fact that employment opportunities have become a rich, fertile ground for the private sector while the public system contracted, shriveled up, and has been made inefficient by costs and work rules imposed by civil service systems. Again, no one could have ever anticipated that residential communities, critical infrastructure, electric, gas and nuclear power plants, corporate complexes, cyber technology, casinos, hospitals, and educational institutions would become an almost exclusive province for the private sector as public participation slowly but surely withered away.

An excellent friend over the last 20 years, K.C. Poulin, who is the CEO of Critical Intervention Services of Tampa, Florida, told me about this dramatic shift while I was working at the State University of New York. He termed what was happening to private security a major "paradigm shift," and I initially reacted as if this claim was a form of self-promotion. I think he was right at the time, but when compared to the present, his argument was understated, for the shift has been tectonic, as if earthly plates of crust were shattering each other's edges. It has been an astounding ride for all of us involved in the private security business, a rollercoaster now at full bore with little signs of slowing up. Private security, for all of its adaptability, will surely be an even more significant player in how justice is meted out in our communities and institutions for generations to come.

15.1.1 History of private security and the American experience

When public policing first came on the scene on the American landscape, it was an odd bird. By 1880, Americans resisted public policing in all shapes and sizes, eventually acquiescing in Western Expansionism and the Industrial Revolution. The standard rationale was that life had become too complicated and socially and communally dependent that self-protection and self-preservation alone could not possibly deliver the needed security and safety of a given community. Americans bought this argument too in the large Northeastern centers such as Philadelphia and New York by the twentieth century.[1]

---

[1] F.R. Prassel, *The Western Peace Officer* 126 (1972); P.J. Stephens, *The Thief-Takers* (W. W. Norton, 1970); J.F. Richardson, *The New York Police* 38 (1970); R. Lane, *Policing the City: Boston: 1822–1885* 7 (1975); S. Bacon, *The Early Development of American Municipal Police* 44 (1939).

However, at no time did the same decision making comfortably allow a "national" or U.S. police force to come to be, for law enforcement in its limited level was mostly a matter of local concern. Indeed, the founding of the FBI was considered controversial by many at the time since it so aggressively preempted local control in favor of a nationalized police model. Surely, the KGB-Stalinist model, where all citizens lived in fear under constant surveillance, is not a model Americans hope for. I pose this not to be controversial but to edify the historic dilemma, that Americans do not like nor crave centralized policing and have historically been self-governing, self-defending, self-protecting, more than the knee-jerk "Let's Call the Police for Anything" model unfortunately witnessed today. Put another way, Americans resist an overzealous police presence; nearly all Americans in many ways suffer a sort of perverse alienation to an active, fully in-your-face type of policing that some community policing experts think to be healthy. Public policing is not part of the American DNA, although it is clear that self-determination and self-defense clearly are. Private security allows Americans room to breathe, to take matters into their own hands, and possibly not be judicially forced to seek one remedy over the other. Public police must march lockstep to standing policies; they have been stripped of most of their discretionary powers; they are victimized by ticket quotas and visits to homeless shelters; they are asked to be everything the rest of our culture appears incapable of doing, and this is a very sorry state of affairs for these dedicated personnel.

Private security has never labored under these restraints or these delusions of performance. Private security is what it says that it is, private first and then communal. On top of this, private security has the power of choice; to pick this or that and to not engage this or that. Or it has the power to divert; to handle by alternative resolution or to seek money over prison in a personal sense. When compared to the public system, the private system is so extraordinarily capable of efficiency. In contrast to the public system, private security is not compelled by the latest fad or social justice initiative invented by out-of-touch politicos and academics. Private security does not live off the public largesse and thus has to be picky and efficacious in its choices. The public system can keep eating at that trough as long as the fad stays alive. The current state of public policing is essentially at odds with our history. This is a nation of independent and very hardy people and in fact, it mostly is still a land of venturers and risk-takers. Given these historical inclinations, private security will continue to grow and flourish.

15.1.2 Private security industry and the constitutional advantage

As was discussed fully in Chapter 5, the legal advantages of the private action or actors in matters of law and justice continue to benefit the private security industry. When compared to the public system, private security personnel are not bogged down in a miasma of constitutional pin splitting involving arrest, search, and seizure questions and nor does it need to fret too much over cruel and unusual punishment standards or the many other constitutional challenges that are hurled at public police each and every day. The constitution expressly, unambiguously, and clearly reserves these constitutional remedies to public policing along in that the language indicates the "No State shall …?" State action means governmental action and those employed by Securitas or Allied Barton are not state agents and no amount of wishful thinking can make it so. Of course, there is nothing to halt bad legal reasoning and the willful rejection of long-standing and self-evident legal maxims—a common condition among contemporary judicial activists who act like social workers rather than jurists. Unfortunately, there are a few cases out there that challenge the status quo simply because that is what these judges want rather than this is what the law requires. This was clearly evident in the Zelinski and Buswell decisions.[2]

Of course, there are occasions when the entanglement between the public and private officers simply becomes too intimate not to find governmental, state action on the part of both parties, but these are the rare situations discoverable in fact and case law. Legal policy is never well founded when based on aberration. For the foreseeable future, the constitutional advantages to the private security industry foretell an even more vibrant future than exists presently.

15.1.3 Privatization of the public sector

Privatized services are a reality that no reasonable observer can deny. To privatize is to transform a once delivered and performed public service to be assumed by a private entity. This has been true with garbage collection, EMT and ambulance services, and security at federal installations, military bases, colleges and universities, cultural institutions, and the like. At one point, nearly all of these services were performed by public employees serving in public

---

[2] State of Minnesota v. Buswell, 449 N.W.2d 471, 474 (Minn. App. 1989); People v. Zelinski, 594 P. 2d 1000 (1979).

police departments. To put it mildly, those days are long over. Privatized services are economically favorable to the town, borough, city, or department seeking to save costs; privatized services are not controlled by union and civil service rules and privatized services can be fine-tuned and flexibly delivered without violating some governmentally entrenched protocol. Public police departments are shackled by some many work rules and restrictions that their services cannot be efficiently and productively delivered. Otherwise, why are federal installations now the province of private security? Why have sports arena and stadiums now largely become protected by private companies and why must governmental authorities contract with private firms, whether based on technology and cyber-science rather than implement their own protocols? The answer is one relating to capacity and skill, for the government cannot invent anything; it cannot innovate and it has little chance adapting. Most of what it will do is reinforce and replay a static and dead playbook and await the innovation that comes from the private sector and then even more importantly, weigh and evaluate the stark difference in approach and delivery. Privatization is a doorway of sorts that permits encounters with the public system and during these exchanges, learns truly the best and most effective ways of carrying out the law enforcement function. Public policing alone cannot achieve its stated ends without active participation from a vibrant and entrepreneurial cohort of private security professionals. In this way, privatization guarantees a brighter than brilliant future for the private security industry.

15.1.4 A customer/consumer-based mentality

Currently, the tension and stresses arising from shootings by police officers, of certain members of the black community, always give pause to consider the methods employed and adopted by law enforcement professionals. Some of these cases, alleged as unjustified, have been confirmed and corroborated as perfectly legitimate and correctly adjudicated in a court of law. Not all allegations of police racism hold water and in fact, when evaluated statistically, the vast, vast majority of police officers carry out their functions with deft professionalism day to day. It seems almost incongruous to claim that three Baltimore City police officers, who were in fact black themselves, would be operating with racial animus. Such a claim borders on absurdity. However, there are in fact cases of police brutality and police racism. These cases are substantiated and very real events. Then too there are cases in which the paranoid alienation that develops between the public system and the very community it hopes to serve eventually blinds rational judgment. As a result, the Thin Blue Line becomes an autonomic defense mechanism—a them versus us mindset—that clouds judgment in the performance of duties. Police grapple with this reality each and every day and those who cannot balance reality with paranoia, as crudely put, start to see the world in adversarial ways rather than ways of serving others. Nothing said here is new to the debate. What is new relates to my argument that private sector police are less prone to move into that wall of separation than their public counterparts and that is because in the private firm, the private officer is driven by customer service mentality more than his or her public counterpart. Making customers and consumers happy is not a dirty idea but a fully creative acceptance that each system seeks different things. On the one hand, the public mentality will go on ad infinitum because it has the funds to do so and hence effective or not, accountable or not, it shall live in perpetuity. When public police speaks of community policing, these ideas are not the province of a public mentality but a private one that hopes to please its constituency—stating it crudely, to make the customer happy since any continuance of service or contract will come to depend on this determination. Communities, businesses, and the like can hire and fire private security at will while the public system erects a protectionist wall that makes improvement and customer service almost an impossibility. In the next few decades, the private security industry will continue to make further inroads into community policing as I predicted in 2005.[3] It will not happen because it wants to; rather, it will happen because it has little other choice, for only the private security industry zeroes in on what consumers, customers, and communities really aspire to. And for that reason alone, the future of private security shall continue its meteoric rise.

Finally, the sweep of this industry, from technology to new markets, from creative solutions to its amazing adaptability to market forces, will further accelerate the dramatic unfolding of the private security industry. In the end, it is a domain of the inventor and pioneer, cutting a swatch across a field of new ideas and innovative methods. None of this happens in a vacuum, but instead, because the private system itself, it represents not only our historical tendencies to dream big and build empires but also because this is system that eventually wins hearts and minds by its very results.

---

[3] C.P. Nemeth & K.C. Poulin, *Private Security and Public Safety: A Community-Based Approach* (Prentice Hall, 2004); C.P. Nemeth & K.C. Poulin, *The Prevention Agency: A Public Safety Model for High Crime Communities in the 21st Century* (California University of PA, 2004).

ALABAMA SECURITY REGULATORY BOARD
COMPANY LICENSE APPLICATION
2777 Zelda Road
Montgomery, AL 36106
(334) 420-7234
Fax (334) 263-6115

CONTRACT SECURITY COMPANY APPLICATION CHECKLIST

❑ Completed ASRB **COMPANY LICENSE APPLICATION** *

    ❑ **CERTIFICATE OF GOOD STANDING** from Alabama Dept. of Revenue (if Domestic Corporation)
    OR
    ❑ **CERTIFICATE OF AUTHORITY** from Alabama Secretary of State (if Foreign Corporation)

❑ Certificate(s) of Insurance (see Code of Alabama, §34-27C-6)

Have the Qualifying Agent complete the following forms:

    ❑ ASRB **PERSONAL LICENSE APPLICATION*** (check the 'Qualifying Agent' box)

        ❑ 2 ea. Recent color pictures, separated, passport-style

        ❑ Military Separation documents if applicable (DD-214 or equivalent)

        ❑ Proof of Age/Citizenship (copy of a current state-issued driver's license/non-driver I.D is sufficient)

    ❑ ASRB **AUTHORIZATION FOR RELEASE OF INFORMATION***

    ❑ ASRB **CERTIFICATION OF EXPERIENCE/TRAINING***

Have the Qualifying Agent complete the following ABI forms:

    ❑ **CRIMINAL HISTORY INFORMATION RELEASE FORM*** (ALEA Form)

    ❑ 2 ea. **APPLICANT** fingerprint cards w/ rolled fingerprints of applicant

Cashier's Checks, Money Orders, or Business Checks from a Board-Licensed Contract Security Company for the following amounts: (Payee: Alabama Security Regulatory Board or ASRB)

    ❑ $250.00: Contract Security Company License fee (Late fee $125.00; Replacement fee $50.00)

    ❑ $50.00: Qualifying Agent Personal License fee (Late fee $25.00; Replacement fee $10.00)

    ❑ $39.75: Background check fee payable to ALEA Records and Identification Division (must be in form of money order or Cashier's check)

Submit all forms and checks to the Board at: Alabama Security Regulatory Board
                                           2777 Zelda Road
                                         Montgomery, AL 36106
                                         www.asrb.alabama.gov

* : Form must be notarized (ALEA Release can be witnessed by 2 persons)

ALABAMA SECURITY REGULATORY BOARD

COMPANY LICENSE APPLICATION

2777 Zelda Road

Montgomery, AL 36106

FOR BOARD USE ONLY	
BY:_____	Approved ☐
DATE:_____	Denied ☐

Each contract security company requesting or renewing a license shall pay a security license fee of **$250.00**. NOTICE: This application must be typed or legibly printed in blue or black ink. All applicable questions must be answered. Indicate not applicable questions by entering "N/A "in the proper field.

Incomplete applications and applications that are not legible will be returned without consideration.

If space provided is not sufficient for complete answers, attach additional sheets as necessary. Number each answer to correspond with the question being answered.

This Application is for: ☐ New License ☐ License Renewal (License #:_____)

1. COMPANY INFORMATION

Company Name (The name under which the Company will be Licensed)

Fictitious/DBA Name (The name under which the Company will be engaged in regulated activities if different than the Company Name)

Business Address (Physical Location) (Street Address, City, ST, ZIP)

Mailing Address (If different from Business Address) (Street Address/P.O. Box #, City, ST, ZIP)

Business Phone	Business Fax	Business E-Mail

Business Type: ☐ Single Owner   ☐ Partnership   ☐ Domestic Corporation   ☐ Foreign Corporation

Domestic Corporations must submit a Certificate of Good Standing from the Alabama Department of Revenue with this Application.

Foreign Corporations must submit a Certificate of Authority from the Alabama Secretary of State with this Application.

(Submitted Certificates must be originals and must be dated less than 30 days prior to the date this Application is received by the Board)

2. COMPANY PERSONNEL

LIST ALL PARTNERS, PRINCIPAL OFFICERS, DIRECTORS, AND BUSINESS MANAGERS OF THE BUSINESS (Use additional sheets if needed).

	Full Name (LAST, First, Middle)	Title/Position	Home Address (Street Address, City, ST, ZIP)
A			
B			
C			
D			
E			
F			
G			
H			

I		
J		

3. QUALIFYING AGENT

Full Name (LAST, First, Middle)	Date of Birth (MM/DD/YYYY)

Home Address (Street Address, City, ST, ZIP)

Home Phone	Cell Phone	E-Mail

Submit the Qualifying Agent's complete "APPLICATION FOR PERSONAL LICENSE" and "CERTIFICATION OF EXPERIENCE" with this Application.

4. AFFIRMATION OF UNDERSTANDINGS

By signing below, the Qualifying Agent affirms they understand the following;

1. After this application is submitted, the Company may continue regulated activities until the Alabama Security Regulatory Board (the Board) notifies the Qualifying Agent of either an approval or denial of the Company license which will occur within a reasonable time following receipt of the application.

2. A certified copy of the completed application as submitted to the Board must be conspicuously posted in ALL offices of the Contract Security Company in the State of Alabama.

3. The Board will conduct a comprehensive review of the Application and may conduct additional checks and verifications as determined by the Board.

4. The Qualifying Agent must ensure that the Company complies with all relevant laws, as well as all rules and regulations promulgated by the Board at all times that the Company is performing any activity regulated by the Board.

5. Licensure with the Board is a privilege, not a right, and a Board license may be revoked for violation of any law, rule, or regulation deemed relevant by the Board.

6. Making false statements or providing false information to the Board is grounds for denial/revocation of licensure.

By signing this document the applicant affirms under penalty of perjury that the information provided is factually truthful.

STATE OF ALABAMA, COUNTY OF _____

SUBSCRIBED AND SWORN TO BEFORE ME THIS

_____ DAY OF _____, _____

_____
NOTARY PUBLIC

MY COMMISSION EXPIRES: _____

_____
SIGNATURE OF QUALIFYING AGENT

_____
DATE

RECEIVED:	REVIEWED:

ALABAMA SECURITY REGULATORY BOARD	FOR BOARD USE ONLY
Qualifying Agent Application 2777 Zelda Road Montgomery, AL 36106	BY:_____ Approved☐ DATE:_____ Denied☐

Each security officer of armed security officer requesting or renewing a license shall pay a nonrefundable security license fee of **$50.00**. ***Check made payable to ASRB*** Submit: **2 color photographs (passport size). Photographs must show the subject in a frontal portrait.**

NOTICE: This application must be typed or legibly printed in blue or black ink. All applicable questions must be answered. Indicate not applicable questions by entering "N/A "(not applicable) in the proper field.

Incomplete applications and applications that are not legible will be returned without consideration.

If space provided is not sufficient for complete answers, attach additional sheets as necessary. Number each answer to correspond with the question being answered.

This Application is for: ☐New License/Certification
☐License Renewal License #:_____

License/Certifications Applied for: ☐ Qualifying Agent Certification

5. PERSONAL INFORMATION

Full Name (LAST, First, Middle)							Date of Birth (MM/DD/YYYY)

Social Security Number	Race	Sex	Height	Weight	Eyes	Hair	Place of Birth (City, ST)

Aliases (any other name you have been known by; e.g., Maiden Name, Married Name, etc... [DO NOT INCLUDE CASUAL NICKNAMES])

Home Phone	Cell Phone	E-Mail

Licensed Security Company Currently Working For: (MANDATORY)	**Co. Lic #: (if available)**

6. RESIDENCES

Current Residence (Street Address, City, ST, ZIP)	How Long?

LIST ALL PRIOR RESIDENTIAL ADDRESSES FOR THE PAST 10 YEARS (Street Address, City, ST, and ZIP). Use additional sheets if needed.

	How Long?
A	
B	
C	
D	

7. MILITARY SERVICE

Have You ever Served in the Military? ☐No ☐Yes (answer questions to the right)	From	To	Type of Discharge

If "Yes": include a copy of you Separation Document(s) (e.g., DD Form 214) with your application to the Board.

8. EMPLOYMENT

STARTING WITH THE MOST RECENT, LIST ALL EMPLOYMENT FOR THE PAST 10 YEARS (including part-time employment). All time must be accounted for. If unemployed for any time indicate by entering "Unemployed" in the 'Employer' field and enter the dates of unemployment.
Use Additional Sheets if needed.

Employer Name, Address, & Telephone #	Dates From	To	Position/Type of Work	Name of Supervisor	Reason for Leaving
A					
B					
C					
D					
E					

9. CRIMINAL HISTORY

Have You ever been arrested or charged with any violation (including traffic citations and UCMJ violations), misdemeanor, or felony? ❑No   ❑Yes

(If 'Yes' provide details below, even if not formally charged, found 'Not Guilty', or if the charge was settled by payment of a fine or by pre-trial diversion)

Date	Jurisdiction	Charge	Final Disposition	Details (Use additional sheet if needed)

10. REFERENCES

LIST THE NAME, ADDRESS AND TELEPHONE NUMBER OF 3 UNRELATED AND DISINTERESTED PERSONS TO BE USED AS REFERENCES FOR BOARD INQUIRIES ABOUT YOUR STANDING, REPUTATION, AND CHARACTER.

1
2
3

11. AFFIRMATION OF UNDERSTANDINGS

By signing this form, I affirm that I understand the following;

7. Licensure with the Alabama Security Regulatory Board (the Board) is a privilege, not a right, and my license may be revoked for violation of any law, rule, or regulation deemed relevant by the Board.

8. Making false statements to or providing false information to the Board is grounds for denial/revocation of licensure.

9. After I submit this application, I may work as a Security Officer or Armed Security Officer until the Board notifies me of either an approval or denial of personal licensure which will occur within a reasonable time following receipt of my application.

10. The Board will conduct a comprehensive background investigation to include a criminal history check and may include additional checks and verifications as determined by the Board.

11. I must keep Temporary License at the bottom of this page on my person at all times that I am performing any service or activity regulated by the Board until the Board either issues or denies my Personal License.

12. If the Board denies my Personal License, I must immediately stop performing any services or activities regulated by the Board upon receipt of notification of license denial.

13. If the Board denies personal licensure, I can appeal the denial decision to the Board following the procedures on the Alabama Administrative Procedures Act.

14. I must comply with all relevant laws, as well as all rules and regulations promulgated by the Board at all times when performing any activity regulated by the Board.

12. MANDATORY SWORN DECLARATIONS

By signing below, I certify and declare that;

1. I am 21 years of age or older if applying for an Armed Security Officer License, or 18 years of age or older if applying for a Security Officer License. (ATTACH PROOF OF AGE)

2. I am a citizen of the United States or a resident alien. (ATTACH PROOF OF CITIZENSHIP OR PROOF OF RESIDENT ALIEN STATUS)

3. I have never been convicted in any jurisdiction of the United States of any Felony or crime involving Moral Turpitude for which a full pardon has not been granted.

4. I have never been declared, by any court of competent jurisdiction, incompetent by reason of mental defect or disease, and competency has not been restored.

5. I am not suffering from habitual drunkenness or from narcotics addiction or dependence.

6. All information I have provided to the Board is true and accurate.

By signing this document the applicant affirms under penalty of perjury that the information provided is factually truthful.

STATE OF ALABAMA, COUNTY OF _____

SUBSCRIBED AND SWORN TO BEFORE ME THIS

_____ DAY OF _____, _____

APPLICANT SIGNATURE

_____

DATE

_____
NOTARY PUBLIC

MY COMMISSION EXPIRES: _____

RECIEVED:	REVIEWED:	CRIMINAL HISTORY REC'D:

-✂-------------------------CUT-------------------------✂-------------------------CUT-------------------------✂-------------------------CUT-------------------------✂-

The person identified on this Temporary License has completed and signed an ASRB Personal License Application to be submitted to the Board.

STATE OF ALABAMA, COUNTY OF _____

SUBSCRIBED AND SWORN TO BEFORE ME THIS

_____ DAY OF _____, _____

_____
NOTARY PUBLIC

MY COMMISSION EXPIRES: _____

F
O
L
D

ALABAMA SECURITY REGULATORY BOARD TEMPORARY PERSONAL LICENSE

Print Full Name

_____
Date of Application
Qualifying Agent Certification

This document meets all ASRB Temporary License requirements ONCE A PERSONAL APPLICATION HAS BEEN SUBMITTED TO THE BOARD. This document must be carried at all times the Applicant is performing any regulated activity. This Temporary License is valid until a Personal License is either granted or denied by the Board.

ALABAMA SECURITY REGULATORY BOARD

AUTHORIZATION FOR RELEASE OF INFORMATION

2777 Zelda Road

Montgomery, AL 36106

NOTICE: This form must be typed or legibly printed in blue or black ink. All applicable questions must be answered. Indicate not applicable questions by entering "N/A "(not applicable) in the proper field.

Incomplete forms and forms that are not legible will be returned without consideration.

If space provided is not sufficient for complete answers, attach additional sheets as necessary. Number each answer to correspond with the question being answered.

1. PERSONAL INFORMATION

Full Name (LAST, First, Middle)   Date of Birth (MM/DD/YYYY)

Aliases (any other name you have been known by; e.g., Maiden Name, Married Name, etc… [DO NOT INCLUDE CASUAL NICKNAMES])

Current Residence (Street Address, City, ST, ZIP)

Home Phone | Cell Phone | E-Mail

2. DECLARATION OF UNDERSTANDINGS

I understand that the Alabama Security Regulatory Board (herein after, "the Board") will conduct any investigation deemed necessary to ensure that I fulfill all requirements for licensure by the Board.

I understand that a FBI and State Background Check will be done.

I understand that inquiry may be made regarding my residential history, employment history (to include disciplinary and training records), school records, financial records, or any other record, information, or knowledge deemed relevant by the Board.

I understand that inquiry may also be made into any history of controlled substance or alcohol abuse by me, and into my mental competency.

3. AUTHORIZATION, WAIVER AND RELEASE

I hereby authorize Alabama Security Regulatory Board (herein after, "the Board") to conduct a background investigation of me to determine my suitability for licensure by the Board.

I hereby waive any provision of law forbidding any court, law enforcement agency, credit reporting agency, employer, school or school official, financial institution, business, or person from disclosing to the Board any record, information, or knowledge concerning me and I give permission without restriction for any court, agency, business, or person to disclose any record, information, or knowledge concerning me to the Board.

I hereby release any court, law enforcement agency, credit reporting agency, employer, school or school official, financial institution, business, or person from any and all claims, demands, losses, suits, and actions of any kind, whether at law, in equity, through litigation or arbitration, in connection with any court, agency, business, or person acting in compliance with any request for records, information, or knowledge about me by the Board.

STATE OF ALABAMA, COUNTY OF _____

SUBSCRIBED AND SWORN TO BEFORE ME THIS   APPLICANT SIGNATURE

_____ DAY OF _____, _____   _____

_____   _____

NOTARY PUBLIC   DATE

MY COMMISSION EXPIRES: _____

ALABAMA SECURITY REGULATORY BOARD

CERTIFICATION OF EXPERIENCE/TRAINING

2777 Zelda Road

Montgomery, AL 36106

NOTICE: This form must be typed or legibly printed in blue or black ink. All applicable questions must be answered. Indicate not applicable questions by entering "N/A "(not applicable) in the proper field.

Incomplete forms and forms that are not legible will be returned without consideration.

If space provided is not sufficient for complete answers, attach additional sheets as necessary. Number each answer to correspond with the question being answered.

Certification Applied for: ❑ Qualifying Agent

4. PERSONAL INFORMATION	
Full Name (LAST, First, Middle)	Date of Birth (MM/DD/YYYY)

5.   REASON FOR CERTIFICATION OF EXPERIENCE

Qualifying Agent for:_____

(Name of Contract Security Company)

❑ I certify that I have a minimum of 3 years' experience as a manager, supervisor, or administrator with a contract security company. (summarize in the 'Qualifying Experience/Training' section)

OR

❑ I certify that I have a minimum of 3 years of supervisory experience with any federal, military, state, county, or municipal law enforcement agency. (summarize in the 'Qualifying Experience/Training' section)

Further;

❑ I certify that I am an employee of the Contract Security Company that I will serve as Qualifying Agent for.

❑ I certify that I am not a Qualified Agent for any other Contract Security Company licensed by the Alabama Security Regulatory Board.

❑ I certify that I understand that I may not serve as the Qualifying Agent for more than one Contract Security Company licensed by the Alabama Security Regulatory Board without prior written approval of the Board.

AND

❑ I understand that I must submit a complete "PERSONAL LICENSE APPLICATION" to the Board.

OR

❑ I am currently licensed by the Board. License #: _____

6.   QUALIFYING EXPERIENCE/TRAINING

Summarize your experience and/or training that is relevant to your application to be a Qualifying Agent.
Provide the Name, Address and telephone number for all persons, businesses, or agencies, referenced in your qualifying experience/training.
Attach any supporting documentation/certificates of training to this form and submit with your Application to the Board.

By signing this document the applicant affirms under penalty of perjury that the information provided is factually truthful.

STATE OF ALABAMA, COUNTY OF _____

SUBSCRIBED AND SWORN TO BEFORE ME THIS

_____ DAY OF _____, _____

_____
NOTARY PUBLIC

MY COMMISSION EXPIRES: _____

_____
APPLICANT SIGNATURE

_____
DATE

RECEIVED:

REVIEWED:

Appendix A – Chapter 265-X-2

ALABAMA LAW ENFORCEMENT AGENCY

Application to Review Alabama Criminal History Record Information

Applicant Information

Full Name (First, Middle, Last, Suffix): _____

Applicant <u>Current</u> Address: _____

City: _____   State: _____   Zip Code: _____

Alias or Nickname(s):   _____   **Sex/Gender:** ☐ Male   ☐ Female

Social Security Number: _____   **Date of Birth:**_____*(month/date/year)*

Race: ☐ White   ☐ Black   ☐ Asian   ☐ Indian   ☐ Other (please specify) _____

Current Driver's License Number:_____   **Issuing State:**   _____

Current e-mail address: _____

Home Phone #: ( )_____   Cell Phone #: (_____)_____

Work Phone #: (___)_____   Extension: _____

Included with my Application are the following items*:
☐   Completed Application signed by applicant and two witnesses *or* notarized.
☐   The required copy of my valid photo identification *(see "Appendix B" for applicant instructions, required documents <u>and</u> accepted forms of identification).*
☐   The required $25.00 administrative fee *(must be in the form of a money order or Cashiers checks made payable to the ALEA Records and Identification Division).*
☐   A classifiable copy of my own fingerprints taken by an authorized law enforcement agency as required *(please see "Appendix C" for instructions).*

I, the above referenced individual, hereby request to Review my Alabama criminal history record information (CHRI) maintained by the Alabama Law Enforcement Agency. By signing below and submitting this application, I hereby verify that the information listed in my application and in the attached documentation is correct. I also acknowledge that I understand that, in accordance with Section 41-9-601 of the Code of Alabama 1975, that any person who willfully requests, obtains or seeks to obtain criminal offender record information under false pretenses, or who willfully communicates or seeks to communicate criminal offender record information to any agency or person without authorization, may be guilty of a felony, and shall be fined not less than $5,000 nor more than $10,000 or imprisoned in the state penitentiary for not more than five years or both. §41-9-601, Code of Ala. (1975).

Applicant Signature_____   Date_____

_Name of Witness _____   Name of Witness _____

Address of Witness _____   Address of Witness _____

City, State and Zip_____   City, State and Zip_____

Sworn to and subscribed before me this ____ day of _____, 20___.

Notary Signature _____   My Commission Expires _____, 20___.

Appendix A-1 – Chapter 265-X-2

ALABAMA LAW ENFORCEMENT AGENCY

Application to Challenge Alabama Criminal History Record Information

Request to Challenge CHRI maintained by ALEA

An individual may Challenge or Appeal any portion of his or her own Criminal History Record Information (CHRI) maintained by the ALEA Records and Identification Division that he or she believes to be **incomplete** or **inaccurate**. This may be requested by completing the *ALEA Application to Challenge AL Criminal History Record Information* and returning it along with the required documentation to ALEA within one calendar year of the date of the ALEA response to the individual's request to review CHRI.

<u>Please **ATTACH IN WRITING** to this completed application the following information regarding EACH arrest and/or disposition you wish to challenge:</u>

1. **The charge and DATE of each** specific arrest or disposition being challenged;

2. **The Name of the ARRESTING AGENCY OR COURT for each** arrest or disposition being challenged;

3. **A listing of each specific arrest or disposition** being challenged;

4. **The details related to why each specific arrest** is incorrect or incomplete;

5. **What the applicant believes to be the correct information for each arrest or disposition** being challenged;

6. **Where the applicant obtained what he/she believes to be the correct supporting information** (if applicable); and

7. **Official documentation from the arresting agency or court (if applicable) to support** each arrest or disposition being challenged.

Please mail your completed application, along with the required documentation to:
  Records & Identification Division
  P.O. Box 1511
  Montgomery, Alabama 36102-1511

The *ALEA Application to Review or Challenge AL Criminal History Record Information* will be reviewed by an ALEA official, along with the documentation provided. The applicant will be notified as promptly as possible of the results of the challenge and you may appeal a decision that is unsatisfactory to you according to the procedures established by the ALEA Commission.

Appendix B – Chapter 265-X-2	**Applicant Instructions** **For completing the ALEA Applications to Review or to Challenge Alabama Criminal History Record Information**

In order for your request to review, challenge or appeal your Alabama criminal history record information to be processed by the Alabama Law Enforcement Agency (ALEA), **you must complete the *ALEA Application to Review or to Challenge AL Criminal History Record Information* in accordance with the following instructions:**

1.   **Your application must include ONE COPY of at least one of the following forms of your own valid photo identification:**
    a. A valid unexpired United States state-issued photo driver license or photo ID (non-driver) card;
    b. A valid unexpired United States Active Duty, Retiree or Reservist military ID card (DD Form 2 or 2A);
    c. A valid unexpired United States Military Dependent ID card (for spouse or children of Active Duty Military personnel);
    d. A valid unexpired United States Citizenship and Immigration Service Documentation, which may include either:
       i. Certificate of Naturalization N-550, N-570, N-578; or
       ii. Certificate of Citizenship N-560, N-561, N-645
    e. A valid unexpired United States Passport; or
    f. A valid unexpired Foreign Passport which meets the following requirements:
       i. A foreign passport must contain a Valid United States Visa or I-94 to be used as a primary proof of identification; or
       ii. A foreign passport, not issued in English, must be translated and accompanied by a Certificate of Accurate Translation. Passports are not acceptable if un-translated into English and/or expired.

2.   **Your application must include the required $25.00 administrative fee in the form of only a cashier's check or a money order** made payable to the "ALEA Records and Identification Division" *(sorry – personal and/or business checks are not accepted).; and*

3.   **Your application must include a classifiable set of your own fingerprints, taken by an authorized law enforcement agency** with an FBI-issued Originating Agency Number (ORI).
    a. The fingerprints accompanying your application should be provided to ALEA on an official FBI-approved "Applicant" fingerprint card or a FBI-approved AFIS printout of an official "Applicant" fingerprint card (i.e., FBI blue card) collected by an approved law enforcement agency with a valid FBI ORI. This permits positive identification and insures that the proper criminal record is reviewed.
    b. Details for the fingerprinting agency may be found in APPENDIX C.

4.   **If your application is to CHALLENGE any part of your CHRI maintained by ALEA, the application must include, at a minimum:**
    a. The charge and DATE of each specific arrest or disposition being challenged;
    b. The Name of the ARRESTING AGENCY OR COURT for each arrest or disposition being challenged;
    c. A listing of each specific arrest or disposition being challenged;
    d. The details related to why each specific arrest is incorrect or incomplete;
    e. What the applicant believes to be the correct information for each arrest or disposition being challenged;
    f. Where the applicant obtained what he/she believes to be the correct supporting information (if applicable); and
    g. Official documentation from the arresting agency or court (if applicable) to support each arrest or disposition being challenged.

5.   **Your completed request and all of the required documentation should be mailed to:**
     Alabama Law Enforcement Agency – Records & Identification Division
     P.O. Box 1511
     Montgomery, Alabama 36102-1511

Please allow a minimum of 5-10 business days from the date the application is received by ALEA for ALEA to process your request for review. Requests to Challenge CHRI information do NOT fall under this timeframe, as they require additional research, contact and verification with the arresting agencies, etc. If you have any questions concerning this procedure, you may contact ALEA by calling (334) 353-4340.

Appendix C – Chapter 265-X-2

Instructions for Law Enforcement Official
Taking the applicant's fingerprints on
FBI "Applicant" Fingerprint Card
FD-258 (Rev 12-10-07)

In accordance with Alabama law and the procedures established in Section 265-X-2 of the *Alabama Administrative Code*, individual citizens may request and may be provided with classifiable sets of their own fingerprints to accompany a request for his/her own Alabama criminal history record information (CHRI) from the Alabama Law Enforcement Agency (ALEA).

1. One of the requirements for an individual to request their own criminal history record information is that the individual to provide ALEA with a classifiable set of his or her own fingerprints (taken by an authorized law enforcement agency with an FBI-issued ORI) with his or her application to Review or Challenge his or her own Alabama criminal history. This permits positive identification and insures that the proper criminal record is reviewed and/or challenged.

1.   The individual you are fingerprinting should provide proper identification to your agency upon request.

2. The individual's fingerprints should be taken by law enforcement on an FBI "Applicant" Fingerprint Card (i.e. blue card). Please insure that your agency's name and ORI, AND your name and telephone number, are included on the completed fingerprint card. A sample of the FBI "Applicant" Fingerprint Card FD-258 (Rev 12-10-07) for your reference purposes is provided below.

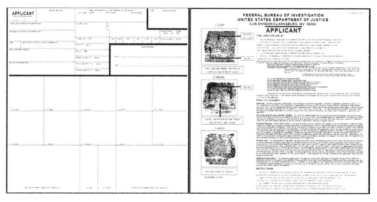

3. **Please return the completed fingerprint card to the applicant,** as it is the APPLICANT's responsibility to mail the completed CHRI request form, along with his/her own fingerprint card and the other required documents to:

> *Alabama Law Enforcement Agency*
>
> *Records and Identification Division*
>
> *P.O. Box 1511*
>
> *Montgomery, Alabama 36102-1511*

4. **If you have any questions,** please call ALEA at (334) 353-4340. **To request blank FBI APPLICANT cards**, your law enforcement agency may contact the FBI's Identification and Investigative Services Section's Customer Service Group at (304) 625-5590 or by e-mail at liaison@leo.gov

EMERGENCY ACTION PLAN

(INSERT NAME AND ADDRESS OF ORGANIZATION HERE)

Version Date: (INSERT DATE HERE)

TABLE OF CONTENTS

WORKPLACE EMERGENCIES

Introduction

This Emergency Action Plan (EAP) establishes guidelines for all reasonably foreseeable workplace emergencies. Because each emergency situation involves unique circumstances, the guidelines provide general guidance only. Thoughtful actions based on situation assessment are always required when responding to an emergency. It is also important to note that emergency guidelines do not necessarily represent sequential series of steps.

> **Special Note:** *Safety and health are the overriding priorities in all emergency situations. Think before you act and… if you see something, say something!*

General Information (Refer to "EAP Position and Personnel Roster")

Emergencies can be identified as Medical, Fire, Severe Weather, Bomb Threats, Chemical Spills, Terrorist Attacks, Criminal Acts, Extended Power Loss, etc. Personnel should identify these emergencies and report them to the Emergency Coordinator and **CALL 911** to alert Police. The local Emergency Services respond to emergencies.

Assembly Area – (INSERT LOCATION)

Alerting Personnel

The following apply during fires and other workplace emergencies requiring evacuation:

- The fire alarm will be activated and personnel will calmly evacuate using designated escape routes giving vocal alarms of "FIRE", etc.
- Personnel will look into rooms as they leave the suite and notify personnel to exit; do not delay your evacuation for this purpose.
- Personnel will assemble and remain in the evacuation Assembly Area. Leaving the group or failing to report to the evacuation Assembly Area can cause unnecessary effort locating personnel believed to be missing.
- Immediately notify your Floor Captain or the Emergency Coordinator of missing or unaccounted for personnel.
- Stay alert and listen for instructions.
- Await guidance to disperse, return to the building or take additional measures.
- In the event of a Medical or other emergency that does NOT require evacuation, **CALL 911** to alert Police and notify the Emergency Coordinator.

ROLES & RESPONSIBILITIES

Refer to "EAP Position and Personnel Roster"

Authority: Emergency Coordinator, Floor Captain, and Aides for Persons with Disabilities are responsible only for evacuating personnel out of the suite and assisting personnel to the Assembly Area. Building Managers assume responsibility once our personnel exit Suite 550. Upon their arrival, Emergency Services (Incident Commander) will assume command.

A. Emergency Coordinator (EC)

Non-Emergency Responsibilities:

- Ensure the dissemination, implementation and updating of the EAP.
- Review and update EAP annually.
- Ensure personnel are assigned to all EAP positions.
- Conduct exercises as needed to optimize our personnel emergency response.
- Conduct and document an After Action Review following any emergency event and provide a copy to the organization's Director.
- The EAP will be maintained in accordance with **(INSERT ALL GUIDANCE TO BE CONSIDERED)** and shall include:

    - Emergency escape procedures and emergency escape route assignments.
    - Procedures to be followed by personnel who remain behind to operate/conduct critical operational requirements before they evacuate.
    - Procedures to account for all personnel following evacuation.

Duties/Responsibility during an Emergency:

- Ensure Floor Captains initiate and complete accountability and/or evacuation.
- Coordinate the orderly evacuation of personnel when needed.
- Obtain accountability for our personnel following the incident and/or evacuation.
- Provide Emergency Response personnel with necessary facility information.
- Notify Building Management & Emergency Response of unaccounted for personnel.

B. Floor Captain (FC)

A minimum of one floor captain will be assigned to each zone (**see Attachment 1**).

Non-Emergency Responsibilities:

- Understand the building's emergency procedures and be prepared to assume his/her responsibilities promptly and calmly in an emergency.

- Maintain an accurate roster of all members assigned to his/her zone, which will be updated at least twice a year and upon the arrival of any new personnel. Provide updated information on personnel in your zone to the EC within 2 business days.

Duties/Responsibilities during an Emergency:

- Put on a vest, take your cellphone and copy of the EAP Position and Personnel Roster and ensure accountability for all personnel in your zone.
- During an evacuation, direct people out of your zone and exit via the stairwells; remind employees NOT to use the elevators, as they will be taken out of service.
- Upon arrival at the Assembly Area, confirm all personnel are present or are otherwise accounted for (e.g., illness, travel, vacation, meetings).
- Immediately notify Emergency Coordinator of unaccounted for/missing personnel.

C. Aide for Persons with Disabilities (APD)

Non-Emergency Responsibilities:

- Understand the building's emergency procedures and be prepared to assume his/her responsibilities promptly and calmly in an emergency.

Duties/Responsibilities during an Emergency:

- Put on vest, take your cellphone and copy of the EAP Position and Personnel Roster.
- Locate the Mobility Impaired Person(s) and assist them in getting to the designated mobility impaired location—the stairwell landing.
- Contact the Emergency Coordinator via the contact information located on your recall roster and let them know what stairwell you are located in and that you have arrived there safely with the person needing assistance.
- Continue to wait on stairwell landing until flashing strobes/alarms have been silenced. Once the alarm has been shut off, assist the person back to their work station.

D. All other Personnel

- Understand all information in the EAP.
- Read updates to the EAP when provided.
- Know the names and contact info for personnel serving as EC/FC/APD, where to find the AED, evacuation routes and procedures, Assembly Area location.

GENERAL INSTRUCTIONS FOR REPORTING EMERGENCIES

Summon emergency assistance by **CALLING 911**

Be prepared to provide the following information:

- Your name and location.

- Phone number from where the call is being made.

- Location of the emergency, including facility name, Bldg #, suite #, full address.

- Type of emergency:

  - Medical
  - Fire
  - Confined Space Rescue
  - Hazardous Material
  - Criminal Act
  - Bomb Threat

- Other important Information:

  - Number and condition of victims.
  - Location and extent of situation, hazard, fire, etc.
  - Involvement of Hazardous Materials (as available, give product name and/or describe any markings, labels or placards).

- What is needed

DO NOT HANG UP FIRST. Let emergency personnel hang up first.

After the call, station someone to direct Emergency Response personnel to the scene of the emergency.

MEDICAL EMERGENCIES

Survey the scene; evaluate personal safety issues.

Request assistance (SHOUT FOR HELP)

Call 911

Provide the following information:
- Number and location of victim(s)
- Nature of injury or illness
- Hazards involved
- Nearest entrance (emergency access point)

Alert trained employees to respond to the victim's location and bring a first aid kit or Automated External Defibrillator (AED).

Location of First Aid Kits and Automated External Defibrillator(s)

First Aid Kit	(INSERT LOCATION)
Automated External Defibrillator	(INSERT LOCATION)

Procedures
- Only trained responders should provide first aid assistance.
- Do not move the victim unless the victim's location is unsafe.
- Take "universal precautions" to prevent contact with body fluids and exposure to bloodborne pathogens.
- Meet the ambulance at the nearest entrance or emergency access point; direct them to victim(s).

FIRES

Fire Emergency Plan

If a fire is reported, pull the fire alarm, (if available and not already activated) to warn occupants to evacuate. Then Dial 911 to alert Fire Department. Provide the following information:

- Business name and street address
- Nature of fire
- Fire location (building and floor)
- Type of fire alarm (detector, pull station, sprinkler waterflow)
- Location of fire alarm (building and floor)
- Name of person reporting fire
- Telephone number for return call

Emergency Coordinator and Floor Captains to direct evacuation of personnel

Evacuation Procedures

- Evacuate building along evacuation routes to primary assembly areas outside.
- Redirect building occupants to stairs and exits away from the fire.
- Prohibit use of elevators.
- Evacuation team to account for all employees and visitors at the Assembly Area.

ACTIVE SHOOTER AND WORKPLACE VIOLENCE

Profile of an Active Shooter

An Active Shooter is an individual actively engaged in killing or attempting to kill people in a confined and populated area, typically through the use of firearms.

How to respond when an Active Shooter is in your vicinity

1. Evacuate	2. Hide Out	3. Take Action
• Have an escape route and plan in mind • Leave your belongings behind • Keep your hands visible	• Hide in an area out of the active shooters view • Block entry to your hiding place and lock doors.	• As a last resort and only when your life is in imminent danger. • Attempt to incapacitate the active shooter • Act with physical aggression and throw items at the active shooter
************************CALL 911 WHEN IT IS SAFE TO DO SO*********************************		

How to respond when Law Enforcement arrives on the scene

How you should react when Law Enforcement Arrives	
• Remain calm and follow officers instructions • Immediately raise hands and spread fingers • Avoid making quick movements towards officers such as attempting to hold on to them for safety	• Avoid pointing, screaming, and/or yelling • Do not stop to ask officers for help or directions when evacuating. Just proceed in the direction from which the officers entered the premises.

Information you should provide to Law Enforcement	
• Location of active shooter • Number of shooters, if more than one • Physical description of shooter(s)	• Number and type of weapon(s) • Number of potential victims at the location

BOMB THREATS

Phone Bomb Threat

- Stay calm – do not alarm others.

- Notify your supervisor who will report the threat to law enforcement by **CALLING 911**. If supervisor is not present, you make the call.

- Fill out the *Bomb Threat Card* (**See Attachment 2**) to assist responding agency.

- Decision to evacuate the building will be made by law enforcement personnel.

- Take the Bomb Threat Card with you if the building is evacuated.

Written Bomb Threat

- Remain calm and leave the message where it is found.

- Do not handle the document any more than necessary to preserve fingerprints and other evidence.

- Do not alarm others.

- Notify your supervisor who will report the threat to law enforcement by **CALLING 911**. If supervisor is not present, you make the call.

- Do not give information to anyone except supervisor and law enforcement personnel.

SEVERE WEATHER
AND NATURAL DISASTERS

Tornado:
- When a warning is issued by sirens or other means, seek shelter inside. The following are recommended locations for shelter:
  - Small interior rooms on the lowest floor and without windows,
  - Hallways on the lowest floor away from doors and windows, and
  - Rooms constructed with reinforced concrete, brick, or block with no windows.
  - When a warning is issued by sirens or other means, seek shelter inside.
- Stay away from outside walls and windows.
- Use arms to protect head and neck.
- Remain sheltered until the tornado threat is announced to be over.

Earthquake:
- Stay calm and await instructions from the Emergency Coordinator.
- Keep away from overhead fixtures, windows, filing cabinets, and electrical power.
- Assist people with disabilities in finding a safe place.
- Evacuate as instructed by the Emergency Coordinator or the designated official.

Flood:
- Be ready to evacuate as directed by the Emergency Coordinator.
- Follow the recommended primary or secondary evacuation routes.
- Climb to high ground and stay there.
- Avoid walking or driving through flood water.
- If car stalls, abandon it immediately and climb to a higher ground.

Blizzard:
- Stay calm and await instructions from the Emergency Coordinator.
- Stay indoors!
- If there is no heat:
  - Close off unneeded rooms or areas.
  - Stuff towels or rags in cracks under doors.
  - Cover windows at night.
- Eat and drink. Food provides the body with energy and heat, and fluids prevent dehydration.

EXTENDED POWER LOSS

In the event of extended power loss to a facility certain precautionary measures should be taken depending on the geographical location and environment of the facility:

- Unnecessary electrical equipment and appliances should be turned off in the event that power restoration would surge causing damage to electronics and effecting sensitive equipment.

- Facilities with freezing temperatures should turn off and drain the following lines in the event of a long-term power loss.
  - o Fire sprinkler system
  - o Standpipes
  - o Potable water lines
  - o Toilets

- Equipment that contain fluids that may freeze due to long term exposure to freezing temperatures should be moved to heated areas, drained of liquids, or provided with auxiliary heat sources.

Upon Restoration of heat and power:

- Electronic equipment should be brought up to ambient temperatures before energizing to prevent condensation from forming on circuitry.

- Fire and potable water piping should be checked for leaks from freeze damage after the heat has been restored to the facility and water turned back on.

PERSONS WITH DISABILITIES

Employee and Supervisor Responsibilities

If you are an employee with a disability, there are critical steps you should take to help ensure that you will be safe during an emergency. First, inform your supervisor if you require assistance in the event of an evacuation. Second, work with your supervisor to develop a plan to ensure your safe evacuation in the event of an emergency. If you do not wish to share your needs with your supervisor you should review the procedures to be followed in an emergency situation affecting your assigned facility and familiarize yourself with your evacuation route and assembly area.

If you are a supervisor, you are responsible for reviewing your facility's EAP with all employees under your supervision, including those with disabilities, to ensure that each employee clearly understands procedures that must be followed during an emergency event. Be proactive in developing emergency plans to meet the needs of employees with a disability. You should also include your employees with disabilities in the decision-making process when selecting special equipment and developing evacuation procedures in collaboration with your building managers. Ensure the "Aide for Persons with Disabilities" (see Attachment 3) is notified of any employee that may require special assistance in the event of evacuation or emergency.

Procedures

Options for disability evacuation include:
- Shelter in Place—Take immediate shelter at the designated location.
- Evacuation Chair or Other Assistive Device—An evacuation chair or escape chair is a lightweight wheelchair used to evacuate a physically disabled person from an area of danger, such as a burning building. The chair is designed to allow an attendant to transfer the person down stairs more safely than could be done with a normal wheelchair. Such chairs may be folded to a small size and stowed in much the same manner as other firefighting equipment such as fire hoses and fire extinguishers.
- Two-person Carry—This is a way to carry a person to safety with the assistance of a partner. The two assistants link arms to form a backrest and grip wrists to from a seat.

Please remember, when making decisions regarding the best way to evacuate individuals with disabilities from your building, you should work closely with your local emergency response personnel and their safety specialists.

ATTACHMENT 1   Zone Listing

(INSERT FACILITY FLOOR PLAN COLOR-CODED BY ZONES)

ATTACHMENT 2

Bomb Threat Card

BOMB THREAT CALL PROCEDURES

Most bomb threats are received by phone. Bomb threats are serious until proven otherwise. Act quickly, but remain calm and obtain information with the checklist on the reverse of this card.

If a bomb threat is received by phone:

1. Remain calm. Keep the caller on the line for as long as possible. DO NOT HANG UP, even if the caller does.
2. Listen carefully. Be polite and show interest.
3. Try to keep the caller talking to learn more information.
4. If possible, write a note to a colleague to call the authorities or, as soon as the caller hangs up, immediately notify them yourself.
5. If your phone has a display, copy the number and/or letters on the window display.
6. Complete the Bomb Threat Checklist (reverse side) immediately. Write down as much detail as you can remember. Try to get exact words.
7. Immediately upon termination of the call, do not hang up, but from a different phone, contact FPS immediately with information and await instructions.

If a bomb threat is received by handwritten note:

- Call _____
- Handle note as minimally as possible.

If a bomb threat is received by email:

- Call _____
- Do not delete the message.

Signs of a suspicious package:

- No return address
- Excessive postage
- Stains
- Strange odor
- Strange sounds
- Unexpected delivery
- Poorly handwritten
- Misspelled words
- Incorrect titles
- Foreign postage
- Restrictive notes

DO NOT:

- Use two-way radios or cellular phone; radio signals have the potential to detonate a bomb.
- Evacuate the building until police arrive and evaluate the threat.
- Activate the fire alarm.
- Touch or move a suspicious package.

WHO TO CONTACT (select one)

- Follow your local guidelines
- Federal Protective Service (FPS) Police
  1-877-4-FPS-411 (1-877-437-7411)
- 911

BOMB THREAT CHECKLIST

Date: _____   Time: _____

Time Caller Hung Up: _____   Phone Number Where Call Received: _____

Ask Caller:

- Where is the bomb located?
  (Building, Floor, Room, etc.)
- When will it go off?
- What does it look like?
- What kind of bomb is it?
- What will make it explode?
- Did you place the bomb?   Yes   No
- Why?
- What is your name?

Exact Words of Threat:

_____
_____
_____
_____

Information About Caller:

- Where is the caller located? (Background and level of noise)
- Estimated age:
- Is voice familiar? If so, who does it sound like?
- Other points:

Caller's Voice	Background Sounds:	Threat Language:
☐ Accent	☐ Animal Noises	☐ Incoherent
☐ Angry	☐ House Noises	☐ Message read
☐ Calm	☐ Kitchen Noises	☐ Taped
☐ Clearing throat	☐ Street Noises	☐ Irrational
☐ Coughing	☐ Booth	☐ Profane
☐ Cracking voice	☐ PA system	☐ Well-spoken
☐ Crying	☐ Conversation	
☐ Deep	☐ Music	
☐ Deep breathing	☐ Motor	
☐ Disguised	☐ Clear	
☐ Distinct	☐ Static	
☐ Excited	☐ Office machinery	
☐ **Female**	☐ Factory machinery	
☐ Laughter	☐ Local	
☐ Lisp	☐ Long distance	
☐ Loud		
☐ **Male**	Other Information:	
☐ Nasal		
☐ Normal		
☐ Ragged		
☐ Rapid		
☐ Raspy		
☐ Slow		
☐ Slurred		
☐ Soft		
☐ Stutter		

Homeland Security

ATTACHMENT 3   SAMPLE Position Matrix

Position	Name	Office Room #	Mobile Phone	Office Phone
Emergency Coordinator				
Alternate #1 Emergency Coordinator				
Alternate #2 Emergency Coordinator				
Zone A Floor Captain				
Alternate Zone A Floor Captain				
Zone B Floor Captain				
Alternate Zone B Floor Captain				
Zone C Floor Captain				
Alternate Zone C Floor Captain				
Aide for Persons with Disabilities				
Aide for Persons with Disabilities				
Alternate Aide for Persons with Disabilities				
Alternate Aide for Persons with Disabilities				

ATTACHMENT 4

SAMPLE Personnel Roster

List Updated as of XX Jan 20XX

FLOOR CAPTAIN

Name	Office Room #	Mobile Phone	Office Phone
Primary			
Alternate			

PERSONNEL

Name	Office Room #	Mobile Phone	Office Phone

Appendix C

Campus/Building Emergency Action Plan

Table of Contents

This Page Intentionally Left Blank

<u>BUILDING DESCRIPTION</u>

ENTER DESCRIPTION OF BUILDING HERE

EMERGENCY CONTACTS/CALL TREE AND DUTIES

❖ **Primary Emergency Coordinator**:
  ➢ Responsible for the implementation and updating of this plan.
  ➢ All emergencies will be reported to the Emergency Coordinator by telephone or by runner.
  ➢ Responsible for ensuring that employees are notified of the emergency.
  ➢ Surveying those present at assembly points to determine whether anyone is potentially missing and possibly still in the building.
  ➢ Meet Emergency Responders when they arrive at the building.
  ➢ Communicate potential issues to Emergency Responders, i.e. occupants who might still be in the building, location of fire, known dangerous situations, etc.
  ➢ Work with the MU News Bureau to handle communications with the news media.
  ➢ Within 24 hours following the emergency, meet with all involved parties to discuss the occurrence and to document the details in written form. The form at the end of the plan is designed to be used during the review.

❖ **Secondary Emergency Coordinator:**
  ➢ Assist the Primary Emergency Coordinator in the execution of the plan during an emergency
  ➢ Assist in surveying those present at assembly points to determine whether anyone is potentially missing and possibly still in the building
  ➢ Assume all responsibilities of the Primary Emergency Coordinator in the absence of the PEC

❖ **Zone/Floor Monitors**
  ➢ Assist occupants in their zone/floor during an emergency, i.e. directing traffic for evacuation, sheltering assistance
  ➢ Work with the Primary Emergency Coordinator and Secondary Emergency Coordinator in surveying those present at assembly points to determine whether anyone is potentially missing and possibly still in the building

Departments/Groups Housed in Building Name	
Department 1	
Department 2	
Department 3	
Department 4	
Department 5	

Building Emergency Contact & Duty Information

Title	Name/Department	Work Number	Home Number	Duties
Primary Building Emergency Coordinator				
☐ Check here if the above is the building coordinator.				
Secondary Building Emergency Coordinator				
☐ Check here if the above is the building coordinator.				
Building Coordinator (If different from above)				
Department 1 Primary Contact				
Department 1 Secondary Contact				
Department 2 Primary Contact				
Department 2 Secondary Contact				
Department 3 Primary Contact				
Department 3 Secondary Contact				
Department 4 Primary Contact				
Department 4 Secondary Contact				
Department 5 Primary Contact				
Department 5 Secondary Contact				

Building Name

Emergency Action Plan
3

Date Revised: XX/XX/XXXX
Reviser Initials: AAA

Zone/Floor Monitor Contact Information

Area of Responsibility	Name/Department	Work Number	Home Number	Zone/Floor Description
Basement Zone A				
Basement Zone B				
1st Floor Zone A				
1st Floor Zone B				
2nd Floor Zone A				
2nd Floor Zone B				
3rd Floor Zone A				
3rd Floor Zone B				
4th Floor Zone A				
4th Floor Zone B				

Building Name

Emergency Action Plan
4

Date Revised: XX/XX/XXXX
Reviser Initials: AAA

Campus Emergency Contact Information		
Department		Phone Number
Campus Facilities	General Information Emergency	XXX-XXXX
Environmental Health and Safety	During Normal Working Hours	XXX-XXXX
	After Hours	XXX-XXXX
University Police	Emergency	911
	Nonemergency	XXX-XXXX
University News Bureau		XXX-XXXX
University Registrar's Office		XXX-XXXX

RESPONSE PROCEDURES FOR EMERGENCIES

NOTE: In all of the circumstances below, it is important to remain calm and follow steps as indicated. If there are any questions regarding these procedures please call the University Police at (XXX-XXXX).

Fire Emergencies

1. If you discover a fire, you should activate the Fire Alarm System.
2. ENTER DESCRIPTION OF FIRE ALARM SYSTEM.
3. From a safe location call the Fire Department (911). Give the nature and location of the fire. DO NOT HANG UP UNTIL 911 STAFF HAVE ALREADY HUNG UP!
4. Evacuate the building utilizing the escape routes outlined in this Plan (Appendix A). You may collect valuables, i.e. purse, coats, etc., if within a reasonable reach and will not interfere with the evacuation of the building. Doors should be closed but not locked upon evacuating. DO NOT use elevators unless directed by emergency personnel.
5. If you come into contact with a student or visitor you should direct them to evacuate the building. If you come into contact with an occupant who is disabled or having difficulty evacuating you should assist those individuals in evacuating the building, if doing so will not endanger the personal health or safety of yourself or the occupant needing assistance.
6. If you are trapped by smoke, stay low, cover your mouth with wet cloth, stay near a window, open the window but do not break it, hang something out the window to let fire personnel know you are there and put something in cracks around the door, phone 911 if possible.
7. Use a fire extinguisher, if feasible to do so without jeopardizing personal well-being.
   - ❖ Never use water on an electrical or flammable liquid fire. Use a dry chemical or carbon dioxide extinguisher only.
   - ❖ When using a dry chemical extinguisher on a flammable liquid fire, stay back a minimum of 10 feet from the fire.
     - ➢ Start at the leading edge of the fire and use a side to side sweeping action to extinguish the fire
     - ➢ Remember the acronym P.A.S.S.
       - ▪ **P**ull the pin.
       - ▪ **A**im at the base of the fire.
       - ▪ **S**queeze the discharge handle.
       - ▪ **S**weep from side to side.
8. If rescue duties are called for, the Fire Department will perform these duties. Please pay attention to the location and status of any person needing rescue and relay that information to the Building Emergency Coordinator who will notify the Fire Department Officer in Charge.

9. Once out of the building, gather at ENTER PRIMARY ASSEMBLY POINT to be surveyed. In the event that the primary assembly area is not safe or available, you should gather at ENTER SECONDARY ASSEMBLY POINT. Zone Monitors and/or the Building Emergency Coordinator will conduct a brief survey of all present to determine if anyone is potentially missing and possibly still in the building. You should not leave the assembly area, either to re-enter the building, go to another area of campus or leave the campus, until advised to do so by the Building Emergency Coordinator.

10. Notify University Police (XXX-XXXX).

11. Notify Campus Facilities (XXX-XXXX).

12. Report to your supervisor.

Medical Emergencies

1. If the individual is unconscious:
   - ❖ Call an ambulance (911). When reporting the emergency provide the following information:
     - ➤ Type of Emergency
     - ➤ Location of the Victim
     - ➤ Condition of the Victim
     - ➤ Any dangerous conditions
     - ➤ Do not move the individual unless authorized by some medical authority, or it is obvious that delay in movement would be detrimental to the individual
2. If the individual is conscious:
   - ❖ Call for an ambulance (911) if requested by the individual. When reporting the emergency provide the following information:
     - ➤ Type of Emergency
     - ➤ Location of the Victim
     - ➤ Condition of the Victim
     - ➤ Any dangerous conditions
   - ❖ If the individual does not request an ambulance, then assist the individual, in the form of transportation, to the proper medical treatment facility.
     - ➤ If the injured party is a University employee, assist them in contacting a care facility authorized by Worker's Compensation (882-7019).
     - ➤ If the individual is a student, the Student Health Services Center (882-7481) located on the 4th floor of the University Physicians Medical Building just east of University Hospital is the proper treatment facility.
3. If the individual is a student and fully conscious, call Student Health Services (XXX-XXXX) and give information.
4. In all cases:
   - ❖ Call University Police (XXX-XXXX).
   - ❖ When an ambulance is called for ask a fellow staff employee or the Building Emergency Coordinator to wait outside the building to flag the ambulance down and direct the emergency personnel to the location of the injured individual.
   - ❖ Notify appropriate supervisors.

<u>Severe Weather</u>

1. HOW IS THE BUILDING NOTIFIED OF A SEVERE WEATHER WARNING

    ❖ OUTDOOR SIRENS ARE USED ONLY AS AN ATTENTION GETTING DEVICE WITH NO WAY TO DETERMINE WHY THE SIRENS ARE SOUNDING.

    ❖ Specific information regarding the actual nature of the emergency will be broadcast by the local media.   <Radio Station> serves as the local emergency broadcast station with a direct link from the City/County Emergency Operation Center.

    ❖ No all clear signal will be sounded; sirens are used only for warnings.

2. HOW ARE THE OCCUPANTS OF THE BUILDING NOTIFIED OF A SEVERE WEATHER WARNING

3. Once you have been notified of a thunderstorm warning, it is not necessary to take any additional steps other than to ensure that you are prepared if the conditions deteriorate.

4. Upon notification of a Tornado Warning, take shelter in one of the areas outlined in Appendix B.

    ❖ If you are unable to seek shelter in one of the designated areas, move away from windows. Stay away from auditoriums, gymnasiums, areas having a wide, free span roof, or the upper levels of a building. Take cover under heavy furniture.

    ❖ If you are outdoors and unable to access an indoor shelter, lie flat in the nearest depression, such as a ditch or ravine. If there is time, move away from the path of the Tornado at a right angle.

5. If you come into contact with a student or visitor you should direct them to take shelter in the building. If you come into contact with an occupant who is disabled or having difficulty taking shelter you should assist the individual in getting or taking shelter.

6. After the danger has passed, you should report to the designated shelter/assembly point to allow the Emergency Coordinator to take a survey of all present to determine if anyone is potentially missing.

<u>Hazardous Materials</u>

1. Evacuate the area to the extent appropriate.
2. Warn fellow workers, supervisors, and the Building Emergency Coordinator.
3. Call Environmental Health and Safety (XXX-XXXX). At night, on weekends, or holidays call University Police (XXX-XXXX).
4. Take action to contain the spill if it is possible to do so without jeopardizing personal safety or health.
5. If it is warranted, evacuate according to the evacuation procedures outlined in this plan (Appendix A).
6. If a medical emergency is created due to the hazardous material incident, then follow the procedures for Medical Emergencies and inform medical personnel that a hazardous materials incident has occurred, including the suspected type of hazardous material involved.
7. ***DO NOT*** call state or national emergency response numbers without prior authorization.

Radiological

Fire Emergencies Involving Radiation:

1. Follow the procedures for fire emergencies **AND**
2. Inform emergency personnel that a radiation hazard may exist **AND**
3. Contact Environmental Health and Safety (XXX-XXXX). At night, on weekends, or holidays call University Police (XXX-XXXX).

Medical Emergencies Involving Radiation:

1. Follow the procedures for medical emergencies **AND**
2. Inform medical personnel that a radiation hazard may exist **AND**
3. Contact Environmental Health and Safety (XXX-XXXX). At night, on weekends, or holidays call University Police (XXX-XXXX).

Release of Radioactive Materials:

1. Evacuate personnel from radiation contaminated area.
2. Assemble all personnel in a nearby safe area until radiation surveys and personnel decontamination are performed by the EHS Radiation Safety Office.
3. Prevent spread of contamination from the site.
4. Use the nearest telephone for communication and avoid walking through buildings.
5. Close off doors and windows and, if convenient, turn off air handling equipment that might transfer radiation contamination throughout the building.
6. Control access to radiation area and place warning signs indicating radiation and contamination hazards.
7. Contact Environmental Health and Safety (XXX-XXXX). At night, on weekends, or holidays call University Police (XXX-XXXX).
8. Decontamination of rooms and buildings shall only be done under EHS Radiation Safety Office supervision.

Earthquake

1. Earthquakes occur without warning. Some earthquakes are instantaneous tremors and others are significant sustained events followed by aftershocks.
2. Stay indoors if already there.
3. If indoors take cover. Suggested locations inside buildings that provide cover include:
   * Standing in a doorway and bracing your hands and feet against each side
   * Getting under sturdy furniture, such as work tables or desks
   * Standing flat against an interior wall
   * DO NOT SEEK COVER UNDER LABROTORY TABLES OR BENCHES, CHEMICALS COULD SPILL AND CAUSE HARM
4. Stay near the center of the building and avoid glass windows and doors.
5. If outdoors, stay in open areas, away from buildings and structures, and a safe distance from utility wires.
6. After tremors have stopped, gather valuables, if doing so will not jeopardize the personal health and safety of yourself and others, and quickly leave the building through the evacuation routes outlined in this Plan (Appendix A). DO NOT USE ELEVATORS.
7. If you come into contact with a student or visitor you should direct them to evacuate the building. If you come into contact with an occupant who is disabled or having difficulty evacuating you should assist the individual in evacuating the building if doing so will not endanger the personal health and safety of yourself and the individual needing assistance.
8. Once out of the building, gather at ENTER PRIMARY ASSEMBLY POINT to be surveyed. In the event that the primary assembly area is not safe or available, you should gather at ENTER SECONDARY ASSEMBLY POINT. Zone Monitors and/or the Building Emergency Coordinator will conduct a brief survey of all present to determine if anyone is potentially missing and possibly remains in the building. You should not leave the assembly area, either to re-enter the building, go to another part of campus or leave the campus, until advised to do so by the Building Emergency Coordinator.
9. After tremors have stopped, stay away from damaged buildings and structures. Avoid going through or near buildings where there is a danger of falling debris.
10. Be prepared for aftershocks. Although smaller than the main shock, aftershocks cause additional damage and may bring weakened structures down. Aftershocks can occur in the first hours, days, weeks, or even months after the quake.

Mechanical Equipment or Other Physical Facility Emergencies

1. Call Campus Facilities (XXX-XXXX).
2. Do not attempt to correct the mechanical emergency.
3. If fire ensues, follow procedures outlined for a Fire Emergency.

Oral or Written Threat to People or Facilities, i.e., Bomb Threat

1. Record time and date of call or receipt of message.
2. If caller, keep on line as long as possible and attempt to determine the following:
   - ❖ Who or what are you attempting to harm?
   - ❖ What is to happen?
   - ❖ When is it to happen?
   - ❖ Where is it to happen?
   - ❖ How is it to happen?
   - ❖ Listen closely for background noises
   - ❖ Listen closely for voice type (male, female, voice quality, accents etc.)
   - ❖ Why are you making the threat?
   - ❖ Note if caller knows area by description of location.
   - ❖ Note caller's phone number if you have a display phone.
3. When the caller hangs up on you call University Police (XXX-XXXX) and report the above information.
4. Notify your immediate supervisor and the Building Emergency Coordinator.
5. A decision will be made by the Building Emergency Coordinator and University Police on whether a building evacuation is warranted. If it is warranted, evacuation should take place as outlined in this Plan (Appendix A).
6. You should not touch any suspicious or unfamiliar objects. Do not conduct any type of search until police personnel arrive on scene.

University Emergency Operations Plan

The University, in accordance with state and federal guidelines, has developed an Emergency Operations Plan (EOP) which will be implemented in the event of a disaster. A disaster is defined for purposes of the EOP as any type of situation that endangers life and property to a degree that a concentrated effort of emergency services be coordinated on a large scale to contain the situation. Disasters are distinguished from emergencies by the greater level of response required.

In the event that a disaster does occur, an Emergency Operations Center (EOC) will be activated to coordinate the implementation of the EOP in responding to and recovering from the disaster. All activities and decisions relating to the disaster will be made from the EOC.

The EOP provides for the dissemination of information about the disaster through the use of Public Information Officer (PIO). The PIO is charged with ensuring that the university community, public, and media are kept informed about the situation. The PIO and the EOC will ensure through whatever communication methods are available that buildings are informed about what additional and further steps, if any, should be taken by the occupants. Until such information is received, the Building Name Emergency Action Plan should be followed.

<u>EMERGENCY PREVENTION TIPS</u>

The following tips when followed will help reduce emergencies:

1. **Smoking:** Careless smoking is a major cause of fire. To minimize this potential fire ignition source, a "NO SMOKING POLICY" is strongly encouraged.

2. **Trash Accumulation:** The accumulation of trash generated in the course of the workday provides an environment conducive to the spread of fire. In order to reduce this potential risk the following steps are to be considered.
   1. All combustible waste material should be kept at least six (6) feet from any heat source. Heat sources would include such things as water heaters, furnaces, etc.
   - All trash containers for combustible materials should be dumped at the end of the shift.
   - Special attention should be given to the location of paper recycling containers.

3. **Improper Storage of Combustible and Flammable Materials:** Improper storage of materials can contribute to the ignition and spread of fire. To reduce this risk the following procedures are to be followed.
   1. All flammable liquids must be stored in approved containers. If flammable liquids are removed from their original container, they are to be stored in an approved safety can which is properly labeled and meeting the requirements of the MU Hazardous Waste Management Program.
   2. Do not store flammable or combustible materials near a heat source. If in doubt of storage requirements, consult the label, the appropriate material safety data sheet or contact EHS.

4. **General Housekeeping:** One of the simplest ways to prevent emergencies is to conduct a good general housekeeping of your workspace, office, and building on a frequent basis. This includes but is not limited to:
   1. Ensuring that doorways, stairways, Fire Department connections, fire extinguishers, fire alarm pull boxes, and emergency exits are not blocked by boxes, furniture, etc.
   2. Keep corridors and stairways free of clutter
   3. Computer and Electrical Cables are kept organized to prevent clutter
   4. Frayed electrical cords should be discarded

<u>PERSONS WHO NEED ASSISTANCE DURING AN EMERGENCY</u>

1. In the event of any emergency there are occupants of the building who will need assistance in evacuating the building, taking shelter, taking cover, etc.

2. If you encounter someone who needs assistance during an emergency you should attempt to assist the individual, if it is possible to do so without jeopardizing the personal safety or health of yourself or the person needing assistance.

3. If you know or have reason to know that you will need assistance during an emergency you should report that information to the Building Emergency Coordinator as soon as possible.

4. More details about emergency evacuation for persons who need assistance can be found in Appendix C.

5. The following people are occupants of the building who have expressed the need for assistance in the event of an emergency to the Building Emergency Coordinator.

Known Persons Needing Assistance			
Name/ Department	**Room Number/ Location**	**Dept. Phone**	**Type of Assistance Needed**

TRAINING:

❖ Before implementing the EAP, the Building Emergency Coordinator and Building Managers/Supervisors shall designate and train a sufficient number of persons to assist in the safe and orderly emergency evacuation of employees.

❖ The EAP must be reviewed with all occupants at the following times: Initially when the plan is developed, whenever the employee's responsibilities or designated action under the plan change, and whenever the plan is changed.

❖ At least annually employee meetings are to be held to train employees of the contents of the EAP and revise the plan as appropriate.

❖ Drills will be conducted and full participation encouraged in March (Severe Weather/Tornado Drill) and October (Fire Drill) of each year.

❖ All training must be documented in writing and copies sent to Environmental Health and Safety.

  ➢ Checklists from Environmental Health and Safety are distributed in March and October for use in the March and October drills.

  ➢ The form included in this plan can be used to document training exercises.

EHS PLAN REVIEW:

1. A copy of the building specific Emergency Action Plan must be sent to the University Safety Professional (XXX-XXXX) at EHS after completion.
2. The EAP will be reviewed during routine fire and safety inspection by EHS.
3. The EAP will be maintained by the Building Emergency Coordinator and made available to all occupants of the building.

ENVIRONMENTAL HEALTH AND SAFETY INCIDENT REPORT

DATE/TIME OF INCIDENT:

DATE/TIME INCIDENT NOTIFICATION RECEIVED:

HOW CONTACTED & BY WHOM (By telephone, in person, by MUPD Dispatch, etc.):

INCIDENT DESCRIPTION (Who/What/When/Where/How):

EHS RESPONSE REQUIRED: Yes ☐   **No** ☐

INCIDENT RESPONSE DESCRIPTION (If no response was required by EHS, but information was provided to/by EHS or spill clean-up procedures were confirmed by EHS, so state in this section):

ITEMIZE EQUIPMENT USED IN RESPONSE:

ITEMIZE ANY ADDITIONAL EQUIPMENT NEEDED FOR RESPONSE OR FOR PERSONAL SAFETY:

COMMENTS (Include any problems or potential problems noted during the incident, recommended improvements in procedures, etc.):

DATE/TIME RESPONSE WAS COMPLETED:

LIST ANY RELATED REPORTS (e.g., Police or Fire reports, EHS documents, etc.):

NAME OF PERSON PREPARING REPORT:

DATE OF REPORT SUBMISSION:

(Use this form to report emergency incidents to Environmental Health and Safety.

Appendix A
<u>EVACUATION ROUTES</u>

LIST THE PRIMARY AND SECONDARY ASSEMBLY POINTS HERE

ATTACH THE EVACUATION ROUTES OF EACH FLOOR TO THE PLAN IN THIS APPENDIX

Appendix B
<u>SHELTER LOCATIONS</u>

LIST POTENTIAL SHELTER LOCATIONS

LIST ASSEMBLY POINT FOR AFTER EMERGENCY

INCLUDE A FLOOR PLAN SHOWING THE SHELTER LOCATIONS IN THE BUILDING

Appendix C
Emergency Evacuation for Persons with Disabilities

General

This appendix provides a general guideline of evacuation procedures for persons with disabilities, which would make exiting difficult, during fire and other building emergencies. Faculty, staff, students, and visitors with disabilities must develop their own facilities' evacuation plans and identify their primary and secondary evacuation routes from each building they use.

❖ Be familiar with evacuation options.
❖ Seek evacuation assistants who are willing to assist in case of an emergency.
❖ Ask supervisors, instructors, building emergency coordinators, or Environmental Health & Safety about evacuation plans for buildings.

Most MU buildings have accessible exits at the ground level floor that can be used during an emergency. In some buildings, it may be possible for people in unaffected wings of the building to remain inside rather than exiting. However, in most MU buildings people will need to use stairways to reach building exits. Elevators cannot be used because they are unsafe to use in an emergency and are normally automatically recalled to the ground floor.

Evacuation Options

Persons with disabilities must evacuate to the nearest exit. Persons with disabilities have four basic evacuation options.

❖ Horizontal
  ➢ Using building exits to the outside ground level
  ➢ Going into unaffected wings of multi-building complexes
❖ Stairway
  ➢ Using steps to reach ground level exits from the building
❖ Stay in Place
  ➢ Unless danger is imminent, remaining in a room with an exterior window, a telephone, and a solid or fire-resistant door.
  ➢ With this approach, the person may keep in contact with emergency services by dialing 911 and reporting his or her location directly. Emergency services will immediately relay this location to on-site emergency personnel, who will determine the necessity for evacuation.
  ➢ Phone lines are expected to remain in service during most building emergencies. If the phone lines fail, the individual can signal from the window by waving a cloth or other visible object.
  ➢ The Stay in Place approach may be more appropriate for sprinkler protected buildings or buildings where an "area of refuge" is not nearby or available.
  ➢ It may also be more appropriate for an occupant who is alone when the alarm sounds.

> A "solid" or fire-resistant door can be identified by a fire label on the jam and frame. Nonlabeled 1 ¾ inch thick solid core wood doors hung on a metal frame also offer good fire resistance

❖ Area of Refuge
> With an evacuation assistant, going to an area of refuge away from obvious danger.
> The evacuation assistant will then go the building evacuation assembly point (Appendix A) and notify the Building Emergency Coordinator or on-site emergency personnel of the location of the area of refuge.
> Emergency personnel will determine if further evacuation is necessary.
> The safest areas of refuge are pressurized stair enclosures common to high-rise buildings, and open-air exit balconies.
> Other possible areas of refuge include: fire rated corridors or vestibules adjacent to exit stairs, and pressurized elevator lobbies.
> Taking a position in a rated corridor next to the stairs is a good alternative to a small stair landing crowded with other building occupants using the stairway.
> For assistance in identifying Areas of Refuge, contact Environmental Health & Safety.

For false or needless alarms or an isolated and contained fire, a person with a disability may not have to evacuate. The decision to evacuate will be made by the Fire Department. The FD will tell the individual their decision or relay the information via the Campus Police Department (CPD).

Disability Guidelines

<u>Mobility Impaired - Wheelchair</u>
Persons using wheelchairs should stay in place, or move to an area of refuge with their assistant when the alarm sounds. The evacuation assistant should then proceed to the evacuation assembly point outside the building and tell FD or CPD the location of the person with a disability. If the person with a disability is alone, he/she should phone emergency services at 911 with their present location and the area of refuge they are headed to.

If the stair landing is chosen as the area of refuge, please note that many campus buildings have relatively small stair landings, and wheelchair users are advised to wait until the heavy traffic has passed before entering the stairway.

Stairway evacuation of wheelchair users should be conducted by trained professionals (FD). Only in situations of extreme danger should untrained people attempt to evacuate wheelchair users. Moving a wheelchair down stairs is never safe.

<u>Mobility Impaired - Non-Wheelchair</u>
Persons with mobility impairments, who are able to walk independently, may be able to negotiate stairs in an emergency with minor assistance. If danger is imminent, the individual should wait until the heavy traffic has cleared before attempting the stairs. If there is no immediate danger (detectable smoke, fire, or unusual odor), the person with

a disability may choose to stay in the building, using the other options, until the emergency personnel arrive and determine if evacuation is necessary.

Hearing Impaired

Some buildings on campus are equipped with fire alarm strobe lights; however, many are not. Persons with hearing impairments may not hear audio emergency alarms and will need to be alerted of emergency situations. Emergency instructions can be given by writing a short explicit note to evacuate.

Reasonable accommodations for persons with hearing impairments may be met by modifying the building fire alarm system, particularly for occupants who spend most of their day in one location.

Visually Impaired

Most people with a visual impairment will be familiar with their immediate surroundings and frequently traveled routes. Since the emergency evacuation route is likely different from the commonly traveled route, persons who are visually impaired may need assistance in evacuating. The assistant should offer their elbow to the individual with a visual impairment and guide him or her through the evacuation route. During the evacuation the assistant should communicate as necessary to assure safe evacuation.

Appendix D

Building Name Emergency Action Plan

POLICY ACKNOWLEDGMENT

I have reviewed the Emergency Action Plan (EAP) for Building Name. I agree to adhere to this policy.

_____

Signature of Building Name University Staff Member   Date

_____

Signature of Building Name Trainer/Staff Member   Date

Property:

Assessor's Name:

Date of Assessment:

Clear Form   Print Form

HOTEL SECURITY AND SAFETY ASSESSMENT FORM

Part One: Background and Property Information

There is increasing interest in the health, safety, and security attributes of hotels. Many companies and organizations are interested in this information to satisfy two overarching managerial responsibilities: Duty of Care and Due Diligence.

Because of this interest, they may request information from a hotel in order to assess the security and safety integrity of the property. Determining what information is relevant to such an assessment is particularly challenging because there are no agreed-upon standards of what security/safety features a hotel should have, nor are there any agreed-upon standards as to what constitutes a "secure" or "safe" property. There are only generally accepted "best practices." Assessing the security/safety of a property is therefore a subjective analysis. Hence, this guide is referred to as an "Assessment" rather than an audit or inspection, which implies an appraisal against a defined standard. And since each hotel company operates its properties according to its own brand operating standards, it is appropriate that the assessment take these factors into consideration.

This assessment guide was created to help corporate security departments, corporate travel and safety departments, event planners, meeting organizers, tour operators, and others (e.g., third-party health, safety, and security assessors) collectively referred to as "Customers," to conduct security, safety, and health surveys and assessments of hotels.

It is important that hotels be able to respond to such requests in a timely, accurate, and customer-friendly manner. While hotels certainly understand the concerns of Customers and wish to cooperate with them as much as possible, there are also important restrictions on what may be provided to them. Therefore, the Loss Prevention Committee of the American Hotel and Lodging Association (AH&LA), in collaboration with the U.S. Department of State Overseas Security Advisory Council (OSAC) and its Common Interest Council (referred to as the Hotel Security Working Group), came together to produce this assessment guide. The guide reflects a common agreement on what security, safety, and health information is generally able to be provided by a hotel in order for Customers to make an assessment of a particular property.

As you can appreciate, to avoid compromising the hotel's security and safety systems, there are limitations on what the property may disclose (e.g., information concerning security camera locations or alarm systems, security staffing information, security procedures) or routinely provide upon demand (e.g., copies of emergency plans or procedures, floor diagrams, property schematics, etc.). These limitations are in the interest of protecting the hotel's guests and staff. The hotel recognizes, however, that a Customer may wish to further discuss the security or safety matters of the hotel. If so, the Customer should contact the Hotel General Manager. Alternatively, the Customer may also contact the Corporate Security department of the respective hotel chain. Contact information for the Corporate Security department may be obtained from the AH&LA or through the OSAC Coordinator for Common Interest Councils.

Hotels are a significant part of the hospitality business. Security and safety considerations have increasingly become integral to the success of a hotel enterprise. Accordingly, members of the AH&LA Loss Prevention Committee and the OSAC Hotel Security Working Group acknowledge this and affirm that:

> *We believe that the comfort and reasonable duty of care of our guests is an inherent responsibility, and that protecting the hotel's Brand and Reputation must be accomplished in a competent and professional manner.*

> *We recognize that the quality of security and safety services at a hotel is a growing concern for corporate business and private travellers, and where there is a choice they will seek out hotel properties that have enhanced security and safety features and services.*

V.2014 Proprietary and Confidential
Please ensure the information contained herein is safeguarded and protected.
Control the dissemination of information contained herein.   Page 1

We safeguard our guests, our staff, and our properties by creating a security and safety environment that promotes hospitality and enhances the guest experience.

We collaborate to promote information sharing that advances the security and safety of our guests, our staff, our properties, and our Customers.

About the AHLA – Security and Safety Committee: The mission of the Committee is to assist industry members in achieving effective and efficient security practices, identifying and adopting appropriate technologies, and providing professional training that promotes a secure and safe operating environment. The Committee also assists the lodging industry in responding to safety and security legislative, regulatory, and code initiatives that could impact the industry.

About The Overseas Security Advisory Council (OSAC): The Council was created in 1985 under the Federal Advisory Committee Act to promote security cooperation between American private sector interests worldwide and the U.S. Department of State.

The OSAC "Council" is comprised of 34 private sector and public sector member organizations that represent specific industries or agencies operating abroad. The Department of State's Bureau of Diplomatic Security (DS) implemented the following recommendations for OSAC: to create the OSAC website, to create a Country Council Program, and to develop a Research and Information Support Center (RISC). A primary goal of OSAC is to develop an effective security communication network; consequently, OSAC invited all U.S. businesses, academia, faith-based groups, and non-governmental organizations to become constituents. There is no cost to become a constituent member.

About the Hotel Security Working Group (HSWG): The HSWG is a sector-specific Working Group within OSAC that focuses on security concerns relevant to the hotel industry operating abroad. The Group was founded in June 2008 by a handful of Security Directors representing various hotel chains to promote the safety and security of guests and employees of member organizations and to protect the assets of the hotel brand. The HSWG accomplishes this by sharing information and best practices, collaborating on educational and training initiatives among its members, and by members networking and benchmarking with security professionals throughout the hospitality industry.

V.2014 Proprietary and Confidential
Please ensure the information contained herein is safeguarded and protected.
Control the dissemination of information contained herein.   Page 2

Assessment Methodology:
(How to use this assessment guide)

Collecting the Data: This assessment guide is divided into three parts.

Part One: Background information about the Hotel Security Assessment program, as well as basic property information considered necessary to enable a Customer to make a security assessment of the property.

Part Two: Essential information a Customer, such as a Corporate Security department, may consider necessary to enable them to assess the general security of the property and arrive at a Duty of Care determination.

Part Three: Ancillary information considered necessary to enable a Customer to make a security and safety assessment of the property. A Customer, such as a tour operator, may consider the information in both Part Two and Part Three necessary to enable them to assess the general security and safety of the property and arrive at a Due Diligence determination.

Part Three also contains information related to airline crew considerations. A Customer, such as an airline operator, may consider the information in Parts Two and Three necessary to enable them to assess the general security and safety of the property and arrive at a Due Diligence determination.

Understanding the Data:

Every property is unique. Depending on the specific operating factors of the hotel, various data elements noted in this assessment guide may or may not apply to the property. For example, a Select Service hotel is a property purposefully managed with a limited staff. Such properties normally do not have an onsite security staff and therefore would not mark many of the data elements in the Guarding Section. Accordingly, the elements checked in this guide and reported by a property will vary. This variance should not imply a derogatory operating environment. It simply connotes a difference in operating environment.

Assessing the Data:

Based on the information reported in this assessment guide, Customers should evaluate the information, based on their own security and safety management systems. Customers should decide for themselves whether the security and safety operations of the property sufficiently satisfy the Duty of Care and Due Diligence considerations of their respective organization.

In this regard, while some organizations may wish to make recommendations to a hotel on measures to implement to improve the security or safety of their property, the hotel is under no obligation to accept them or implement them. In such cases, the Customer may exercise their discretion and be inclined to not use the hotel for their intended business.

Updating the Data:

The data elements of this assessment guide are periodically updated to accommodate changing operating environments and emerging best practices. To suggest data elements for consideration in future editions of this guide, please submit them to:

Staff Liaison – Safety and Security Committee		**Coordinator – Common Interest Councils/HSWG**
American Hotel & Lodging Association (AH&LA)		Overseas Security Advisory Council (OSAC)
1201 New York Avenue, NW, Suite 600	**OR**	Diplomatic Security Service
Washington, DC 20005		U.S. Department of State
		Washington, DC 20522

General Index

PART ONE

Information for general security and safety assessment.

Property Information

    A. Hotel Contact Information

    B. Property General Description

    C. Property Key Attributes

    D. Property Licenses and Documentation

PART TWO
Property Details

    E. Property Fire, Life Safety and Security Information

        1. Fire Systems

        2. Security Systems and Equipment

        3. Lighting

        4. Guarding

        5. Health and Life Safety

        6. Guest Room Security

        7. Elevators/Lifts

        8. Swimming Pool and Fitness Center

        9. Nightclubs and Conference/Function Rooms

       10. Security and Safety Training

       11. Emergency Planning

       12. Emergency Response/Crisis Management

    F. Local Emergency Contact Information

        1. Law Enforcement

        2. Ambulance Service

        3. Fire Brigade

        4. Hospital

    G. Reporting Security or Safety Incidents

    H. Property Operating Environment

PART THREE

(Additional safety considerations to be considered along with the information from Part One, for use by Tour Operators, Airlines, and other third parties)

Further Safety Considerations

    1. Food Hygiene

    2. Premises Hygiene

    3. Gas Safety

    4. Legionella Safety

    5. Swimming Pool Safety

    6. General Safety

    7. Airline Crew Safety

V.2014 Proprietary and Confidential
Please ensure the information contained herein is safeguarded and protected.
Control the dissemination of information contained herein.

Page 4

Property Information

A. Hotel Contact Information

Hotel Name	
General Manager Name/Contact Number	
Director of Rooms Name/Contact Number	
Director of Security Name/Contact Number	
Hotel Street Address	
Hotel City/Country/Postal Code	
Hotel Main Telephone Number	Hotel Fax Number
Hotel E-mail Address	

B. Property General Description

Insert a general description of the Hotel. This section is intended to provide the reader only with sufficient information to understand the location of the property, its general layout, and the general services available at the property.

V.2014 Proprietary and Confidential
Please ensure the information contained herein is safeguarded and protected.
Control the dissemination of information contained herein.   Page 5

C. Property Key Attributes:

Provides relevant information on the key physical attributes of the property

Property Descriptors:

☐ Located in the U.S.   ☐ Located Outside the U.S.

☐ Urban   ☐ Resort   ☐ Multi-Tenant Facility   ☐ Super-Tall Building (>75 floors)

☐ Full Service   ☐ Select Service   ☐ Owned/Managed   ☐ Franchised

Total number of floors in main building:	
Number of upper floors (including ground floor):	
Number of floors below ground:	
Number of stairways in main building suitable for use in an emergency:	
Total number of guest rooms for property:	
Hotel has an emergency generator to support basic infrastructure (lighting, lifts, etc.) ☐ YES ☐ NO	
Approximate duration (in hours) Hotel generator can continuously operate on fuel tank capacity:	

D. Property Licenses and Documentation

Hotel is in possession of the following:

☐	Fire Certificate	
☐	Public Liability Insurance	State the expiry date of the public liability insurance:
☐	Log of inspections for fire alarm system, emergency lighting system, fire extinguishers, hose reels, hydrants, and main electrical system	
☐	Fire Training Log	

V.2014 Proprietary and Confidential
Please ensure the information contained herein is safeguarded and protected.
Control the dissemination of information contained herein.   Page 6

Part Two: Property Details

E. Property Fire, Life Safety, and Security Information

1. Fire Systems

☐ Hotel has a fire emergency plan (including evacuation assembly areas) that may be reviewed at the office of the General Manager.

Hotel has Smoke Detectors connected to the fire alarm system:

☐ • In Guest Rooms

☐ • In Public Areas

Hotel has Sprinklers:

☐ • In Guest Rooms

☐ • In Public Areas

☐ • In Utility Areas

☐ Emergency exit doors are fitted with locks that enable immediate release and opening.

☐ Hotel has systems and procedures to enunciate an alarm in the case of a fire or other emergency.

☐ Hotel fire alarm system is tested on a regular basis.

☐ Fire alarm system has a PA (public address) functionality to enable emergency announcements.

☐ Fire alarm system has stand-by power supplied by batteries/charger.

☐ The Hotel has fire extinguishers on guest floors, in public areas, and in key BOH areas.

☐ Emergency lighting and fire extinguishers comply with local fire code and are regularly inspected.

☐ Emergency stairways have self-closing fire resistant doors.

☐ Emergency stairways are fitted with handrails and kept clear of obstructions.

☐ Emergency egress route end points are locations that discharge persons outside the building.

☐ Exit doors and Final Exit doors are clearly identified with appropriate signage.

☐ Exit doors are unobstructed and Final Exit doors are unobstructed externally.

☐ Corridors and stairways are fitted with emergency lighting units.

☐ Public areas, corridors, and stairways contain signs indicating evacuation routes.

☐ Corridors have no dead end more than 10 meters from evacuation stairway. (A dead end is an area where escape in an emergency is only possible in one direction).

Heat detectors are located in:

☐ • Boiler Room

☐ • Kitchen Areas

☐ • Laundry Area

☐ CO detectors are located where fossil fuel burning devices are located.

☐ CO detectors are hard-wired to the Fire Alarm control panel.

☐ Maintenance/Inspection records for fire system and fire equipment are available for review at the office of the Hotel Engineer.

2. Security Systems and Equipment

☐ Hotel utilizes a CCTV surveillance system.

Hotel CCTV surveillance system covers:

☐ • Parking Facilities (garage and/or parking lots)

☐ • Entrances to Hotel (public and employee)

☐ • Public Areas (lobby, meeting room foyers)

☐ • Guest Room Floors

☐ • Loading Dock and Service Delivery Area

☐ Hotel has video archiving system that retains surveillance video for minimum of 30 days.

☐ Hotel car parks have entry and exit controls.

☐ There is a means to ensure vehicles do not directly approach the hotel without passing a physical barrier.

☐ Measures are in place to stop unauthorized vehicles from parking adjacent to the hotel building.

☐ Hotel has parking facilities adjoining or beneath the hotel.

☐ Hotel has self-parking.

☐ Hotel prohibits parking on the main-entry Porte Cochere.

☐ Hotel conducts vehicle inspections as part of access control procedures.

☐ Loading dock and service delivery areas have separate access that is controlled.

☐ Hotel has key-control protocol for daily accountability of assigned staff keys.

☐ Hotel regularly audits the key-control protocol for accountability of hotel master keys.

☐ Housekeeping keys are segmented to defined or assigned block of rooms.

☐ Access to guest rooms can be electronically audited.

V.2014 Proprietary and Confidential
Please ensure the information contained herein is safeguarded and protected.
Control the dissemination of information contained herein.   Page 7

3. Lighting

☐	Hotel has emergency lighting in public areas and evacuation stairwells.
☐	Parking areas are lighted.
☐	Premises and grounds are lighted.
☐	Hotel guest rooms have a flashlight for emergency use.

4. Guarding

☐	Hotel has onsite security staff 24 hours daily.
☐	Hotel conducts periodic security/safety patrols of hotel and premises on 24-hour basis.
☐	Public access entrances and exits are observed or supervised by hotel staff 24 hours daily.
☐	Hotel staff controls access to the guest floors from public areas.
☐	Hotel has a process for increasing security manpower for meetings or events upon request.
☐	Hotel has a staffed command center that actively monitors hotel access control systems, CCTV system, and fire/life safety systems.
☐	An internal emergency telephone number is available and is continually staffed.
☐	Hotel has an armed guard presence on premises.
☐	Hotel Security staff wear name badges.
☐	Hotel Security staff has means to readily identify themselves to others as premises security.
☐	In the event of an emergency Hotel Security have a marked vest, armband, or other means to be readily identified.

5. Health and Life Safety

☐	Hotel has a food safety management system based on Hazard Analysis Critical Control Point (HACCP) principles.
☐	Hotel conducts regular hygiene inspections.
☐	Hotel has procedures to mitigate Legionella.
☐	Hotel has pest control measures in place that cover Food Control areas, public areas, and guest room areas.
☐	Upon request, a private licensed physician or medical care provider can be summoned to the Hotel.
☐	Hotel staff has received basic First Aid and CPR training.
☐	Hotel has First Aid Kits for emergencies.
☐	Hotel has Medical Trauma Kits for emergencies.
☐	Hotel has AED equipment on premises.

6. Guest Room Security

Guest Rooms have:

☐	• Deadbolt Locks
☐	• Door Chain or Wishbone Latch
☐	• Door Closure Mechanism
☐	• View Ports
☐	Guest room connecting room doors have a deadbolt lock.
☐	Guest rooms are fitted with a convenience safe.
☐	Guest room appliances have instructions for use in English.
☐	Guest rooms have a compendium that contains guidance for guests to follow in case of Fire and other emergencies.
☐	Guest rooms have Safety Exit maps on back of door.
☐	Guest rooms with balconies have internal locking devices to deter forced entry.
☐	Height of guest room balcony surrounds is greater than 1.1 meter (42 inch equivalent).
☐	Guest room balcony surrounds have no gap greater than 100mm (4 inch equivalent).
☐	Guest room windows have restricted opening capability of no greater than 100mm (4 inch equivalent).
☐	Guest rooms have no gas-operated appliances or water heaters.

7. Elevators/Lifts

☐	State the number of elevators/lifts in the hotel. (Operating certificates are available and may be reviewed at the office of the Hotel General Manager)	Total Number
☐	Hotel elevators have regular maintenance inspections.	

Hotel elevators have following notices displayed outside the lift on each floor:

☐	• DO NOT USE IN CASE OF FIRE
☐	• NO SMOKING (in the lift)
☐	• NO UNACCOMPANIED CHILDREN
☐	Hotel elevators are fitted with key-card control to prevent direct access to the guest floors from public areas.
☐	Hotel elevators/lifts have an emergency alarm and communication system.
☐	Hotel elevators are fitted with CCTV cameras.

V.2014 Proprietary and Confidential
Please ensure the information contained herein is safeguarded and protected.
Control the dissemination of information contained herein.

Page 8

8. Swimming Pool and Fitness Center

☐	Pool water is checked as per local regulations for pH and chlorine.
☐	Pool has clearly designated depth markings visible from within the pool and around it.
☐	Buoyancy aids are provided at the pool side.
☐	Pool surround deck/area has non-slip surface.
☐	Pool has general "pool regulations" notice board and signage that advises whether or not there is a lifeguard on duty during operating hours.
☐	Fitness Center has controlled access.
☐	Fitness Center has a phone or alarm system to summon emergency assistance.

9. Nightclubs and Conference Function Rooms

☐	Hotel has nightclub or discotheque on premises.
☐	Hotel has separate access controls/procedures for the nightclub/discotheque.
☐	Exit routes from nightclub/discotheque are clearly signed and permanently illuminated.
☐	Exit doors in the escape route from the nightclub/discotheque open in the direction of travel.
☐	Exit doors from the nightclub/discotheque are immediately operable without the use of a key.
☐	The nightclub/discotheque area is covered by the Hotel fire system.
☐	Hotel is able to secure Conference and Function Rooms to provide "client-only" access.

10. Security and Safety Training

☐	Hotel has a Security Awareness training program for staff.
☐	Hotel staff has undertaken training in Human Trafficking Awareness.
☐	Hotel staff has received training in accident and medical incident response.
☐	All Hotel staff receives training in actions to be taken in the event of a fire and other emergencies.
☐	Key staff receives First Aid and CPR training.
☐	Hotel Security staff receive in-house orientation and job-specific training.
☐	Hotel security staff receives training in control and restraint techniques.
☐	Hotel is periodically reviewed by the brand's Corporate Security department.
Hotel Security Staff trained and certified as:	
☐	• CLSO (AHLA)
☐	• CLSD (AHLA)
☐	• CPP (ASIS)

11. Emergency Planning

☐	The Hotel has emergency response protocols and procedures for security and safety contingencies and safety-related incidents that may be reviewed at the office of the Hotel Manager or Hotel Security Director. ALL BELOW (if not all, check those applicable to property)
☐	Active Shooter
☐	Bomb Threat/Suspicious Package
☐	Natural Disasters relevant to location
☐	Fire/Explosion
☐	Food-Related Illness
☐	Human Trafficking
☐	Medical

12. Emergency Response/Crisis Management

☐	The Hotel has a crisis management protocol and procedures that enables response coordination and support for natural disasters and other contingencies listed below. (if not all, check those applicable to property)
☐	Biological Threat
☐	Civil Unrest/Protest Group/Demonstration
☐	Criminal Activity
☐	HAZMAT Incident
☐	Hostage/Kidnapping/Extortion
☐	Hostile Conflict
☐	Information Technology/Data Breach/Technology & Equipment Theft
☐	Nuclear/Radiological Incident
☐	Pandemic
☐	Regulatory Action
☐	Transportation Disruption
☐	Earthquake
☐	Extreme Heat
☐	Flood
☐	Heavy Snowstorm
☐	Hurricane/Tropical Storm/Typhoon
☐	Tornado/Severe Weather/Thunderstorm
☐	Tsunami
☐	Volcano
☐	Wildfire

V.2014 Proprietary and Confidential
Please ensure the information contained herein is safeguarded and protected.
Control the dissemination of information contained herein.

Page 9

F. Local Emergency Contact Information

Law Enforcement		Fire Brigade	
Authority Name:		Authority Name:	
Authority Address:		Authority Address:	
Authority Telephone Number:		Authority Telephone Number:	
Approximate Distance to Hotel and Travel Time:		Approximate Distance to Hotel and Travel Time:	
Ambulance Service		**Hospital**	
Service Name:		Name:	
Service Address:		Address:	
Service Telephone Number:		Telephone Number:	
Approximate Distance to Hotel and Travel Time:		Approximate Distance From Hotel and Travel Time:	

G. Reporting Security or Safety Incidents – Requesting Immediate Assistance

The security and safety of guests and staff is a top priority for the Hotel. If a health, safety, or security situation arises that should be brought to the Hotel's attention, please observe the following reporting protocol:

EXAMPLE (to be defined specifically for the property) If the situation is an emergency --- dial "55" from any Hotel phone and immediately report it. If the matter is NOT an emergency, dial "4240" from any Hotel phone, ask to speak to the Manager on Duty, and report the matter accordingly.

H. Property Operating Environment

THIS SECTION IS OPTIONAL. This section identifies the general operating environment of the property to evaluate its potential vulnerability to various criminal, terrorist, and other risks.

For properties in the U.S.: There are a number of crime reporting services such the www.fbi.gov/contact-us/field/search-by-zip-code, and CAP Index. The CAP Index is a commercially available tool that provides crime data information for locations in the U.S. by zip code. You can purchase a comprehensive online crime report from CAP Index at: https://www.capindex.com.

Obtain a crime data report for the property location. What is the crime index rating?

For properties outside the US: Obtain the Department of State/U.S. Embassy—Regional Security Office, Crime and Safety report for the city. These reports are available online or through the Overseas Security Advisory Council (OSAC) at: https://www.osac.gov

☐ The hotel is a constituent member of the OSAC local Country Council.

☐ An OSAC Crime and Safety report for this location is attached hereto.

Sections A—H:
I confirm as the responsible person at the property that the information provided in the aforementioned section is an accurate reflection of the security and safety facilities at this property.

Hotel General Manager: INSERT NAME and electronic signature

V.2014 Proprietary and Confidential
Please ensure the information contained herein is safeguarded and protected.
Control the dissemination of information contained herein.   Page 10

Part Three: Further Safety Considerations

To enable tour operators and other third parties to assess the general operating conditions and safety practices of the property, the Hotel is encouraged to provide the following supplementary information as applicable. The requested information observes the recommended best practices of the World Tour Operators Association (WTOA) and its subsidiary members:

1. Food Hygiene

I confirm as the responsible person at the property that the information provided in this section is an accurate reflection of the safety facilities at this property.

Please state the name of the person completing this information:

Please state position held : (e.g., Hotel Executive Chef)

Check all below that apply

Management Control

☐ Property has an established food safety management system (e.g., HACCP).

Food Delivery Controls

☐ Property has a system of assessing food and beverage suppliers.

☐ Property has a documented system for reviewing delivery problems and complaints relating to suppliers.

Frozen Food Storage

☐ Foods are covered.

☐ Foods are within date code.

☐ Staff follow stock rotation procedures.

☐ Frozen food temperatures are recorded.

☐ Freezers maintain food temperatures at or below −10°C (15°F).

Refrigerated Food Storage

☐ Foods are covered.

☐ Foods are within date code.

☐ Staff follow stock rotation procedures.

☐ Refrigerated food temperatures are recorded.

☐ Refrigerators maintain food temperatures at or below 5°C (41°F).

Cooking/Reheating

Temperatures of Cooked Foods:

☐ Temperatures are recorded.

☐ Temperatures are over 75°C (167°F).

Temperatures of Re-heated Foods:

☐ Temperatures are recorded.

☐ Temperatures are over 75°C (167°F).

☐ Procedures are in place to ensure foods are only reheated once.

Cooling

☐ Documented procedures exist for the cooling of food in place.

Service

☐ Documented procedures exist for the hot holding of food.

☐ Hot holding procedures are recorded.

☐ Hot holding units maintain food above 63°C (145°F).

☐ Hot foods are removed from display after 2 hours and discarded.

☐ Documented procedures exist for the cold holding of food.

☐ Cold holding procedures are recorded.

☐ Cold foods on display are removed after 4 hours and discarded.

☐ Cold holding units maintain food below 5°C (41°F).

☐ Foods on display in restaurants and buffets are labelled to describe the food items (content and potential allergen).

Quality of Water:

☐ The water quality is regularly checked and recorded.

☐ Food preparation areas have a constant supply of hot and cold water available.

V.2014 Proprietary and Confidential
Please ensure the information contained herein is safeguarded and protected.
Control the dissemination of information contained herein.   Page 11

Hotel Security and Safety Assessment/Part Three

☐	The temperature of the hot water at taps and faucets in food preparation areas exceeds 50°C (122°F).

Quality of Ice:

☐	The quality of ice is regularly checked and recorded.

2. Premises Hygiene

I confirm as the responsible person at the property that the information provided in this section is an accurate reflection of the safety facilities at this property.

Please state the name of the person completing this information:

Please state position held : (e.g., Engineer)

Check all below that apply

Pest Control

☐	Property has a pest control program including the provision for the eradication of infestations in place.

Structure

☐	Separate hand washing facilities are provided in kitchens and food preparation areas.

Wash Hand Basins Are Provided With:

☐	Hot water
☐	Cold water
☐	Antibacterial soap

Personal Hygiene

☐	Food handling staff and management receive appropriate food hygiene training.
☐	Training records are available.

3. Gas Safety

I confirm as the responsible person at the property that the information provided in this section is an accurate reflection of the safety facilities at this property.

Please state the name of the person completing this information:

Please state position held: (e.g., Director of Engineering)

Check all below that apply

Safety Management

☐	Property has a safety management system for gas supply and storage on premises.

Fuel Used to Produce Hot Water and/or Heating

☐	Natural Gas (Mains Gas)
☐	LPG (Gas from storage vessel/bottle)
☐	Oil/Diesel fuel (Oil from storage vessel)
☐	Solid Fuel (Coal/Wood)
☐	Electric or solar powered. Electric or solar powered, have gas, oil or solid fuels as a secondary fuel (or backup) for hot water or cooking
☐	Boilers and water heaters have been installed by a qualified person in accordance with the manufacturer's instruction.

Please indicate the Manufacturer and Model of Boiler/Water Heater:

MANUFACTURER

MODEL

Location of Boiler

Where is the boiler/water heater located?

☐	Central boiler room is accessed from within the main building but **NOT directly** connected to a guest accommodation.
☐	Central boiler room accessed from within the main building and **directly** connected to a guest accommodation.
☐	Boiler room externally accessed from outside the main building and **directly** connected to a guest accommodation.
☐	Boiler room that is totally separate from the guest accommodation and not attached to any part of the building.
☐	A single boiler/water heater within the guest room or villa (Individual water heater /boiler).

If There Is More Than One Boiler/Water Heater:

☐	If more than one boiler/water heater they are located in the same location or room.
☐	Boiler(s) serve more than one guest room.

V.2014 Proprietary and Confidential
Please ensure the information contained herein is safeguarded and protected.
Control the dissemination of information contained herein.   Page 12

☐	Flue terminates within 3 meters of an opening back into a guest accommodation.
☐	Water heater or boiler has a flue attached that goes directly to outside.
☐	There is gas-operated equipment in the guest room/apartment (gas fireplace, heaters, or a cooking facility).
☐	Boilers/water heaters have been serviced in the past 12 months by a qualified person. Date of Service:
☐	Gas for cooking in guest rooms, is provided from gas bottles located in guest room.
☐	Written instructions are provided for the use of the gas operated facilities.
☐	Gas is used for cooking in the main kitchen of the property.
☐	CO detectors are located in areas where fossil fuel burning devices are located.

4. Legionella Safety

I confirm as the responsible person at the property that the information provided in this section is an accurate reflection of the safety facilities at this property.

Please state the name of the person completing this information:

Please state position held: (e.g., Director of Engineering)

Check all below that apply

Legionella Management

☐	The hotel has a Legionella prevention and control program that includes the ELDS net 14 point plan.
☐	There is a named person responsible for Legionella control.
☐	The named person has received specific training in the control of Legionella.
☐	Hotel water is maintained at a temperature of 50° C to 60°C for hot taps (122°F to 140°F).
☐	Hotel operations standards ensure taps and showers in guest rooms are run for 5 minutes at least once a week if they are unoccupied and always prior to occupation.

Shower Heads and Taps

☐	Shower heads are cleaned quarterly.
☐	Shower heads are kept free from scale.
☐	Cooling towers and associated pipes used in air conditioning systems are cleaned and disinfected regularly - at least twice a year.
☐	Cleaning records of the cooling towers and associated pipes are retained.

Water Heaters (Calorifiers) and Filters

☐	Water heaters are cleaned once a year.
☐	Water heaters are disinfected once a year.
☐	There is documentation that the hot water system is disinfected with high-level (50 mg/L) chlorine for 2–4 hours.
☐	System disinfection is done at least annually.
☐	Disinfection is done following any maintenance work on water heaters.
☐	There is documentation that water filters are cleaned regularly (every 1 to 3 months).
☐	There is documentation that water filters are disinfected regularly (every 1 to 3 months).
☐	Water storage tanks, cooling towers, and visible pipe work are inspected monthly.

Cold Water Tanks

☐	There is documentation that cold water tanks are inspected at least once a year.
☐	There is documentation that cold water tanks are disinfected with 50 mg/L chlorine
☐	There is documentation that cold water tanks are cleaned annually.

Fountains and Decorative Features

☐	Fountains and decorative features are regularly cleaned, at least twice per year.
☐	Fountains and decorative features are chlorinated daily and records retained.

Spa Pools

☐	Hotel has spa pool(s) (also known as whirlpool spas, "Jacuzzis," spa baths).
☐	Spa pools are continuously treated with either 2–3 mg/L chlorine or 3–5 mg/L bromine.
☐	The chemical levels of the spa pools are monitored at least three times a day.

V.2014 Proprietary and Confidential
Please ensure the information contained herein is safeguarded and protected.
Control the dissemination of information contained herein.   Page 13

☐	Records of all spa water treatment readings including temperature and chemical levels are retained.
☐	At least half of the water within the spa pool is replaced each day.
☐	Sand filters for the spa/Jacuzzi are backwashed daily.
☐	The whole spa pool system is cleaned and disinfected at least once a week.

5. Swimming Pool Safety

I confirm as the responsible person for the property that the information provided is an accurate reflection of the safety facilities at this property.

Please state the name of the person completing this information:

Please state position held : (e.g., Director of Engineering)

Check all below that apply

General Pool Information

☐	Premises has a swimming pool.
☐	There is more than one adult pool.
	If there is more than one adult pool, please state how many: _____ number of adult pools
☐	Swimming pools are connected.
☐	Swimming pools are separate.

If the pool is connected to any other adult pool, how is it connected?

☐	By waterfall
☐	By river/stream feature
☐	By slides/slopes
☐	By bridge
☐	By walkway
☐	Pool surrounding area has NO features such as rocks or other decorative features, raised platforms, walkways, urns, or bridges.
☐	Diving is prohibited from the poolside.
☐	There are prominently displayed pictorial "No Diving" signs.

Pool Depths

☐	Pool has prominently displayed depth markings.

There Is a Multi-Board/Safety Notice at Each Pool Indicating:

☐	Pool opening and closing hours.
☐	Children must be supervised at all times.
☐	Emergency action information.
☐	Shower before entering pool.
☐	Details of whether there is a life guard on duty or not.

Lifeguard Supervision and Rescue

☐	Hotel pool has trained dedicated lifeguards on duty at the poolside when the pool is open.
☐	If NO, pool has a "No Lifeguard on Duty" sign posted.

Pool Quality, Management, and Surround

☐	Pool maintenance staff are trained in pool management, including water testing and chemical dosing, and the actions to be taken if test results are outside the required range.

Children's Pool(s)

☐	Hotel has a children's pool.
☐	The distance between the children's pool and main pool is 3 meters or greater.

Additional Pool Features

☐	There is a heated Jacuzzi.
☐	The Jacuzzi has an emergency shutoff feature/switch.
☐	There are water flumes/waterslides over 2m in height.
☐	Slides/flumes are supervised when open.

Pool Water Treatment and Filtration

☐	A record is kept of the chemicals added to the swimming pool water, including dosage, dates and times.
☐	Pool water tests undertaken at intervals throughout the day.
☐	Pool water test results are recorded.

Pool Hygiene

☐	There is a documented procedure for dealing with faecal and vomitus incidents in the swimming pool.

6. General Safety

I confirm as the responsible person at the property that the information provided in this section is an accurate reflection of the safety facilities at this property.

Please state the name of the person completing this information:

Please state position held : (e.g., Hotel Security and Safety Manager)

Check all below that apply

Balconies

- ☐ Height of the balcony is 1.1 m (42 inch equivalent) or higher (e.g., from the floor to the top of the balcony).
- ☐ Balcony railings have gaps no wider than 10 cm (4in).

  If greater than 10 cm, (4in.) please state width cm.

Guest Room Glass Doors and Partitions

- ☐ Full-length glass doors/partitions have identifying warning strips or stickers.
- ☐ Identifying warning strips or stickers are at adult eye level (approx. 1.5 m).
- ☐ Identifying warning strips or stickers are at child eye level (approx. 0.8 m).

Beach and Leisure Facilities

- ☐ Property directly access a beach   .
- ☐ The beach is under the control of the Hotel.
- ☐ The beach uses a flag warning system to indicate surf conditions.

Water Sports

- ☐ The watersport activities are under the direct control of the Hotel.
- ☐ Watersport activities are operated by the Hotel in conjunction with third party supplier(s).
- ☐ Watersports activities are operated exclusively by third-party supplier(s).

Children's Club Room

- ☐ Property operates a children's club.

- ☐ If so, please state floor location (i.e. –2, –1, 0, 1, 2, 3, and 4) of the children's clubroom.
- ☐ The Children's club location is away from potential risk areas such as roadways, swimming pools, water features, etc.

Guest Club Room

- ☐ Access to the guest club room is controlled
- ☐ Club room has kitchen facility that includes ovens and stoves

7. Airline Crew Safety (If the hotel is used by airline crews, please complete this section)

I confirm as the responsible person at the property, that the information provided in this section is an accurate reflection of the safety facilities at this property.

Please state the name of the person completing this information:

Please state position held : (e.g., Hotel Security and Safety Manager)

Check all below that apply

What airline(s) use the hotel (please list):

Transportation Logistics

Name of Company:

Address:

Contact Person:

Office Telephone:

Cell Telephone:

V.2014 Proprietary and Confidential
Please ensure the information contained herein is safeguarded and protected.
Control the dissemination of information contained herein.   Page 15

Type of vehicles used for crew transportation:	
Number of Drivers:	
Approximate drive time to airport:	
How does the crew Identify the driver?	
What is the route to the airport?	
What is the airport drop-off location?	
What is the airport pick-up location?	

☐	Background checks are performed on drivers and regularly updated to revalidate their driving records.
☐	Drivers are properly qualified and licensed to operate a commercial vehicle.
☐	Drivers speak and understand English.

Air Crew Vehicles

☐	Vehicles are equipped with GPS.
☐	Vehicle drivers have cell phones and can communicate with the Hotel.
☐	Vehicles are equipped with seat belts for all passengers.
☐	Vehicles have emergency medical kit.
☐	Vehicles are appropriate size and fitted for secure transportation of crew and luggage.
☐	Maintenance records and inspection records of vehicles are maintained and are current.
☐	Courtesy vehicle transportation is available for locations in close proximity to Hotel.

Miscellaneous Crew Considerations

☐	Telephone calls are routed through the Hotel operator.
☐	Incoming calls are logged.
☐	Guest rooms used by crew have blackout curtains.
☐	Hotel public lobby has shatter-proof glass or protective film laminate.
☐	Hotel has separated crew luggage storage facility.
☐	Hotel has public ATM machine.
☐	Currency exchange is available on premises.
☐	Hotel has gift shop on premises where basic sundries can be purchased.

V.2014 Proprietary and Confidential
Please ensure the information contained herein is safeguarded and protected.
Control the dissemination of information contained herein.   Page 16

Burdeau v. McDowell

256 U.S. 465; 41 S. Ct. 574; 65 L. Ed. 1048 (1921).

Appeal from an order of the District Court requiring that certain books and papers be impounded with the clerk and ultimately returned to the appellee, and enjoining officers of the Department of Justice from using them, or evidence derived through them, in criminal proceedings against him. The facts are stated in the opinion, post, 470.

COUNSEL: The Solicitor General for appellant:

It was not shown that any book, paper, or other document which was the private property of appellee was delivered to or was ever in the possession of appellant.

It is difficult to see how it can be said, with any show of reason, that there was any stealing of books and papers in this case. Certainly there was no invasion of appellee's right of privacy. Everything that was taken into possession was found in the office of the company itself, with the exception of a few papers which were in the private office of appellee, but which it is admitted related to the business of the company, and were, therefore, such papers as the company was entitled to have delivered to it. They were, in fact, delivered to its auditor by appellee's representative.

If the employee has left papers of his own commingled with those of the company, he certainly cannot be said to be the sole judge of whether a particular paper is his or belongs to the company. He has brought about a condition under which the company has the right to inspect everything in the office before allowing anything to be removed. The inspection, therefore, is entirely lawful, and any information of crime or other matters which may be thus acquired is lawfully acquired and may properly be used. In the present case, appellee's representative was allowed to be present and make a list or take copies of all papers examined. A paper furnishing evidence of crookedness in the conduct of the company's affairs certainly relates to a matter in which the company is interested; and if the unfaithful employee has left it in the company's files, or in the company's office, there is no principle of law under which he can lawfully claim the right to have it returned to him. He has parted with the private possession of it, and his surrender of possession has not been brought about by any invasion of his constitutional rights.

Even if it could be said that the company or its representatives stole these papers from the appellee, this would not preclude their use in evidence if they should thereafter come to the hands of the federal authorities. The court found, as the evidence clearly required, that no department of the Federal Government had anything whatever to do with the taking of these papers and that no federal official had any knowledge that an investigation of any kind was being made, nor did such knowledge come to any federal official until several months later. It would scarcely be insisted by anyone that, if the Government should discover that someone has stolen from another a paper which shows that the latter has committed a crime, the thief could not be called as a witness to testify to what he has discovered. If the paper were still in his possession, he could be subpoenaed to attend and produce the paper. The same thing is accomplished when the Government, instead of issuing a subpoena duces tecum, takes the paper and holds it as evidence. The rightful owner, while it is being so held, is no more entitled to its return than one who has been arrested for carrying a pistol is entitled to have the pistol returned to him pending a trial.

It must always be remembered that "a party is privileged from producing the evidence but not from its production." *Johnson v. United States*, 228 U.S. 457, 458.

Moreover, the Fourth Amendment protects only against searches and seizures which are made under governmental authority, real or assumed, or under color of such authority. If papers have been seized, even though wrongfully, by one not acting under color of authority, and they afterwards come to the possession of the Government, they may be properly used in evidence. *Weeks v. United States*, 232 U.S. 383; *Gouled v. United States*, 255 U.S. 298; *Boyd v. United States*, 116 U.S. 616; *Adams v. New York*,192 U.S. 585; *Johnson v. United States*, supra; *Perlman v. United States*, 247 U.S. 7.

Mr. E. Lowry Humes, with whom Mr. A. M. Imbrie and Mr. Rody P. Marshall were on the brief, for appellee:

> The issue in this proceeding was the title and right of possession of certain private papers alleged to have been stolen. The right to private property can be as effectually asserted against the Government as it can against an individual, and the Government has no greater right to stolen property than the private citizen. The receiver of stolen goods has no right superior to the right of the thief and the officer or agent of the Government who receives stolen goods is in no better position to retain the fruits and advantages of the crime than the humble private citizen. *Boyd v. United States*, 116 U.S. 616, 624; *Weeks v. United States*, 232 U.S. 383, 398. The right which the appellee asserted was a right which the court had jurisdiction to recognize and preserve.

The courts of the United States are open to the citizen for the enforcement of his legal and constitutional rights, and the right to private property may be asserted as a mere legal right or it may be asserted under the guarantees of the Constitution.

Abuses of individuals involving the deprivation of the right to the possession, use and enjoyment of private property are adequately redressed by the assertion of the legal rights of the individual in either courts of law or equity. The resort to the limitations of the Constitution may be necessary to curb the excesses of the Government.

In the case at bar there can be no question but that replevin would lie against both the thief and the receiver of the stolen goods to recover the private property of the appellee. But the legal remedy by replevin would have been inadequate as the injury could not be measured in damages. It was necessary to resort to the equitable powers of the court. The fact that the appellant happened to be an officer or employee of the Government provided no immunity to him that could prevent the owner of private property from asserting his legal rights in either a court of law or of equity. Quite to the contrary, the very fact that he was an officer of the court, enlarged rather than diminished the authority of the court to exercise control over and deal with the stolen papers which had come into his possession as such officer of the court.

In this case the proceeding is properly a much more summary proceeding than in a case against a stranger to the court where the formality and difficulty of securing jurisdiction over both the person and the property might be involved.

The right of a court of equity to order and decree the return of private property and papers is well recognized, as is illustrated by the following cases. *McGowin v. Remington*, 12 Pa. St. 56; *Dock v. Dock*, 180 Pa. St. 14; *Pressed Steel Car Co. v. Standard Steel Car Co.*, 210 Pa. St. 464.

This is an independent proceeding having for its purpose the recovery of property in equity. The law side of the court provided no adequate remedy. The court in adjudicating the case properly found that the papers had been stolen; that they were private and personal papers of the appellee, and that they were in the hands of an officer of the court, and that the owner was entitled to their return. Up to this point no constitutional question is involved. It is, however, respectfully submitted that had the court below refused under the evidence and the facts in this case to order the return of the books and papers, and dismissed the proceeding, and if subsequently a criminal proceeding had been instituted against the appellee and the stolen books and papers been admitted in evidence over objection, then appellee would have been denied the constitutional right guaranteed him under the Fifth Amendment to the Constitution in that he would have been "compelled in" a "criminal case to be a witness against himself." If this conclusion is not correct then a means has been found by which private prosecutors and complainants and those personally interested in the prosecution and persecution of alleged offenders can, by the mere acquiescence of the Government, deprive citizens of the United States of the constitutional rights guaranteed to them by both the Fourth and Fifth Amendments.

JUDGES: McKenna, Holmes, Day, Van Devanter, Pitney, McReynolds, Brandeis, Clarke

OPINION BY: DAY

OPINION: MR. JUSTICE DAY delivered the opinion of the court.

J. C. McDowell, hereinafter called the petitioner, filed a petition in the United States District Court for the Western District of Pennsylvania asking for an order for the return to him of certain books, papers, memoranda, correspondence and other data in the possession of Joseph A. Burdeau, appellant herein, Special Assistant to the Attorney General of the United States.

In the petition it is stated that Burdeau and his associates intended to present to the grand jury in and for the Western District of Pennsylvania a charge against petitioner of an alleged violation of § 215 of the Criminal Code of the United States in the fraudulent use of the mails; that it was the intention of Burdeau and his associates, including certain post-office inspectors cooperating with him, to present to the grand jury certain private books, papers, memoranda, etc., which were the private property of the petitioner; that the papers had been in the possession and exclusive control of the petitioner in the Farmers Bank Building in Pittsburgh. It is alleged that during the spring and summer of 1920 these papers were unlawfully seized and stolen from petitioner by certain persons participating in and furthering the proposed investigation so to be made by the grand jury, under the direction and control of Burdeau as special assistant to the Attorney General, and that such books, papers, memoranda, etc., were being held in the possession and control of Burdeau and his assistants; that in the taking of the personal private books and papers the person who purloined and stole the same drilled the petitioner's private safes, broke the locks upon his private desk, and broke into and abstracted from the files in his offices his private papers; that the possession of the books, papers, etc., by Burdeau and his assistants was unlawful and in violation of the legal and constitutional rights of the petitioner. It is charged that the presentation to the grand jury of the same, or any secondary or other evidence secured through or by them, would work a deprivation of petitioner's constitutional rights secured to him by the Fourth and Fifth Amendments to the Constitution of the United States.

An answer was filed claiming the right to hold and use the papers. A hearing was had before the District Judge, who made an order requiring the delivery of the papers to the clerk of the court, together with all copies memoranda and data taken therefrom, which the court found had been stolen from the offices of the petitioner at rooms numbered 1320 and 1321 in the Farmers Bank Building in the City of Pittsburgh. The order further provided that upon delivery of the books, papers, etc., to the clerk of the court the same should be sealed and impounded for the period of ten days, at the end of which period they should be delivered to the petitioner or his attorney unless an appeal were taken from the order of the court, in which event, the books, papers, etc., should be impounded until the determination of the appeal. An order was made restraining Burdeau, Special Assistant Attorney General, the Department of Justice, its officers and agents, and the United States Attorney from presenting to the United States Commissioner, the grand jury or any judicial tribunal, any of the books, papers, memoranda, letters, copies of letters, correspondence, etc., or any evidence of any nature whatsoever secured by or coming into their possession as a result of the knowledge obtained from the inspection of such books, papers, memoranda, etc.

In his opinion the District Judge stated that it was the intention of the Department of Justice, through Burdeau and his assistants, to present the books, papers, etc., to the grand jury with a view to having the petitioner indicted for the alleged violation of § 215 of the Criminal Code of the United States, and the court held that the evidence offered by the petitioner showed that the papers had been stolen from him, and that he was entitled to the return of the same. In this connection the District Judge stated that it did not appear that Burdeau, or any official or agent of the United States, or any of the Departments, had anything to do with the search of the petitioner's safe, files, and desk, or the abstraction therefrom of any of the writings referred to in the petition, and added that "the order made in this case is not made because of any unlawful act on the part of anybody representing the United States or any of its Departments but solely upon the ground that the Government should not use stolen property for any purpose after demand made for its return." Expressing his views, at the close of the testimony, the judge said that there had been a gross violation of the Fourth and Fifth Amendments to the Federal Constitution; that the Government had not been a party to any illegal seizure; that those Amendments, in the understanding of the court, were passed for the benefit of the States against action by the United States, forbidden by those Amendments, and that the court was satisfied that the papers were illegally and wrongfully taken from the possession of the petitioner, and were then in the hands of the Government.

So far as is necessary for our consideration certain facts from the record may be stated. Henry L. Doherty & Company of New York were operating managers of the Cities Service Company, which company is a holding company, having control of various oil and gas companies. Petitioner was a director in the Cities Service Company and a director in the Quapaw Gas Company, a subsidiary company, and occupied an office room in the building owned by the Farmers Bank of Pittsburgh. The rooms were leased by the Quapaw Gas Company. McDowell occupied one room for his private office. He was employed by Doherty & Company as the head of the natural gas division of the Cities Service Company. Doherty & Company discharged McDowell for alleged unlawful and fraudulent conduct in the course of the business. An officer of Doherty & Company and the Cities Service Company went to Pittsburgh in March, 1920, with authority of the president of the Quapaw Gas Company to take possession of the company's office.

He took possession of room 1320; that room and the adjoining room had McDowell's name on the door. At various times papers were taken from the safe and desk in the rooms, and the rooms were placed in charge of detectives. A large quantity of papers were taken and shipped to the auditor of the Cities Service Company at 60 Wall Street, New York, which was the office of that company, Doherty & Company and the Quapaw Gas Company. The secretary of McDowell testified that room 1320 was his private office; that practically all the furniture in both rooms belonged to him; that there was a large safe belonging to the Farmers Bank and a small safe belonging to McDowell; that on March 23, 1920, a representative of the company and a detective came to the offices; that the detective was placed in charge of room 1320; that the large safe was opened with a view to selecting papers belonging to the company, and that the representative of the company took private papers of McDowell's also. While the rooms were in charge of detectives both safes were blown open. In the small safe nothing of consequence was found, but in the large safe papers belonging to McDowell were found. The desk was forced open, and all the papers taken from it. The papers were placed in cases, and shipped to Doherty & Company, 60 Wall Street, New York.

In June, 1920, following, Doherty & Company, after communication with the Department of Justice, turned over a letter, found in McDowell's desk to the Department's representative. Burdeau admitted at the hearing that as the representative of the United States in the Department of Justice he had papers which he assumed were taken from the office of McDowell. The communication to the Attorney General stated that McDowell had violated the laws of the United States in the use of the mail in the transmission of various letters to parties who owned the properties which were sold by or offered to the Cities Service Company; that some of such letters, or copies of them taken from McDowell's file, were in the possession of the Cities Service Company, that the Company also had in its possession portions of a diary of McDowell in which he had jotted down the commissions which he had received from a number of the transactions, and other data which, it is stated, would be useful in the investigation of the matter before the grand jury and subsequent prosecution should an indictment be returned.

We do not question the authority of the court to control the disposition of the papers, and come directly to the contention that the constitutional rights of the petitioner were violated by their seizure, and that having subsequently come into the possession of the prosecuting officers of the Government, he was entitled to their return. The Amendments involved are the Fourth and Fifth, protecting a citizen against unreasonable searches and seizures, and compulsory testimony against himself. An extended consideration of the origin and purposes of these Amendments would be superfluous in view of the fact that this court has had occasion to deal with those subjects in a series of cases. *Boyd v. United States,*116 U.S. 616; *Adams v. New York*, 192 U.S. 585; *Weeks v. United States,* 232 U.S. 383; *Johnson v. United States*, 228 U.S. 457; *Perlman v. United States*, 247 U.S. 7; *Silverthorne Lumber Co. v. United States*, 251 U.S. 385; and *Gouled v. United States*, 255 U.S. 298.

The Fourth Amendment gives protection against unlawful searches and seizures, and as shown in the previous cases, its protection applies to governmental action. Its origin and history clearly show that it was intended as a restraint upon the activities of sovereign authority, and was not intended to be a limitation upon other than governmental agencies; as against such authority it was the purpose of the Fourth Amendment to secure the citizen in the right of unmolested occupation of his dwelling and the possession of his property, subject to the right of seizure by process duly issued.

In the present case the record clearly shows that no official of the Federal Government had anything to do with the wrongful seizure of the petitioner's property, or any knowledge thereof until several months after the property had been taken from him and was in the possession of the Cities Service Company. It is manifest that there was no invasion of the security afforded by the Fourth Amendment against unreasonable search and seizure, as whatever wrong was done was the act of individuals in taking the property of another. A portion of the property so taken and held was turned over to the prosecuting officers of the Federal Government. We assume that petitioner has an unquestionable right of redress against those who illegally and wrongfully took his private property under the circumstances herein disclosed, but with such remedies we are not now concerned.

The Fifth Amendment, as its terms import is intended to secure the citizen from compulsory testimony against himself. It protects from extorted confessions or examinations in court proceedings by compulsory methods.

The exact question to be decided here is: May the Government retain incriminating papers, coming to it in the manner described, with a view to their use in a subsequent investigation by a grand jury where such papers will be part of the evidence against the accused, and may be used against him upon trial should an indictment be returned?

We know of no constitutional principle which requires the Government to surrender the papers under such circumstances. Had it learned that such incriminatory papers, tending to show a violation of federal law, were in the hands of a person other than the accused, it having had no part in wrongfully obtaining them, we know of no reason why a subpoena might not issue for the production of the papers as evidence. Such production would require no unreasonable search or seizure, nor would it amount to compelling the accused to testify against himself.

The papers having come into the possession of the Government without a violation of petitioner's rights by governmental authority, we see no reason why the fact that individuals, unconnected with the Government, may have wrongfully taken them, should prevent them from being held for use in prosecuting an offense where the documents are of an incriminatory character.

It follows that the District Court erred in making the order appealed from, and the same is Reversed.

DISSENT BY: BRANDEIS

DISSENT: MR. JUSTICE BRANDEIS dissenting, with whom MR. JUSTICE HOLMES concurs.

Plaintiff's private papers were stolen. The thief, to further his own ends, delivered them to the law officer of the United States. He, knowing them to have been stolen, retains them for use against the plaintiff. Should the court permit him to do so?

That the court would restore the papers to plaintiff if they were still in the thief's possession is not questioned. That it has power to control the disposition of these stolen papers, although they have passed into the possession of the law officer, is also not questioned. But it is said that no provision of the constitution requires their surrender and that the papers could have been subpoenaed. This may be true. Still i cannot believe that action of a public official is necessarily lawful, because it does not violate constitutional prohibitions and because the same result might have been attained by other and proper means. At the foundation of our civil liberty lies the principle which denies to government officials an exceptional position before the law and which subjects them to the same rules of conduct that are commands to the citizen. And in the development of our liberty insistence upon procedural regularity has been a large factor. Respect for law will not be advanced by resort, in its enforcement, to means which shock the common man's sense of decency and fair play.

Appendix F: Physical security survey checklist

PERIMETER BARRIERS—TRANSIT FACILITIES

Does a fence or other type of physical barrier define the perimeter of the facility?

1. Specify type and height of physical barrier.
2. Describe condition of physical barriers.
3. Is perimeter barrier considered to be a security safeguard?
4. Is perimeter barrier set back 20 feet or more from transit facility property boundary?
5. Is perimeter barrier under surveillance at all times?

If chain link fence is used as the perimeter barrier,

1. Is it constructed of #11 gauge or heavier wire?
2. Is mesh opening no larger than two inches square?
3. Is selvage twisted and barbed at top and bottom?
4. Is bottom of fence extended into the ground?

If masonry wall is used,

1. Is it at least seven feet high with a top guard of barbed wire or at least eight feet high with broken glass set on edge and cemented to top surface?
2. Do building walls, floors, or roofs form a part of the perimeter barrier?
3. Are all openings properly secured?

Note: Openings, with an area of 96 square inches or greater, and located less than 18 feet above the level of the ground outside the perimeter barrier or less than 14 feet from controlled structures outside the perimeter barrier, should be provided with security equivalent to that of the perimeter.

If building forms a part of the perimeter barrier,

1. Does it present a hazard at the point of juncture with the perimeter fence?
2. Does it have any doors, windows, or other openings on perimeter side?

If a river, lake, or other body of water forms any part of the perimeter boundary, are additional security measures provided?

Are openings such as culverts, tunnels, manholes for sewers and utility access, and sidewalk elevators which permit access to the facility secured?

Describe the physical characteristics of each perimeter entrance.

Are all entrance points in perimeter barriers guarded or secured?

Are all perimeter gates of such material and installation as to provide protection equivalent to the perimeter barriers of which they are a part?

Are gates and/or other perimeter entrances which are not in active use frequently inspected by guards or other personnel?

Is the security officer responsible for security of keys to perimeter entrances?

Are keys to perimeter entrances issued to other than facility personnel such as contractor personnel?

Are all normally used pedestrian and vehicle gates and other perimeter entrances lighted so as to assure:

1. Proper identification of individuals and examination of credentials
2. That interiors of vehicles are clearly lighted; and
3. That glare from luminaries is not in guard's eyes.

Are appropriate signs setting forth the provisions of entry conspicuously posted at all principal entrances?

Are "No Trespassing" signs posted on or adjacent to perimeter barriers at such intervals that at least one sign is visible at any approach to the barrier for a minimum distance of 50 yards?

Are clear zones maintained on both sides of the perimeter barrier?

Are automobiles permitted to park against or close to perimeter barriers?

Are lumber, boxes, or other materials allowed to be stacked against, or in close proximity to, perimeter barriers?

Do guards patrol perimeter areas?

Do guards observe and report insecure factors related to perimeter barriers?

Is an interior all-weather perimeter road provided for the use of guard patrol cars? If so, what is the condition?

Are perimeters protected by intrusion alarm devices?

PROTECTIVE LIGHTING

Is the perimeter of the installation protected by lighting?

Does protective lighting provide a means of continuing during the hours of darkness the same degree of protection available during the daylight hours?

Are the cones of illumination from lamps directed downward and away from the facility proper and away from guard personnel?

Are lights mounted to provide a strip of light both inside and outside the fence?

Is perimeter lighting used so that guards remain in comparative darkness?

Are lights checked for proper operation prior to darkness?

Are repairs to lights and replacement of inoperative lamps effected immediately?

Do light beams overlap to provide coverage in case a bulb burns out?

Is additional lighting provided at active gates and points of possible intrusion?

Are gate guard shacks provided with proper illumination?

Are light finishes or stripes used on lower parts of buildings and structures to aid guard observation?

Does the facility have a dependable source of power for its lighting system?

Does the facility have a dependable auxiliary source of power?

Is the protective lighting system independent of the general transit facility lighting or power system?

Is the power supply for lights adequately protected?

Is there provision for standby or emergency lighting?

Is the standby or emergency equipment tested frequently?

Is emergency equipment designed to go into operation automatically when needed?

Is wiring for protective lighting properly mounted?

1. Is it in tamper-resistant conduits?
2. Is it mounted underground?
3. If above ground, is it high enough to reduce possibility of tampering?

Are switches and controls properly located, controlled, and protected?

1. Are they weatherproof and tamper-resistant?
2. Are they readily accessible to security personnel?
3. Are they located so that they are inaccessible from outside the perimeter barrier?
4. Is there a centrally located switch to control protective lighting?

Is adequate lighting for guard use provided on indoor routes?

Are materials and equipment in shipping and storage areas properly arranged so as not to mask security lighting?

PROTECTIVE ALARMS

If an alarm system is used in the facility, what detection device is used?

1. Is it a local alarm system?
2. Is it a central station system?
   a. Is it connected to facility guard headquarters?
   b. Is it connected directly to a headquarters outside the facility proper? Is it a private protection service? Police station? Fire station?

Is the system backed up by properly trained, alert guards?

Is the alarm system for active areas of structures turned off during operational hours?

Is the system tested prior to activating it from nonoperational periods?

Is the alarm system inspected regularly?

Is the system tamper-resistant? Weatherproof?

Is an alternate alarm system provided for use in the event of failure of the primary system?

Is an alternate or independent source of power available for use on the system in the event of power failure?

Is the emergency power source designed to cut in and operate automatically?

Are frequent tests conducted to determine the adequacy and promptness of response to alarm signals?

SECURITY COMMUNICATIONS

Is there a security communications system?

What means of communications are used?

1. Telephone.
   a. Is it a commercial switchboard system?
   b. Is it an independent switchboard?
   c. Is it restricted for guard use only?
   d. Are switchboards adequately guarded?
   e. Are call boxes conveniently located?
   f. Are open wires, terminal boxes, cables, etc. frequently inspected for damage, sabotage, and wire-tapping?
2. Radio.
   a. Is an effective routine code being used? Duress code?
   b. s proper authentication required?

Is security communications equipment in use capable of transmitting instructions to all key posts simultaneously?

Is the equipment in use sufficient for guard to communicate with guard headquarters with minimum delay?

Is there more than one system of security communications available for exclusive use of security personnel?

Does one of these systems have an alternate or independent source?

Is there more than one system of communications restricted to security use available for communicating with outside protective agencies?

Has the communications center been provided with adequate security safeguards?

PERSONNEL IDENTIFICATION AND CONTROL CHECKLIST

Is an identification card or badge used to identify all personnel within the confines of the controlled areas?

Does the identification and control system include arrangements for the following:

1. Protection of coded or printed components of badges and passes.
2. Designation of the various areas requiring special control measures.
3. Controlled issue of identification media.

Are there written procedures for the method of identification at time of entering and leaving controlled area, as applied to both employees and visitors?

1. Details of where, when, and how ID cards shall be carried.
2. Procedures to be followed in case of loss or damage to identification media.
3. Procedure for recovery and invalidation.

If a badge exchange system is used for any controlled area, does the system provide for:

1. Comparison of badge, pass, and personnel?
2. Physical exchange of pass for badge at time of entrance and exit?
3. Security of badges not in use?

Are personnel who are regularly required to enter areas of varying degrees of security interest provided with special identification?

Are personnel who require infrequent access to a critical area and who have not been issued regular security identification for such area treated as "visitors" thereto, and issued either

1. A visitor's badge or pass?
2. A special pass?

Are all personnel required to wear the security identification badge while on duty?

Do guards at control points compare badges to bearers both upon entry and upon exit?

Are badges recorded and controlled by rigid accountability procedures?

Are lost badges replaced with one bearing a different number or one that is otherwise not identical to the one lost?

What are procedures relative to lost, damaged, and/or forgotten badges?

Are rosters of lost badges posted at guard control points?

Are badges of such design and appearance as to enable guards and other personnel to recognize quickly and positively the authorizations and limitations applicable to the bearers?

Do existing procedures insure the return of identification badges upon termination of employment?

What type of badges are issued to outside contractor employees working within the installation?

Are all phases of system under supervision and control of security officer?

Is there a visitor escort procedure established?

Do guards check on visitors' movements to assure that they do not enter areas for which they do not have the required authorization?

Are visitors required to conspicuously display identification on outer garments at all times while in controlled areas?

When visitors leave the installation, are they required to turn in their identification badges?

Is the departure time in each case recorded on the visitor's register?

Are visitors indicating an intention to return at a later time permitted to retain their identification badges?

What procedures are invoked when visitor identification media are not turned in prior to departure of the visitor?

Is there a central receptionist?

> 1. If "yes," specify functions.
> 2. Are functions performed under supervision of security officer?

Are vendors, tradesmen, utility servicemen, special equipment servicemen, etc. issued a special or distinctive type of visitor badge?

What measures are employed, other than the issuance of identification badges, to control the movement of personnel from other transportation companies working within the perimeter of the facility?

Is the transit security officer the responsible official for all aspects of visitor control?

VEHICLE IDENTIFICATION

Is an effective procedure used for control of special vehicles?

> 1. Emergency vehicles.
> 2. VIP vehicles.
> 3. Special courier vehicles.
> 4. Vendor's vehicles.
> 5. Vehicles with loads which are impracticable to search.

Is there coordination between guard headquarters and the activities that handle cargo movements?

Is a regular security education program in effect?

VEHICLE CONTROL

Are vehicles which are allowed regular access to the transit registered with the security officer?

Have definite procedures been established for the registration of private cars?

Do the vehicle registration provisions apply also to motor vehicles owned or operated by: employees of any individual firm, corporation, or contractor engaged in activities at the transit facility and individuals, partnerships, or other business concerns whose business activities require daily or frequent use of their vehicles at the transit facility?

Is annual registration provided for?

Are decalcomania or other registration tags affixed to all registered vehicles?

Do the controls for registration tags include:

---

1. Prohibition against transfer of registration tags for use with a vehicle other than the one for which originally issued?
2. Replacement of lost tags at the registrant's expense?
3. Return of tags to the security officer when vehicle is no longer authorized entry into facility?
4. Destruction of invalidated decalcomania?
5. Is security section notified when employee leaves for over 30 days?

What is the nature and scope of registration records maintained by the security officer?

Do private gate guards make periodic checks to insure that vehicles are operated on the premises only by properly licensed persons?

Is a definite system used to control the movement of commercial trucks and other goods conveyances into and out of the most secure areas of the transit facility?

Are loading and unloading platforms located outside transit operations and separated there/from/by controlled and guard supervised entrances?

Are all trucks and other conveyances required to enter through service gates manned by guards?

If trucks are permitted direct access to the transit maintenance or administrative facility, are truck drivers and vehicle contents carefully examined?

Does the check at entrances cover both incoming and outgoing vehicles?

Are truck registers maintained?

Are registers maintained on all company vehicles entering and leaving the facility?

Does the supervision of loading and unloading operations insure that unauthorized goods or people do not enter or leave the installation via trucks or other conveyances?

Is a temporary tag issued to visitors' vehicles?

Are automobiles allowed to be parked within 50 feet of major transit facilities and stations?

Are parking lots provided?

Are interior parking areas located away from sensitive points?

Are interior parking areas fenced so that occupants of automobiles must pass through a pedestrian gate when entering or leaving the working area?

Are separate parking areas provided for visitors' vehicles?

What is the extent of guard surveillance over interior parking area?

Are there restrictions against employees entering parking areas during duty hours?

Are automobiles allowed to park so close to buildings or structures that they would be a fire threat or obstruct fire fighters?

Are automobiles permitted to be parked close to controlled area fences?

Are parking facilities adequate?

LOCK SECURITY

Has a key control official been appointed, normally a security officer?

Are locks and keys to all buildings and entrances supervised and controlled by a key control official?

Does the key control official have overall authority and responsibility for issuance and replacement of locks and keys?

Are keys issued only to authorized personnel?

Are keys issued to other than transit personnel?

Is the removal of keys from the premises prohibited?

Are keys not in use maintained indicating:

---
1. Buildings and/or entrances for which keys are issued?
2. Number and identification of keys issued?
3. Location and number of master keys?
4. Location and number of duplicate keys?
5. Issue and turn in of keys?
6. Location of locks and keys held in reserve?

Are locks changed immediately upon loss or theft of keys?

If master keys are used, are they devoid of markings identifying them as such?

Are losses or thefts of keys promptly investigated by the key control personnel?

Must all requests for reproduction or duplication of keys be approved by the key control official?

Are locks on inactive gates and storage facilities under seal? Are they checked periodically by guard personnel?

Are padlocks rotated within the installation at least semiannually?

Where applicable, is manufacturer's serial number on combination locks obliterated?

GUARD FORCES

Is a guard force provided?

Indicate authorized and actual strength, broken down by positions.

Is present guard force strength commensurate with degree of security protection required?

Is the use of guard forces reviewed periodically to ascertain effective and economical use?

Is supervisory responsibility for guard force operations vested in the security officer?

Is a guard headquarters area provided?

Does the guard headquarters area contain control equipment and instruments of all alarm, warning, and guard communications systems?

Are guards familiar with communications equipment used?

Does guard headquarters have direct communication with local municipal fire and police headquarters?

Are guards armed while on duty, and if so, with what type of weapon?

Are the weapons kept in arms racks and adequately secured when not in use?

Are ammunition supplies properly secured and issued only for authorized purposes?

Is each member of guard force required to complete a course of basic training?

Are the subjects included in the various training course adequate?

Does the training cover:

1. Care and use of weapons?
2. Common forms of pilferage, theft, and sabotage activity?
3. Types of bombs and explosives?
4. Orientation on the facility emphasis of controlled and vulnerable areas?
5. Location of hazardous materials and processes?
6. Location and use of fire protective equipment, including sprinkler control valves?
7. Location and operation of all important steam and gas valves and main electrical switches?
8. Conditions which may cause fire and explosions?
9. Location and use of first aid equipment?
10. Duties in the event of fire, explosion, natural disaster, civil disturbance, blackout, or air raid?
11. Use of communication system?
12. Proper methods of search?
13. Observation and description?
14. Patrol work?
15. Supervision of visitors?
16. Preparation of written reports?
17. General and special guard orders?
18. Authority to use force, conduct searches, and arrest or apprehend?

Are activities of the guard force consonant with established policy?

Is supervision of the guard force adequate?

Are general and special orders properly posted?

Are guard orders reviewed periodically to insure applicability?

Are periodic inspections and examinations conducted to determine the degree of understanding and compliance with all guard orders?

Do physical, functional, or other changes at the transit agency indicate the necessity for or feasibility of

1. Establishing additional guard posts?
2. Discontinuing any existing posts or patrols?

Is two-way radio equipment installed on all guard patrol cars?

Are duties other than those related to security performed by guard personnel?

Index

Note: Page numbers followed by "*n*" with numbers indicate footnotes.